D1710920

HANDBOOK OF UTILITY THEORY

HANDBOOK OF UTILITY THEORY

Volume 1
Principles

Edited by

SALVADOR BARBERÀ
Universitat Autònoma de Barcelona

PETER J. HAMMOND
Stanford University

CHRISTIAN SEIDL
Christian-Albrechts-Universität zu Kiel

KLUWER ACADEMIC PUBLISHERS
DORDRECHT / BOSTON / LONDON

Library of Congress Cataloging-in-Publication Data

ISBN 0-7923-8174-2

Published by Kluwer Academic Publishers,
P.O. Box 17, 3300 AA Dordrecht, The Netherlands.

Sold and distributed in North, Central and South America
by Kluwer Academic Publishers,
101 Philip Drive, Norwell, MA 02061, U.S.A.

In all other countries, sold and distributed
by Kluwer Academic Publishers,
P.O. Box 322, 3300 AH Dordrecht, The Netherlands.

Printed on acid-free paper

Printed in the Netherlands

Table of Contents

Preface
ix

1 Preference and Utility
1
Ghanshyam B. Mehta

  1   Introduction
2

  2   Preliminaries on Order and Topology
4

  3   Existence of a Utility Function
9

  4   Existence of a Continuous Utility Function on Euclidean Spaces
10

  5   Debreu's Gap Lemma and the Existence of a Continuous Utility Function on Totally Preordered Topological Spaces
17

  6   Existence of a Continuous Utility Function on Partially Ordered Topological Spaces
24

  7   The Urysohn–Nachbin Approach to Continuous Utility Functions
26

  8   Miscellaneous Topics on Utility Functions
30

      8.1   Continuous Utility Functions on Infinite Dimensional Spaces
30

      8.2   Utility Representations for Interval Orders
32

      8.3   Differentiable Utility Functions
34

      8.4   Jointly Continuous Utility Functions
36

      8.5   Existence of a Utility Function with Values in a Lexicographic Product
37

  References
38

2 Separability: A Survey
49
C. Blackorby, D. Primont and R. R. Russell

  1   Introductory Remarks
51

  2   Decentralization and Separability
51

      2.1   Notation
52

      2.2   Decentralization
53

      2.3   Separability and Functional Structure
54

      2.4   Decentralization $\Longleftrightarrow$ Separability
58

  3   Price Aggregation and Budgeting
59

      3.1   Price Aggregation
60

      3.2   Two–Stage Budgeting
61

  4   Separability and Duality
63

      4.1   Dual Representations of Preferences: Indirect Utility, Expenditure, and Distance Functions
64

      4.2   Separability of Dual Representations of Preferences
65

      4.3   Homothetic Separability
68

      4.4   Additive Price Aggregation
69

  5   Additive Structures.
70

      5.1   Complete Separability
71

      5.2   Additivity in a Two–Group Partition.
74

      5.3   Additivity and Duality.
75

  6   Conjunction of Direct and Indirect Separability and Additivity
77

      6.1   Direct and Indirect Additivity
78

      6.2   Direct and Indirect Separability
79

  7   Implicit Separability
82

  8   Concluding Remarks: Extensions and Applications.
87

  References
88

i

3 Recursive Utility and Dynamic Programming   93
Peter A. Streufert
   1   Introduction   94
   2   Stationary Theory   94
       2.1   Decomposing Recursive Utility   94
       2.2   Feasibility   97
       2.3   The Commodity Space and Biconvergence   98
       2.4   Recomposing Recursive Utility   99
       2.5   Dynamic Programming   101
       2.6   Informal Links to Optimal Control   104
   3   Stationary Applications   105
       3.1   Additive Utility   105
       3.2   Deterministic Saving Problems with Additive Utility   106
       3.3   Deterministic Saving Problems with Non–Additive Utility 108
   4   Nonstationary Theory and Applications   109
       4.1   Nonstationary Theory   109
       4.2   Stochastic Saving Problems with Additive Utility   112
       4.3   Intergenerational Models   116
   5   An Extension   118
   References   119

4 Dual Approaches to Utility   123
Martin Browning
   1   Introduction   124
   2   An Optimal Tax Example   125
   3   Mathematical Background   127
   4   The Cost and Indirect Utility Functions   128
   5   The Distance and Profit Functions   132
   6   Mixed Representations   137
   7   Concluding Remarks   139
   References   139

5 Objective Expected Utility   143
Peter J. Hammond
   1   Introduction and Outline   145
   2   The Expected Utility Hypothesis   147
       2.1   Simple Lotteries   147
       2.2   Expected Utility Maximization   148
       2.3   Ratios of Utility Differences   149
       2.4   Cardinally Equivalent Utility Functions 151
   3   Necessary Conditions   152
       3.1   The Ordering Condition   152
       3.2   Independence Conditions   153
       3.3   Lexicographic Preferences   154
       3.4   Continuity Conditions   155

4   Sufficient Conditions   157
     4.1   Ordinality and Independence   157
     4.2   Continuity   159
     4.3   Construction of a Utility Function   161
5   Consequentialist Foundations: Ordinality   164
     5.1   The Consequentialist Principle   164
     5.2   Simple Finite Decision Trees   165
     5.3   Behaviour and Unrestricted Domain   166
     5.4   Continuation Subtrees and Dynamic Consistency   166
     5.5   Consequentialism in Simple Decision Trees   167
     5.6   Consequentialism Implies Ordinality   169
6   Consequentialist Foundations: Independence   172
     6.1   Finite Decision Trees with Chance Nodes   172
     6.2   Consequentialism in Finite Decision Trees   173
     6.3   Consequentialism Implies Independence   174
     6.4   Ordinality and Strong Independence Characterize Consequentialism   177
     6.5   Summary   178
7   Continuous Behaviour and Expected Utility   179
     7.1   Continuous Behaviour   179
     7.2   Dynamic Programming and Continuous Behaviour   181
     7.3   Main Theorem   185
8   Discrete Lotteries, Boundedness, and Dominance   185
     8.1   Discrete Lotteries   185
     8.2   Unbounded Utility   186
     8.3   Bounded Expected Utility   188
     8.4   Dominance   189
     8.5   Sufficient Conditions for the EU Hypothesis   190
     8.6   Continuity   191
     8.7   Consequentialist Motivation for Dominance   193
9   Probability Measures   195
     9.1   Probability Measures and Expectations   195
     9.2   Necessary Conditions for EU Maximization   196
     9.3   Sufficient Conditions for the EU Hypothesis   198
     9.4   Continuity of Expected Utility   200
     9.5   Consequentialism and Probability Dominance   203
10   Summary and Concluding Remarks   205
     References   206

6 Subjective Expected Utility   213
  Peter J. Hammond
1   Introduction and Outline   215
2   Necessary Conditions   219
     2.1   Subjective Expected Utility Maximization   219
     2.2   Contingent Preferences and the Sure Thing Principle   219
     2.3   State Independent Preferences   221
     2.4   A Likelihood Ordering of Events   221
3   Consequentialist Foundations   222

	3.1	Decision Trees with Natural Nodes	222
	3.2	Feasible and Chosen CCFs	223
	3.3	Consequentialism and Contingent Orderings	224
	3.4	Consequentialism and the Sure Thing Principle	225
	3.5	Consequentialism Characterized	226
	3.6	Unordered Events	226
4		Anscombe and Aumann's Axioms	228
	4.1	Horse Lotteries versus Roulette Lotteries	228
	4.2	Ratios of Utility Differences	229
	4.3	Ordinality, Independence and Continuity	229
	4.4	Reversal of Order	230
	4.5	Sure Thing Principle	231
	4.6	State Independence	232
	4.7	Sufficient Conditions for the SEU and SEU* Hypotheses	233
5		Consequentialist Foundations Reconsidered	237
	5.1	Decision Trees with Both Chance and Natural Nodes	237
	5.2	Consequentialism and Contingent Utilities	238
	5.3	Consequentialist Normal Form Invariance and Condition (RO)	239
	5.4	State Independent Consequentialism, No Null Events, and Continuity	240
	5.5	Sufficient Conditions for Consequentialism	241
	5.6	Dynamic Programming and Continuous Behaviour	243
	5.7	Main Theorem	244
6		State–Dependent Consequence Domains	244
	6.1	Evaluation Functions	244
	6.2	Chosen Probabilities and State–Dependent Utilities	247
	6.3	State–Independent Utilities	250
7		Countable Events	254
	7.1	Bounded Preferences	254
	7.2	Event Continuity	254
	7.3	Event Dominance	255
	7.4	Sufficient Conditions for SEU and SEU*	256
8		Subjective Probability Measures	256
	8.1	Measurable Expected Utility	256
	8.2	Sufficient Conditions for SEU and SEU*	259
	8.3	Eleven Sufficient Conditions	265
9		Summary and Conclusions	266
	References		268

7 Stochastic Utility   273
Peter C. Fishburn

1		Introduction	275
2		Structures	278
	2.1	The Universal Set of Objects	279
	2.2	Domains for P	280
	2.3	Domains for p	280
	2.4	Primitive Domains and Axioms	281
3		Representations	284

3.1   Representation Theorems and Uniqueness   284
3.2   Constant Utility and Binary Advantage Representations   286
3.3   Random Utility Representations   286
3.4   Subset Choice and Sequential Reduction   288
3.5   Preview   290
4   Binary Choice Probabilities   291
5   Simple Scalability and Luce's Model   294
6   Random Utility   296
7   The Linear Ordering Polytope   299
8   Rankings: Induced and Primitive   302
8.1   Rankings from Choice Probabilities   302
8.2   Rankings as Primitive   305
8.3   Social Choice Lotteries   306
9   Lotteries and Acts   307
References   311

8 Fuzzy Utility   321
Maurice Salles

1   Introduction   322
2   Fuzzy Preference   323
2.1   Fuzzy Preference: Numerical Values   324
2.2   Fuzzy Preference: Qualitative Values   327
3   Choice and Fuzzy Preference   329
3.1   Exact Choice and Standard Fuzzy Preference   329
3.2   Choice and Soft Preference   333
4   Fuzzy Social Choice   335
4.1   Numerical Fuzzy Social Choice   335
4.2   Social Choice with Qualitative Fuzziness   337
5   Conclusion   341
References   341

9 Lexicographic Utility and Orderings   345
Juan E. Martínez–Legaz

1   Introduction   346
2   Lexicographic Preferences   347
3   The Lexicographic Order in $\mathbb{R}^n$ 350
4   Lexicographic Utility   353
5   Lexicographic Expected Utility   355
6   Lexicographic Subjective Expected Utility   358
7   Lexicographic Probabilities and Game Theory   361
References   365

10 Utility Theory and Ethics   371
Philippe Mongin and Claude d'Aspremont

1   Introduction   373
2   Some Philosophical and Historical Clarifications   376

	2.1	Preliminaries	376
	2.2	Early Utilitarian Views: Utility Related to Pleasure and Pain	379
	2.3	Utility as a Measure of Actual Preference Satisfaction	382
	2.4	Utility and Well–Being: Critical Arguments	388
	2.5	Utility, Well–Being, and Social Ethics: Some Positive Arguments	394
3		Some Definitions and Concepts from Utility Theory	401
	3.1	Utility Functions in the Case of Certainty, and "Economic" Domains	401
	3.2	Von Neumann–Morgenstern Utility Functions	402
	3.3	Anscombe–Aumann Utility Functions	404
	3.4	Interpersonal Utility Differences	407
4		The Aggregative Setting with Interpersonal Comparisons of Utility	408
	4.1	The SWFL Framework	409
	4.2	Invariance Axioms and Interpersonal Comparisons of Utility	411
	4.3	Further Conditions on SWFL	413
	4.4	Utilitarianism Versus Leximin	415
	4.5	Further Rules for Social Evaluation. The Variable Population Case	419
	4.6	Some Conceptual Problems of the Multi–Profile Approach	422
5		The Aggregative Setting with Choice–Theoretic Constraints	425
	5.1	Harsanyi's Approach to Utilitarianism. The Aggregation Theorem	425
	5.2	A SWFL Reconstruction of Harsanyi's Aggregation Theorem	429
	5.3	Further Philosophical Comments on Harsanyi's Utilitarianism	432
	5.4	The Aggregative Approach in the Case of Subjective Uncertainty	437
6		The Impartial Observer, the Original Position, and Fairness	444
	6.1	Impartial–Observer Theories	444
	6.2	State–of–Nature Theories and the "Original Position"	447
	6.3	Harsanyi's Impartial Observer Theorem, and the Problem of "Extended Sympathy"	449
	6.4	Rawls's "Original Position" and "Veil of Ignorance"	455
	6.5	Alternative Notions of Fairness	459
	6.6	Equality of Resources and Welfare	462
7		Concluding Comments	465
	References		467

11 Measures of Economic Welfare — 483
Michael Ahlheim

1		Introduction	484
2		Criteria for the Characterization of Welfare Measures	486
3		Welfare Measurement in a Comparative Static World	488
	3.1	Definitions	489
	3.2	Functional Welfare Measures	495
	3.3	Atomistic Welfare Measures	512
	3.4	Index Measures	515
4		Welfare Measurement with Quantity Constraints	526
	4.1	Definitions	527
	4.2	Measuring Welfare	531
5		Intertemporal Aspects	537
6		Further Topics	543

6.1   Public Goods   543
6.2   Uncertainty   553
6.3   Aggregation   555
References   558

12 Changing Utility Functions   569
Hersh Shefrin

1   Introduction and Outline   569
2   Historical Development   571
3   The Discounted Utility Model   573
4   A Changing Tastes Model   574
5   Hyperbolic Discounting   578
6   Dynamic Consistency as Nash Equilibrium   582
7   Existence and Indifference   590
8   Welfare Implications   594
9   Endogenously Changing Utility Functions   596
10   Changing Tastes and Consumer Theory   599
11   Uncertainty   603
12   Prospect Theory   607
13   Self–Control, Willpower, and Rules   612
14   Concluding Remarks   619
References   623

13 Causal Decision Theory   627
James M. Joyce and Allan Gibbard

1   Introduction   628
2   Dominance and Expected Utility: Two Versions   630
3   Conditionals and their Probabilities   634
4   Ratificationism   642
5   Ratificationism and Causality in the Theory of Games   645
6   Foundational Questions   656
7   Conclusion   663
References   664

Subject Index   667

Name Index   677

Preface

The standard rationality hypothesis is that behaviour can be represented as the maximization of a suitably restricted utility function. This hypothesis lies at the heart of a large body of recent work in economics, of course, but also in political science, ethics, and other major branches of social science. Though this utility maximization hypothesis is venerable, it remains an area of active research. Moreover, some fundamental conceptual problems remain unresolved, or at best have resolutions that are too recent to have achieved widespread understanding among social scientists.

The main purpose of this *Handbook* is to make more widely available some recent developments in the area. The editors selected a number of specific topics, and invited contributions from people whose work had come to our attention. So the list of topics and contributors is largely the editors' responsibility, although some potential contributors did decline our invitation. Each contributor's chapter has also been refereed, and often significantly revised in the light of the referees' remarks.

This is the first volume of what is intended as a complementary pair. Topics which we expect to be included in Volume II are:

14   Alternatives to Expected Utility: Foundations and Concepts
15   Alternatives to Expected Utility: Some Formal Theories
16   State Dependent Utility
17   Extending Preferences to Sets of Alternatives
18   Utility as a Tool in Non–Cooperative Game Theory
19   Utility as a Tool in Cooperative Game Theory
20   Utility in Social Choice
21   Interpersonal Comparisons of Utility
22   Experimental and Empirical Research I: Riskless Utility
23   Experimental and Empirical Research II: Utility under Risk
24   Experimental and Empirical Research III: Utility under Ambiguity
25   Utility Theory in Retrospect

With a couple of exceptions, the book has been prepared from LaTeX input files prepared by the contributors themselves. Authors also suggested what should be included in the index. We started by using Kluwer style files but, as the work proceeded, adapted these to determine the general appearance of each chapter, including equation numbering and the bibliography format. Other details — notably the numbering of theorems, etc. — have been left to the authors' own discretion.

It remains our pleasant duty to thank, apart from the contributors and referees, a number of other people who have made this volume possible. Especially Zachary Rolnik of Kluwer Academic Publishers for his encouragement as we have worked on this project and his patience while we have repeatedly exceeded estimates of the time we would need to complete it. We are also grateful to Christian Seidl's team of able secretaries and assistants at the Institut für Finanzwissenschaft und Sozialpolitik at the University of Kiel, first and foremost to Jens Kintrup, who wrote new macros and worked day and night during the final stages of processing the manuscripts, but also to Gabriele Rahn, Stefan Traub, Sonja Witthöft, Bärbel Habeck, Veronika Grimm, Eileen Kücükkaraca, Felix Streitferdt, and Marco Bach, whose engangement in the administration of this project and the processing of the text made it all possible.

1 PREFERENCE AND UTILITY

Ghanshyam B. Mehta

University of Queensland

Contents

1 Introduction   2

2 Preliminaries on Order and Topology   4

3 Existence of a Utility Function   9

4 Existence of a Continuous Utility Function on Euclidean Spaces   10

5 Debreu's Gap Lemma and the Existence of a Continuous Utility
   Function on Totally Preordered Topological Spaces   17

6 Existence of a Continuous Utility Function on Partially Ordered
   Topological Spaces   24

7 The Urysohn–Nachbin Approach to Continuous Utility Func-
   tions   26

8 Miscellaneous Topics on Utility Functions   30

   8.1 Continuous Utility Functions on Infinite Dimensional
        Spaces   30

   8.2 Utility Representations for Interval Orders   32

   8.3 Differentiable Utility Functions   34

   8.4 Jointly Continuous Utility Functions   36

   8.5 Existence of a Utility Function with Values in a Lexi-
        cographic Product   37

References   38

1

1   Introduction

The objective of this article is to study the problem of preference and utility. This problem has a long, complicated and controversial history. In a sense, it is as old as economics itself. Even at the present time there is no agreement among economists about the "real" meaning of "utility" and the way in which it should be defined.

In this article, we avoid these untoward problems by *defining* preference to be a mathematical relation on a set X. We do not ask about the social or individualistic origins of the preference relation but take it as being given. In a sense this is not a satisfactory procedure because from a philosophical point of view it is by no means obvious that preference relations "exist". Nevertheless, this is what we do because our primary objective is to examine the relationship between preference and utility and not to conduct an ontological and episte-mological study of the "real" meaning of preference. In the same spirit, we do not define "utility". Instead we *define* a utility function f as being an order-preserving function on a set X endowed with a relation R, i.e. we think of f as an order-homomorphism in the sense that it preserves the relational structure R on X.

On both economic and mathematical grounds [see, for example, Chipman (1960)] it may be preferable to consider utility functions with values in some ordered set Y. However, for reasons that are not entirely clear, most economists have traditionally only dealt with the special case in which the codomain Y of the utility function is the real line $\mathbb{R}$ with the natural ordering. This may have something to do with the fact that the general case is difficult to handle from a mathematical point of view. In any event, we will assume in this article, unless there is an explicit statement to the contrary, that the codomain of any utility function is the real line $\mathbb{R}$ with the natural ordering. Therefore, a utility function for us will mean a real-valued order preserving function on an ordered set X.

The fundamental problem with which this article is concerned is that of finding general conditions for the existence (and non-existence) of a real-valued (continuous, differentiable) utility representation on an ordered set X.

We now comment very briefly on the historical origin of the concepts of preference and utility in economics. In an inchoate and nebulous sense these concepts are implicit in Smith's *The Wealth of Nations*, which is considered by some historians as the first scientific work in economics. The first explicit and systematic use of the concept of utility to explain value of commodities is to be found in the classical *Theory of Political Economy* by Jevons in 1871. But Jevons did not distinguish between preference and utility, at least not explicitly. The credit for seeing the difference between the two and for observing that in some sense the concept of preference is more primitive is due to Pareto (1971) who in his *Manual of Political Economy* developed a sophisticated apparatus for studying this problem. Pareto observes (p. 119) that Edgeworth assumes "utility" and derives an indifference curve from it. In contrast to Edgeworth, Pareto does not start with utility or what he calls ophelimity. Instead he proceeds as follows [see Pareto (1971), appendix]. Let (x_0, y_0) be a fixed commodity bundle. Consider variations in the first coordinate. For each x different from x_0 let y be a point such that (x, y) is equivalent (in some primitive sense since at this stage we do not have the concept of ophelimity) to (x_0, y_0). Pareto says that this correspondence defines a function $y = f_0(x)$. We may call this the "indifference function" corresponding to the initial point (x_0, y_0). We then take another point (x_1, y_1) not on the graph of this "indifference function" and repeat the reasoning to get another such function f_1 and so on. Now to each such function f_d we may wish to assign what Pareto calls an "index of ophelimity". These indices have the property (p. 119) that any two points on the graph of the same function are given the same index of ophelimity and (a, b) on the graph of one indifference function is assigned a higher index than (c, d) on the graph of another indifference function if and only if the former point is strictly preferred to the latter point.

It is clear from the above brief description that Pareto clearly distinguishes between preference and utility. But Pareto does not see that the assignment of indices of ophelimity to the graphs of indifference functions is a highly nontrivial problem. The reason for this perhaps lies in the fact that Pareto is keen on showing that the results of demand theory do not depend upon the precise definition of ophelimity. His animadversions upon other economists for being so concerned with the meaning of ophelimity prevented him from seeing that the problem of assigning indices of ophelimity to the graphs of indifference functions is an important problem. The solution of this problem requires one to state precisely certain axioms (or conditions) that preference has to satisfy which guarantee that one can assign indices of ophelimity to the graphs of indifference functions.

This crucial step was undertaken in a fundamental paper of Wold (1943–44). Wold lists axioms for a preference relation and then proves that every preference relation that satisfies the axioms has a real-valued continuous utility representation. Further fundamental progress was made in the classical paper of Debreu (1954). Just as Pareto and Wold did before him, Debreu clearly distinguishes between preference and utility. To underscore the distinction between the two, Debreu even gives an example of a preference relation (the so-called lexicographic preference relation) which does not have a utility representation. This was an important contribution to the subject because even as late as the nineteen fifties many economists did not distinguish clearly between preference and utility. As an example of the confusion that prevailed at that time we may cite Hicks (1956, p. 19) who states that "if a set of items is strongly ordered, it is such that each item has a place of its own in the order; it could, in principle, be given a number". Hicks (1956, pp. 39-40) also states that "a two-dimensional continuum of points cannot be strongly ordered" because $\mathbb{R}^2$ has two dimensions and the real line is one–dimensional!

2   Preliminaries on Order and Topology

NOTATION We will use the logical symbol $\neg$ for negation.

Since 'preference' is a relation on a set X we start by studying relations and their properties. For proofs and further discussion of relations we refer the reader to Bridges and Mehta (1995, Chapter 1) and Roberts (1979). For topological concepts the books by Croom (1989) and Kelley (1955) are recommended.

DEFINITION 2.1 A relation R on a set X is said to be:

1. reflexive if xRx for all x in X;
2. irreflexive if $\neg(xRx)$ for all x in X;
3. symmetric if xRy implies that yRx for all x, y in X:
4. asymmetric if xRy implies $\neg(yRx)$ for all x, y in X;
5. transitive if xRy and yRz imply that xRz for all x, y, z in X;
6. antisymmetric if xRy and yRx imply that $x = y$ for all x, y in X.
7. negatively transitive if $\neg(xRy)$ and $\neg(yRz)$ imply that $\neg(xRz)$ for all x, y, z in X;
8. weakly connected if for all $x \neq y$, either xRy or yRx;
9. connected if for all x, y in X either xRy or yRx;

NOTATION We will use the symbol '$\precsim$' for reflexive relations and the symbol '$\prec$' for irreflexive relations. The reader is warned that some authors do not follow this practice.

DEFINITION 2.2 A relation R on a set X is an *equivalence relation* if it is reflexive, symmetric and transitive.

DEFINITION 2.3 A *preorder* on a set X is a reflexive transitive relation on X. An antisymmetric preorder is called a *partial order*.

A preorder $\precsim$ on a set X gives rise in a natural way to new relations in the following way. If $x, y \in X$ then $x \sim y$ if and only if $x \precsim y$ and $y \precsim x$. The relation $\sim$ is easily seen to be an equivalence relation on X. If $x, y \in X$ then

$x \prec y$ if and only if $x \precsim y$ and $\neg(y \precsim x)$. The relation $\prec$ is irreflexive and transitive. The relation $\prec$ is called the strict part of the relation $\precsim$.

DEFINITION 2.4 A connected preorder on a set X is called a *total* (or *complete* or *linear*) preorder. An asymmetric, transitive and weakly connected relation is called a *strict total order*. An asymmetric negatively transitive relation is said to be a *strict weak order*.

There is a connection between total preorders and strict weak orders. Suppose that $\precsim$ is a total preorder on X. Then the relation $\prec$ induced on X by $\precsim$ is a strict weak order. Conversely suppose that $\prec$ is a strict weak order on X. Define a new relation $\precsim$ on X as follows: if $x, y \in X$ then $x \precsim y$ if and only if either $x \prec y$ or if ($\neg(x \prec y)$ and $\neg(y \prec x)$). Then this relation $\precsim$ on X is a total preorder on X.

DEFINITION 2.5 *A strict partial order* on a set X is an irreflexive and transitive relation on X.

A preference on a set X may be formalized either as a reflexive relation or an irreflexive relation. Suppose that we define a preference relation on a set X to be a preorder $\precsim$ on X. Then it is clear that two points x, y in X are defined to be indifferent if $x \sim y$. On the other hand, suppose that a preference relation is defined to be a strict partial order $\prec$ on X. Then two points x, y are defined to be indifferent if $\neg(x \prec y)$ and $\neg(y \prec x)$. In the former case, the points x and y are indifferent if both (x, y) and (y, x) belong to the relation. In the latter case, they are indifferent if neither (x, y) nor (y, x) belongs to the relation. In economics, there is no agreement among economists as to what "indifference" really means.

DEFINITION 2.6 Let $\precsim$ be a preorder on a set X. Then if $x \in X$ the set $\{ y \in X : y \precsim x \}$ is called the *lower section* (or *lower contour set*) of x. The set $\{ y \in X : x \precsim y \}$ is called the *upper section* (or *upper contour set*) of x. If $\prec$ is a strict partial order on X then in an analogous manner we define the *strict lower sections* and *strict upper sections* of points in X.

Our next objective is to define order–separability conditions in preordered sets and related concepts. We begin with the following definitions.

DEFINITION 2.7 Let $(X, \precsim)$ be a preordered set.

1. The preorder $\precsim$ is said to be *order–separable in the sense of Cantor* if there exists a countable subset Z with the property that for each $x \prec y$ in X there exists $z \in Z$ such that $x \prec z \prec y$.

2. The preorder $\precsim$ is said to be *order–separable in the sense of Debreu* if there exists a countable subset Z with the property that for each $x \prec y$ in X there exists $z \in Z$ such that $x \precsim z \precsim y$.

3. The preorder $\precsim$ is said to be *order–separable in the sense of Jaffray* (or Herden–Jaffray) if there exists a countable subset Z with the property that for each $x \prec y$ in X there exist $z_1, z_2 \in Z$ such that $x \precsim z_1 \prec z_2 \precsim y$.

4. The preorder $\precsim$ is said to be *order–separable in the sense of Birkhoff* if there exists a countable subset Z with the property that for each x, y in $X \setminus Z$ there exists $z \in Z$ such that $x \prec z \prec y$.

In each of these cases, we say that the subset Z is *order–dense* in X in the relevant sense.

It can be proved that if the preorder $\precsim$ is total, then Debreu order-separability is equivalent to Jaffray order-separability. Observe also that if a preorder is order–separable in the sense of Cantor then it is surely order–separable in the sense of Debreu. However, the converse is false. For example, the set of natural numbers with the usual ordering is Debreu order–separable but not Cantor order–separable.

Suppose now that $\prec$ is a strict partial order on X. Define a preorder $\precsim$ on X by declaring $x \precsim y$ in X if and only if either $x \prec y$ or if $x = y$. The preorder $\precsim$ on X defined in this way is clearly the smallest preorder on X that contains the original strict partial order. It is called its reflexive closure. We say that a strict partial order $\prec$ on X is order–separable in one of the senses given above if its reflexive closure is order–separable in that sense.

DEFINITION 2.8 Let $(X, \precsim)$ be a preordered set. A subset F is said to be *decreasing* if $a \in F$ and $b \precsim a$ imply that $b \in F$. Each subset K of X determines uniquely the smallest decreasing subset containing it. This set is denoted by $d(K)$. In an analogous manner one defines an *increasing set* and the smallest increasing subset $i(K)$ containing a subset K.

We introduce now some concepts of topology.

DEFINITION 2.9 Let X be a set and let $\mathcal{T}$ be a family of subsets of X satisfying the following conditions:
(a) The set X and the empty set $\emptyset$ belong to $\mathcal{T}$.
(b) The intersection of any finite family of members of $\mathcal{T}$ is a member of $\mathcal{T}$.
(c) The union of any family of members of $\mathcal{T}$ is a member of $\mathcal{T}$.
Then $\mathcal{T}$ is called a *topology* for X and the members of $\mathcal{T}$ are called *open sets*. The pair $(X, \mathcal{T})$ is called a *topological space*. In general, a set X has many topologies. If only one topology is being considered then we may write "X is a topological space", omitting mention of the topology.

DEFINITION 2.10 Let $(X, \mathcal{T})$ be a topological space and A a subset of X. The *relative* or *subspace topology* β for A determined by $\mathcal{T}$ consists of all sets of the form $U \cap A$ where U is a member of $\mathcal{T}$. The set A with the topology β is said to be a *topological subspace* of $(X, \mathcal{T})$

DEFINITION 2.11 Let $(X, \mathcal{T})$ be a topological space. A subfamily $\mathcal{B}$ of $\mathcal{T}$ is said to be a *basis* for $\mathcal{T}$ if for each U in $\mathcal{T}$ and $x \in U$ there exists V in $\mathcal{B}$ such that $x \in V \subset U$. A topological space $(X, \mathcal{T})$ is said to be *second countable* if it has a *countable basis*.

Consider, for example, the Cartesian space $\mathbb{R}^n$. For each $x \in \mathbb{R}^n$ and $r > 0$, let $B(x, r) = \{ y \in \mathbb{R}^n : d(x, y) < r \}$ be the open ball of radius r and center x where d is the usual metric on $\mathbb{R}^n$. Let $\mathcal{T}$ be the family of subsets of $\mathbb{R}^n$ with the property that for each U in $\mathcal{T}$ and $x \in U$ there exists $B(x, r)$ such that $x \in B(x, r) \subset U$. Then it may be verified that $\mathcal{T}$ is a topology for $\mathbb{R}^n$ which has a countable basis consisting of open balls with rational centres and rational radii.

DEFINITION 2.12 A subset Z of a topological space X is *dense* in X if for each non–empty open set U there exists $z \in Z$ such that $z \in U$. A topological space X is said to be *separable* if it has a countable dense subset.

The real line $\mathbb{R}$ is separable because the countable set of rational numbers is dense in $\mathbb{R}$. In fact, every second countable topological space is separable. Furthermore, every subspace of a second countable space is second countable.

DEFINITION 2.13 A topological space X is *connected* if it is not the disjoint union of two non–empty open subsets A and B.

For example, the space $X = \mathbb{R} \setminus \{0\}$ is not connected. It can be proved that the unit interval $[0, 1]$ is connected!

DEFINITION 2.14 Let K be a subset of a topological space X. An *open cover* of K is a collection $\mathcal{O}$ of open sets whose union contains K. A *subcover* derived from an open cover $\mathcal{O}$ is a subcollection $\mathcal{O}'$ of $\mathcal{O}$ whose union contains K. A topological space X is *compact* if every open cover has a finite subcover.

DEFINITION 2.15 A subset F of a topological space X is *closed* if its complement $X \setminus F$ is open. Let K be an arbitrary subset of X. Then the smallest closed set containing K is called the *closure* of K and is denoted by cl K.

DEFINITION 2.16 A subset K of $\mathbb{R}^n$ is *bounded* if there exists $r > 0$ such that $K \subset B(0, r)$. In $\mathbb{R}^n$ one has the following important characterization of compact sets [Bartle, (1974, p. 85)].

THEOREM 2.17 [Heine–Borel] A subset K of $\mathbb{R}^n$ is compact if and only if it is closed and bounded.

Now we consider the relationship between order and topology on a set X.

DEFINITION 2.18 Let $(X, \mathcal{T})$ be a topological space and $\precsim$ a preorder on X. The preorder is said to be $\mathcal{T}$–*continuous* if for each $x \in X$ the sets $\{y \in X : x \precsim y\}$ and $\{y \in X : y \precsim x\}$ are $\mathcal{T}$–closed in X. Such a topology is also called a *natural topology* and is said to be compatible with the preorder. In general, there is no relationship between a preorder and a topology on a space. However, there is one topology that is inherently connected with a total preorder. It is called the order topology.

DEFINITION 2.19 Let $\precsim$ be a total preorder on a set X. Consider the family of order–intervals of X of the form $\{x \in X : a \prec x \prec b\}$, $\{x \in X : m \precsim x \prec b\}$ if m is the smallest element of X, $\{x \in X : a \prec x \precsim n\}$ if n is the largest element of X, where a, b are arbitrary elements of X. This family of sets is a basis for a topology on X called the *order topology* with respect to the total preorder. Clearly, the order topology is the one naturally induced by the preorder. It is the coarsest natural topology on X.

We now define the important concept of an order–homomorphism.

DEFINITION 2.20 Let (A, R) and (B, S) be two sets with binary relations R and S defined on them. Then a function $f : A \to B$ is said to be an *order homomorphism* if $x, y \in A$ and xRy imply that $f(x)Sf(y)$. A function $f : A \to B$ is said to be an *order monomorphism* (or *order embedding* or *order isomorphism*) if xRy is equivalent to $f(x)Sf(y)$. A bijective order isomorphism is sometimes also called a *similarity mapping*.

DEFINITION 2.21 Let R be a partial (total) preference relation on a set X. Then a *utility function* on X is a real–valued order homomorphism (order monomorphism) on X. A utility function on a topological space $(X, \mathcal{T})$ is *continuous* if the inverse image $f^{-1}(U)$ is $\mathcal{T}$–open in X for every open set U of real numbers.

3   Existence of a Utility Function

In this section we derive necessary and sufficient conditions for the existence of a utility function on a totally preordered set X. Recall that such a set is Jaffray order–separable if and only if it is order–separable in the sense of Debreu. Therefore we may use any one of these conditions of order–separability in the theorem below. We now show that there is a utility function on a totally preordered set X if and only if it is Jaffray order–separable.

THEOREM 3.1 Let $(X, \precsim)$ be a totally preordered set. Then the following are equivalent:

1. There exists a utility function on X.
2. X is Jaffray order–separable.

PROOF Suppose first that f is a utility function on X. For all pairs of rational numbers (p_i, q_i) $(i = 1, 2, \dots)$ such that $p_i < q_i$ for all i, let $A_i = \{ x \in X : f(x) \le p_i \}$ and $B_i = \{ x \in X : q_i \le f(x) \}$. Let G be the set consisting of the smallest element and the greatest element (if any) of X. For each pair of rationals $p_i < q_i$ let M_i be the set of all points x in X such that $p_i < f(x) < q_i$. For each M_i that is nonempty pick an element $x \in M_i$. Let H be the union of all such points. Then H is clearly countable and it is not hard to check that $Z = G \cup H$ is Jaffray order–dense in X.

Conversely, suppose that Z is a countable Jaffray order–dense subset of X. We may write $Z = \{ z_1, z_2, \dots \}$. For each $i \in \mathbb{N}$ let $A_i = \{ x \in X : x \precsim z_i \}$ and $B_i = \{ x \in X : z_i \precsim x \}$. Observe that for each i the set A_i is decreasing and the set B_i is increasing. Now define for each $i \in \mathbb{N}$ an isotone function f_i on X with values in the unit interval $[0, 1]$ by $f_i(x) = 0$ if $x \in X \setminus B_i$ and $f_i(x) = 1$ if $x \in B_i$ for all $x \in X$. Since Z is Jaffray order–separable the function $f = \sum_{i=1}^{\infty} 2^{-i} f_i$ is clearly a utility function on X. ∎

EXAMPLE 3.2 [Debreu (1954)] On $X = \mathbb{R}^2$ define a lexicographic relation as follows. For $x, y \in X$, $x \precsim y$ if $x_1 \le y_1$ or if $x_1 = y_1$ and $x_2 \le y_2$. Observe that for each real number r, the line $x_1 = r$ has a non–trivial order interval of the form (a, b). Therefore, X is not Jaffray order–separable because there are uncountably many such lines. It follows from Theorem 3.1 that X has no utility representation.

For further discussion of lexicographic relations the reader is referred to Candeal and Induráin (1996).

4   Existence of a Continuous Utility Function on Euclidean Spaces

In the preceding section we derived necessary and sufficient conditions for a preference relation to have a utility representation. In many applications one wants to have continuous utility functions. For example, if a consumer has a continuous utility function defined over a compact budget set then one can apply the classical theorem of Weierstrass to conclude that the utility maximization problem has a solution.

In this section we study two classical methods for proving the existence of continuous utility functions on subsets of finite dimensional Euclidean spaces. The first approach is due to Wold (1943–44) and is based on a weak monotonicity assumption on the preference relation. The second approach is due to Arrow and Hahn (1971) and is based on a local non–satiation assumption.

Let us first consider the Wold approach. The characteristic feature of Wold's approach is his use of the weak monotonicity assumption which is defined as follows. But first we need the following notation for vector inequalities in $\mathbb{R}^n$.

NOTATION Let x, y be two points in $\mathbb{R}^n$. We write $x \leq y$ to denote that $x_i \leq y_i$ for all $i = 1, 2, \ldots$. We write $x < y$ to denote that $x \leq y$ and for some $i, x_i < y_i$. We write $x \ll y$ to denote that $x_i < y_i$ for all i.

DEFINITION 4.1 Let $\precsim$ be a total preorder on a subset X of $\mathbb{R}^n$. Then the preorder is said to be *weakly monotonic* if $x < y$ in $\mathbb{R}^n$ implies that y is not strictly worse than x or equivalently if $x \precsim y$. The preorder is said to be *monotonic* if $x < y$ in $\mathbb{R}^n$ implies that x is strictly worse than y, i.e. $x \prec y$.

REMARK 4.2 Observe that a monotonic relation is weakly monotonic but not conversely.

Wold assumes that there is a preference relation that is reflexive, transitive, total, continuous and weakly monotonic. Wold's procedure of listing axioms for a preference relation constituted a decisive step forwards, as has been explained in the introduction, because it implies a realization that the connection between preference and utility is not trivial.

Contrary to what has been supposed in the literature [see Beardon and Mehta (1994b)] Wold only assumes weak monotonicity. Furthermore the difference between weak monotonicity and monotonicity is of great importance as is explained in Beardon and Mehta (1994b). We will return to this point later.

Our objective now is to give a proof of the existence of a continuous utility function using Wold's approach. Since we want to give a *simple* proof we use the monotonicity assumption. In this way we can explain the main ideas of the proof without introducing complications. We will return to the general Wold approach later when we use it to give an elementary proof of the Debreu Gap Lemma.

Before stating the theorem and giving the proof it would be helpful if we describe intuitively the basic ideas involved. Assume that X is the nonnegative orthant of $\mathbb{R}^n$ and that there is a reflexive, transitive, total, continuous and monotonic preference relation defined on it. Let D be the image of the diagonal embedding of the real line in $\mathbb{R}^n$ (what economists call "the 45° line"). The assumption of monotonicity enables one to "create a picture" of the preference relation in D in the sense that as one moves along D from the origin one passes through all levels of preference. The continuity assumption implies that for each $x \in X$ there is at least one point, say $d(x)$, on D such that $x \sim d(x)$ and by monotonicity we may conclude that there is at most one such point. Now the utility of x is defined to be the Euclidean distance from the origin to the point $d(x)$. This is a very natural definition of the utility of a bundle x.

In what follows we present a generalization of this argument. Instead of assuming, like Wold, that preference is strictly increasing along D, we assume that there is a differentiable curve in X along which preference is increasing and we define utility to be the distance along this curve. This generalization does not require any change in the structure of the argument. One advantage of this approach is that we do not have to assume that X is the nonnegative orthant.

DEFINITION 4.3 A *path* $f = (f_1, f_2, \ldots, f_n)$ in a subset X of $\mathbb{R}^n$ is a continuous vector–valued function on an open interval $I = (a, b)$ with values in X. A path $f : I \to \mathbb{R}^n$ is said to be *differentiable* if each component function $f_i, i = 1, 2, \ldots$ is differentiable. The image of the path is said to be the *curve* described by f. The curve described by a path f is said to be a *Jordan arc* if $s \neq t$ implies that $f(s) \neq f(t)$. A path $f : I \to \mathbb{R}^n$ is said to be *regular* if its derivative $f'(t) \neq 0$ for all $t \in I$.

DEFINITION 4.4 Suppose that $f : I \to \mathbb{R}^n$ is a path and $[a, b]$ is a finite closed subinterval of I. Let $P = \{ a = x_0 < x_1 < \ldots < x_n = b \}$ be a partition of $[a, b]$. Then the length of the polygonal path joining the points $f(x_i), i = 0, 1, \ldots, n$ in that order is given by $\ell(P) = \sum_{i=1}^{n} \|f(x_i) - f(x_{i-1})\|$. The *arc–length* of f from $x = a$ to $x = b$ is defined to be the supremum of $\ell(P)$ over all partitions P of $[a, b]$.

It can be proved that if f is a differentiable path the arc–length of f from $x = a$ to $x = b$ is given by the following integral: $\int_a^b \|f'(t)\| dt$ [Rudin, 1976, p. 136)]. Suppose now that $f : I \to \mathbb{R}^n$ is a differentiable path.

We say that a differentiable path $g : J \to \mathbb{R}^n$ is a *reparametrization* of f if there exists a differentiable strictly monotonic function $h : J \to I$ such that $g(s) = f(h(s))$ for $s \in J$.

THEOREM 4.5 Let X be a subset of $\mathbb{R}^n$, $\precsim$ a weak preference relation on X and $f : I \to X$ a regular differentiable path in X such that the following conditions are satisfied:

1. (Continuity) R is a continuous total preorder;
2. (Path monotonicity) If $s < t$ are in I then $f(s) \prec f(t)$.
3. (Bounding condition) For each $x \in X$, there exist $a, b \in I$ such that $f(a) \precsim x \precsim f(b)$.

Then there exists a continuous utility function on X.

PROOF Let C be the curve described by f. Choose a point $x_0 \in C$. We first prove the existence of a continuous utility function on the upper section $B(x_0)$ of x_0.

For $x \in B(x_0)$, let $A^x = \{ y \in B(x_0) : y \precsim x \}$ and $A_x = \{ y \in B(x_0) : x \precsim y \}$. The set A^x is nonempty because $x \in B(x_0)$ and the set A_x is nonempty because of the bounding condition 3. The sets A^x and A_x are closed in $B(x_0)$ for every x by the continuity condition 1. Since f is continuous the curve described by f in $B(x_0)$ is connected. Hence, there exists a point z in the intersection of the sets A^x and A_x. This implies that for each $x \in B(x_0)$ there exists $d(x) \in C$ such that $x \sim d(x)$. The curve $f(I)$ is a Jordan arc by the monotonicity condition 2 whence we may conclude that there is exactly one $m_x \in I$ such that $f(m_x) = d(x)$.

Let t_0 be the unique point in I such that $f(t_0) = x_0$. Consider now the arc–length function $s(t) = \int_{t_0}^{t} ||f'(u)|| du$. Then since the path f is regular, the derivative $\frac{ds}{dt} = ||f'(t)|| \neq 0$. Therefore the arc–length function has a differentiable inverse $t = h(s)$ with $h' > 0$ defined on some interval J. It follows that the path $g : J \to \mathbb{R}^n$ given by $g(s) = f(h(s))$ for $s \in J$ is a reparametrization of the path f.

Now define a real–valued function U on $B(x_0)$ by

$$U(x) = s(m_x) = \int_{t_0}^{m_x} ||f'(u)|| du$$

and observe that the arc–length of the path g from $s(t_0)$ to $s(m_x)$ is just $s(m_x)$ [O'Neill (1966, p. 52)]. It follows [Apostol (1957, pp. 164 and 176)] that the integral is finite. Therefore the function U is well–defined. To prove that U is a utility function let $x, y \in B(x_0)$ and suppose that $x \precsim y$. Then $x \sim f(m_x)$ and $y \sim f(m_y)$ for some m_x, m_y in I. Since $x \precsim y$ we have

$m_x \leq m_y$ by monotonicity whence $U(x) \leq U(y)$. If $x \prec y$ then $m_x < m_y$ again by monotonicity which implies that $U(x) < U(y)$ since the arc–length of a Jordan arc is strictly increasing [Apostol (1957), p. 177)]. We have therefore proved that U is a utility function on $B(x_0)$.

We prove next that U is continuous on $B(x_0)$. Let r be a real number. Then if $\sup\{ U(z) : z \in B(x_0) \} \leq r$, the set $\{ x \in B(x_0) : U(x) \leq r \} = B(x_0)$ and if $r \leq \inf\{ U(z) : z \in B(x_0) \}$ and r is not in the image of U the set $\{ x \in B(x_0) : U(x) \leq r \} = \emptyset$. In either case the set $U^{-1}(-\infty, r]$ is closed in $B(x_0)$. If $r \in U[B(x_0)]$, there exists $z \in B(x_0)$ such that $U(z) = r$. Then $U^{-1}(-\infty, r] = \{ x \in B(x_0) : x \precsim z \}$ which is closed in $B(x_0)$ by the continuity condition. This proves that U is a lower semicontinuous function. Similarly, one proves that U is upper semicontinuous by showing that sets of the form $U^{-1}[r, \infty)$ are closed in $B(x_0)$ for every real number r. We have proved that U is a continuous function on $B(x_0)$.

If X has a smallest element then we can choose x_0 to be that element and the theorem is proved. Suppose now that X does not have a smallest element. In that case, the utility function has only been defined on a proper subset of X. To obtain a continuous utility function on the whole space we proceed as follows. Let $y \in F = \{ a \in X : a \precsim x_0 \}$. For each such y, let $V(y) = - \int_{t_0}^{m_y} \|f'(u)\| \, du$. Arguing as before, we see that V is a continuous utility function on F. Now U and V are two continuous functions on subsets of a topological space X and they agree on the intersection of their domains (both are zero on this set). Therefore, the function g on X defined by $g(x) = U(x)$ if $x \in B(x_0)$ and $g(x) = V(x)$ if $x \in F$ is a continuous function by the Glueing Lemma [Croom (1989, p. 151)]. The function g is the required continuous utility function on X and the theorem is proved. ∎

REMARK 4.6   (a) It should be observed that the theorem not only asserts the existence of a continuous utility function. The proof shows that the utility function can be defined in terms of arc–length along a curve and this arc–length is itself defined in terms of the Euclidean norm. This is a particularly appealing feature of the Wold approach.

(b) Assume that $X = \mathbb{R}_+^n$ and that the curve described by the path f is the diagonal D in X. Then we have a special case of Theorem 4.5 that is frequently cited in this form in the literature and is called Wold's theorem. The reader may verify for herself that in this case the conditions of Theorem 4.5 are indeed satisfied.

(c) Some authors [for example, Aubin (1979) and Aliprantis, Brown and Burkinshaw (1989)] have proved a special case of the theorem by assuming that the function f describes a ray from the origin. Clearly, this is also a special case of the above theorem.

We turn now to the discussion of the Arrow–Hahn approach [Arrow and Hahn (1971)]. In this approach, X is assumed to be any closed convex subset of $\mathbb{R}^n$. Instead of the monotonicity assumption, Arrow and Hahn use a local non–satiation assumption which is defined as follows.

DEFINITION 4.7 A preference relation $\precsim$ on a subset X of $\mathbb{R}^n$ is said to be *locally non–satiated* if for each $x \in X$ and each open ball $B(x, r)$ with center x there is $y \in B(x, r)$ such that $x \prec y$.

The assumption of local non–satiation rules out "thick" indifference sets. A monotonic preference relation is clearly locally non–satiated but not conversely. Observe, however, that weak monotonicity does not imply local non–satiation.

The intuitive idea of the Arrow–Hahn proof is as follows. Since the relation is not monotonic, the Wold method does not work. Instead Arrow and Hahn proceed as follows. Let x_0 be an arbitrary point in X. A function U is defined on the upper section of this point by letting $U(x)$ to be equal to the Euclidean distance between the point x_0 and the upper section of x. Then this function U is shown to be continuous. Finally an extension procedure is used to define a utility function on the whole space X.

We now prove the following theorem in which we *generalize* the Arrow–Hahn method of proof by *defining* the utility of a point x as the Euclidean distance between a nonempty compact subset X_0 of X and the upper section of the point x. The advantage of using this method is explained below.

DEFINITION 4.8 Let K be a nonempty compact subset X of $\mathbb{R}^n$. The *upper section* of K, denoted by $C(K)$, is the set $\{ x \in X : k \precsim x$ for every $k \in K \}$. If $K = \{x\}$ we write $C(x)$ and not $C(\{x\})$.

DEFINITION 4.9 Let A, B be non–empty subsets of $\mathbb{R}^n$. If d denotes the usual metric of $\mathbb{R}^n$, the *distance* between the sets A and B is $d(A, B) = \inf\{ d(x, y) : x \in A$ and $y \in B \}$.

In the proof of the next theorem we use the following simple but important fact (Hu, 1979, p. 118).

PROPOSITION 4.10 Let A and B be non–empty compact subsets of $\mathbb{R}^n$. Then there exist points $a \in A$ and $b \in B$ such that $d(a, b) = d(A, B)$.

THEOREM 4.11 Let X be a closed convex subset of $\mathbb{R}^n$ and $\precsim$ a preference relation on X such that the following conditions are satisfied:

1. The preorder $\precsim$ is total and continuous
2. The preorder $\precsim$ is locally non–satiated.

Then there exists a continuous utility function on X.

PROOF Let X_0 be a nonempty compact subset of X. The first step is to prove the existence of a continuous utility function on $C(X_0)$ which is a closed subset of X. To this end, define a function U on $C(X_0)$ by $U(x) = d(X_0, C(x))$ for each $x \in C(X_0)$, where $d(x, y) = ||a - b||$ is the Euclidean distance. The function U is well–defined. Indeed, let $a \in X_0, b \in C(x)$ and $r = ||a - b||$. Define $K = \cup_{z \in X_0} B[z, r]$ where $B[z, r] = \{ y \in \mathbb{R}^n : d(z, y) \leq r \}$ is the closed ball around z of radius $r > 0$. Then K is compact because X_0 is compact. Furthermore, $K \cap C(x)$ is nonempty and compact. Hence, $d(X_0, C(x)) = d(X_0, K \cap C(x))$ which is well–defined. Thus U is well–defined and assigns to each point x the distance between two compact sets.

Now for each $x \in C(X_0)$, let $M(x) = \{ x' \in C(x) : U(x) = d(X_0, x') \}$. The set $M(x)$ is non–empty by Proposition 4.10. We claim that if $x' \in M(x)$ then $x \sim x'$. To prove this observe that clearly $x \precsim x'$. Suppose that $x \prec x'$. There exists a point $a \in X_0$ such that $d(a, x') \leq d(a, y)$ for every $y \in C(x)$. Consider the line segment $[a, x']$. If this line segment is degenerate then $a = x'$. Since $x \prec x'$ we have $x \prec a$ contradicting the fact that $x \in C(X_0)$ which implies that $a \precsim x$. This contradiction shows that the line segment $[a, x']$ is nondegenerate. Let $z_\lambda = \lambda a + (1 - \lambda)x'$. For small positive $\lambda, x \prec z_\lambda$ by the continuity of the preference relation. Hence, $z_\lambda \in C(x)$ and $d(X_0, z_\lambda) < d(X_0, x') = U(x)$ contradicting the definition of U. This contradiction proves that for each $x' \in M(x)$ we have $x \sim x'$. It is now easily verified that U is a utility function on $C(X_0)$.

We prove next that U is lower semicontinuous on $C(X_0)$. Let (x_n) be a sequence converging to x with $U(x_n) \leq u$ for some real number u. For each n, choose $z_n \in M(x_n)$. Then the sequence (z_n) is a bounded sequence. Therefore, it follows from the Bolzano–Weierstrass theorem [Bartle (1964, p. 76)] that the sequence (z_n) has a convergent subsequence. Without loss of generality we may assume that (z_n) converges to some point z. It is easy to verify that $d(X_0, z) \leq u$. It follows now from the continuity of the preference relation that $U(x) = U(z) \leq u$. Hence, U is lower semicontinuous.

Observe that the local non–satiation assumption has not been used in the proof so far. We now use this property to prove that U is upper semicontinuous on $C(X_0)$. So let (x_n) be a sequence in $C(X_0)$ converging to x such that $u \leq U(x_n)$ for some real number u. Choose $z \in M(x)$ and $z' \in C(x)$ such that $z \prec z'$. This is possible by the local non–satiation condition. Since the preference relation is continuous there exists N such that $x_n \prec z'$ for all $n \geq N$. Now $d(X_0, z') \geq U(z') > U(x_n) \geq u$.

Furthermore, by the local non–satiation condition we may conclude that there is a sequence (z_n) converging to z such that $z \prec z_n$ for all n. Also, the function $f(x) = d(X_0, x)$ is continuous [Hu, (1979, p. 116)]. Hence, $d(X_0, z_n) \to d(X_0, z) = U(z)$. Since for each n, $d(X_0, z_n) \geq u$, we conclude that $U(x) = U(z) = d(X_0, z) = d(X_0, C(z)) = \inf\{ d(X_0, y) : y \in C(z) \} \geq u$. Therefore, the function U is upper semicontinuous.

We have proved that there is a continuous utility function on the closed upper section $C(X_0)$. It remains to "extend" this function to the whole space.

Suppose that X has no smallest element because otherwise there is nothing further to be proved. Let Z be the set of all points in X with all coordinates rational numbers. Then Z is a countable dense set. We may write $Z = \{ z_1, z_2, \ldots \}$. Consider the family $\mathcal{F}$ of closed balls, where $\mathcal{F} = \{ B[z_i, \frac{1}{n}] : i = 1, 2, \ldots ; n = 1, 2, \ldots \}$. This family is countable. Now let $K_{i,n} = B[z_i, \frac{1}{n}] \cap X$. Then $\{ K_{i,n} = 1, 2, \ldots \}$ is a sequence of compact sets in X. We claim that for each $x \in X$ there exist positive integers i, n such that $x \in C(K_{i,n})$. To prove this let $x \in X$. Then $C(x)$ is closed in X by the continuity of $\precsim$. Hence, $X \setminus C(x)$ is a nonempty open subset of X. Since Z is dense in X there exist positive integers i, n such that $(B(z_i, \frac{1}{n}) \cap X) \subset (B[z_i, \frac{1}{n}] \cap X) \subset X \setminus C(x)$. This implies that $x \in C(K_{i,n})$ and completes the proof of the claim.

We now change the indexing of the family of compact sets considered above from $\{ K_{i,n} : n = 1, 2, \ldots \}$ to $\{ K_j : j = 1, 2, \ldots \}$. For each j, there exists a continuous utility function U_j on $C(K_j)$ by the earlier part of the proof. Since the real line is order homeomorphic to the unit interval we may assume without loss of generality that for each j the function U_j takes its values in $[0, 1]$. Now extend the function U_j to V_j on the whole space by defining $V_j(x) = U_j(x)$ if $x \in C(K_j)$ and $V_j(x) = U_j(z)$ if $x \notin C(K_j)$ where z is any point in $C(K_j)$ such that $U_j(z) \leq U_j(y)$ for all $y \in C(K_j)$. The function V_j is isotone and continuous on X by the Glueing Lemma [Croom, (1989, p. 151)].

Now define a function V on X by $V(x) = \sum_{j=1}^{\infty} 2^{-j} V_j(x)$ for each $x \in X$. The series of functions converges uniformly by Weierstrass's M-test. Therefore, the function V is continuous. Clearly, V is isotone. It remains to prove that V is strictly isotone. So let $x, y \in X$ such that $x \prec y$. Since the set $X \setminus C(x)$ is open there exists some j such that $x, y \in C(K_j)$. For this j, $U_j(x) < U_j(y)$, which implies that $V_j(x) < V_j(y)$ whence $V(x) < V(y)$ and the proof of the theorem is finished. ∎

REMARK 4.12   (a) Observe first that if we let $X_0 = \{x_0\}$ then as a special case we get the Arrow–Hahn construction of a utility function.

(b) In the theorem proved above, the utility of x is defined as the distance between a compact set X_0, which is not necessarily a singleton, and the upper section of x. This generalization of the Arrow–Hahn method is useful because it may be applied in understanding certain problems relating to the expenditure function $M(p, x)$ which is a very useful concept in microeconomics. This may be explained as follows. Let $p \gg 0$ be a fixed strictly positive price vector in $\mathbb{R}^n$. Let z be a least-cost commodity bundle at prices p. For each $x \in C(z)$, let $d(H(p), C(x))$ be the Euclidean distance between the hyperplane $H(p)$ containing z and the upper section $C(x)$ of x. Then $U(x) = d(H(p), C(x))$ may be regarded as a measure of the additional expenditure needed to buy a bundle that is at least good as x. It can be proved that the function U is a utility function similar to the utility functions of Wold and Arrow–Hahn [see Mehta, (1995)]. Observe, however, that in order to prove this one needs the full strength of the generalization of the Arrow–Hahn theorem proved above. The method used in the original Arrow–Hahn theorem is not sufficient for this purpose.

(c) In the proof above the utility function is defined in terms of Euclidean distance. In this respect, therefore, the Arrow–Hahn theorem and the theorem proved above share this appealing feature of the Wold approach to utility functions.

5   Debreu's Gap Lemma and the Existence of a Continuous Utility Function on Totally Preordered Topological Spaces

While the theorems proved in the previous section have intuitive appeal, in as much as they are defined explicitly in terms of Euclidean distance, they only apply to subsets of Euclidean spaces. Our objective in this section is to study the classical theorems on the existence of continuous utility functions on topological spaces due to Eilenberg (1941) and Debreu (1954, 1964).

There are, of course, several ways of proving these classical theorems. We will describe here one important approach that may be used to prove these theorems. This approach is based on the famous Gap Lemma and is due to Debreu.

We start by describing intuitively the essential ideas involved in Debreu's approach and his motivation for introducing the idea of a gap. Let S be a subset of the real line. Then a gap of S is a maximal nondegenerate interval (i.e. one that has at least two points) that is disjoint from S and has an upper bound and a lower bound in S.

What is the connection between a gap of a set S and utility functions? The answer is as follows. Consider a real–valued function defined on an interval $[a, b]$ and let c be an interior point of $[a, b]$. It is easy to construct a function

f that is strictly increasing on $[a, b]$ and which is discontinuous exactly at c. The reader is advised to draw a diagram at this point to convince herself of the argument. There is a jump discontinuity at c. Regardless of the way the function f is defined at c, observe that there is an half–open half–closed gap in the image $f([a, b])$ or two adjacent half–open half–closed gaps. So it would appear that a jump discontinuity produces a half-open half-closed gap. Now consider a strictly increasing function g defined on the domain $K = [1, 2] \cup [3, 4]$ such that g has constant slope 1 on [1,2] and constant slope 2 on [3,4]. Again the reader is advised to draw a diagram. Observe, now that there is an open gap in the image $g(K)$ and that the function g is continuous.

From these examples one is led to conjecture the following assertion: a strictly increasing function $f : \mathbb{R} \to \mathbb{R}$ is discontinuous if and only if there is some half–open half–closed gap in its image. One can prove that this is indeed true. It follows that if there is a strictly increasing real–valued function g defined on some subset S of the reals and $g(S)$ has no half–open half–closed gaps then g is continuous. This is the motivation underlying Debreu's concept of a gap. For further discussion, see Beardon (1994a) and Bridges and Mehta (1995, Chapter 3).

DEFINITION 5.1 Let S be an arbitrary subset of the real line. A *lacuna* of S is a nondegenerate interval (i.e. with at least two points) that is disjoint from S and has upper and lower bounds in S. A *gap* is a maximal lacuna.

Now we are in a position to give a precise statement of the Gap Lemma of Debreu.

LEMMA 5.2 (THE GAP LEMMA) Let S be an arbitrary subset of $\mathbb{R}$. Then there exists a strictly increasing function $g : \mathbb{R} \to \mathbb{R}$ such that all the gaps of $g(S)$ are open.

A variant of the Gap Lemma [see Beardon (1992, 1994a)] says that $g(S)$ has no half–open half–closed gaps. It is this version that we prove below.

The Gap Lemma has a very interesting history. It was first stated and "proved" in a classical paper by Debreu (1954). Debreu's idea for a proof is as follows. First, construct a strictly increasing function g on S. Now the image of g may have gaps of the form $(a, b]$ and $[a, b)$. We disregard the open gaps of the form (a, b) because they are "good gaps". We try to remove the other gaps by "sliding" the real line to the left by the length of the gap. For example, if there is only one gap of the form $(3, 5]$ then we subtract an amount equal to $(5 - 3)$ from points x such that $5 < x$. In this way, the "bad gaps" are removed. Now in simple cases (for example, if there are only finitely many gaps) this procedure does work. Unfortunately, the method does not work in general.

A problem arises, for example, when the image $g(S)$ of S is "small" and has Lebesgue measure zero. This problem was recognized by Debreu (1964) who gives a counterexample to show that his earlier proof is false and then gives a long, difficult but quite beautiful proof.

Subsequently, many other proofs of the Gap Lemma have been discovered. We describe some of them briefly here. Bowen (1968) gave a new proof of the lemma using concepts of measure theory. The idea of his proof is to "slide" the relevant set to the left by appropriate amounts and then "expand" what may have been "shrunk" to a subset of Lebesgue measure zero, so that injectivity is maintained. Another proof was given by Jaffray (1975). The idea of Jaffray's proof is to first define a generalization of Debreu's concept of a gap. Let Q be the set of rationals in $[0, 1]$ and consider a mapping f from a countable set A into Q. Suppose there are points $a, b \in A$ such that there is no point in the open order–interval $(f(a), f(b))$ that is also in the image under f of A. Then Jaffray calls such an order–interval a "gap". Roughly speaking, Jaffray proves that there is a mapping of a countable set A into Q that is strictly isotone and has the property that the image $f(A)$ has only open gaps in the Jaffray sense. This result may then be used to yield another proof of the Debreu Gap Lemma. Recently, Beardon (1992) has given a topological proof. The idea of Beardon's proof is first to construct a quotient space from $\mathbb{R}$ by defining a certain equivalence relation. This quotient space with the quotient topology is then shown to be homeomorphic to $\mathbb{R}$. This fact is then used to give another proof of the Gap Lemma.

Proofs of the Gap Lemma of Debreu have also been given by Droste (1987), Herden and Mehta (1996) and others.

Now all these proofs of the Gap Lemma are non–elementary in the sense that each one of them uses a non–trivial result from order theory or topology. Recently, a new proof of the Gap Lemma has been discovered by Beardon and Mehta (1994b). This proof is elementary in the sense that it does not use any difficult result from order theory or topology. It is based on Wold's method for constructing utility functions and uses only some elementary concepts from analysis. We now present this proof in two stages.

We first prove the following theorem due to Wold. We stress the fact that in the following theorem we are only using the weak monotonicity assumption and *not* the monotonicity assumption as we did in the preceding section.

NOTATION Suppose that x belongs to a preordered set X. Then we denote the $\sim$–equivalence class of x by $I(x)$.

THEOREM 5.3 Let $\precsim$ be a weakly monotonic total preorder on $[0,1]$ such that each $\sim$–equivalence class is a closed interval. Then there is an isotone function $u : [0,1] \to [0,1]$ such that $x \sim y$ if and only if $u(x) = u(y)$.

PROOF As in Wold, we construct a sequence (u_n), $n = 1, 2, \dots$ of piecewise linear, non–decreasing continuous functions from $[0,1]$ to itself which satisfies the following property: $|u_{n+1}(x) - u_n(x)| \leq \frac{1}{2^{(n+1)}}$. We define the sequence of functions inductively. First, let $u_0(x) = 0$ if $x \in I(0)$ and $u_0(x) = 1$ if $x \in I(1)$. This defines u_0 on the closed set $E_0 = I(0) \cup I(1)$. We now extend the function u_0 in a canonical way to a piecewise linear non–decreasing continuous function on $[0,1]$ which we also denote by u_0. At this stage we have considered two equivalence classes $\mathcal{E}_0 = \{ I(0), I(1) \}$ and have defined the function u_0 to be constant on these classes.

Now suppose that u_n has been defined in such a way that the following conditions are satisfied:

1. $\mathcal{E}_n$ is a set of $2^n + 1$ equivalence classes whose union is E_n;
2. u_n is constant on each of the equivalence classes in $\mathcal{E}_n$ and the values of u_n on these equivalence classes are $\frac{k}{2^n}$ where $k = 0, 1, \dots, 2^n$;
3. u_n is defined on $[0,1]$ and is the canonical piecewise linear non–decreasing continuous extension of the function in 2.

We define the function u_{n+1} as follows. First, we let u_{n+1} be equal to u_n on E_n. Consider the 2^n intervals in the complement of E_n. Let J be one such interval and c the midpoint of J. Then $I(c)$ is the equivalence class of the point c. Repeat this process for each interval in the complement of E_n. Add the 2^n equivalence classes obtained in this way to $\mathcal{E}_n$ to form $\mathcal{E}_{n+1}$. Thus $\mathcal{E}_{n+1}$ is a set of $2^{n+1} + 1$ closed intervals in $[0,1]$. Let E_{n+1} be the union of these closed intervals. It remains to define the value of u_{n+1} on the intervals in the complement of E_n. Let J be one such interval. The function u_n takes (constant) values $k2^{-n}$ and $(k+1)2^{-n}$ on either side of J. Define $u_{n+1}(x)$ to be equal to the average of these two values—i.e., $u_{n+1}(x) = (2k+1)2^{-(n+1)}$ for all $x \in I(c)$ where c is the midpoint of J. Finally, extend u_{n+1} in a canonical manner to a piecewise linear non-decreasing continuous function on $[0,1]$. This completes the inductive definition of the sequence of functions (u_n).

An important property of the sequence of functions u_n is worth noting. Let $[a,b]$ be a subinterval of $[0,1]$ that meets no equivalence class of positive length. Then each u_n is linear on $[a,b]$ with slope d_n and $d_n \leq d_{n+1}$ for all n. Hence, the image of $[a,b]$ is "stretched out" more and more as n increases.

We claim next that the sequence (u_n) is a uniformly convergent sequence. To that end observe that in order to show that the difference between u_n and u_{n+1} does not become large we only have to consider points not belonging to

E_n since on E_n these functions agree by definition. Let J be one of these open intervals in the complement of E_n with $u_n(a) = k2^{-n}, u_n(b) = (k+1)2^{-n}$. If again we denote the midpoint of J by c we see that

$$u_n(x), u_{n+1}(x) \in [k2^{-n}, (2k+1)2^{-(n+1)}] \text{ if } x \in (a, c] \quad \text{and} \quad (5.1)$$

$$u_n(x), u_{n+1}(x) \in [(2k+1)2^{-(n+1)}, (k+1)2^{-n}] \text{ if } x \in [c, b) \quad (5.2)$$

Since

$$\frac{2k+1}{2^{n+1}} - \frac{k}{2^n} = \frac{1}{2^{n+1}} = \frac{k+1}{2^n} - \frac{2k+1}{2^{n+1}} \quad (5.3)$$

it follows that

$$|u_{n+1}(x) - u_n(x)| \le \frac{1}{2^{n+1}} \quad (5.4)$$

Therefore the sequence of functions (u_n) is uniformly convergent and by a well known theorem of analysis it follows that the function u defined by $u(x) = \lim_{n\to\infty} u_n(x)$ for each x is continuous.

It remains to prove that u is a strictly isotone function. Let x and y be two points such that $x \sim y$. We claim that $u(x) = u(y)$. Let $I(x) = [a, b]$. If $a = b$ the result is immediate. So suppose that $a < b$. Now the length of the intervals in the complement of E_n is at most 2^{-n}. It follows from this that as $n \to \infty$ the closed interval $[a, b]$ will be a subinterval of one of the intervals in $\mathcal{E}_m$ for all $m \ge N$ where N is some large positive integer. This implies that u_m is constant on $[a, b]$ for all $m \ge N$. Therefore, $u(x) = u(y)$. Suppose now that $x \prec y$. If the interval $[x, y]$ does not intersect any equivalence class of positive length, then $0 < (u_0(x) - u_0(y)) \le (u_n(x) - u_n(y))$ for all n because the sequence of (constant) derivatives of the functions u_n is non-decreasing. Therefore, $u(x) < u(y)$. Suppose then that some equivalence class of positive length intersects $[x, y]$ and let us suppose that $u(x) = u(y)$. Clearly, two distinct classes of positive length, say, $I(w)$ and $I(v)$ cannot intersect $[x, y]$ because $u(x) = u(y)$ implies that $u(x) = u(z) = u(y)$ for all $z \in [x, y]$ and u takes different values on distinct classes. Hence only one class, say $I(w)$, intersects $[x, y]$. Since $u(x) = u(y)$ we deduce that $[x, y] \subset I(w)$ which contradicts our supposition that $x \prec y$. This contradiction proves that $x \prec y$ implies that $u(x) < u(y)$. It is easily verified that u is the required continuous isotone function on X and the theorem is proved. ∎

We now use Wold's theorem to prove the Gap Lemma.

PROOF OF THE GAP LEMMA We may assume without loss of generality that $S \subset [0, 1]$. Now define an equivalence relation on $[0, 1]$ as follows. If S has adjacent gaps $[a, b)$ and $(b, c]$ then $[a, c]$ is an equivalence class, i.e. all points in $[a, c]$ are declared to be equivalent to one another. If $[a, b)$ or $(a, b]$ are gaps which have no neighbouring gaps then the equivalence class is $[a, b]$. All other equivalence classes are singletons. Observe that each equivalence class is a closed interval.

All the conditions of Theorem 5.3 are satisfied and we may conclude that there is a function u on $[0, 1]$ such that $u(x) = u(y)$ if $x \sim y$ and $u(x) < u(y)$ if $x \prec y$. We claim that the image $u(S)$ has no half–open half–closed gaps. Suppose that $u(S)$ has a gap of the form $(e, f]$. It follows that there is some $c \in S$ such that $u(c) = e$ and that there is a sequence $(d_n) \in S$ such that $(u(d_n))$ is a strictly decreasing sequence converging to f. Then $\cap_{n=1}^{\infty} \{ x : c < x < d_n \}$ is disjoint from S. Hence, the sequence (d_n) converges to some number d such that $u(d) = f$. This means that $(c, d]$ is a gap in S. Now by the definition of the equivalence relation $\sim$ this implies that u is constant on the equivalence class $[c, d]$ whence $e = f$. This contradiction proves that $u(S)$ has no half–open half–closed gaps and completes the proof of the lemma. ∎

We now use the Gap Lemma to prove the following important theorem.

THEOREM 5.4 Let X be a topological space and $\precsim$ a continuous total preorder defined on it. Then there is a utility function on X if and only if there is a continuous utility function on X.

PROOF The implication in one direction is trivial. So suppose that v is a utility function on X. Since the real line is order homeomorphic to $(0, 1)$ we may assume without loss of generality that v assumes its values in $[0, 1]$. Let $v(X) = S$. Then Wold's theorem implies that there exists a non–decreasing function $u : [0, 1] \to [0, 1]$ that is strictly increasing on S and such that $u(S)$ has no half–open half–closed gaps. Define a function f on X by $f(x) = u(v(x))$ for each $x \in X$. Clearly, the function f is strictly isotone on X. We claim that it is continuous. To prove this let r be a real number. If $r \in f(X)$, there exists $a \in X$ such that $f(a) = r$. Then the set $f^{-1}[r, \infty] = \{ x \in X : a \precsim x \}$ which is closed by the continuity of the preorder. Suppose now that r is not in the image of X under f. If $\sup\{ f(x) : x \in X \} \leq r$ the set $f^{-1}[r, \infty] = \emptyset$ and if $r \leq \inf\{ f(x) : x \in X \}$ the set $f^{-1}[r, \infty] = X$. In either case, the set $f^{-1}[r, \infty)$ is closed. Suppose now that r belongs to an open gap (c, d) so that $c, d \in f(X)$. Then the set $f^{-1}[r, \infty) = f^{-1}[d, \infty) = \{ x \in X : b \precsim x \}$, for some $b \in X$, which is closed by the continuity condition. Finally, suppose that r belongs to a closed gap $[c, d]$. Then $f^{-1}[r, \infty) = \cap\{ f^{-1}[s, \infty) : s \leq c$ and $s \in f(x) \}$ which is closed as an intersection of closed sets. We have proved therefore that the set $f^{-1}[r, \infty)$ is closed in X for every real number r, whence f is upper semicontinuous. Similarly we can prove that the set $f^{-1}(-\infty, r]$ is closed for every real number r showing that f is lower semicontinuous. Therefore, f is continuous and the theorem is proved. ∎

We are now in a position to prove the classical theorems of Eilenberg (1941) and Debreu (1954, 1964). First, we prove the following theorem of Eilenberg on the existence of a continuous utility function on a connected and separable topological space.

THEOREM 5.5 Let $\precsim$ be a continuous total preorder on a connected and separable topological space X. Then there exists a continuous utility function on X.

PROOF We show first that there is a utility function on X. Let $Z = \{z_1, z_2, \ldots\}$ be a countable dense subset of X. Such a set exists because X is topologically separable. For each $x \in X$ let $N(x) = \{n \in \mathbb{N} : z_n \prec x\}$ and define $v(x) = \sum_{n \in N(x)} 2^{-n}$. Now let $x, y \in X$ such that $x \precsim y$. By transitivity of the preorder, $N(x) \subset N(y)$ which implies that $v(x) \leq v(y)$. Suppose now that $x \prec y$. The sets $\{a \in X : a \precsim x\}$ and $\{a \in X : y \precsim a\}$ are disjoint, nonempty and closed (by continuity of $\precsim$). Since X is connected they do not exhaust X. Therefore, the set $\{a \in X : x \prec a \prec y\}$ is nonempty and open. Since Z is dense in X there exists $z_n \in Z$ such that $x \prec z_n \prec y$. Hence, $N(x) \not\subset N(y)$ which implies that $v(x) < v(y)$. We have proved that v is a utility function on X. It now follows from Theorem 5.4 that there is a continuous utility function on X. ∎

We now prove the following theorem of Debreu on the existence of a continuous utility function on a second countable space.

THEOREM 5.6 Let $\precsim$ be a continuous total preorder on a second countable topological space. Then there is a continuous utility function on X.

PROOF As in Theorem 5.5 we first prove that there is a utility function on X. Since X is second countable there is a countable basis $B_1, B_2, \ldots$. For each $x \in X$ let $N(x) = \{n \in \mathbb{N} : y \prec x$ for every $y \in B_n\}$ and define a function v on X by $v(x) = \sum_{n \in N(x)} 2^{-n}$ for each $x \in X$.

If $x \precsim y$ then clearly $N(x) \subset N(y)$ so that $v(x) \leq v(y)$. Now suppose that $x \prec y$. Since the preorder is continuous the set $K = \{a \in X : a \prec y\}$ is open and $x \in K$. Hence there is a member of the countable basis, say B_n, such that $x \in B_n \subset K$. Observe that $n \in N(y)$ but $n \notin N(x)$ because the relation $\prec$ is irreflexive. Therefore $v(x) < v(y)$ and we have proved that v is a utility function on X. Again, Theorem 5.4 implies that there is a continuous utility function on X and the proof of the theorem is finished. ∎

We now mention two important applications of the Eilenberg and Debreu theorems proved above. The first example we have in mind is from general equilibrium theory. In extending the Arrow–Debreu model to an economy with land some conceptual problems have to be overcome. See, for example, the work of Berliant (1982, 1986) for a detailed discussion. In models with land as one commodity the following problem arises. The elements of the "commodity space" are measurable subsets of some set L and a preference relation $\precsim$ is defined on a σ–algebra of subsets of L. In order to prove that such a relation has a continuous utility representation, Berliant defines a certain topology on the σ–algebra and then proves that this topology is connected and separable. Eilenberg's theorem then implies the existence of a continuous utility function. Our second example is from expected utility theory. Let X be a set and $\mathcal{P}(X)$ a set of probability measures on X. We may intuitively think of an element $p \in \mathcal{P}$ as a "lottery" which assigns probabilities to the "prizes" in X. Suppose now that there is a preference relation $\precsim$ defined on the set of probability measures $\mathcal{P}$ which is endowed with a certain topology called the weak topology. Under certain conditions this topology may be shown to be a separable metrizable topology. Since a separable metric space is second countable it follows from Debreu's theorem that there is a continuous utility function representing the preference relation. Such a utility function is called a Bernoulli utility function and may be used to construct continuous von Neumann–Morgenstern utility functions [Grandmont (1972)].

6   Existence of a Continuous Utility Function on Partially Ordered Topological Spaces

We have so far only considered utility functions on totally preordered sets. For both theoretical and empirical reasons it is desirable to prove the existence of continuous utility functions for spaces that may not be totally preordered. A classical theorem of this kind was proved by Peleg (1970). Peleg only assumes that there is an irreflexive and transitive relation $\prec$ on X that may not be total. A utility function f in this context has the property that $x \prec y$ implies that $f(x) < f(y)$. Of course, the converse implication may not hold because the order is not total. In other words, a utility function in this context is an order homomorphism and not an order monomorphism.

Now, in view of the proofs of the theorems of Eilenberg and Debreu, it is tempting to try to prove Peleg's theorem by using the Gap Lemma. However, this approach does not work because the method based on the Gap Lemma is valid only for totally preordered sets. It is not valid, in general, for partially ordered sets. Therefore, a different method has to be used. In fact, Peleg's proof is based on the following classical theorem of Cantor (1955). In order to state Cantor's theorem we need the following definitions.

DEFINITION 6.1 Let $\prec$ be a strict total order on a set X. Then $(X, \prec)$ is *unbordered* if for each $x \in X$ there exist $a, b \in X$ such that $a \prec x \prec b$.

DEFINITION 6.2 Let $\prec$ be a strict total order on a set X. Then $(X, \prec)$ is *dense–in–itself* if $x, y \in X$ with $x \prec y$ then there exists $z \in X$ such that $x \prec z \prec y$.

THEOREM 6.3 Let X be a countable set and $\prec$ a strict total order on X such that the following conditions are satisfied:

1. $(X, \prec)$ is unbordered;
2. $(X, \prec)$ is dense–in–itself.

Then there is an order isomorphism on X onto the set of rational numbers.

PROOF See Cantor (1955), Kamke (1950) or Frankel (1976). ∎

We are now in a position to prove Peleg's theorem.

THEOREM 6.4 Let $\prec$ be an irreflexive and transitive preference relation on a topological space X such that the following conditions are satisfied:

1. (Order–separability) There exists a countable subset Z that is order–dense in the sense of Cantor.
2. (Continuity) For each $x \in X$ the set $L(x) = \{ y \in X : y \prec x \}$ is open in X.
3. (Spaciousness) If $x \prec y$ then $cl L(x) \subset L(y)$.

Then there exists a continuous utility function U on X.

PROOF Let a, b be elements in X such that $a \prec b$. We first show that there exists an isotone function $u : X \to [0, 1]$ such that $x \prec y$ implies $u(x) \leq u(y)$. The order–separability condition (1) implies that there exists a countable unbordered dense–in–itself subset W of Z such that $W \subset (a, b)$. By Cantor's theorem there is an order bijection f from W onto the set of all rational numbers in $(0, 1)$. Now define a function $u : X \to [0, 1]$ by $u(x) = \inf\{ f(s) : x \in L(s)$ and $s \in W \}$ and $u(x) = 1$ if $x \notin L(s)$ for all $s \in W$. Clearly, u is a function on X with values in $[0, 1]$ that is non–decreasing on X, strictly increasing on W and such that $u(a) < u(b)$.

We prove now that u is continuous. To that end, let r be a real number. Let $K = u^{-1}(-\infty, r)$ and $x \in K$. There exists s such that $x \in L(s)$ and $f(s) < r$.

Choose a rational q satisfying $f(s) < q < r$. Since f is bijective there exists $z \in X$ such that $f(z) = q$. Then the set $\{y \in X : y \prec z\}$ is open by the continuity condition 2 and it owns x. Hence, $u^{-1}(-\infty, r)$ is an open set.

We prove next that the set $J = u^{-1}(r, +\infty)$ is an open set. So let $x \in J$. Then $f(x) > r$ so that $x \in L(s)$ for some s and $f(s) > r$. Choose rationals m, n such that $r < m < n < f(s)$.

Since f is bijective there exist $c, d \in X$ such that $f(c) = m$ and $f(d) = n$. Since $c \prec d$, the spaciousness condition 3 implies that cl $L(c) \subset L(d)$. Therefore, $X \setminus$ cl $L(c)$ is an open set and for any $y \in X \setminus$ cl $L(c)$ we have $r < m \leq u(y)$. Therefore $u^{-1}(r, +\infty)$ is an open set. This proves that u is a continuous function.

Now consider all the pairs of points $z_i, z_j \in Z$ such that $z_i \prec z_j$. This set is countable and we may write it in the form $S = \{(a_1, b_1), (a_2, b_2), \ldots\}$. For each positive integer n there exists a continuous non–decreasing function u_n on X such that $u_n(a_n) < u_n(b_n)$. Define a function U on X by $U(x) = \sum_{n=1}^{\infty} 2^{-n} u_n(x)$ for each $x \in X$. Then, clearly, U is a continuous isotone function on X. To prove that it is strictly isotone let $x, y \in X$ such $x \prec y$. Then by the order–separability condition 1 and the indexing of the set S there exists n such that $x \prec a_n \prec b_n \prec y$. It follows that $u_n(x) < u_n(y)$ which implies that $U(x) < U(y)$. Therefore f is the required continuous utility function on X and the proof of the theorem is finished. ∎

7   The Urysohn–Nachbin Approach to Continuous Utility Functions

In this section we describe the essentials of a recently developed approach to the problem of proving the existence of continuous utility functions. See, for example, Mehta (1977a, 1981, 1983a, 1986a,b, 1988, 1992) and Herden (1989a,b,c, 1990, 1993a,b). This new approach is based on the Urysohn–Nachbin separation and extension theorems on topological spaces equipped with a preorder. This approach casts considerable light on the structure of the utility representation problem. In addition to yielding powerful new theorems on the existence of continuous utility functions it also enables us to unify, simplify and generalize the different approaches that have been used to prove the existence of continuous utility functions.

We start by discussing two basic problems in topology: the separation problem and the extension problem. Given a topological space X it is natural to inquire if there is a "rich" family $\mathcal{F}$ of continuous functions on the space that separates subsets A and B in the sense that there is a member $f \in \mathcal{F}$ such that $f(x) = 0$ for $x \in A$ and $f(x) = 1$ for $x \in B$. The classical Urysohn separation theorem (also called Urysohn's lemma) states that if X is a normal space and A, B are disjoint closed subsets of X then there is such a separating function.

The Urysohn separation theorem therefore provides an answer to a separation problem. Consider now an extension problem. Suppose that f is a continuous function defined on a subset K of a topological space. Then under what conditions does there exist a continuous function g on X such that $g(x) = f(x)$ for $x \in K$? The classical Urysohn extension theorem (also called the Lebesgue–Tietze–Urysohn extension theorem) states that if X is a normal space and K is a closed subset of X then every continuous function f on K has a continuous extension to the whole space X.

Suppose now that one has a preorder $\precsim$ on a topological space X. Let a, b be two points in X that are separated by the preorder in the sense that $a \prec b$. Then does there exist a continuous isotone function f on X such that $f(x) < f(y)$? More generally, one may want to know if, given two subsets A, B, there is a continuous isotone function f on X such that $f(x) = 0$ for $x \in A$ and $f(x) = 1$ for $x \in B$. These are separation problems. Now consider an extension problem. Suppose that K is a subset of a preordered topological space X and f is a continuous isotone (or strictly isotone) function on K (as, for example, in the Arrow–Hahn theorem). Then under what conditions does there exist a continuous isotone (or strictly isotone) function g on X that is an extension of f? The separation and extension theorems of Nachbin answer questions of this type.

DEFINITION 7.1 Let X be a topological space equipped with a preorder. Then X is said to be *normally preordered* if for every pair of disjoint closed subsets F_0 and F_1 of X, F_0 being decreasing and F_1 increasing, there exist two disjoint open subsets A_0 and A_1 such that A_0 contains F_0 and is decreasing and A_1 contains F_1 and is increasing.

The concept of a normally preordered space is a generalization of the concept of a normal space. This may be seen as follows. Let X be an arbitrary topological space. Define a relation $\precsim$ on X by the following rule: $a \precsim b$ if and only if $a = b$. Then it is easily verified that $\precsim$ is a partial order. It is called a discrete order. It follows that every topological space may be regarded as a preordered topological space. Under the discrete order every subset of X is decreasing and increasing and it follows that X is normal if and only if it is normally preordered.

Now the Nachbin separation theorem [Nachbin (1965, p. 30)] states that in a normally preordered topological space, disjoint closed subsets A and B, such that A is decreasing and B is increasing, can be separated by a continuous isotone function. The Nachbin extension theorem [Nachbin (1965, p. 36)] states that in a normally preordered space any continuous isotone function f defined on a closed subset K may be extended to a continuous isotone function g on X if a certain separation condition is satisfied.

Why is the Urysohn–Nachbin approach important for utility functions? In order to answer this question let us consider briefly the situation that existed in utility theory in the early nineteen seventies. By this time some important theorems on utility functions had been proved in the literature. Continuous utility representations were known to exist for total continuous preorders on connected and separable or second countable spaces (for example, closed convex subsets of $\mathbb{R}^n$) by the Eilenberg and Debreu theorems. In particular, Debreu's theorem on second countable topological spaces is noteworthy because it implies that a continuous total preorder defined on an *arbitrary* subspace of $\mathbb{R}^n$ has a continuous utility representation. For preference relations on $\mathbb{R}^n$ satisfying some kind of desirability condition (monotonicity or local non–satiation) it was known that one could get utility representations in which utility is defined in terms of the canonical Euclidean metric of $\mathbb{R}^n$. Furthermore, utility representations for certain types of partial order were also known.

Although important progress had been made the *structure* of the utility representation problem had not been elucidated. For example, useful necessary and sufficient conditions for the existence of a continuous utility function were not known. The conditions of connectedness and topological separability (Eilenberg's theorem) and second countability (Debreu's theorem) are sufficient but not necessary for the existence of a continuous utility function. Furthermore, utility representations for total preorders appeared to be "completely different" from those for partial orders since the Gap Lemma can only be used for total preorders. Also, the extension procedure used by Arrow and Hahn was *ad hoc* in the sense that it was not connected with the general separation and extension problems in topology. This state of affairs created the impression that the methods used by Eilenberg, Debreu, Peleg and Arrow and Hahn had no relation to one another.

The use of the Urysohn–Nachbin methods in utility theory has proved that this impression is false. In fact, all these approaches and methods are not different but essentially manifestations of the same underlying phenomenon. We will show now that there is one set of ideas or principles from which all these theorems may be derived as special cases.

These developments are based on the concept of a separable system. This concept is fundamental to the Urysohn-Nachbin approach to utility functions and is a refinement of the ideas used by Urysohn in his seminal work.

DEFINITION 7.2 Let X be a topological space and $\precsim$ a preorder on X. A family $\mathcal{E}$ of open decreasing subsets of X is said to be a *separable system* on X if the following conditions hold:

1. There exist sets $E_1, E_2 \in \mathcal{E}$ such that $\operatorname{cl} E_1 \subset E_2$.

2. For all sets $E_1, E_2 \in \mathcal{E}$ such that $\mathrm{cl}\, E_1 \subset E_2$ there exists some set $E_3 \in \mathcal{E}$ such that $\mathrm{cl}\, E_1 \subset E_3 \subset \mathrm{cl}\, E_3 \subset E_2$.

A separable system is said to be total (or linear) if for $E_1, E_2 \in \mathcal{E}$ either $E_1 \subset E_2$ or $E_2 \subset E_1$.

The concept of a separable system provides the key to the understanding of the utility representation problem and the more general utility extension problem. For the utility representation problem we have the following general theorem due to Herden (1989a, b).

THEOREM 7.3 Let $(X, \precsim)$ be an arbitrary preordered topological space. Then the following are equivalent:

1. There exists a continuous utility function on X.
2. There exists a countable family $\{\, \mathcal{E}_i : i \in \mathbb{N} \,\}$ of separable systems on X such that for each pair (x, y) such that $x \prec y$ there exists i such that $x \in E$, $y \notin E$ for all $E \in \mathcal{E}_i$.
3. There exists a countable linear separable system $\mathcal{E}$ on X such that for all pairs (x, y) in X with $x \prec y$ there exist sets $E_1, E_2 \in \mathcal{E}$ such that $E_1 \subset \mathrm{cl}\, E_1 \subset E_2$, $x \in E_1$ and $y \notin E_2$.

PROOF See Herden (1989a,b). ∎

We now indicate briefly how the major theorems of utility theory are consequences of this general theorem. So suppose that a space $(X, \precsim)$ satisfies the conditions of the Eilenberg theorem. Let $Z = \{\, z_1, z_2, \dots \,\}$ be a countable dense subset. For each $z_i \in Z$, let $E_i = \{\, x \in X : x \prec z_i \,\}$. Then for each $i = 1, 2, \dots$ the set E_i is open and decreasing. The family $\{\, E_i : i \in \mathbb{N} \,\}$ is easily seen to be a countable total separable system on X such that condition 3 of Theorem 7.3 holds. Therefore, X has a continuous utility representation. Suppose now that X satisfies the conditions of Peleg's theorem. We show that condition 2 of the theorem holds. Let S be the countable family of pairs (a_i, b_i) such that $a_i \prec b_i$. For each i, let $\mathcal{E}_i = \{\, L(s) : a_i \prec s \prec b_i \,\}$. Then Peleg's spaciousness condition implies that $\mathcal{E}_i$ is a separable system and it is easily verified that the family $\{\, \mathcal{E}_i : i \in \mathbb{N} \,\}$ of separable systems on X satisfies condition 2. Debreu's theorem may be proved in a similar manner. We see, therefore, that these theorems, while appearing to be different, are in fact special cases of a more general theorem.

What about the method used in the Arrow–Hahn theorem? Recall now that in the Arrow–Hahn theorem the problem is to extend a continuous utility function defined on a closed subset to the whole space. We see now that this problem is just a special case of the extension problem described above. The concept of a separable system also provides the key to the solution of the extension problem. It can be proved [see Herden (1989a,c, 1990, 1993a,b) and Herden and Mehta (1997a) that a continuous isotone (or strictly isotone) function defined on a closed subset K of a preordered topological space X has a continuous isotone (or strictly isotone) extension to a function g on X if and only if there is a separable system on X which satisfies certain "separation" conditions. Due to limitations of space we do not discuss these conditions here. But we stress that it is the idea of a separable system that also provides the key to the understanding of the extension problem.

We conclude by showing that the utility representation problem studied in classical utility theory is itself a special case of the utility extension problem. To see this, suppose that K is a closed subset (perhaps empty) of a preordered topological space X and that f is a continuous isotone (or strictly isotone) function on K. Now the extension problem consists in finding conditions that imply that there exists a continuous isotone (or strictly isotone) extension g, defined on X, of the function f. Therefore, if one has solved the *utility extension problem*, one has automatically solved the *utility representation problem* because one may take K to be the empty set and f the empty function. It follows that the utility existence problem is a special case of the utility extension problem. Using this approach we are now able to see that the classical theorems of Wold, Eilenberg, Debreu, Peleg and Arrow–Hahn are all special cases of general extension theorems. By using the Urysohn–Nachbin approach we are now able to see that all these classical theorems have a common structure. See Herden and Mehta (1997a) and Mehta (1992) for further discussion.

8   Miscellaneous Topics on Utility Functions

8.1   *Continuous Utility Functions on Infinite Dimensional Spaces*

The classical utility representation theorems of Eilenberg and Debreu are very useful. In particular, Debreu's theorem implies the existence of a continuous utility representation on an *arbitrary* subspace of $\mathbb{R}^n$, because such a subspace is second countable. However, both the Eilenberg and Debreu theorems apply only to spaces that are topologically separable. This limits their usefulness in normed linear spaces because such spaces are not, in general, topologically separable. As an example we may mention the space $L^\infty(\mu)$ of μ–essentially bounded μ–measurable functions on a σ–finite measure space. This space is not separable. Infinite dimensional commodity spaces of this type are now commonly encountered in economic theory. It is desirable, therefore, to have utility representation theorems for such spaces since the classical theorems may not apply.

We now discuss some approaches that have been used in this area. The first is due to Mas–Colell (1986), Shafer (1984) and, in its most general form, Monteiro (1987).

DEFINITION 8.1 Let $\precsim$ be a total preorder on a set X. We say that a subset Z *bounds* the preorder $\precsim$ if for each $x \in X$ there exist $a, b \in Z$ such that $a \precsim x \precsim b$. If Z is countable we say that $\precsim$ is *countably bounded*.

LEMMA 8.2 Let X be a path–connected topological space and $\precsim$ a continuous total preorder on X which is countably bounded. Then there exists a connected and separable $F \subset X$ which bounds $\precsim$.

PROOF Let $\{x_n : n = 1, 2, \ldots\}$ be a countable set that bounds $\precsim$. Choose a point $a \in X$ and for each $n \geq 1$ let $f_n : [0, 1] \to X$ be a path connecting a to x_n. Let $F = \cup_{n=1}^{\infty} f_n([0, 1])$. The set F bounds $\precsim$ because $x_n = f_n(1)$ for $n \geq 1$. Clearly, F is connected. Furthermore, F is separable because the rational numbers $Q \subset [0, 1]$ are dense in $[0, 1]$ which implies that $\cup_{n=1}^{\infty} f_n(Q)$ is dense in F. ∎

We now prove the following theorem of Monteiro (1987).

THEOREM 8.3 Let $\precsim$ be a continuous countably bounded total preorder on a path connected topological space X. Then there is a continuous utility function on X.

PROOF The proof is based on Eilenberg's theorem and is similar to the proof of Theorem 4.5. The lemma implies that there is a connected and separable subset F that bounds $\precsim$. For each $x \in X$, consider the sets $A^x = \{y \in F : y \precsim x\}$ and $A_x = \{y \in F : x \precsim y\}$. These sets are closed by the continuity of $\precsim$. They are nonempty because F bounds $\precsim$. Since F is connected it follows that there exists a point $d(x) \in F$ such that $x \sim d(x)$. If the preorder $\precsim$ is restricted to F, we see that F satisfies the conditions of Eilenberg's theorem from which we conclude that there exists a continuous utility function v on F. Now define a function u on X by $u(x) = v(d(x))$. Since $x \precsim y$ if and only if $d(x) \precsim d(y)$ and v is a utility function we see that u is a utility function. The proof that u is continuous is similar to the arguments that have been used earlier and is left to the reader. ∎

REMARK 8.4 Any convex subset of a topological vector space X is path connected. Therefore, the theorem implies that any countably bounded continuous total preorder on a convex subset of X has a continuous utility representation.

In this connection it should be noted that X is countably bounded if X has worst and best points.

Another approach one may take to the problem of proving the existence of continuous utility functions on infinite dimensional spaces is to ask if the Wold and Arrow–Hahn theorems are applicable (or extensible) to such spaces. Since a normed linear space has a canonical metric (the one induced by the norm) and utility in the Wold and Arrow–Hahn theorems is defined in terms of the Euclidean metric this approach looks promising and is worth investigating.

Let us first consider the Wold approach. It can be proved that the special case of Wold's theorem (Theorem 4.5 above) is indeed valid in a Banach space even without any separability assumptions. The idea is to replace the Riemann integral by the Cauchy–Bochner integral of a function with values in a Banach space and then, as before, to define utility in terms of arc–length along a differentiable curve. The reader is referred to Mehta (1993a) for more details.

Now let us turn to the Arrow–Hahn approach. The Arrow–Hahn theorem is valid only in $\mathbb{R}^n$. Indeed, a careful examination of the Arrow–Hahn proof reveals that each of the three parts of the proof is based on the Heine–Borel property of $\mathbb{R}^n$ according to which a closed bounded set is compact. This property does not hold, in general, in an infinite–dimensional Banach space. It should be observed, however, that a conjugate Banach space (that is, one with a predual) has an analogous property: the closed unit ball is compact in the weak *–topology. This suggests that the Arrow–Hahn theorem can be extended to infinite–dimensional conjugate Banach space that may not be topologically separable. Indeed, this can be done. We refer the reader to Bridges and Mehta (1995) and Candeal, Induráin and Mehta (1995a) for further discussion. It should be observed that theorems of this kind are generalizations of the finite–dimensional Arrow–Hahn theorem because the weak *–topology on $\mathbb{R}^n$ is the Euclidean topology. For other infinite–dimensional versions see Candeal, Induráin and Mehta (1995b) and Mehta and Monteiro (1996).

8.2   Utility Representations for Interval Orders

Suppose that $\prec$ is a strict preference relation on X. Then as we have seen a point a is said to be "indifferent" to b if and only if neither point is preferred to the other. Suppose there is a utility function f on X which satisfies $a \prec b$ if and only if $f(a) < f(b)$. It is easily verified that this implies that "indifference" is transitive. Objections to this property of preferences have been raised by Luce (1956) and others and are well known in the literature. See, for example, Roberts (1979). As a result other axiom systems for preferences have been proposed.

DEFINITION 8.5 A relation $\prec$ on a set X is said to be an *interval order* if it is irreflexive and has the property that if $a, b, c, d \in X, (a \prec b)$ and $(c \prec d)$ imply that $(a \prec d)$ or $(c \prec b)$. An interval order is said to be a *semiorder* if in addition it has the property that $a, b, c, d \in X$, $(a \prec b)$ and $(b \prec c)$ imply that $(a \prec d)$ or $(d \prec c)$.

Let us first briefly consider semiorders. One reason why economists and psychologists have maintained that indifference is intransitive is that it is difficult to discern small differences. This suggests that we look for a function f with the property that $a \prec b$ if and only if $f(b)$ exceeds $f(a)$ by a certain "minimal amount". Let α measure this threshold. We then have the following classical theorem of Scott and Suppes (1958). For a proof and further discussion, see Roberts (1979) and Gensemer (1987a, b).

THEOREM 8.6 Let X be a finite set and α a positive number. Then $\prec$ is a semiorder on X if and only if there is a utility function f on X such that $a \prec b$ if and only if $f(a) + \alpha < f(b)$.

Let us now consider interval orders. Observe, first, that an interval order is asymmetric and transitive. One approach to the problem of finding order preserving representations for interval orders is to use *interval-valued* representations [Fishburn (1973, 1985)]. The other approach, which we describe briefly in what follows, is to use *two* real valued functions.

NOTATION If $\prec$ is asymmetric we write $x \precsim y$ to denote $\neg(y \prec x)$.

DEFINITION 8.7 Let $\prec$ be an asymmetric relation on a topological space X. We say that $\prec$ is *continuous* if for each $x \in X$, the sets $\{y \in X : y \prec x\}$ and $\{y \in X : x \prec y\}$ are open. We say that a pair (u, v) of real-valued functions is a (utility) *representation* of $\prec$ if $x \prec y - u(x) < v(y)$. If u and v are continuous on X we say that the representation is continuous.

It is worth observing that if (u, v) is a continuous representation of an interval order $\prec$ then the maximization of either u or v on a budget set leads to a maximal element — i.e. an element to which no other element is strictly preferred.

Suppose that $\prec$ is an interval order on X. The relation $\prec$ induces two relations $\precsim_1$ and $\precsim_2$ as follows: for $x, y \in X$, $x \precsim_1 y$ if and only if [for all $z \in X, z \precsim x \implies z \precsim y$] and $x \precsim_2 y$ if and only if [for all $z \in X, y \precsim z \implies x \precsim z$]. It is easily verified that $\precsim_1$ and $\precsim_2$ are total preorders on X.

We now define a concept of order-separability for interval orders.

DEFINITION 8.8 Let $\prec$ be an asymmetric relation on a set X. We say that $(X, \prec)$ is *strongly order–separable* if there is a countable subset Z of X such that if $x, y \in X$ and $x \prec y$ there exist $a, b \in Z$ such that $x \prec a \precsim b \prec y$.

We now have the following theorem of Chateauneuf (1987) which builds on earlier work of Fishburn (1970a, 1970b, 1973, 1985) and Bridges (1983a, 1983b). See also Bosi and Isler (1995) and Bosi (1996a).

THEOREM 8.9 Let $\prec$ be an asymmetric relation defined on a connected topological space X. Then there exists a continuous representation (u, v) of $\prec$ if and only if the following hold:

1. The relation $\prec$ is an interval order.
2. The relations $\precsim_1$ and $\precsim_2$ are continuous.
3. The interval order is strongly order–separable.

SKETCH OF PROOF The idea of the sufficiency part of the proof is to first consider the total preorder $\precsim_1$ on X induced by the given relation $\prec$. By strong order–separability of $\prec$ (condition 3) we can prove that $\precsim_1$ is Debreu order–separable and this implies that $(X, \precsim_1)$ satisfies the conditions of Eilenberg's theorem. We may conclude from this theorem that there is a continuous utility function u that represents $\precsim_1$. Now define $v : X \to [0, 1]$ by $v(x) = \sup\{ u(y) : y \in X \text{ and } y \prec x \}$ and $v(x) = 0$ if there is no $y \in X$ such that $y \prec x$. It can be proved that this function v is continuous and that it represents the total preorder $\precsim_2$.

Finally, the pair (u, v) may be shown to be a continuous representation of the interval order $\prec$. ∎

REMARK 8.10 It is worth observing that if the "indifference" relation $\sim$ induced by the relation $\prec$ is transitive then the relations $\precsim$, $\precsim_1$ and $\precsim_2$ are all equal. Furthermore, the strong order–separability condition reduces to the Cantor order–separability condition.

8.3 Differentiable Utility Functions

In standard microeconomic theory it is *assumed* that there is a twice continuously differentiable utility function U defined on some subset of $\mathbb{R}^n$. This function is then used to characterize the optimum position of the consumer and to obtain other results in demand theory such as the Slutsky equation. But under what conditions on the preference relation does there exist a differentiable utility function that represents the preference relation? This question was posed and answered in a seminal paper of Debreu (1972). It is true that the study of differentiable preference relations has a long history that goes back to Antonelli [see Chipman *et al.* (1971)]. However, this literature on the so–called "integrability problem" in demand theory did not really address and certainly did not state or answer the question in the form given above. It was Debreu who formulated the problem as a problem in preference and utility theory.

Unfortunately, Debreu's solution of the problem is quite difficult because it uses the methods of differential geometry. Our objective here, therefore, is merely to give the reader an intuitive feeling for Debreu's ideas and methods. For further discussion, see Bridges and Mehta (1995, Chapter 7).

DEFINITION 8.11 Let U and V be open subsets of $\mathbb{R}^n$. A function $f : U \to V$ is said to be *smooth* (or C^∞) if all its partial derivatives of all orders exist and are continuous. If U and V are arbitrary subsets of $\mathbb{R}^n$ then f is called smooth if for each $x \in U$ there is an open set W of $\mathbb{R}^n$ containing x and a smooth function F on W that agrees with f on $W \cap U$. A function $f : U \to V$ is said to be a *diffeomorphism* if f is bijective and both f and f^{-1} are smooth. If such an f exists we say that U and V are diffeomorphic.

DEFINITION 8.12 Let X be a subset of $\mathbb{R}^n$. Then X is said to be a *smooth n–manifold* if for each $x \in X$, there is a neighbourhood U of x in X and an open set V in $\mathbb{R}^n$ such that there is a diffeomorphism h between U and V.

In other words, a smooth n–manifold is a space that is locally like $\mathbb{R}^n$. For example, the 2–sphere in $\mathbb{R}^3$ is a 2–manifold because a neighbourhood of each point on the 2–sphere "looks like" an open set in $\mathbb{R}^2$. Suppose now that $\precsim$ is a continuous total preorder on some open set V in $\mathbb{R}^n$. Consider the set $I = \{ (x,y) \in V \times V : x \sim y \}$. Now I is not an "indifference curve". It is the graph of the indifference relation $\sim$. The crux of Debreu's approach is to use smoothness assumptions on I. More precisely, we have the following definition.

DEFINITION 8.13 Consider a preference relation $\precsim$ on an open subset V of $\mathbb{R}^n$ that is a continuous, monotonic total preorder. We say that the preference relation is smooth if $\precsim$ (or its graph I) is a smooth n–manifold.

We then have the following theorem on the existence of a differentiable function representing a smooth preference relation. The version stated below is based on the work of Debreu and is due to Mas–Colell (1985).

THEOREM 8.14 Let V be an open subset of $\mathbb{R}^n$ and $\precsim$ a preference relation on V that is a locally non–satiated continuous total preorder such that, for each $x \in V$, the indifference set $I_x = \{ y \in X : x \sim y \}$ is connected. Then there is a differentiable utility function f with no critical point representing $\precsim$ if and only if $\precsim$ is a smooth preference relation.

PROOF See Mas–Colell (1985), Bridges and Mehta (1995) and McLennan (1995).
∎

REMARK 8.15 . The proof of Mas–Colell's theorem is not easy. The idea of the proof is as follows. First, a point $x \in V$ is selected. Then a differentiable utility function is constructed on a neighbourhood of x essentially by using the implicit–function theorem. In the second part of the proof, Zorn's Lemma is used to obtain a differentiable utility function on the whole space V. It is also worth observing that the proof of the existence of a differentiable utility function appears to be completely different from the earlier proofs of the existence of continuous utility functions.

8.4   Jointly Continuous Utility Functions

So far we have studied the problem of the existence of a continuous order homomorphism (or order monomorphism) on a topological space $(X, \mathcal{T})$ with *one* relation $\precsim$ or $\prec$ defined on it. Suppose now that instead of one relation there is a set $\Gamma = \{\precsim_i : i \in I\}$ of relations defined on X, say, one for each consumer i in the set I. Suppose that there is some topology $\mathcal{S}$ defined on this set Γ. Then the following problem presents itself. Find conditions on the topological spaces $(X, \mathcal{T})$ and $(\Gamma, \mathcal{S})$ that imply that there is a continuous function $u : X \times \Gamma \to \mathbb{R}$ such that for each $i \in I$, the section $u(\cdot, i)$ is a continuous order homomorphism (or order monomorphism) on X.

Now to prove that there is a continuous function u of the type described above one needs topologies on X and Γ. For simplicity assume that $X \subset \mathbb{R}^n$. Then the concept of "nearness" in X is clear because it is defined by the Euclidean distance. But how does one define "nearness" in the set I of preference relations on X? This is done as follows. A relation $\precsim$ on X is a subset of $X \times X$. Therefore, preference relations are just elements of the set $X \times X$ and "nearness" may be defined in terms of a metric or topology on that set. Various approaches to this problem have been used in the literature. Kannai (1970) was the "first" to define a concept of "nearness" for the set of preference relations. Debreu (1969) introduced a different concept that is based on the concept of Hausdorff distance between two sets.

Hildenbrand (1970) was one of the first economists to introduce the topology of closed convergence in economics. Subsequently, other topologies on the set of preference relations have also been proposed, for example, the order topology (Chichilnisky, 1977). Due to limitations of space we only briefly consider the topology of closed convergence. For further discussion see Bridges and Mehta (1995, Chapter 8).

DEFINITION 8.16 Let X be a topological space. For each compact set K of X and each finite family $\mathcal{E}$ of open subsets of X, let $[K : \mathcal{E}] = \{S \subset X : S$ is closed, $S \cap K = \emptyset$ and $S \cap G \neq \emptyset$ for each $G \in \mathcal{E}\}$. It is easily verified that sets of this type form a basis for a topology called the *topology of closed convergence* on the set of all closed subsets of X.

As an example of the use of this topology we consider a recent theorem of Bridges (1988) on the existence of a jointly continuous utility function. A feature of the approach used by Bridges is that it enables him to write down explicitly a formula for the utility function.

THEOREM 8.17 Let X be a closed convex subset of $\mathbb{R}^n$ and $\mathcal{P}(X)$ a set of irreflexive, transitive locally non–satiated preference relations on X with an open graph. Assume, in addition, that for each $\prec \in \mathcal{P}$ the negation $\precsim$ is transitive. Let $\mathcal{P}(X)$ be endowed with the topology of closed convergence. Then there exists a continuous function $u : X \times \mathcal{P}(X) \to \mathbb{R}$ such that for each $\prec \in \mathcal{P}(X)$ the section $u(\cdot, \prec)$ is a utility function.

The strategy of the proof given by Bridges is as follows. Assume first that there is only one preference relation $\prec$ on X. Using a variant of the method used by Arrow and Hahn, he constructs a continuous utility function $u(B_n, \cdot)$ on, roughly speaking, the upper section of each compact subset B_n of X. This utility function is defined in terms of Euclidean distance. Bridges then proves that the required continuous function is the map taking

$$(\prec, x) \text{ to } u(\prec, x) = \sum_{n=1}^{\infty} 2^{-n} u(\prec, B_n, x)/[1 + u(\prec, B_n, x)] \qquad (8.1)$$

which is the required continuous function.

8.5   *Existence of a Utility Function with Values in a Lexicographic Product*

Hitherto, we have assumed that a utility function is a real–valued order preserving function on an ordered set. We now prove a theorem due to Milgram (1939) [see also Chipman (1960)] on the existence of a utility function on a partially ordered set with values in a set of lexicographically ordered transfinite sequences. In this section, it is assumed that the reader is familiar with the theory of cardinal and ordinal numbers [see, for example, Devlin (1979)].

DEFINITION 8.18 A collection $\mathcal{L}$ of upper sections of a partially ordered set $(X, \precsim)$ is said to be a *separating system* of X if for each pair $a \prec b$ there exists $U \in \mathcal{L}$ such that $b \in U$ and $a \notin U$.

Let β be the cardinal number of a set P. Then β is the least ordinal number that is equinumerous with P. Let D_M denote the set of all (perhaps trans-finite) sequences $a = (a_1, a_2, \ldots, a_n, \ldots)$ of length μ (i.e., n goes through all ordinal numbers less than μ) such that $a_n = 0$ or $a_n = 1$ for all n. Order D_M lexicographically — that is, define $a \prec b$ if and only if there exists i such that $a_i = 0, b_i = 1$ and $a_n = b_n$ for all $n < i$.

THEOREM 8.19 Let $\prec$ be a strict partial order on a set X having a separating system $\mathcal{L}$ of upper sections such that the cardinal number of $\mathcal{L}$ is β. Then there is an order homomorphism f on X with values in D_M.

PROOF By the Well–Ordering Theorem of Zermelo the elements of $\mathcal{L}$ may be written in a well–ordered sequence $U_1, U_2, ., \ldots$. Define a function f on X by $f(p) = (a_1(p), a_2(p), \ldots, a_n(p), \ldots)$ where $a_n(p) = 1$ if $p \in U_n$ and $a_n(p) = 0$ if $p \notin U_n$ for each $p \in X$. If $p \precsim q$, then q belongs to any upper section to which p belongs which implies that $a_n(p) \leq a_n(q)$ for each n. Since $\mathcal{L}$ is a separating system there exists i such that $q \in U_i$ and $p \notin U_i$. For this i, $a_i(p) = 0$ and $a_i(q) = 1$ which implies that $f(p) < f(q)$ and the theorem is proved. ∎

Acknowledgments

Most of the work for this article was done while the author was visiting the Department of Applied Economics at the University of Cambridge, England and the Department of Mathematics at Dalhousie University, Canada in 1992. I should like to thank these institutions for their hospitality and for providing an excellent research environment. I acknowledge the assistance given to me at the Killam Computer Laboratory at Dalhousie University. I am also grateful to an anonymous referee for valuable comments.

References

Alcantud, J. C. R. (1997). Topological Separability and Axioms of Countability in GPO Spaces. *Bulletin of the Australian Mathematical Society*, 55:131–142.

Aliprantis, C., Brown, D., and Burkinshaw, O. (1989). *Existence and Optimality of Competitive Equilibria*. Springer-Verlag, Berlin–Heidelberg.

Arrow, K. J. and Hahn, F. (1971). *General Competitive Analysis*. Holden-Day, Edinburgh.

Aubin, J. (1977). *Applied Abstract Analysis*. Wiley, New York.

Bartle, R. (1964). *The Elements of Real Analysis*. Wiley, New York.

Bartle, R. (1966). *The Elements of Integration*. Wiley, New York.

Beardon, A. F. (1992). Debreu's Gap Theorem. *Economic Theory*, 2:150–152.

Beardon, A. F. (1994a). Utility Theory and Continuous Monotonic Functions. *Economic Theory*, 4:531–538.

Beardon, A. F. (1994b). Totally Ordered Subsets of Euclidean Space. *Journal of Mathematical Economics*, 23:391–393.

Beardon, A. F. and Mehta, G. B. (1994a). Utility functions and the Order Type of the Continuum. *Journal of Mathematical Economics*, 23:387–390.

Beardon, A. F. and Mehta, G. B. (1994b). The Utility Theorems of Wold, Debreu and Arrow–Hahn. *Econometrica*, 62:181–186.

Berliant, M. (1982). *A General Equilibrium Model of an Economy with Land*. PhD thesis, University of California, Berkeley.

Berliant, M. (1986). A Utility Representation for a Preference Relation on a σ-algebra. *Econometrica*, 54:359–352.

Berliant, M. and Ten Raa, T. (1988). A Foundation of Location Theory: Consumer Preferences and Demand. *Journal of Economic Theory*, 44:336–353.

Birkhoff, G. (1948). *Lattice Theory*, volume 25. American Mathematical Society Colloquium Publication.

Boothby, W. (1986). *Introduction to Differentiable Manifolds and Riemannian Geometry*. Academic Press, New York, 2nd edition.

Bosi, G. (1996a). Continuous Representations of Interval Orders based on Induced Preorders. *Rivista di Matematica per le Scienze Economiche e Sociali*, 18:75–81.

Bosi, G. (1996b). A Note on the Existence of Continuous Representations of Homothetic Preferences on Topological Vector Spaces. Preprint.

Bosi, G. (1996c). A Note on the Existence of Semicontinuous Order Preserving Functions. Preprint.

Bosi, G. and Isler, R. (1995). Representing Preferences with Nontransitive Indifference by a Single Real–Valued Function. *Journal of Mathematical Economics*, 24:621–631.

Bosi, G. and Metha, G. B. (1997). Semicontinous Order Preserving Functions and Separable Systems. In preparation.

Bowen, R. (1968). A New Proof of a Theorem in Utility Theory. *International Economic Review*, 9:374.

Bridges, D. S. (1982). Preference and Utility—A Constructive Development. *Journal of Mathematical Economics*, 9:165–185.

Bridges, D. S. (1983a). A Numerical Representation of Preferences with Intransitive Indifference. *Journal of Mathematical Economics*, 11:24–42.

Bridges, D. S. (1983b). Numerical Representation of Intransitive Preferences on a Countable Set. *Journal of Economic Theory*, 30:213–217.

Bridges, D. S. (1985). Representing Interval Orders by a Single Real-Valued Function. *Journal of Economic Theory*, 36:149–155.

Bridges, D. S. (1986). Numerical Representation of an Interval Order on a Topological Space. *Journal of Economic Theory*, 38:160–166.

Bridges, D. S. (1988). The Euclidean Distance Construction of Order Homomorphisms. *Mathematical Social Sciences*, 15:179–188.

Bridges, D. S. and Mehta, G. B. (1995). *Representations of Preference Orderings*. Springer-Verlag, Berlin–Heidelberg.

Candeal, J. C., Hervés, C., and Induráin, E. (1996a). Some Results on Representation and Extension of Preferences. To appear in Journal of Mathematical Economics.

Candeal, J. C. and Induráin, E. (1992). Utility Representations on Partially Ordered Topological Groups. *Proceedings of the American Mathematical Society*, 115:765–767.

Candeal, J. C. and Induráin, E. (1993a). Utility Functions on Chains. *Journal of Mathematical Economics*, 22:161–168.

Candeal, J. C. and Induráin, E. (1993b). Utility Representations from the Concept of Measure. *Mathematical Social Sciences*, 26:51–62.

Candeal, J. C. and Induráin, E. (1994). On the Lebesgue Measure of Indifference Classes. *Cuadernos Aragoneses De Economia*, 4:345–350.

Candeal, J. C. and Induráin, E. (1995). A Note on Linear Utility. *Economic Theory*, 6:519–522.

Candeal, J. C. and Induráin, E. (1996). Lexicographic Behaviour of Chains. Preprint.

Candeal, J. C., Induráin, E., and Mehta, G. B. (1995a). Some Utility Theorems on Inductive Limits of Preordered Topological Spaces. *Bulletin of the Australian Mathematical Society*, 52:235–246.

Candeal, J. C., Induráin, E., and Mehta, G. B. (1995b). Utility Functions on Banach Spaces. Preprint.

Candeal, J. C., Induráin, E., and Mehta, G. B. (1996b). Further Remarks on Totally Ordered Representable Subsets of Euclidean Space. *Journal of Mathematical Economics*, 25:381–390.

Candeal, J. C., Miguel, J. R. D., and Induráin, E. (1996c). Additive Utility on Totally Ordered Topological Semigroups. Preprint.

Candeal, J. C., Miguel, J. R. D., Induráin, E., and Mehta, G. B. (1997). Entropy and Utility. Preprint.

Cantor, G. (1955). *Contributions to the Founding of the Theory of Transfinite Numbers*. Dover, New York.

Chateauneuf, A. (1987a). Continuous Representation of a Preference Relation on a Topological Space. *Journal of Mathematical Economics*, 16:139–146.

Chateauneuf, A. (1987b). Existence of a Continuous Utility Function and Metrizability. Universite de Paris. Preprint.

Chichilnisky, G. (1976). *Manifolds of Preferences and Equilibria — Technical Report No. 27, Project on Efficiency of Decision Making in Economic Systems.* Harvard University.

Chichilnisky, G. (1977). Spaces of Economic Agents. *Journal of Economic Theory,* 15:160–173.

Chichilnisky, G. (1980). Continuous Representation of Preferences. *Review of Economic Studies,* 47:959–963.

Chipman, J. S. (1960). The Foundations of Utility. *Econometrica,* 28:193–224.

Chipman, J. S., Hurwicz, L., Richter, M. K., and Sonnenschein, H. F., editors (1971). *Preferences, Utility and Demand.* Harcourt Brace and Jovanovich, New York.

Cohen, M. and Girard, B. (1971). Preordres et Toplogiies sur un Ensemble Fonction d'Utilite. *Bulletin de Mathematiques Economiques,* 5:7–34.

Conlon, L. (1993). *Differentiable Manifolds: A First Course.* Birkhäuser, Boston.

Croom, F. (1989). *Principles of Topology.* Saunders College Publishing, Philadelphia.

Debreu, G. (1954). Representation of a Preference Ordering by a Numerical Function. In R. Thrall, C. C. and Davis, R., editors, *Decision Processes,* pages 159–166. Wiley, New York.

Debreu, G. (1959). *Theory of Value.* Wiley, New York.

Debreu, G. (1964). Continuity Properties of Paretian Utility. *International Economic Review,* 5:285–293.

Debreu, G. (1969). Neighbouring Economic Agents. In *La Decision,* pages 85–90, Paris. Editions du Centre National de la Recherche Scientifique.

Debreu, G. (1972). Smooth Preferences. *Econometrica,* 40:603–615.

Debreu, G. (1976). Smooth Preferences: A Corrigendum. *Econometrica,* 44:831–832.

Devlin, K. (1979). *Fundamentals of Contemporary Set Theory.* Springer–Verlag, New York.

Droste, M. (1987). Ordinal Scales in the Theory of Measurement. *Journal of Mathematical Psychology,* 31:60–82.

Eilenberg, S. (1941). Ordered Topological Spaces. *American Journal of Mathematics,* 63:39–45.

Estévez, M. and Hervés, C. (1995). On the Existence of Continuous Preference Orderings without Utility Representations. *Journal of Mathematical Economics,* 24:305–339.

Fishburn, P. C. (1970a). Suborders on Commodity Spaces. *Journal of Economic Theory,* 2:321–328.

Fishburn, P. C. (1970b). *Mathematics of Decision Theory.* Mouton, The Hague.

Fishburn, P. C. (1970c). *Utility Theory for Decision Making*. Wiley, New York.

Fishburn, P. C. (1970d). Intransitive Indifference with Unequal Indifference Intervals. *Journal of Mathematical Psychology*, 7:144–179.

Fishburn, P. C. (1973). Interval Representations for Interval Orders and Semiorders. *Journal of Mathematical Psychology*, 19:91–105.

Fishburn, P. C. (1974). Lexicographic Orders, Utilities and Decision Rules. *Management Science*, 20:1442–1471.

Fishburn, P. C. (1983). Utility Functions on Ordered Convex Sets. *Journal of Mathematical Economics*, 12:221–232.

Fleischer, I. (1961). Numerical Representation of Utility. *Journal of the Society for Industrial and Applied Mathematics*, 9:48–50.

Florenzano, M. (1976). Preferences and Utility: A Case of Complete Preorder. Preprint.

Frankel, A. (1976). *Abstract Set Theory*. North Holland, Amsterdam, 2nd edition.

Gensemer, S. (1987a). On Relationships between Numerical Representations of Interval Orders and Semiorders. *Journal of Economic Theory*, 43:157–169.

Gensemer, S. (1987b). Continuous Semiorder Representations. *Journal of Mathematical Economics*, 16:275–289.

Georgescu-Roegen, N. (1936). The Pure Theory of Consumer Behaviour. *Quarterly Journal of Economics*, 50:545–593.

Glustoff, E. (1975). On Continuous Utility: The Euclidean Distance Approach. *Quarterly Journal of Economics*, 89:512–517.

Grandmont, J. (1972). Continuity Properties of von–Neumann–Morgenstern Utilities. *Journal of Economic Theory*, 4:45–57.

Grodal, B. (1974). A Note on the Space of Preference Relations. *Journal of Mathematical Economics*, 1:279–294.

Guillemin, V. and Pollack, A. (1974). *Differential Topology*. Prentice–Hall, Englewood Cliffs, New Jersey.

Herden, G. (1989a). On the Existence of Utility Functions. *Mathematical Social Sciences*, 17:297–313.

Herden, G. (1989b). On the Existence of Utility Functions II. *Mathematical Social Sciences*, 18:107–117.

Herden, G. (1989c). Some Lifting Theorems for Continuous Utility Functions. *Mathematical Social Sciences*, 18:119–134.

Herden, G. (1990). On a Lifting Theorem of Nachbin. *Mathematical Social Sciences*, 19:37–44.

Herden, G. (1991). Topological Spaces for which Every Continuous Total Preorder has a Continuous Utility Function. *Mathematical Social Sciences*, 22:123–136.

Herden, G. (1993a). On the Lifting of Continuous Utility Functions I. Preprint.

Herden, G. (1993b). On the Lifting of Continuous Utility Functions II. Preprint.

Herden, G. (1995). On Some Equivalent Approaches to Mathematical Utility Theory. *Mathematical Social Sciences*, 29:19–31.

Herden, G. and Mehta, G. B. (1994). The Continuous Analogue and Generalization of the classical Birkhoff-Milgram Theorem. *Mathematical Social Sciences*, 28:59–66.

Herden, G. and Mehta, G. B. (1996). Open Gaps, Metrization and Utility. *Economic Theory*, 7:541–546.

Herden, G. and Mehta, G. B. (1997a). Continuous Order Preserving Functions and Lifting Theorems of the Urysohn–Nachbin Type. In preparation.

Herden, G. and Mehta, G. B. (1997b). Is the Debreu Gap Lemma Generalizable? Preprint.

Herden, G. and Mehta, G. B. (1997c). Semicontinuous Order Preserving Functions. Preprint.

Herden, G. and Mehta, G. B. (1997d). The Structure of Separable systems on a Topological Space. Preprint.

Hicks, J. (1956). *A Revision of Demand Theory*. Clarendon Press, Oxford.

Hicks, N. (1965). *Notes on Differential Geometry*. Van Nostrand, New York.

Hildenbrand, W. (1970). On Economies with Many Agents. *Journal of Economic Theory*, 2:161–188.

Hildenbrand, W. (1974). *Core and Equilibria of a Large Economy*. Princeton University Press, Princeton.

Hu, S. (1979). *Introduction to General Topology*. Tata McGraw-Hill, New Delhi.

Jaffray, J. (1974). *Existence, proprietes de continuite, additivite de fonction d'utilite sur un espace partialllement ou totalement ordonne*. These de doctorat d'etat es sciences, Universite de Paris VI.

Jaffray, J. (1975a). Existence of a Continuous Utility Function: An Elementary Proof. *Econometrica*, 43:981–983.

Jaffray, J. (1975b). Semicontinuous Extension of a Partial Order. *Journal of Mathematical Economics*, 2:395–406.

Jameson, G. (1974). *Topology and Normed Spaces*. Chapman and Hall, London.

Jevons, S. (1931). *Theory of Political Economy*. Macmillan, London.

Kamke, E. (1950). *Theory of Sets*. Dover, New York.

Kannai, Y. (1963). Existence of a Utility in Infinite Dimensional Partially Ordered Spaces. *Israel Journal of Mathematics*, 1:229–234.

Kannai, Y. (1970). Continuity Properties of the Core of a Market. *Econometrica*, 38:791–815.

Kannai, Y. (1974). Approximation of Convex Preferences. *Journal of Mathematical Economics*, 1:101–106.

Kelley, J. (1955). *General Topology*. Van Nostrand, New York.

Klein, E. and Thompson, A. (1984). *Theory of Correspondences Including Applications to Mathematical Economics*. Wiley, New York.

Koopmans, T. (1966). Structure of Preference over Time. Cowles Foundation Discussion Paper No. 206.

Kreps, D. (1988). *Notes on the Theory of Choice*. Westview, London.

Lee, L. (1972). The Theorems of Debreu and Peleg for Ordered Topological Spaces. *Econometrica*, 40:1151–1153.

Levin, V. (1983a). Measurable Utility Theorems for Closed and Lexicographic Preference Relations. *Soviet Math. Doklady*, 28:639–643.

Levin, V. (1983b). A Continuous Utility Theorem for Closed Preorders on a σ-Compact Metrizable Space. *Soviet Math. Doklady*, 28:715–718.

Luce, R. D. (1957). Semiorders and a Theory of Utility Discrimination. *Econometrica*, 24:178–191.

Majumdar, M. and Sen, A. K. (1976). A Note on Representing Partial Orderings. *Review of Economic Studies*, 43:403–404.

Mas-Colell, A. (1977a). On the Continuous Representation of Preorders. *International Economic Review*, 18:509–513.

Mas-Colell, A. (1977b). Regular Nonconvex Economies. *Econometrica*, 45:1387–1430.

Mas-Colell, A. (1985). *The Theory of General Economic Equilibrium: A Differentiable Approach*. Cambridge University Press, Cambridge.

Mas-Colell, A. (1986). The Price Equilibrium Existence Problem in Topological Vector Lattices. *Econometrica*, 54:1039–1053.

Mashburn, J. (1995). A Note on Reordering Ordered Topological Spaces and the Existence of Continuous Strictly Increasing Functions. Preprint.

McLennan, A. (1995). On the Representability of C^r Preference Relations by Utility Functions. *Economic Theory*, 6:357–363.

Mehta, G. B. (1977a). Topological Ordered Spaces and Utility Functions. *International Economic Review*, 18:779–782.

Mehta, G. B. (1977b). A Comment on Peleg's Theorem. *Economic Analysis and Policy*, 7:53–57.

Mehta, G. B. (1981). A New Extension Procedure for the Arrow–Hahn Theorem. *International Economic Review*, 22:113–118.

Mehta, G. B. (1983a). Recent Developments in Utility Theory. *Indian Economic Journal*, 30:103–125.

Mehta, G. B. (1983b). Order-Separable Spaces. *Economics Letters*, 12:49–51.

Mehta, G. B. (1983c). Ordered Topological Spaces and the Theorems of Debreu and Peleg. *Indian Journal of Pure and Applied Mathematics*, 14:1174–1182.

Mehta, G. B. (1984). On a Theorem of Peleg. *Indian Journal of Pure and Applied Mathematics*, 15:1072–1074.

Mehta, G. B. (1985). Continuous Utility Functions. *Economics Letters*, 18:113–115.

Mehta, G. B. (1986a). Existence of an Order Preserving Function on a Normally Preordered Space. *Bulletin of the Australian Mathematical Society*, 34:141–147.

Mehta, G. B. (1986b). On a Theorem of Fleischer. *Journal of the Australian Mathematical Society*, Series A, 40:261–266.

Mehta, G. B. (1988). Some General Theorems on the Existence of Order Preserving Functions. *Mathematical Social Sciences*, 15:135–143.

Mehta, G. B. (1991a). The Euclidean Distance Approach to Continuous Utility Functions. *Quarterly Journal of Economics*, 106:975–977.

Mehta, G. B. (1991b). Utility Functions on Preordered Normed Linear Spaces. *Applied Mathematics Letters*, 4:53–55.

Mehta, G. B. (1992). Remarks on Some Recent Developments in Utility Theory. University of Cambridge Economic Theory, Discussion Paper No. 180.

Mehta, G. B. (1993a). Existence of a Continuous Utility Function with Path Monotonicity: the Wold Approach. *Economic Theory*, 3:387–392.

Mehta, G. B. (1993b). Order Extension of Order Monomorphisms on a Preordered Topological Space. *International Journal of Mathematics and Mathematical Sciences*, 16:663–668.

Mehta, G. B. (1995). Metric Utility Functions. *Journal of Economic Behaviour and Organization*, 26:289–298.

Mehta, G. B. (1997). A Remark on a Utility Representation Theorem of Rader. *Economic Theory*, 9:367–370.

Mehta, G. B. and Monteiro, P. K. (1996). Infinite Dimensional Utility Representation Theorems. *Economics Letters*, 53:169–173.

Michael, E. (1956). Continuous Selections I. *Annals of Mathematics*, 6, 3:361–382.

Milgram, A. (1939). Partially Ordered Sets, Separating Systems and Inductiveness. In *Reports of a Mathematical Colloquium*, Second Series, pages 18–30, Paris. University of Notre Dame.

Milgram, A. (1940). Partially Ordered Sets and Topology. In *Reports of a Mathematical Colloquium*, Second Series, pages 3–9. University of Notre Dame.

Milnor, J. (1965). *Topology from a Differentiable Viewpoint*. University of Virginia Press, Charlottesville, Virginia.

Monteiro, P. K. (1987). Some Results on the Existence of Utility Functions on Path Connected Spaces. *Journal of Mathematical Economics*, 16:147–156.

Mount, K. and Reiter, S. (1974). Continuous Representation of Preferences. Centre for Mathematical Studies in Economics and Management Science, Discussion Paper No. 81, Northwestern University, Evanston, Illinois.

Mount, K. and Reiter, S. (1976). Construction of a Continuous Utility Function for a Class of Preferences. *Journal of Mathematical Economics*, 3:227–246.

Munkres, J. (1975). *Topology: A First Course*. Prentice-Hall, Englewood Cliffs, New Jersey.

Nachbin, L. (1965). *Topology and Order*. Van Nostrand, New York.

Neuefeind, W. (1972). On Continuous Utility. *Journal of Economic Theory*, 5:174–176.

Newman, P. and Read, R. (1958). Demand Theory Without a Utility Index - A Comment. *Review of Economic Studies*, 25:197–200.

Newman, P. and Read, R. (1961). Representation Problems for Preference Orderings. *The Journal of Economic Behaviour*, 1:149–169.

O'Neill, B. (1966). *Elementary Differential Geometry*. Academic Press, New York.

Pareto, V. (1971). *Manual of Political Economy*. A. M. Kelley, New York.

Peleg, B. (1970). Utility Functions for Partially Ordered Topological Spaces. *Econometrica*, 38:93–96.

Rader, T. (1963). The Existence of a Utility Function to Represent Preferences. *Review of Economic Studies*, 30:229–232.

Richard, S. and Zame, W. (1986). Proper Preferences and Quasi-Concave Utility Functions. *Journal of Mathematical Economics*, 15:231–247.

Richter, M. K. (1966). Revealed Preference Theory. *Econometrica*, 34:635–645.

Richter, M. K. (1980). Continuous and Semicontinuous Utility. *International Economic Review*, 21:293–299.

Roberts, F. (1979). Measurement Theory. *Encyclopedia of Mathematics*, 7. Addison-Wesley, Reading, Massachusetts.

Robertson, A. and Robertson, W. (1964). *Topological Vector Spaces*. Cambridge University Press, Cambridge.

Royden, H. (1968). *Real Analysis*. Macmillan.

Rudin, W. (1976). *Principles of Mathematical Analysis*. McGraw-Hill, New York, 3rd edition.

Schmeidler, D. (1970). A Condition for the Completeness of Partial Preference Relations. *Econometrica*, 39:403–404.

Scott, D. and Suppes, P. (1958). Foundational Aspects of Theories of Measurement. *Journal of Symbolic Logic*, 23:113–128.

Shafer, W. (1984). Representations of Preorders on Normed Spaces. Preprint.

Simmons, G. (1963). *Introduction to Topology and Modern Analysis*. McGraw-Hill, New York.

Smith, A. (1904). *The Wealth of Nations*. Metheun, London.

Sondermann, D. (1980). Utility Representations for Partial Orders. *Journal of Economic Theory*, 23:183–188.

Sondermann, D. (1982). Revealed Preference Theory. *Econometrica*, 50:777–780.

Vohra, R. (1995). The Souslin Hypothesis and Continuous Utility Functions: A Remark. *Economic Theory*, 5:537–540.

Wakker, P. (1988). Continuity of Preference Relations for Separable Topologies. *International Economic Review*, 29:105–110.

Weymark, J. (1985). Money-Metric Utility Functions. *International Economic Review*, 28:219–232.

Wieczorek, A. (1979). An Elementary Proof of the Measurable Utility Theorem. In Moeschlin, O. and Pallaschke, D., editors, *Game Theory and Related Topics*, pages 253–264. North Holland, Amsterdam.

Wieczorek, A. (1980). On the Measurable Utility Theorem. *Journal of Mathematical Economics*, 7:165–173.

Wold, H. (1943–44). A Synthesis of Pure Demand Analysis I, II and III. *Skandinavisk Actuarietidskrift*, 26:85–118, 220–263, 69–120.

Yokoyama, T. (1956). Continuity Conditions of Preference Orderings. *Osaka Economic Papers*, 4:39–45.

2 SEPARABILITY: A SURVEY

Charles Blackorby*
Daniel Primont**
and R. Robert Russell***

*University of British Columbia and GREQAM
**University at Carbondale, Southern Illinois
***University of California at Riverside

Contents

1	Introductory Remarks		51
2	Decentralization and Separability		51
	2.1	Notation	52
	2.2	Decentralization	53
	2.3	Separability and Functional Structure	54
	2.4	Decentralization $\Longleftrightarrow$ Separability	58
3	Price Aggregation and Budgeting		59
	3.1	Price Aggregation	60
	3.2	Two–Stage Budgeting	61
4	Separability and Duality		63
	4.1	Dual Representations of Preferences: Indirect Utility, Expenditure, and Distance Functions	64
	4.2	Separability of Dual Representations of Preferences	65
	4.3	Homothetic Separability	68
	4.4	Additive Price Aggregation	69

49

5   Additive Structures.   70

      5.1   Complete Separability   71

      5.2   Additivity in a Two–Group Partition.   74

      5.3   Additivity and Duality.   75

6   Conjunction of Direct and Indirect Separability and Additivity   77

      6.1   Direct and Indirect Additivity   78

      6.2   Direct and Indirect Separability   79

7   Implicit Separability   82

8   Concluding Remarks: Extensions and Applications.   87

References   88

1 Introductory Remarks

Separability is a powerful restriction on orderings, requiring that the (conditional) ordering on a subspace be invariant with respect to changes in the values of variables outside that subspace. Various separability conditions impose convenient (additive and non–additive) structures on the (direct and dual) representations of preferences. Direct separability is equivalent to the existence of commodity aggregates, like "food" and "clothing" — constructions that are central to most empirical applications of consumer theory. Dual separability notions are equivalent to the existence of price aggregates, like the "price of food." A separability condition is also equivalent to the optimality of decentralized decision making — e.g., allocating a food budget to food items using only food prices as information, or allocating current expenditure to current consumption commodities without knowing future prices. Stronger conditions rationalize two–stage budgeting — allocating total expenditure to broad categories using price and quantity indices for these categories in the first stage and then allocating the category expenditures to the components of each category.

This survey lays out the fundamentals of separability theory, integrating literature half a century old with recent results. For convenience the results are presented in the guise of consumer theory, but they hold for any organization or agent with a well–behaved preference ordering.

Section 2 develops the connection between separability, simple structures induced by separability, commodity aggregation, and decentralized decision making. Section 3 discusses price aggregation and two–stage budgeting. Section 4 develops the theory of separability of dual representations of consumer preferences (the indirect utility function, the expenditure function, and the distance function) and the relationships between them. Section 5 introduces additive structures and their relationships to separability conditions. Section 6 examines the implications of conjoining direct and indirect separability and additivity. Section 7 discusses "implicit separability" (separability of an arbitrary, implicit representation of preferences) and applies the concept to a problem of second–best planning. Finally, Section 8 concludes with a brief description of additional applications of the theory of separability, referring the reader to the relevant literature for details.

2 Decentralization and Separability

Consumers must make choices among a large number of goods — both consumption and leisure, both present and future. The apparent complexity of their decision–making problems may lead consumers to simplify budgeting practices (short–cuts). Are these procedures consistent with rational behavior? In modeling consumer behavior, economists — theoretical and empirical — employ models that consider only a subset or several subsets of the complete list of goods and services consumed. Can these practices be justified? And, if so, what kinds of restrictions do these rationalizations place on the preferences and the behavior of the consumer. In what follows, we discuss several proposals that address this class of problems and present their solutions.

One way to think about reducing the complexity of the allocation decision is to imagine that the consumer receives a lump sum of money that he or she first allocates to broad classes of commodities, such as food, shelter, and recreation. Detailed decisions about how to spend the money that has been allocated to the food budget are postponed until one is actually in the store buying specific food items.

More formally, if the correct amount of money to spend on food commodities, for example, has been allocated, under what circumstances is the consumer able to dispense the food budget among food commodities knowing only the food prices? If the consumer can arrive at an optimal pattern of food expenditures in this way, preferences are said to be *decentralizable*. It is fairly obvious that, if food commodities were separable from all other commodities, decentralization would be possible. What is somewhat surprising, however, is that separability is necessary as well as sufficient for this practice to be rationalized. We first present more formally the concepts of decentralization and separability and then discuss their equivalence.

2.1   Notation

Define the consumer's consumption space, Ω, as a subset of $\mathbb{R}^N_+$, the N–dimensional nonnegative orthant. We assume that Ω is a closed and convex set with a nonempty interior. A consumption vector is an element of Ω and is denoted by the N-tuple, $x = (x_1, \ldots, x_N)$. We further assume that the consumer has a preference ordering, $\succeq$, defined over the consumption vectors in Ω, and that this preference ordering is complete,[1] transitive,[2] and continuous.[3] The completeness, transitivity, and continuity of the preference ordering ensure the existence of a continuous, real–valued utility function — i.e., a continuous, real–valued function, U, that satisfies

$$U(x) \geq U(x') \quad \text{if and only if} \quad x \succeq x' \quad \text{for all} \quad x, x' \in \Omega. \tag{2.1}$$

In what follows, we partition the commodity indices $I = \{1, 2, \ldots, N\}$ into R subsets $\{I^1, \ldots, I^R\}$. Commodity prices are given by the N–tuple,

---

[1] For all $x, x' \in \Omega$, either $x \succeq x'$ or $x' \succeq x$.

[2] For all $x, x', x'' \in \Omega$ if $x \succeq x'$ and $x' \succeq x''$ then $x \succeq x''$.

[3] For all $x, x' \in \Omega$, the sets, $\{x \mid x \succeq x'\}$ and $\{x \mid x' \succeq x\}$, are closed.

$p = (p_1, \ldots, p_N)$. Given the partition of the commodity indices, we rewrite the quantity and price vectors (in an appropriate permutation of the variable indices) as $x = (x^1, \ldots, x^R)$ and $p = (p^1, \ldots, p^R)$. The consumer's total income (i.e. money income available for consumption) is denoted by y. The consumer's utility–maximization problem,

$$\max_x U(x) \quad \text{subject to} \quad p \cdot x \leq y, \tag{2.2}$$

can be rewritten as

$$\max_x U(x^1, \ldots, x^R) \quad \text{subject to} \quad \sum_{r=1}^{R} p^r \cdot x^r \leq y. \tag{2.3}$$

The solution to (2.2) [or (2.3)] is denoted by[4]

$$\overset{*}{x} = (\overset{*}{x}^1, \ldots, \overset{*}{x}^R) = \big(\Phi^1(y,p), \ldots, \Phi^R(y,p)\big). \tag{2.4}$$

The expenditure on goods in group r is denoted by y_r. Group–r expenditure is optimal if $y_r = p^r \cdot \Phi^r(y,p)$.

2.2 Decentralization

The consumer's utility maximization problem is decentralizable if it is possible for the consumer to optimally allocate the rth group expenditure knowing only the prices of group–r commodities. Formally, we say that the consumer's utility maximization problem is *decentralizable* if there exist functions, $\phi^1, \ldots, \phi^R$, such that

$$\phi^r(y_r, p^r) = \Phi^r(y,p) \quad \text{if} \quad y_r = p^r \cdot \Phi^r(y,p), \quad r = 1, \ldots, R. \tag{2.5}$$

That is, if the consumer knows that it is optimal to spend one hundred and seventy–two dollars on food, decentralization means that only food prices need to be known in order to optimally allocate this sum across the various food items.

As already mentioned, a constrained utility maximization problem is decentralizable if and only if the underlying preferences are separable — a notion to which we now turn.

---

[4]If this solution is not unique, $\overset{*}{x}$ is an arbitrary element in the optimizing set of consumption bundles.

2.3 Separability and Functional Structure

Let $\{I^1, I^2\}$ be a binary partition of the set of the variable indices, I. Corresponding to this partition we write the commodity space as a Cartesian product, $\Omega = \Omega^1 \times \Omega^2$. In the same way, we write the commodity vector (in an appropriate permutation of the variable indices) as $x = (x^1, x^2)$. Define a conditional preference ordering over group–2 commodity vectors, $\succeq^2 (x^1)$, according to

$$x^2 \succeq^2 (x^1) \, \hat{x}^2 \quad \text{if and only if} \quad (x^1, x^2) \succeq (x^1, \hat{x}^2). \tag{2.6}$$

As indicated, this conditional preference ordering depends, in general, on the quantities of commodities in group 1. We say that the commodities in group 2 are *separable* from the commodities in group 1 if the conditional preference ordering, $\succeq^2 (x^1)$, is in fact independent of the quantities of commodities in group 1, in which case it can be written more simply as $\succeq^2$.

This definition of separability is equivalent to the following characterization. Commodities in group 2 are separable from the commodities in group 1 if the following condition holds:

$$U(x^1, x^2) \geq U(x^1, \hat{x}^2) \quad \text{if and only if} \quad U(\bar{x}^1, x^2) \geq U(\bar{x}^1, \hat{x}^2) \tag{2.7}$$

for all $x^1, \bar{x}^1 \in \Omega^1$ and all $x^2, \hat{x}^2 \in \Omega^2$.

We now consider the implications for the utility function of the above separability assumption. It is fairly straightforward to show that the conditional preference ordering for group 2 is complete, transitive, and continuous, since $\succeq$ has these properties. Hence there exists a continuous, real–valued utility function for commodities in group 2; call it U^2. Moreover, under the separability hypothesis, the group–2 utility function, U^2, is independent of x^1. Thus, we conclude that there exists a continuous function, U^2, such that

$$U^2(x^2) \geq U^2(\hat{x}^2) \quad \text{if and only if} \quad x^2 \succeq^2 \hat{x}^2 \tag{2.8}$$

The variable, $u_2 = U^2(x^2)$, can be interpreted as the utility of commodities in group 2 or, more simply, as group–2 utility.

Actually, we know more about the group–2 aggregator function, U^2, than its mere existence. Let O^1 be any fixed vector in Ω^1. Then the group–2 aggregator function may be obtained from the utility function as $U^2(x^2) := U(O^1, x^2)$. Thus U^2 and U are ordinally equivalent representations of group–2 preferences, given the separability hypothesis. This constructive method of determining U^2 makes it clear that the properties of the group–2 aggregator function are inherited directly from the overall utility function. Having determined the aggregator function, we can then define a "macro" function, $\mathcal{U}$, by the following:

$$\mathcal{U}\big(x^1, U^2(x^2)\big) := U(x^1, x^2). \tag{2.9}$$

This leads to the following theorem.

THEOREM 2.1 [Debreu (1959) and Gorman (1968)] Assume that the consumer's preference ordering is complete, transitive, and continuous, and thus is represented by a continuous utility function, U. For the partition, $\{I^1, I^2\}$, commodities in group 2 are separable from the commodities in group 1 if and only if there exist continuous functions, $\mathcal{U}$ and U^2, such that

$$U(x^1, x^2) \equiv \mathcal{U}(x^1, U^2(x^2)), \tag{2.10}$$

where $\mathcal{U}$ is increasing in its last argument.

PROOF The foregoing argument established the structure (2.10) up to the strict monotonicity condition. Demonstration that $\mathcal{U}$ is increasing in $u_2 = U^2(x^2)$ goes as follows:

$$
\begin{aligned}
U^2(x^2) \geq U^2(\hat{x}^2) &\iff x^2 \succeq^2 \hat{x}^2 \quad \text{(by construction)} \\
&\iff (x^1, x^2) \succeq (x^1, \hat{x}^2) \quad \text{(by separability)} \\
&\iff U(x^1, x^2) \geq U(x^1, \hat{x}^2) \quad \text{(by (2.1))} \\
&\iff \mathcal{U}(x^1, U^2(x^2)) \geq \mathcal{U}(x^1, U^2(\hat{x}^2)) \quad \text{(by (2.10)).}
\end{aligned}
\tag{2.11}
$$

Therefore,

$$U^2(x^2) \geq U^2(\hat{x}^2) \iff \mathcal{U}(x^1, U^2(x^2)) \geq \mathcal{U}(x^1, U^2(\hat{x}^2)), \tag{2.12}$$

which implies that $\mathcal{U}$ is increasing in $u_2 = U^2(x^2)$.

A demonstration that the functional structure of the utility function, (2.10), implies separability is as follows:

$$
\begin{aligned}
x^2 \succeq^2 (x^1) \, \hat{x}^2 &\iff (x^1, x^2) \succeq (x^1, \hat{x}^2) \quad \text{(by definition)} \\
&\iff U(x^1, x^2) \geq U(x^1, \hat{x}^2) \quad \text{(by (2.1))} \\
&\iff \mathcal{U}(x^1, U^2(x^2)) \geq \mathcal{U}(x^1, U^2(\hat{x}^2)) \quad \text{(by (2.10))} \\
&\iff U^2(x^2) \geq U^2(\hat{x}^2) \\
&\qquad \text{(by strict monotonicity of } \mathcal{U} \text{ in } u_2\text{).}
\end{aligned}
\tag{2.13}
$$

The last equivalence implies that the conditional ordering over group–2 commodities is independent of group–1 quantities. ∎

An important implication of Theorem 2.1 is that a quantity aggregate, given by $u_2 = U^2(x^2)$, exists for group 2 if and only if group 2 is separable from group 1. Thus, quantity aggregation is equivalent to separability.[5]

---

[5]Unlike a Hicksian composite commodity, the quantity aggregate obtained under the separability hypothesis depends only on group–2 quantities and not on group–2 prices.

This is a good place to discuss the original definition of separability attributable to Leontief (1947a, 1947b) and Sono (1945, 1961). This definition is applicable when the consumer's utility function is increasing in every good and is twice continuously differentiable. Let $U_i(x)$ be the first partial derivative of the utility function with respect to commodity i. We refer to the following as the Leontief–Sono condition:

$$\frac{\partial}{\partial x_k}\left(\frac{U_i(x)}{U_j(x)}\right) = 0.$$

In economic terms, the Leontief–Sono condition says that the consumer's marginal rate of substitution between goods i and j is independent of the level of consumption of good k. Then the set of commodities in group 2 is separable from the set of commodities in group 1 if the Leontief–Sono condition holds for all $i,j \in I^2$ and all $k \in I^1$. We leave it to the reader to show that the functional structure of the utility function given in Theorem 2.1 yields, upon differentiation, the Leontief–Sono separability condition.

EXAMPLE 2.2 Let $I = \{1,2,3,4\}$, $I^1 = \{1,2\}$, and $I^2 = \{3,4\}$. Consider the utility function given by

$$U(x_1, x_2, x_3, x_4) = x_1^{1/3} x_3^{1/3} x_4^{1/3} + x_2^{1/2} x_3^{1/4} x_4^{1/4}.$$

By defining $u_2 = U^2(x_3, x_4) = x_3^{1/3} x_4^{1/3}$ and $\mathcal{U}(x_1, x_2, u_2) = x_1^{1/3} u_2 + x_2^{1/2} u_2^{3/4}$, we observe that

$$U(x_1, x_2, x_3, x_4) = \mathcal{U}(x_1, x_2, u_2),$$

and hence that group 2 is separable from group 1. One may also confirm this fact using the Leontief–Sono conditions. The reader should notice that the choice of the aggregator and macro functions is not unique. An alternative choice would be $u_2 = U^2(x_3, x_4) = x_3^{1/2} x_4^{1/2}$ and $\mathcal{U}(x_1, x_2, u_2) = x_1^{1/3} u_2^{2/3} + x_2^{1/2} u_2^{1/2}$. In this case, the aggregator function is chosen to be homogeneous of degree one. The reader should also notice that group 1 is *not* separable from group 2; separability is not a symmetric concept.

We saw in Theorem 2.1 that, given separability, there exist aggregator and macro functions that are continuous when the utility function is continuous. Of course, the aggregator and macro functions that satisfy

$$U(x^1, x^2) = \mathcal{U}(x^1, U^2(x^2)).$$

are not unique (as the above example pointed out). The theorem states, however, that of all the possible choices for aggregator and macro functions, there exists at least one choice for which the two functions are continuous.

There are several other properties that the aggregator and macro functions can "inherit" whenever the utility function possesses the same property. If, for example, the utility function is nondecreasing ($x \geq x' \Rightarrow U(x) \geq U(x')$) then there exists an aggregator function that is nondecreasing. (Of course, the macro function must be increasing and hence, a fortiori, is nondecreasing.) A (partial) list of properties of the utility function that can be inherited from U by the aggregator and macro functions includes: (i) quasiconcavity;   (ii) strict monotonicity; (iii) homotheticity; (iv) homogeneity of degree one; and (v) concavity. For details, consult Chapter 3 in Blackorby, Primont, and Russell (1978b).

The idea of separability is easily extended to the case of several separable groups. Suppose the set of goods is partitioned into $R+1$ subsets. Denote that partition by

$$\{I^0, I^1, \cdots, I^R\}.$$

Corresponding to this partition, we write

$$x = (x^0, x^1, \ldots, x^R) \quad \text{and} \quad p = (p^0, p^1, \ldots, p^R)$$

(in an appropriate permutation of the variable indices). We can now state

THEOREM 2.3 [Debreu (1959) and Gorman (1968)] Assume that the consumer's preference ordering is complete, transitive, and continuous, and thus is represented by a continuous utility function, U. For the partition, $\{I^0, I^1, \ldots, I^R\}$, group r, $r = 1, \ldots, R$, is separable from all of the other commodities in I if and only if there exist continuous functions, $\mathcal{U}, U^1, \ldots, U^R$, such that

$$U(x) = \mathcal{U}\big(x^0, U^1(x^1), \ldots, U^R(x^R)\big), \qquad (2.14)$$

where the macro function, $\mathcal{U}$, is increasing in the group utilities,

$$u_r = U^r(x^r), \; r = 1, \ldots, R.$$

The form of the utility function in Theorem 2.3, in the absence of I^0, has often been called "weak separability" in the literature. More specifically, we say that U is separable with respect to the partition $(I^1, \ldots, I^R)$ if and only if U can be written as

$$U(x) = \mathcal{U}(U^1(x^1), \ldots, U^R(x^R))$$

where $\mathcal{U}$ is increasing in its arguments.

2.4   Decentralization $\Longleftrightarrow$ Separability

To explore the relationship between separability and decentralization, we use the concept of a conditional indirect utility function, H, defined by

$$H(y_1, \ldots, y_R, \ p) = \max_x \left\{ U(x) \ \middle| \ p^r \cdot x^r \le y_r, \ r = 1, \ \ldots, R \right\}. \qquad (2.15)$$

The conditional indirect utility function yields the maximum utility conditional on an allocation, $y_1, \ldots, y_R$, of total expenditure to the R sectors. Maximization of $H(y_1, \ldots, y_R, p)$ over $y_1, \ldots, y_R$ subject to $\sum_r y_r \le y$ then yields the expenditure–allocation functions,

$$y_r = \theta^r(y, p), \quad r = 1, \ldots, R. \qquad (2.16)$$

Substitution of this solution into H yields the indirect utility function:

$$\begin{aligned} H\big(\theta^1(y,p), \ldots, \theta^R(y,p), p\big) &= W(y,p) \\ &= \max_x \{ U(x) \mid p \cdot x \le y \}, \end{aligned} \qquad (2.17)$$

where the second equality defines the indirect utility function, W, in non–normalised prices and money income. Clearly, $\theta^r(y,p) = p^r \cdot \Phi^r(p,y)$, $r = 1, \ldots, R$.

THEOREM 2.4[6] The direct utility function is separable in the partition $\{I^1, \ldots, I^R\}$, that is,

$$U(x) = \mathcal{U}\big(U^1(x^1), \ldots, U^R(x^R)\big), \qquad (2.18)$$

where $\mathcal{U}$ is increasing in its arguments, if and only if the conditional indirect utility function can be written as

$$H(y_1, \ldots, y_R, p) = \mathcal{U}\big(v^1(y_1, p^1), \ldots, v^R(y_R, p^R)\big). \qquad (2.19)$$

PROOF To see the necessity of (2.19), suppose that U is separable in the partition $\{I^1, \ldots, I^R\}$. Then the conditional indirect utility function is derived by

$$\begin{aligned} &H(y_1, \ldots, y_R, p) \\ &= \max_x \left\{ \mathcal{U}\big(U^1(x^1), \ldots, U^R(x^R)\big) \ \middle| \ p^r \cdot x^r \le y_r, r = 1, \ \ldots, R \right\} \\ &= \mathcal{U}\left(\ldots, \max_{x^r} \left\{ U^r(x^r) \ \middle| \ p^r \cdot x^r \le y_r \right\}, \ldots \right) \\ &= \mathcal{U}\big(v^1(y_1, p^1), \ldots, v^R(y_R, p^R)\big), \end{aligned} \qquad (2.20)$$

---

[6]See Theorem 4.5.1 in Blackorby, Primont, and Russell (1978b).

where we have used the monotonicity of $\mathcal{U}$ in u_r for $r = 1, \ldots, R$. In this representation, $v^r(y_r, p^r)$ is the "conditional indirect utility function" for the rth sector, and it satisfies the usual conditions for indirect utility functions. ∎

The following theorem is proved as Theorem 5.3 in Blackorby, Primont, and Russell (1978b) [see Gorman (1970, 1995) and Primont (1970) for earlier proofs].

THEOREM 2.5 Assume that the consumer's utility function, U, is continuous, increasing and strictly quasi–concave in x. Further assume that the conditional indirect utility function, H, and the expenditure–allocation functions, θ^r, $r = 1, \ldots, R$, are differentiable and that each $\theta^r(p, y) > 0$. Then the consumer's utility maximization problem is decentralizable in the partition $\{I^1, \ldots, I^R\}$ if and only if U is separable in the same partition.

PROOF Sufficiency is immediate. Suppose that the consumer knows y_r and p^r. Then maximising U^r subject to $p^r \cdot x^r \leq y_r$ yields the conditional indirect utility function, $v^r(y^r, p^r)$. The application of Roy's theorem to this conditional indirect utility function yields demand functions that depend only on sector expenditure and prices, namely decentralization (2.5). ∎

3   Price Aggregation and Budgeting

In Section 2, we demonstrated that separability is a necessary and sufficient restriction on preferences for decentralization of the consumer's optimization problem. That is, if sector I^r is separable from its complement in the utility function, then the allocation of total expenditure to this sector can in turn be allocated among its component commodities with no loss in utility, so long as the allocation to the sector is itself optimal. However, the consumer must still determine the optimal expenditure on each sector; substitution of (2.16) into $\overset{*}{x}^r = \phi^r(y_r, p^r)$ makes it is clear that, in general, the allocation depends on all prices and total income. But if the overall optimization problem must be solved in the usual manner to determine optimal sector allocations, little is gained by the decentralization of the optimization problem.

This provides a motivation for finding a method of allocating total expenditure to the sectors that economizes on information — the principal motivation for the classic budgeting papers of Strotz (1957, 1959) and Gorman (1959): they sought a rule, or formula, determining the sectoral expenditure allocations using R sectoral price indices (and total expenditure) as information, rather than all N commodity prices. The answer, maintaining separability, was provided by Gorman (1959) and subsequently generalized by Blackorby and Russell (1997).

If there are to exist rules for determining the optimal expenditure on each group that use less information than all prices and incomes, then it seems reasonable that it should depend on the existence of price aggregates. Hence, we first explore the use of price aggregates in the first–stage expenditure allocation without assuming separability, a result attributable to Gorman (1965, 1995).

3.1 Price Aggregation

Define *price aggregation* as the existence of price aggregator functions (indices), $\Pi^1, \ldots, \Pi^R$, and expenditure–allocation functions, $\Theta^1, \ldots, \Theta^R$, such that the optimal sectoral allocations are given by

$$y_r = \Theta^r\big(y, \Pi^1(p^1), \ldots, \Pi^R(p^R)\big), \ r = 1, \ \ldots, R, \tag{3.1}$$

where Θ^r is positive–valued and strictly essential in its arguments, Π^r is increasing, and both Θ^r and Π^r are continuously differentiable, for all $r = 1, \ldots, R$.

Note that, other than the smoothness and monotonicity conditions, no properties are imposed, *a priori*, on the price aggregates, $\Pi^r, r = 1, \ldots, R$; more pointedly, these aggregates are not assumed to be homogeneous, or even homothetic. Gorman (1959, p. 478), however, has shown that the prices indices *must be* homothetic and hence can be picked to be positively linearly homogeneous.[7] Gorman (1965, 1995) also proved the following theorem on necessary and sufficient conditions for price aggregation:

THEOREM 3.1 Preferences satisfy price aggregation if and only if the indirect utility function can be written as

$$W(y, p) = \mathcal{W}\big(\Psi(y, \Pi^1(p^1), \ldots, \Pi^R(p^R)), p\big), \tag{3.2}$$

where $\mathcal{W}$ is homogeneous of degree zero in p^r for all r.

PROOF As shown below, this condition does not imply, nor is it implied by, separability of the direct utility function and hence it is formally unrelated to the conditions for decentralization. We refer the reader to Gorman for his elegant necessity proof, but proof of the sufficiency of (3.2) for price aggregation is easy and instructive. To ease the notational burden, let

$$\Pi = (\Pi^1(p^1), \ldots, \Pi^R(p^R))$$

and apply Roy's Theorem to (3.2) to obtain the demands for sector–r commodities:

---

[7] An alternative proof is in Blackorby and Russell (1994).

$$\Phi_i(y,p) = -\frac{\mathcal{W}_\Psi\big(\Psi(y,\Pi),p\big)\ \Psi_{\Pi^r}(y,\Pi)\ \Pi_i^r(p^r) + \mathcal{W}_i\big(\Psi(y,\Pi),p\big)}{\mathcal{W}_\Psi\big(\Psi(y,\Pi),p\big)\ \Psi_y(y,\Pi)}, \quad \forall i \in I^r.$$

(3.3)

Multiplication of (3.3) by p_i and summation over all $i \in I^r$ yields

$$
\begin{aligned}
y_r &= -\frac{\mathcal{W}_\Psi\big(\Psi(y,\Pi),p\big)\ \Psi_{\Pi^r}(y,\Pi)\ \sum_{i\in I^r}\Pi_i^r(p^r)\ p_i + \sum_{i\in I^r}\mathcal{W}_i\big(\Psi(y,\Pi),p\big)\ p_i}{\mathcal{W}_\Psi\big(\Psi(y,\Pi),p\big)\ \Psi_y(y,\Pi)}\\[2mm]
&= -\frac{\Psi_{\Pi^r}(y,\Pi)\ \Pi^r(p^r)}{\Psi_y(y,\Pi)} =: \Theta^r\big(y,\Pi^1(p^1),\ldots,\Pi^R(p^R)\big),
\end{aligned}
$$

(3.4)

where the second–to–last identity follows, using Euler's Theorem, from the homogeneity of degree one and zero in p^r of Π^r and $\mathcal{W}$, respectively. Although sector–r expenditures depend only on income and the vector of price indices, this is not the case for the individual demands in each sector. From (3.2) it is clear that the demand for commodity i in sector r depends on income, the vector of prices indices, and directly on the price vector p itself. Thus the consumer can determine the optimal allocation to sector r using only income and price indices, but in order to actually spend this money, all prices must be taken into account. ∎

3.2 Two–Stage Budgeting

Thus far, we have discussed decentralization (which is equivalent to quantity aggregation) and price aggregation separately. Full two–stage budgeting, as introduced by Strotz (1957), requires both. That is, under what conditions can the consumer calculate optimal group expenditure using only group price indices and then spend the allocated funds using only sector–specific prices? Thus, we investigate the conditions that suffice for the conjunction of the two concepts. Proof of the following theorem can be found in Blackorby and Russell (1997):[8]

THEOREM 3.2 If U is separable in the partition $\{I^1,\ldots,I^R\}$ and the conditional indirect utility function, H, is twice continuously differentiable, then price aggregation is equivalent to the following structure for the direct utility function (in an appropriate permutation of the sectoral indices, $1,\ldots,R$): there

---

[8]The proof of this theorem in Blackorby, Primont, and Russell (1978a, 1978b) is incorrect (see Blackorby and Russell (1997). A weaker version of the theorem is in Gorman (1959).

exist continuous, increasing functions F and G and an integer D, $0 \leq D \leq R$ such that

$$U(x) = F\left(\sum_{r=1}^{D} U^r(x^r) + G\big(U^{D+1}(x^{D+1}), \dots, U^R(x^R)\big) \right), \qquad (3.5)$$

where each U^r, $r = D + 1, \dots, R$, is homothetic and hence can be normalized to be homogeneous of degree one, and the sectoral indirect utility functions dual to the first D aggregator functions have the structure,

$$v^r(y_r, p^r) = \nu^r\left(\frac{y_r}{\Pi^r(p^r)} \right) + w^r(p^r), \quad r = 1, \dots, D, \qquad (3.6)$$

where each w^r is homogeneous of degree zero in p^r and each Π^r is homogeneous of degree one in p^r.

PROOF It must be the case that the structure (3.5) is a special case of (3.2). To see that it is, note that the indirect utility function corresponding to (3.5) is obtained by solving

$$W(y, p) = \max_{\{y_r\}} \left\{ F\left(\sum_{r=1}^{D} \left[\nu^r\left(\frac{y_r}{\Pi^r(p^r)} \right) + w^r(p^r) \right] \right. \right.$$
$$\left. \left. + G\left(\frac{y_{D+1}}{\Pi^{D+1}(p^{D+1})}, \dots, \frac{y_R}{\Pi^R(p^R)} \right) \right) \,\middle|\, \sum_{r=1}^{R} y_r = y \right\}. \qquad (3.7)$$

As F is strictly monotonic, the maximizing values do not depend on the additive terms, $w^r(p^r)$, $r = 1, \dots, R$, so that the solution to (3.7) has the form

$$y_r = \Theta^r\big(y, \Pi^1(p^1), \dots, \Pi^R(p^R)\big), \quad r = 1, \dots, R, \qquad (3.8)$$

which, of course, establishes price aggregation. Substitution of (3.8) into the objective function in (3.7) yields a special case of (3.2) (since the functions, w^r, $r = 1, \dots, R$, are homogeneous of degree zero). ∎

The structure (3.6) is referred to as the "Generalized Gorman Polar Form." The "Gorman Polar Form," also referred to as quasi–homotheticity and of considerable significance in the theory of aggregation across agents, is obtained when ν^r is the identity function.[9] The latter is, in turn, a generalization of homotheticity, which holds when $w^r(p^r)$ vanishes. Thus, in words, price aggregation is equivalent to a structure of the utility function in which utility is a monotonic function of the sum of aggregator functions that are generalizations of quasi–homotheticity (and hence homotheticity), plus a (possibly non–additive) function of sectoral utility functions that are homothetic.

---

[9]See Blackorby, Boyce, and Russell (1978) or Blackorby, Primont, and Russell (1978b, Section 8.1.3) for more on the Gorman Polar Form.

An interesting special case of (3.5) is obtained if $D = 0$:

$$U(x) = F\Big(G\big(U^1(x^1), \ldots, U^R(x^R)\big)\Big). \tag{3.9}$$

In this case, the direct utility function is not only separable, but, in addition, each sector–specific aggregator is homothetic (and can be chosen to be homogeneous of degree one). As such, these aggregators look very much like quantity indices that are dual to the price indices whose existence has been assumed. Is the price index, $\Pi^r(p^r)$, the price of the quantity, $U^r(x^r)$, in the sense that

$$\Pi^r(p^r)\, U^r\big(\Phi^r(y, p)\big) = y_r? \tag{3.10}$$

If so, can the first stage of the budgeting algorithm be expressed as choosing $X^1, \ldots, X^R$ to maximize $F(X^1, \ldots, X^R)$ subject to the budget constraint, $\sum_r \Pi^r(p^r)\, X^r = y$? Affirmative answers to both questions would permit two–stage budgeting to be accomplished using only price and quantity aggregates. The existence of quantity aggregates, as we have shown in Section 2, is equivalent to separability restrictions on the direct utility function. In order to construct price aggregates it is natural then to look for similar properties in either the indirect utility function or the expenditure function. It is to this problem that we now turn, postponing the discussion of two–stage budgeting with price and quantity aggregates until after we have resolved the question of the existence of price aggregates with the appropriate properties.

4   Separability and Duality

Although the previous sections have focused on separability and functional structure of the direct utility function, it is clear from the statement of the price aggregation theorems that functional structure is being imposed on other representations of preferences. Houthakker (1960) demonstrated that alternative restrictions are imposed on preferences by restricting dual representations of preferences to satisfy separability conditions. For example, separability of the indirect utility function neither implies nor is implied by separability of the direct utility function. That is, direct and indirect separability are distinct concepts and have different implications for demand systems. In addition, separability (in prices) of the expenditure function — an alternative representation of consumer preferences — constitutes yet a third restriction on consumer preferences. Another representation of consumer preferences, formulated long ago by Malmquist (1953), but overlooked until applications by Blackorby and Russell (1978) and Deaton (1978), is the distance function.[10]   As it turns out,

---

[10]See Russell (1977) for a recent exposition of the distance function and its applications.

separability of the distance function (in quantities) does not provide additional restrictions on preferences, since it is equivalent to separability of the expenditure function (in prices).

Although separability of the direct and indirect utility functions and of the expenditure/distance functions constitute distinct restrictions on preferences, it turns out that *homothetic* separability of the direct and indirect utility functions — that is, separability with homothetic aggregator functions — are equivalent. Moreover, homothetic separability is equivalent to separability of a price sector from the utility scalar as well as other price sectors in the expenditure function and separability of a quantity sector from the utility scalar as well as other quantity sectors in the distance function.

While homothetic separability of preferences implies that both the direct and the indirect utility functions are separable, the converse is not true: the conjunction of direct and indirect separability does not imply homothetic separability. A complete characterization of joint direct and indirect separability, along with a characterization of direct and indirect complete separability (additivity) is provided in Section 6.

4.1 *Dual Representations of Preferences: Indirect Utility, Expenditure, and Distance Functions*

We assume throughout Section 4 that the preference ordering, in addition to satisfying the conditions posited in Section 2, is convex[11] (*i.e.*, that the utility function is quasi–concave[12] and monotonic[13]).

The indirect utility function, defined for all $p \in \mathbb{R}^n_{++}$, by

$$V(p/y) = \max_x \{U(x) \mid p \cdot x \leq y\} \tag{4.1}$$

is continuous, non–increasing, and quasi–convex.[14] The expenditure function, defined by

$$E(u,p) = \min_{x \in \Omega} \{p \cdot x \mid U(x) \geq u \wedge p \in \mathbf{R}^n_{++}\}, \tag{4.2}$$

is (jointly) continuous in (u,p), increasing in u, and nondecreasing, concave, and homogeneous of degree one in p. The distance function, defined by

$$D(u,x) = \max_{\lambda > 0} \{\lambda \mid U(x/\lambda) \geq u\}, \tag{4.3}$$

---

[11] For all $x, x' \in \Omega, x \succ x' \Rightarrow \alpha x + (1-\alpha)x' \succ x' \quad \forall \, \alpha \in (0,1]$.
[12] $U(x) \geq U(x') \Rightarrow U(\alpha x + (1-\alpha)x') \geq U(x') \quad \forall \, \alpha \in [0,1]$.
[13] $x \geq x' \Rightarrow U(x) \geq U(x')$.
[14] $V\left(\frac{p}{y}\right) \leq V\left(\frac{p'}{y}\right) \Rightarrow V\left(\alpha \frac{p}{y} + (1-\alpha)\frac{p'}{y}\right) \leq V\left(\frac{p'}{y}\right) \quad \forall \, \alpha \in [0,1]$.

is (jointly) continuous in (u, x), decreasing in u, and nondecreasing, concave, and homogeneous of degree one in x.[15]

The (direct) utility function, the indirect utility function, the expenditure function, and the distance function are equally valid representations of a continuous, convex preference ordering. Each can be derived from any of the other three with no loss of information about the preference ordering (although closed–form representations often, or even typically, do not exist for some of these functions). Specification of any one satisfying the requisite properties is tantamount to specification of any of the others, and of the preference ordering itself.

The reader is referred to the appropriate duality literature for full descriptions and proofs of these relationships,[16] but for our purposes it will be convenient to note that the distance and expenditure functions are (particular) implicit representations of the direct and indirect utility functions, since

$$u = U(x) - D(u, x) = 1 \qquad (4.4)$$

and

$$u = V(p/y) - E(u, p) = y. \qquad (4.5)$$

In fact, the direct and indirect utility functions are obtained from the distance and expenditure functions by inverting the right–hand sides of the equivalences in (4.4) and (4.5) (exploiting the strict monotonicity in u). A useful property of these particular implicit representations of the direct and indirect utility functions is their first–degree homogeneity in quantities and prices.[17]

4.2 Separability of Dual Representations of Preferences

The indirect utility function induces an ordering on (normalized) price vectors, p/y. This ordering can be used to define price–space separability, analogously to the definition of consumption–space separability in Section 2; in particular, the rth sector is separable from its complement if the conditional ordering on the rth price subspace is invariant with respect to changes in price vectors outside that

---

[15]Proofs of these claims are in the Appendix of Blackorby, Primont, and Russell (1978b).

[16]See, e.g., Diewert (1974), Blackorby, Primont, and Russell (1978b, Chapter 2 and Appendix), or Browning (this volume).

[17]Another important property of the expenditure and distance functions — as we shall see — is their symmetry (or conjugacy). For example, the distance function can be alternatively interpreted as an (imputed) expenditure function, obtained by choosing (shadow) prices to minimize (imputed) expenditure, $p \cdot x$, given (positive) quantities and subject to the constraint that $V(p/y)$ be no greater than u, and the expenditure function can be alternatively interpreted as a distance function in price space. To pursue these notions further, however, would immerse us in some nasty boundary problems that are tangential to our main purpose.

sector. Of some interest is the contrast between direct and indirect separability in terms of the differential (Leontief/Sono) conditions. If V is decreasing and twice differentiable, sector r is separable from its complement if

$$\frac{\partial}{\partial(p_k/y)}\left(\frac{V_i(p/y)}{V_j(p/y)}\right) = 0, \tag{4.6}$$

for all i, j in I^r and for all k in the complement of I^r. Invoking Roy's Theorem,

$$\Phi_i(p/y) = \frac{V_i(p/y)}{\sum_j V_j(p/y)p_j/y}, \tag{4.7}$$

we find that indirect separability of sector r is equivalent to

$$\frac{\partial}{\partial(p_k/y)}\left(\frac{\Phi_i(p/y)}{\Phi_j(p/y)}\right) = 0, \tag{4.8}$$

for all i, j in I^r and for all k in the complement of I^r. Thus, *direct* separability of sector r means that marginal rates of substitution—i.e., sector–r shadow–price ratios—are independent of consumption quantities outside the rth sector; *indirect* separability of sector r means that optimal quantity ratios in this sector are independent of prices outside the sector.

Representation theorems analogous to Theorems 2.1 and 2.3 can be proved for separability of the indirect utility function. In the interest of generality, we will carry along a free (nonseparable) sector in presenting these representation results. For convenience, let us say that a function is "separable in the partition $\{I^0, I^1, \ldots, I^R\}$" if I^r is separable from its complement in $I = \{1, \ldots, N\}$, $r = 1, \ldots, R$.

Separability of the indirect utility function in the partition $\{I^0, I^1, \ldots, I^R\}$ is equivalent to the structure,

$$V(p/y) = \mathcal{V}\left(p^0/y, V^1(p^1/y), \ldots, V^R(p^R/y)\right), \tag{4.9}$$

where $\mathcal{V}$ is increasing in each of the last R arguments (each of the aggregator–function images) or, equivalently,

$$W(y, p) = \mathcal{W}\left(y, p^0, W^1(y, p^1), \ldots, W^R(y, p^R)\right), \tag{4.10}$$

where $\mathcal{W}$ is increasing in its last R arguments. Moreover, each of the aggregator functions, $V^1, \ldots, V^R$, inherits the properties of V. It is tempting, therefore, to interpret these aggregator functions as sectoral indirect utility functions. But it should be stressed that a ("conditional") direct utility function, U^r, derived from V^r cannot be interpreted as representing "the" preference ordering on the

r^{th} commodity subspace. As indirect separability does not imply direct separability, there does not in general exist a unique ordering on the rth commodity subspace; the ordering induced on this subspace by the ordering on Ω depends in general on the consumption quantities in other sectors. [Equivalently, if direct separability pertains, the conditional indirect utility function for the rth sector in (2.20) does not in general imply the existence of the rth element of (4.9).]

We obtain characterizations of separability of the expenditure and distance functions in the partition $\{I^0, I^1, \ldots, I^R\}$ by proceeding much as we did in analyzing separability of the direct and indirect utility functions — with one important exception: we must take account of the utility variable (since it cannot be absorbed in a harmless normalization, as can the expenditure variable in the indirect utility function because of homogeneity of degree zero in prices and expenditure). Thus, in the constructions analogous to those of Section 2, u must be carried along as a "nuisance" variable. The outcome is that the expenditure function is separable in the above partition if and only if it can be written as

$$E(u,p) = \mathcal{E}\big(u, p^0, E^1(u, p^1), \ldots, E^R(u, p^R)\big), \qquad (4.11)$$

where $\mathcal{E}$ is increasing in the last R arguments (the aggregator functions), and the distance function is separable in the above partition if and only if it can be written as

$$D(u,x) = \mathcal{D}\big(u, x^0, D^1(u, x^1), \ldots, D^R(u, x^R)\big), \qquad (4.12)$$

where $\mathcal{D}$ is increasing in the last R arguments.

The aggregator functions in (4.11) and (4.12) inherit most of the salient properties of E and D.[18] Again, however, these aggregator functions are not in general the expenditure and distance functions derived from an ordering on the corresponding consumption subspace or price subspace, since separability of the expenditure and distance functions imply neither direct nor indirect separability (nor is separability of the expenditure and distance functions implied by direct or indirect separability).

As it turns out, however, separability of the expenditure and distance functions are equivalent:

THEOREM 4.1 The separability condition (4.11) holds if and only if the separability condition (4.12) holds (in the same partition).

---

[18]One important property of expenditure and distance functions that is not inherited by aggregator functions is strict monotonicity in the utility variable, u. [See Blackorby, Primont, and Russell (1978b, p. 76).]

Proof of this result can be found in Gorman (1970, 1995), McFadden (1978), and Blackorby, Primont, and Russell (1978b, Theorem 4.2). The key feature of these functions that allows us to derive (4.11) from (4.12) and vice versa, is the homogeneity of degree one in quantities and prices. This suggests that restricting the direct and indirect utility functions to be homothetic (and hence homogeneous of degree one in some normalization), would allow us to derive (4.9) from (2.14) and *vice versa*, and hence render direct and indirect separability equivalent. This turns out to be true, but in fact a weaker condition suffices for the equivalence of direct and indirect separability.

4.3   Homothetic Separability

Preferences satisfy *homothetic separability* in the partition $\{I^0, I^1, \dots, I^R\}$ if they are separable in this partition and the ordering induced on each of the R separable subspaces in the partition is homothetic. In this case, the aggregator functions in (2.14) are homothetic and can be chosen to be homogeneous of degree one in an appropriate normalization (of the macro function, $\mathcal{U}$, as well as the R aggregator functions). Note that homothetic separability does not imply overall homotheticity of preferences (even if the free sector, I^0, is empty). Indirect homothetic separability is defined similarly and allows us to choose the aggregator functions in (4.9) to be homogeneous of degree one.

Proof of the following theorem can be found in Blackorby, Primont, and Russell (1978b, Theorem 4.4):

THEOREM 4.2 Direct and indirect homothetic separability in the same partition are equivalent.

Thus, the structures (2.14) and (4.9), with homothetic aggregator functions, are equivalent. We can therefore refer, without ambiguity, to either/both of these structures as "homothetic separability."

What does homothetic separability imply about the expenditure and distance functions? To answer this question, we extend the set of variable indices to include the utility variable, indexed by 0. This allows us to introduce separability of a sector of prices or consumption quantities from utility as well as other quantities or prices. Thus, we partition the extended set of variable indices, $\{0, 1, \dots, N\}$, into $R+1$ subsets, $\{\{0\} \cup I^0, I^1, \dots, I^r, \dots, I^R\}$. The sectors, $I^1, \dots, I^R$, are separable from their complements in $\{0, 1, \dots, N\}$ in the expenditure and distance functions, respectively, if and only if

$$E(u, p) = \mathcal{E}\big(u, p^0, \Pi^1(p^1), \dots, \Pi^R(p^R)\big), \qquad (4.13)$$

and

$$D(u,x) = \mathcal{D}\big(u, x^0, X^1(x^1), \dots, X^R(x^R)\big). \tag{4.14}$$

As E and D are homogeneous of degree one in prices and quantities, respectively, the aggregator functions in these two representations can be chosen to have the same homogeneity property.

Theorem 4.1 suggests that (4.13) and (4.14) are equivalent, and indeed they are. But a stronger result holds [Blackorby, Primont, and Russell (1978b, Theorem 4.2)]:

THEOREM 4.3 The following are equivalent:

(i) Homothetic separability in the partition $\{I^0, I^1, \dots, I^R\}$ [equations (2.14) and (4.9)].

(ii) Separability of the expenditure function in the partition
$\{\{0\} \cup I^0, I^1, \dots, I^r, \dots, I^R\}$ [equation (4.13)].

(iii) Separability of the distance function in the partition
$\{\{0\} \cup I^0, I^1, \dots, I^r, \dots, I^R\}$ [equation (4.14)].

Having resolved the question of the joint existence of price and quantity aggregates, we return to the question of their use in two–stage budgeting.

4.4   Additive Price Aggregation

If the utility function is separable, then the group utility functions are natural candidates for quantity aggregator functions. If, in addition, price aggregation obtains then we also have price aggregator functions. However, in addition to the existence of these price and quantity aggregates (or indices) we wish to impose the property that the product of the price index and the quantity index for group r be equal to the expenditure on group r commodities.

Define *additive price aggregation* as the existence of price aggregator functions, $\Pi^1, \dots, \Pi^R$, and quantity aggregator functions, $\Gamma^1, \dots, \Gamma^R$, such that

$$\Pi^r(p^r)\,\Gamma^r(x^r) = y_r, \quad r = 1, \dots, R.$$

where $x^r = \phi^r(y_r, p^r)$, $y_r = p^r \Phi^r(y,p)$, and each Γ^r is homogeneous of degree one in x^r.

THEOREM 4.4 [Blackorby, Lady, Nissen, and Russell (1970) and Blackorby, Primont, and Russell (1978b, Theorem 5.8)] If U is separable in the partition

$\{I^1, \ldots, I^r, \ldots, I^R\}$ then additive price aggregation is equivalent to homothetic separability.

PROOF Under homothetic separability, we can always find a representation of the utility function for which each aggregator function U^r is homogeneous of degree one. Then the group–r indirect utility function for U^r can be written as

$$U^r\big(\phi^r(y_r, p^r)\big) = \frac{y_r}{\Pi^r(p^r)}.$$

Thus, for additive price aggregation, Π^r is the required price aggregator function and $U^r = \Gamma^r$ is the required quantity aggregator function. ∎

5 Additive Structures.

Fascination with additive utility functions goes back at least to Gossen (1854). Although many economists reject additive utility as too restrictive a starting point for the explanation of consumer behavior,[19] one frequently encounters problems where the assumption of additivity is usefully employed. Thus it is fruitful to investigate the restrictions on preferences that lead to additive forms of the utility function.

As an example, suppose a Bergson–Samuelson social welfare function is given by

$$U(x) = W\big(U^1(x^1), \ldots, U^R(x^R)\big),$$

where U^r is the utility function of person r in an R–person economy and suppose, in addition, that W is a symmetric function. (Symmetry is equivalent to anonymity — that is, only the individuals' utilities and not their names should matter in social evaluation.) In addition, it often seems natural to suppose that policies that affect only a subset of individuals, such as those in a particular province or state, should be evaluated without considering the utilities of those who are unaffected by these policies. For example, in deciding the nature of an optimal commodity tax in British Columbia one ought to be able to ignore the unchanged wellbeing of the citizens of Nova Scotia. The conjunction of these two plausible – perhaps even innocuous – assumptions has a strong implication: the social welfare function must be additive separable:

$$U(x) = \mathcal{W}\big(U^1(x^1) + \cdots + U^R(x^r)\big).$$

---

[19]See Deaton (1971).

As a second example, consider a consumer who lives for T periods. The intertemporal consumption vector is given by $x = (x^1, x^2, \ldots, x^t, \ldots, x^T)$. Posit the existence of an intertemporal utility function, U, defined over $x \in \Omega$. Consider two intertemporal consumption bundles, x and $\hat{x}$ that satisfy the condition that $x^r = \hat{x}^r$ for all $r \neq t, t+1$. Thus x and $\hat{x}$ differ only in terms of the consumption in time periods t and $t+1$. It seems reasonable to assume that the preference between x and $\hat{x}$ should depend only on those components that differ. For this condition to hold for arbitrary t, it must be the case that the intertemporal utility function can be written as

$$U(x) = \mathcal{U}\big(U^1(x^1) + \ldots + U^T(x^T)\big).$$

We turn now to a discussion of how such simple assumptions can lead to such strong conclusions.

5.1 Complete Separability

Consider once again the partition of the N variables into R groups, which is given by $\{I^1, \ldots, I^R\}$. The utility function is *completely separable* in this partition if every union of groups is separable from all variables in the remaining groups. Clearly, so long as $R > 2$, complete separability is a stronger condition than separability and, as we shall see, implies a more restrictive form of the utility function. Of course, the distinction between separability and complete separability disappears when there are only two groups; thus we shall assume throughout this section that the above partition contains at least three groups.[20]

As a prelude to the characterization of complete separability, we present a powerful theorem attributable to Gorman (1968). This theorem characterizes the utility function when there are two groups of variables that are separable from all of the remaining variables and that have some variables in common. The presence of these two overlapping separable groups leads to a utility function with an additive structure. First, some definitions.

Suppose there are four groups, I^1, I^2, I^3, and I^4. Let I^c be the union of groups 2, 3, and 4 and let $x^c = (x^2, x^3, x^4)$. The first group of variables, I^1, is said to be *essential* if, for every $\hat{x}^1 \in \Omega^1$, the set

$$\{\, x^1 \mid U(x^1, x^c) \neq U(\hat{x}^1, x^c)\,\}$$

is nonempty for at least one point $x^c \in \Omega^2 \times \Omega^3 \times \Omega^4$. Group 1 is said to be *strictly essential* if it is essential for *all* points $x^c \in \Omega^2 \times \Omega^3 \times \Omega^4$. Essentiality and strict essentiality of the other three groups are defined in the same way.

---

[20]Note that, for simplicity, we again set $I^0 = \emptyset$. For more general representation theorems, see Chapter 4 of Blackorby, Primont, and Russell (1978b).

EXAMPLE 5.1 Suppose the commodity space is the four–dimensional nonnegative orthant. Let $U(x) = \min\{x_1, x_2, x_3, x_4\}$ and $I^r = \{r\}$, $r = 1, 2, 3, 4$. Note that group 1 is essential since $U(x_1, x^c) < U(\hat{x}_1, x^c)$ whenever $x_1 < \hat{x}_1 < \min\{x^c\} = \min\{x_2, x_3, x_4\}$. Group 1, however, is not strictly essential, since $U(x_1, x^c) = U(\hat{x}_1, x^c) = 0$ for all $x_1, \hat{x}_1$ when $x^c = (0, 0, 0)$.

Let $I^r = I^1 \cup I^2$ and $I^s = I^2 \cup I^3$. Set differences are given by $I^r - I^s = I^1$ and $I^s - I^r = I^3$. I^r and I^s are the overlapping separable sets in the following theorem.

THEOREM 5.2 [Gorman (1968)] Assume that the utility function is continuous and that all four groups are essential. If (a) I^r and I^s are nonempty and separable from $I^3 \cup I^4$ and $I^1 \cup I^4$, respectively, if $I^r \cap I^s$, $I^r - I^s$, and $I^s - I^r$ are nonempty, and if $I^s - I^r$ is strictly essential, then (b) each of the following sets is separable from all of the remaining variables:

$$I^r \cap I^s, \quad I^r - I^s, \quad I^s - I^r, \quad I^r \cup I^s \quad \text{and} \quad (I^r - I^s) \cup (I^s - I^r).$$

In this case, (c) there exist continuous functions, $\mathcal{U}$, U^1, U^2, and U^3 such that

$$U(x) = \mathcal{U}\big(U^1(x^1) + U^2(x^2) + U^3(x^3), x^4\big),$$

where $\mathcal{U}$ is strictly increasing in its first argument. Thus (a) $\Rightarrow$ (b) and (a) $\Rightarrow$ (c). Moreover, (c) $\Rightarrow$ (a) and (c) $\Rightarrow$ (b).

We are now in a position to state the additive representation theorem.

THEOREM 5.3 [Gorman (1968)] Assume that the consumer's utility function U is continuous. Then U is completely separable in the partition $\{I^1, \ldots, I^r, \ldots, I^R\}$ ($R \geq 3$) if and only if there exist functions, U^r, $r = 1, \ldots, R$, and an increasing function $\mathcal{U}$ such that

$$U(x) = \mathcal{U}\Big(\sum_{r=1}^{R} U^r(x^r)\Big). \tag{5.1}$$

PROOF It should be clear that, in proving this theorem, one can make good use of the Gorman's theorem on overlapping separable sets. If there are just three groups that are completely separable, then $I^1 \cup I^2$ is separable from I^3 and $I^2 \cup I^3$ is separable from I^1. Since these overlapping sets are separable, the additive structure obtains. The rest of the proof extends this result to R groups by induction. As was the case with a separable utility function, the aggregator functions can be constructed directly from the utility function. In particular, the aggregator and macro functions can be normalized so that, for some fixed vector, $O = (O^1, \ldots, O^r, \ldots, O^R)$,

$$U^r(O^r) = 0, \quad r = 1, \ldots, R,$$

and

$$\mathcal{U}(t) = t.$$

Thus,

$$U^r(x^r) = U(O^1, \ldots, O^{r-1}, x^r, O^{r+1}, \ldots, O^R)$$

and

$$U(x) = \sum_{r=1}^{R} U^r(x^r).$$

Thus, the aggregator functions are monotone tranforms of the utility function and, therefore, the aggregator functions inherit from the utility function all properties that are preserved by monotone transforms. [See Blackorby, Primont, and Russell (1978b, pp. 138–140) for details.] ∎

Return for the moment to the social welfare example with which we began this section. Letting $u_r = U^r(x^r)$, the social welfare function can be written as

$$w = W(u_1, \ldots, u_R).$$

Let $\{1, 2\}$ be the subset of individuals who are affected by some set of policies and, as above, suppose that these policies are judged solely by their effect on these two individuals. This implies that $\{1, 2\}$ is separable from its complement in the set of citizens and hence that

$$W(u_1, \ldots, u_R) = \mathcal{W}(F(u_1, u_2), u_3, \ldots, u_R).$$

The fact that W is symmetric means that it can be written as

$$\mathcal{W}(F(u_1, u_2), u_3, \ldots, u_R) = \mathcal{W}(F(u_1, u_3), u_2, u_4, \ldots, u_R).$$

This in turn implies that $\{1, 3\}$ is separable from its complement in the set of citizens. However, these sets have a nonempty intersection, $\{2\}$, and the overlapping theorem implies that the social welfare function can be written as

$$W(u_1, \ldots, u_R) = \mathcal{W}(U^1(u_1) + U^2(u_2) + U^3(u_3), u_4, \ldots, u_R).$$

Proceeding by induction verifies the claim made at the beginning of this section: namely, that W is additive.

A similar argument with respect to the intertemporal preferences above would verify that claim as well.

5.2   Additivity in a Two–Group Partition.

As mentioned above, if there are only two groups, then separability and complete separability are equivalent and the utility function need not have an additive form. But two–group additivity arises in many contexts. One example is the typical additive utility function in overlapping–generations models where each generation's finite lifetime is divided into two periods (often a "work" period and a "retirement" period). A special case of two–group additivity is the quasi–linear utility function that is so critical to the analysis of public goods and incentive compatibility. The stronger conditions required for two–group additivity are based on Sono's (1945, 1961) independence condition, to which we now turn.

Consider a two–group partition $\{I^1, I^2\}$ where $I^1 = \{1\}$ and $I^2 = \{2, \dots, N\}$. Commodity 1 is *Sono independent* of I^2 if

$$\frac{\partial}{\partial x_1} \left(\ln \frac{\partial U(x)/\partial x_i}{\partial U(x)/\partial x_1} \right) = \psi(x_1) \quad \forall \quad i \in I^2. \tag{5.2}$$

LEMMA 5.4 [Blackorby, Primont, and Russell (1978b)] Assume that the utility function, U, is twice continuously differentiable. Then variable 1 is independent of I^2 if and only if there exist functions, $\mathcal{U}$, U^1, and U^2, such that[21]

$$U(x) = \mathcal{U}\big(U^1(x_1) + U^2(x_2, \dots, x_n)\big).$$

The above result can be generalized to allow for more than one good in group 1. A set of variables, I^1, is said to be *independent* of I^2 if there exist functions ψ^{ji}, $i, j, \in I^1$, such that

$$\frac{\partial}{\partial x_i} \left(\ln \frac{\frac{\partial U(x)}{\partial x_k}}{\frac{\partial U(x)}{\partial x_j}} \right) = \frac{\partial}{\partial x_i} \left(\ln \frac{\frac{\partial U(x)}{\partial x_l}}{\frac{\partial U(x)}{\partial x_j}} \right) = \psi^{ji}(x^1) \quad \forall i, j \in I^1, \forall k, l \in I^2.$$

Armed with this definition, we can state

THEOREM 5.5 [Blackorby, Primont, and Russell (1978b)] Assume that the utility function, U, is twice continuously differentiable. Then I^1 is independent of I^2 and is separable from I^2 if and only if there exist functions, $\mathcal{U}$, U^1, and U^2, such that

$$U(x) = \mathcal{U}\big(U^1(x^1) + U^2(x^2)\big).$$

---

[21] Sono (1945, 1961) established the above result under the maintained hypothesis that group 2 is separable from variable 1. Blackorby, Primont, and Russell (1978b) show, however, that the independence of variable 1 from group 2 implies that group 2 is separable from 1. Thus Sono's maintained hypothesis was unnecessary.

SKETCH OF PROOF To prove this theorem, one first exploits the fact that separability of group 1 implies that group–1 variables can be aggregated into a single scalar, u_1. Next, the independence of group 1 is shown to be equivalent to the independence of the scalar variable u_1. It then remains to apply Lemma 5.4 to complete the proof. In the course of proving this theorem, one discovers that the condition that group 1 is independent of group 2 implies the condition that group 2 is separable from group 1.[22]   ∎

5.3   Additivity and Duality.

Complete separability of the indirect utility and cost functions (in prices) and of the distance function (in quantities) also result in additive structures:[23]

$$V\left(\frac{p}{y}\right) = \mathcal{V}\left(\sum_r V^r\left(\frac{p^r}{y}\right)\right), \tag{5.3}$$

$$C(u,p) = \mathcal{C}\left(u, \sum_r C^r(u,p^r)\right), \tag{5.4}$$

and

$$D(u,x) = \mathcal{D}\left(u, \sum_r D^r(u,x^r)\right). \tag{5.5}$$

As in the case of separability and duality, the four additive structures, (5.1) and (5.3)–(5.5), impose only three independent structures on preferences. Analogously to Theorem 4.1 above, we have

THEOREM 5.6 The structures (5.4) and (5.5) are equivalent.

We noted in Section 4.3 that direct and indirect separability with homothetic aggregator functions are equivalent restrictions on preferences. The analog for additive (completely separable) structures is not true: direct additivity (complete separability of U) with homothetic aggregators is not equivalent to indirect additivity (complete separability of V) with homothetic aggregators.

---

[22]Geary and Morishima (1973) also obtain the above result. It appears, however, that they (unnecessarily) assume that both groups 1 and 2 are separable from each other.
[23]See Blackorby, Primont, and Russell (1978b, Sec. 4.8.2) for formal theorem statements and proofs. Because of the homogeneity in prices and quantites of the expenditure and distance functions, additional structure can be imposed on (5.4) and (5.5); see Blackorby, Primont, and Russell (1978b, Corollaries 4.9.4 and 4.9.5).

The intuitive reason for this is that the additive structures implied by complete separability rely critically on separability of unions of sectors of variables; but homotheticity of all R sectors does not imply homotheticity on Cartesian products of the sectoral subspaces. In fact, if preferences on arbitrary Cartesian products of sectoral subspaces are homothetic, then overall preferences are homothetic. Indeed, overall homotheticity is the glue that binds the three alternative complete–separability restrictions. Moreover, overall homotheticity and complete separability induce additional structure on the above representations, (5.1) and (5.3)–(5.5), so that they can be written as CES (constant elasticity of substitution) utility functions (subsuming the Cobb–Douglas limiting case) of the aggregators. We state these duality result as follows:

THEOREM 5.7 Given certain regularity conditions for the direct and indirect utility functions and the cost and distance functions [see Blackorby, Primont, and Russell (1978b, Sections 4.4–4.5)], the following conditions are equivalent:

(i) The (direct) utility function is homothetic and completely separable in the partition $\{I^1, \ldots, I^R\}$, in which case it can be written as

$$U(x) = \mathcal{U}\left[\left(\sum_{r=1}^{m} U^r(x^r)^\rho\right)^{1/\rho}\right], \qquad 0 \neq \rho \leq 1,$$

or

$$U(x) = \mathcal{U}\left(\prod_{r=1}^{m} U^r(x^r)^{\rho^r}\right), \qquad \rho^r > 0 \quad \forall r, \qquad \sum_{r=1}^{R} \rho^r = 1,$$

where each of the aggregator functions, $U^r, r = 1, \ldots, R$, is positively linearly homogeneous.

(ii) The indirect utility function is homothetic and completely separable in the partition $\{I^1, \ldots, I^R\}$, in which case it can be written as

$$V\left(\frac{p}{y}\right) = \mathcal{V}\left[\left(\sum_{r=1}^{m} V^r\left(\frac{p^r}{y}\right)^\rho\right)^{1/\rho}\right], \qquad 0 \neq \rho \leq 1,$$

or

$$V\left(\frac{p}{y}\right) = \mathcal{V}\left(\prod_{r=1}^{m} V^r\left(\frac{p^r}{y}\right)^{\rho^r}\right), \qquad \rho^r > 0 \quad \forall r, \qquad \sum_{r=1}^{R} \rho^r = 1,$$

where each of the aggregator functions, $V^r, r = 1, \ldots, R$, is negatively linearly homogeneous.

(iii) The expenditure function is completely separable in the partition $\{I^1, \ldots, I^R\}$, in which case it can be written as

$$E(u, p) = \Gamma(u)\mathcal{E}\left[\left(\sum_{r=1}^{m} P^r(p^r)^\rho\right)^{1/\rho}\right], \qquad 0 \neq \rho \leq 1,$$

or

$$E(u, p) = \Gamma(u)\,\mathcal{E}\left(\prod_{r=1}^{m} P^r(p^r)^{\rho^r}\right), \qquad \rho^r > 0 \quad \forall r, \qquad \sum_{r=1}^{R} \rho^r = 1,$$

where each of the aggregator functions, $P^r, r = 1, \ldots, R$, is positively linearly homogeneous.

(iv) The distance function is completely separable in the partition $\{I^1, \ldots, I^R\}$, in which case it can be written as

$$D(u, x) = \Gamma(u)\,\mathcal{D}\left[\left(\sum_{r=1}^{m} X^r(x^r)^\rho\right)^{1/\rho}\right], \qquad 0 \neq \rho \leq 1,$$

or

$$D(u, x) = \Gamma(u)\,\mathcal{D}\left(\prod_{r=1}^{m} X^r(x^r)^{\rho^r}\right), \qquad \rho^r > 0 \quad \forall r, \qquad \sum_{r=1}^{R} \rho^r = 1,$$

where each of the aggregator functions, $X^r, r = 1, \ldots, R$, is positively linearly homogeneous.

6 Conjunction of Direct and Indirect Separability and Additivity

It was noted in Section 4 that homothetic separability of *either* the direct or the indirect utility function implies *both* direct and indirect separability and in Section 5 that overall homotheticity and *either* direct or indirect additivity implies *both* direct and indirect additivity. A question that arises is whether either of the converses to these results holds: does the conjunction of direct and indirect separability imply homothetic separability and does the conjunction of direct

and indirect additivity imply overall homotheticity? These converse statements
have sufficient intuitive appeal that each has been stated as a theorem in the
literature on duality and functional structure, yet each has been shown to be
false. In this section, we examine the necessary and sufficient conditions for
the conjunction of direct and indirect additivity (Section 6.1) and of direct and
indirect separability (Section 6.2).

6.1   Direct and Indirect Additivity

The literature on duality and functional structure dates back to Houthakker's
(1960) pioneering examination of the empirical implications of additive preferences (in normalized prices as well as consumption quantities). One of the
conclusions of this paper was that the conjunction of direct and indirect additivity in the individual–commodity partition,

$$U(x) = \sum_{i=1}^{N} u^i(x_i) \tag{6.1}$$

and

$$V\left(\frac{p}{y}\right) = \sum_{i=1}^{N} v^i\left(\frac{p_i}{y}\right), \tag{6.2}$$

implies overall homotheticity. Samuelson (1965), in his formalization of this
result, distinguished between *simultaneous* and *non–simultaneous* direct and
indirect separability. Simultaneous additivity holds if (6.1) and (6.2) represent
the same preferences, whereas non–simultaneous additivity holds if (6.1) and
(6.2) represent the same preferences only after taking an appropriate monotonic
transformation of either the direct or the indirect utility indicator. Samuelson
concluded that simultaneous separability holds if and only if the direct and
indirect utlity functions are Cobb–Douglas and that non–simultaneous additivity holds if and only if the two utility functions are "Bergsonian" (CES with
elasticity of substitution not equal to one).

Hicks (1969), however, provided the following counterexample to Samuelson's result:

$$U(x) = u^1(x_1) + \sum_{i=2}^{N} \beta_i \ln x_i, \tag{6.3}$$

where u^1 is not necessarily homogeneous. It is easy to show that the dual to (6.3) is

$$V\left(\frac{p}{y}\right) = v^1\left(\frac{p_1}{y}\right) - \sum_{i=2}^{N} \beta_i \ln \frac{p_i}{y}. \tag{6.4}$$

Samuelson (1969) acknowledged the error with respect to simultaneous additivity but concluded that his result on the equivalence of non–simultaneous additivity and the Bergsonian structure was correct. Haque (1974) later formalized Samuelson's conclusion about non–simultaneous additivity.

Lau (1969) then extended these results to a groupwise partition:[24]

THEOREM 6.1 [Lau (1969)] The direct and indirect utility functions are both completely separable in a common partition, $\{I^1, \ldots, I^R\}$, if and only if (i) preferences are homothetic, or (ii)

$$U(x) = U^s(x^s) + \sum_{r \neq s} U^r(x^r), \tag{6.5}$$

where U^r is homogenous for all $r \neq s$.

PROOF In case (i), as shown in Theorem 5.7 above, the direct and indirect utility functions are CES (or Cobb–Douglas) functions of the R aggregator functions. In case (ii), the indirect utility function takes the form

$$V\left(\frac{p}{y}\right) = \mathcal{V}\left(V^s\left(\frac{p^s}{y}\right) + \sum_{r \neq s} V^r\left(\frac{p^r}{y}\right)\right), \tag{6.6}$$

where $\mathcal{V}$ is a strictly monotonic function and V^r is homogeneous of degree one for all $r \neq s$. [Of course, case (ii) of Lau's theorem could equivalently be stated in terms of the indirect utility function.] ∎

6.2 Direct and Indirect Separability

As is clear from Theorem 4.2, homothetic separability is sufficient for the conjunction of direct and indirect separability. Hicks's counterexample, as generalized by Lau, shows, however, that the conjunction of direct and indirect separability does not imply homothetic separability since complete separability is a special case of separability. Haque (1981) provided a complete characterization of the conjunction of direct and indirect separability. If there is some

---

[24]Throughout this section, we assume an empty free sector, I^0, in order to simplify notation.

region over which the sector–r preferences are non–homothetic, then the overall function must be, in Haque's terminology, "r–conditionally homogeneous of degree zero" for all consumption bundles in which the rth consumption sub–vector is in this region. (A function F is r–conditionally homogeneous of degree zero if $\sum_{s\neq r} F_s(x)\, x_s = \zeta(x_r)\, F_r(x)$.) Haque partitions the commodity space into $R+1$ regions such that preferences are homothetically separable over one region and, over each of the other R regions, one—and only one—of the groups is non–homothetically separable (in which case the appropriate conditional–homogeneity–of–degree–zero condition holds). Some of these regions may be empty.

Blackorby and Russell (1994) extended Haque's result by providing a closed–form solution (and hence a closed–form characterization of conditional homogeneity of degree zero):

THEOREM 6.2 [Blackorby and Russell (1994)] The following conditions are equivalent:

(i) The sectors $\{I^1,\dots,I^R\}$ are separable from their complements in I in the direct and indirect utility functions, so that

$$U(x) = \mathcal{U}\Big(U^1(x^1),\dots,U^R(x^R)\Big) \tag{6.7}$$

and

$$V\Big(\frac{p}{y}\Big) = \mathcal{V}\Big(V^1\Big(\frac{p^1}{y}\Big),\dots,V^R\Big(\frac{p^R}{y}\Big)\Big). \tag{6.8}$$

(ii) The domain of the direct utility function, Ω, can be partitioned into $R+1$ subsets, $\mathbf{H}_U, \mathbf{C}_U^1,\dots,\mathbf{C}_U^R$, such that

$$U(x) = \hat{U}\Big(X^1(x^1),\dots,X^R(x^R)\Big) \quad \forall\, x \in \mathbf{H}_U, \tag{6.9}$$

where $X^r, r = 1,\dots,R$, are positively linearly homogeneous, and

$$U(x) = \tilde{U}^s\Big(\{U^s(x^s) \times X^r(x^r)\}_{\forall r\neq s}\Big) \quad \forall\, x \in \mathbf{C}_U^s, \tag{6.10}$$

where the X^r ($r \neq s$) are positively linearly homogeneous, $s = 1,\dots,R$.

(iii) The domain of the indirect utility function can be partitioned into $R + 1$ subsets, $\mathbf{H}_V, \mathbf{C}_V^1, \ldots, \mathbf{C}_V^R$, such that

$$V\left(\frac{p}{y}\right) = \hat{V}\left(P^1\left(\frac{p^1}{y}\right), \ldots, P^R\left(\frac{p^r}{y}\right)\right) \quad \forall \frac{p}{y} \in \mathbf{H}_V^s, \tag{6.11}$$

where $P^r, r = 1, \ldots, R$, are positively linearly homogeneous, and

$$V\left(\frac{p}{y}\right) = \tilde{V}^s\left(\left\{V^s\left(\frac{p^s}{y}\right) \times P^r\left(\frac{p^r}{y}\right)\right\}_{\forall r \neq s}\right), \quad \forall \frac{p}{y} \in \mathbf{C}_V^s \tag{6.12}$$

where the P^r $(r \neq s)$ are positively linearly homogeneous, $s = 1, \ldots, R$.

To interpret the non–homothetic structure (6.10) and (6.12), recall the Hicks's (1969) counterexample to the Houthakker (1960) / Samuelson (1965) additivity theorem, as generalized by Lau (1969), Theorem 6.1 above:

$$U(x) = U^s(x^s) + \sum_{r \neq s} U^r(x^r).$$

Renormalize by letting $\bar{U}^s(x^s) = \exp U^s(x^s) - \exp(R-1)$, $\bar{U}^r(x^r) = \exp U^r(x^r)$, and $\bar{U}(x) = \exp U(x)$, to obtain

$$\tilde{U}(x) = \prod_{r \neq s} \tilde{U}^s(x^s) \times \tilde{U}^r(x^r) =: \tilde{U}^s\left(\{\tilde{U}^s(x^s) \times \tilde{U}^r(x^r)\}_{\forall r \neq s}\right).$$

Thus, the Hicks/Lau counterexample has the form (6.10), and it would appear that this structure is the natural generalization, to encompass non–additive structures, of the Hicks/Lau counterexample.

The economic implications of the alternative structure (6.10) are not obvious. Equation (6.10) looks like Hicks–neutral, factor–augmenting technological change, where the augmentation factor, $U^s(U^s)$, applied to the quantities of aggregate inputs, $\{U^r(x^r)\}_{\forall r \neq s}$ in (6.10) depends on the quantities employed of sector–s inputs. This interpretation is also applicable to a household production function, where the homothetic aggregators are characteristics. Equation (6.12) then indicates that this factor–augmentation structure is—using Houthakker's (1965) terminology—"self–dual."[25]

In many applications, the commodity space is a product space (e.g., $\mathbb{R}_+^n$). Blackorby and Russell (1994, Theorem 3) showed that, in this case, the partition

---

[25] Blackorby and Russell (1994, Theorem 2) also characterize the conjunction of direct and indirect separability in terms of restrictions on the expenditure and distance functions.

in Haque (1981) and in Blackorby and Russell (1994) degenerates to a binary partition, **H** and **C**, such that preferences are homothetic on **H** and the Hicksian counterexample (6.10) holds for some (unique) s on **C**. That is, there is a unique sector s such that preferences are non–homothetic on the corresponding commodity subspace for all $x \in$ **C**.

7   Implicit Separability

We now turn to a more general version of separability that has manifested itself in several applied problems: viz., implicit separability.[26] To motivate this notion, we first sketch one of the problems in which implicit separability appears as a necessary and sufficient condition.

The second–best literature addresses a variety of problems that differ in their specification of the distortions in the economy and their assumptions about the policy instruments available to the social planner. Consider the case of irreducible distortions in which one sector of the economy has an exogenous divergence between producer and consumer prices that cannot be changed by the planner. The planner is unable to change either producer or consumer prices in the distorted sector, where consumer prices differ from producer prices. In the rest of the economy, the planner has complete control over consumer prices (for example, through commodity–specific taxes). The planner, unable to control directly any production or consumption decisions, affects these decisions only by selecting the consumer prices for the controlled sector. The problem of the planner is to choose consumer prices optimally in the other sectors of the economy.[27]

Assume a linear technology, so that feasible production vectors, x, satisfy

$$\gamma \cdot x \leq \beta, \tag{7.1}$$

where γ and β are technological coefficients. Assume further that there is productive efficiency in the economy, so that producer prices, p, are equal to the constant marginal cost of producing each commodity. In addition, note that units can be chosen so that $\beta = 1$. Therefore, feasible output vectors are characterized by the following constraint:

$$p \cdot x \leq 1. \tag{7.2}$$

Consumer prices are denoted by q.

---

[26]The notion itself is attributable to Gorman (1965, 1976, 1995), who called it *pseudo-separability*.
[27]We follow the formulation of the second–best problem given in Boadway and Harris (1977), which was used by Jewitt (1981).

Corresponding to the two sectors of the economy, partition the commodity vector and the consumer and producer price vectors as follows: $x = (x^1, x^2)$, $p = (p^1, p^2)$, and $q = (q^1, q^2)$. The planner is able to control the consumer prices in the controlled sector, q^1. The producer prices, p, and the distorted consumer prices, q^2, cannot be affected by the planner. Given the consumer and producer prices, there is an implicit distortion, τ, defined by $\tau = q - p$. The distortion, $\tau^2 = q^2 - p^2$, is exogenous and can not be changed, but the planner can choose the distortion, $\tau^1 = q^1 - p^1$. The planner is assumed to choose consumer prices in the controlled sector to achieve a point on the second–best Pareto frontier, given the consumer and producer prices in the distorted sector.

Suppose for simplicity that there is but one consumer. Market demands can then be expressed in terms of the consumer's expenditure function as

$$\overset{*}{x} = \psi(u, p) = \nabla_q E(u, q). \tag{7.3}$$

The planner's problem is to choose consumer prices in the controlled sector to solve

$$\max_{q^1} u \quad s.t. \quad p \cdot \nabla_q E(u, q) \leq 1. \tag{7.4}$$

This piecemeal policy is optimal if the consumer prices in the controlled sector are chosen to be proportional to the corresponding producer prices and, hence, to marginal costs.

Let the consumer prices in the controlled sector that solve (7.4) be given by

$$\overset{*}{q}^1 = Q^1(u, p, q^2). \tag{7.5}$$

Then piecemeal policy is optimal if there exists a positive scalar k such that

$$Q^1(u, p, q^2) = kp^1 \tag{7.6}$$

where

$$k = K(u, p, q^2), \tag{7.7}$$

for some positive function, K. This guarantees that marginal rates of substitution in sector 1 are equal to marginal rates of transformation in production. Hence, in this subsector, the first–best efficiency conditions are satisfied. Jewitt (1981) showed that this piecemeal policy is optimal if and only if preferences are implicitly separable.[28]

---

[28] See Blackorby, Davidson, and Schworm (1991b) for further discussion and an extension to a multi–consumer economy.

Preferences are *implicitly separable* in the partition $\{I^1, I^2\}$ if there exists an implicit representation, T, and functions T^1 and T^2 such that

$$T(u, x) = 0 \iff u = U(x) \tag{7.8}$$

and

$$T(u, x) = 0 \iff T^1(u, x^1) = T^2(u, x^2). \tag{7.9}$$

Note that, if T^2 is independent of u, then group 2 is directly separable from its complement and, if T^1 is independent of u, then group 1 is directly separable from its complement. Because the quantity aggregates thus defined depend on the utility level, there many alternative representations of implicit separability. In particular, the following are equivalent to (7.9):

$$T(u, x) = \mathcal{T}\left(u, x^1, T^2(u, x^2)\right) = 0,$$

$$T(u, x) = \mathcal{T}\left(u, T^1(u, x^1), x^2\right) = 0,$$

and

$$T(u, x) = \mathcal{T}\left(u, T^1(u, x^1), T^2(u, x^2)\right) = 0.$$

Thus, implicit separability is symmetric: given the partition $\{I^1, I^2\}$, group 2 is implicitly separable from group 1 if and only if group 1 is implicitly separable from group 2.[29]

Implicit separability can also be characterized differentially. Suppose that U is increasing and twice continuously differentiable; then U is implictly separable if and only if either of the following conditions holds:[30]

(i) for all $i, j \in I^1$, the ratio $U_i(x)/U_j(x)$ is a function of x^1 and $U(x)$ alone;

(ii) for all $i, j \in I^1$ and for all $m, n \in I^2$,

$$U_{im}(x)U_j(x)U_n + U_{jn}(x)U_i(x)U_m(x)$$
$$= U_{jm}(x)U_i(x)U_n + U_{in}(x)U_j(x)U_m(x).$$

---

[29] Note the contrast between this and the non–symmetry of explicit separability.
[30] See Blackorby, Davidson and Schworm (1991a, Lemma 4.2).

As with direct separability, the implications of implicit separability are easiest to see in terms of the expenditure function and the compensated demand
functions. Define the conditional expenditure functions,

$$E^1(u, p^1, \xi) := \min\{p^1 \cdot x^1 \mid T^1(u, x^1) \geq \xi\} \tag{7.10}$$

and

$$E^2(u, p^2, \xi) := \min\{p^2 \cdot x^2 \mid T^2(u, x^2) \leq \xi\}. \tag{7.11}$$

$E^1(u, p^1, \xi)$, for example, is the minimum expenditure needed to obtain utility level u, given that the amount of the group-2 aggregate is ξ. Then U is
implicitly separable if and only if the expenditure function can be written as

$$E(u, p) = \min_{\xi}\{E^1(u, p^1, \xi) + E^2(u, p^2, \xi)\}. \tag{7.12}$$

The optimal amount of the intermediate aggregate, $\overset{*}{\xi} = \Xi(u, p)$, is determined
by the first-order condition,

$$E^1_\xi(u, p^1, \overset{*}{\xi}) + E^2_\xi(u, p^2, \overset{*}{\xi}) = 0. \tag{7.13}$$

Using (7.13) and Shephard's lemma, we see that

$$\overset{*}{x}_i = E_i(u, p) = E^1_i(u, p^1, \overset{*}{\xi}) \quad \forall\, i \in I^1 \tag{7.14}$$

and

$$\overset{*}{x}_m = E_m(u, p) = E^2_m(u, p^2, \overset{*}{\xi}) \quad \forall\, m \in I^2. \tag{7.15}$$

Thus sector-2 prices enter the compensated demand for group-1 commodities
only through the aggregator, $\overset{*}{\xi}$. Furthermore, using Euler's theorem, sectoral
expenditures have the same pattern:

$$\sum_{i \in I^1} p_i \cdot x_i = E^1(u, p^1, \overset{*}{\xi})$$

and

$$\sum_{m \in I^2} p_m \cdot x_m = E^2(u, p^2, \overset{*}{\xi}).$$

An alternative but equivalent set of restrictions can be stated in terms of the intersectoral price effects. That is,

$$\frac{\partial \overset{*}{x}_i}{\partial p_m} = a^i(u,p)b^m(u,p) \quad \forall i \in I^1 \quad \wedge \quad \forall m \in I^2 \tag{7.16}$$

for some functions a^i and b^m. Equivalently, the rank of the intersectoral block of the Slutsky matrix, $\nabla_{p^1 p^2} E(u,p)$ is at most 1.

A special case, *implicit homothetic separability* is the solution to an optimal tax problem. Suppose that a planner must raise some tax revenue by means of commodity taxation. Under what circumstances should this tax be proportional? Second–best efficiency is obtained by maximizing the utility of the single consumer subject to his or her budget constraint and subject to a government budget constraint that the government collect enough revenue to pay for a lump–sum transfer, R, by the choice of a tax vector. That is,

$$\max_t u \quad s.t. \quad q^1 \cdot x^1 + q^2 \cdot x^2 \leq \omega^2 \cdot q^2 + R \quad \wedge \quad \sum_{i \in I^1} t_i x_i = R,$$

where $q = p + t$ and ω^2 is a vector of endowments of those commodities that cannot be taxed. The solution is some optimal commodity tax vector. Simmons (1974) and Deaton (1978, 1981) demonstrated that the optimal tax is proportional if and only if the preferences of the consumer are homothetically implicitly separable: that is, (7.9) holds with T^1 homothetic in x^1. Hence, group–1 goods are separable from group 2 in the distance function and, by Theorem 4.1 above, this means that group–1 prices are separable from group–2 prices in the expenditure function. Of course, (7.12) above also holds, with the additional restriction that

$$E^1(u,p^1,\xi) = \hat{E}^1(u,p^1)\xi.$$

Notice that this is more general than homothetic separability. Group 1 is homothetically separable if and only if $\hat{E}^1$ is independent of u.

Finally we note that the above differential restrictions on demand functions can easily be extended from implicit separability to separability itself. Suppose that group 2 is separable from group 1. Then, as already noted, E^2 is independent of u. In addition,[31]

$$\frac{\partial \overset{*}{x}_m}{\partial p_i} = a^i(u,p)b^m(u,p) \quad \forall i \in I^1 \quad \wedge \quad \forall m \in I^2 \tag{7.17}$$

---

[31] See Theorem 4 in Blackorby, Davidson, and Schworm (1991a).

and

$$\frac{\partial \overset{*}{x}_m}{\partial u} = a^u(u,p)b^m(u,p) \qquad \forall m \in I^2 \tag{7.18}$$

for some functions a^u, a^i, and b^m. Equivalently, the rank of the intersectoral block of the Slutsky matrix, $[\nabla_{up^2}E(u,p), \nabla_{p^1p^2}E(u,p)]$ is at most 1. If, in addition, group 1 is also separable from group 2 then[32]

$$\frac{\partial \Phi_m(y,p)}{\partial p_i} = \delta(y,p)\frac{\partial \Phi_i(y,p)}{\partial y}\frac{\partial \Phi_m(y,p)}{\partial y} \qquad \forall i \in I^1 \quad \wedge \quad \forall m \in I^2. \tag{7.19}$$

8 Concluding Remarks: Extensions and Applications.

Separability theory has been extended to infinite–dimensional spaces by Streufert (1995) and has been conjoined with the theory of aggregation over consumers (as well as commodities) by Blackorby and Schworm (1988). Pollak (1972) has introduced a generalised notion of separability, and Mak (1988) has formulated and analysed the notion of approximate separability.

Parametric methods of testing separability restrictions—most using flexible functional forms—have been addressed in Berndt and Christensen (1974), Jorgenson and Lau (1975), Denny and Fuss (1977), Blackorby, Primont, and Russell (1977, 1978b, Chapter 8), Woodland (1978), Lau (1986), Barnett and Choi (1989), Browning and Meghir (1989), Yuhn (1991), Moschini (1992), Driscoll, McGuirk, and Alwang (1992), Driscoll and McGuirk (1992), Conlon (1993), Cooper (1994), Moschini, Moro, and Green (1994), and Diewert and Wales (1995), while Moschini (1991) proposes a semi–parametric method. Revealed–preference methods of testing separability conditions have been developed by Afriat (1970) and Diewert and Parkin (1985) and applied by Swofford and Whitney (1988).

Applications of separability concepts as necessary and/or sufficient conditions abound, as do empirical tests of separability restrictions in particular contexts—most notably, separability of commodities from labor/leisure, the existence of monetary aggregates, and intertemporal separability. A search of EconLit for the period from 1980 to 1995 generated 231 papers in which "separability" appears in the abstract. Most are applications or tests of separability concepts.

---

[32]See Goldman and Uzawa (1964) and Section 7 of Blackorby, Davidson, and Schworm (1991a).

Acknowledgments

Many thanks to Dolors Berga for a very careful reading of this paper. We have also benefited from the comments of a referee. Blackorby has been partially supported by a grant from the SSHRCC.

References

Afriat, S. N. (1970). The Construction of Separable Utility Functions from Expenditure Data. Manuscript, Chapel Hill, N.C: University of North Carolina.

Barnett, W. A. and Choi, S. (1989). A Monte Carlo Study of Tests of Blockwise Weak Separability. *Journal of Business and Economic Statistics*, 7:363–377.

Berndt, E. R. and Christensen, L. R. (1974). Testing for the Existence of a Consistent Aggregate Index of Labor Inputs. *American Economic Review*, 64:391–404.

Blackorby, C., Boyce, R., and Russell, R. R. (1978). Estimation of Demand Systems Generated by the Gorman Polar Form: A Generalization of the S-Branch Utility Tree. *Econometrica*, 46:345–364.

Blackorby, C., Davidson, R., and Schworm, W. (1991a). Implicit Separability: Characterisation and Implications for Consumer Demands. *Journal of Economic Theory*, 55:364–399.

Blackorby, C., Davidson, R., and Schworm, W. (1991b). The Validity of Piecemeal Second-Best Policy. *Journal of Public Economics*, 46:267–290.

Blackorby, C., Lady, G., Nissen, D., and Russell, R. R. (1970). Homothetic Separability and Consumer Budgeting. *Econometrica*, 38:469–472.

Blackorby, C., Primont, D., and Russell, R. R. (1977). On Testing Separability Restrictions with Flexible Functional Forms. *Journal of Econometrics*, 5:195–209.

Blackorby, C., Primont, D., and Russell, R. R. (1978a). An Extension and Alternative Proof of Gorman's Price Aggregation Theorem. In Eichhorn, W., editor, *Theory and Applications of Economic Indices*, pages 109–142. Physica-Verlag, Würzburg–Wien.

Blackorby, C., Primont, D., and Russell, R. R. (1978b). *Duality, Separability, and Functional Structure: Theory and Economic Applications*. North–Holland, New York–Amsterdam.

Blackorby, C. and Russell, R. R. (1994). The Conjunction of Direct and Indirect Separability. *Journal of Economic Theory*, 62:480–498.

Blackorby, C. and Russell, R. R. (1997). Two-Stage Budgeting: An Extension of Gorman's Theorem. *Economic Theory*, 9:185–193.

Blackorby, C. and Schworm, W. (1988). Consistent Commodity Aggregates In Market Demand Equations. In Eichhorn, W., editor, *Measurement in Economics*, pages 577–606. Physica-Verlag, Würzburg–Wien.

Boadway, R. and Harris, R. (1977). A Characterization of Piecemeal Second-Best Policy. *Journal of Public Economics*, 8:167–198.

Browning, M. and Meghir, C. (1991). The Effects of Male and Female Labor Supply on Commodity Demands. *Econometrica*, 59:925–951.

Conlon, J. R. (1993). Separability and Separability Flexibility of the CRESH Function. *Journal of Productivity Analysis*, 4:371–377.

Cooper, R. J. (1994). General Consumer Demand Systems. *Economics Letters*, 44:79–82.

Deaton, A. (1971). A Reconsideration of the Empirical Implications of Additive Preferences. *Economic Journal*, 74:338–348.

Deaton, A. (1978). The Distance Function in Consumer Behaviour with Applications to Index Numbers and Optimal Taxation. *Review of Economic Studies*, 45:391–405.

Deaton, A. (1981). Optimal Taxes and the Structure of Preferences. *Econometrica*, 49:1245–1260.

Debreu, G. (1959). Topological Methods in Cardinal Utility Theory. In Arrow, K., Karlin, S., and Suppes, P., editors, *Mathematical Methods in the Social Sciences*, pages 16–26. Stanford University Press, Stanford, California.

Denny, M. and Fuss, M. (1977). The Use of Approximation Analysis to Test for Separability and the Existence of Consistent Aggregates. *American Economic Review*, 67:404–418.

Diewert, W. E. (1974). Applications of Duality Theory. In Intriligator, M. and Kendrick, K., editors, *Frontiers of Quantitative Economics: Volume II*, pages 160–171. North Holland, New York.

Diewert, W. E. and Parkan, C. (1985). Tests for the Consistency of Consumer Data. *Journal of Econometrics*, 30:127–147.

Diewert, W. E. and Wales, T. J. (1995). Flexible Functional Forms and Tests of Homogeneous Separability. *Journal of Econometrics*, 67:259–302.

Driscoll, P. J. and McGuirk, A. M. (1992). A Class of Separabiliy Flexible Functional Forms. *Journal of Agricultural and Resource Economics*, 17:266–276.

Driscoll, P. J., McGuirk, A. M., and Alwang, J. (1992). Testing Hypotheses of Functional Structure: Some Rules for Determining Flexibility of Restricted Production Models. *American Journal of Agricultural Economics*, 74:100–108.

Geary, P. T. and Morishima, M. (1973). Demand and Supply Under Separability. In Morishima, M. et al., editors, *Theory of Demand: Real and Monetary*, pages 87–147. Clarendon Press, Oxford.

Goldman, S. M. and Uzawa, H. (1964). A Note on Separability and Demand Analysis. *Econometrica*, 32:387–398.

Gorman, W. M. (1959). Separability and Aggregation. *Econometrica*, 27:469–481.

Gorman, W. M. (1965). Consumer Budgets and Price Indices. Unpublished manuscript, published as pages 61–88 in Gorman (1995).

Gorman, W. M. (1968). The Structure of Utility Functions. *Review of Economic Studies*, 32:369–390.

Gorman, W. M. (1970). Two Stage Budgeting. Unpublished manuscript, published as pages 19–30 in Gorman [1995].

Gorman, W. M. (1976). Tricks with Utility Functions. In Artis, M. and Nobay, R., editors, *Essays in Economic Analysis*, pages 211–243. Cambridge University Press, Cambridge.

Gorman, W. M. (1995). *The Collected Works of W. M. Gorman, Volume I*, edited by C. Blackorby and A. Shorrocks. Oxford University Press, Oxford.

Gossen, H. H. (1854). *Entwicklung der Gesetze des menschlichen Verkehrs und der daraus fließenden Regeln für menschliches Handeln*. Braunschweig, 3rd edition 1927, Prager, Berlin.

Haque, W. (1974). Nonsimultaneous Additive Separability. *International Economic Review*, 15:450–457.

Haque, W. (1981). Direct and Indirect Separability. *Journal of Economic Theory*, 25:237–254.

Hicks, J. R. (1969). Direct and Indirect Additivity. *Econometrica*, 37:353–354.

Houthakker, H. S. (1960). Additive Preferences. *Econometrica*, 28:244–257.

Houthakker, H. S. (1965). A Note on Self–Dual Preferences. *Econometrica*, 33:797–801.

Jewitt, I. (1981). Preference Structure and Piecemeal Second-Best Policy. *Journal of Public Economics*, 16:215–231.

Jorgenson, D. C. and Lau, L. J. (1975). The Structure of Consumer Preferences. *Annals of Social and Economic Measurement*, 4:49–101.

Lau, L. (1969). Duality and the Structure of Utility Functions. *Journal of Economic Theory*, 1:374–396.

Lau, L. J. (1986). Functional Forms in Econometric Model Building. In Griliches, Z. and Intriligator, M. D., editors, *Handbook of Econometrics*, pages 1516–1566. North–Holland, Amsterdam.

Leontief, W. W. (1947a). Introduction to a Theory of the Internal Structure of Functional Relationships. *Econometrica*, 15:361–373.

Leontief, W. W. (1947b). A Note on the Interrelation of Subsets of Independent Variables of a Continuous Function with Continuous First Derivatives. *Bulletin of the American Mathematical Society*, 53:343–350.

Mak, K. T. (1988). Approximate Separability and Aggregation. *Journal of Economic Theory*, 45:200–206.

Malmquist, S. (1953). Index Numbers and Indifference Surfaces. *Trabajos de Estatistica*, 4:209–242.

McFadden, D. (1978). Cost, Revenue, and Profit Functions: A Cursory Review. In Fuss, M. and McFadden, D., editors, *Production Economics; A Dual Approach to Theory and Applications*, pages 3–110. North–Holland, Amsterdam.

Moschini, G. (1991). Testing for Preference Change in Consumer Demand: An Indirectly Separable, Semiparametric Model. *Journal of Business and Economic Statistics*, 9:111–117.

Moschini, G. (1992). A Non–nested Test of Separability for Flexible Functional Forms. *Review of Economics and Statistics*, 74:365–369.

Moschini, G., Moro, D., and Green, R. D. (1994). Maintaining and Testing Separability in Demand Systems. *American Journal of Agricultural Economics*, 76:61–73.

Pollak, R. A. (1972). Generalized Separability. *Econometrica*, 40:431–453.

Primont, D. (1970). *Functional Structure and Economic Decision Making*. PhD thesis, University of California, Santa Barbara.

Russell, R. R. (1997). Distance Functions in Consumer and Producer Theory. In Färe, R., Groskopf, S., and Russell, R. R., editors, *Index Number Theory: Essays in Honor of Sten Malmquist*, pages 7–90. Kluwer, Dordrecht.

Samuelson, P. A. (1965). Using Full Duality to Show that Simultaneously Additive Direct and Indirect Utilities Implies Unitary Price Elasticity of Demand. *Econometrica*, 33:781–796.

Samuelson, P. A. (1969). Corrected Formulation of Direct and Indirect Additivity. *Econometrica*, 37:355–359.

Simmons, P. (1974). A Note on Conditions for the Optimality of Proportional Taxation. Manuscript, University of York.

Sono, M. (1945). The Effect of Price Changes on the Demand and Supply of Separable Goods. *Kokumin Keisai Zasshi*, 74:1–51.

Sono, M. (1961). The Effect of Price Changes on the Demand and Supply of Separable Goods. *International Economic Review*, 2:1–51.

Streufert, P. A. (1995). A General Theory of Separability for Preferences Defined on a Countably Infinite Product Space. *Journal of Mathematical Economics*, 24:407–434.

Strotz, R. H. (1957). The Empirical Implications of Utility Tree. *Econometrica*, 25:269–280.

Strotz, R. H. (1959). The Utility Tree—A Correction and Further Appraisal. *Econometrica*, 27:269–280.

Swofford, J. L. and Whitney, G. A. (1988). Comparison of Nonparametric Tests of Weak Separability for Annual and Quarterly Data on Consumption, Leisure, and Money. *Journal of Business and Economic Statistics*, 6:241–246.

Woodland, A. D. (1978). On Testing Weak Separability. *Journal of Econometrics*, 8:383–398.

Yuhn, K. H. (1991). Functional Separability and the Existence of Consistent Aggregates in U.S. Manufacturing. *International Economic Review*, 32:229–250.

3 RECURSIVE UTILITY AND DYNAMIC PROGRAMMING

Peter A. Streufert

University of Western Ontario

Contents

1   Introduction   94
2   Stationary Theory   94
    2.1   Decomposing Recursive Utility   94
    2.2   Feasibility   97
    2.3   The Commodity Space and Biconvergence   98
    2.4   Recomposing Recursive Utility   99
    2.5   Dynamic Programming   101
    2.6   Informal Links to Optimal Control   104
3   Stationary Applications   105
    3.1   Additive Utility   105
    3.2   Deterministic Saving Problems with Additive Utility   106
    3.3   Deterministic Saving Problems with Non–Additive Utility   108
4   Nonstationary Theory and Applications   109
    4.1   Nonstationary Theory   109
    4.2   Stochastic Saving Problems with Additive Utility   112
    4.3   Intergenerational Models   116
5   An Extension   118
References   119

1   Introduction

Economists frequently formulate a dynamic optimization problem in order to study an agent's decision to forgo current benefits for the sake of future benefits. Such agents include consumers who save some of their current income for the sake of future consumption; firms who invest in the reputations of their products; parents who invest in the education of their children; and oligopolists who tacitly cooperate with their competitors for the sake of future cooperation. In formulating and analyzing such a problem, the economist seeks to illuminate the agent's fundamental trade-off between consumption and investment. Toward that end, the economist's formulation must diligently avoid all subsidiary economic issues and all unnecessary mathematical constructions.

The economist must choose between a stationary[1] formulation having an infinite number of time periods and a nonstationary formulation having a finite number of time periods. In short, the economist must choose between stationarity and finite–dimensionality. This choice is unavoidable: one cannot have both stationarity and finite–dimensionality because the first and last periods of a finite–horizon optimization problem must be very different. In most (but not all) circumstances, the economic issues which arise at the end of a finite–dimensional problem are subsidiary or even irrelevant.[2] In such circumstances, the economist must choose the lesser of two evils: the economic and mathematical distractions of a final time period (and the resulting nonstationarity that ripples back into earlier time periods), or the economic and mathematical distractions of an infinite time–horizon.

This chapter explains the economic and mathematical issues which arise from an infinite time–horizon. We believe that when these issues are understood, the distractions of an infinite–horizon model are far less than those of a nonstationary model. In short, infinity is easier to live with than nonstationarity.

2   Stationary Theory

2.1   Decomposing Recursive Utility

Accordingly, we specify an infinite time–horizon by letting $t \in \{1, 2, ...\}$ denote the time period. We then let $a_t \in A$ denote the action taken in period t, where A is the set of all conceivable actions (feasibility is defined in Section

---

[1]In the stochastic environment of Section 4.2, this notion of "stationarity" corresponds to the use of state–contingent value functions.

[2]Note that an uncertain final time period is often best modeled with an infinite number of conceivable periods (see examples in Section 2.1).

2.2). For example, Section 3.2 sets $A = \mathbb{R}_+^2$ so that an action $a = (c, x)$ lists a consumption c and a saving x.

Preferences are specified by an extended–real–valued *utility function U*: $A^\infty \to \bar{\mathbb{R}}$. It gives the utility $U(\mathbf{a}) \in \bar{\mathbb{R}} \equiv [-\infty, +\infty]$ of an action stream $\mathbf{a} = (a_1, a_2, ...)$ beginning in period 1. Such a U is *strictly*[3]*after–1 separable* if

$$(\forall a_1^W, a_1^X)(\forall {}_2\mathbf{a}^Y, {}_2\mathbf{a}^Z)$$
$$U(a_1^W, {}_2\mathbf{a}^Y) \geq U(a_1^W, {}_2\mathbf{a}^Z) \Leftrightarrow U(a_1^X, {}_2\mathbf{a}^Y) \geq U(a_1^X, {}_2\mathbf{a}^Z),$$

where ${}_2\mathbf{a} = (a_2, a_3, ...)$. U is *stationarily*[4]*strictly after–1 separable* if

$$(\forall a_1)(\forall {}_2\mathbf{a}^Y, {}_2\mathbf{a}^Z)$$
$$U(a_1, {}_2\mathbf{a}^Y) \geq U(a_1, {}_2\mathbf{a}^Z) \Leftrightarrow U({}_2\mathbf{a}^Y) \geq U({}_2\mathbf{a}^Z). \tag{2.1}$$

(Stationarity is relaxed in Section 4.) On the other hand, U is *weakly after–1 separable* if

$$(\forall a_1^W, a_1^X)(\forall {}_2\mathbf{a}^Y, {}_2\mathbf{a}^Z)$$
$$U(a_1^W, {}_2\mathbf{a}^Y) > U(a_1^W, {}_2\mathbf{a}^Z) \Rightarrow U(a_1^X, {}_2\mathbf{a}^Y) \geq U(a_1^X, {}_2\mathbf{a}^Z).$$

Weak after–1 separability is weaker than strict after–1 separability because $U(a_1^W, {}_2\mathbf{a}^Y) = U(a_1^W, {}_2\mathbf{a}^Z)$ need not imply $U(a_1^X, {}_2\mathbf{a}^Y) = U(a_1^X, {}_2\mathbf{a}^Z)$. U is *stationarily weakly after–1 separable* if

$$(\forall {}_2\mathbf{a}^Y, {}_2\mathbf{a}^Z)$$
$$[(\forall a_1)U(a_1, {}_2\mathbf{a}^Y) \geq U(a_1, {}_2\mathbf{a}^Z)] \Leftrightarrow U({}_2\mathbf{a}^Y) \geq U({}_2\mathbf{a}^Z). \tag{2.2}$$

The distinction between (2.2) and (2.1) lies in (2.2)'s brackets. While the $\Leftarrow$ half of the biconditionals are identical, the contrapositive of the $\Rightarrow$ half in (2.1) states that

$$U({}_2\mathbf{a}^Y) < U({}_2\mathbf{a}^Z) \quad \text{implies} \quad (\forall a_1)U(a_1, {}_2\mathbf{a}^Y) < U(a_1, {}_2\mathbf{a}^Z),$$

while in (2.2) it states that

$$U({}_2\mathbf{a}^Y) < U({}_2\mathbf{a}^Z) \quad \text{implies} \quad (\exists a_1)U(a_1, {}_2\mathbf{a}^Y) < U(a_1, {}_2\mathbf{a}^Z).$$

---

[3]Koopmans (1960) and Gorman (1968) studied strict separability, while Bliss (1975), Blackorby, Primont, and Russell (1977), and Mak (1986) studied weak separability. A thorough and insightful synthesis is provided by von Stengel (1993).

[4]Stationary strict after–1 separability is equivalent to strict after–1 separability and $(\exists a_1)(\forall {}_2\mathbf{a}^Y, {}_2\mathbf{a}^Z)U(a_1, {}_2\mathbf{a}^Y) \geq U(a_1, {}_2\mathbf{a}^Z) \Leftrightarrow U({}_2\mathbf{a}^Y) \geq U({}_2\mathbf{a}^Z)$. There is no such equivalence for *weak* separability.

THEOREM 2.1 [DECOMPOSITION OF UTILITY] Stationary strict (respectively weak) after–1 separability is equivalent to the existence of an *aggregator* W: $A \times U(A^\infty) \to \mathbb{R}$ which is strictly (respectively weakly) increasing in its second argument and satisfies ($\forall \mathbf{a}$) $U(\mathbf{a}) = W(a_1, U(_2\mathbf{a}))$.[5]

One common example of a stationarily weakly after–1 separable utility function is the stationarily additive utility function $U(\mathbf{a}) = \limsup_{q \to \infty} \Sigma_{t=1}^q \beta^{t-1} G(a_t)$ which is developed in Section 3.1. Here $\beta > 0$ is a discount factor and $G : A \to [-\infty, +\infty)$ is a felicity function; and the aggregator derived from U is $W(a, u_+) = G(a) + \beta u_+$. [Throughout the chapter, read the subscript + as "tomorrow's", the subscript − as "yesterday's", and the absence of a subscript as "today's".] Note that when G can assume both infinite and finite values (as when today's felicity is the logarithm of today's consumption), U is weakly but not strictly after–1 separable (consider $G(a) > -\infty$ and $G(a') = -\infty$) and thus W is weakly but not strictly increasing in tomorrow's utility (consider $G(a) = -\infty$).

The discount factor β is typically less than unity, in which case it can be interpreted in at least two ways: [1] $\beta = (1 + \rho)^{-1}$, where $\rho > 0$ is a taste parameter known as the rate of impatience (more impatience implies a lower discount factor and hence less concern for the future); or [2] β is the probability of surviving until the next period (a lower probability implies less concern for all future time periods).

Additivity is *not* necessary for dynamic programming, and this additional generality has significant economic importance. Consider for example a neo-classical dynamic general equilibrium model in which each consumer i has an additive utility function with discount factor β^i. In a steady–state equilibrium, only those agents with the highest discount factors (*i.e.*, lowest rates of impatience) hold wealth, and there is no restriction on the distribution of wealth among those agents [Becker (1980)]. In short, the stationary wealth distribution is both indeterminate and trivial. On the other hand, we might follow Koopmans, Diamond, and Williamson (1964) and suppose each agent i has a non–additive utility function with aggregator $W(c, u_+) = G(c) + \delta^i \ln(1 + u_+)$ [this is developed formally in Section 3.3]. In this case, steady–state equilibrium uniquely determines the distribution of wealth, and agents with relatively low parameters δ^i can hold wealth [Lucas and Stokey (1984)]. In short, the steady–state wealth distribution is both determinate and nontrivial. These different results arise because the discount factor β (and hence the rate of impatience ρ) is fixed under additivity, while in this non–additive example, increases in future consumption lead to decreases in the discount factor $\partial W / \partial u_+$ (*i.e.*, increases

---

[5] Adapted from Koopmans (1960).

in the rate of impatience $(\partial W/\partial u_+)^{-1} - 1$). Thus variable rates of impatience fundamentally change economic dynamics.

Additivity is discussed at length in a finite–dimensional context by Deaton and Muellbauer (1980, Section 5.3). They note that additivity across different goods (*i.e.*, time periods) implies that all goods are substitutes in the sense that the compensated demand for any good increases with the price of any other good. They argue that this and several other implications of additivity are both restrictive from a theoretical perspective as well as absent from empirical data. These same criticisms of additivity can be leveled in the present dynamic context. For instance, nutritional considerations suggest that the "discount factor" will increase with current consumption as the probability of survival increases. In this case, the compensated demand for consumption in period $t + 2$ might *fall* with an increase in the price of consumption in period $t + 1$ (there's no point saving in period t for consumption in period $t + 2$ if the probability of surviving until period $t + 2$ decreases with the increased price of consumption in period $t + 1$). While such complementarities are precluded by additivity, they are readily specified by non–additive aggregators of the form $W(c, u_+) = G(c) + H(c)u_+$, where $H: \mathbb{R}_+ \to (0, 1)$ is an increasing function giving the survival probability.[6]

2.2 Feasibility

Let the *production correspondence* $\Phi : A \twoheadrightarrow A$ give the set of actions $\Phi(a_-) \subseteq A$ which are feasible today given that yesterday's action was a_-. An action stream **a** is *feasible* from a_- if $a_1 \in \Phi(a_-)$ and $(\forall t \geq 2)a_t \in \Phi(a_{t-1})$. [We prefer a_- over the alternative notation a_0.] For example, in the saving problem of Section 3.2, today's action $a = (c, x) \in \mathbb{R}^2_+$ is feasible if $c + x$ does not exceed the income $F(x_-)$ determined by yesterday's saving x_-. There we define $A = \mathbb{R}^2_+$, write $a = (c, x)$, assume $F: \mathbb{R}_+ \to \mathbb{R}_+$, and define $\Phi : A \twoheadrightarrow A$ by $\Phi(a_-) = \{(c, x)|c + x \leq F(x_-)\}$.

While stationarity may be relaxed at the mere cost of time subscripts on A, Φ, and W (see Section 4.1), the recursivity of Φ and W is essential to the techniques discussed here.[7] Yet many apparently nonrecursive problems can be placed within a recursive framework by reformulating the action space. For instance, after–1 separability directly states that experiences in period 1 cannot

---

[6]This functional form was introduced by Uzawa (1968) and Epstein and Hynes (1983), and used in a nutritional context by Ray and Streufert (1993). See Section 3.3 for a formal development.

[7]Formally, any conceivable nonstationarity or nonrecursivity can be accommodated by reformulating the action set as $\bigcup_{t=1}^{\infty} A^t$, describing an action in period t by $_1\mathbf{a}_t = (a_1, a_2, ...a_t)$, requiring that $\Phi(_1\mathbf{a}_t) \subseteq A^{t+1}$, and only considering streams in $\bar{A}$ (as defined in Section 2.3 below) rather than A^{∞}. There is probably very little value in this awkward reformulation.

shape tastes in period 2. Yet, such acquired tastes can often be accommodated by expanding the action to include a taste variable and then regarding the acquisition of tastes as a matter of technology rather than preference. Similarly, if the feasible set is determined by savings made in the past *two* periods, today's action can be expanded to include yesterday's saving. And finally, if today's feasible set can be affected by committing to future actions, the action can often be expanded to record such commitments.

2.3 The Commodity Space and Biconvergence

Note that if $\mathbf{a}$ is feasible from a_-, then $(\forall t)a_t \in \Phi^t(a_-)$, where Φ^t denotes the composition of Φ with itself t times. In other words, the feasibility of $\mathbf{a}$ from a_- implies that $\mathbf{a} \in \Pi_{t=1}^{\infty}\Phi^t(a_-)$, which we routinely abbreviate as $\Pi_t\Phi^t(a_-)$. Consequently, the set

$$\bar{\mathbf{A}} \equiv \{\mathbf{a}|(\exists a_-)\mathbf{a} \in \Pi_t\Phi^t(a_-)\}$$

contains all feasible streams. We use $\bar{\mathbf{A}}$ rather than A^{∞} as our commodity space because A^{∞} is typically much larger and consequently much less tractable.

Accordingly, the remainder of Section 2 assumes that the utility function U is defined over $\bar{\mathbf{A}}$ and that there exists an aggregator W defined over $\{(a,u)|$ $(\exists \mathbf{a} \in \bar{\mathbf{A}})(a,u) = (a_1, U(_2\mathbf{a}))\}$ such that

A1. $(\forall \mathbf{a} \in \bar{\mathbf{A}})U(\mathbf{a}) = W(a_1, U(_2\mathbf{a}))$, and
A2. W is weakly increasing in its second argument.

These assumptions are weaker than the conclusion of Theorem 2.1 to the extent that $\bar{\mathbf{A}}$ is smaller than A^{∞}.

Biconvergence is defined as the combination of *upper* and *lower convergence*:

AU. $(\forall a_-)(\forall \mathbf{a} \in \Pi_q\Phi^q(a_-)) \lim_{t\to\infty} \sup U(_1\mathbf{a}_t, \Pi_{q\geq t+1}\Phi^q(a_-)) = U(\mathbf{a})$,
AL. $(\forall a_-)(\forall \mathbf{a} \in \Pi_q\Phi^q(a_-)) \lim_{t\to\infty} \inf U(_1\mathbf{a}_t, \Pi_{q\geq t+1}\Phi^q(a_-)) = U(\mathbf{a})$,

where $_1\mathbf{a}_t = (a_1, a_2, ..., a_t)$. Note that the set sequence $\langle(_1\mathbf{a}_t, \Pi_{q\geq t+1}\Phi^q(a_-))\rangle_t$ is monotonically contracting with t. Thus the utility sequence defining upper convergence is weakly decreasing and bounded from below by $U(\mathbf{a})$. Symmetrically, the utility sequence defining lower convergence is weakly increasing and bounded from above by $U(\mathbf{a})$. From the perspective of mathematics, biconvergence is equivalent to the requirement that, for all a_-, U is continuous over the product space $\Pi_t\Phi^t(a_-)$ when each of the coordinate spaces $\Phi^t(a_-)$ is endowed with the discrete topology. From the perspective of economics, biconvergence is a joint restriction on technology and preferences: it is hindered by the "growth" of the "tail" $\Pi_{q\geq t+1}\Phi^q(a_-)$ over time, and it is promoted by the utility function's impatience (which reduces the importance of the tail) and satiation (which penalizes streams in the tail which grow over time). Please see the examples of Sections 3.1, 3.2, 3.3, and 4.2 for further intuition.

2.4   Recomposing Recursive Utility

Section 2.1 showed how a stationarily after–1 separable utility function U uniquely determined an aggregator W. The remainder of this section shows that W uniquely determines U over $\bar{\mathbf{A}}$ if (and almost only if) biconvergence holds. Disinterested readers may comfortably skip to the theory of dynamic programming in Section 2.5.

W defines a functional difference equation known as *Koopmans' equation*

$$(\forall \mathbf{a} \in \bar{\mathbf{A}})(\forall t)U_t(_t\mathbf{a}) = W(a_t, U_{t+1}(_{t+1}\mathbf{a}))$$

which is solved by a possibly nonstationary stream of utility functions $\langle U_t : \bar{\mathbf{A}} \to \bar{\mathbb{R}}\rangle_t$. Koopmans' equation almost always has multiple solutions.

In order to illustrate this and a handful of other points, we consider a classic saving problem known as the "cake–eating" problem, in which an agent having additive preferences can eat any fraction of the cake he saved yesterday while saving the remainder for tomorrow. Formally, define $A = \mathbb{R}_+^2$, write $a = (c, x)$, define $\Phi(a_-) = \{ (c, x) \mid c + x \leq x_- \}$, define $U(\mathbf{a}) = \Sigma_{q=1}^{\infty}\beta^{q-1}c_q$ where $\beta > 0$, and then derive $W(a, u_+) = c + \beta u_+$. Clearly $(U, U, ...)$ solves Koopmans' equation. But then so does the spurious $(U_1, U_2, ...)$ defined by

$$U_t(_t\mathbf{a}) = \begin{cases} U(_t\mathbf{a}) + \beta^{-t} & \text{if } _t\mathbf{a} \text{ is finitely nonzero,} \\ U(_t\mathbf{a}) & \text{if } _t\mathbf{a} \text{ is not finitely nonzero.} \end{cases}$$

To see this, note that if $\mathbf{a}$ is not finitely nonzero, we have $(\forall t)U_t(_t\mathbf{a}) = \Sigma_{q=t}^{\infty}\beta^{q-t}c_q = c_t + \beta[\Sigma_{q=t+1}^{\infty}\beta^{q-(t+1)}c_q] = W(a_t, U_{t+1}(_{t+1}\mathbf{a}))$. On the other hand, if it is finitely nonzero, $(\forall t)U_t(_t\mathbf{a}) = \Sigma_{q=t}^{\infty}\beta^{q-t}c_q + \beta^{-t} = c_t + \beta[\Sigma_{q=t+1}^{\infty}\beta^{q-(t+1)}c_q + \beta^{-(t+1)}] = W(a_t, U_{t+1}(_{t+1}\mathbf{a}))$.

Such multiplicity should be expected: difference equations usually need a "boundary condition" in order to uniquely[8] determine a solution. Such a "boundary condition at infinity" is provided by admissibility: a solution $(U_1, U_2, ...)$ is *admissible* if

$$(\forall a_-)(\exists T)(\forall t \geq T)U_t(\Pi_{q \geq t}\Phi^q(a_-)) \subseteq U(\Pi_{q \geq t}\Phi^q(a_-)).$$

---

[8]The sole purpose of this split infinitive is to thoroughly irritate Peter Hammond.

THEOREM 2.2 [RECOMPOSITION OF UTILITY]

(a) Given A1, A2, and upper convergence (AU), U is the greatest admissible solution to Koopmans' equation.

(b) Given A1, A2, and biconvergence (AU and AL), U is the unique admissible solution to Koopmans' equation.[9]

Theorem 2.2 (b) shows biconvergence is sufficient for a unique solution. It is also necessary: if biconvergence fails and an innocuous technical condition is met, Koopmans' equation will have at least two admissible solutions which are ordinally distinct [Streufert (1993b, Theorems B and C)]. In other words, the "boundary condition" of admissibility has no teeth without biconvergence.

In our cake–eating example, biconvergence holds if and only if $\beta < 1$. If $\beta < 1$, the right–hand side in admissibility's definition is the interval $[0, (1 - \beta)^{-1} x_-]$ for any value of t, and thus the spurious utility function stream is not admissible because the geometric term added to finitely nonzero streams exceeds $(1 - \beta)^{-1} x_-$ in the sufficiently distant future. On the other hand, if $\beta \geq 1$, admissibility is vacuous because its definition's right–hand side is the interval $[0, +\infty]$, and the spurious solution is admissible (as well as a host of other solutions).

Although we cannot obtain uniqueness without biconvergence, Theorem 2.2 (a) obtains something weaker under the weaker assumption of upper convergence.

Stokey and Lucas (1989) and Boyd (1990) employ an alternative approach to recursive utility. First they derive a modulus of contraction from W. It is then critical that this modulus of contraction dominates certain parameters used in the construction of a Banach space containing all feasible action streams. They then derive U as the fixed point of a contraction mapping derived from W and defined over a second Banach space containing utility functions, each defined over the first Banach space containing all feasible action streams (this fixed-point equation in W is a variant of Koopmans' equation). The parameters used in the construction of this second Banach space serve to weed out spurious solutions to the fixed–point equation in W (just as admissibility weeds out spurious solutions to Koopmans' equation).

Arguably, this alternative approach is less elegant. Indisputably, it is less general: [1] a contraction mapping can exist only in biconvergent problems, [2] there are interesting biconvergent problems in which a contraction mapping cannot be readily defined, and [3] there are a great many interesting upper-convergent problems which are not biconvergent. Each of these contentions is easily substantiated: [1] A contraction mapping implies that Koopmans' equation has a unique solution, and uniqueness is both necessary and sufficient

---

[9]Adapted from Streufert (1993b, Theorems B and C).

for biconvergence (as shown immediately below Theorem 2.2), [2] Section 3.3 shows that the parametric assumptions needed for a contraction mapping are substantially less general than those needed for biconvergence, and [3] Section 3.2 exhibits many upper–convergent problems which are not biconvergent (e.g., a problem whose utility function is a discounted sum of logarithms). [And yet, furthermore, contraction mappings require stationarity while convergence properties do not (see Section 4).]

2.5   Dynamic Programming

Assume that

$A3$. Φ is upper semicontinuous,

$A4$. W is upper semicontinuous,[10]and

$A5$. J^+ and J^- exist and are upper semicontinuous,[11]

where the *optimistic* value function J^+: $A \to \bar{\mathbb{R}}$ is defined by $(\forall a_-)J^+(a_-) = \max U(\Pi_t \Phi^t(a_-))$, and the *pessimistic* value function J^-: $A \to \bar{\mathbb{R}}$ is defined by $(\forall a_-)J^-(a_-) = \min U(\Pi_t \Phi^t(a_-))$. Note that we employ Berge's (1963, p. 109) concept of upper semicontinuity which includes compact–valuedness.

In a nutshell, dynamic programming finds the true value function as an admissible solution to Bellman's equation, and then characterizes optima as the recursive optima derived from the true value function.

The *true value function* J^*: $A \to \bar{\mathbb{R}}$ is

$$J^*(a_-) = \max\{U(\mathbf{a})|\mathbf{a} \text{ is feasible from } a_-\}.$$

A stream $\mathbf{a}$ is *optimal* from a_- if it is feasible from a_- and satisfies $U(\mathbf{a}) = J^*(a_-)$ and $(\forall t \geq 2)U(_t\mathbf{a}) = J^*(a_{t-1})$. [Optimality in future time periods is not redundant if U is weakly rather than strictly separable.] The *true policy correspondence* K^*: $A \twoheadrightarrow A$ is

$$K^*(a_-) = \arg\max\{W(a, J^*(a))|a \in \Phi(a_-)\}.$$

[Alternatively, such a policy correspondence is said to be "conserving".] A stream $\mathbf{a}$ is *recursively optimal* from a_- if $a_1 \in K^*(a_-)$ and $(\forall t \geq 2)$ $a_t \in K^*(a_{t-1})$.

---

[10]Streufert (1992, Proposition 3) can be used to derive A4 from the finite–horizon properties of U.

[11]Streufert (1992, Proposition 4) can be used to derive A5 from properties of Φ and U. Note however that the existence of J^- is not essential (admissibility may be defined alternatively as in Streufert, 1992). Furthermore, the upper semicontinuity of J^+ and J^- is needed only to define the terms $B^n J^+$ and $B^n J^-$ used in successive approximations.

A function $J: A \to \bar{\mathbb{R}}$ is an *admissible value function* if it is upper semi-continuous and satisfies $J^- \leq J \leq J^+$. *Bellman's operator* B maps the set of admissible value functions into itself by the formula

$$(\forall a_-)BJ(a_-) = \max\{W(a, J(a))|a \in \Phi(a_-)\}.$$

B is a well-defined operator by the Maximum Theorem [Berge (1963, p. 116, Theorem 2)] used with the upper semicontinuity of Φ (by A3) and $W \circ J$ (by A2, A4, and the admissibility of J); and by the straightforward inequalities $BJ^+ \leq J^+$ and $BJ^- \geq J^-$. J solves *Bellman's equation* if $J = BJ$.

THEOREM 2.3 [DYNAMIC PROGRAMMING]

(a) Assume A1–A5 and upper convergence (AU). Then J^* exists and is the greatest admissible solution to Bellman's equation; optimality is equivalent to recursive optimality; and $J^* = \lim_{n \to \infty} B^n J^+$.

(b) In addition to that, assume lower convergence (AL). Then, in addition, J^* is the unique admissible solution to Bellman's equation; and $J^* = \lim_{n \to \infty} B^n J^-$.[12]

It is often advantageous to restrict one's attention to a subset of the set of admissible value functions. We do this in Sections 3.2 and 4.2 when we consider only value functions that are insensitive to past consumption, and we do it again in Section 4.2 when we consider only value functions that are generated from state–contingent value functions. The restricted subset must meet two qualifications: (a) J^*, J^+, and J^- must all belong to the restricted subset, and (b) Bellman's operator must map the restricted subset into itself. [The use of a restricted subset is rather straightforward, though it should be explicitly mentioned that the greatest solution to Bellman's equation in the restricted subset coincides with the greatest solution to Bellman's equation in the unrestricted set because both equal J^*.]

One can sometimes find an analytic solution to Bellman's equation by [1] guessing the functional form of the solution while leaving a number of coefficients undetermined, [2] applying Bellman's operator to this functional form, and [3] determining the coefficients by equating the result of [2] to the functional form of [1]. For example, the solutions appearing in Sections 3.2 and 4.2 can be found by guessing $J(x) = aG(bx) + c$, where G is the felicity function and a, b, and c are undetermined coefficients. This approach is directly analogous to the way in which differential equations are solved analytically.

---

[12] Adapted from Streufert (1992, Theorems A and B).

Typically, analytic solutions are elusive and numerical techniques are required. Again, one begins with [1] a functional form having undetermined coefficients. Such functional forms may be plausible from the economic structure of the model and/or efficient in the sense of using orthogonal polynomials [Judd (1993)]. The computer algorithm is initiated with (very crude) estimates for the coefficients. These estimates are then iteratively improved by [2] applying Bellman's operator to the functional form with the old estimates and then [3] deriving new estimates by matching the result of [2] to the functional form.

Conceptually, iterative applications of the Bellmann operator B are straightforward because of the monotonicity of B. (a) The sequences $\langle B^n J^+ \rangle_n$ and $\langle B^n J^- \rangle_n$ are monotonic since $BJ^+ \leq J^+$ and $BJ^- \geq J^-$. (b) These two sequences bound J^* since $J^- \leq J^* \leq J^+$ and $BJ^* = J^*$. (c) These same two sequences bound the sequence of "successive approximiations" $\langle B^n J^0 \rangle_n$ initiated with any admissible J^0 since admissibility implies $J^- \leq J^0 \leq J^+$. Theorem 2.3 shows that all these sequences converge to J^* when biconvergence holds.

Note that Theorems 2.1, 2.2 and 2.3 are invariant to any strictly increasing continuous transformation $\delta: U(\bar{A}) \to \bar{\mathbb{R}}$ which transforms U into $\delta \circ U$ and W into $\delta \circ W(\cdot, \delta^{-1}(\cdot))$. (Theorem 3.1 below is invariant to any strictly increasing affine transformation.)

Also note that one could define admissibility with bounds other than the J^+ and J^- which we derived from the product $\Pi_t \Phi^t(a_-)$. In general, tighter bounds require weaker convergence properties, but may well be awkward to apply in practice. The weakest convergence properties could be used when the upper bound is defined by the feasible set rather than the product $\Pi_t \Phi^t(a_-)$, but then the upper bound is indistinguishable from J^* so that admissibility becomes just as hard to calculate as J^*. In the other direction, one could conceivably impose stronger convergence properties that admit looser bounds that are easier to manipulate than J^+ and J^-.

Blackwell (1965) initiated the study of problems that we are calling biconvergent (this area is sometimes called "discounted positive dynamic programming"), and Strauch (1966) initiated the study of problems that we are calling upper–convergent but not lower–convergent (this area is sometimes called "negative dynamic programming"). Puterman (1990) carefully enumerates the ensuing contributions in the dynamic programming literature.

As discussed at the end of Section 2.4, contraction mappings offer an alternative technique. This technique was initiated by Denardo (1967) and has become well-known to economists through Stokey and Lucas (1989). Here one imposes restrictions so that W's modulus of contraction dominates the parameters used to define a Banach space of value functions (in practice this often entails finding a monotonic transformation of the problem such that the modulus of contraction is less than unity and the Banach space is defined with the sup norm). For the reasons discussed in the closing paragraph of Section 2.4, this contraction-mapping technique is much less general than the convergence-property technique used here.

2.6 Informal Links to Optimal Control

Consider the saving problem of Section 3.2, with nonnegative additive preferences. That is, let $A = \mathbb{R}_+^2$ where $a = (c, x)$, let $\Phi(a_-) = \{(c, x) | c + x \leq F(x_-)\}$ where $F : \mathbb{R}_+ \to \mathbb{R}_+$, and let $U(\mathbf{a}) = \Sigma_{t=1}^{\infty} \beta^{t-1} G(c_t)$ where $\beta > 0$ and $G : \mathbb{R}_+ \to [0, +\infty)$. Given that F and G are strictly increasing, consumption variables are redundant and Bellman's equation is equivalent to

$$J(x_-) = \max\{G(F(x_-) - x) + \beta J(x) | x \in [0, F(x_-)]\}.$$

Given suitable concavity, differentiability, and interiority conditions, the elements of $\arg\max\{G(F(x_-) - x) + \beta J(x) | x \in [0, F(x_-)]\}$ are characterized by the first-order condition $G'(F(x_-) - x) = \beta J'(x)$. Further, by the envelope theorem, $J'(x_-) = G'(F(x_-) - x)F'(x_-)$, which by the exchange of today for tomorrow yields $J'(x) = G'(F(x) - x_+)F'(x)$. The combination of these two observations yields $G'(F(x_-) - x) = \beta G'(F(x) - x_+)F'(x)$. When applied at every period, this requires that any optimum satisfies Euler's equation

$$(\forall t) G'(c_t) = \beta F'(x_t) G'(c_{t+1}).$$

Euler's equation replaces Bellman's equation within the technique of optimal control. Euler's equation is simpler than Bellman's equation because it is solved by action streams rather than value functions. However, its usefulness relies upon restrictive assumptions such as concavity, differentiability, and interiority.

Like Bellman's equation, Euler's equation needs a "boundary condition" in order to determine a unique solution. Such a "boundary condition at infinity" is established by means of the *transversality condition*

$$\lim_{t \to \infty} \beta^{t-1} G'(c_t) x_t = 0.$$

Note that by the first-order condition derived earlier, transversality is equivalent to

$$\lim_{t \to \infty} \beta^t J'(x_t) x_t = 0.$$

Since $J'(x_t)x_t$ may be regarded as an approximation of the utility obtained after period t from the saving x_t made in period t, the thrust of transversality is to bound the value of saving. By bounding value functions, admissibility does something similar within the context of dynamic programming.

We wish we could provide the reader with an elegant theorem stating that under biconvergence, the combination of Euler's equation and transversality is both necessary and sufficient for an optimum. However, such a theorem would be somewhat misleading (e.g., optimality can be derived without the full force of biconvergence), and rife with auxiliary assumptions (e.g., interiority is rather complicated with multidimensional investments or non–additive utility). Nonetheless we hope that the reader can see the unifying principle, if not the unifying theorem, linking dynamic programming to optimal control.

3 Stationary Applications

3.1 Additive Utility

The utility functions constructed in Theorem 3.1 below are called *stationarily additive*. The term "additivity" refers to the fact that utility is constructed by summing over time periods. Equivalent terms for additivity are "time–additivity" and "quasi–linearity". The theorem shows that when the utility function is stationarily additive, upper and lower convergence are virtually equivalent to boundedness from above and below.[13] (Such a link between biconvergence and boundedness is *completely* spurious when the utility function is non–additive.)

THEOREM 3.1 [ADDITIVE UTILITY] Suppose that Φ is upper semicontinuous, and that $U(\mathbf{a}) = \limsup_{q \to \infty} \Sigma_{t=1}^{q} \beta^{t-1} G(a_t)$ where $\beta > 0$ and $G : A \to [-\infty, +\infty)$ is upper semicontinuous.[14]

(a) Upper convergence holds if $(\forall a_-) J^+(a_-) < +\infty$. Conversely, upper convergence fails if $(\exists a_-) J^+(a_-) = +\infty$ and $(\exists \mathbf{a} \in \Pi_t \Phi^t(a_-)) U(\mathbf{a}) \in \mathbb{R}$.

(b) $(\forall \mathbf{a} \in \bar{A})\, U(\mathbf{a}) = \Sigma_{t=1}^{\infty} \beta^{t-1} G(a_t)$ if $(\forall a_-) J^+(a_-) < +\infty$ and the sequence $\langle \max G \Phi^t(a_-) \rangle_t$ is ultimately nonpositive or nonnegative.

(c) Biconvergence holds if $(\forall a_-) - \infty < J^-(a_-) \le J^+(a_-) < +\infty$. Conversely, biconvergence fails if $(\forall a_-) \inf G \Phi(a_-) = -\infty$ and $(\exists a_-) J^+(a_-) > -\infty$.[15]

---

[13] The theorem expresses boundedness via J^+ and J^-. We could have alternatively used U and the commodity space $\bar{A}$. The statement $(\forall a_-) J^+(a_-) < +\infty$ is equivalent to $(\forall \mathbf{a} \in \bar{A}) U(\mathbf{a}) < +\infty$. Similarly, the statement $(\forall a_-) - \infty < J^-(a_-) \le J^+(a_-) < +\infty$ implies $(\forall a_-)(\exists v \in \mathbb{R})(\forall \mathbf{a} \in \Pi_t \Phi^t(a_-)) U(\mathbf{a}) \in [v, +\infty)$. The theorem's proof uses this weaker condition to derive biconvergence, and hence does not assume the existence of J^-.
[14] Note that the partial sums defining U could be ill–defined if G could assume both $-\infty$ and $+\infty$.
[15] Proof available from the author.

Note that upper convergence and lower convergence appear in the theorem asymmetrically because G can assume $-\infty$ but not $+\infty$, and because U is defined as an upper limit. Also note that the upper semicontinuity of Φ implies that each $\Phi^t(a_-)$ is compact. Hence the upper semicontinuity of $G : A \to [-\infty, +\infty)$ implies that each max $G\Phi^t(a_-)$ exists and does not equal $+\infty$ [their existence also ensures that $J^+(a_-) = \limsup_{t\to\infty} \Sigma_{q=1}^t \beta^{q-1}$ max $G\Phi^q(a_-)$ exists]. Finally, note that the ultimate expansion or contraction of the sets $\langle \Phi^t(a_-) \rangle_t$ implies the ultimate nonnegativity or nonpositivity of $\langle \max G\Phi^t(a_-) \rangle_t$.

3.2 *Deterministic Saving Problems with Additive Utility*

Consider a stationary deterministic saving problem: Let $A = \mathbb{R}_+^2$, write $a = (c, x)$, and let $\Phi(a_-) = \{(c, x) | c + x \le F(x_-)\}$ where $F : \mathbb{R}_+ \to \mathbb{R}_+$ is a weakly increasing and upper semicontinuous production function. Further suppose stationarily additive utility: Let $U(\mathbf{a}) = \limsup_{q\to\infty} \Sigma_{t=1}^q \beta^{t-1} G(c_t)$ where $\beta > 0$ is the discount factor and $G : \mathbb{R}_+ \to [-\infty, +\infty)$ is a weakly increasing and upper semicontinuous felicity function.

If $\mathbf{a} \in \Pi_t \Phi^t(a_-)$, then c_t is bounded exactly from below by 0 and from above by $F^t(x_-)$, where F^t is the composition of F with itself t times. This $F^t(x_-)$ is the "pure-accumulation" consumption which could actually be consumed in period t if nothing had been consumed in all previous periods. This simple observation implies that

$$(\forall a_-) J^+(a_-) = \max U(\Pi_t \Phi^t(a_-)) = \limsup_{q\to\infty} \Sigma_{t=1}^q \beta^{t-1} G(F^t(x_-)).$$

Thus Theorem 3.1 (a) shows that upper convergence holds if

$$\limsup_{q\to\infty} \Sigma_{t=1}^q \beta^{t-1} G(F^t(x_-)) < +\infty$$

for any initial x_-, and conversely, that upper convergence fails if

$$\limsup_{q\to\infty} \Sigma_{t=1}^q \beta^{t-1} G(F^t(x_-)) = +\infty$$

for some x_- from which finite utility is conceivable. Theorem 3.1 (b) shows that, if $(\forall x_-) \limsup_{q\to\infty} \Sigma_{t=1}^q \beta^{t-1} G(F^t(x_-)) < +\infty$, then, for all $\mathbf{a} \in \bar{\mathbf{A}}$, $U(\mathbf{a})$ is defined by a convergent infinite sum instead of just an upper limit of partial sums. Finally, it is obvious that

$$(\forall a_-) J^-(a_-) = \min U(\Pi_t \Phi^t(a_-)) = \Sigma_{t=1}^\infty \beta^{t-1} G(0).$$

Thus Theorem 3.1 (c) shows that, if $(\forall x_-) \limsup_{q\to\infty} \Sigma_{t=1}^q \beta^{t-1} G(F^t(x_-)) < +\infty$, then lower convergence holds when $G(0) = 0$, and that conversely, lower convergence fails when $G(0) = -\infty$ and finite utility is conceivable.

Economists frequently specify a linear F and an isoelastic G by

$$F(x_-) = Rx_- \qquad \text{and}$$

$$G(x) = \begin{cases} (1-\sigma)^{-1}c^{1-\sigma} \in [0,+\infty) & \text{if } \sigma \in (0,1) \\ \ln(c) \in [-\infty,+\infty) & \text{if } \sigma = 1 \\ (1-\sigma)^{-1}c^{1-\sigma} \in [-\infty,0) & \text{if } \sigma \in (1,+\infty), \end{cases}$$

where $R > 0$ is the gross rate of return on saving, and $\sigma \geq 0$ is the usual measure of intertemporal inelasticity (a relatively large σ implies a relatively large desire to smooth consumption over time). [By analogy with expected–utility theory (identify time periods with states), σ is sometimes called the degree of relative risk aversion.] Note that when $\sigma \neq 1$, the utility of the pure–accumulation stream is readily calculated as

$$\limsup_{q\to\infty} \Sigma_{t=1}^q \beta^{t-1}G(F^t(x_-)) = \limsup_{q\to\infty} \Sigma_{t=1}^q \beta^{t-1}(1-\sigma)^{-1}(R^tx_-)^{1-\sigma}$$

$$= (1-\sigma)^{-1}(Rx_-)^{1-\sigma}\Sigma_{t=1}^\infty(\beta R^{1-\sigma})^{t-1},$$

which is finite iff $\beta R^{1-\sigma} < 1$. When $\sigma = 1$, we have instead that

$$\limsup_{q\to\infty} \Sigma_{t=1}^q \beta^{t-1}G(F^t(x_-)) = \limsup_{q\to\infty} \Sigma_{t=1}^q \beta^{t-1}\ln(R^tx_-)$$

$$= \ln(x_-)[\Sigma_{t=1}^\infty\beta^{t-1}] + \ln(R)[\Sigma_{t=1}^\infty\beta^{t-1}]^2,$$

which is finite iff $\beta < 1$, which is in turn equivalent to $\beta R^{1-\sigma} < 1$ since $\sigma = 1$. Therefore, when $\sigma \in [0,1)$, utility is nonnegative and biconvergence holds iff $\beta R^{1-\sigma} < 1$ (else upper convergence is violated). When $\sigma = 1$, the felicity function is logarithmic, lower convergence fails, and upper convergence holds iff $\beta = \beta R^{1-\sigma} < 1$. When $\sigma \in (1,+\infty)$, utility is nonpositive, lower convergence fails, upper convergence holds without further restrictions, and some stream in $\Pi_t\Phi^t(a_-)$ attains finite utility iff $\beta R^{1-\sigma} < 1$.

Given that $\beta R^{1-\sigma} < 1$, the true value function is

$$J^*(x_-) = (1-\sigma)^{-1}(1-(\beta R^{1-\sigma})^{1/\sigma})^{-\sigma}(Rx_-)^{1-\sigma}$$

in the event that $\sigma \neq 1$ and

$$J^*(x_-) = (1-\beta)^{-1}\ln((1-\beta)Rx_-) + \beta(1-\beta)^{-2}\ln(\beta R)$$

in the event that $\sigma = 1$. When $\sigma \in [0,1)$, this is the unique admissible solution to Bellman's equation. When $\sigma \in [1,+\infty)$, this is the greatest admissible solution to Bellman's equation (another admissible solution is $J(x_-) = -\infty$). In either event, the true policy correspondence derived from J^* dictates that optimal consumption and saving grow by the factor $g \equiv (\beta R)^{1/\sigma}$. [When $\sigma = 0$, set $g = 0$. This is consistent with the formula $g = (\beta R)^{1/\sigma}$ since the requirement $\beta R^{1-\sigma} < 1$ implies $\beta R < 1$ in this case.]

This growth factor entails that the fraction g/R of current income must be saved in each period. The plausible requirement $g/R < 1$ happens to be algebraically identical to the inequality $\beta R^{1-\sigma} < 1$ discussed two paragraphs ago. Hence ill–defined problems correspond to situations in which the "optimal" growth factor g exceeds the gross rate of return R. The upshot is that upper convergence holds almost everywhere that the underlying economic problem is interesting, and that lower convergence fails in a considerable number of interesting cases (in such cases Theorem 2.3 (a) applies and contraction mappings are useless: see the ends of Sections 2.4 and 2.5 for details).

3.3 Deterministic Saving Problems with Non–Additive Utility

Here we modify the last section's saving problem by assuming an aggregator $W \colon \mathbb{R}_+^2 \to \mathbb{R}_+$ which is differentiable and weakly increasing in both arguments. We then define $U(\mathbf{a})$ at each $\mathbf{a}$ in $\bar{\mathbf{A}}$ as the limit of the following weakly increasing sequence of partial compositions: $W(c_1, 0)$, $W(c_1, W(c_2, 0))$, $W(c_1, W(c_2, W(c_3, 0)))$, ... This construction subsumes the familiar definition of an infinite sum as the limit of partial sums, and the additional assumption $W(0, 0) = 0$ would lead to the useful normalization $U(\mathbf{0}) = 0$. Recall that Section 2.1 provided extensive economic motivation for such non–additive preferences.

Derive from W the asymptotic elasticity $\tilde{\sigma}$, the uniform discount factor $\bar{\beta}$, and the asymptotic discount factor $\tilde{\beta}$:

$$
\begin{aligned}
\tilde{\sigma} &= 1 - \inf\{e \in [0,1] \,|\, (\exists \tilde{c})(\forall c > \tilde{c}) W(c, 0) \le c^e\}, \\
\bar{\beta} &= \sup_{u_+ < +\infty} \sup_c (\partial W/\partial u_+)(c, u_+), \text{ and} \\
\tilde{\beta} &= \limsup_{u_+ \to +\infty} \sup_c (\partial W/\partial u_+)(c, u_+).
\end{aligned}
$$

Note that $\tilde{\beta} \le \bar{\beta}$. Streufert (1990) derives A1–A5 and biconvergence from the existence of $\tilde{\sigma}$ and the inequalities $\bar{\beta} < 1$ and

$$
\tilde{\beta}(\limsup_{x \to \infty} F'(x))^{1-\sigma} < 1 \tag{3.1}
$$

(given that F is differentiable and $\limsup_{x \to \infty} F'(x) < +\infty$). For example, consider the isoelastic utility functions of the last section, under the restriction $\sigma \in [0, 1)$. There $W(c, u_+) = (1 - \sigma)^{-1} c^{1-\sigma} + \beta u_+$, $\tilde{\sigma} = \sigma$, and $\bar{\beta} = \tilde{\beta} = \beta$. Thus (3.1) coincides with the inequality $\beta R^{1-\sigma} < 1$ emphasized in the last section.

A more interesting example is the Koopmans–Diamond–Williamson aggregator $W(c, u_+) = (1 - \sigma)^{-1}c^{1-\sigma} + \beta \ln(1 + u_+)$ discussed in Section 2.1. Here $\tilde{\sigma} = \sigma$, $\tilde{\beta} = \beta$, and $\bar{\beta} = 0$. Thus (3.1) holds for *any* (finite) asymptotic gross interest rate $\limsup_{x \to \infty} F'(x)$. This is plausible because the asymptotic discount factor $\tilde{\beta}$, rather than the uniform discount factor $\bar{\beta}$, is relevant at the extremely high levels of consumption which appear in the definition of upper convergence. The Koopmans–Diamond–Williamson aggregator exhibits increasing impatience, that is, its variable discount factor $\partial W/\partial u_+$ falls with increases in utility. As discussed in Section 2.1, increasing impatience is used by Lucas and Stokey (1984) to derive the stability of dynamic general equilibrium. The above observations also apply to any aggregator of the form $W(c, u_+) = (1 - \sigma)^{-1}c^{1-\sigma} + ((1 + u_+)^{\beta} - 1)$ for $\beta \in (0, 1)$. Streufert (1992, Proposition 5) uses asymptotic discount factors to derive biconvergence in much more general models with abstract action spaces.

Finally, note that the contraction mappings used by Boyd (1990) employ the inequality $\bar{\beta}(\limsup_{x \to \infty} F'(x))^{1-\sigma} < 1$. This is less general than (3.1) to the extent that $\bar{\beta}$ exceeds $\tilde{\beta}$.

4   Nonstationary Theory and Applications

The introduction of Section 1 argued that infinity is a lesser evil than nonstationarity. Here we admit nonstationarity as well. Yet, the introduction's lesson is not altogether lost. Rather, Section 4.2 applies the nonstationary theory to stochastic saving problems and derives a more sophisticated sort of stationarity in which the utility function, each admissible value function under consideration, and the Bellman operator are all state–contingent.

4.1   Nonstationary Theory

Consider a stream of action spaces $\langle \hat{A}_t \rangle_{t \geq 0}$ and a stream of utility functions $\langle \hat{U}_t \colon \Pi_{s \geq t} \hat{A}_s \to \bar{\mathbb{R}} \rangle_{t \geq 1}$. Interpret the action space $\hat{A}_0$ as the space from which the exogenously given initial action $\hat{a}_0$ is taken. The utility function stream $\langle \hat{U}_t \rangle_{t \geq 1}$ is *strictly consistent* if

$$(\forall t \geq 1)(\forall \hat{a}_t)(\forall_{t+1}\hat{\mathbf{a}}^Y, \,_{t+1}\hat{\mathbf{a}}^Z)$$
$$\hat{U}_t(\hat{a}_t, \,_{t+1}\hat{\mathbf{a}}^Y) \geq \hat{U}_t(\hat{a}_t, \,_{t+1}\hat{\mathbf{a}}^Z) - \hat{U}_{t+1}(_{t+1}\hat{\mathbf{a}}^Y) \geq \hat{U}_{t+1}(_{t+1}\hat{\mathbf{a}}^Z).$$

Similarly, $\langle \hat{U}_t \rangle_t$ is *weakly consistent* if

$$(\forall t \geq 1)(\forall_{t+1}\hat{\mathbf{a}}^Y, \,_{t+1}\hat{\mathbf{a}}^Z)$$
$$\left[(\forall \hat{a}_t)\hat{U}_t(\hat{a}_t, \,_{t+1}\hat{\mathbf{a}}^Y) \geq \hat{U}_t(\hat{a}_t, \,_{t+1}\hat{\mathbf{a}}^Z) \right] - \hat{U}_{t+1}(_{t+1}\hat{\mathbf{a}}^Y) \geq \hat{U}_{t+1}(_{t+1}\hat{\mathbf{a}}^Z).$$

Note that if $\langle \hat{A}_t \rangle_t$ and $\langle \hat{U}_t \rangle_t$ happen to be stationary, then strict (respectively weak) consistency is identical to stationary strict (respectively weak) after–1 separability as defined in Section 2.1. Thus the following is a straightforward extension of Theorem 2.1.

THEOREM 4.1 [DECOMPOSITION OF UTILITY] Given strict (respectively weak) consistency, there exists an aggregator stream $\langle \hat{W}_t \colon \hat{A}_t \times \hat{U}_{t+1}(\Pi_{s \geq t+1} \hat{A}_s) \to \mathbb{R} \rangle_t$ such that each $\hat{W}_t$ is strictly (respectively weakly) increasing in its second argument and $(\forall t)(\forall_t \hat{\mathbf{a}}) \hat{U}_t({}_t\hat{\mathbf{a}}) = \hat{W}_t(\hat{a}_t, \hat{U}_{t+1}({}_{t+1}\hat{\mathbf{a}}))$.

Also consider a stream of production correspondences $\langle \hat{\Phi}_t \colon \hat{A}_{t-1} \twoheadrightarrow \hat{A}_t \rangle_{t \geq 1}$, and say that ${}_t\hat{\mathbf{a}}$ is feasible from $\hat{a}_{t-1}$ if $(\forall q \geq t)\hat{a}_q \in \hat{\Phi}_q(\hat{a}_{q-1})$. Note that the set of action streams ${}_t\hat{\mathbf{a}}$ which are feasible from some $\hat{a}_{t-1}$ must lie in $\Pi_{q \geq t} \hat{\Phi}_t^q(\hat{a}_{t-1})$, where Φ_t^q is defined as the composition $\hat{\Phi}_q \circ \dots \hat{\Phi}_{t+1} \circ \hat{\Phi}_t$. Thus it will suffice to assume that each utility function $\hat{U}_t$ is defined over $\bigcup_{\hat{a}_{t-1}} \Pi_{q \geq t} \hat{\Phi}_t^q(\hat{a}_{t-1})$, and that there exists $\langle \hat{W}_t \rangle_t$ such that each aggregator $\hat{W}_t$ is defined over $\{(a, u) | (\exists \hat{a}_{t-1})(\exists_t \hat{\mathbf{a}} \in \Pi_{q \geq t} \hat{\Phi}_t^q(\hat{a}_{t-1}))(a, u) = (\hat{a}_t, \hat{U}_{t+1}({}_{t+1}\hat{\mathbf{a}}))\}$ and such that

A$\hat{1}$. $(\forall t)(\forall \hat{a}_{t-1})(\forall_t \hat{\mathbf{a}} \in \Pi_{q \geq t} \hat{\Phi}_t^q(\hat{a}_{t-1})) \hat{U}_t({}_t\hat{\mathbf{a}}) = \hat{W}_t(\hat{a}_t, \hat{U}_{t+1}({}_{t+1}\hat{\mathbf{a}}))$,

A$\hat{2}$.   and $(\forall t)\hat{W}_t$ is weakly increasing in its second argument.

These assumptions on $\langle \hat{W}_t \rangle_t$ are weaker than the conclusions of Theorem 4.1 to the extent that each $\bigcup_{\hat{a}_{t-1}} \Pi_{q \geq t} \hat{\Phi}_t^q(\hat{a}_{t-1})$ is smaller than $\Pi_{q \geq t} \hat{A}_q$. Furthermore, upper and lower convergence may be defined in this nonstationary context by

A$\hat{U}$. $(\forall t)(\forall \hat{a}_{t-1})(\forall_t \hat{\mathbf{a}} \in \Pi_{q \geq t} \hat{\Phi}_t^q(\hat{a}_{t-1}))$
$\lim_{p \to \infty} \sup \hat{U}_t({}_t\hat{\mathbf{a}}_p, \Pi_{q \geq p+1} \hat{\Phi}_t^q(\hat{a}_{t-1})) = \hat{U}_t({}_t\hat{\mathbf{a}})$;

A$\hat{L}$. $(\forall t)(\forall \hat{a}_{t-1})(\forall_t \hat{\mathbf{a}} \in \Pi_{q \geq t} \hat{\Phi}_t^q(\hat{a}_{t-1}))$
$\lim_{p \to \infty} \inf \hat{U}_t({}_t\hat{\mathbf{a}}_p, \Pi_{q \geq p+1} \hat{\Phi}_t^q(\hat{a}_{t-1})) = \hat{U}_t({}_t\hat{\mathbf{a}})$.

Note that we have put hats on the nonstationary primitives $\hat{A}_t$, $\hat{a}_t$, $\hat{U}_t$, $\hat{W}_t$, and $\hat{\Phi}_t$.

The aggregators $\langle \hat{W}_t \rangle_t$ define the nonstationary *Koopmans' equation*

$$(\forall t)(\forall \hat{a}_{t-1})(\forall_t \hat{\mathbf{a}}) U_t({}_t\hat{\mathbf{a}}) = \hat{W}_t(\hat{a}_t, U_{t+1}({}_{t+1}\hat{\mathbf{a}})),$$

which is solved by a utility function stream $\langle U_t \rangle_t$. Such a solution is *admissible* if

$$(\forall t)(\forall \hat{a}_{t-1})(\exists T \geq t)(\forall p \geq T) U_p(\Pi_{q \geq p} \hat{\Phi}_t^q(\hat{a}_{t-1})) \subseteq \hat{U}_p(\Pi_{q \geq p} \hat{\Phi}_t^q(\hat{a}_{t-1})).$$

THEOREM 4.2 [RECOMPOSITION OF UTILITY]

(a) Given $A\hat{1}$, $A\hat{2}$, and $A\hat{U}$, $\langle\hat{U}_t\rangle_t$ is the greatest admissible solution to Koopmans' equation.

(b) Given $A\hat{1}$, $A\hat{2}$, $A\hat{U}$, and $A\hat{L}$, $\langle\hat{U}_t\rangle_t$ is the unique admissible solution to Koopmans' equation.

Theorem 4.2 can be derived from Theorem 2.2 because the present model is stationary if one defines $A = \bigcup_t(\hat{A}_t \times \{t\})$. One can then write an action a as $(\hat{a}_t, t)$; define $\Phi : A \twoheadrightarrow A$ by $\Phi(a) = \hat{\Phi}_{t+1}(\hat{a}_t) \times \{t+1\}$; derive $\bar{A}$ from A and Φ as in Section 2.3; define $U : \bar{A} \to \mathbb{R}$ by $U(\mathbf{a}) = \hat{U}_t({}_t\hat{a})$; and define $W: \{(a, u)|(\exists \mathbf{a} \in \bar{A})a = a_1 \text{ and } u = U({}_2\mathbf{a})\} \to \mathbb{R}$ by $W(a, u) = \hat{W}_t(\hat{a}_t, u)$. Then $A1$, $A2$, AU, and AL are, respectively, equivalent to $A\hat{1}$, $A\hat{2}$, $A\hat{U}$ and $A\hat{L}$, and the domains of definition specified for U and W in Section 2.3 are equivalent to the domains of definition specified for $\langle\hat{U}_t\rangle_t$ and $\langle\hat{W}_t\rangle_t$ above. On the other hand, if $\langle\hat{A}_t\rangle_t$, $\langle\hat{U}_t\rangle_t$, $\langle\hat{\Phi}_t\rangle_t$, and $\langle\hat{W}_t\rangle_t$ are stationary, Theorem 2.2 can be derived from Theorem 4.2. Hence Theorems 2.2 and 4.2 are equivalent.

We will further assume

$A\hat{3}$. $(\forall t)\hat{\Phi}_t$ is upper semicontinuous,
$A\hat{4}$. $(\forall t)\hat{W}_t$ is upper semicontinuous, and
$A\hat{5}$. $(\forall t)J_t^+$ and J_t^- exist and are upper semicontinuous,

where $\langle J_t^+: \hat{A}_{t-1} \to \bar{\mathbb{R}}\rangle_t$ is defined by $J_t^+(\hat{a}_{t-1}) = \max \hat{U}_t(\Pi_{s\geq t}\hat{\Phi}_t^s(\hat{a}_{t-1}))$ and $\langle J_t^-: \hat{A}_{t-1} \to \bar{\mathbb{R}}\rangle_t$ is defined by $J_t^-(\hat{a}_{t-1}) = \min \hat{U}_t(\Pi_{q\geq t}\hat{\Phi}_t^q(\hat{a}_{t-1}))$.

The *true value function* stream $\langle J_t^*: \hat{A}_{t-1} \to \bar{\mathbb{R}}\rangle_t$ is defined by

$$(\forall t)(\forall \hat{a}_{t-1})J_t^*(\hat{a}_{t-1}) = \max\{\hat{U}_t({}_t\hat{a})|_t\hat{a} \text{ is feasible from } \hat{a}_{t-1}\}.$$

A stream $\hat{a}$ is *optimal* from $\hat{a}_0$ if it is feasible from $\hat{a}_0$ and satisfies $(\forall t)\hat{U}_t({}_t\hat{a}) = J_t^*(\hat{a}_{t-1})$. The *true policy correspondence* stream $\langle K_t^*: \hat{A}_{t-1} \twoheadrightarrow \hat{A}_t\rangle_t$ is defined by $(\forall t)(\forall \hat{a}_{t-1})K_t^*(\hat{a}_{t-1}) = \arg\max\{\hat{W}_t(\hat{a}_t, J_{t+1}^*(\hat{a}_t))|\hat{a}_t \in \hat{\Phi}_t(\hat{a}_{t-1})\}$. A stream $\hat{a}$ is *recursively optimal* from $\hat{a}_0$ if $(\forall t)\hat{a}_t \in K_t^*(\hat{a}_{t-1})$.

A value function stream $\langle J_t: \hat{A}_{t-1} \to \bar{\mathbb{R}}\rangle_t$ is *admissible* if each J_t is upper semicontinuous and satisfies $J_t^- \leq J_t \leq J_t^+$. *Bellman's operator* $\hat{B}$ maps the set of admissible value function streams into itself by

$$(\forall t)(\forall \hat{a}_{t-1})[\hat{B}\langle J_t\rangle_t]_t(\hat{a}_{t-1}) = \max\{\hat{W}_t(\hat{a}_t, J_{t+1}(\hat{a}_t))|\hat{a}_t \in \hat{\Phi}_t(\hat{a}_{t-1})\}.$$

$\langle J_t\rangle_t$ solves *Bellman's equation* if $\langle J_t\rangle_t = \hat{B}\langle J_t\rangle_t$.

THEOREM 4.3 [DYNAMIC PROGRAMMING]

(a) Assume $A\hat{1} - A\hat{5}$ and upper convergence $(A\hat{U})$. Then $\langle J_t^* \rangle_t$ exists and is the greatest admissible solution to Bellman's equation; optimality is equivalent to recursive optimality; and $\langle J_t^* \rangle_t = \lim_{n\to\infty} \hat{B}^n \langle J_t^+ \rangle_t$.

(b) In addition assume lower convergence $(A\hat{L})$. Then, in addition, $\langle J_t^* \rangle_t$ is the *unique* admissible solution to Bellman's equation; and $\langle J_t^* \rangle_t = \lim_{n\to\infty} \hat{B}^n \langle J_t^- \rangle_t$.

Theorem 4.3 is a corollary of Theorem 2.3 by means of the definitions and equivalences noted after Theorem 4.2. On the other hand, if $\langle \hat{A} \rangle_t$, $\langle \hat{\Phi}_t \rangle_t$, $\langle \hat{U}_t \rangle_t$, and $\langle \hat{W}_t \rangle_t$ are stationary, Theorem 2.3 can be derived from Theorem 4.3 by restricting attention to the stationary value function streams (recall Section 2.5's discussion of restricted subsets of admissible value functions). Hence Theorems 2.3 and 4.3 are equivalent. Similarly, the following is equivalent to Theorem 3.1.[16]

THEOREM 4.4 [ADDITIVE UTILITY] Suppose that each $\hat{\Phi}_t$ is upper semicontinuous, and that there exists $\langle G_t \colon \hat{A}_t \to [-\infty, +\infty) \rangle_t$ such that each G_t is upper semicontinuous and each $\hat{U}_t(_t\mathbf{a}) = \limsup_{p\to\infty} \Sigma_{q=t}^p G_q(\hat{a}_q)$.

(a) Upper convergence $(A\hat{U})$ holds if $(\forall t, \hat{a}_{t-1}) J_t^+(\hat{a}_{t-1}) < +\infty$. Conversely, upper convergence fails if
$$(\exists t)(\exists \hat{a}_{t-1}) J_t^+(\hat{a}_{t-1}) = +\infty \text{ and } (\exists_t \mathbf{a} \in \Pi_{q \geq t} \Phi^q(\hat{a}_{t-1})) \hat{U}_t(_t\mathbf{a}) \in \mathbb{R}.$$

(b) $(\forall t)(\forall \hat{a}_{t-1})(\forall_t \hat{\mathbf{a}} \in \Pi_{q \geq t} \hat{\Phi}_t^q(\hat{a}_{t-1})) \hat{U}_t(_t\hat{\mathbf{a}}) = \Sigma_{q=t}^\infty G_q(a_q)$ if $J_t^+(\hat{a}_{t-1}) < +\infty$ and the sequence $\langle \max G_q \hat{\Phi}_t^q(\hat{a}_{t-1}) \rangle_{q \geq t}$ is ultimately nonpositive or nonnegative.

(c) Biconvergence holds if $(\forall t, \hat{a}_{t-1}) - \infty < J_t^-(\hat{a}_{t-1}) \leq J_t^+(\hat{a}_{t-1}) < +\infty$. Conversely, biconvergence fails if $(\forall t, \hat{a}_{t-1}) \inf G_t \Phi(\hat{a}_{t-1}) = -\infty$ and $(\exists t, \hat{a}_{t-1}) J_t^+(\hat{a}_{t-1}) > -\infty$.

4.2 Stochastic Saving Problems with Additive Utility

Let S be a finite set of states, let s_1 be the exogenously given state in period 1, and let $p(s_+|s)$ be the probability that tomorrow's state is s_+ when today's state is s.[17] We assume that any state can, given enough time, follow any other state

---

[16]Theorems 4.1, 4.2, and 4.3 are invariant to any stream of strictly increasing continuous transformations $\langle \delta_t \colon \hat{U}_t(\cup_{\hat{a}_{t-1}} \Pi_{q \geq t} \hat{\Phi}_t^q(\hat{a}_{t-1})) \to \bar{\mathbb{R}} \rangle_t$ which transforms each $\hat{U}_t$ into $\delta_t \circ \hat{U}_t$ and each $\hat{W}_t$ into $\delta_t \circ \hat{W}_t(\cdot, \delta_{t+1}^{-1}(\cdot))$. Theorem 4.4 is invariant to any stream of strictly increasing affine transformations.

[17]It is standard to list transition probabilities along with the specification of states and histories. However, these probabilities only affect preferences and might best be regarded as preference parameters.

with positive probability. At each time $t \geq 2$, let the history $_2s_t = (s_2, s_3, ...s_t)$ record all past and current realizations of this Markov process. Note that there are S^{t-1} histories in period t, and that the probability of arriving at history $_2s_t = (s_2, ...s_t)$ given the initial state s_1 is $\Pi_{q=2}^t p(s_q|s_{q-1})$.

In the initial period $t = 1$ and at every history in subsequent time periods $t \geq 2$, the consumer chooses how to divide income between consumption $c \in \mathbb{R}_+$ and saving $x \in \mathbb{R}_+$. A production function F then determines tomorrow's income $F_{s_+}(x) \in \mathbb{R}_+$ as a function of today's saving x and tomorrow's state s_+. To be more explicit, a consumption process $\mathbf{c} = (c_1, c_2, c_3, ...) \in \Pi_{t \geq 1} \mathbb{R}_+^{S^{t-1}}$ is a stochastic process which specifies a consumption $c_1 \in \mathbb{R}_+$ at the initial period $t = 1$ and a consumption $c_t(_2s_t) \in \mathbb{R}_+$ at each history $_2s_t$ in every subsequent period $t \geq 2$. Similarly, a saving process $\mathbf{x} = (x_1, x_2, x_3, ...) \in \Pi_{t \geq 1} \mathbb{R}_+^{S^{t-1}}$ specifies an $x_1 \in \mathbb{R}_+$ at $t = 1$ and an $x_t(_2s_t) \in \mathbb{R}_+$ at each $_2s_t$ in every $t \geq 2$. Let $F: S \times \mathbb{R}_+ \to \mathbb{R}_+$ be such that $(\forall s)F_s: \mathbb{R}_+ \to \mathbb{R}_+$ is weakly increasing and upper semicontinuous. A consumption process $\mathbf{c}$ is *feasible* from initial saving x_0 and initial state s_1 if there exists a corresponding saving process $\mathbf{x}$ such that $c_1 + x_1 \leq F_{s_1}(x_0)$ and $(\forall t \geq 2)c_t + x_t \leq F(x_{t-1})$.

Finally, assume $G_t: \mathbb{R}_+^{S^{t-1}} \to [-\infty, +\infty)$ is defined by $G_t(c_t) = E_{s_1}G(c_t)$, where G is a weakly increasing and upper semicontinuous felicity function and E denotes the expectation operator. Note that $G_t(c_t)$ may be computed explicitly as $\Sigma_{2s_t}\Pi_{q=2}^t p(s_q|s_{q-1})G(c_t(_2s_t))$. Further suppose that the utility of a consumption process $\mathbf{c}$ is defined by $\limsup_{q \to \infty} \Sigma_{t=1}^q \beta^{t-1}G_t(c_t)$. Such a utility function is termed "additive" because it is constructed by summing across not only time (as in Section 3.1) but also across histories. An equivalent term is "time–additive expected–utility".

Although uncertainty has not been mentioned until now, a stochastic problem with additive preferences is a nonstationary application of our abstract deterministic theory. Specifically, let $\hat{A}_t = (\mathbb{R}_+^2)^{S^{t-1}}$, that is, let an action in period t be a pair of vectors $\hat{a}_t = (c_t, x_t)$ which specify a consumption and saving at each of the S^{t-1} histories in period t. The production correspondence stream, utility function stream, and aggregator stream may then be defined by

$$\hat{\Phi}_t(\hat{a}_{t-1}) = \{(c_t, x_t)|c_t + x_t \leq F(x_{t-1})\},^{18}$$
$$\hat{U}_t(_t\hat{\mathbf{a}}) = \Sigma_{q \geq t}\beta^{q-t}E_{s_1}G(c_q), \text{ and}$$
$$\hat{W}_t(\hat{a}_t, u) = E_{s_1}G(c_t) + \beta u.$$

---

[18] Explicitly, $\hat{\Phi}_t(\hat{a}_{t-1}) = \Pi_{2s_t}\{(c_t(_2s_t), x_t(_2s_t))|c_t(_2s_t) + x_t(_2s_t) \leq F_{s_t}(x_{t-1}(_2s_{t-1}))\}$.

The value function streams, policy correspondence stream, and Bellman operator are then

$$J_t^+(x_{t-1}) = \Sigma_{q\geq t}\beta^{q-t}E_{s_1}G(F^{q-(t-1)}(x_{t-1})),$$
$$J_t^-(x_{t-1}) = \Sigma_{q\geq t}\beta^{q-t}G(0) = G(0)(1-\beta)^{-1},$$
$$J_t^*(x_{t-1}) = \max\{\Sigma_{q\geq t}\beta^{q-t}E_{s_1}G(c_t)|(\exists_t\mathbf{x})(\forall q \geq t)c_q + x_q \leq F(x_{q-1})\},$$
$$K_t^*(x_{t-1}) = \arg\max\{E_{s_1}G(c_t) + \beta J_{t+1}^*(x_t)|c_t + x_t \leq F(x_{t-1})\}, \text{ and}$$
$$(\hat{B}\langle J_t\rangle_t)_t(x_{t-1}) = \max\{E_{s_1}G(c_t) + \beta J_{t+1}(x_t)|c_t + x_t \leq F(x_{t-1})\}.$$

Given our assumptions on G and F, the one restriction that

$$(\forall t, x_{t-1})J_t^+(x_{t-1}) < +\infty \tag{4.1}$$

will imply upper convergence (by Theorem 4.4 (a)) and $A\hat{1} - A\hat{5}$ [the upper semicontinuity of each J_t^+ follows from Ozaki and Streufert (1994, Lemma A.3)]. Furthermore, $G(0) = 0$ will imply lower convergence. Thus Theorems 4.2 and 4.3 are at our disposal. Notice that we are considering a restricted subset of the admissible set which contains only value functions that are insensitive to yesterday's consumption.

A further restriction of the admissible set is also advantageous. A value function stream $\langle J_t\rangle_t$ is said to be *generated* from a *state-contingent* value function $J: S \times \mathbb{R}_+ \to \bar{\mathbb{R}}$ if

$$J_1(x_0) = J_{s_1}(x_0) \quad \text{and} \quad (\forall t \geq 2)J_t(x_{t-1}) = E_{s_1}J(x_{t-1}).\text{[19]}$$

For instance, $\langle J_t^+\rangle_t$, $\langle J_t^-\rangle_t$, and $\langle J_t^*\rangle_t$ are respectively generated by

$$J_s^+(x_-) \equiv G(F_s(x_-)) + \Sigma_{t\geq 2}\beta^{t-1}E_sG(F^t(x_-)),$$
$$J_s^-(x_-) \equiv \Sigma_{t\geq 1}\beta^{t-1}E_sG(0) = G(0)(1-\beta)^{-1}, \text{ and} \tag{4.2}$$
$$J_s^*(x_-) \equiv \max\{\Sigma_{t\geq 1}\beta^{t-1}E_sG(c_t)|c_1 + x_1 \leq F_s(x_-)$$
$$\text{and } (\forall t \geq 2)c_t + x_t \leq F(x_{t-1})\}.$$

A state–contingent J is *admissible* if it is upper semicontinuous and lies between J^- and J^+. Note that the admissibility of J implies the admissibility of the

---

[19]Explicitly, $(\forall t \geq 2)J_t(x_{t-1}) = \Sigma_{2^{s_t}}[\Pi_{r=2}^t p(s_r|s_{r-1})]\, J_{s_t}(x_{t-1}(2s_{t-1}))$.

$\langle J_t \rangle_t$ it generates. Also notice that if $\langle J_t \rangle_t$ is generated by J, then

$$
\begin{aligned}
(\forall t) \quad & [\hat{B}\langle J_t \rangle_t]_t(x_{t-1}) \\
= \; & \max\{E_{s_1} G(c_t) + \beta J_{t+1}(x_t) | c_t + x_t \le F(x_{t-1})\} \\
= \; & \max\{E_{s_1} G(c_t) + \beta E_{s_1} J(x_t) | c_t + x_t \le F(x_{t-1})\} \qquad (4.3) \\
= \; & E_{s_1} \max\{G(c_t) + \beta E_{s_t} J(x_t) | c_t + x_t \le F_{s_t}(x_{t-1})\} \\
= \; & E_{s_1} BJ(x_{t-1}),
\end{aligned}
$$

where B maps the set of admissible state–contingent value functions into itself by the rule

$$
(BJ)_s(x_-) = \max\{G(c) + \beta E_s J(x) | c + x \le F_s(x_-)\}.
$$

Therefore, we may restrict attention to value function streams generated by admissible state–contingent value functions because both of the conditions discussed below Theorem 2.3 hold: (a) $\langle J_t^+ \rangle_t$, $\langle J_t^- \rangle_t$, and $\langle J_t^* \rangle_t$ are all in this restricted subset, and (b) $\hat{B}$ maps elements of this subset back into the subset.

State–contingent value functions are extremely convenient. [1] The key restriction (4.1) holds iff $(\forall s)(\forall x_-) J_s^+(x_-) < +\infty$ (by (4.2)). [2] If J generates $\langle J_t \rangle_t$, then $J = BJ$ iff $\langle J_t \rangle_t = B\langle J_t \rangle_t$ (by (4.3)). [3] If J^0 generates $\langle J_t^0 \rangle_t$, then $(\forall n) B^n J^0$ generates $\hat{B}^n \langle J_t^0 \rangle_t$ (again by (4.3)). [4] $\langle K_t^* \rangle_t$ can be derived from J^* by

$$
[K_t^*(x_{t-1})](_2 s_t) = \arg\max\{G(c) + \beta E_{s_t} J^*(x) | c + x \le F_{s_t}(x_{t-1}(_2 s_t))\}.
$$

For example, suppose that each $F_s(x_-) = R_s x_-$ for some $R_s > 0$, that G is isoelastic (as in Section 3.2), and that its parameter $\sigma \ne 1$.[20] The state–contingent upper bound is then

$$
J_s^+(x_-) = (1 - \sigma)^{-1} k_s^+ (R_s x_-)^{1-\sigma},
$$

where each $k_s^+ = \Sigma_{t=1}^{\infty} \beta^{t-1} \mathbf{1}^T (\Gamma^{1-\sigma} P)^{t-1} \mathbf{1}_s$; $\Gamma^{1-\sigma}$ is the diagonal matrix which lists $R_s^{1-\sigma}$ in the sth position; P is the transition matrix in which $p(s_+|s)$ appears on the s_+th row; $\mathbf{1}$ is a vector of ones; and $\mathbf{1}_s$ is a unit vector pointing in the sth direction. Note that every k_s^+ is finite iff the dominant eigenvalue of $\Gamma^{1-\sigma} P$ is less than β^{-1}: this requires that the "average" growth factor is less than the gross rate of impatience [the role of P is nontrivial, as discussed in Streufert (1996)]. Given that every k_s^+ is finite, the state–contingent true value function is

$$
J_s^*(x_-) = (1 - \sigma)^{-1} k_s^* (R_s x_-)^{1-\sigma},
$$

---

[20]If $\sigma = 1$, G is the logarithm. Given that $\beta < 1$, both $J_s^+(x)$ and $J_s^*(x)$ are of the form $A_s \ln(x) + C_s$ for some real constants A_s and C_s. Although these constants can be computed by linear algebra, they aren't pretty.

where each k_s^* is defined to be the sth element of the row vector $\mathbf{k}^*$ which solves the nonlinear system $\mathbf{k}^{*1/\sigma} = \mathbf{1} + \{\beta \mathbf{k}^* \Gamma^{1-\sigma} P\}^{1/\sigma}$. Not surprisingly, this system has a unique solution if the dominant eigenvalue of $\Gamma^{1-\sigma} P$ is less than β^{-1}. [In the event that the transition probabilities $p(s_+|s)$ are independent of today's state s, each $k_s^+ = (1 - \beta E R^{1-\sigma})^{-1}$ and each $k_s^* = (1 - (\beta E R^{1-\sigma})^{1/\sigma})^{-\sigma}$, where $E R^{1-\sigma}$ is the expectation of $R^{1-\sigma}$. These clearly extend Section 3.2's deterministic formulas.]

This section's saving problem is dreadfully simple because the agent faces many states but has only one asset. Additional assets may be straightforwardly included by letting x be a vector. In this extension, it is prudent to restrict attention to value functions which are generated by state–contingent value functions that vary only with today's income (as opposed to other features of yesterday's portfolio). Hakansson (1970) provides analytic solutions to examples with independent transition probabilities.

4.3 Intergenerational Models

Consider the nonstationary model defined by $\langle \hat{A}_t \rangle_t$, $\langle \hat{\Phi}_t \rangle_t$, and $\langle \hat{U}_t \rangle_t$. Here we interpret each $\hat{U}_t$ as the utility function of the generation living in period t. A strategy for generation t is a function $\sigma_t \colon \hat{A}_{t-1} \to \hat{A}_t$ such that $(\forall \hat{a}_{t-1}) \sigma_t(\hat{a}_{t-1}) \in \hat{\Phi}_t(\hat{a}_{t-1})$. A stream of such strategies is a *true equilibrium* if

$$(\forall t)(\forall \hat{a}_{t-1})$$

$$\sigma_t(\hat{a}_{t-1}) \in \arg\max\{\hat{U}_t(\hat{a}_t, \sigma_{t+1}(\hat{a}_t), \sigma_{t+2} \circ \sigma_{t+1}(\hat{a}_t), \ldots) | \hat{a}_t \in \hat{\Phi}_t(\hat{a}_{t-1})\}.$$

Thus true equilibria are subgame–perfect equilibria consisting of Markov strategies in the game of perfect information [Bernheim and Ray (1983), Harris (1985), Leininger (1986), Streufert (1993a)]. If non–Markov strategies were introduced, true equilibria would remain equilibria, but additional non–Markov equilibria might be introduced.[21]

By Theorem 4.1, strict (respectively, weak) consistency implies the existence of an aggregator stream $\langle \hat{W}_t \rangle_t$ which satisfies $(\forall t)(\forall_t \hat{\mathbf{a}}) \hat{U}_t(_t\hat{\mathbf{a}}) = \hat{W}_t(\hat{a}_t, \hat{U}_{t+1}(_{t+1}\hat{\mathbf{a}}))$ and for which each $\hat{W}_t$ is strictly (respectively, weakly) increasing in its second argument. Thus strict (respectively, weak) consistency implies that each generation takes its child's utility as a sufficient statistic for all future actions and finds that its utility strictly (respectively, weakly) increases in its child's utility. This has been termed nonpaternalistic as opposed to paternalistic altruism [Ray (1987)] because the parent is not concerned with *how* the

---

[21] As noted earlier, recursivity (which is called the Markov property here) is a vacuous restriction if period t's action space is redefined (*extremely* awkwardly) as $\Pi_{q=1}^t \hat{A}_q$.

child derives its utility. By Theorem 4.2, upper convergence (respectively, bi-convergence) implies that $\langle \hat{U}_t \rangle_t$ is the greatest (respectively, unique) admissible solution to the Koopmans' equation defined by $\langle \hat{W}_t \rangle_t$.

A strategy stream $\langle \sigma_t \rangle_t$ is an *admissible equilibrium* if there exists an admissible solution to Bellman's equation $\langle J_t \rangle_t$ such that

$$(\forall t)(\forall \hat{a}_{t-1}) \quad \sigma_t(\hat{a}_{t-1}) \in \arg\max\{\hat{W}_t(\hat{a}_t, J_t(\hat{a}_t)) | \hat{a}_t \in \hat{\Phi}_t(\hat{a}_{t-1})\}.$$

This equilibrium concept is not well–founded in game theory because the objective functions are not primitives in the model. Rather, they are of interest primarily because they are easier to calculate than true equilibria.

Assume $A\hat{1}$–$A\hat{5}$ and upper convergence $(A\hat{U})$. Three fundamental observations can then be made (note that they move in a circle).

[1] Every selection from $\langle K_t^* \rangle_t$ is a true equilibrium:

$$(\forall t)(\forall \hat{a}_{t-1})$$
$$\sigma_t(\hat{a}_{t-1}) \in K_t^*(\hat{a}_{t-1}) = \arg\max\{\hat{W}_t(\hat{a}_t, J_t^*(\hat{a}_t)) | \hat{a}_t \in \hat{\Phi}_t(\hat{a}_{t-1})\}$$
$$= \arg\max\{\hat{W}_t(\hat{a}_t, \hat{U}_{t+1}(\sigma_{t+1}(\hat{a}_t), \sigma_{t+2} \circ \sigma_{t+1}(\hat{a}_t), ...)) | \hat{a}_t \in \hat{\Phi}_t(\hat{a}_{t-1})\}$$
$$= \arg\max\{\hat{U}_t(\hat{a}_t, \sigma_{t+1}(\hat{a}_t), \sigma_{t+2} \circ \sigma_{t+1}(\hat{a}_t), ...) | \hat{a}_t \in \hat{\Phi}_t(\hat{a}_{t-1})\}.$$

The first equality is the definition of K_t^*. The second holds since $(\sigma_{t+1}(\hat{a}_t), \sigma_{t+2} \circ \sigma_{t+1}(\hat{a}_t), ...)$ is optimal from any $\hat{a}_t$ by Theorem 4.3 (a) and by the fact that it is recursively optimal (recall every σ_{t+q} is a selection from K_{t+q}^*). The third holds by $A\hat{1}$.

[2] Every true equilibrium is an admissible equilibrium:

$$(\forall t)(\forall \hat{a}_{t-1})$$
$$\sigma_t(\hat{a}_{t-1}) \in \arg\max\{\hat{U}_t(\hat{a}_t, \sigma_{t+1}(\hat{a}_t), \sigma_{t+2} \circ \sigma_{t+1}(\hat{a}_t), ...) | \hat{a}_t \in \hat{\Phi}_t(\hat{a}_{t-1})\}$$
$$= \arg\max\{\hat{W}_t(\hat{a}_t, \hat{U}_{t+1}(\sigma_{t+1}(\hat{a}_t), \sigma_{t+2} \circ \sigma_{t+1}(\hat{a}_t), ...)) | \hat{a}_t \in \hat{\Phi}_t(\hat{a}_{t-1})\}$$
$$= \arg\max\{\hat{W}_t(\hat{a}_t, J_{t+1}(\hat{a}_{t+1})) | \hat{a}_t \in \hat{\Phi}_t(\hat{a}_{t-1})\}.$$

The first equality holds by $A\hat{1}$ and the second defines $\langle J_t \rangle_t$.

[3] An admissible equilibrium is a selection from $\langle K_t^* \rangle_t$ if *either* (a) its $\langle J_t \rangle_t$ is the greatest solution to Bellman's equation *or* (b) lower convergence $(A\hat{L})$ holds. This follows from Theorem 4.3.

These three observations have numerous corollaries. First, true equilibria and admissible equilibria exist (combine [1] and [2] with the existence of $\langle K_t^* \rangle_t$ from Theorem 4.3 (a)). Second, an admissible equilibrium is a true equilibrium if either (a) its $\langle J_t \rangle_t$ is the greatest solution to Bellman's equation or (b) lower convergence $(A\hat{L})$ holds (combine [3] and [1]). Third, a true equilibrium is a selection from $\langle K_t^* \rangle_t$ if either (a) the $\langle J_t \rangle_t$ defined in [2] is the greatest solution to Bellman's equation or (b) lower convergence $(A\hat{L})$ holds (combine [2] and [3]).

The above results may be interpreted in two other ways. First, one could consider the same individual at different points in time rather than a sequence of generations [Hammond (1976)]. In this context, the nonstationarity of $\langle \hat{U}_t \rangle_t$ models an individual's changing tastes. Second, the action stream resulting from a true equilibrium is termed "unimprovable" in the dynamic programming literature. Similarly, the action stream resulting from a selection from $\langle K_t^* \rangle_t$ is termed a "recursive optimum" in Sections 2 and 4.1. Hence the above discussion links unimprovability and recursive optimization.

Finally, we note that the stochastic model of the last section may be interpreted as an intergenerational model in which each individual has multiple children of different types. Each history is an individual, the current state s denotes the individual's type, and $p(s_+|s)$ specifies the weight which a parent of type s attaches to the child of type s_+ (if $p(s_+|s) = 0$, then a type s either cannot produce a type s_+ or cares nothing for the type s_+). In this interpretation, each $\hat{U}_t$ sums the utilities of all individuals in generation t, weighted according to the preferences of the initial individual in period 1 of type s_1. The last section's trick of using state–contingent value functions now employs type–contingent value functions.

5 An Extension

The additive stochastic preferences used in Section 4.2 are very restrictive in that the curvature of the felicity function G must determine both risk aversion and intertemporal inelasticity. In particular, if $G(c) = (1 - \sigma)^{-1} c^{1-\sigma}$, then the one parameter σ is identically equal to both the degree of relative risk aversion and the usual measure of intertemporal inelasticity. As shown by Epstein and Zin (1989), one can break this link by aggregating utility across tomorrow's states by a function other than the expectation operator. Earlier Kreps and Porteus (1978) had noted that such non–additive aggregators affected preferences over the timing of the resolution of uncertainty.

This additional generality cannot be accommodated by the theory of Section 4 because it requires that each $\hat{U}_q$ be vector-valued. In particular, one must list the utility at every history in period t because there is no suitable summary statistic like expectation given s_1. This same obstacle appears in an intergenerational model where a parent aggregates the utilities of its several children in a non-additive fashion. Suitable mathematics for saving problems with non-additive objectives are developed in Ozaki and Streufert (1996).

Acknowledgments

I am especially grateful to Robert Becker, John Boyd, Larry Epstein, Peter Hammond, Mordecai Kurz, Val Lambson, Hiro Ozaki, and Debraj Ray for valuable feedback over many years.

References

Becker, R. A. (1980). On the Long–Run Steady State in a Simple Dynamic Model of Equilibrium with Heterogeneous Households. *Quarterly Journal of Economics*, 95:375–382.

Becker, R. A. and Boyd, III., J. H. (1995). *Capital Theory, Equilibrium Analysis and Recursive Utility*. Mimeo.

Berge, C. (1963). *Topological Spaces*. Oliver and Boyd, Edinburgh.

Bernheim, D. and Ray, D. (1983). Altruistic Growth Economies: I. Existence of Bequest Equilibria. *IMSSS Technical Report No. 419, Stanford.*

Bertsekas, D. P. (1987). *Dynamic Programming: Deterministic and Stochastic Models*. Prentice-Hall, Englewood (New Jersey) and Cambridge.

Bertsekas, D. P. and Shreve, S. (1978). *Stochastic Optimal Control: The Discrete Case*. Academic Press, New York.

Blackorby, C., Primont, D., and Russell, R. R. (1977). Separability vs. Functional Structure: A Characterization of Their Differences. *Journal of Economic Theory*, 15:135–144.

Blackwell, D. (1965). Discounted Dynamic Programming. *Annals of Mathematics and Statistics*, 36:226–235.

Bliss, C. (1975). *Capital Theory and the Distribution of Income*. North-Holland, New York.

Boyd, III., J. H. (1990). Recursive Utility and the Ramsey Problem. *Journal of Economic Theory*, 50:326–345.

Deaton, A. and Muellbauer, J. (1980). *Economics and Consumer Behavior*. Cambridge University Press, Cambridge.

Denardo, E. V. (1967). Contraction Mappings in the Theory Underlying Dynamic Programming. *SIAM Review*, 9:169–177.

Epstein, L. G. and Hynes, J. A. (1983). The Rate of Time Preference and Dynamic Economic Analysis. *Journal of Political Economy*, 91:611–635.

Epstein, L. G. and Zin, S. E. (1989). Substitution, Risk Aversion, and the Temporal Behavior of Consumption and Asset Returns. *Econometrica*, 57:937–970.

Gorman, W. M. (1968). The Structure of Utility Functions. *Review of Economic Studies*, 35:376–390.

Hakansson, N. H. (1970). Optimal Investment and Consumption Strategies under Risk for a Class of Utility Functions. *Econometrica*, 38:587–607.

Hammond, P. J. (1976). Changing Tastes and Coherent Dynamic Choice. *Review of Economic Studies*, 63:159–173.

Harris, C. (1985). Existence and Characterization of Perfect Equilibrium in Games of Perfect Information. *Econometrica*, 53:613–628.

Judd, K. L. (1993). Numerical Methods in Economics. Unpublished manuscript.

Koopmans, T. (1960). Stationary Ordinal Utility and Impatience. *Econometrica*, 28:287–309.

Koopmans, T., Diamond, P. A., and Williamson, R. E. (1964). Stationary Utility and Time Perspective. *Econometrica*, 32:82–100.

Kreps, D. M. and Porteus, E. L. (1978). Temporal Resolution of Uncertainty and Dynamic Choice Theory. *Econometrica*, 46:185–200.

Leininger, W. (1986). The Existence of Perfect Equilibria in a Model of Growth with Altruism between Generations. *Review of Economic Studies*, 53:349–368.

Lucas, jr., R. E. and Stokey, N. L. (1984). Optimal Growth with Many Consumers. *Journal of Economic Theory*, 32:139–171.

Mak, K.-T. (1986). On Separability: Functional Structure. *Journal of Economic Theory*, 40:250–282.

Ozaki, H. and Streufert, P. A. (1996). Dynamic Programming for Non–Additive Stochastic Objectives. *Journal of Mathematical Economics*, 25:391–442.

Puterman, M. L. (1990). Markov Decision Processes. In *Handbooks in Operations Research and Management Science*, volume 2. Elsevier Science Publishers (North Holland), Amsterdam.

Ray, D. (1987). Nonpaternalistic Intergenerational Altruism. *Journal of Economic Theory*, 41:112–132.

Ray, D. and Streufert, P. A. (1993). Dynamic Equilibria with Unemployment due to Undernourishment. *Economic Theory*, 3:61–85.

Stokey, N. L. and Lucas, jr., R. E. (1989). *Recursive Methods in Economic Dynamics*. Harvard University Press, Cambridge.

Strauch, R. (1966). Negative Dynamic Programming. *Annals of Mathematics and Statistics*, 37:871–890.

Streufert, P. A. (1990). Stationary Recursive Utility and Dynamic Programming under the Assumption of Biconvergence. *Review of Economic Studies*, 57:79–97.

Streufert, P. A. (1992). An Abstract Topological Approach to Dynamic Programming. *Journal of Mathematical Economics*, 21:59–88.

Streufert, P. A. (1993a). Markov–Perfect Equilibria in Intergenerational Games with Consistent Preferences. *Journal of Economic Dynamics and Control*, 17:929–951.

Streufert, P. A. (1993b). Abstract Recursive Utility. *Journal of Mathematical Analysis and Applications*, 175:169–185.

Streufert, P. A. (1996). Biconvergent Stochastic Dynamic Programming, Asymptotic Impatience, and 'Average' Growth. *Journal of Economic Dynamics and Control*, 20:385–413.

Uzawa, H. (1968). Time Preference, the Consumption Function, and Optimum Asset Holdings. In Wolfe, J. N., editor, *Value, Capital, and Growth. Papers in Honour of Sir John Hicks*, pages 485–504. University Press, Edinburgh.

Von Stengel, B. (1993). Closure Properties of Independence Concepts for Continuous Utilities. *Mathematics of Operations Research*, 18:346–389.

4 DUAL APPROACHES TO UTILITY

Martin Browning

University of Copenhagen

Contents

1   Introduction   124
2   An Optimal Tax Example   125
3   Mathematical Background   127
4   The Cost and Indirect Utility Functions   128
5   The Distance and Profit Functions   132
6   Mixed Representations   137
7   Concluding Remarks   139
References   139

1   Introduction

There are lots of different ways of describing a convex set; consequently there are lots of different ways of representing convex preferences. Although the usual way to do this is by the direct utility function, this is by no means the most useful representation in most contexts. In this chapter I shall define several ways of representing preferences and give examples of their use. This list is not meant to be exhaustive; indeed the primary "message" of this survey is that the economic problem at hand may require the construction of some new representation that facilitates the analysis. Ideally the economic problem should define how we do the analysis rather than what we can do with conventional tools defining what we actually do.

The notion of duality is not very well defined in economics[1] but it may loosely be given as the art of describing preferences (or technology) to make the analysis easier. An alternative characterisation is given by Gorman (1976): "duality is about the choice of independent variables in terms of which one defines a theory". For example, analyses that start with the direct utility function take quantities as the "independent" variables but in the usual choice situation they are the objects of choice (that is, the "dependent" variables). This leads to all sorts of complications and concerns with horrendous objects like bordered Hessians which may have been of interest to 19th century mathematicians but are surely not of interest to modern economists. All of this is avoided if we take as our independent variables those variables that are parametric to the agent; for example, prices and income (strictly, total expenditure).

To give some idea of how we use duality methods I present an example in Section 2. This examines when a tax on a particular good will not lead to any deadweight loss. Although the example has some intrinsic interest I present it mainly as an example of how choosing the "correct" independent variables makes the analysis easier. The condition required is that the compensated own price elasticity for the good should be zero. This *functional* requirement is impossible to characterise using the direct utility function but it implies a simple structure for the cost function. This is an example of the interaction between duality and separability or functional structural assumptions. Often the import of the latter is impossible to determine using the direct utility function but very simple given the "correct" dual representation. In this chapter I shall not discuss separability explicitly [see the chapter by Blackorby, Primont and Russell (this volume)] but it should be kept in mind that the value of a dual analysis is almost always bound up with drawing out the implications of particular separability assumptions.

---

[1] This contrasts with mathematics where the notion of a dual space and a duality is very precisely defined.

As the first paragraph in this introduction suggests, I think that the best formal way to think of duality is to consider different ways of describing a convex set (in particular, an upper contour set). To emphasise this, in Section 3 I present a short mathematical digression that illustrates most of the important points about the mathematics of duality. This section is largely optional; it may add to the understanding of the later results but it can be skipped by readers who are impatient of mathematical underpinnings. On the other hand, the fact that many results that are useful in duality theory (as used in economics) already exist in the convex analysis literature should not be ignored; there are limits to how many times we wish to re-invent any particular wheel.

After Section 3 I shall dispense almost entirely with formalities and simply state results in a relatively rough and ready form. This is how it should be when we use duality methods; we should not get bogged down in worries about continuity or what is happening at boundaries.[2] This is not to say that such issues are unimportant but rather that they can usually be left for tidying up if the analysis goes anywhere. In keeping with this I shall also assume that all prices and quantities are positive unless otherwise stated.

The duality literature is venerable (dating back, at least, to Hotelling in 1932 and, perhaps, to Antonelli in 1886) and large. There are several good surveys of this literature [see, for example, Diewert (1982), or Blackorby, Primont and Russell (1978)]. Deaton and Muellbauer (1980) also provide a very accessible introduction to the area. There is also a recent text by Cornes (1992) which is highly recommended. Even more highly recommended is Gorman (1976) which gives a tour of some of the main landmarks of duality (and separability) theory by one of the most important contributors to the literature.[3] Given this wealth of previous discussion, I shall devote very little space to the historical roots of the ideas presented here (so that the references omit most of the important innovators in duality theory); neither shall I give many formal proofs. Rather the intent is to give a fairly informal guide to what can be done; this is in line with my belief suggested above that duality is about thinking about how to make the analysis of a specific problem easier.

2   An Optimal Tax Example

It is well established that lump sum taxes are at least as good as commodity taxes for raising revenue. An interesting question is: when is a lump sum tax no better than a tax on a particular commodity? Put another way: when does a

---

[2] As Diewert (1982) remarks "continuity complexities appear to be the only difficult concepts associated with duality theory". I would add that they are also the least important. See Jackson (1986) for results on continuity.

[3] But note that this classic paper does contain some errors.

tax on a particular good not impose any dead weight loss? It turns out that this can be answered completely and simply using the cost function representation.

Let us first develop the standard proof that a lump sum tax is at least as good as a commodity tax. Suppose the tax authority wishes to raise revenue from a single agent. Let us suppose that two instruments are available: a lump sum tax (that is, taking some endowment) or a tax (t) on good 1. Since we are going to make prices ($\mathbf{p}$) and utility (u) parametric for the agent the natural representation the cost function is:

$$c(\mathbf{p}, u) = \min_{\mathbf{q}} \{ \mathbf{p}'\mathbf{q} | u(\mathbf{q}) \geq u \},$$

where $\mathbf{q}$ is a vector of quantities and $u(\cdot)$ is the direct utility function.[4] I shall discuss this representation at greater length below; for now all we need to note about $c(\cdot)$ is that (under suitable regularity conditions) it is concave and increasing in $\mathbf{p}$ and the derivative of $c(\cdot)$ with respect to p_i is equal to the compensated (Hicksian) demand for good i.

Given fixed $(\mathbf{p}, u)$ define:

$$\psi(t) = c(p_1 + t, \mathbf{p}_{-1}, u) - c(\mathbf{p}, u),$$

where $\mathbf{p}_{-1}$ is the vector of prices of all goods other than good 1. Thus $\psi(t)$ is the amount of money the agent needs to compensate her for the commodity tax. The function $\psi(t)$ is concave, increasing and has $\psi(0) = 0$. Moreover, the compensated demand for good 1 with the tax t is given by the derivative of $\psi(t) = \psi'(t)$ so that the tax revenue that the tax authority receives is $t\psi'(t)$. Given the properties of $\psi(t)$ we have:

$$\psi(t) \geq t\psi'(t).$$

Thus starting from a commodity tax of t and no lump sum tax we could raise at least as much revenue and leave the agent indifferent by setting $t = 0$ and imposing a lump sum tax of $\psi(t)$. This completes the demonstration that lump sum taxes are at least as good as commodity taxes.

Now consider when lump sum taxes are no better than a tax on good 1. For this to hold we require that the inequality above be an equality which implies that $\psi(t)$ is linear; this in turn requires that $c(\mathbf{p}, u)$ be linear in p_1:

$$c(\mathbf{p}, u) = a(\mathbf{p}_{-1}, u) + b(\mathbf{p}_{-1}, u)p_1.$$

This condition is necessary and sufficient for a commodity tax on good 1 to be "first best". There are much stronger sufficient conditions that apply to

---

[4] I assume here that the minimum is attained. This places implicit restrictions on $u(\cdot)$; I shall return to this in Section 4 below.

the direct utility representation. For example, if preferences are Leontief then a tax on any good is "first best". This illustrates a theme that runs through the duality literature—whilst direct methods (that is, methods that start from the direct utility function) can often be used to give sufficient conditions for some desired property we generally need to resort to duality methods to give full characterisations. The point of this example is to show that if we set up the problem in the "right" way at the start then the analysis can be relatively trivial. I turn now to the formalities of setting a problem up in the "right" way; that is, to duality methods.

3   Mathematical Background

A function $f : \mathbb{R}^n \to \bar{\mathbb{R}}$ (where $\bar{\mathbb{R}}$ is the extended real line) is convex if its epigraph (the volume above the graph) is a convex set (that is, $\mu f(\mathbf{x}) + (1 - \mu)f(\mathbf{x}') \geq f(\mu \mathbf{x} + (1-\mu)\mathbf{x}')$ for all $\mathbf{x}, \mathbf{x}'$ and $\mu \in [0,1]$). Now define the (convex) conjugate of $f(\cdot)$, denoted $f^* : \mathbb{R}^n \to \bar{\mathbb{R}}$:

$$f^*(\mathbf{y}) = \sup_{\mathbf{x}}\{\mathbf{x}'\mathbf{y} - f(\mathbf{x})\} \qquad (3.1)$$

[see Rockafellar (1970) or Roberts and Varberg (1973)]. The two most important facts about conjugates are:

- Fact 1: For any $f(\mathbf{x})$, $f^*(\mathbf{y})$ is convex.

- Fact 2: If $f(\mathbf{x})$ is convex then $f^{**}(\mathbf{x}) = f(\mathbf{x})$ (where $f^{**}(\mathbf{x})$ is the conjugate of the conjugate).[5]

From Fact 1 we see that no matter what function we start with (convex or not) the conjugate is convex. The second Fact establishes that conjugacy induces a one-one relationship between $f(\cdot)$ and $f^*(\cdot)$ if $f(\cdot)$ is convex. Starting from either function we can recover the other by taking conjugates: $f(\cdot)$ and $f^*(\cdot)$ are "dual" representations of the same structure. We shall see analogs of these facts emerging again and again in the economics below. If $f(\cdot)$ is not convex then we only have $f^{***}(\mathbf{y}) = f^*(\mathbf{y})$. To see that $f(\mathbf{x})$ and $f^{**}(\mathbf{x})$ can be different if $f(\cdot)$ is not convex, consider the function of one variable $f(x) = x^3$. The conjugate of this is $f^*(\mathbf{y}) = +\infty$ with $f^{**}(\mathbf{x}) = -\infty$.

If $f(\cdot)$ is convex and differentiable then a natural way to derive the conjugate is to solve the first order conditions:

$$\mathbf{y} = \nabla f(\hat{\mathbf{x}})$$

---

[5]So long as $f(\cdot)$ satisfies some regularity conditions, see Rockafellar (1970), Section 12.

and then to substitute for $\mathbf{x}$ in equation (3.1).[6] Although this is very natural for economists we can rarely invert the first order conditions so that this is not usually a practical route to deriving conjugates.

Although the conjugate is the most common dual operator for convex functions it is not the only one. Almost as widely used is the polar of $f^0(\cdot)$:

$$f^0(\mathbf{y}) = \max_{\mathbf{x}}\{\mathbf{x}'\mathbf{y}|f(\mathbf{x}) = 1\}.$$

The polarity operator induces a one-one relationship in the class of functions $f(\cdot)$ which are convex, positively linear homogeneous with $f(\mathbf{0}) = 0$ and $f(\cdot)$ positive and finite everywhere else. Although this might seem to be a class of functions that is rather restricted we shall see below that it is an important set in duality theory.

4   The Cost and Indirect Utility Functions

The usual way to represent preferences is by the utility function $u(\mathbf{q})$. In keeping with tradition we shall start from this. In Section 2 we introduced *the cost function* representation (sometimes termed the expenditure function) using the direct representation:

$$c(\mathbf{p}, u) = \min_{\mathbf{q}}\{\mathbf{p}'\mathbf{q}|u(\mathbf{q}) \geq u\}. \tag{4.1}$$

The following assumption on the direct utility function is sufficient to ensure that the minimum in (4.1) is attained for every $\mathbf{p}$:[7]

- *(U1)* $u(\cdot)$ is continuous.

Given this assumption we have the following properties for the cost function (proofs can be found in any of the references given at the end of Section 1):

- *(C1)* $c(\cdot, u)$ is non-decreasing in $\mathbf{p}$;

- *(C2)* $c(\cdot, u)$ is linear homogeneous in $\mathbf{p}$;

- *(C3)* $c(\cdot, u)$ is concave in $\mathbf{p}$.

The statement of properties here brings out an important feature of dual representations that we shall see many more times: the dual does not necessarily "inherit" properties from the direct representation in any obvious way. Thus

---

[6]This procedure is known as the Legendre transform.

[7]So long as u is chosen to be in the range of $u(\cdot)$. I shall assume this condition in all that follows.

the cost function is concave whether or not the direct utility function is quasi–concave. This is an analogue of Fact 1 in Section 3. As another example, differentiability of the cost function is neither necessary nor sufficient for differentiability of the direct utility function.

The usefulness of the cost function derives from the envelope property of optimum value functions [see, for example, Dixit (1990)]. For example, for the convex conjugate given in (3.1) we have:

$$\nabla f^*(\mathbf{y}) = \hat{\mathbf{x}}(\mathbf{y}),$$

so that the optimal function for $\mathbf{x}$ is given by the gradient of the conjugate. Thus to find an optimal value there is no need to equate gradients to zero and then solve a set of non-linear equations. For the cost function we have:

$$\text{Shephard's Lemma: } \frac{\partial c}{\partial p_k}(\mathbf{p}, u) = q_k = h^k(\mathbf{p}, u). \tag{4.2}$$

Since these demands condition on prices and utility they are known as compensated (or Hicksian) demands. The widespread use of the cost (and the indirect utility function defined below) derives from the fact that we can derive demand functions from them by simple differentiation. Since we very often want to move backwards and forwards between preferences and demands this gives dual representations a decisive advantage in many contexts.

In the derivation of the cost function above we started with the direct utility function and defined the cost function. We can also go the other way; indeed, this is the whole point of duality. Thus given any cost function $c(\mathbf{p}, u)$ we can define a new function:

$$u^*(\mathbf{q}) = \max_u \{u | \mathbf{p}'\mathbf{q} \geq c(\mathbf{p}, u), \forall \mathbf{p}\}. \tag{4.3}$$

If $c(\mathbf{p}, u)$ satisfies *(C1)* to *(C3)* then $u^*(\mathbf{q})$ is a "well behaved" utility function. Furthermore, if the original utility function used to derive the costs function is quasi-concave and monotone then the function defined in (4.3) is the "original" utility function $u(\mathbf{q})$; this is the analogue of Fact 2 in Section 3. We shall formalise this as a proposition with a proof. We first specify some assumptions on the direct utility function:

- *(U2)* $u(\mathbf{q})$ is strictly increasing in $\mathbf{q}$

- *(U3)* $u(\mathbf{q})$ is quasi-concave in $\mathbf{q}$.

PROPOSITION 4.1 Given *(U1)-(U3)* the function $u^*(\mathbf{q})$ defined in equation (4.3) is the original utility function $u(\mathbf{q})$ used to construct $c(\mathbf{p}, u)$ in equation (4.1).

PROOF The proof proceeds in two parts; the first part does not need *(U1)–(U3)*.

(i) For arbitrary $\tilde{\mathbf{q}}$ we have:

$$
\begin{aligned}
u^*(\tilde{\mathbf{q}}) &= \max_u \{u | \mathbf{p}'\tilde{\mathbf{q}} \geq c(\mathbf{p}, u), \ \forall \ \mathbf{p}\} \\
&\geq u(\tilde{\mathbf{q}}),
\end{aligned}
$$

since $\mathbf{p}'\tilde{\mathbf{q}} \geq c(\mathbf{p}, u(\tilde{\mathbf{q}}))$, $\forall \ \mathbf{p}$.

(ii) By *(U1)* to *(U3)* for any $\tilde{\mathbf{q}}$ we can find the "supporting" prices $\tilde{\mathbf{p}}$ which give:

$$
\tilde{\mathbf{q}} = \arg\min_{\mathbf{q}} (\tilde{\mathbf{p}}'\mathbf{q} | u(\mathbf{q}) \geq u(\tilde{\mathbf{q}})) .
$$

Thus we have:

$$
\begin{aligned}
u^*(\tilde{\mathbf{q}}) &= \max_u \{u | \mathbf{p}'\tilde{\mathbf{q}} \geq c(\mathbf{p}, u), \ \forall \ \mathbf{p}\} \\
&\leq \max_u \{u | \tilde{\mathbf{p}}'\tilde{\mathbf{q}} \geq c(\tilde{\mathbf{p}}, u)\} \\
&= u(\tilde{\mathbf{q}}) .
\end{aligned}
$$

Combining the two inequalities, we have $u^*(\mathbf{q}) = u(\mathbf{q})$. ∎

From the proof we see that $u^*(\mathbf{q}) \geq u(\mathbf{q})$ whatever the original preferences. The continuity, monotonicity and quasi-concavity of the utility function were needed to prove the reverse inequality. These assumptions allow us to pick out any point on any indifference curve.

The other commonly used dual representation is *the indirect utility function* which is defined as:

$$
V(\mathbf{p}, x) = \max_{\mathbf{q}} \{u(\mathbf{q}) | \mathbf{p}'\mathbf{q} \leq x\}.
$$

Thus $V(\mathbf{p}, x)$ gives the maximum utility level attainable for an agent with income x who faces prices $\mathbf{p}$. An alternative derivation using the cost function defines $V(\mathbf{p}, x)$ implicitly by:

$$
c(\mathbf{p}, V(\mathbf{p}, x)) = x.
$$

Thus the indirect utility function is the inverse of the cost function. This leads to another "duality" between these two representations:

$$
V(\mathbf{p}, c(\mathbf{p}, u)) = u.
$$

Although the cost and indirect utility function are closely connected their properties are very different, as can be seen by comparing the following with (C1) to (C3) above. The indirect utility function satisfies:

- (I1) $V(\cdot)$ is increasing in x and non-increasing in $\mathbf{p}$;

- (I2) $V(\cdot)$ is zero homogeneous in $(\mathbf{p}, x)$;

- (I3) $V(\cdot)$ is quasi-convex in $(\mathbf{p}, x)$.

Given the zero homogeneity we can also define the normalised indirect utility function on normalised price $\mathbf{p}^* = \frac{1}{x}\mathbf{p}$ by $V^*(\mathbf{p}^*) = V(\mathbf{p}^*, 1)$. This function is continuous, decreasing and quasi-convex in normalised prices so it looks like the negative of a direct utility function with properties (U1)-(U3).

To derive uncompensated (or Marshallian) demand functions from the cost function, we use (4.2) above to derive compensated demands and then substitute for $u = V(\mathbf{p}, x)$ to give:

$$q_k = h^k(\mathbf{p}, V(\mathbf{p}, x)) = f^k(\mathbf{p}, x).$$

Alternatively, we can start from the indirect utility function:

$$\text{Roy's Identity:} \quad -\frac{\partial V}{\partial p_k} / \frac{\partial V}{\partial x} = q_k = f^k(\mathbf{p}, x).$$

For many purposes we do not need to specify the functional form for the cost function. For deriving demand systems that can be applied to data, however, we do need to parameterise the cost function. Although any function that satisfies (C1) to (C3) is a valid cost function, experience has shown that particular functional forms are more tractable and flexible. Generally, if we wish to model demands then we start with the cost function and prices; for budget shares it is best to start with the log of the cost function and log prices since the uncompensated budget share is given by:

$$\omega(\mathbf{p}, x) = \nabla \ln c(\ln \mathbf{p}, V(\mathbf{p}, x)),$$

where the gradient is with respect to $\ln \mathbf{p}$. Discussion of the choice of functional forms can be found in Deaton and Muellbauer (1980), Lau (1986), Barnett and Lee (1985), Barnett, Lee and Wolfe (1987), Banks, Blundell and Lewbel (1992) and Diewert and Wales (1993).

As a second illustration of the power of dual arguments (the first was the tax example given in Section 2), consider the following derivation of the Slutsky equation [see Cook (1972) and McKenzie (1957)]. The compensated demand for good j can be derived from the uncompensated demand in the following way:

$$h^j(\mathbf{p}, u) = f^j(\mathbf{p}, c(\mathbf{p}, u)).$$

Taking derivatives of both sides of this with respect to p_k we have:

$$
\begin{aligned}
\frac{\partial q_j}{\partial p_k}(\mathbf{p}, u) &= \frac{\partial q_j}{\partial p_k}(\mathbf{p}, x) + \frac{\partial q_j}{\partial x}(\mathbf{p}, x)\frac{\partial c}{\partial p_k}(\mathbf{p}, u) \qquad (4.4)\\
&= \frac{\partial q_j}{\partial p_k}(\mathbf{p}, x) + q_k \frac{\partial q_j}{\partial p_k}(\mathbf{p}, x).
\end{aligned}
$$

This one line derivation of the Slutsky equation is dramatically simpler than older derivations that use bordered Hessians; on its own it might justify the study of duality methods. Once we have the compensated price response in terms of observable responses we might go further and ask what conditions are implied by the existence of a utility function and its maximisation. This is simply a matter of drawing out the implications of *(C1)* to *(C3)* for the response on the right hand side of (4.4). These are adding up; zero homogeneity; symmetry and "negativity" (the Hessian of $c(\mathbf{p}, u)$ is negative semi–definite in $\mathbf{p}$).

5   The Distance and Profit Functions

Although the cost and indirect utility functions are the most common alternative representations to the direct utility function, they are by no means the only ones. In this section we introduce two other representations that have been quite widely used: *the distance function* and *the profit function*. Both of these representations had their origin in the analysis of producer behaviour but both have turned out to be useful in consumer theory as well. Among other places, discussions of both representations in the consumer context can be found in Gorman (1976) and Cornes (1992). For more extended discussions see Deaton (1979) and Browning, Deaton and Irish (1985) for the distance and profit functions, respectively.

The *distance function* is not strictly a dual representation since it is defined on quantities. It can be defined using either the direct utility function or the cost function:

$$
\begin{aligned}
d(\mathbf{q}, u) &= \max_{\delta}\{\delta | u(\delta^{-1}\mathbf{q}) \geq u\}\\
&= \min_{\mathbf{p}}\{\mathbf{p}'\mathbf{q} | c(\mathbf{p}, u) = 1\}\\
&= \min_{\mathbf{p}}\{\mathbf{p}'\mathbf{q} | V(\mathbf{p}, 1) \geq u\}.
\end{aligned}
$$

From the first definition we see that $d(\mathbf{q}, u)$ is how far we have to go along a ray through $\mathbf{q}$ to reach the indifference curve that has value u. From the second definition, we have that $d(\cdot, u)$ is the polar of the cost function $c(\cdot, u)$ (see Section 3 above) and since the latter is concave in $\mathbf{p}$ we can also move back the other way:

$$c(p, u) = \min_{\mathbf{q}}\{\mathbf{p}'\mathbf{q} | d(\mathbf{q}, u) = 1\},$$

so that the cost and distance function are very closely related. To move from the distance function to the direct utility function we simply define $u(\mathbf{q})$ implicitly by $d(\mathbf{q}, u(\mathbf{q})) = 1$.

Given the close relationship between the cost and distance functions it will come as no surprise that they have similar properties [compare these properties with *(C1)* to *(C3)* above]:

■   *(D1)* $d(\cdot, u)$ is non-decreasing in $\mathbf{q}$;

■   *(D2)* $d(\cdot, u)$ is linear homogeneous in $\mathbf{q}$;

■   *(D3)* $d(\cdot, u)$ is concave in $\mathbf{q}$.

Indeed the "duality" between the cost function and the distance function is so pervasive that we can adopt a slogan: if anything is true of the cost function for prices then it will generally be true of the distance function for quantities. To illustrate, suppose that the cost function has the following separability structure:

$$c(\mathbf{p}^1, \mathbf{p}^2, \dots, \mathbf{p}^T, u) = \chi(\phi^1(\mathbf{p}^1, u), \phi^2(\mathbf{p}^2, u), \dots, \phi^T(\mathbf{p}^T, u), u),$$

where $(\mathbf{p}^1, \mathbf{p}^2, \dots, \mathbf{p}^T)$ is a partition of the price vector $\mathbf{p}$. This restriction on preferences is usually known as quasi-separability; it is independent of the more familiar (weak) separability of the direct utility function. It is straightforward to show that this structure on the cost function implies a similar structure for the distance function:

$$d(\mathbf{q}^1, \mathbf{q}^2, \dots, \mathbf{q}^T, u) = \omega(\sigma^1(\mathbf{q}^1, u), \sigma^2(\mathbf{q}^2, u), \dots, \sigma^T(\mathbf{q}^T, u), u).$$

Moreover, each $\phi^t(\mathbf{p}^t, u)$ has $\sigma^t(\mathbf{q}^t, u)$ as its associated distance function.

To illustrate the use of the distance function, consider the need for a quantity index [see Deaton (1979) or Diewert (1980) for a full discussion]. In the context of consumer theory, a quantity index is simply a function that takes two quantity vectors $\mathbf{q}^0$ (the base year quantity vector) and $\mathbf{q}^1$ (the current year quantity vector) and returns a value that tells us how much "real consumption" has risen. There are many possible candidates. For example, one candidate would be $u(\mathbf{q}^1)/u(\mathbf{q}^0)$. Although this index has the virtue that the index is greater than unity if the bundle $\mathbf{q}^1$ is preferred to the bundle $\mathbf{q}^0$ it suffers from a number of flaws. The most important of these is that unless $u(\cdot)$ is linear homogeneous it fails *the proportionality test* : if $\mathbf{q}^1 = k\mathbf{q}^0$ for some scalar $k > 0$ then the index should equal k. This suggests the following index:

$$Q(\mathbf{q}^0, \mathbf{q}^1, u) = \frac{d(\mathbf{q}^1, u)}{d(\mathbf{q}^0, u)}.$$

This is known as the Malmquist quantity index.

Although the Malmquist index has many attractive features it does have the drawback that it depends on a reference level of utility. Clearly this will not be the case if and only if $d(\mathbf{q}, u) = v(\mathbf{q})u$. This in turn implies that preferences are homothetic (in which case all sensible definitions of quantity indices coincide). Generally, then, the Malmquist quantity index depends on the reference level of utility. Two obvious candidates are $u = u(\mathbf{q}^0)$ and $u = u(\mathbf{q}^1)$, which give the Laspeyres-Malmquist and Paasche-Malmquist quantity indices, respectively.

The other representation we present in this section is the *profit function*.[8] This function is familiar from producer theory:

$$\begin{aligned} \pi(\mathbf{p}, r) &= \max_{\mathbf{q}}\{ru(\mathbf{q}) - \mathbf{p}'\mathbf{q}\} \qquad &(5.1)\\ &= \max_{u}\{ru - c(\mathbf{p}, u)\}. \end{aligned}$$

Thus the profit function gives the "profit" if a cost minimising agent faces "input" prices $\mathbf{p}$ and "sells" utility at a price r.[9] The interpretation of the parameter r follows directly from the first order conditions of either of the maximisation problems in (5.1):

$$r = \frac{p_i}{u_i(\mathbf{q})} \ (\forall i) = c_u(p, u). \qquad (5.2)$$

Thus r is the inverse of the marginal utility of money (the Lagrange multiplier in the usual direct maximisation problem) or the marginal cost (or price) of utility.

---

[8]For reasons that will become clear below it would be easier to work with the negative of the profit function (the "net loss" function) but the use of the profit function is too well entrenched to be worth trying to alter the usual approach.

[9]In the language of convex analysis $-\pi(\mathbf{p}, 1)$ is the (concave) conjugate of the direct representation. Thus the distance and profit functions represent the two most widely used "duals" of the direct utility function in convex analysis - the polar and the conjugate respectively. Note as well that the profit function is the conjugate of the cost function on u.

The main reason that we are interested in the profit function is that it "inherits" additivity from the direct utility function.[10] That is, if the direct utility function is additive then the profit function will also be additive. This inheritance of structure from the direct representation is by no means automatic. Although, for example, separability of the direct utility function implies restrictions on the cost function, it does not imply that the cost function is itself separable. The best illustration of the usefulness of the profit function is in the analysis of intertemporal allocation where we often assume (intertemporal) additivity. Let $\mathbf{q} = (\mathbf{q}^1, \mathbf{q}^2, \dots, \mathbf{q}^T)$ be a stack of n-vectors of quantities in periods $t = 1, 2, \dots, T$. Let $\mathbf{p} = (\mathbf{p}^1, \mathbf{p}^2, \dots, \mathbf{p}^T)$ be the corresponding vector of discounted prices (where all prices are discounted to period 1 using a fixed nominal interest rate). We have:

$$u(\mathbf{q}) = \sum_t \nu^t(\mathbf{q}^t) \text{ if and only if } \pi(\mathbf{p}, r) = \sum_t \varphi^t(\mathbf{p}^t, r).$$

Thus the additivity of the direct utility function is equivalent to the additivity of the profit function in prices. Moreover we have:

$$\varphi^t(\mathbf{p}^t, r) = \max_{\mathbf{q}^t} \left\{ r\nu^t(\mathbf{q}^t) - \mathbf{p}^{t\prime}\mathbf{q}^t \right\}.$$

Thus the sub-profit function is period t is dual to the sub-utility function in t.

The "price" of utility defined in (5.2) depends on the normalisation of the direct utility function so that the profit function representation also depends on the normalisation. This is in contrast to other dual representations. Indeed, we require that the direct utility function in (5.1) be strictly concave to ensure that the profit function is useful; if $u(\cdot)$ exhibits "increasing returns" then $\pi(\cdot)$ can only take on values $\{0, +\infty\}$ which is not very useful. Since not all convex preferences that are representable by a utility function admit of a concave representation this restricts the domain of this dual representation somewhat. In the intertemporal context with an intertemporally additive utility function, however, the normalisation of the sub-utility functions is given by the additivity (up to an affine transformation) which makes the dependence of the profit function on the normalisation undisturbing.

The properties of the profit function are:

- (P1) $\pi(\cdot)$ is convex in $(\mathbf{p}, r)$;

- (P2) $\pi(\cdot)$ is linear homogeneous in $(\mathbf{p}, r)$;

- (P3) $\pi(\cdot)$ is increasing in r and decreasing in $\mathbf{p}$.

---

[10]An additional use is suggested by Cooper (1994) who shows how the profit function representation can be exploited in the choice of functional forms for demand systems.

Just as we can derive Hicksian (or constant utility compensated) demands as derivatives of the cost function, so we can derive Frisch (or constant marginal utility of money) demand functions as (the negative of) the partials of the profit function with respect to prices. Taking the envelope theorem through (5.1) we have:

$$-\frac{\partial \pi}{\partial p_k}(\mathbf{p}, r) = q_k = \tilde{g}^k(\mathbf{p}, r).$$

Thus it is easy to derive Frisch demands from the profit function.

The importance of Frisch demands in intertemporal analysis has been recognised for some time [see, for example, Heckman (1974)]. Primarily this is because if we take the Frisch demand for good k in period t:

$$q_k^t = g^k(\mathbf{p}^t, r) = -\frac{\partial \varphi}{\partial p_k}(\mathbf{p}^t, r) \tag{5.3}$$

(where we have assumed that the within period utility function is the same in each period), then the variable r is a "sufficient statistic" for all extra-period information [see MaCurdy (1981)]. Thus we do not need to know much about what has happened in the past or what the agent believes about the future to model demands. This enormous parsimony in information that the econometrician needs is, however, bought at a price since we need to deal with the unobservable marginal cost of utility. We do this by noting that if there is no uncertainty then r is a fixed effect and if there is uncertainty and perfect capital markets then r^{-1} follows a martingale (that is, $E_t(r_{t+1}^{-1}) = r_t^{-1}$). It is this insight that underpins the radical change in the modelling of consumption and labour supply that followed Hall (1978) and MaCurdy (1981).

The use of the profit function as a potential function for Frisch demands was introduced in Browning, Deaton and Irish (1985). As an example of the use to which we can put this, consider the econometric requirements to estimate the parameters of $g^k(\mathbf{p}, r)$ in (5.3). As discussed above, to overcome the unobservability of the marginal costs of utility we need to parameterise this function in such a way that we can "difference" away r. That is, we need to write:

$$g^k(\mathbf{p}, r) = \xi^k(\mathbf{p}) + \tau_k(r).$$

In Browning et al. (1985) it is shown that this additive-in-r form implies that the within period profit function takes the form:

$$\varphi(\mathbf{p}, r) = \alpha r + \rho(\mathbf{p}) + \sum_k \mu_k p_k \ln\left(\frac{p_k}{r}\right). \tag{5.4}$$

Once we have the characterisation of preferences that give additive–in–r Frisch functions we can then determine exactly what extra restrictions are imposed on preferences by this restriction. For example, since the cost function is the conjugate of the profit function it can be derived from:

$$c(\mathbf{p}, u) = \max_r \{ru - \pi(\mathbf{p}, r)\},$$

which yields (after some manipulations) that for the particular functional form given in (5.4), the cost function takes the form $a(\mathbf{p}) + b(\mathbf{p})u$; that is, preferences are quasi–homothetic (Engel curves are straight lines).

   For the purposes of this survey, the details of the derivations of the additive–in–r Frisch demands above are unimportant. Two general features are, however, of importance. The first of these is that it would be impossible to characterise the preferences that give rise to additive–in–r Frisch demands starting from the direct utility function. This is yet another example of the general theme that runs through this chapter that given some desired structure on observables (demands) it is usually easiest to derive the implications for preferences using duality methods. The second general remark is that having a full characterisation for some given structure often reveals further restrictions that are by no means obvious from just looking at the demands. In this case, the additivity–in–r restriction requires quasi–homotheticity which is quite a strong restriction.

6   Mixed Representations

Up until now we have considered only representations that depend just on prices or quantities (and some measure of welfare). In many contexts, however, it is useful to have representations that depend on the prices of some goods and the quantities of others. This goes back to the remarks by Gorman quoted at the beginning of this survey to the effect that we want to set up the analysis in terms of variables that are exogenous to the agent being considered. To illustrate, suppose that an agent can buy private goods $\mathbf{q}$ at market prices $\mathbf{p}$ and also receives publicly provided (private or public) goods $\mathbf{z}$, where, for convenience, we shall assume that the goods in $\mathbf{z}$ and $\mathbf{q}$ do not overlap (that is, the agent cannot buy any goods that the government provides). Let the direct utility function be $u(\mathbf{q}, \mathbf{z})$. Now define the *conditional (or restricted) cost function*:

$$c^*(\mathbf{p}, \mathbf{z}, u) = \min_{\mathbf{q}} \left\{ \mathbf{p}'\mathbf{q} | u(\mathbf{q}, \mathbf{z}) \geq u \right\}. \tag{6.1}$$

This representation has the properties of a conventional cost function in $(\mathbf{p}, u)$ and looks like (the negative of) a utility function in $\mathbf{z}$.

   Although the inclusion of $\mathbf{z}$ above was motivated by the example of a set of publicly provided goods, it could be a vector of any conditioning variables that affect preferences. One particularly important case is that for which $\mathbf{q}$ is a basket of market goods and $\mathbf{z}$ includes the labour supplies of the members of the household; if labour supply is constrained in some way then labour supply is the exogenous variable rather than the wage.[11]   Alternatively $\mathbf{q}$ could be market goods that are adjustable in the short run whilst $\mathbf{z}$ might be market goods that can only be changed in the long run. A wider interpretation for $\mathbf{z}$ is also possible; for example, $\mathbf{z}$ could include the number of children in the household and the number of bathrooms in the dwelling the household occupies. In the case where $\mathbf{z}$ are goods in the usual sense[12] we can put more structure on this framework. Let $\mathbf{r}$ be a vector of prices for the vector of goods $\mathbf{z}$. If the conditioning goods are available in the market at prices $\mathbf{r}$ then we can define the rationed cost function:

$$\tilde{c}^*(\mathbf{p}, \mathbf{z}, \mathbf{r}, u) = c^*(\mathbf{p}, \mathbf{z}, u) + \mathbf{r}'\mathbf{z}.$$

Thus the rationed[13] cost function is the conditional cost function plus the cost of the vector $\mathbf{z}$ at prices $\mathbf{r}$.

The conditional cost function is not, of course, the only mixed representation that we can define. In some contexts the conditional indirect utility function or the conditional profit function (or other, even more exotic mixed representations) makes the analysis more tractable. For example, it may be that once we condition on the stock of semi-durables, durables and housing then intertemporal preferences can be represented by an additive–over–time utility function on other goods (non-durables and services). If this is the case then the conditional profit function is the obvious representation to use.

Although we defined the conditional cost function in (6.1) in terms of the direct utility function, we could have started from the cost function [see Browning (1983) for details]:

$$c^*(\mathbf{p}, \mathbf{z}, u) = \max_{\mathbf{r}}\{c(\mathbf{p}, \mathbf{r}, u) - \mathbf{r}'\mathbf{z}\},$$

so that $c(\cdot, u)$ and $c^*(., u)$ are (concave) conjugates on $\mathbf{r}/\mathbf{z}$. This implies that starting from the conditional cost function we can derive the (unconditional) cost function:

$$
\begin{aligned}
c(\mathbf{p}, \mathbf{r}, u) &= \min_{z}\{c^*(\mathbf{p}, \mathbf{z}, u) + \mathbf{r}'\mathbf{z}\} \\
&= \min_{z}\left(\tilde{c}^*(\mathbf{p}, \mathbf{z}, \mathbf{r}, u)\right)
\end{aligned}
$$

---

[11] The use of the term exogenous here is meant to indicate that the agent takes labour supply as given. This does not necessarily imply that labour supply is exogenous in the econometric sense [see Browning and Meghir (1991) for a discussion].

[12] And many investigators would include leisure and children in this definition.

[13] There is not much consensus in the literature about what to call these different representations. I prefer the terminology "conditional" for $c^*(\cdot)$ since $\mathbf{z}$ can be any variable that affects preferences and "rationed" for this representation since it captures the idea that agents have to consume $\mathbf{z}$ and pay $\mathbf{r}'\mathbf{z}$ for this bundle of goods.

(note the change in sign in the first maximisation problem). The first order conditions for the first optimisation problem in this derivation yield the important concept of virtual prices:

$$\hat{\mathbf{r}}(\mathbf{p}, \mathbf{z}, u) = -\nabla_z c^*(\mathbf{p}, \mathbf{z}, u)$$

(where ∇_z denotes the gradient vector with respect to $\mathbf{z}$). The prices $\hat{\mathbf{r}}$ are the prices which would induce the agent to purchase $\mathbf{z}$ if she faces prices $\mathbf{p}$ for the other goods and has utility level u. The use of mixed representations has turned out to be fruitful in a wide range of applications; see Cornes (1992), Chapter 7 for an insightful discussion[14] and further references.

7   Concluding Remarks

The primary "message" of this survey is that there are lots of different ways of describing preferences and some are more suitable in some contexts than others. Consequently it is almost always worthwhile spending some time at the beginning of any analysis in thinking about how to think about the problem at hand. This is all very worthy, but of little practical use unless we have some alternative ways of thinking about particular problems. The methods outlined in this survey are the most common alternative methods in consumer theory. As such they are useful items for any microeconomist to have in her or his tool kit.

References

Banks, J., Blundell, R., and Lewbel, A. (1992). Quadratic Engel Curves, Welfare Measurement and Consumer Demand. Institute for Fiscal Studies Working Paper 92/14.

Barnett, W. and Lee, Y. W. (1985). The Global Properties of Miniflex Laurent, Generalised Leontief and Translog Flexible Functional Forms. *Econometrica*, 53:1421–37.

Barnett, W., Lee, Y. W., and Wolfe, M. D. (1987). The Global Properties of the Two Miniflex Laurent Flexible Functional Forms. *Journal of Econometrics*, 36:281–98.

Blackorby, C., Primont, D., and Russell, R. R. (1978). *Duality, Separability and Functional Structure: Theory and Economic Applications*. American Elsevier, New York.

---

[14]Including the use of dual representations in the analysis of allocation under uncertainty, which has been a relatively barren area for duality theory up until now.

Blackorby, C., Primont, D., and Russell, R. R. (1998). Separability: A Survey. In *this volume*, Chapter 2.

Browning, M. J. (1983). Necessary and Sufficient Conditions for Conditional Cost Functions. *Econometrica*, 51:851–856.

Browning, M. J., Deaton, A. S., and Irish, M. (1985). A Profitable Approach to Labor Supply and Commodity Demands Over the Life-Cycle. *Econometrica*, 53:503–543.

Browning, M. J. and Meghir, C. (1991). The Effects of Male and Female Labor Supply on Commodity Demands. *Econometrica*, 59:925–952.

Cook, P. J. (1972). A One-Line proof of the Slutzky Equation. *American Economic Review*, 62:139.

Cooper, R. J. (1994). On the Exploitation of Additional Duality Relationships in Consumer Demand Analysis. *Economics Letters*, 44:73–77.

Cornes, R. (1992). *Duality and Modern Economics*. Cambridge University Press, Cambridge.

Deaton, A. S. (1979). The Distance Function and Consumer Behaviour with Applications to Index Numbers and Optimal Taxation. *Review of Economic Studies*, 46:391–405.

Deaton, A. S. and Muellbauer, J. (1980). *Economics and Consumer Behaviour*. Cambridge University Press, Cambridge.

Diewert, W. E. (1980). The Economic Theory of Index Numbers: A Survey. In Deaton, A., editor, *Essays in the Theory and Measurement of Consumer Behaviour*, pages 163–208. Cambridge University Press, Cambridge.

Diewert, W. E. (1982). Duality Approaches to Microeconomic Theory. In Arrow, K. J. and Intriligator, M. D., editors, *Handbook of Mathematical Economics*, volume II, pages 535–599. North Holland, Amsterdam.

Diewert, W. E. and Wales, T. J. (1993). Linear and Quadratic Spline Models for Consumer Demand Models. *Canadian Journal of Economics*, 36:77–106.

Dixit, A. (1990). *Optimization in Economic Theory*. Oxford University Press, Oxford, second edition.

Gorman, W. M. (1976). Tricks with Utility Functions. In Artis, M. and Nobay, R., editors, *Essays in Economic Analysis*, pages 211–243. Cambridge University Press, Cambridge.

Hall, R. E. (1978). Stochastic Implications of the Life Cycle-Permanent Income Hypothesis: Theory and Evidence. *Journal of Political Economy*, 86:971–987.

Heckman, J. J. (1974). Life Cycle Consumption and Labor Supply: An Explanation of the Relationship Between Income and Consumption Over the Life Cycle. *American Economic Review*, 64:188–194.

Jackson, M. (1986). Continuous Utility Functions in Consumer Theory: A Set of Duality Theorems. *Journal of Mathematical Economics*, 15:63–77.

Lau, L. J. (1986). Functional Forms in Econometric Model Building. In Griliches, Z. and Intriligator, M. D., editors, *Handbook of Econometrics*, volume III, pages 1515–66. North Holland, Amsterdam.

MaCurdy, T. (1981). An Empirical Model of Labor Supply in a Life Cycle Setting. *Journal of Political Economy*, 89:1059–1085.

McKenzie, L. W. (1957). Demand Theory Without a Utility Index. *Review of Economic Studies*, 24:185–189.

Roberts, A. V. and Varberg, D. E. (1973). *Convex Functions*. Academic Press, New York.

Rockafellar, R. T. (1970). *Convex Analysis*. Princeton University Press, Princeton.

5 OBJECTIVE EXPECTED UTILITY: A CONSEQUENTIALIST PERSPECTIVE

Peter J. Hammond

Stanford University

Contents

1	Introduction and Outline		145
2	The Expected Utility Hypothesis		147
	2.1	Simple Lotteries	147
	2.2	Expected Utility Maximization	148
	2.3	Ratios of Utility Differences	149
	2.4	Cardinally Equivalent Utility Functions	151
3	Necessary Conditions		152
	3.1	The Ordering Condition	152
	3.2	Independence Conditions	153
	3.3	Lexicographic Preferences	154
	3.4	Continuity Conditions	155
4	Sufficient Conditions		157
	4.1	Ordinality and Independence	157
	4.2	Continuity	159
	4.3	Construction of a Utility Function	161
5	Consequentialist Foundations: Ordinality		164
	5.1	The Consequentialist Principle	164
	5.2	Simple Finite Decision Trees	165
	5.3	Behaviour and Unrestricted Domain	166

5.4	Continuation Subtrees and Dynamic Consistency	166
5.5	Consequentialism in Simple Decision Trees	167
5.6	Consequentialism Implies Ordinality	169
6	Consequentialist Foundations: Independence	172
6.1	Finite Decision Trees with Chance Nodes	172
6.2	Consequentialism in Finite Decision Trees	173
6.3	Consequentialism Implies Independence	174
6.4	Ordinality and Strong Independence Characterize Consequentialism	177
6.5	Summary	178
7	Continuous Behaviour and Expected Utility	179
7.1	Continuous Behaviour	179
7.2	Dynamic Programming and Continuous Behaviour	181
7.3	Main Theorem	185
8	Discrete Lotteries, Boundedness, and Dominance	185
8.1	Discrete Lotteries	185
8.2	Unbounded Utility	186
8.3	Bounded Expected Utility	188
8.4	Dominance	189
8.5	Sufficient Conditions for the EU Hypothesis	190
8.6	Continuity	191
8.7	Consequentialist Motivation for Dominance	193
9	Probability Measures	195
9.1	Probability Measures and Expectations	195
9.2	Necessary Conditions for EU Maximization	196
9.3	Sufficient Conditions for the EU Hypothesis	198
9.4	Continuity of Expected Utility	200
9.5	Consequentialism and Probability Dominance	203
10	Summary and Concluding Remarks	205
References		206

1   Introduction and Outline

The St. Petersburg game was a problem posed in 1713 by Nicholas Bernoulli to Montfort, another mathematician. It involves tossing a fair coin repeatedly until the first time it lands "heads". If this happens on the kth toss, the prize is 2^k ducats. How much is it worth paying to be allowed to play? The expected winnings are $\sum_{k=1}^{\infty} 2^{-k} . 2^k = +\infty$. But, as Gabriel Cramer (1728) wrote to Daniel Bernoulli, "no reasonable man would be willing to pay 20 ducats as equivalent"—see Bernoulli (1954, p. 33). Both Samuelson (1977, 1983) and Shapley (1977) offer some cogent reasons for this, including the obvious fact that there is an upper bound to the real value of what can actually be paid as a prize.

The expected utility (or EU) hypothesis was formulated in Cramer's (1728) suggestion for resolving this "St. Petersburg paradox". The hypothesis is that one lottery affecting wealth is preferred to another prospect iff its expected utility of wealth or "moral expectation" is higher. This generalizes the earlier hypothesis that a lottery is preferred iff expected (monetary) wealth is greater. For the St. Petersburg game, if a potential player has utility of wealth level w given by $v(w)$ and starts with initial wealth $w_0 > 0$, then the amount a that the player is willing to pay to play the game must satisfy

$$v(w_0) = \sum_{k=1}^{\infty} 2^{-k} \, v(w_0 + 2^k - a). \tag{1.1}$$

Cramer suggested taking $v(w) = \min\{\, w, 2^{24} \,\}$ or $v(w) = \sqrt{w}$; Bernoulli (1738) suggested $v'(w) = 1/w$, implying that $v(w) = \ln w + \text{constant}$. For the last two of these utility functions, as well as for the first provided that $w_0 + 2 - a < 2^{24}$, the right hand side of (1.1) clearly converges and is strictly decreasing as a function of a. So the solution is well defined and finite.[1]

The general EU hypothesis is stated formally in Section 2. Let $v(y)$ be any utility function defined on the consequence domain Y. Let a, b, c be any three consequences in Y, no two of which are indifferent. In this case, following ideas due to Machina (1982, 1983, 1987), it is proved that the ratio $\frac{v(a)-v(c)}{v(b)-v(c)}$ of utility differences must equal the constant marginal rate of substitution between shifts in probability from consequence c to a and shifts in probability from c to b. In Section 2, this result is shown to imply that the familiar result that the utility function is determined up to a unique cardinal equivalence class.

---

[1]For further useful discussion of the St. Petersburg paradox, see Sinn (1983) and Zabell (1987). Also, some of the ideas of EU theory appear earlier, but less explicitly, in the work of Blaise Pascal and his contemporaries in Paris during the 1660s. See Hacking (1975) for a more modern perspective and interpretation.

Expected utility was little used in economics, and little understood by economists, before von Neumann and Morgenstern (1944, 1953). Their axiomatic treatment was intended to ensure that preferences would have an expected utility representation. This treatment constitutes what they and Savage (1954, p. 97) regarded as a digression from their main work on game theory. According to Leonard (1995, p. 753), their axiomatic formulation apparently occupied not much more than two hours in the first place—see also Morgenstern (1979, p. 181). Nevertheless, their fundamental contribution soon led to an explosion of work in economics and related disciplines making use of the EU hypothesis in order to consider decisions under risk. Since their pioneering work, a utility function whose expected value is to be maximized has generally come to be called a **von Neumann–Morgenstern utility function** (here called an NMUF for short).

Fairly soon Marschak (1950), Nash (1950), Samuelson (1952), Malinvaud (1952) and others noticed that actually von Neumann and Morgenstern had left implicit a rather important independence axiom, as has been pointed out by Fishburn (1989) and by Fishburn and Wakker (1995) in particular. Also Marschak (1950), followed by Herstein and Milnor (1953), moved toward a much more concise system of, in the end, just three axioms. These axioms are, respectively, ordinality (O), independence (I), and continuity (C). Different versions of these axioms are introduced in Section 3, and the strongest variants are shown to be necessary for the EU hypothesis. Weaker variants are then used in Section 4 to demonstrate expected utility maximization, following standard proofs such as those to be found in Blackwell and Girshick (1954), Jensen (1967), and Fishburn (1970, 1982), as well as in most of the original works that have already been cited.[2]

Not much later, expected utility theory, especially the independence axiom, was criticized by Allais (1953)—see also Allais (1979a, b). Partly in response to this and many succeeding attacks, but also in order to justify the existence of a preference ordering, it seemed natural to consider the implications of the hypothesis that behaviour in decision trees should have consequences that are independent of the tree structure—see Hammond (1977, 1983, 1988a, b). This hypothesis plays a prominent role in this chapter, and differentiates it from the many other surveys of expected utility theory.[3] In fact the "consequentialist foundations" are taken up in Sections 5 and 6. First, Section 5 concerns the

---

[2]Marschak (1950) has a rather different proof, based on the fact that indifference surfaces are parallel hyperplanes.

[3]It should be added that I have not even covered all attempts to justify the expected utility hypothesis. For example, LaValle and Wapman (1986) assume that there is a preference ordering and show that the property of being able to "roll back" decision trees implies the independence axiom. Somewhat similar arguments arise in Karni and Safra's (1989) discussion of auctions. Finally, Border (1992) also justifies the expected utility hypothesis without

existence of a preference ordering, and then Section 6 shows how the independence axiom can be deduced. The third continuity axiom is the subject of
Section 7.

Next, Section 8 turns to Blackwell and Girshick's extension of EU theory to
accommodate countable lotteries. Obviously, no framework excluding these
permits consideration of the problem that originally motivated EU theory,
namely the St. Petersburg paradox. Blackwell and Girshick imposed an additional dominance axiom. Following their arguments as well as similar ideas
due to Menger (1934), Arrow (1965, pp. 28–44; 1971, ch. 2; 1972), and Fishburn (1967, 1970), it is then shown that generalizations of the St. Petersburg
paradox can only be avoided if each possible von Neumann–Morgenstern utility function is bounded both above and below, as Cramer's first suggestion
$v(w) = \min\{w, 2^{24}\}$ is if wealth is bounded below. Conversely, it will also be
shown that boundedness implies dominance in the presence of the other conditions (O), (I), and (C). Finally, it will be shown that a stronger continuous
preference condition (CP) can replace dominance or boundedness as a sufficient
condition.

Section 9 is the only part of the chapter that relies on measure theory. It
briefly discusses the extension of EU theory to general probability measures on
the space of consequences, showing that this extension is possible if and only
if all upper and lower preference sets and all singleton sets are measurable.
Section 9 also considers the continuity of expected utility w.r.t. changes in
the probability measure, and shows the sufficiency of a particular continuous
preference axiom, in combination with other standard conditions. Actually,
since the results of Section 8 are subsumed in those of Section 9, the main reason
for discussing countable lotteries separately is to allow the most important
complications caused by unbounded utilities to be discussed without the use of
measure theory.

The brief final Section 10 contains a summary and a few concluding remarks.

2   The Expected Utility Hypothesis

2.1   Simple Lotteries

Let Y denote an arbitrary set of possible *consequences*. A typical *simple lottery*
or probability distribution λ is a mapping $\lambda : Y \to [0,1]$ with the properties
that:

---

directly assuming the existence of a preference ordering, but does so for a special domain
allowing the use of stochastic dominance arguments.

(i) there is a finite *support* $K \subset Y$ of λ such that $\lambda(y) > 0$ for all $y \in K$ and $\lambda(y) = 0$ for all $y \in Y \setminus K$;[4]

(ii) $\sum_{y \in K} \lambda(y) = \sum_{y \in Y} \lambda(y) = 1$.

Let $\Delta(Y)$ denote the set of all such simple lotteries. Given any pair $\lambda, \mu \in \Delta(Y)$ and any $\alpha \in [0, 1]$, define the *convex combination*, *compound lottery*, or *mixture* $\alpha\lambda + (1 - \alpha)\mu$ by

$$[\alpha\lambda + (1 - \alpha)\mu](y) := \alpha\lambda(y) + (1 - \alpha)\mu(y)$$

for all $y \in Y$. Note then that $\alpha\lambda + (1 - \alpha)\mu$ also belongs to $\Delta(Y)$. Because it is convex, $\Delta(Y)$ is said to be a *mixture space*.[5]

Given any consequence $y \in Y$, let $1_y \in \Delta(Y)$ denote the degenerate simple lottery in which y occurs with probability one. Then each $\lambda \in \Delta(Y)$ can be expressed in the form

$$\lambda = \sum_{y \in Y} \lambda(y) \, 1_y \tag{2.1}$$

where, because λ has finite support, the sum on the right-hand side of (2.1) has only finitely many non-zero terms.

2.2   Expected Utility Maximization

A standard model of choice is that due to Arrow (1959, 1963), Sen (1970), Herzberger (1973), etc. In this model, a *feasible set* F is any set in a domain $\mathcal{D}$ of non-empty subsets of a given *underlying set* or *choice space* Z. For each $F \in \mathcal{D}$, the *choice set* $C(F)$ is a subset of F, and the mapping $F \mapsto C(F)$ on the domain $\mathcal{D}$ is the *choice function*. It is typically assumed that $\mathcal{D}$ includes all finite non-empty subsets of Z and that $C(F)$ is non-empty for all such sets. But, in case Z is an infinite set, $\mathcal{D}$ can also include some or even all infinite subsets of Z. Also, for some of these feasible sets, $C(F)$ could be empty.

The *expected utility* (EU) *hypothesis* applies to the choice space of lotteries $\Delta(Y)$. It requires the existence of a *von Neumann–Morgenstern utility function* (or NMUF) $v : Y \to \mathbb{R}$ such that, given any feasible set $F \subset \Delta(Y)$, the choice

---

[4] Throughout the chapter, $\subset$ will denote the weak subset relation, so that $P \subset Q$ does not exclude the possibility that $P = Q$.

[5] As discussed by Wakker (1989, pp. 136–7) and especially by Mongin (1996), every convex set is a mixture space, but not every mixture space is a convex set. For this reason, it would be more logical in many ways to focus on the convexity of $\Delta(Y)$. But, following Herstein and Milnor (1953), it has become traditional to regard $\Delta(Y)$ as a mixture space.

set is

$$C(F) = \arg\max_{\lambda} \left\{ \sum_{y \in Y} \lambda(y)v(y) \mid \lambda \in F \right\}. \tag{2.2}$$

That is, $C(F)$ consists of those lotteries $\lambda \in F$ which maximize the *expected utility function* (EUF) defined by

$$U(\lambda) := \mathbb{E}_{\lambda} v := \sum_{y \in Y} \lambda(y)v(y). \tag{2.3}$$

Notice how (2.3) implies that

$$U(\alpha\lambda + (1-\alpha)\mu) = \sum_{y \in Y} [\alpha\lambda(y) + (1-\alpha)\mu(y)]v(y) = \alpha U(\lambda) + (1-\alpha)U(\mu)$$

So $U(\cdot)$ satisfies the **mixture preservation property** (MP) requiring that

$$U(\alpha\lambda + (1-\alpha)\mu) = \alpha U(\lambda) + (1-\alpha)U(\mu) \tag{2.4}$$

for all $\lambda, \mu \in \Delta(Y)$ and all $\alpha \in [0,1]$. That is, the utility of any mixture of two lotteries is equal to the corresponding mixture of the utilities of the lotteries. Conversely, because of (2.1), for any utility function U satisfying (MP) on the domain $\Delta(Y)$ it must be true that $U(\lambda) = \sum_{y \in Y} \lambda(y)U(1_y)$ for all $\lambda \in \Delta(Y)$. Then (2.3) follows if one defines $v(y) := U(1_y)$ for all $y \in Y$. Hence U must be an EUF.

2.3 Ratios of Utility Differences

Suppose that behaviour does satisfy the EU hypothesis, but the NMUF is unknown. What features of the NMUF can be inferred from behaviour, or from revealed preferences? An argument due to Machina (1987, pp. 125–6) allows a straightforward answer.

In fact, suppose that $a, b, c \in Y$ are any three consequences with $v(a) > v(b) > v(c)$. Consider the *Marschak triangle* (Marschak, 1950) in the left-hand part of Figure 2.1. This represents all simple lotteries attaching probability one to the set $\{a, b, c\}$. Obviously the typical member of this triangle is a convex combination of the three degenerate lotteries 1_a, 1_b and 1_c, so can be expressed as $p\,1_a + q\,1_b + (1-p-q)\,1_c$, where $p, q \geq 0$ and $p + q \leq 1$. Under the EU hypothesis, preferences within this triangle give rise to an indifference map in which each indifference curve takes the form

$$p\,v(a) + q\,v(b) + (1-p-q)\,v(c) = \text{constant}.$$

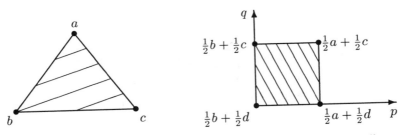

Figure 2.1 Two Indifference Maps for Constant Ratios of Utility Differences

Thus, all indifference curves in the Marschak triangle are parallel straight lines. Their common constant slope is determined by the ratio

$$-\frac{dq}{dp} = \frac{v(a) - v(c)}{v(b) - v(c)} \qquad (2.5)$$

provided that this expression is well defined because $v(b) \neq v(c)$. In fact, this ratio of utility differences is the constant marginal rate of substitution (MRS) between: (i) any increase in the probability p of getting a that is offset by a compensating decrease in the probability $1 - p - q$ of getting c, with q fixed; (ii) any increase in the probability q of getting b that is offset by a compensating decrease in the probability $1 - p - q$ of getting c, with p fixed. For each $a, b, c \in Y$, this common constant ratio can therefore be inferred from hypothetical behaviour.

Equation (2.5) involves a three-way ratio of utility differences. But the four-way ratio $[v(a) - v(b)]/[v(c) - v(d)]$ can also be interpreted as a constant MRS whenever $a, b, c, d \in Y$ are four consequences with $v(c) \neq v(d)$. For consider the square in the right-hand half of Figure 2.1. This represents the two-dimensional set

$$\{ \tfrac{1}{2}p\,1_a + \tfrac{1}{2}(1 - p)\,1_b + \tfrac{1}{2}q\,1_c + \tfrac{1}{2}(1 - q)\,1_d \mid (p,q) \in [0, 1] \times [0, 1] \}$$

of lotteries in which the sets $\{a, b\}$ and $\{c, d\}$ each have fixed probability $\tfrac{1}{2}$. Under the EU hypothesis, the indifference curves in this square are parallel straight lines with

$$\tfrac{1}{2}p\,v(a) + \tfrac{1}{2}(1 - p)\,v(b) + \tfrac{1}{2}q\,v(c) + \tfrac{1}{2}(1 - q)\,v(d) = \text{constant}.$$

So their common constant slope is

$$-\frac{dq}{dp} = \frac{v(a) - v(b)}{v(c) - v(d)}.$$

This is the constant MRS between shifts in probability from consequence b to consequence a and shifts in probability from consequence d to consequence c among lotteries giving all four consequences positive probability.

Thus, ratios of utility differences correspond to constant MRSs between appropriate shifts in probability. As will be shown next, no other features of the NMUF can be inferred from expected utility maximizing behaviour alone.

2.4 Cardinally Equivalent Utility Functions

Behaviour satisfying the EU hypothesis does not determine the corresponding NMUF uniquely. Indeed, let $v : Y \to \mathbb{R}$ and $\tilde{v} : Y \to \mathbb{R}$ be any pair of NMUFs which, for some additive constant δ and multiplicative constant $\rho > 0$, are related by the identity

$$\tilde{v}(y) \equiv \delta + \rho v(y) \tag{2.6}$$

which holds throughout Y. Then, given any pair of lotteries $\lambda, \mu \in \Delta(Y)$, one has

$$
\sum_{y \in Y} [\lambda(y) - \mu(y)] \tilde{v}(y) = \sum_{y \in Y} [\lambda(y) - \mu(y)][\delta + \rho v(y)]
$$

$$
= \rho \sum_{y \in Y} [\lambda(y) - \mu(y)] v(y),
$$

because $\sum_{y \in Y} \lambda(y) = \sum_{y \in Y} \mu(y) = 1$. But $\rho > 0$ and so

$$
\sum_{y \in Y} \lambda(y) \tilde{v}(y) \geq \sum_{y \in Y} \mu(y) \tilde{v}(y) \iff \sum_{y \in Y} \lambda(y) v(y) \geq \sum_{y \in Y} \mu(y) v(y).
$$

For this reason, the pair of NMUFs satisfying (2.6) are said to be **cardinally equivalent**. Furthermore, (2.6) obviously implies that

$$
\frac{\tilde{v}(a) - \tilde{v}(c)}{\tilde{v}(b) - \tilde{v}(c)} = \frac{v(a) - v(c)}{v(b) - v(c)}, \tag{2.7}
$$

and so the MRS given by (2.5) is also the same for all NMUFs in the same cardinal equivalence class. Clearly, any four-way ratio of utility differences of the form $[v(a) - v(b)]/[v(c) - v(d)]$ with $v(c) \neq v(d)$ is also preserved by the transformation (2.6) from $v(y)$ to $\tilde{v}(y)$.

Conversely, if v and $\tilde{v}$ are NMUFs whose expected values represent the same preferences, then both must satisfy (2.5) for the same constant MRS $-dq/dp$. Hence (2.7) is satisfied for all $a, b, c \in Y$. But then

$$
\frac{\tilde{v}(a) - \tilde{v}(c)}{v(a) - v(c)} = \frac{\tilde{v}(b) - \tilde{v}(c)}{v(b) - v(c)}
$$

whenever $v(a) \neq v(c)$ and $v(b) \neq v(c)$. So, for each fixed $y' \in Y$, there must exist a constant ρ such that

$$\frac{\tilde{v}(y) - \tilde{v}(y')}{v(y) - v(y')} = \rho$$

for all $y \in Y$ with $v(y) \neq v(y')$. Moreover, because the expected values of v and $\tilde{v}$ represent identical preferences, it follows that $v(y) > v(y') \iff \tilde{v}(y) > \tilde{v}(y')$ and so $\rho > 0$. Therefore

$$\tilde{v}(y) = \tilde{v}(y') + \rho\,[v(y) - v(y')] = \delta + \rho v(y)$$

for all $y \in Y$, where $\delta := \tilde{v}(y') - \rho v(y')$. This confirms (2.6) for the case when the domain Y is rich enough to include at least two non-indifferent consequences. But (2.6) is trivially valid when all consequences in Y are indifferent.

3   Necessary Conditions

3.1   The Ordering Condition

The EU hypothesis implies three obvious but important properties. The first of these concerns the preference relation $\succsim$ defined by

$$\lambda \succsim \mu \iff \sum_{y \in Y} \lambda(y)v(y) \geq \sum_{y \in Y} \mu(y)v(y). \tag{3.1}$$

Then, for every finite $F \subset \Delta(Y)$, it follows from (2.2) that the choice set is given by $C(F) = \{\lambda \in F \mid \mu \in F \implies \lambda \succsim \mu\}$. In particular, of course, $\lambda \succsim \mu$ iff $\lambda \in C(\{\lambda, \mu\})$.

Evidently, then, the EU hypothesis implies the **ordering condition** (O), requiring the existence of a complete and transitive binary *preference ordering* $\succsim$ on $\Delta(Y)$ satisfying (3.1). As usual, we write $\lambda \succ \mu$ and say that λ is *strictly preferred* to μ when $\lambda \succsim \mu$ but not $\mu \succsim \lambda$; we write $\lambda \sim \mu$ and say that λ is *indifferent* to μ when $\lambda \succsim \mu$ and also $\mu \succsim \lambda$. Also, $\lambda \precsim \mu$ is equivalent to $\mu \succsim \lambda$, and $\lambda \prec \mu$ is equivalent to $\mu \succ \lambda$. Because $\succsim$ is complete, $\lambda \succsim \mu$ is equivalent to $\lambda \nprec \mu$.

For general consequence spaces, such preference orderings, and their representation by utility functions, are discussed in the preceding chapter by Mehta. This chapter concentrates entirely on spaces of consequence lotteries. For preference orderings that violate the EU hypothesis, some of the possible "non-expected" utility functions are discussed in other chapters of this *Handbook*. By contrast, this chapter also concentrates on behaviour patterns corresponding to preference orderings with the special structure that the EU hypothesis entails.

3.2   Independence Conditions

An important second implication of the EU hypothesis is *independence*. Indeed, this is the crucial property that distinguishes preferences satisfying the EU hypothesis from non-expected utility theories.

As Marschak (1950), Samuelson (1952) and Malinvaud (1952) pointed out, von Neumann and Morgenstern had originally left one important axiom implicit. In Samuelson (1983, p. 511), the *independence axiom* is expressed by means of the following **condition** (I′): Whenever $\lambda, \mu, \nu \in \Delta(Y)$ and $0 < \alpha < 1$, then

$$\lambda \succsim \mu \implies \alpha\lambda + (1-\alpha)\nu \succsim \alpha\mu + (1-\alpha)\nu. \tag{3.2}$$

Marschak and Malinvaud stated only the weaker **condition** (I⁰), requiring that

$$\lambda \sim \mu \implies \alpha\lambda + (1-\alpha)\nu \sim \alpha\mu + (1-\alpha)\nu \tag{3.3}$$

under the same hypotheses as for condition (I′). Later Herstein and Milnor (1953), following Samuelson's (1952) idea discussed below in connection with condition (I*), required (3.3) to be true only when $\alpha = \frac{1}{2}$. This is one of Herstein and Milnor's three axioms whose implications are also analysed at length in Fishburn (1982, pp. 13–17).

This chapter, however, will rely on two quite different versions of the independence axiom. Given the other axioms, it will be sufficient to use the following **independence condition** (I), apparently due to Jensen (1967). This requires that, whenever $\lambda, \mu, \nu \in \Delta(Y)$ and $0 < \alpha < 1$, then

$$\lambda \succ \mu \implies \alpha\lambda + (1-\alpha)\nu \succ \alpha\mu + (1-\alpha)\nu.$$

Combining conditions (I) and (I′) into one gives a single condition that, as shown in Lemma 3.1 below, is equivalent to the **finite dominance condition** (FD*). This states that, whenever $\lambda_i, \mu_i \in \Delta^*(Y)$ and $\alpha_i > 0$ with $\lambda_i \succsim \mu_i$ ($i = 1, 2, \ldots m$) and $\sum_{i=1}^{m} \alpha_i = 1$, then $\sum_{i=1}^{m} \alpha_i \lambda_i \succsim \sum_{i=1}^{m} \alpha_i \mu_i$ with strict preference if $\lambda_k \succ \mu_k$ for any k. Condition (FD*) is a simplified version of the infinite dominance condition (D*) due to Blackwell and Girshick (1954, p. 105, H₁) that is discussed in Section 8.4.

Apparently stronger than conditions (I), (I⁰) or (I′) is the **strong independence condition** (I*), requiring the logical equivalence

$$\lambda \succsim \mu \iff \alpha\lambda + (1-\alpha)\nu \succsim \alpha\mu + (1-\alpha)\nu \tag{3.4}$$

to hold whenever $0 < \alpha < 1$. For the case when $\alpha = \frac{1}{2}$, this is equivalent to Samuelson's (1952, p. 672) original "strong independence" axiom. Condition (I*) is not really new, however, because of:

LEMMA 3.1 Provided that condition (O) is satisfied, then condition (FD*), condition (I) combined with (I′), and condition (I*) are all equivalent.

PROOF (i) Suppose condition (FD*) is true. Obviously condition (I′) holds and so therefore does (3.2). Conversely, if $\alpha\lambda + (1-\alpha)\nu \succsim \alpha\mu + (1-\alpha)\nu$ and $0 < \alpha < 1$, then $\alpha\mu + (1-\alpha)\nu \not\succ \alpha\lambda + (1-\alpha)\nu$ by condition (O). So $\mu \not\succ \lambda$ by condition (I), from which it follows that $\lambda \succsim \mu$ by condition (O). Therefore (3.4) holds and condition (I*) is satisfied.

(ii) Suppose condition (I*) is true. Obviously (3.4) implies (3.2), so condition (I′) is true. Also, if $\lambda \succ \mu$, then by condition (O), $\mu \not\succsim \lambda$. Therefore, whenever $0 < \alpha < 1$, condition (I*) implies that $\alpha\mu + (1-\alpha)\nu \not\succsim \alpha\lambda + (1-\alpha)\nu$. Then condition (O) implies that $\alpha\lambda + (1-\alpha)\nu \succ \alpha\mu + (1-\alpha)\nu$, which is condition (I).

(iii) Finally, it is easy to show that conditions (I) and (I′) jointly imply (FD*) when $m = 2$. A routine induction proof establishes the same implication for larger values of m.

Thus, it has been proved that (FD*) $\implies$ (I*) $\implies$ [(I) and (I′)] $\implies$ (FD*). ∎

Finally, when (3.1) is true and $0 < \alpha < 1$, then

$$\alpha\lambda + (1-\alpha)\nu \succsim \alpha\mu + (1-\alpha)\nu$$
$$\iff \sum_{y \in Y} \{[\alpha\lambda(y) + (1-\alpha)\nu(y)] - [\alpha\mu(y) + (1-\alpha)\nu(y)]\}v(y) \geq 0$$
$$\iff \sum_{y \in Y} \lambda(y)\, v(y) \geq \sum_{y \in Y} \mu(y)\, v(y) \iff \lambda \succsim \mu.$$

Thus, (3.1) implies (3.4). So the strongest independence condition (I*) is an implication of the EU hypothesis.

3.3   Lexicographic Preferences

Though conditions (O) and (I*) are implied by the EU hypothesis, they do not characterize it. There are preference orderings which violate the EU hypothesis even though they satisfy (I*) on a domain $\Delta(Y)$.

As an example, consider the consequence domain $Y = \{a, b, c\}$. Furthermore, suppose that $v : Y \to \mathbb{R}$ is an NMUF whose expected value $U(\lambda) = \mathbb{E}_\lambda v$ represents a preference ordering $\succsim$ on $\Delta(Y)$ satisfying $1_a \succ 1_b \succ 1_c$. The corresponding indifference map must be as shown in the Marschak triangle of Figure 2.1 in Section 2.3. Consider the alternative "lexicographic" preference relation $\succsim^*$ on $\Delta(Y)$ defined by

$$\lambda \succsim^* \mu \iff U(\lambda) > U(\mu) \text{ or } [U(\lambda) = U(\mu) \text{ and } \lambda(a) \geq \mu(a)].$$

The preference relation $\succsim^*$ is evidently complete and transitive. It also satisfies condition (I*), as is easily checked. But unlike $\succsim$, the relation $\succsim^*$ is a *total ordering* in the sense that either $\lambda \succ^* \mu$ or $\mu \succ^* \lambda$ whenever $\lambda \neq \mu$. Thus all indifference sets in the Marschak triangle are isolated single points, which is incompatible with the existence of any NMUF whose expected value represents the preference ordering $\succsim^*$. So the EU hypothesis is violated.

3.4   Continuity Conditions

The third and last implication of the EU hypothesis is the requirement that preferences satisfy the following **continuity condition** (C), due to Blackwell and Girshick (1954, p. 106, H$_2$).[6] Whenever $\lambda, \mu, \nu \in \Delta(Y)$ with $\lambda \succ \mu$ and $\mu \succ \nu$, this requires that there exist $\alpha', \alpha'' \in (0,1)$ satisfying

$$\alpha'\lambda + (1-\alpha')\nu \succ \mu \quad \text{and} \quad \mu \succ \alpha''\lambda + (1-\alpha'')\nu. \tag{3.5}$$

Next, define the two preference sets

$$A := \{\alpha \in [0,1] \mid \alpha\lambda + (1-\alpha)\nu \succsim \mu\}$$
$$B := \{\alpha \in [0,1] \mid \mu \succsim \alpha\lambda + (1-\alpha)\nu\}$$

and let $\underline{\alpha} := \inf A$ and $\overline{\alpha} := \sup B$. An alternative **mixture continuity condition** (C*) introduced by Herstein and Milnor (1953) requires that, whenever $\lambda, \mu, \nu \in \Delta(Y)$ with $\lambda \succ \mu$ and $\mu \succ \nu$, both A and B must be closed. Note that, when combined with condition (O), condition (C*) is a strengthening of (C) because of part (i) of the following Lemma 3.2.

Note that the stronger continuity condition (C*) is entailed by the EU hypothesis (2.2) because, for instance, (2.3), (2.4) and (3.1) together imply that

$$A = \{\alpha \in [0,1] \mid \alpha U(\lambda) + (1-\alpha)U(\nu) \geq U(\mu)\}$$
$$= \{\alpha \in [0,1] \mid \alpha \geq \frac{U(\mu) - U(\nu)}{U(\lambda) - U(\nu)}\}$$

given that $U(\lambda) > U(\nu)$. Similarly,

$$B = \{\alpha \in [0,1] \mid \alpha \leq \frac{U(\mu) - U(\nu)}{U(\lambda) - U(\nu)}\}.$$

In fact, there must be a unique number $\alpha^* \in (0,1)$ satisfying the condition that $\alpha^*\lambda + (1-\alpha^*)\nu \sim \mu$ and also:

$$\alpha\lambda + (1-\alpha)\nu \succ \mu \iff \alpha > \alpha^*; \quad \alpha\lambda + (1-\alpha)\nu \prec \mu \iff \alpha < \alpha^*.$$

---

[6]This is sometimes called the *Archimedean axiom* — see, for instance, Karni and Schmeidler (1991, p. 1769).

On the other hand, note that the lexicographic preferences described in Section 3.3 are discontinuous. For suppose that $\lambda, \mu, \nu \in \Delta(Y)$ with $W(\lambda) > W(\mu) > W(\nu)$. Define $\alpha^* \in (0,1)$ as the critical value

$$\alpha^* := \frac{W(\mu) - W(\nu)}{W(\lambda) - W(\nu)}.$$

Then the two sets defined above take the form

$$A = \{\, \alpha \in [0,1] \mid \alpha > \alpha^* \text{ or } [\alpha = \alpha^* \text{ and } \alpha\lambda(y_1) + (1-\alpha)\nu(y_1) \geq \mu(y_1)]\,\},$$
$$B = \{\, \alpha \in [0,1] \mid \alpha < \alpha^* \text{ or } [\alpha = \alpha^* \text{ and } \alpha\lambda(y_1) + (1-\alpha)\nu(y_1) \leq \mu(y_1)]\,\}.$$

With lexicographic preferences, the common boundary point α^* of these two sets generally belongs to only one of them, and so either A or B is not closed. The only exception occurs in the special case when $\alpha^*\lambda(y_1) + (1 - \alpha^*)\nu(y_1) = \mu(y_1)$. Then $\alpha^* \in A \cap B$, so both A and B are closed. But for almost all $\lambda, \mu, \nu \in \Delta(Y)$, such lexicographic preferences exhibit a discontinuity.

The following implication of the preceding definitions plays an important role in Section 4.

LEMMA 3.2 Suppose that condition (O) is satisfied. Then: (i) condition (C*) implies (C); (ii) on the other hand, condition (C) implies that $\underline{\alpha} \in B$ and $\overline{\alpha} \in A$. Also, under the additional hypothesis $\underline{\alpha} = \overline{\alpha} =: \alpha^*$, it follows that $\alpha^*\lambda + (1 - \alpha^*)\nu \sim \mu$.

PROOF Suppose that $\lambda, \mu, \nu \in \Delta(Y)$ with $\lambda \succ \mu$ and $\mu \succ \nu$. The definitions of A and B and condition (O) together imply that $0 \notin A$, $1 \in A$, $0 \in B$, $1 \notin B$.

(i) If condition (C*) is satisfied, then $\underline{\alpha} = \min A$ and $\overline{\alpha} = \max B$, from which it follows that $\underline{\alpha} > 0$ and $\overline{\alpha} < 1$. Choosing any $\alpha', \alpha'' \in (0,1)$ to satisfy $1 > \alpha' > \overline{\alpha}$ and $\underline{\alpha} > \alpha'' > 0$ implies that $\alpha' \notin B$ and $\alpha'' \notin A$. Now (3.5) follows immediately from definition (3.4) and condition (O).

(ii) Whenever $\alpha \in (0,1] \setminus B$, condition (O) implies that $\alpha\lambda + (1 - \alpha)\nu \succ \mu$. Because $\mu \succ \nu$, condition (C) implies the existence of $\alpha' \in (0,1)$ such that

$$\alpha'[\alpha\lambda + (1-\alpha)\nu] + (1 - \alpha')\nu \succ \mu.$$

So $\alpha'\alpha \in A$. But $\alpha > \alpha'\alpha$. Because $\underline{\alpha} = \inf A$, it follows that $\alpha > \underline{\alpha}$ whenever $\alpha \in (0,1] \setminus B$. Therefore $\underline{\alpha} \notin (0,1] \setminus B$ and so $\underline{\alpha} \in B \cup \{0\}$. But $0 \in B$ and so $\underline{\alpha} \in B$ even if $\underline{\alpha} = 0$.

Similarly, when $\alpha \in [0,1) \setminus A$, condition (O) implies that $\mu \succ \alpha\lambda + (1 - \alpha)\nu$. Because $\lambda \succ \mu$, condition (C) implies the existence of $\alpha'' \in (0,1)$ such that

$$\mu \succ \alpha''\lambda + (1 - \alpha'')[\alpha\lambda + (1-\alpha)\nu].$$

So $\alpha'' + (1 - \alpha'')\alpha = \alpha + (1 - \alpha)\alpha'' \in B$. But $\alpha < \alpha + (1 - \alpha)\alpha''$. Because $\overline{\alpha} = \sup B$, it follows that $\alpha < \overline{\alpha}$ whenever $\alpha \in [0, 1) \setminus A$. Therefore $\overline{\alpha} \notin [0, 1) \setminus A$ and so $\overline{\alpha} \in A \cup \{1\}$. But $1 \in A$ and so $\overline{\alpha} \in A$ even if $\overline{\alpha} = 1$.

Under the additional hypothesis $\underline{\alpha} = \overline{\alpha} =: \alpha^*$, it follows that $\alpha^* \in A \cap B$. Obviously, definition (3.4) implies that $\alpha^* \lambda + (1 - \alpha^*)\nu \sim \mu$ in this case.   ∎

The three properties (O), (I), and (C) are important because, as shown by Jensen (1967), they are not only necessary, but also sufficient conditions for the EU hypothesis to hold. This is discussed in the next section. Here it has been shown that the stronger properties (I*) and (C*) are also necessary.

4   Sufficient Conditions

Condition (O) requiring that there be a preference ordering $\succsim$ is, of course, standard in utility theory. The independence condition (I) imposes strong restrictions on the possible form of $\succsim$. And, in combination with the continuity condition (C), it implies EU maximization. This section will be devoted to proving this important result, due to Jensen (1967). Note that, compared to Herstein and Milnor (1953), Jensen uses the stronger independence condition (I) instead of only (I⁰) for $\alpha = \frac{1}{2}$. On the other hand, Jensen uses the weaker continuity condition (C) instead of (C*).

It is worth noting that the proof given here becomes rather easier if one assumes conditions (I*) and (C*) instead of (I) and (C). Indeed, there would be no need to prove Lemmas 4.2 or 4.5, since their only role is to show that (I*) is satisfied.

4.1   Ordinality and Independence

In the following, conditions (O) and (I) will be assumed throughout. Also, though the succeeding Lemmas 4.1–4.7 are stated only for the space $\Delta(Y)$, they are actually true in any convex set or mixture space. This important fact will be used later in Sections 8 and 9, as well as in Chapter 6 on subjectively expected utility.

Notice first that if $\lambda \sim \mu$ for all $\lambda, \mu \in \Delta(Y)$, then the EU hypothesis is trivially satisfied: there must exist a constant $\overline{v} \in \mathbb{R}$ such that $U(\lambda) = \overline{v} = v(y)$ for all $\lambda \in \Delta(Y)$ and all $y \in Y$. So, it will be supposed throughout this section that there exist $\lambda, \mu \in \Delta(Y)$ with $\lambda \succ \mu$.

LEMMA 4.1 For any pair of lotteries $\lambda, \mu \in \Delta(Y)$ with $\lambda \succ \mu$, one has:

(a) (Strict Betweenness) $\lambda \succ \alpha\lambda + (1 - \alpha)\mu \succ \mu$ whenever $0 < \alpha < 1$.

(b) (Stochastic Monotonicity) $\lambda \succ \alpha\lambda + (1 - \alpha)\mu \succ \alpha'\lambda + (1 - \alpha')\mu \succ \mu$ whenever $0 < \alpha' < \alpha < 1$.

(c) (Weak Stochastic Monotonicity) if $\alpha, \alpha' \in [0,1]$, then

$$\alpha\lambda + (1-\alpha)\mu \succsim \alpha'\lambda + (1-\alpha')\mu \iff \alpha \geq \alpha'.$$

PROOF (a) Whenever $0 < \alpha < 1$, condition (I) implies that

$$\lambda = \alpha\lambda + (1-\alpha)\lambda \succ \alpha\lambda + (1-\alpha)\mu \succ \alpha\mu + (1-\alpha)\mu = \mu.$$

(b) If $0 < \alpha' < \alpha < 1$, then there exists $\delta \in (0,1)$ such that $\alpha' = \delta\alpha$. So

$$\delta[\alpha\lambda + (1-\alpha)\mu] + (1-\delta)\mu = \delta\alpha\lambda + (1-\delta\alpha)\mu = \alpha'\lambda + (1-\alpha')\mu.$$

By part (a), $\lambda \succ \alpha\lambda + (1-\alpha)\mu \succ \mu$. Next, applying part (a) a second time to $\delta[\alpha\lambda + (1-\alpha)\mu] + (1-\delta)\mu$ gives

$$\alpha\lambda + (1-\alpha)\mu \succ \delta[\alpha\lambda + (1-\alpha)\mu] + (1-\delta)\mu \succ \delta\mu + (1-\delta)\mu = \mu.$$

Together these statements clearly imply part (b).

(c) Immediate from part (b), given that $\succsim$ is a complete ordering. ∎

In particular, if $\lambda \succ \mu$, then a compound lottery with a higher probability of λ and a lower probability of μ is preferred to one with a lower probability of λ and a higher probability of μ.

LEMMA 4.2 Suppose that $0 < \alpha < 1$ and $\lambda, \mu, \nu \in \Delta(Y)$. Then:

(a) $\alpha\lambda + (1-\alpha)\nu \sim \alpha\mu + (1-\alpha)\nu$ implies $\lambda \sim \mu$;

(b) if $\lambda \succ \alpha\lambda + (1-\alpha)\mu$ or $\alpha\lambda + (1-\alpha)\mu \succ \mu$, then $\lambda \succsim \alpha\lambda + (1-\alpha)\mu \succsim \mu$ and so $\lambda \succ \mu$;

(c) (Betweenness) $\lambda \sim \mu$ implies $\lambda \sim \alpha\lambda + (1-\alpha)\mu \sim \mu$;

(d) $\lambda \sim \mu \sim \nu$ implies $\alpha\lambda + (1-\alpha)\nu \sim \alpha\mu + (1-\alpha)\nu$.

PROOF (a) By condition (I), if $\lambda \nsim \mu$, then $\alpha\lambda + (1-\alpha)\nu \nsim \alpha\mu + (1-\alpha)\nu$.

(b) If $\lambda \succ \alpha\lambda + (1-\alpha)\mu$, then condition (I) implies that

$$\alpha\lambda + (1-\alpha)\mu \succ \alpha[\alpha\lambda + (1-\alpha)\mu] + (1-\alpha)\mu. \tag{4.1}$$

But

$$\alpha[\alpha\lambda + (1-\alpha)\mu] + (1-\alpha)[\alpha\lambda + (1-\alpha)\mu] = \alpha\lambda + (1-\alpha)\mu.$$

Hence, (4.1) is compatible with condition (I) only if $\mu \not\succ \alpha\lambda + (1-\alpha)\mu$, and so $\alpha\lambda + (1-\alpha)\mu \succsim \mu$, by condition (O). Similarly, if $\alpha\lambda + (1-\alpha)\mu \succ \mu$ then condition (I) implies that

$$\begin{aligned}
\alpha\lambda + (1-\alpha)\left[\alpha\lambda + (1-\alpha)\mu\right] &\succ \alpha\left[\alpha\lambda + (1-\alpha)\mu\right] + (1-\alpha)\left[\alpha\lambda + (1-\alpha)\mu\right] \\
&= \alpha\lambda + (1-\alpha)\mu.
\end{aligned}$$

This is compatible with condition (I) only if $\alpha\lambda + (1-\alpha)\mu \not\succ \lambda$, which implies that $\lambda \succsim \alpha\lambda + (1-\alpha)\mu$, because of condition (O). Therefore, if $\lambda \succ \alpha\lambda + (1-\alpha)\mu$ or $\alpha\lambda + (1-\alpha)\mu \succ \mu$, then $\lambda \succsim \alpha\lambda + (1-\alpha)\mu \succsim \mu$. In either case, transitivity of $\succsim$ implies that $\lambda \succ \mu$.

(c) If $\mu \succsim \lambda$, condition (O) and the contrapositive of part (b) together imply that $\mu \succsim \alpha\lambda + (1-\alpha)\mu \succsim \lambda$. Similarly, with λ and μ interchanged, as well as α and $1-\alpha$, it must be true that $\lambda \succsim \mu$ implies $\lambda \succsim \alpha\lambda + (1-\alpha)\mu \succsim \mu$. Therefore, $\lambda \sim \mu$ must imply that $\lambda \sim \alpha\lambda + (1-\alpha)\mu \sim \mu$.

(d) Suppose that $\lambda \sim \mu \sim \nu$. Applying part (c) first to the pair λ, ν and then to the pair μ, ν implies that $\alpha\lambda + (1-\alpha)\nu \sim \nu \sim \alpha\mu + (1-\alpha)\nu$. ∎

4.2 Continuity

Note that both Lemmas 4.1 and 4.2 rely only on conditions (O) and (I). From now on, assume throughout the rest of this section that the continuity condition (C) is also satisfied. Then:

LEMMA 4.3 Suppose that $\lambda, \mu, \nu \in \Delta(Y)$ with $\lambda \succ \mu$ and $\mu \succ \nu$. Then there exists a unique $\alpha^* \in (0,1)$ such that $\alpha^*\lambda + (1-\alpha^*)\nu \sim \mu$.

PROOF Consider the two sets A and B as defined in Section 3.4. Define $\alpha^* := \inf A$. Now whenever $\alpha > \alpha^*$, there exists $\alpha' \in A$ such that $\alpha > \alpha' \geq \alpha^*$. From part (b) of Lemma 4.1 and the definition of A, it follows that

$$\alpha\lambda + (1-\alpha)\nu \succ \alpha'\lambda + (1-\alpha')\nu \succsim \mu.$$

By condition (O), $\alpha \notin B$. This is true whenever $\alpha > \alpha^*$. Therefore $\alpha \in B$ implies $\alpha \leq \alpha^*$. So α^* is an upper bound for B, implying that $\alpha^* \geq \sup B$. But completeness of the preference ordering $\succsim$ excludes the possibility that $\inf A > \sup B$. Hence $\alpha^* = \inf A = \sup B$. By Lemma 3.2, condition (C) then implies that

$$\alpha^*\lambda + (1-\alpha^*)\nu \sim \mu. \tag{4.2}$$

Now apply part (b) of Lemma 4.1 to the pair λ, ν. Whenever the inequalities $1 \geq \alpha' > \alpha^* > \alpha'' \geq 0$ are satisfied, it follows that

$$\alpha'\lambda + (1-\alpha')\nu \succ \alpha^*\lambda + (1-\alpha^*)\nu \succ \alpha''\lambda + (1-\alpha'')\nu. \tag{4.3}$$

Because of (4.2) and (4.3), condition (O) implies that

$$\alpha'\lambda + (1 - \alpha')\nu \succ \mu \succ \alpha''\lambda + (1 - \alpha'')\nu.$$

This shows that α^* is the unique member of $A \cap B$. ∎

COROLLARY 4.4 Suppose that $\lambda, \mu, \nu \in \Delta(Y)$ with $\lambda \succ \nu$ and $\lambda \succsim \mu \succsim \nu$. Then there exists a unique $\alpha^* \in [0, 1]$ such that $\alpha^*\lambda + (1 - \alpha^*)\nu \sim \mu$.

PROOF Lemma 4.3 already treats the case when $\lambda \succ \mu \succ \nu$. Alternatively, if $\lambda \sim \mu$, one can take $\alpha^* = 1$, whereas if $\mu \sim \nu$, one can take $\alpha^* = 0$. ∎

LEMMA 4.5 Suppose that $0 < \alpha < 1$ and that $\lambda, \mu, \nu \in \Delta(Y)$. Then:

(a) $\alpha\lambda + (1 - \alpha)\nu \succ \alpha\mu + (1 - \alpha)\nu$ implies $\lambda \succ \mu$;

(b) Condition (I*) is satisfied.

PROOF (a) *Case 1:* $\lambda \succsim \nu \succsim \mu$.   Here, unless $\lambda \succ \mu$, it must be true that $\lambda \sim \mu \sim \nu$. But then Lemma 4.2(d) would imply $\alpha\lambda + (1-\alpha)\nu \sim \alpha\mu + (1-\alpha)\nu$, a contradiction.

Case 2: $\nu \succ \lambda$.   Here, by Lemma 4.1(a), $\nu \succ \alpha\lambda + (1 - \alpha)\nu$. So, whenever $\alpha\lambda + (1 - \alpha)\nu \succ \alpha\mu + (1 - \alpha)\nu$, Lemma 4.3 implies that there exists $\alpha^* \in (0, 1)$ satisfying

$$\alpha^* [\alpha\mu + (1 - \alpha)\nu] + (1 - \alpha^*)\nu \sim \alpha\lambda + (1 - \alpha)\nu.$$

From this it follows that

$$\alpha[\alpha^*\mu + (1 - \alpha^*)\nu] + (1 - \alpha)\nu = \alpha\alpha^*\mu + (1 - \alpha\alpha^*)\nu \sim \alpha\lambda + (1 - \alpha)\nu.$$

Applying Lemma 4.2(a) and condition (I) gives

$$\lambda \sim \alpha^*\mu + (1 - \alpha^*)\nu \succ \alpha^*\mu + (1 - \alpha^*)\lambda.$$

Because $\succsim$ is transitive, Lemma 4.2(b) then yields $\lambda \succ \mu$.

Case 3: $\mu \succ \nu$.   Here, by Lemma 4.1(a), $\alpha\mu + (1 - \alpha)\nu \succ \nu$. So, whenever $\alpha\lambda + (1 - \alpha)\nu \succ \alpha\mu + (1 - \alpha)\nu$, Lemma 4.3 implies that there exists $\alpha^* \in (0, 1)$ satisfying

$$\alpha^* [\alpha\lambda + (1 - \alpha)\nu] + (1 - \alpha^*)\nu \sim \alpha\mu + (1 - \alpha)\nu.$$

From this it follows that

$$\alpha[\alpha^*\lambda + (1 - \alpha^*)\nu] + (1 - \alpha)\nu = \alpha\alpha^*\lambda + (1 - \alpha\alpha^*)\nu \sim \alpha\mu + (1 - \alpha)\nu.$$

Applying condition (I) and Lemma 4.2(a) gives

$$\alpha^* \lambda + (1 - \alpha^*)\mu \succ \alpha^* \lambda + (1 - \alpha^*)\nu \sim \mu.$$

Because $\succsim$ is transitive, Lemma 4.2(b) then yields $\lambda \succ \mu$.

(b) Because condition (O) implies that $\succsim$ is complete, the contrapositive of part (a) implies (3.2) in Section 3.2, which is condition (I′). If condition (I) is also true, the result follows from Lemma 3.1. ∎

4.3 Construction of a Utility Function

We continue to assume that conditions (O), (I), and (C) are satisfied on $\Delta(Y)$. Now that Lemma 4.3 and condition (I*) have been established, one can show how to construct a utility function. In order to do so, first let $\overline{\lambda}, \underline{\lambda} \in \Delta(Y)$ be any two lotteries with $\overline{\lambda} \succ \underline{\lambda}$. Define the associated *order interval*

$$\Lambda := \{ \lambda \in \Delta(Y) \mid \overline{\lambda} \succsim \lambda \succsim \underline{\lambda} \}. \tag{4.4}$$

LEMMA 4.6 (a) There exists a unique utility function $U : \Lambda \to \mathbb{R}$ which: (i) represents the preference relation $\succsim$ on Λ; (ii) takes the values $U(\overline{\lambda}) = 1$ and $U(\underline{\lambda}) = 0$ at $\overline{\lambda}$ and $\underline{\lambda}$ respectively; and (iii) satisfies the mixture preservation property (MP) for all $\lambda, \mu \in \Lambda$ and all $\alpha \in [0, 1]$.

(b) Suppose $V : \Lambda \to \mathbb{R}$ is any other utility function representing $\succsim$ restricted to Λ which satisfies (MP). Then there exist real constants $\rho > 0$ and δ such that $V(\lambda) = \delta + \rho U(\lambda)$ for all $\lambda \in \Lambda$.

PROOF (a) For each $\lambda \in \Lambda$, Lemma 4.3 and Corollary 4.4 imply the existence of a unique $U(\lambda) \in [0, 1]$ such that

$$U(\lambda) \overline{\lambda} + [1 - U(\lambda)] \underline{\lambda} \sim \lambda. \tag{4.5}$$

Furthermore, $\lambda \sim \overline{\lambda}$ implies $U(\lambda) = 1$, and $\lambda \sim \underline{\lambda}$ implies $U(\lambda) = 0$. Also, if $\lambda, \mu \in \Lambda$, then (4.5) and transitivity of $\succsim$, when combined with Lemma 4.1(c), imply that

$$\lambda \succsim \mu \iff U(\lambda) \overline{\lambda} + [1 - U(\lambda)] \underline{\lambda} \succsim U(\mu) \overline{\lambda} + [1 - U(\mu)] \underline{\lambda} \iff U(\lambda) \geq U(\mu).$$

So $U : \Lambda \to \mathbb{R}$ represents $\succsim$ on Λ. Furthermore, for all $\lambda, \mu \in \Lambda$ and $\alpha \in [0, 1]$, (4.5) and condition (I*) imply that

$$
\begin{aligned}
\alpha \lambda + (1 - \alpha)\mu \ &\sim\ \alpha \{ U(\lambda) \overline{\lambda} + [1 - U(\lambda)] \underline{\lambda} \} + (1 - \alpha)\mu \\
&\sim\ \alpha \{ U(\lambda) \overline{\lambda} + [1 - U(\lambda)] \underline{\lambda} \} \\
&\qquad + (1 - \alpha) \{ U(\mu) \overline{\lambda} + [1 - U(\mu)] \underline{\lambda} \} \\
&=\ [\alpha U(\lambda) + (1 - \alpha) U(\mu)] \overline{\lambda} + [1 - \alpha U(\lambda) - (1 - \alpha) U(\mu)] \underline{\lambda}.
\end{aligned}
$$

Therefore, definition (4.5) implies that

$$U(\lambda\alpha + (1 - \alpha)\mu) = \alpha U(\lambda) + (1 - \alpha)U(\mu).$$

This confirms property (MP).

(b) Given $\overline{\lambda}, \underline{\lambda} \in \Delta(Y)$ and the alternative utility function $V : \Lambda \to \mathbb{R}$ representing $\succsim$, define $\delta := V(\underline{\lambda})$ and $\rho := V(\overline{\lambda}) - V(\underline{\lambda}) > 0$. If V also satisfies (MP), then definition (4.5) implies that

$$V(\lambda) = V\left(U(\lambda)\,\overline{\lambda} + [1 - U(\lambda)]\,\underline{\lambda}\right) = U(\lambda)\,V(\overline{\lambda}) + [1 - U(\lambda)]\,V(\underline{\lambda}) = \delta + \rho\,U(\lambda)$$

for all $\lambda \in \Lambda$. ∎

LEMMA 4.7 There exists a utility function $U : \Delta(Y) \to \mathbb{R}$ which represents $\succsim$ and satisfies (MP). Also, if $V : \Delta(Y) \to \mathbb{R}$ is any other utility function with the same properties, then there exist real constants $\rho > 0$ and δ such that $V(\lambda) = \delta + \rho\,U(\lambda)$ for all $\lambda \in \Delta(Y)$.

PROOF The first simple case occurs when $\overline{\lambda}$ and $\underline{\lambda}$ can be chosen so that, for all $\lambda \in \Delta(Y)$, one has $\overline{\lambda} \succsim \lambda \succsim \underline{\lambda}$. In this case the order interval Λ defined in (4.4) is the whole space $\Delta(Y)$. There is nothing more to prove.[7]

It remains to prove the lemma even when the lotteries $\overline{\lambda}, \underline{\lambda} \in \Delta(Y)$ cannot be chosen to satisfy $\overline{\lambda} \succsim \lambda \succsim \underline{\lambda}$ for all $\lambda \in \Delta(Y)$. In this case, one can still construct the order interval Λ as in (4.4) and the utility function $U : \Lambda \to \mathbb{R}$ to represent $\succsim$ on Λ while satisfying $U(\overline{\lambda}) = 1$, $U(\underline{\lambda}) = 0$, and (MP). Moreover, consider any four lotteries $\mu_1, \mu_2, \nu_1, \nu_2 \in \Delta(Y)$ such that $\mu_i \succsim \overline{\lambda}$ and $\nu_i \precsim \underline{\lambda}$ for $i = 1, 2$, and let Λ_i denote the corresponding order interval $\{ \lambda \in \Delta(Y) \mid \mu_i \succsim \lambda \succsim \nu_i \}$. Now, for $i = 1, 2$, Lemma 4.6(a) implies that there exists a utility function $U_i : \Lambda_i \to \mathbb{R}$ which represents $\succsim$ on Λ_i, while also satisfying $U_i(\mu_i) = 1$, $U_i(\nu_i) = 0$, and (MP).

As discussed in Section 2.4, for $i = 1, 2$, whenever $U_i^*(\lambda) \equiv \delta_i + \rho_i U_i(\lambda)$ for some constants $\rho_i > 0$ and δ_i, the alternative utility function $U_i^* : \Lambda_i \to \mathbb{R}$ will also represent $\succsim$ on Λ_i while satisfying (MP). Furthermore, one can make $U_i^*(\overline{\lambda}) = 1$ and $U_i^*(\underline{\lambda}) = 0$ by choosing ρ_i and δ_i to satisfy

$$\delta_i + \rho_i U_i(\overline{\lambda}) = 1; \quad \delta_i + \rho_i U_i(\underline{\lambda}) = 0.$$

These equations will be satisfied provided that one chooses

$$\rho_i = 1/[U_i(\overline{\lambda}) - U_i(\underline{\lambda})] > 0; \quad \delta_i = -U_i(\underline{\lambda})/[U_i(\overline{\lambda}) - U_i(\underline{\lambda})].$$

---

[7]Of course, many textbooks consider only this easy case.

Then, for all $\lambda \in \Lambda_i$, one has

$$U_i^*(\lambda) = \frac{U_i(\lambda) - U_i(\underline{\lambda})}{U_i(\overline{\lambda}) - U_i(\underline{\lambda})}.$$

Now, both utility functions U_1^* and U_2^* represent the same ordering $\succsim$ and also satisfy (MP) on $\Lambda_1 \cap \Lambda_2$. By Lemma 4.6(b), there must exist constants $\rho > 0$ and δ such that

$$U_2^*(\lambda) = \delta + \rho U_1^*(\lambda)$$

for all λ in the set $\Lambda_1 \cap \Lambda_2$, which obviously has Λ as a subset. But $U_1^*(\underline{\lambda}) = U_2^*(\underline{\lambda}) = 0$, implying that $\delta = 0$. Also $U_1^*(\overline{\lambda}) = U_2^*(\overline{\lambda}) = 1$, implying that $1 = \delta + \rho$ and so $\rho = 1$. This proves that $U_1^* \equiv U_2^*$ on $\Lambda_1 \cap \Lambda_2$.

So, given any $\lambda \in \Delta(Y)$, there is a *unique* $U^*(\lambda)$ which can be found by constructing U_0 to represent $\succsim$ and satisfy (MP) on any order interval Λ_0 large enough to include all three lotteries λ, $\overline{\lambda}$, and $\underline{\lambda}$, then re-normalizing by choosing constants $\rho > 0$ and δ so that the transformed utility function U^* satisfies $U^*(\lambda) \equiv \delta + \rho U_0(\lambda)$ on Λ_0, as well as $U^*(\overline{\lambda}) = 1$, $U^*(\underline{\lambda}) = 0$. Because U_0 satisfies (MP), so does U^*. Evidently $\lambda \succsim \mu$ iff $U^*(\lambda) \geq U^*(\mu)$ because U^* represents $\succsim$ on any order interval large enough to include all four lotteries λ, μ, $\overline{\lambda}$, and $\underline{\lambda}$.

Next, let U be any alternative utility function representing $\succsim$ on the whole of $\Delta(Y)$. Then U also represents it on any non-trivial order interval Λ_0 that includes Λ. So there exist real constants $\rho > 0$ and δ such that throughout Λ_0 one has $U(\lambda) = \delta + \rho U^*(\lambda)$, including for $\lambda = \overline{\lambda}$ and $\lambda = \underline{\lambda}$. Because $U^*(\overline{\lambda}) = 1$ and $U^*(\underline{\lambda}) = 0$, it follows that $U(\underline{\lambda}) = \delta$ and $U(\overline{\lambda}) = \delta + \rho$. Hence $\rho = U(\overline{\lambda}) - U(\underline{\lambda})$. This implies that $U(\lambda) = U(\underline{\lambda}) + [U(\overline{\lambda}) - U(\underline{\lambda})] U^*(\lambda)$ throughout Λ_0 and so, because Λ_0 is arbitrarily large, throughout $\Delta(Y)$. So U^* is unique up to cardinal transformations. ∎

Finally:

THEOREM 4.8 Suppose that conditions (O), (I), and (C) are satisfied on $\Delta(Y)$. Then there exists a unique cardinal equivalence class of NMUFs $v : Y \to \mathbb{R}$ such that

$$\lambda \succsim \mu \iff \sum_{y \in Y} \lambda(y) v(y) \geq \sum_{y \in Y} \mu(y) v(y).$$

PROOF The theorem is a direct implication of Lemma 4.7, provided that $v(y)$ is defined, for each $y \in Y$, as $U(1_y)$. This is because (2.1) and repeated application of (MP) together imply that

$$U(\lambda) = \sum_{y \in Y} \lambda(y) U(1_y) = \sum_{y \in Y} \lambda(y) v(y).$$

Also, uniqueness of U up to cardinal transformations obviously implies that v has the same property. ∎

5 Consequentialist Foundations: Ordinality

5.1 The Consequentialist Principle

There has been frequent criticism of the three axioms (O), (I), and (C) which, as Sections 3 and 4 showed, characterize EU maximization. It is clear that (O) and (I) in particular describe actual behaviour rather poorly—see, for example, the other chapters in this *Handbook* on non-expected utility and on experiments. Utility theorists, however, should be no less interested in whether these axioms are an acceptable basis of normative behaviour. This section and the next will show that at least (O) and (I)—indeed, even condition (I*)—can be derived from another, more fundamental, normative principle of behaviour. This is the "consequentialist principle", requiring behaviour to be entirely explicable by its consequences.

As in Section 2, let Y denote a *consequence domain*, and $\Delta(Y)$ the set of all simple lotteries on Y. It will be convenient to regard the members of $\Delta(Y)$ as *random consequences*, to be distinguished from *elementary consequences* $y \in Y$.

The *consequentialist principle* requires that, given any non-empty finite *feasible set* $F \subset \Delta(Y)$, the set of all possible random consequences of behaviour, called the *behaviour set*, should be the non-empty "revealed" or *implicit choice set* $C(F) \subset F$ that depends only on F. In other words, changes in the structure of the decision problem should have no bearing on the possible consequences $C(F)$ of behaviour, unless they change the feasible set F. At first, this restriction seems very weak, putting no restrictions at all on the *consequentialist choice function* C mapping feasible sets F into choice subsets $C(F) \subset F$.

This consequentialist principle has a long history, especially in moral philosophy. Aristotle can be read as suggesting that the moral worth of an act depended on its results or consequences. St. Thomas Aquinas explicitly attacked this doctrine, suggesting that good acts could remain good even if they had evil consequences, and that evil acts would remain evil even if they happened to have good consequences. Later philosophical writers, especially John Stuart Mill and G.E. Moore, then enunciated clearly a doctrine or principle that flew in the face of Aquinas' assertion, claiming that acts should be judged by their consequences. This doctrine was given the name "consequentialism" by Elisabeth Anscombe (1958), in a critical article. To this day it remains controversial in moral philosophy.[8]

In decision theory, Arrow (1951) stated the principle that acts should be valued by their consequences. Savage (1954) defined an act as a mapping from states of the world to consequences, thus espousing consequentialism implicitly.

5.2 Simple Finite Decision Trees

Consequentialism acquires force only in combination with other axioms, or else when applied in a rather obvious way to decision problems that can be described by decision trees in a sufficiently unrestricted domain. This is my next topic.

A *simple finite decision tree* is a list

$$T = \langle N, N^*, X, n_0, N_{+1}(\cdot), \gamma(\cdot) \rangle \tag{5.1}$$

in which:

(i) N is the finite set of *nodes*;

(ii) N^* is the finite subset of *decision nodes*;

(iii) X is the finite subset of *terminal nodes*;

(iv) n_0 is the unique *initial node*;

(v) $N_{+1}(\cdot) : N \twoheadrightarrow N$ is the *immediate successor correspondence*;

(vi) $\gamma : X \to \Delta(Y)$ is the *consequence mapping* from terminal nodes to their lottery consequences.[9]

Obviously, N is partitioned into the two disjoint sets N^* and X. The set X must always have at least one member for every finite decision tree. For non-trivial decision trees, both N^* and X are non-empty. But in case $n_0 \in X$, then $X = \{n_0\}$ and $N^* = \emptyset$. Generally, of course, $n \in X \iff N_{+1}(n) = \emptyset$.

In order that N should have a tree structure, there must be a partition of N into a finite collection of pairwise disjoint non-empty subsets N_k ($k =$

---

[8]In Hammond (1986, 1996) I have discussed the origins of consequentialism at somewhat greater length, and provided references for the writings cited above, as well as some others. The same issues also receive attention in the contribution by d'Aspremont and Mongin to this *Handbook*.

[9]One could well argue that, strictly speaking, lotteries can only arise in decision trees having chance nodes. Thus, in what I am calling a "simple" decision tree, each $x \in X$ is not really a terminal node, but a chance node where a lottery determines which terminal node and which elementary consequence $y \in Y$ will result from earlier decisions. However, later proofs are facilitated by allowing terminal nodes to have random consequences, which is why I have chosen this more general formulation.

$0, 1, \ldots K)$ such that each N_k consists of all the nodes that can be reached after exactly k steps from n_0 through the decision tree. Thus

$$N_0 = \{n_0\} \quad \text{and} \quad N_k = \bigcup_{n \in N_{k-1}} N_{+1}(n) \ (k = 1, 2, \ldots K).$$

Evidently the last set N_K is a subset of X, but X can also include some members of the sets N_k with $k < K$.

Similarly, starting with any node $n \in N_k$ $(k = 1, 2, \ldots K)$, define

$$N_k(n) := \{n\} \text{ and } N_r(n) = \bigcup_{n' \in N_{r-1}(n)} N_{+1}(n') \ (r = k+1, k+2, \ldots, K(n)),$$

where $K(n) + 1$ is the maximum number of nodes, including the initial node, on any path in T that passes through n. Then $N(n) := \cup_{r=k}^{K(n)} N_r(n)$ is the set of nodes that *succeed* n in the tree T.

Given the consequence domain Y, let $\mathcal{T}(Y)$ denote the collection of all simple finite decision trees given by (5.1).

5.3   Behaviour and Unrestricted Domain

In any simple finite decision tree $T \in \mathcal{T}(Y)$, at any decision node $n \in N^*$, the agent's *behaviour* or a possible course of action is described by the set $\beta(T, n)$ satisfying

$$\emptyset \neq \beta(T, n) \subset N_{+1}(n). \tag{5.2}$$

Thus, any decision in $\beta(T, n)$ takes the form of a move to a node $n' \in N_{+1}(n)$ that immediately succeeds n. When $\beta(T, n)$ is multi-valued, this captures the idea that, among the different members of $\beta(T, n)$, there is no good reason to choose one move rather than another.

The **unrestricted domain** assumption is that $\beta(T, n)$ is defined, and satisfies (5.2), whenever T is a simple finite decision tree in $\mathcal{T}(Y)$ with n as one of its decision nodes. Note that $\beta(T, n)$ must be defined even at nodes that cannot be reached given earlier behaviour in T.

5.4   Continuation Subtrees and Dynamic Consistency

Let T be any simple finite decision tree, as in (5.1), and $n \in N$ any node of T. Then there exists a *continuation subtree*

$$T(n) = \langle N(n), N^*(n), X(n), n, N_{+1}(\cdot), \gamma(\cdot) \rangle$$

with initial node n, and with $N(n)$ consisting of all nodes that succeed n in T. Moreover, $N^*(n) = N(n) \cap N^*$ is the set of decision nodes in $T(n)$, whereas $X(n) = N(n) \cap X$ is the set of terminal nodes. Also, $N_{+1}(\cdot)$ and $\gamma(\cdot)$ in the subtree $T(n)$ are the restrictions to $N(n)$ and $X(n)$ respectively of the same correspondence and mapping in the tree T. In fact, if $n \in N_{k(n)}$, then $N(n) = \cup_{k=0}^{K(n)} N_k(n)$ where

$$N_0(n) \quad = \quad \{n\} \quad = \quad N(n) \cap N_{k(n)},$$

$$\text{and} \quad N_k(n) \quad = \bigcup_{n' \in N_{k-1}(n)} N_{+1}(n') \ = \ N(n) \cap N_{k(n)+k} \quad (k = 1 \text{ to } K(n)).$$

Let $n' \in N^*(n)$ be any decision node in the subtree $T(n)$. In this case $\beta(T(n), n')$ describes behaviour at node n', but so does $\beta(T, n')$. It should make no difference whether n' is regarded as belonging to the whole tree T, or only to the subtree $T(n)$. In fact, because $T(n')$ is the relevant decision tree at node n', behaviour there will ultimately be determined at the very last minute by $\beta(T(n'), n')$. This motivates the **dynamic consistency** assumption that

$$\beta(T, n') = \beta(T(n), n') \text{ whenever } n' \in N^*(n).$$

Note that this is a behavioural dynamic consistency condition, requiring consistency between behaviour at the same decision node of a subtree and of the whole tree. It is quite different from dynamic consistency of planned behaviour, of preferences, or of choice. It also differs from consistency between planned and actual behaviour. These differences have been the source of some misunderstanding which is further discussed at the end of Section 5.5.

5.5 Consequentialism in Simple Decision Trees

Applying the consequentialist principle to simple decision trees requires the feasible set of consequences $F(T)$ to be determined, for each simple finite decision tree T, as well as the *behaviour set* $\Phi_\beta(T)$ of possible consequences of behaviour. Both these sets can be found by backward recursion, starting with terminal nodes and then proceeding in reverse to the initial node. Thus, we can calculate successive sets $F(T, n)$ and $\Phi_\beta(T, n)$ for all $n \in N$ by starting from each $n \in X$ and working backwards, until in the end we are able to define $F(T)$ as $F(T, n_0)$ and $\Phi_\beta(T)$ as $\Phi_\beta(T, n_0)$.

Indeed, at any terminal node $x \in X$, there is no alternative to the uniquely specified consequence $\gamma(x) \in \Delta(Y)$. Because $F(T)$ and $\Phi_\beta(T)$ will be *sets* of consequence lotteries, however, rather than single consequence lotteries, it is natural to construct

$$F(T, x) := \Phi_\beta(T, x) := \{\gamma(x)\} \text{ (all } x \in X). \tag{5.3}$$

Consider any decision node $n \in N^*$. Suppose that for all $n' \in N_{+1}(n)$ the two sets $F(T, n')$ and $\Phi_\beta(T, n')$ have already been constructed and, as the induction hypothesis, that they satisfy

$$\emptyset \neq \Phi_\beta(T, n') \subset F(T, n'). \tag{5.4}$$

After reaching n, by moving to an appropriate node $n' \in N_{+1}(n)$, any consequence in $F(T, n')$ can be made feasible. Hence, $F(T, n)$ is the union of all such sets. But behaviour β allows only moves to nodes $n' \in \beta(T, n)$. Hence, only consequences in $\Phi_\beta(T, n')$ for some $n' \in \beta(T, n)$ can result from behaviour β. Therefore we construct

$$F(T, n) := \bigcup_{n' \in N_{+1}(n)} F(T, n'); \quad \Phi_\beta(T, n) := \bigcup_{n' \in \beta(T,n)} \Phi_\beta(T, n'). \tag{5.5}$$

This construction is essentially the process which LaValle and Wapman (1986) call "rolling back" the decision tree. Now, it is obvious from (5.2) and (5.4) that

$$\emptyset \neq \Phi_\beta(T, n) \subset F(T, n). \tag{5.6}$$

This confirms that the induction hypothesis also holds at n. So, by backward induction, (5.6) holds at any node $n \in N$.

Recalling that $F(T) = F(T, n_0)$ and also $\Phi_\beta(T) = \Phi_\beta(T, n_0)$ in any simple decision tree T, (5.6) implies in particular

$$\emptyset \neq \Phi_\beta(T) \subset F(T). \tag{5.7}$$

The **consequentialist axiom** then requires the existence of an implicit choice function C_β such that, for all simple finite decision trees T, one has

$$\Phi_\beta(T) = C_\beta(F(T)). \tag{5.8}$$

In particular, (5.8) is satisfied if and only if, for any pair of decision trees T, T' with $F(T) = F(T')$, it is true that $\Phi_\beta(T) = \Phi_\beta(T')$. That is, for trees with identical feasible sets of consequences, there must also be identical behaviour sets of consequences.

At this stage it may be useful to note the distinction between (general) behaviour and consequentialist choice. The former is simply a description of what moves might be made at each decision node of a decision tree, as in Section 5.3. It need not involve, even implicitly, any conscious or even unconscious process of choice. By contrast, consequentialism restricts behaviour to yield the same (random) consequences as if there were a conscious choice mechanism C_β making selections from the relevant feasible set $F(T)$ in each tree T.

Now, given any non-empty finite set F, it is easy to construct a decision tree T such that $F(T) = F$. Indeed, it suffices to construct a simple one-stage or "reduced" decision tree T with components as in (5.1) specified by

$$N^* = \{n_0\}; \ X = N_{+1}(n_0) = \{\, x_\lambda \mid \lambda \in F \subset \Delta(Y)\,\}; \ \gamma(x_\lambda) = \lambda \ (\text{all } \lambda \in F). \tag{5.9}$$

Then, because of (5.7) and (5.8), consequentialism implies that

$$\emptyset \neq C_\beta(F) \subset F. \tag{5.10}$$

Finally, some interesting criticisms of consequentialism due to Machina (1989), McClennen (1990) and others should be noted. Recall that dynamic consistency of behaviour requires the behaviour sets $\beta(T, n')$ and $\beta(T(n), n')$ to be the same at all decision nodes $n' \in N^*(n)$, regardless of whether the subtree $T(n)$ is regarded as part of the whole tree T or not. Then, an obvious implication of consequentialism is that the consequences $\Phi_\beta(T, n) = \Phi_\beta(T(n))$ of behaviour in the subtree $T(n)$ must depend only on the set $F(T, n) = F(T(n))$ of consequences that are feasible in the subtree. Machina and McClennen call this property "separability." They dispute the property, however, and claim that it makes an important difference whether a decision node $n' \in N^*(n)$ is treated as part of T or of $T(n)$. Their argument is that consequences that occur in T but not in $T(n)$ may after all be relevant to behaviour in $T(n)$, in which case both consequentialism and this separability property are violated.[10] But if consequences outside the subtree $T(n)$ are relevant to decisions within the tree, it seems clear that consequences have not been adequately described, and that the consequence domain Y needs to be extended. As Munier (1996) in particular has pointed out, an important issue which then arises is whether in practice the consequence domain can be enriched in a way that allows all behaviour to be explained without at the same time making the unrestricted domain assumption implausible.

5.6 Consequentialism Implies Ordinality

Given behaviour β, define the implicit weak preference relation R_β on $\Delta(Y)$ by

$$\lambda \, R_\beta \, \mu \iff \lambda \in C_\beta(\{\,\lambda, \mu\,\}) \tag{5.11}$$

---

[10]Some writers seem to suggest that it is dynamic consistency which is violated. Indeed, unless this dependence of preferences on consequences in $T \setminus T(n)$ is foreseen, there is a sense in which both preferences and choice may have to be dynamically inconsistent — cf. Hammond (1976, 1988c). But I prefer to consider dynamic consistency of behaviour, which is satisfied virtually automatically. So the criticisms apply to the consequentialist hypothesis and the implied property of separability, rather than to the behavioural dynamic consistency condition of Section 5.4.

for all pairs $\lambda, \mu \in \Delta(Y)$. Impose also the reflexivity condition that $\lambda \, R_\beta \, \lambda$ for all $\lambda \in \Delta(Y)$. Thus, R_β is the reflexive binary preference relation revealed by behaviour in decision trees with only a pair of feasible consequence lotteries. Let I_β be the associated *indifference relation* defined by

$$\lambda \, I_\beta \, \mu \iff [\lambda \, R_\beta \, \mu \ \& \ \mu \, R_\beta \, \lambda] \iff C_\beta(\{\lambda, \mu\}) = \{\lambda, \mu\}.$$

and let P_β be the associated *strict preference* relation defined by

$$\lambda \, P_\beta \, \mu \iff [\lambda \, R_\beta \, \mu \ \& \ \text{not} \ \mu \, R_\beta \, \lambda] \iff C_\beta(\{\lambda, \mu\}) = \{\lambda\}.$$

The following is a striking implication of the three axioms set out in Sections 5.3, 5.4 and 5.5 respectively:

THEOREM 5.1 (Consequentialism Implies Ordinality): Let behaviour β be defined for an unrestricted domain of simple finite decision trees, and satisfy both dynamic consistency and consequentialism. Then the implicit preference relation R_β is a (complete and transitive) preference ordering on $\Delta(Y)$. Moreover, the implicit choice function is *ordinal*—i.e., for every non-empty finite set $F \subset \Delta(Y)$, one has

$$C_\beta(F) = \{\lambda \in F \mid \mu \in F \implies \lambda \, R_\beta \, \mu\}. \tag{5.12}$$

For a general choice space, this result was first proved in Hammond (1977) by using Arrow's (1959) characterization of an ordinal choice function. The direct proof provided here seems preferable. It proceeds by way of four lemmas:

LEMMA 5.2   For any finite subset $F \subset \Delta(Y)$, if $\lambda \in C_\beta(F)$ and $\mu \in F$, then $\lambda \, R_\beta \, \mu$.

LEMMA 5.3   For any finite subset $F \subset \Delta(Y)$, if $\lambda \in C_\beta(F)$ and $\mu \in F$ with $\mu \, R_\beta \, \lambda$, then $\mu \in C_\beta(F)$.

LEMMA 5.4   Equation (5.12) is true for any non-empty finite $F \subset \Delta(Y)$.

LEMMA 5.5   The binary relation defined by (5.11) is a (complete and transitive) preference ordering.

Lemmas 5.2 and 5.3 are both proved by considering a particular decision tree T, as illustrated in Figure 5.1. The components specified in (5.1) are given

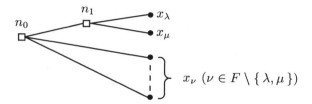

Figure 5.1 Decision Tree Illustrating Ordinality

by:

$$
\begin{aligned}
N^* &= \{n_0, n_1\}; \quad X = \{x_\nu \mid \nu \in F\}; \\
N_{+1}(n_0) &= \{n_1\} \cup \{x_\nu \mid \nu \in F \setminus \{\lambda, \mu\}\}; \\
N_{+1}(n_1) &= \{x_\lambda, x_\mu\}; \\
\gamma(x_\nu) &= \nu \ (\text{all } \nu \in F).
\end{aligned}
\tag{5.13}
$$

In fact, for any non-empty finite subset F of $\Delta(Y)$ with $\lambda, \mu \in F$, the finite tree T can be constructed to satisfy (5.13). By the unrestricted domain hypothesis, $\emptyset \neq \beta(T, n) \subset N_{+1}(n)$ for $n \in \{n_0, n_1\}$. Also, $F(T, x_\nu) = \Phi_\beta(T, x_\nu) = \{\nu\}$ for all $\nu \in F$, by (5.3). Then the construction (5.5) gives

$$
\begin{aligned}
F(T(n_1)) &= F(T, n_1) = F(T, x_\lambda) \cup F(T, x_\mu) = \{\lambda, \mu\}; \\
F(T) &= F(T, n_0) = F(T, n_1) \cup [\cup_{\nu \in F \setminus \{\lambda, \mu\}} F(T, x_\nu)]; \\
&= \{\lambda, \mu\} \cup [F \setminus \{\lambda, \mu\}] = F.
\end{aligned}
$$

Now, $\lambda \in C_\beta(F)$ implies $\lambda \in \Phi_\beta(T)$. But construction (5.5) implies that

$$
\begin{aligned}
\Phi_\beta(T(n_1)) &= \Phi_\beta(T, n_1) = \bigcup_{n' \in \beta(T, n_1)} \Phi_\beta(T, n') = \{\nu \mid x_\nu \in \beta(T, n_1)\}; \\
\Phi_\beta(T) &= \Phi_\beta(T, n_0) = \bigcup_{n' \in \beta(T, n_0)} \Phi_\beta(T, n').
\end{aligned}
\tag{5.14}
$$

Because $\lambda \notin \Phi_\beta(T, n')$ for all $n' \in N_{+1}(n_0) \setminus \{n_1\}$, it follows from $\lambda \in C_\beta(F)$ that $n_1 \in \beta(T, n_0)$ and also that $\lambda \in \Phi_\beta(T, n_1)$. The latter implies that $x_\lambda \in \beta(T, n_1)$.

PROOF OF LEMMA 5.2: Because $x_\lambda \in \beta(T, n_1)$, it follows from dynamic consistency that $x_\lambda \in \beta(T(n_1), n_1)$. But $F(T(n_1)) = \{\lambda, \mu\}$, whereas $\Phi_\beta(T(n_1)) = \Phi_\beta(T, n_1) \ni \lambda$. From this one has $\lambda \in C_\beta(F(T(n_1))) = C_\beta(\{\lambda, \mu\})$. So $\lambda \, R_\beta \, \mu$, by definition (5.11) of R_β. ∎

PROOF OF LEMMA 5.3:   Suppose also that $\mu \; R_\beta \; \lambda$. Then $\mu \in C_\beta(\{\lambda, \mu\}) = \Phi_\beta(T(n_1)) = \Phi_\beta(T, n_1)$. Because it has already been proved that $n_1 \in \beta(T, n_0)$, one has

$$C_\beta(F) = \Phi_\beta(T) = \Phi_\beta(T, n_0) = \bigcup_{n' \in \beta(T, n_0)} \Phi_\beta(T, n') \supset \Phi_\beta(T, n_1) \ni \mu$$

as an implication of (5.14). ∎

PROOF OF LEMMA 5.4:   By Lemma 5.2,

$$C_\beta(F) \subset \{\lambda \in F \mid \mu \in F \implies \lambda \; R_\beta \; \mu\}. \tag{5.15}$$

Conversely, by (5.10) there must exist $\nu \in C_\beta(F)$. Suppose now that $\lambda \in F$ and $\lambda \; R_\beta \; \mu$ for all $\mu \in F$. Then $\lambda \; R_\beta \; \nu$ in particular. Therefore, by Lemma 5.3 with ν and λ replacing λ and μ respectively, it follows that $\lambda \in C_\beta(F)$. This proves that

$$\{\lambda \in F \mid \mu \in F \implies \lambda \; R_\beta \; \mu\} \subset C_\beta(F).$$

Together with (5.15), this confirms (5.12). ∎

PROOF OF LEMMA 5.5 — *Completeness of R_β*:   Given any pair $\lambda, \mu \in \Delta(Y)$, the choice set $C_\beta(\{\lambda, \mu\})$ cannot be empty because of (5.10). Hence, either $\lambda \in C_\beta(\{\lambda, \mu\})$, in which case definition (5.11) implies that $\lambda \; R_\beta \; \mu$, or alternatively $\mu \in C_\beta(\{\lambda, \mu\})$, in which case (5.11) implies $\mu \; R_\beta \; \lambda$.
   — *Transitivity of R_β*:   Suppose $\lambda, \mu, \nu \in \Delta(Y)$ and $\lambda \; R_\beta \; \mu$, $\mu \; R_\beta \; \nu$. Let $F := \{\lambda, \mu, \nu\}$. By (5.10), $C_\beta(F)$ is non-empty. This leaves three possible cases (which need not be mutually exclusive, however):

   (i) If $\lambda \in C_\beta(F)$, then Lemma 5.2 implies that $\lambda \; R_\beta \; \nu$.

   (ii) If $\mu \in C_\beta(F)$, then $\lambda \; R_\beta \; \mu$ and Lemma 5.3 imply that $\lambda \in C_\beta(F)$, so case (i) applies.

   (iii) If $\nu \in C_\beta(F)$, then $\mu \; R_\beta \; \nu$ and Lemma 5.3 imply that $\mu \in C_\beta(F)$, so case (ii) applies.

   Therefore, case (i) always applies. So $\lambda \; R_\beta \; \nu$, as required. ∎

6   Consequentialist Foundations: Independence

6.1   *Finite Decision Trees with Chance Nodes*

Section 5 restricted attention to "simple" finite decision trees, whose non-terminal nodes are all decision nodes. Here the domain of decision trees will be expanded to include trees with a set N^0 of *chance nodes*. Thus, the set N can be partitioned into the three pairwise disjoint subsets N^*, N^0 and X, where as before N^* denotes the set of decision nodes and X the set of terminal nodes. The other new feature will be that (objective) *transition probabilities* $\pi(n'|n)$ are specified for every chance node $n \in N^0$ and for every immediate successor $n' \in N_{+1}(n)$. In particular, the non-negative real numbers $\pi(n'|n)$ $(n' \in N_{+1}(n))$ should satisfy $\sum_{n' \in N_{+1}(n)} \pi(n'|n) = 1$ and so represent a (simple) probability distribution in $\Delta(N_{+1}(n))$.

As before, behaviour β will be described by the sets $\beta(T, n)$ for each finite decision tree T and each decision node $n \in N^*$ of T. The *unrestricted domain* assumption will be that $\beta(T, n)$ is defined as a non-empty subset of $N_{+1}(n)$ for all such pairs (T, n). But there will also be reason to invoke the **almost unrestricted domain** assumption. This requires $\beta(T, n)$ to be specified only for decision trees T in which $\pi(n'|n) > 0$ for all $n' \in N_{+1}(n)$ at any chance node $n \in N^0$. To some extent, this assumption can be justified by requiring all parts of a decision tree that can be reached with only zero probability to be "pruned" off. Such pruning makes good sense in single-person decision theory. But, as discussed in Hammond (1994, 1997), it has unacceptable implications in multi-person game theory.

6.2   Consequentialism in Finite Decision Trees

In this extended domain of finite decision trees that may include chance nodes, most of the analysis set out in Section 5 remains valid. However, rules (5.3) and (5.5) in Section 5.5 for calculating the sets $F(T, n)$ and $\Phi_\beta(T, n)$ by backward recursion need supplementing, in order to deal with chance nodes.

First, given subsets $S_i \subset \Delta(Y)$ and non-negative numbers α_i $(i = 1, 2, \ldots, k)$ with $\sum_{i=1}^k \alpha_i = 1$, define

$$\sum_{i=1}^k \alpha_i S_i = \{\lambda \in \Delta(Y) \mid \exists \lambda_i \in S_i \ (i = 1, 2, \ldots, k) : \lambda = \sum_{i=1}^k \alpha_i \lambda_i\}$$

as the corresponding set of convex combinations or probability mixtures. Then, for all $n \in N^0$, construct the two sets

$$F(T, n) \quad := \quad \sum_{n' \in N_{+1}(n)} \pi(n'|n) \, F(T, n'); \tag{6.1}$$

$$\Phi_\beta(T, n) \quad := \quad \sum_{n' \in N_{+1}(n)} \pi(n'|n) \, \Phi_\beta(T, n'). \tag{6.2}$$

This construction can be explained as follows. Suppose that $\lambda(n') \in F(T, n')$ $(n' \in N_{+1}(n))$ is any collection of lotteries each of which will be feasible after reaching n, provided that chance selects the appropriate node n'. So the *compound lottery* in which first n' is selected with probabilities $\pi(n'|n)$ $(n' \in N_{+1}(n))$ and then a consequence y is selected with probabilities $\lambda(n')(y)$ $(y \in Y)$ must also be feasible. Now we invoke what Luce and Raiffa (1957, p. 26) call the *reduction of compound lotteries* assumption, originally due to von Neumann and Morgenstern (1953, Axiom (3:C:b), p. 26).[11] This states that the above compound lottery reduces to the single lottery $\lambda \in \Delta(Y)$ with $\lambda = \sum_{n' \in N_{+1}(n)} \pi(n'|n)\lambda(n')$. Then (6.1) says that this λ belongs to the feasible set $F(T, n)$ at node n. Conversely, (6.1) requires that, whenever $\lambda \in F(T, n)$, this can only be because there exists a collection of lotteries $\lambda(n') \in F(T, n')$ $(n' \in N_{+1}(n))$ such that $\lambda = \sum_{n' \in N_{+1}(n)} \pi(n'|n)\lambda(n')$. Similarly for $\Phi_\beta(T, n)$, the set of possible consequences of behaviour. See (6.3) below for a specific example.

In this framework, consequentialism still requires $\Phi_\beta(T) = C_\beta(F(T))$ to hold, as in (5.8) of Section 5.5. Only now the domain of finite decision trees includes those with chance nodes at which all probabilities are positive. Also, rules (6.1) and (6.2) are involved in constructing the sets $F(T)$ and $\Phi_\beta(T)$.

Consider the restricted domain of simple decision trees without any chance nodes. Arguing as in Section 5, there must exist an implicit preference ordering R_β on the domain $\Delta(Y)$ of consequence lotteries such that, for all simple decision trees T, one has

$$C_\beta(F(T)) = \{ \lambda \in F(T) \mid \mu \in F(T) \implies \lambda \ R_\beta \ \mu \}.$$

This preliminary result is used throughout the following discussion.

6.3 *Consequentialism Implies Independence*

Once chance nodes are allowed into decision trees, however, ordinality is not the only implication of the three axioms set out in Sections 5.3, 5.4 and 5.5 respectively. The strong independence condition (I*) is as well. To see this,

---

[11] Actually, von Neumann and Morgenstern (p. 28) link this axiom to the absence of "utility for gambling", and write (p. 632) that the "axiom expresses the combination rule for multiple chance alternatives, and it is plausible, that a specific utility or disutility for gambling can only exist if this simple combination rule is abandoned." Luce and Raiffa (p. 26) concur with this interpretation, and also write of there being no "pleasure of suspense". Consequentialism requires that, if it is normatively appropriate for feelings of suspense or the excitement of gambling to affect decision-making, then such psychological variables should be included as part of each possible consequence.

consider the particular decision tree T illustrated in Figure 6.1, with:

$$
\begin{aligned}
N^0 &= \{\, n_0 \,\}; \quad N^* = \{\, n_1 \,\}; \quad X = \{\, x_\lambda, x_\mu, x_\nu \,\}; \\
N_{+1}(n_0) &= \{\, n_1, x_\nu \,\}; \quad N_{+1}(n_1) = \{\, x_\lambda, x_\mu \,\}; \\
\pi(n_1 | n_0) &= \alpha; \quad \pi(x_\nu | n_0) = 1 - \alpha; \\
\gamma(x_\lambda) &= \lambda; \quad \gamma(x_\mu) = \mu; \quad \gamma(x_\nu) = \nu.
\end{aligned}
$$

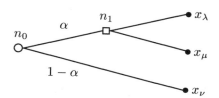

Figure 6.1 Decision Tree Illustrating Independence

Constructions (5.3), (5.5), (6.1) and (6.2) imply that:

$$
F(T, x_\rho) = \Phi_\beta(T, x_\rho) = \{\rho\} \quad (\rho \in \{\, \lambda, \mu, \nu \,\}); \qquad F(T, n_1) = \{\, \lambda, \mu \,\}
$$

and also that

$$
\begin{aligned}
F(T) &= F(T, n_0) = \alpha F(T, n_1) + (1 - \alpha) F(T, x_\nu) \\
&= \alpha\{\, \lambda, \mu \,\} + (1 - \alpha)\{\nu\} \\
&= \{\, \alpha\lambda + (1 - \alpha)\nu, \ \alpha\mu + (1 - \alpha)\nu \,\}; \\
\Phi_\beta(T) &= \Phi_\beta(T, n_0) = \alpha\Phi_\beta(T, n_1) + (1 - \alpha)\Phi_\beta(T, x_\nu) \\
&= \alpha\Phi_\beta(T, n_1) + (1 - \alpha)\{\nu\}.
\end{aligned}
\tag{6.3}
$$

Therefore

$$\lambda \; R_\beta \; \mu \quad \Longleftrightarrow \quad \lambda \in C_\beta(\{\lambda, \mu\}) = C_\beta(F(T, n_1)) = \Phi_\beta(T, n_1)$$
$$\Longleftrightarrow \quad \alpha\lambda + (1 - \alpha)\nu \in \alpha\Phi_\beta(T, n_1) + (1 - \alpha)\{\nu\} = \Phi_\beta(T, n_0)$$
$$\Longleftrightarrow \quad \alpha\lambda + (1 - \alpha)\nu \in C_\beta(F(T, n_0)) \tag{6.4}$$
$$\Longleftrightarrow \quad \alpha\lambda + (1 - \alpha)\nu \; R_\beta \; \alpha\mu + (1 - \alpha)\nu.$$

This is the strong independence condition (I*), but with the crucial difference that (6.4) is valid even when $\alpha = 0$.

Indeed, if $\alpha = 0$ really were allowed in the decision tree T illustrated in Figure 6.1, then (6.4) would imply that

$$\lambda \; R_\beta \; \mu \quad \Longleftrightarrow \quad \nu \; R_\beta \; \nu.$$

But Theorem 5.1 says that R_β is a preference ordering, so $\nu \; R_\beta \; \nu$ is always true because R_β is reflexive. From this it follows that $\lambda \; R_\beta \; \mu$ (and also $\mu \; R_\beta \; \lambda$) for all $\lambda, \mu \in \Delta(Y)$. The implication is that *all* lotteries in $\Delta(Y)$ must be indifferent, and that $\Phi_\beta(T) = F(T)$ in any finite decision tree T. Behaviour must be entirely insensitive.

This explains why it seems natural to invoke only the assumption of an *almost unrestricted domain*, and so to exclude decision trees having any zero transition probability at a chance node. Then (6.4) applies only when $0 < \alpha < 1$, or trivially when $\alpha = 1$, and so it becomes exactly the same as the strong independence condition (I*).

Finally, it should be noted that essentially the same argument for the independence axiom was advanced by LaValle and Wapman (1986). A related argument can also be found in Samuelson (1988). But all these authors *postulate* the existence of a preference ordering, whereas the consequentialist axioms presented here *imply* both the existence of a preference ordering and the independence axiom.

6.4 Ordinality and Strong Independence Characterize Consequentialism

So far, it has been shown that consequentialist and dynamically consistent behaviour on an almost unrestricted domain of finite decision trees must maximize an implicit preference ordering satisfying the strong independence condition (I*). A converse of this result is also true. Given any preference ordering $\succsim$ on $\Delta(Y)$ satisfying condition (I*), there exists consequentialist and dynamically consistent behaviour β on an almost unrestricted domain of finite decision trees such that the implicit preference ordering R_β is identical to the given ordering $\succsim$.

To show this, for any given finite decision tree T, first construct the feasible sets $F(T, n)$ by backward recursion as in (5.3), (5.5) and (6.1). Second, for each $n \in N$, construct the set of preference maximizing lotteries

$$\Psi(T, n) := \{ \lambda \in F(T, n) \mid \mu \in F(T, n) \implies \lambda \succsim \mu \}. \tag{6.5}$$

This set is non-empty because $F(T, n)$ is finite and $\succsim$ is an ordering. Next, for any decision node $n \in N^*$, let $\beta(T, n)$ be any subset of $N_{+1}(n)$ with the property that

$$\bigcup_{n' \in \beta(T,n)} \Psi(T, n') = \Psi(T, n). \tag{6.6}$$

Such a set always exists, because one can obviously put

$$\beta(T, n) = \beta^*(T, n) := \{ n' \in N_{+1}(n) \mid \exists \lambda \in F(T, n') : \lambda \in \Psi(T, n) \}. \tag{6.7}$$

In fact, $\beta^*(T, n)$ is the largest set satisfying (6.6). But $\beta(T, n)$ can be any non-empty set such that $\cup_{n' \in \beta(T,n)} \Psi(T, n') = \cup_{n' \in \beta^*(T,n)} \Psi(T, n')$. However, in order for $n' \in \beta^*(T, n) \setminus \beta(T, n)$ to be possible, it must be true that $\Psi(T, n') \subset \cup_{\tilde{n} \in \beta^*(T,n) \setminus \{n'\}} \Psi(T, \tilde{n})$. Thus, some consequences as good as those in $\Psi(T, n')$ must still be available even if the decision-maker refuses to move to n'.

Now, constructing the behaviour sets $\Phi_\beta(T, n)$ by backward recursion as in (5.3), (5.5) and (6.2) yields the following:

LEMMA 6.1 At any decision node $n \in N$ of any finite decision tree T, one has $\Phi_\beta(T, n) = \Psi(T, n)$, so that β is consequentialist and $R_\beta = \succsim$.

PROOF The proof will proceed by backward induction. First, at any terminal node $x \in X$, (5.3) implies that $\Psi(T, x) = \Phi_\beta(T, x) = F(T, x) = \{\gamma(x)\}$.

Consider any non-terminal node $n \in N \setminus X$. As the induction hypothesis, suppose that $\Phi_\beta(T, n') = \Psi(T, n')$ is true at all nodes $n' \in N_{+1}(n)$. Then two different cases must be considered:

Case 1: $n \in N^*$. Here n is a decision node. Because of (5.5) and the induction hypothesis, it follows from (6.6) that

$$\Phi_\beta(T,n) = \bigcup_{n' \in \beta(T,n)} \Phi_\beta(T,n') = \bigcup_{n' \in \beta(T,n)} \Psi(T,n') = \Psi(T,n).$$

Case 2: $n \in N^0$. Here n is a chance node. So, by (6.2) and the induction hypothesis,

$$\Phi_\beta(T,n) = \sum_{n' \in N_{+1}(n)} \pi(n'|n)\, \Phi_\beta(T,n') = \sum_{n' \in N_{+1}(n)} \pi(n'|n)\, \Psi(T,n'). \quad (6.8)$$

Now suppose that $\lambda \in \Phi_\beta(T,n)$. Consider any $\mu \in F(T,n)$. Then, for all $n' \in N_{+1}(n)$, (6.1) and (6.2) imply that there exist $\lambda(n') \in \Phi_\beta(T,n')$ and $\mu(n') \in F(T,n')$ satisfying

$$\lambda = \sum_{n' \in N_{+1}(n)} \pi(n'|n)\, \lambda(n'), \quad \mu = \sum_{n' \in N_{+1}(n)} \pi(n'|n)\, \mu(n'). \quad (6.9)$$

By the induction hypothesis, for all $n' \in N_{+1}(n)$ one has $\lambda(n') \in \Psi(T,n')$, so $\lambda(n') \succsim \mu(n')$. Because of the hypothesis that $\succsim$ satisfies conditions (O) and (I*), Lemma 3.1 implies that it satisfies (FD*) as well. Therefore, because $\lambda(n') \succsim \mu(n')$ for all $n' \in N_{+1}(n)$, it follows that $\lambda \succsim \mu$. Because this is true for all $\mu \in F(T,n)$, one must have $\lambda \in \Psi(T,n)$.

Conversely, suppose that $\lambda \in \Psi(T,n)$. Because $\lambda \in F(T,n)$, for all $n' \in N_{+1}(n)$ there exists $\lambda(n') \in F(T,n')$ such that $\lambda = \sum_{n' \in N_{+1}(n)} \pi(n'|n)\, \lambda(n')$. Because $\lambda \in \Psi(T,n)$, for any $n' \in N_{+1}(n)$ and any $\mu(n') \in F(T,n')$ it must be true that

$$\begin{aligned}
\lambda &= \pi(n'|n)\, \lambda(n') + \sum_{n'' \in N_{+1}(n)\setminus\{n'\}} \pi(n''|n)\, \lambda(n'') \\
&\succsim \pi(n'|n)\, \mu(n') + \sum_{n'' \in N_{+1}(n)\setminus\{n'\}} \pi(n''|n)\, \lambda(n'').
\end{aligned}$$

Because $\pi(n'|n) > 0$, condition (I*) then implies that $\lambda(n') \succsim \mu(n')$. This is true for all $\mu(n') \in F(T,n')$, so $\lambda(n') \in \Psi(T,n')$. This is true for all $n' \in N_{+1}(n)$. Then (6.8) implies that $\lambda \in \Phi_\beta(T,n)$.

In each of these two cases, it has been proved that $\Phi_\beta(T,n) = \Psi(T,n)$. This completes the backward induction argument. ∎

6.5   Summary

The results of this section can be summarized in:

THEOREM 6.2 (1) Suppose that behaviour β is consequentialist and dynamically consistent for the almost unrestricted domain of finite decision trees with only positive probabilities at all chance nodes. Then β reveals a preference ordering R_β on $\Delta(Y)$ satisfying the strong independence condition (I*).

(2) Conversely, given any ordering $\succsim$ on $\Delta(Y)$ satisfying the strong independence condition (I*), there exists consequentialist behaviour β which is dynamically consistent on the almost unrestricted domain of finite decision trees with only positive probabilities such that the implicit preference ordering R_β on $\Delta(Y)$ is identical to $\succsim$.

7   Continuous Behaviour and Expected Utility

7.1   Continuous Behaviour

As shown in Section 3.3, the ordering and strong independence conditions (O) and (I*) by themselves do not imply EU maximization. So, to arrive at the EU hypothesis, the consequentialist axioms of Sections 5 and 6 need to be supplemented by a continuity condition. To state this condition, consider any infinite sequence of decision trees T^m $(m = 1, 2, \ldots)$ which are all identical except for the positive probabilities $\pi^m(n'|n)$ at each chance node $n \in N^0$. In fact, suppose that at any chance node $n \in N^0$, as $m \to \infty$ one has $\pi^m(n'|n) \to \bar{\pi}(n'|n)$ for all $n' \in N_{+1}(n)$. Let $\bar{T}$ denote the "limit tree" with the probabilities $\bar{\pi}(n'|n)$ at each chance node.

It would be usual to assume that behaviour has the *closed graph property* requiring that, at any decision node n^* belonging to each of the trees T^m $(m = 1, 2, \ldots)$, whenever $n \in \beta(T^m, n^*)$ for all large m, then $n \in \beta(\bar{T}, n^*)$ in the limit tree. Because each set $N_{+1}(n)$ is finite, implying that $\Delta(N_{+1}(n))$ is compact at every chance node n, this is equivalent to upper hemi-continuity of the correspondence from probabilities to behaviour in each decision tree—the condition that is fundamental in, for instance, proving the existence of Nash equilibrium in a multi-peron game where mixed strategies are allowed. However, there is a difficulty here because if $\bar{\pi}(n'|n) = 0$ for some $n' \in N_{+1}(n)$, then node n' and all its successors in the set $N(n')$ should be excluded from the tree $\bar{T}$.

Thus, the closed graph property needs weakening as follows. The limit tree $\bar{T}$ should have exactly the same structure and consequence mapping as each tree T^m in the sequence, except that any subtree following a node n' for which $\bar{\pi}(n'|n) = 0$ should be "pruned off" from the limit tree $\bar{T}$. Let $\bar{N}^*$ denote the set of decision nodes in $\bar{T}$ that remain after any necessary pruning. Now, the **continuous behaviour condition** (CB) requires that the closed graph property should hold at each remaining decision node $n^* \in \bar{N}^*$ when the limit tree $\bar{T}$ is constructed in this special way. Under the consequentialist hypothesis of

Section 6, this condition has the important implication that implicit preferences must be continuous:

LEMMA 7.1 The continuous behaviour condition (CB) implies condition (C*).

PROOF Suppose that $\lambda, \mu, \nu \in \Delta(Y)$ with $\lambda\ P_\beta\ \mu$ and $\mu\ P_\beta\ \nu$. Recall that the stochastic monotonicity Lemma 4.1(b) is true under conditions (O) and (I) alone. So it applies to the ordering R_β and to the pair $\lambda, \nu \in \Delta(Y)$ satisfying $\lambda\ P_\beta\ \nu$. In particular, it implies that

$$\alpha'\lambda + (1 - \alpha')\nu\ P_\beta\ \alpha\lambda + (1 - \alpha)\nu \iff \alpha' > \alpha. \tag{7.1}$$

Consider next the two sets

$$\overline{A} := \{\alpha \in [0, 1] \mid \alpha\lambda + (1 - \alpha)\nu\ R_\beta\ \mu\};$$
$$\underline{A} := \{\alpha \in [0, 1] \mid \mu\ R_\beta\ \alpha\lambda + (1 - \alpha)\nu\}.$$

Because of (7.1) and because R_β is transitive, there must exist a unique common boundary point $\alpha^* := \sup \underline{A} = \inf \overline{A}$ such that $\alpha \in \underline{A}$ whenever $0 \leq \alpha < \alpha^*$, whereas $\alpha' \in \overline{A}$ whenever $\alpha^* < \alpha' \leq 1$. Now, $0 \notin \overline{A}$ and $1 \notin \underline{A}$, so $0 < \alpha^* < 1$. Furthermore:

$$\alpha \in [0, \alpha^*) \implies \mu\ P_\beta\ \alpha\lambda + (1 - \alpha)\nu; \quad \alpha \in (\alpha^*, 1] \implies \alpha\lambda + (1 - \alpha)\nu\ P_\beta\ \mu. \tag{7.2}$$

Consider any two convergent sequences $\underline{\alpha}^m, \overline{\alpha}^m$ $(m = 1, 2, \dots)$ of probabilities which have the common limit α^*, while also satisfying $0 < \underline{\alpha}^m < \alpha^* < \overline{\alpha}^m < 1$ for all m. Let $\underline{T}^m, \overline{T}^m$ $(m = 1, 2, \dots)$ be the two corresponding sequences of decision trees of the form illustrated in Figure 7.1, where $\alpha = \underline{\alpha}^m$ in each tree $\underline{T}^m$, but $\alpha = \overline{\alpha}^m$ in each tree $\overline{T}^m$.

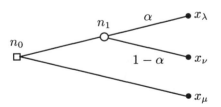

Figure 7.1 Decision Tree Illustrating Continuity

The constant tree structure and consequence mapping for each of these trees are given by:

$$N^* = \{n_0\}; \quad N^0 = \{n_1\}; \quad X = \{x_\lambda, x_\mu, x_\nu\};$$
$$N_{+1}(n_0) = \{n_1, x_\mu\}; \quad N_{+1}(n_1) = \{x_\lambda, x_\nu\};$$
$$\gamma(x_\lambda) = \lambda; \quad \gamma(x_\mu) = \mu; \quad \gamma(x_\nu) = \nu.$$

For each α in the set

$$A^* := \{\underline{\alpha}^m \mid m = 1, 2, \ldots\} \cup \{\overline{\alpha}^m \mid m = 1, 2, \ldots\}$$

the transition probabilities at the chance node n_1 are given by:

$$\pi^\alpha(x_\lambda|n_1) = \alpha; \quad \pi^\alpha(x_\nu|n_1) = 1 - \alpha.$$

Because $A^* \subset (0, 1)$, the common tree structure is valid for all $\alpha \in A^*$, without any need to prune off either of the terminal nodes x_λ or x_ν. Note that for each tree T in the set

$$\{\underline{T}^m \mid m = 1, 2, \ldots\} \cup \{\overline{T}^m \mid m = 1, 2, \ldots\}$$

one has $F(T, x_\rho) = \{\rho\}$ for all $\rho \in \{\lambda, \mu, \nu\}$. It follows that

$$F(T, n_1) = \alpha\{\lambda\} + (1 - \alpha)\{\nu\} = \{\alpha\lambda + (1 - \alpha)\nu\};$$
$$F(T) = F(T, n_0) = F(T, n_1) \cup \{\mu\} = \{\alpha\lambda + (1 - \alpha)\nu, \mu\}.$$

Together with (7.2), the construction of the two sequences $\underline{\alpha}^m, \overline{\alpha}^m$ obviously implies that

$$\beta(\underline{T}^m, n_0) = \{x_\mu\}; \quad \beta(\overline{T}^m, n_0) = \{n_1\}.$$

Evidently, applying condition (CB) to the particular tree T^* with limiting probability $\alpha^* \in (0, 1)$ gives $\beta(T^*, n_0) = \{x_\mu, n_1\}$. Therefore $\alpha^* \in \underline{A} \cap \overline{A}$. It follows that $\underline{A} = [0, \alpha^*]$ and that $\overline{A} = [\alpha^*, 1]$. In particular, the two sets $\underline{A}$ and $\overline{A}$ are both closed, as condition (C*) requires. ∎

7.2 Dynamic Programming and Continuous Behaviour

Let $v : Y \to \mathbb{R}$ be any NMUF. For each $\lambda \in \Delta(Y)$, let $U(\lambda) := \sum_{y \in Y} \lambda(y) v(y)$ denote the expected value of v. Let T be any finite decision tree. Then the node valuation function $w(T, \cdot) : N \to \mathbb{R}$ is calculated by backward recursion, starting with terminal nodes $x \in X$ where $w(T, x) := U(\gamma(x))$. When $n \in N^*$ is a decision node, define

$$w(T, n) := \max_{n'} \{w(T, n') \mid n' \in N_{+1}(n)\},$$

and when $n \in N^0$ is a chance node, define

$$w(T, n) := \sum_{n' \in N_{+1}(n)} \pi(n'|n)\, w(T, n').$$

Evidently, given the continuation subtree $T(n)$ with initial node $n \in N$, the construction by backward recursion ensures that $w(T(n), n') = w(T, n')$ whenever n' is a node of $T(n)$.

An obvious implication of the constructions (6.7) and of Lemma 6.1 is that, if β is behaviour which maximizes expected utility $U(\lambda)$, then

$$\emptyset \neq \beta(T, n) \subset \arg\max_{n'} \{\, w(T, n') \mid n' \in N_{+1}(n) \,\} \tag{7.3}$$

at any decision node $n \in N^*$. Also, at any node $n \in N$, one has

$$\left.\begin{aligned} \Phi_\beta(T, n) &= \arg \\ w(T, n) &= \end{aligned}\right\} \max_\lambda \{\, U(\lambda) \mid \lambda \in F(T, n) \,\}. \tag{7.4}$$

Both these statements can easily be verified by backward induction.

Note that (7.3) and (7.4) together constitute the *principle of optimality* in dynamic programming, stating that an optimal policy at each decision node is to choose an immediately succeeding node in order to maximize the node valuation function. The only difference from the standard theory is that the word "node" has replaced "state".

Now one can prove:

LEMMA 7.2 Suppose that $v : Y \to \mathbb{R}$ is any NMUF. Then there exists behaviour β that maximizes the expected value of v in each finite decision tree T of the almost unrestricted domain $\mathcal{T}(Y)$, and also satisfies condition (CB).

PROOF Let T^m ($m = 1, 2, \dots$) be any infinite sequence of finite decision trees in $\mathcal{T}(Y)$ that are all identical except for the positive probabilities $\pi^m(n'|n)$ at each chance node $n \in N^0$. Suppose that $\pi^m(n'|n) \to \bar\pi(n'|n)$ as $m \to \infty$ for all $n' \in N_{+1}(n)$ at any chance node $n \in N^0$. Let $\bar T$ denote the limit tree, as defined in Section 7.1, with set of nodes $\bar N$ after eliminating those that can be reached only with zero probability. Also, let $\bar T(n)$ denote the corresponding limit of the subtrees $T^m(n)$, rather than the continuation subtree of $\bar T$ that starts from initial node n. The difference is that the limit $\bar T(n)$ is well defined even at those nodes $n \in N \setminus \bar N$ that can only be reached with zero probability in $\bar T$. When $n \in N^0$ is any chance node, note that

$$\bar N_{+1}(n) = \{\, n' \in N_{+1}(n) \mid \bar\pi(n'|n) > 0 \,\}.$$

First it will be confirmed by backward induction that:

INDUCTION HYPOTHESIS (H): At all nodes $n \in N$ of each tree T^m, one has:

(a) (Upper Hemi-continuity) Every sequence satisfying $\lambda^m \in F(T^m, n)$ $(m = 1, 2, \ldots)$ has a convergent subsequence, and the limit λ of any convergent subsequence satisfies $\lambda \in F(\bar{T}(n), n)$.

(b) (Lower Hemi-continuity) Any $\lambda \in F(\bar{T}(n), n)$ is the limit of a sequence satisfying $\lambda^m \in F(T^m, n)$ $(m = 1, 2, \ldots)$.

These two properties are analogous to those required for the "maximum theorem" of Berge (1963, p. 116) or Hildenbrand (1974, p. 29). Note first that (H) is trivially true at any terminal node $x \in X$, where $F(T^m, x) = F(\bar{T}(x), x) = \{\gamma(x)\}$. At any $n \in N \setminus X$, assume that (H) is true at all $n' \in N_{+1}(n)$.

PROOF WHEN $n \in N^*$ IS A DECISION NODE: (a) Suppose that $\lambda^m \in F(T^m, n)$ $(m = 1, 2, \ldots)$. Then there must exist a corresponding sequence of nodes $n^m \in N_{+1}(n)$ such that $\lambda^m \in F(T^m, n^m)$ $(m = 1, 2, \ldots)$. Because $N_{+1}(n)$ is a finite set, there must exist a subsequence n^{m_k} and a limit point $\tilde{n} \in N_{+1}(n)$ such that $n^{m_k} = \tilde{n}$ for all large k. But then $\lambda^{m_k} \in F(T^{m_k}, \tilde{n})$ for all large k. Because (H) holds at $\tilde{n} \in N_{+1}(n)$, the sequence λ^{m_k} must have a convergent subsequence $\lambda^{m'_k}$, which is the required convergent subsequence of λ^m.

It follows that if λ^m converges to λ, then λ is the limit of a subsequence which, for some $\tilde{n} \in N_{+1}(n)$, satisfies $\lambda^{m_k} \in F(T^{m_k}, \tilde{n})$ $(k = 1, 2, \ldots)$. Because (H) holds at $\tilde{n} \in N_{+1}(n)$, the limit $\lambda \in F(\bar{T}(\tilde{n}), \tilde{n})$. Because n is a decision node, $\tilde{n}$ is included in $\bar{T}(n)$, implying that $F(\bar{T}(\tilde{n}), \tilde{n}) = F(\bar{T}(n), \tilde{n}) \subset F(\bar{T}(n), n)$. So $\lambda \in F(\bar{T}(n), n)$.

(b) Suppose that $\lambda \in F(\bar{T}(n), n)$. There must exist $n' \in N_{+1}(n)$ such that $\lambda \in F(\bar{T}(n), n') = F(\bar{T}(n'), n')$. By the induction hypothesis, there exists a sequence $\lambda^m \in F(T^m(n'), n') = F(T^m, n') \subset F(T^m, n)$ $(m = 1, 2, \ldots)$ such that $\lambda^m \to \lambda$ as $m \to \infty$, as required.

PROOF WHEN $n \in N^0$ IS A CHANCE NODE: (a) Suppose that $\lambda^m \in F(T^m, n)$ $(m = 1, 2, \ldots)$. Then

$$\lambda^m = \sum_{n' \in N_{+1}(n)} \pi^m(n'|n)\, \lambda^m(n'),$$

where $\lambda^m(n') \in F(T^m, n')$ for each $n' \in N_{+1}(n)$. Because (H) holds at each $n' \in N_{+1}(n)$, the finite list of sequences $\langle \lambda^m(n') \rangle_{n' \in N_{+1}(n)}$ has a convergent subsequence $\langle \lambda^{m_k}(n') \rangle_{n' \in N_{+1}(n)}$ $(k = 1, 2, \ldots)$. But then the corresponding subsequence

$$\lambda^{m_k} = \sum_{n' \in N_{+1}(n)} \pi^{m_k}(n'|n) \lambda^{m_k}(n') \ (k = 1, 2, \ldots) \tag{7.5}$$

also converges. Denote the limit of $\langle \lambda^{m_k}(n') \rangle_{n' \in N_{+1}(n)}$ by $\langle \lambda(n') \rangle_{n' \in N_{+1}(n)}$. Because (H) holds at each $n' \in N_{+1}(n)$, each limit $\lambda(n') \in F(\bar{T}(n'), n')$. Now, if λ^m converges to λ, of course $\lambda^{m_k} \to \lambda$ as $k \to \infty$. Then, taking the limit of (7.5) as $k \to \infty$ gives

$$\lambda = \sum_{n' \in N_{+1}(n)} \bar{\pi}(n'|n) \lambda(n').$$

Furthermore, whenever $\bar{\pi}(n'|n) > 0$, then n' is included in $\bar{T}(n)$, implying that $n' \in \bar{N}_{+1}(n)$. Hence,

$$\lambda = \sum_{n' \in \bar{N}_{+1}(n)} \bar{\pi}(n'|n) \lambda(n'),$$

which confirms that $\lambda \in F(\bar{T}(n), n)$.

(b) Suppose that $\lambda \in F(\bar{T}(n), n)$. Then

$$\lambda = \sum_{n' \in \bar{N}_{+1}(n)} \bar{\pi}(n'|n) \lambda(n'),$$

where $\lambda(n') \in F(\bar{T}(n), n')$ for each $n' \in \bar{N}_{+1}(n)$. Because (H) holds at each $n' \in \bar{N}_{+1}(n)$, there exists a sequence $\lambda^m(n') \in F(T^m(n'), n')$ $(m = 1, 2, \ldots)$ such that $\lambda^m \to \lambda$ as $m \to \infty$. For each $n' \in N_{+1}(n) \setminus \bar{N}_{+1}(n)$, choose $\lambda^m(n') \in F(T^m(n'), n')$ arbitrarily. Then

$$\lambda^m = \sum_{n' \in N_{+1}(n)} \pi^m(n'|n) \lambda^m(n') \in F(T^m, n) \ (m = 1, 2, \ldots).$$

Also, because $\bar{\pi}(n'|n) = 0$ for all $n' \in N_{+1}(n) \setminus \bar{N}_{+1}(n)$, one has

$$\lambda^m \to \sum_{n' \in N_{+1}(n)} \bar{\pi}(n'|n) \lambda(n') = \sum_{n' \in \bar{N}_{+1}(n)} \bar{\pi}(n'|n) \lambda(n') = \lambda \text{ as } m \to \infty.$$

This completes the proof of (H) by induction. ∎

Next, consider the behaviour β^* defined by (6.7) for all finite decision trees $T \in \mathcal{T}(Y)$ and all decision nodes $n \in N^*$. This behaviour is evidently consequentialist and dynamically consistent. Suppose that n is a decision node of $\bar{T}$, and also that $n^m \in \beta^*(T^m, n)$ $(m = 1, 2, \ldots)$. Because $N_{+1}(n)$ is finite, there exists a subsequence $n^{m_k} \in \beta^*(T^{m_k}, n)$ and $\tilde{n} \in N_{+1}(n)$ such that $n^{m_k} = \tilde{n}$ $(k = 1, 2, \ldots)$. By definition (6.7), there exists a corresponding sequence satisfying $\lambda^k \in F(T^{m_k}, \tilde{n}) \cap \Psi(T^{m_k}, n)$, where $\Psi(T^{m_k}, n)$ is defined by (6.5). Because (H) is true at $\tilde{n}$, there is a convergent subsequence λ^{k_r} $(r = 1, 2, \ldots)$ with limit $\lambda \in F(\bar{T}(n), \tilde{n})$. Let μ be any other lottery in $F(\bar{T}(n), n)$. Because (H) is true at $\tilde{n}$, there is a sequence $\mu^m \in F(T^m, n)$ $(m = 1, 2, \ldots)$ such that $\mu^m \to \mu$ as $m \to \infty$. Then $\lambda^k \in \Psi_\beta(T^{m_k}, n)$ implies that $U(\lambda^k) \geq U(\mu^{m_k})$. Because $U(\lambda)$ is a continuous function of the probabilities $\lambda(y)$ $(y \in Y)$, taking limits as $k \to \infty$ gives $U(\lambda) \geq U(\mu)$. Because μ is any lottery in $F(\bar{T}(n), n)$, it follows that $\lambda \in \Psi(\bar{T}(n), n)$. So $\lambda \in F(\bar{T}(n), \tilde{n}) \cap \Psi(\bar{T}(n), n)$, implying that $\tilde{n} \in \beta^*(\bar{T}(n), n)$. This verifies that β^* satisfies condition (CB), and so completes the proof of Lemma 7.2. ∎

7.3   Main Theorem

Gathering together the results of Sections 3 and 4 with Theorem 6.2 and Lemmas 7.1–7.2 gives the following theorem, which constitutes the main result of this chapter for the case of finite lotteries generated by finite decision trees.

THEOREM 7.3 (1) Let β be consequentialist behaviour satisfying dynamic consistency and continuity condition (CB) for the almost unrestricted domain $\mathcal{T}(Y)$ of finite decision trees with only positive probabilities at all chance nodes. Then there exists a unique cardinal equivalence class of NMUFs $v : Y \to \mathbb{R}$ such that β maximizes expected utility.

(2) Conversely, let $v : Y \to \mathbb{R}$ be any NMUF. Then there exists consequentialist behaviour β satisfying dynamic consistency and condition (CB) on the domain $\mathcal{T}(Y)$ with the property that the implicit preference ordering R_β is represented by the expected value of v.

8   Discrete Lotteries, Boundedness, and Dominance

8.1   Discrete Lotteries

Previous sections have considered only the space $\Delta(Y)$ of simple lotteries on the set Y of possible consequences. For such lotteries, only a finite set of consequences can have positive probability. On the other hand, a *countably infinite lottery* on Y is a mapping $\lambda : Y \to [0, 1]$ with the properties that:

(i) there is a countably infinite *support* $K = \{y_1, y_2, y_3, \ldots\} \subset Y$ of λ such that $\lambda(y) > 0$ for all $y \in K$ and $\lambda(y) = 0$ for all $y \in Y \setminus K$;

(ii) $\sum_{y \in K} \lambda(y) = \sum_{y \in Y} \lambda(y) = 1$.

A *discrete lottery* or probability distribution on Y is either simple or count-ably infinite; in other words, it satisfies (i) and (ii) above for a support K which is either finite or countably infinite. Let $\Delta^*(Y)$ denote the set of all such dis-crete lotteries. Like $\Delta(Y)$, it is convex and so a mixture space. Of course, if Y is a finite set, then $\Delta(Y) = \Delta^*(Y)$; to avoid this uninteresting case, the rest of this chapter will assume that Y is infinite.

Many of the earlier results for the space $\Delta(Y)$ of simple lotteries extend in a straightforward way to the space $\Delta^*(Y)$ of discrete lotteries. This section therefore concentrates on the differences between the results for the two spaces.

8.2   Unbounded Utility

Let $v : Y \to \mathbb{R}$ be any NMUF defined on sure consequences. Unless v is bounded, its expected value may not even be defined for some possible lotteries in $\Delta^*(Y)$. Indeed, suppose that v happens to be unbounded both above and below. Then there exists an infinite sequence of consequences y_k $(k = 1, 2, \dots)$ such that:

$$v(y_{2k-1}) \quad < \quad -4^{2k-1} - \sum_{r=1}^{2k-2} 2^{2k-1-r} |v(y_r)|;$$

$$v(y_{2k}) \quad > \quad 4^{2k} + \sum_{r=1}^{2k-1} 2^{2k-r} |v(y_r)|.$$

Consider now the countable lottery $\lambda = \sum_{r=1}^{\infty} 2^{-r} 1_{y_r} \in \Delta^*(Y)$. Its expected value, if it existed, would be the infinite sum $\sum_{r=1}^{\infty} 2^{-r} v(y_r)$. But for $k = 1, 2, \dots$ the above pair of inequalities imply that:

$$\sum_{r=1}^{2k-1} 2^{-r} v(y_r) \leq \sum_{r=1}^{2k-2} 2^{-r} |v(y_r)| + 2^{1-2k} v(y_{2k-1}) < -2^{2k-1};$$

$$\sum_{r=1}^{2k} 2^{-r} v(y_r) \geq -\sum_{r=1}^{2k-1} 2^{-r} |v(y_r)| + 2^{-2k} v(y_{2k}) > 2^{2k}.$$

It follows that $\sum_{r=1}^{n} 2^{-r} v(y_r)$ has no limit as $n \to \infty$, and so the expected value of v w.r.t. λ is undefined.

Even if v is bounded below, but unbounded above, there is still a problem in applying the EU hypothesis to the whole of $\Delta^*(Y)$. This is the point of Menger's (1934) generalization of the St. Petersburg paradox which was briefly reviewed in Section 1. Indeed, there will be an infinite sequence of consequences $y_1', y_2', y_3', \dots$ such that $v(y_k') > 4^k$ for $k = 1, 2, \dots$. In this case, the expected utility of the lottery $\lambda' = \sum_{r=1}^{\infty} 2^{-r} 1_{y_r'} \in \Delta^*(Y)$ is $+\infty$. Moreover, for k large enough, one certainly has $v(y'_k) > v(y'_1)$. Now, if the independence axiom (I) were satisfied, then

$$\lambda'' = \tfrac{1}{2}\,1_{y'_k} + \sum_{r=2}^{\infty} 2^{-r}\,1_{y'_r} \succ \lambda' = \tfrac{1}{2}\,1_{y'_1} + \sum_{r=2}^{\infty} 2^{-r}\,1_{y'_r}.$$

Yet the expected utility of λ'' is also $+\infty$, of course. So the EU criterion fails to distinguish lotteries which, according to condition (I), should not be regarded as indifferent. Similarly if v is bounded above but unbounded below.

Consider next the upper preference set

$$A := \{\, \alpha \in [0,1] \mid \alpha\,\lambda' + (1-\alpha)1_{y'_1} \succsim 1_{y'_k} \,\}.$$

If the EU hypothesis is satisfied, this set must be the half-open interval $(0,1]$, because the expected utility of $\alpha\,\lambda' + (1-\alpha)\,1_{y'_1}$ is $+\infty$ unless $\alpha = 0$. This contradicts the continuity condition (C) because, even though $\lambda' \succ 1_{y'_k} \succ 1_{y'_1}$, there is no $\alpha'' \in (0,1)$ such that $1_{y'_k} \succ \alpha''\lambda' + (1-\alpha'')\,1_{y'_1}$. A similar contradiction arises if v is bounded above but unbounded below.

In order to avoid such difficulties in applying the EU hypothesis to $\Delta^*(Y)$, it seems natural to assume that $v : Y \to \mathbb{R}$ is bounded both above and below — i.e., that there exist $\underline{v}$ and $\overline{v}$ such that $\underline{v} \le v(y) \le \overline{v}$ for all $y \in Y$. Call this the **boundedness condition** (B). Amongst other implications, this will rule out the St. Petersburg paradox — either as originally stated, or in the generalized form due to Menger (1934). Of course, if any one NMUF is bounded, so is any cardinally equivalent NMUF.

However, unlike the three earlier implications of the EU hypothesis — namely conditions (O), (I), (C) and their variants — condition (B) has not been directly expressed in terms of preferences. Yet it can be. Indeed, in combination with conditions (O), (I), and (C), condition (B) is evidently satisfied iff, for all fixed consequences $b,c \in Y$ with $b \succ c$, the constant MRS given by the ratio $[v(a)-v(c)]/[v(b)-v(c)]$ of utility differences, as defined in (2.5) of Section 2.3, is bounded both above and below as a function of $a \in Y$. This is the *bounded preferences* condition. In the following, however, condition (B) will be assumed directly.

Now recall how Section 3 showed that, applied to the space $\Delta(Y)$, the EU hypothesis implies the three conditions (O), (I*) and (C*). Of course, the same three properties should be implications of the EU hypothesis applied to $\Delta^*(Y)$. But, as has just been shown, there are some difficulties with these properties unless utility is bounded (or unless the EU hypothesis is restricted to lotteries in $\Delta^*(Y)$ whose expected utility is finite). It will turn out too that boundedness entails an additional dominance condition. In this sense, the EU hypothesis can have other implications when applied to the whole of $\Delta^*(Y)$.

Conversely, Section 4 showed that the three conditions (O), (I) and (C) imply the EU hypothesis for the whole of $\Delta(Y)$. But for $\Delta^*(Y)$, even the stronger conditions (O), (I*) and (C*), without any extra assumptions, imply only a weakened version of the EU hypothesis. One possibility is that the preference ordering $\succsim$ is represented by a utility function U defined on the whole of $\Delta^*(Y)$. But then any $\lambda \in \Delta^*(Y) \setminus \Delta(Y)$ is an infinite probability mixture, so the (MP) property cannot be applied to the infinite sum $\lambda = \sum_{y \in Y} \lambda(y) \, 1_y$ in order to argue that $U(\lambda) = \sum_{y \in Y} \lambda(y) \, v(y)$. In other words, the EU hypothesis may not extend to the whole of $\Delta^*(Y)$. A rather complicated example to show this possibility, relying on Zorn's lemma or the equivalent axiom of choice, is provided by Fishburn (1970, pp. 141–2); it seems that no simple example exists.

Alternatively, a second possibility is that only on a convex subset of $\Delta^*(Y)$ which includes $\Delta(Y)$ can $\succsim$ be represented by a utility function U satisfying the mixture preservation property (MP). But then U may not be defined on the whole of $\Delta^*(Y)$. For example, if the NMUF $v : Y \to \mathbb{R}$ is unbounded, one could restrict the definition of U to lotteries in $\Delta^*(Y)$ for which the expected value of v is finite. This excludes some lotteries in $\Delta^*(Y) \setminus \Delta(Y)$. For an exploration of what is then possible, see especially Wakker (1993).[12]

Instead of these two possibilities with an unbounded NMUF, I shall follow the standard literature and concentrate on the third case. This occurs when $\succsim$ is represented on the whole of $\Delta^*(Y)$ by an expected utility function satisfying $U(\lambda) = \sum_{y \in Y} \lambda(y) \, v(y)$ for all $\lambda = \sum_{y \in Y} \lambda(y) \, 1_y$ in $\Delta^*(Y)$, where $v(y) = U(1_y)$ for all $y \in Y$. Moreover, assume that condition (I) is satisfied throughout $\Delta^*(Y)$. Then the arguments above establish that the NMUF $v : Y \to \mathbb{R}$ must be bounded.

8.3   Bounded Expected Utility

The utility function $U : \Delta^*(Y) \to \mathbb{R}$ is said to satisfy the **countable mixture preservation property** (MP*) if, whenever $\lambda_i \in \Delta^*(Y)$ and $\alpha_i \geq 0$ ($i = 1, 2, \dots$) with $\sum_{i=1}^{\infty} \alpha_i = 1$, then

$$U\left(\sum_{i=1}^{\infty} \alpha_i \lambda_i \right) = \sum_{i=1}^{\infty} \alpha_i U(\lambda_i). \tag{8.1}$$

LEMMA 8.1 Suppose that the function $v : Y \to \mathbb{R}$ is bounded. Then the expected value $U(\lambda) := \sum_{y \in Y} \lambda(y) \, v(y)$ of v w.r.t. each $\lambda \in \Delta(Y)$ defines a bounded utility function $U : \Delta^*(Y) \to \mathbb{R}$ satisfying (MP*).

---

[12]See also Wakker (1989, Ch. V) for more on unbounded expected utility where there are uncertain states of the world.

PROOF Suppose that $\bar{v}$ and $\underline{v}$ are respectively upper and lower bounds for v on Y. Now, given any $\lambda = \sum_{r=1}^{\infty} \lambda(y_r) 1_{y_r} \in \Delta^*(Y)$, it must be true that $\sum_{r=1}^{\infty} \lambda(y_r) = 1$, so $\sum_{r=k}^{\infty} \lambda(y_r) \to 0$ as $k \to \infty$. But then

$$\sum_{r=k}^{\infty} \lambda(y_r)\,\underline{v} \leq \sum_{r=k}^{\infty} \lambda(y_r)\,v(y_r) \leq \sum_{r=k}^{\infty} \lambda(y_r)\,\bar{v},$$

and so $\sum_{r=k}^{\infty} \lambda(y_r)\,v(y_r) \to 0$ as $k \to \infty$. It follows that the infinite series $\sum_{r=1}^{\infty} \lambda(y_r)\,v(y_r)$ converges. So the utility function

$$U(\lambda) := \sum_{r=1}^{\infty} \lambda(y_r)\,v(y_r) = \sum_{y \in Y} \lambda(y)\,v(y)$$

is well defined for any $\lambda \in \Delta^*(Y)$. Of course, it must also satisfy (MP) and the inequalities $\underline{v} \leq U(\lambda) \leq \bar{v}$ for all $\lambda \in \Delta^*(Y)$.

Next, suppose $\lambda_i \in \Delta^*(Y)$ and $\alpha_i \geq 0$ $(i = 1, 2, \ldots)$ with $\sum_{i=1}^{\infty} \alpha_i = 1$. For $k = 1, 2, \ldots$ define $\sigma_k := \sum_{i=k+1}^{\infty} \alpha_i = 1 - \sum_{i=1}^{k} \alpha_i$ and $\mu_k := \sum_{i=k+1}^{\infty} (\alpha_i/\sigma_k)\,\lambda_i \in \Delta^*(Y)$. Using this notation, one can write $\sum_{i=1}^{\infty} \alpha_i \lambda_i$ as the finite mixture $\sum_{i=1}^{k} \alpha_i \lambda_i + \sigma_k \mu_k$. Because U satisfies (MP),

$$U\left(\sum_{i=1}^{\infty} \alpha_i \lambda_i\right) = \sum_{i=1}^{k} \alpha_i U(\lambda_i) + \sigma_k U(\mu_k).$$

But $\sum_{i=1}^{\infty} \alpha_i = 1$ implies that $\sigma_k \to 0$ as $k \to \infty$. Because U is bounded on $\Delta^*(Y)$, one has $\sigma_k U(\mu_k) \to 0$, and so (8.1) follows. ∎

Now, by repeating the arguments of Section 3, it is easy to show that when condition (B) is satisfied, then the EU hypothesis really does imply conditions (O), (I*), and (C*) on the whole of $\Delta^*(Y)$.

8.4 Dominance

Another important implication of the EU hypothesis, applied to the whole of $\Delta^*(Y)$, is the **dominance condition** (D) stating that, whenever $\lambda_i, \mu_i \in \Delta^*(Y)$ and $\alpha_i > 0$ with $\lambda_i \succsim \mu_i$ $(i = 1, 2, \ldots)$ and $\sum_{i=1}^{\infty} \alpha_i = 1$, then $\sum_{i=1}^{\infty} \alpha_i \lambda_i \succsim \sum_{i=1}^{\infty} \alpha_i \mu_i$. The **strong dominance condition** (D*) requires strict preference if in addition $\lambda_i \succ \mu_i$ for some i. Condition (D*) was originally formulated by Blackwell and Girshick (1954, p. 105, H_1). It is a natural extension of the finite dominance condition (FD*) discussed in Section 3.2. The following result shows when (D*) is a necessary condition.

LEMMA 8.2 Suppose that the EU hypothesis is satisfied on $\Delta^*(Y)$, and that any NMUF $v : Y \to \mathbb{R}$ is bounded. Then condition (D*) is satisfied.

PROOF Suppose $U(\lambda_i) \geq U(\mu_i)$ and $\alpha_i > 0$ for $i = 1, 2, \ldots$ with $\sum_{i=1}^{\infty} \alpha_i = 1$. Because of Lemma 8.1, the hypotheses imply that (MP*) is satisfied. Hence

$$ U \left(\sum_{i=1}^{\infty} \alpha_i \lambda_i \right) - U \left(\sum_{i=1}^{\infty} \alpha_i \mu_i \right) = \sum_{i=1}^{\infty} \alpha_i \left[U(\lambda_i) - U(\mu_i) \right] \geq 0 $$

with strict inequality if $U(\lambda_i) > U(\mu_i)$ for some i. ∎

Condition (D) evidently implies the following property. Suppose that $\lambda, \mu \in \Delta^*(Y)$ satisfy $\mu(\{ y \in Y \mid 1_y \succsim \lambda \}) = 1$. Then $\mu = \sum_{i=1}^{\infty} \mu(y_i) 1_{y_i}$ where the support of the distribution μ is the set $\{ y_1, y_2, \ldots \}$, and where $1_{y_i} \succsim \lambda$ for $i = 1, 2, \ldots$. Because $\lambda = \sum_{i=1}^{\infty} \mu(y_i) \lambda$, condition (D) implies that $\mu \succsim \lambda$. Similarly, if $\mu(\{ y \in Y \mid 1_y \precsim \lambda \}) = 1$, then $\mu \precsim \lambda$. A related property for probability measures is the probability dominance condition (PD) used in Section 9.2.

8.5 Sufficient Conditions for the EU Hypothesis

It can now be proved that when conditions (O), (I), (C) and (D) apply to the whole of $\Delta^*(Y)$, they are jointly sufficient for the EU hypothesis to hold on $\Delta^*(Y)$, as are conditions (O), (I), (C) and (B). In fact, it will turn out that conditions (B) and (D) are logically equivalent in the presence of the other three. As remarked in Section 8.1, however, the EU hypothesis on the whole of $\Delta^*(Y)$ does not follow from conditions (O), (I) and (C) alone.

LEMMA 8.3 Conditions (O), (I), (C) and (B) imply that there exists a unique cardinal equivalence class of expected utility functions $U : \Delta^*(Y) \to \mathbb{R}$ which represent $\succsim$ and satisfy (MP*) on the whole of $\Delta^*(Y)$.

PROOF Note that Lemma 4.7 is true of the space $\Delta^*(Y)$. So conditions (O), (I), and (C) imply that there exists an expected utility function $U : \Delta^*(Y) \to \mathbb{R}$ which represents $\succsim$ and satisfies (MP) on $\Delta^*(Y)$. Define $v : Y \to \mathbb{R}$ by $v(y) := U(1_y)$ for all $y \in Y$. By condition (B), the function v is bounded. So Lemma 8.1 implies that the function U satisfies (MP*) and is given by $U(\lambda) = \sum_{y \in Y} \lambda(y) v(y)$ for all $\lambda \in \Delta^*(Y)$. ∎

LEMMA 8.4 Conditions (O), (I), (C), and (D) together imply condition (B).

PROOF Let $U : \Delta^*(Y) \to \mathbb{R}$ be the expected utility function and $v : Y \to \mathbb{R}$ the NMUF constructed in the proof of Lemma 8.3. The result here will be proved by showing that when condition (B) is violated, so is condition (D).

Suppose condition (B) is violated because v is unbounded above. Then there exists a sequence of consequences $\langle y_i \rangle_{i=1}^{\infty}$ in Y satisfying $v(y_i) \geq \max\{v(y_1), 2^i\}$ for $i = 1, 2, \ldots$. Define $\pi_k := \sum_{i=1}^{\infty} 2^{-i} 1_{y_{k+i}} \in \Delta^*(Y)$ $(k = 0, 1, 2, \ldots)$. Then $\pi_0 = \sum_{i=1}^{k} 2^{-i} 1_{y_i} + 2^{-k} \pi_k$, so property (MP) implies that $U(\pi_0) = \sum_{i=1}^{k} 2^{-i} v(y_i) + 2^{-k} U(\pi_k)$. Because $v(y_i) \geq 2^i$ for $i = 1, 2, \ldots$ it follows that

$$U(\pi_k) = 2^k \left[U(\pi_0) - \sum_{i=1}^{k} 2^{-i} v(y_i) \right] \leq 2^k [U(\pi_0) - k] < v(y_1)$$

for large k, so $1_{y_1} \succ \pi_k$. Yet $v(y_i) \geq v(y_1)$ and so $1_{y_i} \succsim 1_{y_1}$ for $i = 1, 2, \ldots$. Because $\pi_k(\{y \in Y \mid 1_y \succsim 1_{y_1}\}) = 1$, this shows that condition (D) is violated. The proof when v is unbounded below is similar. ∎

8.6 Continuity

In order to state a continuity condition for preferences on $\Delta^*(Y)$, this space must first be given a topology. In fact, it will be given a metric. To do so, given any pair $\lambda, \mu \in \Delta^*(Y)$, consider the sum defined by

$$d(\lambda, \mu) := \sum_{y \in Y} |\lambda(y) - \mu(y)|.$$

Observe first that this sum of non-negative terms always converges because

$$d(\lambda, \mu) \leq \sum_{y \in Y} [|\lambda(y)| + |\mu(y)|] = \sum_{y \in Y} [\lambda(y) + \mu(y)] = 2.$$

Then d is a metric on $\Delta^*(Y)$ because it satisfies the three conditions:

(i) $d(\lambda, \mu) = 0 \iff \lambda = \mu$; (ii) $d(\lambda, \mu) = d(\mu, \lambda)$; (iii) $d(\lambda, \mu) + d(\mu, \nu) \leq d(\lambda, \nu)$

for all $\lambda, \mu, \nu \in \Delta^*(Y)$. Furthermore,

$$d(\lambda, \mu) = \max_f \{ |\mathbb{E}_\lambda f - \mathbb{E}_\mu f| \ | \ \forall y \in Y : |f(y)| \leq 1 \},$$

because the maximum is attained by choosing $f(y) = \text{sign}(\lambda(y) - \mu(y))$ for all $y \in Y$. It follows that the infinite sequence $\langle \lambda^n \rangle_{n=1}^{\infty}$ in $\Delta^*(Y)$ converges to λ iff $\mathbb{E}_{\lambda^n} f = \sum_y \lambda^n(y) f(y)$ converges to $\mathbb{E}_\lambda f$ for every bounded function $f : Y \to \mathbb{R}$. This implies that the expectation $\mathbb{E}_\lambda f$ of any bounded function f is continuous w.r.t. λ on $\Delta^*(Y)$. Hence, if the EU hypothesis is satisfied and the NMUF v is bounded, then the following **continuous preference condition** (CP) is satisfied: for all $\bar{\lambda} \in \Delta^*(Y)$, the two *preference sets*

$$\{ \lambda \in \Delta^*(Y) \mid \lambda \succsim \bar{\lambda} \} \quad \text{and} \quad \{ \lambda \in \Delta^*(Y) \mid \lambda \precsim \bar{\lambda} \}$$

must both be closed in the metric topology. In particular, because of Lemmas 8.3 and 8.4, the four conditions (O), (I), (C) and (D) together imply (CP).

A converse result has (CP) replace (B) or (D) among the set of sufficient conditions for the EU hypothesis to be satisfied. This is true because of the following two Lemmas:

LEMMA 8.5 Conditions (O) and (CP) imply condition (C*).

PROOF Consider any pair $\lambda, \mu \in \Delta^*(Y)$. Define the convex hull

$$\mathrm{co}\{\lambda, \mu\} = \{\nu \in \Delta^*(Y) \mid \exists \alpha \in [0,1] : \nu = \alpha\lambda + (1-\alpha)\mu\}$$

which is evidently a closed set. Hence, the two preference sets A and B defined in Section 3.4 must both be closed, because each is the intersection of a closed preference set in $\Delta^*(Y)$ with $\mathrm{co}\{\lambda, \mu\}$. This verifies condition (C*). ∎

LEMMA 8.6 Conditions (O), (I*) and (CP) jointly imply conditions (D) and (D*).

PROOF Suppose that $\lambda^* = \sum_{i=1}^{\infty} \alpha_i \lambda_i$ and $\mu^* = \sum_{i=1}^{\infty} \alpha_i \mu_i$, where $\lambda_i, \mu_i \in \Delta^*(Y)$ and $\alpha_i > 0$ with $\lambda_i \succsim \mu_i$ $(i = 1, 2, \dots)$ and $\sum_{i=1}^{\infty} \alpha_i = 1$. Define the two sequences

$$\lambda^k := \sum_{i=1}^{k} \alpha_i \lambda_i + \sum_{i=k+1}^{\infty} \alpha_i \mu_i \in \Delta^*(Y);$$

$$\nu^k := (1 - \alpha_k)^{-1} \left(\sum_{i=1}^{k-1} \alpha_i \lambda_i + \sum_{i=k+1}^{\infty} \alpha_i \mu_i \right) \in \Delta^*(Y);$$

for $k = 1, 2, \dots$, with $\lambda^0 := \mu^*$. Note that $\lambda^k = \alpha_k \lambda_k + (1 - \alpha_k)\nu^k$ whereas $\lambda^{k-1} = \alpha_k \mu_k + (1 - \alpha_k)\nu^k$. Because $\lambda_k \succsim \mu_k$, condition (I*) implies that $\lambda^k \succsim \lambda^{k-1}$ $(k = 1, 2, \dots)$. In particular $\lambda^k \succsim \mu^*$ because $\succsim$ is transitive and $\lambda^0 := \mu^*$. Also, if $\lambda_j \succ \mu_j$ for any j, then condition (I*) implies that $\lambda^k \succsim \lambda^j \succ \lambda^{j-1} \succsim \mu^*$ for all $k \geq j$.

Note too that $\lambda^k(y) - \lambda^*(y) = \sum_{i=k+1}^{\infty} \alpha_i [\lambda_i(y) - \mu_i(y)]$, so

$$d(\lambda^k, \lambda^*) = \sum_{y \in Y} \left| \sum_{i=k+1}^{\infty} \alpha_i [\lambda_i(y) - \mu_i(y)] \right|$$

$$\leq \sum_{i=k+1}^{\infty} \alpha_i \sum_{y \in Y} |\lambda_i(y) - \mu_i(y)|$$

$$= \sum_{i=k+1}^{\infty} \alpha_i \, d(\lambda_i, \mu_i) \leq 2 \sum_{i=k+1}^{\infty} \alpha_i \to 0,$$

because $d(\lambda_i, \mu_i) \leq 2$ and $\sum_{i=1}^{\infty} \alpha_i = 1$. This shows that $\lambda^k \to \lambda^*$ as $k \to \infty$. Because $\lambda^k \succsim \lambda^j$ whenever $k \geq j$, condition (CP) implies that $\lambda^* \succsim \lambda^j \succsim \mu^*$. And if $\lambda_j \succ \mu_j$ for any j, then $\lambda^* \succsim \lambda^j \succ \lambda^{j-1} \succsim \mu^*$, which confirms condition (D*). ∎

The following summarizes the previous results in this section:

THEOREM 8.7 (1) All six conditions (O), (I*), (C*), (B), (D*) and (CP) are necessary if the EU hypothesis is to hold on the whole of $\Delta^*(Y)$, without any violations of either condition (I) or (C).

(2) The four conditions (O), (I), (C) and (D) are sufficient for the EU hypothesis to hold on all of $\Delta^*(Y)$, with a bounded NMUF and an expected utility function that satisfies (MP*) and is continuous on the metric space $\Delta^*(Y)$. Condition (D) can be replaced by (B) in this list of sufficient conditions. Also, provided that (I) is strengthened to (I*), condition (CP) can replace both (C) and (D).

8.7 Consequentialist Motivation for Dominance

Like its close relatives the strong independence axiom (I*) and the finite dominance axiom (FD*) of Section 3.2, the important dominance conditions (D) and (D*) can also be given a consequentialist justification. Indeed, suppose that $\lambda_i, \mu_i \in \Delta^*(Y)$ and $\alpha_i > 0$ with $\lambda_i \succsim \mu_i$ $(i = 1, 2, \ldots)$ and $\sum_{i=1}^{\infty} \alpha_i = 1$. Let λ and μ denote $\sum_{i=1}^{\infty} \alpha_i \lambda_i$ and $\sum_{i=1}^{\infty} \alpha_i \mu_i$ respectively.

Let $\mathcal{N}$ denote the set of natural numbers $\{1, 2, \ldots\}$. Given any subset $J \subset \mathcal{N}$, define the lottery

$$\nu_J := \sum_{i \in J}^{\infty} \alpha_i \lambda_i + \sum_{i \in \mathcal{N} \setminus J}^{\infty} \alpha_i \mu_i \in \Delta^*(Y).$$

Suppose that ν_J were equal to λ for some $J \neq \mathcal{N}$. In this case, one would have $\sum_{i \in \mathcal{N} \setminus J} \alpha_i \lambda_i = \sum_{i \in \mathcal{N} \setminus J} \alpha_i \mu_i$. Now define $K := \mathcal{N} \setminus J$, $\alpha(J) := \sum_{i \in J} \alpha_i$, $\alpha(K) := 1 - \alpha(J)$ and $\nu := \sum_{i \in K} \alpha_i \lambda_i / \alpha(K) = \sum_{i \in K} \alpha_i \mu_i / \alpha(K)$. Then

$$\lambda = \sum_{i \in J} \alpha_i \lambda_i + \alpha(K)\nu \quad \text{and} \quad \mu = \sum_{i \in J} \alpha_i \mu_i + \alpha(K)\nu.$$

Therefore, $\sum_{i \in J} \alpha_i \lambda_i / \alpha(J) \succsim \sum_{i \in J} \alpha_i \mu_i / \alpha(J)$ would imply that $\lambda \succsim \mu$ by condition (I). So one could consider the reduced sequences λ_i, μ_i $(i \in J)$ in the following. Thus, it loses no generality to assume that $\lambda \neq \nu_J$ for any $J \subset \mathcal{N}$ with $J \neq \mathcal{N}$.

Consider now the (countably infinite) decision tree T with initial chance node n_0 at which $N_{+1}(n_0) = \{n_i \mid i = 1, 2, \ldots\}$. Moreover, each transition probability at n_0 should satisfy $\pi(n_i|n_0) = \alpha_i$. Then each node n_i is a decision node at which the agent chooses between two terminal nodes $x_{i\lambda}$ and $x_{i\mu}$. The ensuing lottery consequences in $\Delta^*(Y)$ are given by $\gamma(x_{i\lambda}) = \lambda_i$ and $\gamma(x_{i\mu}) = \mu_i$ $(i = 1, 2, \dots)$ respectively. A typical branch of this tree is represented in Figure 8.1.

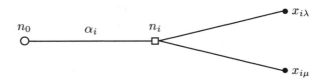

Figure 8.1 One Typical Tree Branch

Because $\lambda_i \succsim \mu_i$, at each decision node n_i $(i = 1, 2, \dots)$ of the tree T it must be true that $\lambda_i \in \Phi_\beta(T, n_i)$ and so $x_{i\lambda} \in \beta(T, n_i)$. But then

$$\lambda \in \Phi_\beta(T) = \Phi_\beta(T, n_0) = \sum_{i=1}^{\infty} \alpha_i \, \Phi_\beta(T, n_i).$$

Also $F(T, n_i) := \{\, \lambda_i, \mu_i \,\}$ for $i = 1, 2, \dots$ and so

$$F(T) = F(T, n_0) = \sum_{i=1}^{\infty} \alpha_i \, F(T, n_i) = \sum_{i=1}^{\infty} \alpha_i \, \{\, \lambda_i, \mu_i \,\} = \{\, \nu_J \mid J \subset \mathcal{N} \,\}.$$

Consider also an alternative decision tree T' with initial decision node n'_0 at which the set $N_{+1}(n'_0)$ consists of a second decision node n'_1 together with terminal nodes x'_J for every proper subset $J \subset \mathcal{N}$ — i.e., for every non-empty subset J which is not equal to $\mathcal{N}$. Suppose that $\gamma(x'_J) = \nu_J$ for all such J. Suppose too that $N_{+1}(n'_1) = \{\, x'_\lambda, x'_\mu \,\}$ where $\gamma(x'_\lambda) = \lambda$ and $\gamma(x'_\mu) = \mu$. This tree is represented in Figure 8.2.

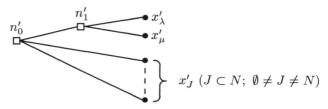

Figure 8.2 Decision Tree Illustrating Dominance

Clearly $F(T') = F(T)$, so extending the consequentialist axiom in an obvious way to the countably infinite decision trees T and T' entails $\Phi_\beta(T') = \Phi_\beta(T)$;

in particular, because $\lambda \in \Phi_\beta(T)$ it must be true that $\lambda \in \Phi_\beta(T')$. But $\nu_J = \lambda$ only if $J = \mathcal{N}$, so this requires that $x'_\lambda \in \beta(T', n'_1)$. Dynamic consistency then implies that $x'_\lambda \in \beta(T'(n'_1), n'_1)$, and so $\lambda \in \Phi_\beta(T'(n'_1), n'_1)$. But $F(T'(n'_1), n'_1) = \{\lambda, \mu\}$. Hence, the implicit preference relation must satisfy $\lambda \succsim \mu$. So condition (D) has been given a consequentialist justification, as promised.

Finally, it is evident that when combined with condition (I*), which also has a consequentialist justification, condition (D) implies condition (D*). So (D*) has a consequentialist justification as well.

9 Probability Measures

9.1 Probability Measures and Expectations

This introductory subsection is designed to remind the reader of a few essential but unavoidably technical concepts from the theory of measure and probability that are needed in order to discuss lotteries in which the range of possible outcomes is uncountable. The presentation is not intended as a substitute for a more thorough treatment of the topic such as Halmos (1950), Royden (1988), Billingsley (1995) or—perhaps more suitable for economists—Kirman (1981).

To avoid trivialities, the consequence domain Y should be an infinite set, as in Section 8. Then a σ-field on Y is a family $\mathcal{F} \subset 2^Y$ of subsets of Y such that: (i) $Y \in \mathcal{F}$; (ii) $B \in \mathcal{F}$ implies $Y \setminus B \in \mathcal{F}$; (iii) if B_i ($i = 1, 2, \ldots$) is a countable collection in $\mathcal{F}$, then $\cup_{i=1}^\infty B_i \in \mathcal{F}$.[13] The pair $(Y, \mathcal{F})$ constitutes a *measurable space*. Obviously, (i) and (ii) imply that $\emptyset \in \mathcal{F}$.

A *probability measure* on $(Y, \mathcal{F})$ is a mapping $\pi : \mathcal{F} \to [0, 1]$ satisfying $\pi(\emptyset) = 0$, $\pi(Y) = 1$, and also the *σ-additivity property* that $\pi(\cup_{i=1}^\infty B_i) = \sum_{i=1}^\infty \pi(B_i)$ whenever B_i ($i = 1, 2, \ldots$) is a countable collection of *pairwise disjoint* sets in $\mathcal{F}$. Let $\Delta(Y, \mathcal{F})$ denote the space of such measures on $(Y, \mathcal{F})$.

A function $v : Y \to \mathbb{R}$ is said to be *$\mathcal{F}$-measurable* if, given any interval $J \subset \mathbb{R}$, the set $v^{-1}(J) := \{y \in Y \mid v(y) \in J\}$ belongs to $\mathcal{F}$.

An $\mathcal{F}$-measurable *step function* $v : Y \to \mathbb{R}$ has the property that, for some finite partition $\cup_{i=1}^k Y_i$ of Y into pairwise disjoint sets $Y_i \in \mathcal{F}$, and some corresponding collection of real constants $v_i \in \mathbb{R}$ ($i = 1, 2, \ldots, k$), one has $v(y) \equiv v_i$ throughout each Y_i. It follows that $v = \sum_{i=1}^k v_i \chi_{Y_i}$, in effect, where χ_{Y_i} is the

---

[13] Royden (1988) does not impose the restriction that $Y \in \mathcal{F}$, but this is useful in probability theory. Also, note that the term σ-algebra is often used instead of σ-field. Halmos (1950) distinguishes between a σ-ring, which need not satisfy $Y \in \mathcal{F}$, and a σ-algebra, which must satisfy this condition.

particular *characteristic* step function defined by

$$\chi_{Y_i}(y) = \begin{cases} 1 & \text{if } y \in Y_i; \\ 0 & \text{otherwise.} \end{cases}$$

Let V_0 denote the set of all such step functions. Given any $v = \sum_{i=1}^{k} v_i \chi_{Y_i}$ belonging to V_0, the *expectation* $\mathbb{E}_\pi v$ of v w.r.t. any probability measure π on $(Y, \mathcal{F})$ is defined as the sum

$$\mathbb{E}_\pi v := \sum_{i=1}^{k} v_i \, \pi(Y_i).$$

A fundamental result in the theory of Lebesgue integration is that the expectation $\mathbb{E}_\pi v$ can also be well defined for *any* bounded measurable $v : Y \to \mathbb{R}$, not just for step functions. In fact, given such a general measurable function, define the "greater" and "lesser" sets of step functions as

$$V_0^+(v) := \{ v_0 \in V_0 \mid \forall y \in Y : v_0(y) \geq v(y) \};$$
$$V_0^-(v) := \{ v_0 \in V_0 \mid \forall y \in Y : v_0(y) \leq v(y) \}.$$

Then one can define

$$\mathbb{E}_\pi v := \int_Y v(y)\pi(dy) := \inf_{v_0} \{ \mathbb{E}_\pi v_0 \mid v_0 \in V_0^+(v) \} = \sup_{v_0} \{ \mathbb{E}_\pi v_0 \mid v_0 \in V_0^-(v) \}.$$
$$(9.1)$$

For a bounded function v, this definition is unambiguous if and only if there is a measurable function $\hat{v} : Y \to \mathbb{R}$ such that $\pi(\{ y \in Y \mid v(y) = \hat{v}(y) \}) = 1$. See Royden (1988, Ch. 4, Prop. 3 and proof) while recalling that Royden uses a more inclusive definition of measurability.

9.2   Necessary Conditions for EU Maximization

As in Sections 3 and 8, I shall begin by considering some key implications of the EU hypothesis. Indeed, suppose that there is a domain D of probability distributions over Y and a preference ordering $\succsim$ on D that can be represented by the expected value of some NMUF defined on Y. What properties must the space D and the ordering $\succsim$ have for such a representation to be possible?

The answer to this question hinges on the definition of "expected value". For simple probability distributions $\pi \in \Delta(Y)$ and discrete probability distributions $\pi \in \Delta^*(Y)$, the answer was unambiguous—in fact, $\mathbb{E}_\pi v = \sum_{y \in Y} \pi(y)v(y)$ for any utility function $v : Y \to \mathbb{R}$. More generally, it is natural to assume that, for some σ-field $\mathcal{F}$ on Y, the domain D is the set $\Delta(Y, \mathcal{F})$ of $\mathcal{F}$-measurable probability distributions on Y, and that $\mathbb{E}_\pi v = \int_Y v(y)\, \pi(dy)$ for all $\pi \in \Delta(Y, \mathcal{F})$. For this integral to be defined, however, the function v has to be $\mathcal{F}$-measurable.

In considering sufficient conditions for such a representation, one should not simply assume that v is $\mathcal{F}$-measurable, because v itself represents preferences. For this reason, it is better to adopt a slightly different approach. In Section 8, conditions for an ordering $\succsim^*$ on $\Delta^*(Y)$ to have an EU representation have already been given. So the most pertinent question is this: For what σ-field $\mathcal{F}$ on Y can $\succsim^*$ on $\Delta^*(Y)$ be extended to an ordering $\succsim$ that also has an EU representation on $\Delta(Y, \mathcal{F})$?

First, for the NMUF $v : Y \to \mathbb{R}$ to be $\mathcal{F}$-measurable, the set $v^{-1}(I)$ must be measurable for every interval I of the real line. This evidently implies that the sets $v^{-1}((-\infty, \alpha))$ and $v^{-1}((\alpha, \infty))$ should be measurable for every real α. In particular, this must be true whenever $\alpha = \mathbb{E}_\pi v$ for some discrete probability distribution $\pi \in \Delta^*(Y)$. Hence, the σ-field $\mathcal{F}$ has to include all upper and lower preference sets of the ordering $\succsim^*$ on $\Delta^*(Y)$. In other words, it must satisfy the **preference measurability condition** (PM) stating that, for every $\bar{\pi} \in \Delta^*(Y)$, the two *preference sets*

$$\{ y \in Y \mid 1_y \succsim \bar{\pi} \}, \quad \{ y \in Y \mid \bar{\pi} \succsim 1_y \} \tag{9.2}$$

are both members of $\mathcal{F}$.

A second desirable property of the σ-field $\mathcal{F}$ will be that $\Delta^*(Y) \subset \Delta(Y, \mathcal{F})$. Now, given any lottery $\lambda \in \Delta^*(Y)$, the probabilities $\lambda(y)$ are well-defined. So, given any $\pi \in \Delta(Y, \mathcal{F})$, it is desirable that the probabilities $\pi(\{y\})$ should be well-defined. Accordingly, the stronger **measurability condition** (M) will be imposed, requiring not only condition (PM), but also that $\{y\} \in \mathcal{F}$ for all $y \in Y$. Because $\mathcal{F}$ is a σ-field, this implies that $K \in \mathcal{F}$ for every finite or countably infinite set $K \subset Y$. So, it will be true that $\Delta^*(Y) \subset \Delta(Y, \mathcal{F})$. The implication of condition (M) is that $\mathcal{F}$ contains the smallest σ-field generated by both the singleton sets $\{y\}$ (all $y \in Y$) and the preference sets defined by (9.2).

Because $\Delta(Y, \mathcal{F})$ extends $\Delta^*(Y)$, the arguments of Section 8.2 apply *a fortiori*. So it will be assumed that condition (B) holds, otherwise the EU hypothesis is inconsistent with condition (I) and with condition (C).

Finally, another obvious necessary condition for $\succsim$ to have an EU representation is the following **probability dominance condition** (PD). This states that for every $\pi \in \Delta(Y, \mathcal{F})$ and $\lambda \in \Delta(Y)$, one has

$$\pi(\{ y \in Y \mid 1_y \succsim \lambda \}) = 1 \quad \Longrightarrow \quad \pi \succsim \lambda;$$
$$\pi(\{ y \in Y \mid 1_y \precsim \lambda \}) = 1 \quad \Longrightarrow \quad \pi \precsim \lambda.$$

Section 8.4 discusses the relationship between condition (PD) applied to $\Delta^*(Y)$ and dominance condition (D).

9.3   Sufficient Conditions for the EU Hypothesis

The main result of this Section is:

THEOREM 9.1 The six conditions (O), (I), (C), (M), (D) and (PD) are sufficient for the EU hypothesis to apply to the whole of $\Delta(Y, \mathcal{F})$.

PROOF Because $\Delta(Y, \mathcal{F})$ is a convex mixture space and conditions (O), (I), and (C) are all satisfied, Lemma 4.7 is applicable. So there exists a utility function $U : \Delta(Y, \mathcal{F}) \to \mathbb{R}$ which represents $\succsim$ and satisfies (MP). Because of (M), the set $\{y\}$ is measurable for all $y \in Y$, so $1_y \in \Delta(Y, \mathcal{F})$. Hence, one can define the NMUF $v : Y \to \mathbb{R}$ so that $v(y) := U(1_y)$ for all $y \in Y$. Because of condition (D), Theorem 8.7 implies that the EU hypothesis is satisfied on $\Delta^*(Y)$, and also that condition (B) is satisfied. So the function v is bounded both above and below. Also, U satisfies the countable mixture preservation property (MP*).

Consider next the two sets $\{y \in Y \mid v(y) \leq r\}$ and $\{y \in Y \mid v(y) \geq r\}$ for any real r. It will be shown that these two sets are $\mathcal{F}$-measurable. First, there are the two trivial cases where: either (a) $v(y) > r$ for all $y \in Y$; or (b) $v(y) < r$ for all $y \in Y$. Then $\{y \in Y \mid v(y) \leq r\}$ and $\{y \in Y \mid v(y) \geq r\}$ are respectively the empty set and the whole of Y in case (a), and *vice versa* in case (b). In either case, both are certainly measurable.

Alternatively, there exist $y_1, y_2 \in Y$ such that $v(y_1) \geq r \geq v(y_2)$. Then, because of (MP), there exists a mixture $\alpha 1_{y_1} + (1-\alpha)1_{y_2} \in \Delta(Y)$ with $0 \leq \alpha \leq 1$ such that

$$U(\alpha 1_{y_1} + (1 - \alpha)1_{y_2}) = \alpha v(y_1) + (1 - \alpha)v(y_2) = r.$$

This implies that

$$\{y \in Y \mid v(y) \leq r\} = \{y \in Y \mid 1_y \precsim \alpha 1_{y_1} + (1 - \alpha)1_{y_2}\};$$
$$\text{and} \quad \{y \in Y \mid v(y) \geq r\} = \{y \in Y \mid 1_y \succsim \alpha 1_{y_1} + (1 - \alpha)1_{y_2}\}.$$

By condition (M), both these sets are measurable. Therefore the function $v : Y \to \mathbb{R}$ is $\mathcal{F}$-measurable. Because v is bounded, it follows that the integral $\mathbb{E}_\pi v$ is well defined for every $\pi \in \Delta(Y, \mathcal{F})$. So it remains only to show that $U(\pi) \equiv \mathbb{E}_\pi v$ on $\Delta(Y, \mathcal{F})$.

As in Section 9.1, let V_0 be the set of all $\mathcal{F}$-measurable step functions — i.e., functions that can be expressed in the form $v_0 \equiv \sum_{i=1}^k v_i \chi_{Y_i}$ for some finite partition $\cup_{i=1}^k Y_i$ of Y into pairwise disjoint sets $Y_i \in \mathcal{F}$, and some corresponding collection of real constants $v_i \in \mathbb{R}$ $(i = 1, 2, \dots, k)$. Also, let $V_0^+(v)$ and $V_0^-(v)$ denote the set of all $v_0 \in V_0$ satisfying respectively $v_0(y) \geq v(y)$ and $v_0(y) \leq v(y)$ for all $y \in Y$.

Suppose that $v_0 \equiv \sum_{i=1}^{k} v_i \chi_{Y_i} \in V_0^+(v)$ is any step function which, for $i = 1$ to k, satisfies $v_0(y) = v_i \geq v(y)$ for all $y \in Y_i$, where $\cup_{i=1}^{k} Y_i$ is a partition of Y. Let y_j $(j = 1, 2, \dots)$ be any infinite sequence of consequences such that $v(y_j)$ increases strictly with j, and $v(y_j) \to \bar{v} := \sup \{ v(y) \mid y \in Y \}$ as $j \to \infty$. Define the sequence of measurable sets

$$
\begin{aligned}
Z_1 &:= \{ y \in Y \mid v(y) \leq v(y_1) \}; \\
\text{and} \quad Z_j &:= \{ y \in Y \mid v(y_{j-1}) < v(y) \leq v(y_j) \} \quad (j = 2, 3, \dots).
\end{aligned}
$$

Now, the sets $\{ Z_1, Z_2, \dots \}$ partition Y. Then the step function defined by $v^+ := \sum_{j=1}^{\infty} v(y_j) \chi_{Z_j}$ satisfies $v^+(y) = v(y_j) \geq v(y)$ for all $y \in Z_j$. Hence, $v^+(y) \geq v(y)$ for all $y \in Y$. So the function defined by $v^* := \min\{ v_0, v^+ \}$ also satisfies $v^*(y) \geq v(y)$ for all $y \in Y$. Moreover,

$$
v^* \equiv \sum_{i=1}^{k} \sum_{j=1}^{\infty} v_{ij}^* \chi_{W_{ij}}, \quad \text{where} \quad v_{ij}^* := \min\{ v_i, v(y_j) \}
$$

$$
\text{and} \quad W_{ij} := Y_i \cap Z_j \quad (i = 1, 2, \dots, k; \ j = 1, 2, \dots). \tag{9.3}
$$

Of course, whenever $W_{ij} = \emptyset$, it is understood that $\chi_{Y_i \cap Z_j}(y) = \chi_\emptyset(y) = 0$ for all $y \in Y$. Now, either $v_{ij}^* = v(y_j)$ or else $v(y) \leq v_{ij}^* = v_i < v(y_j)$ for all $y \in Y_i$. In either case, there exist $y_{ij} \in Y$ and $\alpha_{ij} \in [0, 1]$ such that $v_{ij}^* = U(\lambda_{ij}) = \alpha_{ij} v(y_{ij}) + (1 - \alpha_{ij}) v(y_j)$ where $\lambda_{ij} := \alpha_{ij} 1_{y_{ij}} + (1 - \alpha_{ij}) 1_{y_j} \in \Delta(Y)$. Therefore, for $i = 1$ to k and for $j = 1, 2, \dots$, one has

$$
v_{ij}^* = U(\lambda_{ij}) \geq v(y) \quad \text{for all } y \in W_{ij}. \tag{9.4}
$$

Now, for each variable probability measure $\pi \in \Delta(Y, \mathcal{F})$, as well as some arbitrary fixed measure $\bar{\pi} \in \Delta(Y, \mathcal{F})$, define the associated conditional probability measures $\pi_{ij} = \pi(\cdot | W_{ij}) \in \Delta(Y, \mathcal{F})$ $(i = 1$ to k and $j = 1, 2, \dots)$ by

$$
\pi_{ij}(S) := \begin{cases} \pi(S \cap W_{ij}) / \pi(W_{ij}) & \text{if } \pi(W_{ij}) > 0 \\ \bar{\pi}(S) & \text{if } \pi(W_{ij}) = 0 \end{cases} \tag{9.5}
$$

for every measurable set $S \in \mathcal{F}$. Because $\cup_{i=1}^{k} \cup_{j=1}^{\infty} W_{ij}$ is a partition of Y, it follows that $\cup_{i=1}^{k} \cup_{j=1}^{\infty} (S \cap W_{ij})$ is a partition of S. Therefore σ-additivity of π, combined with (9.5), implies that

$$
\pi(S) = \sum_{i=1}^{k} \sum_{j=1}^{\infty} \pi(S \cap W_{ij}) = \sum_{i=1}^{k} \sum_{j=1}^{\infty} \pi(W_{ij}) \pi_{ij}(S). \tag{9.6}
$$

Next, because of (9.4) and (9.5), for each pair i and j such that $\pi(W_{ij}) > 0$, it follows that $\pi_{ij}(\{\, y \in Y \mid 1_y \precsim \lambda_{ij} \,\}) = \pi_{ij}(W_{ij}) = 1$. Therefore the probability dominance condition (PD) implies that, whenever $\pi(W_{ij}) > 0$, then $\pi_{ij} \precsim \lambda_{ij}$, and so

$$U(\pi_{ij}) \le U(\lambda_{ij}) = v_{ij}^*, \tag{9.7}$$

because of (9.4). Also, $\cup_{j=1}^{\infty} W_{ij}$ is a partition of Y_i $(i = 1, 2, \dots, k)$, so

$$\pi(Y_i) = \sum_{j=1}^{\infty} \pi(W_{ij}). \tag{9.8}$$

Because (9.6) implies that π is the countable mixture $\sum_{i=1}^{k} \sum_{j=1}^{\infty} \pi(W_{ij}) \pi_{ij}$ of the measures π_{ij}, and because U satisfies (MP*), it follows from (9.7), (9.3), and (9.8) that

$$
\begin{aligned}
U(\pi) &= \sum_{i=1}^{k} \sum_{j=1}^{\infty} \pi(W_{ij}) \, U(\pi_{ij}) \;\le\; \sum_{i=1}^{k} \sum_{j=1}^{\infty} \pi(W_{ij}) \, v_{ij}^* \\
&\le \sum_{i=1}^{k} \sum_{j=1}^{\infty} \pi(W_{ij}) \, v_i \;=\; \sum_{i=1}^{k} \pi(Y_i) \, v_i \;=\; \mathbb{E}_\pi v_0
\end{aligned}
$$

by definition of v_0. This is true even when $\pi(W_{ij}) = 0$ for some i and j. Moreover $U(\pi) \le \mathbb{E}_\pi v_0$ holds for all $v_0 \in V_0^+(v)$, so definition (9.1) of the Lebesgue integral implies that $\mathbb{E}_\pi v \ge U(\pi)$.

Similarly, replacing U by $-U$ and v by $-v$ throughout this demonstration shows that $\mathbb{E}_\pi(-v) \ge -U(\pi)$ or $\mathbb{E}_\pi v \le U(\pi)$. This completes the proof that $U(\pi) = \mathbb{E}_\pi v$. ∎

9.4 Continuity of Expected Utility

Here, conditions for an NMUF $v : Y \to \mathbb{R}$ to be continuous will be investigated. So that continuity of v can have meaning, suppose that the consequence domain Y is a *metric space*. That is, there must be a *metric* $d : Y \times Y \to \mathbb{R}_+$ satisfying the three conditions that

(i) $d(x, y) = 0 \iff x = y$; (ii) $d(x, y) = d(y, x)$; (iii) $d(x, y) + d(y, z) \le d(x, z)$

for all $x, y, z \in Y$. Moreover, assume that Y is *separable* in the sense that there exists a countable *dense* subset $S = \{\, y_1, y_2, \dots \}$ whose closure in the metric topology is the whole space Y. That is, for any $y \in Y$, there must exist a sequence $\langle x_k \rangle_{k=1}^{\infty}$ of points in S such that $d(x_k, y) \to 0$ as $k \to \infty$. As will explained further below, the separability of Y plays an important role in ensuring that any probability measure $\pi \in \Delta(Y, \mathcal{F})$ can be approximated arbitrarily closely by a simple probability measure in $\Delta(Y)$.

Let $\mathcal{B}$ denote the *Borel σ-field* — i.e., the smallest σ-field that includes all the open sets of Y. Then $\mathcal{B}$ also includes all closed subsets of Y, and many but not all subsets that are neither open nor closed. The measurability condition (M) of Section 9.2 will now be strengthened to the **Borel measurability condition** (M*), requiring that the σ-field $\mathcal{F}$ is equal to $\mathcal{B}$. In particular, the preference sets specified by (9.2) must belong to the Borel σ-field. Of course, when they are closed sets, this condition is automatically satisfied.

For discrete lotteries in the space $\Delta^*(Y)$, Section 8.6 showed that the continuity condition (C) and dominance condition (D) could be replaced by the single continuous preference condition (CP). Here, for the space of probability measures $\Delta(Y, \mathcal{F})$, it will be shown that (C), (D) and the probability dominance condition (PD) can all be replaced by a single continuous preference condition (CP*) which strengthens (CP).

To discuss continuity of expected utility, the space $\Delta(Y, \mathcal{F})$ must also be given a topology. Following Grandmont (1972) and Hildenbrand (1974), it is customary to use the *topology of weak convergence of measures*. This extends the similar topology on $\Delta^*(Y)$ that was used in Section 8.6. Specifically, say that the sequence $\pi^n \in \Delta(Y, \mathcal{F})$ $(n = 1, 2, \dots)$ *converges weakly* to $\pi \in \Delta(Y, \mathcal{F})$ iff, for every bounded continuous function $f : Y \to \mathbb{R}$, one has $\mathbb{E}_{\pi^n} f \to \mathbb{E}_\pi f$. In this case, write $\pi^n \overset{w}{\to} \pi$. Unlike for the corresponding topology on $\Delta^*(Y)$, here the function $f : Y \to \mathbb{R}$ is required to be continuous. Properties of this topology are fully discussed in Billingsley (1968) — see also Parthasarathy (1967), Billingsley (1971), Huber (1981, ch. 2) and Kirman (1981, pp. 196–8). It turns out that $\pi^n \overset{w}{\to} \pi$ iff $\pi^n(E) \to \pi(E)$ for every set $E \in \mathcal{F}$ whose boundary bd E satisfies $\pi(\text{bd } E) = 0$. Also, that $d(y^n, y) \to 0$ in Y iff $1_{y^n} \overset{w}{\to} 1_y$ in the weak topology on $\Delta(Y, \mathcal{F})$. This implies in turn that the set $\{ 1_y \in \Delta(Y, \mathcal{F}) \mid y \in Y \}$ of degenerate lotteries is closed in the weak topology.

Suppose that the EU hypothesis is satisfied on $\Delta(Y, \mathcal{F})$ for an NMUF $v : Y \to \mathbb{R}$ which is both bounded and continuous. Then it is true by definition that the utility function $U(\pi) = \mathbb{E}_\pi v$ is continuous when $\Delta(Y, \mathcal{F})$ is given the topology of weak convergence. In particular, the induced preference ordering $\succsim$ satisfies the **continuous preference condition** (CP*) requiring that both preference sets

$$\{ \pi \in \Delta(Y, \mathcal{F}) \mid \pi \succsim \bar{\pi} \} \quad \text{and} \quad \{ \pi \in \Delta(Y, \mathcal{F}) \mid \pi \precsim \bar{\pi} \}$$

must be closed, for all $\bar{\pi} \in \Delta(Y, \mathcal{F})$.

More interesting is the converse, which includes (CP*) among a set of sufficient conditions for the EU hypothesis to be true with a continuous NMUF.

LEMMA 9.2 Condition (CP*) implies the corresponding condition (CP) for preferences restricted to $\Delta^*(Y)$.

PROOF Suppose that $\lambda^n \in \Delta^*(Y)$ $(n = 1, 2, \ldots)$ and that, as $n \to \infty$, so $\lambda^n \to \lambda$ in the topology of $\Delta^*(Y)$, as defined in Section 8.6. Then $\mathbb{E}_{\lambda^n} f \to \mathbb{E}_\lambda f$ for all bounded functions, and so for all bounded continuous functions $f : Y \to \mathbb{R}$. Therefore $\lambda^n \overset{w}{\to} \lambda$ as $n \to \infty$. So, if $\lambda^n \succsim \bar{\lambda}$ $(n = 1, 2, \ldots)$, then condition (CP*) implies that $\lambda \succsim \bar{\lambda}$. Similarly, if $\lambda^n \precsim \bar{\lambda}$ $(n = 1, 2, \ldots)$, then $\lambda \precsim \bar{\lambda}$. This confirms condition (CP). ∎

LEMMA 9.3 Conditions (O), (I*) and (CP*) together imply conditions (C*), (D) and (D*).

PROOF Immediate from Lemmas 9.2, 8.5 and 8.6. ∎

LEMMA 9.4 Conditions (O), (I*), (M*) and (CP*) together imply condition (PD).

PROOF Given any $\lambda \in \Delta(Y)$, define the two sets

$$Y^+(\lambda) := \{ y \in Y \mid 1_y \succsim \lambda \} \quad \text{and} \quad Y^-(\lambda) := \{ y \in Y \mid 1_y \precsim \lambda \}.$$

By condition (CP*), the upper weak preference set $P := \{ \mu \in \Delta(Y, \mathcal{F}) \mid \mu \succsim \lambda \}$ is closed. So therefore is $Y^+(\lambda)$, as the intersection of P with the closed set $\{ 1_y \in \Delta(Y, \mathcal{F}) \mid y \in Y \}$. A similar argument shows that $Y^-(\lambda)$ is also closed.

Let $\Delta(Y^+(\lambda), \mathcal{F})$ denote the set of probability measures in $\Delta(Y, \mathcal{F})$ satisfying $\pi(Y^+(\lambda)) = 1$, and let $\Delta(Y^+(\lambda))$ be the subset of simple probability distributions in $\Delta(Y)$.

Suppose that $\pi \in \Delta(Y^+(\lambda), \mathcal{F})$. By Parthasarathy (1967, Theorem 6.3, p. 44), the set $\Delta(Y^+(\lambda))$ is dense in $\Delta(Y^+(\lambda), \mathcal{F})$ when $\Delta(Y, \mathcal{F})$ is given the topology of weak convergence. So π is the weak limit of a sequence of simple distributions $\pi^n \in \Delta(Y^+(\lambda))$ $(n = 1, 2, \ldots)$.[14] By Lemma 3.1, condition (I*) implies (FD*), so $\pi^n \succsim \lambda$ for $n = 1, 2, \ldots$. Therefore condition (CP*) implies that $\pi \succsim \lambda$.

A similar proof shows that, if $\pi(Y^-(\lambda)) = 1$, then $\pi \precsim \lambda$. Hence, condition (PD) is satisfied. ∎

---

[14]In fact, by a trivial application of the Glivenko–Cantelli Theorem (Parthasarathy, 1967, Theorem 7.1, p. 53), for any infinite sequence $\langle y_k \rangle_{k=1}^\infty$ of independently and identically distributed random draws from the probability distribution π on Y, the associated sequence $\pi^n = n^{-1} \sum_{k=1}^n 1_{y_k} \in \Delta(Y^+(\lambda))$ $(n = 1, 2, \ldots)$ of empirical distributions converges weakly to π.

LEMMA 9.5 Conditions (O), (I*), (M*) and (CP*) together imply the EU hypothesis, with a bounded continuous NMUF.

PROOF By Theorem 9.1 together with Lemmas 9.3 and 9.4, the four conditions (O), (I*), (M) and (CP*) together imply that $\succsim$ on $\Delta(Y, \mathcal{F})$ can be represented by an expected utility function $U(\pi)$. Consider any weakly convergent sequence $\pi^n \in \Delta(Y, \mathcal{F})$ ($n = 1, 2, \ldots$) whose limit is $\bar{\pi} \in \Delta(Y, \mathcal{F})$.

Suppose first that there exists $\pi_+ \in \Delta(Y, \mathcal{F})$ for which $\pi_+ \succ \bar{\pi}$. Then (CP*) implies that, for every $\epsilon > 0$, the set

$$
\begin{aligned}
P_\epsilon \ &:= \ \{\, \pi \in \Delta(Y, \mathcal{F}) \mid \epsilon\pi_+ + (1 - \epsilon)\bar{\pi} \succ \pi \succ \bar{\pi} \,\} \\
&= \ \{\, \pi \in \Delta(Y, \mathcal{F}) \mid 0 < U(\pi) - U(\bar{\pi}) < \epsilon\,[U(\pi_+) - U(\bar{\pi})] \,\}
\end{aligned}
$$

is open. In this case there exists an integer $n_+(\epsilon)$ for which, if $n > n_+(\epsilon)$ and $\pi^n \succ \bar{\pi}$, then $\pi^n \in P_\epsilon$ and so $0 < U(\pi^n) - U(\bar{\pi}) < \epsilon\,[U(\pi_+) - U(\bar{\pi})]$.

Alternatively, suppose that there exists $\pi_- \in \Delta(Y, \mathcal{F})$ for which $\pi_- \prec \bar{\pi}$. In this case, reversing the preferences and inequalities in the argument of the previous paragraph shows that there must exist an integer $n_-(\epsilon)$ for which, if $n > n_-(\epsilon)$ and $\pi^n \prec \bar{\pi}$, then $0 > U(\pi^n) - U(\bar{\pi}) > \epsilon\,[U(\pi_-) - U(\bar{\pi})]$.

The last two paragraphs together imply that $U(\pi^n) - U(\bar{\pi}) \to 0$ as $n \to \infty$. Therefore U is continuous when $\Delta(Y, \mathcal{F})$ is given the topology of weak convergence. Also, because $y_n \to y$ as $n \to \infty$ implies that $1_{y_n} \overset{w}{\to} 1_y$, it follows that $v(y_n) = U(1_{y_n}) \to U(1_y) = v(y)$. This shows that the NMUF $v : Y \to \mathbb{R}$ is continuous. ∎

Thus, provided that conditions (I) and (M) are strengthened to (I*) and (M*) respectively, the one condition (CP*) can replace all three conditions (C), (D) and (PD) in the set of sufficient conditions listed in Theorem 9.1. Moreover, the resulting four sufficient conditions (O), (I*), (M*) and (CP*) imply the stronger conclusion that not only is the EU hypothesis satisfied for a bounded NMUF, but in fact any possible NMUF is continuous.

9.5 Consequentialism and Probability Dominance

The probability dominance condition (PD) can be given a consequentialist justification, just as condition (D) was in Section 8.7. Indeed, suppose that $\pi, \bar{\pi} \in \Delta(Y, \mathcal{F})$. Let $H \subset Y$ be any set large enough to satisfy $\pi(H) = 1$; when Y is a topological space and $\mathcal{F}$ coincides with its Borel σ-algebra, it is natural to take H as the *support* of π—i.e., the smallest closed set satisfying $\pi(H) = 1$.

Let $\pi_{|K}$ denote the conditional probability measure that is derived from π given the event K. Suppose that there existed $K \in \mathcal{F}$ with $K \subset H$ and $0 < \pi(K) < 1$ such that $\pi = \pi(K)\,\pi_{|K} + [1 - \pi(K)]\,\bar{\pi}$. Then one could replace

H by K and π by $\pi_{|K}$ in the following. Indeed, because of condition (I), proving that $\pi_{|K} \succsim \bar{\pi}$ guarantees that

$$\pi = \pi(K)\,\pi_{|K} + [1 - \pi(K)]\,\bar{\pi} \succsim \bar{\pi}.$$

Consider the following infinite decision tree T with initial chance node n_0. For each $y \in H$, suppose there exists a unique node n_y, and that $N_{+1}(n_0) = \{\, n_y \mid y \in H \,\}$. Corresponding to the σ-field $\mathcal{F}$ on Y and the set $H \subset Y$, define the collection

$$\mathcal{F}_N(H) := \{\, K_N \subset N_{+1}(n_0) \mid \exists K_Y \in \mathcal{F} : K_Y \subset H, \ K_N = \{\, n_y \mid y \in K_Y \,\} \,\}$$

It is easy to verify that $\mathcal{F}_N(H)$ is a σ-field on $N_{+1}(n_0)$. Moreover, suppose that the transition probabilities at n_0 satisfy

$$\pi(K_N|n_0) = \pi(\{\, y \in Y \mid n_y \in K_N \,\})$$

for every $K_N \in \mathcal{F}_N(H)$. Also, for each $y \in Y$, suppose that n_y is a decision node with $N_{+1}(n_y) = \{\, x_y, \bar{x}_y \,\}$, where x_y and $\bar{x}_y$ are terminal nodes whose lottery consequences are 1_y and $\bar{\pi}$ respectively. This tree is very similar to the one whose typical branch was illustrated in Figure 8.1 of Section 8.7.

Consider also a second decision tree T' with initial decision node n'_0 at which the set $N'_{+1}(n'_0)$ consists of a second decision node n'_1, together with a unique terminal node x'_K corresponding to each measurable set $K \in \mathcal{F}$ with $K \subset H$ and $0 < \pi(K) < 1$. Let $N'_{+1}(n'_1)$ consist of the two terminal nodes x'_π and $x'_{\bar{\pi}}$ whose lottery consequences are $\gamma'(x'_\pi) = \pi$ and $\gamma'(x'_{\bar{\pi}}) = \bar{\pi}$ respectively. Thus $F(T', n'_1) = \{\, \pi, \bar{\pi} \,\}$. Suppose too that, for each $K \in \mathcal{F}$ which satisfies both $K \subset H$ and $0 < \pi(K) < 1$, the lottery consequence $\gamma'(x'_K)$ at the corresponding terminal node x'_K is $\pi(K)\,\pi_{|K} + [1 - \pi(K)]\,\bar{\pi}$. This tree is very similar to the one represented in Figure 8.2 of Section 8.7.

Following the reasoning behind equation (6.1) of Section 6.2, the obvious feasible set $F(T)$ consists of all possible integrals w.r.t. π of integrable selections from the correspondence $y \mapsto F(T, n_y) = \{\, 1_y, \bar{\pi} \,\}$, defined on the domain H —see Hildenbrand (1974, p. 53). That is

$$F(T) = \int_H F(T, n_y)\,\pi(dy) = \int_H \{\, 1_y, \bar{\pi} \,\}\,\pi(dy).$$

Evidently both $F(T)$ and $F(T')$ are equal to the set

$$\{\, \pi, \bar{\pi} \,\} \cup \{\, \pi(K)\,\pi_{|K} + [1 - \pi(K)]\,\bar{\pi} \mid K \in \mathcal{F}, \ K \subset H, \ 0 < \pi(K) < 1 \,\}. \quad (9.9)$$

Suppose that $\pi(\{\, y \in Y \mid y \succsim \bar{\pi} \,\}) = 1$. Then $\pi(\{\, y \in H \mid x_y \in \beta(T, n_y) \,\}) = 1$, and so $\pi = \int_H 1_y\,\pi(dy) \in \Phi_\beta(T)$. From this and (9.9), an obvious extension of the consequentialist hypothesis to the "measurable" trees T and T' implies that $\pi \in \Phi_\beta(T')$. But, because $\pi \neq \pi(K)\,\pi_{|K} + [1 - \pi(K)]\,\bar\pi$ whenever $K \in \mathcal{F}$, $K \subset H$ and $0 < \pi(K) < 1$, this is only possible if $\pi \in \Phi_\beta(T', n_1')$. Because $\bar\pi \in F(T', n_1')$, it follows that the implicit preference ordering must satisfy $\pi \succsim \bar\pi$.

On the other hand, if $\pi(\{\,y \in Y \mid y \precsim \bar\pi\,\}) = 1$, then one has $\pi(\{\,y \in H \mid \bar x_y \in \beta(T, n_y)\,\}) = 1$, and so $\bar\pi = \int_H \bar\pi\,\pi(dy) \in \Phi_\beta(T)$. The rest of the proof is as in the previous paragraph, but with π and $\bar\pi$ interchanged.

In both cases, condition (PD) is satisfied. As promised, it has been given a consequentialist justification.

10 Summary and Concluding Remarks

In Section 2, the EU hypothesis was stated and ratios of utility differences were interpreted as marginal rates of substitution between corresponding probability shifts. Utility is then determined only up to a unique cardinal equivalence class. Thereafter, the chapter has concentrated on necessary and sufficient conditions for the EU hypothesis to be valid for lotteries on a given consequence domain Y, as well as the "consequentialist" axioms that can be used to justify some of these conditions.

For the space $\Delta(Y)$ of simple lotteries with finite support, Sections 3 and 4 showed that necessary and sufficient conditions are ordinality (O), independence (I), and continuity (C). Actually, stronger versions (I*) and (C*) of conditions (I) and (C) were shown to be necessary. These classical results are well known.

The space $\Delta^*(Y)$ of discrete lotteries that can have countably infinite support was considered in Section 8. For this space, a somewhat less well known dominance condition (D) due to Blackwell and Girshick (1954) enters the set of necessary and sufficient conditions. Furthermore, utility must be bounded. Provided that (I*) is satisfied, a continuous preference condition (CP) can replace both conditions (C) and (D).

Finally, Section 9 considered the space $\Delta(Y, \mathcal{F})$ of probability measures on the σ-field $\mathcal{F}$ of measurable sets generated by the singleton and preference subsets of Y. Here two extra conditions enter the list—the obvious measurability condition (M), and a probability dominance condition (PD) that is different from condition (D). When the consequence domain Y is a separable metric space, then provided that conditions (I) and (M) are strengthened somewhat to (I*) and (M*) respectively, it is possible to replace conditions (C), (D) and (PD) with a single continuous preference condition (CP*). Moreover, then each utility function in the unique cardinal equivalence class must be continuous.

The heart of the chapter (Sections 5, 6 and 7) considered the implications of assuming that behaviour in an (almost) unrestricted domain of decision trees could be explained by its consequences while satisfying dynamic consistency in subtrees. This assumption was expressed through three "consequentialist" axioms. These three axioms were shown to imply conditions (O) and (I). By allowing a richer domain of trees, conditions (D) and (PD) could also be given a consequentialist justification. The continuity condition (C) (or (CB)) and measurability condition (M), however, remain as supplementary mathematical hypotheses, without a consequentialist justification. All six conditions play an important role in the succeeding separate chapter on subjectively expected utility. So do the three consequentialist axioms.

When applied to decision trees, the three consequentialist axioms appear natural. Nevertheless, McClennen (1990) and Cubitt (1996) have both offered interesting decompositions of these axioms into a larger set of individually weaker axioms. Moreover, these decompositions invoke the notion of a plan which could differ from actual behaviour.

At least one open problem remains. Theorem 7.3 of Section 7.3 characterizes completely consequentialist behaviour satisfying dynamic consistency and continuity condition (CB) on an almost unrestricted domain of finite decision trees. Still lacking is a similar result for a richer domain of infinite decision trees giving rise to random consequences in the space $\Delta^*(Y)$ or $\Delta(Y, \mathcal{F})$. Indeed, beyond some results in classical decision analysis due to LaValle (1978), there appears to have been little systematic analysis of general infinite decision trees.

Acknowledgments

Work on this chapter was begun with the support of a research award from the Alexander von Humboldt Foundation. This financed a visit to Germany, especially the University of Kiel, during the academic year 1993–4. The chapter has also benefited from the extensive comments of Philippe Mongin, and the opportunity he kindly arranged to give some lectures at C.O.R.E. in February 1994. Also very helpful were the reports of two unusually careful, conscientious, and constructively critical referees, as well as discussion with Peter Wakker during the visit to C.O.R.E., and insightful comments by Mamoru Kaneko, Mark Machina and Ulrich Schmidt. Finally, Roderick Duncan's exceptional alertness during a lecture back at Stanford has saved me from at least one embarrassing error. My thanks to these while absolving them of all responsibility for remaining errors and inadequacies.

References

Allais, M. (1953). Le comportement de l'homme rationnel devant le risque: critique des postulats et des axiomes de l'école américaine. *Econometrica*,

21:503–546. Summary version of paper whose translation appeared as Allais (1979a).

Allais, M. (1979a). The Foundations of a Positive Theory of Choice Involving Risk and a Criticism of the Postulates and Axioms of the American School. In Allais, M. and Hagen, O., editors, *The Expected Utility Hypothesis and the Allais Paradox*, pages 27–145. D. Reidel, Dordrecht.

Allais, M. (1979b). The So–called Allais Paradox and Rational Decisions under Uncertainty. In Allais, M. and Hagen, O., editors, *The Expected Utility Hypothesis and the Allais Paradox*, pages 437–681. D. Reidel, Dordrecht.

Allais, M. (1987). Allais Paradox. In Eatwell, J., Milgate, M., and Newman, P., editors, *The New Palgrave: A Dictionary of Economics*, pages 3–9. Macmillan, London. Reprinted in Eatwell *et al.* (1990).

Allais, M. and Hagen, O., editors (1979). *The Expected Utility Hypothesis and the Allais Paradox*. D. Reidel, Dordrecht.

Anscombe, G. E. M. (1958). Modern Moral Philosophy. *Philosophy*, 33:1–19.

Arrow, K. J. (1951). Alternative Approaches to the Theory of Decision in Risk-Taking Situations. *Econometrica*, 19:404–437. Reprinted in Arrow (1971), ch. 1 and in Arrow (1984), ch. 2.

Arrow, K. J. (1959). Rational Choice Functions and Orderings. *Economica*, 26:121–127. Reprinted in Arrow (1984), ch. 6.

Arrow, K. J. (1963). *Social Choice and Individual Values*. Yale University Press, New Haven, 2nd edition.

Arrow, K. J. (1965). *Aspects of the Theory of Risk-Bearing*. North–Holland, Amsterdam.

Arrow, K. J. (1971). *Essays in the Theory of Risk-Bearing*. Markham/North–Holland, Chicago/Amsterdam.

Arrow, K. J. (1972). Exposition of the Theory of Choice under Uncertainty. In McGuire, C. B. and Radner, R., editors, *Decision and Organization*, chapter 2, pages 19–55. North–Holland, Amsterdam. Reprinted in Arrow (1984), chapter 10.

Arrow, K. J. (1984). *Collected Papers of Kenneth J. Arrow, Volume 3: Individual Choice under Certainty and Uncertainty*. Belknap Press of Harvard University Press, Cambridge, Mass.

Berge, C. (1959). *Espaces Topologiques, fonctions multivoques*. Dunod, Paris. Translated as *Topological Spaces*, Edinburgh, Oliver & Boyd, 1963.

Bernoulli, D. (1738). Specimen theoriae novae de mensura sortis. *Commentarii Academiae Scientiarum Imperialis Petropolitanae*. Translated by L. Sommer, (1954). Exposition of a New Theory on the Measurement of Risk, *Econometrica*, 22:23–36.

Billingsley, P. (1968). *Convergence of Probability Measures*. John Wiley, New York.

Billingsley, P. (1971). *Weak Convergence of Measures: Applications to Probability*. Society for Industrial and Applied Mathematics, Philadelphia.

Billingsley, P. (1995). *Probability and Measure*. John Wiley, New York, 3rd edition.

Blackwell, D. and Girshick, M. A. (1954). *Theory of Games and Statistical Decisions*. John Wiley, New York.

Border, K. C. (1992). Revealed Preference, Stochastic Dominance, and the Expected Utility Hypothesis. *Journal of Economic Theory*, 56:20–42.

Cramer, G. (1728). Letter to Nicholas Bernoulli. Extracts printed in Bernoulli (1738).

Cubitt, R. (1996). Rational Dynamic Choice and Expected Utility Theory. *Oxford Economic Papers*, 48:1–19.

Eatwell, J., Milgate, M., and Newman, P., editors (1987). *The New Palgrave: A Dictionary of Economics*. Macmillan, London.

Eatwell, J., Milgate, M., and Newman, P., editors (1990). *The New Palgrave: Utility and Probability*. Macmillan, London.

Fishburn, P. C. (1967). Bounded Expected Utility. *The Annals of Mathematical Statistics*, 38:1054–1060.

Fishburn, P. C. (1970). *Utility Theory for Decision Making*. John Wiley, New York.

Fishburn, P. C. (1982). *The Foundations of Expected Utility*. D. Reidel, Dordrecht.

Fishburn, P. C. (1989). Retrospective on the Utility Theory of von Neumann and Morgenstern. *Journal of Risk and Uncertainty*, 2:127–157.

Fishburn, P. C. and Wakker, P. (1995). The Invention of the Independence Condition for Preferences. *Management Science*, 41:1130–1144.

Grandmont, J.-M. (1972). Continuity Properties of a von Neumann–Morgenstern Utility. *Journal of Economic Theory*, 4:45–57.

Hacking, I. (1975). *The Emergence of Probability*. Cambridge University Press, Cambridge.

Halmos, P. R. (1950). *Measure Theory*. Van Nostrand Reinhold, New York.

Hammond, P. J. (1976). Changing Tastes and Coherent Dynamic Choice. *Review of Economic Studies*, 43:159–173.

Hammond, P. J. (1977). Dynamic Restrictions on Metastatic Choice. *Economica*, 44:337–350.

Hammond, P. J. (1983). Ex–Post Optimality as a Dynamically Consistent Objective for Collective Choice Under Uncertainty. In Pattanaik, P. K. and Salles, M., editors, *Social Choice and Welfare*, chapter 10, pages 175–205. North–Holland, Amsterdam.

Hammond, P. J. (1986). Consequentialist Social Norms for Public Decisions. In Heller, W. P., Starr, R. M., and Starrett, D. A., editors, *Social Choice and*

Public Decision Making: Essays in Honor of Kenneth J. Arrow, volume I, chapter 1, pages 3–27. Cambridge University Press, Cambridge.

Hammond, P. J. (1988a). Consequentialist Foundations for Expected Utility. *Theory and Decision*, 25:25–78.

Hammond, P. J. (1988b). Consequentialism and the Independence Axiom. In Munier, B. R., editor, *Risk, Decision and Rationality, Proceedings of the 3rd International Conference on the Foundations and Applications of Utility, Risk and Decision Theories*, pages 503–516. D. Reidel, Dordrecht.

Hammond, P. J. (1988c). Orderly Decision Theory: A Comment on Professor Seidenfeld. *Economics and Philosophy*, 4:292–297.

Hammond, P. J. (1994). Elementary Non-Archimedean Representations of Probability for Decision Theory and Games. In Humphreys, P., editor, *Patrick Suppes: Scientific Philosopher*, volume I, chapter 2, pages 25–59. Kluwer Academic Publishers, Dordrecht.

Hammond, P. J. (1996). Consequentialist Decision Theory and Utilitarian Ethics. In Farina, F., Hahn, F., and Vannucci, S., editors, *Ethics, Rationality, and Economic Behaviour*, pages 92–118. Clarendon Press, Oxford.

Hammond, P. J. (1997). Consequentialism, Non-Archimedean Probabilities, and Lexicographic Expected Utility. To appear in Bicchieri, C. and Jeffrey, R. and Skyrms, B. (eds.): *The Logic of Strategy* (Oxford: Oxford University Press).

Harsanyi, J. C. (1977). *Rational Behavior and Bargaining Equilibrium in Games and Social Situations*. Cambridge University Press, Cambridge.

Herstein, I. N. and Milnor, J. (1953). An Axiomatic Approach to Measurable Utility. *Econometrica*, 21:291–297. Reprinted in Newman (1968), pages 264–270.

Herzberger, H. G. (1973). Ordinal Preference and Rational Choice. *Econometrica*, 41:187–237.

Hildenbrand, W. (1974). *Core and Equilibria of a Large Economy*. Princeton University Press, Princeton.

Huber, P. J. (1981). *Robust Statistics*. John Wiley, New York.

Jensen, N. E. (1967). An Introduction to Bernoullian Utility Theory I: Utility Functions. *Swedish Journal of Economics*, 69:163–183.

Karni, E. and Safra, Z. (1989). Dynamic Consistency, Revelations in Auctions and the Structure of Preferences. *Review of Economic Studies*, 56:421–433.

Karni, E. and Schmeidler, D. (1991). Utility Theory with Uncertainty. In Hildenbrand, W. and Sonnenschein, H., editors, *Handbook of Mathematical Economics*, volume IV, chapter 33, pages 1763–1831. North–Holland, Amsterdam.

Kirman, A. P. (1981). Measure Theory with Applications to Economics. In Arrow, K. J. and Intriligator, M. D., editors, *Handbook of Mathematical Economics*, volume I, chapter 5, pages 159–209. North–Holland, Amsterdam.

LaValle, I. (1978). *Foundations of Decision Analysis*. Holt, Rinehart and Winston, New York.

LaValle, I. and Wapman, K. (1986). Rolling Back Decision Trees Requires the Independence Axiom! *Management Science*, 32:382–385.

Leonard, R. J. (1995). From Parlor Games to Social Science: von Neumann, Morgenstern, and the Creation of Game Theory 1928–1944. *Journal of Economic Literature*, 33:730–761.

Luce, R. D. and Raiffa, H. (1957). *Games and Decisions: Introduction and Critical Survey*. John Wiley, New York.

Machina, M. J. (1982). Expected Utility Analysis without the Independence Axiom. *Econometrica*, 50:277–323.

Machina, M. J. (1983). Generalized Expected Utility Analysis and the Nature of Observed Violations of the Independence Axiom. In Stigum, B. P. and Wenstøp, F., editors, *Foundations of Utility and Risk Theory with Applications*, pages 117–136. D. Reidel, Dordrecht. Reprinted in Gärdenfors, P. and N.-E. Sahlin, editors (1988) *Decision, Probability, and Utility*. Cambridge, Cambridge University Press, chapter 12.

Machina, M. J. (1987). Choice under Uncertainty: Problems Solved and Unsolved. *Journal of Economic Perspectives*, 1:121–154.

Machina, M. J. (1989). Dynamic Consistency and Non-Expected Utility Models of Choice Under Uncertainty. *Journal of Economic Literature*, 28:1622–1668.

Malinvaud, E. (1952). Note on von Neumann–Morgenstern's Strong Independence Axiom. *Econometrica*, 20:679. Reprinted in Newman (1968), page 271.

Marschak, J. A. (1950). Rational Behavior, Uncertain Prospects, and Measurable Utility. *Econometrica*, 18:111–141.

McClennen, E. F. (1990). *Rationality and Dynamic Choice: Foundational Explorations*. Cambridge University Press, Cambridge.

Menger, K. (1934). Das Unsicherheitsmoment in der Wertlehre, Betrachtungen im Anschluss an das sogenannte Petersburger Spiel. *Zeitschrift für Nationalökonomie*, 5:459–485. Translated under the title 'The Role of Uncertainty in Economics' in Shubik, M. (ed.) (1967) Essays in Mathematical Economics in Honor of Oskar Morgenstern (Princeton, Princeton University Press), chapter 16, pages 211–231.

Mongin, P. (1996). A Note on Mixture Sets in Decision Theory. Preprint, CORE. Université Catholique de Louvain.

Morgenstern, O. (1979). Some Reflections on Utility. In Allais, M. and Hagen, O., editors, *The Expected Utility Hypothesis and the Allais Paradox*, pages 175–183. D. Reidel, Dordrecht.

Munier, B. (1996). Comment. In Arrow, K. J., Colombatto, E., Perlman, M., and Schmidt, C., editors, *The Rational Foundations of Economic Behaviour*, pages 43–47. Macmillan, London.

Nash, J. F. (1950). The Bargaining Problem. *Econometrica*, 18:155–162.

Newman, P., editor (1968). *Readings in Mathematical Economics, Volume I: Value Theory*. Johns Hopkins Press, Baltimore.

Parthasarathy, K. R. (1967). *Probability Measures on Metric Spaces*. Academic Press, New York.

Royden, H. L. (1968). *Real Analysis*. Macmillan, New York, 2nd edition.

Samuelson, P. A. (1952). Probability, Utility and the Independence Axiom. *Econometrica*, 20:670–678.

Samuelson, P. A. (1977). St. Petersburg Paradoxes Defanged, Dissected, and Historically Described. *Journal of Economic Literature*, 15:24–55.

Samuelson, P. A. (1983). *Foundations of Economic Analysis*, Enlarged Edition. Harvard University Press, Cambridge, Mass.

Samuelson, P. A. (1988). How a Certain Internal Consistency Entails the Expected Utility Dogma. *Journal of Risk and Uncertainty*, 1:389–393.

Savage, L. J. (1954). *The Foundations of Statistics*. John Wiley, New York.

Sen, A. K. (1970). *Collective Choice and Social Welfare*. Holden–Day, San Francisco.

Shapley, L. S. (1977). The St. Petersburg Paradox: A Con Game? *Journal of Economic Theory*, 14:439–442.

Sinn, H.-W. (1983). *Economic Decisions under Uncertainty*. North–Holland, Amsterdam.

von Neumann, J. and Morgenstern, O. (1944). *Theory of Games and Economic Behavior*. Princeton University Press, Princeton. 3rd edition 1953.

Wakker, P. P. (1989). *Additive Representations of Preferences: A New Foundation of Decision Analysis*. Kluwer Academic Publishers, Dordrecht.

Wakker, P. P. (1993). Unbounded Utility for Savage's 'Foundations of Statistics', and other Models. *Mathematics of Operations Research*, 18:446–485.

Zabell, S. L. (1987). Bernoulli, Daniel (1700–1782). In Eatwell, J., Milgate, M., and Newman, P., editors, *The New Palgrave: A Dictionary of Economics*. Macmillan, London. Reprinted in Eatwell et al. (1990), pages 12–14.

6 SUBJECTIVE EXPECTED UTILITY

Peter J. Hammond

Stanford University

Contents

1	Introduction and Outline	215
2	Necessary Conditions	219
	2.1 Subjective Expected Utility Maximization	219
	2.2 Contingent Preferences and the Sure Thing Principle	219
	2.3 State Independent Preferences	221
	2.4 A Likelihood Ordering of Events	221
3	Consequentialist Foundations	222
	3.1 Decision Trees with Natural Nodes	222
	3.2 Feasible and Chosen CCFs	223
	3.3 Consequentialism and Contingent Orderings	224
	3.4 Consequentialism and the Sure Thing Principle	225
	3.5 Consequentialism Characterized	226
	3.6 Unordered Events	226
4	Anscombe and Aumann's Axioms	228
	4.1 Horse Lotteries versus Roulette Lotteries	228
	4.2 Ratios of Utility Differences	229
	4.3 Ordinality, Independence and Continuity	229
	4.4 Reversal of Order	230
	4.5 Sure Thing Principle	231
	4.6 State Independence	232
	4.7 Sufficient Conditions for the SEU and SEU* Hypotheses	233

5   Consequentialist Foundations Reconsidered   237
      5.1   Decision Trees with Both Chance and Natural Nodes   237
      5.2   Consequentialism and Contingent Utilities   238
      5.3   Consequentialist Normal Form Invariance and Condi-
             tion (RO)   239
      5.4   State Independent Consequentialism, No Null Events,
             and Continuity   240
      5.5   Sufficient Conditions for Consequentialism   241
      5.6   Dynamic Programming and Continuous Behaviour   243
      5.7   Main Theorem   244

6   State–Dependent Consequence Domains   244
      6.1   Evaluation Functions   244
      6.2   Chosen Probabilities and State–Dependent Utilities   247
      6.3   State–Independent Utilities   250

7   Countable Events   254
      7.1   Bounded Preferences   254
      7.2   Event Continuity   254
      7.3   Event Dominance   255
      7.4   Sufficient Conditions for SEU and SEU*   256

8   Subjective Probability Measures   256
      8.1   Measurable Expected Utility   256
      8.2   Sufficient Conditions for SEU and SEU*   259
      8.3   Eleven Sufficient Conditions   265

9   Summary and Conclusions   266

References   268

1   Introduction and Outline

The expected utility (EU) hypothesis was originally formulated to be used with specified or "objective" probabilities. Objectively expected utility is the subject of Chapter 5. Not all uncertainty, however, can be described by a specified or objective probability distribution. The pioneering work of Frank Ramsey (1926) and Bruno de Finetti (1937, 1949) demonstrated how, under certain assumptions, "subjective" probabilities could still be inferred from behaviour in the face of such uncertainty.[1] The task of this chapter is to set out some recent developments in this decision–theoretic approach to subjective probability, and in the closely associated theory of subjectively expected utility. As in Chapter 5, an explicitly "consequentialist" perspective will be maintained. A much more thorough survey of earlier developments can be found in Fishburn (1981) — see also Karni and Schmeidler (1991) and Fishburn (1994).

An important body of earlier work, especially that most directly inspired by Savage (1954), will not be covered here. One reason for this omission is that extensive reviews of Savage's particular approach can be found elsewhere, including Arrow (1965, 1971, 1972) and Fishburn (1970, Ch. 14). A second reason is the continuing ready and affordable accessibility of Savage's original work. A third reason is that more recent writers such as Harsanyi (1977, 1983), Myerson (1979) and Fishburn (1982) have chosen, as I do here, to derive subjective probabilities from preferences for state dependent lotteries involving objective probabilities. Of course, this latter approach was first set out in full by Anscombe and Aumann (1963), though earlier related ideas can be found in Rubin (1949), Arrow (1951), Chernoff (1954), Suppes (1956), and Ellsberg (1961).[2]

A rather better reason suggests itself, however. Following Keynes (1921), de Finetti (1937) and many others, Savage (1954, pp. 30–32) used a crucial "ordering of events" assumption in order to derive "qualitative" probabilities. This axiom is described in Section 2.4. Later these qualitative probabilities are made quantitative as a result of additional assumptions. For example, Villegas (1964) and DeGroot (1970) simply assume that, for every $p \in [0, 1]$, there exists an event whose objective probability is p. Then the ordering of events assumption implies that every event E has subjective probability equal to the objective probability of an equally likely event. For surveys of qualitative probability

---

[1] De Finetti, who founds subjective probabilities on the willingness of a risk–neutral agent to take bets, cites the earlier work by Bertrand (1889) using a similar idea. But this concept surely pre–dates Bertrand—see, for example, the original works by Hobbes (1684) and Bayes (1763), as well as the recent commentaries by Hacking (1975, especially p. 48) and Lindley (1987).

[2] Indeed, Ellsberg's "paradox" concerns violations of an extended sure thing principle that had not even been properly formulated before Anscombe and Aumann's pioneering work.

theory, see Narens (1980) and Fishburn (1986). However, in Section 3 it will be shown that without more structure such as objective probabilities, the ordering of events condition cannot be derived from the consequentialist axioms. For this reason, the consequentialist approach followed both in Chapter 5 and here does not lend support to Savage's axiom system.

Instead of objective probabilities, another approach which was pioneered by Ramsey uses a continuum of deterministic consequences and at least one even chance event—see Gul (1992) for a more modern exposition and references to other work. Here, an "even chance event" E has the property that, for all consequences y, y', the prospect of y if E occurs combined with y' if E does not occur is indifferent to the prospect of y' if E occurs combined with y if E does not occur. Thus, the events E and not E are regarded as equally likely, implying that E has a subjective probability of $\frac{1}{2}$, in effect. This condition turns out to be a significant weakening of the ordering of events assumption. In a similar way de Finetti (1937), followed by Pratt, Raiffa and Schlaifer (1964), proposed the *uniformity* axiom requiring that, for $m = 2, 3, \ldots$, there should be m equally likely events. Savage (1954, p. 33) also discusses this approach. Not surprisingly, one can then avoid postulating a continuum of deterministic consequences. Another implication of the examples in Section 3, however, is that neither do such assumptions of equally likely events have any consequentialist justification. Nevertheless, this chapter uses Anscombe and Aumann's assumption requiring objective probabilities to exist, which is in some sense a stronger form of uniformity. The view taken here is that it is more straightforward to assume directly that objective probabilities can appear in decision problems.

Finally, Wakker (1989) has a connected topological space of consequences but no even chance events. Instead, an assumption of "noncontradictory trade-offs on consequences" is used to ensure an appropriate additively separable utility function. Once again, however, the examples in Section 3 show that this assumption lacks a consequentialist justification.

Following this introduction and outline, Section 2 of the chapter presents four key conditions which are necessary for behaviour to correspond to the maximization of subjective expected utility (or SEU)—i.e., expected utility with subjective probabilities attached to events. Actually it will be convenient to distinguish two different versions of the SEU hypothesis. Whereas maximizing SEU in general allows null events whose subjective probabilities must be zero, a stronger version of the hypothesis, called SEU*, excludes null events. Thus, SEU* requires all subjective probabilities to be positive.

Of the four necessary conditions for SEU maximization, the first states that, for each non–null event, there must be a contingent preference ordering over the possible consequences of acts, in Savage's form of "state contingent consequence functions" (or CCFs). Second, these orderings must satisfy Savage's sure thing principle (STP), which is the counterpart for subjectively expected utility theory of the equally controversial independence axiom in objectively expected utility theory. In fact, when SEU* is satisfied, a stronger version of (STP), called (STP*), must hold. Third, when either the state of the world is known, or the consequence is independent of the state of the world, there must be a state independent contingent preference ordering over certain consequences. Fourth and last, preferences over CCFs must induce an ordering of events according to relative likelihood.

Section 3 turns to consequentialist foundations. So that different states of the world may occur, decision trees are allowed to include "natural nodes", at which nature refines the set of possible states. The axioms that were set out in Chapter 5 for finite decision trees are then adapted in a rather obvious way. They imply the existence of a preference ordering over CCFs satisfying (STP*). There need not be an implied ordering of events, however, nor subjective probabilities. Thus, SEU theory cannot be derived by applying consequentialism only to decision trees with natural nodes.

Next, Section 4 turns instead to the Anscombe and Aumann theory of subjective probability and subjectively expected utility. This approach is based on combinations of "horse lotteries", for which probabilities are not specified, with "roulette lotteries", for which they are. In fact, roulette lotteries involve objective probabilities, as considered in Chapter 5, and so implicitly the previously mentioned uniformity axiom must be satisfied. Anyway, a version of Anscombe and Aumann's axioms is set out, and their main theorem proved. This particular proof owes much to Fishburn (1970, Ch. 13) and also to Myerson (1991, Ch. 1).

In Section 5 the discussion returns to consequentialist analysis in decision trees, and a simplified version of the analysis set out in Hammond (1988). Corresponding to the distinction between horse and roulette lotteries, decision trees will contain "natural" nodes at which nature moves but probabilities are not specified, as opposed to chance nodes of the kind considered in Chapter 5, where "objective" probabilities are specified. It will follow that decisions give rise to lotteries over CCFs rather than to sure CCFs. The decision tree which the agent faces will induce a strategic game against both chance and nature. The consequentialist axiom is then somewhat re-formulated so that it becomes normal form invariance in this strategic game. This axiom, together with both a form of state independence and also continuity of behaviour as probabilities vary, will justify the axioms used by Anscombe and Aumann. And actually these conditions imply rather more, since it will also turn out that null events having zero subjective probability are excluded. Thus, consequentialism justifies the stronger SEU* hypothesis.

The theories of Savage and of Anscombe and Aumann both rely on the assumption that there are "constant acts" yielding the same consequence in all states of the world. More precisely, they postulate that the domain of consequences is state independent. But there is a whole class of decision problems where this hypothesis makes no sense — for instance, where there is a risk of death or serious injury. See the chapter in Volume II of this *Handbook* by Drèze and Rustichini as well as Karni (1993a, b). For such cases, Section 6 begins by finding sufficient conditions for behaviour to maximize the expectation of an evaluation function (Wilson, 1968).[3] Then it considers one possible way of deriving subjective probabilities and utilities in this case also. Moreover, the utilities will be state independent in the sense of giving equal value to any consequence that happens to occur in more than one state dependent consequence domain. The key is to consider decision trees having "hypothetical" probabilities attached to states of nature, following the suggestion of Karni, Schmeidler and Vind (1983), and even to allow hypothetical choices of these probabilities, as in Drèze (1961, 1987) and also Karni (1985).

The first part of the chapter will assume throughout that the set S of possible states of the world is finite. Section 7 considers the implications of allowing S to be countably infinite. Extra conditions of bounded utility, event continuity and event dominance are introduced. When combined with the conditions of Section 4, they are necessary and sufficient for the SEU hypothesis to hold. Necessity is obvious, whereas sufficiency follows as a special case of the results in Section 8.

Finally, Section 8 allows S to be a general measurable space, and considers measurable lotteries mapping S into objective probability measures on the consequence domain. For this domain, two more conditions were introduced in Section 9 of Chapter 5—namely measurability of singletons and of upper and lower preference sets in the consequence domain, together with probability dominance. Not surprisingly, these two join the list of necessary and sufficient conditions for the SEU hypothesis. This gives eleven conditions in all, which are summarized in a table at the end of the brief concluding Section 9. Only this last part of the chapter requires some familiarity with measure theory, and with corresponding results for objective probability measures set out in Chapter 5.

---

[3] See also Myerson (1979) for a somewhat different treatment of this issue.

2   Necessary Conditions

2.1   Subjective Expected Utility Maximization

Let Y be a fixed domain of possible *consequences*, and let S be a fixed finite set of possible *states of the world*. No probability distribution over S is specified. An *act*, according to Savage (1954), is a mapping $a : S \to Y$ specifying what consequence results in each possible state of the world. Inspired by the Arrow (1953) and Debreu (1959) device of "contingent" securities or commodities in general equilibrium theory, I shall prefer to speak instead of **contingent consequence functions**, or CCFs for short. Also, each CCF will be considered as a list $y^S = \langle y_s \rangle_{s \in S}$ of contingent consequences in the Cartesian product space $Y^S := \prod_{s \in S} Y_s$, where each set Y_s is a copy of the consequence domain Y.

The *subjective expected utility* (SEU) maximization hypothesis requires that there exist non–negative subjective or personal probabilities p_s of different states $s \in S$ satisfying $\sum_{s \in S} p_s = 1$. Also, there must be a von Neumann–Morgenstern utility function (or NMUF) $v : Y \to \mathbb{R}$, as in the objective expected utility (EU) theory considered in Chapter 5. Moreover, it is hypothesized that the agent will choose a CCF y^S from the relevant feasible set in order to maximize the *subjectively expected utility* function

$$U^S(y^S) := \sum_{s \in S} p_s \, v(y_s). \tag{2.1}$$

As in Chapter 5, the NMUF v could be replaced by any $\tilde{v}$ that is cardinally equivalent, without affecting EU maximizing behaviour. The difference from the earlier theory arises because the probabilities p_s are not objectively specified, but are revealed by the agent's behaviour. The SEU* hypothesis strengthens SEU by adding the requirement that the subjective probabilities satisfy $p_s > 0$ for all $s \in S$.

Obviously, if behaviour maximizes the utility function (2.1), there is a corresponding complete and transitive *preference ordering* $\succsim$ over the domain Y^S. This is the **ordering condition** (O). Let $\succ$ and $\sim$ respectively denote the corresponding strict preference and indifference relations. There is an uninteresting trivial case of *universal indifference* when $y^S \sim \tilde{y}^S$ for all $y^S, \tilde{y}^S \in Y^S$; in the spirit of Savage's P5 postulate, it will usually be assumed in this chapter that there exists at least one pair $\overline{y}^S, \underline{y}^S \in Y^S$ such that $\overline{y}^S \succ \underline{y}^S$.

2.2   Contingent Preferences and the Sure Thing Principle

An *event* E is any non–empty subset of S. Its *subjective probability* is defined as $P(E) := \sum_{s \in E} p_s$.

Given the function $U^S : Y^S \to \mathbb{R}$ defined by (2.1) and any event E, there is a *contingent expected utility* function U^E defined on the Cartesian subproduct $Y^E := \prod_{s \in E} Y_s$ by the partial sum

$$U^E(y^E) := \sum_{s \in E} p_s\, v(y_s). \tag{2.2}$$

Obviously, U^E induces a *contingent preference ordering* $\succsim^E$ on Y^E satisfying

$$y^E \succsim^E \tilde{y}^E \iff U^E(y^E) \geq U^E(\tilde{y}^E)$$

for all pairs $y^E, \tilde{y}^E \in Y^E$. This is intended to describe the agent's preference or behaviour given that E is the set of possible states, so that consequences $y^{S \setminus E} = \langle y_s \rangle_{s \in S \setminus E}$ are irrelevant. Evidently, then, for all pairs $y^E, \tilde{y}^E \in Y^E$ and all $\bar{y}^{S \setminus E} = \langle y_s \rangle_{s \in S \setminus E} \in Y^{S \setminus E} := \prod_{s \in S \setminus E} Y_s$ one has

$$y^E \succsim^E \tilde{y}^E \iff \sum_{s \in E} p_s\, v(y_s) \geq \sum_{s \in E} p_s\, v(\tilde{y}_s).$$

But the right hand side is true iff

$$\sum_{s \in E} p_s\, v(y_s) + \sum_{s \in S \setminus E} p_s\, v(\bar{y}_s) \geq \sum_{s \in E} p_s\, v(\tilde{y}_s) + \sum_{s \in S \setminus E} p_s\, v(\bar{y}_s),$$

and so

$$y^E \succsim^E \tilde{y}^E \iff (y^E, \bar{y}^{S \setminus E}) \succsim (\tilde{y}^E, \bar{y}^{S \setminus E}). \tag{2.3}$$

Furthermore, $(y^E, \bar{y}^{S \setminus E}) \precsim (\tilde{y}^E, \bar{y}^{S \setminus E})$ either for all $\bar{y}^{S \setminus E}$ because $y^E \sim^E \tilde{y}^E$, or else for no $\bar{y}^{S \setminus E}$ because $y^E \succ^E \tilde{y}^E$. It follows that $y^E \succsim^E \tilde{y}^E$ iff $y^E \succsim \tilde{y}^E$ *given* E, in the sense specified in Savage (1954, definition D1).

The requirement that (2.3) be satisfied, with the contingent ordering $\succsim^E$ on Y^E independent of $\bar{y}^{S \setminus E} \in Y^{S \setminus E}$, will be called the **sure thing principle** (or STP). It is a second implication of SEU maximization.[4]

When conditions (O) and (STP) are satisfied, say that the event E is *null* if $y^E \sim^E \tilde{y}^E$ for all $y^E, \tilde{y}^E \in Y^E$. Otherwise, if $y^E \succ^E \tilde{y}^E$ for some $y^E, \tilde{y}^E \in Y^E$, say that E is *non–null*. When the SEU hypothesis holds, event E is null iff its

---

[4]In Savage (1954) there is no formal statement of (STP), though the informal discussion on p. 21 seems to correspond to the "dominance" result stated as Theorem 3 on p. 26. This theorem is a logical consequence of his postulates P1, which is condition (O), together with P2, which is close to what I have chosen to call the "sure thing principle", and P3 which, at least when combined with conditions (O) and (STP), is equivalent to the state–independence condition (SI) set out in Section 2.3 below.

subjective probability $P(E) := \sum_{s \in E} p_s$ satisfies $P(E) = 0$, and E is non–null iff $P(E) > 0$. Note that S is null if and only if there is universal indifference; outside this trivial case, S is non–null. Of course, one also says that the state $s \in S$ is *null* iff the event $\{s\}$ is null, otherwise s is non–null. Obviously, under the SEU hypothesis, state $s \in S$ is null iff $p_s = 0$ and non–null iff $p_s > 0$.

The **strong sure thing principle**, or condition (STP*), requires that no state $s \in S$ be null. Thus, the difference between SEU* and SEU is that SEU* excludes null states and null events, whereas SEU allows them. When SEU* holds, so that no event is null, then condition (STP*) must be satisfied.

Suppose that $E \subset E' \subset S$ and that conditions (O) and (STP) are satisfied. Clearly, for all $y^E, \tilde{y}^E \in Y^E$ and all $\bar{y}^{S \setminus E} \in Y^{S \setminus E}$, it will be true that

$$y^E \succsim^E \tilde{y}^E \quad \Longleftrightarrow \quad (y^E, \bar{y}^{S \setminus E}) \succsim (\tilde{y}^E, \bar{y}^{S \setminus E}) \tag{2.4}$$
$$\Longleftrightarrow \quad (y^E, \bar{y}^{E' \setminus E}) \succsim^{E'} (\tilde{y}^E, \bar{y}^{E' \setminus E}).$$

2.3   State Independent Preferences

Given any event E and any consequence $y \in Y$, let $y\,1^E$ denote the *constant* or *sure consequence* with $y_s = y$ for all $s \in E$. It describes a CCF for which, even though there is uncertainty about the state of the world, the consequence y is certain. Note how (2.2) implies that

$$U^E(y\,1^E) = \sum_{s \in E} p_s\, v(y) = P(E)\, v(y)$$

for all $y \in Y$. Because $P(E) > 0$ whenever E is non–null, there is a preference ordering $\succsim^*$ on Y, independent of the state $s \in S$ or the event $S \subset E$, such that

$$y \succsim^* \bar{y} \iff v(y) \geq v(\bar{y}) \iff y\,1^E \succsim^E \bar{y}\,1^E \text{ (all non–null events } E).$$

This **state independence condition** (SI) is the third implication of SEU maximization.

Under conditions (O), (STP), and (SI), if $y \succ^* \bar{y}$, then $y\,1^E \succ^E \bar{y}\,1^E$ for all non–null events E.

2.4   A Likelihood Ordering of Events

Given two events $E_1, E_2 \subset S$, their respective subjective probabilities induce a clear "likelihood" ordering between them, depending on whether $P(E_1) \geq P(E_2)$ or *vice versa*. When the SEU hypothesis holds, this likelihood ordering can be derived from preferences. Indeed, suppose that $\bar{y}, \underline{y} \in Y$ with $\bar{y} \succ^* \underline{y}$.

Consider then the two CCFs $(\overline{y}\,1^{E_1}, \underline{y}\,1^{S\backslash E_1})$ and $(\overline{y}\,1^{E_2}, \underline{y}\,1^{S\backslash E_2})$. Suppose that the better consequence $\overline{y}$ is interpreted as "winning", and the worse consequence $\underline{y}$ as "losing". Then the first CCF arises when the agent wins iff E_1 occurs and loses iff E_2 occurs; the second when winning and losing are interchanged. The subjective expected utilities of these two CCFs are

$$
\begin{aligned}
U^S(\overline{y}\,1^{E_1}, \underline{y}\,1^{S\backslash E_1}) &= \sum_{s \in E_1} p_s\, v(\overline{y}) + \sum_{s \in S\backslash E_1} p_s\, v(\underline{y}); \\
&= P(E_1)\, v(\overline{y}) + [1 - P(E_1)]\, v(\underline{y}); \\
\text{and}\quad U^S(\overline{y}\,1^{E_2}, \underline{y}\,1^{S\backslash E_2}) &= P(E_2)\, v(\overline{y}) + [1 - P(E_2)]\, v(\underline{y}).
\end{aligned}
$$

respectively. Therefore

$$
U^S(\overline{y}\,1^{E_1}, \underline{y}\,1^{S\backslash E_1}) - U^S(\overline{y}\,1^{E_2}, \underline{y}\,1^{S\backslash E_2}) = [P(E_1) - P(E_2)]\,[v(\overline{y}) - v(\underline{y})],
$$

implying that

$$
(\overline{y}\,1^{E_1}, \underline{y}\,1^{S\backslash E_1}) \succsim^E (\overline{y}\,1^{E_2}, \underline{y}\,1^{S\backslash E_2}) \iff P(E_1) \geq P(E_2).
$$

Moreover, this must be true no matter what the consequences $\overline{y}, \underline{y} \in Y$ may be, provided only that $\overline{y} \succ^* \underline{y}$. So the agent weakly prefers winning conditional on E_1 to winning conditional on E_2 iff E_1 is no less likely than E_2. The implication is the **ordering of events condition** (OE), which requires that a (complete and transitive) likelihood ordering can be inferred from preferences for winning as against losing conditional on those events. This is the fourth implication of SEU maximization. It is equivalent to Savage's (1954) P4 postulate.

The four conditions (O), (STP), (SI) and (OE) do not by themselves imply the SEU hypothesis. For example, they amount to only the first four of Savage's seven postulates — or the first five if one excludes the trivial case of universal indifference. I shall not present the last two postulates, except peripherally in Sections 7.2 and 7.3. Instead, I shall turn to consequentialist axioms like those set out in Section 5 of Chapter 5. It will turn out that these fail to justify (OE). In my view, this detracts considerably from the normative appeal of Savage's approach, though it remains by far the most important and complete theory of decision-making under uncertainty prior to 1960.

3   Consequentialist Foundations

3.1   *Decision Trees with Natural Nodes*

Chapter 5 was concerned with objective EU maximization. There the ordering and independence properties were derived from consequentialist axioms applied to decision trees incorporating chance nodes, at which random moves occurred with specified objective probabilities. Here, similar arguments will be applied to decision trees in which no probabilities are specified. The chance nodes that have specified probabilities will be replaced by natural nodes at each of which nature has a move that restricts the remaining set of possible states of nature.

Formally, then, the finite decision trees considered in this section all take the form

$$T = \langle\, N, N^*, N^1, X, n_0, N_{+1}(\cdot), S(\cdot), \gamma(\cdot)\,\rangle. \tag{3.1}$$

As in Chapter 5, N denotes the set of all nodes, N^* the set of decision nodes, X the set of terminal nodes, n_0 the initial node, $N_{+1}(\cdot) : N \twoheadrightarrow N$ the immediate successor correspondence, and $\gamma(\cdot)$ the consequence mapping. The three new features are as follows.

First, N^1 denotes the set of natural nodes, replacing the earlier set N^0 of chance nodes.

Second, $S(\cdot) : N \twoheadrightarrow S$ denotes the *event correspondence*, with $S(n) \subset S$ as the set of states of the world which are still possible after reaching node n. Within the decision tree the agent is assumed to have perfect recall in the sense that $S(n') \subset S(n)$ whenever node n' follows node n in the decision tree. In fact, the event correspondence should have the properties that: (i) whenever $n \in N^*$ and $n' \in N_{+1}(n)$, then $S(n') = S(n)$ because the agent's decision at node n does not restrict the set of possible states; (ii) whenever $n \in N^1$, then $\cup_{n' \in N_{+1}(n)} S(n')$ is a partition of $S(n)$ into pairwise disjoint events because nature's move at n creates an information partition of $S(n)$.

Third, at each terminal node $x \in X$, where $S(x)$ is the set of states that remain possible, the consequence mapping γ determines a CCF $\gamma(x) \in Y^{S(x)}$ specifying, for each state $s \in S(x)$, a state contingent consequence $\gamma_s(x)$ in the fixed domain Y of possible consequences.[5]

3.2 Feasible and Chosen CCFs

Let T be any decision tree with natural nodes, as defined in (3.1). Then $F(T)$ will denote the set of feasible CCFs in T, whereas $\Phi_\beta(T)$ will denote the possible CCFs which can result from behaviour β. As in Chapter 5, these two sets are respectively equal to the values at $n = n_0$ of the sets

$$F(T, n) := F(T(n)) \quad \text{and} \quad \Phi_\beta(T, n) := \Phi_\beta(T(n)),$$

---

[5]It might seem more natural to define each decision tree so that by the time a terminal node $x \in X$ is reached, all uncertainty must be resolved and so $S(x)$ is a singleton $\{s(x)\}$. I have avoided doing this, not just to increase generality, but more importantly, to allow results in Section 5 of Chapter 5 to be applied directly, especially Theorem 5.1 concerning the existence of a preference ordering.

where $T(n)$ denotes the continuation subtree T that starts with initial node n. Moreover, $F(T,n)$ and $\Phi_\beta(T,n)$ can be constructed by backward recursion, starting at terminal nodes $x \in X$ where

$$F(T,x) := \Phi_\beta(T,x) := \{\gamma(x)\} \subset Y^{S(x)}. \tag{3.2}$$

At a decision node $n \in N^*$, one has $S(n') = S(n)$ (all $n' \in N_{+1}(n)$). Then

$$F(T,n) := \bigcup_{n' \in N_{+1}(n)} F(T,n') \quad \text{and} \quad \Phi_\beta(T,n) := \bigcup_{n' \in \beta(T(n),n)} \Phi_\beta(T,n'), \tag{3.3}$$

where both are subsets of $Y^{S(n)} = Y^{S(n')}$. At a natural node $n \in N^1$, on the other hand, where $S(n)$ is partitioned into the pairwise disjoint sets $S(n')$ $(n' \in N_{+1}(n))$, one has Cartesian product sets of CCFs given by

$$F(T,n) = \prod_{n' \in N_{+1}(n)} F(T,n') \quad \text{and} \quad \Phi_\beta(T,n) = \prod_{n' \in N_{+1}(n)} \Phi_\beta(T,n'). \tag{3.4}$$

Both of these are subsets of $Y^{S(n)} = \prod_{n' \in N_{+1}(n)} Y^{S(n')}$. It is easy to prove by backward induction that, for all $n \in N$, including $n = n_0$, one has

$$\emptyset \neq \Phi_\beta(T,n) \subset F(T,n) \subset Y^{S(n)}. \tag{3.5}$$

3.3 Consequentialism and Contingent Orderings

As in Section 5.5 of Chapter 5, the **consequentialist hypothesis** requires that there exists a consequence choice function specifying how the behaviour set (of possible consequences of behaviour) depends upon the feasible set of consequences. Here, however, any such consequence is a CCF $y^S \in Y^S$. In fact, each different event $E \subset S$ gives rise to a different domain Y^E of possible CCFs. Accordingly, for each event $E \subset S$ there must be a corresponding event–contingent choice function C_β^E defined on the domain of non–empty finite subsets of Y^E, and satisfying

$$\Phi_\beta(T) = C_\beta^E(F(T)) \subset F(T) \subset Y^E \tag{3.6}$$

for all decision trees T such that $S(n_0) = E$ at the initial node n_0 of T.

Consider now any fixed event E, and the restricted domain of all finite decision trees with no natural nodes which have the property that $S(n) = E$ at all nodes $n \in N$, including at all terminal nodes. On this restricted domain, impose the **dynamic consistency** hypothesis that $\beta(T(n),n') = \beta(T,n')$ at any decision node n' of the continuation tree $T(n)$. Then the arguments in Section 5.6 of Chapter 5 apply immediately and yield the result that C_β^E must correspond to a preference ordering R_β^E on the set Y^E. Thus, the family of event–contingent choice functions $\{\, C_\beta^E \mid \emptyset \neq E \subset S\,\}$ gives rise to a corresponding family of *contingent preference orderings* $\{\, R_\beta^E \mid \emptyset \neq E \subset S\,\}$ such that, whenever Z is a non–empty finite subset of Y^E, then

$$C_\beta^E(Z) = \{\, y^E \mid \tilde{y}^E \in Z \implies y^E \, R_\beta^E \, \tilde{y}^E \,\}. \tag{3.7}$$

3.4   Consequentialism and the Sure Thing Principle

In Section 6 of Chapter 5 it was argued that, for decision trees with chance nodes, consequentialism implied the independence axiom. Here, for decision trees with natural nodes, a very similar argument establishes that consequentialism implies the sure thing principle (STP) described in equation (2.3) of Section 2.2. Indeed, suppose that E_1 and E_2 are disjoint events in S, whereas $E = E_1 \cup E_2$, and $a^{E_1}, b^{E_1} \in Y^{E_1}, c^{E_2} \in Y^{E_2}$. Then consider the tree T as in (3.1), with

$$N^* = \{n_1\}; \quad N^1 = \{n_0\}; \quad X = \{\, x_a, x_b, x_c \,\};$$
$$N_{+1}(n_0) = \{\, n_1, x_c \,\}; \quad N_{+1}(n_1) = \{\, x_a, x_b \,\};$$
$$S(n_0) = E; \quad S(n_1) = S(x_a) = S(x_b) = E_1; \quad S(x_c) = E_2;$$
$$\gamma(x_a) = a^{E_1}; \quad \gamma(x_b) = b^{E_1}; \quad \gamma(x_c) = c^{E_2}.$$

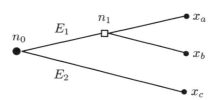

Figure 3.1 Decision Tree Illustrating the Sure Thing Principle

This tree is illustrated in Figure 3.1. Notice how (3.2) and (3.3) imply that

$$F(T, n_1) \;=\; F(T, x_a) \cup F(T, x_b) = \{a^{E_1}\} \cup \{b^{E_1}\} \;=\; \{\, a^{E_1}, b^{E_1} \,\}.$$

Then (3.4) implies that

$$\begin{aligned}
F(T) = F(T, n_0) \;&=\; F(T, n_1) \times F(T, x_c) \\
&=\; F(T, n_1) \times \{c^{E_2}\} = \{\, (a^{E_1}, c^{E_2}), \ (b^{E_1}, c^{E_2}) \,\}.
\end{aligned}$$

Also (3.7), (3.6) and (3.4) together imply that

$$a^{E_1} \, R_\beta^{E_1} \, b^{E_1} \quad \Longleftrightarrow \quad a^{E_1} \in C_\beta(F(T, n_1)) = \Phi_\beta(T, n_1)$$
$$\Longleftrightarrow \quad (a^{E_1}, c^{E_2}) \in \Phi_\beta(T, n_1) \times \{c^{E_2}\} = \Phi_\beta(T, n_1) \times \Phi_\beta(T, x_c)$$
$$= \Phi_\beta(T, n_0) = C_\beta(F(T, n_0))$$
$$\Longleftrightarrow \quad (a^{E_1}, c^{E_2}) \, R_\beta^{E} \, (b^{E_1}, c^{E_2}).$$

This is exactly the sure thing principle (STP), as expressed by (2.4) in Section 2.2, but applied to the contingent orderings $R_\beta^{E_1}$ and R_β^{E} instead of to $\succsim^{E}$ and $\succsim^{E'}$ respectively.

3.5   Consequentialism Characterized

In fact, consequentialist behaviour satisfying dynamic consistency on an unrestricted domain of finite decision trees is possible whenever there exist, for all events $E \subset S$, contingent orderings R_β^{E} that satisfy (STP). To see this, consider *any* family of contingent orderings R^E ($\emptyset \neq E \subset S$) satisfying (STP). Essentially the same arguments as in Section 6.4 of Chapter 5 can then be used to construct behaviour β satisfying the consequentialist axioms whose family of contingent revealed preference orderings satisfies $R_\beta^E = R^E$ whenever $\emptyset \neq E \subset S$. The proof of Lemma 6.1 in that chapter does need extending to deal with one new case, which is when $n \in N^1$ is a natural node. However, this is a routine modification of the proof for when $n \in N^0$ is a chance node, with condition (STP) replacing condition (I). Also, see the subsequent Section 5.5 in this chapter for a proof which applies in a more general setting.

3.6   Unordered Events

It has just been shown that consequentialist behaviour is completely characterized by any family of contingent orderings satisfying (STP). Therefore, no further restrictions on behaviour can be inferred from consequentialism, unless these restrictions are implications of there being a family of orderings satisfying (STP). In particular, the crucial ordering of events condition (OE) is generally violated, implying that consequentialist behaviour does *not* maximize SEU.

To confirm this, it is enough to exhibit a family of contingent preference orderings that fails to induce an ordering of events despite satisfying (STP*). So, let $S = \{s_1, s_2\}$ and $Y = \{a, b, c\}$. Then define the state independent utility function $v : Y \to \mathbb{R}$ so that:

$$v(a) = 1; \quad v(b) = 0; \quad v(c) = -1. \tag{3.8}$$

Now consider the preference ordering on Y^S induced by the specific additive utility function

$$U^S(y^S) = \phi_1(v(y_{s_1})) + \phi_2(v(y_{s_2})),\tag{3.9}$$

where ϕ_1 and ϕ_2 are increasing functions satisfying

$$\begin{array}{llll}
\phi_1(1) & = & 2, & \phi_1(0) & = & 0, & \phi_1(-1) & = & -1; \\
\phi_2(1) & = & 1, & \phi_2(0) & = & 0, & \phi_2(-1) & = & -2.
\end{array}\tag{3.10}$$

Suppose that the two contingent orderings on Y_{s_1} and Y_{s_2} are represented by the utility functions $\phi_1(v(y_{s_1}))$ and $\phi_2(v(y_{s_2}))$ respectively. Neither state is null, because neither $\phi_1(v(y))$ nor $\phi_2(v(y))$ are constant functions independent of y. Because (3.9) has an additive form, (STP*) is evidently satisfied. Moreover, the preferences on Y_{s_1}, Y_{s_2} are even state independent, as are those on the set $Y1^S := \{ (y_{s_1}, y_{s_2}) \in Y_{s_1} \times Y_{s_2} \mid y_{s_1} = y_{s_2} \}$, since all are represented by the same utility function $v(y)$. Nevertheless

$$\begin{array}{llll}
U^S(a,b) & = & 2, & U^S(b,a) & = & 1; \\
U^S(b,c) & = & -2, & U^S(c,b) & = & -1.
\end{array}$$

So the agent's behaviour reveals a preference for winning a in state s_1 to winning it in state s_2, when the alternative losing outcome is b. On the other hand, it also reveals a preference for winning b in state s_2 to winning it in state s_1, when the alternative losing outcome is c. Hence, there is no induced ordering of the events $\{s_1\}$ and $\{s_2\}$.

Savage, of course, introduced other postulates whose effect is to ensure a rather rich set of states — see the later discussion in Section 7.2. Adding such postulates, however, in general will not induce an ordering of events. To see this, suppose that S is the entire interval $[0,1]$ of the real line instead of just the doubleton $\{s_1, s_2\}$. Instead of the additive utility function (3.9), consider the integral

$$\bar{U}^S(y^S) = \int_0^{1/2} \phi_1(v(y(s))) ds + \int_{1/2}^1 \phi_2(v(y(s))) ds$$

with v given by (3.8) and ϕ_1, ϕ_2 by (3.10). Also, so that the integrals are well defined, y^S should be a measurable function from S to Y, in the sense that the set $\{ s \in S \mid y(s) = y \}$ is measurable for all $y \in Y$. Then the particular CCF $y^S = \left(a\,1_{[0,\frac{1}{2}]}, b\,1_{(\frac{1}{2},1]} \right)$ with

$$y(s) = \left\{ \begin{array}{lll} a & \text{if} & s \in [0, \frac{1}{2}] \\ b & \text{if} & s \in (\frac{1}{2}, 1] \end{array} \right.$$

is preferred to the lottery represented by $\left(b\,1_{[0,\frac{1}{2}]},a\,1_{(\frac{1}{2},1]}\right)$ in the same notation. But $\left(c\,1_{[0,\frac{1}{2}]},b\,1_{(\frac{1}{2},1]}\right)$ is preferred to $\left(b\,1_{[0,\frac{1}{2}]},c\,1_{(\frac{1}{2},1]}\right)$. So there is no induced likelihood ordering of the two events $[0,\frac{1}{2}]$ and $(\frac{1}{2},1]$. In fact, it is easy to confirm that this example satisfies Savage's six postulates P1–P3 and P5–P7; only the ordering of events postulate P4 is violated. See Wakker and Zank (1996) for a systematic study of the rather rich extra possibilities which arise when all but P4 of Savage's seven postulates are satisfied.

4   Anscombe and Aumann's Axioms

4.1   Horse Lotteries versus Roulette Lotteries

Anscombe and Aumann's (1963) article is the definitive statement of a different approach to the derivation of subjective probabilities. They allowed subjective probabilities for the outcomes of "horse lotteries" or CCFs to be inferred from expected utility representations of preferences over compounds of horse and "roulette lotteries". Formally, the framework of Section 2 is extended to allow preferences over, not only CCFs of the form $y^E \in Y^E$ for some non–empty $E \subset S$, but also (finitely supported) simple roulette lotteries in the space $\Delta(Y)$, as considered in Chapter 5. And in fact general compound lotteries are allowed, taking the form of simple lotteries $\lambda^E \in \Delta(Y^E)$ attaching the objective probabilities $\lambda^E(y^E)$ to CCFs $y^E \in Y^E$ instead of to consequences $y \in Y$. Then the finite collection of random variables y_s ($s \in E$) has a multivariate distribution with probabilities $\lambda^E(y^E)$.

Within this extended framework, the SEU hypothesis extends that of Section 2 by postulating that there is a preference ordering $\succsim$ over the domain $\Delta(Y^S)$ of mixed lotteries, and that $\succsim$ is represented by the objective expected utility function

$$U^S(\lambda^S) = \sum_{y^S \in Y^S} \lambda^S(y^S)\,v^S(y^S), \qquad (4.1)$$

where $v^S(y^S)$ is the subjective expected utility function defined by

$$v^S(y^S) := \sum_{s \in S} p_s\,v(y_s). \qquad (4.2)$$

Thus $U^S(\lambda^S)$ involves the double expectation w.r.t. both the objective probabilities $\lambda^S(y^S)$ of different CCFs $y^S \in Y^S$ and the subjective probabilities p_s of different states $s \in S$. The SEU* hypothesis implies in addition that $p_s > 0$ for all $s \in S$.

4.2 Ratios of Utility Differences

Let a^S, b^S, c^S be any three CCFs in Y^S with $v^S(b^S) \neq v^S(c^S)$. As in Section 2.3 of Chapter 5, the ratio $[v^S(a^S) - v^S(c^S)]/[v^S(b^S) - v^S(c^S)]$ of utility differences is equal to the constant marginal rate of substitution (MRS) between, on the one hand, an increase in the probability of a^S that is compensated by an equal decrease in the probability of c^S, and on the other hand, an increase in the probability of b^S that is also compensated by an equal decrease in the probability of c^S. Furthermore, because only these ratios of utility differences are uniquely determined, each NMUF v^S is unique only up to a cardinal equivalence class. Also, because of (4.2), one has $v^S(y \, 1^S) = v(y)$ for all $y \in Y$ and

$$v^S(a, b \, 1^{S \setminus \{s\}}) = p_s \, v(a) + (1 - p_s) \, v(b) = v(b) + p_s \, [v(a) - v(b)]$$

for all $a, b \in Y$ and all $s \in S$. Provided that $v(a) \neq v(b)$, it follows that the subjective probability of each state $s \in S$ is given by

$$p_s = \frac{v^S(a, b \, 1^{S \setminus \{s\}}) - v(b)}{v(a) - v(b)} = \frac{v^S(a, b \, 1^{S \setminus \{s\}}) - v^S(b \, 1^S)}{v^S(a \, 1^S) - v^S(b \, 1^S)}. \tag{4.3}$$

It is therefore the constant MRS between an increase in the probability of the CCF $(a, b \, 1^{S \setminus \{s\}})$ that is compensated by an equal decrease in the probability of $b \, 1^S$, and an increase in the probability of $a \, 1^S$ that is also compensated by an equal decrease in the probability of $b \, 1^S$. Note that this MRS must be independent of the two consequences a, b. Of course, the uniqueness of each such MRS implies that each subjective probability p_s ($s \in S$) is unique, even though the utility function is unique only up to a cardinal equivalence class.

One particular advantage of Anscombe and Aumann's version of the SEU hypothesis is that subjective probabilities can be interpreted in this way. No interpretation quite as simple emerges from Savage's version of the theory.

4.3 Ordinality, Independence and Continuity

As obvious notation, let $1_{y^S} \in \Delta(Y^S)$ denote the degenerate lottery which attaches probability 1 to the CCF y^S. Next, define $v^S(y^S) := U^S(1_{y^S})$ for every CCF $y^S \in Y^S$. Note how (4.1) and (4.2) together imply that the preference ordering $v^S(y^S) = \sum_{s \in S} p_s \, v(y_s)$, which is exactly the SEU expression that was introduced in (2.1) of Section 2.1. Equation (4.1) also implies that

$$U^S(\lambda^S) = \sum_{y^S \in Y^S} \lambda^S(y^S) \, v^S(y^S) = \mathbb{E}_{\lambda^S} \, v^S.$$

Hence, the preference ordering $\succsim$ is represented by the objectively expected value of the NMUF $v^S : Y^S \to \mathbb{R}$. So, as discussed in Chapter 5, the following three conditions must be satisfied:

(O) *Ordering.* There exists a preference ordering $\succsim$ on $\Delta(Y^S)$.

(I*) *Strong Independence Axiom.* For any $\lambda^S, \mu^S, \nu^S \in \Delta(Y^S)$ and $0 < \alpha \leq 1$, it must be true that

$$\lambda^S \succsim \mu^S \iff \alpha\lambda^S + (1-\alpha)\nu^S \succsim \alpha\mu^S + (1-\alpha)\nu^S.$$

(C*) *Strong Continuity as Probabilities Vary.* The two sets

$$
\begin{aligned}
A &:= \{\alpha \in [0,1] \mid \alpha\lambda^S + (1-\alpha)\nu^S \succsim \mu^S\} \quad \text{and} \\
B &:= \{\alpha \in [0,1] \mid \alpha\lambda^S + (1-\alpha)\nu^S \precsim \mu^S\}
\end{aligned}
$$

are closed whenever $\lambda^S, \mu^S, \nu^S \in \Delta(Y^S)$ with $\lambda^S \succ \mu^S \succ \nu^S$.

Indeed, these three properties are precisely those that were used to characterize objective EU maximization in Chapter 5. More precisely, conditions (O), (I*) and (C*) were shown to be necessary; for sufficiency, conditions (I*) and (C*) could be replaced by the following two weaker conditions, which both apply for each $\lambda^S, \mu^S, \nu^S \in \Delta(Y^S)$:

(I) *Independence.* Whenever $0 < \alpha \leq 1$, then

$$\lambda^S \succ \mu^S \implies \alpha\lambda^S + (1-\alpha)\nu^S \succ \alpha\mu^S + (1-\alpha)\nu^S.$$

(C) *Continuity.* Whenever $\lambda^S \succ \mu^S$ and $\mu^S \succ \nu^S$, there must exist $\alpha', \alpha'' \in (0,1)$ such that

$$\alpha'\lambda^S + (1-\alpha')\nu^S \succ \mu^S \quad \text{and} \quad \mu^S \succ \alpha''\lambda^S + (1-\alpha'')\nu^S.$$

4.4   Reversal of Order

For each $y \in Y$ and $s \in S$, define $Y_s^S(y) := \{y^S \in Y^S \mid y_s = y\}$ as the set of CCFs yielding the particular consequence y in state s. Then, given any $\lambda^S \in \Delta(Y^S)$ and any $s \in S$, define

$$\lambda_s(y) := \sum_{y^S \in Y_s^S(y)} \lambda^S(y^S). \tag{4.4}$$

Note that $\lambda_s(y) \geq 0$ and that

$$\sum_{y \in Y} \lambda_s(y) = \sum_{y^S \in Y^S} \lambda^S(y^S) = 1.$$

Therefore λ_s is itself a simple probability distribution in $\Delta(Y)$, called the *marginal distribution* of the consequence y_s occurring in state s. Moreover, (4.1), (4.2) and (4.4) imply that

$$U^S(\lambda^S) = \sum_{y^S \in Y^S} \lambda^S(y^S) \sum_{s \in S} p_s \, v(y_s) = \sum_{s \in S} p_s \sum_{y \in Y} \lambda_s(y) \, v(y), \qquad (4.5)$$

thus demonstrating that only the marginal probabilities $\lambda_s(y)$ ($s \in S$, $y \in Y$) matter in the end. So the SEU hypothesis also implies:

(RO) *Reversal of Order.* Whenever $\lambda^S, \mu^S \in \Delta(Y^S)$ have marginal distributions satisfying $\lambda_s = \mu_s$ for all $s \in S$, then $\lambda^S \sim \mu^S$.

This condition owes its name to the fact that there is indifference between: (i) the compound lottery in which a roulette lottery λ^S determines the random CCF y^S before the horse lottery that resolves which state $s \in S$ and which ultimate consequence y_s occur; and (ii) the reversed compound lottery in which the horse lottery is resolved first, and its outcome $s \in S$ determines which marginal roulette lottery λ_s generates the ultimate consequence y.

In particular, suppose that $\mu^S = \prod_{s \in E} \lambda_s$ is the *product lottery* defined, for all $y^S = \langle y_s \rangle_{s \in S} \in Y^S$, by $\mu^S(y^S) := \prod_{s \in S} \lambda_s(y_s)$. Thus, the different random consequences y_s ($s \in S$) all have independent distributions. Then condition (RO) requires λ^S to be treated as equivalent to μ^S, whether or not the different consequences y_s ($s \in S$) are correlated random variables when the joint distribution is λ^S. Only marginal distributions matter. So any $\lambda^S \in \Delta(Y^S)$ can be regarded as equivalent to the list $\langle \lambda_s \rangle_{s \in S}$ of corresponding marginal distributions. This has the effect of reducing the space $\Delta(Y^S)$ to the Cartesian product space $\prod_{s \in S} \Delta(Y_s)$, with $Y_s = Y$ for all $s \in S$.

4.5 Sure Thing Principle

For each event $E \subset S$, there is obviously a corresponding *contingent expected utility function*

$$U^E(\lambda^E) = \sum_{s \in E} p_s \sum_{y \in Y} \lambda_s(y) \, v(y), \qquad (4.6)$$

which represents the contingent preference ordering $\succsim^E$ on the set $\Delta(Y^E)$.

Given $\lambda^E, \mu^E \in \Delta(Y^E)$ and $\nu^{S\backslash E} \in \Delta(Y^{S\backslash E})$, let $(\lambda^E, \nu^{S\backslash E})$ denote the combination of the conditional lottery λ^E if E occurs with $\nu^{S\backslash E}$ if $S \backslash E$ occurs. Similarly for $(\mu^E, \nu^{S\backslash E})$. Then the following extension of the sure thing principle (STP) in Section 2.2 can be derived in exactly the same way as (2.3):

(STP)   *Sure Thing Principle.* Given any event $E \subset S$, there exists a contingent preference ordering $\succsim^E$ on $\Delta(Y^E)$ satisfying

$$\lambda^E \succsim^E \mu^E \iff (\lambda^E, \nu^{S\backslash E}) \succsim (\mu^E, \nu^{S\backslash E})$$

for all $\lambda^E, \mu^E \in \Delta(Y^E)$ and all $\nu^{S\backslash E} \in \Delta(Y^{S\backslash E})$.

The following preliminary Lemma 4.1 shows that the four conditions (O), (I*), (RO) and (STP) are not logically independent, In fact, as Raiffa (1961) implicitly suggests in his discussion of the Ellsberg paradox, condition (STP) is an implication of the three conditions (O), (I*) and (RO) — see also Blume, Brandenburger and Dekel (1991).

LEMMA 4.1 Suppose that the three axioms (O), (I*), and (RO) are satisfied on $\Delta(Y^S)$. Then so is (STP).

PROOF Consider any event $E \subset S$ and also any lotteries $\lambda^E, \mu^E \in \Delta(Y^E)$, $\bar{\nu}^{S\backslash E} \in \Delta(Y^{S\backslash E})$ satisfying $(\lambda^E, \bar{\nu}^{S\backslash E}) \succsim (\mu^E, \bar{\nu}^{S\backslash E})$. For any other lottery $\nu^{S\backslash E} \in \Delta(Y^{S\backslash E})$, axioms (I*) and (RO) respectively imply that

$$\tfrac{1}{2}(\lambda^E, \nu^{S\backslash E}) + \tfrac{1}{2}(\lambda^E, \bar{\nu}^{S\backslash E}) \succsim \tfrac{1}{2}(\lambda^E, \nu^{S\backslash E}) + \tfrac{1}{2}(\mu^E, \bar{\nu}^{S\backslash E})$$
$$\sim \tfrac{1}{2}(\mu^E, \nu^{S\backslash E}) + \tfrac{1}{2}(\lambda^E, \bar{\nu}^{S\backslash E}).$$

But then transitivity of $\succsim$ and axiom (I*) imply that $(\lambda^E, \nu^{S\backslash E}) \succsim (\mu^E, \nu^{S\backslash E})$. This confirms condition (STP). ∎

4.6   State Independence

For each non–null state $s \in S$ there is an associated event $\{s\} \subset S$. Because $p_s > 0$, according to (4.6) the corresponding contingent preference ordering $\succsim^{\{s\}}$ on the set $\Delta(Y)$ is represented by the conditional objectively expected utility function $\sum_{y \in Y} \lambda_s(y)\, v(y)$. This makes the following condition (SI) an obvious implication of the fact that the NMUF v is independent of s:

(SI)   *State Independence.* Given any non–null state $s \in S$, the contingent preference ordering $\succsim^{\{s\}}$ over $\Delta(Y^{\{s\}}) = \Delta(Y)$ is independent of s;

let $\succsim^*$ denote this state independent preference ordering, which must satisfy conditions (O), (I*) and (C*), of course.

To summarize, the SEU hypothesis implies the six conditions (O), (I), (C), (RO), (STP), and (SI). Of course, the stronger SEU* hypothesis has the same implications, except that there can be no null events.

4.7 Sufficient Conditions for the SEU and SEU* Hypotheses

The principal contribution of Anscombe and Aumann (1963) was to demonstrate how, in effect, these six conditions (O), (I), (C), (RO), (STP), and (SI) are sufficient for the SEU hypothesis to hold.[6] In particular, unlike Savage, there was no explicit need for the ordering of events assumption. Nor for the assumption that events can be refined indefinitely. Moreover, they were able to give a much simpler proof, based on the corresponding result for the objective version of the EU hypothesis. Their proof, however, requires that there exist both best and worst consequences in the domain Y. The proof given here relaxes this unnecessary requirement. It proceeds by way of several intermediate lemmas. The key Lemma 4.4 is proved by means of an elegant argument that apparently originated with Fishburn (1970, p. 176).

Of course, the six conditions (O), (I), (C), (RO), (STP), and (SI) are assumed throughout.

LEMMA 4.2 (a) Suppose that $E \subset S$ is an event and that $\lambda^E, \mu^E \in \Delta(Y^E)$ satisfy $\lambda_s \succsim^* \mu_s$ for all $s \in E$. Then $\lambda^E \succsim^E \mu^E$. (b) If in addition $\lambda^E \sim^E \mu^E$, then $\lambda_s \sim^* \mu_s$ for every non–null state $s \in E$.

PROOF The proof is by induction on m, the number of states in E. For $m = 1$, the result is trivial. Suppose that $m > 1$. As the induction hypothesis, suppose that the result is true for any event with $m - 1$ states.

Let s' be any state in E, and let $E' := E \setminus \{s'\}$. If $\lambda_s \succsim^* \mu_s$ for all $s \in E$, then the same is true for all $s \in E' \subset E$, so the induction hypothesis implies that $\lambda^{E'} \succsim^{E'} \mu^{E'}$. But $\lambda_{s'} \succsim^* \mu_{s'}$ also, and so for every $\nu^{S\setminus E'} \in \Delta(Y^{S\setminus E'})$, applying (STP) twice yields

$$(\lambda^E, \nu^{S\setminus E}) = (\lambda^{E'}, \lambda_{s'}, \nu^{S\setminus E}) \succsim (\mu^{E'}, \lambda_{s'}, \nu^{S\setminus E}) \tag{4.7}$$
$$\succsim (\mu^{E'}, \mu_{s'}, \nu^{S\setminus E}) = (\mu^E, \nu^{S\setminus E}).$$

Then (STP) implies $\lambda^E \succsim^E \mu^E$, which confirms that (a) holds for E.

---

[6]In fact Anscombe and Aumann assumed the EU hypothesis directly when the state of the world is known. This has the effect of merging conditions (O), (I) and (C) into one.

To prove (b), suppose in addition that $\lambda^E \sim \mu^E$. Then (STP) implies that $(\lambda^E, \nu^{S\backslash E}) \sim (\mu^E, \nu^{S\backslash E})$. From (4.7) and transitivity of $\succsim$, it follows that

$$(\lambda^{E'}, \lambda_{s'}, \nu^{S\backslash E}) \sim (\mu^{E'}, \lambda_{s'}, \nu^{S\backslash E}) \sim (\mu^{E'}, \mu_{s'}, \nu^{S\backslash E}). \tag{4.8}$$

But then (STP) implies $\lambda^{E'} \sim^{E'} \mu^{E'}$, so the induction hypothesis implies that $\lambda_s \sim^* \mu_s$ for all non–null $s \in E'$. However, (4.8) and (STP) also imply that $\lambda_{s'} \sim^{\{s'\}} \mu_{s'}$ and so, unless s' is null, that $\lambda_{s'} \sim^* \mu_{s'}$. Therefore $\lambda_s \sim^* \mu_s$ for all non–null $s \in E$.

The proof by induction is complete. ∎

Suppose it were true that $\lambda \sim^* \mu$ for all pure roulette lotteries $\lambda, \mu \in \Delta(Y)$. Because S is finite, Lemma 4.2 would then imply that $\lambda^S \sim \mu^S$ for all $\lambda^S, \mu^S \in \Delta(Y^S)$. However, the ordering $\succsim$ could then be represented by the trivial subjective expected utility function $\sum_{s \in E} p_s U^*(\lambda_s)$ for arbitrary subjective probabilities p_s and any constant utility function satisfying $U^*(\lambda) = c$ for all $\lambda \in \Delta(Y)$. So from now on, exclude the trivial case of universal indifference by assuming there exist two pure roulette lotteries $\overline{\lambda}, \underline{\lambda} \in \Delta(Y)$ with $\overline{\lambda} \succ^* \underline{\lambda}$. Equivalently, assume that the set S is not itself a null event.

The key idea of the following proof involves adapting the previous construction of an NMUF for the objective version of the EU hypothesis in Chapter 5. Because $\succsim^*$ satisfies conditions (O), (I) and (C), Lemma 4.5 of Chapter 5 can be applied. It implies that $\succsim^*$ can be represented by a normalized expected utility function $U^* : \Delta(Y) \to \mathbb{R}$ which satisfies

$$U^*(\underline{\lambda}) = 0 \quad \text{and} \quad U^*(\overline{\lambda}) = 1 \tag{4.9}$$

and also the **mixture preservation property** (MP) that, whenever $\lambda, \mu \in \Delta(Y)$ and $0 \le \alpha \le 1$, then

$$U^*(\alpha\,\lambda + (1-\alpha)\,\mu) = \alpha\,U^*(\lambda) + (1-\alpha)\,U^*(\mu). \tag{4.10}$$

As an obvious extension of the notation introduced in Section 2.3, given any event $E \subset S$ and any lottery $\lambda \in \Delta(Y)$, let $\lambda\,1^E$ denote the lottery in $\Delta(Y^E)$ whose marginal distribution in each state $s \in E$ is $\lambda_s = \lambda$, independent of s.

LEMMA 4.3 Given any $\lambda, \mu \in \Delta(Y)$, one has

$$\lambda \succsim^* \mu \iff \lambda\,1^S \succsim \mu\,1^S.$$

PROOF Lemma 4.2 immediately implies that $\lambda \succsim^* \mu \implies \lambda\,1^S \succsim \mu\,1^S$. On the other hand, because the event S cannot be null, Lemma 4.2 also implies that $\mu \succ^* \lambda \implies \mu\,1^S \succ \lambda\,1^S$. But $\succsim^*$ and $\succsim$ are complete orderings, so $\lambda\,1^S \succsim \mu\,1^S \implies \mu\,1^S \not\succ \lambda\,1^S \implies \mu \not\succ^* \lambda \implies \lambda \succsim^* \mu$. ∎

By Lemma 4.3, $\overline{\lambda}1^S \succ \underline{\lambda}1^S$. Because the ordering $\succsim$ on $\Delta(Y^S)$ satisfies conditions (O), (I) and (C), Lemma 4.5 of Chapter 5 shows that $\succsim$ can also be represented by a normalized expected utility function $U^S : \Delta(Y^S) \to \mathbb{R}$ which satisfies

$$U^S(\underline{\lambda}1^S) = 0 \quad \text{and} \quad U^S(\overline{\lambda}1^S) = 1 \tag{4.11}$$

and also (MP). Then Lemma 4.6 of Chapter 5 and Lemma 4.3 above imply that $U^S(\lambda 1^S)$ and $U^*(\lambda)$ must be cardinally equivalent functions of λ on the domain $\Delta(Y)$. Because of the two normalizations (4.9) and (4.11), for all $\lambda \in \Delta(Y)$ one has

$$U^*(\lambda) = U^S(\lambda 1^S). \tag{4.12}$$

Next, define the functions $g_s : \Delta(Y) \to \mathbb{R}$ and constants p_s (all $s \in S$) by

$$g_s(\lambda) := U^S(\underline{\lambda}1^{S\setminus\{s\}}, \lambda) \quad \text{and} \quad p_s := g_s(\overline{\lambda}). \tag{4.13}$$

Evidently, because of the normalization (4.11), it must be true that

$$g_s(\underline{\lambda}) = 0. \tag{4.14}$$

LEMMA 4.4 For all $\lambda^S \in \Delta(Y^S)$ one has

$$U^S(\lambda^S) \equiv \sum_{s \in S} p_s\, U^*(\lambda_s), \tag{4.15}$$

where $p_s = 0$ iff s is null. Also $p = \langle p_s \rangle_{s \in S}$ is a probability distribution in $\Delta(S)$ because $p_s \geq 0$ for all $s \in S$ and $\sum_{s \in S} p_s = 1$.

PROOF Let m be the number of elements in the finite set S. For all $\lambda^S \in \Delta(Y^S)$, the two members

$$\sum_{s \in S} \frac{1}{m}\, (\underline{\lambda}1^{S\setminus\{s\}}, \lambda_s) \quad \text{and} \quad \frac{m-1}{m}\underline{\lambda}1^S + \frac{1}{m}\lambda^S \tag{4.16}$$

of $\Delta(Y^S)$ have the common marginal distribution $(1 - \frac{1}{m})\underline{\lambda} + \frac{1}{m}\lambda_s$ for each $s \in S$. So condition (RO) implies that they are indifferent. Because U^S satisfies (MP), applying U^S to the two indifferent mixtures in (4.16) gives the equality

$$\sum_{s \in S} \frac{1}{m}\, U^S(\underline{\lambda}1^{S\setminus\{s\}}, \lambda_s) = \frac{m-1}{m}\, U^S(\underline{\lambda}1^S) + \frac{1}{m}\, U^S(\lambda^S). \tag{4.17}$$

But $U^S(\underline{\lambda}\,1^S) = 0$ by (4.11), so (4.17) and definition (4.13) imply that

$$U^S(\lambda^S) = \sum_{s\in S} U^S(\underline{\lambda}\,1^{S\setminus\{s\}}, \lambda_s) = \sum_{s\in S} g_s(\lambda_s). \tag{4.18}$$

Because of (4.13) and (4.14), if s is a null state, then $g_s(\lambda) = 0$ for all $\lambda \in \Delta(Y)$. In particular, $p_s = g_s(\overline{\lambda}) = 0$. Otherwise, if s is not null, then (STP) and (4.13) jointly imply that $p_s := g_s(\overline{\lambda}) > 0$.

Because the function U^S satisfies (MP), equations (4.12) and (4.13) evidently imply that the functions U^* and g_s ($s \in S$) do the same. Also, by (STP), $g_s(\lambda)$ and $U^*(\lambda)$ both represent $\succsim^{\{s\}}$ on $\Delta(Y)$ while satisfying (MP). So by Lemma 4.6 of Chapter 5, they must be cardinally equivalent utility functions. By (4.9) and (4.14), $U^*(\underline{\lambda}) = g_s(\underline{\lambda}) = 0$. Hence, there exists $\rho > 0$ for which

$$g_s(\lambda) \equiv \rho\,U^*(\lambda). \tag{4.19}$$

By (4.13), putting $\lambda = \overline{\lambda}$ in (4.19) yields $p_s = g_s(\overline{\lambda}) = \rho\,U^*(\overline{\lambda}) = \rho$, where the last equality is true because $U^*(\overline{\lambda}) = 1$, by (4.9). Therefore (4.19) becomes $g_s(\lambda) \equiv p_s\,U^*(\lambda)$. Substituting this into (4.18) gives (4.15). Finally, (4.11), (4.15) and (4.9) jointly imply that

$$1 = U^S(\overline{\lambda}\,1^S) = \sum_{s\in S} p_s\,U^*(\overline{\lambda}) = \sum_{s\in S} p_s,$$

which completes the proof. ∎

THEOREM 4.5 Under conditions (O), (I), (C), (RO), (STP), and (SI), there exists a unique cardinal equivalence class of NMUFs $v : Y \to \mathbb{R}$ and, unless there is universal indifference, unique subjective probabilities p_s ($s \in S$) such that the ordering $\succsim$ on $\Delta(Y^S)$ is represented by the expected utility function

$$U^S(\lambda^S) \equiv \sum_{s\in S} p_s \sum_{y\in Y} \lambda_s(y)\,v(y).$$

PROOF First, define $v^*(y) := U^*(1_y)$ for all $y \in Y$. Because λ_s is the (finite) mixture $\sum_{y\in Y} \lambda_s(y)\,1_y$ and U^* satisfies (MP), it follows that $U^*(\lambda_s) = \sum_{y\in Y} \lambda_s(y)\,v^*(y)$ for all $s \in S$. But then, by Lemma 4.4, one has

$$U^S(\lambda^S) = \sum_{s\in S} p_s\,U^*(\lambda_s) = \sum_{s\in S} p_s \sum_{y\in Y} \lambda_s(y)\,v^*(y).$$

As in Chapter 5, v^* could be replaced by any cardinally equivalent NMUF $v : Y \to \mathbb{R}$. But, whenever s is non–null, any such replacement leaves the ratio of utility differences on the right hand side of (4.3) in Section 4.2 unaffected. On the other hand, $p_s = 0$ iff s is null. So the subjective probabilities p_s are unique. ∎

When there is no null event, $p_s > 0$ for all $s \in S$, so SEU* is satisfed instead of SEU.

5 Consequentialist Foundations Reconsidered

5.1 Decision Trees with Both Chance and Natural Nodes

Simple finite decision trees were introduced in Section 5.2 of Chapter 5, and trees with chance nodes in Section 6.1 of that chapter. Section 3.1 of this chapter introduced decision trees with natural nodes but no chance nodes. Now, in order to allow both horse and roulette lotteries to arise as consequences of decisions, it is natural to consider decision trees with both natural and chance nodes, like those in Hammond (1988). These take the form

$$T = \langle\, N, N^*, N^0, N^1, X, n_0, N_{+1}(\cdot), \pi(\cdot|\cdot), S(\cdot), \gamma(\cdot)\,\rangle.$$

Compared with (3.1) of Section 3.1, the tree T now has the set of all nodes N partitioned into four instead of only three sets; the new fourth set is N^0, the set of chance nodes. Also, at each $n \in N^0$ the transition probabilities $\pi(n'|n)$ are specified for all $n' \in N_{+1}(n)$, just as in Section 6.1 of Chapter 5. For reasons explained in that chapter, it is assumed that each $\pi(n'|n) > 0$. In addition, at each terminal node $x \in X$ the consequence takes the form of a lottery $\gamma(x) \in \Delta(Y^{S(x)})$ over CCFs.

The construction of the feasible set $F(T)$ and of the behaviour set $\Phi_\beta(T)$ proceeds by backward recursion, much as it did in Sections 5.5 and 6.2 of Chapter 5 and in Section 3.2 of this chapter. When n is a natural node, however, (3.4) needs reinterpreting because the sets

$$\prod_{n' \in N_{+1}(n)} F(T, n') \quad \text{and} \quad \prod_{n' \in N_{+1}(n)} \Phi_\beta(T, n') \tag{5.1}$$

are no longer Cartesian products. Instead, the set $S(n) \subset S$ is partitioned into the disjoint non–empty sets $S(n')$ $(n' \in N_{+1}(n))$, so that $Y^{S(n)}$ is the Cartesian product $\prod_{n' \in N_{+1}(n)} Y^{S(n')}$. Now, given the finite collection of lotteries $\lambda(n') \in \Delta(Y^{S(n')})$ $(n' \in N_{+1}(n))$, their *probabilistic product* $\prod_{n' \in N_{+1}(n)} \lambda(n')$, like the product lottery defined in Section 4.4, is the lottery $\lambda(n) \in \Delta(Y^{S(n)})$ which satisfies

$$\lambda(n)\,(y^{S(n)}) := \prod_{n' \in N_{+1}(n)} \lambda(n')\,(y^{S(n')})$$

for all combinations $y^{S(n)} = \langle y^{S(n')}\rangle_{n' \in N_{+1}(n)} \in Y^{S(n)}$. That is, $\lambda(n)$ is the multivariate joint distribution of $y^{S(n)}$ which arises when each of its components $y^{S(n')}$ $(n' \in N_{+1}(n))$ is an independent random variable with distribution

$\lambda(n')$. Then the sets in (5.1) are *probabilistic product sets* consisting of all the possible probabilistic products of independent lotteries $\lambda(n')$ which, for each $n' \in N_{+1}(n)$, belong to the sets $F(T, n')$ and $\Phi_\beta(T, n')$ respectively.

Furthermore, because $\gamma(x) \in \Delta(Y^{S(x)})$ at each terminal node $x \in X$, from (3.2) and (3.3) it follows that, instead of (3.5), the constructed sets satisfy

$$\emptyset \neq \Phi_\beta(T, n) \subset F(T, n) \subset \Delta(Y^{S(n)})$$

for all $n \in N$ including $n = n_0$.

5.2   Consequentialism and Contingent Utilities

In this new framework, the consequentialist hypothesis of Chapter 5 and of Section 3.3 requires that, for each event $E \subset S$, there must be a contingent choice function C_β^E defined on the domain of non–empty finite subsets of $\Delta(Y^E)$, and satisfying

$$\Phi_\beta(T) = C_\beta^E(F(T)) \subset F(T) \subset \Delta(Y^E) \tag{5.2}$$

for all decision trees T such that $S(n_0) = E$ at the initial node n_0 of T. Suppose also that behaviour is dynamically consistent on the almost unrestricted domain of finite decision trees in which all transition probabilities $\pi(n'|n)$ ($n \in N^0$; $n' \in N_{+1}(n)$) are positive.

Consider the restricted domain of decision trees with no natural nodes. Arguing as in Sections 5.6 and 6.3 of Chapter 5, in the first place each C_β^E must correspond to a contingent revealed preference ordering R_β^E on the set $\Delta(Y^E)$; this is condition (O), of course. Second, each contingent ordering R_β^E must satisfy the strong independence condition (I*).

Moreover, the following *sure thing principle for independent lotteries* must be satisfied. Suppose that the two events $E_1, E_2 \subset S$ are disjoint, and that $E = E_1 \cup E_2$. Then, whenever $\lambda^{E_1}, \mu^{E_1} \in \Delta(Y^{E_1})$, and $\nu^{E_2} \in \Delta(Y^{E_2})$, arguing as in Section 3.4 shows that

$$\lambda^{E_1} \; R_\beta^{E_1} \; \mu^{E_1} \iff \left(\lambda^{E_1} \times \nu^{E_2}\right) \; R_\beta^E \; \left(\mu^{E_1} \times \nu^{E_2}\right), \tag{5.3}$$

where $\lambda^{E_1} \times \nu^{E_2}$ and $\mu^{E_1} \times \nu^{E_2}$ denote probabilistic products. Condition (5.3) remains weaker than (STP). Nevertheless, the next subsection introduces an extra assumption that implies condition (RO). Then (STP) will follow from (5.3) because $\lambda^{E_1} \times \nu^{E_2}$ and $\mu^{E_1} \times \nu^{E_2}$ will be indifferent to $(\lambda^{E_1}, \nu^{E_2})$ and (μ^{E_1}, ν^{E_2}) respectively; only the marginal distributions will matter.

Suppose that behaviour also satisfies the continuity hypothesis discussed in Section 7.1 of Chapter 5. Then, for each non–empty $E \subset S$, there is a unique cardinal equivalence class of NMUFs $v^E : Y^E \to \mathbb{R}$ whose expected values represent the revealed preference ordering R_β^E. The complete family of all possible NMUFs v^E ($\emptyset \neq E \subset S$) is characterized in Hammond (1988).

5.3 Consequentialist Normal Form Invariance and Condition (RO)

One of the six conditions discussed in Section 4 was (RO) — reversal of order. An implication of the results in Hammond (1988) is that this condition cannot be deduced from the other consequentialist axioms introduced so far. But one can argue that it is reasonable to impose it anyway as an additional axiom. Indeed, let λ^S be any lottery in $\Delta(Y^S)$. Then there exist CCFs $y_i^S \in Y^S$ and associated probabilities $q_i \geq 0$ ($i = 1, 2, \ldots, k$) such that $\sum_{i=1}^k q_i = 1$ and $\lambda^S = \sum_{i=1}^k q_i 1_{y_i^S}$. For each $s \in S$ the corresponding marginal distribution is $\lambda_s = \sum_{i=1}^k q_i 1_{y_{is}}$. Now consider two decision trees T and T' described as follows.

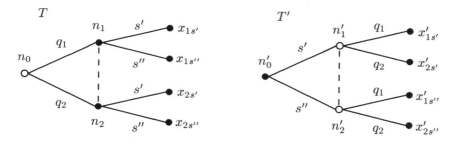

Figure 5.1 Decision trees T and T' (when $k = 2$ and $E = \{ s', s'' \}$)

Tree T begins with the chance node n_0, which is succeeded by the set of natural nodes $N_{+1}(n_0) = \{ n_i \mid i = 1, 2, \ldots, k \}$. The transition probabilities are $\pi(n_i|n_0) = q_i$ ($i = 1, 2, \ldots, k$). Each $n_i \in N_{+1}(n_0)$ is succeeded by the set of terminal nodes $N_{+1}(n_i) = \{ x_{is} \mid s \in S \}$. The tree T is illustrated in the left half of Figure 5.1 for the case when $k = 2$ and $S = \{ s', s'' \}$. The consequences are assumed to be given by $\gamma(x_{is}) = 1_{y_{is}} \in \Delta(Y)$ for $i = 1, 2, \ldots, k$ and $s \in S$.

On the other hand, tree T' begins with the natural node n_0', whose successors form the set $N_{+1}'(n_0') = \{ n_s' \mid s \in S \}$. Then each $n_s' \in N_{+1}'(n_0')$ is a chance node whose successors form the set $N_{+1}'(n_s') = \{ x_{is}' \mid i = 1, 2, \ldots, k \}$ of terminal nodes. The transition probabilities are $\pi'(x_{is}'|n_s') = q_i$ ($i = 1, 2, \ldots, k$). The tree T' is illustrated in the right half of Figure 5.1, again for the case when $k = 2$ and $S = \{ s', s'' \}$. The consequences are assumed to be given by $\gamma'(x_{is}') = 1_{y_{is}} \in \Delta(Y)$ for $i = 1, 2, \ldots, k$ and $s \in S$.

Both trees represent a three–person extensive game between chance, nature, and the decision maker, who actually has no decision to make. In tree T it is natural to assume that $N_{+1}(n_0)$ is a single information set for nature. Similarly, in tree T' it is natural to assume that $N'_{+1}(n'_0)$ is a single information set for chance. Then the extensive form games represented by the two trees will have identical normal forms, in which the decision maker has only one strategy, whereas chance's strategies are indexed by $i \in \{1, 2, \ldots, k\}$ and nature's strategies are indexed by $s \in S$. Furthermore, in either extensive form game, when chance chooses i and nature chooses s, the consequence is $1_{y_{is}}$. In fact, the *consequentialist normal form invariance* condition is that trees like T and T' with identical three–person normal forms should be regarded as giving rise to equivalent feasible sets, and that behaviour should generate equivalent choice sets of consequences in each case. This is a natural extension of the normal form invariance hypothesis which will be discussed in a later chapter on utility in non–cooperative games.

Evidently, in tree T the only feasible consequence is $\lambda^S = \sum_{i=1}^{k} q_i 1_{y_i^S}$, whereas in tree T' it is $\langle \lambda_s \rangle_{s \in S} = \langle \sum_{i=1}^{k} q_i 1_{y_{is}} \rangle_{s \in S}$. Consequentialist normal form invariance requires these consequences to be regarded as equivalent. So only the marginal distributions $\sum_{i=1}^{k} q_i 1_{y_{is}}$ ($s \in S$) are relevant. By the remark after Theorem 4.5 this is precisely condition (RO), as stated in Section 4.4.

5.4   State Independent Consequentialism, No Null Events, and Continuity

Let T and T' be two finite decision trees such that $S(n) = \{s\}$ for all $n \in N$ and $S'(n') = \{s'\}$ for all $n' \in N'$, so only a single state of nature is possible in each tree. Thus, there is really no uncertainty about the state. Suppose also that the feasible sets $F(T)$ and $F(T')$ of random consequences are equal when regarded as subsets of the set $\Delta(Y)$. Then a very minor extension of the consequentialist hypothesis (5.2), to be called *state independent consequentialism*, requires that the behaviour sets $\Phi_\beta(T)$ and $\Phi_\beta(T')$ should be equal subsets of $F(T) = F(T') \subset \Delta(Y)$. Thus, because only consequences matter and the state is certain, that state should not affect the consequences of behaviour. Equivalently, there must be a state independent consequence choice function C_β^* satisfying $C_\beta^* = C_\beta^{\{s\}}$ for all $s \in S$. Obviously, this implies that the preference orderings $R_\beta^{\{s\}}$ are state independent, so condition (SI) of Section 4.6 must be satisfied—i.e., there must exist R_β^* such that $R_\beta^{\{s\}} = R_\beta^*$ for all $s \in S$.

Next, note that $s \in S$ will be a null state iff $\lambda \, I_\beta^{\{s\}} \, \mu$ for all $\lambda, \mu \in \Delta(Y)$. Now, state independent consequentialism implies that C_β^* must equal $C_\beta^{\{s\}}$ for all $s \in S$, not only for all non-null $s \in S$. In particular, the indifference relation $I_\beta^{\{s\}}$ must be state independent. It follows that, if any state $s \in S$ is null, then all states are null. Because S is finite, Lemma 4.2 implies that then we must be in the trivial case of universal indifference throughout the domain $\Delta(Y^S)$, with $\Phi_\beta(T) = F(T)$ for every finite decision tree T. This is similar to the result noted in Section 6.3 of Chapter 5 that, if zero probabilities are allowed into decision trees, the consequentialist axioms imply universal indifference. Outside this trivial case, therefore, state independent consequentialism implies that there can be no null events.

As for the continuity conditions (C) and (C*) of Section 4.3, the stronger condition (C*) follows provided that behaviour satisfies the continuity hypothesis set out in Section 7.1 of Chapter 5. Then all six conditions of Section 4 in this chapter must be satisfied. It has therefore been shown that the usual consequentialist axioms, supplemented by the continuity hypothesis of Chapter 5 and by the above state independence hypothesis, imply that all six conditions of Theorem 4.5 are met and also that null events are impossible. By the remark after Theorem 4.5, the SEU* hypothesis must be satisfied.

5.5 Sufficient Conditions for Consequentialism

State independent consequentialist behaviour that is dynamically consistent on the almost unrestricted domain of finite decision trees is completely characterized by the existence of a preference ordering $\succsim$ on $\Delta(Y^S)$ satisfying conditions (I*), (RO), (STP), and (SI), as well as the absence of null states. It has been shown that these conditions are necessary. Conversely, if these conditions are all satisfied, then consequentialist and dynamically consistent behaviour β can be defined on an almost unrestricted domain of finite decision trees in order to satisfy the property that, for each event $E \subset S$, the contingent revealed preference ordering R_β^E is equal to the contingent preference ordering $\succsim^E$ on $\Delta(Y^E)$. This can be proved by essentially the same argument as in Chapter 5. Indeed, for each node n of each finite decision tree T, define

$$\Psi(T,n) := \{ \lambda \in F(T,n) \mid \mu \in F(T,n) \implies \lambda \succsim^{S(n)} \mu \} \qquad (5.4)$$

as in Section 6.4 of Chapter 5. Also, for any decision node $n \in N^*$, let $\beta(T(n), n)$ be any subset of $N_{+1}(n)$ with the property that

$$\bigcup_{n' \in \beta(T(n),n)} \Psi(T, n') = \Psi(T, n).$$

As was argued in Chapter 5, $\Psi(T,n) \neq \emptyset$ for all $n \in N$, and $\beta(T,n) \neq \emptyset$ at every decision node n of tree T. Obviously, to make β dynamically consistent, put $\beta(T,n^*) = \beta(T(n^*),n^*)$ whenever n^* is a decision node of tree T.

Now Lemma 6.1 of Chapter 5 can be proved almost as before, showing in particular that $\Phi_\beta(T,n) = \Psi(T,n)$ everywhere. This last equality evidently implies that $R_\beta^{S(n)} = \succsim^{S(n)}$. Apart from minor changes in notation, with $\succsim^{S(n)}$ replacing $\succsim$ throughout, the only new feature of the proof by backward induction is the need to include an extra case 3, when $n \in N^1$ is a natural node. The following proof is a routine modification of that for when $n \in N^0$ is a chance node.

When $n \in N^1$ is a natural node, the relevant new version of the induction hypothesis used in proving Lemma 6.1 of Chapter 5 is that $\Phi_\beta(T,n') = \Psi(T,n')$ for all $n' \in N_{+1}(n)$. Recall too that

$$\Phi_\beta(T,n) = \prod_{n' \in N_{+1}(n)} \Phi_\beta(T,n') \quad \text{and} \quad F(T,n) = \prod_{n' \in N_{+1}(n)} F(T,n'), \quad (5.5)$$

where, as in (5.1) of this chapter, the products are probabilistic.

Suppose that $\lambda \in \Phi_\beta(T,n)$ and $\mu \in F(T,n)$. By (5.5), for all $n' \in N_{+1}(n)$ there exist $\lambda(n') \in \Phi_\beta(T,n') = \Psi(T,n')$ and $\mu(n') \in F(T,n')$ such that

$$\lambda = \prod_{n' \in N_{+1}(n)} \lambda(n'), \quad \mu = \prod_{n' \in N_{+1}(n)} \mu(n'). \quad (5.6)$$

For all $n' \in N_{+1}(n)$, because $\lambda(n') \in \Psi(T,n')$, one has $\lambda(n') \succsim^{S(n')} \mu(n')$. By repeatedly applying condition (STP) as in the proof of Lemma 4.2, it follows that $\lambda \succsim^{S(n)} \mu$. This is true for all $\mu \in F(T,n)$, so (5.4) implies that $\lambda \in \Psi(T,n)$.

Conversely, suppose that $\lambda \in \Psi(T,n)$. For all $n' \in N_{+1}(n)$, there must then exist $\lambda(n') \in F(T,n')$ such that $\lambda = \prod_{n' \in N_{+1}(n)} \lambda(n')$. So for any $n'' \in N_{+1}(n)$ and any $\mu(n'') \in F(T,n'')$ it must be true that

$$\lambda = \prod_{n' \in N_{+1}(n)} \lambda(n') \succsim^{S(n)} \mu(n'') \times \prod_{n' \in N_{+1}(n) \setminus \{n''\}} \lambda(n'). \quad (5.7)$$

Applying condition (STP) to (5.7) implies that $\lambda(n'') \succsim^{S(n'')} \mu(n'')$. Since this holds for all $\mu(n'') \in F(T,n'')$, it follows that $\lambda(n'') \in \Psi(T,n'')$. But this is true for all $n'' \in N_{+1}(n)$. Hence, by the induction hypothesis, $\lambda(n') \in \Psi(T,n') = \Phi_\beta(T,n')$ for all $n' \in N_{+1}(n)$. So (5.5) and (5.6) together imply that $\lambda \in \Phi_\beta(T,n)$.

Therefore $\Phi_\beta(T,n) = \Psi(T,n)$ also when $n \in N^1$. The proof by induction is complete for this third case as well.

5.6 Dynamic Programming and Continuous Behaviour

Suppose that there are no null states in S. Suppose too that, for each event $E \subset S$, the contingent preference ordering $\succsim^E$ is represented by the *conditional expected utility function*

$$\sum_{s \in E} p_s \left[\sum_{y \in Y} \lambda_s(y)\, v(y) \right] \Bigg/ \sum_{s \in E} p_s.$$

This is proportional to $U^E(\lambda^E)$ given by (4.6) in Section 4.5, but with the strictly positive subjective probabilities p_s replaced by conditional probabilities $p_s / \sum_{s \in E} p_s$. Let T be any finite decision tree. As in Section 7.2 of Chapter 5, a node valuation function $w(T, \cdot) : N \to \mathbb{R}$ can be constructed by backward recursion. The process starts at each terminal node $x \in X$, where $w(T, x)$ is simply the conditional expected utility of the random consequence $\gamma(x) = \langle \gamma_s(x) \rangle_{s \in S(x)} \in \Delta(Y^{S(x)})$. That is,

$$w(T, x) := \sum_{s \in S(x)} p_s \sum_{y \in Y} \gamma_s(x)(y)\, v(y) \Bigg/ \sum_{s \in S(x)} p_s.$$

As in Section 7.2 of Chapter 5, at any decision node $n \in N^*$ one has

$$w(T, n) := \max_{n'} \{\, w(T, n') \mid n' \in N_{+1}(n) \,\},$$

while at any chance node $n \in N^0$ one has

$$w(T, n) := \sum_{n' \in N_{+1}(n)} \pi(n' | n)\, w(T, n').$$

Now, at any natural node $n \in N^1$ one constructs in addition

$$w(T, n) := \sum_{n' \in N_{+1}(n)} P(S(n') | S(n))\, w(T, n'),$$

where $P(S(n') | S(n)) := \sum_{s \in S(n')} p_s / \sum_{s \in S(n)} p_s$ is the well defined conditional subjective probability that nature will select a state in the set $S(n')$, given that a state in $S(n)$ is already bound to occur after reaching node n. As in Section 7.2 of Chapter 5, the principle of optimality in dynamic programming still holds, with subjective expected utility maximizing behaviour β satisfying

$$\emptyset \neq \beta(T, n) \subset \arg\max_{n'} \{\, w(T, n') \mid n' \in N_{+1}(n) \,\} \tag{5.8}$$

at any decision node $n \in N^*$. Also, at any node $n \in N$, one has

$$
\left.\begin{array}{rcl}
\Phi_\beta(T,n) & = & \arg \\
w(T,n) & = &
\end{array}\right\} \max_\lambda \left\{ U^{S(n)}(\lambda) \mid \lambda \in F(T,n) \right\}. \tag{5.9}
$$

The proof of Lemma 7.2 in Chapter 5 can then be adapted easily to show that SEU behaviour β must satisfy continuity condition (CB). Indeed, it is only necessary to realize that each natural node $n \in N^1$ can be replaced with an equivalent chance node where nature moves to each node $n' \in N_{+1}(n)$ with positive conditional probability $P(S(n')|S(n))$.

5.7 Main Theorem

Corresponding to the main result in Section 7.3 of Chapter 5 is the following:

THEOREM 5.1 (1) Let β be non–trivial state independent consequentialist behaviour which, for the almost unrestricted domain of finite decision trees with only positive probabilities at all chance nodes, satisfies consequentialist normal form invariance, dynamic consistency, and the continuous behaviour condition (CB) stated in Section 7.1 of Chapter 5. Then there exists a unique cardinal equivalence class of NMUFs $v : Y \to \mathbb{R}$ and unique strictly positive subjective probabilities such that β maximizes subjectively expected utility.

(2) Conversely, let $v : Y \to \mathbb{R}$ be any NMUF, and p_s ($s \in S$) any strictly positive subjective probabilities. Then state independent consequentialist behaviour β satisfying consequentialist normal form invariance, dynamic consistency and condition (CB) can be defined on the almost unrestricted domain of finite decision trees with only positive probabilities at all chance nodes in order that the associated preference ordering R_β revealed by behaviour β should be represented by the subjective expected value of v.

6 State–Dependent Consequence Domains

6.1 Evaluation Functions

Up to this point, it has been assumed throughout that there is a fixed consequence domain Y, independent of the state of the world $s \in S$. Yet, as discussed in the later chapter on state–dependent utility, this is a poor assumption in many practical examples — for example, if some states lead to the death or permanent impairment of the decision maker. Consequences arising in such disastrous states seem quite different from those that can be experienced while the decision maker still enjoys good health. Accordingly, this section considers the implications of allowing there to be a consequence domain Y_s that depends on the state of the world $s \in S$. Also, in contrast to Karni (1993a, b), it will not be assumed that consequences in different state–dependent consequence domains are in any way related through "constant valuation acts" or "state invariance". Evidently, the state independence condition (SI) must be dropped.

Eventually, Lemma 6.1 in this Section will demonstrate what happens when the five axioms of Sections 4.3–4.5 are applied to the domain $\Delta(Y^S)$, where Y^S is now the Cartesian product $\prod_{s \in S} Y_s$ of state dependent consequence domains, and S is once again the finite domain of possible states of the world. In order to state the result, first define the *union domain* $\hat{Y} := \cup_{s \in S} Y_s$ of all consequences that can occur in some state of the world. Then let

$$Y_S := \cup_{s \in S}(\{s\} \times Y_s) = \{(s, y) \in S \times \hat{Y} \mid y \in Y_s\} \qquad (6.1)$$

be the *universal domain* of state–consequence pairs. This is an obvious generalization of the domain of "prize–state lotteries" considered by Karni (1985) — see also the later chapter on state–dependent utility.

Second, define an **evaluation function** (Wilson, 1968; Myerson, 1979) as a real–valued mapping $w(s, y)$ on the domain Y_S with the property that the preference ordering $\succsim$ on $\Delta(Y^S)$ is represented by the expected total evaluation, which is defined for all $\lambda^S \in \Delta(Y^S)$ with associated marginal distributions $\lambda_s \in \Delta(Y_s)$ $(s \in S)$ by

$$U^S(\lambda^S) = \sum_{s \in S} \sum_{y_s \in Y_s} \lambda_s(y_s) \, w(s, y_s). \qquad (6.2)$$

Evaluation functions will be distinguished from state–dependent utility functions because the latter are separate from and independent of subjective probabilities, whereas the former conflate utility functions with subjective probabilities. Also, say that two evaluation functions $w(s, y)$ and $\tilde{w}(s, y)$ are *co–cardinally equivalent* if and only if there exist real constants $\rho > 0$, independent of s, and δ_s $(s \in S)$, such that

$$\tilde{w}(s, y) = \delta_s + \rho \, w(s, y). \qquad (6.3)$$

In this case the alternative expected evaluation satisfies

$$\tilde{U}^S(\lambda^S) = \sum_{s \in S} \sum_{y_s \in Y_s} \lambda_s(y_s) \, \tilde{w}(s, y_s) = \sum_{s \in S} \delta_s + \rho \, U^S(\lambda^S), \qquad (6.4)$$

because $\sum_{y_s \in Y_s} \lambda_s(y_s) = 1$ for each $s \in S$. Hence $\tilde{U}^S$ and U^S are cardinally equivalent, so both represent the same contingent preference ordering on $\Delta(Y^S)$.

Conversely, suppose that (6.2) and (6.4) both represent the same ordering $\succsim$ on $\Delta(Y^S)$. Let s, s' be any pair of states in S, and $a, b \in Y_s$, $c, d \in Y_{s'}$ any four consequences with $w(s,a) \neq w(s,b)$ and $w(s',c) \neq w(s',d)$. As was argued in Section 2.3 of Chapter 5 as well as in connection with (4.3) of Section 4.2, the common ratio

$$\frac{w(s,a) - w(s,b)}{w(s',c) - w(s',d)} = \frac{\tilde{w}(s,a) - \tilde{w}(s,b)}{\tilde{w}(s',c) - \tilde{w}(s',d)} \tag{6.5}$$

of evaluation differences is the constant MRS between shifts in probability from consequence b to a in state s and shifts in probability from consequence d to c in state s'. So for all such configurations of s, s', a, b, c, d there must exist a constant ρ such that

$$\frac{\tilde{w}(s,a) - \tilde{w}(s,b)}{w(s,a) - w(s,b)} = \frac{\tilde{w}(s',c) - \tilde{w}(s',d)}{w(s',c) - w(s',d)} = \rho. \tag{6.6}$$

Moreover $\rho > 0$ because the non–zero numerator and denominator of each fraction in (6.6) must have the same sign. Then (6.3) follows, so $\tilde{w}(s,y)$ and $w(s,y)$ must be co–cardinally equivalent functions on the domain Y_S.

For the rest of this section, assume that for every state $s \in S$ there exist $\bar{\lambda}_s, \underline{\lambda}_s \in \Delta(Y_s)$ such that the contingent ordering $\succsim^{\{s\}}$ on $\Delta(Y_s)$ satisfies $\bar{\lambda}_s \succ^{\{s\}} \underline{\lambda}_s$. This loses no generality because, by (STP), states without this property are null states which can be omitted from S without affecting preferences. Obviously, $\bar{\lambda}^S \succ \underline{\lambda}^S$, as can be shown by repeated application of condition (STP).

LEMMA 6.1 Under the five conditions (O), (I), (C), (RO) and (STP), there exists a unique co–cardinal equivalence class of evaluation functions $w(s,y)$ such that the expected sum $U^S(\lambda^S)$ defined by (6.2) represents the corresponding preference ordering $\succsim$ on $\Delta(Y^S)$.

PROOF Because the ordering $\succsim$ satisfies conditions (O), (I) and (C), Theorem 4.8 of Chapter 5 shows that $\succsim$ can be represented by a unique cardinal equivalence class of expected utility functions $U^S : \Delta(Y^S) \to \mathbb{R}$ which satisfy the mixture property (MP) on $\Delta(Y^S)$ (like (4.10) in Section 4.7). Then normalize U^S so that

$$U^S(\underline{\lambda}^S) = 0 \quad \text{and} \quad U^S(\bar{\lambda}^S) = 1. \tag{6.7}$$

Next, for each state $s \in S$ and lottery $\lambda \in \Delta(Y_s)$, define

$$u_s(\lambda) := U^S(\underline{\lambda}^{S\backslash\{s\}}, \lambda). \tag{6.8}$$

Note that whenever $s \in S$ is a null state, then $(\underline{\lambda}^{S \setminus \{s\}}, \lambda) \sim \underline{\lambda}^S$ for all $\lambda \in \Delta(Y_s)$. In this case, it follows from (6.8) and (6.7) that $u_s(\lambda) \equiv 0$ on $\Delta(Y_s)$.

Let m be the number of elements in the finite set S. By an argument similar to that used in the proof of Lemma 4.4, for all $\lambda^S \in \Delta(Y^S)$, condition (RO) implies that the two members

$$\sum_{s \in S} \frac{1}{m} (\underline{\lambda}^{S \setminus \{s\}}, \lambda_s) \quad \text{and} \quad \frac{m-1}{m} \underline{\lambda}^S + \frac{1}{m} \lambda^S \tag{6.9}$$

of $\Delta(Y^S)$ are indifferent because for each $s \in S$ they have the common marginal distribution $(1 - \frac{1}{m}) \underline{\lambda}_s + \frac{1}{m} \lambda_s$. Because U^S satisfies (MP), applying U^S to the two indifferent mixtures in (6.9) gives the equality

$$\sum_{s \in S} \frac{1}{m} U^S(\underline{\lambda}^{S \setminus \{s\}}, \lambda_s) = \frac{m-1}{m} U^S(\underline{\lambda}^S) + \frac{1}{m} U^S(\lambda^S). \tag{6.10}$$

But $U^S(\underline{\lambda}^S) = 0$ by (6.7), so (6.10) and (6.8) together imply that

$$U^S(\lambda^S) = \sum_{s \in S} U^S(\underline{\lambda}^{S \setminus \{s\}}, \lambda_s) = \sum_{s \in S} u_s(\lambda_s). \tag{6.11}$$

Finally, define $w(s, y) := u_s(1_y)$ for each $s \in S$ and $y \in Y_s$. Because U^S satisfies (MP), (6.8) implies that so does each function u_s on the corresponding domain $\Delta(Y_s)$. It follows that $u_s(\lambda_s) \equiv \sum_{y \in Y_s} \lambda_s(y) w(s, y)$ and so, because of (6.11), that $U^S(\lambda^S)$ is given by (6.2).

The fact that there is a unique co–cardinal equivalence class of the functions $w(s, y)$ follows easily from the discussion preceding the lemma. ∎

6.2 Chosen Probabilities and State–Dependent Utilities

An extreme case occurs if the state–dependent consequence domains Y_s and $Y_{s'}$ are disjoint whenever $s \neq s'$. In this case, there seems no hope of inferring subjective probabilities from behaviour. To see why, suppose that an agent's behaviour is observed to maximize the SEU function

$$U^S(y^S) = \sum_{s \in S} p_s \, v(y_s),$$

where $p_s > 0$ for all $s \in S$. Then the same behaviour will also maximize the equivalent SEU function

$$U^S(y^S) = \sum_{s \in S} \tilde{p}_s \, \tilde{v}(y_s)$$

for *any* positive subjective probabilities $\tilde{p}_s$ satisfying $\sum_{s \in S} \tilde{p}_s = 1$, provided that $\tilde{v}(y) = p_s\, v(y_s)/\tilde{p}_s$ for all $y \in Y_s$. Without further information, there is no way of disentangling subjective probabilities from utilities.

Following a suggestion of Karni, Schmeidler and Vind (1983), such additional information could be inferred from hypothetical behaviour when probabilities p_s $(s \in S)$ happen to be specified. The idea is that, though the agent does not know the true probabilities of the different states of the world, nevertheless it should be possible for coherent decisions to emerge if the agent happened to discover what the true probabilities are. In particular, if those true probabilities happen to coincide with the agent's subjective probabilities, the agent's behaviour should be the same whether or not these true probabilities are known.[7]

A somewhat extreme version of this assumption will be used here. Following Karni (1985, Section 1.6), Schervish, Seidenfeld and Kadane (1990), and also Karni and Schmeidler (1991), it will be assumed that the decision–maker can handle problems involving not only hypothetical probabilities, but also hypothetical choices of probabilities. Take, for instance, problems where the states of nature are indeed natural disasters, weather events, etc. It will be assumed that the decision–maker can rank prospects of the following general kind: A probability of 2% each year of a major earthquake? Or 1% each year of a devastating hundred year flood? Or 4% each year of a serious forest fire set off by lightning? More specifically, the assumption is that the decision–maker can resolve such issues within a coherent framework of decision analysis. Certainly, if the SEU hypothesis holds, it can be applied to decide such issues. Drèze's (1961, 1987) theory of "moral hazard" is based on a somewhat related idea. But Drèze assumes that the agent can influence the choice of state, as opposed to the choice of probabilities of different states.

For this reason, it will be assumed that there exists an additional preference ordering $\succsim_S$ on the whole extended lottery domain $\Delta(Y_S)$, where Y_S, defined by (6.1), is the universal state–consequence domain of pairs (s, y). Thus, $\succsim_S$ satisfies condition (O). Furthermore, assume that $\succsim_S$ satisfies the obvious counterparts of conditions (I) and (C) for the domain $\Delta(Y_S)$. Obviously, these conditions (O) and (I) can be given a consequentialist justification, along the lines of that in Sections 5 and 6 of Chapter 5, by considering a suitably extended domain of decision trees in which natural nodes become replaced by chance nodes, and there are even several copies of natural nodes so that opportunities to affect the probabilities attached to states of nature are incorporated in the tree. Arguing as in that chapter, there must exist a unique cardinal equiva-

---

[7]Recently Mongin (1998), then Karni and Mongin (1997) have pointed out a serious defect with the approach due to Karni, Schmeidler and Vind. The problem is that alternative specifications of the "hypothetical" probabilities p_s $(s \in S)$ can easily lead to different subjective probabilities, in general.

lence class of extended NMUFs v_S on the domain Y_S whose expected values all represent the ordering $\succsim_S$ on $\Delta(Y_S)$. Because the function $v_S(s, y)$ has both the state $s \in S$ and the consequence $y \in Y_s$ as arguments, for each fixed $s \in S$ the NMUF $v_S(s, \cdot)$ is a state–dependent utility function on the domain Y_s.

Note next that when any state $s \in S$ is certain, and assuming that everything relevant to each decision is included within each consequence $y \in Y_s$, the spaces Y_s and $Y_{Ss} := \{s\} \times Y_s$ are effectively equivalent consequence domains. Thus, each $\Delta(Y_s)$ is effectively the same as the set

$$\Delta(Y_{Ss}) := \{\, \lambda \in \Delta(Y_S) \mid \lambda(\{s\} \times Y_s) = 1 \,\} \tag{6.12}$$

of lotteries attaching probability one to the state $s \in S$. So, after excluding states in which the contingent preference ordering $\succsim^{\{s\}}$ on $\Delta(Y_s)$ is trivial, as in Section 6.1, it will be assumed that each $\succsim^{\{s\}}$ is identical to the ordering $\succsim_S$ restricted to the corresponding set $\Delta(Y_{Ss})$. But these orderings are represented by the expected values of the two respective NMUFs $w(s, y)$ and $v_S(s, y)$ on the common domain Y_s. So these NMUFs are cardinally equivalent functions of y. Hence, there must exist constants $\rho_s > 0$ and δ_s such that on Y_s one has

$$w(s, y) \equiv \delta_s + \rho_s \, v_S(s, y). \tag{6.13}$$

Now define $\rho := \sum_{s \in S} \rho_s > 0$ and, for all $s \in S$, the ratios $p_s := \rho_s / \rho$. Clearly each $p_s > 0$ and $\sum_{s \in S} p_s = 1$. Therefore the ratios p_s can be interpreted as subjective probabilities. Furthermore, because $\succsim$ on $\Delta(Y^S)$ is represented by the expected total evaluation (6.2), it is also represented by the expectation of the cardinally equivalent NMUF $v^S(y^S) := \sum_{s \in S} p_s \, v_S(s, y_s)$.

Given the CCF $y^S \in Y^S$ and consequence $y \in \hat{Y} = \cup_{s \in S} Y_s$, let

$$E(y^S, y) := \{\, s \in S \mid y_s = y \,\}$$

be the set of states in which y occurs. Then the CCF $y^S \in Y^S$ is subjectively equivalent to the lottery $\lambda \in \Delta(\hat{Y})$ with the objective probability of each consequence $y \in \hat{Y}$ given by $\lambda(y) = \sum_{s \in E(y^S, y)} q_s$.

Because of (6.13), one has $w(s, \tilde{y}_s) - w(s, y_s) = \rho_s [v_S(s, \tilde{y}_s) - v_S(s, y_s)]$ for any state $s \in S$ and any pair of consequences $y_s, \tilde{y}_s \in Y_s$. Therefore,

$$\frac{p_s}{p_{s'}} = \frac{\rho_s}{\rho_{s'}} = \frac{w(s, \tilde{y}_s) - w(s, y_s)}{w(s', \tilde{y}_{s'}) - w(s', y_{s'})} \cdot \frac{v_S(s', \tilde{y}_{s'}) - v_S(s', y_{s'})}{v_S(s, \tilde{y}_s) - v_S(s, y_s)}. \tag{6.14}$$

This formula enables ratios of subjective probabilities to be inferred uniquely in an obvious way from marginal rates of substitution (MRSs) between shifts in objective probability, expressed in the form of ratios of utility differences. The first term of the product is the MRS between changes in the probabilities of consequences in two different states of the kind considered in (6.5). The second term is a four–way ratio of utility differences that equals the MRS between shifts in probability from $(s', \tilde{y}_{s'})$ to $(s', y_{s'})$ and shifts in probability from $(s, \tilde{y}_s)$ to (s, y_s).

To summarize the results of the above discussion:

LEMMA 6.2 Suppose that:

1. conditions (O), (I), and (C) apply to the ordering $\succsim_S$ on the domain $\Delta(Y_S)$;

2. conditions (O), (I), (C), (RO) and (STP) apply to the ordering $\succsim$ on $\Delta(Y^S)$;

3. for each $s \in S$, the contingent preference ordering $\succsim^{\{s\}}$ on $\Delta(Y_s)$ is identical to the restriction of the ordering $\succsim_S$ to this set, regarded as equal to $\Delta(Y_{Ss})$ defined by (6.12);

4. for each $s \in S$, there exist $\bar{\lambda}_s, \underline{\lambda}_s \in \Delta(Y_s)$ such that $\bar{\lambda}_s \succ^{\{s\}} \underline{\lambda}_s$.

Then there exist unique positive subjective probabilities p_s $(s \in S)$ and a unique cardinal equivalence class of state–dependent NMUFs $v_S : Y_S \to \mathbb{R}$ such that the ordering $\succsim$ on $\Delta(Y^S)$ is represented by the expected utility function

$$U^S(\lambda^S) \equiv \sum_{s \in S} p_s \sum_{y_s \in Y_s} \lambda_s(y_s) \, v_S(s, y_s).$$

6.3 State–Independent Utilities

So far, no attention has been paid to the possibility of the same consequence arising in different states of the world. Apart from being unrealistic, this also means that the theory set out in the previous sections of this chapter has not really been generalized. Instead of one extreme of identical consequence domains in all states, as in the classical theory, we have merely gone to the other extreme of consequence domains in different states being treated as if they were pairwise disjoint. Here the implications of treating the same consequence in a different state of the world as really the same consequence will be explored.

First, note that there is a natural embedding $\phi : \Delta(Y_S) \to \Delta(\hat{Y})$ from lotteries λ_S over the universal domain Y_S defined by (6.1) to lotteries over the union domain $\hat{Y} = \cup_{s \in S} Y_s$. After adopting the convention that $\lambda_S(s, y) = 0$ whenever $y \notin Y_s$, this embedding can be defined by

$$\phi(\lambda_S)(y) := \sum_{s \in S} \lambda_S(s, y) \tag{6.15}$$

for all $\lambda_S \in \Delta(Y_S)$ and all $y \in \hat{Y}$. Thus, $\phi(\lambda_S)(y)$ is the total probability of all state–consequence pairs (s, y) in which the particular consequence y occurs. Evidently, for all $\lambda_S, \mu_S \in \Delta(Y_S)$ and all $\alpha \in (0, 1)$, definition (6.15) implies that

$$\phi(\alpha\,\lambda_S + (1 - \alpha)\,\mu_S) = \alpha\,\phi(\lambda_S) + (1 - \alpha)\,\phi(\mu_S). \tag{6.16}$$

LEMMA 6.3 The mapping $\phi : \Delta(Y_S) \to \Delta(\hat{Y})$ is onto.

PROOF Given any $\lambda \in \Delta(\hat{Y})$, let $K_\lambda := \{ y \in \hat{Y} \mid \lambda(y) > 0 \}$ denote the (finite) support of the distribution λ. For each consequence $y \in K_\lambda$, choose any state $s(y) \in S$ with the property that $y \in Y_{s(y)}$; at least one such state always exists. Then define $\lambda_S \in \Delta(Y_S)$ so that $\lambda_S(s(y), y) = \lambda(y)$ for all $y \in K_\lambda$, but $\lambda_S(s, y) = 0$ unless both $y \in K_\lambda$ and $s = s(y)$. Evidently $\phi(\lambda_S)(y) = \lambda_S(s(y), y) = \lambda(y)$ for all $y \in K_\lambda$, and $\phi(\lambda_S)(y) = \lambda(y) = 0$ for all $y \notin K_\lambda$. This shows that $\phi(\lambda_S) = \lambda$. ∎

The pre–image correspondence $\Phi_S : \Delta(\hat{Y}) \twoheadrightarrow \Delta(Y_S)$ of ϕ can be defined, for all $\lambda \in \Delta(\hat{Y})$, by

$$\Phi_S(\lambda) := \{ \lambda_S \in \Delta(Y_S) \mid \phi(\lambda_S) = \lambda \}.$$

Because of Lemma 6.3, $\Phi_S(\lambda)$ is never empty. In this framework, it now seems natural to impose the requirement that, given any pair $\lambda_S, \mu_S \in \Delta(Y_S)$ for which the induced consequence lotteries $\phi(\lambda_S), \phi(\mu_S) \in \Delta(\hat{Y})$ are the same, the state s in which each state–consequence pair $(s, y) \in Y_S$ occurs is irrelevant. In particular, this suggests the following:

(GSI) *Generalized State Independence.* For all pairs $\lambda_S, \mu_S \in \Delta(Y_S)$ one has $\lambda_S \sim_S \mu_S$ whenever $\phi(\lambda_S) = \phi(\mu_S)$.

Thus, for each $\lambda \in \Delta(\hat{Y})$, the set $\Phi_S(\lambda)$ must be an indifference class for the relation $\succsim_S$. So there must exist a "state–independent consequence" preference relation $\succsim_Y$ on $\Delta(\hat{Y})$ defined by

$$\lambda \succsim_Y \mu \iff [\forall \lambda_S \in \Phi_S(\lambda); \forall \mu_S \in \Phi_S(\mu) : \lambda_S \succsim_S \mu_S]. \tag{6.17}$$

Equivalently, for all pairs $\lambda_S, \mu_S \in \Delta(Y_S)$, it must be true that

$$\lambda_S \succsim_S \mu_S \iff \phi(\lambda_S) \succsim_Y \phi(\mu_S).$$

In the special case of a state independent consequence domain, with $Y_s = Y$ for all $s \in S$, condition (GSI) evidently implies that $\succsim_S$ reduces to an ordering on $\Delta(Y)$. But condition (GSI) can also hold when the domains Y_s depend on the state; they could even be pairwise disjoint.

LEMMA 6.4 Suppose that conditions (O), (I), (C) and (GSI) apply to the ordering $\succsim_S$ on the domain $\Delta(Y_S)$. Then the relation $\succsim_Y$ satisfies conditions (O), (I), and (C) on $\Delta(\hat{Y})$.

PROOF Throughout the following proof, given any three lotteries $\lambda, \mu, \nu \in \Delta(\hat{Y})$, let $\lambda_S, \mu_S, \nu_S \in \Delta(Y_S)$ denote arbitrarily chosen members of $\Phi_S(\lambda)$, $\Phi_S(\mu)$ and $\Phi_S(\nu)$ respectively. That is, suppose $\lambda = \phi(\lambda_S)$, $\mu = \phi(\mu_S)$, and $\nu = \phi(\nu_S)$. Because of (6.16), it follows that

$$\phi(\alpha \lambda_S + (1 - \alpha) \nu_S) = \alpha \lambda + (1 - \alpha) \nu;$$
$$\text{and} \quad \phi(\alpha \mu_S + (1 - \alpha) \nu_S) = \alpha \mu + (1 - \alpha) \nu. \tag{6.18}$$

Condition (O). Because (GSI) implies that each set $\Phi_S(\lambda)$ ($\lambda \in \Delta(\hat{Y})$) must be an indifference class for the preference ordering $\succsim_S$, definition (6.17) obviously implies that $\succsim_Y$ is reflexive, complete, and transitive. So $\succsim_Y$ is a preference ordering.

Condition (I). Suppose that $0 < \alpha < 1$. Because $\succsim_S$ satisfies condition (I), it follows from (6.17) and (6.18) that

$$\lambda \succ_Y \mu \quad \Longrightarrow \quad \lambda_S \succ_S \mu_S \quad \Longrightarrow \quad \alpha \lambda_S + (1 - \alpha) \nu_S \succ_S \alpha \mu_S + (1 - \alpha) \nu_S$$
$$\Longrightarrow \quad \alpha \lambda + (1 - \alpha) \nu \succ_Y \alpha \mu + (1 - \alpha) \nu.$$

Therefore $\succsim_Y$ also satisfies condition (I).

Condition (C). Suppose that $\lambda \succ_Y \mu$ and $\mu \succ_Y \nu$. Then $\lambda_S \succ_S \mu_S$ and also $\mu_S \succ_S \nu_S$. Because $\succ_S$ satisfies condition (C), it follows that there exist $\alpha', \alpha'' \in (0, 1)$ such that $\alpha' \lambda_S + (1 - \alpha') \nu_S \succ_S \mu_S$ and $\mu_S \succ_S \alpha'' \lambda_S + (1 - \alpha'') \nu_S$. Then (6.16) and (6.18) together imply that $\alpha' \lambda + (1 - \alpha') \nu \succ_Y \mu$, and also that $\mu \succ_Y \alpha'' \lambda + (1 - \alpha'') \nu$. Therefore $\succsim_Y$ also satisfies condition (C). ∎

The following is the main result in this chapter for state–dependent consequence domains:

THEOREM 6.5 Suppose that:

1. conditions (O), (I), (C) and (GSI) apply to the ordering $\succsim_S$ on the domain $\Delta(Y_S)$ of lotteries over state–consequence pairs (s, y) satisfying $s \in S$ and $y \in Y_s$;

2. conditions (O), (I), (C), (RO) and (STP) apply to the ordering $\succsim$ on the domain $\Delta(Y^S)$;

3. for each $s \in S$, the contingent preference ordering $\succsim^{\{s\}}$ on $\Delta(Y_s)$ is identical to the restriction of the ordering $\succsim_S$ to this set, regarded as equal to $\Delta(Y_{Ss})$, with $Y_{Ss} := \{s\} \times Y_s$ as in (6.12);

4. for each $s \in S$, there exist lotteries $\underline{\lambda}_s, \overline{\lambda}_s \in \Delta(Y_s)$ such that $\overline{\lambda}_s \succ^{\{s\}} \underline{\lambda}_s$.

Then there exists a unique cardinal equivalence class of state–independent NMUFs $\hat{v}$ defined on the union consequence domain $\hat{Y}$, as well as unique positive subjective probabilities p_s ($s \in S$) such that, for every $\hat{v}$ in the equivalence class, the ordering $\succsim$ on $\Delta(Y^S)$ is represented by the expected value of

$$v^S(y^S) \equiv \sum_{s \in S} p_s \, \hat{v}(y_s). \tag{6.19}$$

PROOF By the first hypothesis and Lemma 6.4, the associated ordering $\succsim_Y$ on $\Delta(\hat{Y})$ satisfies conditions (O), (I), and (C). So Lemma 4.7 in Chapter 5 implies that there exists a unique cardinal equivalence class of utility functions $\hat{U} : \Delta(\hat{Y}) \to \mathbb{R}$ which represent $\succsim_Y$ while satisfying the mixture property (MP). Define $\hat{v}(y) := \hat{U}(1_y)$ for all $y \in \hat{Y}$. Then $\hat{v}$ is state independent and belongs to a unique cardinal equivalence class. Because $\hat{U}$ satisfies (MP), condition (GSI) implies that $\succsim_S$ on $\Delta(Y_S)$ must be represented by the expected utility function U_S defined by

$$
\begin{aligned}
U_S(\lambda_S) \quad := \quad \hat{U}(\phi(\lambda_S)) \quad &= \quad \sum_{y \in Y} \phi(\lambda_S)(y) \, \hat{v}(y) \\
&= \quad \sum_{s \in S} \sum_{y \in Y_s} \lambda_S(s, y) \, \hat{v}(y),
\end{aligned}
$$

where the last equality follows from (6.15).

By the second hypothesis and Lemma 6.1, the ordering $\succsim$ on $\Delta(Y^S)$ is represented by the expected total evaluation given by (6.2) in Section 6.1.

Let $s \in S$ be any state. Because of the third hypothesis of the theorem, the two expected utility functions of λ_s defined by $\sum_{y \in Y_s} \lambda_s(y) \, \hat{v}(y)$ and by $\sum_{y \in Y_s} \lambda_s(y) \, w(s, y)$ must be cardinally equivalent on the domain $\Delta(Y_s)$. This implies that for each state $s \in S$, there exist constants $\rho_s > 0$ and δ_s such that $w(s, y) \equiv \delta_s + \rho_s \, \hat{v}(y)$ on Y_s.

Now define $p_s := \rho_s / \rho$, where $\rho := \sum_{s \in S} \rho_s > 0$. Then each $p_s > 0$ and $\sum_{s \in S} p_s = 1$, so the constants p_s ($s \in S$) are probabilities. Also, $w(s, y) \equiv \delta_s + \rho \, p_s \, \hat{v}(y)$. Therefore, by (6.2) and Lemma 6.1 in Section 6.1, the preference ordering $\succsim$ on $\Delta(Y^S)$ is represented by the expected value of

$$v^S(y^S) := \sum_{s \in S} w(s, y_s) = \sum_{s \in S} \delta_s + \rho \sum_{s \in S} p_s \, \hat{v}(y_s).$$

Because $\rho > 0$, it follows that $\succsim$ is also represented by the objectively expected value of the NMUF (6.19).

Finally, the subjective conditional probabilities p_s ($s \in S$) are unique because each ratio $p_s/p_{s'}$ is given by the unique corresponding ratio (6.14) of utility differences. ∎

7   Countable Events

7.1   Bounded Preferences

Up to now, the set S of possible states of the world has been finite throughout. Here, this assumption will be relaxed to allow both S and some conditioning events $E \subset S$ to be countably infinite. The Anscombe and Aumann framework of Section 4 will still be used. Then the SEU hypothesis remains unchanged except that the summation $\sum_{s \in S}$ in (4.2) may be over infinitely many states. Of course, the six conditions that were set out in Section 4 all remain necessary.

Suppose that the set S is countably infinite and that p_s ($s \in S$) are any subjective probabilities. Then any $\lambda^S \in \Delta(Y^S)$ is subjectively equivalent to the lottery λ with $\lambda(y) = \sum_{s \in S} p_s \lambda_s(y)$. Because $\lambda(y)$ can be positive for infinitely many $y \in Y$, it follows that λ is not in general a member of $\Delta(Y)$, the set of simple or finitely supported lotteries on Y. Instead, λ belongs to $\Delta^*(Y)$, the set of all discrete lotteries over Y, whose support can be countably infinite rather than finite. In order to extend the objective EU hypothesis to $\Delta^*(Y)$, Section 8.2 of Chapter 5 introduced the **boundedness condition** (B), requiring each NMUF $v : Y \to \mathbb{R}$ to be bounded. Thus, following the argument of that section, if subjective expected utility is to be well defined for all possible $\lambda^S \in \Delta(Y^S)$, even when S is infinite, then condition (B) must hold. But also necessary is the appropriately reformulated **dominance condition** (D) requiring that, whenever $\lambda_i, \mu_i \in \Delta^*(Y)$ and $\alpha_i > 0$ with $\lambda_i \succsim^* \mu_i$ ($i = 1, 2, \ldots$) and $\sum_{i=1}^{\infty} \alpha_i = 1$, then $\sum_{i=1}^{\infty} \alpha_i \lambda_i \succsim^* \sum_{i=1}^{\infty} \alpha_i \mu_i$. Section 8.5 of Chapter 5 shows how (D) can replace (B) in the set of sufficient conditions, and Section 8.7 of that chapter shows how (D) can be given a consequentialist justification. For this reason, condition (D) will be included in the following discussion, but condition (B) will be excluded.

7.2   Event Continuity

However, the seven conditions (O), (I*), (C*), (RO), (STP), (SI) and (D) are not sufficient on their own for the SEU hypothesis to hold. Indeed, there exist utility functions $U^E(\lambda^E)$ ($E \subset S$) satisfying (MP) such that, whenever E and E' are infinite sets but $E \setminus E'$ and $E' \setminus E$ are finite, then

$$U^{E \cup E'}(\lambda^{E \cup E'}) = U^E(\lambda^E) = U^{E'}(\lambda^{E'}) = U^{E \cap E'}(\lambda^{E \cap E'}),$$

whereas, whenever E_1 and E_2 are disjoint sets, then

$$U^{E_1 \cup E_2}(\lambda^{E_1 \cup E_2}) = U^{E_1}(\lambda^{E_1}) + U^{E_2}(\lambda^{E_2}).$$

In this case, each individual state of the world $s \in S$ and each finite event $E \subset S$ must be null. In particular, any subjective probabilities must satisfy $p_s = 0$ for all $s \in S$. Therefore, except in the trivial case of universal indifference, it cannot be true that $U^S(\lambda^S) = \sum_{s \in S} p_s U^*(\lambda_s)$ when S is infinite.

One attempt to exclude such awkward possibilities would be to postulate, following Savage (1954, p. 39, P6), that if E is any infinite subset of S, and if $\lambda^E, \mu^E \in \Delta(Y^E)$ satisfy $\lambda^E \succ^E \mu^E$, then for any $\nu \in \Delta(Y)$ there is a finite partition $\cup_{k=1}^r E_k$ of E into r small enough pairwise disjoint subsets such that, for $k = 1, 2, \ldots, r$, both $(\lambda^{E \setminus E_k}, \nu 1^{E_k}) \succ^E \mu^E$ and $\lambda^E \succ^E (\mu^{E \setminus E_k}, \nu 1^{E_k})$. However, as shown by Fishburn (1970, ch. 14), this axiom implies that S must be uncountably infinite and also that $p_s = 0$ for all $s \in S$.

So a more suitable alternative seems to be the following condition, suggested by Fishburn (1982, p. 126, axiom F7). Suppose that

$$E_1 \subset E_2 \subset \ldots \subset E_k \subset E_{k+1} \subset \ldots \subset S \quad \text{and} \quad E^* = \cup_{k=1}^\infty E_k. \qquad (7.1)$$

Then the **event continuity condition** (EC) requires that, for all events E and all $\lambda, \mu \in \Delta(Y)$ satisfying both $\lambda \succ^* \mu$ and $(\lambda 1^{E^*}, \mu 1^{S \setminus E^*}) \succ (\lambda 1^E, \mu 1^{S \setminus E})$, there must exist a finite k such that $(\lambda 1^{E_k}, \mu 1^{S \setminus E_k}) \succ (\lambda 1^E, \mu 1^{S \setminus E})$.

To see why this condition is necessary for the SEU hypothesis to hold, first let $P(E) := \sum_{s \in E} p_s$ denote the subjective probability of each event $E \subset S$. Then note how the hypotheses of condition (EC) imply that $U^*(\lambda) > U^*(\mu)$ and also that

$$P(E^*) U^*(\lambda) + [1 - P(E^*)] U^*(\mu) > P(E) U^*(\lambda) + [1 - P(E)] U^*(\mu).$$

Hence $P(E^*) > P(E)$. But $E^* = E_1 \cup [\cup_{k=1}^\infty (E_{k+1} \setminus E_k)]$, where E_1 and $E_{k+1} \setminus E_k$ $(k = 1, 2, \ldots)$ are all pairwise disjoint events. So

$$P(E^*) = P(E_1) + \sum_{k=1}^\infty [P(E_{k+1}) - P(E_k)] = \lim_{k \to \infty} P(E_k).$$

From this it follows that, for all large enough k, one has $P(E_k) > P(E)$ and so $(\lambda 1^{E_k}, \mu 1^{S \setminus E_k}) \succ (\lambda 1^E, \mu 1^{S \setminus E})$. This confirms condition (EC).

7.3   Event Dominance

One other condition will be needed in order to establish the SEU hypothesis for a countably infinite state space. This is the **event dominance condition**

(ED) requiring that, whenever the lotteries $\mu^S \in \Delta^*(Y^S)$ and $\lambda \in \Delta(Y)$ are given, then $\mu_s \succsim^* \lambda$ (all $s \in S$) implies $\mu^S \succsim \lambda 1^S$, and $\mu_s \precsim^* \lambda$ (all $s \in S$) implies $\mu^S \precsim \lambda 1^S$. Clearly, this condition is closely related to the probability dominance condition (PD) discussed in Section 9 of Chapter 5. It even has a similar consequentialist justification. Moreover, Savage's (1954) postulate P7 is analogous—it requires that whenever y^S, $z^S \in Y^S$, then $y^S \succsim z_s 1^S$ (all $s \in S$) implies $y^S \succsim z^S$, and $y^S \precsim z_s 1^S$ (all $s \in S$) implies $y^S \precsim z^S$. In fact, a postulate which evidently strengthens both (ED) and Savage's P7 is the **strong event dominance condition** (ED*) requiring that, whenever $\lambda^S, \mu^S \in \Delta^*(Y^S)$ are given, then $\mu_s \succsim^* \lambda_s 1^S$ (all $s \in S$) implies $\mu^S \succsim \lambda^S$, and $\mu_s \precsim \lambda_s 1^S$ (all $s \in S$) implies $\mu^S \precsim \lambda^S$.

Obviously, condition (ED*) is necessary for the SEU hypothesis to hold when S is countably infinite.

7.4 Sufficient Conditions for SEU and SEU*

Whenever S is a countably infinite set, the nine conditions (O), (I), (C), (RO), (STP), (SI), (D), (EC), and (ED) are sufficient for the SEU hypothesis to be valid on the domain $\Delta^*(Y^S)$. This will not be proved here, however, since it is an obvious corollary of a more general result in the next section, and much of the proof would then have to be repeated there.

8   Subjective Probability Measures

8.1 Measurable Expected Utility

In this section, the set S of possible states of the world can be an infinite set, not necessarily even countably infinite. However, S will be equipped with a σ-field $\mathcal{S}$, to use the standard terminology set out in Section 9.1 of Chapter 5. Thus the pair $(S, \mathcal{S})$ constitutes a measurable space. So, in this section, an *event* E will be defined as any member of $\mathcal{S}$, implying that all events are measurable.

As in Section 9.2 of Chapter 5, let $\mathcal{F}$ denote the σ-field generated by the singleton sets $\{y\}$ ($y \in Y$) together with the particular upper and lower preference sets of the state–independent preference ordering $\succsim^*$ defined by (9.2) of Chapter 5. Indeed, the **measurability condition** (M) of that chapter states precisely that all sets in $\mathcal{F}$ should be measurable. Finally, let $\Delta(Y, \mathcal{F})$ denote the set of (countably additive) probability measures on the σ-field $\mathcal{F}$.

Next, for any event $E \in \mathcal{S}$, let $\mathcal{S}^E$ denote the σ-field consisting of all sets $G \in \mathcal{S}$ such that $G \subset E$. Of course $\mathcal{S}^S = \mathcal{S}$. Then define $\Delta(Y^E, \mathcal{F})$ as the set of mappings $\pi^E : E \to \Delta(Y, \mathcal{F})$ with the property that, for every measurable set $K \in \mathcal{F}$, the real–valued mapping $s \mapsto \pi(s, K)$ on the domain E is measurable when E is given the σ-field $\mathcal{S}^E$ and the real line is given its

Borel σ–field. In other words, given any Borel measurable set $B \subset [0,1]$, the set $\{\, s \in E \mid \pi(s,K) \in B \,\}$ must belong to $\mathcal{S}$. The following result is important later in Section 8.2:

LEMMA 8.1 The set $\Delta(Y^S, \mathcal{F})$ is a convex mixture space.

PROOF (cf. Fishburn, 1982, p. 134) Suppose that $\pi^S, \tilde{\pi}^S \in \Delta(Y^S, \mathcal{F})$ and $0 < \alpha < 1$. Given any $\delta \in [0,1]$ and any $K \in \mathcal{F}$, define the two sets

$$
\begin{aligned}
A_\delta^+ &:= \{\, s \in S \mid \alpha\, \pi(s,K) + (1-\alpha)\, \tilde{\pi}(s,K) > \delta \,\}; \\
A_\delta^- &:= \{\, s \in S \mid \alpha\, \pi(s,K) + (1-\alpha)\, \tilde{\pi}(s,K) < \delta \,\}.
\end{aligned}
$$

Clearly, in order to show that $\alpha\, \pi^S + (1-\alpha)\, \tilde{\pi}^S \in \Delta(Y^S, \mathcal{F})$, it is enough to prove that, for all $\delta \in [0,1]$, both A_δ^+ and A_δ^- are measurable sets in $\mathcal{S}$. In fact, it will be proved that $A_\delta^+ \in \mathcal{S}$; the proof that $A_\delta^- \in \mathcal{S}$ is similar.

Let $Q \subset \mathbb{R}$ denote the set of rational numbers. Given any pair $r, \tilde{r} \in Q$ with $r + \tilde{r} > \delta$, define

$$
E(r, \tilde{r}) := \{\, s \in S \mid \pi(s,K) > r/\alpha \quad \text{and} \quad \tilde{\pi}(s,K) > \tilde{r}/(1-\alpha) \,\}.
$$

Note that $E(r, \tilde{r})$ is measurable as the intersection of two measurable sets in $\mathcal{S}$. Obviously $E(r, \tilde{r}) \subset A_\delta^+$ whenever $r + \tilde{r} > \delta$. Also, for all $s \in A_\delta^+$, there exist rational numbers $r, \tilde{r}$ satisfying $r + \tilde{r} > \delta$ such that $\alpha\, \pi(s,K) > r$ and $(1-\alpha)\, \tilde{\pi}(s,K) > \tilde{r}$. Therefore

$$
A_\delta^+ = \bigcup_{r, \tilde{r} \in Q} \{\, E(r, \tilde{r}) \mid r + \tilde{r} > \delta \,\}.
$$

Because A_δ^+ is the union of a subfamily of the countable family of measurable sets $E(r, \tilde{r})$ with r and $\tilde{r}$ both rational, A_δ^+ must also be measurable. ∎

The SEU hypothesis requires that there exist an NMUF $v : Y \to \mathbb{R}$ and a subjective probability measure $P(\cdot)$ defined on $\mathcal{S}$ such that the preference ordering $\succsim$ on the domain $\Delta(Y^S, \mathcal{F})$ is represented by a subjective expected utility function in the form of the double integral

$$
U^S(\pi^S) = \int_Y \left[\int_S \pi(s, dy)\, P(ds) \right] v(y).
$$

A standard result in the theory of integration is Fubini's theorem, stating that the order of integration in a double integral is immaterial. A useful extension of this result, due to Halmos (1950, Section 36, exercise 3), here implies that the mapping $s \mapsto U^*(\pi(s)) := \int_Y \pi(s, dy) \, v(y)$ is measurable, and moreover

$$U^S(\pi^S) = \int_S \left[\int_Y \pi(s, dy) \, v(y) \right] P(ds) = \int_S U^*(\pi(s)) \, P(ds). \qquad (8.1)$$

Next, for any measurable event $E \in \mathcal{S}$, the contingent ordering $\succsim^E$ on the domain $\Delta(Y^E, \mathcal{F})$ is represented by the double integral

$$U^E(\pi^E) = \int_Y \int_E \pi(s, dy) \, P(ds) \, v(y) = \int_E U^*(\pi(s)) \, P(ds).$$

In an obvious extension of previous notation, for any measurable event $E \in \mathcal{S}$ and any $\pi \in \Delta(Y, \mathcal{F})$, let $\pi \, 1^E \in \Delta(Y^E, \mathcal{F})$ denote the state independent measure with $\pi(s, K) = \pi(K)$ for all $s \in E$ and all $K \in \mathcal{F}$. Observe that, for all $\pi \in \Delta(Y, \mathcal{F})$, one has

$$U^E(\pi \, 1^E) = P(E) \int_Y \pi(dy) \, v(y) = P(E) \, U^*(\pi) \qquad (8.2)$$

and in particular, $U^S(\pi \, 1^S) = U^*(\pi)$.

Note that the previous state independence condition (SI) should be changed because when S is uncountably infinite, it is possible for every state to be null without being forced into the trivial case of universal indifference. Instead, a reformulated **non–null state independence condition** (SI) will require the existence of a state independent preference ordering $\succsim^*$ on $\Delta(Y, \mathcal{F})$ with the property that, for all pairs $\pi, \tilde{\pi} \in \Delta(Y, \mathcal{F})$ and any non–null event $E \in \mathcal{S}$, one has $\pi \succsim^* \tilde{\pi}$ iff $\pi \, 1^E \succsim^E \tilde{\pi} \, 1^E$. Then (8.2) implies that the expected utility function U^* must represent the preference ordering $\succsim^*$ on $\Delta(Y, \mathcal{F})$. Furthermore, note that the **probability dominance condition** (PD) of Chapter 5 is satisfied—i.e., whenever $\pi \in \Delta(Y, \mathcal{F})$ and $\lambda \in \Delta(Y)$, then:

$$\pi(\{ y \in Y \mid 1_y \succsim^* \lambda \}) = 1 \implies \pi \succsim \lambda;$$
$$\pi(\{ y \in Y \mid 1_y \precsim^* \lambda \}) = 1 \implies \pi \precsim \lambda.$$

The event continuity condition (EC) of Section 7.2 and the event dominance condition (ED) of Section 7.3 will also be slightly modified so that they apply to probability measures. Indeed, the reformulation of condition (EC) in Section 7.2 requires that, whenever $E_1 \subset E_2 \subset \ldots \subset E_k \subset E_{k+1} \subset \ldots \subset S$, $E^* = \cup_{k=1}^\infty E_k$ and $\pi, \tilde{\pi} \in \Delta(Y, \mathcal{F})$ satisfy both $\pi \succ^* \tilde{\pi}$ and $(\pi \, 1^{E^*}, \tilde{\pi} \, 1^{S \setminus E^*}) \succ (\pi \, 1^E, \tilde{\pi} \, 1^{S \setminus E})$, then there must exist a finite k such that $(\pi \, 1^{E_k}, \tilde{\pi} \, 1^{S \setminus E_k}) \succ (\pi \, 1^E, \tilde{\pi} \, 1^{S \setminus E})$. On the other hand, suppose that the event $E \subset S$, the measure

$\pi^E \in \Delta(Y^E, \mathcal{F})$, and the simple lottery $\lambda \in \Delta(Y)$ are all given. The reformulated condition (ED) will then require that $\pi(s) \succsim^* \lambda$ (all $s \in E$) implies $\pi^E \succsim^E \lambda 1^E$, and also that $\pi(s) \precsim^* \lambda$ (all $s \in E$) implies $\pi^E \precsim^E \lambda 1^E$.

Finally, arguing as in Sections 4 and 7 above and as in Chapter 5, the eleven conditions (O), (I), (C), (RO), (STP), (SI), (D), (EC), (ED), (M) and (PD), appropriately modified so that they apply to the domain $\Delta(Y^S, \mathcal{F})$, are clearly necessary for the SEU hypothesis to extend to suitable probability measures.

8.2 Sufficient Conditions for SEU and SEU*

The purpose of this section is to prove that the eleven conditions (O), (I), (C), (RO), (STP), (SI), (D), (EC), (ED), (M) and (PD) are together sufficient for the SEU hypothesis to apply to $\Delta(Y^S, \mathcal{F})$. Much of the proof below is adapted from Fishburn (1982, ch. 10).

First, suppose that $\bar{\pi}, \underline{\pi} \in \Delta(Y, \mathcal{F})$ satisfy $\bar{\pi} \succ^* \underline{\pi}$. If no such pair existed, there would be universal indifference, in which case any subjective probabilities and any constant NMUF would allow the SEU hypothesis to be satisfied. Now, arguing as in Section 4 and using the result of Lemma 8.1, conditions (O), (I), and (C) imply that there exist a real–valued expected utility function U^S defined on the mixture space $\Delta(Y^S, \mathcal{F})$ which represents $\succsim$ while satisfying the mixture preservation property (MP). Moreover, U^S can be normalized to satisfy

$$U^S(\bar{\pi} 1^S) = 1 \quad \text{and} \quad U^S(\underline{\pi} 1^S) = 0. \tag{8.3}$$

Then define the *revealed subjective probability* of each event $E \in \mathcal{S}$ by

$$p(E) := U^S(\bar{\pi} 1^E, \underline{\pi} 1^{S\backslash E}). \tag{8.4}$$

Later, Lemma 8.4 will confirm that this definition does yield a countably additive probability measure on the σ–field $\mathcal{S}$.

LEMMA 8.2 Suppose that the events E_k $(k = 1, 2, \ldots)$ and E^* in $\mathcal{S}$ satisfy the conditions that $E_1 \subset E_2 \subset \ldots \subset E_k \subset E_{k+1} \subset \ldots \subset S$ and $E^* = \cup_{k=1}^{\infty} E_k$, as in (7.1) of Section 7.2. Then for any event E satisfying $p(E) < p(E^*)$, one has $p(E) < p(E_k)$ for some finite k.

PROOF The proof involves applying condition (EC) for probability measures to the pair of lotteries $\bar{\pi}, \underline{\pi} \in \Delta(Y, \mathcal{F})$. Because of (8.4), for any event E satisfying $p(E) < p(E^*)$ one has $U^S(\bar{\pi} 1^{E^*}, \underline{\pi} 1^{S\backslash E^*}) > U^S(\bar{\pi} 1^E, \underline{\pi} 1^{S\backslash E})$. Then condition (EC) implies that for some finite k one has $U^S(\bar{\pi} 1^{E_k}, \underline{\pi} 1^{S\backslash E_k}) > U^S(\bar{\pi} 1^E, \underline{\pi} 1^{S\backslash E})$ and so, because of (8.4), that $p(E_k) > p(E)$. ∎

For the following lemmas, let $U^* : \Delta(Y, \mathcal{F}) \to \mathbb{R}$ be the normalized expected utility function satisfying $U^*(\pi) = U^S(\pi \, 1^S)$ for all $\pi \in \Delta(Y, \mathcal{F})$. Then U^* satisfies (MP) because U^S does. Next, let $v : Y \to \mathbb{R}$ satisfy $v(y) = U^*(1_y)$ for all $y \in Y$. Then, as in Theorem 9.1 of Chapter 5, because conditions (O), (I), (C), (D), (M) and (PD) are satisfied on $\Delta(Y, \mathcal{F})$, it will be true that $U^*(\pi) = \int_Y \pi(dy) \, v(y)$ for all $\pi \in \Delta(Y, \mathcal{F})$. Also, for any $\pi^S \in \Delta(Y^S, \mathcal{F})$, the mapping $s \mapsto U^*(\pi(s)) := \int_Y \pi(s, dy) \, v(y)$ must be measurable, as was argued in Section 8.1 when demonstrating (8.1).

LEMMA 8.3 Let $\{ E_k \mid k = 1, 2, \ldots, r \}$ be a partition of S into a finite collection of pairwise disjoint measurable subsets. Whenever $\pi_k \in \Delta(Y, \mathcal{F})$ $(k = 1, 2, \ldots, r)$ one has

$$U^S \left(\langle \pi_k \, 1^{E_k} \rangle_{k=1}^r \right) = \sum_{k=1}^r p(E_k) \, U^*(\pi_k). \tag{8.5}$$

PROOF Argue as in Lemma 4.4 of Section 4.7, but with the finite set of states $s \in S$ replaced by the finite collection of events E_k $(k = 1, 2, \ldots, r)$, and the lotteries λ_s replaced by the measures π_k. ∎

LEMMA 8.4 The function $p(E)$ on the domain $\mathcal{S}$ of measurable subsets of S is a (countably additive) probability measure.

PROOF First, it is obvious from definition (8.4) and the normalizations in (8.3) that $p(S) = 1$ and $p(\emptyset) = 0$. So, from (8.2) and (8.3), it follows that

$$U^*(\overline{\pi}) = U^S(\overline{\pi} \, 1^S) = 1 \quad \text{and} \quad U^*(\underline{\pi}) = U^S(\underline{\pi} \, 1^S) = 0. \tag{8.6}$$

Also, given any $E \in \mathcal{S}$, because of (8.4) and (8.3), (STP) implies that

$$p(E) = U^S(\overline{\pi} \, 1^E, \underline{\pi} \, 1^{S \setminus E}) \geq U^S(\underline{\pi} \, 1^S) = 0.$$

Next, given any disjoint pair E_1, E_2 of measurable events, by (8.4), (8.5) and (8.6) one must have

$$
\begin{aligned}
p(E_1 \cup E_2) &= U^S(\overline{\pi} \, 1^{E_1 \cup E_2}, \underline{\pi} \, 1^{S \setminus (E_1 \cup E_2)}) = U^S(\overline{\pi} \, 1^{E_1}, \overline{\pi} \, 1^{E_2}, \underline{\pi} \, 1^{S \setminus (E_1 \cup E_2)}) \\
&= [p(E_1) + p(E_2)] \, U^*(\overline{\pi}) + p(S \setminus (E_1 \cup E_2)) \, U^*(\underline{\pi}) \\
&= p(E_1) + p(E_2).
\end{aligned}
$$

An easy induction argument now shows that, whenever $r > 2$ and the events E_k $(k = 1, 2, \ldots, r)$ are pairwise disjoint, then $p(\cup_{k=1}^r E_k) = \sum_{k=1}^r p(E_k)$. Therefore $p(\cdot)$ is finitely additive.

Next, suppose that G is the countable union $\cup_{k=1}^{\infty} G_k$ of pairwise disjoint events $G_k \in \mathcal{S}$. For $r = 1, 2, \ldots$, define $E_r := \cup_{k=1}^{r} G_k$. Then G and all the sets E_r are measurable. Also,

$$E_1 \subset E_2 \subset \ldots \subset E_k \subset E_{k+1} \subset \ldots \subset S \quad \text{and} \quad G = \cup_{k=1}^{\infty} E_k.$$

Because $p(\cdot)$ is finitely additive, $p(E_r) = \sum_{k=1}^{r} p(G_k)$. Because each $p(G_k) \geq 0$, the sequence $p(E_r)$ $(r = 1, 2, \ldots)$ is non–decreasing. Define p^* as the supremum of the probabilities $p(E_r)$ $(r = 1, 2, \ldots)$. Then

$$p^* = \lim_{r \to \infty} p(E_r) = \sum_{k=1}^{\infty} p(G_k) \leq p(G). \tag{8.7}$$

In particular, $p(G_k) \to 0$ as $k \to \infty$.

Now, one possibility is that, for some finite r, one has $p(G_k) = 0$ for all $k > r$. Then $p(E_r) = \sum_{k=1}^{r} p(G_k) = \sum_{k=1}^{\infty} p(G_k) = p^*$. In particular, $p(E_r) \geq p(E_k)$ for $k = 1, 2, \ldots$. By Lemma 8.2, $p(E_r) < p(G)$ would imply that $p(E_r) < p(E_k)$ for some finite k, a contradiction. Therefore $p^* = p(E_r) \geq p(G)$ in this first case.

Because $p(G_k) \to 0$, the only other possibility is that, for every $\epsilon > 0$, there exists r (which depends on ϵ) such that $0 < p(G_r) < \epsilon$. Because $p(G \setminus G_r) = p(G) - p(G_r)$, it follows that

$$p(G) > p(G \setminus G_r) > p(G) - \epsilon. \tag{8.8}$$

Then Lemma 8.2 implies that, for some finite k, one has

$$p(E_k) > p(G \setminus G_r). \tag{8.9}$$

Yet the definition of p^* implies that $p^* \geq p(E_k)$. So from (8.8) and (8.9) one has

$$p^* \geq p(E_k) > p(G \setminus G_r) > p(G) - \epsilon.$$

But this is true for all $\epsilon > 0$, so $p(G) \leq p^*$ in this case as well.

Thus, $p(G) \leq p^*$ in both cases. But then (8.7) implies that $p(G) = p^* = \sum_{k=1}^{\infty} p(G_k)$, verifying that p is countably additive. ∎

For the next lemma, given any $\pi^S \in \Delta(Y^S, \mathcal{F})$, define the two bounds

$$\underline{U}(\pi^S) := \inf_s \{ U^*(\pi(s)) \mid s \in S \}, \quad \text{and} \quad \overline{U}(\pi^S) := \sup_s \{ U^*(\pi(s)) \mid s \in S \}. \tag{8.10}$$

LEMMA 8.5 *For all $\pi^S \in \Delta(Y^S, \mathcal{F})$ one has $\underline{U}(\pi^S) \leq U^S(\pi^S) \leq \overline{U}(\pi^S)$.*

PROOF First, by Lemma 8.4 of Chapter 5, the bounded utility condition (B) is also satisfied. Therefore U^* must be bounded both above and below. So (8.10) implies that $-\infty < \underline{U}(\pi^S) \leq \overline{U}(\pi^S) < \infty$.

The general case occurs when there exists $\mu \in \Delta(Y)$ such that $U^*(\mu) < \overline{U}(\pi^S)$. Then there must exist an infinite sequence of lotteries λ_k ($k = 1, 2, \ldots$) in $\Delta(Y)$ such that $U^*(\lambda_k)$ is increasing and $U^*(\lambda_k) \to \overline{U}(\pi^S)$ as $k \to \infty$. Clearly, then $U^*(\lambda_k) > U^*(\mu)$ for k large enough. In this case, define

$$\alpha_k := \frac{U^*(\lambda_k) - U^*(\mu)}{\overline{U}(\pi^S) - U^*(\mu)}.$$

Then, whenever $0 < \alpha < \alpha_k$, one has $U^*(\lambda_k) > \alpha \overline{U}(\pi^S) + (1 - \alpha) U^*(\mu)$. Because $U^*(\pi(s)) \leq \overline{U}(\pi^S)$ for all $s \in S$, it follows that $\lambda_k \succ^* \alpha \pi(s) + (1 - \alpha) \mu$. By condition (ED), $\lambda_k 1^S \succsim \alpha \pi^S + (1 - \alpha) \mu 1^S$ and so

$$\alpha U^S(\pi^S) + (1 - \alpha) U^*(\mu) \leq U^*(\lambda_k) \leq \overline{U}(\pi^S).$$

Now, as $k \to \infty$, so $\alpha_k \to 1$, implying that $\alpha U^S(\pi^S) + (1 - \alpha) U^*(\mu) \leq \overline{U}(\pi^S)$ for all $\alpha < 1$. Therefore $U^S(\pi^S) \leq \overline{U}(\pi^S)$.

The other, special, case is when $U^*(\mu) \geq \overline{U}(\pi^S)$ for all $\mu \in \Delta(Y)$. Given any fixed $\bar{s} \in S$, note that $\overline{U}(\pi^S) \geq U^*(\pi(\bar{s})) = \int_Y \pi(\bar{s}, dy) v(y)$. So, given any $\epsilon > 0$, there certainly exists a simple lottery $\lambda_\epsilon \in \Delta(Y)$ such that

$$U^*(\lambda_\epsilon) = \sum_{y \in Y} \lambda_\epsilon(y) v(y) \leq \overline{U}(\pi^S) + \epsilon. \tag{8.11}$$

But $v(y) = U^*(1_y) \geq \overline{U}(\pi^S)$ for all $y \in Y$. Hence $U^*(\lambda_\epsilon) \geq \overline{U}(\pi^S) \geq U^*(\pi(s))$ and so $\lambda_\epsilon \succsim^* \pi(s)$ for all $s \in S$. By condition (ED), it follows that $\lambda_\epsilon 1^S \succsim \pi^S$. Because of (8.11), this implies that $\overline{U}(\pi^S) + \epsilon \geq U^*(\lambda_\epsilon) \geq U^S(\pi^S)$. This is true for all $\epsilon > 0$. Hence, $U^S(\pi^S) \leq \overline{U}(\pi^S)$ in this second case as well.

The proof that $U^S(\pi^S) \geq \underline{U}(\pi^S)$ is similar, with each inequality sign reversed. ∎

LEMMA 8.6 *For all $\pi^S \in \Delta(Y^S, \mathcal{F})$ one has $U^S(\pi^S) = \int_S U^*(\pi(s)) \, p(ds)$.*

PROOF Let $\underline{U}(\pi^S)$ and $\overline{U}(\pi^S)$ be as in (8.10). Then, for $n = 2, 3, \ldots$, define:

$$\delta_n := \tfrac{1}{n} [\overline{U}(\pi^S) - \underline{U}(\pi^S)]; \quad J_{1n} := [\underline{U}(\pi^S), \underline{U}(\pi^S) + \delta_n];$$
$$J_{in} := (\underline{U}(\pi^S) + (i - 1) \delta_n, \underline{U}(\pi^S) + i \delta_n] \quad (i = 2, 3, \ldots, n);$$
$$\text{and} \quad E_{in} := \{ s \in S \mid U^*(\pi(s)) \in J_{in} \} \quad (i = 1, 2, \ldots, n).$$

The sets J_{in} $(i = 1, 2, \ldots, n)$ are pairwise disjoint intervals of the real line, whose union is the closed interval $[\underline{U}(\pi^S), \overline{U}(\pi^S)]$. Also, as remarked in connection with showing (8.1) in Section 8.1, the mapping $s \mapsto U^*(\pi(s))$ is measurable.

Hence, each set E_{in} is also measurable. But the family E_{in} $(i = 1, 2, \ldots, n)$ is a partition of S into n pairwise disjoint events, so Lemma 8.4 implies that

$$\sum_{i=1}^{n} p(E_{in}) = 1. \tag{8.12}$$

For each $i = 1, 2, \ldots, n$, let λ_i be any lottery in $\Delta(Y)$ with the property that $U^*(\lambda_i) \in J_{in}$. By Lemma 8.5, it must be true that

$$(i - 1)\,\delta_n \leq U^S\left(\pi^{E_{in}}, \lambda_i 1^{S \setminus E_{in}}\right) - \underline{U}(\pi^S) \leq i\,\delta_n. \tag{8.13}$$

Also, condition (RO) implies that the two members of $\Delta(Y^S, \mathcal{F})$ specified by

$$\frac{1}{n}\sum_{i=1}^{n}\left(\pi^{E_{in}}, \lambda_i 1^{S \setminus E_{in}}\right),\ \frac{1}{n}\pi^S + \frac{n-1}{n}\left\langle \frac{1}{n-1}\left(\sum_{j \neq i}\lambda_j\right)1^{E_{in}}\right\rangle_{i=1}^{n}, \tag{8.14}$$

respectively, are indifferent because, for each state $s \in S$, the common marginal measure is $(1 - \frac{1}{n})\lambda_i + \frac{1}{n}\pi(s)$. But then, because U^S satisfies (MP), and because of Lemma 8.3, applying U^S to the two indifferent prospects in (8.14) gives

$$\frac{1}{n}\sum_{i=1}^{n} U^S\left(\pi^{E_{in}}, \lambda_i 1^{S \setminus E_{in}}\right)$$

$$= \frac{1}{n}U^S(\pi^S) + \frac{n-1}{n}\sum_{i=1}^{n} p(E_{in}) \cdot \frac{1}{n-1}\sum_{j \neq i} U^*(\lambda_j).$$

Therefore, because of (8.12),

$$U^S(\pi^S) = \sum_{i=1}^{n} U^S\left(\pi^{E_{in}}, \lambda_i 1^{S \setminus E_{in}}\right) - \sum_{i=1}^{n} p(E_{in})\sum_{j \neq i} U^*(\lambda_j)$$

$$= \sum_{i=1}^{n} U^S\left(\pi^{E_{in}}, \lambda_i 1^{S \setminus E_{in}}\right) - \sum_{i=1}^{n} [1 - p(E_{in})]\,U^*(\lambda_i),$$

which implies that

$$U^S(\pi^S) - \underline{U}(\pi^S) = \sum_{i=1}^{n}\left[U^S\left(\pi^{E_{in}}, \lambda_i 1^{S \setminus E_{in}}\right) - \underline{U}(\pi^S)\right]$$

$$- \sum_{i=1}^{n} [1 - p(E_{in})]\,[U^*(\lambda_i) - \underline{U}(\pi^S)] \tag{8.15}$$

To simplify notation later, define

$$Q_n := \sum_{i=1}^{n} i\, p(E_{in}). \tag{8.16}$$

First, consider what happens when, for each $i = 1, 2, \ldots, n$, the lottery $\lambda_i \in \Delta(Y)$ with $U^*(\lambda_i) \in J_{in}$ satisfies the extra restriction

$$U^*(\lambda_i) - \underline{U}(\pi^S) \leq \left(i - 1 + \frac{1}{n-1}\right)\delta_n. \tag{8.17}$$

Then (8.15), (8.13), (8.17), (8.12) and (8.16) together imply that

$$
\begin{aligned}
U^S(\pi^S) &- \underline{U}(\pi^S) \\
&\geq\ \delta_n \sum_{i=1}^{n}(i-1) - \delta_n \sum_{i=1}^{n}\left(i-1+\frac{1}{n-1}\right)[1 - p(E_{in})] \\
&=\ -\delta_n \sum_{i=1}^{n}\frac{1}{n-1}[1 - p(E_{in})] + \delta_n \sum_{i=1}^{n}(i-1)\, p(E_{in}) \\
&=\ -2\,\delta_n + \delta_n\, Q_n. \tag{8.18}
\end{aligned}
$$

Alternatively, consider what happens when, for each $i = 1, 2, \ldots, n$, the lottery $\lambda_i \in \Delta(Y)$ with $U^*(\lambda_i) \in J_{in}$ satisfies the extra restriction

$$\left(i - \frac{1}{n-1}\right)\delta_n \leq U^*(\lambda_i) - \underline{U}(\pi^S). \tag{8.19}$$

Then (8.15), (8.13), (8.19), (8.12) and (8.16) together imply that

$$
\begin{aligned}
U^S(\pi^S) - \underline{U}(\pi^S) &\leq\ \delta_n \sum_{i=1}^{n} i - \delta_n \sum_{i=1}^{n}\left(i-\frac{1}{n-1}\right)[1 - p(E_{in})] \\
&=\ \delta_n \sum_{i=1}^{n}\frac{1}{n-1}[1 - p(E_{in})] + \delta_n \sum_{i=1}^{n} i\, p(E_{in}) \\
&=\ \delta_n + \delta_n\, Q_n. \tag{8.20}
\end{aligned}
$$

But the definitions of the intervals J_{in} and of the Lebesgue integral imply that

$$\delta_n \sum_{i=1}^{n}(i-1)\, p(E_{in}) \leq \int_S U^*(\pi(s))\, p(ds) - \underline{U}(\pi^S) \leq \delta_n \sum_{i=1}^{n} i\, p(E_{in}).$$

So, by (8.12) and (8.16), it follows that

$$-\delta_n + \delta_n\, Q_n \leq \int_S U^*(\pi(s))\, p(ds) - \underline{U}(\pi^S) \leq \delta_n\, Q_n. \tag{8.21}$$

Now subtract the second inequality in (8.21) from (8.18), and the first from (8.20). These two operations lead to the double inequality

$$-2\,\delta_n \leq U^S(\pi^S) - \int_S U^*(\pi(s))\,p(ds) \leq 2\,\delta_n. \tag{8.22}$$

Finally, because $\delta_n = \frac{1}{n}[\overline{U}(\pi^S) - \underline{U}(\pi^S)]$, the result follows from taking the limit of (8.22) as $n \to \infty$ and so $\delta_n \to 0$. ∎

8.3   Eleven Sufficient Conditions

THEOREM 8.7 Conditions (O), (I), (C), (RO), (STP), (SI), (D), (EC), (ED), (M) and (PD) are sufficient for the SEU hypothesis to apply to $\Delta(Y^E, \mathcal{F})$.

PROOF Lemma 8.6 shows that the ordering $\succsim$ on $\Delta(Y^S, \mathcal{F})$ is represented by the utility integral $U^S(\pi^S) = \int_S U^*(\pi(s))\,p(ds)$, where $U^*(\pi(s))$ is defined by $\int_Y \pi(s, dy)\, v(y)$. So $U^S(\pi^S)$ takes the form (8.1), as required. Also, by Lemma 8.4, p is a probability measure on the space $(S, \mathcal{S})$. ∎

The above result used eleven sufficient conditions for the SEU model. With so many conditions, it may help to group them in order to assess the contribution each makes to the overall result. This is done in Table 1.

domain of probability distributions	simple	discrete	measures
domain	$\Delta(Y)$	$\Delta^*(Y)$	$\Delta(Y, \mathcal{F})$
conditions for objective EU	(O), (I), (C) [3 conditions]	+ (D) [4 conditions]	+ (M), (PD) [6 conditions]
domain	$\Delta(Y^S)$	$\Delta^*(Y^S)$	$\Delta(Y^S, \mathcal{F})$
extra conditions for subjective EU	+ (RO), (STP), (SI) [6 conditions]	+ (EC), (ED) [9 conditions]	_____ [11 conditions]

(*Extra conditions enter as one moves either down or to the right.*)

Table 6.1   Eleven Sufficient Conditions for Expected Utility Maximization

First come the three conditions that were introduced in Chapter 5 as sufficient for objectively expected utility with simple lotteries. These are **ordinal-**

ity **(O)**, **independence (I)**, and **continuity (C)**. Second, the same chapter introduced one extra condition for objectively expected utility with discrete lotteries: **dominance (D)**. Third, the same chapter also introduced two extra conditions for objectively expected utility with probability measures: **measurability (M)** and **probability dominance (PD)**. It was noted that conditions (O), (I), (C) and (D) imply that utility is bounded.

This chapter first introduced three extra conditions (in addition to (O), (I) and (C)) for subjectively expected utility with simple lotteries. These are **reversal of order (RO)**, the **sure thing principle (STP)**, and **state independence (SI)**. Second, it introduced two extra conditions (in addition to (O), (I), (C), (D), (RO), (STP) and (SI)) for subjectively expected utility with discrete lotteries and an infinite set of states of the world: **event continuity (EC)** and **event dominance (ED)**. Finally, adding the two conditions (M) and (PD) that had already been included for objectively expected utility with probability measures gives the entire list of all eleven conditions that are sufficient for subjectively expected utility with probability measures over both states and consequences—no further conditions need be added.

Note that the eight conditions (O), (I), (D), (RO), (STP), (SI), (PD) and (ED) are all justified by consequentialism (or weak extensions). Only the domain condition (M) and two continuity conditions (C) and (EC) lack a consequentialist justification.

9 Summary and Conclusions

In Section 2, the subjective expected utility (or SEU) hypothesis was stated for the case when there are no events with objective probabilities. It was shown to imply the ordering of events condition (OE) in particular. Turning to sufficient conditions like those in Chapter 5 for the EU hypothesis, Section 3 showed how consequentialist axioms justify the existence of a preference ordering satisfying (STP), which is a form of Savage's sure thing principle. Furthermore, the axioms rule out null events, but they fail to justify condition (OE), and so do not imply the SEU hypothesis.

After this essentially false start, Section 4 turned to the framework inspired by Anscombe and Aumann (1963), with roulette as well as horse lotteries. Particular ratios of utility differences can then be interpreted as subjective probabilities. For the space $\Delta(Y^S)$ whose members are simple lotteries with finite support on the space Y^S of contingent consequence functions, Section 4 showed that necessary and sufficient conditions for the SEU hypothesis are ordinality (O), independence (I), continuity (C), reversal of order (RO), the sure–thing principle (STP), and state independence (SI). In fact, as in Chapter 5, stronger versions of conditions (I) and (C) are also necessary.

In order to provide a consequentialist justification for conditions (O), (I), (RO), (STP), and even (SI), Section 5 considered decision trees including moves made by chance which have objective probabilities, as well as moves made by nature which lack objective probabilities. It was also shown that these conditions exhaust all the implications of consequentialism because consequentialist behaviour is always possible whenever conditions (O), (I), (RO), (STP), and (SI) are all satisfied.

Next, Section 6 considered conditions for the SEU model to apply with state dependent consequence domains, but with state independent utility for consequences which arise in more than one state of the world. These conditions involve the hypothetical choice of the objective probabilities which might apply to different states of the world.

The corresponding space $\Delta^*(Y^S)$ of discrete lotteries on Y^S that can have countably infinite support was considered in Section 7. In addition, S was allowed to be an arbitrary infinite set. Apart from the dominance condition (D) that was introduced in Chapter 5, two new conditions of event continuity (EC) and event dominance (ED) enter the set of necessary and sufficient conditions for the SEU hypothesis to hold.

Finally, Section 8 considered the space $\Delta(Y^S, \mathcal{F})$ of measurable mappings from states of the world $s \in S$ to probability measures on the σ–field $\mathcal{F}$ of measurable sets generated by the singleton and preference subsets of Y^S. Here, as in Chapter 5, two extra conditions enter the list — the obvious measurability condition (M), and a probability dominance condition (PD) that is different from condition (D).

Acknowledgments

My work on this chapter was supported by a research award from the Alexander von Humboldt Foundation. This financed a visit to Germany, especially the University of Kiel, during the academic year 1993–4 when work on this chapter was begun. During a lecture I gave at C.O.R.E. in February 1994, Jean–François Mertens suggested how to justify the reversal of order assumption more directly than previously. Philippe Mongin not only arranged for me to give lectures at C.O.R.E., but also offered useful comments, especially on Section 6 concerning state dependence. Kenneth Arrow shared his recollections of some important precursors to the Anscombe and Aumann approach, and indirectly encouraged me to retain Section 6.3. Last but certainly not least, two diligent referees have produced many pertinent comments that have led to many significant corrections, improvements, and even re–formulations. My thanks to all of these while absolving them of all responsibility for remaining errors and inadequacies.

References

Anscombe, F. J. and Aumann, R. J. (1963). A Definition of Subjective Probability. *Annals of Mathematical Statistics*, 34:199–205.

Arrow, K. J. (1951). Alternative Approaches to the Theory of Decision in Risk-Taking Situations. *Econometrica*, 19:404–437. Reprinted in Arrow, 1971, ch. 1 and in Arrow, 1984, ch. 2.

Arrow, K. J. (1953, 1964). Le rôle des valeurs boursières pour la répartition la meilleure des risques. In *Économétrie*, pages 41–48. Centre National de la Recherche Scientifique, Paris. Translation of English original, The Role of Securities in the Optimal Allocation of Risk-bearing, later published in *Review of Economic Studies*, 31, 91–96; reprinted in Arrow (1983) ch. 3.

Arrow, K. J. (1965). *Aspects of the Theory of Risk-Bearing*. North–Holland, Amsterdam.

Arrow, K. J. (1971). *Essays in the Theory of Risk-Bearing*. Markham, North–Holland, Chicago and Amsterdam.

Arrow, K. J. (1972). Exposition of the Theory of Choice under Uncertainty. In McGuire, C. B. and Radner, R., editors, *Decision and Organization*, chapter 2, pages 19–55. North–Holland, Amsterdam. Reprinted in Arrow (1984), ch. 10.

Arrow, K. J. (1983). *Collected Papers of Kenneth J. Arrow, Vol. 2: General Equilibrium*. Belknap Press of Harvard University Press, Cambridge, Mass.

Arrow, K. J. (1984). *Collected Papers of Kenneth J. Arrow, Vol. 3: Individual Choice under Certainty and Uncertainty*. Belknap Press of Harvard University Press, Cambridge, Mass.

Bayes, T. (1763). An Essay toward Solving a Problem in the Doctrine of Chances. *Philosophical Transactions of the Royal Society*, 53:370–418. Reprinted with biographical note by G. A. Barnard (1958) in *Biometrika*, 45:293–315; reprinted in S. James, editor, *Bayesian Statistics: Principles, Models and Applications*. New York, John Wiley, 1989.

Bertrand, J. (1889). *Calcul des probabilités*. Gauthier-Villars, Paris.

Blume, L., Brandenburger, A., and Dekel, E. (1991). Lexicographic Probabilities and Choice Under Uncertainty. *Econometrica*, 59:61–79.

Chernoff, H. (1954). Rational Selection of Decision Functions. *Econometrica*, 22:422–443.

De Finetti, B. (1937). La prévision: ses lois logiques, ses sources subjectives. *Annales de l'Institut Henri Poincaré*, 7. Translated as 'Foresight: Its Logical Laws, Its Subjective Sources', in Kyburg and Smokler (1964), pages 93–158.

De Finetti, B. (1949). Sull'impostazione assiomatica del calcolo delle probabilità. *Annali Triestini dell'Università di Trieste*, 19:29–81. Translated as 'On the Axiomatization of Probability Theory', in B. De Finetti, editor, (1972),

Probability, Induction and Statistics: The Art of Guessing (New York, John Wiley), ch. 5, pages 67–113.

Debreu, G. (1959). *Theory of Value: An Axiomatic Analysis of Economic Equilibrium*. John Wiley, New York.

DeGroot, M. H. (1970). *Optimal Statistical Decisions*. McGraw-Hill, New York.

Drèze, J. H. (1961). Fondements logiques de la probabilité subjective et de l'utilité. In *La Décision*, pages 73–87. CNRS, Paris. Translated as 'Logical Foundations of Cardinal Utility and Subjective Probability' with postscript in J. H. Drèze, editor, (1987) *Essays on Economic Decisions under Uncertainty* (Cambridge, Cambridge University Press), ch. 3, pages 90–104.

Drèze, J. H. (1987). Decision Theory with Moral Hazard and State–Dependent Preferences. In Drèze, J. H., editor, *Essays on Economic Decisions under Uncertainty*, chapter 2, pages 23–89. Cambridge University Press, Cambridge.

Ellsberg, D. (1961). Risk, Ambiguity, and the Savage Axioms. *Quarterly Journal of Economics*, 75:643–669. Reprinted in Gärdenfors and Sahlin (1988), ch.13.

Fishburn, P. C. (1970). *Utility Theory for Decision Making*. John Wiley, New York.

Fishburn, P. C. (1981). Subjective Expected Utility: A Review of Normative Theories. *Theory and Decision*, 13:139–199.

Fishburn, P. C. (1982). *The Foundations of Expected Utility*. D. Reidel, Dordrecht.

Fishburn, P. C. (1986). Axioms of Qualitative Probability Theory and Rejoinder with comments by I. J. Good, P. Suppes, J. O. Berger, T. L. Fine, T. Seidenfeld, M. Stone and W. D. Sudderth. *Statistical Science*, 1:335–358.

Fishburn, P. C. (1994). Utility and Subjective Probability. In Aumann, R. J. and Hart, S., editors, *Handbook of Game Theory with Economic Applications*, volume II, chapter 39, pages 1397–1435. North–Holland, Amsterdam.

Gärdenfors, P. and Sahlin, N.-E. (1988). *Decision, Probability, and Utility*. Cambridge University Press, Cambridge.

Gul, F. (1992). Savage's Theorem with a Finite Number of States. *Journal of Economic Theory*, 57:99–110. Erratum (1993), *Journal of Economic Theory*, 61:184.

Hacking, I. (1975). *The Emergence of Probability*. Cambridge University Press, Cambridge.

Halmos, P. R. (1950). *Measure Theory*. Van Nostrand Reinhold, New York.

Hammond, P. J. (1988). Consequentialist Foundations for Expected Utility. *Theory and Decision*, 25:25–78.

Harsanyi, J. C. (1977). *Rational Behavior and Bargaining Equilibrium in Games and Social Situations*. Cambridge University Press, Cambridge.

Harsanyi, J. C. (1983). Bayesian Decision Theory, Subjective and Objective Probabilities, and Acceptance of Empirical Hypotheses. *Synthese*, 57:341–365.

Hobbes, T. (1684). *Humane Nature, or the Fundamental Elements of Policy*, 3rd edition, Printed for Matthew Gilliflower, Henry Rogers, and Tho. Fox, London.

Karni, E. (1985). *Decision Making under Uncertainty: The Case of State–Dependent Preferences*. Harvard University Press, Cambridge (Mass.).

Karni, E. (1993a). A Definition of Subjective Probabilities with State–Dependent Preferences. *Econometrica*, 61:187–198.

Karni, E. (1993b). Subjective Expected Utility Theory with State–Dependent Preferences. *Journal of Economic Theory*, 60:428–438.

Karni, E. and Mongin, P. (1997). More on State–Dependent Preferences and the Uniqueness of Subjective Probability. Preprint.

Karni, E. and Schmeidler, D. (1991). Utility Theory with Uncertainty. In Hildenbrand, W. and Sonnenschein, H., editors, *Handbook of Mathematical Economics*, volume IV, chapter 33, pages 1763–1831. North–Holland, Amsterdam.

Karni, E., Schmeidler, D., and Vind, K. (1983). On State Dependent Preferences and Subjective Probabilities. *Econometrica*, 51:1021–1031.

Keynes, J. M. (1921). *A Treatise on Probability*. Macmillan, London.

Kyburg, H. E. and Smokler, H. E., editors (1964). *Studies in Subjective Probability*. John Wiley, New York.

Lindley, D. V. (1987). Bayes, Thomas (1702–1761). In Eatwell, J., Milgate, M., and Newman, P., editors, *The New Palgrave: A Dictionary of Economics*. Macmillan, London. Reprinted in Eatwell, J., Milgate, M. and P. Newman (eds.), *The New Palgrave: Utility and Probability* (London, Macmillan, 1990) pages 10–11.

Mongin, P. (1998). The Paradox of Bayesian Experts and State–Dependent Utility Theory. *Journal of Mathematical Economics*, 29:331–362.

Myerson, R. B. (1979). An Axiomatic Derivation of Subjective Probability, Utility, and Evaluation Functions. *Theory and Decision*, 11:339–352.

Myerson, R. B. (1991). *Game Theory: Analysis of Conflict*. Harvard University Press, Cambridge, Mass.

Narens, L. (1980). On Qualitative Axiomatizations of Probability Theory. *Journal of Philosophical Logic*, 9:143–151.

Pratt, J. W., Raiffa, H., and Schlaifer, R. (1964). The Foundations of Decision under Uncertainty: An Elementary Exposition. *Journal of the American Statistical Association*, 59:353–375.

Raiffa, H. (1961). Risk, Ambiguity, and the Savage Axioms: Comment. *Quarterly Journal of Economics*, 75:690–694.

Ramsey, F. P. (1926). Truth and Probability. In *The Foundations of Mathematics and Other Logical Essays*, pages 156–198. Kegan Paul, 1931, London. Reprinted in Kyburg and Smokler (1964) and in Gärdenfors and Sahlin (1988), ch. 2.

Rubin, H. (1949). Postulates for the Existence of Measurable Utility and Psychological Probability. *Bulletin of the American Mathematical Association*, 55:1050–1051. (Abstract).

Savage, L. J. (1954, 1972). *The Foundations of Statistics*. John Wiley and Dover Publications, New York.

Schervish, M. J., Seidenfeld, T., and Kadane, J. B. (1990). State–Dependent Utilities. *Journal of the American Statistical Association*, 85:840–847.

Suppes, P. (1956). The Role of Subjective Probability and Utility in Decision Making. In Neyman, J., editor, *Proceedings of the Third Berkeley Symposium on Mathematical Statistics and Probability 1954-1955*, volume 5, pages 61–73. University of California Press, Berkeley.

Villegas, C. (1964). On Qualitative Probability σ-Algebras. *Annals of Mathematical Statistics*, 35:1787–1796.

Wakker, P. P. (1989). *Additive Representations of Preferences: A New Foundation of Decision Analysis*. Kluwer Academic Publishers, Dordrecht.

Wakker, P. P. and Zank, H. (1996). State–Dependent Expected Utility for Savage's State Space; Or: Bayesian Statistics without Prior Probabilities. Preprint, CentER, Univ. of Tilburg.

Wilson, R. B. (1968). The Theory of Syndicates. *Econometrica*, 36:119–132.

7 STOCHASTIC UTILITY

Peter C. Fishburn

AT&T Research, Florham Park, NJ

Contents

1	Introduction		275
2	Structures		278
	2.1	The Universal Set of Objects	279
	2.2	Domains for P	280
	2.3	Domains for p	280
	2.4	Primitive Domains and Axioms	281
3	Representations		284
	3.1	Representation Theorems and Uniqueness	284
	3.2	Constant Utility and Binary Advantage Representations	286
	3.3	Random Utility Representations	286
	3.4	Subset Choice and Sequential Reduction	288
	3.5	Preview	290
4	Binary Choice Probabilities		291
5	Simple Scalability and Luce's Model		294
6	Random Utility		296
7	The Linear Ordering Polytope		299
8	Rankings: Induced and Primitive		302
	8.1	Rankings from Choice Probabilities	302
	8.2	Rankings as Primitive	305

8.3   Social Choice Lotteries   306

9   Lotteries and Acts   307

References   311

1 Introduction

Traditional utility theories assume that preferences are deterministic, that their utility representations use nonrandom real–valued functions determined up to a group of order–preserving transformations, and that choices from feasible sets maximize utility or expected utility and are unique except when two or more alternatives have equal maximizing utilities. *Stochastic utility*, broadly interpreted, refers to theories of preference or choice that violate one or more of these assumptions. As a consequence, preferences or choices exhibit probabilistic, stochastic or random behavior. This is most evident when variable choices are made in a series of similar situations, but it can also apply to a single choice when the chooser is uncertain about which alternative he or she most prefers. The following multiattribute example illustrates the latter case.

EXAMPLE 1.1 Fran's team has just won the championship and Fran has been named MVP. It was announced before the competition began that the MVP would win a car to be chosen as desired from the following four:

1. Red Ferarri, automatic transmission;
2. White Ferarri, standard transmission;
3. Red Porsche, standard transmission;
4. White Porsche, automatic transmission.

Cars 1 and 2 are alike in all other respects, as are 3 and 4. Fran tends to prefer red to white, and automatic to standard. If the choice were between 1 and 2, it is highly probable that Fran would choose 1. The choice is less obvious if limited to 3 or 4, but Fran leans toward 4 here since the transmission differential seems slightly more important than the color difference. Other things equal, Fran has a vague preference for Porsches over Ferarris, but the feature advantages of 1 compared to 3 and 4 makes the choice between a Ferarri and a Porsche a virtual toss–up.

In a deterministic approach, we might record Fran's feelings for these binary comparisons as a preference for 1 over 2, a preference for 4 over 3, and indifference between 1 and 3, and so forth. However, this fails to capture the uncertainty of Fran's situation, which could be expressed more accurately by the use of binary choice probabilities. For example, probabilities of 0.95, 0.70 and 0.50 for the choices of 1 from 1 or 2, 4 from 3 or 4, and 1 from 1 and 3, respectively, would be consistent with the deterministic approach while accommodating expressions of uncertainty about what Fran might actually do.

The scope of stochastic utility will be suggested in the rest of this introduction by interpretations of random or variable preference and choice. It should be remarked that terms such as "stochastic utility", "random utility", and "probabilistic choice" are not entirely standard and may be used differently by different authors. We have chosen "stochastic utility" to denote the general subject, and tend to use other terms more selectively, but some flexibility is presumed. The next two sections provide a classification scheme for theories of stochastic preference and choice, and later sections discuss representations and axioms in greater detail.

Many explanations of randomness or variability of preferences and choices have been proposed. A particular explanation is usually associated with a *process* by which an individual or group arrives at a choice. Some processes or parts of processes are largely unobservable, such as what goes on in a person's head when he or she contemplates a difficult decision. Other aspects of processes are integral to a choice model. An example is a specific counting rule for determining the winner of an election from ballot data.

The most common locus of randomness for stochastic utility may be preference comparisons between complex objects that are difficult to compare because of multiple attributes, environmental uncertainties, and incomplete specification. Vague preferences and wavering judgments about better, best, or merely satisfactory alternatives lead naturally to theories based on probabilistic preference and probabilistic choice.

Throughout the chapter, we let $\mathcal{A}$ denote the set of potential objects of choice. We assume in the rest of this introduction that $\mathcal{A}$ is finite, but will relax this later.

Probabilities of preferences and choices are described by two types of probability functions. We use P to denote probabilities of preference relations, and p to denote choice probabilities. Function P is a probability distribution on a set $\mathcal{R}$ of mutually disjoint binary relations on $\mathcal{A}$ whose members are assumed to include all possible preference relations that an individual might have on $\mathcal{A}$. Thus $P(R)$ for $R \in \mathcal{R}$ is the probability that preference relation R obtains, and

$$\sum_{R \in \mathcal{R}} P(R) = 1 \ .$$

Choice probabilities are defined on a set $\mathcal{C}$ of ordered pairs (A, B) of subsets of $\mathcal{A}$ with $A \subseteq B$ and $B \neq \emptyset$. We let $p(A, B)$ denote the probability that an individual will choose an alternative or object in A when the choice is restricted to set B. We could allow A to be the empty set $\emptyset$ to accommodate distinctly the possibility of no choice, such as abstention in voting. When A is a singleton, we often write $p(x, B)$ instead of $p(\{x\}, B)$. Then, for each relevant B,

$$p(\emptyset, B) + \sum_{x \in B} p(x, B) = 1 \ ,$$

with $\sum_{x \in B} p(x, B) = 1$ when $p(\emptyset, B) = 0$, as in a forced choice situation. In the very restrictive but prominent binary comparison context, we abbreviate $p(\{x\}, \{x, y\})$ for $x \neq y$ as $p(x, y)$. Under forced choice between x and y, $p(x, y)$ is the probability that x will be chosen, and

$$p(x, y) + p(y, x) = 1 .$$

EXAMPLE 1.2 Let $\mathcal{A} = \{x, y, z\}$ and assume that $p(\emptyset, B) = 0$ for every nonempty $B \subseteq \mathcal{A}$. Let

$$\mathcal{R} = \{xyz, xzy, yxz, yzx, zxy, zyx\} ,$$

the set of linear orders or rankings on $\mathcal{A}$. We interpret xyz as: x is preferred to y and z, and y is preferred to z. One process for binary choices supposes that an individual selects a ranking in $\mathcal{R}$ according to some probability distribution P and then chooses a from $\{a, b\}$ precisely when a is preferred to b in the selected ranking. Thus

$$p(x, y) = P(xyz) + P(xzy) + P(zxy) ,$$

and similarly for the other binary choice probabilities. Marschak (1960) asked what must be true of the binary choice probabilities so that there exists a P that induces those probabilities in the manner just indicated. His answer was that p must satisfy the triangle inequality

$$p(a, c) \leq p(a, b) + p(b, c)$$

for all distinct a, b and c in $\mathcal{A}$. Moreover, this condition is sufficient as well as necessary for the existence of P in the three–alternative case. The triangle inequality is also sufficient for the existence of P when $\mathcal{A}$ has four or five alternatives, but not when it is larger. We say more about this in Section 7.

As discussed by Block and Marschak (1960) and Luce and Suppes (1965), $p(x, y)$ is often estimated by the relative frequency with which x is hypothetically or actually chosen from $\{x, y\}$ in a series of trials that embed instances of x versus y in a long run of forced binary choices. We do not know of course that preferences on each trial are not deterministic, but in the absence of discernable choice patterns brought on by learning or boredom, the randomness interpretation seems reasonable.

There are, however, interpretations of individual probabilistic choice that have fully deterministic preferences. As one example, suppose a person strictly prefers x to y, y to z, and z to x. Let $\succ$ denote strict preference. Then we have the cyclic preference triple $x \succ y \succ z \succ x$. Although this violates canons of economic rationality, it is plausible in situations that involve multiple attributes or uncertainties [Tversky (1969), MacCrimmon and Larsson (1979), Fishburn (1991)].

Given $x \succ y \succ z \succ x$, the person might choose from $B = \{x, y, z\}$ by using a random device that assigns probability $1/3$ to each object. Hence $p(x, B) = p(y, B) = p(z, B) = 1/3$. We note later that deliberate randomization has a preference–maximizing explanation. Moreover, there is no obvious connection between this explanation and the reasons for deliberate randomization in experimental design or in mixed strategies in game theory.

Choice probabilities and probability distributions over preference relations arise also in group processes. Consider an election among a set of two or more candidates that involves many voters. Here $P(R)$ could denote the proportion of voters who have relation R on the candidates, or the probability that a randomly chosen voter has preference ranking R. And $p(x, y)$ could be the probability that a randomly chosen voter will vote for x in an election between x and y. An interpretation that includes vote counting rules takes $p(x, C)$ as the probability that x will be elected from a set C of candidates when a specified election system is used. In other economic settings, including consumer behavior and equilibrium analyses, $p(A, B)$ could be the proportion of a population that will choose from A when B is the available set, or the probability that a social outcome in A will occur when B is the set of possible social outcomes.

The start of the next section provides access to the rest of the chapter. General treatments of stochastic utility relied on extensively here are Block and Marschak (1960), Luce and Suppes (1965), Luce (1977), and Suppes, Krantz, Luce and Tversky, (1989, Chapter 17). Other extended discussions appear in Luce (1959), Marschak (1960), Indow (1975), Fishburn (1977), Colonius (1984), Machina (1985), Falmagne (1985), Train (1986), Marley (1991), and De Soete and Carroll (1991). Lucid summaries of experimental findings are included in Luce and Suppes (1965) and Luce (1977). McFadden (1976, 1981) and Amemiya (1981) emphasize economic concerns, including models often used in econometric analysis, Critchlow, Fligner and Verducci (1991) reviews probabilistic ranking models, Fishburn (1992) surveys the relationship of binary choice probabilities to random utility, Marley (1992) describes models that integrate reaction time into the stochastic choice picture, and Dagsvik (1995) provides an analysis of the important class of generalized extreme value random utility models developed by McFadden (1981).

2   Structures

This section describes structures that initiate a delineation and classification of stochastic utility theories. We begin with A and the domains of probability functions P and p, then comment on primitive domains and axioms. The next section discusses types of representations that characterize primitive domains, either totally or partially, in alternative languages. In Example 1.2, p

on $\{(a, B) : a \in B \subseteq \{x, y, z\}, |B| = 2\}$ describes a primitive domain for binary choice probabilities, and $(\mathcal{R}, P)$ is an alternative language for characterizing p by P sums in a total representation that is valid if and only if p satisfies the triangle inequality. Example 2.1 at the end of this section describes a natural procedure for defining choice probabilities when $(\mathcal{R}, P)$ is taken to be the primitive domain.

Later sections say more about specific representations and axioms on primitive domains that imply the representations. A guide to those sections appears under the *Preview* heading at the end of Section 3. Throughout, interpretations for individuals can be augmented by interpretations for groups of people when appropriate.

2.1   The Universal Set of Objects

A large part of the theoretical contributions to stochastic utility presume no particular structure for the universal set $\mathcal{A}$ of objects apart from its cardinality. The most prominent cardinality assumption is that $\mathcal{A}$ is finite with at least three members, but denumerable and nondenumerable object sets also occur.

Specific structures for $\mathcal{A}$ that arise frequently in traditional utility theories and have had some bearing on stochastic utility include multiattributed structures $\mathcal{A} \subseteq \mathcal{A}_1 \times \cdots \times \mathcal{A}_m$ for which each object is described by m relevant attributes or aspects. Example 1.1 has $m = 3$ for make of car, color, and transmission type. Special algebraic and topological structures [Fishburn (1970), Krantz, Luce, Suppes and Tversky (1971), Wakker (1989)], with or without multiple attributes, may also be used to describe $\mathcal{A}$.

Two traditional structures that have received modest attention in stochastic utility are lottery sets and act sets. $\mathcal{A}$ is a *lottery set* if its objects are probability distributions or measures defined on an algebra of subsets of an *outcome set* $\mathcal{O}$. An example of a lottery is a wager in which you win \$200 with probability 1/3 and lose \$50 with probability 2/3. $\mathcal{A}$ is an *act set* if each object is a function f on a set S of *states of the world* that assigns an outcome $f(s)$ in $\mathcal{O}$ to each $s \in S$. An example of an act f is the decision to acquit a person accused of murder. There are two states: $s_1 =$ the person committed the murder; $s_2 =$ the person did not commit the murder. Then $f(s_1)$ is the outcome of acquitting a murderer, and $f(s_2)$ is the outcome of acquitting an innocent person. Lottery sets and act sets play a minor role in the chapter until the final section, where additional definitions of these sets and their relationships to stochastic utility are described.

2.2 Domains for P

A binary relation R on $\mathcal{A}$ is a *weak order* if it is transitive (xRy and $yRz \Rightarrow xRz$) and strongly connected (xRy or yRx, for *all* $x, y \in \mathcal{A}$), and a *linear order* or *ranking* if it is an antisymmetric (xRy and $yRx \Rightarrow x = y$) weak order. When R is denoted by $\succsim$ (preferred or indifferent to), we define strict preference $\succ$ and indifference $\sim$ by

$$x \succ y \quad \text{if} \quad x \succsim y \quad \text{and} \quad \text{not}(y \succsim x) \, ,$$

$$x \sim y \quad \text{if} \quad x \succsim y \quad \text{and} \quad y \succsim x \, .$$

When R is a weak order, $\sim$ on $\mathcal{A}$ is an *equivalence relation* (transitive, symmetric: $x \sim y \Rightarrow y \sim x$, and reflexive: $x \sim x$) that partitions $\mathcal{A}$ into equivalence classes of indifferent objects. If R is a ranking, each $\sim$ class is a singleton. One can think of a weak order as a ranking that allows ties.

The most common domains $\mathcal{R}$ for P in stochastic utility are sets of linear orders or rankings on $\mathcal{A}$. In this case we refer to $\mathcal{R}$ as a *ranking domain*. When $\mathcal{R}$ is a set of weak orders, we say that it is a *weak order domain*. A domain that contains all binary relations of a specified type is *complete*. In Example 1.2, $\mathcal{R}$ is a complete ranking domain. Domains that are not complete for the class of weak orders are sets of weak orders restricted by a monotonicity, additivity or single–peaked condition as discussed, for example, in Fishburn (1970, 1973b).

Other types of domains are sets of partial orders and families of tournaments. A *partial order* is similar to a weak order except that its indifference relation $\sim$ is not assumed to be transitive, as when $x \sim y$ and $y \sim z$ but $x \succ z$. A *tournament* is a strongly connected and antisymmetric binary relation. It has $x \succ y$ or $y \succ x$ whenever $x \neq y$. A transitive tournament is a ranking. If every one of an odd number of voters has a preference ranking on a set C of candidates, and if $x \succsim y$ means that as many voters prefer x to y as prefer y to x, then $\succsim$ on C is a tournament.

2.3 Domains for p

Given domain $\mathcal{C}$ for a choice probability function p let

$$\mathcal{B} = \{B : (A, B) \in \mathcal{C} \text{ for some } A \subseteq \mathcal{A}\} \, .$$

We refer to $\mathcal{B}$ as the *base* of $\mathcal{C}$, and to each $B \in \mathcal{B}$ as a *base set*. If every base set has exactly two objects then $\mathcal{B}$ is a *binary* base. If every base set is finite then $\mathcal{B}$ is a *finitary* base. A base that contains every set (with at least two objects) of the indicated cardinality is *complete*. Because it is usually assumed that some object in B will be chosen when B is the feasible set, singleton base sets are of secondary interest.

If it seems important to ensure *logically* that something in B must be chosen when B is the feasible set, a null option ("none of the above") can be included in base sets. For mathematical convenience, *we assume for (C, p) that either a null option different than the empty set $\emptyset$ is included in each base set, or else that the forced choice paradigm applies, so in both cases*

$$p(\emptyset, B) = 0 \quad \text{for all} \quad B \in \mathcal{B} .$$

For each base set B let

$$\mathcal{C}(B) = \{A : (A, B) \in \mathcal{C}\} .$$

It is usually assumed that $\mathcal{C}(B)$ is a Boolean algebra of subsets of B, i.e., $\mathcal{C}(B)$ contains B and is closed under finite unions, $(A, A' \in \mathcal{C}(B) \Rightarrow A \cup A' \in \mathcal{C}(B))$ and complementation $(A \in \mathcal{C}(B) \Rightarrow B \setminus A \in \mathcal{C}(B))$. Then p_B, defined by

$$p_B(A) = p(A, B) \quad \text{for all} \quad A \in \mathcal{C}(B) ,$$

is a *finitely additive probability measure* on a Boolean algebra. That is, $p_B(\emptyset) = 0$, $0 \le p_B(A) \le 1$ for all $A \in \mathcal{C}(B)$, and $p_B(A \cup A') = p_B(A) + p_B(A')$ whenever A and A' are disjoint members of $\mathcal{C}(B)$.

When B is finite, we assume unless noted otherwise that $\mathcal{C}(B)$ is the set of all subsets of B. Then p_B is completely determined by additivity from its singleton choice probabilities $p(x, B)$, or $p_B(x)$, with

$$p_B(A) = \sum_{x \in A} p_B(x) \quad \text{for every} \quad A \subseteq B .$$

When B is infinite, singletons may or may not be included in $\mathcal{C}(B)$. If they are and if p_B is completely determined by the $p_B(x)$ and the preceding summation formula, we say that p_B is *point–summable*. A point–summable measure defined on a σ–algebra (Boolean algebra closed under countable unions) is discrete. Probability measures on σ–algebras that are not point–summable include uniform measures on bounded intervals and normal or Gaussian measures on finite–dimensional Euclidean spaces.

2.4 Primitive Domains and Axioms

The *primitive domain* of a utility theory is a pair (Ω, α) in which Ω is the domain set and α is a primitive notion or set of primitive notions on Ω, interpreted in terms of preference or choice. Primitives can be relational or numerical. The relational primitive domain $(\mathcal{A}, \succsim)$ is used in most traditional theories; the numerical mode is predominant in stochastic theories. For example, most deterministic or "traditional" theories of preference and utility (von Neumann and Morgenstern (1944), Savage (1954), Luce and Raiffa (1957), Debreu (1959), Lancaster (1966), Fishburn (1970, 1988, 1994b), Karni and Schmeidler (1991)) begin by assuming that $\succsim$ is an ordering relation on a set $\mathcal{A}$ of consumption opportunities, commodity bundles or other multiattribute alternatives, risky prospects or lotteries, acts that explicitly recognize exogeneous uncertainty, and so forth. Additional assumptions about the behaviour of $\succsim$ on $\mathcal{A}$ then lead to representations of preference expressed by order–preserving utilities on $\mathcal{A}$. On the other hand, the types of data generated by econometric studies, observations of individual choice behavior, and other contexts subject to statistical analysis are usually numerical. Whether the data apply to the choices of an individual over repeated trials or to the choices of many people in a designated population, they are often expressed as relative frequencies or choice probabilities and therefore fit most naturally into a numerically–based stochastic utility format.

There are, however, several quite different primitive domains that have been used in stochastic theories, including $(\mathcal{C}, p)$, $(\mathcal{R}, P)$, $(\mathcal{A}, \succsim)$ and $(\mathcal{C}, \succsim)$. The first of these, $(\mathcal{C}, p)$, is by far the most common and will be emphasized in this chapter. We use $(\mathcal{A}, \succsim)$ when preferences are primitive and deterministic but choice has a probabilistic interpretation. Examples with $\mathcal{A}$ as a lottery set and members of $\mathcal{O}$ as the basic objects of choice appear in Machina (1985), Fishburn (1988), and Section 9 below. The primitive domain $(\mathcal{C}, \succsim)$ is a qualitative precursor [Narens (1990)] of $(\mathcal{C}, p)$ in which

$$(A, B) \succsim (A', B') \quad \text{for} \quad (A, B), (A', B') \in \mathcal{C}$$

indicates that the propensity to choose from A given B is at least as great as the propensity to choose from A' given B'.

The *axioms* of a stochastic preference or choice theory are usually formulated in the language of its primitive domain. An example for $(\mathcal{C}, p)$ with binary base $\mathcal{B}$ is the triangle inequality $p(x, z) \leq p(x, y) + p(y, z)$. Another is *moderate stochastic transitivity*: if $p(x, y) \geq 1/2$ and $p(y, z) \geq 1/2$ then

$$p(x, z) \geq \min\{p(x, y), p(y, z)\} ,$$

for all distinct $x, y, z \in \mathcal{A}$. An example for finitary $\mathcal{B}$ is the following part of *Luce's choice axiom* (Luce (1959): if all binary choice probabilities are positive and $x \in A \subseteq B$, then
$$p(x, B) = p(x, A)p(A, B) .$$

In words, if $x \in B$ then for *every* A that contains x and is included in B, the probability of choosing x from B (i.e., when choice is restricted to B) is the product of the probabilities of choosing x from A and of choosing something in A from B. We consider these conditions and many others like them in later sections.

Suppose A is finite and R is a complete ranking domain. Let R_{xy} be the set of rankings that have x and y adjacent and $x \succ y$. Define $\succ_{yx}$ for $\succ \in R_{xy}$ as the ranking obtained from $\succ$ by interchanging x and y. An axiom for primitive domain (R, P) is

$$P(\succ) > P(\succ_{yx}) \Leftrightarrow P(\succ') > P(\succ'_{yx})$$

for all distinct $x, y \in A$ and all $\succ, \succ' \in R_{xy}$. Thus, if $P(rxys) > P(ryxs)$ when r and s are linear orders on the parts of a two–part partition of the objects in $A \setminus \{x, y\}$, then the inequality holds for all such r and s. The weaker version, $P(\succ) > P(\succ_{yx}) \Rightarrow P(\succ') \geq P(\succ'_{yx})$, accommodates cases in which $P(\succ') = 0$.

Axioms for the deterministic primitive domain $(A, \succsim)$ are similar to those of traditional theories. Stochastic choice arises from assumptions of how choices relate to $(A, \succsim)$. Suppose final choices in a lottery setting employ the probabilities in preference–maximizing lotteries. Then, if preference is maximized by a lottery that has probability $3/4$ for x and $1/4$ for y, we have $p(x, A) = 3/4$ and $p(y, A) = 1/4$.

Narens (1990) characterizes Luce's choice axiom by conditions on a primitive domain $(C, \succsim)$ when A is infinite and B is the complete finitary base. His initial axiom is a monotonicity condition which says that the propensity of choosing x decreases as its base set expands:

$$(x, A) \succ (x, B) \quad \text{if} \quad x \in A \quad \text{and} \quad A \subset B .$$

Because other primitives can often be defined in natural ways from a given primitive domain, the choice of a primitive domain for a stochastic theory is not always straightforward. Narens's theory offers an avenue to (C, p) through $(C, \succsim)$. The following example identifies natural routes from rankings to other primitives.

EXAMPLE 2.1 Assume that A is finite, $|A| \geq 3$, and R is a complete ranking domain. Given primitive domain (R, P), define p on C as follows:

$$
\begin{aligned}
R(x, B) &= \{\succ \in R : x \succ y \text{ for all } y \in B \setminus \{x\}\}; \\
p(x, B) &= \sum_{\succ \in R(x,B)} P(\succ) \quad \text{for } x \in B; \\
p(A, B) &= \sum_{x \in A} p(x, B) \quad \text{for } A \subseteq B .
\end{aligned}
$$

This defines choice probabilities by the traditional idea of maximizing preference. Given p, we can then define $\succsim$ on C in the obvious way by

$$(A, B) \succsim (A', B') \quad \text{if} \quad p(A, B) \geq p(A', B') .$$

Under the usual convention that $p(x, x) = 1/2$, it is natural also to define a preference relation $\succsim$ on $\mathcal{A}$ by

$$x \succsim y \quad \text{if} \quad p(x, y) \geq 1/2 \ .$$

Then $\succsim$ on $\mathcal{A}$ is strongly connected but not necessarily transitive.

3   Representations

A *representation* for primitive domain (Ω, α) is a characterization of aspects of α in an alternative language L. Many alternative languages involve utilities in the set $\mathbb{R}$ of real numbers, but other L's can be used. We say that a representation is *total* if α can be recovered fully from the information given by L in the representation. Otherwise it is *partial*.

We begin with widely–discussed representations for binary choice probabilities and work up to more inclusive representations.

EXAMPLE 3.1 Let $(\Omega, \alpha) = (\mathcal{C}, p)$ with complete binary base $\mathcal{B}$. Three representations for binary choice probabilities are, for all $x, y, z, w \in \mathcal{A}$:

R1. $p(x, y) \geq 1/2 \Leftrightarrow x \succsim y$, where $\succsim$ is a weak order on $\mathcal{A}$;

R2. $p(x, y) \geq p(z, w) \Leftrightarrow u(x) - u(y) \geq u(z) - u(w)$, where $u : \mathcal{A} \to \mathbb{R}$;

R3. $p(x, y) = \varphi(u(x) - u(y))$, where $u : A \to \mathbb{R}$ and φ is a nondecreasing function from $\mathbb{R}$ into $[0, 1]$ for which $\varphi(0) = 1/2$ and $\{a < b < c, 0 < \varphi(b) < 1\} \Rightarrow \varphi(a) < \varphi(b) < \varphi(c)$.

R3 is total, but R1 and R2 are partial since the information provided by the weak order $\succsim$ or the utility function u is not sufficient to identify p completely.

3.1   Representation Theorems and Uniqueness

A *representation theorem* specifies axioms for (Ω, α) that imply the existence of the L constructs and their relationship to α given by the representation. If the axioms are implied by the representation, they are *necessary* as well as sufficient.

A necessary and sufficient axiom for R1 is *weak stochastic transitivity*: for all $x, y, z \in \mathcal{A}$,

$$\{p(x, y) \geq 1/2, p(y, z) \geq 1/2\} \Rightarrow p(x, z) \geq 1/2 \ .$$

Debreu (1958) gives sufficient conditions for R2, and Scott (1964) [see also Suppes (1961)] identifies necessary and sufficient conditions for R2 when $\mathcal{A}$ is finite.

Representation R3 is sometimes referred to as a Fechnerian model [Block and Marschak (1960), Luce and Suppes (1965)] after the nineteenth century psychophysicist Gustav Fechner. It is also called a linear model [David (1988), Stern (1992)]. If R2 holds, we can define φ to satisfy R3. However, R3 is more powerful than R2 since it accommodates thresholds at the extremes of p. If utility differences can be large but $p(x, y) = 1$ whenever $u(x) - u(y) \geq 1$, R3 can account for this. Note also that the convention $p(x, x) = 1/2$ follows from the representation, and that $\varphi(a) + \varphi(-a) = 1$.

We are usually interested in the extent to which the L constructs in a representation are unique. In R1, $\succsim$ on $\mathcal{A}$ is unique with respect to a given p for which R1 holds. In the general case of R2, and especially when $\mathcal{A}$ is finite, there may be substantial flexibility in defining u, and its uniqueness status can not be easily expressed other than by a set of inequalities on u differences. However, some axiomatizations of R2, including Debreu's, imply that u is *unique up to positive affine transformations*. This means that if $\mathcal{U}$ is the set of all $u : \mathcal{A} \to \mathbb{R}$ which satisfy R2 for a given p, and if $u \in \mathcal{U}$, then $v \in \mathcal{U}$ if and only if there are numbers $a > 0$ and b such that

$$v(x) = au(x) + b \quad \text{for all} \quad x \in \mathcal{A}.$$

A similar uniqueness status may hold for u in R3. Given u there, φ is uniquely determined at all differences $u(x) - u(y)$, but will not be unique overall if there are gaps in the utility difference set.

A stronger uniqueness conclusion obtains in a representation for $(\mathcal{C}, p)$ with finitary $\mathcal{B}$ under Luce's choice axiom. Given $u : \mathcal{A} \to \mathbb{R}$, define u on $\mathcal{B}$ by additive extension:

$$u(B) = \sum_{x \in B} u(x).$$

We suppose that $\mathcal{B}$ is complete and consider

R4. $p(x, B) = u(x)/u(B)$, where $u : A \to \mathbb{R}$ and u is strictly positive.

This representation is variously known as the *strict utility model* [Block and Marschak (1960), Luce and Suppes (1965)], the *BTL model* [after Bradley and Terry (1952) and Luce (1959)] and *Luce's model*. When $\mathcal{A}$ is finite and p is strictly positive, Luce's choice axiom for positive p implies the existence of u that satisfies R4. Moreover, u is unique up to *proportionality transformations*: if $u \in \mathcal{U}$, then $v \in \mathcal{U}$ if and only if there is a number $a > 0$ such that

$$v(x) = au(x) \quad \text{for all} \quad x \in \mathcal{A}.$$

Narens's axiomatization [Narens (1990)] extends the ratio representation of R4 to infinite $\mathcal{A}$ with

$$(x, A) \succsim (y, B) \Leftrightarrow u(x)/u(A) \geq u(y)/u(B) \quad u > 0.$$

His u is also unique up to proportionality transformations. It therefore allows the unambiguous definition of p as $p(x, B) = u(x)/u(B)$.

3.2 Constant Utility and Binary Advantage Representations

Representations R1 and R2 are referred to by Suppes et al. (1989, Section 17.2) as *ordinal representations* because they involve only binary choice probabilities and are partial representations. Representations R2–R4 have been called *constant utility models* for choice probabilities [Block and Marschak (1960), Luce and Suppes (1965), Suppes et al. (1989, Section 17.4)] because each uses a single u with a fixed or "constant" value $u(x)$ for each object.

Marley (1991) discusses representations of $p(x, B)$ based on a bivariate function $\eta(x, y) \geq 0$ rather than on a univariate function $u(x)$. We view $\eta(x, y)$ as a generalization of $p(x, y)$ that measures the relative advantage of x over y. The principal representation axiomatized in Marley (1991), which generalizes a model in Rotondo (1986), is, for $x \in B$ with B finite and $|B| \geq 2$,

$$p(x, B) = \frac{\prod\limits_{y \in B \setminus \{x\}} \eta(x, y)^{\theta(B)}}{\sum\limits_{z \in B} \left[\prod\limits_{y \in B \setminus \{z\}} \eta(z, y)^{\theta(B)} \right]},$$

where η and θ are nonnegative real–valued functions. Rotondo's model has $\theta(B) = 1/(|B| - 1)$. Besides being examples of binary advantage models, these forms are *context–dependent* because of $\theta(B)$, which in Rotondo's case depends only on the cardinality of B. Marley (1991) shows that these models are not random utility models as defined in the next subsection. Related advantage models in the lottery context are described in Fishburn (1976) and Shafir, Osherson and Smith (1989). We say more about this in Section 9.

3.3 Random Utility Representations

In distinction to the preceding designations, a *random utility model* uses a set U of $u : \mathcal{A} \to \mathbb{R}$ along with a probability distribution or measure μ for 'choosing' a member of U. It is generally assumed that not all members of U induce the same ordering of $\mathcal{A}$. In process terms, we imagine that an individual 'chooses' a utility function in U according to μ and then selects a utility–maximizing object from the relevant base set B, i.e., selects an object in B that maximizes preference in the weak order induced by the 'chosen' u.

A common language L for a random utility representation of choice probabilities is provided by a *probability space* $(V, \mathcal{V}, \mu)$ in which V is the set of all $u : \mathcal{A} \to \mathbb{R}$, $\mathcal{V}$ is the Borel algebra for V [see Section 6], and μ is a probability measure on $\mathcal{V}$. That is, $\mu : \mathcal{V} \to [0, 1]$, $\mu(V) = 1$ and $\mu(V_1 \cup V_2) = \mu(V_1) + \mu(V_2)$ whenever V_1 and V_2 are disjoint sets in $\mathcal{V}$. If

$$\mu \left(\bigcup_{i \in I} V_i \right) = \sum_{i \in I} \mu(V_i)$$

whenever I is a countable set and the V_i are mutually disjoint sets in $\mathcal{V}$, then μ is *countably additive*.

Define V_{AB} for each $(A, B) \in \mathcal{C}$ as the Borel set in $\mathcal{V}$ of all $u \in V$ for which some $x \in A$ maximizes utility in B:

$$V_{AB} = \{u \in V : u(x) \geq u(y) \text{ for some } x \in A \text{ and all } y \in B\} .$$

Then a *random utility representation* for choice probabilities is, for all $(A, B) \in \mathcal{C}$,

R5. $p(A, B) = \mu(V_{AB})$, where $(V, \mathcal{V}, \mu)$ is a probability space.

Thurstone (1927) developed this model for binary probabilities modeled by samples from normal distributions, and Daniels (1950) extended its use to complete rankings.

Suppose $B = \{x, y\}$ in the total representation R5. Then, since $p(x, y) + p(y, x) = 1$, we require $\mu = 0$ on the V subset in which $u(x) = u(y)$. Similarly, for any finite base set B, R5 implies that $\mu = 0$ on the set of utility functions in which distinct x and y in B jointly maximize μ within B. In other words,

$$\{x, y \in B, x \neq y\} \Rightarrow \mu(V_{\{x\}B} \cap V_{\{y\}B}) = 0 .$$

Various probability measures, including the normals used by Thurstone and Daniels, satisfy this requirement.

Suppose $\mathcal{A}$ is finite. It then follows [Block and Marschak (1960, Theorem 3.1)] that if $\mathcal{B}$ is a complete binary or finitary base, R5 is equivalent to, for all $x \in B$ and all $B \in \mathcal{B}$,

R6. $p(x, B) = P(\mathcal{R}(x, B))$, where P is a probability distribution on the complete ranking domain $\mathcal{R}$, and $\mathcal{R}(x, B) = \{\succ \in \mathcal{R} : x \succ y \text{ for all } y \in B \setminus \{x\}\}$.

For example, given μ for R5, P satisfies R6 when

$$P(\succ) = \mu\{u \in V : \text{ for all } x, y \in A, \ u(x) > u(y) - x \succ y\} .$$

This partly accounts for the popularity of ranking domains in stochastic utility theory.

Differences between the alternative languages of $(V, \mathcal{V}, \mu)$ and $(\mathcal{R}, P)$ for R5 and R6 are illustrated in Block and Marschak (1960), Falmagne (1978), and Barberá and Pattanaik (1986). Assume that $\mathcal{B}$ is the complete finitary base for finite $\mathcal{A}$. Falmagne (1978) shows that conditions on p that derive from Block and Marschak (1960, p. 115) are necessary and sufficient for the existence of a μ that satisfies R5. The sufficiency proof, however, uses the correspondence noted above for R5 and R6. Barberá and Pattanaik (1986) prove directly that the same conditions are necessary and sufficient for the existence of a P on $\mathcal{R}$ that satisfies R6.

3.4 Subset Choice and Sequential Reduction

We now turn briefly to cases in which subsets of objects rather than single objects are viewed — either ultimately or in transition — as the units of choice. Examples of subsets for choice are committees, banquet entrees, and research projects for next year's budget. The probability that A is the *subset* chosen from among the subsets of B is denoted by $\mathbf{p}(A, B)$. Although we could cast subset choice situations in the earlier p language by formulating A as a family of subsets rather than as a collection of individual objects, it is often useful to retain the latter orientation.

Assume that $\mathcal{A}$ is finite, $\mathcal{C} = \{(A, B) : A \subseteq B \subseteq \mathcal{A}, A \neq \emptyset\}$ and, for each $B \in \mathcal{B}$, $\mathbf{p}(A, B) \geq 0$ for all nonempty A in B, and

$$\sum_{A \in \mathcal{C}(B)} \mathbf{p}(A, B) = 1 .$$

This assumes that some *nonempty* subset of B will be the chosen subset when B is the available set. When a committee of three people is to be chosen from B, $\mathbf{p}(A, B) = 0$ if $|A| \neq 3$.

Barberá and Pattanaik (1986) examine a representation of primitive domain $(\mathcal{C}, \mathbf{p})$ by maximum preference in weak orders. The representation is, for all $(A, B) \in \mathcal{C}$,

R7. $\mathbf{p}(A, B) = P(\mathcal{R}(A, B))$, where P is a probability distribution on the complete weak order domain $\mathcal{R}$, and $\mathcal{R}(A, B) = \{\succsim \in \mathcal{R} : x \sim y \succ z$ for all $x, y \in A$ and all $z \in B \setminus A\}$.

By analogy to R5 and R6, R7 is a *subset random utility model*. Barberá and Pattanaik identify restrictions on $\mathbf{p}$ that are necessary and sufficient for the existence of a P that satisfies R7. The restrictions are similar to those noted in Section 6 for R6. Corbin and Marley (1974) and Marley and Colonius (1992) also discuss the subset choice model.

The subset choice idea is used in single–object choice situations to describe sequential processes that reduce the available set by steps until only a single object remains. At each step, objects retained from the preceding step are those that possess one or more valued aspects or attributes. A weighting scheme for aspects determines probabilistically which aspects will govern the reduction. Tversky's elimination by aspects (EBA) model [Tversky (1972a,1972b)] has become a standard paradigm. It was preceded by related ideas for binary choice in Restle (1961) and Eisler (1964), and has been explored further in Marley (1981a,1988) and Busemeyer, Forsyth and Nozawa (1988). Similar reduction notions, but not necessarily in the probabilistic format, can be seen in voting processes [Black (1958), Farquharson (1969)], consumer choice theory [Lancaster (1966)], and in a variety of branch–and–bound algorithms in combinatorial optimization and sorting techniques for data search and analysis.

Suppes et al. (1989) devotes Section 17.8 to EBA and related sequential processes. With C, p and $\mathbf{p}$ as above, their fundamental connection between p and $\mathbf{p}$ is

$$p(x, B) = \sum_{\{A : A \subseteq B\}} \mathbf{p}(A, B) p(x, A) , \qquad x \in B \subseteq \mathcal{A} ,$$

with the additional stipulation that $\mathbf{p}(B, B) < 1$ when $|B| \geq 2$ to ensure that the process ends with the choice of a single object. One useful way of visualizing this connection is to imagine that $\mathbf{p}(A, B)$ describes an initial editing phase that reduces B to a subset A for further consideration. The final choice is then made from A, and the overall probability $p(x, B)$ of choosing x is computed as the sum of the probabilities of the ways that x can be chosen by the two–step process.

When this holds for some P that satisfies R7, it is referred to as a *random–elimination model*. If, in addition, it is possible to define P so that $P(\succsim) > 0$ only if $\succsim$ on $\mathcal{A}$ has one or two indifference classes, then the model is a *Boolean random–elimination model*. A similar restriction on weak orders is used in the approval voting procedure [Brams and Fishburn (1983)] in social choice theory.

We note two important theoretical results for random–elimination models: see Suppes et al. (1989) for additional contributions. First, Corbin and Marley (1974) shows that if (C, p) satisfies a random–elimination model then it also has a random utility representation as in R5 or R6. In other words, the preceding equation coupled with a weak order domain for R7 can be used to define a ranking domain for R6. Representation of the more specific EBA model as a random utility model is described in Marley (1981b).

The second result involves a *proportionality* property for $\mathbf{p}$ defined by, for all $A, C \subseteq B \subseteq \mathcal{A}$,

$$\frac{\mathbf{p}(A,B)}{\mathbf{p}(C,B)} = \frac{\displaystyle\sum_{\{D:D\cap B=A\}} \mathbf{p}(D,\mathcal{A})}{\displaystyle\sum_{\{D:D\cap B=C\}} \mathbf{p}(D,\mathcal{A})}$$

provided that the denominators are positive and, if one denominator vanishes then so does the other. It follows [Tversky (1972b), Suppes et al. (1989)] that if a random–elimination model has a $\mathbf{p}$ that satisfies proportionality, then there exists a nonnegative real–valued function $\mathbf{u}$ on the subsets of $\mathcal{A}$ such that, for all $x \in B \subseteq \mathcal{A}$, $|B| \geq 2$,

$$p(x,B) = \frac{\displaystyle\sum_{C \in F(B)} \mathbf{u}(C) p(x, B \cap C)}{\displaystyle\sum_{C \in F(B)} \mathbf{u}(C)} \, ,$$

where $F(B) = \{C \subseteq \mathcal{A} : C \cap B \neq \emptyset, \ C \cap B \neq B\}$. Moreover [Suppes et al. (1989, p. 440)], the Boolean random–elimination model, the random–elimination model that satisfies proportionality, and the EBA model are mutually equivalent.

3.5 Preview

With the exception of Narens's primitive domain $(\mathcal{C}, \succsim)$, a few brief mentions of $(\mathcal{A}, \succsim)$ for the lottery setting, and $(\mathcal{C}, \mathbf{p})$ for subsets, the representations discussed above use $(\mathcal{C}, p)$ as their primitive domain. This reflects the common practice of axiomatizing stochastic utility theories on the basis of choice probability as the primitive concept, and we shall follow it in the next four sections. Sections 4 and 7 focus on binary choice probabilities, and the intervening sections say more about constant and random utility models for finitary bases. Section 4 considers versions of stochastic transitivity, threshold representations and multiattribute binary choice. Section 5 discusses the simple scalability basis of constant utility models along with Luce's strict utility model. Section 6 discusses Falmagne's (1978) theorem and describes Cohen's (1980) generalization to infinite $\mathcal{A}$. Section 7 continues with random utility but returns to the binary base of Section 4 to look at the unsolved problem of identifying restrictions on binary p that are necessary and sufficient for the existence of P for $R6$ restricted to the binary context.

Section 8 comments on rankings induced by choice probabilities and on $(\mathcal{R}, P)$ as a primitive domain in its own right. The literature on the latter topic comes mainly from social choice theory rather than stochastic utility.

Section 9 concludes the chapter with remarks on lottery sets and act sets in stochastic utility theory, including deliberate randomization as a preference–maximizing operation.

4 Binary Choice Probabilities

The rest of this chapter surveys specific topics in stochastic utility. References for further study are provided. We assume in the present section that $(\mathcal{C}, p)$ is a primitive domain with complete binary base $\mathcal{B}$. In addition, $p(x, x) = 1/2$ for all $x \in \mathcal{A}$.

Many simple conditions on binary p have been studied [Block and Marschak (1960), Krantz (1964), Luce and Suppes (1965), Tversky and Russo (1969), Roberts (1971), Fishburn (1973a), Luce (1977), Suppes et al. (1989), especially Sections 16.4 and 17.2]. We note several, including types of stochastic transitivity (ST), that relate to ordering. For each $1/2 \leq \lambda < 1$, define $\succ_\lambda$ on $\mathcal{A}$ by

$$x \succ_\lambda y \text{ if } p(x, y) > \lambda .$$

Since $\gamma > \lambda \Rightarrow \succ_\gamma \subseteq \succ_\lambda$, $\{\succ_\lambda\}$ is a nested family of asymmetric binary "decisiveness" relations on $\mathcal{A}$. A member $\succ$ of the family is a *strict weak order* if it is *negatively transitive* ($x \succ z \Rightarrow x \succ y$ or $y \succ z$), and is an *interval order* if, for all $a, b, x, y \in \mathcal{A}$,

$$\{a \succ x, b \succ y\} \Rightarrow [a \succ y \text{ or } b \succ x] .$$

When $\mathcal{A}$ is countable, $\succ$ is a strict weak order if and only if it has a deterministic utility representation $x \succ y \Leftrightarrow u(x) > u(y)$, and $\succ$ is an interval order if and only if there is a mapping I from $\mathcal{A}$ into bounded closed real intervals such that $x \succ y \Leftrightarrow \min I(x) > \max I(y)$. See Fishburn (1970, 1985), Monjardet (1988), and Suppes et al. (1989, Chapter 16) for proofs, generalizations and additional references.

The conditions in the following list were motivated in part by the traditional notion of transitivity and its application to orders $\succ_\lambda$ as defined above from p, and by representations for p such as R2 through R4. Their specificity to the binary choice setting can be seen from the fact, noted shortly, that the weakest version of stochastic transitivity, c1, does not generally hold for the random utility model of R5 or R6. The final four conditions in the list offer different perspectives on strict stochastic transitivity since they are mutually equivalent [Tversky and Russo (1969)]. Each of the first six is implied by its successors except that c2 and c3 are logically independent, as are c5 and c6 [Fishburn (1973a)].

c1 (weak ST). $\min\{p(x, y), p(y, z)\} \geq 1/2 \Rightarrow p(x, z) \geq 1/2$.

c2 (moderate ST).

$\min\{p(x,y), p(y,z)\} \geq 1/2 \Rightarrow p(x,z) \geq \min\{p(x,y), p(y,z)\}.$

c3 (interval ST). $\max\{p(a,x), p(b,y)\} \geq \min\{p(a,y), p(b,x)\}.$

c4 (strong ST). $\min\{p(x,y), p(y,z)\} \geq 1/2 \Rightarrow p(x,z) \geq \max\{p(x,y), p(y,z)\}.$

c5 (negative ST). $p(x,z) > 1/2 \Rightarrow \max\{p(x,y), p(y,z)\} \geq p(x,z).$

c6 (strict ST).

c4, and $\min\{p(x,y), p(y,z)\} > 1/2 \Rightarrow p(x,z) > \min\{p(x,y), p(y,z)\}.$

c7 (independence). $p(a,x) \geq p(b,x) \Leftrightarrow p(a,y) \geq p(b,y).$

c8 (substitutability). $p(a,x) \geq p(b,x) \Leftrightarrow p(a,b) \geq 1/2.$

c9 (binary simple scalability). There are real–valued functions u on $\mathcal{A}$ and F on $u(\mathcal{A}) \times u(\mathcal{A})$ such that $p(x,y) = F[u(x), u(y)]$ with F strictly increasing (decreasing) in its first (second) argument.

The final condition gives a total constant utility model for p that holds if and only if p satisfies c6. In addition:

c1 $\Leftrightarrow \succ_{1/2}$ is a strict weak order ;

c3 $\Leftrightarrow \succ_\lambda$ is an interval order for every $1/2 \leq \lambda < 1$;

c5 $\Leftrightarrow \succ_\lambda$ is a strict weak order for every $1/2 \leq \lambda < 1$.

See, for example, Fishburn (1973a). Although random utility models need not satisfy even c1—consider

$$P(xyz) = 0.1 \qquad P(yzx) = 0.32$$
$$P(xzy) = 0.1 \qquad P(zxy) = 0.32$$
$$P(yxz) = 0.1 \qquad P(zyx) = 0.06 ,$$

Tversky's EBA model and its equivalents noted at the end of the preceding section satisfy c2. For more on this, see Tversky (1972b), Sattath and Tversky (1976), Luce (1977, p. 228) and Suppes et al. (1989, Section 17.8.2).

The robustness of c1–c6 depends on various factors. In some cases, none holds.

EXAMPLE 4.1 [Tverksy (1969), Fishburn (1991)] Professor Jones is about to change jobs. Salary will be most important if two offers are far apart; otherwise department prestige becomes crucial. Jones receives three offers,

$$x : \quad \$65,000 \quad \text{and low prestige}$$

$$y : \quad \$50,000 \quad \text{and high prestige}$$

$$z : \quad \$58,000 \quad \text{and medium prestige} ,$$

and concludes that $\min\{p(x,y), p(y,z), p(z,x)\} > 1/2$. Then c1 fails, so c1–c6 all fail.

Less extreme examples, many of which stem from Debreu (1960), challenge c4 and c3 but not c2. It is plausible for the cars of Example 1.1 that $p(1,2) = 1$, $p(2,3) = 0.6$ and $p(1,3) = 0.7$, where $p(1,2) = 1$ records a transparent feature–dominating preference between similar objects. Then c4 fails. In the same setting it is not unreasonable to suppose that

$$p\,(\text{car } 1 + \$50, \text{ car } 1) = p\,(\text{car } 3 + \$50, \text{ car } 3) = 1 \, ,$$

$$\max\{p\,(\text{car } 1 + \$50, \text{ car } 3), \, p\,(\text{car } 3 + \$50, \text{ car } 1)\} < 1 \, ,$$

in which case c3 fails. Other examples of failures of stochastic transitivity appear in Houston (1991) and references cited there.

Moderate stochastic transitivity c2, but not c4 or c6, is supported reasonably well by empirical data discussed in Block and Marschak (1960), Luce and Suppes (1965), Tversky and Russo (1969), Tversky (1972a) and Luce (1977) among others. The ability of c2 to account for similarities between objects as well as differences in utility is emphasized in Carroll and De Soete (1991) and De Soete and Carroll (1991). The latter paper discusses models for binary choice probabilities that have the general form

$$p(x,y) = \varphi\left(\frac{u(x) - u(y)}{d(x,y)}\right)$$

in which d is a distance function for dissimilarity between objects, u is a utility function, and φ is strictly increasing with $0 \leq \varphi(a) \leq 1$ and $\varphi(a) + \varphi(-a) = 1$. Their models, which are like R3 with the added dissimilarity feature, satisfy c2.

Models for binary choice probabilities for multiattributed objects in which utilities take special forms have been considered. With $\mathcal{A} \subseteq \mathcal{A}_1 \times \mathcal{A}_2 \times \cdots \times \mathcal{A}_n$, an example patterned on additive conjoint measurement [Krantz et al. (1971), Fishburn (1970), Wakker (1989)] is

$$p(x,y) = \varphi\left[f\left(\sum_{i=1}^{n} u_i(x_i)\right) - f\left(\sum_{i=1}^{n} u_i(y_i)\right)\right]$$

for $x = (x_1, \ldots, x_n)$ and $y = (y_1, \ldots, y_n)$, where φ and f are strictly increasing. This has been examined by Falmagne and co–authors [see Falmagne (1979, 1985)] for $n = 2$, but is similar to R3 and therefore subject to the same empirical criticisms as R3. A more robust form patterned after Tversky's additive–difference model [Tversky (1969)] is axiomatized in Suppes et al. (1989, Section 17.2.4). Its representation is

$$p(x,y) \geq p(z,w) \Leftrightarrow \sum_{i=1}^{n} \varphi_i[u_i(x_i) - u_i(y_i)] \geq \sum_{i=1}^{n} \varphi_i[u_i(z_i) - u_i(w_i)]$$

in which u_i is a real–valued function on $\mathcal{A}_i$, and each φ_i is strictly increasing and satisfies $\varphi_i(a) + \varphi_i(-a) = 0$.

The question of conditions on binary p for the existence of a random utility representation is addressed in Section 7.

5   Simple Scalability and Luce's Model

We assume in this section that $|\mathcal{A}| = n \geq 3$, and that the primitive domain is $(\mathcal{C}, p)$ with complete finitary base $\mathcal{B}$. Two conditions are used in Suppes et al. (1989, pp. 410–412) to introduce a general class of constant utility models. The first is

c10 (order–independence). For all $A, B \in \mathcal{B}$, all $x, y \in B \setminus A$ and all $z \in A$,

$$p(x, B) \geq p(y, B) \Leftrightarrow p(z, A \cup \{x\}) \leq p(z, A \cup \{y\}),$$

provided the choice probabilities on the two sides of either inequality are not both 0 or 1.

Given $x, y \in B$, the $p(x, B) \geq p(y, B)$ part of c10 says that x is as good as y in the context of B. With $z \in A$ and neither x nor y in A, the other part, $p(z, A\cup\{x\}) \leq p(z, A\cup\{y\})$, says that z is as attractive in the context of $A\cup\{y\}$ as in the context of $A \cup \{x\}$. The intuition for this part is that the potentially greater attraction for x relative to y can only reduce the choice probabilities for objects in A when x rather than y is appended to A. Because A and B can vary in c10 for fixed x, y and z when $|A| \geq 4$, the condition is quite strong and can be expected to have strong consequences.

The second condition from Suppes et al. (1989) is

c11 (simple scalability). There are real–valued functions u on $\mathcal{A}$ and φ_{k+1} on $[u(\mathcal{A})]^{k+1}$, $k = 1, \ldots, n - 1$, such that, for all (x, B) with $x \in B \in \mathcal{B}$, if $B = \{x, b_1, \ldots, b_k\}$ and $|B| = k + 1$ then

$$p(x, B) = \varphi_{k+1}[u(x), u(b_1), \ldots, u(b_k)],$$

with φ_{k+1} symmetric in its last k arguments. In addition:

(i) if $p(x, B) \in \{0, 1\}$, then φ_{k+1} is nondecreasing in its first argument and nonincreasing in the other arguments;

(ii) if $0 < p(x, B) < 1$, then $\varphi_{k+1}(\alpha, \beta_1, \dots, \beta_k) \geq \varphi_{k+1}(\alpha', \beta_1', \dots, \beta_k')$ if $\alpha \geq \alpha'$ and $\beta_i \leq \beta_i'$ for $i = 1, \dots, k$, with $>$ in the φ_{k+1} inequality if at least one of the α, β inequalities is strict.

Simple scalability, an outgrowth of binary simple scalability c9, identifies a broad class of total constant utility models for $(\mathcal{C}, p)$. Suppes et al. (1989, pp. 412 and 419–420) proves that c11 and c10 are equivalent, thus providing testable implications for simple scalability. One of these, implicit in c10 and c11, is that for all $x, y \in A \cap B$,

$$p(x, A) \geq p(y, A) \Leftrightarrow p(x, B) \geq p(y, B),$$

provided that the four probabilities are in $(0, 1)$. Another, under the same condition on the probabilities, is that for $a \in A$, $b \in B$ and $\{x, y\} \cap (A \cup B) = \emptyset$,

$$p(a, A \cup \{x\}) \geq p(a, A \cup \{y\}) \Leftrightarrow p(b, B \cup \{x\}) \geq p(b, B \cup \{y\}).$$

These are brought together in c10.

Simple scalability is liable to criticisms mentioned after Example 4.1 in the preceding section and in Suppes et al. (1989, p. 413) and has therefore stimulated work on less–vulnerable models, including Tversky's EBA model, the models in De Soete and Carroll (1991), and others described in McFadden (1976, 1981a, 1981b) and Manski (1977). But it has also clarified the class of constant utility models and illuminated work on specific models in this class. By far the best known of these is Luce's strict utility model R4, which under the assumption that all choice probabilities are positive is equivalent to each of the following:

c12 (Luce's choice axiom). For all $x \in A \subseteq B \subseteq \mathcal{A}$, $|B| \geq 2$, $p(x, B) = p(x, A)p(A, B)$.

c13 (constant–ratio rule). For all $x, y \in B \subseteq \mathcal{A}$, $|B| \geq 2$,

$$\frac{p(x, y)}{p(y, x)} = \frac{p(x, B)}{p(y, B)}.$$

The full situation that allows choice probabilities equal to zero is described in Luce (1959) and summarized in Suppes et al. (1989, p. 417). Luce's own words [Luce (1977, p. 226)] in regard to examples and empirical studies that refute simple scalability are noteworthy:

These results are deeply disturbing because their variety of domains make it difficult to see in what domain simple scalability, let alone the choice axiom, may hold. And at the same time, all of the data reported are in large part consistent with simple scalability, and so it is difficult to abandon the idea completely.

The depth to which Luce (1959) has influenced stochastic utility theory is evident in Luce (1977) and Suppes et al. (1989, Chapter 17). We mention two related results that involve random utility and illustrate the use of specific functional forms. First, R4 is a random utility model with independent components [Block and Marschak (1960)]. In particular, with $p(x, B) = v(x)/v(B)$ for R4, when μ for R5 is defined by a probability density function $\prod_{x \in \mathcal{A}} f_x(u(x))$ in which

$$f_x(t) = \begin{cases} v(x)e^{v(x)t} & t \geq 0 \\ 0 & \text{otherwise ,} \end{cases}$$

it follows easily that $p(x, B) = \mu(V_{\{x\}B})$. Luce and Suppes (1965, p. 338) credits this proof to Eric Holman and A. A. J. Marley. By a change of variable in the preceding equation, the result also follows when each f_x is a double exponential with cumulative distribution function

$$F_x(t) = e^{-e^{-[t-v(x)]}} \, , \quad \text{all real } t \, .$$

The second result, due to Yellott (1977), says that if (i) p satisfies a random utility model with independent components, (ii) the distribution functions for the components differ only in their means (a shift family), and (iii) choice probabilities are invariant under k–fold replications of all objects, then the distribution functions (strictly increasing on the line) must be double exponentials and, as a corollary, R4 and Luce's choice axiom hold.

6   Random Utility

We continue to assume that $(\mathcal{C}, p)$ with complete finitary base $\mathcal{B}$ is the primitive domain and that $|\mathcal{A}| \geq 3$. Other restrictions on the cardinality of $\mathcal{A}$ will be noted in context. For convenience here we let $\mathcal{B}$ be the family of all nonempty finite subsets of $\mathcal{A}$. This section pursues the theme of random utility by considering Falmagne's theorem for the existence of a random utility representation R5 or R6 when $\mathcal{A}$ is finite. We then comment on its extension to infinite $\mathcal{A}$, followed by remarks on independent random utility models that augment those in the preceding paragraph.

We approach Falmagne's conditions for p by recalling the regularity property discussed by Block and Marschak (1960, p. 108) among others.

c14 (regularity). For all $x \in B \subseteq A \subseteq \mathcal{A}$, $p(x, B) \geq p(x, A)$.

This asserts that x's probability of being chosen does not increase when the available containing set is enlarged, and is regarded as eminently reasonable when chaotic disturbances such as cognitive overload do not obtain. Corbin and Marley (1974) notes that it will be violated by 'second–best' choosers, e.g. people who in deference to a host select the second most expensive menu entree, but I am aware of no substantial empirical results that contradict c14.

Regularity can be rewritten as $p(x, B) - p(x, B \cup C_1) \geq 0$. When two $C_i \subseteq \mathcal{A}$ are considered, a natural extension is

$$p(x, B) - [p(x, B \cup C_1) + p(x, B \cup C_2)] + p(x, B \cup C_1 \cup C_2) \geq 0 .$$

Continuation in an inclusion–exclusion format leads to Falmagne's conditions. Let $\begin{bmatrix} k \\ j \end{bmatrix}$ denote the collection of all j–element subsets of $\{1, 2, \ldots, k\}$, and for a k–list $(C_1, C_2, \ldots, C_k)$ of sets in $\mathcal{B}$ and $h \in \begin{bmatrix} k \\ j \end{bmatrix}$ let

$$C(h) = \bigcup_{i \in h} C_i .$$

Define $M(x, B)$ with respect to $(C_1, C_2, \ldots, C_k)$ by

$$M(x, B) = p(x, B) + \sum_{j=1}^{k} (-1)^j \sum_{h \in \begin{bmatrix} k \\ j \end{bmatrix}} p(x, B \cup C(h)) .$$

We then have the following condition from Falmagne (1978).

c15 (nonnegativity). For all $x \in B \subseteq \mathcal{B}$, all $k = 1, 2, \ldots$, and all k–lists $(C_1, \ldots, C_k)$ of sets in $\mathcal{B}$,

$$M(x, B) \geq 0 .$$

Falmagne's theorem says that, when $\mathcal{A}$ is finite, $(\mathcal{C}, p)$ has a random utility representation if and only if c15 holds. As mentioned earlier, Falmagne (1978) proves this in the language of R5 with assistance from R6, and Barberà and Pattanaik (1986) proves it directly in the language of R6. Monderer (1992) uses a game-theoretic approach to prove the same theorem. The papers by Falmagne and Barberá and Pattanaik comment on the fairly relaxed uniqueness properties of the representations. Falmagne proves that if μ and ν on $\mathcal{V}$ satisfy R5 then, for all $x, y, z \in \mathcal{A}$, $\mu(\{u \in V : u(x) > u(y) > u(z)\}) = \nu(\{u \in V : u(x) > u(y) > u(z)\})$. Barberá and Pattanaik claim that for $\mathcal{A} = \{x, y, z, w\}$, P_1 and P_2 represent the same $(\mathcal{C}, p)$:

$$P_1(xyzw) = P_1(wzyx) = 1/2 ;$$
$$P_2(xyzw) = P_2(xzyw) = P_2(wyzx) = P_2(wzyx) = 1/4 .$$

However, the claim is false since $p_1(x, \{x, y, z\}) = P_1(z \succ \{x, y\}) = 1/2$ and $p_2(z, \{x, y, z\}) = P_2(z \succ \{x, y\}) = 1/4$. A correct example consistent with Falmagne's result is

$$P_1(xyzw) = P_1(yxwz) = 1/2$$
$$P_2(xywz) = P_2(yxzw) = 1/2 \; .$$

In considering extensions to infinite $\mathcal{A}$, it seems unprofitable to work with the set of all linear orders as such since this set can be extremely complex [Rosenstein (1982)]. A more tractable approach is provided by a probability space $(V, \mathcal{V}, \mu)$ in which V is the set of all real–valued functions on $\mathcal{A}$ and $\mathcal{V}$ is the Borel algebra for V, defined as follows. [See, for example, Loève (1960).]

Let $\mathcal{D}$ be the minimal Boolean algebra (closed under finite unions and complementation) of subsets of $\mathbb{R}$ that contains every real interval and is closed under countable unions. Thus $\mathcal{D}$ is a σ–algebra that comprises the *Borel sets* in $\mathbb{R}$. Let $\mathcal{D}_x$ denote the family of Borel sets in $\mathbb{R}$ for index $x \in \mathcal{A}$. For *finite* $J \subseteq \mathcal{A}$ and $D_j \in \mathcal{D}_j$ for each $j \in J$, the subset of V that contains $(u_x : x \in \mathcal{A})$ if and only if $u_j \in D_j$ for each $j \in J$ is a *cylinder*, or an *interval*, in V with sides D_j, $j \in J$. We define the *product algebra* of the $\mathcal{D}_x$, $x \in \mathcal{A}$, as the set of all finite unions of cylinders or intervals. It is easily seen to be a Boolean algebra of subsets of V. Then the *Borel algebra* $\mathcal{V}$ for V is the minimal σ–algebra that includes the product algebra. It is also called the *product σ–algebra*. Because cylinders are based on finite subsets of $\mathcal{A}$, $\mathcal{V}$ is a natural context for representations of choice probability functions with finitary bases.

This type of approach is used in Cohen (1980) to extend Falmagne's theorem to infinite $\mathcal{A}$. As a convenience for the choice–probability setting, Cohen works with the Borel algebra $\mathcal{V}_{[0,1]}$ for the set $V_{[0,1]}$ of all real–valued functions on $\mathcal{A}$ with values in $[0, 1]$. The definition of $\mathcal{V}_{[0,1]}$ parallels that of the preceding paragraph with $[0, 1]$ in place of $\mathbb{R}$. Cohen (1980) proves that c15 is necessary and sufficient for the existence of $(V_{[0,1]}, \mathcal{V}_{[0,1]}, \mu)$ that satisfies R5, with μ countably additive if $\mathcal{A}$ is countable. A countably additive representation is also obtained from c15 for arbitrary $\mathcal{A}$ when a measurability requirement is relaxed, but additional conditions are needed for the general case when the measurability requirement is imposed.

For the rest of this section we assume that $\mathcal{A}$ is finite. Several sources, including Sattath and Tversky (1976), Suppes et al. (1989, p. 424) and Marley (1992), observe that conditions on p that are necessary and sufficient for representation in a random utility model *with independent components*, where μ on each cylinder is the product of the marginals of μ on each side, are not known. This appears to be one of the main open problems in stochastic utility theory. The following testable implication of independence (plus continuity) has been noted:

c16 (multiplicative inequality).

For all $x \in A, B \subseteq A$, $p(x, A \cup B) \geq p(x, A)p(x, B)$.

Sattath and Tversky (1976) prove that c16 holds if $(\mathcal{C}, p)$ has a random utility representation with independent components that have continuous cumulative distribution functions. Together, c14 and c16 bound $p(x, A \cup B)$ with $p(x, A)p(x, B) \leq p(x, A \cup B) \leq \min\{p(x, A), p(x, B)\}$.

Additional information on independent random utility models and uniqueness for special cases can be found in Yellott (1977), Strauss (1979), Marley (1981a, 1982a) and Dagsvik (1983).

7   The Linear Ordering Polytope

We now bring together the themes of Sections 4 and 6 to consider the set $\mathbf{P_n}$ of all p for primitive domain $(\mathcal{C}, p)$ with complete binary base and $|\mathcal{A}| = n \geq 3$ that have a random utility representation R6. For convenience, let $\mathcal{A} = \{1, 2, \ldots, n\}$, denote $p(i, j)$ as p_{ij}, and let $\mathcal{R}_n$ be the complete ranking domain for $\mathbf{n} = \{1, 2, \ldots, n\}$. Also let $\mathcal{R}_n(i, j)$ be the set of all $r \in \mathcal{R}_n$ in which i precedes j. Then a binary choice probability function p for $\mathbf{n}$ is in $\mathbf{P_n}$ if and only if there is a probability distribution P on $\mathcal{R}_n$ for which

$$p_{ij} = P(\mathcal{R}_n(i, j)) = \sum_{r \in \mathcal{R}_n(i,j)} P(r) \quad \text{for all distinct} \quad i, j \in \mathbf{n} .$$

By earlier assumptions, for all distinct $i, j \in \mathbf{n}$,

$$p_{ij} \geq 0 \quad \text{and} \quad p_{ij} + p_{ji} = 1 .$$

We are interested in further restrictions on p that are necessary, or necessary and sufficient, for $p \in \mathbf{P_n}$.

Two largely separate literatures on the problem of characterizing $\mathbf{P_n}$ have evolved. The first, in psychology and economics, uses the language of this chapter. It is exemplified in Marschak (1960), Fishburn and Falmagne (1989), McFadden and Richter (1990) and Cohen and Falmagne (1990). The second, from the mathematical areas of combinatorial optimization and the theory of polytopes, is represented in Grötschel, Jünger and Reinelt (1985a, 1985b), Leung and Lee (1990) and Suck (1992). The latter literature refers to $\mathbf{P_n}$ as the linear ordering polytope for $\mathbf{n}$. We say more about it shortly. A joint review of the two literatures appears in Fishburn (1992).

Example 1.2 mentioned the pre–eminent necessary condition for $p \in \mathbf{P_n}$ [Guilbaud (1953), Marschak (1960)]:

c17 (triangle inequality). For all distinct $i, j, k \in \mathbf{n}$, $p_{ik} \leq p_{ij} + p_{jk}$.

This is necessary for $p \in \mathbf{P_n}$. It is also sufficient [Dridi (1980)] if and only if $n \leq 5$. The following counterexample to the sufficiency of c17 for $n = 6$ was known as early as 1970 [McFadden and Richter (1990)]. It was rediscovered independently in Dridi (1980), Campello de Souza (1983), Fishburn (1987), and Cohen and Falmagne (1990) among others. The inequalities in Example 7.1 and the two that follow the example are instances of facet defining inequalities for $\mathbf{P_n}$, as we explain shortly. Roughly speaking, the equality parts of facet defining inequalities identify extreme boundary cases of p functions in $\mathbf{P_n}$, and all such inequalities must hold for p to be in $\mathbf{P_n}$. Example 7.1 shows that when $n \geq 6$, a p function can satisfy all instances of the triangle inequality yet lie outside $\mathbf{P_n}$ because it violates some other facet defining inequality.

EXAMPLE 7.1 The inequality

$$(p_{aj} + p_{ak} + p_{bi} + p_{bk} + p_{ci} + p_{cj}) + (p_{ia} + p_{jb} + p_{kc}) \leq 7$$

for disjoint 3–sets $\{a, b, c\}$ and $\{i, j, k\}$ in $\mathbf{n}$ can be shown to be necessary for $p \in \mathbf{P_n}$ when $n \geq 6$. That is, if P is any probability distribution on $\mathcal{R}_n$ then the inequality must hold. However, it is not implied by the triangle inequality, which can be rewritten in a similar form as

$$p_{ij} + p_{jk} + p_{ki} \leq 2 .$$

Let $p_{15} = p_{16} = p_{24} = p_{26} = p_{34} = p_{35} = 1$ and $p_{51} = \cdots = p_{53} = 0$, and set $p_{ij} = 1/2$ for all other $i \neq j$. Then it is easily checked that c17 holds, but

$$(p_{15} + p_{16} + p_{24} + p_{26} + p_{34} + p_{35}) + (p_{41} + p_{52} + p_{63}) = 7.5 .$$

There are two other inequalities necessary for $p \in \mathbf{P_n}$ when $n \geq 6$ that are not implied by those in Example 7.1. Up to reassignments of the six indices, they are

$$(p_{12} + p_{13} + p_{24} + p_{34} + p_{35} + p_{26} + p_{45} + p_{46}) + (p_{41} + p_{52} + p_{63}) \leq 8 ,$$
$$(p_{13} + p_{23} + p_{24} + p_{15} + p_{34} + p_{35} + p_{46} + p_{56}) + (p_{41} + p_{52} + p_{63}) \leq 8 .$$

Reinelt (1991) verified by computer that these two in conjunction with c17 and the leading inequality of Example 7.1 are sufficient for $p \in \mathbf{P_6}$. They are not jointly sufficient for larger n where other necessary inequalities have been identified.

$\mathbf{P_n}$ is known in mathematics as the *linear ordering polytope* for $\mathbf{n}$; inequalities like those that characterize $\mathbf{P_6}$ describe facets of the polytope. To explicate this, let $N = n(n - 1)$, index the coordinates of $\mathbb{R}^N$ by the N ordered pairs (i, j), $1 \leq i \neq j \leq n$, and for each $r \in \mathcal{R}_n$ define $p^r \in \mathbb{R}^N$ by

$$p^r_{ij} = \begin{cases} 1 & \text{if } i \text{ precedes } j \text{ in } r \\ 0 & \text{otherwise .} \end{cases}$$

Each p^r represents a ranking in $\mathcal{R}_n$. The convex hull of the vertex set $\{p^r : r \in \mathcal{R}_n\}$ is $\mathbf{P_n}$, i.e.,

$$\mathbf{P_n} = \left\{ \sum_{\mathcal{R}_n} \lambda_r p^r : \lambda_r \geq 0 \text{ for all } r, \; \sum \lambda_r = 1 \right\},$$

where λ_r corresponds to $P(r)$ in our earlier definition. Thus $\mathbf{P_n}$ is a bounded convex polyhedron in $\mathbb{R}^N$. It has dimension $N/2 = \binom{n}{2}$ and is determined by the *minimal equation system* $\{p_{ij} + p_{ji} = 1\}$ and a finite set of *facet defining* inequalities of the form

$$\langle a, p \rangle \leq b \quad \text{for} \quad a \in \mathbb{R}^N, \; b \in \mathbb{R}; \quad \langle a, p \rangle = \sum a_{ij} p_{ij} .$$

Each *facet* of $\mathbf{P_n}$ is a maximum–dimension proper face that lies in a bounding hyperplane $\{p : \langle a, p \rangle = b\}$ and contains $\binom{n}{2}$ linearly independent vertices of $\mathbf{P_n}$. The intersection of the closed halfspaces $\{p : \langle a, p \rangle \leq b\}$ for the facet defining inequalities is $\mathbf{P_n}$.

In view of the minimal equation system, it suffices to consider explicitly only facet defining inequalities that are *canonical* in the sense that

(i) for all $i \neq j$, $a_{ij} a_{ji} = 0$;

(ii) $b > 0$ and $a_{ij} > 0$ for some $i \neq j$;

(iii) all a_{ij} are nonnegative integers that have no common integer divisor ≥ 2.

The canonical inequalities for $n \leq 5$ are $p_{ij} \leq 1$ and the triangle inequalities $p_{ij} + p_{jk} + p_{ki} \leq 2$. The others written above for $n \geq 6$ are in canonical form.

Various facet defining inequalities and families of such inequalities are established in Grötschel, Jünger and Reinelt (1985a), McLennan (1990), Leung and Lee (1990, 1992), Gilboa and Monderer (1992), and Koppen (1995). Many of these along with an important inequality in Gilboa (1990) are summarized in Fishburn (1992). They are given names such as fences, wheels, bracelets, and Möbius ladders in reference to directed graphs on $\mathbf{n}$ with edge weights $a_{ij} > 0$ (in canonical form) that describe them in a visual format. Examples of fences in canonical form are, for $k \geq 3$, disjoint k–sets A and B in $\mathbf{n}$, a bijection τ from A onto B, $h \in \mathbf{n} \setminus (A \cup B)$, and $t \geq 2$:

$$k\text{–fences:} \quad \sum_{i \in A} \sum_{j \in B \setminus \{\tau_j\}} p_{ij} + \sum_{i \in A} p_{\tau_i i} \leq k^2 - k + 1 \ ;$$

augmented k–fences [McLennan (1990)]:

$$\sum_{i \in A} \sum_{j \in B \setminus \{\tau_j\}} p_{ij} + \sum_{i \in A} p_{\tau_i i} + (k - 2) \left[\sum_{i \in A} p_{hi} + \sum_{j \in B} p_{jh} \right]$$
$$\leq 2k^2 - 3k + 1 \ ;$$

t–reinforced k–fences [Gilboa (1990), Leung and Lee (1990)]:

$$\sum_{i \in A} \sum_{j \in B \setminus \{\tau_i\}} p_{ij} + t \sum_{i \in A} p_{\tau_i i} \leq k^2 - k + \frac{t(t + 1)}{2} \ .$$

The leading inequality in Example 7.1 is a 3–fence facet defining inequality.

Open questions on the linear ordering polytope problem include complete lists of the facet defining inequalities for $\mathbf{P_7}$, $\mathbf{P_8}$, ..., more powerful proof techniques to verify such lists, and questions about properties of the a_{ij} coefficients in canonical inequalities.

8   Rankings: Induced and Primitive

This section comments on three themes for relationships between choice probabilities and probability distributions on binary relations. The first continues along the line of ranking probabilities based on choice probabilities as in R6. The others examine ideas for defining choice probabilities from a primitive domain $(\mathcal{R}, P)$.

8.1   Rankings from Choice Probabilities

Critchlow, Fligner and Verducci (1991) [see also Fligner and Verducci (1993)] offers an extensive interpretive review of probability models on rankings that have appeared in the statistical and psychological literature. The paper describes four main methods of constructing $(\mathcal{R}, P)$ for a complete ranking domain $\mathcal{R}$ and analyzes the methods and particular models from the viewpoint of interesting properties that P might exhibit. One main method is based on the random utility ideas that evolved from Thurstone (1927) and Daniels (1950). Another, which emanated from Babington Smith (1950) with major contributions from Mallows (1957), is based on pairwise comparison data or binary choice probabilities. Its basic model takes $P(r_1 r_2 \cdots r_n)$ as a normalizing constant times the product of all $p(r_i, r_j)$ for $i < j$. The other two main methods are based on notions of distances between rankings and on multistage decompositions. The latter class is related to earlier ideas developed by Luce (1959, 1960), Block and Marschak (1960), Marley (1965, 1968) and others that we consider next.

We focus on two primitive domains, $(\mathcal{C}, p)$ and $(\mathcal{C}, q)$, with complete finitary bases and with finite $\mathcal{A}$, $|\mathcal{A}| = n \geq 3$. We interpret $p(x, B)$ as before, whereas $q(x, B)$ denotes the probability that x is the *least* desirable object in B. We refer to $q(x, B)$ as a *rejection* probability and write $q(x, \{x, y\})$ as $q(x, y)$. As in the last section, let $\mathcal{R}_n$ be the set of all rankings of $\mathcal{A}$. For a ranking $r = r_1 r_2 \cdots r_n$ let

$$r^j = \{r_j, \ldots, r_n\} \quad \text{and} \quad {}^j r = \{r_1, \ldots, r_j\} .$$

Also, for $x \notin A \subseteq \mathcal{A}$, let $x[A]$ denote the set of all rankings in $\mathcal{R}_n$ that have x before all objects in A (which can be in any order), and let $[A]x$ be the set of all rankings in $\mathcal{R}_n$ in which x follows all objects in A.

Luce and others define top–down ranking probabilities $P(r)$ based on p, and bottom–up ranking probabilities $Q(r)$ based on q as follows:

$$\begin{aligned} P(r) &= p(r_1, r^1) p(r_2, r^2) \cdots p(r_{n-1}, r^{n-1}) \\ Q(r) &= q(r_n, {}^n r) q(r_{n-1}, {}^{n-1} r) \cdots q(r_2, {}^2 r) . \end{aligned}$$

In the first of these, r is formed by choosing r_1 in $\mathcal{A} = r^1$ according to p, then choosing r_2 in $\mathcal{A} \setminus \{r_1\}, \ldots$, on down to the binary choice of r_{n-1} from $\{r_{n-1}, r_n\}$. In the second, we first select a worst object r_n from $\mathcal{A} = {}^n r$ according to q, then select r_{n-1} from $\mathcal{A} \setminus \{r_n\}, \ldots$, on up to r_2 from $\{r_1, r_2\}$.

Depending on p and q, the ranking probabilities may or may not be *congruent* in the sense that $P = Q$. Moreover, they may or may not adhere to the random utility paradigm. We say that P satisfies a *random utility model* if

$$p(x, B) = P(x[B \setminus \{x\}]) \quad \text{for all} \quad x \in B \subseteq \mathcal{A} ,$$

and that Q satisfies a *random disutility model* if

$$q(x, B) = Q([B \setminus \{x\}]x) \quad \text{for all} \quad x \in B \subseteq \mathcal{A} .$$

EXAMPLE 8.1 Suppose $\mathcal{A} = \{x, y, z\}$ and all choice and rejection probabilities are positive. We have

$$P(xyz) = p(x, \mathcal{A}) p(y, z) \qquad\qquad Q(xyz) = q(z, \mathcal{A}) q(y, x)$$
$$P(xzy) = p(x, \mathcal{A}) p(z, y) \qquad\qquad Q(xzy) = q(y, \mathcal{A}) q(z, x)$$

and so forth by the preceding definitions of P and Q. If $P = Q$, we can solve for q in terms of p to obtain

$$q(a, A) = p(b, A)p(c, a) + p(c, A)p(b, a)$$

$$q(a, b) = \frac{p(b, A)p(a, c)}{p(b, A)p(a, c) + p(a, A)p(b, c)}$$

for all $a, b \in A$, with $\{a, b, c\} = \{x, y, z\}$. It does *not* follow that $p(a, b) = q(b, a)$.

If, in addition to $P = Q$, the binary choice and rejection probabilities are *congruent* in the sense that $p(a, b) = q(b, a)$ for all distinct $a, b \in A$, then for all $a \in A$ with $\{a, b, c\} = A$,

$$p(a, A) = kp(a, b)p(a, c)$$
$$q(a, A) = kp(b, a)p(c, a) = kq(a, b)q(a, c) ,$$

$k = [p(x, y)p(x, z) + p(y, x)p(y, z) + p(z, x)p(z, y)]^{-1}$, so choice and rejection probabilities from A have simple expressions in the binaries. This places no special restrictions on the binaries: any choices of $p(x, y)$, $p(x, z)$ and $p(y, z)$ in $(0, 1)$ yield a valid system.

Suppose, however, that it is true also that P satisfies a random utility model. Then the binary equations

$$p(a, b) = P(abc) + P(acb) + P(cab)$$

lead to the conclusion that

$$p(a, B) = q(a, B) = \frac{1}{|B|} \quad \text{for all} \quad a \in B \subseteq A ,$$

which "is unacceptable on empirical grounds" [Luce and Suppes (1965, p. 358)].

Block and Marschak (1960, pp. 109–111) and Luce and Suppes (1965, pp. 354–358) prove two important results for P and Q as defined above when choice and rejection probabilities are positive. First, if P satisfies a random utility model then Luce's choice axiom c12 holds. By symmetry, if Q satisfies a random disutility model then Luce's axiom c12 holds with q in place of p. Second, as indicated by Example 8.1, if P and Q are congruent ($P = Q$), if $p(x, y) = q(y, x)$ for all distinct $x, y \in A$, and if P and Q satisfy random utility and random disutility models, respectively, then

$$p(x, B) = q(x, B) = \frac{1}{|B|} \quad \text{for all} \quad x \in B \subseteq A .$$

See Luce and Suppes (1965, p. 358) for comments on the latter result.

Additional results that supplement these two are proved in Luce (1960), Marley (1965, 1968, 1981a) and Strauss (1979). Two noteworthy conditions on probabilities are Marley's concordance condition: for all distinct $x, y \in B \subseteq A$,

c18 (concordance). $p(x, B)q(y, B \setminus \{x\}) = q(y, B)p(x, B \setminus \{y\})$,

which posits probabilistic equivalence for "choose x, reject y" and "reject y, choose x", and Luce's condition

$$p(x, B) = \sum_{y \in B \setminus \{x\}} q^*(y, B)p(x, B \setminus \{y\})$$

in which $q^*(y, B)$ is a *discard probability* that could differ from $q(y, B)$. Luce (1960) proves that c12 and the latter condition imply

$$q^*(x, B) = \frac{1 - p(x, B)}{|B| - 1} \ .$$

A stronger result for $q^*(x, B)$ that does not assume c12 is proved in Marley (1965). Marley (1968) proves that the extension of $P = Q$ to rankings on subsets of A implies c18, and that concordance implies $q = q^*$.

8.2 Rankings as Primitive

A slightly different perspective emerges when we assume that $(\mathcal{R}_n, P)$ with $\mathcal{R}_n$ a complete ranking domain is the primitive domain. Let this be so, and assume for convenience that $P(r) > 0$ for all $r \in \mathcal{R}_n$. When A and B are nonempty disjoint subsets of A and s and t are rankings of A and B respectively, let st denote the ranking of $A \cup B$ formed by juxtaposition: $(s = s_1 \cdots s_j, t = t_1 \cdots t_k) \to st = s_1 \cdots s_j t_1 \cdots t_k$. The following condition [Fishburn (1994a)] is tantamount to the L–decomposability condition in Critchlow, Fligner and Verducci (1993, p. 298).

c19 (split–and–splice). For all disjoint $A, B \subseteq A$ with $A \cup B = A$, $|A| \geq 2$ and $|B| \geq 2$, and for all rankings s, s' of A and t, t' of B,

$$P(st)P(s't') = P(st')P(s't) \ .$$

For example, if $n = 7$, $A = \{1, 3, 5, 7\}$ and $B = \{2, 4, 6\}$, c19 says that
$P(3715 \mid 426)P(5137 \mid 642) = P(3715 \mid 642)P(5137 \mid 426)$.

Suppose c19 holds. Then there are "choice" probabilities $p(x, B)$ and "rejection" probabilities $q(x, B)$ such that, for all $r = r_1 \cdots r_n \in \mathcal{R}_n$,

$$
\begin{aligned}
P(r) &= p(r_1, r^1)p(r_2, r^2) \cdots p(r_{n-1}, r^{n-1}) \\
&= q(r_n, {}^n r)q(r_{n-1}, {}^{n-1} r) \cdots q(r_2, {}^2 r) \ .
\end{aligned}
$$

We do not use Q here since P on $\mathcal{R}_n$ is taken as the sole primitive. Moreover, we hesitate to call $p(x, B)$ a choice probability since there is no assurance that $p(x, B) = P(x[B \setminus \{x\}])$. Another condition which implies this is noted in Fishburn (1994a): when it holds along with c19, Luce's axiom c12 for p follows. If we assume also that $q(x, B) = P([B \setminus \{x\}]x)$, then $p(x, B) = q(x, B) = 1/|B|$ for all $x \in B \subseteq \mathcal{A}$, and therefore

$$P(r) = 1/n! \quad \text{for all} \quad r \in \mathcal{R}_n .$$

8.3 Social Choice Lotteries

Choice probabilities in the setting of group decision making arise when lotteries on candidates or alternatives are used to identify a probability distribution in the set $\mathcal{A}$ of probability distributions on an outcome (candidate) set $\mathcal{O}$ that will be used to make the final choice. The types of voter or individual preference data that have been suggested as input include individual choice probabilities [Intriligator (1973), Fishburn and Gehrlein (1977)], binary comparison data, including rankings and weak orders, on the outcome set $\mathcal{O}$ [Barberá and Sonnenschein (1978), Fishburn (1984), Clark (1992), Marley (1993)], and von Neumann–Morgenstern and related forms of individual utility functions on $\mathcal{A}$ [Zeckhauser (1969), Fishburn (1973b, Chapter 18), and Howard (1992)].

One quite practical method [Kreweras (1965), Fishburn (1984)] is based solely on the *vote differential function* d, where for distinct $x, y \in \mathcal{O}$, $d(x, y)$ is the number of votes (preferences) for x over y minus the number of votes for y over x. Thus $d(x, y) + d(y, x) = 0$. For probability distributions $a, b \in \mathcal{A}$ let

$$\Delta(a, b) = \sum_{x \in \mathcal{O}} \sum_{y \in \mathcal{O}} a(x)b(y)d(x, y) .$$

It then follows from von Neumann's minimax theorem [von Neumann (1928), Luce and Raiffa (1957), Fishburn (1988)] that the set

$$C(d) = \{a \in \mathcal{A} : \ \Delta(a, b) \geq 0 \ \text{ for all } \ b \in \mathcal{A}\}$$

is a nonempty polytope in $\mathcal{A}$. Kreweras's proposal is to use a lottery in $C(d)$ to make the final choice.

This proposal and all methods in a more general class in Fishburn (1984) satisfy properties often considered desirable for social choice. One of these [Smith (1973)] says that if $\{\mathcal{O}_1, \mathcal{O}_2\}$ is a nontrivial partition of $\mathcal{O}$ such that $d(x, y) > 0$ for all $(x, y) \in \mathcal{O}_1 \times \mathcal{O}_2$, then nothing in $\mathcal{O}_2$ will ever be chosen. Another says that if there is any list of weak orders on $\mathcal{O}$ that could have generated d by sincere voting, and if $x \succsim y$ for every order in the list, with $x \succ y$ for at least one order, then y has probability 0 of being chosen.

9   Lotteries and Acts

We recall from Section 2 that $\mathcal{A}$ is a lottery set if its objects are probability distributions or measures defined on an algebra of subsets of an outcome set $\mathcal{O}$. Utility theories for deterministic preferences in the tradition of von Neumann and Morgenstern (1944) use lottery sets.

In addition, $\mathcal{A}$ is an act set if each object is a function f on a set S of states that assigns an outcome $f(s)$ in $\mathcal{O}$ to each $s \in S$. Following Savage (1954), we refer to f as an *act* and to each subset of S as an *event*. The outcome set $\mathcal{O}$ for an act set might be a lottery set. We assume that exactly one state in S obtains, that the individual is uncertain which it will be, and that the chosen act will not affect its occurrence. It is usually assumed that the relevant event set is a Boolean algebra $\mathcal{E}$.

We assume here for lotteries that probability distributions $a, b, \dots$ on $\mathcal{O}$ have finite supports, and for acts $f, g, \dots$ that $S = \{s_1, s_2, \dots, s_N\}$. Then the expected utility representation for lotteries [von Neumann and Morgenstern (1944), Herstein and Milnor (1953), Fishburn (1970)] is

$$a \succsim b \Leftrightarrow \langle a, u \rangle \geq \langle b, u \rangle, \quad \langle a, u \rangle = \sum_{x \in \mathcal{O}} a(x) u(x) \ ,$$

and for acts [Savage (1954), Fishburn (1970)] is

$$f \succsim g \Leftrightarrow \langle \pi, u(f) \rangle \geq \langle \pi, u(g) \rangle, \quad \langle \pi, u(f) \rangle = \sum_{j=1}^{N} \pi(s_j) u(f(s_j)) \ .$$

Here u on $\mathcal{O}$ is a utility function unique up to positive affine transformations, and π is a unique subjective probability distribution on S.

We conclude by considering two main approaches to probabilistic choice for lottery sets and act sets that are motivated by failures of traditional expected utility theories to account for choice behavior in these settings, either because of stochastic choice as discussed above [Edwards (1954, 1956), Taub and Myers (1961), Myers, Reilly and Taub (1961), Luce and Shipley (1962), Becker, De-Groot and Marschak (1963a, 1963b), Suydam (1965), Luce and Suppes (1965), Lee (1971)] or because of systematic violations of the axioms of traditional theories such as independence and transitivity [Allais (1953), Ellsberg (1961), Tversky (1969), MacCrimmon and Larsson (1979), Kahneman and Tversky (1979), Slovic and Lichtenstein (1983)]. The following two examples illustrate such violations.

EXAMPLE 9.1 Let $\mathcal{A}$ denote a set of lotteries with monetary outcomes, and for $a, b \in \mathcal{A}$ and $0 \leq \lambda \leq 1$ let $\lambda a + (1 - \lambda)b$ denote the lottery that assigns probability $\lambda a(x) + (1 - \lambda)b(x)$ to each $x \in \mathcal{O}$. A standard independence axiom of von Neumann–Morgenstern utility theory says that if $a, b, c \in \mathcal{A}$, $0 < \lambda < 1$, and $a \succ b$, then $\lambda a + (1 - \lambda)c \succ \lambda b + (1 - \lambda)c$. Examples initiated by Allais (1953) reveal frequent violations of this axiom. Consider, for example, the following four lotteries from Kahneman and Tversky (1979):

> a: get \$3000 with certainty;
> b: get \$4000 with probability 0.8, and nothing otherwise;
> a':   get \$3000 with probability 0.25, and nothing otherwise;
> b':   get \$4000 with probability 0.20, and nothing otherwise.

More than half of the 95 respondents in an experiment involving these lotteries had $a \succ b$ and $b' \succ a'$. This pair of preferences violates independence because, when c is the lottery that yields \$0 with certainty and $\lambda = 1/4$, $a' = \lambda a + (1 - \lambda)c$ and $b' = \lambda b + (1 - \lambda)c$.

EXAMPLE 9.2 Let $\mathcal{A}$ denote an act set with four states in S and monetary outcomes. The states correspond to the four possible results of the next two flips of a fair coin, i.e., HH, HT, TH and TT, where H = "heads" and T = "tails". Consider four acts:

	HH	HT	TH	TT
f_1	\$6000	\$5000	\$4000	\$3000
f_2	\$5000	\$4000	\$3000	\$6000
f_3	\$4000	\$3000	\$6000	\$5000
f_4	\$3000	\$6000	\$5000	\$4000

Because f_1 has a larger return than f_2 in three of the four states, it is plausible for some people that $f_1 \succ f_2$. For the same reason, those people will have $f_2 \succ f_3$, $f_3 \succ f_4$, and $f_4 \succ f_1$. But then $\succ$ is intransitive and the expected utility representation for acts cannot hold.

The first main approach to probabilistic choice in this section factors $\mathcal{A}$'s lottery or act structure into stochastic choice models similar to those in earlier sections. Representatives include Edwards (1956), Luce (1958), Becker, De-Groot and Marschak (1963a, 1963b), Luce and Suppes (1965, Sections 7 and 8.4) and Fishburn (1976, 1978). For lottery set $\mathcal{A}$ and choice probability function p, Luce and Suppes (1965, pp. 360–361) define stochastic EU (expected utility) models that include:

> weak EU: $p(a, b) \geq 1/2 \Leftrightarrow \langle a, u \rangle \geq \langle b, u \rangle$,
>
> strict EU: $p(a, B) = \langle a, u \rangle / \sum_{b \in B} \langle b, u \rangle$, $u > 0$, B finite,
>
> random EU: $p(a, B) = \mu(\{u : \langle a, u \rangle \geq \langle b, u \rangle \text{ for all } b \in B\})$, $|B|$ finite and $(V, \mathcal{V}, \mu)$ a probability space for $V = \{u : \mathcal{O} \to \mathbb{R}\}$.

Data reviewed in Luce and Suppes (1965, Section 8.4) that include the findings in Becker, DeGroot and Marschak (1963b) on the random EU model indicate limited success of stochastic EU models to account for probabilistic choice.

Another tack for binary choice considers interlocking aspects of lotteries [Edwards (1956), Fishburn (1976, 1978)]. One model is structured as follows. Let $\mathcal{O}$ be a real interval with increasing u. For $a, b \in \mathcal{A}$ with joint support $x_1 > x_2 > \cdots > x_n$, define cumulative probability differences and incremental utility advantages as

$$
\begin{aligned}
\Delta_k(a,b) &= a(\{x \geq x_k\}) - b(\{x \geq x_k\}) \\
U(a,b) &= \sum_{\{k : \Delta_k(a,b) > 0\}} \Delta_k(a,b)[u(x_k) - u(x_{k+1})] .
\end{aligned}
$$

Then binary p is an *incremental EU advantage model* if there is an increasing $u : \mathcal{O} \to \mathbb{R}$ and an increasing $\rho : [0, \infty) \cup \{\infty\} \to [0, \infty) \cup \{\infty\}$ with $\rho(\infty) = \infty$ such that for all $a \neq b$ in $\mathcal{A}$,

$$
\frac{p(a,b)}{p(b,a)} = \rho\left(\frac{U(a,b)}{U(b,a)}\right) .
$$

The model is axiomatized in Fishburn (1978). It satisfies moderate stochastic transitivity, gives $p(a,b) = 1$ when a first–degree stochastically dominates b, and is reasonably consistent with experimental data [Fishburn (1976)].

Models for choice probabilities in the act–set context can be formulated by analogy to the preceding lottery–set models. A new issue in this case is whether π is nonrandom, or whether probability judgments are stochastic. A model for the former case that has antecedents in Edwards's (1956) relative expected loss minimization rule and Suydam's (1965) expected loss ratio rule, is described in Fishburn (1976). Its formulation is similar to that for the incremental EU advantage model. An example of analyses that feature stochastic judgment of event probabilities as well as outcome utilities is Luce (1958), with further discussion in Luce (1959, pp. 78–86) and Luce and Suppes (1965, pp. 362–367). An interesting independence axiom used by Luce applies to all $x, y \in \mathcal{O}$ and all events D and E in S. With xDy the act that yields x if D obtains and y otherwise, and with $\theta(D, E)$ a judgment probability that D is more likely than E, the axiom is

c20 (decomposition). $p(xDy, xEy) = p(x,y)\theta(D,E) + p(y,x)\theta(E,D)$.

This posits statistical independence between the binary choice process for outcomes and the judgment process for relatively likelihoods, and is used extensively in further analyses.

The second main approach to probabilistic choice for lotteries and acts uses $(\mathcal{A}, \gtrsim)$ as the primitive domain. Here preferences are deterministic and choice probabilities arise from deliberate preference–maximizing randomization. One lottery model for $(\mathcal{A}, \gtrsim)$ that accommodates nontransitive preferences and failures of the independence axiom [Allais (1953), Kahneman and Tversky (1979)] is the SSB (skew symmetric bilinear) model of Kreweras (1961) and Fishburn (1982, 1988) that has

$$a \gtrsim b \Leftrightarrow \sum_{x \in \mathcal{O}} \sum_{y \in \mathcal{O}} a(x)b(y)\delta(x,y) \geq 0$$

for a skew symmetric δ $[\delta(x,y) + \delta(y,x) = 0]$ on $\mathcal{O} \times \mathcal{O}$, with δ unique up to proportionality transformations. For any nonempty subset B of $\mathcal{A}$ let $\mathcal{A}_B$ denote the set of lotteries in $\mathcal{A}$ formed as convex combinations of members of B. It then follows from the SSB model and von Neumann's minimax theorem that for each finite B, the set

$$\max(\mathcal{A}_B) = \{a \in \mathcal{A}_B : a \gtrsim b \text{ for all } b \in \mathcal{A}_B\}$$

of preference–maximizing lotteries in $\mathcal{A}_B$ is a nonempty polytope in $\mathcal{A}_B$. This applies to tournaments on $\mathcal{O}$ for the underlying preference structure on objects as well as other potentially nontransitive relations.

EXAMPLE 9.3 Let $\mathcal{O} = \{x, y, z\}$ with $x \succ y \succ z \succ x$. Assume that the SSB model holds, so each of $\delta(x,y)$, $\delta(y,z)$ and $\delta(z,x)$ is positive. Then $\max(\mathcal{A}_\mathcal{O}) = \{a^*\}$ with

$$a^* = (a^*(x),\ a^*(y),\ a^*(z)) = (\delta(y,z)/d,\ \delta(z,x)/d,\ \delta(x,y)/d)\ ,$$

where $d = \delta(x,y) + \delta(y,z) + \delta(z,x)$. If $(\delta(x,y), \delta(y,z), \delta(z,x)) = (1,2,3)$ then $a^* = (2/6, 3/6, 1/6)$. Hence, in choosing from $\mathcal{O}$, if we roll a die and pick x if 1 or 2, y if 3, 4 or 5, and z if 6, then preference is maximized ex ante.

A ramification of the SSB model for act sets [Loomes and Sugden (1982, 1987), Fishburn and LaValle (1987), Fishburn (1988, 1990), whose axioms are similar to Savage's (1954)] without full transitivity, has

$$f \gtrsim g \Leftrightarrow \sum_{j=1}^{N} \pi(s_j)\delta f(s_j), g(s_j)) \geq 0\ .$$

This also allows preference cycles and can be embedded in a lottery superstructure so that every finite subset of acts admits a lottery that is preferred or indifferent to every other lottery defined on those acts.

Machina (1985) discusses deliberate randomization for a lottery set primitive domain $(\mathcal{A}, \succsim)$ in which $\succsim$ is a weak order represented by $v : \mathcal{A} \to \mathbb{R}$:

$$a \succsim b \Leftrightarrow v(a) \geq v(b) .$$

Suppose $\mathcal{O} = \{x, y, z\}$, $v(a) = a(x)a(y)a(z)$ and

$$B = \{b, c\} \text{ with } b(x) = b(y) = \tfrac{1}{2} \text{ and } c(z) = 1.$$

A lottery on B that has probability λ for b and $1-\lambda$ for c yields $v = \lambda^2(1-\lambda)/4$. This is maximized by $\lambda = 2/3$. The corresponding lottery in $\mathcal{A}$ has $a(x) = a(y) = a(z) = 1/3$. Machina goes on to explore preference–maximizing choices for generalizations of the von Neumann–Morgenstern expected utility model, including his own model [Machina (1982b)], which has a local structure much like expected utility but violates the EU linear form in the large. A subsequent analysis of failures of stochastic transitivity is in Segal (1994).

Clark (1990) provides additional insight into the relationship between choice probabilities and determinate utilities. Let $\mathcal{A}$ be the set of all lotteries on finite $\mathcal{O}$, let p be a choice probability function on $\{(x, B) : x \in B \subseteq \mathcal{O}\}$ with $p_B(x) = p(x, B)$, and let $\mathcal{R}'$ be the complete ranking domain on $\mathcal{O}$. Among other things, Clark proves that if a random utility representation R6 holds for p, i.e., if there is a probability distribution P on $\mathcal{R}'$ such that

$$p_B(x) = P(x[B \setminus \{x\}]) \quad \text{for all} \quad x \in B \subseteq \mathcal{O} ,$$

then there is a $v : \mathcal{A} \to \mathbb{R}$ such that, for all $\emptyset \subset B \subseteq \mathcal{O}$,

$$p_B \in \{a \in \mathcal{A}_B : v(a) \geq v(b) \quad \text{for all} \quad b \in \mathcal{A}_B\} .$$

Hence every random utility model for finite $\mathcal{O}$ with complete finitary domain has a maximum–utility representation with respect to a determinate utility function defined on the set of lotteries on $\mathcal{O}$.

References

Allais, M. (1953). Fondements d'une théorie positive des choix comportant un risque et critique des postulats et axiomes de l'école américaine, Colloques Internationaux du Centre National de la Recherche Scientifique. *Économétrie*, XL:257–332. Translated and augmented as "The Foundations of a Positive Theory of Choice Involving Risk and a Criticism of the Postulates and Axioms of the American School", in: Allais and Hagen (1979), pp. 27–145.

Allais, M. and Hagen, O., editors (1979). *Expected Utility Hypotheses and the Allais Paradox*. Reidel, Dordrecht, Holland.

Amemiya, T. (1981). Qualitative Response Models: A Survey. *Journal of Economic Literature*, 19:1483–1536.

Babington Smith, B. (1950). Discussion on Professor Ross's Paper. *Journal of the Royal Statistical Society*, 12:153–162. Series B.

Barberá, S. and Pattanaik, P. K. (1986). Falmagne and the Rationalizability of Stochastic Choices in Terms of Random Orderings. *Econometrica*, 54:707–715.

Barberá, S. and Sonnenschein, H. (1978). Preference Aggregation with Randomized Social Orderings. *Journal of Economic Theory*, 18:244–254.

Becker, G. M., DeGroot, M. H., and Marschak, J. (1963a). Stochastic Models of Choice Behavior. *Behavioral Science*, 8:41–55.

Becker, G. M., DeGroot, M. H., and Marschak, J. (1963b). An Experimental Study of Some Stochastic Models for Wagers. *Behavioral Science*, 8:199–202.

Black, D. (1958). *The Theory of Committees and Elections*. Cambridge University Press, Cambridge.

Block, H. D. and Marschak, J. (1960). Random Orderings and Stochastic Theories of Responses. In Olkin, I., Ghurye, S. G., Hoeffding, W., Madow, W. G., and Mann, H. B., editors, *Contributions to Probability and Statistics: Essays in Honor of Harold Hotelling*, pages 97–132. Stanford University Press, Stanford, CA.

Bradley, R. A. and Terry, M. E. (1952). Rank Analysis of Incomplete Block Designs I: The Method of Paired Comparisons. *Biometrika*, 39:324–345.

Brams, S. J. and Fishburn, P. C. (1983). *Approval Voting*. Birkhäuser, Boston.

Busemeyer, J. R., Forsyth, B., and Nozawa, G. (1988). Comparisons of Elimination by Aspects and Suppression of Aspects Choice Models Based on Choice Response Time. *Journal of Mathematical Psychology*, 32:341–349.

Campello de Souza, F. M. (1983). Mixed Models, Random Utilities, and the Triangle Inequality. *Journal of Mathematical Psychology*, 27:183–200.

Carroll, J. D. and Soete, G. D. (1991). Toward a New Paradigm for the Study of Multiattribute Choice Behavior: Spatial and Discrete Modeling of Pairwise Preferences. *American Psychologist*, 46:342–351.

Clark, S. A. (1990). A Concept of Stochastic Transitivity for the Random Utility Model. *Journal of Mathematical Psychology*, 34:95–108.

Clark, S. A. (1992). The Representative Agent Model of Probabilistic Social Choice. *Mathematical Social Sciences*, 23:45–66.

Cohen, M. A. (1980). Random Utility Systems — the Infinite Case. *Journal of Mathematical Psychology*, 22:1–23.

Cohen, M. A. and Falmagne, J.-C. (1990). Random Utility Representation of Binary Choice Probabilities: A New Class of Necessary Conditions. *Journal of Mathematical Psychology*, 34:88–94.

Colonius, H. (1984). *Stochastische Theorien individuellen Wahlverhaltens.* Springer–Verlag, Berlin.

Corbin, R. and Marley, A. A. J. (1974). Random Utility Models with Equality: An Apparent, but not Actual, Generalization of Random Utility Models. *Journal of Mathematical Psychology,* 11:274–293.

Critchlow, D. E., Fligner, M. A., and Verducci, J. S. (1991). Probability Models on Rankings. *Journal of Mathematical Psychology,* 35:294–318.

Dagsvik, J. K. (1983). Discrete Dynamic Choice: An Extension of the Choice Models of Thurstone and Luce. *Journal of Mathematical Psychology,* 27:1–43.

Dagsvik, J. K. (1995). How Large Is the Class of Generalized Extreme Value Random Utility Models? *Journal of Mathematical Psychology,* 39:90–98.

Daniels, H. E. (1950). Rank Correlation and Population Models. *Biometrika,* 33:129–135.

David, H. A. (1988). *The Method of Paired Comparisons.* Griffin, London, second edition.

De Soete, G. and Carroll, J. D. (1991). Probabilistic Multidimensional Models of Pairwise Choice Data. In Ashby, F. G., editor, *Multidimensional Models of Perception and Cognition.* Erlbaum, Hillsdale, N.J.

Debreu, G. (1958). Stochastic Choice and Cardinal Utility. *Econometrica,* 26:440–444.

Debreu, G. (1959). *Theory of Value.* Wiley, New York.

Debreu, G. (1960). Review of R. D. Luce, Individual Choice Behavior: A Theoretical Analysis. *American Economic Review,* 50:186–188.

Dridi, T. (1980). Sur les distributions binaires associees a des distributions ordinales. *Mathematiques et Sciences Humaines,* 69:15–31.

Edwards, W. (1954). The Theory of Decision Making. *Psychological Bulletin,* 51:380–417.

Edwards, W. (1956). Reward Probability, Amount, and Information as Determiners of Sequential Two-alternative Decisions. *Journal of Experimental Psychology,* 52:177–188.

Eisler, H. (1964). A Choice Model for Paired Comparison Data Based on Imperfectly Nested Sets. *Psychometrika,* 29:363–370.

Ellsberg, D. (1961). Risk, Ambiguity, and the Savage Axioms. *Quarterly Journal of Economics,* 75:643–669.

Falmagne, J.-C. (1978). A Representation Theorem for Finite Random Scale Systems. *Journal of Mathematical Psychology,* 18:52–72.

Falmagne, J.-C. (1979). On a Class of Probabilistic Conjoint Measurement Models: Some Diagnostic Properties. *Journal of Mathematical Psychology,* 19:73–88.

Falmagne, J.-C. (1985). *Elements of Psychophysical Theory*. Oxford University Press, London and New York.

Farquharson, R. (1969). *Theory of Voting*. Yale University Press, New Haven, CT.

Fishburn, P. C. (1970). *Utility Theory for Decision Making*. Wiley, New York.

Fishburn, P. C. (1973a). Binary Choice Probabilities: On the Varieties of Stochastic Transitivity. *Journal of Mathematical Psychology*, 10:327–352.

Fishburn, P. C. (1973b). *The Theory of Social Choice*. Princeton University Press, Princeton, N.J.

Fishburn, P. C. (1976). Binary Choice Probabilities Between Gambles: Interlocking Expected Utility Models. *Journal of Mathematical Psychology*, 14:99–122.

Fishburn, P. C. (1977). Models of Individual Preference and Choice. *Synthese*, 36:287–314.

Fishburn, P. C. (1978). A Probabilistic Expected Utility Theory of Risky Binary Choices. *International Economic Review*, 19:633–646.

Fishburn, P. C. (1982). Nontransitive Measurable Utility. *Journal of Mathematical Psychology*, 26:31–67.

Fishburn, P. C. (1984). Probabilistic Social Choice Based on Simple Voting Comparisons. *Review of Economic Studies*, 51:683–692.

Fishburn, P. C. (1985). *Interval Orders and Interval Graphs*. Wiley, New York.

Fishburn, P. C. (1987). Decomposing Weighted Digraphs into Sums of Chains. *Discrete Applied Mathematics*, 16:223–238.

Fishburn, P. C. (1988). *Nonlinear Preference and Utility Theory*. Johns Hopkins University Press, Baltimore.

Fishburn, P. C. (1990). Skew Symmetric Additive Utility with Finite States. *Mathematical Social Sciences*, 19:103–115.

Fishburn, P. C. (1991). Nontransitive Preferences in Decision Theory. *Journal of Risk and Uncertainty*, 4:113–134.

Fishburn, P. C. (1992). Induced Binary Probabilities and the Linear Ordering Polytope: A Status Report. *Mathematical Social Sciences*, 23:67–80.

Fishburn, P. C. (1994a). On 'Choice' Probabilities Derived from Ranking Distributions. *Journal of Mathematical Psychology*, 38:274–285.

Fishburn, P. C. (1994b). Utility and Subjective Probability. In Aumann, R. J. and Hart, S., editors, *Handbook of Game Theory*, volume 2, pages 1397–1435. Elsevier, Amsterdam.

Fishburn, P. C. and Falmagne, J.-C. (1989). Binary Choice Probabilities and Rankings. *Economics Letters*, 31:113–117.

Fishburn, P. C. and Gehrlein, W. V. (1977). Towards a Theory of Elections with Probabilistic Preferences. *Econometrica*, 45:1907–1924.

Fishburn, P. C. and LaValle, I. H. (1987). A Nonlinear, Nontransitive and Additive–probability Model for Decisions under Uncertainty. *Annals of Statistics*, 15:830–844.

Fligner, M. A. and Verducci, J. S., editors (1993). *Probability Models and Statistical Analysis of Ranking Data*. Number 80 in Lecture Notes in Statistics. Springer–Verlag, Heidelberg.

Gilboa, I. (1990). A Necessary but Insufficient Condition for the Stochastic Binary Choice Problem. *Journal of Mathematical Psychology*, 34:371–392.

Gilboa, I. and Monderer, D. (1992). A Game–Theoretic Approach to the Binary Stochastic Choice Problem. *Journal of Mathematical Psychology*, 36:555–572.

Grötschel, M., Jünger, M., and Reinelt, G. (1985a). Facets of the Linear Ordering Polytope. *Mathematical Programming*, 33:43–60.

Grötschel, M., Jünger, M., and Reinelt, G. (1985b). Acyclic Subdigraphs and Linear Orders: Polytopes, Facets, and a Cutting Plane Algorithm. In Rival, I., editor, *Graphs and Order*, pages 217–264. Reidel, Dordrecht, Holland.

Guilbaud, G. T. (1953). Sur une difficulté de la théorie du risque. *Econometrie*, 40:19–25. Colloques Internationaux de Centre National de Recherche Scientifique.

Herstein, I. N. and Milnor, J. (1953). An Axiomatic Approach to Measurable Utility. *Econometrica*, 21:291–297.

Houston, A. (1991). Violations of Stochastic Transitivity on Concurrent Chains: Implications for Theories of Choice. *Journal of the Experimental Analysis of Behavior*, 55:323–335.

Howard, J. V. (1992). A Social Choice Rule and its Implementation in Perfect Equilibrium. *Journal of Economic Theory*, 56:142–159.

Indow, I. (1975). On Choice Probability. *Behaviometrika*, 2:13–31.

Intriligator, M. D. (1973). A Probabilistic Model of Social Choice. *Review of Economic Studies*, 45:553–560.

Kahneman, D. and Tversky, A. (1979). Prospect Theory: An Analysis of Decision under Risk. *Econometrica*, 47:263–291.

Karni, E. and Schmeidler, D. (1991). Utility Theory with Uncertainty. In W., H. and Sonnenschein, H., editors, *Handbook of Mathematical Economics*, volume IV, pages 1763–1831. Elsevier, Amsterdam.

Koppen, M. (1995). Random Utility Representation of Binary Choice Probabilities: Critical Graphs Yields Critical Necessary Conditions. *Journal of Mathematical Psychology*, 39:21–39.

Krantz, D. H. (1964). *The Scaling of Small and Large Color Differences*. University microfilms no. 65-5777, University of Pennsylvania.

Krantz, D. H., Luce, R. D., Suppes, P., and Tversky, A. (1971). *Foundations of Measurement*, volume I. Academic Press, New York.

Kreweras, G. (1961). Sur une possibilité de rationaliser les intransitivités. *La Décision*, pages 27–32. Colloques Internationaux du Centre National de la Recherche Scientifique.

Kreweras, G. (1965). Aggregation of Preference Orderings. In Sternberg, S. et al., editors, *Compilers, Mathematics and Social Sciences*, volume I, pages 73–79. Mouton, Paris.

Lancaster, K. J. (1966). A New Approach to Consumer Theory. *Journal of Political Economy*, 74:132–157.

Lee, W. (1971). The Effects of Expected Value Differences and Expected Regret Ratio on Preference Strength. *American Journal of Psychology*, 84:194–204.

Leung, J. and Lee, J. (1990). Reinforcing Old Fences Gives New Facets. Technical Report 90–22, Department of Operations Research, Yale University, New Haven, CT.

Leung, J. and Lee, J. (1992). More Facets from Fences for Linear Ordering and Acyclic Subgraph Polytopes. Preprint, Department of Operations Research, Yale University, New Haven, CT.

Loève, M. (1960). *Probability Theory*. Van Nostrand, Princeton, NJ, 2nd edition.

Loomes, G. and Sugden, R. (1982). Regret Theory: An Alternative Theory of Rational Choice under Uncertainty. *Economic Journal*, 92:805–824.

Loomes, G. and Sugden, R. (1987). Some Implications of a More General Form of Regret Theory. *Journal of Economic Theory*, 41:270–287.

Luce, R. D. (1958). A Probabilistic Theory of Utility. *Econometrica*, 26:193–224.

Luce, R. D. (1959). *Individual Choice Behavior: A Theoretical Analysis*. Wiley, New York.

Luce, R. D. (1960). Response Latencies and Probabilities. In Arrow, K. J., Karlin, S., and Suppes, P., editors, *Mathematical Methods in the Social Sciences*, pages 298–311. Stanford University Press, Stanford, CA.

Luce, R. D. (1977). The Choice Axiom after Twenty Years. *Journal of Mathematical Psychology*, 15:215–233.

Luce, R. D. and Raiffa, H. (1957). *Games and Decisions*. Wiley, New York.

Luce, R. D. and Shipley, E. F. (1962). Preference Probability between Gambles as a Step Function of Event Probability. *Journal of Experimental Psychology*, 63:42–49.

Luce, R. D. and Suppes, P. (1965). Preference, Utility, and Subjective Probability. In Luce, R. D., Bush, R. R., and Galanter, E., editors, *Handbook of Mathematical Psychology*, volume III, pages 249–410. Wiley, New York.

MacCrimmon, K. R. and Larsson, S. (1979). Utility Theory: Axioms Versus 'Paradoxes'. In Allais, M. and Hagen, O., editors, *Expected Utility Hypotheses and the Allais Paradox*, pages 333–409. Reidel, Dordrecht, Holland.

Machina, M. J. (1982). 'Expected Utility' Analysis without the Independence Axiom. *Econometrica*, 50:277–323.

Machina, M. J. (1985). Stochastic Choice Functions Generated from Deterministic Preferences over Lotteries. *Economic Journal*, 95:575–594.

Mallows, C. L. (1957). Non-null Ranking Models I. *Biometrika*, 44:114–130.

Manski, C. F. (1977). The Structure of Random Utility Models. *Theory and Decision*, 8:229–254.

Marley, A. A. J. (1965). The Relation between the Discard and Regularity Conditions for Choice Probabilities. *Journal of Mathematical Psychology*, 2:242–253.

Marley, A. A. J. (1968). Some Probabilistic Models of Simple Choice and Ranking. *Journal of Mathematical Psychology*, 5:311–332.

Marley, A. A. J. (1981a). Joint Independent Random Utility Models where One of the Choice Structures Satisfies the Strict Utility Model. *Journal of Mathematical Psychology*, 23:257–272.

Marley, A. A. J. (1981b). Multivariate Stochastic Processes Compatible with 'Aspect' Models of Similarity and Choice. *Psychometrika*, 46:421–428.

Marley, A. A. J. (1982). Random Utility Models with All Choice Probabilities Expressible as 'Functions' of the Binary Choice Probabilities. *Mathematical Social Sciences*, 3:39–56.

Marley, A. A. J. (1988). Random Utility Models with Binary Tree Decomposable Rank Orders Satisfy Tversky's Elimination–by–Aspects Model. *Journal of Mathematical Psychology*, 32:436–448.

Marley, A. A. J. (1991). Context Dependent Probabilistic Choice Models Based on Measures of Binary Advantage. *Mathematical Social Sciences*, 21:201–231.

Marley, A. A. J. (1992). A Selective Review of Recent Characterizations of Stochastic Choice Models Using Distribution and Functional Equation Techniques. *Mathematical Social Sciences*, 23:5–29.

Marley, A. A. J. (1993). Aggregation Theorems and the Combination of Probabilistic Rank Orders. In Fligner, M. A. and Verducci, J. S., editors, *Probability Models and Statistical Analysis of Ranking Data*, volume 80 of *Lecture Notes in Statistics*, pages 216–240. Springer–Verlag, Heidelberg.

Marley, A. A. J. and Colonius, H. (1992). The 'Horse Race' Random Utility Model for Choice Probabilities and Reaction Times, and its Competing Risks Interpretation. *Journal of Mathematical Psychology*, 36:1–20.

Marschak, J. (1960). Binary-choice Constraints and Random Utility Indicators. In Arrow, K. J., Karlin, S., and Suppes, P., editors, *Mathematical Methods in the Social Sciences*, pages 312–329. Stanford University Press, Stanford.

McFadden, D. (1976). Quantal Choice Analysis: A Survey. *Annals of Economic and Social Measurement*, 5:363–390.

McFadden, D. (1981). Econometric Models of Probabilistic Choice. In Manski, C. F. and McFadden, D., editors, *Structural Analysis of Discrete Data with Econometric Applications*, pages 198–272. MIT Press, Cambridge, MA.

McFadden, D. and Richter, M. K. (1990). Stochastic Rationality and Revealed Stochastic Preference. In Chipman, J. S., McFadden, D., and Richter, M. K., editors, *Preferences, Uncertainty, and Optimality*, pages 161–186. Westview Press, Boulder, CO.

McLennan, A. (1990). Binary Stochastic Choice. In Chipman, J. S., McFadden, D., and Richter, M. K., editors, *Preferences, Uncertainty, and Optimality*, pages 187–202. Westview Press, Boulder, CO.

Monderer, D. (1992). The Stochastic Choice Problem: A Game-theoretic Appraoch. *Journal of Mathematical Psychology*, 36:547–554.

Monjardet, B. (1988). Intervals, Intervals, ... *Order*, 5:211–219.

Myers, J. L., Reilly, R. E., and Taub, H. A. (1961). Differential Cost, Gain, and Relative Frequency of Reward in a Sequential Choice Situation. *Journal of Experimental Psychology*, 62:357–360.

Narens, L. (1990). Additive Choice Representations. Preprint, Department of Cognitive Science, University of California, Irvine.

Reinelt, G. (1991). Personal Communication to P. C. Fishburn.

Restle, F. (1961). *Psychology of Judgment and Choice: A Theoretical Essay*. Wiley, New York.

Roberts, F. S. (1971). Homogeneous Families of Semiorders and the Theory of Probabilistic Consistency. *Journal of Mathematical Psychology*, 8:248–263.

Rosenstein, J. G. (1982). *Linear Orderings*. Academic Press, New York.

Rotondo, J. (1986). A Generalization of Luce's Choice Axiom and a New Class of Choice Models. (Abstract), Psychometric Society.

Sattath, S. and Tversky, A. (1976). Unite and Conquer: A Multiplicative Inequality for Choice Probabilities. *Econometrica*, 44:79–89.

Savage, L. J. (1954). *The Foundations of Statistics*. Wiley, New York.

Scott, D. (1964). Measurement Structures and Linear Inequalities. *Journal of Mathematical Psychology*, 1:233–247.

Segal, U. (1994). Stochastic Transitivity and Quadratic Representation Functions. *Journal of Mathematical Psychology*, 38:102–114.

Shafir, E. B., Osherson, D. N., and Smith, E. E. (1989). An Advantage Model of Choice. *Journal of Behavioral Decision Making*, 2:1–23.

Slovic, P. and Lichtenstein, S. (1983). Preference Reversals: A Broader Perspective. *American Economic Review*, 73:596–605.

Smith, J. H. (1973). Aggregation of Preferences with Variable Electorate. *Econometrica*, 41:1027–1041.

Stern, H. (1992). Are All Linear Paired Comparison Models Empirically Equivalent? *Mathematical Social Sciences*, 23:103–117.

Strauss, D. (1979). Some Results on Random Utility Models. *Journal of Mathematical Psychology*, 20:35–52.

Suck, R. (1992). Geometric and Combinatorial Properties of the Polytope of Binary Choice Probabilities. *Mathematical Social Sciences*, 23:81–102.

Suppes, P. (1961). Behavioristic Foundations of Utility. *Econometrica*, 29:186–202.

Suppes, P., Krantz, D. H., Luce, R. D., and Tversky, A. (1989). *Foundations of Measurement*, volume II. Academic Press, New York.

Suydam, M. M. (1965). Effects of Cost and Gain Ratios, and Probability of Outcome on Ratings of Alternative Choices. *Journal of Mathematical Psychology*, 2:171–179.

Taub, H. A. and Myers, J. L. (1961). Differential Monetary Gains in a Two-choice Situation. *Journal of Experimental Psychology*, 61:157–162.

Thurstone, L. L. (1927). A Law of Comparative Judgment. *Psychological Review*, 34:273–286.

Train, K. (1986). *Qualitative Choice Analysis: Theory, Econometrics, and an Application*. MIT Press, Cambridge, MA.

Tversky, A. (1969). Intransitivity of Preferences. *Psychological Review*, 76:31–48.

Tversky, A. (1972a). Elimination by Aspects: A Theory of Choice. *Psychological Review*, 79:281–299.

Tversky, A. (1972b). Choice by Elimination. *Journal of Mathematical Psychology*, 9:341–367.

Tversky, A. and Russo, J. E. (1969). Substitutability and Similarity in Binary Choices. *Journal of Mathematical Psychology*, 6:1–12.

von Neumann, J. (1928). Zur Theorie der Gesellschaftsspiele. *Mathematische Annalen*, 100:295–320.

von Neumann, J. and Morgenstern, O. (1944). *Theory of Games and Economic Behavior*. Princeton University Press, Princeton.

Wakker, P. P. (1989). *Additive Representations of Preferences*. Kluwer, Dordrecht, Holland.

Yellott, J. I., J. (1977). The Relationship between Luce's Choice Axiom, Thurstone's Theory of Comparative Judgment, and the Double Exponential Distribution. *Journal of Mathematical Psychology*, 15:109–144.

Zeckhauser, R. (1969). Majority Rule with Lotteries on Alternatives. *Quarterly Journal of Economics*, 83:696–703.

8 FUZZY UTILITY

Maurice Salles

Université de Caen

Contents

1	Introduction	322
2	Fuzzy Preference	323
	2.1 Fuzzy Preference: Numerical Values	324
	2.2 Fuzzy Preference: Qualitative Values	327
3	Choice and Fuzzy Preference	329
	3.1 Exact Choice and Standard Fuzzy Preference	329
	3.2 Choice and Soft Preference	333
4	Fuzzy Social Choice	335
	4.1 Numerical Fuzzy Social Choice	335
	4.2 Social Choice with Qualitative Fuzziness	337
5	Conclusion	341
	References	341

1   Introduction

Can a concept be inexact? Can a concept be vague? There is some disagreement among philosophers on the answer to give to these questions [see for recent examples Williamson and Simmons (1992)]. Though trying to answer to these questions is, I believe, very important and I intend to get back to them in the future, I will, in this paper, make two rather heroic assumptions: vagueness exists and can be dealt with by using fuzzy set theory.

When considering such a quality as thinness (to take an example of Williamson) or redness, there might be situations that are unclear. Is Mr. x thin? Is this sweater red? When we come to preferences, it might even be more obvious. As a presidential candidate, I may prefer Mr. a to Mr. b a little, or very much. I may very much prefer the third Brahms piano quartet to the first one, or just prefer it slightly. Preferences over a set of options for a given individual can be the result of an analysis of the options according to different points of view or criteria. For instance the preference over cars can be based on their looks, comforts, fuel consumptions, prices etc. Can we expect to have a clear-cut preference in such a case for all cars in the set?

Philosophers have very often associated vagueness with what is called the "sorites paradox" [see for instance Burns (1991), Dummett (1975), Sainsbury (1988) and Sorensen (1988)]. This paradox amounts to an intransitivity of implication (via an induction principle). In some sense, the posssible intransivity of indifference is of the same kind. It appears to me that a common feature of all these difficulties is not only vagueness but also the existence of threshold effects (perhaps as a consequences of vagueness).

Microecomic theory has treated the individuals (consumers) as very crude, but at the same time very rational people. They are characterized by a preference over a consumption set and an initial endowment which defines their budget set over which they maximize this preference (it is very slightly more complicated when production and firms are considered). The preference is given by what is now generally called a total (or complete) preorder which amounts, for a finite subset of the consumption set, to the ability to rank all the elements in the subset, with the possibility of having tied elements. Of course, some economists have considered other assumptions, like semi-orders, partial orders etc. to represent preferences, as well as the introduction of uncertainty and risk. But the standard model is still the one described above.

If I had to single out an economist for having criticized the standard assumptions, I would choose Amartya K. Sen. For a recent example, consider the following, which is taken from *Inequality reexamined*:

> ...Indeed, the nature of interpersonal comparisons of well-being as well as the task of inequality evaluation as a discipline may admit incompleteness as a regular part of the respective exercises. An approach that can rank the well-being of every person against that of every other in a

straightforward way, or one that can compare inequalities without any room for ambiguity or incompleteness, may well be at odds with the nature of these ideas. Both well-being and inequality are broad and partly opaque concepts. Trying to reflect them in the form of totally complete and clear-cut ordering can do less than justice to the nature of these concepts. There is a real danger of overprecision here.

In so far as there is genuine incompleteness, disparity, or ambivalence in relative weights, they should be reflected in corresponding ambiguities in the characterization of the weighted value of well-being. This relates to a methodological point, which I have tried to defend elsewhere, that if an underlying idea has an essential ambiguity, a *precise* formulation of that idea must try to *capture* that ambiguity rather than lose it.

The use of partial ordering has two different types of justification in interpersonal comparison or in inequality evaluation. First, as has been just discussed, the ideas of well-being and inequality may have enough ambiguity and fuzziness tomake it a mistake to look for a complete ordering of either. This may be called the 'fundamental reason for incompleteness'. Second, even if it is not a mistake to look for one complete ordering, we may not be able in practice to identify it. While there may be disagreements about parts of that ordering and disputes as to how we should deal with those parts, there could still be agreements on other parts. The 'pragmatic reason for incompleteness' is to use whatever parts of the ranking we manage to sort out unambiguously, rather than maintaining complete silence until everything has been sorted out and the world shines in dazzling clarity. (pages 48–49).

If I agree with Sen regarding the interest of considering partial orders, I do not believe that it is the best way to deal with ambiguity. Sen himself uses the word fuzziness in its non-formal sense. It is not completely innocent since he mentions on page 47 some works on fuzzy set theory and some papers applying fuzzy set theory to inequality.

After introducing the concept of fuzzy preference in Section 2, I will devote Section 3 to individual choice theory and Section 4 to the aggregation problem.

2   Fuzzy Preference

In (naive) set theory, given a set X and an element x either $x \in X$ or $x \notin X$. Belonging can be defined by a function b from X to $\{0,1\}$. $x \in X$ is then equivalent to $b(x) = 1$ and $x \notin X$ is equivalent to $b(x) = 0$. If the set X refers to the description of some semantic concepts, be they events or phenomena or statements, there might be no clear-cut way to assert that an element is or is not in the set. Classical examples are the set of tall men, the set of intelligent women or the set of beautiful men. This kind of vagueness cannot be in some sense treated by using probabilities since the elements are clearly not well defined. The basic idea of replacing $\{0, 1\}$ by $[0,1]$ as the set where the membership function b takes its values is due to Zadeh. However, the real origin of this is probably ancient, at least as ancient as Lukasiewicz. An excellent introductory textbook on fuzzy set theory is Zimmermann (1991); for an encyclopedic treatment of the subject at the date of publication, I recommend Dubois and Prade (1980).

For fuzzy binary relations, of course, the membership function associates a number in $[0, 1]$ to every ordered pair of elements. To associate a number α in $[0, 1]$ to an ordered pair (x, y), if the semantic concept underlying the binary relation is preference, would mean that x is preferred to y with degree α. Even if α is strictly positive, this does not have to imply that we must assign zero to (y, x). For instance, if I must compar some interpretation of Schumann's piano quintet with another one, I may have mixed or conflicting feelings. For instance, I will prefer Christian Zacharias with the Cherubini quartet to Arthur Rubinstein with the Guarneri quartet for the precision of the rendering of the score to some extent, but, from the point of view of the sense of progression of the interpretation, I will at the same time prefer Rubinstein and the Guarneris to Zacharias and the Cherubinis. On the basis of this example it seems also clear that it is rather odd to describe fuzziness by assigning a precise number. As rightly observed by Alasdair Urquhart [Urquhart (1986)]: " One immediate objection which presents itself to this line of approach is the extremely artificial nature of the attaching of precise numerical values to sentences like '73 is a large number' or 'Picasso's *Guernica* is beautiful'. In fact, it seems plausible to say that the nature of vague predicates precludes attaching precise numerical values just as much as it precludes attaching precise classical truth values ".

One way to avoid this difficulty is to replace $[0, 1]$ (ordered by $\geq$) by some set of qualitative elements ordered by a complete preorder $\succeq$ (for instance, to give some intuition to these elements, elements meaning "not at all", "insignificantly", "a little", "much", "very much", "definitely" ...).

We will consider these two approaches to fuzziness in succession.

2.1   Fuzzy Preference: Numerical Values

Let X be a set (of alternatives).

DEFINITION 2.1   A fuzzy binary (preference) relation over X is a function r from $X \times X$ to $[0, 1]$.

We first list several properties of fuzzy binary relations.

DEFINITION 2.2 r satisfies

(a) reflexivity if for all $x \in X$, $r(x,x) = 1$

(b) irreflexivity if for all $x \in X$, $r(x,x) = 0$.

This is probably the only case where the concepts have a single definition.[1] When r is reflexive, the intuitive meaning of $r(x,y)$ for some $(x,y) \in X \times X$ would be x is at least as good as y with degree $r(x,y)$. One already sees the difficulty in having a satisfying meaning in this case. Since the introduction of fuzzy sets was supposed to reduce the gap between the models and the reality, I believe we must essentially work with irreflexive r. However, since there is an important literature on reflexive r, I will describe some of the results obtained with this assumption.

DEFINITION 2.3 r is

(a) max–min transitive if for all $x,y,z \in X$, $r(x,z) \geq \min(r(x,y), r(y,z))$;

(b) mix–transitive if there exists $\alpha \in]0,1[$ such that for all distinct $x,y,z \in X$, if $r(x,y) > 0$ and $r(y,z) > 0$ then $r(x,z) \geq \alpha \max(r(x,y), r(y,z)) + (1 - \alpha) \min(r(x,y), r(y,z))$;

(c) mean–transitive if for all distinct $x,y,z \in X$ for which $r(x,y) > 0$ and $r(y,z) > 0$, $r(x,z) \geq \frac{1}{2}(r(x,y) + r(y,z))$;

(d) pos–transitive if for all distinct $x,y,z \in X$, if $r(x,y) > 0$ and $r(y,z) > 0$ then $r(x,z) > 0$;

(e) bin–transitive if for all $x,y,z \in X$, if $r(x,y) \geq r(y,x)$ and $r(y,z) \geq r(z,y)$, then $r(x,z) \geq r(z,x)$.

We can give other definitions (others will be given in the sequel). I just wanted to show that there was a very large number of possible and meaningful definitions. Such is the case also for connectedness.

---

[1] However, according to Billot's interesting book (1992), there exists a demarcation line between a so-called French school and an Anglo–Saxon school. For the French school, $r(x,y)$ describes the relative qualities of x when viewed in relation to y. Then reflexivity is defined by $r(x,x)$ being any number in $[0,1]$ and, given x the specific number associated to $r(x,x)$ describes the intrinsic qualities of x, whatever that means. I am afraid that according to Billot's partition, I belong to the Anglo–Saxon world. This is not very surprising since, as everyone knows, the links between Normandy and England have been very strong indeed, since at least 1066!

DEFINITION 2.4 r is

(a) connected if for all $x, y \in X$, $r(x,y) + r(y,x) \geq 1$;

(b) weakly connected if for all distinct $x, y \in X$, $r(x,y) > 0$ or $r(y,x) > 0$.

An irreflexive fuzzy preference p can be defined as a basic concept (and this solution is the one I prefer) or derived from the reflexive fuzzy preference r. Then we have $p(x,y)$ meaning that x is preferred to y with degree $p(x,y)$. A number of derivations of p and also of fuzzy indifference i have been proposed, in particular by Ovchinnikov (1981), Dutta (1987) and Banerjee (1994). For instance, in Dutta (1987), given some conditions, one gets:

$$p(x,y) = \begin{cases} r(x,y) \text{ if } r(x,y) > r(y,x), \\ 0 \text{ otherwise,} \end{cases}$$

$$i(x,y) = \min(r(x,y), r(y,x)).$$

But again, it must be clear that there no clear–cut way of deriving indifference and strict preference relations from r.[2] By the way, what is the meaning of, say, $i(x,y) = 0.8$? Can we have a high degree of indifference?

A utility function is a numerical representation of a complete preorder (in principle). Is there anything to gain, if starting from a numerical information on ordered pairs, we derive a numerical information on elements (or even a preference structure on elements)? There exists, in fact, a literature which has been, I believe, totally ignored by fuzzy set theorists [Fishburn (1970, 1988), Krantz, Luce, Suppes and Tversky (1971)]. A binary relation is defined over $X \times X$ and is interpreted as a comparison of strength of preference. A preference over X is then defined by x is preferred to y if the strength of preference of x over y exceeds the strength of preference of y over y. Again, I must say that I cannot see what is the meaning of the strength of preference of y over y. However, in the literature mentioned above, the interesting feature is that the binary relation over ordered pairs gives rise to some utility representation for comparable differences. On the other hand, Billot (1992) defines a utility for alternative x by taking the maximum of $r(x,y)$ over some set. The danger of such a definition is to have in this set a sufficiently bad alternative y to have $r(x,y) = 1$, and this for each x so that the utility function is a constant function. Obviously, if we want to progress in this, we will have to begin with the impressive work of measurement theorists.

---

[2]There already is an abundant literature on the foundations of fuzzy preference, for instance Banerjee (1993, 1994), Basu (1984), Billot (1987, 1992), Dasgupta and Deb (1991), Dutta (1987), Dutta, Panda and Pattanaik (1986), Jain (1990), Orlovski (1978), Ovchinnikov (1981), Ovchinnikov and Roubens (1991, 1992), Ponsard (1990).

2.2 Fuzzy Preference: Qualitative Values

When using numerical values, we have seen that some assumptions have clearly a cardinal nature, i.e., sums are sometimes made to define completeness or transitivity. As long as the real numbers are used only with their order structure, they are just an easy way to represent the preference structure. Otherwise, the information used to define some concepts may be meaningless. The idea of using qualitative values is due to Goguen (1967). In the following definition, borrowed from Basu, Deb and Pattanaik (1992), it is applied to $X \times X$.

DEFINITION 2.5

(1) An L–set theoretic structure on $X \times X$ is a triple $(\xi, \succeq_*, L)$ where L is a nonempty set with $\# L \geq 2$; $\succeq_*$ is a reflexive, transitive and antisymmetric binary relation over L; ξ is a nonempty set of functions from $X \times X$ to L; there exists a unique $\succeq_*$ greatest element $\bar{d}$ in L and a unique $\succeq_*$-least elements $\underline{d}$ in L; and for all $A \subseteq X \times X$, there exists $f \in \xi$ such that for all $(x, y) \in A$, $f(x, y) = \bar{d}$ and for all $(z, w) \in X \times X - A$, $f(z, w) = \underline{d}$.

(2) An L–set theoretic structure $(\xi, \succeq_*, L)$ is proper if for every $f \in \xi$, the restriction of $\succeq_*$ to $f(X \times X)$ is complete.

(3) $(\xi, \succeq_*, L)$ is complete if ξ is the set of all functions from $X \times X$ to L.

(4) $(\xi, \succeq_*, L)$ is normal if L is a lattice under the meet and join operations induced by $\succeq_*$ on L.

Intuitively L is the set of the degrees of preference (a little, much, very much ...), $\bar{d}$ corresponds to "definitely" and $\underline{d}$ to "not at all". Properness indicates that it is always possible to compare the degrees of preference for any ordered pairs.

Basu, Deb, Pattanaik (1992) introduce the related notion of soft preference.

DEFINITION 2.6

(1) A soft set theoretic structure on $X \times X$ is a triple $(\psi, g, \succeq)$ such that ψ is a nonempty set with $\# \psi \geq \#2^{X \times X}$; g is a one–to–one function from $2^{X \times X}$ to ψ; $\succeq$ is a reflexive and transitive binary relation on $(X \times X) \times \psi$;[3] for all $A \in \psi$, $(x, y), (z, w) \in X \times X$, and $B \subseteq X \times X$, if $(x, y) \in B$ and $(z, w) \in X \times X - B$, then $((x, y), g(B)) \succeq ((z, w), A) \succeq ((z, w), g(B))$ and $((x, y), g(B)) \succ ((z, w), g(B))$.

---

[3]Given a reflexive binary relation $\succeq$, $\succ$ is the asymmetric part of $\succeq$ and $\sim$ its symmetric part.

(2) $(\psi, g, \succeq)$ is proper if for all $A \in \psi$ (called soft sets), the restriction of $\succeq$ to $(X \times X) \times A$ is complete.

(3) Given $(\psi, g, \succeq)$, two soft sets $A, B \in \psi$ are said to be identical if for all $(x,y), (z,w) \in X \times X$ for all $C \in \psi$, $((x,y), A) \succeq ((z,w), C)$ iff $((x,y), B) \succeq ((z,w), C)$ and $((z,w), C) \succeq ((x,y), A)$ iff $((z,w), C) \succeq ((x,y), B)$.

g specifies the exact sets in the set ψ of soft sets, i.e., the exact binary relations in the set of soft binary relations. $((x,y), A) \succeq ((z,w), B)$ intuitively means that the extent to which (x,y) belongs to A is at least as great as the extent to which (z,w) belongs to B. $((x,y), g(B)) \succeq ((z,w), A) \succeq ((z,w), g(B))$ means that the extent to which (z,w) belong to A always lies (since A is "soft") between "definitely" and "not at all". Definition 2.6 (2) is clear enough. Definition 2.6 (3) means that the two soft sets A and B are impossible to distinguish. If we take $(z,w) = (x,y)$ and $C = A$, we have $((x,y), A) \succeq ((x,y), A) \iff ((x,y), B) \succeq ((x,y), A)$. Since $\succeq$ is reflexive, we have $((x,y), B) \succeq ((x,y), A)$. Then by taking $C = B$, we get $((x,y), A) \succeq ((x,y), B)$ and $((x,y), A) \sim ((x,y), B)$.

DEFINITION 2.7   Let $(\psi, g, \succeq)$ be a proper soft set theoretic structure on $(X \times X)$. Then $(\psi, g, \succeq)$ is complete if for all $A \in \psi - \{g(X \times X, g(\emptyset)\}$, for all $(x,y) \in X \times X$ and for every complete preorder T over $(X \times X) \times A \bigcup \{((x,y), g(X \times X)), ((x,y), g(\emptyset))\}$ where $((x,y), g(X \times X))$ is a T–greatest element and $((x,y), g(\emptyset))$ is a T– least element, there exists $B \in \psi$ such that for all $(z,w), (s,t) \in X \times X$,

$((z,w), A)T((s,t), A)$ iff $((z,w), B) \succeq ((s,t), B)$;

$((x,y), g(X \times X))T((z,w), A)$ iff $((x,y), g(X \times X)) \succeq ((z,w), B)$;

$((z,w), A)T((x,y), g(X \times X))$ iff $((z,w), B) \succeq ((x,y), g(X \times X))$;

$((x,y), g(\emptyset))T((z,w), A)$ iff $((x,y), g(\emptyset)) \succeq ((z,w), B)$;

and $((z,w), A)T((x,y), g(\emptyset))$ iff $((z,w), B) \succeq ((x,y), g(\emptyset))$.

This definition is somewhat complicated. It means that, in the case we cannot compare soft sets, the structure cannot be expanded by adding to ψ a soft set which is not identical (in the sense of Definition 2.6) to one of the soft sets already in ψ.

Each soft set in ψ is called a soft binary relation (SBR) over X. An exact soft binary relation (ESBR) over X is an SBR R such that $R = g(A)$ for some subset A of $X \times X$. $g(X \times X)$ will be denoted by $\bar{R}$ and $g(\emptyset)$ by $\underline{R}$. For $R \in \psi$, $((x, y), R)$ will be denoted by $R(x, y)$.

DEFINITION 2.8   A soft ordering (SO) over X is an SBR R over X which verifies

(a) reflexivity: for all $x \in X$, $R(x, x) \sim \bar{R}(x, x)$;

(b) connectedness: for all distinct $x, y \in X$, if $R(y, x) \sim \underline{R}(x, x)$, then $R(x, y) \sim \bar{R}(x, x)$;

(c) max–min transitivity: for all $x, y, z \in X$, $R(x, y) \succeq \inf(\{R(x, y), R(y, z)\})$.

(The infimum is defined from $\succeq$).

Reflexivity is the analogue of $r(x, x) = 1$ in the numerical context; connectedness, the analogue of $r(x, y) > 0$ or $r(y, x) > 0$ and, of course, max–min transitivity, the analogue of $r(x, z) \geq \min(r(x, y), r(y, z))$.

3   Choice and Fuzzy Preference

A choice function associates to a subset of X the chosen elements in this subset. A choice function can be generated by a binary relation on X. Given specific assumptions on the binary relation, we obtain different properties of the choice function. Inversely, given a choice function, one can define a binary relation from it. Then assumptions on the choice function will generate properties of the binary relation. The analysis of these relations between choice functions and the binary relation belong to what economists call "the theory of revealed preference". The literature on this topic originated in papers by Houthakker and Samuelson [Houthakker (1950), Samuelson (1950)] in which X is some economic space and the considered subspaces of X are defined by economic parameters [see also Chipman, Hurwicz, Richter and Sonnenschein (1971) and in particular the paper by Uzawa in this book]. A more abstract setting was introduced by Arrow (1959) with further results obtained by Sen (1971), Suzumura (1975), Schwartz (1976), and Deb (1977) among others.

The individual, even though his preference is fuzzy, will have to make a choice, necessarily exact. In this section, I will essentially consider the exact choice generated by a fuzzy preference, first numerically, then ordinally defined. Alternatively, one can try to define the "closest", in a specific sense, exact preference from a fuzzy preference and use the standard theory [see Ok (1994)].

3.1   Exact Choice and Standard Fuzzy Preference

This subsection will be based upon a paper by Barrett, Pattanaik and Salles (1990).

Let r be a fuzzy binary relation over X which is reflexive, and connected. The set of these fuzzy relations will be denoted by G. If r is further max–min transitive, r will be called a fuzzy ordering. The set of fuzzy orderings will be denoted by H. Furthermore, we assume that X is finite and $\#X \geq 4$.

DEFINITION 3.1   A choice function C is a function from K to $2^X - \emptyset$ (where $K \subseteq 2^X - \emptyset$ and $K \neq \emptyset$) for which $C(A) \subseteq A$ for all $A \in K$.

I will assume in this subsection that $K = 2^X - \emptyset$.

NOTATION   Let $B \in K$, $r \in G$ and suppose $x \in B$. Then we denote

$$MF(x, B) = \max_{y \in B-\{x\}} r(x, y), \ mF(x, B) = \min_{y \in B-\{x\}} r(x, y);$$

$$MA(x, B) = \max_{y \in B-\{x\}} r(y, x), \ mA(x, B) = \min_{y \in B-\{x\}} r(y, x);$$

$$SF(x, B) = \sum_{y \in B-\{x\}} r(x, y), \ SA(x, B) = \sum_{y \in B-\{x\}} r(y, x);$$

$$MD(x, B) = \max_{y \in B-\{x\}} (r(x, y) - r(y, x));$$

$$mD(x, B) = \min_{y \in B-\{x\}} (r(x, y) - r(y, x));$$

$$SD(x, B) = \sum_{y \in B-\{x\}} (r(x, y) - r(y, x));$$

M is for "max", m for "min", F for "for", A for "against", S for "sum", D for "difference".

DEFINITION 3.2   Let C be a choice function, $B \in 2^X - \emptyset$ and $r \in G$

(i) C is max–MF if $C(B) = \{x \in B : MF(x, B) \geq MF(y, B) \text{ for all } y \in B - \{x\}\}$;

(ii) C is max–mF if $C(B) = \{x \in B : mF(x, B) \geq mF(y, B) \text{ for all } y \in B - \{x\}\}$;

(iii) C is max–SF if $C(B) = \{x \in B : SF(x, B) \geq SF(y, B) \text{ for all } y \in B - \{x\}\}$;

(iv) C is min–MA if $C(B) = \{x \in B : MA(x, B) \leq MA(y, B) \text{ for all } y \in B - \{x\}\}$;

(v) C is min–mA if $C(B) = \{x \in B : mA(x,B) \le mA(y,B)$ for all $y \in B - \{x\}\}$;

(vi) C is min–SA if $C(B) = \{x \in B : SA(x,B) \le SA(y,B)$ for all $y \in B - \{x\}\}$;

(vii) C is max–MD if $C(B) = \{x \in B : MD(x,B) \ge MD(y,B)$ for all $y \in B - \{x\}\}$;

(viii) C is max–mD if $C(B) = \{x \in B : mD(x,B) \ge mD(y,B)$ for all $y \in B - \{x\}\}$;

(xi) C is max–SD if $C(B) = \{x \in B : SD(x,B) \ge SD(y,B)$ for all $y \in B - \{x\}\}$.

A choice function which has been much discussed in the literature is due to Orlovsky(1978) [See also Banerjee (1993)].

NOTATION Let $B \in K$, $r \in G$, and $x \in B$. Then

$$OV(x,B) = \min_{y \in B - \{x\}} \min(1 - r(y,x) + r(x,y), 1).$$

DEFINITION 3.3 A choice function C is max–OV if $C(B) = \{x \in B : OV(x,B) \ge OV(y,B)$ for all $y \in B - \{x\}\}$.

A first result shows that max–mD choice functions are identical to max–OV functions (Orlovsky's choice functions).

THEOREM 3.4 A choice function C is max–mD iff it is max–OV.

I first introduce conditions for choosing an element of X.

DEFINITION 3.5 Let $B \in K$, $r \in G$ and $x \in B$. C satisfies reward for pairwise weak dominance (RPWD) if $[r(x,y) \ge r(y,x)$ for all $y \in B - \{x\}]$ implies $x \in C(B)$. C satisfies reward for pairwise strict dominance (RPSD) if $[r(x,y) > r(y,x)$ for all $y \in B - \{x\}]$ implies $x \in C(B)$.

THEOREM 3.6

(i) Let $r \in H$ and C be either max–MF or max–SF or min–MA or min–SA or max–MD or max–SD. Then C violates RPWD and RPSD.

(ii) Let $r \in G$ and C be either max–MF or max–mF or max–SF or min–MA or min–mA or min–SA or max–MD or max–SD. Then C violates RPWD and RPSD.

(iii) If C is max–mD, then C satisfies RPWD and RPSD.

(iv) If $r \in H$ and C is either max–mF or min–mA or max–mD, then C satifies RPWD and RPSD.

I now introduce conditions for rejecting alternatives.

DEFINITION 3.7 Let $B \in K$, $r \in G$ and $x \in B$. C satisfies strict rejection (SR) if $[r(y, x) \geq r(x, y)$ for all $y \in B-\{x\}$ and $r(y, x) > r(x, y)$ for some $y \in B-\{x\}]$ implies $x \notin C(B)$. C satisfies weak rejection (WR) if $[r(y, x) \geq r(x, y)$ for all $y \in B - \{x\}]$ implies $x \notin C(B)$.

THEOREM 3.8

(i) If $r \in H$ and C is either max–mF or min–MA or min–SA, then C violates WR. Also, if C is either max–MF or max–mF or max–SF or min–MA or min–mA or min–SA, then C violates SR.

(ii) If $r \in G$ and C is either max–mF or max–SF or min–MA or min–SA or max–mD, then C violates WR. Also, if C is either max–MF or max–mF or max–SF or min–MA or min–mA or min–SA or max–mD, then C violates SR.

(iii) If C is either max–MD or max–SD, then C satisfies SR, and if C is either max–MF or min–mA or max–MD or max–SD, then C satisfies WR.

(iv) If $r \in H$ and C is either max–MD or max–mD or max–SD, then C satifies SR. Also, if C is either max–MF or max–SF or min–mA or max–MD or max–mD or max–SD, then C satisfies WR.

Suppose that there exist alternatives which are the best in B in the exact sense, i.e., say x in B satisfies $r(x, y) = 1$ for every $y \in B$. We may require that if an alternative is exactly best, it must be chosen. Inversely, we may require that if an alternative is chosen, it must be an exactly best alternative (if there is one). In Barrett, Pattanaik and Salles (1990), these properties are called faithfulness (upper or lower) and are shown to be satisfied very often, when $r \in H$ (satisfied by all choice functions in the case of lower faithfulness, i.e., when it is required that all exactly best alternatives be chosen).

DEFINITION 3.9 Let $B \in K$ and $r \in G$. An alternative $x \in B$ is pairwise optimal in B if $r(x, y) \geq r(y, x)$ for all $y \in B$.

In Barrett, Pattanaik and Salles (1990), it is proved that if $r \in H$, $T(B) = \{x \in B : x$ is pairwise optimal in $B\}$ is nonempty.

DEFINITION 3.10 Let $r \in H$. A choice function C is PO if $C(B) = T(B)$.

The following result is due to Jain (1994).[4]

THEOREM 3.11 Let $B \in K$ and $r \in H$. Then C is PO iff it is max–mD.

I will not consider the rationalizability literature [see Dutta, Panda and Pattanaik (1986), and Dasgupta and Deb (1991)]. Concerning rationalizability with exact choice, the conclusion of Dutta, Panda and Pattanaik is that the hypothesis of a fuzzy preference explains a wider range of choice behaviour than the hypothesis of an exact preference ordering (a complete preorder). However, when considering reflexive, complete binary relations, the asymmetric components of which are transitive (this property is sometimes called quasi–transitivity), this advantage disappears. Dasgupta and Deb study fuzzy choice functions and provide characterizations of rationalizability of such functions using fuzzy preferences. That paper is remarkable, but, again, if from a mathematical viewpoint the notion of fuzzy choice function is as clear as it is interesting, I cannot see the intuitive meaning of it.

As a concluding remark to Section 3.1, I will repeat what is written in Barrett, Pattanaik and Salles: "... our results may be interpreted as suggesting that our usual notions of rational choice behaviour have to be modified when the agent has fuzzy preferences (symptomatic of unresolved conflicts, in the agent's mind, between different criteria for judging the alternatives), unless these fuzzy preferences are assumed to satisfy some fairly stringent, and, intuitively, not quite obvious, property such as transitivity".

3.2 Choice and Soft Preference

With an exact soft ordering R, we have the usual case of a choice function generated by R, i.e., $C(A) = \{x \in A : R(x,y) = \bar{R}(x,x) \text{ for all } y \in A\}$. However, if the soft ordering is not exact, there are several different notions, none of which seems to be more plausible than the others.

NOTATION Let R be a soft ordering and $x^*, y^* \in X$. Then

$$H^1(A) \;=\; \{x \in A : R(x,y) \succeq R(x^*,y^*) \text{ for all } y \in A\};$$
$$H^2(A) \;=\; \{x \in A : R(x,y) \succeq R(y,x) \text{ for all } y \in A\}.$$

---

[4]A part of this result is in Barrett, Pattanaik and Salles (1990): they show that if C is max-mD, then it is PO. The equivalence is due to Jain (1990).

DEFINITION 3.12   The choice function C is an H^1- choice function if there exists a soft ordering R such that for some $(x^*, y^*) \in X \times X$, $R(x^*, y^*) \succ \underline{R}(x^*, x^*)$ and for all $A \in K$, $C(A) = H^1(A)$. The choice function is an H^2- choice function if there exists a soft ordering R such that for all $A \in K$, $C(A) = H^2(A)$.

For H^1–choice functions, the intuition is the following: the individual fixes an ordered pair (x^*, y^*) (for which he finds x^* at least as good y^* to some extent), then he chooses the alternatives x in A for which for all y in A the extent to which x is at least as good as y is at least as great as the extent to which x^* is at least as good as $y*$ (the extent to which x^* is at least as good as y^* being then some kind of "satisficing" principle). H^2–choice function are rather simple: it is the analogue in the soft case of PO–choice functions. Basu, Deb and Pattanaik (1992) introduced another choice function similar in some sense to max–mF of the previous subsection, but this choice function does not behave very well in terms of exact soft relations.

THEOREM 3.13   Let $K = 2^X - \emptyset$. Then C is an H^1–choice function iff there exists an exact soft ordering R' such that for all $A \in K$, $C(A) = \{x \in A : R'(x, y) \sim \bar{R}(x, x)$ for all $y \in A\}$.

This theorem is rather deceiving, since it says that the agent's choice behaviour can be explained in the simpler framework of exact orderings.

DEFINITION 3.14   An exact soft binary relation R satisfies exact quasi–transitivity if for all $x, y, z \in X$, $[R(x, y) \sim \bar{R}(x, x)$ and $R(y, x) \sim \underline{R}(x, x)$ and $R(y, z) \sim \bar{R}(x, x)$ and $R(z, y) \sim \underline{R}(x, x)]$ implies $[R(x, z) \sim \bar{R}(x, x)$ and $R(z, x) \sim \underline{R}(x, x)]$.

THEOREM 3.15 C is an H^2–choice function iff there exists an exact soft binary relation R' which is reflexive, connected and exactly quasi–transitive such that for all $A \in K$, $C(A) = \{x \in A : R'(x, y) \sim \bar{R}(x, x)$ for all $y \in A\}$.

Again the result is deceiving. The only difference with the previous theorem regarding the explanation of the agent's behaviour is that the transitivity of the exact binary relation has been replaced by quasi–transitivity. Basu, Deb and Pattanaik (1992) also consider demand theory, i.e., the case where the choice function is defined on budgets sets.

I am afraid that my concluding remark to Subsection 3.1 could also be used for this subsection.

4   Fuzzy Social Choice

In this section I will consider Arrovian social choice theory when preferences are fuzzy. If you accept our assumption that individual preferences and value judgments are vague and consequently fuzzy, there does not seem to be any compelling reason why one should assume that social preferences, eventually representing ethical judgments about the relative desirability of social states, at least in social choice theory, be exact. Even if individual preferences are exact, one may consider vague social preference to have a more flexible framework to aggregate conflicting preferences [see Puppe (1994)].

One could expect that taking fuzziness into account could have a "smoothing" effect so that negative results [Arrow (1963), Gibbard (1969), Mas–Colell and Sonnenschein (1972)] could be avoided.[5] In fact, the picture obtained is far from clear. Depending on the assumptions one gets negative or positive results. In particular whether you consider "strict" fuzzy preference or a "weak" version and whether you allow for different transitivity conditions,[6] you obtain dramatically different solutions.

I will follow the dichotomy introduced in Section 3 and consider first numerical fuzziness, then qualitative fuzziness.

4.1   Numerical Fuzzy Social Choice

This subsection is mainly based on Barrett, Pattanaik and Salles (1986). I will consider "strict" (irreflexive) fuzzy preferences.

Let $N = \{1, ..., n\}$, $n \geq 2$ be the finite set of individuals and X, $\#X \geq 3$, be the set of alternatives.

DEFINITION 4.1   Let p be a fuzzy irreflexive ("strict") preference. p is ex-asymmetric if for all distinct $x, y \in X$, $p(x, y) = 1 \implies p(y, x) = 0$.

I will consider fuzzy strict preferences which are ex–asymmetric, and pos–transitive and, in some cases, weakly connected. It must be stressed that pos–transitivity is a rather weak concept. It is clearly implied by max–min transitivity. Ex–asymmetry is clear enough. I only require an asymmetry property in the exact case.

---

[5]Sen's theorem on the Paretian liberal (1970, 1970 a) has also been considered by Subramanian (1987, 1993).

[6]On vagueness and transitivity see Barrett and Pattanaik (1985) and Dasgupta and Deb (1993, 1996).

NOTATION FB is the set of fuzzy strict binary relations, FSO, the set of fuzzy strict binary relations which are ex–asymmetric and pos–transitive, FSOC the subset of FSO, the elements of which are weakly connected.

DEFINITION 4.2 A fuzzy aggregation rule (FAR) is a function $f : \bar{FB}^n \to FB$ where $\bar{FB} \subseteq FB$ and $\bar{FB} \neq \emptyset$.

The elements of $\bar{FB}^n$ are n–lists $(p_1, ..., p_n)$.

DEFINITION 4.3 Let $f : \bar{FB}^n \to FB$ be an FAR. f satisfies

(i) Independence of irrelevant alternatives (IIA) if for all $(p_1, ..., p_n)$, $(p'_1, ..., p'_n) \in \bar{FB}^n$, and all distinct $x, y \in X[p_i(x, y) = p'_i(x, y)$ for each $i \in N$ and $p_i(y, x) = p'_i(y, x)$ for each $i \in N]$ implies $[p(x, y) = p'(x, y)$ and $p(x, y) = p'(y, x)]$ where $p = f(p_1, ..., p_n)$ and $p' = f(p'_1, ..., p'_n)$; and

(ii) Pareto criterion (PC) if for all $(p_1, ..., p_n) \in \bar{FB}^n$, all distinct $x, y \in X$ and all $t \in [0, 1]$, $[p_i(x, y) \geq t$ for all $i \in N]$ implies $[p(x, y) \geq t]$, where $p = f(p_1, ..., p_n)$.

IIA and PC are the fuzzy counterpart of well known Arrovian conditions IIA is a rather weak condition in this framework since there is no reason to imagine that the antecedent of the implication in the condition can be realized The following theorems show that given our assumptions we obtain results reminiscent of Gibbard (1969) and Arrow (1963). (Throughout this subsection I assume that the FAR's satisfy conditions IIA and PC.)

THEOREM 4.4 Let f be an FAR defined on FSO^n and taking its values in FSO.[7] Then, there exists a unique coalition C^* such that for all distinct $x, y \in X$ and all $(p_1, ..., p_n) \in FSO^n$ if $[p_i(x, y) > 0$ and $p_i(y, x) = 0$ for every $i \in C^*]$ then $p(x, y) > 0$, and if $[p_j(x, y) > 0$ and $p_j(y, x) = 0$ for some $j \in C^*]$, then $p(y, x) = 0$.

C^* can be viewed as the counterpart of Gibbard's oligarchy. If C^* is small there is clearly a strong concentration of power which may be considered unde sirable. (With a small C^*, individuals in C^* acting unanimously seems normal. If C^* is large, since unanimously fuzzy preference within C^* could be rare, it i the second result which will be effective: every individual having a veto power the collective decision system will be paralyzed.

---

[7]The unrestricted domain condition as stated here is not necessary to obtain the results. It i sufficient for this that the definition set of the function be rich enough (see Barrett, Pattanai and Salles (1986)).

THEOREM 4.5 Let f be an FAR defined on FSO^n and taking its values in FSOC. Then C^* of the previous theorem is a singleton, i.e., there exists an individual $i \in N$ such that for all distinct $x, y \in X$ and all $(p_1, ..., p_n) \in FSO^n$, if $[p_i(x,y) > 0$ and $p_i(y,x) = 0]$, then $p(x,y) > 0$ and $p(y,x) = 0$.

Dutta (1987) showed that if the n–lists are made of reflexive, connected fuzzy binary relations satisfying the following transitivity condition: for all $x, y, z \in X$, $r(x,z) \geq r(x,y) + r(y,z) - 1$, and if the social fuzzy relation also satisfies these properties, then there exists a fuzzy aggregation procedure which satisfies neutrality, anonymity, a strict monotonicity property, and, of course, suitable modified version of IIA and PC. It is defined by: for all $x, y \in X$ and all $(r_1, ..., r_n)$ in the n fold Cartesian product of the set of fuzzy binary relations which are reflexive, connected and transitive in the previous sense, $r(x,y) = \frac{1}{n} \sum_{i \in N} r_i(x,y)$. [On this see also Ovchinnikov (1991).]

A. Banerjee (1994) gives an excellent description of the problems posed by using several different transitivity conditions and alternative derivation of strict preference from weak preference.[8] In particular, he shows that even in Dutta's framework, if $p(x,y) = 1 - r(x,y)$, there exists a dictator, i.e., an individual i such that for any x, y, $p(x,y) > 0$ whenever $p_i(x,y) > 0$.

4.2 Social Choice with Qualitative Fuzziness

In this subsection, I consider strict fuzzy orderings where fuzziness is not given by a number in $[0,1]$ but by an element in a finite set with a complete preorder $\succeq$. I assume further that L has a unique $\succeq$–maximum, noted d^*, and a unique $\succeq$–minimum, noted d_*. This, of course, is very similar to Guogen L–fuzzy sets, the only difference being that I am not imposing antisymmetry.

DEFINITION 4.6 An ordinally fuzzy strict binary relation is a function $P : X \times X \to L$ such that for all $x \in X$, $P(x,x) = d_*$.

An ordinally fuzzy strict binary relation P satisfies ex–asymmetry if for all distinct $x, y \in X$, $P(x,y) = d^* \implies P(y,x) = d_*$.

An ordinally fuzzy strict binary relation P satisfies ex–transitivity if for all distinct $x, y, z \in X$, $P(x,y) = d^* \implies P(x,z) \succeq P(y,z)$, and $P(y,z) = d^*$ implies $P(x,z) \succeq P(x,y)$.

Ex–transitivity means that if x is definitely preferred to y then the degree of the preference of x over z must be as great as the degree of the preference of y over z. Since I definitely prefer Bartok's concerto for Orchestra to Gorecki's

---

[8]For a deep mathematical treatment using algebraic and order–theoretic analysis of fuzzy aggregation see Leclerc (1984, 1991) and Leclerc and Monjardet (1995).

third Symphony, the degree of my preference for Bartok's Concerto over Dutilleux's first Symphony (which is, I must say, mild since I like both) must be as
great as the degree of my preference for Gorecki's Symphony over Dutilleux's
Symphony (the degree of which is, I must confess, null).

NOTATION Let OFSO denote the set of ordinally fuzzy strict binary relations
which satisfy ex–asymmetry and ex–transitivity.

Following Barrett, Pattanaik and Salles (1992), I will define an Arrovian
framework in the fuzzy ordinal case, propose several transitivity conditions
and examine the effects of taking these transitivity conditions into account.

DEFINITION 4.7 An ordinally fuzzy aggregation rule is a function $g : G^n \rightarrow$
$OFSO$, where $G \subseteq OFSO$ and $G \neq \emptyset$.

This means that g associates to an n–list $(P_1, ..., P_n)$ of elements in OFSO
an element P in OFSO: $P = g(P_1, ..., P_n)$.

DEFINITION 4.8 Let g be an ordinally fuzzy aggregation rule. g satisfies

(i) unanimity (U) if for all $x, y \in X$ and for all $(P_1, ..., P_n) \in G^n$, there exists
$i \in N$ such that $P_i(x, y) \succeq P(x, y)$, and there exists $j \in N$ such that
$P(x, y) \succeq P_j(x, y)$;

(ii) Independence of irrelevant alternatives (IIA) if for all $x, y \in X$ and for all
$(P_1, ..., P_n), (P_1', ..., P_n') \in G^n$, $[P_i(x, y) \sim P_i'(x, y)$ and $P_i(y, x) \sim P_i'(y, x)$
for each $i \in N]$ implies $[P(x, y) \sim P'(x, y)$ and $P(y, x) \sim P'(y, x)]$.

Condition U may seem curious. It is, in fact, a sort of Pareto criterion.
Consider an n–list $(P_1, ..., P_n) \in G^n$, two alternatives $x, y \in X$; the set $\{\max_k$
$P_k(x, y)\}^9$ contains some degree α. Then the first part of the conditon means
that since there is some $i \in N$ such that $P_i(x, y) = \alpha$, $\alpha \succeq P(x, y)$. The
two parts of the condition amount to say that $\alpha \succeq P(x, y) \succeq \beta$ with $\alpha \in$
$\{\max_k P_k(x, y)\}$ and $\beta \in \{\min_k P_k(x, y)\}$. If for two alternatives $x, y \in X$, the
degrees of preference of the individuals are all above, say, "a little", or precisely
at that level, and below "much", or precisely at that level, the degree of the
social preference cannot be below "a little" and above "much".

IIA is the ordinal version of IIA in the previous subsection.

I now introduce four transitivity conditions.

---

[9] Since $\succeq$ is a complete preorder, we have not excluded the possibility that two differen
elements represent the same degree of preference (for instance, say, "mildly" and "a little")
Then $\max_k P_k(x, y)$ is not necessarily a single element.

DEFINITION 4.9   Let $P \in OFSO$. P satisfies

(i) restricted max–min transitivity if for all $x, y, z \in X$, $[P(x,y) \succeq P(y,x)$ and $P(y,z) \succeq P(z,y)]$ implies $[P(x,z) \succeq P(x,y)$ or $P(x,z) \succeq P(y,z)]$;

(ii) quasi–transitivity if for all $x, y, z \in X$, $[P(x,y) \succ P(y,x)$ and $P(y,z) \succ P(z,y)]$ implies $P(x,z) \succ P(z,x)$;

(iii) acyclicity if there does not exist a subset $\{x_1, ..., x_k\} \subseteq X$ $(k > 1)$ such that $P(x_1, x_2) \succ P(x_2, x_1)$ and ... and $P(x_{k-1}, x_k) \succ P(x_k, x_{k-1})$ and $P(x_k, x_1) \succ P(x_1, x_k)$;

(iv) simple transitivity if for all $x, y, z \in X$, $[P(x,y) \succ d_*$ and $P(y,x) = d_*$ and $P(y,z) \succ d_*$ and $P(z,y) = d_*]$ implies $[P(x,z) \succ d_*$ and $P(z,x) = d_*]$.

The following example justifies these transitivity properties. Consider three alternatives: a sum of money, m, $m+\delta$ $(\delta > 0)$ with δ small and x (unspecified). One might observe the following $P \in OFSO$: $P(m + \delta, m) = d^*$, $P(m, x) = d$ and $P(x, m + \delta) = d'$ with $d^* \succ d \succ d_*$ and $d^* \succ d' \succ d_*$. If we consider the ordinal version of max–min transitivity, i.e., for all $x, y, z \in X$, $P(x, z) \succeq P(x, y)$ or $P(x, z) \succeq P(y, z)$, we should obtain $P(m, m+\delta) \succeq d$ or $P(m, m+\delta) \succeq d'$. Since $P(m + \delta, m) = d^*$, $P(m, m + \delta) = d_*$ by ex–asymmetry, max–min transitivity is then violated. The same is true for the ordinal version of pos–transitivity, i.e., for all $x, y, z \in X$, $[P(x,y) \succ d_*$ and $P(y,z) \succ d_*]$ implies $P(x, z) \succ d_*$. However, this example is compatible with our four transitivity properties.

NOTATION   Let G_1, G_2, G_3 and G_4 be the subsets of OFSO the elements of which satisfy respectively restricted max–min transitivity, quasi–transitivity, acyclicity and simple transitivity.

THEOREM 4.10 $G_1 \subseteq G_2 \subseteq G_3$.

According to the different transitivity properties and other specific conditions on the set of alternatives, one obtains the five following results.

THEOREM 4.11   Let $\#X \geq n$ and let $g : G^n \to G_3$, where $G_1 \subseteq G$, be an ordinally fuzzy aggregation rule satisfying U and IIA. Let $d \in L$, $d \succ d_*$. Then there exists an individual $j \in N$ for which, for all $a, b \in X$ and for all $(P_1, ..., P_n) \in G^n$, $[P_j(a, b) \succeq d \succ P_j(b, a)$ and $d \succeq P_i(b, a)$ for all $i \in N - \{j\}]$ implies $P(a, b) \succeq P(b, a)$.

This is clearly an expression of a veto power. This veto power can even be strengthened if the number of alternatives is increased.

THEOREM 4.12   Let $\#X \geq 2n$ and let $g : G^n \to G_3$, where $G_1 \subseteq G$, be an ordinally fuzzy aggregation rule satisfying U and IIA. Let $d \in L$, $d \succ d_*$. Then there exists an individual $j \in N$ such that, for all $a, b \in X$ for all $(P_1, ..., P_n) \in G^n$, $P_j(a, b) \succeq d \succ P_j(b, a)$ implies $P(a, b) \succeq P(b, a)$.

THEOREM 4.13   Let $g : G^n \to G_2$, where $G_1 \subseteq G$, be an ordinally fuzzy aggregation rule satisfying U and IIA and let $d \in L$, $d \succ d_*$. Then, there exists a coalition C such that:

(1) for all $a, b \in X$ and for all $(P_1, ..., P_n) \in G^n$, $[P_i(a, b) \succeq d \succ P_i(b, a)$ for all $i \in C]$ implies $P(a, b) \succ P(b, a)$;

(2) for all $i \in C$, for all $a, b \in X$ and for all $(P_1, ..., P_n) \in G^n$, $P_i(a, b) \succeq d \succ P_i(b, a)$ implies $P(a, b) \succeq P(b, a)$.

THEOREM 4.14   Let $g : G^n \to G_1$, where $G_1 \subseteq G$, be an ordinally fuzzy aggregation rule satisfying U and IIA and let $d \in L$, $d \succ d_*$. Then, there exists a coalition C such that:

(1) for all $a, b \in X$ and for all $(P_1, ..., P_n) \in G^n$, $[P_i(a, b) \succeq d \succ P_i(b, a)$ for all $i \in C]$ implies $P(a, b) \succeq d \succ P(b, a)$;

(2) for all $i \in C$, for all $a, b \in X$ and for all $(P_1, ..., P_n) \in G^n$, $P_i(a, b) \succeq d \succ P_i(b, a)$ implies $[P(a, b) \succeq d$ or $d \succ P(b, a)]$.

Because of the Theorem 4.10, G_1 or G_2 can replace G_3 in Theorems 4.11 and 4.12.

THEOREM 4.15   Let $g : G^n \to G_4$, where $G_1 \subseteq G$, be an ordinally fuzzy aggregation rule satisfying U and IIA. Then there exists a coalition C such that

(1) for all $a, b \in X$ and for all $(P_1, ..., P_n) \in G^n$, $[P_i(a, b) \succ d_*$ and $P_i(b, a) = d_*$ for all $i \in C]$ implies $[P(a, b) \succ d_*$ and $P(b, a) = d_*]$;

(2) for all $i \in C$, for all $a, b \in X$ and for all $(P_1, ..., P_n) \in G^n$, $[P_i(a, b) \succ d_*$ and $P_i(b, a) = d_*]$ implies $[P(a, b) \succ d_*$ or $P(b, a) = d_*]$.

Note that the conclusion of Theorem 4.15 is slightly weaker than the corresponding result in Theorem 4.4 (the difference is in (2) where we obtain $P(a, b) \succ d_*$ or $P(b, a) = d_*$).

Even though the IIA condition in Section 4 is very mild, our results show that Arrow-type impossibilities are very robust. Considering an ordinal framework does not improve the whole picture and the comments and conclusion to the previous subsection could be repeated here.

5   Conclusion

I would like here to make some final remarks. First, on the assumption that we accept the fuzzy set–theoretic treatment of utility, preferences, social choice... one can consider standard economic spaces. This has been done to some extent by K. Basu (1984) and Basu, Deb and Pattanaik (1992). In that case, assuming continuity of membership functions does not appear to be a strong assumption. Second, a recent paper by Dasgupta and Deb (1994) suggest that fuzzy set theory can be used to prove results in the exact framework. This is similar to proving results in standard analysis with techniques of nonstandard analysis. Third, supposing that vagueness exists, there should be other ways to deal with it. For instance, one can consider many–valued logic. Also, but I believe that this could be equivalent to soft sets or L–fuzzy sets, we could, in preference theory, assume that the individual is endowed with a family of binary relations connected by transitivity-like properties.

But, more importantly, we must base our work about vagueness on a more fundamental analysis. A number of articles by philosophers have recently explored this domain, and these could be for us – social scientists, economists etc. – a good place to start our reflection.

Acknowledgments

I am very grateful to Richard Barrett and Prasanta Pattanaik for our joint work on this topic over the years. Also, conversations or correspondence with Kaushik Basu, Antoine Billot, Bhaskar Dutta, Neelam Jain, Efe Ok, Claude Ponsard, Clemens Puppe, among others, were very helpful. Finally, I have a special debt toward Richard Barrett who commented on an earlier version of this chapter. Most of his comments have been taken into account in the present version.

References

Arrow, K. J. (1959). Rational Choice Functions and Orderings. *Economica*, 26:121–127. Reprinted in *Collected Papers of Kenneth J. Arrow* (1984), Blackwell, Oxford.

Arrow, K. J. (1963). *Social Choice and Individual Values*. Wiley, New York, 2nd edition.

Banerjee, A. (1993). Rational Choice under Fuzzy Preferences: The Orlovsky Choice Function. *Fuzzy Sets and Systems*, 53:295–299.

Banerjee, A. (1994). Fuzzy Preferences and Arrow–type Problems in Social Choice. *Social Choice and Welfare*, 11:121–130.

Barrett, C. R. and Pattanaik, P. K. (1985). On Vague Preferences. In Enderle, G., editor, *Ethik und Wirtschaftswissenschaft*, pages 69–84. Duncker & Humblot, Berlin.

Barrett, C. R., Pattanaik, P. K., and Salles, M. (1986). On the Structure of Fuzzy Social Welfare Functions. *Fuzzy Sets and Systems*, 19:1–10.

Barrett, C. R., Pattanaik, P. K., and Salles, M. (1990). On Choosing Rationally when Preferences Are Fuzzy. *Fuzzy Sets and Systems*, 34:197–212.

Barrett, C. R., Pattanaik, P. K., and Salles, M. (1992). Rationality and Aggregation of Preferences in an Ordinally Fuzzy Framework. *Fuzzy Sets and Systems*, 49:9–13.

Basu, K. (1984). Fuzzy Revealed Preference. *Journal of Economic Theory*, 32:212–227.

Basu, K., Deb, R., and Pattanaik, P. K. (1992). Soft Sets: An Ordinal Formulation of Vagueness with Some Applications to the Theory of Choice. *Fuzzy Sets and Systems*, 45:45–58.

Billot, A. (1987). *Préférence et utilité floues: Applications à la théorie de l'équilibr partiel du consommateur*. Presses Universitaires de France, Paris.

Billot, A. (1992). *Economic Theory of Fuzzy Equilibria*. Springer, Berlin.

Burns, C. (1991). *Vagueness: An Investigation into Natural Languages and the Sorites Paradox*. Kluwer, Dordrecht.

Chipman, J. S., Hurwicz, L., Richter, M. K., and Sonnenschein, H., editors (1971). *Preferences, Utility, and Demand*. Harcourt, Brace, Jovanovich, New York.

Dasgupta, M. and Deb, R. (1991). Fuzzy Choice Functions. *Social Choice and Welfare*, 8:171–182.

Dasgupta, M. and Deb, R. (1993). Factoring Fuzzy Transitivity. Unpublished Typescript.

Dasgupta, M. and Deb, R. (1994). F–decomposable Social Aggregation Rules and Acyclic Choice. *Journal of Mathematical Economics*, 23:33–44.

Dasgupta, M. and Deb, R. (1996). Transitivity and Fuzzy Preferences. *Social Choice and Welfare*, 13:305–318.

Deb, R. (1977). On Schwartz's Rule. *Journal of Economic Theory*, 16:103–110.

Dubois, D. and Prade, H. (1980). *Fuzzy Sets and Systems: Theory and Applications*. Academic Press, New York.

Dummett, M. (1975). Wang's Paradox. *Synthese*, 30:301–324. Reprinted in Michael Dummett,*Truth and Other Enigmas*, Duckworth, 1978, London.

Dutta, B. (1987). Fuzzy Preferences and Social Choice. *Mathematical Social Sciences*, 13:215–229.

Dutta, B., Panda, C., and Pattanaik, P. K. (1986). Exact Choice and Fuzzy Preferences. *Mathematical Social Sciences*, 11:53–68.

Fishburn, P. C. (1970). *Utility Theory for Decision Making.* Wiley, New York.

Fishburn, P. C. (1988). *Nonlinear Preference and Utility Theory.* Wheatsheaf, Brighton.

Gibbard, A. (1969). Intransitive Social Indifference and the Arrow Dilemma. Unpublished Typescript.

Goguen, J. A. (1967). L–fuzzy Sets. *Journal of Mathematical Analysis and Applications*, 18:145–174.

Houthakker, H. S. (1950). Revealed Preference and the Utility Function. *Economica*, 41:159–174.

Jain, N. (1990). Transitivity of Fuzzy Relations and Rational Choice. *Annals of Operations Research*, 23:265–278.

Krantz, D. H., Luce, R. D., Suppes, P., and Tversky, A. (1971). *Foundations of Measurement.* Academic Press, New York.

Leclerc, B. (1984). Efficient and Binary Consensus Functions on Transitively Valued Relations. *Mathematical Social Sciences*, 8:45–61.

Leclerc, B. (1991). Aggregation of Fuzzy Preferences: A Theoretic Arrow–like Approach. *Fuzzy Sets and Systems*, 43:291–309.

Leclerc, B. and Monjardet, B. (1995). Latticial Theory of Consensus. In W. Barnett, H. Moulin, M. S. and Schofield, N., editors, *Social Choice, Welfare and Ethics*, pages 145–160. Cambridge University Press, Cambridge.

Mas-Colell, A. and Sonnenschein, H. (1972). General Possibility Theorems for Group Decisions. *Review of Economic Studies*, 39:185–192.

Ok, E. A. (1994). On the Approximation of Fuzzy Preferences by Exact Relations. *Fuzzy Sets and Systems*, 67:173–179.

Orlovsky, S. A. (1978). Decision–making with a Fuzzy Preference Relation. *Fuzzy Sets and Systems*, 1:155–167.

Ovchinnikov, S. V. (1981). Structure of Fuzzy Binary Relations. *Fuzzy Sets and Systems*, 6:169–195.

Ovchinnikov, S. V. (1991). Social Choice and Lukasiewicz Logic. *Fuzzy Sets and Systems*, 43:275–289.

Ovchinnikov, S. V. and Roubens, M. (1991). On Strict Preference Relations. *Fuzzy Sets and Systems*, 43:319–326.

Ovchinnikov, S. V. and Roubens, M. (1992). On Fuzzy Strict Preference, Indifference and Incomparability Relations. *Fuzzy Sets and Systems*, 49:15–20.

Ponsard, C. (1990). Some Dissenting Views on the Transitivity of Individual Preference. *Annals of Operations Research*, 23:279–288.

Puppe, C. (1994). Rational Choice Based on Vague Preferences. *Annals of Operations Research*, 52:67–81.

Sainsbury, R. M. (1988). *Paradoxes*. Cambridge University Press, Cambridge.

Samuelson, P. A. (1950). The Problem of Integrability in Utility Theory. *Economica*, 41:355–385. Reprinted in J. E. Stiglitz, editor, *The Collected Scientific Papers of Paul A. Samuelson*, volume 1, 1966, MIT Press, Cambridge, Mass.

Schwartz, T. (1976). Choice Functions, "Rationality" Conditions and Variations on the Weak Axiom of Revealed Preference. *Journal of Economic Theory*, 13:414–427.

Sen, A. K. (1970). The Impossibility of a Paretian Liberal. *Journal of Political Economy*, 78:152–157.

Sen, A. K. (1970 a). *Collective Choice and Social Welfare*. Holden–Day, San Francisco.

Sen, A. K. (1971). Choice Functions and Revealed Preference. *Review of Economic Studies*, 38:307–317. Reprinted in A. K. Sen, *Choice, Welfare and Measurement* (1982), Blackwell, Oxford.

Sen, A. K. (1992). *Inequality Reexamined*. Russell Sage Foundation, New York, and Clarendon Press, Oxford.

Simmons, P. (1992). Vagueness and Ignorance. *The Aristotelian Society*, 66:163–177. Supplementary Volume.

Sorensen, A. (1988). *Blindspots*. Clarendon Press, Oxford.

Subramanian, S. (1987). The Liberal Paradox with Fuzzy Preferences. *Social Choice and Welfare*, 4:213–218.

Subramanian, S. (1993). Liberty, Equality, and Impossibility: Some General Results on the Space of 'Soft' Preferences. Unpublished Typescript.

Suzumura, K. (1975). Rational Choice and Revealed Preference. *Review of Economic Studies*, 43:149–158.

Urquhart, A. (1986). Many-valued logic. In Gabbay, D. and Guenthner, F., editors, *Handbook of Philosophical Logic, Volume III, Alternatives to Classical Logic*, pages 71–116. Reidel, Dordrecht.

Uzawa, H. (1971). Preference and Rational Choice in the Theory of Consumption. In *Preferences, Utility, and Demand*, pages 7–28. Harcourt, Brace, Jovanovich, New York.

Williamson, T. (1992). Vagueness and Ignorance. *The Aristotelian Society*, 66:145–162. Supplementary Volume.

Zimmermann, H.-J. (1991). *Fuzzy Set Theory and its Applications*. Kluwer, Boston.

9 LEXICOGRAPHIC UTILITY AND ORDERINGS

Juan E. Martínez–Legaz

Universitat Autònoma de Barcelona

Contents

1	Introduction	346
2	Lexicographic Preferences	347
3	The Lexicographic Order in $\mathbb{R}^n$	350
4	Lexicographic Utility	353
5	Lexicographic Expected Utility	355
6	Lexicographic Subjective Expected Utility	358
7	Lexicographic Probabilities and Game Theory	361
References		365

1 Introduction

This article explains the role of lexicographic orders in utility theory. In the context of decision making, a lexicographic order appears when the alternatives are compared according to a set of criteria which present a sharp hierarchical structure. In addition, lexicographic utility representations of preference relations arise when the continuity condition that is required to obtain the existence of a real valued utility function is dropped. Likewise, the classical theories of expected utility in decision–making under risk and uncertainty admit lexicographic extensions dealing with the case in which no Archimedean axiom is assumed. The lexicographic probability systems that appear in a lexicographic subjective expected utility theory permit one to consider conditioning on "events with probability zero". Furthermore, they can be used to define lexicographic Nash equilibria for noncooperative games in normal form in such a way that perfect and proper equilibria are characterized in terms of belief systems of the players. Thus, lexicographic probabilities provide a new insight into equilibrium refinements and open the way to discovering new appropriate concepts of this kind.

The literature on lexicographic utility up to 1974 is reviewed in the excellent survey paper of Fishburn (1974). This chapter reproduces the main results presented in that paper. I strongly recommend its reading to anybody wishing more comprehensive information about the foundations of lexicographic utility and its role in decision theory. Most topics discussed in the following sections correspond to developments carried out over the last twenty years, some of them very recent.

Section 2 deals with lexicographic preferences. After giving the main definitions related to lexicographic preorders, brief descriptions of the lexicographic additive model of Luce (1978) and of its additive–difference modification by Fishburn (1980) are presented. In Section 3, the main properties of the lexicographic order in $\mathbb{R}^n$ and its connections with linear algebra and convexity theory are reviewed. The next section discusses lexicographic utility representations of preference relations, including some recent work of Clark (1993) on lexicographic utility rationality of choice correspondences. Lexicographic expected utility is the object of Sections 5 and 6, in the context of decisions under risk and under uncertainty, respectively. The article ends with a section on the role of the lexicographic order in game theory, with special emphasis in the lexicographic characterizations of perfect and proper equilibria of noncooperative games in normal form obtained recently by Blume, Brandenburger and Dekel (1991b).

Because of lack of space some related topics are not included, e.g., lexicographic optimization. A rather satisfactory theory already exists in the linear case [Isermann (1982)]; nonlinear problems with some particular structure have been also considered in the literature [Behringer (1977), Luptáčik and Turnovec (1991)] but there seem to be essential difficulties encountered in constructing a sufficiently rich nonlinear theory. Likewise, the role of the lexicographic order in social choice theory, in rules such as the leximin rule for aggregation of preference orderings [Sen (1970)], will not be discussed here. Let us only mention that characterizations of the leximin rule can be found in d'Aspremont and Gevers (1977), Deschamps and Gevers (1978) and Barberà and Jackson (1988). Some further papers related to the use of the lexicographic order in social choice are those of Hammond (1976), Pattanaik and Peleg (1984), Nieto (1992) and Krause (1995). For bargaining problems, lexicographic solutions have been studied by Imai (1983), Chun (1989) and Chun and Peters (1991).

2   Lexicographic Preferences

A binary relation $\preceq$ on a set X is a preorder if it is reflexive and transitive, i.e., if $x \preceq x$ for all $x \in X$ and the relations $x \preceq y$ and $y \preceq z$ imply $x \preceq z$. If $x \preceq y$ but not $(y \preceq x)$ then we write $x \prec y$; when we have both $x \preceq y$ and $y \preceq x$ we write $x \sim y$. The preorder $\preceq$ may be regarded as a (nonstrict) preference relation between the elements of X; in this sense, we interpret $x \preceq y$ as "x is less preferred than y", $x \prec y$ as "x is strictly less preferred than y" and $x \sim y$ as "x and y are indifferent". Notice that the relation $\prec$ is asymmetric, i.e., $x \prec y$ implies not $(y \prec x)$, and transitive while $\sim$ is reflexive, symmetric (that is, $x \preceq y$ implies $y \preceq x$) and transitive (or, briefly, $\sim$ is an equivalence relation). The preorder $\preceq$ is called complete if any two elements $x, y \in X$ can be compared, i.e., either $x \preceq y$ or $y \preceq x$ (or both); a partial preorder is a preorder which is not complete (that is, there exist at least two incomparable elements). The term order applies to a preorder for which the associated indifference relation $\sim$ reduces to the identity (i.e., $x \sim y$ only if $x = y$). A well ordered set is a set X endowed with an order relation $\preceq$ such that any nonempty subset $Y \subset X$ has a first element — that is, an $x \in Y$ such that $x \preceq y$ for all $y \in Y$.

DEFINITION 2.1 Let $(I, \leq)$ be a nonempty well ordered set each of whose elements i is associated with a nonempty set X_i endowed with a complete preorder $\preceq_i$ and let $X = \prod_{i \in I} X_i$ be the Cartesian product of the X_i's, which consists of all families $x = (x_i)_{i \in I}$ with $x_i \in X$ for all $i \in I$. The lexicographic preorder $\leq_L$, relative to the $\preceq_i$'s and $\leq$, is the binary relation on X defined by $x \leq_L y$ iff either $x_i \sim_i y_i$ for all $i \in I$ or $x_k <_k y_k$, with k being the first element of the set $\{i \in I : \text{not}\,(x_i \sim_i y_i)\}$; by $\sim_i$ we denote here the indifference relation associated with $\preceq_i$.

One can easily check that $\leq_L$ is a complete preorder; it is an order iff all the $\preceq_i$'s are orders.

Lexicographic orders appeared for the first time in the scientific literature in the mathematical works of Cantor (1895) on transfinite numbers. More than fifty years elapsed before the lexicographic order was considered in the context of decision theory [Debreu (1954), Hausner (1954)].

A lexicographic preorder admits the following interpretation. Suppose X is a set of alternatives over which one has to establish a preference relation. Each alternative $x \in X$ is identified with a family of attributes $(x_i)_{i \in I}$, each x_i belonging to a set X_i, the preferences of the decision maker over which are represented by $\preceq_i$. The well ordering $\leq$ on I expresses the fact that there is a hierarchy among the criteria. To compare two alternatives, the lexicographic preorder looks at the most important criterion for which the attributes of the two alternatives are not indifferent. The term lexicographic refers to the way the words are ordered in a dictionary: to decide whether one word precedes another, one has to compare their initial letters; if they coincide then one looks at the second letters, and so on.

Of course, in most applications the index set I is finite and, without loss of generality, one assumes that $I = \{1, \ldots, n\}$ and that it is ordered in the natural way. An important theoretical issue is to characterize axiomatically those preference relations on $X = \prod_{i=1}^{n} X_i$ which are lexicographic, maybe after a reordering of the factors X_i. Two results in this direction are Theorems 1 and 2 in Fishburn (1974).

The lexicographic model has been criticized on the basis that the hierarchical structure of the criteria is too rigid. In practical situations, it is hard to believe that the first criterion is so important that one regards an alternative as better than another because it exhibits a slightly better first attribute even if the remaining attributes are much worse than the corresponding ones of the second alternative. More often, there exist tradeoffs between the criteria such that a small difference in favour of one alternative according to the most important criterion can be compensated by big differences in favour of the remaining criteria. A particular model which tries to reconcile this observation with the lexicographic principle has been proposed by Luce (1978). In this approach, there are two factors, the first of which is more important in the sense that it is decisive in case of sufficiently large differences, but when the difference on the first factor is not too large then one has to consider tradeoffs between the two factors. Luce gave a set of axioms for this model from which he derived a representation theorem. If $X = X_1 \times X_2$ and $\preceq$ is a binary relation on X satisfying the axioms, then there exist three functions, $\phi_1, \delta : X_1 \longrightarrow \mathbb{R}$ and $\phi_2 : X_2 \longrightarrow \mathbb{R}$, such that for all $x_1, y_1 \in X_1$ and $x_2, y_2 \in X_2$

$(x_1, x_2) \preceq (y_1, y_2)$ iff either $\phi_1(y_1) - \phi_1(x_1) > \delta(x_1)$ or
$$- \delta(y_1) \leq \phi_1(y_1) - \phi_1(x_1) \leq \delta(x_1) \text{ and}$$
$$\phi_1(x_1) + \phi_2(x_2) \leq \phi_1(y_1) + \phi_2(y_2).$$

In this representation, ϕ_1 and ϕ_2 can be regarded as utility functions on X_1 and X_2, respectively, while δ associates to $x_1 \in X_1$ the amount of utility by which y_1 has to exceed x_1 for it to be considered so much better than x_1 as to allow us to ignore the second factor. Only when the difference between x_1 and y_1 is so small that they are regarded as virtually indifferent does one compare the complete utility of the two alternatives to decide which one is preferred. The model so obtained is thus a combination of the lexicographic and the additive models. It is easy to give examples showing that a binary relation admitting the representation above need not be transitive.

A modification of Luce's model has been proposed by Fishburn (1980), which essentially consists in replacing the additive component by an additive–difference model, similar to that of Tversky (1969). Unlike the Luce model, Fishburn's is symmetric in the sense that neither factor is regarded as more important than the other a priori. Fishburn identified three axioms for a strict preference relation $\prec$ on $X = X_1 \times X_2$ under which it can be represented as follows: there exist $i_0 \in \{1, 2\}, \phi_i : X_i \longrightarrow \mathbb{R}$ $(i = 1, 2)$, two symmetric (with respect to the origin) real intervals $I_i \subseteq \{\phi_i(x_i) - \phi_i(x_i') : x_i, x_i' \in X_i\}$ $(i = 1, 2)$ and two continuous strictly increasing functions $f_1 : I_1 \longrightarrow I_2$, $f_2 : I_2 \to I_1$ which are inverses of each other and such that for all $x_1, y_1 \in X_1$ and $x_2, y_2 \in X_2$ one has $(x_1, x_2) \prec (y_1, y_2)$ iff either

(1) $\phi_i(y_i) - \phi_i(x_i) \notin I_i$ $(i = 1, 2)$ and $\phi_{i_0}(y_{i_0}) > \phi_{i_0}(x_{i_0})$ or
(2) there exists $i \in \{1, 2\}$ with $\phi_i(y_i) - \phi_i(x_i) \in I_i$ and
$f_i[\phi_i(y_i) - \phi_i(x_i)] + \phi_j(y_j) - \phi_j(x_j) > 0$, where $j \in \{1, 2\}$
with $j \neq i$.

As in Luce's model, ϕ_i can be regarded as a utility function on X_i; the role of the interval I_i is to indicate that y_i is significantly better than x_i when $\phi_i(y_i) - \phi_i(x_i) > 0$ and $\phi_i(y_i) - \phi_i(x_i) \notin I_i$. Concerning f_i, it serves to compare the increase in utility $\phi_i(y_i) - \phi_i(x_i)$ when passing from (x_1, x_2) to (y_1, y_2) with a corresponding possible decrease in utility $\phi_j(x_j) - \phi_j(y_j)$ for the other factor. The index i_0 identifies the most important factor; when y_{i_0} is significantly better than x_{i_0} then $(x_1, x_2) \prec (y_1, y_2)$ regardless of the utilities of the other components of these pairs. Indeed, to simplify notation suppose that $i_0 = 1$ and $\phi_1(y_1) - \phi_1(x_1) \notin I_1$ with $\phi_1(y_1) - \phi_1(x_1) > 0$. If $\phi_2(y_2) - \phi_2(x_2) \notin I_2$ then, by (1), $(x_1, x_2) \prec (y_1, y_2)$; if, on the contrary,

$\phi_2(y_2) - \phi_2(x_2) \notin I_2$ then $f_2[\phi_2(y_2) - \phi_2(x_2)] \in I_1$ whence, as I_1 is a symmetric interval, $f_2[\phi_2(y_2) - \phi_2(x_2)] + \phi_1(y_1) - \phi_1(x_1) > 0$ and therefore, by (2), we also get $(x_1, x_2) \prec (y_1, y_2)$. One can easily prove that a binary relation admitting a representation of this type is necessarily asymmetric but need not be transitive. We refer to Fishburn (1980) for a detailed discussion of the model, showing that some other more particular models (in particular, the completely lexicographic one) fits this general pattern.

A common feature of Luce and Fishburn models is that they assume independent preferences, in the sense that, for all $x_1, y_1 \in X_1$ and $x_2, y_2 \in X_2$,

$$(x_1, x_2) \prec (y_1, x_2) \text{ iff } (x_1, y_2) \prec (y_1, y_2)$$

and

$$(x_1, x_2) \prec (x_1, y_2) \text{ iff } (y_1, x_2) \prec (y_1, y_2).$$

3   The Lexicographic Order in $\mathbb{R}^n$

In this section we review the main properties of the lexicographic order in $\mathbb{R}^n$ and its applications to utility theory. It corresponds to the particular case of Definition 2.1 in which $I = \{1, \dots, n\}$, the relation $\le$ is the natural order on I and $(X_i, \preceq_i)$ is $(\mathbb{R}, \le)$ $(i = 1, \dots, n)$, the set of real numbers with the usual ordering. An element $x = (x_1, \dots, x_n) \in \mathbb{R}^n$ will be regarded as a column vector whenever it is involved in matrix operations. According to Definition 2.1, for all $x, y \in \mathbb{R}^n$ one has

$$x \le_L y \text{ iff either } x = y \text{ or } x_k < y_k, \text{ where } k = \min\{i | x_i \ne y_i\}.$$

The symbols $<_L$, $\ge_L$ and $>_L$ will have the obvious meanings.

In view of some applications discussed later, it is necessary to define a lexicographic order for real matrices.

DEFINITION 3.1 Let $A = (a_1, \dots, a_n)$ and $B = (b_1, \dots, b_n)$ be two $m \times n$ real matrices (with columns a_j and b_j, $j = 1, \dots, n$, respectively). A is said to be (columnwise) lexicographically less than or equal to B, in symbols $A \le_L B$, iff $a_j \le_L b_j$ for all $j = 1, \dots, n$.

Notice that, when $n = 1$, this definition coincides with that of the lexicographic order on $\mathbb{R}^m$. Definition 3.1 is just its columnwise extension to matrices. The next theorem gives a characterization of the lexicographically nonnegative matrices in terms of a decomposition property.

THEOREM 3.2 [Martínez–Legaz (1984)] Let A be an $m \times n$ real matrix. Then A is lexicographically nonnegative, $A \geq_L 0$, iff there exist an $m \times m$ unitary lower triangular matrix L and a termwise nonnegative $m \times n$ matrix P, $P \geq 0$, such that $A = LP$.

Recall that for L to be lower triangular means that it is square and all entries above the main diagonal are zero; unitary means here that all the diagonal elements are equal to one.

Since $A \leq_L B$ is equivalent to $B - A \geq_L 0$ and the inverse of a unitary lower triangular matrix exists and is unitary lower triangular too, from Theorem 3.2 one easily gets

COROLLARY 3.3 Let A and B be two $m \times n$ real matrices. Then $A \leq_L B$ iff there exists a unitary lower triangular matrix L such that $LA \leq LB$.

The interest of Corollary 3.3 lies in that it relates the lexicographic order to the termwise order.

The following result generalizes the classical Farkas (1902) theorem by considering lexicographic (instead of scalar) linear inequalities that are consequences of a given linear inequality system. The standard Farkas theorem is recovered by setting $p = 1$.

THEOREM 3.4 [Martínez–Legaz (1984)] Let A and C be two real matrices of sizes $m \times n$ and $p \times n$, respectively. Then $Cx \geq_L 0$ for every $x \in \mathbb{R}^n$ satisfying $Ax \geq 0$ iff there exists a $p \times m$ matrix $W \geq_L 0$ such that $WA = C$.

Applying Theorem 3.4 to the particular case when A is the identity matrix implies that C transforms termwise nonnegative vectors into lexicographically nonnegative vectors (i.e., $Cx \geq_L 0$ for every $x \geq 0$) iff $C \geq_L 0$. This can also be easily proved directly from Definition 3.1. A related natural question is to characterize those (not necessarily square) matrices that preserve lexicographic nonnegativity. For this, a useful concept is the lexicographic index studied in Martínez–Legaz and Singer (1990).

DEFINITION 3.5 The lexicographic index $\alpha(x)$ of $x \in \mathbb{R}^n$ is

$$\alpha(x) = \begin{cases} \min\{j \in \{1, \ldots, n\} : x_j \neq 0\} & \text{if } x \neq 0, \\ +\infty & \text{if } x = 0. \end{cases}$$

THEOREM 3.6 [Martínez–Legaz and Singer (1990)] Let $A = (a_1, \ldots, a_n)$ be a $m \times n$ real matrix. Then $Ax \geq_L 0$ for every $x \geq_L 0$ iff $A \geq_L 0$ and, for each $j = 2, \ldots, n$ such that $a_j \neq 0$, $\alpha(a_{j-1}) < \alpha(a_j)$.

From Theorem 3.6 it is easy to show that a matrix A satisfying the conditions in the statement preserves lexicographic (strict) positivity iff all of its columns are nonzero and then, necessarily, $m \geq n$. In the case of a square matrix A, it turns out that $Ax >_L 0$ for every $x >_L 0$ iff A is lower triangular and all of its diagonal entries are strictly positive.

Some related results such as characterizations of the matrices which preserve, do not increase or do not decrease the lexicographic index are given in Martínez–Legaz and Singer (1990).

The mathematical importance of the lexicographic order in $\mathbb{R}^n$ is mainly due to its role in representing compatible complete preorders. Recall that $\preceq$, a complete preorder on $\mathbb{R}^n$, is said to be compatible (with the vector space structure) if

$$
\begin{aligned}
x \preceq y, \quad x' \preceq y' &\implies x + x' \preceq y + y', \\
x \preceq y, \quad \lambda \geq 0 &\implies \lambda x \preceq \lambda y.
\end{aligned}
$$

For any compatible complete preorder on $\mathbb{R}^n$, the nonpositive cone

$$
C_{\preceq} = \{ x \in \mathbb{R}^n : x \preceq 0 \}
$$

is a convex set with convex complement (satisfying $x \in C_{\preceq}$ or $-x \in C_{\preceq}$ for all $x \in \mathbb{R}^n$) which contains all the relevant information about $\preceq$ since one has $x \preceq y$ iff $x - y \in C_{\preceq}$ for any $x, y \in \mathbb{R}^n$. Convex sets with convex complements are called hemispaces [Jamison–Waldner (1982)]. A representation theorem for hemispaces given in Martínez–Legaz and Singer (1988) leads to the following characterization of compatible complete preorders.

THEOREM 3.7 [Martínez–Legaz and Singer (1991)] A compatible preorder $\preceq$ on $\mathbb{R}^n$ is complete iff there exist a unique $r \in \{0, 1, \dots, n\}$ and a unique $r \times n$ orthogonal matrix A (with $AA^T = I$, the identity matrix) such that

$$
x \preceq y \text{ iff } Ax \leq_L Ay.
$$

From this theorem one can easily classify all compatible complete preorders in terms of their "ranks"; the rank $r(\preceq)$ of $\preceq$ is defined as the unique $r \in \{0, 1, \dots, n\}$ associated with $\preceq$ as in Theorem 3.7. Namely, given two compatible complete preorders on $\mathbb{R}^n$, $\preceq$ and $\preceq'$, there is an isomorphism $v : (\mathbb{R}^n, \preceq) \longrightarrow (\mathbb{R}^n, \preceq')$ of preordered vector spaces iff $r(\preceq) = r(\preceq')$; in this case, v can be chosen to be a linear isometry (i.e., a distance preserving isomorphism) of the form $v(x) = Ax$ for some orthogonal matrix A. Thus, for the class of compatible preorders on $\mathbb{R}^n$ of a given rank r, there is a canonical representation $\preceq^r$ defined by

$$
x \preceq^r y \text{ iff } (x_1, \dots, x_r) \leq_L (y_1, \dots, y_r).
$$

Clearly, $\preceq^r$ is an order iff $r = n$ and therefore the lexicographic order on $\mathbb{R}^n$ is, up to a (unique) linear isometry, the unique compatible complete order on $\mathbb{R}^n$. An equivalent version of this result, stating that any finite–dimensional ordered vector space can be represented as a lexicographic function space, was proved by Hausner and Wendel (1952). This fact shows the importance of the lexicographic order.

Theorem 3.7 was used in Martínez–Legaz and Singer (1991) to prove that any compatible preorder $\preceq$ on $\mathbb{R}^n$ is the intersection of its compatible complete extensions having the same indifference subspace. Recall that the intersection of a family of binary relations on a given set is defined as that relation whose graph is the intersection of the graphs of the relations in the family. Also, an extension of a binary relation is another relation with a (not necessarily strictly) larger (in the sense of inclusion) graph. And the indifference subspace of $\preceq$ is $\{ x \in \mathbb{R}^n : x \sim 0 \}$. In particular, any compatible order on $\mathbb{R}^n$ is the intersection of its extensions to compatible complete orders (since the compatible orders are those compatible preorders whose indifference subspace reduces to the origin). These results can be regarded as versions, for compatible preorders, of the classical extension theorem of Szpilrajn (1930) for general partially ordered sets.

Many other results on lexicographic orders in $\mathbb{R}^n$, including separation theorems for convex sets, can be found in Klee (1969), Borwein (1980), Martínez–Legaz (1983, 1984, 1985, 1988a, 1988b, 1991), Singer (1984), Gorokhovik (1986) and Martínez–Legaz and Singer (1987a, 1987b, 1988, 1990, 1991).

4   Lexicographic Utility

One of the first appearances of the lexicographic order (in $\mathbb{R}^n$) in the literature on decision theory was in a Debreu's (1954) example of a preference relation that could not be represented by a real–valued utility function. This is easy to prove; indeed, take, e.g., $n = 2$ and suppose that one could find $u : \mathbb{R}^2 \longrightarrow \mathbb{R}$ such that, for any $x, y \in \mathbb{R}^2$, $x \leq_L y$ iff $u(x) \leq u(y)$. This would entail the existence of an uncountable family of pairwise disjoint open intervals, namely, $\{ (u(r, 0), u(r, 1)) \}_{r \in \mathbb{R}}$. Yet there can only be countably many such intervals because each must intersect the countable set of all rational numbers.

In view of the preceding example, it is natural to ask which complete order relations can be represented by lexicographic utility functions. The somewhat surprising but nevertheless rather trivial answer to this question is provided by an old result due to Cuesta Dutari (1943, 1947) and Sierpiński (1949):

THEOREM 4.1 Every completely ordered set $(X, \preceq)$ admits a lexicographic utility representation into some power set $(\{0, 1\}^I, \leq_L)$, where I is a set of the same cardinality as X, endowed with a well ordering $\leq$.

This theorem is a straightforward consequence of Zorn's Lemma, according to which any set X admits a well ordering $\leq$. Then one can define $u : X \longrightarrow \{0, 1\}^X$ by $u(x) = (u_i(x))_{i \in X}$, with $u_i(x) = 0$ if $x \prec i$ and $u_i(x) = 1$ if $i \preceq x$. It readily follows that, for any $x, y \in X$, one has $x \preceq y$ iff $u(x) \leq_L u(y)$, the lexicographic order $\leq_L$ being that relative to the natural order in $\{0, 1\}$ and the well ordering $\leq$ in X.

The main value of Theorem 4.1 lies in its generality, as it is valid for any totally ordered set, but this is also the reason why the lexicographic utility representation it asserts is frequently much more complicated than other possible representations (there might exist, e.g., a real-valued utility function). Nevertheless, there are some examples showing that the cardinality of I cannot generally be reduced [Fishburn (1974), p. 1455)].

As Debreu's example illustrates, the need for lexicographic utility representations appears when the Archimedean property (see the next section) fails to hold. Although the Archimedean axiom looks quite reasonable in most situations, there are some cases in which such an assumption would be inapplicable. The reader can find some examples in consumer choice theory illustrating this point in Chipman (1960, p. 221). Another approach to non–Archimedean utility, using concepts of Nonstandard Analysis, is developed in the book of Skala (1975). Some other references on non–Archimedean structures can be found in Narens (1974, 1985).

In a recent article, Clark (1993) has characterized lexicographic utility rationality of choice correspondences. Given a set of actions X and a collection β of nonempty subsets of X, a choice correspondence is a multi–valued mapping $\Phi : \beta \longrightarrow X$. The interpretation is the following: when the decision–maker must choose an action belonging to the constraint set $B \in \beta$, his choice belongs to $\Phi(B)$, which is assumed to be a nonempty subset of B. In this way, Φ describes the decision–maker's behavior. If $\wp$ denotes some property of a utility function, one says that Φ is lexicographic $(\wp)$ utility rational if there exist a natural number m and a function $u : X \longrightarrow \mathbb{R}^m$ satisfying $\wp$ such that, for each $B \in \beta$,

$$\Phi(B) = \{ x \in B : u(x) \geq_L u(y) \ \forall y \in B \}.$$

Lexicographic utility rationality is characterized in terms of the so–called revealed weak preference relation V. This is defined so that, given $x, y \in X$, one has $x V y$ iff there exists some $B \in \beta$ such that $x \in \Phi(B)$ and $y \in B$. The revealed strict preference relation V^* is defined by replacing the condition $y \in B$ by $y \in B \setminus \Phi(B)$ in the preceding definition. The choice correspondence Φ is said to satisfy the weak axiom of revealed preference [Arrow (1959)] if there are no actions $x, y \in X$ such that $x V y$ and $y V^* x$. A function $u : X \longrightarrow \mathbb{R}^m$ is called a one–way lexicographic $(\wp)$ utility representation of V if the following two conditions hold:

(i) $x \, V \, y$ and not $y \, V \, x$ imply $u(x) >_L u(y)$,

(ii) $x \, V \, y$ and $y \, V \, x$ imply $u(x) = u(y)$.

THEOREM 4.2 [Clark (1993)] A choice correspondence $\Phi : \beta \longrightarrow X$ is lexicographic ($\wp$) utility rational iff it satisfies the weak axiom of revealed preference and V has a one–way lexicographic ($\wp$) utility representation.

5   Lexicographic Expected Utility

The well known expected utility theory for decision making under risk, as developed by Von Neumann and Morgenstern (1944), establishes conditions for the existence of a utility function on an outcome set X such that a given preference relation on the set of probability distributions with finite support on X is represented by the associated expected utility. See also Chapter 2. The axioms on which the theory is based consist in assuming that the preference relation over the lotteries is a complete preorder satisfying a continuity or Archimedean property and an independence condition. As observed by Narens (1985), the role of the Archimedean axiom in single person decision theory is merely technical — namely, to ensure the existence of a real valued utility function, so that from the foundational point of view it is important to examine the consequences of removing this axiom. In game theory, however, existence of a Nash equilibrium may depend on such an axiom. On the other hand, on some occasions there may exist some hierarchies among the criteria invalidating the Archimedean axiom (see Section 2). As will be seen next, dropping this assumption modifies classical expected utility theory by allowing lexicographic utilities of the form initially considered by Hausner (1954) and Chipman (1960). The convenience of this extension was already considered in the appendix to the second edition (1947) of the book by Von Neumann and Morgenstern (1944). Here we will follow the approach of Fishburn (1971, 1982).

The set of probability measures with finite support or, more briefly, of lotteries on X will be denoted by $\wp$. Given $P, Q \in \wp$ and $\alpha \in [0, 1]$, the convex combination $\alpha P + (1 - \alpha)Q$ is well defined and also belongs to $\wp$. Recall that a weak order on $\wp$ is a binary relation $\prec$ which is irreflexive (not $P \prec P$) and negatively transitive (not $P \prec Q$ and not $Q \prec R$ imply not $P \prec R$). The indifference relation $\sim$ associated with $\prec$ is defined by $P \sim Q$ iff not $P \prec Q$ and not $Q \prec P$. We write $P \preceq Q$ when either $P \prec Q$ or $P \sim Q$. The relation $\sim$ is an equivalence and $\preceq$ is a complete preorder. We will say that $\prec$ is nontrivial if $P \prec Q$ for some $P, Q \in \wp$. The weak order $\prec$ satisfies the independence condition if $P \prec Q$ implies

$\alpha P + (1 - \alpha)R \prec \alpha Q + (1 - \alpha)R$ for all $R \in \wp$ and all $\alpha \in (0, 1)$. The independence condition for $\sim$ is defined similarly. Let $\mathcal{A}_\prec$ denote the set of all nonempty preference intervals $PR = \{Q \in \wp : P \preceq Q \preceq R\}$ with $P \prec R$. The following lemma can be easily proved, as discussed in Chapter 2.

LEMMA 5.1 [Fishburn (1971, 1982)] Let $\prec$ be a nontrivial weak order on $\wp$ and let $\sim$ be the associated indifference relation. Suppose that $\prec$ and $\sim$ satisfy the independence condition. Then for any $PR \in \mathcal{A}_\prec$ and $Q \in PR$ there exists a unique $\mu \in [0, 1]$ such that

$$\alpha R + (1 - \alpha)P \prec Q \quad \text{for all} \quad \alpha \in [0, \mu),$$

$$Q \prec \alpha R + (1 - \alpha)P \quad \text{for all} \quad \alpha \in (\mu, 1].$$

The preceding lemma suggests introducing a function $f_{PR} : PR \longrightarrow [0, 1]$, defined by $f_{PR}(Q) = \mu$. Consider the relation $<_0$ on $\mathcal{A}_\prec$ given by $PQ <_0 RS$ iff $PQ \subseteq RS$ and $f_{RS}(P) < f_{RS}(Q)$. One can prove that it is a preorder. Let $=_0$ be the relation on $\mathcal{A}_\prec$ defined by $PQ =_0 RS$ iff $PQ <_0 PS \cup RQ$ and $RS <_0 PS \cup RQ$. It is an equivalence relation [Fishburn (1971, p. 674)]. Notice that, under the usual Archimedean axiom, $=_0$ reduces to the trivial equivalence relation (all intervals in $\mathcal{A}_\prec$ are equivalent). Let $\mathcal{A}_\prec^0 = \mathcal{A}_\prec/=_0$ and denote by $\wp(A)$ the union of all intervals belonging to $A \in \mathcal{A}_\prec^0$. Then $<_0$ induces a strict order relation $<$ on $\mathcal{A}_\prec^0$ which is defined by setting $A < B$ iff $\wp(A) \subset \wp(B)$. Based on $<$, define the relations $<_k$ on $\mathcal{A}_\prec^0$, $k \geq 1$, recursively by

$$A <_1 B \text{ iff } A < B \text{ and there is no } C \in \mathcal{A}_\prec^0 \text{ with } A < C < B,$$

$$A <_k B \text{ iff } A <_1 C \text{ and } C <_{k-1} B \text{ for some } C \in \mathcal{A}_\prec^0.$$

The lexicographic representation theorem requires the following axiom, depending on a natural number $n > 1$.

AXIOM $L = n$. If $A < B$ then $A <_k B$ for some $k \in \{1, \ldots, n - 1\}$. There exist $C, D \in \mathcal{A}_\prec^0$ such that $C <_{n-1} D$.

The interpretation of axiom $L = n$ is that there are exactly n levels in the lexicographic hierarchy.

THEOREM 5.2 [Hausner (1954), Fishburn (1971)] Let $\prec$ satisfy the assumptions of Lemma 5.1 and suppose that axiom $L = n$ holds. Then there exists

$u : \wp \longrightarrow \mathbb{R}^n$ such that, for all $P, Q \in \wp$,

$$P \prec Q \quad \text{iff} \quad u(P) <_L u(Q) \quad \text{and}$$

$$u(\alpha P + (1 - \alpha)Q) = \alpha u(P) + (1 - \alpha)u(Q) \quad \text{for all} \quad \alpha \in [0, 1].$$

Moreover, another function $v : \wp \longrightarrow \mathbb{R}^n$ satisfies these conditions iff there exist a lower triangular matrix A with strictly positive diagonal elements and a vector $b \in \mathbb{R}^n$ such that

$$v(P) = A u(P) + b \quad \text{for all} \quad P \in \wp.$$

In fact, the assumptions of Lemma 5.1 are necessary for $\prec$ to admit such a lexicographic utility representation, as one can easily check. However, the axiom $L = n$ is superfluous when X is finite; in this case, the lexicographic utility representation holds for some $n \leq |X| - 1$ [Fishburn (1979, p. 254)].

Let $E(u, P)$ denote the expected value of $u : X \longrightarrow \mathbb{R}^n$ with respect to $P \in \wp$. Then Theorem 5.2 has the following corollary:

COROLLARY 5.3 Under the assumptions of Theorem 5.2, there exists $u : X \longrightarrow \mathbb{R}^n$ such that, for all $P, Q \in \wp$, $P \prec Q$ iff $E(u, p) <_L E(u, Q)$. Moreover, another function $v : X \to \mathbb{R}^n$ satisfies this condition iff there exist a lower triangular matrix A with strictly positive diagonal elements and a vector $b \in \mathbb{R}^n$ such that

$$v(x) = A u(x) + b \quad \text{for all} \quad x \in X.$$

In fact Theorem 5.2 is valid for any mixture space $\wp$, an abstract structure introduced by Hausner (1954) which contains, as a special case, convex sets in vector spaces. A still more general notion is that of a mixture set, considered by Herstein and Milnor (1953). Then a weaker version of the existence part of Theorem 5.2, consisting in replacing the "linearity" property of u by that of u_j (where j denotes the lexicographic index of $u(P) - u(Q)$, in the sense of Definition 3.5), can be found in Fishburn (1971, p. 676; 1982, Ch. 4). The role of mixture structures in expected utility theories is discussed in Fishburn and Roberts (1978). For the existence of one–way lexicographic utility representations of partial orders in vector spaces, the reader may consult Aumann (1962) and Kannai (1963). A related result appears in Fishburn (1979, p. 253); see also Lemma 5 in Clark (1993).

In the case when the outcome set is a Cartesian product, $X = X_1 \times \ldots \times X_m$ (with $m \geq 2$), independence conditions for lexicographic utility representations have been studied in LaValle and Fishburn (1991) and Fishburn and LaValle (1992). The X_i are said to be value independent if for all $p, q \in \wp$, one has $p \sim q$ whenever $(p_1, \ldots, p_n) = (q_1, \ldots, q_n)$, where p_i and q_i $(i = 1, \ldots, n)$ denote the marginal distributions of p and q, respectively, on X_i. The set of all lotteries on X_i will be represented by $\wp_i$.

THEOREM 5.4 [Fishburn and LaValle (1992)] Let $u : \wp \longrightarrow \mathbb{R}^n$ be a lexicographic utility representation of a weak order on $\wp$. Then the X_i are value independent iff there exist $u_i : \wp_i \longrightarrow \mathbb{R}^n$ $(i = 1, \ldots, n)$ such that, for all $p \in \wp$,

$$u(p) = u_1(p_1) + \ldots + u_n(p_n).$$

It is easy to prove that the u_i must satisfy the same "linearity" property as u.

One can derive from Theorem 5.4 a statement on expected utility in a similar way as Corollary 5.3 follows from Theorem 5.2. We omit the details.

Other independence conditions for lexicographic utility representations have been discussed in Fishburn and LaValle (1992).

Suppose that X is a convex subset of Y, a finite–dimensional real vector space. We close this section by stating a characterization of lexicographic linear utility choice correspondences on X, as obtained recently by Clark (1993). To do this, we need to introduce the linear closure $\bar{V}$ of the revealed weak preference relation V defined in Section 4. Given $x, y \in X$, one sets $x \bar{V} y$ iff there exist $x_1, \ldots, x_n, y_1, \ldots, y_n \in X$ and positive $\lambda_1, \ldots, \lambda_n \in \mathbb{R}$ such that $x_i V y_i$ $(i = 1, \ldots, n)$ and $x - y = \sum_{i=1}^n \lambda_i (x_i - y_i)$. The choice correspondence Φ is said to satisfy the linear axiom of revealed preference if $x \bar{V} y \implies$ not $y V^* x$.

THEOREM 5.5 [Clark (1993)] A choice correspondence $\Phi : \beta \longrightarrow X$ is lexicographic linear utility rational iff it satisfies the linear axiom of revealed preference.

Since the set of lotteries on a finite outcome set is convex and finite-dimensional, as a consequence of Theorem 5.5 one can easily obtain a characterization of those choice correspondences (on the set of lotteries) induced by lexicographic expected utility maximization.

6   Lexicographic Subjective Expected Utility

The classical subjective expected utility theory for decision making under uncertainty established by Savage (1954) also admits a lexicographic version for the case when one drops the usual Archimedean axiom [LaValle and Fishburn

(1991, 1992, 1996), Fishburn and LaValle (1994)], in a spirit similar to that of the model presented in the preceding section. For simplicity, we will describe here the more restrictive approach of Blume, Brandenburger and Dekel (1991a), which follows Fishburn's (1982) version of the model due to Anscombe and Aumann (1963), and will be pursued in the next section in connection with equilibrium refinements of noncooperative games.

The model consists of a finite set of states Ω and a set of consequences C. Let $\wp$ be the set of all probability distributions with finite support (lotteries) on C. The set of acts is $\wp^\Omega$. Thus, an act is regarded as a function $x : \Omega \longrightarrow \wp$ assigning a lottery $x_\omega \in \wp$ to each possible state $\omega \in \Omega$. The decision maker has preferences over acts, represented by a complete preorder $\preceq$ on $\wp^\Omega$. The lexicographic expected utility considered by Blume, Brandenburger and Dekel (1991a) is expressed in terms of lexicographic probability systems, defined as K–tuples $\rho = (p_1, \ldots, p_K)$ of probability distributions on Ω for some integer K. Given a utility function $\bar{u} : \wp \to \mathbb{R}$ on the set of lotteries, the expected utility of an act $x \in \wp^\omega$ relative to the lexicographic probability system ρ is the K-dimensional vector

$$E(\tilde{u}, \rho, x) = \left(\sum_{\omega \in \Omega} p_k(\omega)\, \tilde{u}(x_\omega) \right)^K_{k=1}.$$

A subjective expected utility representation of this type requires the following axioms.

AXIOM OI (Objective Independence). $x \prec y$ implies $\alpha x + (1 - \alpha)z \prec \alpha y + (1 - \alpha)z$ and $x \sim y$ implies $\alpha x + (1 - \alpha)z \sim \alpha y + (1 - \alpha)z$ for all $x, y, z \in \wp^\Omega$ and $\alpha \in (0, 1)$.

AXIOM NT (Nontriviality). $x \prec y$ for some $x, y \in \wp^\Omega$.

To state the next axiom, we need to introduce conditional preferences. Given $S \subset \Omega$ and $x, y \in \wp^\Omega$, one defines $x \preceq_S y$ iff $(x_S, z_{-S}) \preceq (y_S, z_{-S})$ for some $z \in \wp^\Omega$, where the notation (x_S, z_{-S}) is used to represent the act $v \in \wp^\Omega$ such that $v_\omega = x_\omega$ if $\omega \in S$ and $v_{\omega'} = z_{\omega'}$ if $\omega' \in \Omega \backslash S$. We will abbreviate $\{\omega\}$ by writing simply ω.

AXIOM CA (Conditional Archimedean Property). For all $x, y, z \in \wp$ and $\omega \in \Omega$, $x \prec_\omega y \prec_\omega z$ implies $\beta x + (1 - \beta)z \prec_\omega y \prec_\omega \alpha x + (1 - \alpha)z$ for some $0 < \alpha < \beta < 1$.

This is a weakening of the usual Archimedean Property, required in the classical subjective expected utility representation obtained by Anscombe and Aumann (1963), because it is stated for $\prec$ instead of $\prec_\omega$.

One says that $S \subset \Omega$ is Savage–null if $x \sim_S y$ for all $x, y \in \wp^\Omega$.

AXIOM NSI (Non–null State Independence). $x \preceq_\omega y$ iff $x \preceq_{\omega'} y$ for all constant acts $x, y \in \wp^\Omega$ and all states $\omega, \omega' \in \Omega$ which are not Savage–null.

THEOREM 6.1 [Blume, Brandenburger and Dekel (1991a)] Let $\preceq$ be a complete preorder on $\wp^\Omega$. If axioms OI, NT, CA and NSI hold then there exist a nonconstant function $u : C \longrightarrow \mathbb{R}$ and a lexicographic probability system $\rho = (p_1, \ldots, p_K)$ on Ω such that $x \preceq y$ iff $E(\tilde{u}, \rho, x) \leq_L E(\tilde{u}, \rho, y)$ for all $x, y \in \wp^\Omega$, where $\tilde{u} : \wp \longrightarrow \mathbb{R}$ denotes the extension of u defined by $\tilde{u}(l) = \sum_{c \in C} u(c) l(c)$ for every lottery $l \in \wp$.

Furthermore, u is unique up to positive affine transformations. There is a minimal K less than or equal to the cardinality of Ω. Among lexicographic probability systems of minimal length K, $\rho = (p_1, \ldots, p_K)$ generates the same preferences as $\rho' = (p_1', \ldots, p_K')$ iff $\rho' = L\rho$, where ρ and ρ' are regarded as column vector functions and L is a lower triangular matrix with strictly positive diagonal elements. Finally, $p_k(S) = 0$ for all k iff S is Savage–null.

One can easily prove that any binary relation $\preceq$ on $\wp^\Omega$ admitting the lexicographic subjective expected utility representation of Theorem 6.1 is necessarily a complete preorder and satisfies axioms OI, NT, CA and NSI.

The interpretation of the lexicographic probability system ρ in the statement of Theorem 6.1 is that it represents the decision maker's belief about the true state of the world, according to a hierarchy structure: p_1 is the primary theory, p_2 is the secondary theory, and so on.

As already observed at the beginning of this section, the model just described is a particular case of the LaValle and Fishburn (1991, 1992, 1996) approach, where Archimedean axioms are almost entirely avoided thus leading to lexicographic expected utility on the constant acts and obtaining matrix probabilities which can be regarded as generalizing the vector probabilities of Theorem 6.1. These matrix probabilities are lexicographic nonnegativity preserving and therefore have the structure described in Theorem 3.6.

Lexicographic probability systems have their own interest beyond subjective expected utility theory. The following definition will lead us to consider conditioning on events with probability zero.

DEFINITION 6.2 A lexicographic probability system $\rho = (p_1, \ldots, p_K)$ on Ω has full support if for each $\omega \in \Omega$ there exists $k \in \{1, \ldots, K\}$ such that $p_k(\omega) > 0$.

DEFINITION 6.3 Let $\rho = (p_1, \ldots, p_K)$ be a lexicographic probability system on Ω and let S be a nonempty subset of Ω. The conditional lexicographic probability system given S is $\rho_S = (p_{k_1}(\cdot \mid S), \ldots, p_{k_L}(\cdot \mid S))$, where the indices $k_1 < \ldots < k_L$ are those $k \in \{1, \ldots, K\}$ for which $p_k(S) > 0$, and $p_{k_i}(\cdot \mid S)$ is given by the usual definition of conditional probability.

When axiom NSI is replaced by the following stronger axiom SI, conditional lexicographic probabilities represent conditional preferences, as shown in Theorem 6.4 below.

AXIOM SI (State Independence). $x \preceq_\omega y$ iff $x \preceq_{\omega'} y$ for all constant acts $x, y \in \wp^\Omega$ and all states $\omega, \omega' \in \Omega$.

THEOREM 6.4 [Blume, Brandenburger and Dekel (1991a)] Let $\preceq$ be a complete preorder on $\wp^\Omega$. If axioms OI, NT, CA and SI hold and u, ρ and $\tilde{u}$ are as in Theorem 6.1 then for any nonempty set $S \subset \Omega$ one has
$$x \preceq_S y \text{ iff } E(\tilde{u}, \rho_S, x) \leq_L E(\tilde{u}, \rho_S, y)$$
for all $x, y \in \wp^\Omega$.

Analogously to the observation following Theorem 6.1, any binary relation $\preceq$ on $\wp^\Omega$ admitting the representation of Theorem 6.4 is necessarily a complete preorder and satisfies axioms OI, NT, CA and SI.

7 Lexicographic Probabilities and Game Theory

The lexicographic order also plays a role in game theory. It appears, for instance, in the definition of the nucleolus, one of the main solution concepts for cooperative games [Schmeidler (1969)]. The literature on noncooperative games has also considered the possibility that the utilities be non–Archimedean or, in particular, lexicographic. Fishburn (1971/72) observed that a finite two–person zero–sum game with non–Archimedean utilities may lack equilibria and the players may have no minimax strategies. It may also happen that the players possess minimax strategies but they do not define an equilibrium of the game. However, Weyl (1950) provided a proof of Von Neumann's minimax theorem which did not require any Archimedean condition so that it applies also to games whose payoff matrix has its entries in a nonstandard model of the real numbers provided that the components of the mixed strategies are allowed to take values in the same model [see also Skala (1974)].

Blume, Brandenburger and Dekel (1991b) used lexicographic subjective expected utility (see Section 6) as a basis for equilibrium refinements of noncooperative games. In this approach, players' beliefs are lexicographic probability systems. We devote this section to describe this model.

A finite N–person game in normal form consists of N players, $i = 1, \ldots, N$, each of which has a finite set of pure strategies A^i and a utility function $u^i : \prod_{j=1}^{N} A^j \longrightarrow \mathbb{R}$. Player i's beliefs are described by a lexicographic probability system $\rho^i = (p_1^i, \ldots, p_{K^i}^i)$, for some integer K^i, on the set $A^{-i} = \prod_{j \neq i} A^j$. A collection $\mu = (\rho^1, \ldots, \rho^N)$ of beliefs, one for each player, is called a belief system. For player j, the expected payoff when he adopts strategy $b^j \in A^j$ and his beliefs are represented by ρ^j is the K^j–dimensional vector

$$E_j(\rho^j, b^j) = \left(\sum_{a^{-j} \in A^{-j}} p_k^j(a^{-j}) u^j(b^j, a^{-j}) \right)_{k=1}^{K^j}.$$

The set of mixed strategies of player i (that is, probability measures on A^i) will be denoted by $\Delta(A^i)$. The marginal on A^j of p_k^i, with $j \neq i$, will be represented by p_k^{ij}. We set $\rho^{ij} = (p_1^{ij}, \ldots, p_K^{ij})$.

DEFINITION 7.1 A strategy profile $\sigma = (\sigma^1, \ldots, \sigma^N) \in \prod_{j=1}^{N} \Delta(A^j)$ is a Nash equilibrium iff for all $i = 1, \ldots, N$ and $\tau = (\tau^1, \ldots, \tau^N) \in \prod_{j=1}^{N} \Delta(A^j)$:

$$\sum_{a=(a^1,\ldots,a^N) \in \prod_{j=1}^{N} A_j} \left(\prod_{j=1}^{N} \sigma^j(a^j) \right) u^i(a)$$

$$\geq \sum_{a=(a^1,\ldots,a^N) \in \prod_{j=1}^{N} A_j} \left(\prod_{j \neq i} \sigma^j(a^j) \right) \tau^i(a^i) u^i(a).$$

Thus, a Nash equilibrium is a strategy profile such that no player can increase expected utility by a unilateral change of strategy.

DEFINITION 7.2 Let μ be a belief system and $\sigma = (\sigma^1, \ldots, \sigma^N) \in \prod_{i=1}^{N} \Delta(A^i)$. The pair (μ, σ) is a lexicographic Nash equilibrium iff for all $i = 1, \ldots, N$ and $j \neq i$:
  (i) $p_1^{ij}(a^j) > 0$ implies $E_j(\rho^j, a^j) \geq_L E_j(\rho^j, b^j)$ for all $b^j \in A^j$;
  (ii) $p_1^i(a^{-i}) = \prod_{j \neq i} \sigma^j(a^j)$ for all $a^{-i} \in A^{-i}$.

Condition (i) says that player i assigns positive probability (in his first order belief) only to those pure strategies of player j that are lexicographically optimal in the sense of the expected utility relative to the belief system. Condition (ii) expresses the fact that first order beliefs are consistent with mixed strategies.

One can easily prove that a strategy profile σ is a Nash equilibrium iff (μ, σ) is a lexicographic Nash equilibrium for some belief system μ. Indeed, when $K^j = 1$ for each $j = 1, ..., N$, Definition 7.2 reduces to Definition 7.1. The interest of Definition 7.2 lies in that, by imposing appropriate conditions on the belief system μ, the associated Nash equilibria become perfect or proper. In this connection, recall that a strategy profile σ is a perfect equilibrium [Selten (1979)] if it is the limit as $\varepsilon \to 0$ of a sequence of Nash equilibria $\sigma(\varepsilon)$ in the modified game where each player is restricted to choosing a mixed strategy in the set $\Delta_\varepsilon(A^j) = \{\sigma^j \in \Delta(A^j) : \sigma^j(a^j) \geq \varepsilon$ for all $a^j \in A^j\}$, that is, each player must attach probability at least ε to each pure strategy whether or not it is a best response to the other players' mixed strategies. Also, recall that σ is a proper equilibrium [Myerson (1978)] if it is the limit as $\varepsilon \to 0$ of a sequence of Nash equilibria $\sigma(\varepsilon)$ in the modified game where each player j much attach a probability of at least ε to at least two pure strategies, a probability of at least ε^2 to a third pure strategy, then at least ε^3 to a fourth pure strategy and so on until every strategy is given a small positive probability. See also the game theory textbooks by Fudenberg and Tirole (1991) and by Osborne and Rubinstein (1994).

To characterize perfect and proper equilibria in terms of lexicographic Nash equilibria, we need some definitions.

DEFINITION 7.3 A belief system $\mu = (\rho^1, \dots, \rho^N)$ has full support iff each ρ^i $(i = 1, \dots, N)$ has full support.

DEFINITION 7.4 A belief system $\mu = (\rho^1, \dots, \rho^N)$ satisfies the Common Prior Assumption iff there exists one lexicographic probability system ρ on $\prod_{i=1}^N A^i$ such that each player's ρ^i is the marginal on A^{-i} of ρ.

The Common Prior Assumption implies that the beliefs of any two players over any other player coincide.

DEFINITION 7.5 A belief system $\mu = (\rho^1, \dots, \rho^N)$ satisfies strong independence iff for each ρ^i $(i = 1, \dots, N)$ there is a sequence $r^i(n) \in (0, 1)^{k-1}$ with $r^i(n) \longrightarrow 0$ such that $r^i(n) \square \rho^i$ is a product measure for every n, where the notation $r \square \rho$ represents the probability measure q_K obtained recursively according to $q_1 = p_K$, $q_j = (1 - r_{K-j+1})p_{K-j+1} + r_{K-j+1}q_{j-1}$ $(j = 2, \dots, K)$, for $r = (r_1, \dots, r_K) \in (0, 1)^{K-1}$ and $\rho = (p_1, \dots, p_K)$.

The strong independence condition is satisfied iff each ρ^i admits an equivalent probability measure taking values in a non–Archimedean ordered–field extension of $\mathbb{R}$ that is a product measure.

THEOREM 7.6 [Blume, Brandenburger and Dekel (1991b)] A strategy profile σ is a perfect equilibrium iff (μ, σ) is a lexicographic Nash equilibrium for some belief system μ that has full support and satisfies the Common Prior Assumption and strong independence.

The characterization of proper equilibria requires an additional condition, for which we introduce the following definitions.

DEFINITION 7.7 Player i believes that $b^j \in A^j$ is not infinitely more likely than $a^j \in A^j$, in symbols $a^j \geq_{\rho^{ij}} b^j$, iff $\alpha(\rho^{ij}(a^j)) \geq \alpha(\rho^{ij}(b^j))$, where $\rho^{ij}(a^j) = (p_1^{ij}(a^j), \ldots, p_{K^i}^{ij}(a^j))$ for any $a^j \in A^j$ and α denotes lexicographic index (see Definition 3.5).

DEFINITION 7.8 A belief system $\mu = (\rho^1, \ldots, \rho^N)$ respects preferences iff for all $i = 1, \ldots, N$ and $j \neq i$, $E_j(\rho^j, a^j) \geq_L E_j(\rho^j, b^j)$ for all $a^j, b^j \in A^j$ with $a^j \geq_{\rho^{ij}} b^j$.

The meaning of this condition is rather obvious, as it says that, when player j strictly prefers action b^j to action a^j, the belief of any other player i is that b^j is infinitely more likely than a^j.

THEOREM 7.9 [Blume, Brandenburger and Dekel (1991b)] A strategy profile σ is a proper equilibrium iff (μ, σ) is a lexicographic Nash equilibrium for some belief system μ that has full support, respects preferences and satisfies the Common Prior Assumption and strong independence.

In the same context of noncooperative games in normal form, Okada (1988), has introduced a notion of lexicographic domination of strategies in such a way that perfect equilibrium points are lexicographically undominated (and conversely in the case of two players). In a subsequent paper, Okada (1991) has extended this notion to extensive games in such a way that lexicographically undominated equilibrium points are subgame perfect in the case of extensive games with perfect recall.

A comparison between the lexicographic Nash equilibrium concept and the notion of sequential equilibrium for games in extensive form of Kreps and Wilson (1982) is made in Blume, Brandenburger and Dekel (1991b, p. 86).

Acknowledgments

This work has been partially supported by the Dirección General de Investigación Científica y Técnica (DGICYT), Project PB95–0679 and by the Comissionat per Universitats i Recerca de la Generalitat de Catalunya, Grant SGR96–75. I am very grateful to Peter J. Hammond for many useful suggestions leading to a substantial improvement of the presentation of this chapter. I also thank Andrew Vladimirov for some helpful bibliographical remarks as well as an anonymous referee for useful comments.

References

Anscombe, F. and Aumann, R. J. (1963). A Definition of Subjective Probability. *Annals of Mathematical Statistics*, 34:199–205.

Arrow, K. J. (1959). Rational Choice Functions and Orderings. *Economica*, 26:121–127.

Aumann, R. J. (1962). Utility Theory without the Completeness Axiom. *Econometrica*, 30:445–462.

Barberà, S. and Jackson, M. O. (1988). Maximin, Leximin and the Prospective Criterion. *Journal of Economic Theory*, 46:34–44.

Behringer, F. A. (1977). Lexicographic Quasiconcave Multiobjective Programming. *Zeitschrift für Operations Research*, 21:103–116.

Blume, L., Brandenburger, A., and Dekel, E. (1991a). Lexicographic Probabilities and Choice under Uncertainty. *Econometrica*, 59:199–205.

Blume, L., Brandenburger, A., and Dekel, E. (1991b). Lexicographic Probabilities and Equilibrium Refinements. *Econometrica*, 59:81–98.

Borwein, J. M. (1980). Lexicographic Multipliers. *Journal of Mathematical Analysis and Applications*, 78:309–327.

Cantor, G. (1895/1897). Beiträge zur Begründung der transfiniten Mengenlehre. *Mathematische Annalen*, 46/49:481–512/207–246.

Chipman, J. S. (1960). The Foundations of Utility. *Econometrica*, 28:193–224.

Chun, Y. (1989). Lexicographic Egalitarian Solution and Uncertainty in the Disagreement Point. *ZOR–Methods and Models of Operations Research*, 33: 259–266.

Chun, Y. and Peters, H. (1991). The Lexicographic Equal–Loss Solution. *Mathematical Social Sciences*, 22:151–161.

Clark, S. A. (1993). Revealed Preference and Linear Utility. *Theory and Decision*, 34:21–45.

Cuesta Dutari, N. (1943). Teoría decimal de los tipos de orden. *Revista Matemática Hispano–Americana*, 3:186–205, 242–268.

Cuesta Dutari, N. (1947). Notas sobre unos trabajos de Sierpiński. *Revista Matemática Hispano–Americana*, 7:128–131.

D'Aspremont, C. and Gevers, L. (1977). Equity and the Informational Basis of Collective Choice. *Review of Economics Studies*, 44:199–209.

Debreu, G. (1954). Representation of a Preference Order by a Numerical Function. In Thrall, R. M., Coombs, C. H., and Davis, R. L., editors, *Decision Processes*, pages 159–166. Wiley, New-York.

Deschamps, R. and Gevers, L. (1978). Leximin and Utilitarian Rules: A Joint Chararacterization. *Journal of Economic Theory*, 17:143–163.

Farkas, J. (1902). Über die Theorie der einfachen Ungleichungen. *Journal für die reine und angewandte Mathematik*, 124:1–24.

Fishburn, P. C. (1971). A Study of Lexicographic Expected Utility. *Management Science*, 17:672–678.

Fishburn, P. C. (1971/72). On Foundations of Game Theory: The Case of Non–Archimedean Utilities. *International Journal of Game Theory*, 1:65–71.

Fishburn, P. C. (1974). Lexicographic Orders, Utilities and Decision Rules: A Survey. *Management Science*, 20:1442–1471.

Fishburn, P. C. (1979). On the Nature of Expected Utility. In Allais, M. and Hagen, O., editors, *Expected Utility Hypotheses and the Allais Paradox*, pages 243–257. Reidel, Dordrecht.

Fishburn, P. C. (1980). Lexicographic Additive Differences. *Journal of Mathematical Psychology*, 21:191–218.

Fishburn, P. C. (1982). *The Foundations of Expected Utility*. Reidel, Dordrecht.

Fishburn, P. C. and LaValle, I. H. (1992). Multiattribute Expected Utility Without the Archimedean Axiom. *Journal of Mathematical Psychology*, 36: 573–591.

Fishburn, P. C. and LaValle, I. H. (1994). On Matrix Probabilities in Nonarchimedean Decision Theory. *Journal of Risk and Uncertainty*, 8:283–299.

Fishburn, P. C. and Roberts, F. S. (1978). Mixture Axioms in Linear and Multilinear Utility Theories. *Theory and Decision*, 9:161–171.

Fudenberg, D. and Tirole, J. (1991). *Game Theory*. M.I.T. Press, Cambridge, MA.

Gorokhovik, V. (1986). Dual Characteristics of Minimality in Preordered Vector Spaces. In *Internationale Tagung Mathematische Optimierung — Theorie und Anwendungen, Book of Abstracts*, pages 58–61, Eisenach.

Hammond, P. J. (1976). Equity, Arrow's Conditions, and Rawls' Difference Principle. *Econometrica*, 44:793–804.

Hausner, M. (1954). Multidimensional Utilities. In Thrall, R. C. C. and Davis, R., editors, *Decision Processes*, pages 167–180. Wiley, New York.

Hausner, M. and Wendel, J. G. (1952). Ordered Vector Spaces. In *Proceedings of the American Mathematical Society*, volume 3, pages 977–982.

Herstein, I. N. and Milnor, J. (1953). An Axiomatic Approach to Measurable Utility. *Econometrica*, 21:291–297.

Imai, H. (1983). Individual Monotonicity and Lexicographic Maxmin Solution. *Econometrica*, 51:389–401.

Isermann, H. (1982). Linear Lexicographic Optimization. *O.R. Spektrum*, 4:223–228.

Jamison-Waldner, R. E. (1982). A Perspective on Abstract Convexity: Classifying Alignments by Varieties. In Kay, D. C. and Breen, M., editors, *Convexity and Related Combinatorial Geometry*, pages 113–150. Marcel Dekker, New York.

Kannai, Y. (1963). Existence of a Utility in Infinite Dimensional Partially Ordered Spaces. *Israel Journal of Mathematics*, 1:229–234.

Klee, V. (1969). Separation and Support Properties of Convex Sets—A Survey. In Balakrishnan, A. V., editor, *Control Theory and the Calculus of Variations*, pages 235–303. Academic Press, New York.

Krause, U. (1995). Essentially Lexicographic Aggregation. *Social Choice and Welfare*, 12:233–244.

Kreps, D. and Wilson, R. (1982). Sequential Equilibria. *Econometrica*, 50:863–894.

LaValle, I. H. and Fishburn, P. C. (1991). Lexicographic State–Dependent Subjective Expected Utility. *Journal of Risk and Uncertainty*, 4:251–269.

LaValle, I. H. and Fishburn, P. C. (1992). State–Independent Subjective Expected Lexicographic Utility. *Journal of Risk and Uncertainty*, 5:217–240.

LaValle, I. H. and Fishburn, P. C. (1996). On the Varieties of Matrix Probabilities in Nonarchimedean Decision Theory. *Journal of Mathematical Economics*, 25:33–54.

Luce, R. D. (1978). Lexicographic Tradeoff Structures. *Theory and Decision*, 9:187–193.

Luptáčik, M. and Turnovec, F. (1991). Lexicographic Geometric Programming. *European Journal of Operational Research*, 51:259–269.

Martínez-Legaz, J. and Singer, I. (1988). The Structure of Hemispaces in $\mathbb{R}^n$. *Linear Algebra and Its Applications*, 110:117–179.

Martínez-Legaz, J. E. (1983). Exact Quasiconvex Conjugation. *Zeitschrift für Operations Research*, 27:257–266.

Martínez-Legaz, J. E. (1984). Lexicographical Order, Inequality Systems and Optimization. In Thoft-Christensen, P., editor, *System Modelling and Optimization*, pages 203–212. Springer, Berlin.

Martínez-Legaz, J. E. (1985). Some News Results on Exact Quasiconvex Duality. *Methods of Operations Research*, 49:47–62.

Martínez-Legaz, J. E. (1988a). Quasiconvex Duality Theory by Generalized Conjugation Methods. *Optimization*, 19:603–652.

Martínez-Legaz, J. E. (1988b). Lexicographical Order and Duality in Multi-objective Programming. *European Journal of Operational Research*, 33:342–348.

Martínez-Legaz, J. E. (1991). Characterizations of Efficient Solutions Under Polyhedrality Assumptions. *Zeitschrift für Operations Research*, 35:221–230.

Martínez-Legaz, J. E. and Singer, I. (1987a). Lexicographical Separation in $\mathbb{R}^n$. *Linear Algebra and Its Applications*, 90:147–163.

Martínez-Legaz, J. E. and Singer, I. (1987b). Surrogate Duality for Vector Optimization. *Numerical Functional Analysis and Optimization*, 9:547–568.

Martínez-Legaz, J. E. and Singer, I. (1990). Lexicographical Order, Lexicographical Index, and Linear Operators. *Linear Algebra and Its Applications*, 128:65–95.

Martínez-Legaz, J. E. and Singer, I. (1991). Compatible Preorders and Linear Operators on $\mathbb{R}^n$. *Linear Algebra and Its Applications*, 153:53–66.

Myerson, R. (1978). Refinements of the Nash Equilibrium Concept. *International Journal of Game Theory*, 1:73–80.

Narens, L. (1974). Measurement without Archimedean Axioms. *Philosophy of Science*, 41:374–393.

Narens, L. (1985). *Abstract Measurement Theory*. M.I.T. Press, Cambridge, MA.

Nieto, J. (1992). The Lexicographic Egalitarian Solution on Economic Environments. *Social Choice and Welfare*, 9:203–212.

Okada, A. (1988). Perfect Equilibrium Points and Lexicographic Domination. *International Journal of Game Theory*, 17:225–239.

Osborne, M. J. and Rubinstein, A. (1994). *A Course in Game Theory*. M.I.T. Press, Cambridge, MA.

Pattanaik, P. K. and Peleg, B. (1984). An Axiomatic Characterization of the Lexicographic Maximin Extension of an Ordering over a Set to the Power Set. *Social Choice and Welfare*, 1:113–123.

Savage, L. J. (1954). *The Foundations of Statistics*. Wiley, New York.

Schmeidler, D. (1969). The Nucleolus of a Characteristic Function Game. *SIAM Journal of Applied Mathematics*, 17:1163–1170.

Selten, R. (1975). Reexamination of the Perfectness Concept for Equilibrium Points in Extensive Games. *International Journal of Game Theory*, 4:25–55.

Sen, A. K. (1970). *Collective Choice and Social Welfare*. Holden-Day, San Francisco.

Sierpiński, W. (1949). Sur une propriété des ensembles ordonnés. *Fundamenta Mathematicae*, 36:56–67.

Singer, I. (1984). Generalized Convexity, Functional Hulls and Applications to Conjugate Duality in Optimization. In Hammer, G. and Pallaschke, D., editors, *Selected Topics in Operations Research and Mathematical Economics*, pages 49–79. Springer, New-York.

Skala, H. J. (1974). Nonstandard Utilities and the Foundation of Game Theory. *International Journal of Game Theory*, 3:67–81.

Skala, H. J. (1975). *Non–Archimedean Utility Theory*. Reidel, Dordrecht.

Szpilrajn, E. (1930). Sur l'extension de l'ordre partiel. *Fundamenta Mathematica*, 16:386–389.

Tversky, A. (1969). Intransitivity of Preferences. *Psychological Review*, 76:31–38.

Von Neumann, J. and Morgenstern, O. (1944). *Theory of Games and Economic Behavior*. Princeton University Press.

Weyl, H. (1950). Elementary Proof of a Minimax Theorem Due to Von Neumann. In Kuhn, H. and Tucker, A., editors, *Contributions to the Theory of Games I*, pages 19–25. Princeton University Press, Princeton.

10 UTILITY THEORY AND ETHICS

Philippe Mongin*
and Claude d'Aspremont**

*THEMA, Centre National de la Recherche Scientifique, and
Université de Cergy–Pontoise
**CORE, Université Catholique de Louvain

Contents

1	Introduction	373
2	Some Philosophical and Historical Clarifications	376
	2.1 Preliminaries	376
	2.2 Early Utilitarian Views: Utility Related to Pleasure and Pain	379
	2.3 Utility as a Measure of Actual Preference Satisfaction	382
	2.4 Utility and Well–Being: Critical Arguments	388
	2.5 Utility, Well–Being, and Social Ethics: Some Positive Arguments	394
3	Some Definitions and Concepts from Utility Theory	401
	3.1 Utility Functions in the Case of Certainty, and "Economic" Domains	401
	3.2 Von Neumann–Morgenstern Utility Functions	402
	3.3 Anscombe–Aumann Utility Functions	404
	3.4 Interpersonal Utility Differences	407
4	The Aggregative Setting with Interpersonal Comparisons of Utility	408
	4.1 The SWFL Framework	409

4.2   Invariance Axioms and Interpersonal Comparisons of Utility   411

4.3   Further Conditions on SWFL   413

4.4   Utilitarianism Versus Leximin   415

4.5   Further Rules for Social Evaluation. The Variable Population Case   419

4.6   Some Conceptual Problems of the Multi–Profile Approach   422

5   The Aggregative Setting with Choice–Theoretic Constraints   425

5.1   Harsanyi's Approach to Utilitarianism. The Aggregation Theorem   425

5.2   A SWFL Reconstruction of Harsanyi's Aggregation Theorem   429

5.3   Further Philosophical Comments on Harsanyi's Utilitarianism   432

5.4   The Aggregative Approach in the Case of Subjective Uncertainty   437

6   The Impartial Observer, the Original Position, and Fairness   444

6.1   Impartial–Observer Theories   444

6.2   State–of–Nature Theories and the "Original Position"   447

6.3   Harsanyi's Impartial Observer Theorem, and the Problem of "Extended Sympathy"   449

6.4   Rawls's "Original Position" and "Veil of Ignorance"   455

6.5   Alternative Notions of Fairness   459

6.6   Equality of Resources and Welfare   462

7   Concluding Comments   465

References   467

1   Introduction

The technical sense of "utility", as in "utility theory", can be traced back to the work of 18th century British empiricists and, of course, of 19th century utilitarians. These writers began to use the word in a sense different from the common sense meaning of "usefulness" but did not agree upon a clear–cut explicit or even implicit definition. The emergence of Paretian microeconomics in the first half of the 20th century, and the later developments of utility theory as a quasi–separate field of study, brought with them further connotations, so that despite its short history of technical use, the word "utility" is now richly ambiguous. As a result, the relevance of utility theory to ethics cannot be taken for granted without prior clarification.

Section 2 of this chapter attempts to provide the needed clarification. We begin by distinguishing two received notions of "utility" in the technical context: (i) pleasure and pain, and (ii) the satisfaction of the individual's *actual* preferences. We then enquire whether utility can represent more generally: (iii) the individual's well–being. All of the three interpretations of utility have been endorsed, at least implicitly, by some ethical theories. Today's predominant philosophical view is that (i) and (ii) are not relevant in an ethical context of application. We shall restate this critique, and examine whether it leaves room for an ethical application of the utility concept. If utility can fully represent (iii), it becomes a relevant concept to use by all those ethical systems in which well–being is the underlying notion of good. We shall emphasize one particular strategy to confirm that utility can indeed represent well–being. It consists in interpreting utility as measuring: (iv) the satisfaction of *rational and well–informed* preferences, and then arguing that this interpretation essentially coincides with (iii).

Once the semantic ground has been cleared, it becomes possible to discuss various applications of utility theory. Section 3 introduces definitions and notation. Sections 4, 5 and 6 then investigate the ethical consequences of imposing various axiomatic restrictions on the utility concept, such as the von Neumann–Morgenstern (VNM) axioms of risky choice, and the Savage (or related) axioms of uncertain choice. The importance of these standard constructions for investigating ethical theories can be defended most easily on the background of the last mentioned interpretation—i.e., (iv) above. If one insists on an ethically relevant notion of utility that makes crucial reference to the rational formation of preferences, one is naturally led to consider the ethical consequences of adopting the definitions of rationality provided by utility theory.

The present survey will be essentially restricted to the better known parts of the theory. Having adopted the classic distinction between three contexts of rational choice—i.e., certainty, risk, and uncertainty—we shall apply the following standard constructions to them: the theory of choice under certainty, as in consumer microeconomics; von Neumann–Morgenstern expected utility theory; and subjective expected utility theory, respectively.

This chapter will also be narrowed down for a different and perhaps less defensible reason. Except in the rather general Section 2, we shall most of the time restrict the problems of ethics to those of the proper foundations of collective life. We are keenly aware that a majority of ethical systems would reject this identification—Bentham's utilitarianism being arguably an exception. To mention a few standard doctrines, hedonism, perfectionism, eudemonism, and Kantianism are conceptions of *both* individual and social ethics. Accordingly, the connection between utility theory and ethics should be explored also at a strictly individual level. For example, the famous and unresolved question of whether or not individuals should entertain time–preferences can be interpreted as being, or at least involving, an ethical question, and has been discussed as such among utilitarian circles [see Parfit (1984)]. The content of individual preferences—e.g., time–preferences and egoism—as well as the various formal constraints that have been imposed on them—e.g., the maximization principle or the sure–thing postulate—raise significant ethical questions. These issues will hardly be addressed here. What will occupy the forefront are the issues of. distributive justice, and more generally those raised by *the evaluation of social states of affairs*. The expression "social ethics" provides a loose delineation of our subject matter.[1] In sum, we are concerned with the logic and normative strength of a particular class of value judgements. For expository purposes, it is convenient to attribute these judgements to some ideal "social evaluator" (or "observer") who may or may not be also a "social planner". This ambiguity is typical of welfare economics and social choice theory, on which we heavily rely in this chapter. These two fields deliver not just technical explorations of normative principles, but also broad guidelines for public decisions; they connect with both political philosophy and prescriptive economics. More often than not, the theories presented below do not resolve the ambiguity between the "evaluator" and the "planner".

Even granting the scope restrictions just discussed, the ethical connections of utility theory can be appraised in a variety of ways. This chapter will emphasize the distinction between the *aggregative setting*, on the one hand, and the *original position* and *impartial observer* devices, on the other. In either case, the aim is to determine the nature of the ethical observer's evaluation rule from (among other things) antecedent rationality constraints that have been imposed on the individuals' preferences or utility functions. An important point for dis-

---

[1] Some writers would use "morality" to refer to that part of ethics which is "other–regarding" (as against "self–regarding"). We do not adopt this terminology here, and use "moral" and "ethical" more or less interchangeably.

cussion within either framework is whether the ethical observer himself should be subjected to identical rationality constraints. In the aggregative setting, which is the topic of Sections 4 and 5, one or more axioms determine the functional relations holding between the individuals' relevant characteristics and the observer's. Section 4 reviews some ethically relevant concepts and results in the theory of "social welfare functionals" (SWFL), as expounded by Sen and others in 1970–1980. Section 5 elaborates on Harsanyi's Aggregation Theorem, the *ex ante* versus *ex post* debate in welfare economics, and the many results connected with these topics. Section 6 moves on to original position and impartial observer theories. The general device investigated in this section consists in identifying the ethical observer's preference, or utility, with those of the individuals when the latter are deprived of part of their information. Harsanyi's Impartial Observer Theorem and Rawls's "veil of ignorance" construction are the key references here. These and related theories provide an indirect derivation of ethical rules which is in some sense more constructive and concrete than the aggregation procedures of Sections 4 and 5. Both the aggregative and original position or impartial observer types of analysis have received extensive treatment in the literature, so that we might perhaps be excused for not offering an exhaustive survey.[2] As to the distinction between the aggregative theories of Section 4 and Section 5, respectively, it depends in part on the chosen conceptual and technical frameworks, in part on the underlying information context (i.e., pure certainty in the former, and risk or uncertainty in the latter).

Most of the work surveyed in this chapter involves the philosophically questionable thesis of *welfarism*—i.e., that individual utility values contain all the information required to derive collective evaluation rules. This thesis has come under increasing criticism in recent years, notably in the wake of Rawls and Sen. New constructions have emerged that either make no reference at all to the utility concept or (more usually) employ it just as a subordinate device. We shall echo this recent debate in virtually every section of this chapter but more particularly in Section 2, which states a qualified defence of welfarism.

---

[2]The recent years have witnessed book–length presentations of collective choice theory and normative economics broadly speaking. To date, Fleurbaey's (1995) is the most comprehensive. Binmore's (1994), Kolm's (1995), Moulin's (1988, 1995) and Roemer's (1996) also contain useful material. Hausman and McPherson (1996) provide a non–technical introduction to part of the field. The philosophical background of this chapter is covered in Singer's (1991) and Canto–Sperber's (1996) encyclopaedias of ethics.

2   Some Philosophical and Historical Clarifications

2.1   Preliminaries

This section surveys several influential interpretations of the utility concept, in order to see whether the latter can be made relevant to social ethics. The discussion will be organized around three notions of utility. The first is utility as related to the individual's pleasure and pain, a notion introduced by 19th century utilitarians (see Section 2.2). The second notion is utility as a measure of the individual's preference satisfaction, as in most of 20th century economic theory (see Section 2.3). We then inquire whether utility can represent the individual's welfare or well–being, a third and more general interpretation which is arguably more relevant (see Section 2.4). To prepare the ground for the discussion, some philosophical terminology must first be introduced.

We need the classic distinction between two types of ethical theories, *teleological* theories on the one hand, and *deontological* ones on the other. This distinction is usually understood in terms of the two concepts that are perhaps most basic to ethical reasoning at large, i.e., the *right* and the *good*. In teleological theories the good has conceptual priority over the right. Typically, they define what it means for a thing or a state of affairs to be good, and then what it means for an act or a life to be morally right. As Rawls (1971, p. 25) insists, a crucial point is that "in a teleological theory, the good is defined *independently* from the right". A possibly no less crucial point is that in such a theory, no considerations other than the good contribute to the definition of the right, i.e., the latter can be *entirely* derived in terms of the former. Consequently, nonteleological theories are exactly those which either dispute that there can be an ethically relevant independent definition of the good, or else do not dispute that but introduce considerations other than the good in order to determine their concept of rightness. Nonteleological ethical doctrines are commonly referred to as deontological. This terminology conveys the fact that nonteleological ethics generally emphasizes the notion of a duty or a moral obligation.

Since at least Kant's (1785, 2nd section) classic discussion, the example of promise–keeping has been used to illustrate the contrast between deontological and teleological views of morality. Following a typically deontological analysis, when we say that it is wrong to break promises, we mean that it is *intrinsically* wrong to do so. This moral judgement derives—or so the argument goes—from the correct understanding of the rightness/wrongness distinction. It is supposed to be independent of whether or not promise–keeping is a good thing (and in particular, of whether or not it leads to good consequences). Following the equally banal, though opposite interpretation, which is held by many teleologists, we predicate that the action of promise–keeping is morally right just because it is good for society under normal circumstances. Note emphatically that the conflict between teleological and nonteleological views is compatible with the endorsement of one and the same maxim of action.[3] Here, as in many other relevant applications, ethical disagreements relate to the proper way of founding commonsense morality. It is however not difficult to conceive of particular cases in which deontologically oriented and teleologically oriented moralists would give conflicting recommendations. The most famous representative of the former school, Kant, insists that promises should be kept in all and every circumstances, whereas moralists of the latter school typically make exceptions to the rule (i.e., whenever the consequences of following the rule involve a net harm rather than net benefit).

Teleological ethics is best represented by utilitarianism, a doctrine which will receive much attention in this chapter. Roughly speaking, classical utilitarianism is associated with the views that: (i) pleasure is the relevant concept of the individual's good; (ii) the right action is that which maximizes the total sum of individual amounts of good. By and large, contemporary utilitarianism has faithfully maintained principle (ii), while often rejecting (i) in favour of alternative definitions of the individual's good. Adherence to (ii) should be qualified in view of the distinction between *act–utilitarianism* and *rule–utilitarianism*. Strictly speaking, (ii) is the act–utilitarian's maxim, whereas the rule–utilitarian's would read as follows: (ii') the right action is that which follows from the rule maximizing the total sum of individual amounts of good.[4] Utilitarianism is a pervasive doctrine, but teleological ethics has a much wider coverage as well as deeper historical roots. Plato's *Republic*, and more strikingly, Aristotle's *Nichomachean Ethics* count as the historical sources of teleological ethics at large.

Kant's practical philosophy is the classic example of deontological ethics. This tradition too has deep historical roots: Kantianism has often been described as a systematic and laicized version of Christian ethics.[5] Following the *Groundwork of the Metaphysics of Morals* (1785), the defining conditions for the right action are, for one, that it accords to duty, and for another, it is

---

[3]"Maxim of action" will be used here in the Kantian sense of the subjective principle underlying the action; see the *Critique of Practical Reason* (1788) and the comments by Verneaux (1973, 2, pp. 177–178).
[4]This classic distinction permeates the utilitarian tradition. Harrod (1936) and Harsanyi (1977c) endorse rule utilitarianism. Brandt (1958, 1992), Lyons (1965), and Hare (1981) have discussed it. Smart (1973) dismisses rule utilitarianism by claiming that when properly understood, it reduces to act utilitarianism.
[5]Kant's Categorical Imperative, to be discussed below, is distinct from, but definitely related to the Golden Rule of Jewish and Christian Ethics: "What you dislike don't do to others; that is the whole Torah" [B.T. Schabbat 31a, cited in Singer ed. (1991, p. 87)], "Always treat others as you would like them to treat you" (Matt. 7:12).

taken for no other reason than its conformity with duty (it is performed "out of duty"). For instance, if I keep my promise because I feel that false promising would have disadvantageous consequences, my action satisfies the former condition, but not the latter, and thus does not count as a right action. On Kant's view, then, the nature of motives is crucial to the moral judgement. Since outward behaviour is uninformative, and motives are largely inscrutable, it must be extremely difficult to ascertain whether or not a particular act is right. In the *Critique of Practical Reason* (1788) Kant himself had to recognize that perhaps not any single right action had ever been performed since the beginning of mankind, and many critics have eventually rejected his ethical system as being aloof from human concerns and virtually impracticable. At any rate, Kant's approach very clearly illustrates the priority of the concepts of right and duty in nonteleological ethics.

Some of Kant's conceptions have proved remarkably influential, even among non–Kantian philosophers.[6] The *Groundwork* is justly famous for introducing the following test for something to count as a moral principle: the maxim of an action is a moral principle only if it is *universalizable*. This condition is contained in the so–called Categorical Imperative: "Act only on the maxim through which you can at the same time will that it be a universal law". To elaborate again on the previous example, actions resulting from the maxim of promising falsely fail the universality test, because it is impossible to "will this maxim as a universal law". To break promises systematically has the effect of destroying trust, without which the very notion of promise becomes meaningless. Crucially, the Categorical Imperative does not only demand that we formulate some universal principle under which the particular act–description can be subsumed, but also that the "covering" principle be, for one, free from any contradiction, and for another, related to the agent's actual motive. We will mention examples of non–Kantian theories in which motives play no role but at least the non–contradiction requirement is kept, and even strongly emphasized (see 6.1 on Hare's "universal prescriptivism" and Harsanyi's reinterpretation of Kant). The *Groundwork* also states the Categorical Imperative in the following alternative form: "treat humanity in your own person, or in the person of any other, never simply as a means but always at the same time as an end". This Formula of the End in Itself makes respect (for oneself as well as others) a condition for the right action. Like the above mentioned Formula of Universal Law, it has exerted considerable influence. It indirectly suggests an appeal to

---

[6]This paragraph discusses only the influence of Kant's ethics. Picavet (1996) has recently uncovered another connection between Kant's philosophy and the subject matter of this chapter. He argues that several important themes in Bayesian decision theory are foreshadowed in the first *Critique*.

consent on which some contemporary theories are explicitly based (see Sections 6.1 and 6.2).

There are modern examples of theories in social ethics which are deontological, or at least clearly nonteleological. Rawls repeatedly claims that his own doctrine, "justice as fairness", prioritizes the right over the good (e.g., 1971, p. 451). Accordingly, it should be counted as a nonteleological doctrine. This holds regardless of the fact that the notion of the individual's good, as defined by his own ends and pursuits, is pervasive in Rawls's *Theory of Justice*. As a further illustration, Nozick's (1974, pp. 28–29) conception of "moral constraints" versus "moral goals" is best ranked among the deontological theories. After many others, Nozick is particularly concerned with protecting the exercise of *rights*, in the sense of the individual's rights to property and other "natural rights". A case can be, and was indeed sometimes, made for individual rights along the teleological line that they serve the collective good. But this is not the deontologist's argument. Rather, he would claim that rights are primitive concepts, and their recognition is to be viewed as a "side–constraint" (Nozick's expression) on any social arrangements.[7]

Utility theory plays a more important role in the context of teleological than of nonteleological ethics. This privileged connection emerges from the early developments of the field, since the rudiments of modern utility theory date back to classical utilitarianism.

2.2 Early Utilitarian Views: Utility Related to Pleasure and Pain

In daily parlance "utility" and "usefulness" are near synonyms.[8] Thus, "utility" refers to the property of actually serving, or of being able to serve, an end or purpose. Like "usefulness", "utility" is normally predicated of concrete things; but it can also be employed for persons, actions or states of affairs whenever they are envisaged from the viewpoint of an end they serve. When we say that a thing is useful, we presumably mean that it does not only serve an idle purpose: the commonsense notion of utility seems to imply the view that some ends are relevant and some are not. Also, the property referred to as "utility", in the sense of usefulness, often conflicts with pleasurableness. This much is implied by the French cliché: "joindre l'utile à l'agréable".

---

[7]Sen (1982) discusses Nozick's notion of right as side–constraints while defending his own conception of rights.

[8]See for instance *Webster's New Dictionary of Synonyms*. Importantly, English is exceptional in having two words. Both "utility" and "usefulness" are translated into a single word in French, German or Italian ("utilité", "Nützlichkeit", "utilità"). This linguistic fact has attracted attention since the early days of utilitarianism. The duality of "utility" and "usefulness" in ordinary English has no doubt facilitated the separation of technical and nontechnical uses of the utility concept, but it has also created a semantic problem of its own.

By and large, the commonsense meaning of utility prevailed in ethical and political philosophy until utilitarians began to employ this word in a special sense. Bentham's early writings, such as the *Introduction to the Principles of Morals and Legislation* (1789), signal a major change in use. We shall argue that early utilitarianism manifests a crucial shift in emphasis—since with Bentham, utility becomes the foundation of a whole system—but only a partial shift in meaning.

Here is the beginning of the *Introduction*:

"Nature has placed mankind under the governance of two sovereign masters, *pain* and *pleasure*. It is for them alone to point out what we ought to do, as well as to determine what we shall do. On the one hand the standard of right and wrong, on the other the chain of causes and effects, are fastened to their throne ... The *principle of utility* recognises this subjection, and assumes it for the foundation of that system, the object of which is to rear the fabric of felicity by the hands of reason and of law" (1789, pp. 1–2).

Since pleasure and utility are normally viewed as noncoincident, and even divergent concepts, there is a definite semantic shift in these famous lines. But in another crucial respect, Bentham does *not* depart from the commonsense meaning of "utility": he employs it to refer to a particular instrumental property of things—i.e., that they serve the purpose of producing pleasure or avoiding pain. Consider Bentham's definition in the same passage (ib., p. 2): "By utility is meant that property in any object, whereby it tends to produce benefit, advantage, pleasure, good, or happiness". This and many other supporting passages show that Bentham employs "utility" in the sense of "usefulness", but with a twist.[9] Contrary to the popular reconstruction among historians of economics, he does not identify "utility" and "pleasure" directly with each other. These words refer to mutually related but distinct concepts: a subjective feeling, on the one hand; a property of things, acts, or states of affairs, on the other.

Whenever utility is conceived of as a property of things, it becomes an *objective* concept in the various accepted senses of this word.[10] Thus understood, it has to do with the relation of man in general—instead of some particular individual—to external objects. It would then hardly make sense to predicate utility of people, as in today's economists' phrase: "Given a consumer x endowed with a utility function ...". It follows that the problem of interpersonal comparisons of utility, which will be an acute one in the later subjective value theories, hardly arises in Bentham's framework. To illustrate this, consider the

---

[9]The present interpretation follows Broome's (1991b). See also Little (1950, p. 7): "Utility was a power in objects which would normally create satisfaction".
[10]This paragraph and the next are based on Mongin (1995b).

passage from the *Pannomial Fragments*,[11] in which he anticipates the "law of diminishing marginal utility". This passage shows that Bentham understands functional reasoning, as well as the mathematical property of a decreasing first derivative. However, Bentham's function here is not a utility function in the sense of subjective value theories. Rather, it is a money–to–pleasure mapping, and crucially, this mapping is *not* indexed by individuals.

No doubt, the misunderstanding that Bentham's utility *is* pleasure minus pain was fostered by the fact that he endows the pleasure and pain concepts with a rich numerical structure, as in contemporary utility theories. Here again, however, one should be careful to avoid retrospective misunderstandings. Schumpeter's (1954, p. 409) claim that Bentham's "felicitic calculus" lays down the essentials of 20th-century value theory is inaccurate. For one thing, Bentham explicates pleasure and pain in terms of several (viz., seven) dimensions or "circumstances" (1789, Chapter 4). He borrows from Beccaria's *Dei delitti e delle pene* (1764) the basic distinction between intensity, duration, certainty, and proximity, and he complicates it with a further distinction of his own between fecundity, purity, and extent (i.e., the number of persons to whom the pleasure or pain extends). Bentham normally does not assume that there is a complete system of exchange rates between them. That is to say, his analysis of pleasure and pain remains truly pluridimensional and partly qualitative. For another thing, Bentham repeatedly emphasizes that material gains have different psychological consequences from material losses.[12] To formalize this claim, one could possibly resort to the following nonstandard assumption in the style of Kahneman and Tversky (1979): the net pleasure aggregate is a function of net variations in, rather than absolute levels of, current wealth, and this function exhibits different concavity properties on gains and losses.

To investigate the later utilitarians' work in any detail would lead beyond the scope of this chapter. Suffice it to say that their analysis manifests a general trend towards simplification. The semantic shift in the use of the word "utility" is already complete in the following excerpt from John Stuart Mill:

"Those who know anything about the matter are aware that every writer, from Epicurus to Bentham, who maintained the theory of utility, meant by it, not something to be contradistinguished from pleasure, but *pleasure itself, together with exemption from pain*" (1861, Chapter 2, p. 5, our emphasis).

Even more obviously, in Jevons (1871) and Edgeworth (1881), "utility" stands for "pleasure" rather than for the "tendency of objects to produce pleasure".

---

[11] In Bowring (1838, vol. 33, pp. 228–229). For a discussion of this important passage, see Halévy (1901–1904, I, pp. 83–84) and Stigler (1965, Chapter 5).

[12] This insight played a crucial role in the early utilitarians' conservative assessment of property rights and income distribution. On the political economy of early utilitarianism, see the classic discussions by Stephen (1901), Halévy (1901–1904), and Viner (1949).

Contemporary readers have become so accustomed to this definition, even to reject it, that they might overlook the gap between them and the early utilitarians' still colloquial understanding of utility.

A further accompanying simplification in the late utilitarians' work is related to the metric of pleasure and pain. In fact, Bentham never consistently used his distinction between seven "circumstances". Most of his reasonings in penal theory can be reconstructed by restricting attention to intensity, duration, certainty and proximity (the two of which can be identified with each other), and extent. Even this simplified list has its conceptual problems; along with the search for tractable physical analogies, this might explain why Jevons and Edgeworth just retained the two dimensions of "intensity" and "time". Moreover, late utilitarians lost interest in Bentham's insight that pain and pleasure had distinctive measurement properties.[13]

2.3   Utility as a Measure of Actual Preference Satisfaction

Following the most popular interpretation among 20th century writers, utility is a measure of actual preference satisfaction. "Actual" is meant to contrast the individual's preference underlying his behaviour with his rationally formed preferences. This interpretation underlies standard texts in economic theory, and pervades other social sciences as well as philosophy. Most of the time, it seems to be regarded as a stipulation rather than a substantial claim, and it is not stated very clearly. It can be made precise in a number of different ways but the crucial point that all these formulations share is this: the utility of a thing or an action reflects the extent to which that thing or action is preferred to others, and has no meaning beyond that. Thus, the modern technical sense of "utility" not only excludes the commonsense notion of utility as usefulness, but also supersedes the old technical sense of utility as being related to pleasure and pain. More generally, the modern sense conflicts with any conception which would take the utility concept as primitive. This rejection of established interpretations has led some to suggest that "utility", as in "utility theory" or "utility function", is just a misnomer, a confusing remainder from 19th century economics. What is important is that numerical values can be attached to objects in a way expressive of the individual's preferences between these objects. What matters in "utility function" is the second word, not the first.

---

[13] J.S. Mill's multi–dimensional conception of pleasure (and derivatively, utility) strongly departs from Bentham's. Mill is famous for claiming that pleasures have different *kinds*, as well as different *intrinsic values*, a conception which has often been rebutted as being inconsistent with utilitarianism. On this issue, see, e.g., Riley (1988). Sen (1980–81) compares different senses in which utility can be said to be "plural".

Since it is claimed to be the true primitive, the notion of preference is in need of explication. In ordinary parlance, the word refers to a wide range of subjective comparisons between objects: I prefer Burgundy to Bordeaux wines, a studio in Paris to a house in Paris (Texas), an adventurous to a quiet life, peace to war, etc. My tastes, as well as my goals, interests and values, might contribute to explaining why I prefer x to y. Nothing in the ordinary linguistic use appears to exclude that I prefer x to y from one point of view (for instance my tastes today), and y to x from another point of view (for instance my tastes tomorrow, or my permanent values). Although this has been suggested by some philosophers, it does not seem to be a matter of definition that my preferences comply with a global structure. Notice also that the objects that are compared with each other can be of many kinds. I can entertain preferences over states of affairs and things, as well as over actions. Hence, there is no privileged connection between preferring and choosing, at least if one understands choice as action rather than just as a determination to act.

Here as elsewhere, economists have shifted the ordinary meaning of words, and to some extent have become unaware of the shift. For one, today's economists put in it more structure than is normally implied. They assume that there is a preference *scale* underlying (and perhaps causing) the individual's preferential comparisons. What this scale exactly consists of is a matter for technical investigations, but all economists agree that it is structured and enjoys some form of permanence. Significantly, "the agent's preferences" is increasingly used to abbreviate "the agent's preference scale", i.e., the same word is used to refer both to the comparisons and their explanatory factor. For another, preferences in the economists' sense have to do with *choices between objects or actions*; they would not normally consider preferences between states of affairs in general. This double change is apparent in the following excerpt from Hicks (1956, pp. 17–18):

"We have to make some assumption about the principles governing (the consumer's) behaviour. The assumption of behaviour according to a scale of preferences comes in here as the simplest hypothesis (...) What I mean by action according to a scale of preferences is the following. The ideal consumer (...) chooses that alternative, out of the various alternatives open to him, which he most prefers, or ranks most highly. In one set of market conditions he makes one choice, in others other choices; but the choices he makes always express the same ordering, and must therefore be consistent with one another."[14]

---

[14] At least, Hicks is careful enough not to conflate "preference" with "scale of preference". Some of the philosophers' technical elaborations of the preference concept are more faithful to ordinary language connotations than are the economists'. For instance, Jeffrey's (1965) system defines preferences and utility over *logical propositions*, and is therefore capable of encompassing preferences, typically over states of affairs, which are unrelated to choices.

The notion of preference exemplified by this passage goes along with the methodological conviction that the theoretician should not take a position on the content of preferences, but only on their formal or structural properties. Another deep–seated conviction among 20th century economists is that preferences are specific to the particular individual, so that interpersonal comparisons appear to be inherently problematic. In sum, the standard doctrine of preference is at the same time *formalistic* and *relativistic*. It is against this conceptual background that one should appreciate the polemics against utilitarianism that are typical of early expositions of modern economics. Since preferential behaviour, in the formal conception, does not have to be pleasure–oriented, the utility theory of Bentham and his followers has been rejected as being all too specific. Also, the ease with which 19th century utilitarians take for granted that preference intensities are identical from one individual to another has aroused puzzlement and irritation, given the prevailing relativism. Among others, Robbins (1932) and Schumpeter (1954) are emphatic on the rejection of utilitarianism, both at the individual and the collective levels.[15]

The preference satisfaction view of utility can be traced back to Pareto. In the *Cours d'économie politique* (1896–7) and the *Manuel* (1909) he made it clear that utility is a formal concept, although he expressed this in a psychologistic language which sounds old–fashioned to today's readers. The most important feature of his conception is that he does not regard utility as being *itself* a feeling (or any mental state): utility is one step remote from its psychological substratum, *la sensation*. Pareto was equally clear about the relativistic nature of the utility concept. The *Manuel* introduces the celebrated notion of an optimum in a purely technical way, leaving the philosophical interpretations open.[16] But it distinguishes clearly between intra– and interpersonal comparisons of satisfactions, and emphasizes that the latter belong to an underdeveloped area of social sciences [see (1909, p. 149)]. The Paretian conception is perhaps most clearly stated in the passage in which he contrasts *utilité* in the ordinary sense with *utilité économique* (or *ophélimité*). The former, it is claimed, is concerned with the relation of mankind to external objects and has therefore an objective sta-

---

[15]The former insisted that utility theory should be rid of "the accidental deposit of the historical association of Economics with Utilitarianism" (1932, p. 141). The latter somewhat aggressively condemned "the unholy alliance between economics and Benthamite philosophy" (1954, p. 831). Similar complaints underlie the contributions of the "new welfare economics" in the 1930's. Most of the writings of the time betray a confusion between the *utilitarian type* of interpersonal comparisons of utility and the *general* possibility of making such comparisons.

[16]See Appendix 89 on *Maximum d'ophélimité* (1909, pp. 617–619). This primarily mathematical passage is compatible with virtually any conception of utility, which might have been a source of conceptual misunderstandings. In his *Traité de sociologie générale* (1917–1919) Pareto is more explicit about the meaning of a collective optimum.

tus; the latter is concerned with the particular individual under consideration and is therefore irreparably subjective (1909, p. 157).

Pareto makes limited use of the preference concept.[17] It was left for later writers of his school first to clarify, second to formalize it, as the structural feature that accounts for the individual's choice activity. Hicks's prewar studies of consumer theory and his *Value and Capital* (1939) might signal its first systematic occurrence as an *explicans* of utility. At a later stage, Arrow's *Social Choice and Individual Values* (1951) popularized the formalism of binary relations, and it is probably only then that preference was fully recognized as a distinctive technical entity. The fact that preference can be endowed with a mathematical structure no less precise than that of utility has had far–reaching consequences on developments in the field. Today's utility theory is essentially concerned with establishing *representation theorems*, i.e., equivalences that connect various properties of the preference relation with numerical properties of the "representing" utility functions.[18] The technical turn of the theory approximately coincided with the conquest of its autonomy. The rather large body of representation theorems and related results that have become available by now goes far beyond the theoretical needs of microeconomics. So it is more appropriately referred to as *decision* or *choice theory*, a relabelling which conveys the broad scope of application and avoids the misleading allusion to utility.[19]

Before closing this retrospective we need to emphasize that the actual preference satisfaction interpretation of utility is more general than two views with which it has often been associated: (i) the view that utility is a purely ordinal concept, and (ii) revealed preference theory. Concerning (i), the Paretians are famous for being critical not only of the strong utilitarian assumption that utility differences are *inter*personally comparable, but also of the weaker assumption that they are *intra*personally meaningful. Definitionally, this amounts to denying that utility functions can be "cardinal". All the information they convey is about the ordering of alternatives: they are just "ordinal". This conclusion was endorsed by Arrow in his 1951 book; it is still very influential

---

[17]Texts in history of economics perhaps underrate this fact. In the next paragraph our (all too brief) account departs from standard historiography on another score: we emphasize that the modern conception of preference is more general than both "ordinalism" and revealed preference theory. Compare, with, e.g., Blaug (1980), or Screpanti and Zamagni (1993).

[18]The abstract structure of representation theorems is investigated in Krantz, Luce, Suppes and Tversky (1971). Under the name "measurement theory", these authors have developed mathematical tools to analyze the relations holding between qualitative (i.e., set–theoretic) structures and the numbers that represent them. The resulting algebra can be applied to problems in physical measurement as well as to the representation theorems that are specific to utility theory. For an introduction, see Suppes (1981).

[19]Arrow [e.g. (1984, 3, p. 56)] discusses this terminological change.

among economists. It should be clear that its conflation with the view that utility measures actual preference satisfaction is a matter of historical coincidence, not of logic. It is perfectly possible to adhere to the latter view while claiming a cardinal interpretation for the utility function. This position is perhaps best understood in terms of Suppes and Winet's (1955) axiomatic construction. These authors state axiomatic conditions on preference relations that give a meaning to the notion of preference differences (e.g., I prefer x to y more strongly than I prefer w to z), and then show that these conditions are equivalent to the existence of a cardinal utility representation. Prominent writers like Allais (1953) [see also Allais and Hagen (1994)] or Harsanyi (1977b) appear to adhere to both a cardinal interpretation *and* the standard representation–of–preference view of utility. Their conception seems to be implicitly grounded in the Suppes–Winet axiomatization. Section 5 will further elaborate on Harsanyi's cardinalism.[20]

A somewhat related warning applies to (ii). As expounded by Samuelson (1938), revealed preference theory is an attempt to extract the empirically testable content of Paretian consumer theory and axiomatize it in terms of relevant observable concepts. The (supposedly observable) "revealed preference relation" is the building block in Samuelson's reconstruction. More broadly, and somewhat loosely, revealed preference theory is the methodological claim that the preference concept receives its meaning from, and is completely expressed in, the agent's choices between objects. The standard conception, as exemplified above by Hicks, says that preference is the factor underlying the individual's actual choices. This is an altogether different claim from that of revealed preference theory. Actually, the two claims are not only different but openly conflict with each other. In the standard conception, preference has an existence of its own and assumes conceptual (and perhaps causal) priority relative to choice; in revealed preference theory, only choice exists in a substantial sense, and preference is just an abbreviative concept for the latter. Again, it is a matter of coincidence if some writers on economics or choice theory make the simultaneous claims that utility represents the individual's actual preferences *and* that these preferences are just another name for the individual's choices. Even when it is assumed that actions are the only objects of preference, which we said earlier is a significant restriction, the former claim does *not* logically imply the latter.[21]

---

[20] The conception of cardinal *preference* suggested here should be contrasted with the following other two positions: (i) cardinal *utility* makes sense but cardinal preference does not, so that cardinalism can be defined only if utility is the primitive concept; (ii) neither cardinal preference nor cardinal utility makes sense. As an example of (i), see Loomes and Sugden (1982). Position (ii) is the more common of the two.

[21] The technical side and analytical history of revealed preference theory are covered in Chipman et al. (1971). Sen (1973a) provides a thorough critical discussion of revealed preference theory in the broad methodological sense.

It is important to realize that actual preference satisfaction is the notion of utility underlying contemporary welfare economics. The object of welfare economics is to rank economic states of affairs, in particular those involving distributional consequences, public goods, and state provisions, in terms of "better" or "worse". To do so, the discipline needs a concept of good: officially, it is "welfare" or "well–being", presumably in some appropriately restricted interpretation. Since Pigou's pioneering *Economics of Welfare* (1920), specialists in the field have generally emphasized that they were concerned only with "economic" well–being. Abstracting from the (non–trivial) problem created by this restriction, it would appear that welfare economists should interpret utility functions as measuring individual welfare or well-being (in this chapter we shall not attempt to distinguish between these two words). Some important papers in the field suggest that this is indeed the case: for instance, Lange's (1942) classic piece on the computation of Pareto optima.[22] But even if individual welfare or well–being is theoretically at the centre of welfare economists' concerns, they are nearly silent about what this notion consists of. At least after Paretian economics established its grip on the field, the definition of utility effectively used in welfare economics, as against the official definition, went in terms of actual preference satisfaction—i.e., the very same definition as that which underlies *positive* theorizing.

A respected textbook in its time, Graaff's, resolved the tension between the two notions of utility by identifying them *by way of stipulation*:

"a person's welfare map is defined to be identical with his preference map— which indicates how he would choose between different situations, if he were given the opportunity for choice. To say that his welfare would be higher in *A* than in *B* is thus no more than to say that he would choose *A* rather than *B*, if he were allowed to make the choice" (1957, p. 5).

Modern treatments are more cautious, but the conceptual difficulty remains. What Graaff made part of a definition, Boadway and Bruce explicate more lucidly as an informal, important and questionable postulate, as a "value judgement" (1984, p. 8). They also suggest that the relevant starting point of welfare economics is not so much objective welfare as "the household's view of welfare" (ibid.). This seems to be how it should be stated: welfare economics *assumes* that the the relevant agents' conceptions of well–being are conveyed by a de-

---

[22] He states that "welfare economics is concerned with the conditions which determine the total economic welfare of a community". Throughout his paper, Lange identifies "utility" with "welfare". In particular, he reinterprets utilitarianism as being that doctrine which equates "total welfare" with the sum of individual "welfares", and rejects it on the basis of this interpretation.

scription of their actual preferences. This is a strongly loaded claim, and it is undefended within welfare economics itself.[23]

2.4   Utility and Well–Being: Critical Arguments

Is utility theory relevant to social ethics applications? In this subsection we shall review some recent arguments, in particular by Rawls and Sen, to the effect that it is, at best, very little relevant. Some of these arguments assume a teleological framework in which the good is equated with individual well–being. Others are either teleological in another sense or quite clearly deontological. Most of the arguments discussed here are overtly critical of the "utility–based" approach in general. However, some are really directed towards the *standard interpretations*: their actual target is utility in either of the two received senses, i.e., pleasure minus pain and actual preference satisfaction, and the essential point made is that utility thus understood cannot really represent the individual's well–being. Other arguments are more disturbing because they suggest rejecting the utility concept *even if it could somehow be made to represent the individual's well–being.* This section attempts at recapitulating the negative case for the ethical use of utility theory, whereas the next subsection will attempt to make a positive case.[24]

Rawls and Sen are prominent among those writers on social ethics who have criticized the use of the utility concept in social ethics. Rawls's (1971, 1982) arguments are difficult to appreciate independently of his overall construction of the "well–ordered society". Sen's arguments are easier to detach. One of them is condensed in the following passage:

"The choice–approach to well–being is really a nonstarter. But the other two—more classical and more reasonably defended—views of utility, viz., happiness and desire–fulfilment, are indeed serious candidates for serving as the basis of a theory of well–being ... [But] a person who is illfed, undernourished, unsheltered and ill can still be high up in the scale of happiness or desire–fulfilment if he or she has learned to have 'realistic' desires and to take pleasure in small mercies. The physical conditions of a person do not enter the view of well–being seen entirely in terms of happiness or desire–fulfilment, except

---

[23] For an early statement of this criticism, see Broome (1978). To make the household, rather than the individual, the relevant unit of analysis is to add another questionable assumption. In this chapter we do not discuss the nature of agents but are most of the time concerned with individuals in the ordinary sense.

[24] If we were also concerned with *individual* ethics, our discussion would follow a different path. For instance, utility in the pleasure–pain interpretation is relevant to the assessment of a famous system of individual ethics, *hedonism*. We could restate in the language of utility the classic formulations and refutations of hedonism to be found in, e.g., Sidgwick (1884), but we shall not undertake that here.

insofar as they are *indirectly* covered by the mental attitudes of happiness or desire. And this neglect is fortified by the lack of interest, of these two perspectives, in the person's own valuation as to what kind of a life would be worthwhile" (1985, pp. 20–21).

In this passage Sen assumes a teleological framework of social ethics, in which the relevant notion of good is the individual's well–being.[25] The "choice-approach to well–being" is what we called earlier revealed preference theory in the broad methodological sense. It seems permissible to identify the "happiness" and "desire-fulfilment" views with those discussed in Sections 2.2 and 2.3, respectively.[26] Hence, Sen's passage is intended to dispose at once of the more popular interpretations of the utility concept. That revealed preference theory has nothing to say about well–being can be argued as follows: the choices made by an individual might or might not be directed towards his good; by themselves, they indicate nothing about the causes and attainment of his well-being. Naturally, choices specifically directed towards his good are relevant; but revealed preference theory is concerned with choices in general, not with that particular class, and cannot explain how to draw the line. The argument just stated would be too sweeping if it were made against the "happiness" (i.e., pleasure and pain) and "desire–fulfilment" (i.e., preference satisfaction) views. At least, these two notions refer to particular goods.

The point against the "more reasonably defended" interpretations of utility is that well–being has crucial objective components, such as enjoying good health, which can be taken into account only *accidentally* by these views. If I find no enjoyment in smoking, if I prefer taking strolls in a clean countryside to lying on sun–burned and overcrowded beaches, so much the better for me, but plainly in this example, the achievement of better health coincides with higher enjoyment, or higher preference satisfaction, just by chance. I could have altogether different idiosyncrasies. It is important to understand that by making this point, Sen and his followers revert to commonsense considerations that earlier writers in the field—both in the utilitarian and Paretian traditions—had in some way examined, and concluded to be irrelevant. Both in the pleasure and preference satisfaction interpretations, utility was implicitly claimed to capture not particular goods but an overall conception of the individual's well–being. To concentrate on the preference satisfaction version: if I

---

[25] Elsewhere he has emphasized freedom as one crucial aspect of the individual's good; see below. Sen (1982b) has also discussed "rights and agency" in a way which does not fit so easily with the teleological versus deontological distinction.

[26] The conflation of happiness with pleasure was not part of the Greek and classical philosophers' tradition but has become common since the beginning of utilitarianism. Desire–fulfilment and preference satisfaction are not really identical objectives, but have been identified with each other in 20th century economics. Pigou (1920) was aware of the conceptual distinction but claimed that it could be ignored for the purpose of his welfare analysis.

prefer smoking to non–smoking, despite the fact that by smoking I will impoverish my health, then it must be said that smoking is after all better for me than non–smoking. On this view, it is implicit that preference comparisons are made *all things being considered*. Preference satisfaction can take care— *indirectly* but not *accidentally*—of any other factor pertaining to the individual's well–being. This conception is deeply subjectivist. If all things considered, I continue to smoke heavily, those who claim that I thus promote my own good put more weight on the individual's assent to his own fate than on his objective status. It is never said in this conception that there are objective goods; rather, that there are objective factors, which are somehow taken into account by the subjective good.

We might interpret Sen's critical point as stating that those earlier writers on utility had not properly thought through their case. First, like clauses *ceteris paribus* in typical reasonings of positive economics, the clause *all things being considered* is the name of a problem, not its solution. In the absence of a proper analysis, Sen suggests, it is better to rely on our commonsense intuitions of what is objectively good for the individual. Second, not just any set of preference judgements satisfies the clause, even if it happens to meet standard formal requirements of utility theory, such as transitivity and completeness. This simple observation has important negative consequences. It was just explained that standard welfare economics relies on the notion of utility as representing *actual* preference satisfaction. By pointing out that only considered preferences appropriately represent the individual's good or well–being, one casts doubts on the ethical relevance of the welfare economics exercise. The crucial assumption mentioned at the end of Section 2.3 could prove to be not a "value judgement", but a brute logical *non sequitur*. Not all of those, mostly Paretian, writers who insist that preferences should be understood as considered preferences have thought through the damaging consequences of this claim for the existing normative theory.

Elsewhere, Sen argues again against utility as "happiness" or as "desire–satisfaction", but on partly different grounds: any utility–based approach involving either of these interpretations

"is a restrictive approach to taking note of individual advantage in two distinctive ways: it ignores freedom and concentrates only on achievements, and it ignores achievements other than those reflected in one of these mental metrics" (1992, p. 6).

The critical point made here is again that the utility–based approach contains an inadequate account of the individual's good; but it also introduces the consideration of freedom, with a view of connecting it with the earlier criticism. Sen is not so much concerned with free will as such, as he is with the *objectively defined* conditions of its exercise—then, with "real freedom" as against the formal notions provided by metaphysics or legal theory.[27] In his recent positive work he has come to emphasize the twin notions of *functionings*, to wit, "what the person succeeds in doing with the commodities and characteristics at his or her command" (1985, p. 10), and of *capabilities*, understood as the set of functionings actually available to the person. For instance, "bicycling" is a functioning; it should of course be kept distinct from the commodity "bicycle" to which it relates. The corresponding capability is the set of bicycling possibilities, which evidently varies from one individual to another. Sen argues that the individual's well–being can be measured by a suitable index of functionings (1985, p. 25). He also emphasizes that normative economics cannot be based solely on a concept of *achievement*, be it the functioning concept, but crucially needs a concept of *opportunity*; capability is then said to be the relevant one. This notion constitutes the seed of Sen's current project in social ethics. We see this project as belonging to teleological ethics, albeit in the sense of some enlarged notion of the good: real freedom, as well as (and perhaps more crucially than) well–being, contributes to defining the good.

The various arguments made thus far share the following common component: they point out that the utility concept is *too limited or too narrow* in order to properly capture the notion of well–being. They can be read either as completely dismissive arguments, or much less strongly, as critical arguments. For instance, if pleasure or happiness is construed as a functioning, there might remain a relevant technical role for utility theory; it would provide a metric for at least one among the functionings, and perhaps also for the corresponding capability.

The further group of arguments to be reviewed now are critical or dismissive in a different, and actually nearly opposite way: they suggest that the utility–based approach is *too broad and too flexible*. The approach registers the effect on utility values of too many factors, including those which seem to be irrelevant from the ethical point of view. By and large, contrary to the arguments in the previous group, the arguments below do not dispute that utility values represent individual well–being; rather, they aim at showing that while being perhaps an appropriate representation of well–being, utility functions provide either worthless or insufficient information.

Zealous aspirations have long been an embarrassment to utilitarian writers. If the fanatic's pleasure or satisfaction outweighs the pain or dissatisfaction of the victims of his policies, then the ordinary intuition notwithstanding, the fanatic should have his way.[28] This unpleasant conclusion plagues not only

---

[27] Or Kantianism for that matter. Kant's *Freiheit* excludes any empirical determination: it is the unrestricted exercise of the will in accord with pure reason.

[28] Hare (1976, 1981) has repeatedly addressed this problem. Notice that *rule* utilitarianism might eschew it, contrary to *act* utilitarianism.

utilitarianism but any theory in which utility, in either of the two senses, would be retained as a significant quantity. For the sake of the argument, let us conceive of a theory in which utility values are balanced against some non–utility–based index, say a relevant index of the individual's capabilities. It is unlikely that such a theory will ever recommend the fanatic's policies, but it might have to pay a taxing price in order to escape from this implication. The fanatic would have to be "compensated", and this might influence resource allocation to a disproportionate extent. This argument suggests that there are cases in which, perhaps, utility values should not be included *at all* in the social ethics evaluation. In the same spirit, and somewhat surprisingly, Harsanyi (1977a,b,c) has recommended to "censor" utility functions before computing the utilitarian sum. [29] Neither the argument nor the conclusion needs modifying when the standard interpretations of utility are replaced with well–being.

Handicaps have often been mentioned to illustrate another alleged failure of the utility-based approach. A handicapped person needs more resources than an able person to reach the same level of utility; or equivalently, he or she reaches lower utility values when given the same amount of resources. Utilitarian rules will automatically imply that the handicapped person will receive fewer resources than the able one. This intuitively unattractive consequence is very likely to follow from utility-based social rules more generally than just utilitarianism. The problem here with utility values is not that they are altogether irrelevant, as in the fanatic's case, but rather that they are not sufficiently informative to guide the social evaluator. What should be made out of X's low utility value for going to museums and art exhbitions? X might be a philistine, but it might also be the case that X has refined artistic tastes and is disabled, while museums are not well-equipped with ramps, so that he is simply not fit to go. To ration X's access to art just on the grounds of his low utility value for art is to deal with these two possibilities as if they were identical from the ethical point of view. Many contemporary writers find this implication shocking. The counterexample is effective against the standard interpretations of utility but appears to work as well, if utility is construed as measuring well-being.

A formally related problem has been discussed in relation to expensive tastes. The general point is aptly summarized by Rawls: "Desires and wants, however intense, are not by themselves reasons in matter of justice" (1982, p. 171). More clearly than the previous two cases, the expensive taste example leads to assessing whether the individual is *responsible* for his particular utility values. A person who has expensive tastes is like a handicapped person, in that an average amount of resources would leave him or her with a below–the–average amount of utility. (In this argument also, utility can be taken as representing

---

[29] See also Goodin's (1986) review of various cases of "laundering preferences".

well–being.) But there is a difference between the two cases. Only if those with expensive tastes are *not* responsible for these tastes can they be treated as they were handiccaped, and thus claim a higher than average amount of resources. Notice the deontological assumption underlying this argument: it relies on our intuition of what a *right* distribution of resources is, irrespective of what its implications for the individuals' good may be.

Given this deontological undertone, it is perhaps not surprising that responsibility has come to play a major role in Rawls's later work. He discusses it as follows:

"It is not by itself an objection to (a theory of justice) that it does not accommodate those with expensive tastes. One must argue in addition that it is unreasonable, if not unjust, to hold such persons responsible for their preferences and to require them to make out the best they can. But to argue this seems to presuppose that citizens' preferences are beyond their control as propensities or cravings that just happen. Citizens seem to be regarded as passive carriers of desires" (ibid., pp. 168–69).[30]

Whether or not one is prepared to regard individuals as responsible for their expensive tastes depends in part on the purpose and scope of the theory. Under Rawls's "veil of ignorance", "citizens" decide about their plans of life and about the society which would best make them mutually compatible. From this *ex ante* perspective, it might be reasonable to regard individuals as responsible for their preferences. But from an *ex post* point of view, a case by case discussion seems unavoidable. In 1920, the underpaid professional taxi driver in Paris and the Russian immigrant aristocrat who had to drive a cab for his living were in similar objective situations. Presumably, because of his acquired tastes, the latter did much worse than the former in welfare terms. It is not easy to decide to what extent the Russian was responsible for his preferences, and whether this should influence the *ex post* social evaluation.[31]

Recent normative economics has been much concerned with the issues of expensive tastes, handicaps, and the counterpart of handicaps, talents. These issues have been on the agenda since *A Theory of Justice* (1971). From Rawls's own admission, his book abstracted almost entirely from the problems of handicaps and talents, and accordingly could provide only a first approximation of the desired theory of "justice as fairness". Besides the Rawlsian connection, all these issues have been discussed in relation to a time–honoured question recently revived by Sen (1980), "Equality of what?". We shall give here only a coarse sketch of some of the literature. Crucial to the work of Sen (1985, 1987,

---

[30]Responsibility for one's preferences was previously discussed in Scanlon (1975).
[31]Since responsibility is usually not a matter of all–or–nothing, a more appropriate wording is perhaps *to what extent* it should influence the *ex post* social evaluation.

1992), Arneson (1989), Cohen (1989), Roemer (1994, 1996) and others, is the notion of the individual's relevant *achievement*, which these authors envisage variously, and normally do *not* describe in terms of a utility function. Arneson (1989) might be the only writer who retains a utility–based notion of achievement while distancing himself from the traditional approach; his is a borderline case. Roughly speaking, these writers analyze individual achievement in terms of three explanatory variables, i.e., physical or economic resources r, talents or handicaps t, and "will" w — a catchword to refer to those factors which are under the individual's own control. While the chosen notion of resource is borrowed from standard microeconomics and regarded as unproblematic, the distinction between talents and handicaps, on the one hand, and "will" on the other, is variously construed and has led to active controversies. The point of the whole construction is to define an appropriate redistributive process. The above–mentioned writers agree with each other that the t factor should be compensated by transfers in r, on the grounds that individuals are not responsible for t, while they are for w, and that differences in achievements can be tolerated only if they can be traced to differences in factors for which individuals are responsible. How the redistributive process takes place is again a matter for discussion, but there are *prima facie* two broad schools of thought, one of which aims at equalizing the individuals' sets of possible achievements, the other is primarily concerned with factors and somehow tries to equalize the individuals' extended resource vectors (r, t).[32] These divergences can be accounted for in terms of different philosophical answers to Sen's question. Like responsibility, equality is of the keywords to the recent work in normative economics.

2.5   *Utility, Well–Being, and Social Ethics: Some Positive Arguments*

As usually defined in recent normative economics and moral philosophy, *welfarism* is the thesis that the utility concept provides all the information required to construct a social evaluation rule. To the best of our knowledge, welfarism was never defended explicitly by any writer. But as an underlying assumption, it is clearly shared by utilitarianism (both modern and classical), Paretian welfare economics, as well as a significant part of social choice theory. To reject welfarism is to reject all those approaches at once. Sen (1979) introduced this new concept to capture what he thought was a severe common limitation to all of them.[33]   Welfarism is an "informational constraint" imposed on ethi-

---

[32] Typical representatives of each school are Arneson and Dworkin, respectively. For further elucidation the reader is referred to Fleurbaey's (1994) survey (on which the present paragraph is based). See also the accounts by Arneson (1990a), Hausman and McPherson (1996), and Roemer (1996).

[33] See also Sen (1977, reprinted in 1982a, Chapter 11). Sen's "liberal paradox", as first stated in *Collected Choice and Social Welfare* (1970), is an early occurrence of his critique of

cal judgements: if all the utility–relative information about two social states is known, one can judge them without knowing anything more about those states. Why this restriction might be exacting has been explained in the last subsection. Some of the arguments reviewed above point towards the conclusion that utility information is relevant, though insufficient. This seems to have been the essence of Sen's position at the early stage of his critique. Rather than being excluded from the analysis, utility values would have to be supplemented by direct descriptions of the states of affairs under examination. Other arguments point towards the stronger conclusion that utility information might be altogether irrelevant. Accordingly, we should distinguish between several positions among the "antiwelfarists". It is convenient (though no doubt oversimplifying) to classify them in terms of the achievement-factor model of Section 2.4:

- One position retains utility as *the* relevant index of achievement but relies on a factor analysis of utility values, in particular when it comes to asssessing the role of handicaps, talents and expensive tastes; it is minimally antiwelfarist.

- Another position makes utility one among several indexes of achievements, for instance along with various "capability" indexes, and then proceeds to the factor analysis of each of these achievement concepts.

- Still another position is to exclude utility from the list of relevant achievement indexes; hence is maximally antiwelfarist.[34]

Whatever its scope, the antiwelfarist critique crucially depends on the chosen interpretation of the utility concept. Enough has been said in Section 2.4 to suggest that the *two received senses*, i.e., the pleasure and the actual preference–satisfaction interpretations, have little ethical import. They are relevant only as a roundabout way of referring to individual well–being, so it seems appropriate to consider the latter interpretation only. However, some important objections were raised in connection with this interpretation, too. It is by no means clear that today's utility theorists can *fully* meet the antiwelfarists' challenge. But something can be said in favour of a continuing use of choice-theoretic methods in social ethics. We shall sketch three lines of defence.

First, one could further elaborate on the contrast between actual and considered preferences, with a view to showing that the latter relate to individual

---

welfarism. On this paradox, see Sen's (1976) and (1987) further elaboration and discussion of the extensive secondary literature. As to the word "welfarism", it was first used by Hicks, but with an altogether different meaning.

[34]Some writers, like Kagan (1992), have addressed "the limits of well–being" without really discussing the utility concept. It would not be so easy to fit them in the present classification of antiwelfarist positions.

well–being in an ethically relevant way. One key notion in Griffin's book *Well–Being* is that of "informed desire", to wit, a desire put through criticism and reflection, a desire "formed by appreciation of the nature of its object" (1986, p. 14). This deliberative conception clashes with that of ordinary economics, which views preference as a fixed attribute of the individual, and thus must regard desire, to the extent that it determines preference, as also being fixed. The "informed desire" view goes against a broader tradition, of which economics is the late offspring, that claims that deliberation is only of the means, not of the ends (*Nichomachean Ethics*, 1112b 12). Griffin follows an alternative tradition. The Kantians have been arguing that ends fall within the jurisdiction of reason. The ordinary meta–ethical intuition probably endorses the point that deliberation is of ends (if ethics excludes deliberations of that sort, what then is it about?). One strength of the "informed desire" view is that, in principle it can take into account those objective components of well–being which Sen wanted to emphasize against standard welfare economics. One apparent weakness of this conception, however, is that it is roundabout, and perhaps even redundant: can we not directly consider the objects of our reasoned desires, such as enjoying good health, improving our knowledge, and the like? Griffin's answer is summarized here:

"The advantages of the informed desire account, therefore, seem to be these. It provides the material needed to encompass the complexity of prudential value. It has the advantages of scope and flexibility over explanations of 'well–being' in terms of desirability features. It has scope because all prudential values, from objects of simple varying tastes to objects of universal informed agreement, register somewhere in informed preferences. It has flexibility, because not everyone's well–being is affected in the same way by a certain desirability feature, and we want a notion sensitive to these differences. We want to know not only that something is valuable, but how valuable it is, and how valuable to different persons" (1986, pp. 30–31).

One implication of this passage is that well–being has an irreducibly subjective aspect. This could well be the grain of truth contained in the utilitarian and Paretian writers' work — even if they overemphasized it to the point of absurdity. Another suggestion is methodological in character: a desire account of well–being avoids the charge of being unduly specific, a charge to which purely objective accounts are clearly open. The objection of undue specificity, if not of arbitrariness, has been raised against Rawls's list of "primary goods", as well as against Sen's examples of "functionings". We cannot here bring this methodological debate to its close, but are implying that the preference–based conception of well–being is probably in no worse predicament than the conception of well–being in terms of objective achievement lists.

To make progress with the previous account of well–being, the connection between the latter and preference satisfaction should be worked out more precisely. We suggest trying the following:

> (*) x is better than y for individual i if and only if were i rational and well–informed, i would prefer x to y.

Notice that the conditional occurring after the "if and only if" is a counterfactual. It would be inappropriate to resort to *material implication*, as in the following statement:

> x is better than y for individual i if and only if whenever i is rational and well–informed, i prefers x to y.

Here are the reasons why the material implication variant does not do the required job. If one takes the view that no agent is ever rational and well–informed, the variant is vacuously true. If one takes the less extreme view that agents are not always rational and well–informed, one is led to the paradoxical conclusion that sometimes x is better than y, sometimes x is not, for reasons that we cannot intuitively connect to a change in relative "betterness". Importantly, (*) is meant to convey not a definition of what the individual's good consists of, but a criterion to recognize it. To distinguish here between an *essential definition* and a *criterion* is one way of trying to set welfare economics on its feet. It is clearly wrong to claim, as de Graaff does, that well–being *is* preference satisfaction. The link between the two concepts is at best an external one. (In the same way, very roughly, that choices can be linked to preferences: under certain conditions, choices make it possible to identify the individual's preferences, but choices never define what preferences are.) The welfare economists' further, and no less serious, mistake was to use actual, rather than rational and well–informed, preferences as their implicit criterion.

Some writers constrain the preference notion even further than we have just done in order to tie it to the notion of the individual's good. They insist that other–regarding desires should be kept aside. Accordingly, "self–interested" should be added to "rational" and "well–informed" in statement (*).[35] To add this proviso has much plausibility in the present context of discussion, where individual well–being is taken to be the relevant notion of good. (There are other teleological frameworks, such as perhaps Aristotle's ethics, in which the proviso would not make much sense.) However, one might argue that if self–interest

---

[35]See Broome (1991, p. 133), who however distances himself from the rational–preference–satisfaction theory of the good in whatever version. Griffin's own account of "informed desire" does not emphasize self–interest.

is construed narrowly, for instance so as to exclude any impersonal motives,[36] the proviso will be unduly restrictive. A sufficiently encompassing definition of what it means for the individual to be rational and well–informed might very well account for the kind of long–term interests that one would intuitively like to connect with individual well–being. This leads to asking whether (*) should be construed as involving only *formal*, or also substantial rationality constraints. If "self–interested" is not added to the statement, rationality con- straints should clearly be of the latter type. One should also inquire whether the agent's information should be complete and correct, or just partial and cor- rect, and in particular how far it should be extended beyond general knowledge of a law–like sort. In brief, there are a number of ways in which formula (*) can be made precise. To state and compare them would lead us beyond the purview of this chapter, while we just want to argue for the general plausibility of this formula.[37]

There is a second line of argument available. Most of the discussion thus far has assumed a teleological framework of ethics, in which the relevant notion of good is the individual's well–being. But there are alternative notions of good that are relevant to social ethics. We already mentioned that Sen has enlarged his framework of teleological analysis to make room for real freedom. Indepen- dently of this, he has sometimes also distinguished between two notions of good, i.e., well-being and "advantage" [e.g., Sen (1992)]. Actually, the whole list of well-received definitions of the good in moral philosophy (pleasure, happiness, human perfection, harmonious civic life, etc.) is *prima facie* relevant to social ethics. Rather than examining each in turn, one might be willing to abstract from particular definitions and attempt directly to comprehend the features *all* notions of good have in common. One might argue that educated people recog- nize at least broadly what the sensible use of the word "good" is, although they employ it in various senses and lack a theory to account for underlying regu- larities in their own use. Philosophers might then rely on the rich information provided by ordinary language and sketch the missing theory.[38] If this method works, it is unlikely to lead to a theory like, say, hedonism: it will be a *formal* theory, not a substantial one. To illustrate, when we say that x is better than y, and y better than z, we presumably take for granted that x is better than z. Hence, transitivity appears to be implied by our understanding of the word

---

[36]That impersonal motives should be excluded has been defended by some utilitarians, but on different grounds: the proviso would be necessary to avoid *circularity* in defining moral rules; on this argument see Brandt (1979).

[37]For a discussion of self–regarding versus other–regarding preferences, see Collard (1978) and Kolm (1984). Incidentally, the restriction to self–regarding preferences is a classic way of escape from Sen's "Paretian liberal" paradox; see Gibbard (1974) and Hammond (1995).

[38]This type of analysis can probably be traced to Moore's *Principia Ethica* (1903).

"good".[39] This seems like a meagre result, but it suggests that the same method may be applied in less obvious directions. What is relevant for our purposes is that transitivity is an axiom from utility theory: the concept of good might be similarly scrutinized from the vantage point of *any* axiom of that theory. In brief, by adopting a formal stand in teleological ethics, one creates room for an ethical application of utility theory, at least as a mathematical framework of analysis.

The method sketched in the last paragraph has recently been illustrated by Broome. His *Weighing Goods* (1991a) makes two major claims: one can investigate the essential properties of good (or rather, the betterness relation) without adhering to any specific substantial theory, and the technical apparatus of preference and utility is relevant to that investigation. The two claims are mutually supporting: if he had not arrived at choice–theoretic conclusions about the structure of good, Broome would have had to face the charge that his ethical formalism is empty; in order to remain within teleology, he would have had to fall back on one of the substantial notions of good. His most significant conclusion is that the good satisfies the technical property of *separability*. This property will be defined below in Section 3.1. Among other things, it implies a warrant to utilitarianism, in the special interpretation of utility as referring to the individual's good. A remarkable feature of his analysis, Broome does not want initially to limit the scope of the good to the individual's good: persons are said to be "locations" of good in a way no different from times and states of nature. In order to argue that good is separable in its three locations, he investigates the properties of the betterness relation as if it were a preference relation. It is found to satisfy the "sure–thing principle", which is the technical expression for the separability property when that property concerns states of nature. Related arguments are intended to take care of separability relative to times and to persons. We do not mean to endorse these conclusions, but only to illustrate how the general method works.

To elaborate on the methodological point from a slightly different angle, remember that the basic structure of a teleological theory results from answering the following questions in succession: (i) How does the particular theory define the good? (ii) How does it relate goodness to rightness? Leaving aside question (i) and assuming a pretheoretic understanding of the good, there remains question (ii), which we argue utility–theoretic methods can help illuminate. The standard way of thinking of (ii) goes as follows: first, the chosen notion of good is attached to states of affairs; second, the rightness of actions is determined by the goodness of their consequences, which are particular states of affairs. Ethical theories based on this two–stage process are said to be *consequentia-*

---

[39]However, even this has been called into question; see Temkin (1987).

list. Teleological systems of ethics are consequentialist.[40] Now, part of utility theory is precisely concerned with the problem of how to evaluate a prospect in terms of the evaluation of its outcomes. *Prima facie*, there are many ways of constructing an overall evaluation for prospects. Rawls appears to skip over this problem when he simply states that in teleological systems, "the right is defined as that which maximizes the good" (1971, p. 24). It is a matter for technical investigation to formulate a maximization principle which takes into account the two–stage structure of consequentialist reasoning. Among other things, the present chapter is concerned with this issue. It will surface when we discuss Harsanyi's assumption that the social observer should obey the axioms of expected utility theory.

Finally, there is a third line of argument, which goes beyond the confines of teleological ethics. Typically, a non–teleological or deontological theory is one which does not determine the right action from the consideration of the good alone. In Kantian ethics, reason alone—without any role played by the good—determines the right action. In most other deontological systems, especially in the contemporary ones, such as Rawls's, the right action is derived by reason in the light of some consideration of the good. Understood one way or another, rationality plays a crucial role in deontological theories—a role in some sense more explicit than in teleological theories. So one wonders whether utility theory could not become relevant to the deontologist too, as a tool for clarifying his rationality concept. To make this claim precise would involve one in distinguishing between several notions of rationality. Choice theory— a better expression than "utility theory" in this context—deals only with *prudential* rationality, which is known to be of no major concern to Kantian ethics but is relevant to most other deontological systems. Choice theory is restrictive in another, more exacting sense: it is usually said to be "formal", in that it does not take any position on the individuals' aims, but just on the proper way of attaining them.[41] That choice theory leaves aside rationality considerations of interest to the deontologist is beyond doubt. But there is room for the use in deontological ethics of choice theory at least as a subordinate device—i.e., *qua* formal theory of prudential rationality. The main example in this chapter consists in Rawls's (cautious) reliance on choice theory when he derives the principles of justice from the "original position".

The first of the three lines of reasoning sketched above provides us with an interpretation of the *individuals'* utility functions for the welfarist constructions reviewed in this chapter. Note emphatically that collective choice theories do

---

[40] Much of the discussion of teleological versus nonteleological ethics has indeed been concerned with the merits and demerits of consequentialism. See in particular Williams (1973) and Scheffler (1982, 1988).

[41] This claim cannot be accepted without qualification; see Mongin (1984).

not necessarily have to make the restrictions of a "rational", "well–informed", and (if needed at all) "self–interested" preference explicit in the formalism: some do, but others do not, while becoming nonetheless relevant once the technical notions of utility and preference receive the suggested interpretation. Utility–theoretic restrictions, such as the ordering axiom (always) or the expected utility axioms (sometimes) will also be imposed on *the evaluating observer himself.* To account for these technical restrictions we think that one of the last two interpretations should come into play. The axioms will either serve as tools to investigate the structure of consequentialism, or else refer to primitive rationality constraints that the observer should satisfy. By making these various interpretative points in favour of welfarism, we do not mean, of course, to imply that all the welfarist constructions reviewed below deliver good ethical theories. Each will have to be assessed on its own merits. What we claim at this stage is simply that they belong to the province of ethics, and should be discussed as such.

3   Some Definitions and Concepts from Utility Theory

Throughout, we shall denote the set of alternatives by X and the relevant domain of utility functions by $\mathcal{U} \subset \mathbb{R}^X$ (where $\mathbb{R}^X$ is the set of real functions on X). Most of the formal results of this chapter depend on assuming that there is a fixed population of n numbered individuals; denote $\{1, \cdots, n\}$ by N. We shall normally consider the elements of $\mathcal{U}$ as our primitives. We want the technical developments of this and the following sections to be compatible with both the now prevailing notion that utility functions represent preferences of some kind and those earlier theories which exclusively relied on the utility concept. However, a brief reminder of axiomatic justifications of utility in terms of preferences is to the point in this preliminary section. There will be three major cases.

3.1   Utility Functions in the Case of Certainty, and "Economic" Domains

As explained in microeconomics textbooks, consumer theory takes the set of alternatives X to be $\mathbb{R}^p$ or some suitably restricted subset of $\mathbb{R}^p$, where p is the number of commodities, and it takes $\mathcal{U}$ to be the set of continuous functions on X. An element in $\mathcal{U}$ is then seen as a representation of the consumer's preference over commodity vectors. Given an *ordering* (i.e., transitivity and completeness) and a *continuity* axiom imposed on the binary preference relation, the existence (and uniqueness up to strictly increasing transformations) of $u \in \mathcal{U}$ follows from a classic representation theorem by Debreu (1960). It is also known that further axiomatic restrictions on the preference relation can be translated into corresponding properties of u. *Monotonicity* properties of preferences directly translate into monotonocity properties of utility representations. *Convex* and *satiable* preferences lead to representations which are quasi–concave and bounded from above, respectively. Another particular case of interest is *separability*. When the preference relation over $X = \mathbb{R}^p$ induces well–behaved preference relations over each component or each subset of components, it is said to be "weakly" or "strongly" separable, respectively. These properties lead to special utility representations; typically, strong separability leads to additive representations with respect to the components.[42]

The more basic axioms of choice under certainty—i.e., the two ordering axioms, transitivity and completeness—have been accepted by most economists and a large number of philosophers and social scientists as being compelling for any rational agent. As the formal theory of choice functions demonstrates,[43] these two axioms essentially exhaust the meaning of "optimization"—i.e., of the notion that the agent's choice maximizes some preference relation—and "optimization" is widely seen as unproblematic.[44] Most writers regard continuity as a purely technical requirement; it serves to bridge the mathematical gap between the preference binary relation and its numerical representation. As to the other conditions, such as monotonicity and separability, they play only an occasional role in the theory of choice under certainty. They enter the definition of specific "economic" domains of utility functions that have been investigated in both social choice theory and normative economics (see 6.5 for an illustration).

3.2   Von Neumann–Morgenstern Utility Functions

In von Neumann–Morgenstern (VNM) theory the typical objects of choice are lottery tickets, as in games of chance, or rather some idealization of them. A standard formalization assumes that there is a measurable space of final outcomes Γ and that the alternative set is $X = \Delta_s(\Gamma)$, i.e., the set of *simple* probabilities on Γ. (A simple probability has a finite number of values.) Clearly, this variant as well as the more general one in which $X = \Delta(\Gamma)$—i.e., the set of *all* probabilities on Γ—takes for granted that the material presentation of lottery tickets, or lotteries for short, does not matter. For instance, compound lotteries are unproblematically identified with simple lotteries.

---

[42]See Gorman's (1968) classic paper and the chapter by Blackorby, Primont and Russell in this volume.
[43]See for instance Richter's (1971) survey.
[44]For a dissenting view, see Mongin (1984, 1994b).

The basic utility notion in VNM theory is expected utility, which can be formalized in either of the following ways. Granting the standard identification of outcomes γ with sure lotteries, any x on X gives rise to a function v on Γ; the latter is defined to be the restriction of u to Γ. Then, the VNM property is the familiar one that u is *expectational*: i.e., for all $x \in X$,

$$u(x) = \sum_{\gamma \in \Gamma} v(\gamma) x(\gamma).$$

Following an alternative definition, the VNM property states that u is mixture–preserving (MP): i.e., for all $x, y \in X$, all $\lambda \in [0,1]$,

$$u(x\lambda y) = \lambda u(x) + (1 - \lambda)u(y),$$

where $x\lambda y$ stands for the convex combination $\lambda x + (1 - \lambda)y$. This shorthand will be used throughout. (Of course, $x\lambda y$ is itself a probability.)

In either formalization the algebraic restriction on u translates the well–known VNM independence axiom, to the effect that the preference between x and y is equivalent to the preference between mixtures $x\lambda z$ and $y\lambda z$ (for $\lambda \neq 0$ and any z). When added to the usual ordering and continuity requirements, this axiom implies that there is a utility representation satisfying the VNM property in either the expectional or the mixture–preserving sense, depending on the properties of the set X. It is also the case that the VNM representation, in either formalization, is unique up to a positive affine transformation. For this classic result the reader is referred in particular to Luce and Raiffa (1957, chapter 2) and Herstein and Milnor (1953). Fishburn (1970, 1982, 1988) provides up–to–date presentations.[45] The expectional definition of VNM utility functions always implies the MP one but the converse need not hold in the more general versions of the theory. At least, whenever $X = \Delta_s(\Gamma)$, it is readily seen (by finite induction) that the two definitions are equivalent.[46] We shall denote the set of VNM utility functions on X by $\mathcal{V}(X)$.

That the VNM axioms are compelling for rational agents has been argued in various ways, and similarly disputed. The average opinion leans towards acceptance of this claim. Hammond's (1988a) "consequentialist" reconstruction provides a normative argument for the ordering and independence axioms; see his chapter on "objective" expected utility, and see also McClennen's (1990) thorough critique. Allais (1953) is famous among those who deny that VNM independence is normatively compelling.

---

[45] A number of technical variants have evolved from von Neumann and Morgenstern's (1944) initial theorem; see Fishburn (1989) for a historically oriented survey.
[46] See Hammond's chapter on "objective" expected utility for this and other results in VNM utility theory.

3.3   Anscombe–Aumann Utility Functions

In terms of a time–honoured distinction the VNM theory describes the individual's choice under *risk* rather than under *uncertainty*. That is to say, it takes probabilities in $\Gamma(\Delta)$, or $\Delta_s(\Gamma)$, as *given*, be they objective in the technical sense of expressing relative frequencies, or—more broadly—derived in some antecedent and unspecified way. The former sense is a particular case of the latter, which is the relevant one to consider here: VNM theory *per se* does not take any position on the origin of probabilities. In a multi–individual context, the use of VNM utility theory is tantamount to assuming that probabilities have somehow been agreed upon. Again, the theory does not explain why agreement should prevail among individuals. This puts a severe limitation on the use of VNM theory in social ethics. Roughly speaking, it is inappropriate in any context where the agents have reasons to differ in their assessment of factual matters as well as ultimate objectives.

In contrast, the more thorough Subjective Expected Utility (SEU) theory both provides an explicit derivation of probabilities and allows for disagreements between individuals. Essentially, it views the existence of probability assignments as reflecting coherent preferences over betting schemes. According to the celebrated *Dutch Book* argument, a probability assignment exists if and only if the individual cannot be involved in a system of bets which would leave him with a net loss, whatever the actual state of the world turns out to be. The argument can be phrased in such a way that it ensures not only existence, but also uniqueness of the subjective probability assignment. Crucially, it does not prescribe specific probability values. Starting with Ramsey (1931) and de Finetti (1937), writers in the SEU framework have always insisted that the individual's probability values depend on his particular information. For instance, he might or might not take relative frequencies into account. SEU theorists normally take for granted that whatever the individual's incoming information, he should process it according to Bayes's rule any time that the latter applies meaningfully (i.e., whenever the prior probability of the conditioning event is nonzero). This further piece of doctrine is only loosely connected with the Dutch book argument. Despite this fact, we shall follow a widespread practice and also refer to SEU theory as "Bayesianism", especially in contexts where the existence of subjective probabilities is the important feature to emphasize (as in 5.4).[47]

In the main, there are three axiomatizations of SEU in current use— Savage's (1954 and 1972), Anscombe and Aumann's (1963), and Jeffrey's (1965

---

[47]SEU theory should also be seen as part of the philosophical and statistical tradition of subjective probability theory which developed independently of choice theory. For this important connection see, e.g., Fine (1973), or the more accessible survey by Fishburn (1986).

and 1983). Each of the three starts from the preference concept as a primitive, and derives both a unique subjective probability and an expected utility representation of preferences, where the expectation is taken with respect to the (endogenous) subjective probablity. As in VNM theory, the SEU representation is unique up to positive affine transformations. In Jeffrey's system the objects of preference are *propositions* in the logician's sense. Accordingly, the set X of all propositions is endowed with a Boolean algebra structure. Jeffrey's axiomatization has become the classic version of SEU theory among English–speaking philosophers. Economists usually rely on Savage's or Anscombe and Aumann's axiomatizations, in which the assumed objects of choice are altogether different from Jeffrey's.[48] Given a set Ω of states of the world and a set C of consequences, the individual's objects of choice are functions $a : \Omega \to C$. Clearly, these state-dependent functions are meant to represent subjective lotteries—i.e., lotteries which assign consequences (prizes) to each state *without* specifying the state probabilities. It is also appropriate to view state–dependent functions as those acts which are available to the agent. The intuition underlying the latter interpretation is roughly this: a consequence is entirely determined by the joint data of the individual's action and the state of nature; hence, to choose an action is tantamount to selecting a particular way in which states influence consequences. Savage insists on the "act" interpretation of state–dependent functions, whereas Anscombe and Aumann just regard them as subjective lottery tickets. (They call subjective lottery tickets "horse lotteries" and contrast them with the "roulette lotteries" of VNM theory, which carry given probabilities.) We shall always refer to the a functions as *acts*, even in the context of Anscombe–Aumann applications, thus avoiding any possible confusion between two kinds of lotteries. Notice that any consequence c can be identified with a relevant *constant act*, i.e., that act a_c which has constant value c across states.

A remarkable common feature of these three systems is that each involves a seemingly irrelevant structural assumption relative to the alternative set X. Jeffrey requires the Boolean algebra of propositions to be "atomless". A related condition appears as (P6) in Savage's axioms: it says in effect that the event space $(\Omega, \mathcal{A})$ is infinitely divisible; in particular, there must be infinitely many states in Ω. The corresponding mathematical restriction in Anscombe and Aumann is that the consequence set C is convex; typically (though not necessarily), it is a probability set. Contrary to Savage, Anscombe and Aumann can deal with acts having finite domains; but they have to constrain the range of acts somewhat artificially, by requiring it to be convex. There are deep— and by now, well–recognized—logical difficulties surrounding the axiomatiza-

---

[48]To the best of our knowledge, Broome's (1990) axiomatization of utilitarianism is the only application of Jeffrey's theory in the field of economics at large.

tion of SEU theory in a completely general context.[49] By and large, there is a gap between the preference axioms and the numerical data (i.e., the probability and utility functions) representing them. To bridge the gap, a restriction on the structure of the alternative set turns out to be unavoidable. This fact has serious implications for the philosophical assessment of SEU theory. For the axioms are meant to express the rationality justifications of the expected utility formula. Ideally, they should not exceed the logical content of the latter. No such difficulty occurred in the simpler case of VNM theory.

Conceptually, Savage's axiomatization is the most interesting among the three. It involves the widely discussed *sure–thing principle* which can be seen —very roughly speaking—as the subjective lottery variant of VNM's independence axiom. The sure–thing principle—Savage's (P2)—plays a crucial role in the derivation of both the additive property of subjective probabilities and the expectational form of the utility representation. As was mentioned earlier, most normative discussions of SEU theory have focused on the sure–thing principle. However, another important component in Savage's axiomatization —i.e., postulates (P3), (P4) and (P5)—has to do in effect with the Dutch book argument and the possibility of deriving the individual's subjective probability uniquely. Despite—or perhaps because of—its explicitness, Savage's approach is less elegant than Jeffrey's and less handy than Anscombe and Aumann's. In this chapter we shall base our technical developments on the latter, and only allude to the other two.

As in Anscombe and Aumann (AA), we introduce a finite state set Ω and a consequence set $\mathcal{C}$ endowed with the following special structure: $\mathcal{C} = \Delta_s(\Gamma)$ for some measurable set Γ, i.e., $\mathcal{C}$ is the set of lottery tickets—in the VNM sense— over some given set of final outcomes. This heavy but convenient restriction made it possible for AA to use antecedent results from VNM theory in order to derive their representation theorem. Notice that the chosen definition implies that $\mathcal{C}$ is convex. The alternative set is $X = \mathcal{C}^{\Omega}$, i.e., the set of all acts. Given the above–mentioned identification of c with a_c, any function u on X gives rise to a function v over $\mathcal{C}$. The AA axioms imposed on the preference relation imply that there is a unique probability p on Ω, and a utility u on X having the expectational form: for any $a \in X$,

$$u(a) = \sum_{\omega \in \Omega} p(\omega)v(a(\omega)).$$

As in VNM theory, the set of positive affine transformations of u is exactly the set of all utility representations having the expectational form. We shall denote the set of Anscombe–Aumann utility representations on $\mathcal{C}^{\Omega}$ by $\mathcal{A}(X)$.

---

[49]See Krantz et al. (1971) or the more accessible discussion in Suppes (1981). Wakker (1989, IV.6) also provides comments, extensions and references.

Importantly, both Savage's and Anscombe and Aumann's axiom systems deliver *state–independent* SEU representations, i.e., expected utility representations in which the v function depends on states ω only through the chosen act $a(\cdot)$. The above AA representation should be contrasted with the following, more general variant:

$$u(a) = \sum_{\omega \in \Omega} p(\omega)v(\omega, a(\omega)).$$

It is not difficult to axiomatize this *state–dependent* SEU representation, but the resulting preference axioms will imply that the subjective probability p is essentially indeterminate. In other words, the Dutch book procedure for identifying subjective probabilities is no longer operative in the state-dependent case. This well-known difficulty explains why most writers in choice theory have preferred to avoid it altogether in spite of the serious loss of generality implied by state-independence.[50]

That the axioms of SEU theory are compelling for rational agents has been both strongly argued for and strongly disputed, with the dissenters typically going in one of these two directions: either they retain the expected utility property but take the expectation with respect to a non–standard ("non–additive") concept of probability distribution; or they retain probability but apply a non–expected utility formula to it. As for VNM theory, the average opinion is biased towards acceptance of the normativity claim. Hammond's (1988a) consequentialism encompasses SEU theory and therefore provides an argument for it; see Chapter 6 on subjective expected utility in this volume. The dissenters often base their case on a famous counterexample by Ellsberg (1954). The normative appraisal of the Dutch Book argument has led to lively discussions among philosophers.[51]

3.4   Interpersonal Utility Differences

At some point we shall have to formally express the assumption that the individuals' utilities strongly differ from each other. A attractive rendering is to say that for each individual, there is a pair of alternatives such that he is not indifferent over this pair while the other individuals are. Formally, if $f_1, \cdots, f_n$ denote the individuals' utility functions over X, we shall require that:

(*) $(\forall \, j \in N)(\exists \, x_j, y_j \in X)f_j(x_j) > f_j(y_j)$ and $f_i(x_j) = f_i(y_j)$, $i \neq j$.

This requirement should be compared with the more abstract property that:

(**) $f_1, \cdots, f_n$ are affinely independent.

---

[50]On the topic of this paragraph, Fishburn (1970) and the survey by Schervish, Seidenfeld and Kadane (1990) are good sources.

[51]See in particular Howson and Urbach (1989).

Recall that a family of real–valued functions $f_1, \cdots, f_n$ is said to be *affinely independent* if whenever $\sum \alpha_i f_i + \beta = 0$, then $\alpha_1 = \cdots = \alpha_n = \beta = 0$; otherwise, it is said to be affinely dependent. Equivalently, define the f_i to be affinely dependent if there is $j \in N$ such that f_j can be written as an affine combination of the remaining f_i; and define the f_i to be affinely independent if otherwise. Clearly, affine independence strengthens the more familiar concept of linear independence, and the two concepts collapse into each other in the particular case where the f_i are probabilities. Now, it follows from the definitions that $(*) \Rightarrow (**)$. It turns out that whenever the f_i are expected utility representations, the implication $(**) \Rightarrow (*)$ also holds.[52] Hence, for most of the technical developments of the present chapter, the interpretable property $(*)$ and the less transparent (but mathematically handy) property $(**)$ turn out to be identical. This fact will be put to use in Section 5.[53]

4   The Aggregative Setting with Interpersonal Comparisons of Utility

This section discusses the connection between social ethics and utility theory within a particular aggregative setting that has been provided by social choice theory. Whereas Arrow's celebrated *Social Choice and Individual Values* (1951) considered only preference relations and embodied the assumption that these preferences are noncomparable, Sen's *Collective Choice and Social Welfare* (1970) opened the way to a more general kind of social choice–theoretic investigation involving utility as well as preference, and allowing for both comparability and noncomparability assumptions.[54] The crucial step was to redefine Arrow's aggregative process appropriately. The Arrovian *social welfare function* (SWF) maps individual preference relations into the binary relation that models the collective preference relation. Sen and his followers' major tool of analysis is the *Social Welfare Functional* (SWFL), which maps individual utility functions to a collective preference. In this framework, Arrow's noncomparability assumption, as well as the various comparability assumptions that suggest themselves, can be captured under the guise of particular *invariance principles*. Arrow's impossibility theorem can then be restated and compared

---

[52] This result was proved by Fishburn (1984) in the VNM case and by Mongin (1995a) for SEU representations.

[53] Notice this perhaps not very intuitive implication of defining different utility functions in terms of either $(*)$ or $(**)$: opposite utility representations (i.e., such that $u_j = -u_i$) will *not* be treated as being "different".

[54] Arrow's approach is implicitly related to the welfare economics of the Paretian school, as it took shape in the 1930s. Sen (1970) and d'Aspremont (1995) discuss this connection. Arrow's later work (e.g., 1973a) shows that he became less adamant in his rejection of interpersonal comparisons.

with possibility results which follow from selecting weaker *invariance* principles than noncomparability; prominent among the latter are characterizations of utilitarian rules. Most of the results of SWFL theory can be obtained by a two–step process, one leading to technical welfarism (as defined in Section 4.1), the other to the specific formula (e.g., utilitarian) according to which the individuals' utilities are to be combined (see Sections 4.2 and 4.3). Since this material has been extensively reviewed elsewhere,[55] we will restrict technicalities to essentials and lay the emphasis on interpretations (in particular in Sections 4.4 and 4.6).

4.1   The SWFL Framework

The notation will be in keeping with that of Section 3. It is meant to suggest relevant connections between SWFL theory and individual utility theory. As before, X will refer to the alternative set, which is taken here to be identical for the various individuals and the social observer. This is not an insignificant assumption. When the bearer of collective preference refers to the state, its alternative set is obviously non–coincident with those of the members of society (which might themselves differ from each other). To reduce a situation of initially heterogeneous alternative sets to the present framework is not logically impossible, but might require some care. For any given set $\mathcal{U}$ of utility functions, we define a social welfare functional, or SWFL, to be a function:

$$F : \mathcal{U}^n \to 2^{X \times X},$$

such that for every $U = (u_1, \cdots, u_n) \in \mathcal{U}^n$, $F(U)$ is a weak ordering on X (i.e., it is a transitive, reflexive and complete binary relation). $F(U)$ refers to the collective weak preference. Denote the induced strict preference and indifference relations by $P(U)$ and $I(U)$, respectively.

The following axioms belong to standard SWFL theory.

AXIOM **I** (Independence of Irrelevant Alternatives)

$\forall\, U, U' \in \mathcal{U}^n, \forall\, x, y \in X,$
$U(x) = U'(x)$
$U(y) = U'(y) \quad \Rightarrow \quad xF(U)y$ iff $xF(U')y.$

---

[55] In particular by Sen (1982a, 1986), Blackorby, Donaldson and Weymark (1984), d'Aspremont (1985), Moulin (1988). The reader is referred to Bossert and Weymark's chapter in volume II on utility in social choice for a complete exposition of SWFL theory.

AXIOM **PI** (Pareto Indifference)

$\forall\, U \in \mathcal{U}^n, \forall\, x, y \in X,$
$U(x) = U(y) \;\Rightarrow\; xI(U)y.$

AXIOM **PWP** (Pareto Weak Preference)

$\forall\, U = (u_1, \cdots, u_n) \in \mathcal{U}^n, \forall\, x, y \in X,$
$u_i(x) \geq u_i(y), i = 1, \cdots n$ [denoted as $U(x) \geq U(y)$]
$\Rightarrow\;\; xF(U)y.$

AXIOM **WP** (Weak Pareto)

$\forall\, U = (u_1, \cdots, u_n) \in \mathcal{U}^n, \forall\, x, y \in X,$
$u_i(x) > u_i(y), i = 1, \cdots n$ [denoted as $U(x) \gg U(y)$]
$\Rightarrow\;\; xP(U)y.$

AXIOM **Strict P** (Strict Pareto)

$\forall\, U = (u_1, \cdots, u_n) \in \mathcal{U}^n, \forall\, x, y \in X,$
$u_i(x) \geq u_i(y), i = 1, \cdots n \;\&\; \exists\, j : u_j(x) > u_j(y)$
[denoted as $U(x) > U(y)$]
$\Rightarrow\;\; xP(U)y.$

AXIOM **SP** (Strong Pareto)

$\equiv$ (Strict P) & (PI).

Clearly, **(Strict P)** $\Rightarrow$ **(WP)** and **(PWP)** $\Rightarrow$ **(PI)**. The vector inequality notation introduced above will be used throughout this chapter.

Standard SWFL theory deals with the case in which X is any set of at least three elements and $\mathcal{U} = \mathbb{R}^X$. This domain restriction leads to a classic lemma which says in effect that all the information relevant to the ethical preference is contained in the *set of values* taken by all utility function vectors U. Formally, the problem of ranking alternatives in X is reduced to the problem of ranking elements in the set $\cup\{Range\, U/U \in \mathcal{U}n\}$, which is readily seen to be equal to $\mathbb{R}^n$. Could we rely on a similar lemma in SWFL theory when VNM restrictions are assumed, i.e., when $X = \Delta_s(\Gamma)$ for some outcome set Γ, and $\mathcal{U} = \mathcal{V}(X)$? The answer is in the affirmative, provided that a (weak) dimensionality condition holds. We state formally the standard result as well as its VNM variant:

LEMMA 4.1 [WELFARISM LEMMA] Assume that F is a SWFL, and either of the following domain definitions holds:

(i) Either X is any set of at least three elements, and $\mathcal{U} = \mathbb{R}^X$;

(ii) Or $X = \Delta_s(\Gamma)$ has (vector space) dimension at least 2, and $\mathcal{U} = \mathcal{V}(X)$.

Then F satisfies **(I)** and **(PI)** if and only if the binary relation relation R^* on $\mathbb{R}^n$ defined by

$$aR^*b - \exists\ U \in \mathcal{U}^n, \exists\ x, y \in X \text{ s.t. } U(x) = a, U(y) = b \ \text{ and } \ xF(U)y$$

is an ordering.[56]

The R^* relation defined in this lemma will be called a *social welfare ordering* (SWO), and used extensively below. We denote by P^* and I^* its asymmetric and symmetric parts, respectively.

The present notion of welfarism is a purely technical one. It is important to distinguish it from the *philosophical* notion of welfarism, which has been discussed in Section 2. The latter does not assume any specific formalization such as the SWFL framework used here. Being purely mathematical, the former would be compatible with any interpretation of the u_i symbol referring to other concepts than utility *if for that other interpretation, the underlying axioms* **(I)** *and* **(PI)** *could be defended*. For example, Kelsey (1987) applies the axioms of technical welfarism to "criteria" which might not be utilities in one of the received senses, and Roberts (1995) constructs a modified SWFL framework which allows for comparisons of *ways of comparing utilities* as well as for straightforward utility comparisons. Notice that within the SWFL framework, one can envisage mathematical definitions of welfarism of varying strength.[57] The definition here is the most common and the simplest among those available.

4.2   *Invariance Axioms and Interpersonal Comparisons of Utility*

The classical invariance axioms of SWFL theory must now be introduced:

AXIOM **CC** (Cardinality and Full Comparability)

$$\forall\ U \in \mathcal{U}^n, \forall\ \alpha > 0, \forall\ \beta \in \mathbb{R} \text{ s.t. } \alpha U + (\beta, \cdots, \beta) \in \mathcal{U}^n,$$
$$F(U) = F(\alpha U + (\beta, \cdots, \beta)).$$

---

[56]For a proof of (i), see d'Aspremont (1985, Theorem 2.1). For (ii), see Mongin (1994a, Lemmas 1 and 2).

[57]For instance, Roberts (1980b, pp. 425ff.) states a notion of welfarism for SWFL satisfying **(I)** and **(WP)**. Alternatively, axiom **(I)** rather than the Pareto conditions can be weakened to derive further technical notions of welfarism. See also the variant presented in Section 4.6.

AXIOM **CU** (Cardinality and Unit Comparability)

$$\forall\, U \in \mathcal{U}^n, \forall\, \alpha > 0, \forall\, \beta \in \mathbb{R}^n \text{ s.t. } \alpha U + \beta \in \mathcal{U}^n,$$
$$F(U) = F(\alpha U + \beta).$$

AXIOM **CN** (Cardinality and Noncomparability)

$$\forall\, U \in \mathcal{U}^n, \forall\, \alpha = (\alpha_1, \cdots, \alpha_n) \in \mathbb{R}^n_{++}, \ \forall\, \beta = (\beta_1, \cdots, \beta_n) \in \mathbb{R}^n$$
$$\text{s.t. } (\alpha_1 u_1 + \beta_1, \cdots, \alpha_n u_n + \beta_n) \in \mathcal{U}^n,$$
$$F(U) = F(\alpha_1 u_1 + \beta_1, \cdots, \alpha_n u_n + \beta_n).$$

In the statement of the following two axioms $\varphi_1, \cdots, \varphi_n, \varphi$ stand for arbitrary strictly increasing functions from suitably defined subsets of $\mathbb{R}$ to $\mathbb{R}$, and $\varphi \circ u$ stands for the operation of composing functions φ and u.

AXIOM **OC** (Ordinality and Comparability)

$$\forall\, U \in \mathcal{U}^n, \forall\, \varphi \text{ s.t. } (\varphi \circ u_1, \cdots, \varphi \circ u_n) \in \mathcal{U}^n,$$
$$F(U) = F(\varphi \circ u_1, \cdots, \varphi \circ u_n).$$

AXIOM **ON** (Ordinality and Noncomparability)

$$\forall\, U \in \mathcal{U}^n, \forall\, (\varphi_1, \cdots, \varphi_n) \text{ s.t. } (\varphi_1 \circ u_1, \cdots, \varphi_n \circ u_n) \in \mathcal{U}^n,$$
$$F(U) = F(\varphi_1 \circ u_1, \cdots, \varphi_n \circ u_n).$$

Clearly, **(ON)** $\Rightarrow$ **(OC)** $\Rightarrow$ **(CC)** and **(ON)** $\Rightarrow$ **(CN)** $\Rightarrow$ **(CU)** $\Rightarrow$ **(CC)**. The consequences of these axioms in terms of two classes of social choice rules will be spelled out below. This is not an exhaustive list. (For a more detailed analysis, see Bossert and Weymark's chapter. Their labelling of invariance conditions may occasionally differ from ours.)

Invariance axioms are intended to capture the *impossiblity* of certain interpersonal comparisons of utility. For instance, **(CU)** implies that the ethical observer cannot compare the *levels* of cardinal utility functions. The comparisons which are possible (though not compulsory, of course) are exactly those which are not excluded by the given invariance axiom. For instance, **(CU)** allows for comparison of *measurement units* of cardinal utility functions. A well–recognized consequence of the invariance formalism is that the stronger the chosen axiom is, the narrower the basis for interpersonal comparisons on the observer's part. At one end of the spectrum, to assume a pure SWFL framework without any invariance axiom is tantamount to assuming that *any* interpersonal comparison is possible. At the other end, the strong axiom **(ON)** says in effect that no comparison is possible. Many social choice theorists conclude that the invariance based approach to SWFL leads to the following paradox: the *ethical* content of social choice theories is inversely proportional to their *logical* content.[58] It should be emphasized that the paradox depends on the prior philosophical assumption that interpersonal utility comparisons, rather than the lack of them, are a problem. Such an assumption underlies Arrow's (1951) pioneering work, as well as (although to a lesser degree) his followers' contributions, but cannot be accepted uncritically. Our discussion of Bentham and Pareto in Section 2 provides some historical perspective on this problem. To pursue the issue of interpersonal comparisons of utility, the reader is referred to Hammond's chapter as well as his extensive (1991) survey and the many references listed in these two papers.

4.3   Further Conditions on SWFL

Once technical welfarism holds, all unanimity axioms stronger than Pareto indifference, as well as all of the invariance axioms above, are automatically translated into corresponding conditions on the set of utility values, i.e., $\mathbb{R}^n$. For instance, using the definition of the R^* relation in the Welfarism Lemma, **(PWP)** becomes equivalent to:

CONDITION PWP^*

$$\forall\, a, b \in \mathbb{R}^n, a \geq b \;\Rightarrow\; aR^*b,$$

and so forth for the remaining Pareto axioms. Similarly, **(CC)** becomes equivalent to:

CONDITION CC^*

$$\forall\; a, b \in \mathbb{R}^n, \forall\, \alpha > 0, \forall\, \beta \in \mathbb{R},$$
$$aI^*b \;-\; \alpha a + (\beta, \cdots, \beta)I^* \alpha b + (\beta, \cdots, \beta),$$

and so forth for the remaining invariance axioms. In the sequel the starred name of an axiom should always be understood as referring to the translation of that axiom in terms of the R^* relation. Starred conditions are more tractable than their initial counterparts in terms of social welfare functionals. This well–known technical advantage is put to use in the expositions of SWFL theory by Blackorby, Donaldson and Weymark (1984) and d'Aspremont (1985). If only for expository purposes, these writers assume the conclusion of the Welfarism Lemma to hold throughout.

---

[58]See the discussion of this point in Blackorby, Donaldson and Weymark (1984).

The following axioms will be used in the sequel. One is the well–known axiom of Anonymity:

Axiom **A**

> For any permutation $\sigma(\cdot)$ of $N = \{1, \cdots, n\}$ and any $U \in \mathcal{U}^n$,
> $F(U) = F(u_{\sigma(1)}, \cdots, u_{\sigma(n)})$.

When technical welfarism holds, **(A)** is translated into:

Condition A^*

> For any permutation $\sigma(\cdot)$ of N and any $a = (a_1, \cdots, a_n) \in \mathbb{R}^n$,
> $a I^*(a_{\sigma(1)}, \cdots, a_{\sigma(n)})$.

At the general level, **(A)** stipulates that individuals should receive equal treatment in utility terms. The exact implications of this condition depend on whether and which (if any) interpersonal comparisons of utility are allowed. For instance, in the presence of technical welfarism and the utilitarian invariance principle, it will imply that each individual's utility *differences* are treated equally.

The most extreme case of unequal treatment is perhaps when one individual alone dictates the social preference. Following Arrow's (1951) definition, dictatorship prevails when one individual dictates the social *strict* preference. This leaves the social preference undetermined when the dictator is indifferent between two alternatives.[59] Restating Arrow's notion in the SWFL framework, we define *Nondictatorship* as follows:

Axiom **ND**

> There is no $i \in N$ such that for all $x, y \in X$ and $U \in \mathcal{U}^n$,
> $u_i(x) > u_i(y) \Rightarrow x P(U) y$.

Obviously, **(A)** $\Rightarrow$ **(ND)**, and under technical welfarism the latter condition will be translated into

Condition ND^*

> There is no $i \in N$ such that for all $a, b \in \mathbb{R}^n$, $a_i > b_i \Rightarrow a P^* b$.

---

[59] One possible strengthening of Arrow's notion is to introduce a *hierarchy* of dictators, where the $(n+1)$-th dictator rules if the n-th one is indifferent [Gevers (1979)].

The last condition is Continuity, to be defined here directly in terms of the R^* relation:[60]

CONDITION C^*

> For all $a \in \mathbb{R}^n$, the sets $\{a' \mid a' \in \mathbb{R}^n \text{ and } a'R^*a\}$ and $\{a' \mid a' \in \mathbb{R}^n \text{ and } aR^*a'\}$ are closed in $\mathbb{R}^n$.

LEMMA 4.2 For whichever domain restriction stated in Lemma 4.1, the following holds: if F satisfies **(I)** and **(PI)**, then each starred condition is equivalent to the corresponding axiom on SWFL, and: **(A)** & **(CU)** $\Rightarrow$ (C^*).

4.4   Utilitarianism Versus Leximin

We shall now restate and discuss some classic characterizations of social–choice–theoretic rules. The most famous among the utilitarian rules is the Benthamite *sum utilitarianism* rule:

$$\forall\, U = (u_1, \cdots, u_n) \in \mathcal{U}^n, \forall x, y \in X,$$
$$xF(U)y \quad - \quad \sum u_i(x) \geq \sum u_i(y).$$

A relevant variant is *mean utilitarianism*, where the equivalence just stated is replaced with:

$$xF(U)y \quad - \quad 1/n \sum u_i(x) \geq 1/n \sum u_i(y).$$

Obviously, the two rules coincide when the size n of the population is fixed. Henceforth, the expression *standard utilitarianism* will refer to either of these classic rules.

At least for technical reasons, we need to introduce weaker variants than those of standard utilitarianism. After d'Aspremont (1985, p. 46), we define *generalized utilitarianism* as follows: there are nonnegative numbers $\alpha_1, \cdots, \alpha_n$, one of which is strictly positive, such that:

RULE GU

$$\forall\, U = (u_1, \cdots, u_n) \in \mathcal{U}^n, \forall\, x, y \in X,$$
$$\sum \alpha_i u_i(x) \geq \sum \alpha_i u_i(y) \quad - \quad xF(U)y.$$

---

[60]For brevity, we follow the standard exposition [see Maskin (1978)], but it would be more consistent to define continuity in terms of the primitive notion F.

A further variant is *weak utilitarianism*. It is defined by replacing (GU) with:

RULE WU

$$\sum \alpha_i u_i(x) > \sum \alpha_i u_i(y) \quad \Rightarrow \quad xP(U)y.$$

When $\alpha_i = 0$ for all except but one i, (WU) reduces to dictatorship in Arrow's sense, while (GU) delivers a different dictatorship concept.[61] Rule (WU) is hardly weaker than (GU). Using completeness of the social preference $F(U)$, it can be checked that only one piece of information should be added to (WU) in order to recover (GU):

$$\sum \alpha_i u_i(x) = \sum \alpha_i u_i(y) \quad \Rightarrow \quad xI(U)y.$$

Another widely explored social–choice–theoretic rule is the *leximin principle*. It says that alternatives x and y will be socially ranked according to the minimum individual utility values in each alternative; if the worst–off individual in x and the worst–off in y happen to have the same amount of utility, the rule prescribes to compare the minimum utility values in the remaining population, and so on. That is to say, it gives lexicographic priority to the worse–off (in utility terms).

Formally, given any utility vector $U(x) = (u_1(x), \cdots, u_n(x))$ define $\hat{U}(x) = (\hat{u}_1(x), \cdots, \hat{u}_n(x))$ to be any permutation of $U(x)$ which ranks the individual utility levels in a weakly increasing order, i.e., $\hat{u}_1(x) \leq \hat{u}_2(x) \leq \cdots \leq \hat{u}_n(x)$. Now, the *leximin rule* can be defined as follows:

RULE L

$$\forall\, U \in \mathcal{U}^n, \forall\, x, y \in X,$$
$$xP(U)y \quad - \quad \exists\, m \in N \text{ s.t. } \forall\, h < m, \hat{u}_h(x) = \hat{u}_h(y), \text{ and } \hat{u}_m(x) > \hat{u}_m(y).$$

Like symmetric utilitarian rules, leximin implies that x and y are socially indifferent whenever $U(x)$ and $U(y)$ are identical up to a permutation.[62] Unlike

---

[61]If $\alpha_i = 0$ for all except but one i, and (GU) rather than (WU) holds, i imposes not only his strict preference but also his indifference relation. This is another strengthening of Arrow's definition of a dictator.

[62]All these rules also imply that x is socially strictly preferred to y if any permutation of the $U(x)$ vector Pareto–dominates $U(y)$ (in the **(Strict P)** sense). This property is Suppes's (1966) *grading principle*. It has sometimes been defended as a minimum equity principle for welfaristic contexts [e.g., Suzumura, (1983)].

symmetric utilitarian rules, leximin is not compatible with any further indifference case. It should be clear that (L) requires that utility levels be comparable from one individual to the other: unsurprisingly, **(OC)** will emerge as part of the characterization of this rule. Another — intuitively unattractive — concept must be introduced for formal purposes: define the *leximax principle* as that rule which gives lexicographic priority to the better–off.

Sen (1970, Chapter 9, and 1974) introduced the notion of leximin in the course of discussing Rawls's conception of justice.[63] He noted that Rawls's (1958, 1967) work pointed towards the simpler principle of *maximin*, which consists in giving priority to the worst-off (without paying attention to any higher ranks). For instance, if two alternatives x and y are described by utility vectors (1, 4, 7) and (5, 1, 8) respectively, maximin would declare x and y to be socially indifferent. The example illustrates a gross violation of the Pareto principle (in the **(Strict P)** version). This is why Sen (1970, p. 138) argued for a refined, iteratively defined concept. Relevant SWFL characterizations of leximin were provided by Hammond (1976), Strasnick (1976), and d'Aspremont and Gevers (1977). The latter writers rely on some of the SWFL axioms explained above, as well as the following added principle of *separability*:

AXIOM **SE**

> $\forall\, U, U' \in \mathcal{U}^n$, $F(U) = F(U')$ if $\exists\, M \subset N$ s.t.
> (i) $\forall\, i \in M$, $u_i = u'_i$
> (ii) $\forall\, j \in N \setminus M$, u_j and u'_j are constant functions.

In this statement, individuals in $N \setminus M$ can be said to be *unconcerned* by which alternative is chosen. Hence, it says that unconcerned individuals do not influence the social preference. D'Aspremont and Gevers's result states that leximin and leximax together are characterized by Independence of Irrelevant Alternatives, Strong Pareto, Ordinality and Comparability, Anonymity, and Separability. A complementary result by Deschamps and Gevers (1978) shows that if Ordinality and Comparability **(OC)** is *weakened* into Cardinality and Full Comparability **(CC)**, and if leximax is excluded by assumption, the set of admissible rules is exactly leximin *and* weak utilitarianism. We restate here these two results together:

---

[63] Kolm (1972, 1974) also contributed to introduce leximin under the label *justice pratique*. However, Kolm applies leximin to "fundamental preferences" which (by construction) are identical from one individual to the other (see Section 6.3). Consistently with his leximin approach, Kolm (1993) strongly argues against utilitarianism.

PROPOSITION 4.3 Take any SWFL which satisfies (I), (SP), (A), (SE) and does not coincide with leximax. Then:

(i) It coincides with either leximin or weak utilitarianism (with equal coefficients) if and only if it satisfies (CC).

(ii) It coincides with leximin if and only if it satisfies (OC).

(iii) It coincides with standard utilitarianism if and only if it satisfies (CU).[64]

Part (i) comes close to saying that assuming the welfarism framework, an apparently modest requirement of separability and a sufficiently general axiom of interpersonal utility comparisons imply that there are no rules *other than egalitarianism (in the sense of leximin) and utilitarianism*. The difference between this loose wording and part (i) reflects the technical difference between weak utilitarianism and standard utilitarianism. In the case in which $\sum \alpha_i u_i(x) = \sum \alpha_i u_i(y)$, the conclusion that $xI(U)y$ does not necessarily follow; for instance, it would be permissible to break the tie by applying leximin. However, the loose wording captures the essential message of the Deschamps–Gevers theorem — arguably, one of the philosophically most instructive contributions of SWFL theory. This result makes it possible to construe utilitarianism and leximin as being *exhaustive* alternatives. In other words, it gives a formal explanation of why the debate between Rawls and Harsanyi is absolutely central to social ethics.

The above discussion of maximin and leximin is typical of the *welfaristic* reconstruction of Rawls's *Theory of Justice* (1971), a reconstruction which was authorized not only by Sen's early work, but also by Arrow's comments on Rawls (1973a, 1973b), and which quickly gained acquiescence among economists.[65] As is well-recognized by now, this interpretation leaves aside several crucial aspects of Rawls's conception. Both Rawls himself (1982) and his commentators have insisted that "justice as fairness" leads to rejecting the utility concept as a way of assessing the members of society's positions, and that accordingly, the welfarist reconstruction is inadequate. An "index of primary goods" should be used instead of utility functions. This distinction will be revisited in 6.4. At least, the SWFL framework used here has the didactic advantage of illuminating one important claim in Rawls's doctrine: he admits of no trade-off when it comes to the individuals' essential interests. His strongest disagreement with utilitarianism stems from the fact that the latter requires the sacrifice of the

---

[64]For(i), see the proof of Theorem 2 in Deschamps and Gevers (1978). For (ii) and (iii), see the proof of Theorem 7 in d'Aspremont and Gevers (1977).

[65]Arrow reviews *A Theory of Justice* in (1973a), while in (1973b) he critically investigates the dynamic properties of Rawls's theory, again by using a welfarist model.

individual's interests whenever this is necessary for the greatest happiness of all. "Utilitarianism does not take seriously the distinction between persons" (1971, p. 27).[66]

4.5   Further Rules for Social Evaluation. The Variable Population Case

By introducing weaker invariance axioms than those just considered, more scope is given to interpersonal comparisons. Consider for example:

Axiom **RS** (Ratio Scale Comparability)

$$\forall\, U \in \mathcal{U}^n, \forall\, \alpha > 0, F(U) = F(\alpha U).$$

This axiom has been used in the theory of income inequality, which in part connects with SWFL theory.[67] Under **(RS)**, **(I)**, **(SP)**, **(A)** and (C^*), restricting the domain $\mathcal{U}^n$ to positive–valued utility functions, one gets a large class of social welfare orderings, namely all orderings R^* that are representable by some increasing, symmetric, homothetic[68] and continuous "social–evaluation function" W from $\mathbb{R}^n_{++}$ to $\mathbb{R}$: $aR^*b - W(a) \geq W(b)$.

More generally, one could even assume *extreme* comparability — i.e., no invariance axiom at all. Then, under the same other axioms, one would obtain an even larger class of rules: all social welfare orderings (SWO) R^* that are representable by some increasing, symmetric and continuous "social–evaluation function" W from $\mathbb{R}^n$ to $\mathbb{R}$. There is one representation of particular interest: the *equally distributed equivalent* utility function w, which is uniquely defined by the equation:

$$W(a) = W(w(a), w(a), \cdots, w(a)),$$

for every a in the domain of definition of W. This notion is relevant to the theory of inequality measurement. A related concept will be mentioned in the context of fairness theory (see Section 6.5).

The equally distributed equivalent representation turns out to be useful also in some extensions of welfarism to the variable–population case. The ethical

---

[66] Some critics (such as Temkin, 1993, and Glannon, 1995) have argued that Rawls is concerned only about the distinction between persons among the worst off, since maximin (and to a lesser extent, leximin) leads to the neglect of losses, however large, when they are incurred by the better off.

[67] See in particular Blackorby and Donaldson (1978). The recent survey by Blackorby, Bossert and Donaldson (1995a) also explores various connections between the two theories.

[68] Homotheticity means that W can be written as a composed function $\varphi \circ \lambda$, where λ is homogeneous of degree 1 and φ is monotonic.

problems involved in population policies, life–saving social decisions, transfers to future generations, and so on, go far beyond the scope of this chapter.[69] We want, however, to indicate what new axioms are required to derive welfarist rules in this novel context. This exposition is limited to the particular approach introduced by Blackorby and Donaldson (1984). Like these authors, we assume that utility values are defined for the individual's life taken as a whole, not for each period of his life: this is the "lifelong utility" assumption, which by–passes the problems involved in constructing this aggregate from more elementary utility data.

The Pareto conditions, (PI) and (SP), and the independence axiom (I) will remain unchanged. But they might have new implications when applied to alternatives involving populations of different sizes. Blackorby and Donaldson argue that (PI) rules out social discounting of future utilities, a consequence which many authors would find undesirable. Axiom (A) should be formally modified to deal with comparisons involving two populations of the same size but with different individuals: under these circumstances, utility vectors that are identical up to a permutation will be declared to be socially indifferent. These axioms lead back to welfarism, but the social–evaluation function is now denoted by W^n, since the size n of the population determines the dimension of the utility vector. Then, assuming (C^*), we can again define the equally distributed equivalent utility function as an alternative representation of W^n; denote it by w^n.

The rules considered here will be variable population variants of utilitarianism. All involve the notion of a *minimal utility level*, to be interpreted as the level attached to a life which is just worth living, and normalized to zero. A first rule to consider is the extension of sum–utilitarianism: for any positive integer n and any $a \in \mathbb{R}^n$, $W^n(a) = \sum_{i=1}^{n} a_i$. The corresponding equally distributed equivalent is defined by average utility: $w^n(a) = 1/n \sum_{i=1}^{n} a_i$. For any two utility vectors, $a \in \mathbb{R}^n$ and $b \in \mathbb{R}^m$, aR^*b if and only if $W^n(a) = \sum_{i=1}^{n} a_i \geq W^m(b) = \sum_{i=1}^{m} b_i$, or equivalently in terms of averages, $nw^n(a) \geq mw^m(a)$. After the philosopher Parfit (1984), this utilitarian rule has been criticized for leading to the so–called *repugnant conclusion*: for any two positive average utility levels, assigning the lower one, however low, to a large enough population, will be preferred to assigning the larger one to a smaller population.

Mean utilitarianism provides one way to overcome this difficulty. Formally, (variable population) mean utilitarianism amounts to taking as a social evaluation function the equally distributed equivalent of (variable population) sum–utilitarianism. Namely, for any two utility vectors, $a \in \mathbb{R}^n$ and $b \in \mathbb{R}^m$,

---

[69] See in particular the collection by Sikora and Barry (1978), Parfit's (1984) important book, and the continuing discussion on the latter. Among others, Hammond (1988b), Cowen (1989) and Broome (1992, 1996) discuss population issues.

$$aR^*b \text{ if and only if } 1/n \sum_{i=1}^{n} a_i \geq 1/m \sum_{i=1}^{m} b_i.$$

Blackorby and Donaldson (1984) provide a simple characterization in terms of standard utilitarian axioms, i.e., **(SP)**, **(A)**, **(CU)**, and the following specific condition that they attribute to the early 20th century economist Wicksell.

WICKSELL POPULATION PRINCIPLE:

For any two utility vectors $a \in \mathbb{R}^n$ and $b \in \mathbb{R}^{n+1}$ such that $a_i = b_i$ for $i = 1, 2, \cdots, n$, bR^*a if and only if $b_{n+1} \geq w^n(a)$.

However, Blackorby and Donaldson choose to avoid the "repugnant conclusion" by defending a less "elitist" population principle than mean utilitarianism. They propose the following two principles, the first of which involves a critical utility level which they take to be positive, the other being a separability condition:

α–PARETO POPULATION PRINCIPLE $(\alpha > 0)$:

For any two utility vectors $a \in \mathbb{R}^n$ and $b \in \mathbb{R}^{n+1}$ such that $a_i = b_i$ for $i = 1, 2, \cdots, n$, bR^*a if and only if $b_{n+1} \geq \alpha$.

POPULATION SUBSTITUTION PRINCIPLE:

For any two utility vectors $a \in \mathbb{R}^n$ and $b \in \mathbb{R}^m$, $w^{n+m}(a, b) = w^{n+m}(w^n(a), \cdots, w^n(a), b)$.

The point of taking α positive is to avoid the "repugnant conclusion". (However, one should note than an "α–repugnant conclusion" can be opposed to critical–level utilitarianism.) In the presence of axioms **(SP)**, **(A)** and (C^*), these two principles characterize the class of SWO represented by *Critical–Level Generalized Utilitarian* rules (with the critical level fixed by α):

$$W^n(a) = h[\sum_{i=1}^{n}(g(a_i)) - g(\alpha))],$$

for some monotonic transformations h and g (where g is continuous).

Implicitly, the role of the weighting function $g(\cdot)$ is to take account of the social evaluator's attitude to inequalities in the utility distribution; typically, welfare inequalities will be smoothed out by one's choice of a concave $g(\cdot)$. The definition of generalized utilitarianism here is not the same as that used in Section 4.4; the weighting function can be (and typically is) non–linear.

This result, as well as the above characterization of mean utilitarianism, corresponds to a *static* framework of social choice. The only difference between this setting and that of Section 4.4 is that alternatives now involve populations of variable size. There is still no time dimension involved in the social choice problem. Blackorby, Bossert and Donaldson (1995) attempt to remedy this by constructing a framework of dated individuals and principles. The main innovation in their framework is the principle of *Independence of the Utility of the Dead* (IUD), which states that the ranking of two alternatives remains unchanged when the dead are removed from these alternatives.[70] Principles like this make it possible to distinguish between individuals according to their birth and death dates, so that history matters to a certain extent. Technically, (IUD) plays in the intertemporal setting a role similar to the α–Pareto Population and the Population Substitution Principle taken together, so that this new axiom is the basis for another axiomatization of critical–level generalized utilitarianism.[71]

4.6 Some Conceptual Problems of the Multi–Profile Approach

In 4.1 we emphasized the difference between Arrow's preference–based notion of a social welfare function (SWF) and Sen's and his followers' notion of a social welfare functional (SWFL). However, the two concepts share an important common feature: they belong to the *multi–profile* approach of social choice theory. In the *single–profile* approach only one vector of individual utilities or preferences is considered at a time. Then, it is hardly relevant to consider the collective preference as a "function" or "functional" of individual items (although, trivially, a function can be defined on a singleton domain). By contrast, the multi–profile approach makes it possible to consider *several* vectors of individual utilities or preferences at a time, and accordingly to relate these items to the collective preference in a truly functional way. To express the distinction between the two kinds of approaches in completely formal terms is a delicate task.[72] But it is normally easy to recognize whether a particular axiom belongs to one or the other (or both). A moment's thought shows that the Pareto principle can be expressed in both frameworks. The conclusions it

---

[70] Hammond (1988b) had also used a version of this principle.

[71] Loosely related to the theme of this subsection is the recent discussion of infinite utility streams, as in Nelson (1991), Vallentyne (1994), and Van Liedekerke and Lauwers (1997). These and other writers investigate the Pareto principle, the anonymity axiom, as well as several variants of utilitarianism, in the case of *infinite–dimensional* vectors of utility values — a mathematically natural extension of the welfarism framework which may be relevant to population issues. To avoid the paradoxes of infinity, standard axioms and social choice rules have to be reformulated using abstract methods; see in particular Lauwers (1995).

[72] See Rubinstein's (1984) elucidation in terms of mathematical logic.

implies about collective preference depend on just considering *one* profile of individual utilities or preferences at a time. Conceptually, the Pareto principle is of the single–profile type. But it can also be expressed unproblematically in the multi–profile language of SWF or SWFL theory (as in Section 4.1 above). By contrast, Independence of Irrelevant Alternatives, as first introduced by Arrow (1951, p. 26), is a specifically multi–profile axiom. The conclusions it implies depend on comparing *two* profiles with each other; it states a law of variation of collective preference in terms of the relevant individual variables.

In the early days of social theory, objections were often raised against the multi–profile approach.[73] Since these objections hit the SWFL and the SWF frames of analysis with equal force, they should be reviewed here, albeit sketchily. The critics' common theme was that "laws of variation", such as Arrow's Independence axiom, assumed that analogies and disanalogies in individual preference profiles can be ascertained meaningfully, which they claimed was impossible. As Little put it forcefully:

"we do not require that the difference between the new and the old ordering should bear any particular relation to the changes of taste which have occurred. We have, so to speak, a new world and a new order, and we do not demand correspondence between the change in the world and the change in the order" (1952, p. 423).

Even if one restricts the interpretation of preferences to tastes, as Little does in this famous comment, the critical point appears to be questionable. It is hard to see why tastes could not be compared with each other. A given individual's tastes in profiles 1 and 2 can be compared to the extent, for instance, that they lead to the same preference for wine over bread. Arrow's independence axiom does not require more than unproblematic comparisons of that sort. Presumably, Little's conviction that different individual preference profiles are like incommunicable worlds depends on the deeper point that there is no sense in considering individuals apart from the preferences they actually have. He is in effect questioning the meaning of the expression "a given individual's tastes in profiles 1 and 2" in the last sentence. The social choice theorist should not be misled by his use of the same index i in profiles 1 and 2. Different *profiles*, the argument goes, refer to different *populations*. This line of criticism leads to the conclusion that Arrow's independence axiom involves a misunderstanding of the individualistic foundations of welfare economics. Once it is rephrased in this way, the Little-Bergson attack on the independence axiom becomes a conceptually relevant objection (though its exact force remains to be assessed). Notice that it appears not to depend on a taste interpretation of individual preference.

---

[73]See Little (1952), Bergson (1954), and Samuelson (1967).

When technical welfarism is assumed right from the beginning, the distinction between the single–profile and the multi–profile approaches becomes largely irrelevant. Any social welfare ordering R^* might derive from either a multi–profile framework *or a suitably enriched single–profile framework*. Formally, take $\overline{U}$ to be any given profile of utility functions in $\mathcal{U}^n$, and $[\overline{U}]$ to be the class of relevant transforms of $\overline{U}$ (according to some chosen invariance condition). We introduce a SWFL restricted to $[\overline{U}]$ and require it to be constant on this domain. Now, we impose a "richness" condition on the domain, as well as a condition intended to play the role of Independence of Irrelevant Alternatives in SWFL theory. Respectively:

AXIOM *Unrestricted Utility Profile:*

For all a, b and c in $\mathbb{R}^n$ there exist x, y and z in X such that for some $U \in [\overline{U}]$,
$U(x) = a, U(y) = b$, and $U(z) = c$,

and:

AXIOM *Relative Neutrality:*

$\forall\, U, U' \in [\overline{U}], \forall\, x, y, x', y' \in X,$
$U(x) = U'(x')$ and $U(y) = U'(y') \quad \Rightarrow \quad x F(U) y$ iff $x' F(U') y'$.

These two axioms together imply that F can be extended to the complete domain $\mathcal{U}^n$ in such a way that both **(I)** and **(PI)** hold (see d'Aspremont, 1985, for a proof).[74] It then follows (by applying Lemma 4.1) that technical welfarism can be recovered in the *enlarged single–profile* framework just introduced. This demonstrates that the welfarist approach of this section does not need the full force of the multiprofile approach, and thus has broader applicability than standard SWFL theory.

---

[74] An extension result can also be proved for a profile of VNM utility functions. For further elaboration of the enlarged single–profile approach sketched in this paragraph, see Roberts (1980b), d'Aspremont (1985), and the earlier contributions referenced in these papers.

5 The Aggregative Setting with Choice–Theoretic Constraints

5.1 Harsanyi's Approach to Utilitarianism. The Aggregation Theorem

Harsanyi's contribution to ethics is contained in two seminal papers (1953, 1955), his book *Rational Behavior and Bargaining Equilibrium* (1977a), and a number of philosophical or interpretative papers (in particular 1977b; see also his 1977c *Essays* and his 1992 restatement). The classic three-page 1953 article states Harsanyi's version of the "original state" or "veil of ignorance", to be compared with Rawls's (1971) altogether different version. This approach led Harsanyi to formulate the Impartial Observer Theorem: assuming that individuals value social positions as if they did not know who will hold them, and that this ignorance is captured by the VNM theory of risk, as applied to equiprobable lotteries, he concludes that the mean rule of utilitarianism prevails. The equally classic 1955 article states the following Aggregation Theorem: assuming a profile of individual utilities and a social or ethical utility, all of which are VNM functions on a lottery set, the Pareto-Indifference condition implies generalized utilitarianism, i.e., that the social utility is a weighted sum of the individuals' utilities. Harsanyi takes up the two theorems in his (1977a) book, where he also provides a direct philosophical defence of utilitarian interpersonal comparisons of utility. The common theme of the three piece is, of course, utilitarianism, although the mathematical form of the rule is not quite the same from one to the other—a technical problem which will be addressed below. Harsanyi's philosophy, if not always his formalism, leans towards *symmetric* utilitarian rules, and more particularly the mean rule which he thinks is superior to the more popular sum rule.[75]

The crucial philosophical problems raised by Harsanyi's two theorems are that, for one, they do not state explicitly the interpersonal comparison axiom that is necessary for utilitarian rules to hold; for another, they are not clearly connected with any ethically relevant concept of utility. These two criticisms have led Sen (1986) and Weymark (1991) to the strong negative conclusion that Harsanyi's theorems had no ethical relevance after all. We shall here take the more moderate view that the theorems are ethically significant, but that a nontrivial argument is needed to bridge the gap between the formal results and utilitarian ethics. This conclusion is common to Broome (1991a), Ham-

---

[75]However, Harsanyi does not normally discuss the variable population case. He also claims to be a rule– rather than an act–utilitarianism (e.g., 1977c), and provides philosophical arguments in favour of the former variant, but this distinction appears to play no role in the interpretation of his two theorems. (To the best of our knowledge this distinction is not discussed in the choice–theoretic literature.)

mond (1987), and Mongin (1994a), even if they differ in their interpretations of Harsanyi's contribution.

A further important point for discussion is Harsanyi's method of deriving ethical conclusions from decision–theoretic premisses. He goes as far as to claim that "ethics is a branch of the general theory of rational behavior" (1977b, p. 42). Specifically, the crucial premiss in both the Impartial Observer and the Aggregation Theorems is that the individuals as well as the observer are VNM decision–makers. We shall reserve the discussion of the former theorem for Section 6. The present section is concerned with the latter and its numerous variants, applications and criticisms. It is interesting to record Harsanyi's own judgement on the relative strengths of his two major contributions: "[the Aggregation Theorem] yields a lesser amount of philosophically interesting information about the nature of morality than [the Impartial Observer Theorem], but it has the advantage of being based on much weaker—almost trivial— philosophical assumptions" (1977b, p. 48).

Formally:

PROPOSITION 5.1 [HARSANYI'S AGGREGATION THEOREM] Assume that the set of alternatives is $X = \Delta_s(\Gamma)$ or $X = \Delta(\Gamma)$ for some outcome set Γ. Assume also that the individual utilities $U = (u_1, \cdots, u_n)$ and the social utility u_0 are VNM functions on X. Then, the following condition holds:

(PI') $\forall \, x, y \in X, U(x) = U(y) \;\Rightarrow\; u_0(x) = u_0(y)$

if and only if there exist real numbers $\alpha_1, \cdots, \alpha_n, \beta$ such that:

$$u_0 = \sum_{i=1}^{n} \alpha_i u_i + \beta.$$

Harsanyi's initial proof lacked definiteness, while his later argument (1977a, 4.8) involved irrelevant algebraic independence restrictions. Uselessly complicated constructions have been erected around Harsanyi's result, which can be proved most simply, as the following shows.

PROOF [Coulhon and Mongin (1989)] Denote $(u_1, \cdots, u_n)$ by U. Condition **(PI')** is equivalent to the property that $u_0 = f \circ U$ for some function f: Range $U \rightarrow \mathbb{R}$. The following shows that f is mixture–preserving (MP): for any $Y, Y' \in$ Range U, there are $y, y' \in X$ such that $U(y) = Y, U(y') = Y'$, and

$$f(\lambda Y + (1 - \lambda)Y') = f(\lambda U(y) + (1 - \lambda)U(y'))$$

$$= f(U(y\lambda y')) = u_0(y\lambda y')$$

$$= \lambda u_0(y) + (1-\lambda)u_0(y') = \lambda f(Y) + (1-\lambda)f(Y').$$

(Notice the role of the assumption that both U and u_0 are MP.) From the MP property of U, it is clear that Range U is convex. It is a fact that if a real function is MP on some convex subset of $\mathbb{R}^n$, it is affine on that subset. We conclude that u_0 is affine in terms of the u_i. ∎

For simplicity we took X to be a lottery set but the proof carries through without change to the more general case in which X is a convex subset of any vector space whatever.[76] This last observation delivers an interesting *non-stochastic* variant of Harsanyi's Aggregation Theorem. Take the alternative set X to be some convex subset of $\mathbb{R}^p$, as in consumer theory, and take the utility set $\mathcal{U}$ to be the set of all affine functions on X. These assumptions define a particular "economic" domain in the sense of Section 3.1; utility functions are strongly separable in each commodity. Now, if $u_0, u_1, \cdots, u_n \in \mathcal{U}$ satisfy (**PI'**), we can conclude that u_0 is affine in terms of the u_i, exactly as in the VNM case.[77]

The following features of Proposition 5.1 should be carefully recorded: (i) the derived coefficients $\alpha_1, \cdots, \alpha_n$ can be of any sign; (ii) they can be of any magnitude; (iii) the result is a single–profile one, i.e., the coefficients $\alpha_1, \cdots, \alpha_n$ depend on the given utility profile $u_0, u_1, \cdots, u_n$. Hence the conclusion reached above is still at a distance from Harsanyi's theoretical target, which was to derive the mean rule of utilitarianism. Feature (i) is the most troublesome of all. Utilitarianism can hardly remain an interesting ethical doctrine, if it is extended to the point of involving negative weights for some individuals. Feature (ii) would be compatible with the more plausible concept of *generalized utilitarianism*, which was introduced within the SWFL framework in Section 4.4. However, this is *not* Harsanyi's brand of utilitarianism, which follows a longstanding tradition in requiring weights to be equal. Finally, (iii) raises the equally important question of whether or not the individuals' weights should just depend on their identity (which is represented here by the index i) or *also on their utility functions*, as is the case in Harsanyi's own version of the Aggregation Theorem. Problem (iii) is already part of Sen's (1986) assessment of the ethical significance of Harsanyi's theorems. Except for this overlapping

---

[76] Actually the proof above applies to the even more general case in which X is a *mixture set* [in the sense of Herstein and Milnor (1953)].
[77] Hammond (1996) provides another nonstochastic variant of Harsanyi's Aggregation Theorem in which individual utilities $u_1, \cdots, u_n$ are defined on endowment vectors but depend only on the individual's own component.

point, the discussion just sketched should be seen as a technical prerequisite to the Sen–Weymark critique.[78]

In both (1955) and (1977a) Harsanyi suggested that in order to remedy problem (i), it was enough to use a more demanding condition than the rather weak Pareto Indifference condition **(PI')**. The further results stated below clarify this intuition. We define the following strengthening of **(PI')**:

AXIOM **SP'**

$$\textbf{(SP')} \equiv \textbf{(PI')} \ \& \ \textbf{(Strict P')}, \text{ where } \textbf{(Strict P')} \text{ is}$$

$$\forall \ x, y \in X, U(x) > U(y) \ \Rightarrow \ u_0(x) > u_0(y).$$

It will also be interesting to investigate **(Strict P')** in isolation, as well as:

AXIOM **WP'**

$$\forall \ x, y \in X, U(x) \gg U(y) \ \Rightarrow \ u_0(x) > u_0(y).$$

Neither **(Strict P')** nor **(WP')** implies **(PI')**. As their labelling suggests, the various Pareto conditions introduced here exactly parallel those of Section 4.

Now, the following proposition shows that **(SP')** exactly conforms with Harsanyi's intuition. But to reach similar results under **(WP')** and **(Strict P')**, a restriction of *minimum agreement among individuals* — **(MA)** below — must be added:

PROPOSITION 5.2 [HARSANYI'S AGGREGATION THEOREM WITH STRONGER PARETO CONDITIONS][79] Assume that the individual utilities $U = (u_1, \cdots, u_n)$ and the social utility u_0 are VNM functions on $X = \Delta_s(\Gamma)$ or $X = \Delta(\Gamma)$.

1. If **(SP')** holds, there exist positive numbers $\alpha_1, \cdots, \alpha_n$, and a real number β such that $u_0 = \sum_{i=1}^{n} \alpha_i u_i + \beta$.

---

[78]This critique questions the philosophical relevance of the two theorems, but at leat takes for granted that they are successful technically, i.e., that they derive rules which are *formally* identical to standard utilitarian rules. As just explained, the conclusion of Proposition 5.1 falls short of this requirement.

[79]This proposition is borrowed from De Meyer and Mongin (1994). It is proved using convex analysis.

2. Assume further that:

    (MA) There are $x, y \in X$ with the property that $u_i(x) > u_i(y), i = 1, \cdots, n$.

Then, if **(WP')** [**(Strict P')**] holds, there exist nonnegative numbers, not all of them zero [resp. positive numbers] $\alpha_1, \cdots, \alpha_n$, and a real number β such that $u_0 = \sum_{i=1}^{n} \alpha_i u_i + \beta$.

Interestingly (and somewhat counterintuitively), the weak agreement condition **(MA)** can be derived from the assumption that individual utilities strongly differ from each other, or more technically, are affinely independent.[80]

We still have to deal with two technical issues among the three listed after Proposition 5.1. As it turns out, the technical problems (ii) and (iii) can be addressed at the same time by shifting from Harsanyi's initial framework to a SWFL one.[81]

5.2   A SWFL Reconstruction of Harsanyi's Aggregation Theorem

As in Mongin (1994a), the present reconstruction relies on the following social–choice–theoretic concepts: $X = \Delta_s(\Gamma)$ or $X = \Delta(\Gamma)$ for some outcome set Γ; X is required to have (vector space) dimension at least 2; and $\mathcal{U} = \mathcal{V}(X)$, i.e., the set of VNM functions on X. The SWFL

$$F : \mathcal{U}^n \to 2^{X \times X}$$

will be investigated under the special assumption that for all $U \in \mathcal{U}^n$, $F(U)$ satisfies VNM properties. Thus, we shall incorporate into the SWFL framework Harsanyi's assumption that both the individuals and the social aggregate are VNM maximizers. Let us define formally:[82]

---

[80]See Weymark (1993, Proposition 5.2). Mongin (1995a) proves the corresponding statement for SEU theory (i.e., when the alternatives are acts).

[81]Among further relevant *single–profile* variants of Propositions 5.1 and 5.2, Zhou (1997) extends Proposition 5.1 to the case of an infinite population, and Blackorby, Donaldson and Weymark (1996) investigate a variant of Proposition 5.1 in which VNM lotteries are replaced with subjective probabilities which are identical from one individual to another. This last modelling is really a borderline case between Harsanyi's VNM aggregative framework and the SEU framework discussed at length in Section 5.4.

[82]These two axioms are adapted from one among the many axiomatizations of expected–utility representations. Of the two, **(VNM2)** is clearly the crucial one from the conceptual point of view. Axiom **(VNM1)** is introduced here as elsewhere for the well–known reason that numerical representations of preferences require some continuity condition to hold.

AXIOM **VNM1**

> For all $U \in \mathcal{U}^n$, $F(U)$ satisfies the following continuity property:
> $\forall \, x, y, z \in X, \{\lambda \in [0,1] : zF(U)(x\lambda y)\}$ and
> $\{\lambda \in [0,1] : (x\lambda y)F(U)z\}$ are closed subsets of $[0,1]$.

AXIOM **VNM2**

> For all $U \in \mathcal{U}^n$, $F(U)$ satisfies VNM–independence, i.e.:
> $\forall \, x, y, z \in X, \forall \, \lambda \in]0,1], xF(U)y \quad - \quad (x\lambda z)F(U)(y\lambda z).$

In order to complete the literal translation of Harsanyi's assumptions into the new framework, it is enough to add that F satisfies **(PI)** or some alternative Pareto axiom. However, if one stopped at that, the SWFL exercise would plainly be useless. The whole point of shifting to the SWFL framework is that it makes it possible to formulate axioms and (hopefully) results which, unlike **(VNM1)**, **(VNM2)** and the Pareto conditions, relate to *several* utility profiles at a time. This is the essence of the *multi–profile* approach to social choice theory (see Section 4.6). Two relevant axioms are the already defined Independence of Irrelevant Alternatives **(I)** and Anonymity **(A)**. By adding them to the literal translation of Harsanyi's assumptions, one can hope to strengthen his results in the right direction. Specifically, it is likely that by adding **(I)**, one will cancel the dependence of individual weights a_i on the given utility profile, and by further adding **(A)**, one will derive a symmetric summation rule, as required by standard utilitarianism. In brief, the SWFL approach is tailor–made to supersede the technical problems that remained unsolved in view of Propositions 5.1 and 5.2. The following proposition fulfils these expectations, while clarifying the connection between Harsanyi's VNM assumptions with earlier utilitarian conditions:

PROPOSITION 5.3 Take X and $\mathcal{U}$ as defined in the VNM case, and assume throughout that F satisfies **(I)** and **(PI)**. Then:

(i) F satisfies **(VNM1)** and **(VNM2)** if and only if there exists a vector $(\alpha_1, \cdots, \alpha_n) \in \mathbb{R}^n$, unique up to a positive scale factor, such that for all $U = (u_1, \cdots, u_n) \in \mathcal{U}^n$,

$$\forall \, x, y \in X, \ xF(U)y \quad - \quad \sum \alpha_i u_i(x) \geq \sum \alpha_i u_i(y).$$

(ii) Assuming **(Strict P)**, the following holds:

(ii.1) **(CU)** and **(VNM2)** are equivalent to each other, and equivalent to Weak Utilitarianism (with strictly positive coefficients);

(ii.2) The two pairs of conditions **(CU)** & **(C)** and **(VNM1)** & **(VNM2)** are equivalent to each other, and each is equivalent to Generalized Utilitarianism (with strictly positive coefficients).

(iii) Standard utilitarianism follows from adding **(A)** to any of these restatements of Generalized Utilitarianism.[83]

Thus, Proposition 5.3 solves the two remaining technical difficulties surrounding Harsanyi's formulation of the Aggregation Theorem. Its merit lies with its simplicity. Its weakness is that the **(I)** axiom, for one, appears to be external to Harsanyi's initial problem-situation; for another, it gives rise to criticisms in its own right. In connection with the former point, we note that Hammond (1987) has also argued for a reconciliation of Arrow's social choice theory with Harsanyi's brand of utilitarianism. Such a *rapprochement* has the heuristic advantage of making comparisons easier, especially when it comes to discussing interpersonal comparisons of utility in Harsanyi's approach. In connection with the latter point, relevant criticism of Independence of Irrelevant Alternatives have already been raised in Section 4.6.

At least the following simple fact about the SWFL analysis should be clear. It appears to be impossible to derive classical, i.e., equal weights utilitarianism, without imposing either axiom **(A)**, or some variant *which must again be an interprofile axiom*. Hence, if not SWFL theory itself, an enriched single–profile approach, as introduced at the end of Section 4.6, is indispensable if one wants to move from Harsanyi's weighted sum formula to one which makes sense from the point of view of utilitarian philosophy. In the initial version of Harsanyi's theorem, which is purely single–profile, symmetric additive rules have — allegedly — been derived from suitable rescalings of individual utilities. From the axiomatic point of view this is a highly unsatisfactory procedure. The primitives of the reasoning are *fixed* numerical representations $u_0, u_1, \cdots, u_n$; they can be replaced with representations $u'_0, u'_1, \cdots, u'_n$ only if there is an invariance axiom to warrant their replacement. Whatever its exact wording, such an axiom cannot be insignificant, since it will indicate something about permissible and impermissible interpersonal comparisons of utility. We conclude that the usual "derivation" of symmetric rules is faced with a dilemma: either it relies on (some variant of) Proposition 5.3 above, or it should be objected to as being an *ad hoc* procedure.[84]

---

[83] For part (i), see Mongin (1994a), noticing the application of technical welfarism to the special VNM domain, as in Lemma 4.1 (ii) above. Part (ii) can be checked directly, which then leads to a variant proof of d'Aspremont and Gevers's (1977) **(CU)**-based characterization of utilitarian rules.

[84] This comment applies to Harsanyi's initial argument as well as to Broome's (1991a, chapter 10) exposition.

5.3   Further Philosophical Comments on Harsanyi's Utilitarianism

A major objection raised against the ethical relevance of Harsanyi's Aggregation Theorem is that he implicitly relies on an interpersonal comparison assumption, but fails to make it clear which assumption it is. As we shall argue, this objection is misconceived. The whole point of Harsanyi's approach is to show that if some choice–theoretic (i.e., VNM) and social–choice theoretic (i.e., Paretian) assumptions hold, then the collective preference conforms with a utilitarian interpersonal comparison principle. That is to say, the Aggregation Theorem is interesting just because it *derives* the relevant principle. Recall Harsanyi's own judgement as restated in Section 5.1: he regards the choice– and social–choice–theoretic premises of the theorem as "trivial". No doubt, he does not regard the principle of utilitarian interpersonal comparisons as "trivial"; hence the interest in a formal proof that the former implies the latter. Harsanyi might be wrong in believing that his premises are unproblematic; this would be a fair criticism. But to insist on reformulating the premises so as to make the role of interpersonal comparisons apparent right from the beginning is, in our opinion, to miss the fine point of the Aggregation Theorem completely.

Admittedly, Harsanyi's initial single–profile formulation does not facilitate the analysis of underlying interpersonal utility comparisons. The SWFL reformulation is clearer than the initial one in this respect as well as in others. The essential message of the Aggregation Theorem is perhaps best summarized in Proposition 5.3 (ii.1): granting the decision–theoretic and social–choice–theoretic axioms, to assume that the social preference satisfies the VNM independence axiom is tantamount to assuming that it conforms with the utilitarian invariance principle **(CU)**. There are several ways in which this logical equivalence can be turned into an ethical argument. For instance, Proposition 5.3 "could be used against anybody who would be prepared to swallow **(I)** and **(SP)**, make VNM assumptions on the individuals and the [social] utilities— allegedly, because these assumptions reflect individual rationality—and, say, turn Rawlsian, or hostile to any interpersonal comparison whatsoever, when it comes to assessing income distribution" (Mongin, 1994a, p. 349).[85]

The discussion above suggests that Harsanyi's critics should redirect their attack towards his *explicit* assumptions. Both Sen (1986) and Weymark (1991)

---

[85] Broome's (1991a, pp. 219–220) interpretation is different, though compatible with the view that Harsanyi's derivation involves a "surprise effect". This interpretation emphasizes the role of the *completeness* axiom imposed on social preference. The latter assumption implies that the ideal observer can rank situations of conflicting individual preferences (i.e., situations x and y such that i strictly prefers x over y and j strictly prefers y over z). This suggests a close connection between completeness and the admission of interpersonal comparisons of utility. Importantly, the completeness axiom does not indicate what *kind* of comparisons— i.e., utilitarian or otherwise—are made.

indeed follow this strategy by questioning Harsanyi's exclusive reliance on VNM utility representations of social and individual preferences.[86] To analyze this further objection, one should carefully distinguish between two kinds of theoretical commitments, one to the VNM axioms imposed on the *preference relation*, the other to the use of VNM *utility functions* as representations of the underlying preference relation.

Philosophically, this distinction is in accord with Harsanyi's own view of utility as representing preferences of some kind. Harsanyi (e.g., 1977b, p. 54) has emphatically rejected the early utilitarian writers' interpretation in terms of net pleasure. He claims to be a *preference* utilitarian, not a *hedonistic* utilitarian, as was Bentham, or an *ideal* utilitarian, as Moore is sometimes described. This is not to say that he follows the welfare economists' footsteps in defining utility as representing *actual* preferences. To the contrary, he adheres to—and in our opinion should count as a major representative of—that philosophical school we discussed in Section 2.5 which takes utility functions to be relevant to the ethical exercise only if they represent *improved* rather than actual preferences. In Harsanyi's special terminology, "moral" preferences are constructed by aggregating "personal" preferences only after the latter have been "corrected" and "censored" (see, e.g., 1977a, pp. 61–62). Correction is needed because some preference judgements might depend on factual errors; the ideal observer does not make these mistakes, and should thus appropriately modify the individual's preference ranking. Harsanyi mentions the example of an individual who wrongly believes that a certain drug is efficacious when it is not. There are trickier cases than this one, and it is not clear where an enlighted observer should stop improving "personal" preferences in this way. Harsanyi suggests that at least in principle, it is possible to draw a line: the observer "will be justified in using a corrected utility function (for j) only if he thinks that j himself would approve of this" (1977a, pp. 61–62). Notice the recurring methodological theme: the preference concept relevant to ethical applications can only be delineated in terms of some counterfactual experiment (see Section 2.5).

As to censoring "personal" preferences, à la Harsanyi, this does not simply mean that irreflective preference comparisons, or those resulting from the individual's weakness of the will, should not be considered by the observer. Presumably, such a preliminary laundering of "personal" preferences can be taken for granted. It can be analyzed in terms of a counterfactual clause modelled after

---

[86]Weymark (1991) also suggests restating Harsanyi's theorems by including among the axioms some *very general* comparability assumption (such as Cardinality and Full Comparability). This restatement is again compatible with the view that the added value or "surprise effect" of the Aggregation Theorem consists in deriving the *utilitarian* form of comparison. Formally, it would require moving to a SWFL or related framework.

the previous one: under suitable circumstances, the individual *himself* would approve of the observer's overruling his initial preference. Censure refers to a deeper problem: some *considered* preference judgements are, Harsanyi claims, ethically inadmissible. The observer "will be perfectly justified in disregarding j's actual preferences in cases where the latter are based on clearly antisocial attitudes, e.g., on sheer hostility, malice, envy, and sadism" (1977a, p. 62).[87] As critics have noted, it seems unsatisfactory to recommend preference censoring, and Harsanyi himself sometimes comes close to recognizing that there is a serious difficulty here. But is is important to bear in mind that this is a general difficulty with *any welfarist approach* to social ethics. The sadist plagues Harsanyi's theory in the same way, roughly, as the fanatic does Hare's (see Section 2.4). In other words, if Harsanyi's defence of utilitarianism strikes one as being inconsequent, there is nothing here that is specific to him, nor even to the particular brand of utilitarianism he adopts. As we suggested earlier, there are ethical objections that welfarism appears to be inherently incapable of answering. The inadequacy of Harsanyi's recommendation of censoring "personal preferences reflects one of the "limits of well–being".

Moving on to the technical side of the utility–preference distinction, we remind the reader that the uniqueness part of the VNM representation theorem does *not* say that *only* expectational (or mixture–preserving) functions represent those relations which satisfy the ordering, continuity and VNM–independence axioms [see Fishburn (1970) and (1982), and Hammond's chapter on "objective" expected utility]. Actually, any nonlinear, strictly increasing transform of the VNM representation provided by the theorem also represents the given binary relation. Sen and Weymark are then asking: Why should Harsanyi restrict attention to VNM representations only?

An answer to this question can be sketched along the following lines. What is crucial about VNM representations is that those, and only those representations, preserve the risk-attitude properties of the VNM decision maker. For instance, it is well known that the Arrow-Pratt coefficient of absolute risk-aversion remains invariant if and only if expectational representations are used to represent the VNM preference.[88] Now, following the heuristic underlying Harsanyi's approach in both the Aggregation and Impartial Observer Theorems, risk–attitude properties are ethically important data to record. In Harsanyi's opinion there is a close connection between the amount of risk that the VNM decision maker is willing to take in order possibly to receive x, and the strength of his desire for x. As he stated most clearly, "The VNM

---

[87] Notice the following variant: Harsanyi (1992, p. 704) has recently recommended censoring *all* other-regarding preferences, including benevolent ones, whereas he initially meant to exclude only malevolent ones.

[88] See Pratt (1964) or any textbook on the economics of risk.

utility functions do express people's attitudes to risk–taking (in gambling, buying insurance, investing and other similar activities). But they do not merely express these attitudes; rather they try to explain them in terms of the relative importance (relative utility) people attach to possible gains and possible losses of money and other economic and noneconomic assets" [Harsanyi (1977b) in Sen and Williams (1982, pp. 52–53)]. After other writers in the field, Harsanyi essentially claims that VNM indexes provide *cardinal* information on the individuals' and ideal observer's preferences that can be used *universally*, i.e., in the contexts of both risky and riskless choices. We are not suggesting that this strong claim should be endorsed, but just stressing that it is Harsanyi's most likely response to the Sen-Weymark critique. At least his position is internally consistent. Granting his prior conviction that VNM theory delivers cardinally relevant information, there would be no point for him to enlarge the set of utility representations beyond the class of VNM functions.[89]

The further question is, why should one accept Harsanyi's conviction that VNM theory delivers cardinally relevant information? Starting with the early days of expected–utility theory,[90] there has been an active debate about the meaning of cardinality (or "measurability", in some writers' terminology) in VNM theory. Two simple lessons can be drawn from this ever lively discussion. For one, the fact that VNM indexes are unique up to positive affine transformations just defines a mathematical notion of cardinality. It does not in itself lean towards any psychological interpretation. For another, there are two *prima facie* psychologically relevant interpretations of cardinality in the VNM context: one is Harsanyi's; the other is the—by and large now prevailing—opposite view that the numerical information contained in VNM indexes is relevant to *risky choices only*, and thus irrelevant to such issues as income distribution among the members of society (in which no chance mechanism is involved).[91]

We have separated interpretative questions pertaining to VNM indexes from those pertaining to the VNM preference axioms. The question now arises, whether or not these axioms should have been assumed in the first place. Even granting the point that they embody a normatively compelling modeling of rationality, and the further philosophical point that the ideal observer should aggregate *rationally formed* rather than empirically given individual preferences, it could be asked, why should the ideal observer *himself* comply with the VNM axioms? This last requirement turns out to be crucial to the utilitarian-

---

[89]An irrelevant objection here would be that Harsanyi cannot be at the same time a *preference* utilitarian and a cardinalist. We explained in Section 2.3 that the preference concept can receive a cardinal interpretation, as in Suppes and Winet (1955).

[90]See in particular Luce and Raiffa's discussion of "Fallacy 2" (1957, p. 32).

[91]We refer the reader to Fishburn (1970, 1989) and Bouyssou and Vansnick (1990) for careful reviews of these conflicting doctrines.

like results of Harsanyi's two theorems. As far as the Aggregation Theorem is concerned, the equivalences stated in Proposition 5.3 (ii) make the technical contribution of **(VNM2)** very clear: this axiom carries with it the exact force of the utilitarian principle of comparison. In the context of both the Aggregation and the Impartial Observer Theorems, several writers have questioned the assumption that the social preference—as against individual preferences —should be subjected to VNM independence. Their criticism usually runs as follows. When it comes to evaluating social arrangements, one is interested in the *exact distribution* of utility over the individuals. It is not enough to know the *mathematical expectation* of that utility distribution [e.g., Sen (1970, p. 143); see also Sen (1973b, 1986)]. When stated in this way, the objection to VNM independence becomes a variant of the classic objection against the distributional consequences of utilitarianism, an objection which is also endorsed by Rawls (1971).

A related but more specific argument results from a classic example of Diamond (1967). This example relies on a two–person society, and two lotteries x and y involving some equal chance device, say tossing a fair coin. Under x, whatever the result of tossing, individual gets everything, and j gets nothing. Under y, i gets everything if heads, and j gets everything if tails. The ethical intuition, Diamond believes, recommends ranking lottery y higher than lottery x, and at the same time, to express indifference between the following two outcomes: i has everything while j has nothing, j has everything while i has nothing. But a moment's thought shows that this conclusion violates VNM independence, which thus could not apply to the ethical observer's choices. This ingenious example has attracted considerable interest.[92] It broadens the discussion of the normative standing of VNM independence (as well as related axioms, such as Savage's sure–thing principle) to the different issue of *fair lotteries*.[93]

The positive argument in favour of imposing VNM independence on the social preference is, of course, *coherence*. Why should the observer be exempted from the rationality axioms to which individuals are subjected? This question has also been raised with respect to the Savage (or related) axioms of uncertain choice. Since the latter are—in a sense—more general than the VNM axioms of risky choice, we might as well postpone the required discussion to the end of Section 5.4.

---

[92] See in particular the comments by Sen (1970), Harsanyi (1975), Hammond (1983), Broome (1991a), Epstein and Segal (1992), and Karni (1996).

[93] On the issue of fair lotteries, see Broome (1990–1991), Wasserman (1996), and the references listed in the latter paper.

5.4   *The Aggregative Approach in the Case of Subjective Uncertainty*

Harsanyi's reliance on the VNM axioms implies that he takes the relevant state probabilities as given. Although several interpretations can be devised for this assumption, as suggested in Section 3.2, his aggregative approach is inherently incapable of dealing with public or moral situations in which not only utility assessments but factual opinions significantly differ from one individual to another. To be accurate, there are cases in which the role of factual disagreements can plausibly be chanelled through utility functions. For instance, one might conceive of the individual's diverging conditional expectations of lifespan as being appropriately reflected in their time preferences. But such construals should be used with much care. They clearly do not apply to the largest number of cases of relevant factual disagreements. Consider public debates over tax reform, illness prevention schemes, or environmental programmes. Each of these policies is likely to lead to significant discrepancies in the citizens' expectations of their practical consequences, independently of their valuations of consequences. Notice also that Harsanyi's recommendation of "correcting" preference judgements when they depend on mistaken beliefs can attenuate the citizen's differences of opinion, but is unlikely to eliminate them altogether. Following the Bayesian tenet, such truly factual and substantial disagreements can, and even should, be formalized by assuming that individuals entertain different subjective probabilities. Accordingly, SEU theory becomes the relevant frame of analysis to pursue Harsanyi's aggregative approach to social ethics.

Several writers have followed this line of inquiry: Hylland and Zeckhauser (1979), Hammond (1981, 1983), Broome (1990, 1991a), Seidenfeld et al. (1989), Mongin (1995a). The general lesson from this lively strand of literature is that Harsanyi's aggregative approach runs into severe difficulties, as soon as one replaces his own VNM assumption with any axiomatization of SEU theory. Essentially, the Pareto conditions clash with the requirement that both the individuals and the aggregate follow the SEU axioms. The authors just mentioned either properly demonstrate, or illustrate in the case of a two–agent society, impossibility theorems to the effect that only special cases, such as dictatorial rules or uniform probability and/or utility profiles, satisfy the two subsets of conditions at the same time. The last paper in the list has perhaps achieved maximum generality in stating these various impossibilities. The above contributions differ from each other not only in their chosen auxiliary assumptions, but also in more crucial axiomatic respects. Hylland and Zeckhauser's (1979) —which might count as the historical source of the present literature—uses a rich axiomatic framework of social choice theory but no axiomatization of SEU theory *per se*. The same comment applies to Hammond's (1983). The remaining contributions share the common feature that they do not use the language of social choice theory, but—sometimes implicitly—assume some axiomatic framework of Bayesianism. Mongin's (1995a) is based on Savage's axiomatization of SEU theory, but its results carry through without significant loss of content to the more accessible Anscombe–Aumann version. We shall follow this convenient variant here.

The notation will be the same as in Section 3.3. Each individual will thus be endowed with an AA–representation: for $i = 0, 1, \cdots, n$ and any act a,

$$(*) \qquad u_i(a) = \sum_{\omega \in \Omega} p_i(\omega) v_i(a(\omega)).$$

For technical reasons, we introduce the following assumption of *Minimal Agreement on Consequences*:

ASSUMPTION **MAC**

$\exists \ c, c' \in \mathcal{C}$ s.t. $\forall \ i \in N, v_i(c) > v_i(c')$.

This added assumption amounts to strengthening the nontriviality requirement which enters any SEU axiomatization for rather obvious reasons.[94] We should now appropriately reformulate the various *Pareto conditions* envisaged by Harsanyi. To do so, it is enough to revert to the definitions of **(PI')**, **(SP')** and **(WP')** in Section 5.1, and everywhere replace $x, y \in X$ with $a, b \in X = \mathcal{C}^\Omega$. Thus reformulated, the Pareto conditions have an *ex ante* interpretation: if all individuals agree on the ranking of two state–dependent functions (or, more pictorially, bets) a and b, so does the social observer. This stipulation holds before uncertainty is resolved, and should carefully be distinguished from *ex post* versions of the Pareto principle, which will be discussed below. Notice that **(MAC)** has the effect of making **(WP')**, hence also **(SP')**, nonvacuous.

The impossibility theorem below involves various concepts of dictatorship. We shall say that there is a *utility dictator* if $v_0 = v_j$ (up to a positive affine transformation) for some $j \in N$, and an *inverse utility dictator* if $v_0 = -v_j$ (up to a positive affine transformation) for some $j \in N$. Similarly, there is a *probability dictator* if $p_0 = p_j$ for some $j \in N$. The negative conclusions of the theorems depend on assuming affine independence of either the probabilities or the utilities or both. We explained in Section 3.4 that affine independence is an algebraic rendering of interindividual diversity.

---

[94]Without it preferences between acts would not reveal the agent's subjective probability. What **(MAC)** adds to this standard requirement is that the nonconstancy of the U_i can be checked on a *uniform* choice of c, c'. A minimal agreement assumption was already used in the VNM context of Proposition 5.2.

PROPOSITION 5.4 The following assumptions hold. There is a finite state set Ω, a consequence set $\mathcal{C} = \Delta(\Gamma)$ for some outcome set Γ, and the alternative set is $X = \mathcal{C}^\Omega$. The individuals and social observer have Anscombe–Aumann (AA) preferences that are represented by utility functions $U = (u_1, \cdots, u_n)$ and u_0 respectively, as in (*) above. The utility functions satisfy **(PI')**. Then,

(i) If the p_i, $i = 1, \cdots, n$, are affinely independent, there is a utility or inverse utility dictator j; if furthermore the v_i, $i = 1, \cdots, n$, are pairwise affinely independent, j is also a probability dictator.

(ii) Symmetrically, if the v_i, $i = 1, \cdots, n$, are affinely independent, there is a probability dictator j; if furthermore the p_i, are pairwise distinct, j is also a utility or inverse utility dictator.

PROPOSITION 5.5 The assumptions are as in Proposition 5.4, plus **(MAC)**. Then, if **(WP')** holds, the conclusions are as in Proposition 5.4 (i) and (ii), except that inverse dictatorship becomes impossible. Assume now that **(Strict P')** holds. Then,

(i) If the $p_i, i = 1, \cdots, n$, are affinely independent, the v_i, $i = 1, \cdots, n$, must be pairwise dependent.

(ii) If the v_i, $i = 1, \cdots, n$, are affinely independent, the p_i, $i = 1, \cdots, n$, must be identical.

Propositions 5.4 and 5.5 should be compared with their VNM counterparts, i.e., Propositions 5.1 and 5.2 above. It turns out that in the case of the weaker Pareto conditions — i.e., **(PI')** and **(WP')** — Harsanyi's utilitarian–like aggregation rule degenerates into a form of dictatorship (which is stronger than Arrow's). The conclusion is even more negative in the case of the strongest of the Pareto conditions considered here, i.e., **(Strict P')**. Then, the assumptions are shown to impose a constraint on the *data* of the aggregative problem rather than its *solution*. Under **(Strict P')** even dictatorship might fail to provide an aggregative rule. This further impossibility is not so much in the style of Arrow's as of those social choice results which state that some "natural" set of assumptions involves an outright logical contradiction. To make this clear, we may formulate the essential conclusion of Proposition 5.5 in a slightly different way. The following weaker, but perhaps more transparent statement holds:

PROPOSITION 5.6 [THIS IS A VARIANT OF PROPOSITION 5.5] Assume the following. There are n individuals; they, as well as the social observer, have AA preferences represented by utility–probability pairs $(v_1, p_1), \cdots (v_n, p_n)$, and (v_0, p_0), respectively. **(MAC)** holds, as well as the following Interindividual Diversity condition: the p_i and the v_i are affinely independent. Then, if **(WP')** holds, there is an individual $j \in N$ who is both a probability and a utility dictator. To impose **(Strict P')** instead of **(WP')** would lead to a logical contradiction

Subjective probability measures p_i and utility functions v_i play completely symmetric roles in Propositions 5.4 and 5.5. Some variants of Proposition 5.5 (ii) above have been discussed earlier under the label "probability agreement theorem", mostly by Broome (1989), (1990) (1991a)]. This expression is slightly misleading because it might wrongly suggest a constructive interpretation for the theorem. Contrary to convergence results in Bayesian statistics and the economics of information, the theorem here does not state *reasons* why subjective probabilities should become equal. In the other results, asymptotic equalization of subjective probabilities is due to shared information between individuals and successive revising of posterior probabilities in view of this common information. In the present framework, the involved probabilities can be interpreted as being either prior probabilities or posterior probabilities in a context of differing private information. Conceptually, there is absolutely no reason why they should be equal; this is why the result must be interpreted as an impossibility theorem.[95]

Propositions 5.4 and 5.5 are derived by adapting the proof of their counterparts in Savage's framework (Mongin, 1995a, Propositions 5 and 7).[96] The technical argument need not be pursued here. Suffice it to say that the crucial properly to use in the AA framework is the lottery (or convexity) property of the consequence set $\mathcal{C}$. By and large, this property will play the same role as did Savage's (1954) divisibility postulate (P6) in the corresponding proof. These alternative mathematical restrictions are worth emphasizing for the following two reasons. First, in the absence of them, it is possible to construct counterexamples to Propositions 5.4 and 5.5.[97] Second, they happen to be the very same mathematical restrictions that utility theorists need in order to derive SEU representations from axioms on preferences over acts.[98] Hence, there is a tight connection between the paradoxes of collective Bayesianism, as restated here, and the *axiomatic* versions of that doctrine. It follows that at least in the present version, they are paradoxes of *preference* rather than of *utility* theory.

---

[95] For modelling purposes, economists often assume that prior probabilities are equal. It is important to realize that this "common prior assumption" is introduced for methodological reasons and does not have any choice–theoretic foundation. The interested reader is referred to Morris (1995).

[96] For more details on the AA variant, see Mongin (1996).

[97] Mongin (1995a, p. 337).

[98] The fact that special (and seemingly irrelevant) properties of Ω or $\mathcal{C}$ are needed to prove the SEU representation theorem is well–recognized and was explained above in Section 3.3.

On the face of it, they concern *improved* preference theories no less than *actual* preference theories.

We have been stressing the connection between Propositions 5.4 and 5.5 and Harsanyi's research programme in ethics, but these propositions can receive an alternative and equally relevant interpretation in terms of a classic problem of welfare economics. When uncertainty rather than risk prevails, even assuming SEU theory as the relevant theory of choice under uncertainty, it remains to choose between two families of collective evaluation rules. *Ex ante* rules result from aggregating the individuals' Bayesian preferences or SEU functionals over acts. Such rules take the individuals' subjective probabilities into account since these probabilities are embodied in the aggregated characteristics. By contrast, *ex post* rules are obtained by first constructing a probability measure and a utility function on consequences for the collective entity, and second combining these two items in the way prescribed by SEU theory. Each type of rules give rise to specific variants of the Pareto principle. *Ex ante* Pareto conditions relate individual to social preferences or utility representations before uncertainty is resolved. *Ex post* Pareto conditions relate the former to the latter after uncertainty is resolved—i.e., only in terms of consequences. Given the usual identification of consequences with a particular subset of acts, *ex ante* conditions are logically stronger than their *ex post* counterparts. It is also true that each family of rules relies on a distinctive application of SEU theory. The *ex ante* point of view applies the theory to individual preferences, while the *ex post* point of view applies it to collective preference as well.

In sum, either type has good credentials in terms of either Paretianism or Bayesianism, but can at best be described as a partial application of these two doctrines. The question then arises of whether or not an *ex ante* rule can also be *ex post*. Since Hammond's work (1981, 1983), the technical answers to this question by welfare economists and social choice theorists have regularly been negative. Propositions 5.4 and 5.5 might be interpreted as stating a further version of the clash between *ex ante* and *ex post* rules. To see that, notice that the assumptions made in the above propositions are that: (i) the individuals are Bayesian; (ii) the Pareto principle holds in an *ex ante* sense; and (iii) the collective preference itself is Bayesian. We have just explained that (i) and (ii) together define the *ex ante* approach, whereas (i), (iii), and an appropriate weakening of (ii) together define the *ex post* approach. Hence the assumptions of Propositions 5.4 and 5.5 can be understood as formalizing the requirement that an *ex ante* Paretian rule be also *ex post*. The conclusions spell out the precise sense in which this requirement fails.

From the Bayesian point of view, only (i) is completely indispensable, and indeed most of the positive contributions to the *ex post* versus *ex ante* debate can be classified according as they sacrifice (ii) or (iii). The *ex post* school of welfare economics, as it has come to be called, expresses theoretical preference for (iii) over (ii).[99] Its basic objection against the *ex ante* version of the Pareto principle is that it applies the principle to the wrong set of preferences. The underlying argument can be reconstructed as follows. There are various defences of the Pareto principle, based on different interpretations of preference and utility, but all of them involve a basic distinction between factual and normative considerations. One way or another, the individuals are proclaimed to be sovereign about *normative* matters. This appears to mean two things: for one, "collective" normative judgements are derivative; for another, the individuals cannot be mistaken in normative judgements of their own. "Normative" here might be variously understood by reference to values, objectives, or even simply tastes, as in the famous "consumer sovereignty" doctrine. No defence of the Pareto principle has ever involved similar claims in terms of *factual* judgements. This hardly comes as a surprise: it would not make such sense to claim that collective factual judgements are derivative; it is of course grossly untrue that the individuals cannot be mistaken in their factual judgments. *Ex post* oriented writers are aware of the distinction between normative and factual judgements, and of the important implication that unanimity is compelling at most in terms of the former, never in terms of the latter. This is why these writers accept (and indeed recommend) applying the Pareto principle of preferences over *consequences*, but reject it when it comes to preferences over *acts*. Essentially, they see preferences over acts as relying on a critical mixture of factual and normative judgements which blocks the application of the Pareto principle. At the same time, they construe preferences over consequences as reflecting only normative judgements, which, in this case, leads to an unproblematic application of the principle.

The negative case against the *ex ante* version of the Pareto principle seems compelling, but let us reconsider the positive case for the *ex post* version. The underlying argument seems to be this: if the preference concept is suitably restricted, the Pareto principle can reap the benefits of the normative versus factual distinction. But is it possible to restrict the scope of individual preferences to the point where factual considerations do not matter anymore, or at least influence every individual preference identically? A moment's thought shows that this must be very difficult. In real life, judgements about consequences of acts are infected with factual considerations, which typically diverge from one individual to another. It is only because they must stop the analysis somewhere that decision theorists, such as Savage, have introduced unstructured consequence sets. The formalism of the theory should not mislead its

---

[99] A leading exponent is Hammond: he recommends "that a policy–maker maximize expected *ex post* welfare based on the best information available to him" (1983, p. 176); see also the conceptual comments in his 1982 article.

users. In any concrete application, the properties of the consequence set will become relevant, and the claim that the Pareto principle applies to this or that particular consequence set might well founder on the very same argument that earlier refuted the *ex ante* application. On reflection, the *ex post* version is not immune to the difficulties surrounding the *ex ante* version.[100]

Those who find the *ex post* versus *ex ante* debate inconclusive will be inclined to go back to the list of assumptions above and relax (iii) rather than (ii).[101] But a serious obstacle to this way of escape is Harsanyi's already mentioned coherence principle, to the effect that rationality principles are recognized once and for all, and apply to both the individuals' and the observer's preferences (see Section 5.3). Harsanyi expressed this principle as follows: "welfare economists are no more at liberty to reject the sure–thing principle or the other Bayesian axioms of rationality than are people following lesser professions" (1975, p. 67). If anything, "welfare economists" should aim at *higher* standards of rationality than ordinary people. This wording takes for granted that the bearer of social preference is an individual—an assumption which can be disputed. It might well be an appropriate assumption to make in the context of Harsanyi's own ethical theory. He endows each individual with *two* utility functions, or preference maps, one of which (the "personal" one) expresses the individual's tastes and interests, the other (the "moral" or "social" one) his views about the interests of society as a whole.[102] There are no further utility or preference concepts to be considered in Harsanyi's system. Hence, the only interpretation left for "the social observer", "the bearer of collective preference", and like expressions, is: *any* individual in the society, whenever he adopts a "moral" rather than a "personal" point of view.

Granting this analysis, the coherence principle under discussion strikes one as relatively easy to defend. But there are alternative available notions of "the social observer". Following the tradition initiated by Arrow (1951), social choice theory describes the passive result of aggregating individual normative judgements. The properties of collective preference relations are entirely endogenous

---

[100]This paragraph echoes Broome (1990 and 1991a, Chapter 7). See also Hausman and McPherson's comment: "why should one believe that people in general are better at forecasting the consequences of lung cancer than the likelihood of getting it?" (1994, p. 398). For another discussion of the *ex post* Pareto principle, see Hild, Jeffrey and Risse (1997). These authors argue that the *ex post* principle is at odds with a basic requirement of adequacy for collective preference (i.e., that collective preference should remain consistent with earlier descriptions of preferences when these descriptions are progressively refined).

[101]In the context of risky choice, some writers [e.g., Myerson (1981); Kolm (1997)] have recommended the use of *concave* social welfare functions, and therefore implicitly rejected the analogue of assumption (iii), i.e., VNM independence. In the same context, Epstein and Segal (1992) have explored the implications of adopting a quasi–concave quadratic social welfare function.

[102]See, e.g., Harsanyi (1975, pp. 65–66) and similar passages in his (1977a and b).

—they may or may not turn out to be well behaved. As far as collective preferences are concerned, some properties might be *desirable*, but not *normatively compelling* in the way they would be if applied to individual preferences. Accordingly, one should not insist on endowing the collective entity with these properties if this contradicts the more basic requisits of the social choice problem. Transitivity is the most famous example of a requirement on collective preference that Arrovian theorists regard as desirable, though not indispensable.[103] A similar argument could be made for the sure–thing principle in those cases in which the bearer of social evaluation is not a concrete individual, but an abstract entity or a pure aggregate.

For the sake of completeness, we should mention that there are alternative ways of approaching the difficulties of collective Bayesianism. One of them consists in changing the meaning of "Bayesianism" in assumptions (i) and (ii), and more particularly to relax the property of *state–independence* which we explained in Section 3.3 is crucial to both the Savage and Anscombe–Aumann versions of SEU theory. This solution is explored in Schervish et al. (1991) as well as in Mongin (1996). It can be shown that the negative results of Propositions 5.4 and 5.5 disappear from the pure state–dependent version of SEU theory but reemerge (though in a more complex form) when the theory allows for a mixture of state–dependence and state–independence. Thus, given relevant qualifications, state–dependent utility theory does *not* appear to be the way out of the predicament of collective Bayesianism. The impossibility of "consistent Bayesian aggregation" is a robust theorem.[104]

6   The Impartial Observer, the Original Position, and Fairness

6.1   *Impartial–Observer Theories*

Following a long–standing tradition, *impartiality* is a distinctive feature of moral judgements on collective life—notably, when it comes to deciding whether or not a social situation or an institution is just. That is to say, these judgements should not depend on the individuals' identities and other particular circumstances. They should remain the same if the individuals and surrounding circumstances concerned are, *mutatis mutandis*, replaced by others. There are two distinctive currents of thought in which this general

---

[103]On the status of transitivity in social choice theory, see in particular Arrow (1951, pp. 118–120), Buchanan (1954) and Sen (1970, 1982a).

[104]Levi (1990) provides another discussion which does not fit in with the previous pattern of choice between the *ex post* point of view and rejection of Harsanyi's coherence. Levi rejects the *ex ante* principle but does not restrict it as drastically as does the *ex post* school; he is concerned about justifiable unanimity in a truly *ex ante* context. The technical implications of Levi's justifiability criterion need to be sorted out.

principle has been defended. One is typical of the Scottish writer of the 18th century, in particular Hume, Hutcheson and Smith, while the other is associated with Kant's practical philosophy.

The former current leads to the celebrated construction of the "sympathetic but impartial observer" in Smith's *Theory of Moral Sentiments* (1759). In Hutcheson's earlier formulation, "benevolence"—rather than "sympathy" or "impartiality"—was the key notion:

"This universal Benevolence toward all men, we may compare to that Principle of Gravitation, which perhaps extends to all Bodys in the Universe: but, like the Love of Benevolence, increases as the Distance is diminished and is strongest when Bodys come to touch each other." (1725, paragraph 145)

This definition suggests that one and the same feeling is at work whether the individual is concerned with himself or the others—the difference between the two cases being only a matter of degree. "Universal benevolence" was Hutcheson's suggested foundation for morality. It can be argued that it is a shaky foundation. Benevolence is just a *feeling*. Although it might be compatible with the exercise of judgement, it by no means implies that a judgement, let alone a moral judgement, is passed. Besides, even if it is "universal" in Hutcheson's sense of embracing all mankind and varying by degrees, benevolence is only a coarse approximation to the impartiality requirement of traditional morality. That I am moved by others' situations, and willing to act on their behalf, is no evidence that I am a moral person. Benevolent people, if they are just benevolent, lack the disinterestedness which is typical of morality. Hume's notion of "sympathy" has much in common with Hutcheson's "benevolence": it is an all–embracing feeling, the intensity of which varies monotonically with propinquity. However, more clearly than "benevolence", "sympathy" involves the exercise of judgement:

"My sympathy with another may give me the sentiment of pain and *disapprobation*, when any object is presented, that has a tendency to give him uneasiness tho' I may not be willing to sacrifice anything of my own interest, nor cross any of my passions, for his satisfaction." (1736, p. 586, our italics)

Even if sympathy in Hume's sense is an admixture of feeling and judgement, one can argue that it is not yet an appropriate foundation for morality, because, like benevolence, it lacks disinterestedness. To act out of sympathy for my neighbour is not, in a deep sense, to act morally. One can interpret Smith as clarifying this when he recommends that the moral observer should balance *sympathy* and *impartiality* with each other. The crucial point is that sympathy must be corrected by impartiality; in particular, we should avoid biasing our judgements towards those whose life we share, or those who resemble us. Conversely—but this seems to be a secondary theme—impartiality is stimulated, and in some sense preceded, by sympathy. Smith apparently believed that judgements of morality would simply be impossible—i.e., they would not really exist as acts of the mind—once separated from the psychological substratum of sympathy. By and large, this *sentimentalist* stand towards morality was shared by all of the 18th century Scottish writers.[105]

Another, altogether different connection between morality and impartiality can be found in Kantian philosophy. On this view, the notion that the moral law is impartial must be explicated in terms of its conformity to reason. Kant is well known for emphasizing universality as a criterion of conformity to reason. The way in which he does is highly restrictive. He distinguishes between the conditional universality of *hypothetical* imperatives (which tell you what to do if you have certain ends) and the unconditional universality of the *categorical* imperative (see Section 2.1 above). Only the latter has the formal character that Kant claims to be the distinctive feature of reason. Hence, only the latter is said to be relevant to morality. Prudential reasoning, which relies on the former kind of imperatives, is declared to be void of ethical content. Many later philosophers have retained from Kant's *Groundwork* and *Critique of Practical Reason* the important claim that the status of a maxim of action as a moral law can be tested by examining whether and how it can be universalized. But a majority of these philosophers have also rejected the extreme formalistic stance of Kantian ethics. They have denied that the distinction between two kinds of imperatives can consistently be made, while still insisting that universalization provides a usable criterion for moral reasoning. This updated—some would say watered–down—style of Kantianism underlies Harsanyi's reconstruction of "Ethics in Terms of Hypothetical Imperatives" (1958). Rawls's (1980) reconstruction of Kantianism also tampers with Kant's initial distinction between two kinds of imperatives.

Contemporary impartial observer theories appear to borrow from both the Scottish and the Kantian sources. One way or another, these theories elaborate on Smith's basic idea that one should judge one's actions as if they were observed by some hypothetical other. But they appear also to rely on Kant's universalization device, if not on his sharp division between the intelligible and the empirical realms, or between the two kinds of imperatives. The connecting link is as follows: the action that is declared to be best from the impartial observer's point of view can also be said to have successfully passed the universalization test.

As a first application, consider Hare's (1976, 1981) "universal prescriptivism". It relies on the following idea of interpersonal permutations: the same moral prescriptions should apply to all situations obtained from a given one by per-

---

[105]The quotations of this paragraph are borrowed from Collard (1978). For other relevant extracts of the British moralists, see Monroe (1972).

muting individuals. The observer should first evaluate any social situation by adopting the identity of every individual in turn, and then weighting the resulting evaluations equally, in order to derive his final evaluation. Although Hare's theory does not provide any formal derivation, it is meant to be a defence of utilitarianism. Hence, it must be a teleological theory. However it also has a deontological side, since it is based on everybody's right to receive an impartial treatment. Universal prescriptivism "is nothing but a restatement of the requirement that moral principles be universalizable" [Hare (1981, p. 154)]. A weakness of Hare's theory is that it does not specify the defining properties of individual identities, and thus leaves relatively undefined the nature of the many evaluations that should be weighted against each other.

Other writers have brought the Impartial Observer approach to a higher degree of precision by calling upon the methods of utility theory. One prominent example, to be reviewed in Section 6.3, is Harsanyi in his 1953 Impartial Observer Theorem.

6.2 State–of–Nature Theories and the "Original Position"

Impartial observer theories have often been contrasted with state–of–nature theories. The latter claim that the basic principles of society derive from its members' *voluntary agreement*: the concept of a "state of nature" then refers to that particular situation which precedes and brings about the agreement. This important tradition of analysis is more closely linked to political than to moral philosophy. The writers who initiated it in the 17th and 18th centuries —Hobbes (1651), Locke (1690), and Rousseau (1755, 1761), to mention only the most famous ones—were primarily concerned with justifying the existence and defining the limits of political institutions. However, they also wanted to illuminate the contrast between the primitive and fully socialized stages of human life, so that their analysis can be read from other angles than just political theory. They can also be viewed as providing an ideal genesis of morality, a point well emphasized by Gauthier (1986, p. 10). The common feature to all of the 17th and 18th century notions of the state of nature is that they put special constraints on individual interactions before the founding agreement takes place. Depending on the particular author, these constraints can go in opposite directions: Rousseau's state of nature keeps individual interactions to a bare minimum, but Hobbes's and Locke's constructions admit of wide–ranging interactions (which led Rousseau to complain that hey had failed to capture the true meaning of a state of *nature*).[106] The classics were unanimous in considering

---

[106]In Hobbes's state–of–nature individuals have unlimited claims to self–preservation and property, which leads to universal war. By contrast, in Locke's state–of–nature individual freedom and property rights are grounded in, and limited by Natural Law, and peace and

the individuals' agreement on political institutions as a full–fledged *contract*; they modelled it after the corresponding notion in positive law. Hence the label "contractarianism" for these writers' and their followers' theories. Another important feature that is common to the classics is that they accounted for the transition from the state of nature to the political state in quasi-historical terms. Admittedly, their works are essays in *conjectural* rather than in real history. But the fact remains that their argument for justifying and assessing institutions cannot be stated without the device of a temporal set–up, however interpreted.

Those contemporary philosophers, such as Rawls (1971) or Gauthier (1986), who endorse the 17th and 18th contractarian philosophers' tradition, have distanced themselves from them in a number of respects. To the best of our knowledge, no contemporary writer has ever really endorsed the notions of a state of nature and of the ensuing contract—even in the conjectural history interpretation. Two definitely weaker concepts are used instead: respectively, that of a *reference situation* from which relevant institutions and aspects of collective life have counterfactually been eliminated, and that of a (possibly tacit and informal) *agreement* between the individuals.

Gauthier's (1986) construction of the reference situation and the ensuing agreement is based on the formal theory of bargaining—more precisely, on Kalai and Smorodinsky's (1975) solution to the bargaining problem. This and other constructions are representative of a whole class of state–of–nature theories which are formulated in terms of game–theoretic concepts (be they cooperative or non–cooperative), and thus go beyond the purview of this chapter.[107] By contrast, Rawls's reference situation—the "original position"—is not phrased in game–theoretic terms. Rawls requires unanimity to hold for the building up of collective institutions. The citizens' unanimous decision could well result from some preexisting negotiation, but Rawls construes it differently: individual choices are made separately, under special conditions of ignorance, which explain why these separate choices happen to coincide. This famous restatement of the "original position" in terms of a "veil of ignorance" links

---

mutual assistance prevail. For a thorough account of 17th and 18th centuries state–of–nature theories, in particular Rousseau's, the reader is referred to Dérathé (1951).

[107]On Gauthier's contractarianism, see Vallentyne's (1991) collection, and for reviews of bargaining theory, see Kalai (1985), Gaertner and Klemisch–Ahlert (1992), and Thomson (1995). (The latter extends the basic definitions to the variable population case.) Gauthier is not the only contemporary writer to base an ethical construction on bargaining theory. Binmore (1994) also does that, while expressing theoretical preference for Nash's (1950) original solution to the bargaining problem. Yaari (1981) also investigates Nash's solution viewed as a theory of justice. In an innovative empirical study, Yaari and Bar–Hillel (1984) compare respondents' attitudes towards several well–known bargaining solutions. Roemer (1994, Essay 9) questions the relevance of the bargaining approach as a whole to the theory of justice. His critique is largely directed against the informational limitation (i.e., the welfarism assumption) underlying this approach.

Rawls's construction to the theory of individual choice under risk and uncertainty; hence it fully belongs to our subject matter.[108]

6.3   Harsanyi's Impartial Observer Theorem, and the Problem of "Extended Sympathy"

Harsanyi's 1953 theorem, as further clarified in (1977a and b), is perhaps the simplest recent example in the class of impartial observer theories. Harsanyi adheres to Smith's notion that "the moral point of view is essentially the point of view of a *sympathetic* but *impartial* observer" (1977a, p. 49), while occasionally claiming for his theory the benefit of Kant's universalization maxim. He appears to recognize the difference between the hypothetical experiments involved in his quasi–Smithian construction, and the hypothetical histories that are typical of the state–of–nature approach. His novel contribution to the Smithian–Kantian tradition is twofold: he argues first that the observer's judgements can be reproduced as any individual's choices in a relevant situation of ignorance (i.e., "complete ignorance of what his own position, and the position of those near to his heart, would be within the system chosen", 1953, p. 4), and second that this makes utility theory the relevant tool of analysis to resort to ("choice in that hypothetical case would be a clear instance of a 'choice involving risk'", ibid.). In Harsanyi's argument, the connecting link between complete ignorance and risky choice is *equiprobability*. If the individual does not know what his own "position" is, he should give equal probabilities to the various "positions" he can conceivably hold. This is a significant and disputable step in Harsanyi's argument. Bayesian statisticians often take for granted that complete ignorance should be rendered by a uniform prior, but SEU axiomatizations of Bayesianism, such as Savage's and Anscombe and Aumann's, do not logically imply this principle. Also, Harsanyi claims to provide an ethical system rather than just a theory of justice. His notion of ethics is restrictive in one sense, because he unexceptionally identifies the "moral" and "social" points of view, and thus appears to leave no room for private ethics. In another sense, his conception is an encompassing one, because it supposedly covers *all* ethical aspects of social relations.

Even assuming that the theory of risky choices and the equiprobability model are relevant here, one gets different formalizations, and possibly different ethi-

---

[108]Nozick's (1974) libertarian conception also involves a primitive reference situation and a founding agreement. The former is characterized by an "original acquisition of holdings". The latter results only in a "minimal" state. The current property distribution is justified only if it results from successive free transfers starting from the reference situation, but there is a —unanimously agreed—"Lockean clause" whereby this process should not worsen anyone's subsistence level.

cal implications, depending on how one draws the line between what is known and what is unknown to the individuals in the hypothetical experiment. Lerner (1944) and Vickrey (1945) are sometimes given credit for anticipating Harsanyi, but they were imprecise in this respect as well as in others. Vickrey seemed to have in mind that the members of society should ignore their position on the *income distribution* ladder.[109] Harsanyi's 1953 article is still unclear. It can be understood in terms of Vickrey's interpretation, as well as of a richer (and philosophically more challenging) notion of what in the individual's position should be unknown to him. From Harsanyi's later comments, the wider interpretation emerges as the only relevant one:

"Individual i's choice among alternative social situations would certainly satisfy (the) requirement of impartiality and impersonality, if he simply did not know in advance what his own social position would be in each situation — so that he would not know *whether he himself would be a rich man or a poor man, a motorist or a pedestrian, a teacher or a student, a member of one social group or a member of another social group, and so forth*" (1977a, pp. 49–50, our emphasis).

This apparently indefinite list points towards the following interpretation: the information to be cancelled relates to everything that constitutes i's individuality — a point well clarified in Pattanaik's (1968) comparison of Harsanyi with Vickrey.

To formalize Harsanyi's point, one might want to borrow from the following, independently developed construction of social choice theory. In various social choice contexts, Arrow (1951 and 1963, 1977), Suppes (1966), Sen (1970, chapter 9), Kolm (1972, 1995), Suzumura (1983, 1994) and others have discussed versions of "extended sympathy"—Arrow's term. Essentially, these authors assume that each member of the society i is endowed not only with an actual preference relation defined on some alternative set X, but also with an "extended preference" relation defined on suitably modified alternatives, having the typical form (x, j). In these "extended alternatives" both the individuals' identities and the initial alternatives are treated as choice or evaluation variables. That i can make extended preference judgements is not a weak assumption. It means that given any two members of the society, j, k, individual i can decide which is better from these two: either to be faced with x while being j, or to be faced with x while being k.[110] Sen (1970, pp. 149–150) has

---

[109] According to Vickrey, society should choose as would any individual, on the understanding that "once he selects a given economy *with a given distribution of income*, he has an equal chance of landing in the shoes of each member of it" (1945, p. 329; our emphasis). See also Vickrey (1960).

[110] Of course, $i = j$ and $i = k$ are logical possibilities in this statement. "Alternative", here might refer to individual actions, as in Sen's example, as well as to social states of affairs.

provided a two–individual illustration in which j is a devout Muslim and k is a devout Hindu, and x means "to eat pork" and y "to eat beef". Any member of the society should be able, in effect, to decide whether breaking Hindu law is better or worse than breaking Muslim law. This famous example was not primarily meant to illustrate the demanding nature of extended preference judgements, but it does.

Like Harsanyi himself in his later work, we shall borrow the special preference concept just outlined, and formalize his Impartial Observer approach accordingly. However, our extended preference relation will be defined on elements (x, t_j), where t_j denotes individual j's type. This notation is meant to convey the particular interpretation of extended preference that is suited to Harsanyi's approach: i will be assumed to "land in the shoes" of j by deducing what his choices or evaluations are, given j's relevant characteristics. To say that i records j's choices or evaluations directly would be to make an altogether different assumption.[111] Harsanyi (1977a, pp. 58–59) makes it clear that he is concerned with the former, not the latter, Accordingly, the second variable of our extended utility functions will not be an index of individuals but a symbol of their relevant characteristics. As in Harsanyi's (1967–68) classic exposition of incomplete information games, the notion of a type t_j will refer to the (supposedly meaningful) complete list of such characteristics.[112]

Formally, let us denote the set of all individuals' types by $T_N = \{t_1, \cdots, t_n\}$ and the initial alternative set by X. Then, $X \times T_N$ is the set of extended alternatives. We also need to introduce the set $\Delta_s(X \times T_N)$ of extended lotteries: they will be the objects of extended preference in our formalization. Of special significance are the following equiprobable extended lotteries: for any $x \in X$,

$$L_x = (1/n(x, t_1), \cdots, 1/n(x, t_n)).$$

In words, L_x promises alternative x with equal probabilities of being awarded any of the available types. Each individual $i \in N$ is endowed with three utility functions: a personal utility u_i on X, a moral utility w_i also defined on X, and an extended utility v_i, which represents his extended preferences on $\Delta_s(X \times T_N)$. We make the technical assumption that X itself is a lottery set. This will make it possible to apply the VNM axioms to u_i and v_i.

Our first axiom, to be called *Equal Chance*, is Harsanyi's account of the impartial but sympathetic observer:

---

[111] A related distinction is discussed in Suzumura (1983, pp. 133–136).

[112] D'Aspremont and Gérard–Varet (1991) elaborates on the connection between Harsanyi's Impartial Observer construction and his concept of a type in games of incomplete information. They restate the former in terms of Bayesian implementation theory.

Axiom **EC**

$$\forall \ x, y \in X, \ \forall i \in N, w_i(x) \geq w_i(y) \text{ iff } v_i(L_x) \geq v_i(L_y).$$

It says in effect that to compare x and y morally is to be ignorant of one's own identity, in the special sense of giving equal probability to each available type. This axiom should be compared with the symmetry requirements of social choice theory, such as **(A)**. While the Anonymity axiom used in Section 4 can receive only an ethical interpretation, the present one has both an ethical and an epistemic connotation.

(EC) connects the moral preferences with the extended ones. The second axiom, or *Principle of Acceptance*, will connect extended with personal preferences:

Axiom **PA**

$$\forall \ x, y \in X, \ \forall i, j \in N, v_i(x, t_j) \geq v_i(y, t_j) \text{ iff } u_j(x) \geq u_j(y).$$

On the face of it, this seems another axiom about the impartial but sympathetic observer. In the extended sympathy literature (e.g., Suzumura, 1983), a similar condition has been defended as embodying *nonpaternalism*: when i compares two options by mentally occupying j's position, he should reach exactly the same conclusions as does j himself. This interpretation of **(PA)** is suitable for other philosophical contexts, but would miss the essential point here. Axiom **(PA)** expresses Harsanyi's conviction that personal utilities u_j can be reconstructed from knowledge of j's type t_j. In (1977a) he assumes in effect that there are sufficiently precise psychological laws, as well as sufficiently widespread knowledge of these laws, to make the deduction of the u_j function unproblematic for any observer i. This (very strong) assumption is metaphysical rather than ethical in character. It might well involve similar practical consequences to, but does not follow from, the purely ethical attitude of nonpaternalism.

Our third axiom, to be called *Fundamental Preference*, says that extended preference comparisons are the same from one individual to the other. Conceptually, we are only interested in the individual's preferences over extended *alternatives*. But for reasons that the proof below will make clear, we state Fundamental Preference as the requirement that preference comparisons between extended *lotteries* be uniform across individuals.

AXIOM **FP**

$$\forall \, p, p' \in \Delta_s(X \times T_N), \ \forall i, j \in N, v_i(p) \geq v_i(p') \text{ iff } v_j(p) \geq v_j(p').$$

That some uniformity assumption is needed to derive Harsanyi's conclusion of a *unique* moral utility function has been recognized by his commentators.[113] There is no doubt about the mathematical point. Whether **(FP)**, or similar strong uniformity assumptions, can be justified conceptually is another matter. When the objects of extended preference are pairs of initial alternatives and *individualities* (rather than types), there is no reason why uniformity of judgement should prevail. Remember La Fontaine's fable: the poor shoemaker fancies himself happier in the role of the successful moneymaker, whereas the latter holds the exactly opposite view. The whole point of introducing the type notion, and Harsanyi's strong assumption about objectively known laws, is precisely to make uniformity of judgements plausible. But even in this interpretation, the argument for **(FP)** remains open to doubts.[114]

PROPOSITION 6.1 [HARSANYI'S IMPARTIAL OBSERVER THEOREM] Assume that the personal utilities $u_1, \cdots, u_n$ and moral utilities $w_1, \cdots, w_n$, are VNM functions on X, and that the extended utilities $v_1, \cdots, v_n$ are VNM functions on $\Delta_s(X \times T_N)$. If **(EC)**, **(PA)** and **(FP)** hold, there is a common function w such that each w_j is a positive affine transformation of w, and:

$$\forall \, x \in X, \quad w(x) = 1/n \sum_{i=1}^{n} u_i'(x),$$

where $u_1', \cdots, u_n'$ are positive affine transformations of $u_1, \cdots, u_n$, respectively.

Notice carefully that without **(FP)**, the conclusion would simply be this: each individual moral function w_j is some positive affine transformation (PAT) of $1/n \sum_{i=1}^{n} u_{ij}'(x)$, where u_{ij}' is a PAT of u_i which depends *on the particular* j. Note also that if **(FP)** were restricted to preference comparisons between extended alternatives, the argument would not carry through. Extended lotteries are needed if one is to apply the VNM machinery. To make the argument

---

[113]See Pattanaik (1968), Sen (1970), Kaneko (1984), MacKay (1986), and Suzumura (1994).
[114]The intricacies of the argument are illustrated by Broome's (1993) discussion of Harsanyi's and Kolm's claims that extended preference judgements must be made in the same way by different individuals. Broome rejects this claim even in Harsanyi's version. His main point is that extended preference constructions confuse with each other the two notions of an *object* of preference and of a *cause* of preference. Kolm (1994) denies that this constitutes a relevant objection.

straightforward, we have assumed that extended preferences are defined on the set of *all* extended lotteries, but this assumption could be weakened.[115]

Contrary to the Aggregation Theorem, which leads to nontrivial variants, the Impartial Observer Theorem has little technical interest. But it provides an important argument for *mean rule* utilitarianism,[116] as well as a framework in which a number of conceptual issues can be addressed. The first objection raised against the other theorem, to the effect that it does not state the relevant axiom of interpersonal comparisons, would be equally inappropriate here. The above axiomatic decomposition makes it clear that Harsanyi wants to assume the *general* possibility of interpersonal utility comparisons: this much is implied by the conjunction of **(PA)** with the technical assumption of a well–defined extended preference. Exactly like the Aggregation Theorem, the Impartial Observer Theorem derives the *specific* utilitarian form of utility comparisons from the assumption that they are possible in general, and various other assumptions. The second objection against the other theorem, to the effect that Harsanyi should not have exclusively relied on VNM utility representations of moral and personal preferences, applies here with equal force. We refer the reader to the relevant discussion of the Sen-Weymark critique in Section 5.3. This discussion can be reproduced word for word, except for the words "individual" and "social", which should now be replaced by "personal" and "moral", respectively.

Some further philosophical problems are specific to the Impartial Observer Theorem. Most writers in the extended preference literature have followed Arrow (1977) in defining this concept ordinally. Accordingly, some of these writers, like Kolm (1972), have taken Harsanyi to task for *cardinalizing* extended preferences by defining them on a domain of VNM lotteries. Their criticism appears to be based on the view that preference (in whatever context) is an exclusively ordinal concept. We have argued in Section 2.3 against the latter view: it is too restrictive, because "ordinalism" does not analytically follow from the definition of preference. Hence, we do not see cardinality of extended preferences as constituting a problem *per se*. That Harsanyi's specific procedure for cardinalizing extended (as well as other kinds of) preferences by a VNM device may not be appropriate is a different issue, with which part of the Sen–Weymark critique was precisely concerned.

When reviewing early variants of the Impartial Observer theorem, we suggested that there is room for disagreements in the analysis of the individual's position, and of what in his position should be assumed to be unknown. Indeed,

---

[115]Karni and Weymark (1996) derive the Impartial Observer Theorem from a more parsimonious domain assumption.

[116]Although, of course, this rule is equivalent to sum utilitarianism when the population size is fixed.

part of Rawls's (1971) critique of Harsanyi reflects a disagreement of this sort. Another part has to do with the modelling of ignorance and the way of coping with it. In particular, **(EC)** is questionable. Rather than maximizing expected utility with respect to an equiprobable lottery, Rawls contends, agents should apply the alternative model of *maximin*, which implies extreme caution on their part. That component of the Rawls–Harsanyi debate has already surfaced in the framework of social welfare functionals (see Section 4.4). The *maximin* approach does not make use of subjective probabilities, which has led to severe criticisms on the Bayesian writers' part. We said earlier that they do not have to endorse **(EC)**, but this line of thinking has attracted little attention.[117]

Further discussions of the Impartial Observer Theorem relate in effect to axioms **(FP)** and **(PA)**, and mostly to the former. We mentioned the misgivings caused by Harsanyi's claim that extended preference judgments are the same from one individual to another. Pattanaik (1968) suggests applying Harsanyi's Aggregation Theorem in order to amalgamate VNM extended utility functions that do not represent the same fundamental preferences. Using a classical framework of social choice theory, Suzumura (1994) shows that aggregation of extended preference judgments, as formalized by binary relations, lead to difficulties of the Arrow type. These two writers are in effect exploring the consequences of dispensing with axiom **(FP)**.

6.4   Rawls's "Original Position" and "Veil of Ignorance"

As is well known, Rawls's device of putting the individual behind the "veil of ignorance" is meant to explain why it is rational to accept his "two principles of justice". They are:

1. Each person has an equal right to the most extensive basic liberty compatible with the same liberty for others.

2. Social and economic inequalities must be (a) to the greatest benefit of the least advantaged members of the society, and (b) attached to positions open to all.

Rawls has repeatedly claimed that the first principle is to have priority over the second, and part (b) of the second principle over part (a) (which he labels the difference principle). For some time, economists knew Rawls primarily

---

[117]It is possible to devise subjective probability variants of the Impartial Observer Theorem. One simple method is to exploit the formal analogies between Harsanyi's construction of the original position and Anscombe and Aumann's construction of SEU in the single individual case (see Section 3.3). In the resulting model, lotteries will be replaced by uncertain prospects, while individuals will be formally analyzed in the same way as are states of the world in the AA context.

through the formal reconstruction of Section 4, and therefore tended to ignore the broader perspective of his philosophy, which is primarily concerned with basic liberties and equal chances of promoting the individual's own conception of good. That is to say, one should be careful not to emphasize the "economic" part of the doctrine, even when restricting attention to the second principle. Apart from this overemphasis, the early reading involved the already mentioned procedure of discussing Rawls in terms of standard utility functions without properly justifying this restatement.

All this has come to be recognized, and a perhaps more genuine interchange between Rawls and the economists has recently taken place. In particular, it addresses Rawls's notion of primary goods and the problems raised by its formalization. Rawls has described primary goods as "all–purpose" means for the person's promoting his own conception of the good. "Primary goods are things which it is supposed a rational man wants whatever else he wants" (1971, p. 92). The way to define them is closely related to the statement of the two justice principles. The principles are best understood as regulating the distribution of primary goods among citizens at the ideal founding stage of the "well–ordered society". More precisely, Rawls (1982, 1988) defines them in terms of the following list:

1. The basic liberties, in particular freedom of thought, freedom of association, and political liberties.

2. Freedom of movement and of choice of occupation.

3. Powers and prerogatives.

4. Income and wealth.

5. "The social bases of self–respect".

The relative importance of these goods is roughly conveyed by their numbering, and mirrors the respective importance of each principle, or subprinciple, of justice. Because of his lexicographic ranking, Rawls is not prepared to consider trade–offs between all the five groups: the fundamental liberties should be equally distributed, and there should be fair equality of opportunities; only the last three groups are susceptible of being balanced against each other. Rawls (1971, pp. 93–95) appears to recognize that weights should be defined for at least the non–prioritized goods, if the notion of an "index of primary goods" is to make sense at all, but neither in *A Theory of Justice* nor in his later articles (e.g., 1982, 1988) does he come out with a satisfactory formulation. He has himself come to recognize the full difficulty of the indexing problem, as will be explained shortly.

The two principles of justice—or equivalently, the distribution of primary goods they prescribe—are supposed to result from every person's choice under the "veil of ignorance". Notice carefully that the Rawlsian choice is concerned with principles, not with social states, a point which elementary presentations sometimes overlook. A primary good distribution is not a social state in the ordinary sense, since it does not specify the individuals' circumstances entirely. This feature of Rawls's theory reflects the claim that the members of society's make entirely personal use of their primary goods assignments. It makes a significant difference from Harsanyi's theory, which entails an assessment of principles *only indirectly*, i.e., as a result of initially assessing the states. Harsanyi's impartial observer is utilitarian not because he chooses to be so, but because his choices among states turn out to satisfy the utilitarian criterion. The philosophical demarcation here can be understood in terms of the initial contrast of this section between impartial–observer and state–of–nature theories. The Rawlsian "original position" is a state of nature, at least in the following sense: it (ideally) precedes any social state. The impartial observer's position is just distinct from, but not conceptually prior to, the social states. As a state–of–nature theory, Rawls's makes it possible to determine only the society's most general principles, whereas Harsanyi's impartial observer theory supposedly provides a ranking of all social states. Another relevant contrast is that between a mostly deontological and an exclusively teleological analysis: Rawls does not want to make the notion of justice hinge on an evaluation of consequences, whereas Harsanyi wants to do precisely that. All in all, the philosophical differences are so overwhelming that it seems to be less important than has often been suggested to compare Harsanyi and Rawls in terms of the particular choice-theoretic features of their ideal positions.

The Rawlsian veil of ignorance is thick. It obscures not only the individual's place in society (typically, his wealth and income) and his defining characteristics (such as his talents and handicaps), but also his own conception of good. The individual does not know either in what kind of society he will live; he has no idea of the property regime, the income and wealth statistics, etc. On the other hand, he is aware of the basic facts of human nature and has extensive knowledge of a general kind. Under these conditions, Rawls argues, the individuals will tend to form their expectations in terms of an identical primary good index. It will function as "a publicly recognized measure" (1971, p. 95). When revisiting the issue, Rawls (1982) makes it clear that the choice of the index reflects the informational constraints of the original position, and that it has to be common knowledge between the participants. As a further step, he claims that the safe–playing attitude that is inevitable under the veil must lead each to choose the distribution of primary goods recommended by the two justice principles. It is here that the famous maximin "analogy" (1971, p. 152) comes in; it is just an analogy, because, again, the relevant unit of evaluation is the index, not the individuals's utility.

Even leaving aside the basic liberties and conditions of fair opportunity, the commensurability problem raised by Rawls's index is an acute one. Rawls (1971, p. 94) initially attempted to circumscribe the problem by requiring a weighting of primary goods only for the least advantaged, but this is unsatisfactory, as he came to recognize. How could one identify the least favoured group? There seems to be no way of identifying it, except in terms of an index defined for all in the society. Besides, the indexing problem arises not only because one should balance the last three groups of goods against each other, but already because one has to aggregate goods within two of these groups, namely "powers and prerogatives" and "the social bases of self-respect". For lack of a better solution, Rawls (1982) has eventually resigned himself to taking monetary wealth as a proxy for the index.

We shall sketch an alternative argument here. *To assume that the index can be constructed is, formally, to assume that there is a utility function.* This function is essentially unknown, but it will inherit at least some recognizable properties from the preceding philosophical argument. First, it must be unique, since, by assumption, all individuals share the same index. Second, it must be strictly increasing in each of its arguments, which are quantities of (eminently desirable) primary goods. More specific properties than these two do not follow as a matter of logic. But quasi–concavity (diminishing rates of substitution along indifference curves) and other standard microeconomic properties are not logically excluded either.

We can go one step further and inquire whether Rawls's philosophical framework can agree with *technical welfarism*, i.e., the formal notion of welfarism defined in Section 4. There would be little philosophical sense in introducing a multi–profile setting of utility functions. Rather, Rawls's argument points towards a single–profile setting (in the special case in which the n individual utility functions are identical). In order to reap the benefits of the Welfarism Lemma, it is enough to be able to accept the Unrestricted Profile and Relative Neutrality assumptions that make it possible to extend technical welfarism to the single–profile framework (see Section 4.6). The former is a richness–of–domain assumption, which must now be assessed in terms of a primary goods interpretation. The latter (conceptually more crucial) assumption says in essence that the social evaluation of any primary goods allocation will depend only on the distribution of numerical values taken by the index. Both assumptions can be defended in Rawlsian terms. Once the conclusion of the Welfarism Lemma is granted, the discussion can proceed along the lines of SWFL theory. Comparability holds by assumption, and the general philosophical argument favours Ordinality. Thus, we have gone a long way towards the earlier reconstruction of the economic part of the "difference principle" in Section 4, but there remain two differences: for one, the individuals share the same utility function, and for another, the case for leximin (as opposed to any other rule compatible with Ordinality and Comparability) has not been settled. In view of Proposition 4.3 above, to accept leximin at this stage is tantamount to accepting Anonymity and Separability, while rejecting Leximax.

6.5 Alternative Notions of Fairness

Choice theorists have often rejected maximin, as well as leximin, on the grounds that being non–probabilistic, these criteria clash with the Bayesian axioms of rational choice. A related point against maximin, which can be found in Arrow (1973a), is that it is just a limiting case of an expectational approach to uncertainty: it amounts to giving an infinite weight to the worst outcome. These criticisms fully apply to the welfarist reconstruction of Rawls's original position, but do not lose their force when redirected against alternative construals of the primary goods index, such as Rawls's use of a monetary proxy. Another strand of criticisms relates to the Ordinality and Comparability assumption. The recent work in normative economics has often revived the assumption of Ordinality and Non–Comparability that Arrow had emphatically endorsed in *Social Choice and Individual Values*. Despite this heavy informational restriction, the recent work shares much in common with Rawls's project of founding a notion of distributive justice, and significantly borrows Rawlsian expressions such as *fairness* or *equity* to refer to the looked-for foundation. To dismiss Ordinality and Comparability has the effect of shaking the logical basis of maximin comparisons. Thus, at least implicitly, the new social choice rules take the earlier choice-theoretic critique of Rawls into account.

Among these new rules, we shall emphasize the *no–envy criterion* and its cognates. It was mentioned by Tinbergen, but first explored by Foley (1967) and Kolm (1972; see also 1995), who turned it into a general notion of distributive justice. Varian (1974) is very clear in arguing that envy–free efficient allocations (which he initially labelled *fair* allocations) constitute an alternative to the Rawlsian outcome of the original position. These three writers, and most of their followers, count as a theoretical strength the weak informational demand made by these concepts.[118]

Suppose that there are n individuals and a given vector $\bar{\omega} = (\bar{\omega}_1, \cdots, \bar{\omega}_m)$ of goods is to be distributed between them ($\bar{\omega}_h > 0, h = 1, \cdots, m$). By assumption, individual utility functions $u_i(x_i)$ are ordinal and non–comparable. The

---

[118]For further relevant contributions to the issue of no–envy, see Thomson (1982), Thomson and Varian (1985), and the references discussed in Ansperger's (1994) and Thomson's (1994) extensive surveys. See also Moulin's (1995) discussion and further elaboration.

set of feasible allocations is:

$$X = \{x \in \mathbb{R}^{mn}_+ : \sum_{i=1}^{n} x_{ih} = \overline{\omega}_h, h = 1, 2, \cdots, m\}.$$

A feasible allocation x is said to be *envy–free* if it satisfies the condition that:

$$u_i(x_i) \geq u_i(x_j), \quad \forall\, i, j, i \neq j.$$

In words, every individual is at least as well–off with his own allocation as he would be with any other individual's. Whenever the reverse strict inequality holds for two individuals i, j, we shall say that i *envies* j. The equal endowment allocation, i.e., $\omega = (\omega^1, \cdots, \omega^n)$, with $\omega^i = \overline{\omega}/n$ for $i = 1, \cdots, n$, is clearly envy–free. A feasible allocation will be said to be *efficient* if it is Pareto–optimal in the strong sense; that is to say, if no other feasible allocation satisfies the antecedent clause of the Strict Pareto condition (see Sections 4 and 5). In the special (Rawlsian) case in which the individuals' utility functions are identical, the equal endowment allocation is not only envy–free, but also efficient. More generally, it might lack the efficiency property.

Consider now an exchange economy, with initial endowments $\omega = (\omega^1, \cdots, \omega^n)$, and suppose that it satisfies the following assumptions for the existence of a competitive equilibrium (x, p): preferences are continuous orderings, hence representable by utility functions $u_1, \cdots, u_n$, and are strictly increasing and convex, so that these utility functions are strictly increasing in each argument and quasi–concave (see Section 2.1). From the definition of a competitive equilibrium, x is a feasible allocation, and p is a price vector, such that:

$$x_i \in \underset{x_i'}{\mathrm{argmax}}\{u_i(x_i') : px_i' \leq p\omega^i\} \text{ for all } i.$$

If we now make the assumption that the initial endowments ω^i are equal, it immediately follows that the competitive equilibrium allocation x is envy–free. (Suppose it is not; then, there are i, j such that $u_i(x_i) < u_i(x_j)$; from the equilibrium property of x_i, it must be the case that x_j exceeds i's income; but since incomes must be equal at the equilibrium, it also exceeds j's income—a contradiction with the equilibrium property of x_j.) It can also be proved that the equilibrium allocation x is efficient. This strong version of the "first fundamental theorem of welfare economics" follows here from the assumption that preferences are strictly increasing. Thus, we had just proved the existence of an envy–free efficient allocation:[119]

---

[119]The reasoning of this paragraph echoes Varian (1974, Theorems 2.2 and 2.3). The assumption of strictly increasing preferences was introduced by Varian for convenience reasons.

PROPOSITION 6.2 Consider an exchange economy with equal initial endowments and such that individual utility functions are strictly increasing in each argument, continuous, and quasi–concave. This economy has a competitive equilibrium which is envy–free and efficient.

(Under the same assumptions, the leximin allocation with identical utility functions would also be envy–free efficient. This holds because it would ensure equal utility amounts to each individual.)

The simultaneous realization of envy–freeness and efficiency is not a robust microeconomic property. Following an informal argument due to Foley (1967), Pazner and Schmeidler (1974) have shown that the existence conclusion of Proposition 6.2 depended on assuming an exchange economy. An example in their paper illustrates the lack of existence in a production economy. We state another example in the (Rawlsian) particular case of a common utility function:

EXAMPLE 6.3 There are two individuals who produce one good out of their labour. For $i = 1, 2$, denote i's consumption and labour by x_i and ℓ_i, respectively. Suppose that the two individuals have identical Cobb–Douglas utility functions, i.e.,

$$u(x_i, \ell_i) = x_i^\alpha \ell_i^{(1-\alpha)}, \ 0 < \alpha < 1, \ i = 1, 2,$$

and that their production function is given by:

$$x_1 + x_2 = (1 - \ell_1) + \varepsilon(1 - \ell_2), \text{ with } 0 < \varepsilon < 1.$$

This equation implies that 2's productivity is lower than 1's. Now, we equalize the marginal rate of substitution with the marginal rate of transformation for each individual. Hence the following two equations that an efficient allocation should satisfy in addition to the production equation:

$$x_1 = \alpha/(1 - \alpha)\ell_1, \quad x_2 = \varepsilon\alpha/(1 - \alpha)\ell_2.$$

The corresponding utility values are:

$$u(x_1, \ell_1) = (\alpha/(1 - \alpha))^\alpha \ell_1, \quad u(x_2, \ell_2) = \varepsilon^\alpha (\alpha/(1 - \alpha))^\alpha \ell_2.$$

Because $\varepsilon^\alpha < 1$, we see that for every efficient allocation:

$$u(x_1, \ell_1) > u(x_2, \ell_2).$$

The weaker (but less transparent) assumption of "local non–satiation" would imply the same conclusions. On this assumption and the further microeconomic notions used in Sections 6.5 and 6.6, see for instance the text by Mas–Colell, Whinston and Green (1995).

Hence, utility values can never by equalized (even when $\ell_2 = 1$. Individual 2 is worse off because of his low productivity. There exists no envy-free efficient allocation.

Considering how severe the existence problem is, Pazner and Schmeidler (1978) proposed the novel concept of an *efficient egalitarian equivalent allocation* (EEEA). This concept involves introducing a generally fictitious state, which would be perfectly egalitarian. More precisely, an allocation is said to be *egalitarian–equivalent* if there exists a state in which individual consumptions — including leisure — are equal, and each individual enjoys the same utility as in the actual allocation. To define an EEEA, let X denote the set of feasible allocations in the actual economy, as generated by the set $Z \subset \mathbb{R}^m$ of productive production plans z (where positive and negative coordinates denote outputs and inputs, respectively) and by a vector of aggregate initial resources $\overline{\omega} \in \mathbb{R}_+^m$, i.e.,

$$ X = \{x \in \mathbb{R}_+^{mn} : \sum_i x_i \in \{\overline{\omega} + Z\}\}. $$

An allocation x is said to be EEEA if it is efficient and if, for some consumption bundle $x_0 \in \mathbb{R}_+^M$, not necessarily in $\{\overline{\omega} + Z\}$,

$$ u_i(x_i) = u_i(x_0) \text{ for all } i. $$

Pazner and Schmeidler (1978) prove the following existence result:

PROPOSITION 6.4 Assume that each utility function u_i is continuous and strictly increasing in each argument. Assume also that the set X of feasible allocations is compact and comprehensive (i.e., $x' \leq x \in X \Rightarrow x' \in X$), and has non–empty interior. Then, there exists an efficient egalitarian–equivalent allocation.[120]

6.6   Equality of Resources and Welfare

The EEEA concept has an interest of its own, but the existence problem of the initial no–envy criterion remains unsolved. This difficulty derives from an even deeper reason than the role of production, to wit, the *non–exchangeability of some individual characteristics*. Handicaps could have played the role of the individuals' productivities in Example 1. In relation to the non–exchangeability problem, Dworkin (1981) has introduced the distinction between "external resources" and "internal resources", and claimed that both should be taken into

---

[120]For further discussion and a generalization of the EEEA solution, see Moulin (1995, 1996). Moulin also introduces several alternative ordinal criteria, such as the "stand alone test", which prescribes that each individual's utility should not exceed the utility he would obtain if he were the only agent in the economy.

account in solving the problem of distributive justice. In effect, Rawls considers only external resources. Whether the original position device succeeds in establishing principles of justice crucially depends on how resources are delineated.

In order to equalize resources, both internal and external, across individuals, Dworkin has proposed two famous procedures, each of which is based on a distinctive notion of the original position.[121] The starting point for Dworkin's first procedure is the property underlying Proposition 6.2: in any "well–behaved" exchange economy (i.e., when all resources are tradeable and there are no externalities), any competitive equilibrium implying an equal income distribution passes the "envy test" successfully. At the equilibrium, no one would like to exchange his final bundle of resources with someone else's bundle. One way of extending this conclusion to internal resources is to make them tradeable *notionally*, that is to say, to give every individual equal rights on all the members of society's external *and* internal resources. As long as individual i's internal resources have the effect of increasing only i's utility, efficient allocations will automatically imply that these resources are not consumed or used as inputs by any other individual. From the "second fundamental theorem of welfare economics", we know that under standard assumptions, any efficient allocation can be decentralized by some competitive equilibrium. In the particular context, this means that there will be implicit prices for both internal and external resources in the society. The reasoning of Proposition 6.2 may now be applied to the fictitious exchange economy just constructed.

To illustrate, let us go back to Example 6.3. The two individuals have different productivities (1 and ε respectively), a case of differing internal resources. Suppose that "rights to consume leisure" are created, one for the leisure of 1, the other for the leisure of 2, and that the two individuals receive equal shares of these rights. Suppose also that these rights are tradeable. A competitive equilibrium will involve three prices, i.e., the price of the produced good (which we normalize to 1) and the prices of both types of leisure. From the equilibrium condition, the latter should be equal to the respective productivities. Does this equilibrium ensure that individual 2 will be compensated for his low productivity? The equilibrium solutions are:

$$x_1 = x_2 = \alpha(1+\varepsilon)/2, \ \ell_1 = (1-\alpha)(1+\varepsilon)/2, \ \ell_2 = (1-\alpha)(1+\varepsilon)/2\varepsilon.$$

Intuitively, individual 2 is now *overcompensated* for his lower productivity. A similar consequence had been noted in the different context of optimal taxation (Mirrlees, 1974, 1982). In Dworkin's opinion, this "slavery of the talented" is highly undesirable, which leads him to explore an alternative way of equalizing resources.

---

[121]These mechanisms have been extensively investigated, in particular by Roemer (1985, 1994, 1996), Varian (1985) and van Parijs (1990).

Dworkin's second method is to construct "an hypothetical insurance market, which assumes equal initial assets and equal risk". Individuals will be able to hedge against the lack of sufficient internal resources. Formally, it seems best to understand Dworkin's second mechanism in terms of a three–stage procedure, which involves a novel concept of the original position. At the first stage—the original position proper—the individuals do not know what their own type will be and insure against the implied risk. At the second stage, any individual i's is associated with a type, say t_k, in the set T_N of available types; this fixes i's endowment of internal resources. By assumption, types are drawn from an equiprobable lottery, i.e., $p(t_k) = 1/n$. At the third stage, the resulting competitive equilibrium is computed. Due to the presence of internal resources, the individual equilibrium external resources $x_1, x_2, ..., x_n$ will not be equal, and hence the corresponding utility values $u(x_1, t_1), u(x_2, t_2), \cdots, u(x_n, t_n)$ will not be equal either. It is against the risk of eventually getting a low utility value that individuals insure in the first place. Under the VNM assumptions, this three–stage mechanism leads to an additive rule which is formally similar to Harsanyi's. This analogy is noted in Roemer's (1985 and 1994) analysis of Dworkin's two mechanisms, to which the reader is referred for more detail.

Dworkin's project should be assessed against the background of the ethically relevant distinction between two groups of individual characteristics: those describing "tastes", for which the individuals should bear responsibility and there should be no insurance; and those describing either "talents" or "handicaps", which should be insured against. Such a partitioning is intended to take care of the problems inhering in the use of "subjective preferences" in judgements of justice. Like Rawls (see Section 2.5), Dworkin rejects differences in tastes as being a fair basis for unequal resource allocations. Rawls goes very far by eliminating *all* individual characteristics and introducing the supposedly objective index of primary goods. In some sense, Dworkin adopts an intermediate position between Rawls's and the welfarists', since he is willing to include *some* of the individual characteristics, while excluding the others. By doing so, he becomes open to criticisms from both the Rawlsian and the welfarist points of views. Roemer has complained that he assumes clarity where there is none: "Where does one draw the line on this slippery slope, which separates those traits of a person which should properly be deemed part of his preferences, from those which are part of his resource endowment?" (1985, in 1994, p. 146). When discussing expensive tastes and handicaps in Section 2.5, we suggested that sometimes they should be treated the same, sometimes not. There is no obvious rule to overcome this indeterminacy. This failure of human reason to implement an ethically important distinction suggests that there is perhaps no stopping point between complete admission of individual characteristics, leading to some form of welfarism, and complete rejection of them, leading to strong antiwelfarism.

7   Concluding Comments

This chapter has reviewed a number of constructions in social ethics, which share the common feature of applying the apparatus of utility theory to a collective (though not an interactive) setting. We have classified them into three broad categories. The constructions in the first group belong to that part of social choice theory which takes individual utility functions (rather than preference relations) as primitives, i.e., the theory of social welfare functionals. Interpersonal comparisons of utility are the main topic of this theory, which has provided illuminating axiomatizations of utilitarianism and egalitarianism (in the sense of the Rawlsian leximin). In the second group, which is exemplified by Harsanyi's and his followers' work, choice–theoretic restrictions imposed on the observer's utility functions play—roughly speaking—the role of interpersonal comparison assumptions in the first group. While discussing these choice–theoretic assumptions at length, we have emphasized the formal connection between Harsanyi's expected–utility approach to utilitarianism and earlier results in the theory of social welfare functionals. The contributions in the third group typically derive the observer's rule from constructing an ideal, ethically–loaded reference position. Philosophically, the latter refers to either the Impartial Observer's vision of the society, or to a State of Nature which (logically, if not factually) precedes society; this distinction is the bequest of 17th and 18th century writers to contemporary political and moral philosophy. The reference position is typically analyzed as a state of relative ignorance among individuals, and thus becomes amenable to standard utility–theoretic methods. We have lumped with the last group some recent notions of "fairness", such as the no–envy concept, because they can be viewed as alternatives to Rawls's use of leximin to resolve the ignorance prevailing in the State of Nature.

Even granting our initial scope restriction to *social* ethics, the present survey is far from being exhaustive. An important topic for both utility theory and social ethics is the role of preference externalities, in particular of benevolent and malevolent preferences. It has indeed been extensively discussed within the first group of theories in relation to Sen's Paretian Liberal Paradox. Another topic which has recently attracted the normative economists' interest is population ethics, and more generally the dynamic side of the more familiar social choice rules, i.e. leximin and utilitarianism. We have only touched on these issues. While laying special emphasis on the second and third groups of theories, we said nothing about the following relevant questions. Would it make ethical sense to extend Harsanyi's aggregative approach (or Rawls's and

Harsanyi's analyses of the reference position) by assuming non–expected or non–probabilistic utility theories rather than the von Neumann–Morgenstern and subjective expected utility theory? Among the various models of bargaining which have found their way into social ethics, which one is the most appropriate philosophically, and what does the bargaining approach add to the standard aggregative approach?

Despite these—and other—missing topics, we hope that there is enough in this chapter to document the conflicting positions taken among both philosophical and economic circles on "welfarism". After sketching the pros and cons in the welfarism debate in Section 2, we have found that utility theory remains a relevant tool of analysis in social ethics, *provided that it receives an appropriate interpretation.* The first and perhaps most attractive interpretation results from this simple observation: there is a tight connection between the individual's well–being and his considered or improved preferences. The latter notion needs clarifying, and may or may not exhaust the former. This is a topic for serious philosophical discussion, but there is little doubt about the broad fact that the two notions are linked to each other. To the extent that they represent rational, well-informed, and (on some construals) self–interested preferences, utility functions can *also* represent the individual's well–being. Given that the alternative, purely objective accounts of well–being are still at the tentative stage, it would be methodologically objectionable to dispense with this utility-based approach to well–being. This is not to say that non–utility information is irrelevant. It should play a role for two reasons, i.e. (i) well–being is *not* all what the social good, let alone social ethics, is about; (ii) even restricting oneself to a teleological framework in which well–being is the only notion of good, non–utility information, typically information on handicaps, talents, and acquisition of preferences, might be necessary in order to derive the observer's rule. Our brief analysis of Dworkin's theory suggests that to combine utility with non–utility information in one and the same model is not an easy task; however, the difficulties encountered here might lie with the implementation, rather than the substance, of the programme. Our tentative conclusions do not preclude work along the lines of minimal and moderate antiwelfarism (in the terminology of Section 2.5). Elsewhere, we reached a more determinate result of a negative sort. We claimed that the approach typically followed by welfare economists equivocates between several interpretations of utility that cannot easily be reconciled. The improved preference interpretation *cannot* coincide with the actual preference interpretation which welfare economists have borrowed from positive microeconomics. Put bluntly, if welfarism can be salvaged philosophically, traditional welfare economics cannot.

Second, we have introduced a notion of *technical* welfarism as against the (mostly polemical) philosophical definitions in current use. Technical welfarism

CHAPTER 10: UTILITY THEORY AND ETHICS   467

is perhaps best understood as that branch of measurement theory which is concerned with comparisons between personal characteristics. Well–being comparisons are one example, but there are also comparisons of other sorts. An easy (perhaps too easy) application of technical welfarism to a philosophically non–welfarist doctrine is our discussion of Rawls's "primary goods". The analysis of "justice as fairness" in terms of a utility–like index is not so widely off the mark as was claimed by some antiwelfarists. We are not returning to the initial state of the discussion of leximin versus utilitarianism, but rather emphasizing this simple contrast: the primary goods index does not represent well–being, but nonetheless shares several properties in common with a utility–function index of well–being.

Some readers will perhaps be dissatisfied with the semantic manoeuvre that consists in preserving the constructions of utility theory while referring them to a special (i.e., rational and well–informed) kind of preferences. These readers have a point, which leads us to our third and last comment. The formal part, if perhaps not the substantial part, of the rationality concept, can be made explicit *within utility theory itself* under the guise of well–known axioms. In other words, the chosen interpretation can influence the formal constructions. Methodologically, this internalization of semantics appears to be desirable. One application in this chapter was the analysis (in Section 5 and part of 6) of aggregative issues under strong choice–theoretic restrictions imposed on the individuals' preferences. That impossibility theorems follow from systematizing this approach remains a challenge to our understanding of collective rationality.

References

Allais, M. (1953). Le comportement de l'homme rationnel devant le risque: Critique des postulats et axiomes de l'Ecole Américaine. *Econometrica*, 21:503–546.

Allais, M. and Hagen, O., editors (1994). *Cardinalism*. Kluwer, Dordrecht.

Anscombe, F. and Aumann, R. (1963). A Definition of Subjective Probability. *Annals of Mathematical Statistics*, 34:199–205.

Aristotle. The Nichomachean Ethics. In Barnes, J., editor, *The Complete Works of Aristotle: The Revised Oxford Translation*. Princeton University Press, Princeton, 1984.

Arneson, R. J. (1989). Equality and Equal Opportunity for Welfare. *Philosophical Studies*, 56:77–93.

Arneson, R. J. (1990a). Liberalism, Distributive Subjectivism, and Equal Opportunity for Welfare. *Philosophy and Public Affairs*, 19:159–194.

Arneson, R. J. (1990b). Primary Goods Reconsidered. *Nous*, 24:429–454.

Arnsperger, C. (1994). Envy–Freeness and Distributive Justice. *Journal of Economic Surveys*, 8:155–186.

Arrow, K. J. (1951). *Social Choice and Individual Values*. Yale University Press, New Haven. 2nd revised edition, 1963.

Arrow, K. J. (1973a). Some Ordinalist–Utilitarian Notes on Rawls's Theory of Justice. *Journal of Philosophy*, 70:245–263. Reprinted in K. J. Arrow (1984a), chapter 8.

Arrow, K. J. (1973b). Rawls's Principle of Just Saving. *Swedish Journal of Economics*, 75:323–335. Reprinted in K. J. Arrow (1984a), chapter 10.

Arrow, K. J. (1977). Extended Sympathy and the Possibility of Social Choice. *American Economic Review, Papers and Proceedings*, 67:219–229. Reprinted in K. J. Arrow (1984a), chapter 11.

Arrow, K. J. (1984a). *Collected Works, Volume 1: Social Choice and Justice*. Harvard University Press, Cambridge, Mass.

Arrow, K. J. (1984b). *Collected Works, Volume 3: Individual Choice Under Certainty and Uncertainty*. Harvard University Press, Cambridge, Mass.

D'Aspremont, C. (1985). Axioms for Social Welfare Orderings. In L. Hurwicz, D. S. and Sonnenschein, H. F., editors, *Social Goals and Organization*, pages 19–76. Cambridge University Press, Cambridge.

D'Aspremont, C. (1995). Economie du bien-être et utilitarisme. In Gérard-Varet, L. A. and Passeron, J. C., editors, *Le modèle et l'enquête. Les usages du principe de rationalité en sciences sociales*, pages 217–241. Editions de l'E.H.E.S.S., Paris.

D'Aspremont, C. and Gevers, L. (1977). Equity and the Informational Basis of Collective Choice. *Review of Economic Studies*, 44:199–209.

D'Aspremont, C. and Gérard-Varet, L. A. (1991). Utilitarian Fundamentalism and Limited Information. In Elster, J. and Roemer, J. E., editors, *Interpersonal Comparisions of Well–Being*, pages 371–385. Cambridge University Press, Cambridge.

Barry, B. (1989). *Theories of Justice*. Harvester, London.

Barry, B. (1995). *Justice as Impartiality*. Clarendon Press, Oxford.

Beccaria, C. (1764). *Dei delitti e delle pene*. Rizzoli, 1994, Milan.

Bentham, J. (1776). A Fragment on Government. In Bowring, J., editor (1838), *The Works of Jeremy Bentham*, volume 1, pages 221–295. Reprinted by Russell and Russell, New York, 1968.

Bentham, J. (1789). *An Introduction to the Principles of Morals and Legislation, The Hafner Library of Classics*. MacMillan, 1948, New York.

Bergson, A. (1954). On the Concept of Social Welfare. *Quarterly Journal of Economics*, 68:233–252.

Binmore, K. (1994). *Game Theory and the Social Contract*, volume 1. The M.I.T. Press, Cambridge, Mass.

Blackorby, C., Bossert, W., and Donaldson, D. (1995a). Income Inequality Measurement. To appear in J. Silbert (ed.), *Income Inequality Measurement: From Theory to Practice*, Dordrecht, Kluwer.

Blackorby, C., Bossert, W., and Donaldson, D. (1995b). Interpersonal Population Ethics: Critical-Level Utilitarian Principles. *Econometrica*, 63:1303–1320.

Blackorby, C. and Donaldson, D. (1978). Measures of Relative Equality and Their Meaning in Terms of Social Welfare. *Journal of Economic Theory*, 18:59–80.

Blackorby, C. and Donaldson, D. (1984). Social Criteria for Evaluating Population Changes. *Journal of Public Economics*, 25:13–33.

Blackorby, C., Donaldson, D., and Weymark, J. (1984). Social Choice with Interpersonal Utility Comparisons: A Diagrammatic Introduction. *International Economic Review*, 25:327–356.

Blackorby, C., Donaldson, D., and Weymark, J. (1996). Harsanyi's Social Aggregation Theorem for State-Contingent Alternatives. Discussion Paper n° 96-26, Department of Economics, University of British Columbia, Vancouver.

Blaug, M. (1980). *Economic Methodology*. Cambridge University Press, Cambridge.

Boadway, R. W. and Bruce, N. (1984). *Welfare Economics*. Blackwell, Oxford.

Bouyssou, D. and Vansnick, J. (1990). Utilité cardinale dans le certain et choix dans le risque. *Revue Economique*, 6:979–1000.

Bowring, J., editor (1838). *The Works of Jeremy Bentham*, volume 3. Reprinted by Russell and Russell, New York, 1962.

Brandt, R. (1959). *Ethical Theory*. Prentice-Hall, Englewood Cliffs, N.J.

Brandt, R. (1979). *A Theory of the Good and the Right*. Clarendon, Oxford.

Brandt, R. (1992). *Morality, Utilitarianism and Rights*. Cambridge University Press, Cambridge.

Broome, J. (1978). Choice and Value in Economics. *Oxford Economic Papers*, 30:313–333.

Broome, J. (1989). Should Social Preferences Be Consistent? *Economics and Philosophy*, 5:7–17.

Broome, J. (1990). Bolker–Jeffrey Expected Utility Theory and Axiomatic Utilitarianism. *Review of Economic Studies*, 57:477–502.

Broome, J. (1990-91). Fairness. *Proceedings of the Aristotelian Society*, 91:87–102.

Broome, J. (1991a). *Weighing Goods*. Blackwell, Oxford.

Broome, J. (1991b). Utility. *Economics and Philosophy*, 7:1–12.

Broome, J. (1992). *Counting the Cost of Global Warming*. White Horse, Cambridge.

Broome, J. (1993). A Cause of Preference Is Not an Object of Preference. *Social Choice and Welfare*, 10:57–68.

Broome, J. (1996). The Welfare Economics of Population. *Oxford Economic Papers*, 48:177–193.

Buchanan, J. M. (1954). Individual Choice in Voting and the Market. *Journal of Polititcal Economy*, 62:334–343.

Canto-Sperber, M., editor (1996). *Dictionnaire d'éthique et de philosophie morale* Presses Universitaires de France, Paris.

Chipman, J. S., Hurwicz, L., Richter, M. K., and Sonnenschein, H. F., editors (1971). *Preferences, Utility and Demand.* Harcourt Brace Jovanovich, New York.

Cohen, G. A. (1989). On the Currency of Egalitarian Justice. *Ethics*, 99:906–944.

Collard, D. (1978). *Altruism and Economy.* Martin Robertson, Oxford.

Coulhon, T. and Mongin, P. (1989). Social Choice Theory in the Case of von Neumann-Morgenstern Utilities. *Social Choice and Welfare*, 6:175–187.

Cowen, T. (1989). Normative Population Theory. *Social Choice and Welfare*, 6:33–43.

Daniels, N., editor (1989). *Reading Rawls.* Stanford University Press, Stanford.

de Finetti, B. (1937). La prévision, ses lois logiques, ses sources subjectives. *Annales de l'Institut Henri Poincaré*, 7:1–68.

De Meyer, B. and Mongin, P. (1995). A Note on Affine Aggregation. *Economics Letters*, 47:177–183.

Debreu, G. (1960). Topological Methods in Cardinal Utility Theory. In K. J. Arrow, S. K. and Suppes, P., editors, *Mathematical Methods in the Social Sciences*, pages 16–26. Stanford University Press, Stanford.

Deschamps, R. and Gevers, L. (1978). Leximin and Utilitarian Rules: A Joint Characterization. *Journal of Economic Theory*, 17:143–163.

Diamond, P. A. (1967). Cardinal Welfare, Individualistic Ethics, and Interpersonal Comparisons of Utility: A Comment. *Journal of Polititcal Economy*, 75:765–766.

Dérathé, R. (1951). *Jean-Jacques Rousseau et la science politique de son temps.* Vrin, Paris.

Dworkin, R. (1981). What is Equality, I: Equality of Welfare, and What is Equality, II: Equality of Resources. *Philosophy and Public Affairs*, 10:185–246 and 283–345.

Edgeworth, F. Y. (1881). *Mathematical Psychics.* Kegan Paul, London. Reprinted by A.M. Kelley, New York, 1967.

Ellsberg, D. (1954). Classic and Current Notions of 'Measurable Utility'. *Economic Journal*, 64:528–556.

Elster, J. and Roemer, J. E., editors (1991). *Interpersonal Comparisons of Well-Being*. Cambridge University Press, Cambridge.

Epstein, L. G. and Segal, U. (1992). Quadratic Social Welfare Functions. *Journal of Political Economy*, 100:691–712.

Fagot-Largeault, A. (1991). Réflexions sur la notion de qualité de la vie. *Archives de philosophie du droit*, Droit et science, 26:135–153. English translation in L. Nordenfelt (ed.), Concepts and Measurement of Quality of Life in Health Care, Dordrecht, Kluwer, 1992, pages 135–160.

Fine, T. (1973). *Theories of Probability*. Academic Press, New York.

Fishburn, P. C. (1970). *Utility Theory for Decision Making*. Wiley, New York.

Fishburn, P. C. (1982). *The Foundations of Expected Utility*. D. Reidel, Dordrecht.

Fishburn, P. C. (1984). On Harsanyi's Utilitarian Cardinal Welfare Theorem. *Theory and Decision*, 17:21–28.

Fishburn, P. C. (1986). The Axioms of Subjective Probability. *Statistical Science*, 1:335–358.

Fishburn, P. C. (1988). *Nonlinear Preference and Utility Theory*. The John Hopkins University Press, Baltimore.

Fishburn, P. C. (1989). Retrospective on the Utility Theory of von Neumann and Morgenstern. *Journal of Risk and Uncertainty*, 2:127–158.

Fleurbaey, M. (1995). Equal Opportunity or Equal Social Outcomes. *Economics and Philosophy*, 11:25–55.

Fleurbaey, M. (1996). *Théories économiques de la justice*. Economica, Paris.

Foley, D. (1967). Ressource Allocation and the Public Sector. *Yale Economic Essays*, 7:45–98.

Gaertner, W. and Klemisch-Ahlert, M. (1992). *Social Choice and Bargaining Perspectives on Distributive Justice*. Springer, Berlin.

Gauthier, D. (1986). *Morals by Agreement*. Clarendon Press, Oxford.

Gérard-Varet, L. A. and Passeron, J. C., editors (1995). *Le modèle et l'enquête. Les usages du principe de rationalité en sciences sociales*. Editions de l'Ecole des Hautes Etudes en Sciences Sociales, Paris.

Gevers, L. (1979). On Interpersonal Comparability and Social Welfare Orderings. *Econometrica*, 47:75–89.

Gibbard, A. (1974). A Pareto-Consistent Libertarian Claim. *Journal of Economic Theory*, 7:388–410.

Gibbard, A. (1979). Disparate Goods and Rawls' Difference Principle: A Social Choice Theoretic Treatment. *Theory and Decision*, 11:267–288.

Glannon, W. (1995). Equality, Priority, and Numbers. *Social Theory and Practice*, 21:427–455.

Goodin, R. E. (1986). Laundering Preferences. In Elster, J. and Hylland, A., editors, *Foundations of Social Choice Theory*, pages 75–101. Cambridge University Press, Cambridge.

Gorman, W. M. (1968). The Structure of Utility Functions. *Review of Economic Studies*, 35:367–390.

Graaff, J. d. V. (1957). *Theoretical Welfare Economics*. Cambridge University Press, Cambridge.

Griffin, J. (1986). *Well-Being*. Clarendon Press, Oxford.

Halévy, E. (1901-1904). *La Formation du Radicalisme Philosophique, 3 volumes*. Félix Alcan, Paris. New edition, Paris, Presses Universitaires de France, 1995.

Hammond, P. J. (1976). Equity, Arrow's Conditions and Rawls's Difference Principle. *Econometrica*, 44:793–804.

Hammond, P. J. (1981). Ex–ante, and Ex–post, Welfare Optimality Under Uncertainty. *Economica*, 48:235–250.

Hammond, P. J. (1982). Utilitarianism, Uncertainty and Information. In Sen, A. K. and Williams, B. (1982), pages 85–102.

Hammond, P. J. (1983). Ex–post Optimality as a Dynamically Consistent Objective for Collective Choice Under Uncertainty. In Pattanaik, P. and Salles, M., editors, *Social Choice and Welfare*, pages 175–205. North-Holland, Amsterdam.

Hammond, P. J. (1987). On Reconciling Arrow's Theory of Social Choice With Harsanyi's Fundamental Utilitarianism. In Feiwel, G., editor, *Arrow and the Foundations of the Theory of Economic Policy*, pages 79–221. New York University Press, New York.

Hammond, P. J. (1988a). Consequentialist Foundations for Expected Utility Theory. *Theory and Decision*, 25:25–78.

Hammond, P. J. (1988b). Consequentialist Demographic Norms and Parenting Rights. *Social Choice and Welfare*, 5:127–145.

Hammond, P. J. (1991). Interpersonal Comparisons of Utility: Why and How They Should Be Made. In Elster, J. and Roemer, J. E., editors, *Interpersonal Comparisons of Well-Being*, pages 200–254. Cambridge University Press, Cambridge.

Hammond, P. J. (1995). Social Choice of Individual and Group Rights. In Barnett, W. A., Moulin, H., Salles, M., and Schofield, N. J., editors, *Social Choice, Welfare, and Ethics*, pages 55–77. Cambridge University Press, Cambridge.

Hammond, P. J. (1996). Consequentialist Decision Theory and Utilitarian Ethics. In Farina, F., Hahn, F., and Vanucci, S., editors, *Ethics, Rationality and Economic Behaviour*, pages 92–118. Clarendon Press, Oxford.

Hare, R. M. (1976). Ethical Theory and Utilitarianism. In Lewis, H. D., editor, *Contemporary British Philosophy*. Reprinted in A. K. Sen and B. Williams (1982), pages 23–38.

Hare, R. M. (1981). *Moral Thinking: Its Levels, Method and Point*. Clarendon Press, Oxford.

Harrod, R. F. (1936). Utilitarianism Revised. *Mind*, 45:137–156.

Harsanyi, J. C. (1953). Cardinal Utility in Welfare Economics and in the Theory of Risk-Taking. *Journal of Political Economy*, 61:434–435. Reprinted in J. C. Harsanyi (1976), chapter 1.

Harsanyi, J. C. (1955). Cardinal Welfare, Individualistic Ethics, and Interpersonal Comparisons of Utility. *Journal of Political Economy*, 63:309–321. Reprinted in J. C. Harsanyi (1976), chapter 2.

Harsanyi, J. C. (1958). Ethics in Terms of Hypothetical Imperatives. *Mind*, 67:305–316. Reprinted in J. C. Harsanyi (1976), chapter 3.

Harsanyi, J. C. (1967–1968). Games With Incomplete Information Played by 'Bayesian' Players. *Management Science*, 14:159–182, 320–334, and 486–502.

Harsanyi, J. C. (1975). Nonlinear Social Welfare Functions: Do Welfare Economists Have a Special Exemption from Bayesian Rationality? *Theory and Decision*, 6:311–332. Reprinted in J. C. Harsanyi (1976), chapter 5.

Harsanyi, J. C. (1976). *Essays on Ethics, Social Behavior, and Scientific Explanation*. D. Reidel, Dordrecht.

Harsanyi, J. C. (1977a). *Rational Behavior and Bargaining Equilibrium in Games and Social Situations*. Cambridge University Press, Cambridge.

Harsanyi, J. C. (1977b). Morality and the Theory of Rational Behavior. *Social Research*. 44. Reprinted in A. K. Sen and B. Williams (1982), pages 39–62.

Harsanyi, J. C. (1977c). Rule Utilitarianism and Decision Theory. *Erkenntnis*, 11:25–33.

Harsanyi, J. C. (1979). Bayesian Decision Theory, Rule Utilitarianism, and Arrow's Impossibility Theorem. *Theory and Decision*, 11:289–317.

Harsanyi, J. C. (1992). Games and Decision–Theoretic Models in Ethics. In Aumann, R. and Hart, S., editors, *Handbook of Game Theory*, volume 1, chapter 19, pages 669–707. North–Holland, Amsterdam.

Hausman, D. and McPherson, M. (1994). Preference, Belief, and Welfare. *American Economic Review. Papers and Proceedings*, 84:396–400.

Hausman, D. and McPherson, M. (1996). *Economic Analysis and Moral Philosophy*. Cambridge University Press, Cambridge.

Herstein, I. N. and Milnor, J. (1953). An Axiomatic Approach to Measurable Utility. *Econometrica*, 21:291–297.

Hicks, J. R. (1939). *Value and Capital*. Oxford University Press, Oxford. 2nd edition, 1946.

Hicks, J. R. (1956). *A Revision of Demand Theory*. Clarendon Press, Oxford.

Hild, M., Jeffrey, R., and Risse, M. (1997). Problems of Preference Aggregation. forthcoming in Salles, M. and Weymark, J., editors, *Justice,Political Liberalism and Utilitarianism: Themes from Harsanyi and Rawls*, Cambridge University Press, Cambridge.

Hobbes, T. (1651). *Leviathan*. Blackwell, Oxford.

Howson, C. and Urbach, P. (1989). *Scientific Reasoning. The Bayesian Approach*. Open Court, Peru, Ill. Revised edition, 1993.

Hume, D. (1736). Treatise on Human Nature. Reprinted 1896 by Clarendon Press, Oxford.

Hurwicz, L., Schmeidler, D., and Sonnenschein, H. F., editors (1985). *Social Goals and Social Organization*. Cambridge University Press, Cambridge.

Hutcheson, F. (1725). *On the Nature and Conduct of the Passions and Affections*. Foulis, Glasgow.

Hylland, A. and Zeckhauser, R. (1979). The Impossibility of Bayesian Group Decision Making with Separate Aggregation of Beliefs and Values. *Econometrica*, 47:1321–1336.

Jeffrey, R. C. (1965). *The Logic of Decision*. University of Chicago Press, Chicago. 2nd revised edition, 1983.

Jevons, S. (1871). *The Theory of Political Economy*. Macmillan, London.

Kagan, S. (1992). The Limits of Well-Being. In Paul, E., Miller, F., and Paul, J., editors, *The Good Life and the Human Good*, pages 169–189. Cambridge University Press, Cambridge.

Kahneman, D. and Tversky, A. (1979). Prospect Theory: An Analysis of Decisions Under Risk. *Econometrica*, 47:263–291.

Kalai, E. (1975). Solutions to the Bargaining Problem. In Hurwicz, L., Schmeidler, D. and Sonnenschein, H. F. (1985), chapter 3.

Kalai, E. and Smorodinsky, M. (1975). Other Solutions to Nash's Bargaining Problem. *Econometrica*, 47:1623–1630.

Kaneko, M. (1984). On Interpersonal Utility Comparisons. *American Economic Review. Papers and Proceedings*, 1:165–175.

Kant, I. (1785). Grundlegung zur Metaphysik der Sitten. English translation by H. J. Paton, *The Moral Law*. Hutchinson, London, 1953.

Kant, I. (1788). Kritik der Praktischen Vernunft. English translation by L.W. Beck, *Critique of Practical Reason*. Bobbs–Merril, Indianapolis, 1977.

Karni, E. (1996). Social Welfare Functions and Fairness. *Social Choice and Welfare*, 13:487–496.

Karni, E. and Weymark, J. (1996). An Informationally Parsimonious Impartial Observer Theorem. Discussion Paper No. 96-15, Department of Economics, University of British Columbia, Vancouver. Forthcoming in *Social Choice and Welfare*, 1998.

Kelsey, D. (1987). The Role of Information in Social Welfare Judgments. *Oxford Economic Papers*, 39:301–317.

Kolm, S. C. (1972). *Justice et équité*. Editions du Centre National de la Recherche Scientifique, Paris.

Kolm, S. C. (1974). Sur les conséquences économiques de principes de justice et de justice pratique. *Revue d'économie politique*, 84:80–107.

Kolm, S. C. (1984). *La bonne économie. La réciprocité générale*. Presses Universitaires de France, Paris.

Kolm, S. C. (1993). The Impossibility of Utilitarianism. In Koslowski, P. and Shionoya, Y., editors, *The Good and the Economical*, pages 30–66. Springer, Berlin.

Kolm, S. C. (1994). The Meaning of 'Fundamental Preferences'. *Social Choice and Welfare*, 11:193–198.

Kolm, S. C. (1995). *Modern Theories of Justice*. The M.I.T. Press, Cambridge, Mass.

Kolm, S. C. (1997). Chance and Justice: Social Policies and the Harsanyi–Vickrey–Rawls Problem. forthcoming in *European Economic Review*.

Krantz, D. H., Luce, R. D., Suppes, P., and Tversky, A. (1971). *Foundations of Measurement*, volume 1. Academic Press, New York.

Lange, O. (1942). The Foundations of Welfare Economics. *Econometrica*, 10:215–228.

Lauwers, L. (1995). Time–Neutrality and Linearity. *Journal of Mathematical Economics*, 24:347–351.

Lerner, A. (1944). *The Economics of Control*. Macmillan, London.

Levi, I. (1990). Pareto Unanimity and Consensus. *Journal of Philosophy*, 87:481–492.

Little, I. M. D. (1950). *A Critique of Welfare Economics*. Clarendon Press, Oxford.

Little, I. M. D. (1952). Social Choice and Individual Values. *Journal of Political Economy*, 60:422–432.

Locke, J. (1690). Second Treatise of Civil Government. In P. Laslett, editor (1960), *Two Treatises of Government*, Cambridge University Press, Cambridge.

Loomes, G. and Sugden, R. (1982). Regret Theory: An Alternative to Rational Choice Under Uncertainty. *Economic Journal*, 92:805–824.

Luce, R. D. and Raiffa, H. (1957). *Games and Decisions*. Wiley, New York.

Lyons, D. (1965). *Forms and Limits of Utilitarianism*. Clarendon Press, Oxford.

Markowitz, H. (1952). The Utility of Wealth. *Journal of Political Economy*, 60:151–158.

Mas-Colell, A., Whinston, M., and Green, J. (1995). *Microeconomic Theory*. Oxford University Press, New York.

Maskin, E. (1978). A Theorem on Utilitarianism. *Review of Economic Studies*, 45:93–96.

McClennen, E. F. (1990). *Rationality and Dynamic Choice*. Cambridge University Press, Cambridge.

McKay, A. F. (1986). Extended Sympathy and Interpersonal Utility Comparisons. *Journal of Philosophy*, 83:305–322.

Mill, J. S. (1859). On Liberty. In H. B. Acton (1972), *Utilitarianism, Liberty, Representative Government*, pages 65–170. Dent Dutton, London.

Mill, J. S. (1863). Utilitarianism. In H. B. Acton (1972), *Utilitarism, Liberty, Representative Government*, pages 1–61. Dent Dutton, London.

Mirrlees, J. A. (1974). Notes on Welfare Economics, Information and Uncertainty. In Balch, M., McFadden, D., and Wu, S., editors, *Essays on Economic Behavior Under Uncertainty*, pages 243–258. North Holland, Amsterdam.

Mirrlees, J. A. (1982). The Economic Use of Utilitarianism. In Sen, A. K., and Williams, B. (1982), pages 63–84.

Mongin, P. (1984). Modèle rationnel ou modèle économique de la rationalité? *Revue Economique*, 35:9–64.

Mongin, P. (1994a). Harsanyi's Aggregation Theorem: Multi-Profile Version and Unsettled Questions. *Social Choice and Welfare*, 11:331–354.

Mongin, P. (1994b). L'optimisation est-elle un critère de rationalité individuelle? *Dialogue*, 33:191–222. Reprinted in L. A. Gérard-Varet and J. C. Passeron (1995), pages 279–307.

Mongin, P. (1995a). Consistent Bayesian Aggregation. *Journal of Economic Theory*, 66:131–351.

Mongin, P. (1995b). L'utilitarisme originel et le développement de la théorie économique. Postface to the new edition of E. Halévy (1901–1904). Also published in *La Pensée Politique*, 3:341–361.

Mongin, P. (1996). The Paradox of the Bayesian Experts and State-Dependent Utility Theory. C.O.R.E. Discussion Paper 9626, Université Catholique de Louvain. Forthcoming in *Journal of Mathematical Economics*, 1988.

Monroe, D. H., editor (1972). *A Guide to the British Moralists*. Fontana, London.

Moore, G. E. (1903). *Principia Ethica*. Cambridge University Press, Cambridge.

Morris, S. (1995). The Common Prior Assumption. *Economics and Philosophy*, 11:227–253.

Moulin, H. (1988). *Axioms of Cooperative Decision Making*. Cambridge University Press, Cambridge.

Moulin, H. (1995). *Cooperative Microeconomics*. Princeton University Press, Princeton.

Moulin, H. (1996). Stand Alone and Unanimity Tests: A Reexamination of Fair Division. In Farina, F., Hahn, F., and Vanucci, S., editors, *Ethics, Rationality and Economic Behaviour*, pages 121–142. Clarendon Pres, Oxford.

Myerson, R. B. (1981). Utilitarianism, Egalitarianism, and the Timing Effect in Social Choice Problems. *Econometrica*, 49:883–897.

Nagel, T. (1970). *The Possibility of Altruism*. Oxford University Press, Oxford.

Nash, J. F. (1950). The Bargaining Problem. *Econometrica*, 18:155–162.

Nelson, M. (1991). Utilitarian Eschatology. *American Philosophical Quarterly*, 28:339–347.

Nozick, R. (1974). *Anarchy, State and Utopia*. Basic Books, New York.

Pareto, V. (1896-97). *Cours d'économie politique*. In *Oeuvres Complètes*, volume 1. Droz, 1964, Genève.

Pareto, V. (1909). *Manuel d'économie politique*. In *Oeuvres Complètes*, volume 7. Droz, 1966, Genève.

Pareto, V. (1917-1919). *Traité de sociologie générale*. In *Oeuvres complètes*, volume 12. Droz, 1968, Genève.

Parfit, D. (1984). *Reasons and Persons*. Clarendon Press, Oxford.

Pattanaik, P. K. (1968). Risk, Impersonality, and the Social Welfare Function. *Journal of Political Economy*, 76:1152–1169.

Pazner, E. A. and Schmeidler, D. (1978). Egalitarian–Equivalent Allocations: A New Concept of Economic Equity. *Quarterly Journal of Economics*, 92:671–687.

Picavet, E. (1996). *Choix rationnel et vie publique*. Presses Universitaires de France, Paris.

Pigou, A. C. (1920). *The Economics of Welfare*. Macmillan, London, 4th revised, 1932 edition.

Plato. Republic. English translation by Grube, (1974). Hackett, Indianapolis.

Pratt, J. W. (1964). Risk Aversion in the Small and in the Large. *Econometrica*, 32:122–136.

Ramsey, F. P. (1931). Truth and Probability. In Braithwaite, R. B., editor, *The Foundation of Mathematics and Other Logical Essays*, pages 156–198. Harcourt and Brace, New York.

Rawls, J. (1958). Justice as Fairness. *Philosophical Review*, 67:164–194.

Rawls, J. (1971). *A Theory of Justice*. Harvard University Press, Cambridge, Mass.

Rawls, J. (1980). Kantian Constructivism in Moral Theory. *Journal of Philosophy*, 77:515–572.

Rawls, J. (1982). Social Unity and Primary Goods. In Sen, A. K., and Williams, B. (1982), pages 159–185.

Rawls, J. (1988). The Priority of Right and Ideas of the Good. *Philosophy and Public Affairs*, 17:251–276.

Richter, M. (1971). Rational Choice. In Chipman, J. S., Hurwicz, L., Richter M. K., and Sonnenschein, H. F. (1971), pages 29–58.

Riley, J. (1988). *Liberal Utilitarianism. Social Choice Theory and J.S. Mill's Philosophy.* Cambridge University Press, Cambridge.

Robbins, L. (1932). *An Essay on the Nature and Significance of Economics.* MacMillan, London, 2nd revised edition. 1937.

Roberts, K. W. S. (1980a). Interpersonal Comparability and Social Choice Theory. *Review of Economic Studies,* 47:421–439.

Roberts, K. W. S. (1980b). Social Choice Theory: The Single and Multi-Profile Approaches. *Review of Economic Studies,* 47:441–450.

Roberts, K. W. S. (1980c). Possibility Theorems with Interpersonally Comparable Welfare Levels. *Review of Economic Studies,* 47:409–420.

Roberts, K. W. S. (1995). Valued Opinions and Opinionized Values: The Double Aggregation Problem. In Basu, K., Pattanaik, P., and Suzumura, K., editors, *Choice, Welfare and Development,* pages 141–165. Oxford University Press, Oxford.

Roemer, J. E. (1985). Equality of Talent. *Economics and Philosophy,* 1:151–181. Reprinted in Roemer (1994), essay 6.

Roemer, J. E. (1986). The Mismarriage of Bargaining Theory and Distributive Justice. *Ethics,* 97:88–110. Reprinted in Roemer (1994), essay 9.

Roemer, J. E. (1994). *Egalitarian Perspectives.* Cambridge University Press, Cambridge.

Roemer, J. E. (1996). *Theories of Distributive Justice.* Harvard University Press, Cambridge, Mass.

Rousseau, J. J. (1755). Discours sur l'origine de l'inégalité. In Dérathé, R. et al., editors, *Oeuvres complètes,* volume 3. NRF, Bibliothèque de la Pléiade, Paris. English translation in "The Social Contract and Discourses", by Cole, G. D. H. (1950). Dutton, New York.

Rousseau, J. J. (1761). Du contrat social. In Dérathé, R. et al., editors, *Oeuvres complètes,* volume 3. NRF, Bibliothèque de la Pléiade, Paris. English translation in "The Social Contract and Discourses", by Cole G. D. H. (1950), Dutton, New York.

Rubinstein, A. (1984). The Single Profile Analogues to Multi-Profile Theorems: Mathematical Logic's Approach. *International Economic Review,* 25:719–730.

Samuelson, P. A. (1967). Arrow's Mathematical Politics. In Hook, S., editor, *Human Values and Economic Policy,* pages 41–50. New York University Press, New York.

Savage, L. J. (1954). *The Foundations of Statistics.* Wiley, New York, 2nd revised, 1972 edition.

Scanlon, T. M. (1975). Preference and Urgency. *Journal of Philosophy,* 72:655–669.

Scheffler, S. (1982). *The Rejection of Consequentialism*. Oxford University Press, Oxford.

Scheffler, S., editor (1988). *Consequentialism and Its Critics*. Oxford University Press, Oxford.

Schervish, M. J., Seidenfeld, T., and Kadane, J. B. (1990). State–Dependent Utilities. *Journal of the American Statistical Association*, 85:840–847.

Schervish, M. J., Seidenfeld, T., and Kadane, J. B. (1991). Shared Preferences and State–Dependent Utilities. *Management Science*, 37:1575–1589.

Schumpeter, J. (1954). *History of Economic Analysis*. Macmillan, London.

Screpanti, E. and Zamagni, S. (1993). *History of Economic Thought*. Oxford University Press, Oxford.

Seidenfeld, T., Kadane, J. B., and Schervish, M. J. (1989). On the Shared Preferences of Two Bayesian Decision Makers. *Journal of Philosophy*, 86:225–244.

Sen, A. K. (1970). *Collective Choice and Social Welfare*. North Holland, Amsterdam.

Sen, A. K. (1973a). Behaviour and the Concept of Preference. *Economica*, 40:241–259. reprinted in Sen (1982a), chapter 2.

Sen, A. K. (1973b). *On Economic Inequality*. Clarendon Press, Oxford.

Sen, A. K. (1974). Rawls versus Bentham: An Axiomatic Examination of the Pure Distribution Problem. *Theory and Decision*, 4:301–309.

Sen, A. K. (1976). Liberty, Unanimity and Rights. *Economica*, 43:217–245. Reprinted in Sen (1982a), chapter 14.

Sen, A. K. (1979). Utilitarianism and Welfarism. *Journal of Philosophy*, 76:463–489.

Sen, A. K. (1980). *Equality of What? Tanner Lectures on Human Values*, volume 1. Cambridge University Press, Cambridge. Reprinted in Sen (1982a), chapter 16 and in Sen (1992), pages 12–30.

Sen, A. K. (1980-81). Plural Utility. *Proceedings of the Aristotelian Society*, 81:193–215.

Sen, A. K. (1982a). *Choice, Welfare and Measurement*. Blackwell, Oxford.

Sen, A. K. (1982b). Rights and Agency. *Philosophy and Public Affairs*, 11:3–39. Reprinted in Scheffler, S. (1988).

Sen, A. K. (1985). *Commodities and Capabilities*. North Holland, Amsterdam.

Sen, A. K. (1986). Social Choice Theory. In Arrow, K. J. and Intriligator, M. D., editors, *Handbook of Mathematical Economics*, volume III, pages 1073–1181. North Holland, Amsterdam.

Sen, A. K. (1987). *On Ethics and Economics*. Blackwell, Oxford.

Sen, A. K. (1992). *Inequality Reexamined*. Clarendon Press, Oxford.

Sen, A. K. and Williams, B., editors (1982). *Utilitarianism and Beyond*. Cambridge University Press, Cambridge.

Sidgwick, H. (1884). The Method of Ethics. MacMillan, London, 7th revised edition, 1907.

Sikora, R. and Barry, B., editors (1978). *Obligations To Future Generations.* Temple, Philadelphia.

Singer, P., editor (1991). *A Companion to Ethics.* Blackwell, Oxford.

Smart, J. J. C. (1974). An Outline of a System of Utilitarian Ethics. In Smart, J. J. C. and Williams, B., editors, *Utilitarianism: For and Against,* pages 3–74. Cambridge University Press, Cambridge.

Smith, A. (1759). The Theory of Moral Sentiments. Revised 1790. New edition by Raphael, D. D., and Macfie, A. L. Oxford University Press, Oxford.

Stephen, L. (1901). The English Utilitarians. Reprinted 1968 by A. M. Kelley, New York.

Stigler, G. J. (1965). *The History of Economics.* The University of Chicago Press, Chicago.

Strasnick, S. (1976). Social Choice and the Derivation of Rawls' Difference Principle. *Journal of Philosophy,* 73:184–194.

Suppes, P. (1966). Some Formal Models of Grading Principles. *Synthese,* 6:284–306. Reprinted in Suppes, P. (1969). *Studies in Methodology and Foundations of Science,* Dordrecht, Reidel.

Suppes, P. (1981). *Logique du probable.* Flammarion, Paris.

Suppes, P. and Winet, M. (1955). An Axiomatization of Utility Based on the Notion of Utility Differences. *Management Science,* 1:259–270.

Suzumura, K. (1983). *Rational Choice, Collective Decisions and Social Welfare.* Cambridge University Press, Cambridge.

Suzumura, K. (1994). Interpersonal Comparisons of the Extended Sympathy Type and the Possibility of Social Choice. Discussion Paper No. 295, Institute of Economic Research, Hitotsubashi University. Published in Arrow, K. J., Sen, A. K., and Suzumura K., editors (1996). *Social Choice Re-Examined,* volume 2, pages 202–229. London, MacMillan.

Temkin, L. (1987). Intransitivity and the Mere Addition Paradox. *Philosophy and Public Affairs,* 16:138–187.

Temkin, L. (1993). *Inequality.* Oxford University Press, New York.

Thomson, W. (1982). Equity in Exchange Economies. *Journal of Economic Theory,* 18:217–244.

Thomson, W. (1994). L'absence d'envie: une introduction. *Recherches économique de Louvain,* 60:43–61.

Thomson, W. (1995). Population Monotonic Allocation Rules. In Barnett, W. A., Moulin, H., Salles, M., and Schofield, N. J., editors, *Social Choice, Welfare, and Ethics,* pages 79–124. Cambridge University Press, Cambridge.

Thomson, W. and Varian, H. (1985). Theories of Justice Based on Symmetry. In Hurwicz, L., Schmeidler, D., and Sonnenschein, H. F. (1985), pages 107–129.

Vallentyne, P., editor (1991). *Contractarianism and Rational Choice*. Cambridge University Press, Cambridge.

Vallentyne, P. (1994). Infinite Utility and Temporal Neutrality. *Utilitas*, 6:193–199.

Van Liedekerke, L. and Lauwers, L. (1997). Sacrificing the Patrol. *Economics and Philosophy*, 13:159–174.

Van Parijs, P. (1990). Equal Endowments as Undominated Diversity. *Recherches économiques de Louvain*, 56:327–355.

Van Parijs, P. (1991). *Qu'est-ce qu'une société juste ?* Le Seuil, Paris.

Varian, H. (1974). Equity, Envy and Efficiency. *Journal of Economic Theory*, 9:63–91.

Varian, H. (1985). Dworkin on Equality of Resources. *Economics and Philosophy*, 1:110–125.

Verneaux, R. (1971). *Le vocabulaire de Kant*. Aubier-Montaigne, Paris.

Vickrey, W. (1945). Measuring Marginal Utility by Reaction to Risk. *Econometrica*, 13:319–333.

Vickrey, W. S. (1960). Utility, Strategy, and Social Decision Rules. *Quarterly Journal of Economics*, 74:507–535.

Viner, J. (1949). Bentham and J. S. Mill. *American Economic Review*, 39:360–382.

von Neumann, J. and Morgenstern, O. (1944). *Theory of Games and Economic Behavior*. Princeton University Press, Princeton. 2nd edition, 1947, 3rd edition, 1953.

Wakker, P. (1989). *Additive Representation of Preferences*. Kluwer, Dordrecht.

Wasserman, D. (1996). Let Them Eat Chances: Probability and Distributive Justice. *Economics and Philosophy*, 12:29–49.

Weymark, J. (1991). A Reconsideration of the Harsanyi–Sen Debate on Utilitarianism. In Elster, J. and Roemer, J. E. (1991), pages 255–320.

Weymark, J. (1993). Harsanyi's Social Aggregation Theorem and the Weak Pareto Principle. *Social Choice and Welfare*, 10:209–221.

Williams, B. (1973). A Critique of Utilitarianism. In Smart, J. J. C. and Williams, B., editors, *Utilitarianism: For and Against*, pages 77–150. Cambridge University Press, Cambridge.

Yaari, M. E. (1981). Rawls, Edgeworth, Shapley, Nash: Theories of Distributive Justice Re–Examined. *Journal of Economic Theory*, 24:1–39.

Yaari, M. E. and Bar-Hillel, M. (1984). On Dividing Justly. *Social Choice and Welfare*, 1:1–24.

Zhou, L. (1997). Harsanyi's Utilitarianism Theorems: General Societies. *Journal of Economic Theory*, 72:198–207.

11 MEASURES OF ECONOMIC WELFARE

Michael Ahlheim

Technische Universität Cottbus

Contents

1	Introduction		484
2	Criteria for the Characterization of Welfare Measures		486
3	Welfare Measurement in a Comparative Static World		488
	3.1	Definitions	489
	3.2	Functional Welfare Measures	495
	3.3	Atomistic Welfare Measures	512
	3.4	Index Measures	515
4	Welfare Measurement with Quantity Constraints		526
	4.1	Definitions	527
	4.2	Measuring Welfare	531
5	Intertemporal Aspects		537
6	Further Topics		543
	6.1	Public Goods	543
	6.2	Uncertainty	553
	6.3	Aggregation	555
References			558

483

1   Introduction

In a democratic society the success and political survival of government depends to a great extent on the approval of its policy by the public. Therefore, it is of considerable importance for the government to know how its activities affect the well–being or welfare of the citizens concerned. As the true sovereign of a democratic society, the people, have the right to call government to account for the way it directs or influences the use of the resources of the economy under consideration. This influence can be exerted either directly by buying or selling goods and factors in the respective markets or indirectly by taxes, subsidies, regulations or other legislative measures. One possibility for government to justify its economic activities (and to prevent political problems) is to assess the effects which the government actions under consideration have on the well-being or welfare of the people concerned by these actions. The theoretical instruments which are used to determine changes in the well-being of individuals or of society as a whole are called welfare measures. The purpose of this article is to discuss different kinds of welfare measures from both a theoretical and an empirical point of view. This means that our interest in the welfare measures considered here is twofold: on the one hand we want to analyse the theoretical properties and the economic interpretation of these measures, and on the other, we want to investigate the possibilities of computing them on the basis of observable data.

Before we start our analysis we have to specify in more detail the object in which we are interested, namely the economic welfare of society. If we talk about the welfare of a democratic society we have to realise that this social welfare cannot be taken as independent of the welfare of the single individuals who form this society. Therefore, to evaluate the welfare effects of a certain government project like a tax reform or a public spending program we have to look first at the individual welfare changes induced by this project. In a second step we can try to aggregate these individual welfare effects to arrive at a social welfare judgement. If the individual welfare of all members of the society under consideration increases as a consequence of a certain government project, the social valuation of this project is unambiguous: it is socially favourable and should therefore be carried out. An analogously unambiguous case is given if the welfare of all individuals decreases as a consequence of a government project. But, unfortunately, such cases of uniform welfare changes for all individuals are rather uncommon. Usually, welfare will increase for some individuals and decrease for some others. In such cases there arises a trade–off between the welfare gains of the winners and the welfare losses of the losers because a decision for or against the implementation of the project under consideration implies a decision in favour of the winners or of the losers of this project, respectively. Such a trade-off cannot be solved objectively within the framework of ordinal utility theory because this would imply interpersonal utility comparisons, which are not possible within this framework.

In this article we shall deal with ordinal welfare measures only, i.e. with welfare measures that are based on the existence of individual preference orderings, because the assumptions of cardinal utility theory seem to be much too restrictive and unrealistic from our point of view. Since Arrow's (1963) Impossibility Theorem it is clear that under reasonable conditions there does not exist a uniquely determined social preference ordering which can be derived from individual preference orderings and which allows us to solve the conflict between winners and losers of a certain project in an "objective" and democratic (i.e. non–dictatorial) manner. There have been innumerable attempts to overcome this problem but a satisfactory solution which holds under fairly general and plausible conditions has not yet been found. The proposals for social welfare measures made in the literature on welfare measurement are either contradictory in themselves or not uniquely determined or they imply the use of more or less arbitrary welfare weights, which is not compatible with ordinal utility theory.[1] For these reasons, and since the problems of interpersonal utility comparisons and of social choice are dealt with elsewhere in this volume, we shall concentrate on the measurement of individual welfare in this article and neglect the aggregation problem in what follows.

The main problem with welfare is that it is not an objective magnitude like the GNP (which can be measured by computing "given" facts) but a subjective one that depends crucially on the personal perceptions and valuations of different individuals, i.e. on their personal preference orderings. Therefore, the measurement of welfare implies not only statistical but also psychological aspects. The simplest method to assess the welfare change that a certain individual experiences as a consequence of a certain government project would be to ask her or him. This direct method of welfare measurement is used (in more or less modified versions) if no other method can be applied, e.g. because the necessary data are not available. The decisive disadvantage of these direct interview methods is that, typically, there exist considerable incentives for the individuals to give wrong or exaggerated answers for strategic reasons, so that a direct welfare analysis always bears the risk of a strategic bias. Therefore, the indirect methods of welfare measurement are used if this is possible. A characteristic of these methods is that the preference ordering of an individual is inferred indirectly from her or his market behaviour. The typical procedure

---

[1]Much about the restrictedness of the environment in which aggregate welfare measures are valid can be learned e.g. from Blackorby and Donaldson (1985), Slesnick (1991), Campbell (1992), Hammond (1990a, 1990b, 1991), Blackorby et al. (1993) or from Blackorby and Shorrocks (1995).

is that first the individual market demand functions are estimated and then they are integrated (if possible) to one of the mathematical functions which describe the preference ordering of the individual under consideration. It is these indirect methods of welfare measurement that we shall deal with in this article.

The paper is organised as follows: in the next section some basic criteria are introduced which allow us to classify the different kinds of welfare measures according to the range of their applicability. In Section 3 the general problems of welfare measurement in a comparative static world with perfect markets are examined and the traditional measures of individual welfare are analysed. Among these are the "classical" consumer's surplus measures by Marshall and Hicks as well as a less well–known measure based on the distance function. The relation between these functional welfare measures on the one hand and the statistical or atomistic welfare measures on the other is also analysed in this section. Last but not least, the importance of price and quantity indices for the measurement of welfare is examined. Section 4 deals with the measurement problems which arise if the supply of some commodities is rationed. In Section 5 the intertemporal aspects of welfare measurements are analysed. Section 6 deals with some special topics, each of which would deserve to be treated in a separate paper: the welfare effects of public goods, welfare measurement under uncertainty and the aggregation problem, i.e. the question how individual welfare measures can be aggregated to construct a measure of social welfare. In this paper, of course, only a few brief remarks on these issues are possible.

2   Criteria for the Characterization of Welfare Measures

In this section we present four basic criteria that a reliable welfare measure should fulfil. These criteria help us to characterize the various welfare measures to be discussed below by the specific functions they can assume within the general framework of welfare measurement. Of course, an ideal welfare measure of universal applicability should meet all of these criteria, but for many concrete practical purposes only one or two special properties are needed. Therefore, the following catalogue of criteria can be regarded as a means for the classification of different welfare measures according to their special capacities.

Our first criterion simply requires that a welfare measure should indicate if the welfare of an individual increases, decreases or remains constant when we move from an initial situation 0 to a new situation $k \in \{1, 2, ..., K\}$. For this purpose we have to fix an arbitrary scalar as a "neutral point" which indicates that individual welfare or utility did not change. Traditionally this neutral point is the "0" for the so–called variation measures of welfare which we treat here. Therefore, our first criterion can be formulated as

Indicator criterion:

$$W_{0k} \gtreqless 0 \iff U_k \gtreqless U_0 \quad (k \in \{1, 2, ..., K\}), \tag{2.1}$$

where we denote the welfare measure for the change from situation 0 to situation k by W_{0k} and the utility levels for these situations by U_0 and U_k, respectively.

As a second criterion we require that a welfare measure should be able to simultaneously rank an arbitrary number of projects in accordance with the individual's preference ordering. We call this our

Ranking criterion:

$$W_{0k} \gtreqless W_{0j} \iff U_k \gtreqless U_j \quad (k, j \in \{1, 2, ..., K\}). \tag{2.2}$$

The fulfilment of this criterion is of importance only if the government has the choice between a set of alternative projects which all start from the same initial situation. If there is only one project to be evaluated it is sufficient for the welfare measure to fulfil the indicator criterion.

While the first two criteria require consistency in a comparative statics context our third criterion refers to intertemporal consistency. If we evaluate a project that lasts, say, three time periods we can either compute the overall welfare measure W_{03} or we can compute the periodical welfare measures W_{01}, W_{12} and W_{23} and add them up. Our third criterion requires that both ways lead to the same result, no matter how many time periods are concerned. The general formulation of this criterion is given by the

Circularity criterion:

$$W_{0j} + W_{jk} = W_{0k} \quad (k, j \in \{1, 2, ..., K\}), \tag{2.3}$$

which requires that the value of a welfare measure shall be the same no matter whether we evaluate a certain project lasting for several time periods in one step or whether we compute the respective measures for each time period separately and add up these periodical measures afterwards. This criterion is based on the classical circularity test by Fisher (1927) who constructed a whole system of formal tests for statistical or "atomistic" indices [for a detailed discussion of these tests cf. Samuelson and Swamy (1974)]. Most of these tests are more or less irrelevant for our special purpose of welfare measurement (and as a whole they are even contradictory, as Frisch already showed in 1936) but the above stated weak version of the circularity test is useful in the context of intertemporal welfare measurement, as we shall see below.

The above mentioned criteria refer to the theoretical consistency of a welfare measure and mark the bounds within which it can be interpreted. But these criteria which are also fulfilled, e.g. by an ordinary utility function, do not contain the one distinctive property of a welfare measure with respect to a utility index: its empirical observability and computability. Therefore, we demand the

Computability criterion:

> A welfare measure must be uniquely computable on the basis of empirically observable data. $\qquad$ (2.4)

This criterion can be regarded as a *conditio sine qua non* for a welfare measure because a welfare measure that cannot be computed empirically cannot serve its essential purpose: the detection of an individual's preferences from her or his economic actions.

In the main part of this article we shall examine the different welfare measures from the perspective of the four reliability criteria developed in this section, where, of course, the circularity criterion will be applied in an intertemporal context only.

3   Welfare Measurement in a Comparative Static World with Perfect Markets

In this section we study the measurement of welfare for households with given lump–sum incomes who face fixed prices and buy consumption goods in perfect markets. The assumption of given lump–sum incomes can be justified by the observation that for the average household neither the number of working hours nor the wage rate is a decision variable that can be chosen freely like e.g. the quantities of the consumption goods. On the contrary, at least the breadwinner of a typical household is tied down by a working contract where working hours and wages are completely fixed. At the first stage of our analysis we also abstract from the existence of government policy instruments like the supply of public goods or public in–kind programs where the latter, typically, result in rationed markets. The evaluation of benefits ensuing from the employment of these government instruments will be considered in a later section of this article. Further, the analysis of this section will be a comparative static one, i.e. we compare two or more household equilibria from a welfare point of view without considering the respective processes of adaptation. In a later section of this paper we shall explicitly incorporate time into our analysis. In a comparative static framework as used here there is no incentive to save and, therefore, capital income is regarded as a part of the (fixed) lump-sum income of the household and is not mentioned explicitly here. Last but not least, for this first approach to the measurement of welfare we neglect the problem of uncertainty, which will be included into our analysis at a later stage. Before we start with our treatment of welfare measures we introduce some useful definitions to clarify our notation and the theoretical instruments we shall employ below.[2]

3.1 Definitions

We assume that the preferences of a consumer with respect to the quantities $x_n(n = 1, 2, ..., N)$ of N consumption goods can be described by his preference ordering which is defined on the nonnegative orthant of the N–dimensional Euclidean space $\mathbb{R}_+^N$. We further assume that this preference ordering is complete, reflexive, transitive, continuous, monotonous, strictly convex[3] and smooth for $x \in \mathbb{R}_+^N$. As is well known, such a preference ordering can be represented by the consumer's direct utility function $u : \mathbb{R}_+^N \to \mathbb{R}$ which is defined up to a continuous, strictly monotonically increasing transformation only. The functions $u(x)$ are strictly monotonically increasing, strictly quasiconcave, and twice continuously differentiable with respect to commodity bundles x.

Maximizing the direct utility function subject to the consumer's budget constraint yields his indirect utility function $v : \mathbb{R}_+^{N+1} \to \mathbb{R}$

$$v(p, I) \equiv \max_{x \in \mathcal{X}(p,I)} u(x), \quad \mathcal{X}(p, I) = \{x | x \in \mathbb{R}_+^N, \ px \leq I, \ p \in \mathbb{R}_{++}^N, I \in \mathbb{R}_{++}\},[4]$$

$$(3.1)$$

where $p_n(n = 1, 2, ..., N)$ are the prices of the consumption goods, I is the consumer's lump–sum income and $\mathcal{X}(p, I)$ is his budget set.[5] As a solution of this maximization problem one obtains the Marshallian demand functions which describe the optimal consumption bundle x^* as a function of prices p and income I

$$x^* = x(p, I) \tag{3.2}$$

and the Lagrangean multiplier λ^* which can be interpreted as the marginal utility of income at the household equilibrium:

$$\lambda^* = \lambda(p, I). \tag{3.3}$$

---

[2]For a more detailed discussion of the duality concepts and results presented in this section see e.g. Blackorby, Primont and Russell (1978), Diewert (1982), Cornes (1992), and Chapter 4 of this *Handbook*.

[3]From the monotony and strict convexity of the preference ordering, it follows that it is also strictly monotonous.

[4]For the sake of simplicity we do not use different notations for column vectors and row vectors as long as no confusion is possible (so, by px we mean the scalar product of the price vector p and the quantity vector x). By $\mathbb{R}_{++}^N$ we denote the strictly positive orthant of the N–dimensional Euclidean space. Analogously, $\mathbb{R}_+$ ($\mathbb{R}_{++}$) is the nonnegative (positive) 1–dimensional Euclidean space.

[5]Strictly speaking, we obtain the indirect utility function $v(p, I)$ from the maximization problem (3.1) only for strictly positive prices p and incomes I but we can extend the indirect utility function v by continuity to $\mathbb{R}_+^{N+1}$.

Substituting the optimal consumption bundle x^* from (3.2) into the objective function $u(x)$ of the maximization problem (3.1) yields the indirect utility function as

$$v(p, I) \equiv u(x(p, I)). \tag{3.4}$$

The indirect utility function $v(p, I)$ is continuous and strictly monotonically increasing in I, monotonically decreasing, quasiconvex and twice continuously differentiable with respect to p, and homogeneous of degree 0 in $[p, I]$. It is related to the Marshallian demand functions by Roy's Identity [cf. Roy (1942)]:[6]

$$x(p, I) \equiv -\frac{\nabla_p v}{\partial v/\partial I}(p, I) \equiv \frac{\nabla_p v}{\lambda}(p, I). \tag{3.5}$$

For some uses it is more convenient to work with the normalized version of the indirect utility function $\hat{v}(\hat{p}) : \mathbb{R}_+^{N+1} \to \mathbb{R}$ according to

$$\hat{v}(\hat{p}) \equiv \max_{x \in \mathcal{X}(\hat{p},1)} u(x), \quad \mathcal{X}(\hat{p}, 1) = \{x | x \in \mathbb{R}_+^N, \ \hat{p}x \leq 1, \ \hat{p} \in \mathbb{R}_{++}^N\}, \tag{3.6}$$

where $\hat{p} = I/p$ is the vector of normalized prices. By minimizing the normalized indirect utility function with respect to normalized prices $\hat{p}$ we can reconstruct the direct utility function:[7]

$$u(x) \equiv \min_{\hat{p} \in \mathcal{P}(x)} \hat{v}(\hat{p}), \quad \mathcal{P}(x) = \{\hat{p} | \hat{p} \in \mathbb{R}_+^N, \ \hat{p}x \leq 1, \ x \in \mathbb{R}_{++}^N\}. \tag{3.7}$$

As a solution of this minimization problem we obtain the vector of inverse demand functions

$$\hat{p}^* = \hat{p}(x). \tag{3.8}$$

---

[6]By $\nabla_p v(p, I)$ we denote the gradient of the indirect utility function with respect to p. By differentiating identity (3.4) with respect to lump-sum income I and making use of the optimality conditions of our utility maximization problem we can show that the Lagrangian multiplier λ is identical with the marginal utility of income $\partial v/\partial I$ at the same household equilibrium, i.e. $\lambda(p, I) \equiv (\partial v/\partial I)(p, I)$.

[7]As before, from (3.6) we obtain the normalized indirect utility function only for strictly positive prices. But, again, we can extend the indirect utility function by continuity to $\mathbb{R}_+^N$, so that it can be used as an objective function for the optimization problem (3.7). In what follows we shall employ this technique of extending a function by continuity without explicitly mentioning it because all functions dealt with here are continuous so that this extension is always possible [for a more detailed treatment of this problem see e.g. Blackorby, Primont and Russell (1978, p. 17 ff.)].

According to the Hotelling-Wold Identity these functions can also be obtained by differentiating the direct utility function with respect to commodities x:

$$\hat{p} \equiv \frac{\nabla u(x)}{x \nabla u(x)}. \qquad (3.9)$$

In a model where all consumption goods are traded in perfect markets the inverse demand functions of a consumer are identical with his willingness–to–pay or shadow price functions. These functions are of some importance for the measurement of welfare, as we shall see below.

Another possibility to describe the consumer's preferences by a mathematical function is given by his expenditure function $e : \mathbb{R}_+^{N+1} \to \mathbb{R}$

$$e(p, U) \equiv \min_{x \in \mathcal{U}(U)} px, \quad \mathcal{U}(U) = \{x | x \in \mathbb{R}_+^N, u(x) \geq U\}, \quad p \in \mathbb{R}_{++}^N. \qquad (3.10)$$

The function $e(p, U)$ indicates the minimum amount of money the consumer must spend at prices p to achieve the utility level U. Therefore, this function is also often called his "cost–of–utility function". As a solution of the expenditure minimization problem (3.10) we obtain the Hicksian or income–compensated demand functions

$$x^* = \xi(p, U). \qquad (3.11)$$

Substitution into our objective function px yields

$$e(p, U) \equiv p\xi(p, U). \qquad (3.12)$$

The expenditure function is a generalized version of a support function to the consumer's upper contour sets. It is continuous and strictly monotonously increasing in U, and concave, monotonously increasing, linearly homogeneous and twice continuously differentiable with respect to p. The expenditure function is directly related to the Hicksian demand functions by Shephard's Lemma:

$$\xi(p, U) \equiv \nabla_p e(p, U). \qquad (3.13)$$

This implies that the Hessian matrix of the expenditure function with respect to prices is identical with the Jacobian matrix of the Hicksian demand function $\xi(p, U)$ which is the Slutsky matrix. From the twice continuously differentiability of the expenditure function it follows then by Young's Theorem that this matrix is symmetric so that the cross price derivatives of the Hicksian demand functions are symmetric, too.

From the duality between the utility maximization problem (3.1) and the expenditure minimization problem (3.8) we obtain the identities

$$e(p, v(p, I)) \equiv I, \quad v(p, e(p, U)) \equiv U, \qquad (3.14)$$

which establish the duality between the indirect utility function and the expenditure function.

The expenditure function is the basis for the definition of the money–metric utility functions which exist in a direct and an indirect version. The indirect money–metric utility function $m : \mathbb{R}^{N+1}_+ \to \mathbb{R}$ is defined as[8]

$$m(p^R; p, I) \equiv e(p^R, v(p, I)), \tag{3.15}$$

where $p^R \in \mathbb{R}^N_{++}$ is a vector of given parameters. According to (3.15) the value of the money–metric utility function $m(p^R; p, I)$ equals the minimum amount of money the consumer must spend if he wants to realize the utility level $U = v(p, I)$ with prices p^R. The prices p^R are the reference prices. They refer to an arbitrary situation R, which might be the initial situation 0 or the final situation k or a "fictive" situation that is never attained in reality. If we substitute the direct utility function $u(x)$ for the utility level U in the expenditure function we obtain the direct money–metric utility function $\tilde{m} : \mathbb{R}^N_+ \to \mathbb{R}$

$$\tilde{m}(p^R; x) \equiv e(p^R, u(x)), \tag{3.16}$$

which indicates the minimum amount of money the consumer must spent if he wants to realize the utility level $U = u(x)$ with prices p^R.

Because of the strict monotonicity of the expenditure function in utility U these functions are specific monotonic transformations of the indirect and the direct utility function, respectively, which allow us to express utility in monetary units.[9] The interpretation of utility in monetary terms is often considered the main advantage of the money–metric utility concept compared to ordinary utility functions because it makes the whole idea of utility functions better communicable to non–economists and, especially, to politicians. On the other hand this simple transformation of utility into money is often a source of misinterpretation because it implies a mapping from utility space which everybody respects as "ordinal" to the money space which everybody knows as being "cardinal" from his everyday experience. Therefore, the temptation to switch from an ordinal to a cardinal interpretation of utility without even noticing is considerable in connection with money–metric utility functions and must not be underestimated [this problem is pointed out in more detail by Samuelson (1974, p. 1266)].

From definitions (3.15) and (3.16) and from the strict monotonicity of the expenditure function in utility U it follows that the functions $\tilde{m}$ and m are

---

[8]This definition must not be confused with Weymark's (1985, p. 230) definition of an indirect money–metric utility function which is equivalent to our distance function to be defined below
[9]The concept of the money–metric utility function goes back to Lionel McKenzie (1957). For a detailed analysis of these functions and their properties see e.g. Samuelson and Swamy (1974), Weymark (1985) or Blackorby and Donaldson (1988).

utility functions themselves where $\tilde{m}(p^R; x)$ has the typical properties of a direct utility function and $m(p^R; p, I)$ has the general properties of an indirect utility function. From its definition it follows that the indirect money–metric utility function has another property which is of great importance for its empirical computation: from (3.14) and (3.15) we obtain for $p = p^R$ that

$$m(p^R; p^R, I) \equiv e(p^R, v(p^R, I)) \equiv I. \tag{3.17}$$

Differentiation of both sides of this identity with respect to lump–sum income I yields

$$\frac{\partial m}{\partial I}(p^R; p^R, I) \equiv 1, \quad \frac{\partial^j m}{(\partial I)^j}(p^R; p^R, I) \equiv 0 \quad (j = 2, 3, ...). \tag{3.18}$$

This result says that in a situation where the consumer is confronted with the reference prices p^R his marginal utility of income is identical to 1 and, more importantly: it is constant. This property is of considerable importance for the utilization of the indirect money–metric utility function as an empirical welfare measure as we shall see below.

In addition to the expenditure function, the direct and the indirect utility function there exists a fourth possibility for the representation of the consumer's preference ordering by a mathematical function, the distance function $d: \mathbb{R}^{N+1}_+ \to \mathbb{R}$

$$d(x, U) \equiv \max_{\gamma \in \Gamma(x,U)} \gamma, \quad \Gamma(x, U) = \{\gamma | \gamma \in \mathbb{R}_{++}, \ u(x/\gamma) \geq U, \ x \in \mathbb{R}^N_+\}. \tag{3.19}$$

The distance function was introduced into the economic literature by Shephard (1953) though the idea behind this function was already employed by Debreu (1951).[10] From definition (3.19) it follows that the distance function is simply a metric in commodity space. It is the symmetric dual of the expenditure function as can be seen from Shephard's Duality Theorem (1953 and 1970) by which[11]

$$d(x, U) \equiv \min_{\hat{p} \in \mathcal{V}(U)} \hat{p}x, \quad \mathcal{V}(U) = \{\hat{p} | \hat{p} \in \mathbb{R}^N_+, \ \hat{v}(\hat{p}) \leq U, \ x \in \mathbb{R}^N_{++}\}. \tag{3.20}$$

From the duality of the expenditure function and the distance function it follows that the properties of the distance function with respect to the normalized prices $\hat{p}$ are analogous to the properties of the the expenditure function with

---

[10]For a more detailed discussion of the distance function see e.g. Blackorby, Primont and Russell (1978), Diewert (1982), Deaton (1979), Deaton and Muellbauer (1980) or Cornes (1992).

[11]Simple proofs of this theorem are given by Jacobsen (1972) and by Field (1976).

respect to the quantities x: it is concave, monotonously increasing, linearly homogeneous and twice continuously differentiable with respect to $\hat{p}$. Further, it is continuous and strictly monotonously decreasing in U. As a solution of the minimization problem (3.20) we obtain the compensated inverse demand functions

$$\hat{p}^* = \phi(x, U) \tag{3.21}$$

which can be interpreted as inverse Hicksian demand functions. According to the Shephard-Hanoch Lemma these demand functions can also be derived by taking the partial derivatives of the distance function with respect to quantities x:

$$\phi(x, U) \equiv \nabla_x d(x, u) \tag{3.22}$$

This implies that the Hessian matrix of the distance function with respect to quantities x is identical with the Jacobian matrix of the compensated inverse demand functions $\phi(x, U)$. This matrix, which is known as the Antonelli matrix, must be symmetric (because of the twice continuously differentiability of the distance function) so that the cross quantity derivatives $\partial \phi_n / \partial x_j$ of the compensated inverse demand functions are symmetric as well. From definition (3.19) of the distance function we obtain the relation

$$d(x, U) \gtreqless 1 \quad \Longleftrightarrow \quad u(x) \gtreqless U \tag{3.23}$$

between the value of the direct utility function and of the distance function which implies the identities

$$\text{(a)} \quad d(x, U(x)) \equiv 1, \quad \text{(b)} \quad u\left(\frac{x}{d(x, U)}\right) \equiv U. \tag{3.24}$$

From (3.24b) and from the definition of the expenditure function it follows that

$$d(x, U) \cdot e(p, U) \leq p \cdot x \quad \forall x \in \mathbb{R}^N_{++}, \quad \forall p \in \mathbb{R}^N_{++} \tag{3.25}$$

because $[x/d(x, U)] \in \mathcal{U}(U)$. This inequality is useful if we want to compare the magnitudes of welfare measures based on the distance function and welfare measures based on the expenditure function as will be shown below.

We have now four alternative possibilities to describe the preference ordering of a consumer by a mathematical function: the expenditure function, the distance function, the direct and the indirect utility function. The money–metric utility function has been shown to be just a special case of a utility function.

It is not surprising that the deliberate construction of a welfare measure always starts from one of these functions because the measurement of welfare by definition aims at the preferences of a consumer. While these functions perfectly fulfil our criteria of theoretical consistency (2.1) to (2.3) their empirical computation is far from being straightforward and often it is not possible at all. But since computability is the essence of a welfare measure our main concern in the following sections will be the possibility of calculating the different welfare measures on the basis of empirical data. While this computability problem is predominant in connection with the functional welfare measures, i.e. measures which were constructed explicitly for the purpose of welfare measurement, the situation is just reversed with the atomistic or statistical welfare measures, which were originally constructed for statistical purposes only. These measures are easy to compute on the basis of observable data but their theoretical significance is rather limited, as will be shown below. We shall start our analysis with the class of functional welfare measures in the next section and turn to the statistical measures of welfare later.

3.2   Functional Welfare Measures

In a household consumption model like the one presented above, without public goods and without rationing, government policy affects private welfare via the price-income vector $[p, I]$ which determines the household's utility. Such a change in commodity prices and/or lump-sum income can be effectuated either directly by imposing taxes or granting subsidies or indirectly by the market effects of some government activity.

3.2.1   Welfare Measures Based on the Utility Function

The most obvious approach to measuring the welfare effect of a change in prices and income is to employ the individual's indirect utility function $v(p, I)$ which expresses the household's welfare as a function of exactly these variables. If we consider a change of the price–income vector from $[p^0, I_0]$ to $[p^k, I_k]$ (where $k \in \{1, 2, ..., K\}$ is some index of government activities[12]) the resulting change in utility is given by

$$\Delta u_{0k} = v(p^k, I_k) - v(p^0, I_0). \tag{3.26}$$

This measure obviously fulfils the theoretical consistency criteria (2.1) to (2.3). The question of whether it also fulfils the computability criterion (2.4) is much

---

[12]Since it makes no sense to specify for each example the concrete event that could have caused the actual change of the parameters $[p, I]$ we shall speak in what follows quite generally of "project k" (which could be a public expenditure program, a tax reform project or any other event from "outside" our partial household model).

less easy to answer. Since the utility function $v(p, I)$ itself cannot be observed empirically we have to express Δu_{0k} by observable magnitudes, e.g. by the Marshallian demand functions.

Making use of the Second Fundamental Theorem of Integral Calculus [cf. Apostol (1974, p. 162 f.)] and of Roy's Identity (3.5) we obtain

$$\Delta u_{0k} = \int_{p^0, I_0}^{p^k, I_k} \left[\nabla_p v(p, I), \frac{\partial v}{\partial I}(p, I) \right] \cdot \begin{bmatrix} dp \\ dI \end{bmatrix} \tag{3.27}$$

$$= \int_{p^0, I_0}^{p^k, I_k} \lambda(p, I) \cdot [-x(p, I), 1] \cdot \begin{bmatrix} dp \\ dI \end{bmatrix}$$

where $\lambda(p, I)$ is the marginal utility of income. While the Marshallian demand functions $x(p, I)$ can be estimated empirically this is not possible for the marginal utility of income since $\lambda(p, I)$ is a partial derivative of the consumer's (unobservable) indirect utility function. Therefore, it is very tempting to treat λ as a constant so that it can be eliminated from (3.27). But, unfortunately, under the usual non–satiation assumption (also met here) λ cannot be constant with respect to all its arguments. As a partial derivative of the indirect utility function which is homogeneous of degree 0 the function $\lambda(p, I)$ is homogeneous of degree (-1) with respect to $[p, I]$. From Euler's Theorem it follows that

$$\sum_{n=1}^{N} \frac{\partial \lambda}{\partial p_n}(p, I) \cdot p_n + \frac{\partial \lambda}{\partial I}(p, I) \cdot I \equiv -\lambda(p, I).$$

Since the marginal utility of income is strictly positive under our non–satiation assumption the terms on the left side of this identity cannot all be zero simultaneously. Therefore, the marginal utility of income cannot be independent of all its arguments at the same time, but it can be independent of N of the $(N + 1)$ variables $[p, I]$. So we have two possibilities: either λ is independent of all prices and varies only with income I, or λ is independent of $(N - 1)$ prices and of income and varies only with the remaining price. These two cases will now be analysed in more detail.

Case 1: $\lambda = \lambda(I)$

If λ depends only on lump–sum income I we multiply the new price–income vector $[p^k, I_k]$ by I_0/I_k and obtain

$$[\tilde{p}^k, I_0] = \frac{I_0}{I_k} \cdot [p^k, I_k], \tag{3.28}$$

where $\tilde{p}^k = (I_0/I_k) \cdot p^k$ and $v(\tilde{p}^k, I_0) = v(p^k, I_k)$ because of the homogeneity of degree 0 of the indirect utility function. Therefore, we can express Δu as

$$\Delta u_{0k} = v(\tilde{p}^k, I_0) - v(p^0, I_0) = \int_{p^0}^{\tilde{p}^k} -\lambda(I_0) \cdot x(p, I_0) dp. \qquad (3.29)$$

Now the marginal utility of income $\lambda(I_0)$ is a constant because lump–sum income I does not change as a result of our normalisation (3.28). Dividing both sides of (3.29) by $\lambda(I_0)$ we obtain the first version of the **Marshallian measure** of utility

$$MA_{0k}^1 = \frac{\Delta u_{0k}}{\lambda(I_0)} = -\int_{p^0}^{\tilde{p}^k} x(p, I_0) dp. \qquad (3.30)$$

The division of Δu_{0k} by the constant $\lambda(I_0)$ is just a monotonic transformation which converts the utility difference Δu_{0k} into monetary terms.[13] Therefore, MA_{0k} has the same theoretical properties as Δu_{0k} and, especially, fulfils the theoretical consistency conditions (2.1) to (2.3).

The idea of measuring utility changes by the integral over the (empirically observable) Marshallian demand functions goes back to Jules Dupuit (1844) and Alfred Marshall (1890). Both of them interpreted the demand functions as willingness–to–pay functions and denoted the difference between the integral over the demand function for a specific good at a given quantity and the consumer's payment for that quantity of the good as "consumer's surplus". Changes of this consumer's surplus as a consequence of a price change were interpreted as a money measure of the welfare effect induced by this price change. While Dupuit paid no attention to the question of constancy of the marginal utility of income, Alfred Marshall was aware of this problem but his discussion of this question was rather unclear and confusing. The first to present a clear and comprehensive analysis of the economic implications of the seemingly innocent assumption of a constant marginal utility of income was Samuelson (1942). It is his line of argument that will be followed here.

If we want to explore the economic implications of the assumption of a marginal utility of income which is constant with respect to all prices we have to start from Roy's Identity (3.5) which says that

$$x_n(p, I) \cdot \lambda(p, I) \equiv \frac{\partial v}{\partial p_n}(p, I) \qquad (n = 1, 2, ..., N). \qquad (3.31)$$

---

[13]The marginal utility of income λ can be interpreted as a kind of "conversion factor": one can convert a monetary expression into utility by multiplication with λ (as is known from the utility maximization conditions of household theory) and vice versa.

Differentiating this identity with respect to a price $p_j (j \in \{1, 2, ..., N\})$ and taking into account the symmetry of the Hessian matrix of the indirect utility function we obtain

$$\frac{\partial x_n}{\partial p_j} \cdot \lambda + x_n \cdot \frac{\partial \lambda}{\partial p_j} \equiv -\frac{\partial^2 v}{\partial p_n \partial p_j} \equiv -\frac{\partial^2 v}{\partial p_j \partial p_n} \equiv \frac{\partial x_j}{\partial p_n} \cdot \lambda + x_j \cdot \frac{\partial \lambda}{\partial p_n} \quad .$$

Since λ is assumed to be constant with respect to all prices, its partial price derivatives are all zero so that

$$\frac{\partial x_n}{\partial p_j}(p, I) = \frac{\partial x_j}{\partial p_n}(p, I) \qquad (n, j = 1, 2, ..., N), \tag{3.32}$$

i.e., the (uncompensated) Marshallian price effects must be symmetric here. As is well known from microeconomic theory the fulfilment of this condition is equivalent to the homotheticity of the underlying preference ordering. So, the assumption that the marginal utility of income is independent of all prices implies that we have a homothetic preference ordering with linear Engel curves and with all income elasticities being equal to one. Conversely, we see from (3.32) to (3.31) that the assumption of a homothetic preference ordering is compatible with the existence of a marginal utility of income which is independent of all prices; i.e., the assumption of a homothetic preference ordering implies that there exists at least one monotonic transformation of the indirect utility function which has a price–independent income derivative. It should be mentioned that the fulfilment of the symmetry conditions (3.32) is also necessary and sufficient for the path–independence of the integral (3.30).[14] In other words, if we assume that the consumer under consideration has a homothetic preference ordering then we have ensured (1) that there exists a λ which depends on income only, so that we can measure utility changes by MA_{0k}^1, and (2) that the integral over the Marshallian demand functions is path–independent and, therefore, uniquely determined.

Let us now turn to the second kind of "constancy" of the marginal utility of income, where λ depends on only one commodity price, say p_j. This case can be treated in strict analogy to the previous one.

Case 2: $\lambda = \lambda(\mathbf{p_j})$ $(\mathbf{j} \in \{\mathbf{1, 2, ..., N}\})$

To facilitate our notation let us define a truncated price vector $p_\square$ which does not contain the element p_j, i.e.

$$p_\square = [p_1, p_2, ..., p_{j-1}, p_{j+1}, ..., p_N]. \tag{3.33}$$

---

[14] A continuously differentiable vector function $x(y)$ with $x \in \mathbb{R}^N$ and $y \in \mathbb{R}^N$ is uniquely integrable if and only if its cross derivatives are symmetric, i.e. if and only if $\partial x_n / \partial y_j = \partial x_j / \partial y_n$ for all $n, j \in 1, 2, ..., N$ [cf. Apostol (1969, p. 339 and 351)].

Then we can partition our price vector according to

$$p = [p_j, p_\square]. \qquad (3.34)$$

If λ depends only on p_j we multiply the new price–income vector $[p^k, I_k]$ by p_j^0/p_j^k and obtain

$$[p_j^0, \bar{p}_\square^k, \bar{I}_k] = \frac{p_j^0}{p_j^k} \cdot [p^k, I_k], \qquad (3.35)$$

where $\bar{p}_\square^k = (p_j^0/p_j^k) \cdot p_\square^k$. This normalisation does not change the value of the indirect utility function for the new situation because of its homogeneity of degree zero, i.e.,

$$v(p_j^0, \bar{p}_\square^k, \bar{I}_k) = v(p^k, I_k).$$

Applying the Second Fundamental Theorem of Integral Calculus to (3.26) we obtain the welfare effect Δu as

$$\Delta u_{0k} = v(p_j^0, \bar{p}_\square^k, \bar{I}_k) - v(p_j^0, p_\square^0, I_0) = \int_{p_\square^0, I_0}^{\bar{p}_\square^k, \bar{I}_k} \lambda(p_j^0) \cdot \left[-x_\square(p_j^0, p_\square, I), 1 \right] \cdot \begin{bmatrix} dp_\square \\ dI \end{bmatrix},$$
$$\qquad (3.36)$$

where $x_\square = [x_1, x_2, ..., x_{j-1}, x_{j+1}, ..., x_N]$. Since λ is constant with respect to the integration variables $[p_\square, I]$, we can divide both sides of (3.36) by $\lambda(p_j^0)$. This leads us to the second version of the Marshallian consumer's surplus measure

$$MA_{0k}^2 = \frac{\Delta u_{0k}}{\lambda(p_j^0)} = \int_{p_\square^0, I_0}^{\bar{p}_\square^k, \bar{I}_k} \left[-x_\square(p_j^0, p_\square, I), 1 \right] \cdot \begin{bmatrix} dp_\square \\ dI \end{bmatrix}, \qquad (3.37)$$

which is also a monotonic transformation of Δu_{0k}. To analyse the economic implications of the assumption that λ depends on one commodity price only, we have to differentiate Roy's Identity (3.31) with respect to lump–sum income I. We obtain

$$\frac{\partial x_n}{\partial I} \cdot \lambda + x_n \cdot \frac{\partial \lambda}{\partial I} \equiv -\frac{\partial^2 v}{\partial p_n \partial I} \equiv -\frac{\partial^2 v}{\partial I \partial p_n} \equiv -\frac{\partial \lambda}{\partial p_n}.$$

The income derivative of λ is zero and the price derivatives for all prices except p_j are also zero (because λ is constant with respect to these variables) so that

$$\frac{\partial x_n}{\partial I} = 0 \qquad (\forall n \neq j). \qquad (3.38)$$

This means that the demand for all commodities except for commodity j is independent of income and every increase in income is completely spent on commodity j. A preference ordering with this characteristic is called quasilinear in commodity j because it can be represented by a utility function of the general form

$$u(x) = a + b \cdot x_j + f(x_\square), \tag{3.39}$$

which is quasilinear in x_j. The demand system that can be derived from such a preference ordering has the general form

$$x_\square = x_\square(p); \quad x_j = \frac{1}{p_j} \cdot [I - p_\square \cdot x_\square(p)] = x_j(p, I). \tag{3.40}$$

It is obvious that such a demand system is even more unrealistic than the one derived from a homothetic preference ordering with its linear Engel curves. Therefore, this second possibility for a constant marginal utility of income is of no importance at all for empirical work.

If we consider (3.38) together with the Slutsky equation we find that the Marshallian price effects for all commodities except commodity j are symmetric: the income effects are zero for these goods and, therefore, their Marshallian price effects equal the respective Hicksian substitution effects which are always symmetric. So, we have

$$\frac{\partial x_n}{\partial p_m}(p, I) = \frac{\partial x_m}{\partial p_n}(p, I) \qquad (\forall n, m \neq j). \tag{3.41}$$

Together with (3.38) these conditions ensure the path independence of the integral (3.37). Therefore, (3.37) can be rewritten as

$$MA_{0k}^2 = -\int_{p_\square^0}^{p_\square^k} x_\square(p_j^0, p_\square, I) \cdot dp_\square + (I_k - I_0). \tag{3.42}$$

It has been shown that the assumption of a quasilinear preference ordering is necessary and sufficient to guarantee that the marginal utility of income λ is independent of income and of all commodity prices except one, and that the integral which determines MA_{0k}^2 is path–independent.

Summing up the results of this section, we conclude that the Marshallian consumer's surplus measure can be applied only in two rather unrealistic special cases, namely, when preferences are either homothetic or quasilinear. In all other cases this measure cannot be assessed empirically. Equivalently, if preferences are neither homothetic nor quasilinear the consumer's Marshallian demand functions are not integrable so that consumer's surplus according to

(3.30) and (3.42) cannot be computed in these cases. So the idea of measuring changes in individual welfare by using the indirect utility function which led us to the Marshallian consumer's surplus turned out not to be practicable under tolerably realistic assumptions. Therefore we have to try other ways. In the next section we shall analyse the possibilities of constructing welfare measures on the basis of the consumer's expenditure function.

3.2.2   Welfare Measures Based on the Expenditure Function

From the brief microeconomic introduction to this section we know that the consumer's expenditure function $e(p, U)$ is strictly monotonically increasing in utility U. This means that for constant prices p there is a strictly positive correlation between the utility level U and the minimum amount of money $e(p, U)$ the consumer has to spend to achieve this utility level at prices p. So, for given reference prices p^R the expenditure or cost–of–utility function $e(p^R, U)$ can be interpreted as a specific monotonic transformation of the consumer's utility function which measures utility in monetary terms. A welfare measure based on the expenditure function has the general form

$$\Delta e_{0k} = e(p^R, U_k) - e(p^R, U_0),\qquad(3.43)$$

where p^R is an arbitrary price vector. For a specific project which takes the consumer from an initial situation 0 to a final situation k there are two "natural" choices for the reference price vector p^R: the price vector p^0 of the initial situation and the price vector p^k of the final household equilibrium.

If we choose the price vector p^0 as a reference price vector, we arrive at the well–known Hicksian **equivalent variation**

$$EV_{0k} = e(p^0, U_k) - e(p^0, U_0).\qquad(3.44)$$

The equivalent variation measures the welfare effect of a government project k by the difference between the minimum expenditures the consumer has to make at initial prices p^0 to achieve the new utility level U_k and the initial utility level U_0, respectively. So, the equivalent variation EV_{0k} indicates the variation in lump–sum income that would generate the same welfare effect as project k, i.e., it is "equivalent" to the kth project from a utility point of view. This can be seen from part (a) of Figure 3.1 where commodity 1 is chosen as a numéraire with $p_1 = 1$. In Figure 3.1(a) the equivalent variation of a subsidy on commodity 2 is shown. As a consequence of this subsidy the budget line becomes flatter and its horizontal intercept shifts outward. The consumer now chooses the consumption bundle x^k instead of x^0 and his utility rises from U_0 to U_k. The value of the expenditure function for the initial situation $e(p^0, U_0)$ is equal to the consumer's initial income I_0 and is given by the vertical intercept

Figure 3.1

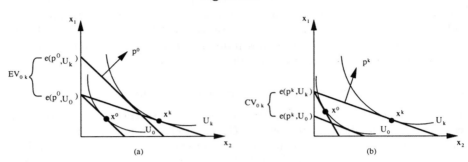

(a)   (b)

of the initial budget line. The value $e(p^0, U_k)$ of the expenditure function is given by the vertical intercept of a "fictitious" budget line which has the same normal vector p^0 as the initial one but is tangential to the new indifference curve for utility level U_k.

If we choose the new price vector p^k as a reference price vector we obtain the Hicksian **compensating variation**[15]

$$CV_{0k} = e(p^k, U_k) - e(p^k, U_0). \tag{3.45}$$

The compensating variation measures the welfare effect of project k by the difference between the expenditures the consumer has to incur at new prices p^k to achieve the new utility level U_k and the old level U_0, respectively. The CV can be interpreted as the amount that could be deducted from an individual's income after a change in prices and income so as to leave him as well off as before this change. In other words, the CV is the income variation that would compensate the individual for a utility gain $(CV > 0)$ or a utility loss $(CV < 0)$ after prices and income have been changed. In Figure 3.1(b) the compensating variation is shown for the same project as before where, again, commodity 1 is chosen as a numéraire.

From the strict monotonicity of the expenditure function it follows that the Hicksian variation measures both fulfil the indicator criterion (2.1), so that

$$EV_{0k} \gtreqless 0 \iff U_k \gtreqless U_0 \qquad (k \in \{1, 2, ..., K\}), \tag{3.46}$$

---

[15]The compensating variation was first proposed by J.R. Hicks in his book on *Value and Capital* (1939). Later [in Hicks (1942)] he added the concept of the equivalent variation.

and

$$CV_{0k} \gtreqless 0 \quad \Longleftrightarrow \quad U_k \gtreqless U_0 \qquad (k \in \{1, 2, ..., K\}). \qquad (3.47)$$

So, both measures indicate correctly whether the kth project generates a welfare improvement or not. The ranking criterion demands that a welfare measure should be capable of ranking in accordance with the consumer's preference ordering an arbitrary number of projects which all start from the same initial situation 0. Taking the difference

$$EV_{0k} - EV_{0j} = e(p^0, U_k) - e(p^0, U_j),$$

we see that this difference is positive if and only if $U_k > U_j$ so that the equivalent variation fulfils the ranking criterion

$$EV_{0k} \gtreqless EV_{0j} \quad \Longleftrightarrow \quad U_k \gtreqless U_j \qquad (k, j \in \{1, 2, ..., K\}). \qquad (3.48)$$

This result is possible because the equivalent variation has the same reference price vector p^0 for all projects starting from situation 0. If we evaluate the same projects with the compensating variation we have p^k as a reference price vector for CV_{0k} and p^j for CV_{0j}, so that these two compensating variations are not compatible. Therefore, the compensating variation does not fulfil the ranking criterion—at least not in general[16]—and can only be used for binary welfare comparisons. I.e. if we want to rank two projects k and j we would have to calculate CV_{0k}, CV_{0j} and—if both CVs have the same sign—also CV_{kj}.

The circularity criterion (2.3) demands that the equivalent and the compensating variation fulfil the conditions

$$EV_{0j} + EV_{jk} = EV_{0k} \quad \text{and} \quad CV_{0j} + CV_{jk} = CV_{0k} \quad (j, k \in \{1, 2, ..., K\}).$$

Neither the EV nor the CV fulfil this criterion because the reference price vectors of these measures are not constant with respect to the different projects to be evaluated, so that e.g. EV_{0j} and EV_{jk} are not compatible and do not add up to EV_{0k} in general.

Turning to the computability criterion we have to answer the question if the equivalent and the compensating variation can be computed on the basis of observable data. Since both Hicksian measures can be treated analogously

---

[16] As Chipman and Moore (1980) showed there are two special cases for which the CV also fulfils the ranking criterion: The first case is that of a homothetic preference ordering and the second is the case of quasilinear preferences.

with respect to this criterion we shall concentrate on the equivalent variation here. Remembering that $e(p^0, U_0) = I_0$ we obtain

$$EV_{0k} = e(p^0, U_k) - I_0$$

from definition (3.44). Our empirical problem reduces to the determination of the hypothetical (and, therefore, not observable) income $e(p^0, U_k)$ which the consumer would need to achieve the new utility level U_k at initial prices p^0. The expenditure function $e(p, U)$ itself cannot be estimated directly because it contains the utility level U as an argument. The traditional and most obvious method for the empirical determination of the expenditure function is to first specify a concrete functional form for the consumer's utility function and then estimate econometrically the parameters of the corresponding Marshallian demand functions. These parameters are then used to calculate the desired value of the expenditure function.

The fundamental flaw of this method is that one does not derive the consumer's (unobservable) preferences from his (observable) market behaviour (as one should expect in an empirical analysis) but, on the contrary, the crucial features of the consumer's preference ordering are prespecified before looking at the data. This a priori specification of the preferences means a severe limitation of the generality of the whole analysis. One often finds that the observed data do not fit well into the consumption pattern which is predetermined by the postulated utility function and that a consumer's behaviour can be much better represented by a class of demand functions for which a corresponding closed form of a utility or expenditure function is not available. Therefore, welfare economists searched for alternative procedures for the empirical computation of the equivalent variation which depend only on the knowledge of the consumer's demand functions irrespective of whether the corresponding expenditure function is known or exists as a closed form.

One important approach goes back to McKenzie and Pearce (1976) who express the equivalent variation in terms of the indirect money–metric utility function (3.15). Using the initial price vector p^0 as reference price vector they define

$$EV_{0k} = m(p^0; p^k, I_k) - m(p^0; p^0, I_0). \tag{3.49}$$

McKenzie and Pearce approximate this difference by a Taylor series. They assume that (1) the consumer's preferences can be represented by an analytic utility function (i.e. by a function which has infinitely many derivatives) and (2) that the absolute value of the remainder term monotonically tends towards zero as the order of the Taylor series approaches infinity. These two assumptions ensure that the accuracy of the approximation improves as the order of the Taylor series increases.

The main features of this method can be sketched by using a Taylor series of second order [for a more detailed treatment see McKenzie (1983, p. 41 ff.)]. From (3.49) it follows that

$$EV_{0k} \approx \nabla m(p^0; p^0, I_0) \cdot \begin{bmatrix} \Delta p \\ \Delta I \end{bmatrix} + \frac{1}{2} \cdot [\Delta p, \Delta I] \cdot \nabla^2 m(p^0; p^0, I_0) \cdot \begin{bmatrix} \Delta p \\ \Delta I \end{bmatrix} + \frac{1}{6} \cdots ,$$

where $\Delta p = [p^k - p^0]$, $\Delta = I_k - I_0$, and $\nabla^2 m(p^0; p^0, I_0)$ is the Hessian matrix of the function $m(p^0; p, I)$ with respect to non–reference prices p and income I in situation $[p^0, I_0]$. Making use of the special properties (3.17) and (3.18) of the money–metric utility function in the reference situation $[p^0; p^0, I_0]$ and remembering that it is a just a special monotonic transformation of the consumer's indirect utility function which fulfils Roy's Identity as

$$\frac{\partial m}{\partial p_n}(p^0; p^0, I_0) \equiv -x(p^0, I_0) = -x_n^0 \qquad (n = 1, 2, ..., N),$$

we obtain the second order approximation of the equivalent variation as

$$
\begin{aligned}
EV_{0k} \approx{} & \Delta I - \sum_{n=1}^{N} x_n^0 \cdot \Delta p_n - \sum_{n=1}^{N} \frac{\partial x_n}{\partial I} p^0, I_0) \cdot \Delta p_n \cdot \Delta I \\
& + \frac{1}{2} \cdot \sum_{n=1}^{N} \sum_{j=1}^{N} \Delta p_n \cdot \left(x_n^0 \cdot \frac{\partial x_n}{\partial I}(p^0, I_0) - \frac{\partial x_n}{\partial p_j}(p^0, I_0) \right) \cdot \Delta p_j \\
& + \frac{1}{6} \cdots
\end{aligned}
$$

Thanks to the special properties of the money–metric utility function it is possible to express the equivalent variation in terms of the Marshallian demand functions and other observable magnitudes. Theoretically, this procedure can be carried on to infinity and, therefore, the McKenzie/Pearce method is rated as an "exact" technique in the economic literature.

Another approach to the empirical computation of the equivalent variation by using the consumer's demand functions would be to apply the Second Fundamental Theorem of Integral Calculus as we did before when we wanted to compute the Marshallian consumer's surplus. Using Shephard's Lemma (3.13) and observing that $e(p^0, U_0) = I_0$ and $e(p^k, U_k) = I_k$ we obtain from definition (3.44)

$$EV_{0k} = - \int_{p^0}^{p^k} \xi(p, U_k)dp + \Delta I, \qquad (3.50)$$

where $\xi(p, U_k)$ is the vector of the Hicksian demand functions for the new utility level U_k. The (first) price derivatives of the Hicksian demand functions are the second price derivatives of the expenditure function because of Shephard's Lemma (3.13). The Hessian matrix of the expenditure function is symmetric by Young's Theorem because $e(p, U)$ is twice continuously differentiable in p so that the integrability conditions for (3.50)

$$\frac{\partial \xi_n}{\partial p_j} = \frac{\partial \xi_j}{\partial p_n} \qquad (n, j = 1, 2, ..., N) \tag{3.51}$$

are fulfilled. So, the integral (3.50) is path–independent and, therefore, uniquely determined. However, the Hicksian demand functions like the expenditure function itself cannot be observed empirically because they also contain the utility level U as an argument.

This problem was solved by Vartia (1983) who generalized an approach by Hausman (1981) and constructed an algorithm for the integration of compensated demand functions which is based on the knowledge of the Marshallian demand functions. This method was developed further and refined by McKenzie and Ulph (1986) and by Breslaw and Smith (1995a). The integration problem is reduced (3.50) to a problem of solving a series of simple first–order ordinary differential equations; all the empirical information needed for this procedure is the old and new price–income vectors $[p^0, I_0]$ and $[p^k, I_k]$ and the consumer's Marshallian demand functions. The calculation can be carried out on every modern personal computer with a program for solving first–order ordinary differential equations [for a detailed description of the algorithm see McKenzie and Ulph (1986)]. Though, of course, the numerical solution of differential equations always means an approximation we can, nevertheless, speak of an "exact" method here because the precision of the results depends on the length of the computing time only and can—theoretically—be increased infinitely. So, with the McKenzie/Pearce method on the one hand and the Vartia, McKenzie and Ulph algorithm on the other we have now two techniques for the (quasi–) exact numerical calculation of the equivalent or compensating variation on the basis of Marshallian demand functions.

If the consumer's Marshallian demand functions are not known completely but, instead, we know the price and income elasticities for the new situation k we can still approximate the equivalent variation by a Taylor series of second order: After reformulating definition (3.44) according to

$$EV_{0k} = \Delta I + e(p^0, U_k) - e(p^k, U_k),$$

we obtain as a second order approximation

$$EV_{0k} \approx \Delta I - \nabla_p e(p^k, U_k) \cdot \Delta p + \frac{1}{2} \cdot \Delta p \cdot \nabla_{pp}^2 e(p^k, U_k) \cdot \Delta p,$$

where $\nabla_p e(p, U)$ is the gradient of the expenditure function with respect to prices and $\nabla_{pp}^2 e(p, U)$ is the respective Hessian matrix. From Shephard's Lemma (3.13) it follows that $\nabla_{pp}^2 e(p^k, U_k)$ is identical with the consumer's Slutsky matrix for the new situation k. Substituting the elasticity form of the Slutsky equation yields

$$EV_{0k} \approx \sum_{n=1}^{N} p_n^0 \cdot \Delta x_n + \frac{1}{2} \sum_{n=1}^{N} \sum_{j=1}^{N} \Delta p_n \cdot \frac{x_n^k}{p_j^k} \cdot \left(\eta_{nj}^k + \frac{p_j^k x_j^k}{I_k} \cdot \varepsilon_n^k \right) \cdot \Delta p_j,$$

where η_{nj}^k is the price elasticity of commodity n with respect to p_j in situation k and ε_n^k is the income elasticity of commodity n in situation k.

All that is needed to compute this second order approximation of the equivalent variation are the initial and new prices and quantities and the point elasticities of the Marshallian demand functions with respect to prices and income. The calculation itself is so simple that it can be performed with a pocket calculator. If instead of ε_n^k and η_{nj}^k these elasticities are known for the initial situation 0 one can compute the compensating variation analogously.

So, we have shown in this section that the Hicksian equivalent variation fulfils the indicator criterion as well as the ranking criterion and can therefore be used without reservation in a comparative static welfare analysis. It has also been demonstrated that this measure can be computed exactly on the basis of a consumer's Marshallian demand functions and approximately if only the point elasticities of these demand functions are known. The Hicksian compensating variation can be used for binary welfare comparisons only since it does not fulfil the ranking criterion while its empirical qualities are the same as those of the equivalent variation. In the context of an intertemporal welfare analysis the problem arises that neither the equivalent nor the compensating variation fulfils the circularity criterion which concerns the intertemporal consistency of a welfare measure.

3.2.3 Welfare Measures Based on the Distance Function

From our microeconomic introduction we know that the consumer's distance function is strictly monotonically decreasing in utility U. So, for constant consumption quantities x this function can be interpreted as a (negatively) monotonic transformation of the consumer's utility function. Therefore, with the distance function we have another candidate for constructing a suitable welfare measure. In analogy to the Hicksian variation measures we define

$$\Delta d_{0k} = d(x^R, U_0) - d(x^R, U_k) \tag{3.52}$$

as the general form of a welfare measure based on the distance function. The vector x^R is an arbitrary but fixed consumption vector which we shall call the reference consumption vector.

Again, there are two "natural" choices for x^R: the initial consumption vector x^0 and the new consumption vector x^k. Choosing x^0 as a reference consumption vector we get our **distance variation** as

$$DV_{0k}^0 = d(x^0, U_0) - d(x^0, U_k) = 1 - d(x^0, U_k), \qquad (3.53)$$

where the second equality of (3.53) follows from (3.24a). Alternatively, we can choose the new consumption vector x^k as a reference vector and obtain the version

$$DV_{0k}^k = d(x^k, U_0) - d(x^k, U_k) = d(x^k, U_0) - 1 \qquad (3.54)$$

of the distance variation. Obviously, the relation between DV_{0k}^0 and DV_{0k}^k is the same as between the equivalent and the compensating variation. Because of the analogy between the two measures we shall concentrate on the version DV_{0k}^0 of the distance variation in most of what follows.

The DV_{0k}^0 simply measures the relative distance of the indifference curves for the utility levels U_k and U_0 from the origin along a ray emanating from the origin and passing through x^0. This can be seen from Figure 3.2(a).

Definition (3.19) of the distance function says that $d(x^0, U_k)$ is the maximum scalar by which the initial consumption vector x^0 can be scaled up or down so that the resulting vector $[x^0/d(x^0, U_k)]$ generates at least the new utility level U_k, i.e. $d(x^0, U_k) = 0A/0B$. So we get

$$DV_{0k}^0 = 1 - \frac{0A}{0B} = \frac{0B - 0A}{0B} > 0.$$

Figure 3.2

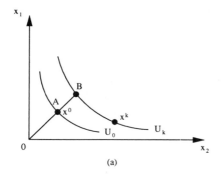

(a)

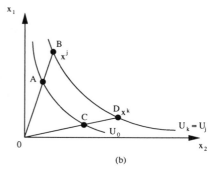

(b)

From the (strictly negative) monotonicity of the distance function in utility it follows that both versions of the distance variation according to (3.53) and (3.54) fulfil the indicator criterion (2.1), i.e.

$$DV_{0k}^0 \gtreqqless 0 \quad \Longleftrightarrow \quad U_k \gtreqqless U_0; \tag{3.55}$$

$$DV_{0k}^k \gtreqqless 0 \quad \Longleftrightarrow \quad U_k \gtreqqless U_0 \quad (k \in \{1, 2, ..., K\}).$$

Taking the difference

$$DV_{0k}^0 - DV_{0j}^0 = d(x^0, U_j) - d(x^0, U_k)$$

we see that the version DV_{0k}^0 of the distance variation also meets the ranking criterion

$$DV_{0k}^0 \gtreqqless DV_{0j}^0 \quad \Longleftrightarrow \quad U_k \gtreqqless U_j \quad (k, j \in \{1, 2, ..., K\}).$$

This does not hold for the version DV_{0k}^k according to (3.54) as can be seen from the counterexample in Figure 3.2(b): here we have

$$DV_{0k}^k = \frac{0D - 0C}{0C} > \frac{0B - 0A}{0A} = DV_{0j}^j$$

though $U_k = U_j$. Like the compensating variation the DV_{0k}^k fails to meet the ranking condition: its reference vector varies with the respective new situation so that the two measures DV_{0k}^k and DV_{0j}^j are not compatible.

Since the reference consumption vector of the distance variation depends on the respective initial situation of the project under consideration it is obvious that this version of the distance variation does not fulfil the circularity criterion either, i.e.

$$DV_{0j}^j + DV_{jk}^j = 1 - d(x^0, U_j) + 1 - d(x^j, U_k) \neq 1 - d(x^0, U_k) = DV_{0k}^0.$$

Analogously, it can be shown that the version DV_{0k}^k of the distance variation does not fulfil the circularity criterion, either.

If we want to compute the distance variation empirically we have, in principle, the same possibilities as in the case of the Hicksian variation measures. The most conventional method would be to start from an a priori specification of the consumer's utility function and estimate econometrically the respective demand functions. The parameters thus determined can then be used to calculate the distance variation. The disadvantages of this method which predetermines the consumer's preferences before looking at the data were discussed at length in the preceding section. If we want to work with more flexible forms of the consumer's demand functions which need not be integrable to a closed form of a utility function we can start from

$$DV_{0k}^0 = d(x^k, U_k) - d(x^0, U_k) = \int_{x^0}^{x^k} \phi(x, U_k)dx, \qquad (3.56)$$

which follows from definition (3.53) by using (3.24a), the Second Fundamental Theorem of Integral Calculus, and the Shephard-Hanoch Lemma (3.22). This integral is path–independent since the cross derivatives $\partial\phi_n/\partial x_j$ of the compensated inverse demand functions are symmetric. It cannot be computed directly because the inverse compensated demand functions are not observable. But, as in the case of the Hicksian measures, we can use an algorithm which is based on Vartia's (1983) method to calculate this integral. The only empirical information needed is the inverse demand functions $\hat{p}(x)$ which can be estimated econometrically. A detailed description of the version of the Vartia algorithm to be applied here is given in Ahlheim and Wagenhals (1988). The advantage of this method compared to the conventional method of prespecifying the consumer's utility function is a higher degree of freedom in estimating the consumer's (inverse) demand functions.

If we do not know the complete inverse demand system but have information on the point elasticities for the new situation k only, then we can approximate the distance variation by a Taylor series of second order as we did in the case of the Hicksian equivalent variation.

Observing that $d(x^0, U_0) = d(x^k, U_k) = 1$ we can reformulate the distance variation (3.53) as

$$DV_{0k}^0 = d(x^k, U_k) - d(x^0, U_k).$$

As a second order approximation of this term we obtain

$$DV_{0k}^0 \approx \nabla_x d(x^k, U_k) \cdot \Delta x - \frac{1}{2} \cdot \Delta x \cdot \nabla_{xx}^2 d(x^k, U_k) \cdot \Delta x,$$

where $\nabla_x d(x^k, U_k)$ is the gradient of the distance function with respect to quantities x and $\nabla_{xx}^2 d(x^k, U_k)$ is the respective Hessian matrix. From the Shephard-Hanoch Lemma (3.22) it follows that $\nabla_{xx}^2 d(x^k, U_k)$ is identical with the consumer's Antonelli matrix for the new situation k. Substituting the elasticity form of the Antonelli equation[17]

$$\frac{\partial \phi_n}{\partial x_j} = \frac{\partial \hat{p}_n}{\partial x_j} - \hat{p}_j \cdot \sum_{m=1}^{n} \frac{\partial \hat{p}_n}{\partial x_m} \cdot x_m$$

for the inverse substitution effects $\partial \phi_n / \partial x_j$ yields as an approximation of the distance variation

$$DV_{0k}^0 \approx \sum_{n=1}^{N} p_n^k \cdot \Delta x_n - \frac{1}{2} \cdot \sum_{n=1}^{N} \sum_{j=1}^{N} \Delta x_n \cdot \frac{\hat{p}_n^k}{x_j^k} \cdot \left(\hat{\eta}_{nj}^k - \hat{p}_j^k x_j^k \cdot \sum_{m=1}^{N} \hat{\eta}_{nm}^k \right) \cdot \Delta x_j,$$

where the expressions

$$\hat{\eta}_{nj}^k = \frac{\partial \hat{p}_n}{\partial x_j}(x^k) \cdot \frac{x_j^k}{\hat{p}_n^k} \quad (n, j = 1, 2, ..., N)$$

are the quantity elasticities of the inverse demand functions for situation k.

For the computation of this second order approximation of the distance variation we only need the point elasticities of the inverse demand functions for the new situation k and, of course, the price and quantity data. If we know these elasticities for the initial situation 0 instead of situation k we can calculate the version $d(x^k, U_0) - d(x^k, U_k)$ of the distance variation which also fulfils the indicator criterion but fails to fulfil the ranking criterion so that, like the Hicksian compensating variation, it can only be used for binary welfare comparisons.

In this section we have shown that the two versions of the distance variation have, in principle, the same theoretical properties and virtues as the Hicksian equivalent and compensating variations. The difference between the two kinds of measures lies in the empirical basis needed for their respective computation. The Hicksian measures are computed on the basis of the Marshallian demand system (or its price and income elasticities) while for the computation of the distance variations we need the inverse demand functions or their elasticities. So, in the context of the simple household model used here the decision which measure should be chosen depends simply on the kind of empirical information that is available for the concrete project. The specific theoretical and empirical advantages of the distance variation will become apparent in the context of the more complex models of rationed households which will be discussed in a later section.

---

[17]The Antonelli equation is the analogue to the Slutsky equation for inverse demand functions. It decomposes the effect of a marginal increase in quantity x_j on the willingness to pay for the nth commodity $\partial \hat{p}_n / \partial x_j$ into the (inverse) substitution effect $\partial \phi_n / \partial x_j$ and the scale effect. For a detailed analysis of the Antonelli equation see Ahlheim (1988).

Another difference between the distance variation on the one hand and the Marshallian consumer's surplus and the Hicksian variation measures on the other is that the latter are all expressed in monetary terms while the distance variation has no dimension. But this is a merely formal difference because the economic content of both kinds of measures is the same in the framework of ordinal welfare theory where the intensity of welfare changes cannot be assessed and interpersonal welfare comparisons are strictly forbidden.

Up to now we have been dealing with functional welfare measures. These measures are based on household theory and were designed especially for the purpose of welfare measurement. They combine the advantage of theoretical consistency with the disadvantage that they are rather awkward to compute. If, for example, we choose the exact methods for the empirical computation of the Hicksian variation measures or of the distance variation we have to know the consumer's complete demand system. Since the econometric estimation of complete demand systems (for a household with, let's say, five hundred commodities) is rather troublesome and expensive there have been many efforts to create welfare measures which are less powerful from a theoretical point of view but which are easier to compute empirically. These are the atomistic or statistical welfare measures which will be studied in the next section.

3.3   Atomistic Welfare Measures

While a typical functional welfare measure is constructed on a household theoretical basis, the construction of an atomistic welfare measure is characterized by a merely mechanistic or technical relation between the price and quantity data to be analysed. Normally, these measures are only approximations to a "true", i.e. functional, welfare measure but their attractiveness lies in the simplicity of their computability. The distinction between atomistic and functional measures goes back to Ragnar Frisch (1936) who differentiated between atomistic and functional index numbers.[18] The only atomistic variation measures which have reached a certain popularity are the Laspeyres variation and the Paasche variation, as defined by Hicks (1942). These measures are closely related to the well-known quantity indices by Laspeyres and Paasche, to be dealt with below.

The Laspeyres and Paasche variation measures evaluate the change from an initial situation 0 to a new situation k by the weighted sum of the corresponding changes in the consumption quantities. The Laspeyres variation uses the initial prices p^0 as weights while the Paasche variation uses the new prices p^k.

---

[18]Frisch (1936, p. 3) characterized atomistic measures as treating prices and quantities as two independent sets of variables while functional measures assume certain specific relations to exist between prices and quantities.

Figure 3.3

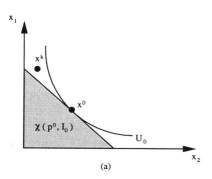

(a)

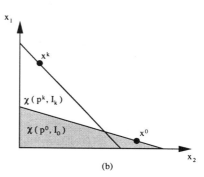

(b)

Therefore, the **Laspeyres variation** is defined as

$$LAV_{0k} = p^0 \cdot [x^k - x^0] = p^0 x^k - I_0 \quad (k \in \{1, 2, ..., K\}). \tag{3.57}$$

Obviously, a non–positive value of the Laspeyres variation implies that the consumer could have bought the new consumption bundle x^k already in the initial situation 0 since in this case x^k is an element of the consumer's initial budget set $\mathcal{X}(p^0, I_0)$. The fact that he chose x^0 instead of x^k shows us that he prefers x^0 to $x^k (\neq x^0)$ according to the theory of revealed preferences,[19] i.e.

$$LAV_{0k} \leq 0 \;\Rightarrow\; p^0 x^k \leq I_0 \;\Rightarrow\; x^k \in \mathcal{X}(p^0, I_0) \;\Rightarrow\; x^0 \succ x^k \;\Rightarrow\; u(x^0) > u(x^k).$$

On the other hand a positive value of the Laspeyres variation indicates that the consumption bundle x^k is not in the initial budget set $\mathcal{X}(p^0, I_0)$. But this does not automatically imply that the consumer prefers x^k to x^0, as can be seen from Figure 3.3(a).

In this counterexample the new consumption bundle x^k is not an element of $\mathcal{X}(p^0, I_0)$ since $p^0 x^k > I_k$ but, nevertheless, x^k lies below the indifference curve for the initial utility level U_0 so that the new utility level U_k must be lower than U_0. Hence, the Laspeyres variation fulfils only one part of our indicator criterion (2.1):

$$
\begin{aligned}
LAV_{0k} \;&\leq\; 0 \;\Rightarrow\; U_k < U_0 \quad (x_k \neq x_0) \\
LAV_{0k} \;&>\; 0 \;\not\Rightarrow\; U_k > U_0 \quad (k \in \{1, 2, ..., K\}).
\end{aligned}
\tag{3.58}
$$

---

[19]The strict preference $x^0 \succ x^k$ for $x^0 \neq x^k$ is valid also if $LAV = 0$. This follows from the strict convexity of the consumer's preferences which implies that x^0 is strictly preferred to all other consumption bundles on the initial budget hyperplane $p^0 x = I_0$.

It is therefore a one-sided welfare measure which can indicate decreases in utility only. Under these circumstances it is superfluous to check the remaining theoretical consistency criteria (2.2) and (2.3).

Comparing the Laspeyres variation (3.57) and the equivalent variation (3.44) we see that these measures differ only in their first element because $e(p^0, U_0) = I_0$. Approximating the first element of the EV by a Taylor series of first order we obtain

$$e(p^0, U_k) \approx e(p^k, U_k) + \nabla_p e(p^k, U_k) \cdot [p^0 - p^k] = p^0 x^k \qquad (3.59)$$

because of Shephard's Lemma (3.13). Therefore, the Laspeyres variation can be interpreted as a first–order Taylor approximation to the Hicksian equivalent variation. From definition (3.10) of the expenditure function it follows that

$$e(p^0, U) \equiv \min_{x \in \mathcal{U}(U_k)} p^0 x \leq p^0 x^k \quad \text{(since } u(x^k) = U_k),$$

so that the value of the Laspeyres variation is an upper bound for the value of the corresponding equivalent variation:

$$LAV_{0k} \geq EV_{0k} \qquad (k = 1, 2, ..., K). \qquad (3.60)$$

Analogously, it can be shown that the **Paasche variation**

$$PAV_{0k} = p^k \cdot [x^k - x^0] = I_k - p^k x^0 \qquad (k \in \{1, 2, ..., K\}) \qquad (3.61)$$

is a first–order Taylor approximation to the Hicksian compensating variation (3.45) where the value of the Paasche variation for a project k is a lower bound for the value of the corresponding CV, i.e.

$$PAV_{0k} \leq CV_{0k} \qquad (k = 1, 2, ..., K). \qquad (3.62)$$

This implies that the Paasche variation is also a one–sided welfare measure which can indicate only increases in welfare correctly. Using a counterexample analogous to the one given in Figure 3.3(a) it can be shown that a negative value of the Paasche variation does not necessarily imply a decrease in utility so that the PAV fulfils only one direction of the indicator criterion according to

$$\begin{aligned} PAV_{0k} &\geq 0 \quad \Rightarrow \quad U_k > U_0 \quad (x^k \neq x^0); \\ PAV_{0k} &< 0 \quad \nRightarrow \quad U_k < U_0 \quad (k \in \{1, 2, ..., K\}). \end{aligned} \qquad (3.63)$$

Since the Laspeyres variation correctly indicates decreases in utility and the Paasche variation correctly indicates increases in utility, one could think that the theoretical properties of these two measures are complementary to each other in the sense that one of them can be applied if the other fails. But, unfortunately, this is not the case. The applicability of these measures depends on the fact that either the new consumption bundle x^k lies in the initial budget set (then the LAV can be applied) or the initial consumption bundle x^0 lies in the new budget set (then the PAV can be applied). But if neither $x^k \in \mathcal{X}(p^0, I_0)$ nor $x^0 \in \mathcal{X}(p^k, I_k)$ as is the case in Figure 3.3(b) then the consumer never has the choice between x^0 and x^k and we cannot derive his preference for one of these two consumption bundles from his market behaviour. In such a case we find ourselves in the so-called "zone of ignorance" and no welfare theoretical judgement is possible on the basis of the atomistic variation measures.

The main advantage of the atomistic welfare measures by Laspeyres and Paasche is that their empirical computation is quite simple. All that is needed are the consumption data for the household under consideration and the reference prices. The computation itself can be performed on a pocket calculator or even with a pencil and a sheet of paper. Thus, the computability criterion (2.4) is perfectly fulfilled by these atomistic variation measures, and this is the reason why they are still very popular even though their theoretical qualities are rather poor, as has been shown.

3.4   Index Measures

The theory of index numbers has a long history in economics. Its beginnings date back to the year 1707 when Fleetwood's *Chronicon Preciosum* appeared. Those early versions of index numbers were used to measure the development of prices and took the form of simple arithmetic or geometric means of the observed data. The interest in index numbers increased during the nineteenth century when the seminal articles of Laspeyres (1864) and of Paasche (1874) appeared. The use of index numbers has always been hotly debated (see, e.g., the controversy between Pierson and Edgeworth (1896) in the *Economic Journal*) and as late as in 1951 M.J. Moroney held that "index numbers are a widespread disease of modern life" and "their regular calculation must be regarded as a widespread compulsion neurosis" [Moroney (1951, p. 48 and 49/50)]. Nevertheless, index numbers have become an essential factor in modern economics where their importance for the field of welfare economics started with Pigou's (1920) *Economics of Welfare*.

The purpose of an index number is to aggregate the relative changes of heterogeneous magnitudes into a single scalar. In principle, such index numbers may refer to macroeconomic as well as to microeconomic data, but here we are interested only in changes of such figures that are relevant for a single household. In this context we can distinguish between three different kinds of index numbers: quantity indices, price or cost-of-living indices and real-income indices. A typical (individual) **quantity index**

$$Q_{0k} = Q(x^0, x^k) \qquad (k \in \{1, 2, ..., K\}) \qquad (3.64)$$

combines the change in the quantities a household consumes from a situation 0 to a situation k into a scalar. The idea of using such a quantity index as a welfare measure is rather obvious because a consumer's level of satisfaction or utility is uniquely determined by his or her consumption vector as we know from the concept of the direct utility function. Therefore, a quantity index is a (potential) welfare measure.

A typical **price** or **cost–of–living index**

$$P_{0k} = P(p^0, p^k) \qquad (k \in \{1, 2, ..., K\}) \qquad (3.65)$$

is a scalar that describes the change in prices from a situation 0 to a situation k. Obviously, a price index alone can never be a welfare measure because the welfare effect of any price change can be offset by an appropriate change in income. But we can use a price index to deflate the ratio I_k/I_0 of a consumer's income in situations 0 and k (which could be interpreted as a kind of nominal–income index) to obtain his **real–income index**

$$Y_{0k} = \frac{I_k/I_0}{P(p^0, p^k)} = Y(p^0, I_0, p^k, I_k) \qquad (k \in \{1, 2, ..., K\}). \qquad (3.66)$$

This index aggregates the changes in prices and income from situation 0 to a situation k into a single number. Thus, a real–income index is a potential welfare measure, too, because a consumer's level of utility is uniquely determined by the prices he has to pay together with his income.

The concepts of quantity indices on the one hand and real–income indices on the other are linked by the **weak factor–reversal test** [for details see Samuelson and Swamy (1974, p. 572 ff.)]

$$P(p^0, p^k) \cdot Q(x^0, x^k) = I_k/I_0, \qquad (3.67)$$

which tests the theoretical compatibility of a particular quantity index and a price index for a household with income ratio I_k/I_0. Dividing both sides of (3.67) by the price index $P(p^0, p^k)$ we get

$$Q(x^0, x^k) = \frac{I_k/I_0}{P(p^0, p^k)} = Y(p^0, I_0, p^k, I_k). \qquad (3.68)$$

This means that by deflating a consumer's nominal income ratio I_k/I_0 by a particular price index $P(p^0, p^k)$ we obtain a real income index $Y(p^0, I_0, p^k, I_k)$

which, for the change from situation 0 to a situation k, shows the same value as the quantity index $Q(x^0, x^k)$ that is connected with $P(p^0, p^k)$ by the weak factor reversal test (3.67). Therefore, we can describe the welfare change from situation 0 to a situation k either by a quantity index or by the respective real-income index while the role of a price index is restricted to that of a deflator. The relation between $Q(x^0, x^k)$ and $Y(p^0, I_0, p^k, I_k)$ is comparable to the relation between the direct and the indirect utility function.

While the variation measures dealt with in the preceding sections normally take the mathematical form of a difference of two expressions (e.g. of two values of the consumer's expenditure function), the index measures are usually constructed as ratios. This explains why we have to reformulate our reliability criteria (2.1) to (2.3) with respect to the special mathematical form of the index numbers. If an index IND_{0k} is to be used as a welfare measure it should at least fulfil the

Indicator criterion:

$$IND_{0k} \gtreqless 1 \quad \Longleftrightarrow \quad U_k \gtreqless U_0 \quad (k \in \{1, 2, ..., K\}). \qquad (3.69)$$

We see that the "indifference value" of an index measure which indicates that welfare did not change is now "1" instead of "0". The other two theoretical consistency criteria now become the

Ranking criterion:

$$\frac{IND_{0k}}{IND_{0j}} \gtreqless 1 \quad \Longleftrightarrow \quad U_k \gtreqless U_j \quad (k, j \in \{1, 2, ..., K\}) \qquad (3.70)$$

and the

Circularity criterion:

$$IND_{0j} \cdot IND_{jk} = IND_{0k} \quad (k, j \in \{1, 2, ..., K\}). \qquad (3.71)$$

The formulation of the computability criterion (2.4) is, of course, independent of the mathematical form of the welfare measure under consideration and, therefore, remains unchanged.

From our short description of the three main kinds of economic indices it follows that only quantity indices and real–income indices can (potentially) fulfil the theoretical reliability criteria (3.69) to (3.71) while this is impossible for a price index. We shall now first take a brief look at the quantity indices and then turn to price index numbers and the related real-income indices.

3.4.1   Quantity Indices

In the context of welfare measurement a quantity index $Q_{0k} = Q(x^0, x^k)$ is supposed to indicate the change of the standard of living from situation 0 to a situation k. If the standard of living for situations 0 and k is represented by the corresponding utility levels $u(x^0)$ and $u(x^k)$ we speak of a functional quantity index, while an index which interprets the standard of living as the respective consumption vectors x^0 and x^k is called an atomistic quantity index. Looking at the most popular quantity indices we find that they can be interpreted as monotonic transformations of the variation measures discussed above. For example Allen (1949) proposed two functional quantity indices that are strictly analogous to the Hicksian variation measures. The general form of these **Allen index** measures is

$$AL_{0k}^R = \frac{e(p^R, u(x^k))}{e(p^R, u(x^0))} \qquad (k \in \{1, 2, ..., K\}), \qquad (3.72)$$

where p^R is some reference price vector. Allen proposes to choose either p^0 or p^k as reference price vector and obtains

$$AL_{0k}^0 = \frac{e(p^0, u(x^k))}{e(p^0, u(x^0))} = \frac{e(p^0, U_k)}{I_0} \qquad (k \in \{1, 2, ..., K\}), \qquad (3.73)$$

which is the quotient version of the equivalent variation and

$$AL_{0k}^k = \frac{e(p^k, u(x^k))}{e(p^k, u(x^0))} = \frac{I_k}{e(p^k, U_0)} \qquad (k \in \{1, 2, ..., K\}), \qquad (3.74)$$

which is the quotient version of the Hicksian compensating variation. Both measures fulfil the indicator criterion (3.69), but only AL_{0k}^0 also fulfils the ranking condition (3.70). Both indices fail to meet the circularity criterion (3.71) because AL_{0j} and AL_{jk} have divergent reference price vectors no matter which version we choose and are, therefore, not compatible. Things are different if we have homothetic preferences so that the expenditure function is separable between the utility level U and prices p and can take on the mathematical structure

$$e(p, U) = U \cdot e_p(p). \qquad (3.75)$$

In this case both Allen index measures are independent of the respective reference price vectors so that they are identical and fulfil all three of our theoretical consistency criteria.

Deaton (1979) proposed to define a quantity index based on the distance function with a constant reference consumption vector analogous to the distance variation discussed above. The general form of the **Deaton index** is given by

$$DEA_{0k}^{R} = \frac{d(x^R, u(x^0))}{d(x^R, u(x^k))} \qquad (k \in \{1, 2, ..., K\}), \qquad (3.76)$$

where x^R is the reference consumption bundle. Though we could choose any commodity vector as a reference consumption vector there are, again, two natural choices, namely x^0 and x^k. According to which of these vectors we choose we obtain the versions

$$DEA_{0k}^{0} = \frac{d(x^0, u(x^0))}{d(x^0, u(x^k))} = \frac{1}{d(x^0, U_k)} \qquad (k \in \{1, 2, ..., K\}) \qquad (3.77)$$

or

$$DEA_{0k}^{k} = \frac{d(x^k, u(x^0))}{d(x^k, u(x^k))} = d(x^k, U_0) \qquad (k \in \{1, 2, ..., K\}) \qquad (3.78)$$

of the Deaton index. The properties of these index measures are analogous to those of the two versions of our distance variation. The first index DEA_{0k}^{0} fulfils the indicator and the ranking criterion while DEA_{0k}^{k} fulfils the ranking criterion only in the case of homothetic preferences when the distance function is separable between U and x and takes on the general form

$$d(x, U) = U^{-1} \cdot d_x(x). \qquad (3.79)$$

In this special case both measures are identical and fulfil not only the indicator and ranking criteria but also the circularity criterion (3.71).

From inequality (3.25) we obtain the fundamental relations between the values of the Allen indices and the Deaton indices for the same project as

$$AL_{0k}^{0} \leq DEA_{0k}^{0}, \quad DEA_{0k}^{k} \leq AL_{0k}^{k} \qquad (k \in \{1, 2, ..., K\}). \qquad (3.80)$$

So, for the same project AL_{0k}^{k} is an upper bound to the version DEA_{0k}^{k} of the Deaton index and AL_{0k}^{0} is a lower bound to DEA_{0k}^{0}.

Another quantity index which is based on the distance function was defined by Malmquist (1953). This index treats some reference utility level U_R as fixed and measures the relative distance of the initial consumption vector x^0 and of the new consumption vector x^k from the indifference surface for the utility level U_R, so that

$$MAL_{0k}^{R} = \frac{d(x^k, U_R)}{d(x^k, U_R)} \qquad (k \in \{1, 2, ..., K\}). \qquad (3.81)$$

The choice of the reference utility level is not arbitrary here as can be seen from Figure 3.4, where the **Malmquist index**

$$MAL_{0k}^R = \frac{0D/0C}{0B/0A} > 1$$

indicates an increase in welfare though utility has decreased from situation 0 to situation k. Wrong indications like this are ruled out if the reference utility level U_R lies between U_0 and U_k, so that either $d(x^k, U_R)$ is greater than one and $d(x^0, U_R)$ is less than one, or vice versa. The simplest way to secure this condition is to choose either U_0 or U_k as reference utility level. According to which of these two possibilities we choose, we obtain one of the following versions of the Malmquist index:

$$MAL_{0k}^0 = \frac{d(x^k, U_0)}{d(x^0, U_0)} = d(x^k, U_0) \qquad (k \in \{1, 2, ..., K\}); \qquad (3.82)$$

$$MAL_{0k}^k = \frac{d(x^k, U_k)}{d(x^0, U_k)} = \frac{1}{d(x^0, U_k)} \qquad (k \in \{1, 2, ..., K\}). \qquad (3.83)$$

Obviously, for these special choices of the reference utility level the Malmquist indices take the same values as the corresponding versions of the Deaton index, i.e.

$$MAL_{0k}^0 = DEA_{0k}^k \quad \text{and} \quad MAL_{0k}^0 = DEA_{0k}^k \quad (k \in \{1, 2, \ldots, K\}). \qquad (3.84)$$

Checking our reliability criteria (3.69) to (3.71) we find that both versions of the Malmquist index fulfil the indicator criterion (3.69) while only MAL_{0k}^k (which equals DEA_{0k}^0) meets also the ranking criterion (3.70). Both versions of the Malmquist index fulfil the circularity criterion (3.71) only for homothetic preferences, but not in general.

The functional quantity indices we have discussed up to now fulfil at least the indicator criterion and are, therefore, suited at least for binary welfare comparisons, i.e. for the welfare theoretical evaluation of a single project. If preferences are homothetic so that the distance function can be expressed by (3.79) while the expenditure function can be represented by (3.75) then the two Allen indices, the Deaton indices and the Malmquist indices are all equal, i.e.

$$AL_{0k}^0 = AL_{0k}^k = DEA_{0k}^0 = DEA_{0k}^k = MAL_{0k}^0 = MAL_{0k}^k$$

and fulfil the complete set of our theoretical consistency criteria (3.69) to (3.71). The disadvantage of the functional index measures is that for their empirical

Figure 3.4

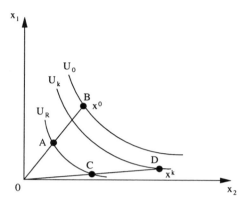

computation, normally, the estimation of a complete demand system is necessary, as has been shown above in the context of the functional variation
measures. The estimation of complete demand systems is always troublesome,
and it is especially difficult if the number of commodities is high compared to
the number of observations. In these cases one often prefers to work with the
atomistic welfare measures already mentioned which are less sophisticated from
a theoretical point of view, but which are much easier to compute empirically.
The two best known atomistic quantity indices are the **Laspeyres quantity
index**

$$LAQ_{0k} = \frac{p^0 x^k}{p^0 x^0} = \frac{p^0 x^k}{I_0} \qquad (k \in \{1, 2, ..., K\}) \qquad (3.85)$$

due to Laspeyres (1864) and the **Paasche quantity index**

$$PAQ_{0k} = \frac{p^k x^k}{p^k x^0} = \frac{I_k}{p^k x^0} \qquad (k \in \{1, 2, ..., K\}) \qquad (3.86)$$

which goes back to Paasche (1874). These two indices are monotonic transformations of the Laspeyres variation and the Paasche variation discussed in
Section 3.3 and they have the same theoretical properties. So, the Laspeyres
quantity index is able to indicate decreases in welfare, i.e.,

$$LAQ_{0k} \leq 1 \quad \Rightarrow \quad U_k < U_0 \qquad (k \in \{1, 2, ..., K\}), \qquad (3.87)$$

while the Paasche quantity index indicates increases in welfare correctly according to

$$PAQ_{0k} \geq 1 \quad \Rightarrow \quad U_k > U_0 \qquad (k \in \{1, 2, ..., K\}). \qquad (3.88)$$

If neither x^k is an element of the initial budget set $\mathcal{X}(p^0, I_0)$ nor x^0 is an element of $\mathcal{X}(p^k, I_k)$ we find ourselves in the "zone of ignorance" where none of these two index measures can be applied so that another (possibly a functional) welfare measure must be employed.

From the definition of the expenditure function it follows that the atomistic index measures of Laspeyres and Paasche are upper and lower bounds of the two versions of the Allen index, i.e.,

$$PAQ_{0k} \leq AL_{0k}^k \quad \text{and} \quad AL_{0k}^0 \leq LAQ_{0k} \qquad (3.89)$$

while the fundamental inequality (3.25) together with (3.84) implies that LAQ and PAQ also form upper and lower bounds to the corresponding versions of the Deaton and Malmquist index according to

$$PAQ_{0k} \geq DEA_{0k}^0 = MAL_{0k}^0 \quad \text{and} \quad MAL_{0k}^k = DEA_{0k}^k \leq LAQ_{0k}. \qquad (3.90)$$

As was shown above the atomistic welfare measures of Paasche and Laspeyres can be interpreted as first–order approximations to the corresponding functional welfare measures.

Time has not stood still since the days of Paasche and Laspeyres and the search went on for welfare measures which are tolerably exact on the one hand but easier to compute than the functional welfare measures on the other. A great deal of effort has been made especially by Diewert [see e.g. Diewert (1976), (1981) and (1990)] to explore the possibilities for the use of atomistic or, as he calls them, "mechanical" index numbers for the measurement of welfare. Diewert [see e.g. Diewert (1981, p. 181)] calls a (quantity) index IND_{0k} "exact" for a homothetic preference ordering if it fulfils the condition

$$IND_{0k} = \frac{U_k}{U_0} \qquad (k \in \{1, 2, ..., K\}). \qquad (3.91)$$

From (3.75) and (3.79) it becomes obvious that all functional quantity indices discussed above are exact in the sense of Diewert. In contrast to exact index numbers Diewert calls an index "superlative" if it is exact with respect to a utility function which can provide a second–order approximation to an arbitrary twice continuously differentiable linear homogeneous utility function [see Diewert (1976, p. 117), (1981, p. 185) or (1990, p. 98)]. In his studies Diewert develops the formulae of several superlative index numbers which sometimes have rather complicated mathematical structures but which are all computable on the basis of point observations only. Therefore, for the computation of superlative index numbers the empirical estimation of complete demand systems is not necessary. The disadvantage of all index numbers based on point observations is that they only provide approximations to the consumer's "true" utility function and that most of the results depend on the assumption of a homothetic preference ordering which is not very plausible from an empirical point of view.

3.4.2 Cost–of–Living Indices

A cost-of-living or price index $P_{0k} = P(P^0, p^k)$ aggregates the change in prices from situation 0 to a situation k into a single scalar. Normally, it is defined as the ratio of the (minimum) expenditures a consumer must make to attain a given constant standard of living under the two price regimes p^0 and p^k. If this "constant standard of living" is interpreted as a constant reference utility level U_R we speak of a functional cost–of–living index (which is based on household theory) and if it is represented by a constant reference consumption vector x^R we speak of an atomistic or mechanical cost–of–living index. As mentioned above, a price index alone cannot indicate welfare changes but it is used to deflate a nominal–income index I_k/I_0 to construct a real–income index which describes the changes in prices and in income and, therefore, is a potential welfare indicator.

The characteristic properties of a typical price or cost-of-living index originate from the famous consistency tests postulated by Fisher (1927). Frisch showed in 1936 that no single index could pass the whole set of Fisher's tests at the same time because they are contradictory. Nevertheless, even today some of these tests are used as axioms to characterize the general properties of a typical price index [see e.g. Eichhorn and Voeller (1990)]. The minimum requirements a price or cost–of–living index should meet are the following [cf. Pollak (1990, p. 13)]:

(a) $P(p^0, p^0) \equiv 1$ (Identity axiom)

(b) $p^k > p^j \Rightarrow P(p^0, p^k) > P(p^0, p^j)$ (Monotonicity axiom)

(c) $P(p^0, \alpha p^k) = \alpha \cdot P(p^0, p^k)$ (Linear-homogeneity axiom)

$\quad\quad P(\alpha p^0, p^k) = (1/\alpha) \cdot P(p^0, p^k) \quad (\alpha > 0)$

(d) $P(\alpha p^0, \alpha p^k) = P(p^0, p^k) \quad (\alpha > 0)$ (Dimensionality axiom).

$$(3.92)$$

The identity axiom fixes the "neutral" point, i.e. that value of a price index which signals that no price has changed. The monotonicity axiom requires that there is a strictly positive correlation between price changes and the value of a price index while the linear–homogeneity axiom demands that a proportional change in all new (initial) prices leads to a change of the index value by the same (reciprocal) factor of proportionality. Last but not least the dimensionality axiom requires that the value of a price index must be independent of the dimension in which the prices are measured, i.e., the value of a price index must be the same no matter if we express the prices in Dollars or in Swiss Francs.

The most popular functional price index is the **"True Index of the Cost of Living"** by **Konüs** (1924) which is defined as the ratio of the minimum expenditures that are required if the consumer under consideration wants to attain a certain reference utility level U_R with initial prices p^0 and with new prices p^k, respectively:

$$KO_{0k}^R = \frac{e(p^k, U_R)}{e(p^0, U_R)} \qquad (k \in \{1, 2, ..., K\}). \tag{3.93}$$

According to which of the utility levels U_0 or U_k we choose as a reference utility level we obtain either the version

$$KO_{0k}^0 = \frac{e(p^k, U_0)}{e(p^0, U_0)} = \frac{e(p^k, U_0)}{I_0} \qquad (k \in \{1, 2, ..., K\}), \tag{3.94}$$

or the version

$$KO_{0k}^k = \frac{e(p^k, U_k)}{e(p^0, U_k)} = \frac{I_k}{e(p^0, U_k)} \qquad (k \in \{1, 2, ..., K\}) \tag{3.95}$$

of the Konüs index. If we construct the corresponding real–income indices Y_{0k} according to (3.66) we find that these indices coincide with the two versions of the Allen quantity index discussed above, i.e.:

$$Y(KO^0)_{0k} = \frac{I_k/I_0}{KO_{0k}^0} = \frac{I_k}{e(p^k, U_0)} = AL_{0k}^k \qquad (k \in \{1, 2, ..., K\}); \tag{3.96}$$

$$Y(KO^k)_{0k} = \frac{I_k/I_0}{KO_{0k}^k} = \frac{e(p^0, U_k)}{I_0} = AL_{0k}^0 \qquad (k \in \{1, 2, ..., K\}). \tag{3.97}$$

From (3.96) and (3.97) we see that the real–income index $Y(KO^k)_{0k}$ that is based on the Konüs index with U_k as reference utility level fulfils the indicator criterion and the ranking criterion, while $Y(KO^0)_{0k}$ meets the indicator criterion only. In the case of a homothetic preference ordering both real–income indices are identical and fulfil all of our theoretical consistency criteria (3.69) to (3.71). Their empirical computation poses the same problems as the corresponding quantity indices and the Hicksian variation measures, i.e. for their exact computation we need the consumer's complete Marshallian demand system.

In analogy to the atomistic quantity indices by Laspeyres and Paasche there are two atomistic price indices which are defined by the ratio of the expenditures necessary to buy a constant reference commodity basket at initial prices p^0 and at new prices p^k, respectively. The motivation for using these simple mechanical price indices instead of the more sophisticated Konüs indices is, again, that atomistic index measures are extremely easy to compute empirically compared to the functional indices. If we choose the initial consumption bundle x^0 as a reference commodity vector, we obtain the **Laspeyres price index**

$$LAP_{0k} = \frac{p^k x^0}{p^0 x^0} = \frac{p^k x^0}{I_0} \qquad (k \in \{1, 2, ..., K\}), \qquad (3.98)$$

and if we choose x^k as reference commodity bundle we arrive at the Paasche price index

$$PAP_{0k} = \frac{p^k x^k}{p^0 x^k} = \frac{I_k}{p^0 x^k} \qquad (k \in \{1, 2, ..., K\}). \qquad (3.99)$$

The atomistic price indices by Laspeyres and Paasche can be interpreted as first–order Taylor approximations to the respective Konüs indices, and from the definition of the expenditure function it follows that they represent the upper and lower bounds for the values of these functional measures, i.e.:

$$PAP_{0k} \le KO_{0k}^k \qquad \text{and} \qquad KO_{0k}^0 \le LAP_{0k} \qquad (k \in \{1, 2, ..., K\}). \quad (3.100)$$

The real–income indices which are based on the Laspeyres and the Paasche price indices equal the Paasche and Laspeyres quantity indices, respectively:

$$Y(LAP)_{0k} = \frac{I_k/I_0}{LAP_{0k}} = \frac{I_k}{p^k x^0} = PAQ_{0k} \qquad (k \in \{1, 2, ..., K\}); \qquad (3.101)$$

$$Y(PAP)_{0k} = \frac{I_k/I_0}{PAP_{0k}} = \frac{p^0 x^k}{I_0} = LAQ_{0k} \qquad (k \in \{1, 2, ..., K\}). \qquad (3.102)$$

The real–income indices which are constructed on the basis of the Laspeyres and Paasche price indices are one–sided welfare indicators like the corresponding quantity indices, i.e. $Y(LAP)_{0k}$ indicates increases in welfare correctly while $Y(PAP)_{0k}$ is a reliable indicator for welfare reductions.

While the Laspeyres and Paasche price indices are only first-order approximations to the true price indices of the Konüs type, Erwin Diewert (1976)
(1981), (1990)] suggested a number of superlative price index numbers which
lead to much better real–income indices, i.e. to real–income indices which are
closer approximations to the consumer's utility function. The motivation for
the construction of these mechanical index numbers is, again, that for their empirical computation it is not necessary to know a consumer's complete demand
system. Therefore, the econometric effort that is necessary for the computation
of Diewert's superlative index numbers is much smaller than for the computation of the true index numbers. The price we have to pay for this econometric
convenience is that the superlative index numbers are less reliable than the true
index numbers under general assumptions.

To sum up, we can say that the theoretical properties of index numbers as
welfare measures are analogous to the properties of the corresponding variation
measures we discussed in the preceeding section. We saw that quantity indices
and real–income indices, in principle, can be used as welfare indicators while
price indices merely play an auxiliary part as deflators for the transformation
of a nominal income index I_k/I_0 into a real-income index. Besides the "true"
index number measures of welfare which fulfil at least our indicator criterion
(3.69) we find atomistic or mechanical index numbers in the literature which
are less exact but much easier to compute empirically than the true indices.

In this section we have been concerned with the measurement of welfare
under "ideal" and also rather restrictive conditions so that the general features
and problems of welfare measurement could be elaborated. We shall now turn to
some special problems of welfare measurement under more realistic assumptions
in the course of the following sections.

4   Welfare Measurement with Quantity Constraints

Up to now our discussion of welfare measurement has been based on household
consumption models where the consumer can buy arbitrary quantities of all
goods at given prices. This assumption cannot be maintained if we want to
measure the welfare effects of in–kind subsidy programs where government
gives selected (normally poor) households the opportunity to consume limited
quantities of certain goods at prices below the corresponding market prices.
For the government programs to be analysed here it is characteristic that the
goods under consideration are purely private goods by nature and are also
traded on free markets. Typical examples of this kind of government aid are
housing programs offering low income households a limited dimension of living
space at a rent much lower than they would have to pay on the free housing
market. This leads to the typical rationed household "equilibrium" where the

marginal utilities (in monetary terms) of the rationed goods are higher than their (subsidised) prices so that the consumer would like to consume more of these goods than he is allowed to. The behaviour of rationed households was studied especially during and after the Second World War when the essentials of life were rationed in many countries. The most prominent publications of this period are Rothbarth (1940–41), Tobin and Houthakker (1950–51) and Tobin (1952). The interest in rationing theory was awakened again in the eighties for two reasons: first, the new techniques of duality theory were broadly established in microeconomics and made the analysis of complex problems like rationing much easier than before and, second, government aid programs, by subsidising limited quantities of essential goods, gained a new importance at that time. General treatments of rationing theory from this period are Neary and Roberts (1980), Mackay and Whitney (1980), Deaton (1981), Madden (1991) and Jackson (1991), while, among others, Cornes and Albon (1981), De Borger (1986, 1989), Lankford (1988), Pauwels (1988), Schwab (1985) and Breslaw and Smith (1995b) focused on the problems of measuring welfare under quantity constrained regimes. Before we start our analysis of the measurement of welfare under rationing we have to extend our basic model used in Section 3 to allow for the existence of rationed goods.

4.1 Definitions

In this section we assume that the consumer under consideration takes part in a government program where he has the possibility to buy $(N - M)$ commodities that are also traded on free markets at subsidised prices $q \in \mathbb{R}_{++}^{N-M}$. The quantities which the consumer can buy at these prices are restricted to $y \in \mathbb{R}_{+}^{N-M}$ and we assume that all of these restrictions are binding. This seems to be plausible since the rationing prices q are lower than the respective market prices so that the consumer will want to buy more of these goods than the rationing quantities y. We further assume that consumers buy either in the rationed or in the free markets but do not mix, so that we do not have to consider kinked budget constraints in our analysis. In addition to the rationed goods the consumer is supposed to buy M private goods at market prices in the free markets. Hence, we can now partition the household's consumption vector $x \in \mathbb{R}_{+}^{N}$ and the price vector $p \in \mathbb{R}_{++}^{N}$ into rationed and unrationed "subvectors" according to

$$
\begin{aligned}
x &= [x_{\#}, y] = [x_1, ..., x_M, y_{M+1}, ..., y_N], &\quad (4.1) \\
p &= [p_{\#}, q] = [p_1, ..., p_M, q_{M+1}, ..., q_N],
\end{aligned}
$$

where $p_{\#} \in \mathbb{R}_{++}^{M}$ and $x_{\#} \in \mathbb{R}_{+}^{M}$ are the prices and quantities of the unrationed market goods. The rationed consumer maximises his direct utility function

$u(x)$ subject to the quantity constraints and his budget restriction where the expenditures for the rationed goods are fixed. This leads us to the quantity–constrained or restricted indirect utility function

$$\tilde{v}(p, y, I) \equiv \max_{x_\# \in \mathcal{Y}(p,y,I)} u(x), \quad \mathcal{Y}(p, y, I) = \{x_\# | x_\# \in \mathbb{R}^M_+, p_\# x_\# \leq I - qy\}. \quad (4.2)$$

As a solution to this maximization problem we obtain the consumer's rationed or restricted Marshallian demand functions for the unrationed market goods $x_\#$ and the Lagrangean multiplier which equals the marginal utility of income:

$$
\begin{aligned}
x^*_\# &= \text{æ}(p, y, I), &(4.3)\\
\mu^* &= \mu(p, y, I).
\end{aligned}
$$

Substitution of the optimal demands in the direct utility function yields the restricted indirect utility function as

$$\tilde{v}(p, y, I) \equiv u(\text{æ}(p, y, I), y). \quad (4.4)$$

This function is continuous and strictly monotonically increasing in I, twice continuously differentiable, monotonically decreasing and strictly quasi–convex in $p = [p_\#, q]$, twice continuously differentiable, strictly monotonically increasing and strictly quasi–concave in y, and homogeneous of degree 0 in p and I.

Minimizing the consumer's expenditures for a minimum standard of living represented by the utility level U and observing the quantity constraints produces his restricted expenditure function

$$
\begin{aligned}
E(p, y, U) &\equiv \min_{x_\# \in \mathcal{W}(U,y)} px, \quad \mathcal{W}(U, y) = \{x_\# | x_\# \in \mathbb{R}^M_+, u(x_\#, y) \geq U\}\\
&\equiv qy + \min_{x_\# \in \mathcal{W}(U,y)} p_\# x_\#\\
&\equiv qy + \tilde{e}(p_\#, y, U), &(4.5)
\end{aligned}
$$

where qy are the consumer's (fixed) expenditures for the rationed goods and

$$\tilde{e}(p_\#, y, U) \equiv \min_{x_\# \in \mathcal{W}(U,y)} p_\# x_\# \quad (4.6)$$

is his variable expenditure function. The variable expenditure function is continuous and strictly monotonically increasing in U, twice continuously differentiable, monotonically increasing, concave and linearly homogeneous in $p_\#$, and twice continuously differentiable, strictly convex and strictly monotonically decreasing in y. As a solution of the minimization problem (4.6) we obtain the rationed Hicksian demand functions

$$x_{\#}^* = \zeta(p_{\#}, y, U).$$ (4.7)

The relation between the restricted indirect utility function and the restricted expenditure function is given by the identities

$$\tilde{v}(p, y, E(p, y, U)) \equiv U \quad \text{and} \quad E(p, y, \tilde{v}(p, y, I)) \equiv I.$$ (4.8)

From these identities we obtain some useful derivative properties of the expenditure function. The partial derivatives of the quantity–constrained expenditure function with respect to the prices turn out to be

$$\nabla_{p_{\#}} E(p, y, U) \equiv \nabla_{p_{\#}} \tilde{e}(p_{\#}, y, U) \equiv \zeta(p_{\#}, y, U)$$ (4.9)

$$\nabla_q E(p, y, U) \equiv y$$ (4.10)

in analogy to Shephard's Lemma. Taking the derivatives with respect to the rationing quantities y we obtain from (4.8)

$$\nabla_y E(p, y, U) \equiv q + \nabla_y \tilde{e}(p_{\#}, y, U) \equiv q - \pi(p_{\#}, y, U) = q - \pi^*,$$ (4.11)

where

$$\pi^* = \nabla_y u(x_{\#}^*, y)/\mu^*$$ (4.12)

is the vector of shadow prices of the rationed goods. These shadow prices indicate the "true" value of the rationed goods to the consumer or his true willingness–to–pay for these goods in the rationed consumer "equilibrium". Under our assumptions the shadow prices are higher than the subsidised prices q that he actually does pay. The functions

$$\pi(p_{\#}, y, U) \equiv -\nabla_y \tilde{e}(p_{\#}, y, U) \quad [= \pi^*]$$ (4.13)

can be interpreted as his "income–compensated" shadow price functions. As mentioned above we assume that the rationed commodities are also traded on private markets so that often there exist data from the time before the household under consideration took part in the government's subsidy program. These data can be used to estimate the consumer's unrationed Marshallian demand system according to (3.2). This is important because there is no possibility to estimate a consumer's rationed demand system directly. The usual procedure is to postulate a direct utility function first and then estimate the relevant parameters of the corresponding unrationed Marshallian demand functions. These are needed to derive the rationed demand system on the basis of the relations presented here [for specific examples for this procedure see Deaton (1981a, p. 60 ff.)]. The theoretical link between the rationed and the unrationed demand system of a consumer is provided by the virtual price system, i.e. "the price system which makes the quantities actually consumed under rationing an optimum" [Rothbarth (1940–41, p. 100)]. So, the virtual prices of a rationed situation are those prices that support the actual consumption vector $[x_\#^*, y]$. The virtual prices of the private goods are their market prices $p_\#$ and the virtual prices of the rationed goods are equal to their shadow prices π^*, as was shown by Neary and Roberts (1980, p. 28 f.). According to (4.12) the shadow price vector π^* is collinear to the gradient of the direct utility function with respect to y in the respective rationing equilibrium, so that the price vector

$$[p_\#, \pi^*] = - \nabla u(x_\#^*, y)/\mu^* \tag{4.14}$$

supports the rationed household equilibrium $[x_\#^*, y]$ and, therefore, is the virtual price vector for this choice of consumption goods. This implies that at these prices the consumer's rationed and unrationed Hicksian demand functions are identical:

$$\xi(p_\#, \pi^*, U) = \zeta(p_\#, \pi(p_\#, y, U), U) \equiv [\xi(p_\#, y, U), y], \tag{4.15}$$

where π^* was substituted from (4.13). The same holds for the rationed and unrationed Marshallian demand functions if the consumer is equipped with a suitable "virtual" income that enables him to pay the (higher) virtual prices for the rationed goods at given quantities y. This virtual income is given by

$$I^* = I + [\pi^* - q] \cdot y, \tag{4.16}$$

so that

$$x(p_\#, \pi^*, I^*) \equiv [æ(p_\#, q, y, I), y], \tag{4.17}$$

where the shadow prices π^* of the rationed goods must now be expressed as uncompensated functions according to

$$\pi^* = \pi(p_\#, y, \tilde{v}(p_\#, q, y, I)) \tag{4.18}$$

to make (4.17) an identity. The fundamental relation between the rationed and the unrationed expenditure function is given by

$$e(p_\#, \pi^*, U) \equiv E(p_\#, q, y, U) + [\pi^* - q] \cdot y \tag{4.19}$$

with π^* expressed as an income–compensated function according to (4.13).

Now we have the tools which are needed to explore the possibilities to measure welfare under conditions of rationing. As shown in the third section the idea of constructing a welfare measure on the basis of the indirect utility function is not very promising since such a measure is applicable only under very restrictive conditions. These conditions are even more restrictive if we have to take quantity constraints into account [cf. Ahlheim (1993, p. 158 ff.)]. Therefore, we shall concentrate here on welfare measures which are based either on the expenditure function or on the distance function.

4.2   Measuring Welfare

The most obvious way to extend the concept of the expenditure–function–based Hicksian variation measures to the case of rationed households is to define the **rationed equivalent variation** on the basis of the quantity constrained expenditure function as

$$REV_{0k} = E(p^0, y^0, U_k) - E(p^0, y^0, U_0) = E(p^0, y^0, U_k) - I_0, \qquad (4.20)$$

and, analogously, the **rationed compensating variation** as

$$RCV_{0k} = E(p^k, y^k, U_k) - E(p^k, y^k, U_0) = I_k - E(p^k, y^k, U_0), \qquad (4.21)$$

where $p_0 = [p_\#^0, q^0]$ and $p^k = [p_\#^k, q^k]$. The rationed equivalent variation is illustrated in Figure 4.1 for a government project k which implies a reduction of the rationing quantity y with all other parameters being constant. As we already know, both measures fulfil the indicator criterion (2.1) while only the EV also fulfils the ranking criterion (2.2) and none of these two meets the circularity criterion (2.3). So, the only question that has to be answered here is how we can compute these measures under the special conditions of rationing. Since this problem is the same for both Hicksian measures, we shall concentrate on the equivalent variation in what follows.

As mentioned above there is no possibility to estimate a consumer's rationed demand functions directly. Therefore, a necessary condition for the computation of any welfare measure for a rationed consumer is the knowledge of his unrationed demand system from which we can derive his rationed demand functions. The traditional approach to the empirical computation of the equivalent variation is first to postulate a specific function form for the consumer's utility function and then derive his unrationed Marshallian demand functions which can be estimated econometrically. The parameters of these demand functions are needed to calculate the corresponding quantity constrained expenditure function. Since this method, which is proposed among others by

Figure 4.1

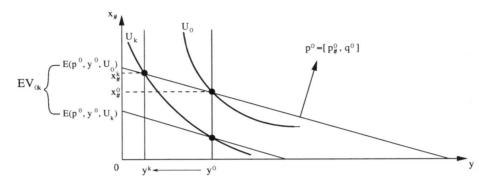

Deaton (1981), is still the most promising one for the computation of the Hicksian measures in the case of rationed households, we shall illustrate it in some more detail.

To make things simple we assume that the consumer's preferences can be described by a Stone–Geary utility function

$$u(x) = \prod_{n=1}^{N} (x_n - \gamma_n)^{\alpha_n}, \quad 0 \leq \gamma_n \leq x_n, \quad \alpha_n > 0, \quad \sum_{n=1}^{N} \alpha_n = 1. \quad (4.22)$$

The corresponding unrationed Marshallian demand functions are then given by the well–known linear expenditure system (LES) according to

$$x_n(p, I) = \gamma_n + \frac{\alpha_n}{p_n}(I - p\gamma) \qquad (n = 1, 2, ..., N), \quad (4.23)$$

where $\gamma \in \mathbb{R}_+^N$ is the vector of the minimum consumption quantities γ_n. These demand functions are estimated econometrically on the basis of the unrationed demand data for all commodities. It is essential that these data are also available for the rationed goods (from the time before the rationing program started) to obtain all parameters which are needed to calculate the rationed equivalent or compensating variation. If we want to assess the REV according to (4.20) for our Stone-Geary utility function, we must express the REV as a function of the parameters estimated above.

For the calculation of the REV according to (4.20) we must know the functional form of the restricted expenditure function $E(p_\#, q, y, U)$ which is related to the unrationed expenditure function $e(p, U)$ by identity (4.19). To derive the unrationed expenditure function for our Stone–Geary utility function we substitute the unrationed Marshallian demand functions (4.23) in the direct utility function (4.22). We obtain the unrationed indirect utility function $v(p, I)$ which is needed to obtain the unrationed expenditure function from identity (3.14) as

$$e(p, U) = U \cdot \prod_{n=1}^{N} \left(\frac{p_n}{\alpha_n} \right)^{\alpha_n} + p\gamma. \tag{4.24}$$

We now assume that the consumer takes part in a government program where he is allowed to buy the quantity y of commodity N at the subsidised price $q < p_N$, while all other commodities are sold under market conditions. In this case with one rationed good the consumer's price and quantity vectors can be written as

$$p = [p_1, ..., p_{N-1}, q] = [p_\#, q] \quad \text{and} \quad x = [x_1, ..., x_{N-1}, y] = [x_\#, y].$$

The rationed and the unrationed expenditure function are connected by the virtual prices, as we know from (4.19). Therefore we need the functional form of the shadow price of the rationed good (which is identical to its virtual price, as we already know). From Shephard's Lemma (3.13) and from identity (4.15) we obtain

$$\frac{\partial e}{\partial p_n}(p_\#, \pi^*, U) \equiv \xi_N(p_\#, \pi^*, U) \equiv y. \tag{4.25}$$

By applying this identity to (4.24) and solving for π^* we get the shadow prices as functions of the market prices $p_\#$, the quantity constraint y and the utility level U:

$$\pi^* = \pi(p_\#, y, U) \equiv \alpha_N \cdot \left(\frac{U}{y - \gamma_N} \prod_{n=1}^{N-1} \left(\frac{p_n}{\alpha_n} \right)^{\alpha_N} \right)^{\frac{1}{1-\alpha_N}}. \tag{4.26}$$

Substitution of (4.24) and (4.26) in (4.19) yields us the functional form of the restricted expenditure function

$$E(p_\#, q, y, U) \equiv (1 - \alpha_N) \cdot \left(\frac{U}{(y - \gamma_N)^{\alpha_N}} \prod_{n=1}^{N-1} \left(\frac{p_n}{\alpha_n} \right)^{\alpha_N} \right)^{\frac{1}{1-\alpha_N}} + \sum_{n=1}^{N-1} p_n \gamma_n + qy, \tag{4.27}$$

which can be used to attain the restricted indirect utility function from identity (4.8) as

$$\tilde{v}(p_\#, q, y, U) \equiv \left(\frac{I - \sum_{n=1}^{N-1} p_n \gamma_n - qy}{1 - \alpha_N} \right)^{1-\alpha_N} \cdot (y - \gamma_n)^{\alpha_N} \cdot \prod_{n=1}^{N-1} \left(\frac{p_n}{\alpha_n} \right)^{\alpha_n}. \tag{4.28}$$

If we substitute (4.28) for the unobservable utility level U in (4.27) we obtain the consumer's restricted expenditure function as a function of observable data only so that the rationed equivalent variation for our Stone–Geary utility function becomes

$$REV_{0k} = \left(\left(\frac{y^k - \gamma_n}{y^0 - \gamma_n} \right)^{\alpha_N} \cdot \prod_{n=1}^{N-1} \left(\frac{p_n^0}{p_n^k} \right)^{\alpha_N} \right)^{\frac{1}{1-\alpha_N}}$$
$$\cdot \left(I_k - \sum_{n=1}^{N-1} p_n^k \gamma_n - q^k y^k \right) - \left(I_0 - \sum_{n=1}^{N-1} p_n^0 \gamma_n - q^0 y^0 \right). \tag{4.29}$$

This formula of the REV can be calculated on the basis of empirically observable data if we know the consumer's unrationed Marshallian demand functions (4.23) for all commodities.

This traditional method to calculate the equivalent variation depends on the postulation of a prespecified Marshallian demand system like the LES in our example that can be derived from a closed–form direct utility function. As mentioned above, one often finds that the empirically assessed data do not fit well into the demand scheme postulated ex-ante. Therefore, it seems more attractive from an empirical point of view to estimate a more flexible functional form of a (well-behaved) demand system, whether or not there exists a specific closed-form utility function from which this demand system can be derived. In the context of the unrationed household model of Section 3 it was shown that there exists a method developed by Vartia (1983) and McKenzie and Ulph (1986) which makes it possible to calculate the equivalent variation empirically on the basis of an arbitrary econometrically estimated demand system, regardless of whether it corresponds to the specific functional form of a utility function or not. If we want to apply this method to a rationed household we have to reformulate the rationed equivalent variation (4.20) by applying the Second Fundamental Theorem of Integral Calculus and the rationed versions of Shephard's Lemma (4.9) and (4.13) to obtain

$$
\begin{aligned}
REV_{0k} &= E(p^0, y^0, U_k) - I_0 \\
&= \tilde{e}(p_\#^0, y^0, U_k) - \tilde{e}(p_\#^k, y^k, U_k) + \Delta I + q^0 y^0 - q^k y^k \\
&= \int_{p_\#^k, y^k}^{p_\#^0, y^0} \left[\nabla_{p_\#} \tilde{e}(p_\#, y, U_k), \nabla_y \tilde{e}(p_\#, y, U_k) \right] \begin{bmatrix} dp_\# \\ dy \end{bmatrix} \\
&\quad + \Delta I + q^0 y^0 - q^k y^k \\
&= \int_{p_\#^k}^{p_\#^0} \zeta(p_\#, y^k, U_k) dp_\# - \int_{y^k}^{y^0} \pi(p_\#^0, y, U_k) dy \\
&\quad + \Delta I + q^0 y^0 - q^k y^k. \tag{4.30}
\end{aligned}
$$

It is obvious that in this case the Vartia method must fail because the functions to be integrated here are not only compensated (Hicksian) demand functions as in the unrationed case but they are also rationed. So, the empirical problems which arise here are twofold: the first kind of problems arises from the fact that we have to compute the integrals of income–compensated demand functions which are not directly observable. This problem can be overcome by using the Vartia method, which allows us to calculate the integral over compensated demand functions from the knowledge of the consumer's Marshallian demand system. The second kind of problems arises from the fact that the demand functions to be integrated are also rationed demand functions, and rationed demand functions cannot be observed empirically, no matter whether they are income compensated or not. Therefore, the Vartia method is of no use here because the rationed Marshallian demand functions cannot be assessed empirically.

There have been attempts to calculate the unrationed equivalent variation in analogy to (3.44) for rationed households by using the concept of virtual prices. The first to explore this possibility was Schwab (1985) whose analysis was restricted to the two–good case. This approach was generalized to the case of more than two goods by De Borger (1989) who employed a modified version of the Vartia algorithm. Unfortunately, De Borger's method only works under the assumption that the prices of all private goods remain constant. Clearly, this method is also far from being satisfactory, since the prices of the private goods are not controlled by the government, but are determined endogenously by the supply and demand behaviour of the private agents in the free markets. This means that there is no possibility for the welfare analyst to guarantee the fulfilment of De Borger's conditions by whatever kind of assumption regarding the government project or the consumer's preferences. So there is no realistic chance to apply this method in practice.

From our considerations up to now we must conclude that the only realistic possibility for an empirical computation of the equivalent variation in the case of household rationing is to prespecify the functional form of a household's utility function and to estimate the corresponding unrationed Marshallian demand functions which are then used to calculate the equivalent variation. All attempts to calculate the equivalent variation on the basis of freely estimated demand functions by using the Vartia method must fail because the equivalent variation — rationed or not — is based on the consumer's expenditure function. The expenditure function implies optimal behaviour of the consumer and, therefore, depends on the market conditions under which the consumer makes his choice. It is not suited for the construction of a welfare measure that is to be applied to quantity constrained regimes because in this special case there is no method of calculation which leads from the empirically observed data to the expenditure function without meeting additional assumptions with respect to the functional structure of the demand system or even with respect to the values of the market prices.

For the case of rationed households it makes more sense to construct a welfare measure on the basis of a simple utility index like the direct utility function or the distance function, because these concepts are independent of both the consumer's optimization behaviour and the market conditions so that they need no specific adaptation for the case of rationing. This leads us directly to the distance variation (3.53) or (3.54) since we already know that welfare measures that are based on a utility function can only be used under very special assumptions with respect to the consumer's preference ordering. The distance variation is independent of the specific market conditions because it just measures the relative distance of the new and the old indifference surface from the origin. Therefore, we can apply the distance variation to the case of rationed households without any modification. If we adjust our notation to the rationing case according to (4.1) our distance variation (3.53) with the initial consumption bundle as reference commodity vector becomes

$$DV_{0k}^0 = d(x_\#^0, y^0, U_0) - d(x_\#^0, y^0, U_k) = 1 - d(x_\#^0, y^0, U_k). \qquad (4.31)$$

The reader should note that the only difference between (3.53) and (4.31) is a change in notation to distinguish the vector y of the rationed goods while the measure itself is the same as in the unrationed case. The distance variation measures the relative distance of two indifference curves from the origin along a ray from the origin, and it doesn't matter at all under which market conditions the consumer attains the respective utility levels. This is the decisive difference to all measures which are based on the expenditure function. In Figure 4.2 the distance variation is illustrated for the same project as shown in Figure 4.1, namely a reduction in the rationing quantity from y^0 to y^k. The value of the distance variation is $DV_{0k}^0 = 1 - 0A/0B = (0B - 0A)/0B < 0$ in this case.

The empirical calculation of the distance variation is the same in the rationed as in the unrationed case. From the Shephard-Hanoch Lemma (3.22) we know that the partial derivatives of the distance function with respect to the quantities x are identical to the consumer's compensated inverse demand functions $\phi(x, U)$ so that the application of the Fundamental Theorem of Integral Calculus to the distance variation leads us to (3.56) which can now be written as

$$DV_{0k}^0 = \int_{x_\#^0, y^0}^{x_\#^k, y^k} \phi(x_\#, y, U_k) \begin{bmatrix} dx \\ dy \end{bmatrix}, \qquad (4.32)$$

where $\phi(x_\#, y, U_k)$ is the vector of the unrationed (!) inverse compensated demand functions for all commodities. So we can apply Vartia's algorithm

Figure 4.2

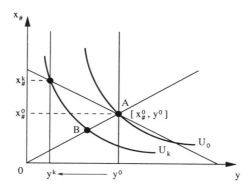

here without any modification and without any additional assumptions if we just know the consumer's unrationed inverse demand functions $\hat{p}(x)$ according to (3.8).

From the considerations of this section it follows that in quantity constrained regimes welfare changes can be measured either by using modified versions of the Hicksian variation measures or by the (unmodified) distance variation. It turned out that the empirical calculation of the Hicksian measures can be accomplished only on the basis of prespecified functional forms for the consumer's utility function and for his demand system. The application of the Vartia algorithm to an independently estimated demand system as in the unrationed case is not possible here unless we make sure that all market prices are constant (which is not possible). If we want to work with demand systems that are estimated with no regard to the existence of a corresponding closed–form utility function we have to employ the distance variation which is the same for the rationed and for the unrationed case. The calculation of this measure depends only on the knowledge of the unrationed inverse demand functions for all commodities which can be estimated on the basis of demand data from the time before the in–kind government program under consideration. Without such data none of the methods mentioned here for the measurement of welfare under rationing can be applied.

5 Intertemporal Aspects

Thus far we have dealt with the measurement of welfare in a static world where time does not matter or, alternatively, where only a single period of time is considered. Many public projects, however, affect a household's utility for more than one period so that our atemporal models are not sufficient for the assessment of the resulting welfare effects. To capture these intertemporal welfare effects we have to employ a household model that describes the consumer's optimization problem over several time periods.

First of all it is necessary to adjust our terminology and notation with respect to the extended scope of our analysis. In this section we shall attach slightly different meanings to some of our previously used variables to avoid excessive notation. We assume that the household under consideration plans for T periods $t = 1, 2, ..., T$ after the tax reform or government project $k \in \{1, 2, ..., K\}$ has started. By p we now denote the vector of the present values of all prices according to

$$p = [p_1, p_2, ..., p_T] \in \mathbb{R}_{++}^{N \cdot T} \tag{5.1}$$
$$\text{with} \quad p_t = [p_{1t}, p_{2t}, ..., p_{Nt}] \in \mathbb{R}_{++}^N \quad (t = 1, 2, ..., T),$$

where p_t is the vector of the present values of the N commodity prices in period $t \in \{1, 2, ..., T\}$. Analogously, we denote the consumer's lifetime consumption vector by

$$x = [x_1, x_2, ..., x_T] \in \mathbb{R}_+^{N \cdot T} \tag{5.2}$$
$$\text{with} \quad x_t = [x_{1t}, x_{2t}, ..., x_{Nt}] \in \mathbb{R}_+^N \quad (t = 1, 2, ..., T),$$

where x_t is the vector of quantities of the N goods consumed in period t. Further, we define the present value of the consumer's lump–sum income in period t by I_t and the present value of his lifetime income by

$$I = \sum_{t=1}^T I_t. \tag{5.3}$$

The consumer's lifetime utility level U is determined by his lifetime utility function $u : \mathbb{R}_+^{N \cdot T} \to \mathbb{R}$ according to

$$U = u(x) = u(x_{11}, x_{21}, ..., x_{N1}, x_{12}, x_{22}, ..., x_{N2}, \quad \cdots \quad , x_{1T}, x_{2T}, ..., x_{NT}), \tag{5.4}$$

so that his lifetime expenditure function $e : \mathbb{R}_+^{N \cdot T + 1} \to \mathbb{R}$ can be defined as

$$e(p, U) = \min_{x \in \mathcal{U}(U)} px, \quad \mathcal{U}(U) = \{x | x \in \mathbb{R}_+^{N \cdot T}, u(x) \geq U\}. \tag{5.5}$$

We now assume that the present values of the commodity prices change from p^0 to p^k as a consequence of a government project $k \in \{1, 2, ..., K\}$ and that the present values of the consumer's period incomes $I_t (t = 1, 2, ..., T)$ change from I_t^0 to I_t^k, so that the present value of his lifetime income according to (5.3) shifts from I^0 to I^k. This induces the consumer to adjust his lifetime consumption vector from x^0 to x^k so that his lifetime utility becomes $U^k = u(x^k)$ instead of $U^0 = u(x^0)$.

To measure this change in utility we can extend the Hicksian variation measures to the intertemporal context. For this purpose we define the intertemporal equivalent variation as

$$EV^{0k} = e(p^0, U^k) - e(p^0, U^0) = e(p^0, U^k) - I^0, \qquad (5.6)$$

and the intertemporal compensating variation as

$$CV^{0k} = e(p^k, U^k) - e(p^k, U^0) = I^k - e(p^k, U^0). \qquad (5.7)$$

The analogy to the atemporal case is obvious: Both measures fulfil the indicator criterion (2.1), i.e., both are "true" measures in the sense that they can evaluate single projects in accordance with the consumer's preference ordering. The essential formal difference between the atemporal Hicksian measures (3.44) and (3.45) on the one hand and their intertemporal pendants (5.6) and (5.7) on the other is the meaning of the price variables p which have to be interpreted as present value prices in the intertemporal case.

While the lifetime Hicksian variations (5.6) and (5.7) are "true" intertemporal welfare measures from a theoretical point of view they are not used in general for practical studies because of the empirical problems arising from their computation. Instead, the equivalent or compensating variations are calculated for each single period $t = 1, 2, ..., T$ in present value terms and then added up over all t. The sum of these period–specific or instantaneous variations is then interpreted as a measure of intertemporal welfare change. As has been shown by Blackorby et al. (1984) and by Keen (1990) this procedure can lead to wrong results since the sums of the instantaneous Hicksian variation measures do not equal the (true) overall variation measures (5.6) and (5.7) in general: the sume of the instantaneous equivalent variations can be greater than the lifetime equivalent variation while the sum of the instantaneous compensating variations can be smaller than the lifetime compensating variation. From this it follows that the sums of the period–specific variations can be interpreted as one–sided welfare measures only, where a negative sum of the instantaneous equivalent variations indicates a (true) decrease in utility while a positive sum of the instantaneous compensating variations indicates an increase in utility.

For the verification of this result we have to assume that our consumer's intertemporal utility function u is at least weakly separable with respect to his period–specific utility levels U_t because, otherwise, the instantaneous equivalent or compensating variations do not exist. In many empirical studies on intertemporal household behaviour the even stronger assumption of additivity in U_t is used since this simplifies the analysis without great (additional) loss of generality compared to the weakly separable case [for a discussion of possibilities to weaken the separability assumption see Browning (1991)]. If we define the consumer's instantaneous utility functions $u_t : \mathbb{R}_+^N \to \mathbb{R}$ by

$$U_t = u_t(x_t) \qquad (t = 1, 2, ..., T), \tag{5.8}$$

we can now express his lifetime utility function (5.4) in its separable form as

$$U = u(u_1(x_1), u_2(x_2), ..., u_T(x_T)) = u(\{u_t(x_t)\}) = u(\{U_t\}). \tag{5.9}$$

This makes it possible to identify the consumer's instantaneous expenditure functions

$$e_t(p_t, U_t) = \min_{x_t \in \mathcal{U}_t(U_t)} p_t x_t; \tag{5.10}$$

$$\mathcal{U}_t(U_t) = \{x_t | x_t \in \mathbb{R}_+^N, \quad u_t(x_t) \geq U_t, \quad u(\{U_t\}) \geq U\}.$$

As a consequence of the separability assumption the consumer's lifetime expenditure minimization problem (5.5) can be decomposed theoretically into two (fictitious) steps: In the first step the consumer chooses the instantaneous utility levels U_t that he wants to realize in the different periods $t = 1, 2, ..., T$ (and which produce his lifetime utility level U); in the second step he chooses the period–specific consumption bundles x_t which generate the instantaneous utility levels U_t at minimal costs according to (5.10).

We can now define the instantaneous equivalent variations as

$$EV_t^{0k} = e_t(p_t^0, U_t^k) - e_t(p_t^0, U_t^0) \qquad (t = 1, 2, ..., T), \tag{5.11}$$

and the instantaneous compensating variations as

$$CV_t^{0k} = e_t(p_t^k, U_t^k) - e_t(p_t^k, U_t^0) \qquad (t = 1, 2, ..., T), \tag{5.12}$$

where p_t^k are the period–specific price vectors if the kth project is realised and p_t^0 are the period–specific price vectors without this project. The consistency between the lifetime measures (5.6) and (5.7) on the one hand and the period–specific variation measures (5.11) and (5.12) on the other is secured by the fact (following from definition (5.10)) that the period–specific utility levels U_t^0 and U_t^k in (5.11) and (5.12) generate for $t = 1, 2, ..., T$ at least the lifetime utility levels U^0 and U^k, respectively, which are presumed in the overall measures (5.6) and (5.7). I.e.,

$$u\left(\{U_t^0\}\right) = u\left(\{u_t(x_t^0)\}\right) \geq U^0 \quad \text{and} \quad u\left(\{U_t^k\}\right) = u\left(\{u_t(x_t^k)\}\right) \geq U^k. \tag{5.13}$$

Now we want to prove that

$$\text{(a)} \quad \sum_{t=1}^{T} EV_t^{0k} \geq EV^{0k} \qquad \text{and} \qquad \text{(b)} \quad \sum_{t=1}^{T} CV_t^{0k} \geq CV^{0k}. \qquad (5.14)$$

The period–specific utility levels $\{U_t^0\}$ are—by definition—optimally chosen with respect to prices p^0 and lifetime income I^0. The same is true for the choice of $\{U_t^k\}$ for the situation when the kth project is realised and the consumer is faced with prices p^k and lifetime income I_k. This implies that

$$\text{(a)} \quad \sum_{t=1}^{T} e_t(p_t^0, U^0) = I^0 \qquad \text{and} \qquad \text{(b)} \quad \sum_{t=1}^{T} e_t(p_t^k, U^k) = I^k. \qquad (5.15)$$

Comparing (5.6) with (5.11) and (5.7) with (5.12) it follows from (5.15) that (5.14) holds if and only if

$$\text{(a)} \quad \sum_{t=1}^{T} e_t(p_t^0, U^k) \geq e(p^0, U^k) \qquad \text{and} \qquad \text{(b)} \quad \sum_{t=1}^{T} e_t(p_t^k, U^0) \geq e(p^k, U^0).$$
$$(5.16)$$

From (5.5) we obtain the values $e(p^0, U^k)$ and $e(p^k, U^0)$ of the lifetime expenditure function as

$$e(p^0, U^k) \equiv \min_{x \in \mathcal{U}(U^k)} p^0 \cdot x, \quad \mathcal{U}(U^k) = \{x | x \in \mathbb{R}_+^{N \cdot T}, \quad u(x) \geq U^k\}; \qquad (5.17)$$

$$e(p^k, U^0) \equiv \min_{x \in \mathcal{U}(U^0)} p^k \cdot x, \quad \mathcal{U}(U^0) = \{x | x \in \mathbb{R}_+^{N \cdot T}, \quad u(x) \geq U^k\}. \qquad (5.18)$$

The values of the respective instantaneous expenditure functions $e(p_t^0, U_t^k)$ and $e(p_t^k, U_t^0)$ result from (5.10) and (5.13):

$$e(p_t^0, U_t^k) = \min_{x_t \in \mathcal{U}_t(U_t^k)} p_t^0 \cdot x_t; \qquad (5.19)$$

$$\mathcal{U}_t(U_t^k) = \{x_t | x_t \in \mathbb{R}_+^N; \ u_t(x_t) \geq U_t^k, \ u(\{U_t^k\}) \geq U^k\};$$

$$e(p_t^k, U_t^0) = \min_{x_t \in \mathcal{U}_t(U_t^0)} p_t^k \cdot x_t; \qquad (5.20)$$

$$\mathcal{U}_t(U_t^0) = \{x_t | x_t \in \mathbb{R}_+^N, \ u_t(x_t) \geq U_t^0, \ u(\{U_t^0\}) \geq U^0\}.$$

Comparing (5.17) with (5.19) and (5.18) with (5.20) we find that

$$\bigcup_{t=1}^{T} \mathcal{U}_t(U_t^k) \subseteq \mathcal{U}(U^k) \qquad \text{and} \qquad \bigcup_{t=1}^{T} \mathcal{U}_t(U_t^0) \subseteq \mathcal{U}(U^0), \qquad (5.21)$$

i.e., the union of the instantaneous constraint sets $\mathcal{U}_t(U_t^k)$ is a subset of the overall constraint set $\mathcal{U}(U^k)$, and the union of the sets $\mathcal{U}_t(U_t^0)$ is a subset of $\mathcal{U}(U^0)$. This is a consequence of the fact that for the successive solution of the instantaneous expenditure minimization problems (5.19) and (5.20) not only the respective lifetime utility levels U^k or U^0 are given as for the overall minimization problems (5.17) and (5.18), but also the choice of the period–specific utility levels $\{U_t^k\}$ or $\{U_t^0\}$ is fixed. This means the imposition of additional constraints with respect to the (sequential) solution of the instantaneous cost–minimization problems (5.19) and (5.20) so that (5.21) must hold. Therefore, the result of the sequential cost–minimization problems (5.19) cannot be better than the result of the less restricted overall cost minimization problem (5.17) and the results of (5.20) cannot be better than the result of (5.18) so that (5.16) must hold. This proves our proposition (5.14).

The essential relations for this proof are the inequalities (5.16). The economic explanation e.g. for (5.16a) is that although the imposed period–specific utility levels $\{U_t^k\}$ are by definition optimal for the realisation of lifetime utility U^k if the present-value prices are p^k, they are not necessarily optimal if prices p^0 prevail. On the contrary, if the consumer is faced with prices p^0 he is likely to rearrange his choice of instantaneous utility levels U_t though his overall utility level U^k must remain unchanged. Therefore, the fact that the sums of the instantaneous Hicksian variation measures differ from their overall pendants is due to the possibility of intertemporal substitution with respect to consumption and—equivalently—with respect to utility. Keen (1990) shows how the difference between the sum of the instantaneous compensating variations on the one hand and the lifetime compensating variation on the other can be computed empirically. In the context of ordinal utility theory, however, this information is irrelevant since only the signs of ordinal welfare measures matter while their exact values are of no importance at all. Or, as Keen (1990, p. 54) himself states: "... the desirability of a reform depends only on the sign of CV, since it is this that indicates whether or not lifetime utility is increased."

From (5.14) it follows that the sums of the period–specific Hicksian variation measures can be interpreted as one–sided welfare measures only, where a negative sum of the instantaneous equivalent variations indicates a (true) decrease in utility, while a positive sum of the instantaneous compensating variations indicates an increase in utility:

$$\text{(a)} \quad \sum_{t=1}^T EV_t^{0k} \le 0 \quad \Longrightarrow \quad U^k \le U^0; \tag{5.22}$$
$$\text{(b)} \quad \sum_{t=1}^T CV_t^{0k} \ge 0 \quad \Longrightarrow \quad U^k \ge U^0.$$

Since only the lifetime Hicksian variation measures EV^k and CV^k are "true" welfare measures, no welfare theoretical conclusions can be drawn from a positive sum of the instantaneous equivalent variations or from a negative sum of the instantaneous compensating variations.

The analysis of this section shows that if we want to assess the lifetime welfare effects of a government project by a true welfare measure in the sense of our indicator criterion (2.1) we have to employ the overall Hicksian equivalent or compensating variation. To avoid severe empirical difficulties it is often more advantageous to compute the instantaneous Hicksian variation measures for all single periods of the consumer's life and then add them up. In this case we can use the period–specific demand functions for our empirical work instead of the lifetime demand functions. The instantaneous demand functions are much easier to estimate econometrically than the lifetime demand functions because under our assumption of separable preferences the demand function for one period is independent of all data concerning any other period, which simplifies their mathematical structure considerably. However, as has been shown in this section, this empirical advantage of the sums of the instantaneous Hicksian variation measures is partly invalidated by their theoretical weakness which makes them one–sided welfare indicators only. Nevertheless, for applied work in the context of intertemporal studies there seems to be no realistic alternative to the use of instantaneous variation measures. This, of course, should be no problem as long as they are interpreted correctly according to (5.22).

6   Further Topics

This section deals with three special topics of welfare measurement each of which would deserve to be treated in a whole paper for itself. These topics are in turn the welfare effects of public goods, welfare measurement under uncertainty and the aggregation of individual welfare measures. Of course, within the framework of this article we cannot offer much more than a brief sketch of these problems.

6.1   Public Goods

A typical field of application for welfare measures is the supply of social goods by the government. The characteristic properties of social goods like national defence, environmental quality or natural amenities are nonrivalry in consumption and nonexcludability. Nonrivalry means that "each individual's consumption of such a good leads to no subtraction from any other individual's consumption of that good" [Samuelson (1954, p. 387)]. This implies that several people can consume the same unit of a social good at the same time without disturbing each other. The nonexcludability property refers to the fact that it is impossible or at least extremely expensive to exclude individual households from the consumption of a good. Because of the nonexcludability and nonrivalry of social goods it would be difficult and inefficient to charge a price for the consumption of these goods, so that a private supply of social goods is always disadvantageous. Therefore, social goods are supplied free of charge as "public goods" by the government in most countries today.

If we want to consider public goods within the framework of our household model we have to define a vector $z \in \mathbb{R}_+^L$ which describes the quantities z_l ($l = 1, 2, \ldots, L$) of these goods. The variables z_l do not appear in the consumer's budget constraint, since we assume that the public goods are supplied free of charge by the government.[20] To avoid excessive notation we retain our previously used symbols for the utility and expenditure functions $u(\cdot)$, $v(\cdot)$ and $e(\cdot)$, though these functions now depend on L more arguments than in our basic model. The same is true for the Marshallian and Hicksian demand functions $x(\cdot)$ and $\xi(\cdot)$. The consumer maximises his direct utility function $u : \mathbb{R}_+^{N+L} \to \mathbb{R}$ with respect to the quantities x of the private goods to obtain his indirect utility function $v : \mathbb{R}_+^{N+L+1} \to \mathbb{R}$:

$$v(p, z, I) \equiv \max_{x \in \mathcal{X}(p,I)} u(x, z), \tag{6.1}$$

$$\mathcal{X}(p, I) = \{x | x \in \mathbb{R}_+^N, px \leq I, p \in \mathbb{R}_{++}^N, I \in \mathbb{R}_{++}\}.$$

The optimal private consumption vector x^* and the marginal utility of income λ^* are now functions of the private good prices p, of income I and of the quantities z of the public goods:

$$x^* = x(p, z, I), \tag{6.2}$$

$$\lambda^* = \lambda(p, z, I). \tag{6.3}$$

Substitution of the optimal private consumption vector x^* in (6.1) yields

$$v(p, z, I) \equiv u(x(p, z, I), z). \tag{6.4}$$

From the differentiation of the adding–up condition

$$p \cdot x(p, z, I) \equiv I \tag{6.5}$$

with respect to the quantity z_l of a public good we get

$$\sum_{n=1}^{N} p_n \frac{\partial x_n}{\partial z_l} \equiv 0 \qquad (l = 1, 2, \ldots, L). \tag{6.6}$$

---

[20]This does, of course, not mean that the consumer does not have to pay indirectly in one way or the other for the supply of public goods (e.g. by commodity taxes which raise p or by an income tax which lowers I). But since this is a partial model there is no direct connection between his consumption of public goods on the one hand and his tax payments on the other.

Differentiating identity (6.4) with respect to z and considering (6.6) we find that the partial derivatives of the direct and the indirect utility function with respect to the public good quantities z are identical:

$$\nabla_z v(p, z, I) = \nabla_z u(x(p, z, I), z). \tag{6.7}$$

This identity says that $\nabla_z v(p, z, I)$ is the vector of the marginal utilities of the public goods in the household equilibrium characterized by the consumption vector $[x(p, z, I), z]$.

The expenditure function $e : \mathbb{R}_+^{N+L+1} \to \mathbb{R}$ is defined in strict analogy to the pure private good case as

$$e(p, z, U) \equiv \min_{x \in \mathcal{U}(z, U)} px, \qquad \mathcal{U}(z, U) = \{x | x \in \mathbb{R}_+^N, u(x, z) \geq U\}. \tag{6.8}$$

The expenditure minimizing private consumption vector x^* is now a function of p, z and U, i.e.

$$x^* = \xi(p, z, U), \tag{6.9}$$

where $\xi(p, z, U)$ is the vector of the Hicksian demand functions in the presence of public goods. Substitution in (6.8) yields

$$e(p, z, U) \equiv p \cdot \xi(p, z, U). \tag{6.10}$$

The utility maximization problem (6.1) and the expenditure minimization problem (6-8) are mirrored optimization problems so that the identities

$$e(p, z, v(p, z, I)) \equiv I \quad \text{and} \quad v(p, z, e(p, z, U)) \equiv U \tag{6.11}$$

hold. Differentiating (6.11) with respect to the private good prices and observing Roy's identity leads us to this slightly modified version of Shephard's Lemma:

$$\nabla_p e(p, z, U) \equiv \xi(p, z, U). \tag{6.12}$$

If we differentiate (6.11) with respect to the public good quantities we obtain

$$\nabla_z e(p, z, U) \equiv -\frac{\nabla_z v(p, z, e(p, z, U))}{\lambda(p, z, e(p, z, U))}. \tag{6.13}$$

The numerator of this fraction is the vector of marginal utilities of the public goods according to (6.7) while the denominator is the marginal utility of income. The division of $\nabla_z v(p, z, e(p, z, U))$ by λ transforms the marginal utilities of the public goods into monetary terms, so that $\nabla_z e(p, z, U)$ can be interpreted as the vector of the income compensated shadow price functions of the public goods which we denote by $\rho(p, z, U)$. Version (6.13) of Shephard's Lemma, therefore, tells us that the partial derivatives of the expenditure function with respect to the quantities of the public goods are identical with the negative of the (income compensated) shadow price functions of these goods:

$$\nabla_z e(p, z, U) \equiv -\rho(p, z, U). \tag{6.14}$$

If we want to measure the welfare effects of a government program k we have to take into account that at least potentially all of the parameters p, z and I might change from $[p^0, z^0, I_0]$ to $[p^k, z^k, I_k]$. The most obvious approach to the measurement of the resulting change of welfare would be to calculate the difference $\Delta u_{0k} = v(p^k, z^k, I_k) - v(p^0, z^0, I_0)$. This approach leads us to the Marshallian measure

$$\Delta u_{0k} = \int_{p^0, z^0, I_0}^{p^k, z^k, I_k} \lambda(p, z, I) \cdot [-x(p, z, I)dp + dI + \rho(p, z, v(p, z, I))dz], \tag{6.15}$$

if we consider (6.13), (6.14) and Roy's Identity. The problem here is the same as in the private good case: the marginal–utility–of–income function $\lambda(p, z, I)$ is neither observable nor is it constant with respect to all integration variables (so it cannot be eliminated from the integral). Therefore, the Marshallian measure is not a suitable measure for the assessment of the welfare effects of public goods.

As an alternative we can turn to the Hicksian equivalent variation $e(p^0, z^0, U_k) - e(p^0, z^0, U_0)$ which equals $e(p^0, z^0, U_k) - e(p^k, z^k, U_k) + I_k - I_0$, so that the Second Fundamental Theorem of Integral Calculus together with (6.14) yields the equivalent variation as

$$\begin{aligned} EV_{0k} &= e(p^0, z^0, U_k) - e(p^0, z^0, U_0) \tag{6.16} \\ &= \int_{p^0, z^0}^{p^k, z^k} [-\xi(p, z, U_k)dp + \rho(p, z, U_k)dz] + I_k - I_0. \end{aligned}$$

If we want to compute this expression we can make use of the fact that under our assumptions the expenditure function is twice continuously differentiable so that the integral in (6.16) is path–independent. Choosing an appropriate path of integration we obtain

$$EV_{0k} = \int_{z^0}^{z^k} \rho(p^0, z, U_k)dz - \int_{p^0}^{p^k} \xi(p, z^k, U_k)dp + I_k - I_0. \tag{6.17}$$

The second integral of (6.17) can be calculated by using Vartia's algorithm if the Marshallian demand functions $x(p, z, I)$ according to (6.2) are known. For the computation of the first integral we need the consumer's (compensated) shadow price functions. These functions are, of course, not known in general. In applied cost–benefit analysis one often treats the shadow price functions $\rho(p, z, U)$ as constants so that the equivalent variation (for unchanged private prices $p^k = p^0$) becomes

$$EV_{0k} = \rho \cdot [z^k - z^0] \tag{6.18}$$

where ρ is a vector of constants. In this case the problem of computing the equivalent variation reduces to the determination of the shadow prices for the public goods at a given household equilibrium. There exists an enormous body of literature with proposals on how to solve this problem, and it would be impossible to review even only a small fraction of it within the framework of this article. Therefore, we shall content ourselves with some short remarks on the main ideas which are presented in this discussion.

The crucial problem of public goods is that they are not traded in free markets so that no ordinary demand functions can be estimated. This means that a consumer's preferences for a certain public good cannot be deduced from his observed market behaviour as in the case of a private good. Therefore, alternative and — in most cases — less reliable techniques for the empirical computation of the equivalent (or compensating) variation have to be found. In principle, we can distinguish between direct and indirect methods of preference revelation. If direct methods are used the consumer is actively involved in the process of preference determination, while the indirect methods try to deduce his preferences for a public good from his market demand for private goods which are somehow related to the consumption of the public good in question.

The indirect methods assess a consumer's preferences for a public good by evaluating market data referring to private goods which are in whatever way related to the public good under consideration. Some of these methods try to infer a consumer's willingness to pay (WTP) for a public good from his expenditures for a private good that is a complement or a substitute for the public good in question. The expenditures for skiing equipment and skiing holidays, for example, can be used to assess a consumer's preferences for the creation of a new skiing area, or his expenditures and time spent on bathing trips can be interpreted as an indicator for his WTP for the preservation of a bathing lake. These are examples for the application of the travel cost method which has been very popular among welfare theorists since a long time. An example for the substitutability case would be the use of the consumer's expenditures for an alarm system or a private security service to estimate his WTP for an increase in the frequency of police controls in his living area. Comprehensive and easy-to-read treatments of these methods can be found e.g. in Freeman (1979, 1993), Pommerehne (1987) or Bockstael (1995).

Another indirect method which is very popular today is the hedonic price method (HPM), which goes back to H.S. Rosen's (1974) seminal article. This method is based on the idea that the total utility a consumer derives from a certain good is generated by the several characteristics of that good. The utility he derives, for example, from an apartment or house can, according to this method, be explained by the utility he derives from the living space, from his neighbourhood, from the view, the traffic noise (or absence of noise), the air quality and so on. Consequently, the price or rent he pays for that house can be decomposed into the prices he implicitly pays for the several characteristics of the house. These implicit prices reflect his WTP for these characteristics. The HPM tries to infer the consumer's WTP for special characteristics of non-homogeneous goods from the price differences between these goods. If there were two identical houses at different prices, one of which has an ocean view while the other has not, the HPM would conclude that the price difference equals the buyer's WTP for the ocean view. So the HPM is based on real markets (for houses, apartments etc.) and tries to derive from these markets the WTP for non-market goods like ocean view, air quality, environmental amenities etc. It creates fictive markets for these non-marketed characteristics and tries to derive "offer functions" of the suppliers and "bid functions" of the demanders of these characteristics. The HPM is especially often applied to assessing the WTP for environmental investments of the government. The problems arising in the context of HPM surveys are considerable: how do individuals perceive the changes in environmental quality to be evaluated? Are they at all aware of these changes? How can these changes be measured or scaled objectively (to derive the offer and bid functions)? In addition, the theoretical assumptions with respect to the consumer's preferences which have to be met for the derivation of the bid curves are highly questionable [cf. Palmquist (1991)]. Therefore, in spite of its actual popularity the HPM must be looked upon with considerable reserve [for a more detailed treatment of the HPM see e.g. Freeman III (1995)].

The most important disadvantage of the indirect methods of welfare measurement is that they depend on the existence of observable market transactions or utilisation activities of the households the preferences of which are to be assessed. Therefore, the indirect methods can measure only the use value of a public good, e.g. the utility a household derives from an active use of the respective good. As is well known now, there is a second kind of utility a household can typically derive from a public good and this utility is completely independent of any observable activity or market demand. The idea that the mere existence of a public good like a public park might generate utility or represent a value that is not "produced" by any household activity like swimming or hiking was already discussed by Weisbrod (1964) and Krutilla (1967). Such a park can be of value for a person even if he has never gone for a walk there because, for example, the existence of this park preserves for him the option to enjoy it any time he wants or because he is happy that his grandchildren might play there in the distant future. Such nonuse values of public goods like the existence value, the option value or the bequest value mentioned in our examples cannot be measured by the indirect methods of welfare measurement. Nor can they deal with public goods that do not yet exist because they are still at the planning stage. Since most public goods generate use and nonuse values at the same time, the use of the indirect methods of welfare measurement leads to a systematic underestimation of their true social value [for more detailed treatments of the relationship between use and nonuse values see e.g. Michell and Carson (1989, p. 67 ff.) or Shechter and Freeman (1994)]. The only methods of welfare measurement that comprise the use values of an environmental good as well as their nonuse values are the direct methods.

A characteristic property of the direct methods of preference assessment is that they rely on the construction of simulated or hypothetical markets for public goods, i.e. of markets that do not exist in reality. The most popular direct techniques today are subsumed under the category of the contingent valuation methods (CVM). These methods aim either at the consumer's willingness to pay (WTP) for the consumption of a public good or at his willingness to accept (WTA) compensation for not consuming it.

The structure of a CVM interview can be divided into three main steps. At the first step the public good to be valued by the respondent must be described to him. At the second step the market conditions must be explained and at the third step his willingness to pay for the good must be elicited. The main problem at the first step is that the CVM is often used for an *ex ante* assessment of the prospective benefits of a planned project. That means that the public good to be valued does not yet exist at the time when the interview takes place so that the respondents have to value a good they have never seen before. In a cost-benefit analysis for a planned project to reduce smog and improve visibility in a certain area, for example, respondents cannot test the prospective improvement in visibility before the interview to get an idea of how much this project will increase their utility. Therefore, an exact description of the planned project is of great importance for the success of a contingent valuation study. The use of photographs or photomontages, video films, detailed verbal descriptions, background information on potential consequences of the planned project for the health of residents and other means of instruction have become very important. If the respondent gets a wrong or inexact picture of the public good the resulting information bias may render the whole study worthless. It is also of great importance that the respondent interprets the interviewer's description of the situations to be valued in exactly the same way as the interviewer does.

Surveys on the evaluation of potential air quality improvements and other "intangible" public goods made the significance of this information bias evident [cf. Carson (1991, p. 147 ff.) or Graves (1991, p. 215 f.)].

At the second step the market design must be explained to the respondents. This implies mainly two different tasks. One concerns the determination of the conditions under which the project will be realised. The other refers to the relation between the WTP expressed by a respondent and the payment (he believes) he actually has to make if the project is realised. It is of great importance that the created market mechanism appears plausible to the respondents.

The last step consists of the elicitation of the households' WTP. The main problem in this context is that the constructed or contingent markets for public goods are completely different from the normal markets people are used to. In a supermarket the characteristics of the commodities are well known to the consumers and the commodity prices are fixed. The consumer typically has the choice either to buy a certain good at its fixed price or to leave it on the shelf. In contingent markets people have to "buy" commodities which they have no experience with. Since there does not exist a market for the public goods in reality the consumer has no idea of the range of prices that are realistic or "fair" for the goods in question. Therefore, the direct question method, where respondents are simply asked "What is the highest price you are willing to pay for that good?" leads to rather unreliable results. With this method it occurs rather frequently that respondents refuse to answer at all or choose their answer by chance, without even trying to produce a correct response, so that this method is very likely to end up with a great number of extreme, i.e. implausibly high or implausibly low responses.

More realistic results are expected from the "bidding game" method which was developed by Randall, Ives, and Eastman (1974). Here the interviewer starts with some amount of money and asks the respondent if he would be willing to pay this price for the public good in question. If the answer is "yes" he repeats his question with a higher amount. This procedure is repeated until the respondent answers with "no". The consumer's WTP is then supposed to equal the amount of money where he answered "yes" for the last time. If even the first question was answered with "no" the bidding game is played in the other direction, i.e. with decreasing amounts of money. The advantage of the bidding game method is that it can exclude extreme responses by a proper choice of the starting value. A severe disadvantage of this method is that the results are very likely to be biased by the choice of the starting point, which might influence the consumer's idea of what the "true" value of the public good is supposed to be.

This "starting point bias" does not occur if the payment card method is applied. Here respondents are given a card with a series of alternative payment amounts in ascending order starting at zero. Respondents are asked to mark their maximum WTP on that card. Of course, it cannot be ruled out that the range of payments printed on the payment card might influence the respondents' answers. Because of this "range bias" the payment card method is rejected by a number of economists [see e.g. Carson (1991, p. 141)].

No matter which of these open–ended elicitation methods we choose we always have the problem that respondents find themselves in a market situation with which they have no experience. Instead of being confronted with fixed commodity prices as they are used to they have to "choose" the prices of the public goods themselves in contingent markets. As an alternative to the open–ended elicitation methods Bishop and Heberlein (1979) proposed the dichotomous choice method that has become increasingly popular during the last years. Here every test subject is asked only one question. He is asked whether he would prefer to pay a certain amount of money for the public good in question or do without that good. This method, which is also known as the discrete response or referendum method, tries to simulate the standard consumer choice situation where a consumer is confronted with a fixed commodity price at which he can buy a certain good or leave it. Respondents are already familiar with this kind of take-it-or-leave-it situation from their everyday shopping experience. Therefore, the results of a dichotomous choice study are expected to be more accurate than those of one of the open-ended surveys. Since each person is asked only one take-it-or-leave-it question it is, of course, not (or only by chance) possible to assess each respondent's personal maximum WTP for the public good in question. Instead something like an aggregate WTP function is estimated from the WTP distribution that results from the percentage of respondents who are willing to pay the different amounts asked for in the hypothetical "referendum".

The dichotomous choice method does, of course, also have some disadvantages. Among other defects it has turned out that dichotomous choice studies lead to an overestimation of the true WTP because many people have a strong tendency of "yeah"–saying [see e.g. Hoevenagel (1994, pp. 206 ff.) or Brown et al. (1996)]. Another disadvantage of that method is that one needs larger samples than for open-ended studies to obtain reliable results. In spite of these problems most CVM studies today employ the dichotomous choice method.

Careful planning of the three steps described above—description of the public good, explanation of the contingent market mechanism, elicitation of the respondents' WTP—is essential for the success of a CVM study. It is also important to enclose a number of follow–up questions to ensure the respondents' understanding of the choice they have to make and the scenario they have to value. Most surveys contain additional questions to get some information on the socio–economic and educational background of the respondents.

Equally important as the three points treated above is the choice of the type of interview. The most appropriate but also most expensive type is the in–person interview performed at the respondent's home. The in–person interview has the advantage that the interviewer can explain in detail the characteristics of the public good and the market scenario. He can use visual aids as photographs or video films and, most important, the respondent can ask the interviewer if he does not understand any details. The interviewer can realise if he was misunderstood by the respondent and he can suit his style of expressing himself to the intellectual capacities of the respondent. He can also control the attention and concentration of the respondent and he can judge his seriousness.

Cheaper but less reliable is a telephone interview. Visual aids to elucidate the public project cannot be used here and the interviews must be much shorter than with the in–person type of interview because one cannot keep a respondent on the phone for a long time. Still cheaper is a mail survey. It has the advantage that such visual aids as photographs can be used here and that there is no time limit. On the other hand there is no personal contact between the interviewer and the test subjects so that respondents cannot ask for further particulars if they did not understand the explanations in the questionnaire. The cheapest and least reliable type of interview is the so-called mall-stop interview where people are randomly accosted in the street (or in a shopping mall). Since these interviews always have to be performed in great haste, their scientific significance is near zero.

From our preceding considerations it follows that a successful CVM survey should be performed as an in–person interview and that the elicitation method should be of the dichotomous choice type. This also conforms with the suggestions made by the NOAA panel for a meaningful use of the CVM for damage assessment after environmental accidents [for details cf. National Oceanic and Atmospheric Administration (1993) or Portney (1994, p. 9)].

The CVM has attracted a lot of criticism, especially after it had been officially recommended in the United States as a reliable valuation technique for damage assessment in the context of environmental accidents. One of the reasons for the harsh criticism the VCM had to face might be that it makes it possible now to also measure nonuse values of environmental goods in addition to the use values, which makes compensation more expensive for polluters. Many of the most important critical arguments against the CVM can be found in Hausman (1993). It would be hopeless to try to summarise the whole discussion about the CVM here. Already in 1994 Michael Hanemann counted more than 1,600 contributions with respect to the validity and reliability of the CVM [cf. Hanemann (1994, p. 21)]. The main points of criticism and the rejoinders of the advocates of the CVM can be found in Diamond and Hausman (1993, 1994) and in Hanemann (1994, 1995). For more detailed presentations of the different views of both sides see Mitchell and Carson (1989), Hausman (1993), Ahlheim (1995), Bateman and Turner (1995) or Bjornstad and Kahn (1996).

To sum up, we can say that the measurement of the welfare effects of public goods is far more problematic and far less straightforward than the assessment of the welfare effects of private goods. Since no real markets exist for these goods the consumer's WTP for public goods must be derived by auxiliary methods which are often very inexact and highly problematic from a theoretical point of view. Nevertheless, since public goods are, usually, paid for by the government out of the general budget an analysis of the resulting welfare effects must be viewed as a necessary and useful instrument of democratic budget control.

6.2   Uncertainty

Thus far we have assumed that prices, income and other possible parameters which determine the "state of the world" are known with certainty. Of course, this assumption is not always realistic. Especially if we have to evaluate long-run projects which influence these economic parameters for several years, it is often not certain *ex ante* which future values these parameters will assume.

To make things clearer let us assume that a consumer has a (cardinal) indirect utility function $v : \mathbb{R}_+^{N+2} \to \mathbb{R}$ which describes utility U as a function of prices p, income I and a random variable s which represents the "state of the world" (e.g. the weather), so that

$$U = v(p, I, s). \tag{6.19}$$

Let us further assume that two alternative sets of parameters, $[p^1, I^1, s^1]$ and $[p^2, I^2, s^2]$, are expected and that situation 1 will occur with probability $\Theta < 1$ while situation 2 will occur with probability $(1 - \Theta)$, so that the consumer's expected utility is

$$EU = \Theta \cdot v(p^1, I^1, s^1) + (1 - \Theta) \cdot v(p^2, I^2, s^2). \tag{6.20}$$

A government project $k \in \{1, 2, ..., K\}$ is assumed to change the consumer's expected utility from

$$EU_0 = \Theta \cdot v(p_0^1, I_0^1, s_0^1) + (1 - \Theta) \cdot v(p_0^2, I_0^2, s_0^2). \tag{6.21}$$

to

$$EU_k = \Theta \cdot v(p_k^1, I_k^1, s_k^1) + (1 - \Theta) \cdot v(p_k^2, I_k^2, s_k^2). \tag{6.22}$$

Graham (1981) uses in this context the example of a farmer whose income depends on whether the weather is wet ($[I^1, s^1]$) or dry ($[I^2, s^2]$). The pair of alternative incomes changes from I_0^1 and I_0^2 to I_k^1 and I_k^2 if a dam is built which serves for flood control in wet years and provides irrigation water in dry years. In the generalized case a government project may potentially influence not only income but also the other parameters, as is assumed in (6.21) and (6.22).

The early literature on welfare measurement under uncertainty proposed basically two alternative magnitudes as measures for the welfare effect of such a government project [cf. Bishop (1982)], viz. the expected surplus and the option price. Graham (1981) generalized these concepts and showed that there exists a willingness–to–pay locus with an infinity of alternative *state dependent* compensation payment vectors $[m^1, m^2]$ which all leave the consumers *ex ante* indifferent as to whether the project under consideration is implemented or not, so that

$$\Theta \cdot v(p_k^1, I_k^1 - m^1, s_k^1) + (1 - \Theta) \cdot v(p_k^2, I_k^2 - m^2, s_k^2) \qquad (6.23)$$
$$= \Theta \cdot v(p_0^1, I_0^1, s_0^1) + (1 - \Theta) \cdot v(p_0^2, I_0^2, s_0^2).$$

The traditional concepts of the option price and the expected consumer's surplus are special cases of Graham's general WTP concept. The option price of the government project is the *state independent* compensation payment that leaves the consumer indifferent with respect to the question if the project is realised or not. Therefore, the option price concept requires in addition to condition (6.23) that the compensation payment is the same for situation 1 and situation 2, i.e. $m^1 = m^2$. The option price OP of the project under consideration can, therefore, be defined implicitly by the condition

$$\Theta \cdot v(p_k^1, I_k^1 - OP, s_k^1) + (1 - \Theta) \cdot v(p_k^2, I_k^2 - OP, s_k^2) \qquad (6.24)$$
$$= \Theta \cdot v(p_0^1, I_0^1, s_0^1) + (1 - \Theta) \cdot v(p_0^2, I_0^2, s_0^2).$$

The expected surplus ES of this project is another special case of Graham's WTP concept. It introduces state dependent compensation payments m_{ES}^1 and m_{ES}^2 according to the conditions

$$v(p_k^1, I_k^1 - m_{ES}^1, s_k^1) = v(p_0^1, I_0^1, s_0^1) \quad \text{and} \quad v(p_k^2, I_k^2 - m_{ES}^2, s_k^2) = v(p_0^2, I_0^2, s_0^2), \qquad (6.25)$$

which imply that (6.23) is always fulfilled. These conditions require that the consumer is indifferent between the realisation or non–realisation of the project in each of the two possible situations. The expected surplus ES equals the weighted sum of the two state dependent payments m_{ES}^1 and m_{ES}^2 according to

$$ES = \Theta \cdot m_{ES}^1 + (1 - \Theta) \cdot m_{ES}^2. \qquad (6.26)$$

The difference between option price and expected surplus is known in the literature as the option value OV of the project:

$$OV = OP - ES. \tag{6.27}$$

It should be noted that the option value need not be positive in general, but can also be zero or negative. Graham (1981) analysed the relative appropriateness of the option price and the expected surplus for welfare measurement under uncertainty with respect to the applicability of the potential Pareto improvement tests for a many-consumer economy. He discovered that the answer to the question of which measure is best depends crucially on the risk distribution between the individuals. Graham's (1981) article started a still continuing debate on the "true" welfare measure for uncertain projects and initiated an enormous number of papers on this subject which tried to extend or generalise his results [see among many others e.g. Marshall (1989), Freeman (1991), Meier and Randall (1991), Chavas (1991), Graham (1992), Svento (1994) and Ready (1995)]. Besides these problems it should not be overlooked that the success of practical welfare measurement depends to a great extent on the question of whether it is possible to assess reasonable estimates for the hypothetical price and income parameters and for the respective probabilities. It should, further, be kept in mind that the price for explicitly including uncertainty in our welfare analysis is that we have to switch from ordinal to cardinal utility theory (because an ordinal indirect utility function $v(p, I, s)$ would render the concept of expected utility meaningless). Therefore, the decision whether or not to consider uncertainty in a concrete welfare analysis always also implies a trade-off between theoretical refinement and economic plausibility.

6.3   Aggregation

Up to now our analysis has focused on the measurement of individual welfare only. After the welfare effects caused by a certain government project are assessed for each individual, government has to decide if the project is to be implemented or not. The solution to this problem is straighforward if the requirements for the application of the Pareto criterion are met: the Pareto criterion holds that a new state of society is to be preferred (is Pareto–superior) to the initial state if no individual is worse off in the new state while at least one individual is better off. In this case the social decision process is not controversial. Unfortunately, projects to which the Pareto criterion can be applied are very few. Most projects generate winners as well as losers and a social decision procedure for such cases of ambiguous welfare changes has to be found.

From Arrow (1950 and 1963) we know that under ethically and economically acceptable conditions there does not exist a social preference ordering that leads to a uniquely determined and consistent ordering of social states. As a consequence of Arrow's non–existence or impossibility theorem, in principle, two ways of handling this problem have emerged: one group of welfare economists tries to define social welfare functions on the basis of weakened versions of Arrow's axioms [see e.g. Hammond (1976) and (1991) or Campbell (1992)], while another group prefers to work with modified versions of the Pareto criterion, instead.

The proposals for the construction of social welfare functions are manifold. All of these different types of welfare functions have in common that their domain includes the utility levels of all individuals (measured in utility or in monetary terms) as arguments and that they are monotonically increasing in these arguments. The definition of a social welfare function always implies interpersonal welfare comparisons since welfare weights are—explicitly or implicitly—attached to the individuals whenever a specific mathematical form is chosen for a welfare function. Therefore, the question is not how we can avoid interpersonal welfare comparisons but rather, what kinds of interpersonal comparisons we are willing to accept [cf. Hammond (1991, p. 1)]. Consequently, the preference for a special class of social welfare functions is—among other factors—determined by the analyst's own idea of distributional justice. Since personal ethics may differ widely it is not surprising that a vast body of literature has developed over the years and many debates about social justice have taken place.

Of course, it would be futile to try to review the literature on social welfare functions within the framework of this article. It should only be mentioned that recently a tendency has emerged to construct social welfare functions with the individual money–metric utility functions (cf. Section 3) as their domain. Roberts (1980) showed that the distributional pattern determined by social aggregator functions based on individual money–metric functions depends on the choice of the reference price vector at which they are computed. The reference–price dependence of money–metric social welfare measures has been the object of much research and of many publications since Roberts started the debate and it may still be reckoned among the relevant problems of welfare economics [see also Slesnick (1991, p. 129 ff.), Blackorby, Laisney and Schmachtenberg (1993) or Johansson (1994); for a more general criticism of money–metric utility based social welfare functions see Blackorby and Donaldson (1988)].

The second class of welfare prescriptions mentioned above does without the construction of welfare functions but relies instead on a weakened version of the Pareto criterion, the so–called potential Pareto improvement (PPI) criterion. The PPI criterion says that a situation k after the implementation of a government project is to be preferred to the initial situation 0 if the gainers of the project are—theoretically—able to compensate the losers so that the losers are not worse off than in the initial situation while at least one of the gainers is better off. In practice, where no compensations are paid, this leads to the Hicks–Kaldor compensation test [cf. Kaldor (1939)] where the individual equivalent or compensating variations are summed across all individuals and a project is declared to be favourable if the respective sum is positive. The problems arising in the context of these PPI tests are twofold. One class of problems is due to the fact that these tests are not always consistent but can lead to contradictory results under special circumstances, as was shown by Scitovsky (1941) and by Boadway (1974). The other class of problems arises from the ethical judgements implied by the tests. Since the compensations are not paid in actual fact, the PPI criterion implies interpersonal welfare comparisons, which are not permitted within the framework of ordinal utility theory. The simple mathematical device of summing up positive and negative individual Hicksian variations implies that every dollar of compensation is weighted equally ("a dollar is a dollar") no matter whether it serves for the compensation of a rich or a poor member of society. This, of course, contradicts not on only the spirit of ordinal utility theory (where only the signs and not the amounts of the Hicksian compensated or equivalent variations are considered) but also the ethical foundations of most modern societies. Therefore, the use of the PPI criterion is to be rejected for theoretical as well as for ethical reasons [see also Blackorby and Donaldson (1985) and (1990)].

Since neither the construction of social welfare functions nor the use of the PPI test is consistent with the spirit of ordinal utility theory the question arises of how a government decision with respect to the realisation or rejection of a given project should be assessed. Of course, this is a normative question that cannot be answered objectively. My favourite idea is that economists confine themselves to the computation of the individual welfare changes for all members affected by the project under consideration. A tableau with these individual welfare changes (where the corresponding socio-economic data or the corresponding frequency distributions could be added) should then be presented to the politician who has to decide if the project is implemented or rejected. This procedure, which is, in principle, also favoured by Hammond (1990, p. 17f.), leaves the politician with the responsibility for the distributional effects of the project. The politician has no possibility here to hide behind some complex mathematical formula of a social welfare function, but has to make his distributional judgements explicit, instead. In a democratic society the distributional decisions of the politicians should be made transparent for the public, in my view, and this can be accomplished only if the political and the scientific sphere are kept strictly separate from each other.

References

Afriat, S. N. (1978). *The Price Index.* Cambridge University Press, Cambridge.

Ahlheim, M. (1988). On the Economics of the Antonelli Equation. *European Journal of Political Economy*, 4:539–552.

Ahlheim, M. (1993). *Zur Theorie rationierter Haushalte, Ein Beitrag über die Berücksichtigung limitierter staatlicher Subventionsprogramme in der Haushaltstheorie.* Studies in Contemporary Economics. Physica Verlag, Heidelberg.

Ahlheim, M. (1994). On the Use of the Distance Function for Measuring Welfare in Regimes with Quantity Constraints and Public Goods. In Eichhorn, W., editor, *Models and Measurement of Welfare and Inequality*, pages 469–490. Springer Verlag, Heidelberg.

Ahlheim, M. (1995). Nutzen–Kosten–Analyse und kontingente Evaluierung bei der Bewertung von Umweltprojekten. *Staatswissenschaften und Staatspraxis*, 3:317–357.

Ahlheim, M. and Wagenhals, G. (1988). Exakte Wohlfahrtsmaße in der Nutzen–Kosten–Analyse. *Zeitschrift für Wirtschafts- und Sozialwissenschaften*, 108:169–193.

Allen, R. G. D. (1949). The Economic Theory of Index Numbers. *Economica*, 16:186–209.

Allen, R. G. D. (1975). *Index Numbers in Theory and Practice.* Macmillan, London.

Anderson, R. W. (1980). Some Theory of Inverse Demand for Applied Demand Analysis. *European Economic Review*, 14:281–290.

Apostol, T. M. (1969). *Calculus*, volume II. Wiley, New York, 2nd edition.

Apostol, T. M. (1974). *Mathematical Analysis.* Addison Wesley, Reading, Mass, 2nd edition.

Arrow, K. J. (1950). A Difficulty in the Concept of Social Welfare. *Journal of Political Economy*, 58:328–346.

Arrow, K. J. (1963). *Social Choice and Individual Values.* Wiley, New York, 2nd edition.

Auerbach, A. J. (1985). The Theory of Excess Burden and Optimal Taxation. In Auerbach, A. J. and Feldstein, M., editors, *Handbook of Public Economics*, volume I, pages 61–86. North Holland, Amsterdam.

Auerbach, A. J. and Rosen, H. S. (1980). Will the Real Excess Burden Please Stand Up? (or, Seven Measures in Search of a Concept). Discussion Paper 767, Harvard University, Cambridge, Mass.

Ballard, C., Shoven, B. J., and Whalley, J. (1985). General Equilibrium Computations of the Marginal Welfare Costs of Taxes in the United States. *American Economic Review*, 75:128–138.

Bateman, I. and Turner, R. (1995). Valuation of the Environment, Methods and Techniques: The Contingent Valuation Method. In Turner, K., editor, *Sustainable Environmental Economics and Management: Principles and Praxis*, pages 120–191. John Wiley and Sons, Chichester.

Baye, M. R. and Black, D. A. (1986). *Consumer Behaviour, Cost of Living Measures, and the Income Tax*. Springer Verlag, Berlin.

Bergson, A. (1975). A Note on Consumer's Surplus. *Journal of Economic Literature*, 13:38–44.

Bishop, R. C. (1982). Option value: An Exposition and Extension. *Land Economics*, 58:1–15.

Bishop, R. C. and Heberlein, T. A. (1979). Measuring Values of Extra-Market Goods: Are Indirect Measures Biased? *American Journal of Agricultural Economics*, 61, 926–930.

Bjornstad, D. and Kahn, J., editors (1996). *The Contingent Valuation of Environmental Resources: Methodological Issues and Research Needs*. Edward Elgar, Cheltenham, UK.

Blackorby, C. and Donaldson, D. (1985). Consumers' Surpluses and Consistent Cost–Benefit Tests. *Social Choice and Welfare*, 1:251–262.

Blackorby, C. and Donaldson, D. (1988). Money Metric Utility: A Harmless Normalisation? *Journal of Economic Theory*, 46:120–129.

Blackorby, C. and Donaldson, D. (1990). A Review Article: The Case Against the Use of the Sum of Compensating Variations in Cost–Benefit Analysis. *Canadian Journal of Economics*, 23:471–494.

Blackorby, C., Donaldson, D., and Moloney, D. (1984). Consumer's Surplus and Welfare Change in a Simple Dynamic Model. *Review of Economic Studies*, pages 171–176.

Blackorby, C., Laisney, F., and Schmachtenberg, R. (1993). Reference–Price–Independent Welfare Prescriptions. *Journal of Public Economics*, 50:63–76.

Blackorby, C., Primont, D., and Russell, R. R. (1978). *Duality, Separability, and Functional Structure: Theory and Economic Applications*. North Holland, New York.

Blackorby, C. and Shorrocks, A. F. (1995). *Separability and Aggregation: Collected Works of W. M. Gorman*, volume 1. Clarendon Press, Oxford.

Blundell, R. (1988). Consumer Behaviour: Theory and Empirical Evidence — A Survey. *Economic Journal*, 98:16–65.

Boadway, R. W. (1974). The Welfare Foundations of Cost–Benefit Analysis. *Economic Journal*, 84:926–939.

Boadway, R. W. and Bruce, N. (1984). *Welfare Economics*. Basil Blackwell, Oxford.

Bockstael, N. E. (1995). Travel Cost Models. In Bromley, D. W., editor, *Handbook of Environmental Economics*, pages 655–671. Blackwell, Oxford.

Bohm, P. (1972). Estimating Demand for Public Goods. *European Economic Review*, 3:111–130.

Bohm, P. (1979). Estimating Willingness to Pay: Why and How? *Scandinavian Journal of Economics*, 81:142–153.

Bohm, P. (1984). Revealing Demand for an Actual Public Good. *Journal of Public Economics*, 24:131–151.

Bowen, H. R. (1948). *Toward Social Economy*. Rinehart & Co., New York.

Breslaw, J. A. and Smith, J. B. (1995a). A Simple and Efficient Method for Estimating the Magnitude and Precision of Welfare Changes. *Journal of Applied Econometrics*, 10:313–327.

Breslaw, J. A. and Smith, J. B. (1995b). Measuring Welfare Changes when Quantity is Constrained. *Journal of Business & Economic Statistics*, 13:95–103.

Brown, T. C., Champ, P. A., Bishop, R. C., and McCollum, D. W. (1996). Which Response Format Reveals the Truth about Donations to a Public Good? *Land Economics*, 72:152–166.

Browning, M. (1991). A Simple Nonadditive Preference Structure for Models of Household Behavior Over Time. *Journal of Political Economy*, 99:607–637.

Brubaker, E. R. (1984). Demand Disclosures and Conditions on Exclusion: An Experiment. *Economic Journal*, 94:536–553.

Campbell, D. E. (1992). Implementation of Social Welfare Functions. *International Economic Review*, 33:525–533.

Carson, R. T. (1991). Constructed Markets. In Braden, J. B. and Kolstad, C. D., editors, *Measuring the Demand for Environmental Quality*, pages 120–162. North Holland, Amsterdam.

Chavas, J. P. (1991). On Welfare Analysis Under Temporal Uncertainty. *Land Economics*, 67:37–48.

Chipman, J. S. and Moore, J. C. (1980). Compensating Variation, Consumer's Surplus, and Welfare. *American Economic Review*, 70: 933–949.

Clarke, E. H. (1971). Multipart Pricing of Public Goods. *Public Choice*, 11:17–33.

Clarkson, K. W. (1976/77). Welfare Benefits of the Food Stamp Program. *Southern Economic Journal*, 43:864–878.

Cornes, R. (1992). *Duality and Modern Economics*. Cambridge University Press Cambridge.

Cornes, R. and Albon, R. (1981). Evaluation of Welfare Change in Quantity-Constrained Regimes. *The European Record*, 57:186–190.

Cronin, F. J. (1983). The Efficiency of Demand–Oriented Housing Programs. *Journal of Human Resources*, 18:100–125.

De Borger, B. (1986). The Relation Between Alternative Benefit Measures for Quantity Cnstrained Pice Subsidies. *European Economic Review*, 30:893–907.

De Borger, B. (1989). Estimating the Welfare Implications of In–Kind Government Programs, A General Numerical Approach. *Journal of Public Economics*, 38:215–226.

Deaton, A. (1979). The Distance Function in Consumer Behaviour with Applications to Index numbers and Optimal Taxation. *Review of Economic Studies*, 46:391–405.

Deaton, A. (1980). The Measurement of Welfare: Theory and Practical Guidelines. LSMS Working Paper 7, World Bank Development Research Center, Washington.

Deaton, A. (1981). Theoretical and Empirical Approaches to Consumer Demand Under Rtioning. In Deaton, A., editor, *Essays in the Teory and Measurement of Consumer Behaviour*, pages 55–72. Cambridge University Press, Cambridge.

Deaton, A. and Muellbauer, J. (1980). *Economics and Consumer Behavior*. Cambridge University Press, Cambridge.

Debreu, G. (1951). The Coefficient of Resource Utilization. *Econometrica*, 19:273–292.

Debreu, G. (1954). A Classical Tax–Subsidy Problem. *Econometrica*, 22:14–22.

Debreu, G. (1972). Smooth Preferences. *Econometrica*, 40:603–615.

Diamond, P. and McFadden, D. (1974). Some Uses of the Expenditure Function in Public Finance. *Journal of Public Economics*, 3:3–21.

Diamond, P. A. and Hausman, J. A. (1993). On Contingent Valuation Measurement of Nonuse Values. In Hausman, J. A., editor, *Contingent Valuation: A Critical Assessment*, pages 3–38. Elsevier, Amsterdam.

Diamond, P. A. and Hausman, J. A. (1994). Contingent valuation: Is Some Number Better Than No Number? *Journal of Economic Perspectives*, 8:45–64.

Diewert, W. E. (1976). Exact and Superlative Index Numbers. *Journal of Econometrics*, 4:115–145.

Diewert, W. E. (1981). The Economic Theory of Index Numbers: A Survey. In Deaton, A., editor, *Essays in the Theory and Measurement of Consumer Behaviour*, pages 163–208. Cambridge University Press, Cambridge.

Diewert, W. E. (1982). Duality Approaches to Microeconomic Theory. In Arrow, K. J. and Intriligator, M. D., editors, *Handbook of Mathematical Economics*, volume II, pages 535–599. North Holland, Amsterdam.

Diewert, W. E. (1990). The Theory of the Cost–of–Living Index and the Measurement of Welfare Change. In Diewert, W. E., editor, *Price Level Measurement*, pages 79–147. North Holland, Amsterdam.

Dooley, P. C. (1983). Consumer's Surplus: Marshall and His Critics. *Canadian Journal of Economics*, 16:26–38.

Dupuit, J. (1844). De la mésure de l'utilité des travaux publics. *Annales des ponts et chaussées*, 8:332–375. translated in Arrow, K. J. and T. Scitovsky, eds. (1969): 'On the Measurement of the Utility of Public Works', A. E. A. Readings in Welfare Economics, pages 255–283. Irwin, Homewood (Ill.).

Ebert, U. (1987a). Axiomatic Foundations of Hicksian Measures of Welfare Change. *Journal of Public Economics*, 33:115–124.

Ebert, U. (1987b). *Beiträge zur Wohlfahrtsökonomie, Effizienz und Verteilung.* Springer Verlag, Berlin.

Edgeworth, F. Y. (1896). A Defense of Index Numbers. *The Economic Journal,* 6:132–142.

Eichhorn, W. (1978). What is an Economic Index? An Attempt of an Answer. In Eichhorn, W., Henn, R., Opitz, O., and Shephard, R. W., editors, *Theory and Applications of Economic Indices*, pages 3–42. Physica Verlag, Würzburg.

Eichhorn, W. and Voeller, J. (1976). *Theory of the Price Index. Fisher's Test Approach and Generalizations.* Springer Verlag, Berlin.

Eichhorn, W. and Voeller, J. (1990). Axiomatic Foundation of Price Indexes and Purchasing Power Parities. In Diewert, W. E., editor, *Price Level Measurement*, pages 321–356. North Holland, Amsterdam.

Field, C. A. (1976). A Note on Shephard's Duality Theorem. *Journal of Economic Theory*, 12:494–495.

Fisher, F. M. and Shell, K. (1972). *The Economic Theory of Price Indices.* Academic Press, New York.

Fisher, I. (1927). *The Making of Index Numbers, A Study of Their Varieties, Tests, and Reliability, 3rd edition.* Houghton Mifflin, Boston. reprinted in 1967.

Fleetwood, W. (1707). *Chronicon Preciosum.* A. M. Kelley, London.

Freeman, III. A. M. (1991). Welfare Measurement and the Benefit–Cost Analysis of Projects Affecting Risks. *Southern Economic Journal*, 58:65–76.

Freeman, III. A. M. (1993). *The Measurement of Environmental and Resource Values. Theory and Methods.* Resources for the Future, Washington D.C.

Freeman, III, A. M. (1979). *The Benefits of Environmental Improvement, Theory and Practice.* Johns Hopkins University Press, Baltimore.

Freeman, III, A. M. (1995). Hedonic Pricing Methods. In Bromley, D. W., editor, *Handbook of Environmental Economics*, pages 672–686. Blackwell, Oxford.

Frisch, R. (1936). Annual Survey of General Economic Theory: The Problem of Index Numbers. *Econometrica*, 4:1–39.

Funke, H., Hacker, G., and Voeller, J. (1979). Fisher's Circular Test Reconsidered. *Schweizerische Zeitschrift für Volkswirtschaft und Statistik*, 115:677–688.

Genser, B. (1984). Zur Messung der Wohlfahrtseffekte der Steuerpolitik. In Bös, D., Rose, M., and Seidl, C., editors, *Beiträge zur neueren Steuertheorie*, pages 116–138. Springer Verlag, Berlin.

Genser, B. (1988). Measuring the Burden of Taxation: An Index Number Approach. In Eichhorn, W., editor, *Measurement in Economics, Theory and*

Applications of Economic Indices, pages 499–518. Springer Verlag, Heidelberg.

Graham, D. A. (1981). Cost–Benefit Analysis Under Uncertainty. *American Economic Review*, 71:715–725.

Graham, D. A. (1992). Public Expenditure Under Uncertainty: The Net–Benefit Criteria. *American Economic Review*, 82:822–846.

Graves, P. E. (1991). Aesthetics. In Braden, J. B. and Kolstad, C. D., editors, *Measuring the Demand for Environmental Quality*, pages 213–226. North Holland, Amsterdam.

Groves, T. (1973). Incentives in Teams. *Econometrica*, 41:617–631.

Hammond, P. J. (1976). Equity, Arrow's Conditions, and Rawls' Difference Principle. *Econometrica*, 44:793–804.

Hammond, P. J. (1990). Theoretical Progress in Public Economics: A Provocative Assessment. *Oxford Economic Papers*, 42:6–33.

Hammond, P. J. (1991). Independence of Irrelevant Interpersonal Comparisons. *Social Choice and Welfare*, 8:1–19.

Hanemann, W. M. (1994). Valuing the Environment Through Contingent Valuation. *Journal of Economic Perspectives*, 8:19–43.

Hanemann, W. M. (1995). Contingent Valuation and Economics. In Willis, K. G. and Corkindale, J. T., editors, *Environmental Valuation — New Perspectives*, pages 79–117. CAB International, Wallingford.

Hanoch, G. (1978). Symmetric Duality and Polar Production Functions. In Fuss, M. and McFadden, D., editors, *Production Economics: A Dual Approach to Theory and Applications*, volume 1, pages 111–131. North Holland, Amsterdam.

Hause, J. C. (1975). The Theory of Welfare Cost Measurement. *Journal of Political Economy*, 83:1145–1182.

Hausman, J. A. (1981). Exact Consumer's Surplus and Deadweight Loss. *American Economic Review*, 71:662–676.

Hausman, J. A. (1993). *Contingent Valuation: A Critical Assessment*. North Holland, Amsterdam.

Hicks, J. R. (1939). *Value and Capital*. Oxford University Press, London.

Hicks, J. R. (1941). The Rehabilitation of Consumer's Surplus. *Review of Economic Studies*, 8:108–116.

Hicks, J. R. (1942). Consumer's Surplus and Index Numbers. *Review of Economic Studies*, 9:126–137.

Hicks, J. R. (1943). The Four Consumer's Surpluses. *Review of Economic Studies*, 11:31–41.

Hicks, J. R. (1946). The Generalized Theory of Consumer's Surpluses. *Review of Economic Studies*, 15:27–33.

Hicks, J. R. (1956). *A Revision of Demand Theory.* Oxford University Press, Oxford.

Hoevenagel, R. (1994). An Assessement of the Contingent Valuation Method. In Pethig, R., editor, *Valuing the Environment: Methodological and Research Issues*, pages 195–227. Kluwer Academic Publishers, Dordrecht.

Hotelling, H. (1935). Demand Functions with Limited Budgets. *Econometrica*, 3:66–78.

Hotelling, H. (1938). The General Welfare in Relation to Problems of Taxation and of Railway and Utility Rates. *Econometrica*, 6:269–272.

Howard, D. H. (1977). Rationing, Quantity Constraints, and Consumption Theory. *Econometrica*, 45:399–412.

Hurwicz, L. and Uzawa, H. (1971). On the Integrability of Demand Functions. In Chipman, J. S., Hurwicz, L., Richter, M. K., and Sonnenschein, H. F., editors, *Preferences, Utility and Demand*, pages 114–148. Harcourt Brace Jovanovich, New York.

Jackson, W. A. (1991). Generalized Rationing Theory. *Scottish Journal of Political Economy*, 38:335–342.

Jacobsen, S. E. (1972). On Shephard's Duality Theorem. *Journal of Economic Theory*, 4:458–464.

Jehle, G. A. (1991). *Advanced Microeconomic Theory.* Prentice Hall, Englewood Cliffs.

Johansson, P.-O. (1987). *The Economic Theory and Measurement of Environmental Benefits.* Cambridge University Press, Cambridge.

Johansson, P.-O. (1994). Valuation and Aggregation. In Pethig, R., editor, *Valuing the Environment: Methodological and Measurement Issues*, pages 59–80. Kluwer Academic Publishers, Dordrecht.

Jorgenson, D. W. and Slesnick, D. T. (1984). Aggregate Consumer Behaviour and the Measurement of Inequality. *Review of Economic Studies*, 51:369–392.

Kaldor, N. (1939). Welfare Propositions and Interpersonal Comparisons of Utility. *Economic Journal*, 49:549–552.

Kay, J. A. (1980). The Deadweight Loss From a Tax System. *Journal of Public Economics*, 13:111–120.

Kay, J. A. and Keen, M. (1988). Measuring the Inefficiencies of Tax Systems. *Journal of Public Economics*, 35:265–287.

Keen, M. (1990). Welfare Analysis and Intertemporal Substitution. *Journal of Public Economics*, 42:47–66.

King, M. A. (1983). Welfare Analysis of Tax Reforms Using Household Data. *Journal of Public Economics*, 21:183–214.

Konüs, A. A. (1924). The Problem of the True Index of the Cost of Living (in Russian). *The Economic Bulletin of the Institute of Economic Conjuncture*, 9–10:64–71. English translation (1939) in *Econometrica*, 7: 10–29.

Krutilla, J. (1967). Conservation Reconsidered. *American Economic Review*, 56:777–786.

Kurz, M. (1974). An Experimental Approach to the Determination of the Demand for Public Goods. *Journal of Public Economics*, 3:329–348.

Lancaster, K. (1966). A New Approach to Consumer Theory. *Journal of Political Economy*, 74:132–157.

Lankford, R. H. (1988). Measuring Welfare Changes in Settings with Imposed Quantities. *Journal of Environmental Economics and Management*, 15:45–63.

Laspeyres, E. (1864). Hamburger Warenpreise 1850–1863. *Jahrbücher für Nationalökonomie und Statistik*, 3:81–118.

Latham, R. (1980). Quantity Constrained Demand Functions. *Econometrica*, 48:307–313.

Mackay, R. J. and Whitney, G. A. (1980). The Comparative Statics of Quantity Constraints and Conditional Demands: Theory and Applications. *Econometrica*, 48:1727–1744.

Madden, P. (1991). A Generalization of Hicksian q Substitutes and Complements with Application to Demand Rationing. *Econometrica*, 59:1497–1508.

Malmquist, S. (1953). Index Numbers and Indifference Surfaces. *Trabajos de Estatistica*, 4:209–242.

Marshall, A. (1920). *Principles of Economics*. Macmillan, London, 8th edition. (1st edition 1890).

Marshall, J. M. (1989). Welfare Analysis Under Uncertainty. *Journal of Risk and Uncertainty*, 2:385–403.

Mayo, S. K. (1981). Theory and Estimation in the Economics of Housing Demand. *Journal of Urban Economics*, 10:95–116.

Mayshar, J. (1990). On Measures of Excess Burden and Their Application. *Journal of Public Economics*, 43:263–289.

McKenzie, G. W. (1983). *Measuring Economic Welfare: New Methods*. Cambridge University Press, Cambridge.

McKenzie, G. W. and Pearce, I. F. (1976). Exact Measures of Welfare and the Cost of Living. *Review of Economic Studies*, 43:465–468.

McKenzie, G. W. and Pearce, I. F. (1982). Welfare Measurement — A Synthesis. *American Economic Review*, 72:669–682.

McKenzie, G. W. and Ulph, D. (1986). Exact Welfare Measures. *Economic Perspectives*, 4:1–43.

McKenzie, L. (1957). Demand Theory Without a Utility Index. *Review of Economic Studies*, 24:185–189.

Meier, C. E. and Randall, A. (1991). Use Value Under Uncertainty: Is There a 'Correct' Measure? *Land Economics*, 67:379–389.

Mishan, E. J. (1981). *Economic Efficiency and Social Welfare.* Unwin Hyman, London.

Mitchell, R. C. and Carson, R. T. (1989). *Using Surveys to Value Public Goods: The Contingent Valuation Method.* Resources for the Future, Washington (D.C.).

Mohring, H. (1971). Alternative Welfare Gain and Loss Measures. *Western Economic Journal,* 9:349–368.

Morey, E. R. (1981). The Demand for Site–Specific Recreational Activities: A Characteristics Approach. *Journal of Environmental Economics and Management,* 8:345–371.

Morey, E. R. (1985). Characteristics, Consumer Surplus, and New Activities, A Proposed Ski Area. *Journal of Public Economics,* 26:221–236.

Moroney, M. J. (1951). *Facts From Figures.* Viking Press, London.

Mosak, J. L. (1944). *General Equilibrium Theory in International Trade.* Principia Press, Bloomington (Ind.).

Musgrave, R. A. (1992). Social Contract, Taxation and the Standing of Deadweight Loss. *Journal of Public Economics,* 49:369–381.

National Oceanic and Atmospheric Administration (1993). *Report of the NOAA Panel on Contingent Valuation.* National Oceanic and Atmospheric Administration. Federal Register 58/10, pages 4602–4614.

Neary, J. P. and Roberts, K. W. S. (1980). The Theory of Household Behaviour Under Rationing. *European Economic Review,* 13:25–42.

Olsen, E. O. and Barton, D. M. (1983). The Benefits and Costs of Public Housing in New York City. *Journal of Public Economics,* 20:299–332.

Paasche, H. (1874). Über die Preisentwicklung der letzten Jahre. *Jahrbücher für Nationalökonomie und Statistik,* 23:168–178.

Palmquist, R. B. (1991). Hedonic methods. In Braden, J. B. and Kolstad, C. D., editors, *Measuring the Demand for Environmental Quality,* pages 77–120. North Holland, Amsterdam.

Pauwels, W. (1988). Measuring Welfare Changes in Quantity Constrained Regim In Bös, D., Rose, M., and Seidl, C., editors, *Welfare and Efficiency in Public Economics,* pages 49–70. Springer Verlag, Berlin.

Pierson, N. G. (1896). Further Considerations on Index–Numbers. *The Economic Journal,* 6:127–131.

Pigou, A. C. (1920). *The Economics of Welfare.* Macmillan, London.

Pollak, R. A. (1978). Welfare Evaluation and the Cost–of–Living Index in the Household Production Model. *American Economic Review,* 68:285–299.

Pollak, R. A. (1983). The Treatment of 'Quality' in the Cost of Living Index. *Journal of Public Economics,* 20:25–53.

Pollak, R. A. (1990). The Theory of the Cost–of–Living Index. In Diewert, W. E., editor, *Price Level Measurement*, pages 5–77. North Holland, Amsterdam.

Pommerehne, W. W. (1987). *Präferenzen für öffentliche Güter, Ansätze zu ihrer Erfassung*. J. C. B. Mohr (Paul Siebeck), Tübingen.

Portney, P. R. (1994). The Contingent Valuation Debate: Why Economists Should Care. *Journal of Economic Perspectives*, 8:3–17.

Randall, A., Ives, B. C., and Eastman, C. (1974). Bidding Games for Valuation of Aesthetic Environmental Improvements. *Journal of Environmental Economics and Management*, 1:132–149.

Randall, A. and Stoll, J. R. (1980). Consumer's Surplus in Commodity Space. *American Economic Review*, 70:449–455.

Ready, R. (1995). Environmental Valuation Under Uncertainty. In Bromley, D. W., editor, *The Handbook of Environmental Economics*, pages 568–593. Basil Blackwell Ltd.

Roberts, K. (1980). Price–Independent Welfare Prescriptions. *Journal of Public Economics*, 13:277–297.

Rosen, H. S. (1974). Hedonic Prices and Implicit Markets: Product Differentiation in Pure Competition. *Journal of Political Economy*, 82:34–55.

Rothbarth, E. (1940–41). The Measurement of Changes in Real Income Under Conditions of Rationing. *Review of Economic Studies*, 8:100–107.

Roy, R. (1942). *De l'utilité*. Herman, Paris.

Samuelson, P. A. (1942). Constancy of the Marginal Utility of Income. In Lange, O., McIntire, F., and Yntema, T. O., editors, *Studies in Mathematical Economics and Econometrics*, pages 75–91. University of Chicago Press, Chicago.

Samuelson, P. A. (1954). The Pure Theory of Public Expenditure. *Review of Economics and Statistics*, 36:387–389.

Samuelson, P. A. (1974). Complementarity — An Essay on the 40th Anniversary of the Hicks–Allen Revolution in Demand Theory. *Journal of Economic Literature*, 12:1255–1289.

Samuelson, P. A. and Swamy, S. (1974). Invariant Economic Index Numbers and Canonical Duality: Survey and Synthesis. *American Economic Review*, 64:566–593.

Schwab, R. M. (1985). The Benefits of In–Kind Government Programs. *Journal of Public Economics*, 27:195–210.

Scitovsky, T. (1941). A note on welfare propositions in economics. *Review of Economic Studies*, 9:77–88.

Shechter, M. and Freeman, S. (1994). Nonuse Value: Reflections on the Definition and Measurement. In Pethig, R., editor, *Valuing the Environment:*

Methodological and Measurent Issues, pages 171–194. Kluwer Academic Publishers, Dordrecht.

Shephard, R. W. (1953). *Cost and Production Functions*. Princeton University Press, Princeton. Reprinted in: Lecture Notes in Economics and Mathematical Systems, No. 194, Berlin 1981.

Shephard, R. W. (1970). *The Theory of Cost and Production Functions*. Princeton University Press, Princeton.

Slesnick, D. T. (1991). Aggregate Deadweight Loss and Money Metric Social Welfare. *International Economic Review*, 32:123–146.

Smith, V. K. (1977). The Principle of Unanimity and Voluntary Consent in Social Choice. *Journal of Political Economy*, 85:1125–1139.

Smith, V. K. and Desvousges, W. H. (1986). *Measuring Water Quality Benefits*. Kluwer, Boston.

Stuart, C. E. (1984). Welfare Costs Per Dollar of Additional Tax Revenue in the United States. *American Economic Review*, 74:352–362.

Stutzer, M. J. (1982). Another Note on Deadweight Loss. *Journal of Public Economics*, 18:277–284.

Svento, R. (1994). Welfare Measurement Under Uncertainty. In Pethig, R., editor, *Valuing the Environment: Methodological and Measurement Issues*, pages 129–168. Kluwer Academic Publishers, Dordrecht.

Tobin, J. (1952). A Survey of the Theory of Rationing. *Econometrica*, 20:521–553.

Tobin, J. and Houthakker, H. S. (1950–51). The Effects of Rationing on Demand Elasticities. *Review of Economic Studies*, 18:140–153.

Vartia, Y. O. (1983). Efficient Methods of Measuring Welfare Change and Compensated Income in Terms of Ordinary Demand Functions. *Econometrica*, 51:79–98.

Weisbrod, B. A. (1964). Collective–Consumption Services of Individual Consumption Goods. *Quarterly Journal of Economics*, 78:471–477.

Weymark, J. (1985). Money–Metric Utility Functions. *International Economic Review*, 26:219–232.

Wold, H. (1944). A Synthesis of Pure Demand Analysis. *Skandinavisk Aktuarietidskrift*, 27:69–120.

12 CHANGING UTILITY FUNCTIONS

Hersh Shefrin

Santa Clara University

Contents

1	Introduction and Outline	569
2	Historical Development	571
3	The Discounted Utility Model	573
4	A Changing Tastes Model	574
5	Hyperbolic Discounting	578
6	Dynamic Consistency as Nash Equilibrium	582
7	Existence and Indifference	590
8	Welfare Implications	594
9	Endogenously Changing Utility Functions	596
10	Changing Tastes and Consumer Theory	599
11	Uncertainty	603
12	Prospect Theory	607
13	Self–Control, Willpower, and Rules	612
14	Concluding Remarks	619
	References	623

1   Introduction and Outline

Intertemporal choice concerns the tradeoffs faced by an individual between consumption at different points of time. The standard way to evaluate such tradeoffs is by means of a utility function. This chapter addresses issues which arise when the utility function changes over time. Changes to utility functions can occur in conjunction with the instantaneous utility functions, as well as the function which evaluates the entire intertemporal profile.

This chapter deals with three ways in which utility functions can change over time:

(1) changes in respect to *intertemporal* substitution;

(2) changes in respect to substitution between *different commodities*; and

(3) changes in respect to substitution between *alternative lotteries*.

A core notion underlying all three is the fact that changes take place in a moving frame of reference. In this respect, there are two central issues. The first issue is to identify the characteristics which define the frame of reference. The second issue concerns a *relativity* principle. Relativity requires that relative relationships among events appear to be preserved as the frame of reference moves. The change to the utility function can be said to be germane when the relativity principle is violated.[1]

The following questions underlie the discussion throughout the chapter. As an empirical matter, do utility functions change over time? If they do change, then does the relativity principle hold? If the relativity principle is violated, then what are the positive implications associated with the way that individuals make intertemporal choices? And what are the welfare implications attached to their choices, given that there may well be conflicts between the preferences held by a single individual at different points of his life?

The remainder of the chapter is organized as follows. Section 2 contains a discussion of the historical development of intertemporal choice theory, which led to the discounted utility model (Section 3). This sets the stage for the first formal treatment of changing utility, namely Strotz's pioneering paper on dynamic consistency and exponential discounting (Section 4). Experimental evidence suggests that the discount function is hyperbolic rather than exponential. Section 5 is devoted to the properties of the hyperbolic discount function. Section 6 describes the properties of a consistent plan for the hyperbolic discount function case. Section 7 sets out conditions under which a consistent plan exists. The existence issue involves some subtle aspects concerning indifference. Having discussed existence, I turn next to the welfare implications associated with consistent plans. Section 8 establishes that the consistent plan

---

[1] The terms frame of reference and relativity are borrowed from physics. Although they can be interpreted in analagous fashion, the parallel should not be taken too far. For instance, there need be no counterpart to the Lorentz transformations, which in physics, reconcile variations across all frames of reference.

is Pareto–inefficient in the hyperbolic discount function case. That is, there are plans which are judged to dominate the consistent plan, from the perspective of *all* utility functions held by the individual over his lifetime. Section 9 indicates how the character of the consistent plan is affected when the utility function depends on past consumption. Most of the analysis in this chapter assumes that there is a single consumption good. Section 10 also discusses the influence of past consumption on utility, but in a multi–commodity setting. Section 11 extends the discussion of changing tastes from the certainty framework to the uncertainty framework. Section 11 describes the structure of prospect theory, a descriptive theory of decision making under uncertainty developed by cognitive psychologists. A key feature of the analysis concerns the connection between uncertainty framing effects and dynamic inconsistency. Section 12 discusses the way that prospect theory has also been used to deal with the role of framing in intertemporal choice. Section 13 describes how the notions of self–control and willpower can provide useful economic insights into savings behavior. The final section is a conclusion. The conclusion is intended to serve three purposes: (1) to summarize the main discussion points; (2) to emphasize how the various strands of the literature relate to one another; and (3) to suggest some challenges and possible future directions.

2   Historical Development

This section contains a brief overview of the way that ideas about intertemporal choice have evolved in economics. This evolution has featured a pattern of ebbs and flows in its emphasis on the relative importance of particular issues. The writings of early economists stressed the importance of will in delaying gratification, as well as cognitive imperfections in weighing future benefits against present ones. Both of these concepts were later downplayed, as the formal utility framework was applied to intertemporal choice. However, as we shall see, issues of will and cognition returned as central issues in the consideration of changing utility functions.

Early economists, such as Adam Smith (1776), focused on capital accumulation as the critical ingredient for explaining differences in the standard of living across demographic groups and over time. Rae (1834) was especially concerned with understanding the determinants of differences in the rate at which capital has accumulated. He argued that the rate at which capital accumulates depends on the willingness of the public to defer gratification from the present to the future. In particular, Rae identified four factors which he felt underlie this willingness to defer. The four are: *(1) uncertain lifetime; (2) abstinence, meaning the psychological discomfort of deferral; (3) the bequest motive; and (4) prudence.* The fourth category dealt with "the extent of intellectual powers, and the consequent power of habits of reflection" (1834, p. 58). Notice that the first two of Rae's factors favor present consumption over future consumption, with the third and fourth providing some offset to this tendency.

The economist N.W. Senior (1836) first suggested that abstinence was priced in the market, noting that this seemed to be the reason why the rate of interest was positive rather than zero. In Senior's treatment, a postive interest rate provided compensation for abstaining from current consumption, which he described as "among the most painful exertions of human will" (1836, p. 60). It is interesting to note the central role played by the psychological factor abstinence in the writings of Rae and Senior, as these were to be downplayed as the theory of intertemporal choice was developed by those who followed.

Using a Benthamite perspective, in which individuals are regarded as being both self–centered and centered in the present relative to other points in time, Jevons (1871) asked why individuals do not act completely myopically? Why, he wondered, do they attach any weight at all to future consumption? Jevons suggested that the weight which individuals attach to future consumption stems from the *present anticipation* of future pleasure. In other words, at any point in time, the individual decides how to allocate his wealth between present pleasure (currently experienced) and the anticipation of future pleasure (*also* currently experienced). However, Jevons did not go so far as to argue that the ability to anticipate future pleasure was perfectly calibrated, stating instead that future pleasures do not all "act upon us with the same force as if they were present" (1871, p. 76). Unlike Senior and Rae, who viewed abstinence as resulting from the psychological pain of delaying gratification, Jevons viewed the asymmetry between present and future consumption in terms of a cognitive imperfection: the anticipated pleasure from future consumption is a downward biased indicator of the future pleasure that it prefigures.

Böhm–Bawerk modified Jevon's approach in a way which set the stage for modern intertemporal choice theory, in which there is a single intertemporal utility function. Böhm–Bawerk rejected Jevon's view that individuals are capable of feeling emotions in advance, and suggested instead that a person acts as a referee in respect to the intertemporal allocation of pleasure over time. Böhm–Bawerk's individuals trade off satisfactions at different points in time, and these are regarded as being placed upon a single cognitive plane on which they can be compared. This view provides the conceptual framework underlying the single utility function theory of intertemporal choice. Nevertheless, Böhm–Bawerk also recognized the presence of a cognitive imperfection concerning the treatment of present consumption relative to future consumption, noting a "systematic tendency to underestimate future wants" (1889, p. 268-269).

Unlike Rae and Senior who emphasized the contribution of abstinence as a factor in intemporal choice, Jevons and Böhm–Bawerk rested their arguments on the cognitive weighting of present and future consumption. Yet Böhm–Bawerk was well aware that abstinence was an important issue, and invoked it in his welfare analysis. Specifically, he discusses an injudicious decision by an individual to favor the present over the future, as a result of giving in to weakness, "which he knows immediately that he is going to regret on the morrow." Ironically, although it is Böhm–Bawerk who first puts forward the conceptual framework underlying intertemporal choice theory based upon a single utility function, his recognition of anticipated "regret on the morrow" clearly reflects his appreciation of changing utility.

The quantification of Böhm–Bawerk's conceptual framework is due to Irving Fisher (1930). Fisher presented the tradeoff between present and future consumption in a two–date model involving indifference curves over consumption at the two dates. These indifference curves (or "willingness lines" as Fisher called them), were not symmetric, with the asymmetry capturing the notion of "impatience". The reasons put forward by Fisher to explain why an individual would be impatient for present consumption are similar to the ones discussed by his predecessors, although he did emphasize imperfect foresight and a failure to display self–control.

3   The Discounted Utility Model

Fisher's indifference curves can be regarded as the level lines of an intertemporal utility function $U(c_1, c_2)$, where c_1 denotes present consumption and c_2 denotes future consumption. Samuelson (1937) developed the notion of intertemporal utility in the form of a discounted utility model over intertemporal consumption profiles of the form $c = (c_1, c_2, \cdots, c_T)$. In Samuelson's formulation, lifetime discounted utility has the form:

$$U(c_1, c_2, \cdots, c_T) = \sum_{t=1}^{T} u(c_t)\delta^{t-1}, \qquad (3.1)$$

where $u(c_t)$ is the instantaneous utility derived at date t from consuming c_t and δ^t is the discount factor, $0 < \delta < 1$. In this formulation, it is assumed that $u' > 0$ and $u'' < 0$. Equation (3.1) has become the standard utility functional for comparing alternative consumption profiles, especially for continuous time where c_t is replaced by $c(t)$, and (3.1) takes the integral form:

$$U(c) = \int_0^T e^{-pt} u(c(t)) dt. \qquad (3.2)$$

Equation (3.1) indicates that intertemporal utility is additively separable in its arguments. Samuelson recognized that this assumption is quite restictive, in that instantaneous utility depends only on consumption at that moment, not on the memory of past consumption or the anticipation of future consumption. Moreover, future utility is discounted back to the present as if it were the same as future cash flow, and δ is treated as if it were the interest rate.[2] Nevertheless, the additively separable form has been used extensively in the literature on changing tastes. Although this has largely been to simplify the analysis, it does raise questions about the extent to which various the conclusions from the model can be generalized. As we shall see, the central results in this literature apply outside the additively separable framework.

4   A Changing Tastes Model

The seminal article on changing utility functions is by Robert Strotz (1956). In the single utility function intertemporal model, an individual's utility function $U( )$ remains invariant throughout his lifetime. The tradeoffs evaluated at age twenty are evaluated in exactly the same way at age seventy. This feature struck Strotz as being inconsistent with casual observation. He noted that some individuals appeared to have difficulty in avoiding what earlier economists had called abstinence. Moreover, he noted that other individuals engage in *precommitment* behavior, whereby they constrained their future choice set of consumption profiles.

Strotz provided a wide ranging set of examples to illustrate what he meant by precommitment. He began his article with the following well known quotation from Homer's classic *The Odyssey* in which Ulysses precommits himself, lest he be tempted by the wail of the Sirens into wrecking his ship upon the rocks:

> ... but you must bind me hard and fast, so that I cannot stir from the spot where you will stand me ... and if I beg you to release me, you must tighten and add to my bonds.

In the body of his article, he mentions a variety of precommitment strategies, such as: the use of "insurance policies and Christmas Clubs which may often be hard to justify in view of the low rates of return"; having one's academic salary dispensed on a twelve month basis instead of nine; and joining the army. These

---

[2] Koopmans (1960) provided a set of axioms which establish conditions for the intertemporal utility function to be additive in instantaneous utilities $u_t(c_t)$. His axioms can be organized into three groups. The first, *independence* states that if two profiles share a common consumption value at any date t, then preference between the two profiles is determined by consumption levels at the other dates. The second, *stationarity* assumes that if date 1 consumption is the same for two profiles, then preference between them will be preserved by dropping the first period, and shifting the profiles forward in time. The third group, *completeness* are a set of technical axioms.

are all viewed as devices to cope with the *mañana* effect, continually putting off until tomorrow what is unpleasant to do today.

In what might be viewed as a "back to Jevons" argument, Strotz reintroduced the notion that individuals are centered in the present, and he relaxed the requirement that the discount function be exponential, as it is in (3.1). Imagine that the present means date τ, with date t occuring after τ, i.e. $t > \tau$. In Strotz's framework, instantaneous utility stemming from date t consumption continues to be $u(c_t)$. However, when the present is date τ, the discount factor[3] applied to $u(c_t)$ is $\lambda_\tau(t)$ rather than δ^{t-1}. Strotz assumes that the discount function $\lambda_1()$ is maintained, but shifts forward in time. In other words, $\lambda_\tau(t)$ is an invariant function of the difference $|t - \tau|$. Since τ parameterizes the moving frame of reference, it can be termed a *reference date*.

With a forward shifting discount function, past consumption is also discounted relative to present consumption. In this sense, the utility function changes whenever the discount function $\lambda_\tau()$ is nonconstant in τ. However, because time is unidirectional, the individual at date τ must accept his past consumption choices.

What interested Strotz was whether the forward shifting discount function resulted in a meaningful change in utility function, in respect to the consumption choices from date τ on? Would the shifting discount function induce a change in the rank ordering of consumption profiles from τ through T?

Formally, consider an individual whose problem is to allocate lifetime wealth q over T consumption dates. The individual's utility function $U_\tau(c)$ has the form:

$$U_\tau(c) = \sum_{t=1}^{T} u(c_t)\lambda_\tau(t), \tag{4.1}$$

where the shifting discount function feature is captured by the condition:

$$\lambda_\tau(t) = \lambda_1(|t - \tau + 1|) \tag{4.2}$$

and $\lambda_1(1)$ is normalized to unity. Budget feasibility is specified by the constraint:

$$\sum_{t=1}^{T} c_t \le q. \tag{4.3}$$

For simplicity, a zero interest rate is assumed in (4.3). In addition, equality is assumed rather than weak inequality because of the nonsatiation condition $u' > 0$.

---

[3]Which is indexed by τ.

Consider the individual at date 1. Denote by c^1 the profile which maximizes lifetime utility (4.1) (for $\tau = 1$), subject to the budget constraint (4.3). The standard first order optimizing condition for c^1 is that for all t and s:

$$\lambda_1(t)u'(c_t^1) \geq \lambda_1(s)u'(c_s^1) \tag{4.4}$$

with equality in (4.4) if and only if c_t^1 and c_s^1 are both positive.

Assume that at date 1, the individual is free to select date 1 consumption c_1, but must defer the implementation of later consumption c_τ until date τ. Suppose that at date 1, the individual selects $c_1 = c_1^1$, believing that at date τ, he will select $c_\tau = c_\tau^1$. Of course, this belief may be naive, because the individual's utility function at date τ will have changed from U_1 to U_τ. For instance, at date 2, the individual will have remaining wealth $q_2 = q - c_1^1$. He is free to compute the profile c^2 which maximizes $U_2(c)$ subject to the constraints:

$$c_1^2 = c_1^1$$

and

$$\sum_{t=2}^{T} c_t^2 = q_2.$$

With the passage of time, this procedure results in the naive consumption profile $c^N = (c_1^1, c_2^2, \cdots, c_T^T)$.

Strotz was interested in characterizing the conditions under which the shifting discount function did not cause the individual to change his mind about the profile selected at date 1. In other words, under what conditions will $c_t^\tau = c_t^1$? He established:[4]

THEOREM 4.1 The equality $c_t^\tau = c_t^1$ holds for all τ if and only if $\lambda_\tau()$ has the exponential form:

$$\lambda_\tau(t) = \delta^{t-\tau}. \tag{4.5}$$

PROOF The proof of the theorem follows from the optimality condition for the U_τ optimization problem:

$$\lambda_\tau(t)u'(c_t^1) = \lambda_\tau(s)u'(c_s^1), \tag{4.6}$$

which is equivalent to:

$$u'(c_t^1)/u'(c_t^1) = \lambda_\tau(s)/\lambda_\tau(t). \tag{4.7}$$

---

[4]Strotz made the argument for a continuous time model.

The optimality of c^1 under U_τ, for all τ, requires that condition (4.7) hold for all τ. However, for $\tau = 1, 2$ and $t, s = 2, 3$, this implies:

$$\lambda_1(3) = \lambda_1(2) \times \lambda_2(3).$$

Moreover, the shifting discount function condition (4.2) implies that $\lambda_1(2) = \lambda_2(3)$. Therefore

$$\lambda_1(3) = (\lambda_1(2))^2$$

which, applying the argument recursively implies that $\lambda_1()$ is exponential. ∎

Notice that exponential discounting gives rise to a relativity principle. That is, people with exponential discount functions whose past plans were formulated by maximizing their initial utility functions U_1 would have no desire to revise those plans with the passage of time, even though their utility functions have changed. Put somewhat differently, such people would have no motive to enter into commitments which would constrain their own behavior in the future. Their future behavior and present utility functions are *dynamically consistent*. The passage below indicates Strotz's thinking on the subject:

> Special attention should be given, I feel, to a discount function ... which differs from a logarithmically linear one in that it "overvalues" the more proximate satisfactions relative to the more distant ones. p. 177.

The people who have the potential to display dynamically inconsistent behavior are the ones whose discount functions are not exponential. For instance, suppose an individual discounts the future in such a way that:

$$\lambda_2(3) < \frac{\lambda_1(3)}{\lambda_1(2)}.$$

Such an individual weighs the relative merits of date 3 consumption and date 2 consumption quite differently at date 2 than he does at date 1. For him, date 2 consumption is relatively more important at date 2 than it is at date 1. The rate at which he discounts the future decreases as a function ot the time delay. Consequently, when date 2 arrives, he will wish to consume more c_2 than he had planned under c^1. This feature has come to be known as the *common difference effect* [Loewenstein and Prelec (1992)]. As the following passage demonstrates, for Strotz, this is the cause, not only of overspending on present consumption relative to the future, but a wide range of social ills.

> ... [T]here are no doubt some who, either through lack of training or insight, have never learned to behave consistently and for whom the intertemporal tussle remains unsolved. These people we call "spendthrifts".

By contrast, those who have taken on log–linear discount functions have learned to be "thrifty".

Spendthriftiness, in the general sense of inconsistent or imprudent planning, is by no means insignificant. It is especially among the lower–income classes, where education and training are commonly blighted, that one would expect to find imprudent behaviour of this sort. In America, lower income people tend to gorge themselves with food after pay–day; overheat their homes when they have money for a bucket of coal; are extravagant, going on sprees on pay–day, not budgeting their money, and engaging in heavy instalment buying; do not keep their children in school; and are freer in the expression of their sexual and agressive impulses. Their high birth rate is well-known. All these behaviour characteristics can be explained as a failure to cope intelligently with the problem of the intertemporal tussle. (p. 178)

5   Hyperbolic Discounting

Strotz' work stimulated both economists and psychologists to examine the way that people discount the future. The most compelling experimental evidence that utility functions change over time involves the common difference effect. Some representantive articles which address this issue are Ainslie (1974, 1975, 1985), Thaler (1981), Horowitz (1988), Benzion, Rapoport, and Yagil (1989), and Loewenstein and Prelec (1992). Interestingly, Ainslie (1974) discusses experimental evidence involving animals.

Consider a mutually exclusive choice between receiving *A) $1 today; and B) $2 tomorrow.* Suppose an individual prefers A over B. Now let us ask that same individual to choose between two other mutually exclusive choices involving the receipt of *(C) $1 25 days from now*; and *(D) $2 26 days from now.* One of the Koopmans (1960) axioms underlying discounted expected utility is *stationarity*, and it stipulates that A is preferred to B if and only if C is preferred to D. The violation of stationarity leads to the common difference effect. The common difference effect gets its name from the fact that the time difference in the two choices, in this example one day, is common.

More formally, imagine that an individual is consuming an amount c at two dates t and s, $t < s$. Suppose that he is indifferent to receiving incremental amounts x at date t and $y > x$ at date s. Then with exponential discounting, we have:

$$u(c+x)\delta^t + u(c)\delta^s = u(c)\delta^t + u(c+y)\delta^s,$$

which implies that:

$$u(c+x) - u(c) = (u(c+y) - u(c))\delta^{s-t},$$

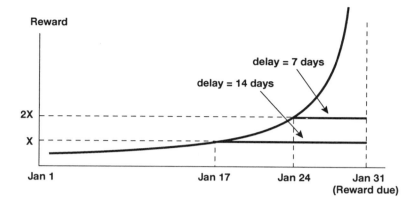

Figure 5.1   Reward value at t as a function of time delay

so that the only aspect of time which is relevant here is the delay $s - t$, but not the dates t and s themselves. In other words, exponential discounting is inconsistent with the common difference effect.

A useful way of depicting the difference between exponential and nonexponential discounting is to graph reward value against time delay: see Figure 5.1. Consider a reward of Z to be received at the current date $\tau = 0$. The X-axis represents time. As we move to the right in the figure, there is a delay until a reward is received. The curve in the figure reprents the size of reward which is required to leave the individual indifferent between Z at $\tau = 0$ and a larger reward at each future time t. Imagine that the current date τ is January 1, and that an individual is indifferent between a $1.00 reward on January 25 and $1.20 reward on January 28.[5] Then the points (25, 1) and (28, 1.2) will lie on the same curve in Figure 5.1. Let time advance and consider how the individual feels on January 25 when the $1 reward is due. An individual who discounts exponentially will continue to be indifferent between (25, 1) and (28, 1.2). Such an individual would not shift his indifference curve in Figure 5.1. However, a nonexponential discounter would exhibit a different indifference curve on January 25, and for example, would regard $2 on January 28 as exact compensation for waiting another 3 days. This individual's indifference curves would cross, with the January 25 indifference curve lying above the January 1 curve to the right of January 25. See Figure 5.2.

One discount function which has received considerable attention in the psychology literature is known as *Herrnstein's matching law* [Herrnstein (1961)].

---

[5]This example is taken from Frank (1992).

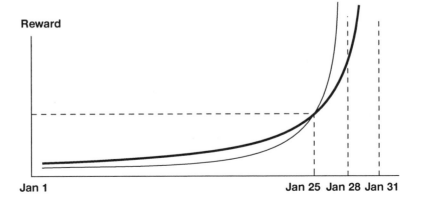

Figure 5.2   Indifference curves which cross: dynamic inconsistency

This discount function has performed well in experiments, with both human and with animal subjects. Economist Robert Frank (1992) writes that the "matching law is apparently part of the hard wiring of most animal nervous systems". The function in question has, as its arguments the present value V, size of reward A, and delay $(t - \tau)$ until the reward is received. The function itself is:

$$V = \frac{A}{K + \alpha(t - \tau)}, \tag{5.1}$$

where K and α are parameters. The role of K is to prevent V from approaching infinity as the delay goes to zero. V denotes the present value at date τ of reward A to be received after a delay of $t - \tau$); see Ainslie and Haslam (1992). The discount function is, of course,

$$\lambda_\tau(t) = \frac{1}{K + \alpha(t - \tau)}. \tag{5.2}$$

Equation (5.1) is known as hyperbolic discounting because it traces out hyperbolic curves. Under the matching law,[6] indifference curves cross in the manner of Figure 5.2: future rewards are heavily discounted, and present ones loom large. Notice from (5.1) that, except for delays close to zero, V is roughly inversely proportional to the length of the delay.

---

[6] The term matching law arises from Herrnstein's prediction that effort will be allocated across rewards in order that effort match reward.

Loewenstein and Prelec (1992) provide an enlightening discussion of the generalized hyperbolic discount function, based upon Prelec (1989). The generalized hyperbola has the form:

$$\lambda(t) = (1 + \alpha t)^{-\beta/\alpha}. \tag{5.3}$$

Notably, the exponential function $e^{-\beta t}$ occurs as the limit of (5.3) when $\alpha \to 0$.

Consider an individual who is indifferent between reward x at $\tau = 0$ and reward $y > x$ at some later date s. Formally,

$$u(x) = u(y)\lambda(s)$$

Suppose that both rewards are delayed by the same amount t. The inequality

$$u(x)\lambda(t) \leq u(y)\lambda(t + s)$$

indicates that preference has shifted to the later reward, with the inequality being strict for the nonexponential case. That is, the indifference before the delay results in strict preference for the later reward y in the presence of the delay. Therefore restoration of indifference requires that the time of arrival of y be delayed even further from $(t + s)$ to $(kt + s)$, where k depends only on x and y, but not on t or s.

THEOREM 5.1 If for all x and y,

$$u(x) = u(y)\lambda(s)$$

implies that for all t,

$$u(x)\lambda(t) = u(y)\lambda(kt + s), \tag{5.4}$$

then

$$\lambda(t) = (1 + \alpha t)^{-\beta/\alpha}.$$

PROOF For any t', and $\gamma t + (1 - \gamma)t'$, (5.4) implies that

$$u(x)\lambda(t') = u(y)\lambda(kt' + s) \tag{5.5}$$

and

$$
\begin{aligned}
u(x)\lambda(\gamma t + (1 - \gamma)t') \\
&= u(y)\lambda(k(\gamma t + (1 - \gamma)t') + s) \\
&= u(y)\lambda(\gamma(kt + s) + (1 - \gamma)(kt' + s)) \\
&= u(y)\lambda(\gamma\lambda^{-1}(u(x)\lambda(t)/u(y)) + (1 - \gamma)\lambda^{-1}(u(x)\lambda(t')/u(y))).
\end{aligned}
\tag{5.6}
$$

Define $r = u(x)/u(y)$, $w = \lambda(t)$, $z = \lambda(t')$, and $v = \lambda^{-1}$. Substitution of these variables into (5.6) leads to the functional equation:

$$rv^{-1}(\gamma v(w) + (1-\gamma)v(z)) = v^{-1}(\gamma v(rw) + (1-\gamma)v(rz)). \qquad (5.7)$$

Equation (5.7) is a functional equation in v. From Aczél (1966, p. 152, equation (18)), the only solutions to this equation are:

$$v(t) = c\log(t) + d$$

and

$$v(t) = ct^{\mu} + d.$$

Since $\lambda(t) = v^{-1}(t)$, the discount function must be either hyperbolic or exponential. In particular, it must have the form (5.3). ∎

6 Dynamic Consistency as Nash Equilibrium

If hyperbolic discounting is the norm, then the individual will not be able to implement the plan c^1 which is optimal under his preferences at date 1. Pollak (1968) develops a particularly insightful example of a naive consumption plan. His example features the case of logarithmic utility. Consider the date τ plan which is optimal for the situation when the individual's discount function is given by $\lambda_\tau(\ )$. As is well known, maximizing logarithmic utility leads to the constant budget share condition. Define

$$\phi_{\tau,t} = \frac{\lambda_\tau(t)}{\sum_{s \geq \tau}^{T} \lambda_\tau(s)}. \qquad (6.1)$$

Let $t \geq \tau$. At date τ, the individual's naive plan calls for date t consumption to be allocated the share $\phi_{\tau,t}$ of remaining wealth q_τ. As Theorem 4.1 established, these budget shares will be the same at each date if and only if the discount function is exponential. In particular, if the discount function is hyperbolic, then the individual will readjust the budget shares every period. It is straightforward to use recursion in order to compute the naive plan c^N. Date 1 consumption is just $\phi_{1,1}q$. Date 2 consumption is $\phi_{2,2}q_2$, which is $\phi_{2,2}(1-\phi_{1,1})q$. Date 3 consumption is $\phi_{3,3}q_3$, which is

$$\phi_{3,3}(1-\phi_{2,2})q_2 = \phi_{3,3}(1-\phi_{2,2})(1-\phi_{1,1})q, \qquad (6.2)$$

and so on.

An individual who has a hyperbolic discount function would prefer to pre-commit the choices of his future selves, and select c^1 as their consumption profile. However, precommitment may not be a feasible option, in which case a far sighted individual will consider the behavior of his future self when selecting current consumption.

A convenient way to think about this situation is as a game with T players, one for each date τ. In this case, player τ's preferences are represented by U_τ. Given lifetime wealth q, player 1's strategy is to choose c_1. Given remaining wealth $q_1 = q - c_1$, player 2's strategy is to choose c_2. In general, a strategy for player τ is a function $\rho_\tau(\ )$ which specifies the rate of consumption $c_\tau = \rho_\tau(q_{\tau-1})$ from remaining wealth $q_{\tau-1}$. A plan c^* which corresponds to a *sub-game perfect Nash equilibrium* for this game is known as a *Strotz–Pollak equilibrium*. Such a plan is dynamically consistent. As I discuss in the next section, the conditions under which a Strotz–Pollak equilibrium exist are quite general.

For expositional purposes, I confine attention to the case $T = 3$ in the remainder of this section.[7] At date 1, player 1 considers the reaction of the other players to a particular selection c_1. If he knows $\rho_2(\ )$ and $\rho_3(\ )$, then he can compute both c_2 and c_3, both as functions of c_1. That is, $c_2(c_1) = \rho_2(q-c_1)$ and $c_3(c_1) = \rho_3(q_1 - c_2)$. Therefore player 1's perfect Nash equilibrium behavior is to select c_1 to maximize:

$$u(c_1) + \sum_{t=2}^{3} \lambda_1(t) u(c_t(c_1)).$$

Put somewhat differently, player 1 trades off two utilities, $u(c_1)$ from current consumption c_1 and $V_1(q_1)$ from his bequest q_1. Here $V_1()$ is given by:

$$V_1(q_1) = \sum_{t=2}^{3} \lambda_1(t) u(c_t(c_1)).$$

A similar maximizing statement holds for player 2, and player 3 simply sets $c_3 = q_2$. Perfection follows because the reaction functions are computed in reverse order, from $T = 3$ back to $\tau = 1$.

Consider the dynamically consistent plan in Pollak's logarithmic utility example. Given q_2, we already know that consumption levels at dates 2 and 3 are determined by the budget shares $\phi_{2,2}, \phi_{2,3}$ respectively. At date 1, the individual's dynamically consistent choice of c_1 maximizes:[8]

$$\lambda_{1,1}\ln(c_1) + \lambda_{1,2}\ln(\phi_{2,2}(q-c_1)) + \lambda_{1,3}\ln(\phi_{2,3}(q-c_1)). \qquad (6.3)$$

---

[7]The arguments are easily generalized.

[8]The constant elasticity of intertemporal substitution function has the form $u(c) = c^{1-\theta}/(1-\theta)$. Logarithmic utility corresponds to the degenerate case $\theta = 1$. Applying the argument associated with (6.3) to $u(c)$ establishes that logarithmic utility is a knife edge case. When $\theta > 1$ the ratio $c_1/(q_1 - c_1)$ is higher for the naive case than the sophisticated case. But the inequality reverses when $\theta < 1$.

Notice that maximizing (6.3) is the same as maximizing:

$$\phi_{1,1} \ln(c_1) + (\phi_{1,2} + \phi_{1,3}) \ln(q - c_1). \tag{6.4}$$

Hence, the maximizing choice of c_1 is actually invariant to the budget shares selected at future dates. By repeating the argument recursively, we can conclude that when the utility function is logarithmic, the dynamically consistent plan actually coincides with the naive plan.[9] Of course, this does not mean that at date 1, the individual is indifferent to the budget shares chosen by his future self. The level of date 1 total utility will vary with the budget shares used at future dates, and will lead to maximum date 1 utility when they coincide with $[\phi_{1,t}]$. However, while the total utility function will shift, the marginal utility function will not, and this is why the maximizing choice of c_1 does not vary with the budget shares used at future dates.

The case of logarithmic utility can also be used to provide some insight into a hypothesis proposed by Strotz (1956). Strotz put forward a condition which he thought characterized a dynamically consistent plan in a continuous time model. This condition involves, at each moment t, the local approximation of the true discount function $\lambda(z - t)$ by an exponential function e^{-pt}. Recall that the continuous time version of Theorem 4.1 indicates that naive choice will be dynamically consistent when the discount function takes this form. Strotz hypothesized that, at each moment, the consistent rate of consumption would be given by the rate along the naive path associated with the local exponential approximation. Pollak (1968) suggested that this hypothesis is counterintuitive. He reasoned that at any given moment, the rate of consumption at a given moment along a sophisticated plan would take into account the entire future time path. In contrast, Strotz's hypothesis indicates that the rate of consumption is determined only by the local features of the discount function. Pollak used a counterexample with logarithmic utility to demonstrate that Strotz's hypothesis is false. In the counterexample, $\dot{c}(t)/c(t) = -p$ at moment t along the path obtained by using the local exponential approximation. However, $\dot{c}(t)/c(t) \neq -p$ along the sophisticated plan. Rather:[10]

$$\frac{\dot{c}(t)}{c(t)} = \frac{\lambda(T - t) - 1}{\int_t^T \lambda(z - t)dz} \tag{6.5}$$

---

[9]From this example, one could draw the conclusion that a naive plan need not be dynamically inconsistent. However, the naive plan should be understood as a process. Certainly, the process of choosing a plan naively leads to sequential revision of the plan selected at date 1.
[10]This is one of several places in the chapter where counterexamples to claims are presented. In such cases I have decided to omit proofs. See also Goldman's discussion of the Peleg-Yaari example in Section 7, and Pollak's discussion of von Weizsäcker's model in Section 10.

along the sophisticated plan, which is also the naive plan in the case of logarithmic utility. The last equation reflects the fact that the rate of consumption is determined by taking the entire future path into consideration, not just the local discount rate.[11]

A consistent plan is self–enforcing. Even an individual with a hyperbolic discount function will not find himself tempted to deviate from a consistent plan over time. However, a consistent plan is not the same as the precommited plan c^1. An individual typically consumes at entirely different rates along the two profiles. For example, in the logarithmic utility example with hyperbolic discounting, date 2 consumption is higher along the consistent plan than along the precommited plan. Therefore we need to ask whether it is generally the case that the act of following a consistent plan, although it may resolve Strotz' "intertemporal tussle", will still lead to spendthrift behavior? When the discount function is hyperbolic, a key question is whether the consistent value c_1^* is always larger than its precommited counterpart c_1^1? The next theorem provides a negative answer to this question. In addition, the proof describes structural features which play a part in later discussion.

THEOREM 6.1 There are utility functions and parameter specifications for which $c_1^* > c_1^1$ and parameter specifications for which $c_1^* < c_1^1$.

PROOF Let $\tilde{c}_2$ be defined by the expression

$$u'(\tilde{c}_2) - \lambda_2(3)u'(0) = 0.$$

If $u'(0) = \infty$, then $\tilde{c}_2$ is undefined. Observe that if $q_1 < \tilde{c}_2$, then $c_2^*(q_1) = q_1$ and $c_3^*(q_1) = 0$. Let y_2 be defined as $1/\lambda_2(3)$. Clearly, $\tilde{c}_2$ is an increasing function of y_2. Consider the case in which $q_1 > \tilde{c}_2$. Then a consistent plan satisfies:

$$y_2 u'(c_2^*) = u'(q_1 - c_2^*), \tag{6.6}$$

so that

$$\frac{dc_2}{dq_1} = \frac{u''(q_1 - c_2)}{y_2 u''(c_2) + u''(q_1 - c_2)}, \tag{6.7}$$

and

$$\frac{dc_3}{dq_1} = \frac{y_2 u''(c_2)}{y_2 u''(c_2) + u''(q_1 - c_2)}. \tag{6.8}$$

---

[11] Notice that (6.5) is the continuous time counterpart to the relation implied by (6.1) and (6.2).

Observe from (6.7) that dc_2/dq_1 is decreasing in y_2 and dc_3/dq_1 is increasing in y_2. However for fixed q_1, (6.6) implies that $dc_2/dy_2 > 0$.

Define $y_1 = \lambda_1(2)/\lambda_1(3)$. Because the discount function is hyperbolic, $y_2 > y_1$, which implies:

$$y_1 u'(c_2^*) < u'(c_3^*). \tag{6.9}$$

This inequality indicates that date 1 preferences would prefer a reallocation of the bequest q_1 from date 2 consumption to date 3. Since this is not possible, the next question concerns the impact on the selection of c_1. Observe that the left hand derivative $V'^-(\tilde{c}_2)$ is equal to $\lambda_1(2)u'(\tilde{c}_2)$. The right hand derivative $V'^+(\tilde{c}_2)$ is given by

$$\lambda_1(2)u'(\tilde{c}_2)\frac{dc_2}{dq_1} + \lambda_1(2)u'(0)\frac{dc_2}{dq_1}. \tag{6.10}$$

It follows that $V'^+(\tilde{c}_2) > V'^-(\tilde{c}_2)$. Furthermore, $u'' < 0$ implies that V' is decreasing in q_1 except at $\tilde{c}_2$. Hence, V' has the shape depicted in Figure 6.1.

Figure 6.1 illustrates how the optimal value of q_1 is selected along the consistent path. The right hand origin is the zero point for c_1 and the left is the zero point for q_1. Since $c_1 + q_1 = q$, the total distance between the origins is q. The optimal value of q_1 must satisfy $u'(c_1) = V'(q_1)$. If the u' curve intersects the V' curve at only one such point, then that point is c_1^*. However, there may be two such points, on account of the discontinuity in V'. This is the case illustrated in Figure 6.1, where the two points are denoted q_1^L and q_1^U. Date 1 preferences select q_1^U over q_1^U if the area of triangle B in the figure exceeds that of triangle A.

Focus attention on Figure 6.2 which compares two marginal utility functions V' and W', where the latter is the counterpart to V' when $U_\tau = U_1$ at every date τ. Define $\bar{c}_2$ such that: $\lambda_1(2)u'(\bar{c}_2) = \lambda_1(3)u'(0)$. Observe that $\bar{c}_2 < \tilde{c}_2$. Therefore when $\bar{c}_2 < q_1 < \tilde{c}_2$ we have $W'(q_1) > V'(q_1)$.

At $q_1 = \bar{c}_2$, Figure 6.2 portrays the value of V' jumping up above the value of W'. To understand how this inequality can come about, observe that when $q_1^* = q_1^L$, $c_1^* > c_1^1$, but when $q_1^* = q_1^L$, $c_1^* < c_1^1$. This situation provides us with the case required to establish the theorem.

It remains to demonstrate that V' can lie above W' in a region of the discontinuity point $\tilde{c}_2$ of V'. Using (6.6), (6.7), (6.8), and the definition of V, obtain the following equation for V':

$$\frac{u'(c_2)(y_2/y_1)y_2 u''(c_3)}{y_1(y_2 u''(c_2)) + u''(c_3)}. \tag{6.11}$$

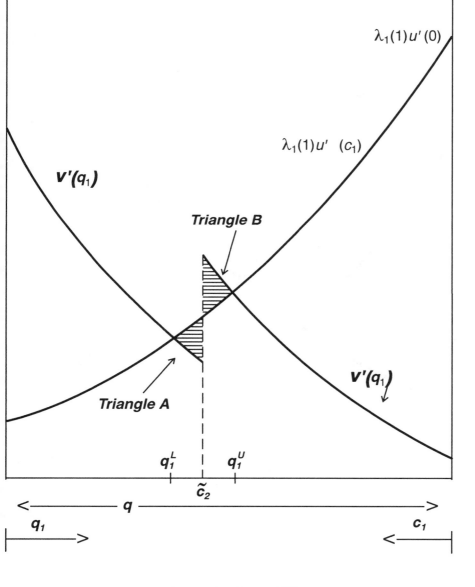

Figure 6.1   Shape of V'

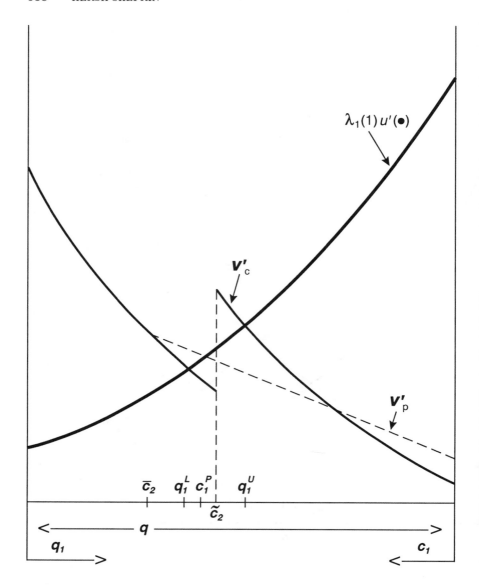

Figure 6.2   Comparison of V' and W'

At the point of discontinuity $q_1 = \tilde{c}_2$, we have $u'(\tilde{c}_2) = u'(0)/y_2$. Therefore equation (6.11) for V' becomes:

$$\frac{u'(0)}{y_2 y_1} \frac{(y_2/y_1) y_2 u''(\tilde{c}_2)) + u''(0)}{y_2 u''(c(\tilde{c}_2)) + u''(0)}. \tag{6.12}$$

Let $c_1^1(q_1)$ be the optimal precommited value of c_2 as a function of the date 1 bequest q_1. Observe that:

$$W'(q_1) = u'(c_2(q_1))/y_1.$$

When $q_1 = \tilde{c}_2$, $y_1 u'(c_2) = u'(0)$. Recall that when q_1 lies between $\bar{c}_2$ and $\tilde{c}_2$, $c_2^1(q_1) > \bar{c}_2$. Since u is concave, $u'(0) > y_1 u'(c_2^1(q_1))$ in this interval of q_1. It follows that:

$$u'(0)/y_1^2 > u'(c_2^1(q_1))/y_1 = W'(q_1).$$

Observe that when $y_1 = y_2$, the value of (6.12) reduces to $u'(0)/y_1^2$. Since the right hand side of (6.11) is continuous in y_2 and q_1, the preceding paragraph implies that we can find a value of $y_2 > y_1$ such that $V'(q_1) > W'(q_1)$ in a region of $\tilde{c}_2$. ∎

When $T = 3$, (6.6) represents the Euler equation for a standard intertemporal optimization involving a nonchanging utility function. The Euler equation for the sophisticated plan is given by $u'(c_1) = V'(q_1)$. Recently, Laibson (1996, 1997) has developed the Euler condition associated with a dynamically consistent plan when the discount function mimics the hyperbolic function in a particular way. He analyzes the following discount function which was introduced by Phelps and Pollak (1968):

$$\lambda_\tau(t) = \beta \delta^{t-\tau}, \tag{6.13}$$

where $0 \le \beta \le 1$ and $t > \tau$. As before, $\lambda_\tau(t) = 1$.

Observe that relative to current date τ consumption, the discount factor applied to date t consumption is $\beta \delta^{t-\tau}$. However for two future dates t and s, where $s > t$, the relative weights attached to consumption at these two dates is δ^{t-s}. Notice that exponential discounting is associated with the condition $\beta = 1$. However, if $\beta < 1$, then the individual always discounts the future more heavily relative to the current date than he does relative to any future date. This is the essential feature of the hyperbolic discount function.

Laibson argues that the Euler equation associated with the preceding discount function has the following form:

$$u'(c_t) = \delta u'(c_{t+1})[1 + ((\beta - 1)\partial c_{t+1}/\partial q_{t-1})]. \tag{6.14}$$

It follows that when $\beta < 1$, the marginal utility of c_τ is less than that of c_t for all $t > \tau$.

7   Existence and Indifference

Recall that in the discussion concerning Figure 6.1, we discussed the possibility of there being multiple local maxima (q_1^L and q_1^U). Indifference between these two maxima occurs along the consistent plan when, in Figure 6.1, the area of triangle B equals that of triangle A. The presence of indifference can be important. From the perspective of early preferences, an individual will typically care about how his later self would resolve future points of indifference. Specifically, his early choices may be premised on the tie–breaking mechanism his future self will use. Therefore it is important to be clear about the extent to which the current self is aware of the way its later self will resolve future indifference.

In the absence of indifference, the existence of a Strotz–Pollak equilibrium follows from backward induction, under the assumption that the utility function is continuous. However, the presence of indifference interferes with the use of this argument as a means of establishing indifference. Nevertheless, as Goldman (1980) demonstrated, indifference does not prevent the existence of a Strotz–Pollak equilibrium. His result is discussed below.

Previous to Goldman's work, there was some confusion about whether an equilibrium can be guaranteed to exist in this type of game. Recall that in the model under discussion, the date t self only games forward. That is, it takes the past as given, and bases its choice upon the anticipated reaction of the selves which follow. Peleg and Yaari (1973) present an example in which the date t self games in both directions. That is the date t self chooses its reaction function with a view to influencing the choice of its earlier self, as well as its future self. Peleg and Yaari argue that an equilibrium does not exist for their example. In their general model, Peleg and Yaari use the Nash concept of equilbrium. That is, each date t self chooses a reaction function, and in a Nash equilibrium, the chosen functions are best responses to the reaction functions of all the other selves. Goldman argues that the equilibrium concept which Peleg and Yaari discuss in the context of their example is non–Nash, and hence at odds with their general model. Moreover, he asserts that the example does actually possess a Nash equilibrium.[12]

Goldman's existence theorem is quite general. In addition to admitting indifference, the utility function at each date need not be additively separable, and can have as its domain the entire consumption path. Consequently, the proof will also cover the case of endogenously changing tastes, which is discussed in section 9. Below I sketch Goldman's existence proof.

---

[12]In the Peleg–Yaari model, there is no requirement that the Nash equilibrium be perfect. Goldman raises the concern that as a result, when considering the implications of choosing a non–equilbrium strategy, the date t self may make erroneous assumptions about the behavior of its future self.

THEOREM 7.1 Let the utility function at each date be continuous in c. Then a Strotz–Pollak equilibrium exists.

PROOF At date t, the individual observes the history c^{t-1} defined as $(c_1, \cdots, c_{t-1})$, and chooses c_t. In turn, this produces the history $c^t = (c^{t-1}, c_t)$. Define $X^t(c^t)$ as the set of full T–length consumption paths c which can emerge, given history c^t and subsequent optimizing behavior. Because of indifference, $X^t(c^t)$ need not be a singleton. Observe that for given c^{t-1}, each choice of c_t in $[0, q_{t-1}]$ has an associated $X^t(c^t)$. Define Y^t as $\cup X^t(c^t)$, where the union is over all c^t such that $q_t \geq 0$.

The claim is that both $X^t(c^t)$ and Y^t are compact and nonempty. The argument for this claim is based upon backward induction. For $t = T$, the case is clear. $X^T(c^T)$ can only be c^T, and Y^T must be the set of all budget feasible consumption paths. Next proceed inductively from $t + 1$ to t, assuming that X^{t+1} and Y^{t+1} are both nonempty and compact.

Since $X^{t+1}(c^{t+1})$ is compact, its elements can be ordered by date $t + 1$ preferences. Define $W^{t+1}(c^{t+1})$ as the worst consumption paths in $X^{t+1}(c^{t+1})$. These are the worst consumption paths which might result after c_{t+1} has been chosen at date $t+1$. With c^t fixed, vary c_{t+1} to find the best consumption path in the closure of the union $\cup W^{t+1}(c^{t+1})$. Call this the maximin set $B^{t+1}(c^t)$.

Formally, $X^t(c^t)$ may be defined as the set of consumption paths faced by the date $t + 1$ self which are at least as good as those in B^{t+1}. Since the upper contour set to b and $\cup X^{t+1}(c^{t+1})$ are both closed and the intersection is nonempty, it follows that $X^t(c^t)$ is nonempty and compact.

Clearly Y^t is nonempty. To see that it is also compact, consider a sequence $\{{}^n c\}$, where ${}^n c \in X^t({}^n c^t)$, such that ${}^n c$ converges to $\bar{c}$. The claim is that $\bar{c}$ belongs to Y^t. Recall that ${}^n c \in X^t({}^n c^t)$ implies that date $t + 1$ preferences rank ${}^n c$ at least as highly as the elements in the union of all worst point sets which could be generated by the budget feasible choices at date $t+1$. Therefore date $t+1$ preferences rank $\bar{c}$ at least as highly as the elements in the set of cluster points attached to sequences selected from the worst point sets $W^{t+1}(\bar{c}^t, c_{t+1})$ where c_{t+1} is budget feasible. Recall that budget feasible means that $c_{t+1} \in [0, q_t]$. It follows that $\bar{c}$ is at least as good as any maximin path in $B^{t+1}(\bar{c}^t)$. Hence $\bar{c}$ belongs to Y^t, which establishes compactness.

Apply the induction process to obtain X^1, which is compact and nonempty. The claim is that any member c^* of X^0 is a consumption path for some Strotz–Pollak equilibrium. To prove the claim, we need to construct reaction functions which constitute a perfect Nash equilibrium for the game. Let the reaction function for date 1 specify the choice c_1^*. Now assign each budget feasible choice of c_1 to a full path $s^1(c_1)$ in Y^1, such that s^1 maps c_1^* to c^* and all other budget feasible elements to the dominated paths $W^1(c_1)$.

Define the reaction function for the date 2 self as the second component of s^1. This means that if the date 1 self chooses c_1^*, then the date 2 self responds with c_2^*. However, suppose that the date 1 self chooses something other than c_1^*. Then if the date 2 self can both maximize its own utility, and simultaneously punish the date 1 self, it will do so. In other words, if because of indifference, the date 2 self has multiple optimal responses to the date 1 choice $c_1 \neq c_1^*$, then it will choose an optimal response which punishes date 1.

Proceeding inductively, we obtain a sequence of reaction functions which together form a perfect Nash equilibrium. The strategy is Nash because given these reaction functions, at no date t does the individual perceive himself to benefit by deviating from the strategy in question. If he does, he anticipates that his future selves will punish him if they can by choosing a path in $W^t(c^t)$. The equilbrium is subgame perfect because the X^t sets were constructed using backward recursion. ∎

Notice that in Goldman's proof, indifference is resolved by punishing past preferences for deviations from a particular reaction function. In recent unpublished work, von Auer (1995a, 1995b) has explored some of the structural issues arising from indifference. His work deals with the characteristics of four specific sophisticated choice mechanisms.

In order to define these mechanisms, consider the following example due to Hammond (1976a). In Figure 7.1, a decision maker faces a two period decision tree with two decision nodes n_0 and n_1, and three possible intertemporal outcomes a, b, and c. At the initial date (0), the decision maker's preferences are $bPcPa$. However, date 1 preferences feature $aPbPc$. At each decision node, the decision maker must select exactly one branch. Observe that a naive decision maker would select the top branch at node n_0 with the intent of achieving outcome b, only to find themselves selecting a at node n_1. Hence a represents naive choice (c^N), and b represents precommitment(c^1). A sophisticated decision maker will understand the full implications of selecting the top branch at n_0, and will choose the lower branch instead, thereby leading to outcome c. That is, c represents consistent choice (c^*).

Consider the use of backward induction to arrive at the choice sets attached to each node. For instance, when n_1–preferences feature aPb, then $C(n_1) = \{a\}$. In such a case, von Auer (1995) states that b can be termed irrelevant for the choice at n_0: only a and c are relevant. If n_0–preferences feature cPa, (written $cP(n_0)a$), then by induction, $C(n_0) = \{c\}$.

The generation of choice sets through backward induction enables us to specify which outcomes are eliminated through strict preference. In the absence of indifference, all choice sets are singletons. This is not generally true when indifference is involved.

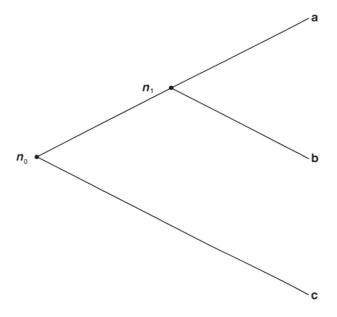

Figure 7.1 Hammond Decision Tree

Consider an example involving indifference. For instance, let $aI(n_1)b$, $bP(n_0)c$, and $cP(n_0)a$. Here $C(n_1) = \{a, b\}$. What will an individual do if his earlier self chose the top branch, thereby confronting him with indifference at n_1? If he resolves the indifference by assigning his earlier (or earliest) preferences seniority, then von Auer labels his choice mechanism as being *dogmatic*. Hence dogmatic choice in this example stipulates that the tie at n_1 be broken in favor of b, since b is strictly preferred at n_0.

Dogmatic choice is the first of four sophisticated mechanisms described by von Auer. It uses seniority to achieve resolution among relevant options. The second is *sagacious choice*. This rule uses the seniority of $bP(n_0)a$ to eliminate a from $C(n_0)$ *only if* a and b split at n_0. In this example, a and b emanate from the same branch at n_0, and so a would not be eliminated by appeal to b. Of course, $cP(n_0)a$, and c does split from a at n_0.

A third mechanism, even less restrictive, is *lenient choice*. Here a will not be eliminated as long as it is relevant, and it emanates from the same branch as some other option which is undominated in the set of relevant options. In this case $C(n_0)$ would contain both a and b, meaning that the decision maker understands that he could end up at either terminal node when he chooses the upper branch.

The last mechanism proposed by von Auer is *cautious choice*. When this mechanism is used, the decision maker at n_0 proceeds as follows. Branch by branch, he ascertains what would be the worst possible way, from the perspective of his n_0 preferences, that his future self might break an indifference tie. He then selects the branch offering the best of the worst cases. In other words, he invokes the maximin principle.

Of the four sophisticated choice mechnisms, von Auer establishes that three produce choice sets consistent with subgame perfect equilibria. The exception is leniency, and it is easy to see how subgame perfection would be violated in this case. Let $aP(n_0)cP(n_0)b$ and $aI(n_1)b$. Then lenient choice permits b to belong to $C(n_0)$. But the decision maker would definitely select c at n_0, if he anticipated that the upper branch would lead to b.

The preceding analysis can be extended to cover the case of uncertainty, for which von Auer establishes a series of general results. In Section 11, I discuss some of the issues which arise when tastes change in an uncertainty framework.

8   Welfare Implications

In the proof of Theorem 6.1, we encountered the choice problem of an individual who takes full account of how his future self will behave. The proof involved an explicit comparison of the dynamically consistent plan c^* with the plan c^1 which is optimal from the perspective of the date 1 utility function U_1. Whereas the individual judges c^1 to be superior to c^* under utility function U_1, his future self will typically disagree, since his future self uses different utility functions. Consequently, it is no longer possible to speak unambiguously about *the individual's* choice as being optimal.

One may wonder whether the consistent choice can be regarded as optimal relative to some meaningful aggregate of the utility functions experienced over the individual's lifetime? The general answer is no. Hammond (1976a) makes the argument that when an individual has an interest in precommitting his future self, then his choice function does not conform with an underlying preference ordering.

Consider the sophisticated decision maker's choice function $C()$ in Hammond's example (Figure 7.1). Recall that at the initial date (0), the decision maker's preferences feature $bPcPa$, but at date 1 preferences feature $aPbPc$. Confronted with the full set $\{a, b, c\}$ of alternatives, the decision maker selects $C(\{a, b, c\}) = \{c\}$. However, consider a subset of alternatives, say $\{b, c\}$. In this case, the decision maker is precluded from selecting a at n_1. Hence the sophisticated decision maker can initially select the top branch, knowing that the choice will conclude with b. That is, $C(\{b,c\}) = \{b\}$.

If the decision maker's choice is to conform with an underlying long run preference ordering, then it is necessary that his choice function conform with Sen's condition of α–rationality [Sen (1971)]. In the context of this example, α–rationality states the following: if c is in the choice set $C(\{a,b,c\})$, and c belongs to a subset X of $\{a,b,c\}$, then c must lie in the choice set $C(X)$. In the preceding example α–rationality is violated, with $X = \{b,c\}$.

Hammond's example illustrates an additional point about the decision maker's choice function. It may feature Pareto–inefficiency. Notice that from the perspective of *both* preference orderings, the precommitted choice b is preferred to sophisticated choice $C\{a,b,c\} = \{c\}$. As we shall now see, Pareto–inefficiency is a general feature of intertemporal choice when the discount function is hyperbolic. Specifically, we have:

THEOREM 8.1 Under hyperbolic discounting, there exists a comparison path c' which satisfies $\sum_{t=1}^{T} c'_t = q$, involves lower consumption at all dates before T, and Pareto–dominates the consistent plan c^*. That is, for all $\tau \leq T$, c' is judged superior to c^* under utility function U_τ.

PROOF We provide the proof for the case $T = 3$. The general case easily follows. Observe that along a consistent path, c_1 is selected to maximize:

$$u(c_1) + \lambda_1(2)u(c_2(q_1) + \lambda_1(3)u(c_3(q_1)), \tag{8.1}$$

so that

$$u'(c_1) = \lambda_1(2)u'(c_2)\frac{dc_2}{dq_1} + \lambda_1(3)u'(c_3)\frac{dc_3}{dq_1} \tag{8.2}$$

along c^*.

Now (6.9) and (8.2) imply that:

$$\lambda_1(2)u'(c_2^*) < u'(c_1^*) < \lambda_1(3)u'(c_3^*). \tag{8.3}$$

The second inequality implies that a transfer from date 1 to date 3 is regarded as an improvement from the perspective of the date 1 utility function. This transfer would also be regarded as an improvement as judged by the utility functions U_2 and U_3. This establishes that c^* is Pareto–inefficient. Finally notice that there is some sufficiently small transfer from date 2 to date 3 which, when combined with the transfer from date 2 to date 3, leaves the individual better off from the perspective of U_2. ∎

Goldman (1979) proves a result similar to Theorem 8.1, but under different hypotheses. In particular, his framework relaxes the assumption of additive separability, and replaces it with a set of restrictions on the reaction functions. One of these restrictions states that "an increase in the first generation's consumption would result in a decrease in the consumptions of all later generations at a rate bounded away from zero" (p. 622). As we saw earlier, this restriction does not hold as a general condition in the present framework.

9 Endogenously Changing Utility Functions

The discounted utility model assumes that instantaneous utility $u(c_t)$ is not directly affected by past consumption levels. An intriguing model with endogenously changing utility functions was proposed by Yaari (1977). In his model, the utility function at each date τ has the form

$$U_\tau = \int_\tau^\infty e^{-p(\tau)t} u(c(t)) dt, \tag{9.1}$$

where $p(\tau)$ is endogenously determined. Specifically, $p(0)$ is given at $\tau = 0$, and $p(\tau)$ is assumed to evolve according to:

$$p(\tau) = p(0) + \int_0^\tau c(t) dt. \tag{9.2}$$

In consequence the individual begins with impatience parameter $p(0)$ and concludes with an impatience parameter $p(0) + q$, after having consumed the entire wealth q. Since $\dot{p} = c(\tau)$, the level of impatience is endogenous: it not only rises continuously as wealth is depleted, but it is rises with the size of each "bite". For this reason Yaari describes q as an "appetite–arousing cake".

Notably, the appetite–arousing cake model features the common difference effect, and in this respect is similar to the hyperbolic discounting model. Yaari discusses this property in terms of naive planning. Let $\hat{T}(p, q)$ be the length of time an individual with impatience parameter p would plan to consume a cake of size q, under the naive belief that his impatience parameter will remain invariant at p over time. Yaari assumes that $0 < u' < \infty$, which implies that $\hat{T}(p, q) < \infty$. Let $T(p, q)$ be the actual time it takes for a naive individual to consume a cake of size q, when his initial impatience parameter is p. Yaari demonstrates that $T(p(\tau), q(\tau)) < \hat{T}(p(\tau), q(\tau))$ for every τ featuring a positive consumption rate. In other words, the cake will be consumed faster than was called for by any of the naive plans formulated by the individual.[13]

---

[13]In Yaari's continuous time model, $c(t)$ is given by $(\partial T / \partial q)^{-1}$. This relationship implies that the precommitment plan features slower consumption rates at each moment than the consistent plan.

In a discrete time version of the appetite arousing cake problem, let $\lambda_\tau(t) = (1/y_\tau)^{t-\tau}$, where y_τ is a positive, monotone increasing function of past consumption $\sum_{t<\tau} c_t$. Yaari's result holds in the discrete version of the model, but in the following slightly weakened form.[14]

THEOREM 9.1 Let T_C and T_P be the minimum length of time needed to consume wealth q completely along the precommited and consistent plans respectively. Then: $T_C \le T_P < \infty$. There are parameter specifications for which the inequality is strict, and there are parameter specifications for which equality holds.

PROOF The first order condition associated with the precommitment path is:

$$u'(c_1) \ge \lambda_1(t)u'(c_t) \qquad (9.3)$$

for all t with strict inequality holding if $c_t = 0$.

Recall that ρ_τ is a reaction function associated with the consistent plan. I now show that there exists a monotone sequence $\bar{q}_0, \bar{q}_1, \cdots, \bar{q}_t, \cdots$, such that when $\bar{q}_t < q < \bar{q}_{t+1}$, one has $\rho_\tau(q) > 0$ for $\tau \le t+1$ and $\mu_\tau(q) = 0$ for $\tau > t+1$. Fix $\gamma > 0$. Define a function $f_t()$ as follows. If $\lambda_1(t)u'(c_t) = \gamma$ then $f_t(\gamma) = c_t$. That is, c_t is the value of date t consumption for which the associated marginal utility is γ. If $\lambda_1(t)u'(0) \le \gamma$, let $f_t = 0$. It follows from (9.3) that the precommitment plan c^1 can be obtained by finding a γ for which:

$$\sum_{t=1}^{\infty} f_t(\gamma) = q,$$

and setting $c_t^1 = f_t(\gamma)$. Consider $\bar{\gamma}_t = \lambda_1(t)u'(0)$. Let $\bar{q}_0 = 0$ and define $\bar{q}_t = \sum_{\tau=1}^{\infty} f_\tau(\bar{\gamma}_{\tau+1})$. It is easily verified that $\bar{q}_0, \bar{q}_1, \cdots$ is the claimed sequence.

Write $c_t(q)$ for $\rho_{t,\tau}(q_\tau)$. Suppose it were true that $T_C > T_P$. Then $c_t^1 > 0$ when $t = T_P + 1$. Hence there must be a τ for which $c_\tau^1 < c_\tau^P$ and $c_t^1 > c_t^P$ for all $t > \tau$. If this were not the case, then $c_t^1 > c_t^P$ for all t, which would contradict (4.3). It follows that $u'(c_t^1) < u'(c_t^P)$ for all $t > \tau$, since $c_t^1 > c_t^P$. Furthermore, $u'(c_\tau^1) > u'(c_\tau^P)$ since $c_\tau^1 < c_\tau^P$. But by (9.3), this implies

$$u'(c_\tau^1) > (\lambda_1(t)/\lambda_1(\tau))u'(c_t^P)$$

for all $t \ne \tau$. Using the monotonicity of the $\{y_t\}$ sequence, obtain

---

[14]Yaari also established the Pareto–inefficiency theorem for his model. An interesting feature of his result is that the comparison of the dynamically consistent path and Pareto dominating comparison path is accomplished from the utility functional corresponding to each impatience parameter p, rather than the utility function at each time t. Under the endogeneity property, these are not the same.

$$u'(c_\tau^1) > (\lambda_\tau(t)/\lambda_\tau(\tau))u'(c_t^P) > (\lambda_\tau(t)/\lambda_\tau(\tau))u'(c_t^C) \tag{9.4}$$

for all $t > \tau$. Let $V_\tau(q) = \sum_{t>\tau} \lambda_\tau(t)u(c_t(q))$. Recall that c_t^1 maximizes:

$$\lambda_\tau(\tau)u(c_\tau) + V_\tau(q_{\tau-1} - c_\tau),$$

where

$$V_\tau(q_\tau) = \sum_{t>\tau} \lambda_\tau(t)u(\rho_{t,\tau}(q_\tau)).$$

But the solution to the latter optimization could never satisfy (9.4), which contradicts the original hypothesis that $T_C > T_P$.

The remainder of the theorem follows from the proof of Theorem 6.1. ∎

A careful reading of the proof of the preceding theorem reveals that it does not depend on the endogeneity of the impatience parameter. All that is required is that the impatience parameters be monotone increasing. What endogeneity does add is an adjustment for anticipated appetite arousal. To see why, call the period 1 individual the current self. Consider how the current self arrives at a consumption decision along the consistent path. Recall that there are two variables to be compared: the utility attached to current consumption c_1 and the utility attached to the bequest q_1 which is consumed by the future self. Since the future self is more impatient than the current self, the former does not behave as the latter would like. Suppose that the future self consumes more rapidly than the current self would prefer. Suppose further that the rate at which the future self overconsumes is an increasing function of its degree of impatience. Then it seems clear that there is a sense in which the current self would wish to decrease its own rate of consumption in order to gain the benefits associated with a lower degree of future impatience. In this case, endogeneity contributes a moderating influence on intertemporal consumption choice.

The preceding issues can be seen formally in the case when $T_C = 3$. It follows from (6.7) and (6.8) that:

$$\begin{aligned} V'(q_1) =&(\lambda_1(2)u'(c_2^*)u''(q_1 - c_2^*) + \lambda_1(3)u'(q_1 - c_2^*)u''(c_2^*)y_2(c_1^*)) \\ &- [\lambda_1(3)u'(q_1 - c_2^*) - \lambda_1(2)[u'(c_2^*)]y_2'(c_1^*u'(c_2^*) \times \\ &[y_2(c_1)u''(c_2^*) + u'(q_1 - c_2^*]^{-1}. \end{aligned} \tag{9.5}$$

Notice that this equation is the sum of three terms. By (6.9), the third term being subtracted in the numerator is positive in the endogenous case, but zero in the exogenous case. Since the denominator is negative, endogeneity serves to make $V'(q_1)$ larger than it would be in the case where y_t is exogenously given by $y_t(c_t^*)$. Ceteris paribus, this makes the bequest q_1 more attractive from the perspective of date 1 preferences.

10   Changing Tastes and Consumer Theory

Until now, I have focused on the case in which there is a but a single commodity. However, changing tastes have also played a role in the development of consumer choice theory. In Section 6, I discussed an example due to Pollak in which utility is logarithmic in intertemporal consumption. In this section, I describe a multi–commodity model in which utility is logarithmic across commodities.

Let p_i be the price of commodity i, x_i the quantity consumed of the i–th commodity, and M the consumer's total expenditure (income). Consider a utility function of the form:

$$U(x_1, x_2, \ldots, x_n) = \sum_{k=1}^{n} a_k \ln(x_k - b_k), \tag{10.1}$$

where for all k, $a_k > 0$, $x_k > b_k$, and $\sum a_k = 1$. Notice that with this utility function, the consumer's utility becomes infinitely negative as x_k approaches b_k. For this reason, b_k can be regarded as a subsistence level. With this interpretation of b, we can view the preceding utility function as being logarithmic (i.e., Cobb–Douglas) in increments over and above subsistence. That is, the consumer first allocates the portion $\sum_k b_k p_k$ of income M to subsistence. He then allocates the residual $M - \sum_k b_k p_k$ according to the constant budget share rule which characterizes maximum logarithmic utility. Hence, the demand function corresponding to the preceding utility function is:

$$x_i = b_i - \frac{a_i}{p_i} \sum_k b_k p_k + \frac{a_i}{p_i} M, \tag{10.2}$$

which has come to be known as the Klein–Rubin–Stone–Geary linear expenditure system. Observe that this demand system exhibits linear Engel curves, a feature which plays a prominent role in one of the key results described below.

It appears that Stone (1954) may have been the first to suggest that the linear expenditure system could accommodate habit formation by letting some of the parameters depend on past consumption. In Pollak's (1971) model of habit formation, the subsistence level $b_{i,t}$ in the linear expenditure system takes the following form:

$$b_{i,t} = b_i^* + \beta_i x_{i,t-1}. \tag{10.3}$$

In Pollak's formulation, the individual becomes habituated to an amount which varies as a linear function of the previous level at which he consumed commodity i. Pollak suggests that the reference consumption level b_i^* can be thought of as the "physiologically necessary" component of $b_{i,t}$, and $\beta_i x_{i,t-1}$ as the "psychologically necessary" component. With this modification, the linear expenditure system gives rise to demand functions which are contingent on the consumption levels at the previous date. These demand functions are termed *short term*. Notice that in the multi–commodity setting, $b_{i,t}$ plays the role of a *reference bundle* in respect to the individual's moving frame of reference.[15]

The literature on habit formation has been concerned with the question of whether demands $x_{i,t}$ converge to steady state levels x_i when prices and expenditure levels remain invariant over time. Such steady state values are termed *long term demands*. Recall that for the short term demand functions, the reference consumption level for commodity i depends upon the past consumption of no other commodity save i. However, this is not so for long term demands, where reference consumption for *every* commodity i depends on the previous consumption levels of all commodities. This is because in the steady state, the budget constraint forces the process of habituation for each commodity to depend on the consumption levels of the other commodities.

The existence of long run demand functions gave rise to the question of whether there might be a long run utility function which would rationalize these long run demands. Peston (1967) considered a two–commodity model with logarithmic (Cobb–Douglas) utility, and derived a long run utility function which rationalizes his long run demand function. Gorman (1967) considered a more general model with n commodities in which short run utility depends on both a quantity vector and a vector of taste parameters. He presents a set of conditions under which a long run demand function can be represented by a long run utility function.

The existence of long run utility functions immediately raises questions about long term welfare. Von Weizsäcker (1971) addressed this issue in a two commodity model. His short run demand system can be expressed as:

$$x_{i,t} = f_i(p_1, p_2, M, x_{1,t-1}, x_{2,t-1}) \tag{10.4}$$

for $i = 1, 2$. Let

$$g_{i,j} = \partial x_{i,t}/\partial x_{j,t-1}. \tag{10.5}$$

Von Weizsäcker proves if $|g_{1,1} + g_{2,2}| < 1 - \epsilon$ for some $\epsilon > 0$, then there is a unique steady state point (x_1, x_2). In this case, there is a long run utility function over the set of steady state solutions.

---

[15]Stigler and Becker (1977) propose a model of habit formation (addiction) in which past consumption leads to the creation of capital. For example, listening to music in the past leads to the production of music capital. This capital increases the current utility produced from a given quantity of current musical input, just as more physical capital enables labor to be more productive. Their model is similar in structure to the habit formation models described here, although they offer a different interpretation of the factors underlying addiction.

Changing tastes can give rise to myopic behavior in which a sequence of short term improvements leads to a worsening long run situation. Figure 10.1 from von Weizsäcker (1971) illustrates a sequence of consumption points, and the indifference curves on which they appear. Notice that the consumer appears to move to a higher indifference curve from one date to the next. However, the sequence of points is moving to the origin. It is because of pathological examples such as these that von Weizsäcker suggests using long run preferences as the *real* indicators of welfare, rather than the short term preferences. In particular, he shows the following. Let $0 < g_{1,1} + g_{2,2} < 1$, and consider two steady state points x^1 and x^2. If x^2 has higher long run utility than x^1, then it will be possible to move from x^1 to x^2 through a sequence of short run choices, in which short run utility improves at every transition along the sequence.

Pollak (1976) argues that there are at least two serious difficulties with the welfare portion of von Weizsäcker's (1971) argument. The first difficulty is that x^2 may not appear to be a short run improvement over x^1 when x^1 is the previous consumption point. To illustrate his concern, Pollak provides an example using the linear expenditure habit formation system in which:

$$b_{i,t} = 1/2 x_{i,t-1} \tag{10.6}$$

and $a_k = 1/2$ for all k. The long run utility function turns out to be the product of the two demands. Let $x^1 = (6,4)$ and $x^2 = (4,7)$. It is easily verified that x^2 is the preferred steady state bundle, but it appears inferior in the short run if x^1 is consumed. Pollak contends basing welfare comparisons on the existence of a particular history leading from x^1 to x^2 is simply too fragile.

The second of Pollak's concerns involves the special nature of the assumption that there are only two commodities. Pollak argues that once there are three or more commodities, a long run utility function which rationalizes the long run demand function may not exist. He makes the argument for the class of linear Engel curve systems with linear habit formation. If the short run utility functions are additively separable, then the long run demand functions can, in fact, be rationalized by a long run utility function which also is additively separable. However, the case of additively separable short run utility curves is the *only* case for which there is a corresponding long run utility function. For linear Engel curve systems generated by short run utility functions which are not additively separable, such as the CES, no long run utility function will exist to rationalize the long run demand function. Welfare analysis based upon a long run utility function will just not be possible.

Hammond (1976b) uses choice theory to analyze the general relationship among short term preferences exhibiting path dependence, the acyclicity of long run preferences, and the global stability of long run choice. One of the key concepts in Hammond's analysis is that of a *conservative sequence*. To

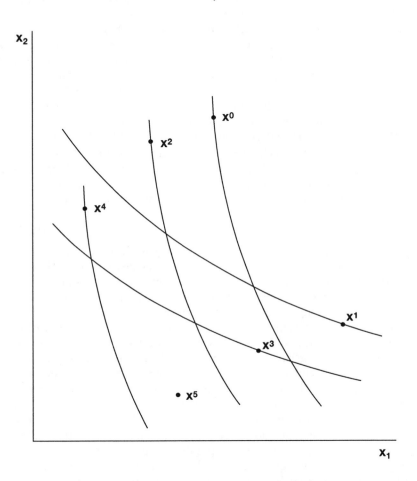

Figure 10.1   Short run improvement – Long run deterioration

understand what is meant by such a sequence, suppose that there is some date at which the individual cannot do better than make the same choice that he did at the preceding date. If he does so, then the sequence is conservative. Hammond shows that the long run choices from any compact set A are the cluster points of all conservative sequences. However, this result is consistent with multiple long run choices because "any cluster point of a conservative sequence is a long run choice. Oscillations between the neighborhoods of multiple long–run choices are still possible." (p. 338). This can be so despite the long run preference relation being acyclic. Indeed Hammond provides an example in which this property holds despite there being a continuous long run utility function. In the example, the objects of choice are real numbers. The utility of an object is its distance from the interval $[2,4]$. Imagine a sequence of points which alternately approach $[2,4]$ from the left of 2, and the right of 4. Let each point be closer to the interval $[2,4]$ than its predecessor, and let 2 and 4 be cluster points of the sequence. Then both cluster points are in the choice set, and the preference relation is acyclic.

11   Uncertainty

There is a close formal analogy between intertemporal choice and decision making under uncertainty. Notably, a profile of state–contingent outcomes is similar to a profile of time–contingent outcomes, and discount weighting is similar to probability weighting. The following extension of (3.1) illustrates a framework which incorporates both intertemporal and uncertainty elements.

$$U(c) = \sum_{t,i} \delta^{t-1} p_i u(c_{t,i}), \qquad (11.1)$$

where $c_{t,i}$ denotes consumption at date t conditional on the occurence of event i, and p_i denotes the probability attached to event i. Observe that in (11.1) utility $u(c_{t,i})$ is discounted by $\delta^{t-1} p_i$. An individual with time invariant preferences represented by (11.1) will exhibit dynamically consistent behavior.

Despite the formal similarities between the intertemporal and uncertainty elements of choice, there are important and subtle differences. Consequently, I begin with some examples to fix ideas. Consider yourself to be in a situation where you are presented with three pairs of lotteries, and asked to express your preference in respect to each pair. For each pair, imagine that you have an opportunity to choose to play exactly one member from each pair on a one–time only basis. The first two pairs $(1A, 1B)$ and $(2A, 2B)$ are as follows:

1A. A 90 percent chance of winning \$2000, and a 10 percent chance of zero.

1B. A 45 percent chance of winning \$4000, and a 55 percent chance of zero.

2A. A 0.2 percent chance of winning $2000, and a 99.8 percent chance of zero.

2B. A 0.1 percent chance of winning $4000, and a 99.9 percent chance of zero.

The third choice pair involves compound lotteries consisting of two stages. In the first stage, the probability of winning a prize is 2/900 (that is, 2.22 percent). Now imagine that you have won at the first stage, and must choose among two lotteries to be played at the second stage:

3A. A lottery ticket to 1A (described above).

3B. A lottery ticket to 1B (described above).

The three binary choices just presented are taken from Kahneman and Tversky (1979). In an experimental setting, Kahneman and Tversky elicited individual preferences for all three. They report that there is a systematic tendency among their subjects to choose in a particular way. Specifically, A tends to be favored over B in both the first and third choice pairs, while 2B tends to be favored over 2A.

Imagine someone who expresses the preceding preference pattern. McClennen (1990) states that this pattern reflects dynamic inconsistency. Notably, the compound lottery associated with 3A is equivalent to 2A, and the compound lottery associated with 3B is equivalent to 2B. Consequently, at the first stage the individual acts as if he prefers 2B over 2A, but reverses this preference at the second stage. To complete the analogy with the certainty case, consider the following modification to the third choice pair.

Imagine that at the first stage of the compound lottery you face a choice. You may play the compound lottery described above, or you may play the following simple lottery:

2A+. A 0.2 percent chance of winning $2001, and a 99.8 percent chance of zero.

Observe that 2A+ stochastically dominates 2A in that it offers a prize which is $1 dollar more. We view $1 as an ϵ which is sufficiently small so that 2B is preferred to 2A+ as well as to 2A.

Figure 11.1 portrays the choice situation. Consider the analogue to naive choice. At the first stage the agent favors 2B, which emanates from the top branch at stage 1, over 2A+, which emanates from the bottom branch at stage 1. Naive choice implies that during the first stage, the agent believes that if he selects the top branch and subsequently wins at the first stage, then he will choose to play 1B over 1A at the second stage. Of course, if the agent manages to end up facing this choice at the second stage, he will choose 1A, not 1B.

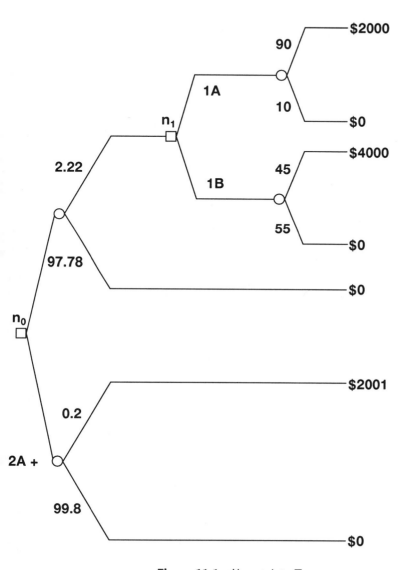

Figure 11.1 Uncertainty Tree

Consequently, naive choice leads the individual to actually choose to play the compound lottery $2A$ over $2A+$.

Recall that $2A+$ actually stochastically dominates $2A$. Consequently, sophisticated choice would involve the selection of $2A+$ at the first stage, since the sophisticated agent makes his choice by taking proper account of his future self's choice behavior.

Keep in mind that the intertemporal certainty framework has been extended to accomodate uncertainty. This extension essentially involves the recasting of time from the single variable t to the ordered pair (t, s), where s is a state of nature. Hence the root of dynamic inconsistency in the intertemporal setting will carry forward to the uncertainty setting. Moreover, the additively separable intertemporal utility function has expected utility as its uncertainty analogue: both involve weighted sums of sub–utilities.

In the certainty model with intertemporally additive utility, a nonexponential discount function lies at the root of the divergence between naive choice and precommitted choice. Consider the same question in connection with the uncertainty framework.[16] In other words, if we take the discount function to be exponential, then what is the root cause of dynamic inconsistency in choices over lotteries? This question brings us to the overlap of ideas between the present chapter and Chapters 3, 5, 6, and 13. Hammond has forcefully argued that in a consequentialist setting, it is the independence axiom associated with expected utility which lies at the root of the issue.

In order to illustrate the key aspect underlying the connection between expected utility and dynamic inconsistency, consider the example discussed above. Let the agent's preferences satisfy the axioms of expected utility. Then the agent possesses a utility function u on the set of consequences. For simplicity, we normalize u and set $u(0) = 0$ and $u(4000) = 1$. Then preferences over gambles are represented by expected utility. Since in the example $1A$ is preferred to $1B$, $1A$ must have a higher expected utility than $1B$. This holds if and only if $u(2000) > 0.5$. However, this last inequality implies that $2A$ must be preferred to $2B$, in contrast to the preference pattern assumed in the example.

The independence axiom underlies the representation of preferences over lotteries by means of an expected utility functional. It should come as no surprise that the independence axiom is central to the issue of dynamic consistency. The independence axiom is a statement about compound lotteries. Let A, B, and C be lotteries, with A being at least as good as B. The independence axiom pertains to two compound lotteries: AC, which is A with probability q and C probability $1 - q$, and BC which is B with probability q and C probability $1 - q$. The independece axiom asserts that since A is at least as good as B, then

---

[16]Von Auer's treatment of the subtleties associated with indifference extends to the uncertainty case as well.

AC must be at least as good as BC. As McClennen's example makes clear, the menu of lotteries at any node in the uncertainty tree comprises compound lotteries based upon lotteries attached to future nodes. Therefore the independence axiom effectively imposes dynamic consistency across the tree.

Note that the preceding example illustrates one of the well known Allais paradoxes, in which preferences are inconsistent with expected utility. See Chapter 6. Notably, if $2A$ is preferred to $2B$, then there is no conflict between the agent's preference ordering at the two stages. Lottery $2A+$ would be selected, regardless of whether the choice mechanism were naive, sophisticated, or precommitted.

12   Prospect Theory

Experimental evidence suggests that dynamic inconsistency is prevalent. If so, then it is important to understand why this is the case. Economists and psychologists have a common interest in this question. Recall the passages quoted in Section 4 from Strotz (1956) which dealt with the general shape of the discount function. Subsequent to the appearance of his article, psychologists proposed that most individuals exhibit dynamic inconsistency because they discount the future using hyperbolic functions. In this section, I discuss the contributions of psychologists Kahneman and Tversky to the analogous question of why individuals exhibit dynamic inconsistency when facing uncertainty. In addition, I describe how their work has been used to provide additional insight into dynamically inconsistent intertemporal choice.

Kahneman and Tversky (1979) have developed a framework to describe the character of the heuristics which lead many people to exhibit preferences such as those described in the examples discussed in the previous section. They call their framework *prospect theory*. Recall that in the examples described in the previous section, dynamic inconsistency leads to the selection of a stochastically dominated lottery under naive choice. Indeed it is common for prospect theoretic individuals to choose stochastically dominated lotteries. Prospect theory seeks to describe why this can occur, but hardly suggests that such behavior is normatively desireable. Nevertheless, Kahneman and Tversky's findings suggest that dynamic inconsistency among individuals is quite prevalent.[17]

---

[17]This feature leads to question of whether all those choosing stochastically dominated lotteries can be subjected to a money pump which leads them to lose all their wealth in short order. An affirmative answer does not follow automatically, and it may not follow at all. There are many complex issues which can interfere with the operation of money pumps, such as: transaction costs, customizing the money pump to individual preference patterns, whether individuals learn when they recognize a sequence of losses, and stop particating without adjusting their preferences, institutional structure and securities market regulation.

Prospect theory involves two stages. In the first stage, a decision problem is decomposed into a series of subproblems. Kahneman and Tversky refer to this stage as *editing*. The editing phase results in the establishment of what can be termed *mental accounts*. These record the outcomes associated with the various subproblems. In the second stage, the *evaluation stage*, the alternatives in each mental account are evaluated by means of a weighted sum of utilities. The actual decision is assumed to maximize the value of the weighted sum. I note that although the weights are functions of the probability distribution, they are not identical to probabilities. In particular, Kahneman and Tversky suggest that individuals tend to overweight low probability events relative to high probability events. The nonuniform weighting function lies at the heart of the breakdown of expected utility across the first and second pairs of lotteries in the preceding example.

The formal structure of prospect theory involves the specification of the mental accounting structure, reference points, utility function, and probability weighting function. Define a general prospect (x, p) in terms of the two vectors x and p. Here p_i denotes the probability attached to the occurence of event i, and x_i represents the outcome attached to this event. Consider a decomposition of x into J subvectors x^j, where:

$$x = \sum_{j=1}^{J} x^j, \tag{12.1}$$

Consider the prospects (x^j, p). A decision maker who faces concurrent prospects (x^j, p), $j = 1, \ldots J$, effectively faces the overall prospect (x, p). A mental account consists of a prospect together with a reference point ρ^j, and hence can be expressed as a triple (x^j, p, ρ^j). If event i occurs then this mental account registers a net gain of $x_i^j - \rho^j$. The prospect theoretic counterpart to expected utility is a function:

$$\sum_i f_i(p)v(x_i^j - \rho^j), \tag{12.2}$$

where v is a utility function over the domain of net gains. Kahneman and Tversky call v a *value function*.

By defining v as a function of $x_i^j - \rho^j$, utility is taken to be defined over the domain of gains and losses, rather than final outcome. Notably, Kahneman and Tversky postulate that utility is concave in gains but convex in losses. That is, $v(x_i^j - \rho^j)$ is concave when $x_i^j - \rho^j$ is positive, and convex when $x_i^j - \rho^j$ is negative. To see the implications of this assumption, consider the following example. Consider the following two pairwise choices. First, choose between:

4A. A 100 percent chance of winning $1800; and

4B. A 45 percent chance of winning $4000, and a 55 percent chance of zero.

Second, choose between:

5A. A 100 percent chance of losing $1800; and

5B. A 45 percent chance of losing $4000, and a 55 percent chance of losing zero.

Because 4A and 4B have the same expected payoff, none of the probabilities lie at the extreme ends of the spectrum, and the lotteries are defined in the domain of gains, a prospect theoretic individual would select 4A. The same is true for 5A and 5B, except that here the two lotteries are defined in terms of losses. Consequently, a prospect theoretic individual would select 5B over 5A, whereas a risk averse individual would select 5A.

Expected utility requires that $f_i(p) = p_i$. In the Kahneman–Tversky (1979) treatment of prospect theory, the function $f_i(p)$ is a function $\pi(p_i)$. In addition, f satisfies $f_i(p) > p_i$ for positive p_i near zero, and $f_i(p) < p_i$ for p_i near unity. This specification has some attendant difficulties with violation of stochastic dominance. The issue motivated Quiggin (1982) to suggest a *rank dependent* structure for f based upon the cumulative density function.

Consider a specific mental account (x^j, p, ρ^j), and order the events i so that x_i^j is lowest in event 1 and monotonically increases over events $2, 3, \ldots$ Rank dependent utility involves the cumulative probability distribution C, where $C(y)$ is the probability (given p) that the random payoff x^j to mental account j is y or less. Let $F(C(x))$ be a transformed cumulative function, with $[f_i]$ being the associated density function. If f_i is obtained in this way, then f_k and f_l need not be equal, even if $p_k = p_l$. In their (1992) version of prospect theory, called cumulative prospect theory, Kahneman and Tversky adopt the rank dependent formulation.[18]

In general, there may be several ways to decompose or frame a particular decision problem. Consequently, the reference point which is used as a basis for computing gains and losses may fail to be unique. This feature can give rise to *framing* effects, in which the decision taken is sensitive to the way that the decision problem is framed. For example, an individual who receives a coincident payment of $2000 when facing pair 5, may factor this payment into his evaluation of the two lotteries. If he does, then he frames his choice as a gamble involving gains, and this would lead him to select 5A. If he views the coincident payment of $2000 to be independent of the gamble, and therefore ignores it when making his choice, then he frames his choice in the domain of

---

[18]In cumulative prospect theory, there are two transformation functions, one for gains and the other for losses

losses and chooses $5B$. Therefore, prospect theoretic individuals are vulnerable to *static inconsistency* as well as dynamic inconsistency. Notice that the core issue is not so much the violation of expected utility as the absence of a consequentialist framework. The domain over which utility (or value v) is defined concerns lottery outcomes rather than final consequences.

The terminology of framing and reference points explicitly links prospect theory to the notion of moving frames of reference. In effect, the reference point serves as a degenerate (certainty) reference lottery, against which the alternatives are compared.[19]

Loewenstein and Prelec (1992) use prospect theory to develop an intertemporal choice model without uncertainty. Their model is designed to accomodate a variety of empirical regularities which have been observed about the way that people discount future outcomes. Notably, such discounting is a function of the way that outcomes are transformed into utility as well as the extent to which future utility is discounted to the present. Consider the *equivalent variation E* associated with a reward of X at time t. That is, E satisfies:

$$u(E) = \lambda(t)u(X).$$

Notice that the ratio E/X can be considered the discount factor applied to X being received at t.[20] If u were linear, then E/X would just be $\lambda(t)$. However if u is strictly concave, then it is easily demonstated that $E/X < \lambda(t)$.

In addition to the common difference effect described in sections 4 and 5, Loewenstein and Prelec discuss three other effects which are inconsistent with the discounted utility model. They are:

The gain–loss asymmetry where gains are discounted at higher rates than losses; and

The absolute magnitude effect where small amounts are discounted at a higher rates than large amounts;[21]

The delay–speedup asymmetry in which the valuation placed upon a change in timing of receipt depends upon whether it is framed as a delay or as a speedup.

The following example illustrates some of the features with which Loewenstein and Prelec are concerned. Two groups of subjects are presented with different descriptions of the *same* decision problem involving the instalment

---

[19]The reference lottery need not be degenerate.
[20]We could also have used the compensating variation in place of the equivalent variation.
[21]This property is actually consistent with the discounted utility model, but becomes anomolous in combination with the gain–loss asymmetry.

purchase of a television set. The first group is told that they must choose between:

A. A payment this week of $160 and a second payment of $110 in six months; and

B. A payment this week of $115 and a second payment of $160 in six months.

The second group is told that the plan normally calls for two equal payments of $200, one this week and one in six months. However, because of a promotional sale, there are rebates which will be applied to both payments, and timed to coincide with the payments themselves. The second group can choose between two rebate schedules, namely:

C. A rebate of $40 on the initial payment and a rebate of $90 on the later payment.

D. A rebate of $85 on the initial payment and a rebate of $40 on the later payment.

Notice that alternatives A and C are equivalent to each other as are B and D. Nevertheless in experimental settings, there is a systematic preference for A over B, but D over C. Loewenstein and Prelec explain this finding in terms of their model as follows. The participants in the first group frame the decision problem as a choice between two loss schedules, where as the participants in the second group frame the problem in terms of gains. Because losses are discounted less than gains, A is selected on the basis of a lower total payment. However, the second frame features *both* gains *and* smaller magnitudes. Therefore the later rebate is discounted highly, and this leads to the preference for D over C.

There is a well documented phenomenon known as *preference reversal* which was discovered in connection with decision making under uncertainty but also applies to intertemporal choice. Tversky and Thaler (1990) survey the literature on this phenomenon. Imagine that an individual is asked for two pieces of information about a pair of lotteries, such as $1A$ and $1B$ in Section 11. The first piece of information is how he ranks the pair. The second piece of information is the value of each certainty equivalent $CE(1A)$ and $CE(1B)$.[22] If an individual claims to favor $1A$ over $1B$, but attaches a higher certainty equivalent to $1B$ than to $1A$, then he is said to commit preference reversal. This leads to a preference cycle since $CE(1A)$ is indifferent to $1A$, $1A$ is preferred to $1B$, $1B$ is indifferent to $CE(1B)$, and $CE(1B)$ is preferred to $CE(1A)$.

---

[22]Let the individual own the lottery ticket, so that the certainty equivalent refers to the lowest amount they would accept in order to voluntarily sell the ticket.

Tversky and Thaler suggest three possible explanations of preference reversal: (1) intransitive preferences; (2) violation of the independence axiom; and (3) cognitive mispricing. Although the evidence suggests that there is more than one single explanation for what causes the phenomenon, Tversky and Thaler indicate that mispricing appears to the most prevalent. Specifically, many individuals are prone to attach too high a certainty equivalent to a lottery such as $1B$. They do this because in their computation of $CE(1B)$, they overweight the importance of the \$4000 payoff relative to the probability of its occurence. Tversky and Thaler indicate that such errors are not confined to uncertainty. Similar reversals occur when delayed rewards are being compared, and their equivalent variations computed. The phenomenon of preference reversal raises the question of whether individuals can even be said to have intact preference orderings. Tversky and Thaler suggest that what they have instead is a set of basic value principles, which they use to construct preferences each time that a choice needs to be made. If so, then preference reversal may reflect systematic cognitive errors in reconstructing the relevant potion of the preference ordering from the underlying value primitives.

13   Self–Control, Willpower, and Rules

The game theoretic model of changing tastes treats the individual as a time sequence of different players. The final topic in this chapter concerns an alternative to the game theoretic formulation of changing tastes. The alternative model is known as *the behavioral life cycle hypothesis (BLC)* [Shefrin and Thaler (1988)].[23] The BLC differs from the game theoretic formulation in several major respects. Most importantly, it postulates that although individuals have long run utility functions, they must simultaneously deal with a variety of elements emphasized in the psychology literature.

McClennen (1990) struggles with the game theoretic characterization of the changing self. He proposes the notion of *resolute choice*, which essentially means that the agent ignores his momentary preferences, and instead chooses the precommited plan. A resolute person manages to persuade himself to ignore the preferences he 'feels' at the moment, and act in accordance with what he currently recognizes that he felt earlier.

Resolute choice assigns priority to preference orderings according to seniority. Is this sensible? Does this mean that the individual's lot is improved by being beholden to his previous tastes? In the game theoretic framework, where an individual is treated as a time sequence of different players, the assignment

---

[23] Although the BLC framework covers the case of many commodities and uncertainty, this section deals only with intertemporal issues. Addiction is usually commodity specific. Perhaps the most vivid self–control problem in an uncertainty context is *compulsive gambling*.

of priority on the basis of seniority seems rather arbitrary. However, resolute choice strikes us as being more compelling if we take a somewhat different view as to what constitutes an individual who has to deal with internal conflict.

Let me suggest that instead of thinking of the source of conflict as being separated by time, we think of the conflict as coincident in time. That is, the individual must simultaneously deal with distinct preference components which may not be aligned with respect to prescribed choice. For instance, one set of preference components stems from what he *thinks*, and another stems from how he *feels*. An individual may think he should save more today, but when physically faced with the array of choice in the shops, feels like spending more.

Incorporating the way an individual feels, as distinct from how they think, reflects the role of emotion in choice. By and large, economists have been slow to recognize the impact of emotion. See Frank (1988).

Temptation operates on how we feel. Individuals who decide on the basis of how they feel rather than on what they think, may be regarded as suffering from weakness of will. Willpower connotes the idea that an individual wills himself to overrule the choice recomended by his feelings and instead choose in accordance with what he thinks.

The preferences associated with what an individual thinks need not be constant over time. Nevertheless, I suggest that adults with coherent personalities, have beliefs about themselves which are fairly constant over reasonable timespans. Moreover, when viewed in relative time, the preferences associated with how they feel may also be fairly constant. For instance, every day, an individual may *experience the urge* to overindulge, even as he *thinks* he should stop smoking.

I would argue that an individual who behaves resolutely with respect to past preferences, is being resolute in respect to preferences which reflect what he thinks, rather than what he feels. Moreover, what confers priority on these past preferences is their stability over time. In this sense, past preferences are a proxy. Because what an individuals thinks is reasonably stable, he is being resolute relative to what he thinks at the moment. Indeed this is what strikes me as being the most compelling aspect of resolute choice. The individual displays willpower, and resolves to behave in accordance with what he thinks, even when it conflicts with what he feels.

The difference in perspective between simultaneous conflict and intertemporally separated conflict is nontrivial, both in terms of positive and normative considerations. Notably, there is a psychological dimension which introduces the possibility of significant framing effects. That is, two situations which differ in form, but appear to be identical in substance, do not lead to the same behavior. This means that the specification of utility functions and intertemporal budget sets may not be sufficient to determine the choice sets. Germane psychological variables must also be identified.

Besides reference point issues, psychological studies offer additional insights into intertemporal choice. Mischel, Shoda, and Rodriguez (1992) describe the techniques used by children to delay gratification. In their work, children are offered the choice between a small immediate reward and a larger delayed reward. Those who announce their preference for the delayed reward are allowed an opportunity to change their mind while they wait, and can call for the smaller reward at any time. The challenge these children face is in implementing their stated preference, by not giving in to the temptation to change their minds. Some are successful while others are not. Mischel, Shoda, and Rodriguez provide insights into the willpower techniques children employ in order to exhibit self–control.

Ainslie and Haslam (1992) discuss self–control in the broader context of impulse control. The central issue here is that the exercise of willpower requires effort, and that people rely on personal rules and reward mechanisms to overcome temptation. There is more going on here than the execution of a Strotz–Pollak equilibrium from the different utility functions held by the individual over the course of his lifetime. We are back to Rae's concern about "abstinence".

Saving for retirement is a self–control exercise for adults. They too must defer immediate gratification in order to receive a larger, delayed reward. They too employ techniques in order to exhibit the self–control required to accumulate wealth for retirement. Shefrin and Thaler (1988) discuss some of these techniques, and provide a model to explain why these techniques work. Empirically, virtually no retirement saving is accomplished through discretionary means. Those who successfully accumulate retirement wealth do so through their reliance upon institutionalized programs. Pension plans, whole life insurance, Social Security, and Individual Retirement Accounts are the primary vehicles used by Americans to save. The Japanese use a system of regular, forecastable bi–annual bonuses. Interestingly, Americans appear to simulate the bonus pattern of payment by having excessive amounts withheld by the Internal Revenue Service, which is returned to them in the form of a lump sum income tax refund. There is also great reliance upon rules of thumb such as 'don't dip into capital'. Shefrin and Statman (1984) document the reluctance of people to dip into their stock portfolios, even in times of financial difficulty.

The *behavioral life cycle model* (BLC) was proposed by Shefrin and Thaler (1988) as a framework for dealing with the way people save for retirmement over the life cycle. It focuses on the character of second–best rules which are used to generate and protect wealth earmarked for retirement. The alternative to using rules in the BLC is to rely on discretion, and discretion maximizes the individual's exposure to self–control conflicts.[24]

The structure of the BLC model is as follows. The implementation of a consumption decision is assumed to require effort. Let θ_t be the degree of willpower effort exerted at date t. Consumption level c_t is taken to result from the interaction of θ_t and the rule R being followed by the individual. We can denote this feature in terms of a function $c_t = f(\theta_t, R)$. There is an intertemporal utility function U which is *unchanging* over time. Willpower effort is taken to be costly in the sense that $\partial U/\partial \theta_t < 0$.

A rule R can be regarded as a set of *self–imposed liquidity constraints*. In the formal BLC model, individuals make choices about the form of their income stream, degree of willpower, and consumption stream in order to maximize lifetime utility U. This optimization is constrained by the lifetime budget constraint, and a series of liquidity constraints implied by the rule R.

The BLC framework draws on prospect theory in relying on the concept of mental accounts as the foundation for a savings rule R. Specifically, the BLC model postulates that an individual decomposes his wealth into a series of mental accounts which correspond respectively to current income, a series of current assets, and future wealth. All of these accounts represent possible sources of funds to finance current consumption. However, the individual's internal decision technology imposes a utility entry cost (a "fence") for "invading" an account for this purpose.

In the BLC, an individual copes with the urge for immediate gratification in two ways. First, he employs willpower. Second, he chooses the form of his income stream and the arrangement of his wealth so that it receives protection from these fences. For instance, he tends to finance consumption entirely from his current income account, and only when that account is exhausted turns to another account, such as liquid savings. This leads the marginal propensity to consume out of wealth to depend on the form in which wealth is held. The marginal propensity to consume out of current income is highest, and out of future income the lowest. Funds earmarked for retirement are protected by using mechanisms such as pension plans that automatically deduct contributions, thereby allocating such wealth to an asset account[25] rather than to the current income account.

A prudent rule, such as "don't dip into capital", corresponds to the use of a mental accounting fence. However, the BLC does not make the self–imposed

---

[24]There are other approaches to modeling internal conflict besides the BLC. For example, Schelling (1992) provides an insightful discussion of "self–command", in which individuals experience alternating intertemporal utility functions. This view of intertemporal conflict has the form of a game, in which players make alternating moves. Schelling's concern is with the strategic implications associated with being involved in such a game with oneself.

[25]Featuring a low marginal propensity to consume.

constraint "hard". There may be circumstances in which the costs of maintaining the rule outweigh the benefits of breaking it. The BLC permits the breaching of a rule, although it requires that a utility cost be incurred for invading a new mental account

The BLC incorporates many of the features addressed in the writings of the early economists which were summarized at the outset of the chapter. Rae's concept of abstinence occupies center stage. In line with Böhm–Bawerk, the individual has an unchanging intertemporal utility function U. This function represents the way an individual thinks, and as such serves as *one* of the cognitive components underlying preferences over the choices available at any given date t. The cognitive component which represents the impulses an individual feels might be represented by hyperbolic discounting, with its disproportionate weighting of the present and near future. In line with the preceding discussion about preference reversal, the individual's preferences over his date t choices will be constructed from the primitive components. In so doing, he will exert effort θ_t in order to reconcile the conflict between what he thinks is best and what his impulses are urging him to do.[26] Self–control, after all, boils down to impulse control.

In order to understand the formal structure which reflects the properties described above, consider the following BLC model. Imagine an individual who lives for T dates. At the beginning of date t he holds nonnegative liquid assets A_t, and receives take home income y_t. For ease of exposition, let the interest rate be zero. At the beginning of t, the individual's future wealth is:

$$F_t = \sum_{\tau \geq 1} y_\tau - \sum_{\tau < t} c_\tau + (A_1 - A_t). \tag{13.1}$$

The value of F_t is required to be nonnegative. Assume that the capital markets permit the individual to borrow against some fraction α of his future wealth, where $0 < \alpha < 1$.[27] Date t consumption is c_t. Imagine that this individual has three mental accounts at each date, one for current income, one for liquid assets, and one for future income.

At date t, the budget constraint on c_t is:

$$c_t \leq y_t + A_t + \alpha F_t. \tag{13.2}$$

The budget constraint is a market constraint. From the market point of view, it is the sum, not the decomposition of the right hand side of (13.2) which is

---

[26] In the Strotz–Pollak framework, preferences over the current choice set must also be computed out, because individuals must anticipate the reaction of their future selves.

[27] Student loans, unsecured personal credit lines, and credit cards offer examples of limited borrowing against future income.

germane. In other words, the decomposition is a matter of form, not substance. However, for reasons having to do with temptation, the decomposition may be substantive for the individual. For instance, having the entire right hand side concentrated into y_t may call for considerable willpower in order to avoid consumption c_t from becoming excessive. Irving Fisher described this issue as one of excessive spending on payday.[28]

An example of a rule R is the "pension–pecking order rule" for funding consumption. The pension portion of the rule involves a retirement date r, and a pension deduction rate δ. The rule stipulates that at each pre–retirement date, the individual receives take home pay $(1 - \delta)y_t$ rather than y_t. The deducted amount then becomes part of future income. The pecking order portion of the rule prioritizes the source of funding for consumption. First spend from current take home income. Only when current take home income is exhausted, can assets be used to finance consumption. Only when assets are exhausted, can future income be accessed through borrowing. Likewise, when the individual is engaged in positive saving at some date t, meaning that $c_t < (1 - \delta)y_t$, then this saving is first applied to pay down any borrowing from the future income account.[29] Only when this debt is paid off, can the individual accumulate assets in his asset account.

Loosely speaking, the pension pecking order rule can be thought of as a habit. In Section 9, the term habit was understood in the sense of habituated consumption levels. Here habit is to be understood as routinized behavior. Specifically, the pension pecking order habit involves saving a fixed fraction of one's income, and only consuming from take home pay. People who are extremely reluctant to borrow against future income are said to follow the "debt ethic". The rule "don't dip into capital" falls into this category. In the BLC, such rules are enforced through habit, but may be broken in exceptional circumstances, at the individual's discretion. In a period of low current income (e.g., unemployment), the individual may prefer to break the rule, and consume from his liquid assets. However, because the habit is enforced by the utility fence described above, a fixed utility entry fee is incurred. Hence, individuals decide whether the cost of entry outweighs the utility benefit from higher consumption during the low income period.

For a fixed pension deduction rate δ, the consumption plan c and rule R determine how the mental account balances evolve through time. In the BLC, consumption c is not chosen directly. Rather the individual decides which

---

[28]Some athletes and actors find that the bulk of their income arrives early in their lives.

[29]This rule implies that at each date there is a threshold value for the future income account specifying the zero debt point. This threshold value is total lifetime income minus total cumulative takehome pay to date. If the future income account balance lies below this threshold, the individual has borrowed against his future income.

accounts will be used to finance consumption at each date, and what corresponding level of willpower θ to exert. In conjunction with the mental account balances, these decisions determine c.

As in standard theory, intertemporal utility U is a function of c. However, in the BLC utility also depends on the level of willpower exerted at each date, and on the accounts used to finance consumption at each date. Willpower θ enters the arguments of U to reflect the fact that willpower is costly to use. The identity of the accounts used to finance c enters the arguments of U because of the way that internal rules (or habits) are enforced. If $c_t > (1 - \delta)y_t$, then the individual will either have to use some of his assets to finance consumption or borrow against future income. Since this requires the invasion of an account, a utility cost is incurred. This cost is fixed, meaning it does not vary with the degree to which this account is used to finance consumption.

The resulting constrained optimization problem leads to the choice of a consumption plan. If the individual has the opportunity to select from several pension plans, then δ becomes one more optimizing variable. Because the problem involves some fixed costs, the optimization problem will have nonconvex elements. This entails the comparison of multiple local optima. In particular, at low income dates, the individual will have to compare the utility received from two alternatives. In the first alternative, consumption is set equal to take home pay, and no willpower is required. In the second alternative, at least one of the accounts is accessed to finance current consumption and utility costs are incurred.

Consider a date in which the individual decides to consume less than his current income. What does he do with the difference? Does he accumulate assets in his asset account? Does he repay outstanding debt? In the BLC, the immediate willpower cost is the same for both, since it pertains to the reduction of current consumption below current income. However, future willpower costs need not be the same. Under rule R, assets are more easily accessed than future income. The decision to repay debt places a portion of wealth in the future income account, which offers more protection. At the same time the cost of accessing that wealth increases, should circumstances require. If current income is highly variable, then the individual may anticipate having to access that wealth on a regular basis, and therefore may prefer to accumulate assets instead of paying down debt. Hence the decision about whether to pay or accumulate more assets typically depends on the shape of the income stream.

In concluding this section, consider the meaning of discounting. Putting uncertainty aside, what does it mean to discount utility when future pleasures are equivalent in intensity to present ones? All else being the same, is the favoring of early consumption over later consumption a reflection of rational preference or of cognitive imperfection? Even if we are all hard wired to apply hyperbolic discounting, is that something we think should be respected? Or does it represent impulses to be controlled, just as human society has striven to overcome other primitive impulses?

These are questions that extend beyond the BLC. However, they arise in the BLC in connection with the form of U. Is it appropriate to employ the time discounting of instantaneous utility in U? It turns out that even if U is neutral in respect to the timing of consumption, discounting enters the model through the self–control technology. Because of the link between current consumption and future willpower costs, even individuals who are impartial to the timing of consumption from the perspective of U, will choose to favor early consumption to later consumption in order to minimize the costs of self–control. This actually is very much in the spirit of Irving Fisher (1930) who used the terms "impatience" and "self–control" to describe time discounting.

14   Concluding Remarks

This section provides a brief recapitulation of the main points in this chapter, along with some integrating remarks.[30] We speak of changing tastes as a situation in which an individual's utility function changes over time. An individual whose tastes change over time may find that the preferences he holds at one date are in conflict with preferences he held in the past. If he alters a plan which his previous self anticipated would be followed, then his behavior is said to be dynamically inconsistent.

The discussion in this chapter has involved three different ways in which tastes are said to change: (1) changes in respect to intertemporal substitution; (2) changes in respect to substitution between different commodities; and (3) changes in respect to substitution between alternative lotteries. A common theme in all three classes is the notion of a *moving frame of reference* without a *relativity principle*. In the case of intertemporal substitution, the change in tastes stems from the combination of nonexponential discounting and a shifting *reference date* τ. In the multicommodity framework, the change in tastes stems from a shifting *reference consumption bundle*. In the uncertainty case, the change in tastes results from the combination of a change in *reference lottery* and the violation of the independence axiom of expected utility.

The starting point for the discussion of dynamic consistency is a model featuring a single commodity and no uncertainty. In this model, the root cause of dynamic inconsistency has two elements. First, the discount function is centered on the present as reference date, and therefore continually shifts forward in time. Second the discount function is nonexponential. When the discount function is exponential, the consumption plan exhibits dynamic consistency.

---

[30]In order to emphasize the pivotal ideas, references are omitted in this section.

Dynamic inconsistency is an area which is of interest to both economists and psychologists. Experimental evidence in psychology suggests that many people appear to possess a hyperbolic time shifting discount function. The hyperbolic discount function induces individuals to place disproportionate weight on the present and immediate future relative to the more distant future.

An individual who knows how his tastes will evolve over time may seek to take the behavior of his future self into account when he makes his current choice. If he does so, we call the resulting consumption plan sophisticated. A sophisticated plan is a subgame perfect Nash equilbrium of the game in which the individual plays against his future selves. Consequently, a sophisticated plan exhibits dynamic consistency.

The character of choice under changing tastes does not always conform to intuition. For instance, consider whether an individual whose discount function is hyperbolic consumes at too rapid a rate, relative to what his initial preferences call for. The discussion in Section 6 illustrates that the answer is yes for some utility functions, and no for others. If the intertemporal utility function is time additively separable in the logarithm of consumption, and the individual does not precommit his consumption plan, then the answer is yes. This statement holds both for naive choice and sophisticated choice. However, Theorem 6.1 demonstrates conditions under which the answer is no.

The circumstances described in Theorem 6.1, whereby consumption may be slower at some date relative to that called for under the precommitment plan involve indifference by the preferences of the individual's future self. The possibility of indifference at a future date raises questions for the current self, when the current self's preferences do not feature the same indifference. In particular, the current self may care how future ties would be broken by his future self, since this typically affects how he would make his current choice. This raises a variety of subtle issues about the nature of tie–breaking mechanisms which are consistent with subgame perfect Nash equilibrium. These were discussed in Section 7.

The second section of the chapter provides a brief history of the development of intertemporal utility theory. By and large, the economics approach to choice has been to cast choice as the outcome of a utility maximizing exercise. From this perspective, it is natural to ask whether individual choice is consistent with the exisitence of a long run utility function which is being maximized? Such a long run utility function could be viewed as aggregating the various utility functions held by the individual over the course of his lifetime. The answer turns out to be no, in general. The discussion in Section 8 indicates that no long run choice mechanism consistent with a preference ordering exists, whenever the individual favors precommitment over sophisticated choice or naive choice. Moreover, under quite general conditions, the sophisticated consumption plan is Pareto–dominated relative to all the long run utility functions held by the individual over the course of his lifetime.

The first nine sections of the chapter deal with a single commodity model, in which the subject of conflict is the rate of consumption over time. There is also a literature dealing with multiple commodities and habit formation. Here a habit is modelled as a reference commodity bundle. In this literature, the subject of conflict concerns the way that current choices lead to habits being formed, with habits subsequently affecting future preferences in respect to budget share allocation. Analgous to the approach taken in the single commodity model, we are led to ask whether the sequence of short run demand functions generated during the habit formation process converge to a long run demand function which can be rationalized by a long run utility function? Although there are specific cases where such a result can be established, it does not hold as a general proposition. Indeed even when short run demand functions do converge to a long run demand function, the latter may not be rationalized by a long run utility function.

Another extension of the dynamic consistency framework involves the addition of uncertainty to the basic single commodity intertemporal model. The major issue here involves the way that preference orderings in respect to future lotteries change with the passage of time. Notably, there is an uncertainty analogue to the role played by exponential discounting in the certainty framework. The uncertainty analogue of exponential discounting is the independence axiom of expected utility. Typically, the naive choice mechanism will be dynamically inconsistent if either of these two conditions is violated. As in the certainty framework, the welfare implications attached to dynamic inconsistency in the uncertainty framework are unfavorable. In particular, an individual whose choice mechanism is both naive and dynamically inconsistent will be prone to choosing stochastically dominated lotteries, even though this is undesirable according to all of his short term preference relations.

Some of the psychologists who study dynamic inconsistency have sought to identify the heuristics which individuals use to guide them in making decisions when cognitive limitations preclude choice which is fully rational. Prospect theory is one particular framework which has been put forward by psychologists and has received considerable attention from economists. Prospect theory proposes that individuals use particular editing heuristics to simplify complex intertemporal lotteries into manageable subproblems which are framed in terms of gains and losses. Notably, gains and losses are defined relative to a reference point, or more generally a reference lottery. Once a problem has been edited, and the menu of choices laid out, the individual then makes his selection using a value function which is concave in gains and convex in losses. Because decisions are based on the use of heuristics rather than full optimization, the resulting choices are dynamically inconsistent. Moreover, these heuristics give rise to dynamically inconsistent behavior which is frame sensitive. Attitudes to risk can be risk averse or risk seeking depending on how problems are framed. Framing a problem in terms of losses instead of gains induces risk seeking behavior instead of risk averse behavior. Framing a problem in terms of losses instead of gains induces low discount rates instead of high discount rates.

Psychological studies of intertemporal choice and self–control underlie behavioral life cycle theory. Behavioral life cycle theory extends standard life cycle models to accomodate elements of several psychological studies. For instance, it incorporates the notion of mental accounting from prospect theory, and bases its treatment of willpower upon psychological studies of the techniques people use to help themselves display patience.

The second section of the chapter traces out the development of intertemporal choice theory, as developed by economists. The last sections of the chapter discuss insights about choice offered by psychologists. What are the fundamental differences in approach between the disciplines?

General economic models of choice are grounded in the framework of constrained optimization. The constraints define the menu of choices, and a utility function represents the preference relation over this choice menu. In intertemporal choice, the menu is a set of alternative intertemporal consumption paths. The utility function ranks alternative intertemporal paths. In the changing tastes literature, the general constrained optimization framework is modified to accomodate a time sequence of preference orderings. However, only utility can vary with time; the constraints are unmodified.

The psychological perspective differs from its economic counterpart in several key respects. One key difference is the emphasis on framing. Most economic models assume that choice should not depend on how the constraint set is described. Description is *form*, the actual set is *substance*, and in standard economic models substance matters but form does not. This is as true for changing taste models, as it is for models with stable preferences. On the other hand, psychological models emphasize that framing is substantive, and should not be dismissed as mere form.

Framing presents a challenge to economic theorists. It plays a pivotal role in actual choice, but is absent in most economic models. This suggests that the standard paradigm of the way that people make choices, elegant and powerful though it may be, is deficient in at least one serious respect. The foundation concepts of preference orderings and constraint sets may be inadequate, or at least insufficient, to the task of describing the basis of intertemporal choice.

The last two sections of the chapter describe models where framing is a key element in the analysis. In both sections, mental accounting structures provide the infrastructure which house the choice menus. These are explicitly set out. Although preference relations are used as a basis for choosing from the choice menu, they have characteristics different from those of the preference relations used in standard economic models. For instance, prospect theory preferences deal with changes relative to a reference point, rather than the overall consequence experienced by the decision maker. In the behavioral life cycle model, preference reflects the amount of willpower that must be exercised in conjuction with a particular choice, and this typically depends on the mental accounting structure. For example, most employees in the U.S. consciously choose to have much more withheld from their paychecks than required to meet their income tax obligations. Many do so with the purpose of receiving a large income tax refund. Given the opportunity to engage in short term borrowing, overwitholding does very little to change the actual budget set. However, in the model it lowers the amount of willpower which needs to be exercised in order to achieve the resulting consumption path.

The phenomenon of preference reversal raises fundamental questions about individuals' abilities to rank order the alternatives they confront at a given moment. Even without framing effects, nonexponential discounting and violations of expected utility theory lead to choice which is dominated in some respect, (e.g., Pareto, stochastic). Notably, the term *dominated* cannot be treated as equivalent to *suboptimal* in this context, because suboptimal implies the existence of an optimum. When tastes change there may be no optimum. In prospect theory, the restricted domain on which preferences are defined may not even allow the notion of a full optimum to be well defined. It may be that future work in this area will involve a more extensive treatment of positive choice, but in a framework which limits the extent to which normative conclusions are possible.

References

Aczél, J. (1966). *Lectures on Functional Equations and Their Applications.* Academic Press, New York.

Ainslie, G. (1974). Impulse Control in Pigeons. *Journal of the Experimental Analysis of Behavior*, 4:485–489.

Ainslie, G. (1975). Specious Reward: A Behavioral Theory of Impulsiveness and Impulse Control. *Psychological Bulletin*, 82:463–496.

Ainslie, G. (1985). Beyond Microeconomics. Conflict Among Interests in a Multiple Self as a Determinant of Value. In Elster, J., editor, *The Multiple Self*, pages 133–175. Cambridge University Press, Cambridge, U.K.

Ainslie, G. and Haslam, N. (1992). Self-Control. In Lowenstein, G. and Elster, J., editors, *Choice over Time*, pages 57–92. Russell Sage Foundation, New York.

Becker, G., Grossman, M., and Murphy, K. (1992). Rational Addiction and the Effect of Price on Consumption. In Lowenstein, G. and Elster, J., editors, *Choice over Time*, pages 361–370. Russell Sage Foundation, New York.

Becker, G. and Murphy, K. (1988). A Theory of Rational Addiction. *Journal of Political Economy*, 96:675–700.

Benzion, U., Rapoport, A., and Yagil, J. (1989). Discount Rates Inferred from Decisions: An Experimental Study. *Management Science*, 35:270–284.

Böhm-Bawerk, E. (1889). *Capital and Interest.* South Holland. IL: Libertarian Press 1889, 1970.

Constantinides, G. (1990). Habit Formation: A Resolution of the Equity Premium Puzzle. *Journal of Political Economy*, 98:519–543.

Fisher, F. M. (1977). On Donor Sovereignty and United Charities. *American Economic Review*, 67.

Fisher, I. (1930). *The Theory of Interest.* MacMillan, New York.

Frank, R. (1988). *Passions Within Reason: The Strategic Role of the Emotions.* W. W. Norton and Co., New York.

Frank, R. (1992). The Role of Moral Sentiments in the Theory of Intertemporal Choice. In Loewenstein, G. and Elster, J., editors, *Choice over Time*, pages 265–284. Russell Sage Foundation, New York.

Goldman, S. (1979). Intertemporally Inconsistent Preferences and the Rate of Consumption. *Econometrica*, 47:621–626.

Goldman, S. (1980). Consistent Plans. *Review of Economic Studies*, 47:533–538.

Gorman, W. M. (1967). Tastes, Habits, and Choices. *International Economic Review*, 8:218–222.

Hammond, P. J. (1976a). Changing Tastes and Coherent Dynamic Choice. *Review of Economic Studies*, 43:159–173.

Hammond, P. J. (1976b). Endogenous Tastes and Stable Long-Run Choice. *Journal of Economic Theory*, 13:329–340.

Herrnstein, R. (1961). Relative and Absolute Strengths of Response as a Function of Frequency of Reinforcement. *Journal of the Experimental Analysis of Behavior*, 4:267–272.

Horowitz, J. K. (1988). Discounting Money Payoffs: An Experimental Analysis. Working Paper Department of Agricultural and Resource Economics.

Jevons, W. S. (1871). *Theory of Political Economy.* Macmillan, London.

Kahneman, D. and Tversky, A. (1979). Prospect Theory: An Analysis of Decision Under Risk. *Econometrica*, 47:263–292.

Kahneman, D. and Tversky, A. (1992). Advances in Prospect Theory: Cumulative Representation of Uncertainty. *Journal of Risk and Uncertainty*, 5:297–323.

Koopmans, T. (1960). Stationary Ordinal Utility and Impatience. *Econometrica*, 28:287–309.

Laibson, D. (1996). Hyperbolic Discount Functions, Undersaving, and Savings Policy. Working Paper # 5635, National Bureau of Economic Research.

Laibson, D. (1997). Golden Eggs and Hyperbolic Discounting. *Quarterly Journal of Economics*, 112:443–477.

Loewenstein, G. (1992). The Fall and Rise of Psychological Explanantions in Intertemporal Choice. In Lowenstein, G. and Elster, J., editors, *Choice over Time*, pages 3–34. Russell Sage Foundation, New York.

Loewenstein, G. and Prelec, D. (1992). Anomalies in Intertemporal Choice: Evidence and Interpretation. In Lowenstein, G. and Elster, J., editors, *Choice over Time*, pages 119–145. Russell Sage Foundation, New York.

McClennen, E. (1990). *Rationality and Dynamic Choice: Foundational Explorations*. Cambridge University Press, Cambridge, United Kingdom.

Mischel, W., Shoda, Y., and Rodriguez, M. (1992). Delay of Gratification in Children. In Lowenstein, G. and Elster, J., editors, *Choice over Time*, pages 147–164. Russell Sage Foundation, New York.

Peleg, B. and Yaari, M. (1973). On the Existence of a Consistent Course of Action when Tastes are Changing. *Review of Economic Studies*, 35:514–579.

Peston, M. (1967). Changing Utility Functions. In Shubik, M., editor, *Essays in Mathematical Economics, Essays in Honor of Oskar Morgenstern*, pages 233–236. Princeton University Press, Princeton, NJ.

Phelps, E. S. and Pollak, R. A. (1968). On Second-Best National Saving and Game-Equilibrium Growth. *Review of Economic Studies*, 35:185–199.

Pollak, R. (1971a). Habit Formation and Dynamic Demand Functions. *Journal of Political Economy*, 78:745–763.

Pollak, R. (1971b). Habit Formation and Long-Run Utility Functions. *Journal of Economic Theory*, 13:272–297.

Pollak, R. A. (1968). Consistent Planning. *Review of Economic Studies*, 35:201–208.

Prelec, D. (1989). Decreasing Impatience: Definition and Consequences. Harvard Business School Working Paper.

Quiggin, J. (1982). A Theory of Anticipated Utility. *Journal of Economic Behavior and Organization*, 3:323–343.

Rae, J. (1834). *The Sociological Theory of Capital*. MacMillan, London. Reprint of Original 1834 Edition.

Samuelson, P. (1937). A Note on Measurement of Utility. *Review of Economic Studies*, 4:155–161.

Schelling, T. (1992). Self-Command: A New Discipline. In Lowenstein, G. and Elster, J., editors, *Choice over Time*, pages 167–209. Russell Sage Foundation, New York.

Sen, A. (1971). *Collective Choice and Social Welfare*. Oliver and Boyd, Edinburgh.

Senior, N. W. (1836). *An Outline of the Science of Political Economy.* Clowes and Son, London.

Shefrin, H. and Statman, M. (1984). Explaining Investor Preference for Cash Dividends. *Journal of Financial Economics*, 13:253–282.

Shefrin, H. and Statman, M. (1992). *Ethics, Fairness, Efficiency, and Financial Markets.* Research Foundation of Institute of Chartered Financial Analysts, Charlottesville, Virginia.

Shefrin, H. and Thaler, R. (1988). The Behavioral Life Cycle Hypothesis. *Economic Inquiry*, 26:609–643.

Smith, A. (1776). *The Wealth of Nations.* George Bell and Sons, London.

Stone, R. (1954). Linear Expenditure Systems and Demand Analysis. *Economic Journal*, 64:511–527.

Strotz, R. H. (1956). Myopia and Inconsistency in Dynamic Utility Maximization. *Review of Economic Studies*, 23:165–180.

Thaler, R. (1981). Some Empirical Evidence on Dynamic Inconsistency. *Economics Letters*, 8:201–207.

Tversky, A. and Thaler, R. H. (1990). Preference Reversals. *The Journal of Economic Perspectives*, 4:201–211.

von Auer, L. (1995a). Dynamic Choice Mechanisms. Working Paper Number 46, Institut für Finanzwissenschaft und Sozialpolitik, Universität Kiel.

von Auer, L. (1995b). Revealed Dynamic Preferences under Uncertainty. Working Paper Number 51, Institut für Finanzwissenschaft und Sozialpolitik, Universität Kiel.

von Weizsäcker, C. C. (1971). Notes on Endogenous Changes of Tastes. *Journal of Economic Theory*, 3:345–372.

Yaari, M. (1977). Consistent Utilization of an Exhaustible Resource or How to Eat an Appetite-Arousing Cake. Research Memorandum No. 26, Hebrew University, Jerusalem.

13 CAUSAL DECISION THEORY

James M. Joyce and Allan Gibbard

University of Michigan

Contents

1	Introduction	628
2	Dominance and Expected Utility: Two Versions	630
3	Conditionals and their Probabilities	634
4	Ratificationism	642
5	Ratificationism and Causality in the Theory of Games	645
6	Foundational Questions	656
7	Conclusion	663
References		664

1   Introduction

EXAMPLE 1.1 [Prisoner's Dilemma with Twin (PDT)] You are caught in a standard, one–shot prisoner's dilemma, and the other player is your twin. You don't know for sure what twin will do, but you know that twin is amazingly like you psychologically. What you do, he or she too will likely do: news that you were going to rat would be good indication that twin will rat, and news that you were going to keep mum would be a good sign that twin will keep mum. Your sole goal is to minimize your own time in jail: Family feelings affect you not, and you care not a whit about loyalty, returning good for good, or how long twin spends in jail. What course of action is rational for you in pursuit of your goals?

	Mum	Rat
Mum	$-1,-1$	$-10,0$
Rat	$0,-10$	$-9,-9$

Prisoner's Dilemma

Many will find the answer easy—though they may disagree with each other on which the answer is. A standard line on the prisoner's dilemma rests on *dominance:* What you do won't affect what twin does. Twin may rat or keep mum, but in either case, you yourself will do better to rat. Whichever twin is doing, you would spend less time in jail if you were to rat than if you were to keep mum. Therefore the rational way to minimize your own time in jail is to rat.

Another line of argument leads to the opposite conclusion. Assess each act by its *auspiciousness,* by how welcome the news would be that you were about to perform it. News that you're about to rat would indicate that twin is likewise about to rat. That's bad news; it means a long time in jail, for you as well as for twin. News that you're about to keep mum, on the other hand, would be good news: It indicates that twin is likewise about to keep mum, and your both keeping mum will mean a short time in jail. Keeping mum, then, is the *auspicious* act, and so—in terms of your selfish goals—you achieve best prospects by keeping mum.[1]

The two lines of reasoning, then, lead to opposite conclusions. One or the other, to be sure, may strike a reader as obviously wrong. Still, if one of them is cogent and the other not, decision theory should tell us why. Standard theories haven't spoken, though, with one voice on this matter. Savage himself [Savage (1972)] was mostly silent on issues that would decide between the two lines: his system could be read in more than one way, and the few pertinent remarks he left us point in opposing directions. Various other decision–theoretic systems do have implications for this matter. Some imply that the argument from auspiciousness is correct: the principle of dominance, these systems entail, doesn't properly apply to a case like PDT, the prisoner's dilemma with twin. Taking the other side, a group called—perhaps somewhat misleadingly—*causal* decision theorists have formulated systems according to which the principle of dominance does apply to this case, and the rational thing to do is to rat.

"Causal" theorists maintain that decision theory requires a notion of causal dependency, explicit or implicit. Otherwise, they say, the theory will yield the wrong prescription for cases like PDT. We touch below on how causal notions might be made explicit for decision theorists' purposes, and how causality might be vindicated as empirically respectable. Auspiciousness theorists—or *evidential* decision theorists, as they are called in the literature—have no need for causal terms in their theory: they manage everything with standard subjective probabilities and conditional probabilities. Some evidential theorists deny that their theory, properly construed or developed, really does say not to rat in PDT. They deny, then, that causal notions must be introduced into decision theory, even if causal theorists are right about what to do in this case. We touch below on debates between "causal" theorists and this camp of "evidential" theorists, but mostly stick with the "causal" theory, explaining it and examining its potentialities.[2]

Cases with the structure of PDT can't be rare. The prisoner's dilemma itself is a parable, but economics, politics, war, and the like will be full of cases

---

[1] An interesting model of Prisoner's Dilemma with a twin can be found in Howard (1988). Howard, who endorses a version of the auspiciousness argument, shows how to write a Basic program for playing the game which is capable of recognizing and cooperating with programs that are copies of itself.

[2] Nozick (1969) introduced PDT and other cases of this kind, focusing his discussion on Newcomb's problem, which he credits to physicist William Newcomb. He makes many of the points that causal theorists have come to accept, but recognizes only one kind of expected utility, the one we are calling auspiciousness. Stalnaker originated causal expected utility in a 1972 letter published only much later [Stalnaker (1981)]. Gibbard and Harper (1978) proselytize Stalnaker's proposal, and Lewis (1981) gives an alternative formulation which we discuss below. Gibbard and Harper (1978) and Lewis (1979b) also discuss PDT along with Newcomb's problem.

where one's own acts suggest how others are acting. Consider, for instance, a sophisticated speculator playing a market. Mustn't he reasonably take himself to model other sophisticated players? Why should he be unique? A rational agent interacting with others must escape the hubris of thinking that only he is smart and insightful—but then he'll have to take himself as a likely model for the schemings and reasonings of others. In such cases, different versions of decision theory may prescribe incompatible actions.

2   Dominance and Expected Utility: Two Versions

Savage (1972) encoded decision problems as matrices, with columns indicating "states of the world". For a Savage matrix with states $S_1, \ldots, S_n$, the expected utility of an act A is calculated by the Savage formula

$$\mathcal{V}(A) = \sum_{i=1}^{n} \rho(S_i) u(A, S_i), \tag{2.1}$$

where $u(A, S_i)$ is the utility of act A for state S_i and $\rho(S_i)$ is the subjective probability of S_i. From (2.1) follows a principle which we'll call the *Unqualified Principle of Dominance*, or *UPD*:

■   UPD: If for each S_i, $u(A, S_i) > u(B, S_i)$, then $\mathcal{V}(A) > \mathcal{V}(B)$.

Which Savage matrix correctly represents a problem, though, must be decided with care, as is shown by a spoof due to Jeffrey (1967), p. 8:

EXAMPLE 2.1 [Better Red Than Dead (BRD)] I'm an old–time American cold warrior with scruples, deciding whether or not my country is to disarm unilaterally. I construct a matrix as follows: My two possible states are that the Soviets invade and that they don't. In case they invade, better red than dead; in case they don't, better rich than poor. In either case, unilateral disarmament beats armament, and so by dominance, I conclude, it is rational to disarm.

Now whether or not unilateral disarmament would be rational all told, this argument from "dominance" treats these considerations as irrelevant—even if the Soviets are sure to invade if we disarm and to hold back if we arm.
a scenario in which they don't invade is better than one in which they do. The argument from "dominance" treats these considerations as irrelevant — even if the Soviets are sure to invade if we disarm and to hold back if we arm.

Savage's states, then, must be act–independent: They must obtain or not independently of what the agent does. How, then, shall we construe this requirement? The first answer was developed, independently, by Jeffrey (1967) and by Luce and Krantz (1971): For dominance correctly to apply, they say, the states must be stochastically (or probabilistically) independent of acts. Where acts $A_1 \ldots A_m$ are open to the agent and $\rho(S/A_j)$ is the standard conditional probability of S given A_j,[3] S is stochastically act–independent iff

$$\rho(S/A_1) = \rho(S/A_2) = \ldots = \rho(S/A_m) = \rho(S). \tag{2.2}$$

The probabilities in question are subjective, or at any rate epistemic. Formula (2.2), then, means roughly that learning what one's going to do won't affect one's credence in S. One's act won't be evidence for whether S obtains. Requirement (2.2), then, is that any state S be *evidentially* act–independent. Theories that entail that (2.2) is what's needed for the principle of dominance to hold good we can thus call *evidential* theories of decision.

As applied to the prisoner's dilemma with your twin, evidential decision theory must treat the dominance argument as bad. Twin's act fails to be independent of yours evidentially. Let proposition C_t be that twin cooperates, let C_y be that you cooperate, and let D_y be that you defect. C_t is not evidentially independent of what you do: $\rho(C_t/C_y)$ is high whereas $\rho(C_t/D_y)$ is low, since your cooperating is good evidence that she is cooperating, whereas your defecting is good evidence that she is defecting. Condition (2.2), then, won't hold for this case.

Evidential decision theory holds that the Savage formula (2.1) applies when condition (2.2) holds—that is, when the states of the matrix are evidentially act–independent. Requirements of act–independence, though, could be dropped if we changed formula (2.1) for computing expected utility. Use as weights not the probability of each state, as in (2.1), but its conditional probability—its probability conditional on the act's being performed. In this more general formulation, we have

$$\mathcal{V}(A) = \sum_{i=1}^{n} \rho(S_i/A) u(A, S_i). \tag{2.3}$$

The Savage formula (2.1) is then a special case of (2.3), for conditions of evidential act–independence.[4] Since UPD follows from (2.1), it follows from (2.3) plus condition (2.2) of evidential act–independence. Evidential decision theory, then, has (2.3) as its general formula for expected utility. Its version of the principle of dominance is UPD qualified by condition (2.2) of evidential act–independence. In general, it recommends using "auspiciousness" to guide choices: a rational agent should select an act whose performance would be

---

[3]More precisely, A_i is the *proposition* that one performs a particular one of the alternative acts open to one in one's circumstances. We reserve the notation $\rho(S \mid A_j)$ for a more general use later in this chapter.

[4]Formula (2.1) is introduced by Jeffrey (1967) and by Luce and Krantz (1971).

best news for him—roughly, an act that provides best evidence for thinking desirable outcomes will obtain.

Evidential theory has the advantage of avoiding philosophically suspect talk of causality: Its general formula (2.3) sticks to mathematical operations on conditional probabilities, and likewise, its requirement (2.2) of evidential act–independence—its condition, that is, for the Savage formula (2.1) to apply to a matrix—is couched in terms of conditional probabilities.

The causal theorist, in contrast, maintains that to apply a principle of dominance correctly, one can't avoid judgments of causality. One must form degrees of belief as to the causal structure of the world; one must have views on what is causally independent of what. Belief in twin's causal isolation is a case in point. Dominance applies to PDT, their contention is, because you and your twin are causally isolated—and you know it. What you do, you know, will in no way affect what twin does. The argument, then, invokes a causal notion: the notion of what will and what won't causally *affect* what else. Causal decision theory then recommends using causal efficacy to guide choices: It holds, roughly, that a rational agent should select an act whose performance would be likely to bring about desirable results.

The causal decision theorist's requirement on a state S of a Savage matrix, then, is the following: The agent must accept that nothing he can do would causally affect whether or not S obtains. For each act A open to him, he must be certain that S's obtaining would not be causally affected by his doing A.

Can the causal theorist find a formula for expected utility that dispenses with this requirement of believed causal act–independence? A way to do so was proposed by Stalnaker (1968); see also Gibbard and Harper (1978). It requires a special conditional connective, which we'll render '$\square\!\!\rightarrow$'. Read '$A \square\!\!\rightarrow B$' as saying, "If A obtained then B would." In other words, either A's obtaining would cause B to obtain, or B obtains independently (causally) of whether or not A obtains. Then to say that S is causally independent of which act $A_1 \ldots A_n$ one performs is to say this: Either S would hold whatever one did, or whatever one did S would fail to hold. In other words, for every act A_i, we have $A_i \square\!\!\rightarrow S$ iff S. We can now generalize the Savage formula (2.1) for the causal theorist's kind of expected utility. Use as weights, now, the probabilities of conditionals $\rho(A \square\!\!\rightarrow S_i)$, as follows:

$$\mathcal{U}(A) = \sum_{i=1}^{n} \rho(A \square\!\!\rightarrow S_i) u(A, S_i). \tag{2.4}$$

Call this $\mathcal{U}(A)$ the *instrumental expected utility* of act A. The Savage formula

$$\mathcal{U}(A) = \sum_{i=1}^{n} \rho(S_i) u(A, S_i), \qquad (2.5)$$

is then (2.4) for the special case where the following condition holds:

$$\text{For each } S_i, \ \rho(A \,\square\!\!\rightarrow S_i) = \rho(S_i). \qquad (2.6)$$

A sufficient condition for this to hold is that, with probability one, S_i is causally independent of A — in other words, that

$$\text{For each } S_i, \ \rho\Big([A \,\square\!\!\rightarrow S_i] \longleftrightarrow S_i\Big) = 1. \qquad (2.7)$$

Note that for the prisoner's dilemma with twin, condition (2.7) does hold. Twin, you know, is causally isolated from you. You know, then, that whether twin would defect if you were to defect is just a matter of whether twin is going to defect anyway. In other words, you know that $D_y \,\square\!\!\rightarrow D_t$ holds iff D_t holds, and so for you, $\rho([D_y \,\square\!\!\rightarrow D_t] \longleftrightarrow D_t) = 1$. This is an instance of (2.7), and similar informal arguments establish the other needed instances of (2.7) for the case.

In short, then, causal decision theory can be formulated taking formula (2.4) for instrumental expected utility as basic. It is instrumental expected utility as given by (2.4), the causal theorist claims, that is to guide choice. The Savage formula is then a special case of (2.4), for conditions of known causal act–independence — where (2.7) holds, so that for each state S_i, $\rho(A \,\square\!\!\rightarrow S_i) = \rho(S_i)$. The Unqualified Principle of Dominance for $\mathcal{U}$ is

- UPD: If for each S_i, $u(A, S_i) > u(B, S_i)$, then $\mathcal{U}(A) > \mathcal{U}(B)$.

Causal decision theory, in this formulation, has (2.4) as its general formula for the instrumental expected utility that is to guide choice, and its own version of the principle of dominance: UPD qualified by condition (2.7) of known causal act–independence.

Evidential and causal decision theorists, in short, accept different general formulas for the expected utility that is to guide choice, and consequently, they accept different conditions for the Savage formula to apply, and different principles of dominance. Causal theory — in the formulation we've been expounding — adopts (2.4) as its formula for expected utility, wheras evidential theory adopts (2.3). Causal theory, in other words, weighs the values of outcomes by the probabilities of the relevant conditionals, $\rho(A \,\square\!\!\rightarrow S_i)$, whereas evidential theory weighs them by the relevant conditional probabilities $\rho(S_i/A)$. Different conditions, then, suffice, according to the two theories, for the Savage formula correctly to apply to a matrix, and consequently for UPD to apply. That makes for distinct principles of dominance: For the causal theorist, UPD qualified by condition (2.7) of known causal act–independence, and for the evidential theorist, UPD qualified by condition (2.2) of evidential act–independence.

3   Conditionals and their Probabilities

What, then, is the contrast on which all this hinges: the contrast between the probability $\rho(A \mathbin{\square\!\!\rightarrow} S)$ of a conditional $A \mathbin{\square\!\!\rightarrow} S$ and the corresponding conditional probability $\rho(S/A)$? Where probability measure ρ gives your *credences* —your degrees of belief—conditional probability $\rho(S/A)$ is the degree to which you'd believe S if you learned A and nothing else. In the prisoner's dilemma with your twin, then, $\rho(D_t/D_y)$ measures how much you'd expect twin to rat on learning that you yourself were about to rat. If $\rho(D_t/D_y) \neq \rho(D_t/C_y)$, that doesn't mean that D_t is in any way causally dependent on whether D_y or C_y obtains. It just means that your act is somehow *diagnostic* of twin's. Correlation is not causation. Probability $\rho(D_y \mathbin{\square\!\!\rightarrow} D_t)$, on the other hand, is the degree to which you believe that if you were to defect, then twin would. There are two circumstances in which this would obtain: Either twin is about to defect whatever you do, or your defecting would cause twin to defect. To the degree to which $\rho(D_y \mathbin{\square\!\!\rightarrow} D_t) > \rho(D_y \mathbin{\square\!\!\rightarrow} C_t)$, you give some credence to the proposition $[D_y \mathbin{\square\!\!\rightarrow} D_t]\&\neg[D_y \mathbin{\square\!\!\rightarrow} C_t]$, that twin would defect if you did, but not if you cooperated. This is credence in the proposition that your act will make a causal difference.

In daily life, we guide ourselves by judgments that seem to be conditional: What would happen if we did one thing, or did another? What would be the effects of the various alternatives we contemplate? We make judgments on these matters and cope with our uncertainties. Classic formulations of decision theory did not explicitly formalize such notions: notions of causal effects or dependency, or of "what would happen if". In Ramsey's and Savage's versions, causal dependency may be implicit in the representational apparatus, but this formal apparatus is open to interpretation. Other theorists had hoped that whatever causal or "would" beliefs are involved in rational decisions could be captured in the structure of an agent's conditional probabilities for non–causal propositions or events.

This last maneuver might have great advantages if it worked, but causal decision theorists argue that it doesn't. Causal or "would" notions must somehow be introduced into decision theory, they claim, if the structure of decision is to be elucidated by the theory. The introduction can be explicit, as in the general formula (2.4) for $\mathcal{U}$ above, or it can be in the glosses we give—say, in interpretations of the Savage formula (2.1) or (2.5). If causal theorists are right, then, the theory of subjective conditional probability won't give us all we need for describing the beliefs relevant to decision. We'll need some way of displaying such beliefs and theorizing about them.

Causal theorists have differed, though, on how causal beliefs are best represented. So far, we've spoken in Stalnaker's terms, but we need to say more on what his treatment consists in, and what some of the alternatives might be for representing causal decision theory.

First, some terminology. Savage spoke of "states" and "events", and distinguished these from "acts" or "strategies". The philosophers who developed causal decision theory often speak of "propositions", and include as propositions not only Savage's "events" and "states", but also acts and strategies. That is to say, propositions can characterize not only what happens independently of the agent, but also what the agent does — or even what he *would* do in various eventualities. A proposition can say that I perform act a or adopt strategy s. Such propositions can be objects of belief and of desire, and so can be assigned credences (subjective probabilities) and utilities.

Let A, then, be the proposition that I perform act a. Stalnaker constructs a conditional proposition $A \boxright B$, which we read as "If I did a, then B would obtain." How does such a conditional proposition work? Much as Savage treats an event as a set of states, so Stalnaker treats a proposition as a set of *possible worlds* or maximally specific ways things might have been. Abstractly, the connective '$\boxright$' is a two–place propositional function: To each pair of propositions it assigns a proposition.

Stalnaker hoped originally that this conditional function $\boxright$ could be defined so that the probability of a conditional is always the corresponding conditional probability: So that whenever $\rho(C/A)$ is defined, $\rho(A \boxright C) = \rho(C/A)$. Lewis (1976) proved that — with trivial exceptions — no such equality will survive conditionalization. Read ρ_A, in what follows, as probability measure ρ conditioned on A, so that by definition, $\rho_A(C) = \rho(C/A)$. What Lewis showed impossible is this: that for all propositions A, C and B for which $\rho(A\&B) > 0$, one has $\rho_B(A \boxright C) = \rho_B(C/A)$. For if this did obtain, then one would have both $\rho_C(A \boxright C) = \rho_C(C/A)$ and $\rho_{\neg C}(A \boxright C) = \rho_{\neg C}(C/A)$. But then

$$
\begin{aligned}
\rho(A \boxright C) &= \rho_C(A \boxright C)\rho(C) + \rho_{\neg C}(A \boxright C)\rho(\neg C) \\
&= \rho_C(C/A)\rho(C) + \rho_{\neg C}(C/A)\rho(\neg C) \\
&= 1 \cdot \rho(C) + 0 \cdot \rho(\neg C) \\
&= \rho(C).
\end{aligned}
$$

We'd have $\rho(A \boxright C) = \rho(C/A)$, then, at most when $\rho(C) = \rho(C/A)$. No such equality can survive conditionalization on an arbitrary proposition.

How, then, should we interpret the probability $\rho(A \mathrel{\Box\!\!\!\rightarrow} C)$ of a conditional proposition $A \mathrel{\Box\!\!\!\rightarrow} C$, if it is not in general the conditional probability $\rho(C/A)$. Many languages contrast two forms of conditionals, with pairs like this one:[5]

> If Shakespeare didn't write *Hamlet*, someone else did.   (3.1)

> If Shakespeare hadn't written *Hamlet*, someone else would have.   (3.2)

Conditionals like (3.1) are often called *indicative*, and conditionals like (3.2) *subjunctive* or *counterfactual*. Now indicative conditional (3.1) seems epistemic: To evaluate it, you might take on, hypothetically, news that Shakespeare didn't write Hamlet. Don't change anything you now firmly accept, except as you would if this news were now to arrive. See, then, if given this news, you think that someone else did write Hamlet. You will, because you are so firmly convinced that Hamlet was written by someone, whether or not the writer was Shakespeare. The rule for this can be put in terms of a thinker's subjecive probabilities—or her *credences*, as we shall say: indicative conditional (3.1) is acceptable to anyone with a sufficiently high conditional credence $\rho(E/D)$ that someone else wrote Hamlet given that Shakespeare didn't. Subjunctive conditional (3.2) works differently: If you believe that Shakespeare did write Hamlet, you will find (3.2) incredible. You'll accept (3.1), but have near zero credence in (3.2). Your conditional credence $\rho(E/D)$ in someone else's having written Hamlet given that Shakespeare didn't will be high, but your credence $\rho(D \mathrel{\Box\!\!\!\rightarrow} E)$ in the subjunctive conditional proposition (3.2) will be near zero. Here, then, is a case where one's credence in a conditional proposition (3.2) diverges from one's corresponding conditional credence. Speaking in terms of the subjective "probabilities" that we have been calling credences, we can put the matter like this: the probability $\rho(D \mathrel{\Box\!\!\!\rightarrow} E)$ of a subjunctive conditional may differ from the corresponding conditional probability $\rho(E/D)$.

The reason for this difference lies in the meaning the $\mathrel{\Box\!\!\!\rightarrow}$ operator. Stalnaker (1968) puts his account of conditionals in terms of alternative "possible worlds". A world is much like a "state" in Savage's framework (except that it will include a strategy one might adopt and its consequences). Think of a possible world as a maximally specific way things might have been, or a maximally specific consistent proposition that fully describes a way things might have been. Now to say what the proposition $A \mathrel{\Box\!\!\!\rightarrow} C$ is, we have to say what conditions must obtain for it to be true. There is no difficulty when the antecedent A obtains, for then, clearly, $A \mathrel{\Box\!\!\!\rightarrow} C$ holds true if and only if C obtains. The puzzle is for cases where A is false. In those situations, Stalnaker proposes that we imagine the possible world w^A in which A is true, and that otherwise is most *similar* to our actual world in relevant respects. $A \mathrel{\Box\!\!\!\rightarrow} C$, then, holds true iff C holds

---

[5] Adams (1975) examines pairs like this.

in this world w^A. Stalnaker and Thomason offered a rigorous semantics and representation theorem for this explication. Stalnaker's distinctive axioms are these:[6]

- *Intermediate strength:* If A necessitates B, then $A \, \square\!\!\rightarrow B$, and if $A \, \square\!\!\rightarrow B$, then $\neg(A \& \neg B)$.

- *Conditional non–contradiction:* For possible A, $\neg[(A \, \square\!\!\rightarrow B) \& (A \, \square\!\!\rightarrow \neg B)]$.

- *Distribution:* If $A \, \square\!\!\rightarrow (B \vee C), then (A \, \square\!\!\rightarrow B) \vee (A \, \square\!\!\rightarrow C)$.

- *Suppositional equivalence:* If $(A \, \square\!\!\rightarrow B)$ and $(B \, \square\!\!\rightarrow A)$, then $(A \, \square\!\!\rightarrow C)$ iff $(B \, \square\!\!\rightarrow C)$.

All this leaves mysterious the notion of *relevant similarity* invoked by Stalnaker's account. Formal axioms are easy: Stalnaker speaks of a *selection function* f which assigns a world $f(A, w) = w^A$ to each proposition A that has the possibility of being true. A compelling logic for $\square\!\!\rightarrow$ can be developed on this basis.

How, though, do we interpret the notion of "relevant similarity" when applying this formal apparatus to real–life decision problems? Intuitive overall likeness of worlds won't do. Nixon, imagine, had in the Oval Office a red button to launch the missiles.[7] In his despair he considered pushing it, but drew back. We can say, "If Nixon had pushed the button, nuclear holocaust would have ensued." This is true, we would judge, if the apparatus was in working order and without safeguards. Of the worlds in which Nixon pushes the button, though, the one most similar overall to the actual world would be not one in which all was destroyed, but one in which the apparatus malfunctioned—a wire became temporarily nonconducting, say. After all, a world in which the missiles were launched would surely have a future radically different from the actual world. Little in any city would look the same.

Clearly, then, we cannot look to overall similarity of worlds to cash out the type of "relevant" similarity needed in the evaluation of subjunctive conditionals. Rather, we want to know what would have ensued from initial conditions that were much like those that actually obtained, but differed in some slight respect in Nixon's decision–making apparatus—differed in such a way that by natural laws, the outgrowth of those modified initial conditions would have been nuclear holocaust. Thus, the rough idea is that one evaluates $A \, \square\!\!\rightarrow C$ by considering a world in which A obtains that is as much like the actual world as possible both with regard to particular facts about the past as well as general

---

[6]Stalnaker (1968) p. 106, Stalnaker and Thomason (1970), slightly modified.
[7]Fine (1975) gives this example to make roughly this point.

facts about what might follow causally from what in the future. Lewis (1979a) attempts a general account of the kind of "relevant similarity" that fits our causal judgments, and derives from it an account of the regularities that give time its direction. As decision theorists, though, we need not be concerned whether such lofty philosophical ambitions can be fulfilled. We need only understand that where w_0 is the actual world, the value $f(A, w_0)$ of the Stalnaker selection function is the world as it would be if A obtained. It is that world, with all its ensuing history. In many situations, it will be clear that agents do have subjective probabilities for what that world would be like, and so the application of Stalnaker's apparatus to an agent's decision situation will be clear enough.[8]

Stalnaker's framework allows us to be more precise about how probabilities of subjunctive conditionals differ from ordinary conditionals probabilities. It is useful to think of both $\rho(A \,\square\!\!\rightarrow C)$ and $\rho(C/A)$ as capturing a sense of *minimal* belief revision. $\rho(C/A)$, as we have seen, is the credence that an agent with prior ρ should assign C if she gets pure and certain news of A's truth. Thus, the function $\rho_A = \rho(\bullet /A)$ describes the outcome of a belief revision process in which an agent learns that A. This revision is minimal in the sense that it changes ρ so as to make A certain without thereby altering any ratios of the form $\rho(X \& A) : \rho(Y \& A)$. In terms of possible worlds, ρ_A is obtained from ρ by setting the credence of $\neg A$ equal to zero, and spreading the residual probability uniformly over the worlds in which A obtains—thus leaving undisturbed any evidential relationships that might obtain among propositions that entail A. The function $\rho^A = \rho(A \,\square\!\!\rightarrow \bullet)$ defines a rather different sort of minimal belief revision, *imaging* [Lewis (1976), (1981)] or better, *imagining*. Instead of distributing the probability of $\neg A$ uniformly over the A-worlds, spread it with an eye to relevant similarities among worlds. Transfer the probability of each world w in which A is false to w^A, the A-world most similar to w, adding this probability to the probability w^A has already.

This whole treatment, though, rests on an assumption that is open to doubt: that there always exists a unique "most similar" world w^A. Perhaps there's no one definite way the world would be were I, say, now to flip this coin. The world might be indeterministic, or the supposition that I now flip the coin might be indeterminate—in that the exact force and manner in which I'd be flipping the coin isn't specified and isn't even under my control. It may then be the case neither that definitely were I to flip the coin it would land heads, nor that definitely were I to flip the coin it would not land heads. The law of *conditional*

---

[8]Shin (1991a), for instance, devises a metric that seems suitable for simple games such as "Chicken".

excluded middle will be violated:

$$(F \mathbin{\square\!\!\rightarrow} H) \vee (F \mathbin{\square\!\!\rightarrow} \neg H). \tag{3.3}$$

Conditional excluded middle obtains in Stalnaker's model. There are models and logics for conditionals in which it does not obtain.[9] In a case like this, however, the right weight to use for decision is clearly not the probability $\rho(F \mathbin{\square\!\!\rightarrow} H)$ of a conditional proposition $F \mathbin{\square\!\!\rightarrow} H$. If I'm convinced that neither $F \mathbin{\square\!\!\rightarrow} H$ nor $F \mathbin{\square\!\!\rightarrow} \neg H$ obtains, then my subjective probability for each is zero. The weight to use if I'm betting on the coin, though, should normally be one–half.

A number of ways have been proposed to handle cases like these. One is to think that with coins and the like, there's a kind of conditional chance that isn't merely subjective: the chance with which the coin would land heads were I to flip it. Write this $\pi_F(H)$. Then use as one's decision weight the following: one's *subjectively expected value for* this *objective conditional chance*. Suppose you are convinced that the coin is loaded, but don't know which way: You think that the coin is loaded either .6 toward heads or .6 toward tails, and have subjective probability of .5 for each of these possibilities:

$$\rho\Big(\pi_F(H) = .6\Big) = .5 \quad \text{and} \quad \rho\Big(\pi_F(H) = .4\Big) = .5. \tag{3.4}$$

Your subjectively expected value for $\pi_F(H)$, then, will be the average of .6 and .4. Call this appropriate decision weight $\epsilon_F(H)$. We can express this weighted averaging in measure theoretic terms, so that in general,

$$\epsilon_A(C) = \int_0^1 x \cdot \rho\Big(\pi_A(C) \in dx\Big). \tag{3.5}$$

$\epsilon_A(C)$ thus measures one's subjective expectation of C's obtaining were A to occur: the sum of (i) the degree to which A's obtaining would tend to bring it about that C obtained, plus (ii) the degree to which C would tend to hold whether or not A obtained.

We can now write formulas for $\mathcal{U}$ using $\epsilon_A(C)$ where we had previously used $\rho(A \mathbin{\square\!\!\rightarrow} C)$. Formula (2.4) above for instrumental expected utility now becomes

$$\mathcal{U}(A) = \sum_{i=1}^{n} \epsilon_A(S_i) u(A, S_i). \tag{3.6}$$

---

[9]Lewis (1973) constructs a system in which worlds may tie for most similar, or it may be that for every A–world, there is an A–world that is more similar. He thus denies Conditional Excluded Middle: It fails, for instance, when two A–worlds tie for most similar to the actual world, one a C–world and the other a $\neg C$–world.

Lewis (1981) gives an alternative formulation of causal decision theory, which is equivalent to the Stalnaker formulation we've been presenting whenever the Stalnaker framework applies as intended. He speaks of *dependency hypotheses:* complete hypotheses concerning what depends on what and how. Which dependency hypothesis obtains is causally independent of what the agent does, and so a Lewis dependency hypothesis can serve as a "state" in the Savage framework. He allows dependency hypotheses to contain an element of objective chance.[10]

Can an empiricist believe in such things as objective conditional chance or objective dependencies? This is a hotly debated topic, mostly beyond the scope of this article. Some philosophers think that objective dependency can be defined or characterized, somehow, in purely non–causal terms. Others doubt that any such direct characterization is possible, but think that a more indirect strategy may be available: Characterize a thinker's *beliefs* in causal dependencies—or his *degrees* of belief, his subjective probabilities, or as we have been calling them, his *credences.* His credences in causal propositions, this contention is, can be cashed out fully in terms of complex features of his credences in non–causal propositions—propositions that don't involve causal notions.

We ourselves would argue that causal propositions are genuine propositions of their own kind, basic to thinking about the world. They can't be fully explained in other terms, but they can be vindicated. We can be just as much empiricists about causes as we can about other features of the layout of the world. A rational thinker forms his credences in causal propositions in much the same Bayesian way he does for any other matter: He updates his subjective probabilities by conditionalizing on new experience. He starts with reasonable prior credences, and updates them. Subjective probability theorists like de Finetti long ago explained how, for non–causal propositions, updating produces convergence. The story depends on surprisingly weak conditions placed on the thinker's prior credence measure. The same kind of story, we suspect, could be told for credences in objective chance and objective dependence.

Lewis (1980) has told a story of this kind for credence in objective chance. His story rests on what he labels the "Principal Principle", a condition which characterizes reasonable credences in objective chances. Take a reasonable credence measure ρ, and a proposition about something that hasn't yet eventuated —say, that the coin I'm about the flip will land heads. Let me conditionalize his credences on the proposition that as of now, the objective probability of this coin's landing heads is .6. Then his resulting conditional credence in the

---

[10]Skyrms (1980) offers another formulation, invoking a distinction between factors that are within the agent's control and factors that aren't. Lewis (1981) discusses both Skyrms and unpublished work of Jordan Howard Sobel, and Skyrms (1984), 105–6, compares his formulation with those of Lewis (1981) and Stalnaker (1981).

coin's landing heads, the principle says, will likewise be .6. Many features of reasonable credence in objective chance follow from from this principle. From a condition on reasonable prior credences in objective chance follows an account of how one can learn about them from experience.

A like project for objective dependency hasn't been carried through, so far as we know, but the same broad approach would seem promising. In the meantime, there is much lore as to how experience can lead us to causal conclusions — and even render any denial of a causal depencency wildly implausible. The dependence of cancer on smoking is a case in point. Correlation is not causation, we all know, and a conditional probability is not a degree of causal dependence. [In the notation introduced above, the point is that $\rho(C/A)$ need not be $\epsilon_A(C)$, the subjectively expected value of the objective chance of C were one to do a.] Still, correlations, examined with sophistication, can *evidence* causation. A chief way of checking is to "screen off" likely common causes: A correlation between smoking and cancer might arise, say, because the social pressures that lead to smoking tend also to lead to drinking, and drinking tends to cause cancer. A statistician will check this possibility by separating out the correlation between smoking and cancer among drinkers on the one hand, and among non–drinkers on the other. More generally, the technique is this: A correlation between A and C, imagine, is suspected of being spurious—suspected *not* to arise from a causal influence of A on C or *vice versa*. Let F be a suspected common cause of A and C that might account for their correlation. Then see if the correlation disappears with F held constant. Econometricians elaborate such devices to uncover causal influences in an economy. The methodological literature on gleaning causal conclusions from experience includes classic articles by Herbert Simon [see Simon (1957), chapters 1–3].

Screening off is not a sure test of causality. A correlation might disappear with another factor held constant, not because neither factor depends causally on the other, but because the causal dependency is exactly counterbalanced by a contrary influence by a third factor.[11] Such a non–correlation might be robust, holding reliably with large sample sizes. But it will also be a coincidence: opposing tendencies may happen to cancel out, but we can expect such cases to be rare. Lack of correlation after screening off is *evidence* of lack of causal influence, but doesn't *constitute* lack of causal influence.

When controlled experiments can be done, in contrast, reasonable credences in a degree of objective dependency can be brought to converge without limit as sample size increases. Subjects are assigned to conditions in a way that we all agree has no influence on the outcome: by means of a chance device, say, or a table of pseudo–random numbers. Observed correlations then evidence

---

[11] Gibbard and Harper (1978), 140–2, construct an example of such a case.

causal dependence to whatever degree we can be confident that the correlation is no statistical fluke. With the *right* kind of partition, then, screening off does yield a reliable test of causality. But what makes a partition suitable for this purpose, we would claim, must be specified in terms that somehow invoke causality—in terms, for instance, of known causal independence.

How we can use evidence to support causal conclusions needs study. Standard statistical literature is strangely silent on questions of causation, however much the goals of statistical techniques may be to test and support causal findings. If we are right, then one class of treatments of causality will fail: namely, attempts to characterize causal beliefs in terms of the subjective probabilities and the like of non–causal propositions. Correct treatments must take causality as somehow basic. A constellation of relations—cause, chance, dependence, influence, laws of nature, what would happen if, what might likely happen if— are interrelated and may be intercharacterizable, but they resist being characterized purely from outside the constellation. Our hope should be that we can show how the right kind of evidence lets us proceed systematically from causal truisms to non–obvious causal conclusions. Fortunately, much of decision and game theory is already formulated in terms that are causal, implicitly at least, or that can be read or interpreted as causal. (When games are presented in normal form, for instance, it may be understood that no player's choice of strategies depends causally on the choice of any other.) A chief aim of causal decision theory is to make the role of causal beliefs in decision and game theory explicit.

4   Ratificationism

While some proponents of auspiciousness maximization have taken the heroic course and tried to argue that cooperating in Prisoner's Dilemma with Twin is rational,[12] most now concede that only defection makes sense. Nevertheless, the promise of an analysis of rational choice free from causal or counterfactual entanglements remains appealing. A number of writers have therefore sought to modify the evidential theory so that it endorses the non–cooperative solution in PDT and yet does not appeal any unreconstructed causal judgements. The hope is that one will be able to find statistical techniques of the sort discussed toward the end of the last section to distinguish causal relationships from suprious correlations, and then employ these techniques to formulate a decision theory that can be sensitive to causal considerations without making explicit use of causal or subjunctive notions. The most influential of these attempts are found in Eells (1982) and Jeffrey (1983). Since the two approaches are similar, we focus on Jeffrey.

---

[12]See, for example, Horgan (1981).

As we have seen, statisticians sometimes use "screening off" techniques to detect the effects of a common cause. Jeffrey's strategy is based on the insight that an agent's ability to anticipate her own decisions typically screens off any purely evidential import that her actions might possess. Prior to performing an act she will generally come to realize that she has decided on it. The act itself then ceases to be a piece of evidence for her since she has already discounted it. Letting Δ^A denote the decision to do a, we can put Jeffrey's claim like this:

- *Screening.* The decision to perform A screens off any purely evidential correlations between acts and states of the world, in the sense that $\rho(S/B\&\Delta^A) = \rho(S/\Delta^A)$ for all acts B and states S.

To ensure that these conditional credences are well–defined, Jeffrey must assume that the agent always assigns some positive probability to the prospect that she will fail to carry out a decision—due to a "trembling hand", a lack of nerve, or other factors beyond her control—so that $\rho(B\&\Delta^A)$ is non–zero for all acts B.

To see what happens when screening is introduced into PDT, imagine that during the course of your deliberations but prior to performing any act, you become certain that you will decide to cooperate, so that your credence in Δ_y^C moves to one. Since you are likely to carry out whatever decision you make, your probability for C_y also moves close to one, which gives you strong grounds for thinking your twin will cooperate. Indeed, if Screening obtains, you will have strong evidence for thinking that twin is about to cooperate, no matter what news you get as to what you yourself are about do, because $\rho(C_t/C_y\&\Delta_y^C) = \rho(C_t/D_y\&\Delta_y^C) = \rho(C_t/\Delta_y^C) \approx 1$. Condition (2.2) is thus satisfied. You can then correctly apply the evidential dominance principle to conclude that defection is your most auspicious option. In this way, Screening ensures that if you are certain that you will eventually decide to cooperate, then you will assign defecting a higher auspiciousness than cooperating. On the other hand, if you are certain that you will decide to defect, you then have strong reason to suspect that twin is about to defect, whatever you learn that you yourself are about to do—and again, defecting turns out to be the more auspicious option. Therefore, no matter how auspicious cooperating might seem *before* you make up your mind about what to do, defecting is sure to look more auspicious *afterwards*—and this will be true no matter what decision you have made. Jeffrey proposes to use this basic asymmetry—between what one decides and what one does—to argue that defection in PDT is the only rational course of action for an auspiciousness maximizer.

The case has already been made for an agent who is already certain about what she will decide. But what about agents who have yet to made up their minds? Here things get dicey. If you have not yet decided what to do, then the probabilities you assign to Δ_y^C and Δ_y^D will be far from one. This puts the auspiciousness values of C_y and D_y near those of $(C_y \& \Delta_y^C)$ and $(D_y \& \Delta_y^D)$ respectively, and since $\mathcal{V}(C \& \Delta_y^C) > \mathcal{V}(D \& \Delta_y^D)$, evidential decision theory tells you to choose cooperation. However, as soon as you make this choice, you will assign Δ_y^D a credence close to one, and as we have seen, you will then favor defection. Thus, the pursuit of good news forces you to make choices that you are certain to rue from the moment you make them—clearly something to avoid.

Jeffrey hopes to circumvent this difficulty by denying that evidential decision theory requires one to maximize auspiciousness as one *currently* estimates it. If you are savvy, he argues, you will realize that any choice you make will change some of your beliefs, thereby altering your estimates of auspiciousness. Thus, given that you want to make decisions that leave you better off for having made them, you should aim to maximize auspiciousness not as you currently estimate it, but as you *will* estimate it once your decision is made. You ought to, "choose for the person you expect to be when you have chosen,"[13] by maximizing expected utility computed relative to the personal probabilities you will have *after* having come to a firm decision about what to do. This is only possible if your choices conform to the maxim

- *Evidential Ratifiability.* An agent cannot rationally choose to perform A unless A is *ratifiable*, in the sense that $\mathcal{V}(A \& \Delta^A) \geq \mathcal{V}(B \& \Delta^A)$ for every act B under consideration.

This principle advises you to ignore your current views about the evidentiary merits of cooperating versus defecting, and to focus on maximizing future auspiciousness by making choices that you will regard as propitious from the epistemic perspective you will have once you have made them. Since in the presence of Screening, defection is the only such choice, the maxim of Evidential Ratifiability seems to provide an appropriately "evidentialist" rationale for defecting in PDT.

Unfortunately, though, the Screening condition need not always obtain. There are versions of PDT in which the actual performance of an act provides better evidence for some desired state than does the mere decision to perform it. This would happen, for example, if you and twin are bumblers who tend to have a similar problems carrying out your decisions. The fact that you were able to carry out a decision would then be evidentially correlated with you twin's act, and this correlation would not be screened off by the decision it-

---

[13] Jeffrey (1983) p. 16.

self. In such cases the evidential ratifiability principle sanctions cooperation.[14] Therefore, the Jeffrey/Eells strategy does not always provide a satisfactory evidentialist rationale for defecting in PDT. We regard this failure as reinforcing our contention that any adequate account of rational choice must recognize that decision makers have beliefs about causal or counterfactual relationships, beliefs that cannot be cashed out in terms of ordinary subjective conditional probabilities—in terms of conditional credences in non–causal propositions.

5   Ratificationism and Causality in the Theory of Games

Despite its failure, the Jeffrey/Eells strategy leaves the theory of rational choice an important legacy in the form of the Maxim of Ratifiability. We will see in this section that it is possible to assimilate Jeffrey's basic insight into casual decision theory, and that so understood, it codifies a type of reasoning commonly employed in game theory. Indeed, the idea that rational players always play their part in a Nash equilibrium is a special case of ratificationism.

The notion of a ratifiable act makes sense within any decision theory with the resources for defining the expected utility of one act given the news that another will be chosen or performed. In causal decision theory the definition would be this:

$$\mathcal{U}(B/A) = \sum_{i=1}^{n} \rho((B \,\square\!\!\rightarrow S_i)/A)u(B, S_i).$$

Jeffrey's insight then naturally turns into the maxim,

- *Causal Ratifiability.* An agent cannot rationally choose to perform act A unless $\mathcal{U}(A/A) \geq \mathcal{U}(B/A)$ for every act B under consideration.

This says that a person should never choose A unless once she does, her expectation of A's efficacy in bringing about desirable results is at least as great as that for any alternative to A. Notice that one no longer needs a "trembling hand" requirement to define the utility of one act conditional on another, since the conditional credence $\rho(B \,\square\!\!\rightarrow S/A)$ is well–defined even when A and B are incompatible. This means that an agent who is certain that she will perform A can still coherently wonder about how things *would* have gone *had* she done B—even though she can no longer wonder about how things are set to go if she's *going* to do B. This ability to assign utilities to actions that definitely will not be performed can be used to used to great advantage in game theory, for instance, when considering subgames and subgame perfection.

---

[14] Jeffrey, in his original published treatment of ratificationism (1983), 20, gives this counterexample and credits it to Bas van Fraassen. Shin (1991b) treats cases in which the respective players' "trembles" are independent of each other.

	HEADS	TAILS
HEADS	$-1, 1$	$1, -1$
TAILS	$1, -1$	$-1, 1$

Matching Pennies

To see how an act might fail to be causally ratifiable, imagine yourself playing Matching Pennies with an opponent who you think can predict your move and will make a best response to it (see table). Neither pure act then turns out to be ratifiable. Suppose that you are strongly inclined to play [HEADS], so that $\rho(H_y)$ is close to one. Since your conditional probability for Twin playing heads given that you do is high, it also follows that your subjective probability for H_t will be high. Thus by recognizing that you plan to play [HEADS], you give yourself evidence for thinking that Twin will also play [HEADS]. Note, however, this does nothing to alter the fact that you still judge Twin's actions to be causally independent of your own; your subjective probabilities still obey

$$\rho((H_y \mathbin{\Box\!\!\rightarrow} H_t)/H_y) = \rho((T_y \mathbin{\Box\!\!\rightarrow} H_t)/H_y).$$

Since $\rho(H_t) \approx 1$, your overall position is this: because you are fairly sure that you will play heads, you are fairly sure that Twin *will* play heads too; but you remain convinced that she *would* play heads even if (contrary to what you expect) you were to play tails. Under these conditions, the conditional expected utility associated with [TAILS] larger than that associated with [HEADS] on the supposition that [HEADS] is played. That is to say, [HEADS] is unratifiable. Similar reasoning shows that tails is also unratifiable. In fact, the only ratifiable act this game is the mixture $1/2$ [HEADS] $+$ $1/2$ [TAILS].[15]

---

[15] Piccione and Rubinstein (1997) present another kind of case in which considerations of ratifiability may be invoked: the case of the "absent–minded driver" who can never remember which of two intersections he is at. One solution concept they consider (but reject) is that of being "modified multi–selves consistent". In our terms, this amounts to treating oneself on other occasions as a twin, selecting a strategy that is ratifiable on the following assumption: that one's present strategy is fully predictive of one's strategy in any other situation that is

	C_1	C_2
R_1	1 , 1	0 , 4
R_2	4 , 0	$-15 , -15$

Chicken

It is no coincidence that this mixture also turns out to be the game's unique Nash equilibrium; there is a deep connection between ratifiable acts and game–theoretic equilibria. Take any two–person game, such as Matching Pennies, for which the unique Nash equilibrium consists of mixed strategies (which the players in fact adopt). If a player has predicted the other's strategy correctly and with certainty, then by playing the strategy she does, she maximizes her expected utility. But this isn't the only strategy that, given her credences, would maximize her expected utility; any other probability mixture of the same pure strategies would do so too. The strategy she adopts is unique, though, in this way: it is the only strategy that could be ratifiable, given the assumption that her opponent has predicted her strategy and is playing a best response to it. It should be clear that this argument extends straightforwardly to the n–person case. In any Nash equilibrium, all players perform causally ratifiable acts.

In fact, the least restrictive of all equilibrium solution concepts—Aumann's correlated equilibrium—can be understood as a straightforward application of the maximum of ratifiability.[16] Aumann sought to generalize the Nash equilibrium concept by relaxing the assumption—implicit in most previous game–theoretic thinking—that players in normal–form games believe that everyone acts independently of everyone else. Take a game of Chicken. The table shown might give the utilities of drivers traveling along different roads into a blind intersection, who must decide whether to stop and lose time (R_1 and C_1) or to drive

---

subjectively just like it. This turns out to coincide with the "optimal" strategy, the stratgy one would adopt if one could choose in advance how to handle all such situations.
[16]More precisely, correlated equilibrium is the weakest equilibrium solution concept which assumes that all players have common beliefs. When this assumption is relaxed one obtains a subjectively correlated equilibrium. For details see Aumann (1974), (1987).

	C_1	C_2
R_1	pq	$p(1-q)$
R_2	$(1-p)q$	$(1-p)(1-q)$

Table 1

	C_1	C_2
R_1	$p+q-1$	$1-q$
R_2	$1-p$	0

Table 2

straight through and risk an accident (R_2 and C_2). Let the players assume that they will choose, respectively, strategies $p \cdot R_1 + (1-p) \cdot R_2$ and $q \cdot C_1 + (1-q) \cdot C_2$. What credences will they give to the various joint pure actions they may end up performing?

Game theorists have traditionally assumed that the players will treat the chance devices that implement their mixed strategies as evidentially independent, ascribing the credences in Table 1. Aumann imagines that they might ascribe the credences of Table 2: To see how the correlations in Table 2 might arise, imagine a "managed" game of Chicken in which, to minimize the chances of a disastrous outcome, things have been arranged so that an impartial arbitrator will throw a fair die and illuminate a traffic light at the intersection according to the "Arbitrator's Scheme" shown in the table. If each player intends to heed the signal, stopping on red and driving through on green, and believes his opponent intends to do so as well, then both will have the correlated priors of Table 2. Aumann showed how to define an equilibrium solution concept even when players' acts are correlated in this way. An *adapted* strategy is a rule s which dictates a unique pure act $s(A)$ for each act A signalled by the arbitrator: for instance, "Stop on red and go on green" or "Run all lights." A correlated equilibrium is simply a pair of adapted strategies r and c such that,

	one	two	three	four	five	six
ROW	Red	Red	Red	Red	Green	Green
COL	Red	Red	Green	Green	Red	Red

Arbitrator's Scheme

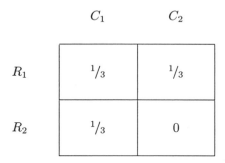

	C_1	C_2
R_1	$^1/_3$	$^1/_3$
R_2	$^1/_3$	0

Table 3

for all alternatives r^* and c^*, the following condition holds (call it CE):

$$\sum_{ij} \rho(R_i \& C_j) \cdot \mathcal{U}_{\text{row}}(r(R_i), C_j) \geq \sum_{ij} \rho(R_i \& C_j) \cdot \mathcal{U}_{\text{row}}(r^*(R_i), C_j);$$

$$\sum_{ij} \rho(R_i \& C_j) \cdot \mathcal{U}_{\text{col}}(R_i, c(C_j)) \geq \sum_{ij} \rho(R_i \& C_j) \cdot \mathcal{U}_{\text{col}}(R_i, c^*(C_j)).$$

Thus, r and c constitute a correlated equilibrium iff no player has reason to deviate from her adapted strategy given her beliefs and the signal she receives. The reader may verify that, when things are as described in Table 3, both players' resolving to obey the light is a correlated equilibrium, whereas there is no correlated equilibrium in which either player decides to run red lights.

Definition CE makes it appear as if the existence of correlated equilibria depends on the availability of external signaling mechanisms. This was the view presented by Aumann in Aumann (1974), but in Aumann (1987), he shows that acts themselves can serve as appropriate signals. Specifically, Aumann established that a common probability distribution[17] ρ defined over strategy combinations comprises a correlated equilibrium iff given any pair of acts R and C assigned positive probabilities, one has CE^*:

$$\sum_{j} \rho(C_j/R) \cdot \mathcal{U}_{\text{row}}(R, C_j) \geq \sum_{j} \rho(C_j/R) \cdot \mathcal{U}_{\text{row}}(R^*, C_j);$$

$$\sum_{i} \rho(R_i/C) \cdot \mathcal{U}_{\text{col}}(R_i, C) \geq \sum_{i} \rho(R_i/C) \cdot \mathcal{U}_{\text{col}}(R_i, C^*).$$

for all alternatives R^* and C^*. CE^* requires, then, that agents assign zero prior probability to any act, either of their own or of their adversaries', that does not maximize expected utility on the condition that it will be performed. Aumann regards this condition as "an expression of Bayesian rationality," since players satisfy it by maximizing expected utility at the time they act.

As a number of authors have noted, CE^* is an application of the maxim of ratifiabilty.[18] It requires players to give zero credence to non–ratifiable acts. Hence for a group of players to end up in a correlated equilibrium, it is necessary and sufficient that all choose ratifiabile acts and expect others to do so as well. Aumann's "Bayesian rationality" thus coincides with the notion of rationality found in Jeffrey's ratificationism. More specifically, we contend that Aumann is requiring rational players to choose *causally* ratifiable actions.

---

[17]Note that such a distribution determines a unique mixed act for each player. Thus, it makes no difference whether one talks about the players' acts or the players' beliefs being in equilibrium.
[18]Shin (1991b), Skyrms (1990).

While Aumann has rather little to say about the matter, he clearly does not mean the statistical correlations among acts in correlated equilibrium to reflect causal connections. This is particularly obvious when external signaling devices are involved, for in such cases each player believes that his opponents would heed the arbitor's signal whether or not he himself were to heed it. Each player uses his knowledge of the arbitor's signal to him to make inferences about the signals given to others, to form beliefs about what his opponents expect him to do, and ultimately to justify his own policy of following the arbitor's signal. What he does not do is suppose that the correlations so discovered *would* continue to hold no matter what he decided to do. For example, if [ROW]'s credences are given in Table 3, it would be a mistake for him to run a red light in hopes of making it certain that [COLUMN] will stop; [COLUMN]'s action, after all, is determined by the signal she receives, not by what [ROW] does. Notice, however, that a straightforward application of evidential decision theory recommends running red lights in this circumstance—further proof that the view is untenable. In cases, then, where correlations are generated via external signaling, a causal interpretation of CE* clearly is called for. To make this explicit, we can rewrite CE* as the following condition CE^{**}:

$$\sum_j \rho((R \mathbin{\square\!\!\rightarrow} C_j)/R) \cdot \mathcal{U}_{\text{row}}(R, C_j) \;\geq\; \sum_j \rho((R^* \mathbin{\square\!\!\rightarrow} C_j)/R) \cdot \mathcal{U}_{\text{row}}(R^*, C_j);$$

$$\sum_i \rho((C \mathbin{\square\!\!\rightarrow} R_i)/C) \cdot \mathcal{U}_{\text{col}}(R_i, C) \;\geq\; \sum_i \rho((C^* \mathbin{\square\!\!\rightarrow} R_i)/C) \cdot \mathcal{U}_{\text{col}}(R_i, C^*).$$

This reduces to CE* on the assumption that [ROW] and [COLUMN] cannot influence each other's acts, so that both $\rho((R^* \mathbin{\square\!\!\rightarrow} C_j)/R) = \rho(C_j/R)$ and $\rho((C^* \mathbin{\square\!\!\rightarrow} R_i)/C) = \rho(R_i/C)$ hold for all R^* and C^*.

The situation is not appreciably different in cases where the correlation arises without any signaling device. Imagine playing [ROW] in the coordination game in Table 4, and consider the correlated equilibrium described by Table 5: These correlations need not have arisen through signaling. You might find the (R_1, C_1) equilibrium salient because it offers the vastly higher payoff, and, knowing that your opponent can appreciate its salience for you, you might conclude that she expects you to play it. That makes C_1 the better play for her, which reinforces your intention to play R_1 and your belief that she will play C_1, and so on. It would not be unreasonable under these conditions for the two of you to end up in the correlated equilibrium of Table 5. Still, there is no suggestion here that your initial inclination to play R_1 is somehow responsible causally for your opponent's credences. Her credences are what they are because she suspects that you are inclined to play R_1, but neither your decision to play R_1 nor your actually playing of R_1 is the cause of these suspicions—she develops them solely on the basis of her knowledge of the game's structure. As in the

	C_1	C_2
R_1	25 , 1	0 , 0
R_2	0 , 0	1 , 2

Table 4

	C_1	C_2
R_1	0.7	0.01
R_2	0.01	0.28

Table 5

signaling case, the acts in a correlated equilibrium are evidentially correlated but causally independent.

This explicitly causal reading of Aumann's discussion helps to clear up a perplexing feature of correlated equilibria. CE only makes sense as a rationality constraint if agents are able to treat their own actions as bits of information about the world, for it is only then that the expressions appearing to the right of the "$\geq$" signs can be understood as giving utilities for the starred acts. As Aumann notes, his model (like that of Jeffrey before him)

> does away with the dichotomy usually perceived between uncertainty about acts of nature and of personal players.... . In traditional Bayesian decision theory, each decision maker is permitted to make whatever decision he wishes, after getting whatever information he gets. In our model this appears not to be the case, since the decision taken by each decision maker is part of the description of the state of the world. This sounds like a restriction on the decision maker's freedom of action. [Aumann (1987, p. 8)]

The problem here is that the utility comparisons in CE seem to portray acts as things that happen to agents rather than things they do. Moreover, it is not clear why an agent who learns that he is surely going to perform R should need to compare it with other acts that he is sure he will not perform. Aumann tries to smooth things over by suggesting that CE describes the perspective of agents, not as choosers, but as "outside observers." He writes,

> The "outside observer" perspective is common to all differential information models in economics.... . In such models, each player gets some information or "signal"; he hears only the signal sent to him, not that of others. In analyzing his situation, [the] player must first look at the whole picture as if he were an outside observer; he cannot ignore the possibility of his having gotten a signal other than he actually got, even

though he knows that he actually did not get such a signal. This is because the other players do not know what signal he got. [He] must take the ignorance of the other players into account when deciding on his own course of action, and he cannot do this if he does not explicitly include in the model signals other than the one he actually got. [Aumann (1987, p. 8)]

The problem with this response is that it does not tell us how a player is supposed to use the knowledge gained from looking at things "externally" (i.e., as if he were not choosing) to help him with his "internal" decision (where he must choose how to act). The point is significant, since what's missing from the outside observer standpoint is the very thing that makes something a decision problem—the fact that a choice has to be made.

In our view, talk about outside observers here is misleading. Aumann's third–person, "outside observer" perspective is the first–person *subjunctive* perspective: a view on what *would* happen if *I were to do* something different. It is an advantage of causal decision theory that it allows one to assess the rationality of acts that certainly will not be performed in the same way as one assesses the rationality of any other option. One simply appeals to whatever facts about objective chances, laws of nature, or causal relations are required to imagine the "nearest" possible world in which the act is performed, the one most similar, in relevant respects, to the actual world in which one won't perform the act. One then sees what would ensue under those circumstances. Even, for instance, if one assigns zero credence to the proposition that one will intentionally leap off the bridge one is crossing, it still makes sense on the causal theory to speak of the utility of jumping. Indeed the abysmally low utility of this action is the principal reason why one is certain not perform it. When we interpret correlated equilibria causally, then, along the lines of CE**, there is no need for an "external" perspective in decision making. All decisions are made from the first–person subjunctive perspective of "What would happen if I performed that act?"

A number of other aspects of game–theoretic reasoning can likewise be analyzed in terms of causal ratifiability.[19] Some of the most interesting work in this area is due to Harper, who has investigated the ways in which causal decision theory and ratifiability can be used to understand extensive–form games Harper (1986), (1991). This is a natural place for issues about causation to arise, since players' choices at early stages in extensive–form games can affect other players' beliefs—and thus their acts—at later stages.

Harper proposes using the maxim of ratifiability as the first step in an analysis of game–theoretic reasoning that is "eductive" or "procedural", an analysis

---

[19]See Shin (1991b), for instance, for an interesting ratificationist gloss on Selten's notion of a "perfect" equilibrium.

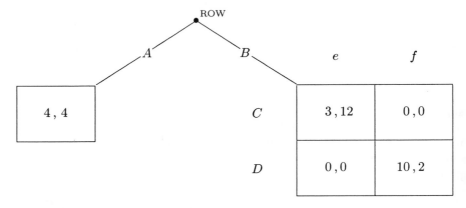

Harsanyi-Selten Game

that seeks to supply a list of rules and deliberative procedures that agents in states of indecision can use in order to arrive at an intuitively correct equilibrium choice.[20]   Rational players, he suggests, should choose actions that maximize their unconditional causal expected utility *from among the ratifiable alternatives.* (Harper regards cases where no ratifiable strategies exist as genuinely pathological.) The idea is not simply to choose acts that maximize unconditional expected utility, since these need not be ratifiable. Nor is it to choose acts with maximal expected utility on the condition that they are performed, since these may have low unconditional utility. Rather, one first eliminates unratifiable options, and then maximizes unconditional expected utility with what is left. In carrying out the second step of this process, each player imagines her adversaries choosing among their ratifiable options by assigning zero probability to any option that wouldn't be ratifiable.

Harper shows that both in normal and in extensive–form games, players who follow these prescriptions end up choosing the intuitively "right" act in a wide range of cases. In extensive–form games, his method produces choices that are in sequential equilibrium — and perhaps most interesting, the method seems to promote a strong form of "forward induction." To illustrate the latter point, and to get a sense of how Harper's procedure works in practice, consider the game of Harsanyi and Selten (1988) shown here. [ROW]'s act A yields fixed payoffs, whereas [ROW]'s act B leads to a strategic subgame with [COLUMN]. Harsanyi and Selten argue that (C, e) is the unique rational solution to the subgame, and they use backwards induction to argue that (AC, e) is the only

---

[20] On the need for such "eductive" procedures see Binmore (1987).

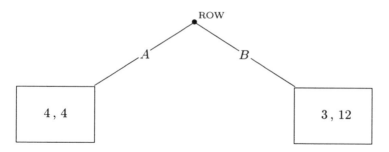

Truncation Game

rational solution in the full game. Their thought is that at the initial choice point [ROW] will know that (C, e) would be played if the subgame were reached, so he actually faces the "truncated game" as shown below, which makes A the only rational choice.

Kohlberg and Mertens (1986) have objected to this reasoning on the grounds that [ROW] can perform B as a way of signaling [COLUMN] that he has chosen BD (since it would be crazy to pass up A for C), and can thus force [COLUMN] to play f rather than e. Harsanyi and Selten respond by claiming that [COLUMN] would have to regard [ROW]'s playing B as a mistake since, "before deciding whether ROW] can effectively signal his strategic intentions, we must first decide what strategies are rational for the two players in the subgame, and accordingly what strategy is the rational strategy for [ROW] in the truncation game" [Harsanyi, Selten (1988, p. 353) (see table)]. Thus, we have a dispute over what sorts of effects the playing of B would have on [COLUMN]'s beliefs at the second choice point, and thereby on her decision. This is just the sort of case where causal decision theory can be helpful.

Harper's procedure endorses Kohlberg's and Mertens' contention. Harsanyi and Selten's preferred act for [ROW] will be unratifiable, so long as each player knows that the other chooses only ratifiable options. For A to be ratifiable, it would at least have to be the case that

$$U(A/A) = 4 \geq U(BD/A) = \rho((BD \boxdot\!\!\rightarrow e)/A) \cdot 0 + \rho((BD \boxdot\!\!\rightarrow f)/A) \cdot 10. \tag{5.1}$$

However, since [COLUMN] must choose at the third choice point knowing that ROW] has played B, but without knowing whether he has played C or D, it follows that [ROW]'s credence for $BC \boxdot\!\!\rightarrow f$ must be $\rho(f/B)$. Now at the final choice point, [COLUMN] would know that [ROW] had chosen either BC or BD or some mixture of the two, and she would have to assume that the option chosen was ratifiable (if such an option is available). BC clearly cannot be ratifiable, since it is dominated by A. Harper also shows, using a somewhat involved argument, that no mixture of BC and BD can be ratifiable.[21] BD, however, is ratifiable, provided that $\rho(BD \,\square\!\!\rightarrow f/BD) = \rho(f/B) \geq {}^4/_{10}$. Thus, since only one of [ROW]'s B–acts can be ratifiable, [COLUMN] would have to assign it a probability of one if she were to find herself at the second choice point. [ROW], knowing all this and knowing that f is [COLUMN]'s only ratifiable response to BD, will indeed assign a high value to $\rho(f/B)$, viz. $\rho(f/B) = 1$. This in turn ensures that $\mathcal{U}(BD/A) > \mathcal{U}(A/A)$, making A unratifiable. BD is thus the only ratifiable solution to the Harsanyi/Selten game. Hence, if Harper is correct, it seems that Kohlberg and Mertens were right to reject the backwards induction argument and to think that [ROW] can use B to warn [COLUMN] of his intention to play D.

We hope this example gives the reader something of the flavor of Harper's approach. Clearly his proposal needs to be elaborated more fully before we will be able to make an informed judgment on its merits. We are confident, however that any adequate understanding of game–theoretic reasoning will rely heavily on causal decision theory and the maxim of ratifiability.

6   Foundational Questions

Before any theory of expected utility can be taken seriously, it must be supplemented with a representation theorem that shows precisely how its requirements are reflected in rational preference. To prove such a theorem one isolates a small set of axiomatic constraints on preference, argues that they are requirements of rationality, and shows that anyone who satisfies them will automatically act in accordance with the theory's principle of expected utility maximization. The best known result of this type is found in Savage (1972), where it was shown that any agent whose preferences conform to the well–known Savage axioms will maximize expected utility, as defined by equation (1), relative to a (unique) probability ρ and a (unique up to positive linear transformation) utility u. Unfortunately, this result does not provide a fully satisfactory foundation for either CDT or ETD, because, as we have seen, Savage's notion of expected utility is ambiguous between a causal and an evidential interpretation. This leaves some important unfinished business for evidential and causal decision theorists, since each camp has an obligation to present a representation theorem that unambiguously captures its version of utility theory.

Evidential decision theorists were first to respond to the challenge. The key mathematical result was proved in Bolker (1966), and applied to decision theory in Jeffrey (1967). The Jeffrey/Bolker approach differs from Savage's in two

---

[21]Harper (1991, p. 293).

significant ways: First, preferences are defined over a σ–algebra of propositions that describe not only states of the world, but consequences and actions as well. Second, Savage's "Sure–thing" Principle (his postulate P3) is replaced by the weaker

- *Impartiality Axiom:* Let X, Y and Z be non–null propositions such that (a) Z is incompatible with both X and Y, (b) X and Y are indifferent in the agent's preference ordering, and (c) $(X \vee Z)$ is indifferent with $(Y \vee Z)$ but not with Z. Then, $(X \vee Z^*)$ must be indifferent with $(Y \vee Z^*)$ for any proposition Z^* incompatible with both X and Y.

In the presence of the other Bolker/Jeffrey axioms, which do not differ substantially from those used by Savage, Impartiality guarantees that the agent's preferences can be represented by a function that satisfies equation (2.3).[22] It also ensures that the representation will be *partition independent* in the sense that, for any partitions $\{X_i\}$ and $\{Y_j\}$ and any act A, one will always have $\mathcal{V}(A) = \sum \rho(X_i/A)\mathcal{V}(A\&X_i) = \sum \rho(Y_j/A)V(A\&Y_j)$. Thus, in EDT it does not matter how one chooses the state partition relative to which expected utilities are computed.

This contrasts sharply with Savage's theory. Formula (2.1) shows how to compute expected utilities with respect to a single partition of states, but it gives no guarantee that different choices of partitions yield the same value for $\mathcal{V}(A)$. As a consequence, Savage had to place restrictions on the state partitions that could be legitimately employed in well–posed decision problems. Strictly speaking, he said, his axioms only apply to *grand–world* decisions whose act and state partitions slice things finely enough to ensure that each act/state pair produces a consequence that is sufficiently detailed to decide every question the agent cares about. Thus, on the official view, we can only be confident that (2.1) will yield the correct value for $\mathcal{V}(A)$ when applied to state partitions in "grand–world" decisions. Savage recognized this as a significant restriction on his theory, since owing to the extreme complexity of grand–world decisions, no actual human being can ever contemplate making one. He tried to make this restriction palatable by suggesting that his axioms might be usefully applied to certain "small–world" decisions, and expressing the hope that there would be only a "remote possibility" of obtaining values for $\mathcal{V}(A)$ inconsistent with those obtained in the grand–world case. This hope, however, was never backed–up by any rigorous proof. We take it as a mark in favor of EDT that it is can solve this "problem of the small–world" by giving such a proof.

---

[22]This representation will not be unique (except in the rare case where $\mathcal{V}$ is unbounded), for, as a simple calculation shows, if the function $\mathcal{V}(A) = \sum \rho(S_i/A)u(A, S_i)$ represents a preference ordering, and if k is such that $1 + k\mathcal{V}(X) > 0$ for all propositions X in the algebra over which $\mathcal{V}$ is defined, then $V_k(A) = \sum \rho_k(S_i/A)u_k(A, S_i)$ will also represent the ordering, when $\rho_k(X) = \rho(X)(1 + k\mathcal{V}(X))$ and $\mathcal{V}_k(X) = [\mathcal{V}(X)(1 + k)]/(1 + k\mathcal{V}(X))$.

The easiest way to prove a representation result for CDT is to co–opt Savage's theorem by stipulating that well–posed decision problems must be based on partitions of states that are certain to be causally independent of acts, and then imposing Savage's axioms on such problems. A number of causal decision theorists have endorsed the view that there is a "right" partition of states to be used for computing instrumental expected utility.[23] The Lewis (1981) formulation of CDT in terms of dependency hypotheses mentioned in Section 2 above is an example of this strategy. Minor intramural squabbles aside, the idea is that each element in the privileged partition, often denoted $\mathbf{K} = \{K_j\}$ following Skyrms (1980), should provide a maximally specific description of one of the ways in which things that the agent cares about might depend on what she does.[24] It is characteristic of such partitions that they will be related to the agent's subjective probability by[25]

- *Definiteness of Outcome:* For any proposition O that the agent cares about (in the sense of not being indifferent between O and $\neg O$), any act A, and any $K_j \in \mathbf{K}$, either $\rho((A \,\square\!\!\rightarrow O)/K_j) = 1$ or $\rho((A \,\square\!\!\rightarrow \neg O)/K_j) = 1$.

- *Instrumental Act Independence:* $\rho([A \,\square\!\!\rightarrow K_j] \leftrightarrow K_j) = 1$ for all acts A and states K_j.

The first of these ensures that $u(A, S_i)$ has the same value for each Savage–state S_i in K_j, and thus that

$$\mathcal{U}(A) = \sum_i \rho(A \,\square\!\!\rightarrow S_i) u(A, S_i) = \sum_j \rho(A \,\square\!\!\rightarrow K_j) \mathcal{U}(A, K_j).$$

The second condition then guarantees that $\mathcal{U}(A) = \sum_j \rho(K_j) \mathcal{U}(A, K_j)$. Since this equation has the form (2.5), it follows that if there exists a partition $\mathbf{K}$ that meets these two requirements, then one can appropriately apply the Savage axioms to actions whose outcomes are specified in terms of it. Fortunately, the required partition is certain to exist, because it is always possible to find a $\mathbf{K} = \{K_i\}$ such that (i) K_j entails either $(A \,\square\!\!\rightarrow O)$ or $(A \,\square\!\!\rightarrow \neg O)$ for every O the agent cares about, and (ii) $([A \,\square\!\!\rightarrow K_j] \leftrightarrow K_j)$ is a truth of logic for

---

[23] See, for example, Skyrms (1980), Lewis (1981), Armendt (1986).

[24] Notice that states are being viewed here as functions from acts to outcomes, whereas acts are taken as unanalyzed objects of choice (that is, as propositions the agent can make true or false as she pleases). This contrasts with Savage's well–known formalization in which acts are protrayed as functions from states to outcomes, and states are left as unanalyzed objects of belief. Less hangs on this distinction than one might think. When one adopts the perspective of Jeffrey (1967), (1983) and interprets both states and actions as propositions, and views outcomes as conjunctions of these propositions, the two analyses become interchangeable.

[25] Here we are following Gibbard (1986).

all A and K_j.[26] The general existence of such partitions lets us use Savage's representation theorem as a foundation for CDT, subject to the proviso that the Savage axioms should only be applied to decisions framed in terms of a **K**–partition.

The trouble with this strategy is that the partition dependence of Savage's theory is carried over into CDT. The need for a partition–independent formulation of CDT has been argued by Sobel (1989), and Eells (1982) has suggested that EDT should be preferred to CDT on this basis alone. The main difficulty is the problem of "small–worlds", which threatens to make the theory inapplicable, in the strictest sense, to all the decision problems people actually consider. Gibbard (1986) goes a certain distance toward alleviating this difficulty by, in effect, showing how to find the smallest **K**–partition for a given decision problem, but his partition is still rather "grand", and a fully partition–invariant version of CDT would still be desirable.

Armendt (1986) proves a representation result that does provide a formulation of CDT that is partition–independent, even though it does not do away with the notion of a **K**–partition. He takes the conditional decision theory of Fishburn (1974) as his starting point. The basic concept here is that of the utility of a prospect X on the hypothesis that some condition C obtains. If $\{C_1, C_2, \ldots, C_n\}$ is a partition of C, these conditional utilities are governed by the (partition independent) equation:

$$\mathcal{U}(X/C) = \sum \rho(C_i/C)\mathcal{U}(X/C_i) \qquad (6.1)$$

which shows how X's utility given C depends on its utilities given the various ways in which C might be true. Notice that (6.1) allows for a distinction between an act A's unconditional utility and its utility conditional on its own performance. These are given respectively by

$$\mathcal{U}(A) = \mathcal{U}(A/A \vee \neg A) = \sum \rho(S_i)\mathcal{U}(A/S_i),$$
$$\mathcal{U}(A/A) = \sum \rho(S_i/A)\mathcal{U}(A/A \& S_i),$$

where the state partition may be chosen arbitrarily. In a suggestion that bears some similarities to Jeffrey's ratificationist proposal, Armendt argues that decision problems in which an agent's unconditional preference for A differs from her preference for A conditional on itself are just the kinds of cases in which A's auspiciousness diverges from its instrumental expected utility. This suggests a way of characterizing **K**–partitions directly in terms of the agent's preferences. Armendt's thought is that the elements of an appropriate **K**–partition should "screen–off" differences in value between unconditional A and A–conditional–on–A, so that the agent is indifferent between

---

[26] An explicit construction of **K** can be found in Gibbard and Harper (1978).

A given K_i and A given $(A\&K_i)$ for every i. When this is so, we will have $\sum \rho(K_i)\mathcal{U}(A/K_i) = \sum \rho(K_i/A)\mathcal{U}(A/K_i)$, and Armendt shows that the conditional utilities $\mathcal{U}(A/K_i)$ can be eliminated in favor of the unconditional news values $\mathcal{V}(A\&K_i)$ as long as there exists at least one partition of "consequences" $\mathbf{O} = \{O_j\}$ such that the agent's unconditional utility for $(A\&O_j\&K_i)$ is equal to her utility for A conditional on $(A\&O_j\&K_i)$. When such a $\mathbf{K}$ and $\mathbf{O}$ exist, we have $\mathcal{U}(A) = \sum \rho(K_i)\mathcal{V}(A\&K_i)$, which is precisely the condition in which CDT and EDT coincide. What Armendt shows, then, is that an appropriate representation theorem for CDT can be obtained by supplementing Fishburn's conditional decision theory with the assumption that every act A can be associated with a $\mathbf{K}$–partition such that $A/K_i \approx A/(A\&K_i)$ for all i, and a partition of consequences $\mathbf{O}$ (dependent on A and $\mathbf{K}$) such that $(A\&O_j\&K_i) \approx A/(A\&O_j\&K_i)$.

This is a nice result. Since Fishburn's theory is partition independent, it follows that CDT will be as well, provided that at least one pair of partitions $\mathbf{K}$, $\mathbf{O}$ exist for each act A. The crucial questions are whether such partitions do exist in general, and whether we should think that the condition that defines $\mathbf{K}$ really does guarantee that $\mathcal{U}(A)$ and $\mathcal{V}(A)$ coincide. On this latter point we have our doubts, but even if it is granted, it seems unlikely to us, in the absence of further argument, that the appropriate $\mathbf{K}$–partitions will exist in all cases where we would want to apply CDT. Indeed, it would be useful to have a representation theorem for CDT that does not need to assume the existence of any special partition of states or any canonical form for a decision problem to take.

A representation theorem with these desirable features is proven in Joyce (forthcoming). Joyce sees both EDT and CDT as instances of an abstract conditional expected utility whose basic concept is that of the utility of an act A on the supposition that some condition C obtains. Joyce begins by characterizing supposition, or provisional belief revision, in terms sufficiently general to subsume Bayesian conditioning and Lewis's imaging as special cases. Given a subjective probability ρ defined over a σ–algebra Ω, and a distinguished subset $\mathcal{C}$ of *conditions* in Ω,[27] a *supposition for* ρ *relative to* $\mathcal{C}$ is a function $\rho(\bullet \mid \bullet)$ from $\Omega \times \mathcal{C}$ into the real numbers that satisfies

a) $\rho(\bullet \mid C)$ is a countably additive probability on Ω for every $C \in \mathcal{C}$.

b) $\rho(C \mid C) = 1$ for all $C \in \mathcal{C}$.

c) $\rho(X \mid C \vee \neg C) = \rho(X)$ for all $X \in \Omega$.

---

[27]The set $\mathcal{C}$ always takes the form $\mathcal{C} = \Omega \sim I$, where the *ideal* I is a collection of Ω-propositions that contains the contradictory event $(X\&\neg X)$, is closed under countable disjunctions, and which contains $(X\&Y)$ whenever $X \in I$ and $Y \in \Omega$.

d) $\rho(X \mid B\&C) \geq \rho(X\&B \mid C)$ for all $X \in \Omega$ whenever $(B\&C) \in \mathcal{C}$.

The reader can verify that the ordinary conditional probability $\rho(X/C)$—that is, $\rho(X\&C)/\rho(C)$—is a supposition for ρ relative to $\mathcal{C} = \{C \in \Omega : \rho(C) > 0\}$. In fact, for any set of conditions C (even those containing conditions with zero prior probability), one can show that any map $\rho(\bullet \mid \bullet)$ defined on $\Omega \times \mathcal{C}$ that satisfies (a)–(b) plus

■   *Bayes's Law:* $\rho(B \mid C)\rho(X \mid B\&C) = \rho(X \mid C)\rho(B \mid X\&C)$ whenever we have $(B\&C)$, $(X\&C) \in C$,

is a supposition.[28] The imaging function $\rho^C = \rho(C \,\square\!\!\rightarrow\, \bullet)$ associated with a similarity relation among possible worlds is also a supposition, but not typically one that satisfies Bayes's Law. There are also suppositions that are neither Bayesian nor instances of imaging.

Joyce, impressed by the need for partition–independent formulations of utility theories, uses the notion of a supposition to define an abstract conditional expected utility to be thought of as "utility under a supposition". Its (partition independent) basic equation is

$$\mathcal{V}(A|C) \;=\; \sum_i \frac{\rho(S_i \& A \mid C)}{\rho(A|C)} u(A, S_i) \qquad\qquad (6.2)$$

$$=\; \sum_i \frac{\rho(X_i \& A \mid C)}{\rho(A|C)} \mathcal{V}(A\&X_i \mid C) \quad \text{for any partition } \{X_i\},$$

where $\rho(\bullet \mid \bullet)$ might be any supposition function for ρ defined relative to a set of conditions $\mathcal{C}$ that contains propositions describing all an agent's actions (as well as other things). Since (6.2) is just EDT's (2.3) with $\rho(\bullet \mid C)$ substituted in for $\rho(\bullet)$, $\mathcal{V}(A|C)$ gives A's auspiciousness on the supposition that condition C obtains, where this supposition may be any provisional belief revision that satisfies (a)–(d).

As with Fishburn's theory, there is no guarantee that A's unconditional utility, which is now just $\mathcal{V}(A)$, will coincide with its utility conditional on itself,

$$\mathcal{V}(A|A) = \sum_i \rho(S_i \mid A)u(A, S_i).$$

The sole exception occurs when $\rho(\bullet \mid \bullet)$ is Bayesian, for in that case we have $\mathcal{V}(A) = \mathcal{V}(A \mid A)$, because $\rho(S_i \mid A) = \rho(S_i\&A)/\rho(A)$ for all i. Given that

---

[28]These Bayesian suppositions were defined in Renyi (1955), and have come to be called "Popper measures" in the philosophical literature, after Popper (1959). Interested readers may consult van Fraassen (1995), Hammond (1994), and McGee (1994) for informative discussions of Popper measures.

$\mathcal{V}(A)$ and $\mathcal{V}(A\,|\,A)$ can differ in general, it becomes a live question whether a decision maker should choose acts that maximize her unconditional expected utility or choose acts that maximize expected utility conditional on the supposition that they are performed. Joyce argues, on grounds having nothing to do with the conflict between CDT and EDT, that a choiceworthy action is always one that maximizes expected utility on the condition that it is performed. The rational decision maker's objective, in other words, should always be to choose an A such that $\mathcal{V}(A\,|\,A) \geq \mathcal{V}(B\,|\,B)$ for all alternatives B. Neither evidential nor causal decision theorists will dispute this point, since the former endorse the prescription to maximize $\mathcal{V}(A\,|\,A)$ when the supposition function is $\rho(X\,|\,C) = \rho_C(A)$, which makes $\mathcal{V}(A\,|\,A)$ equal A's auspiciousness, and the latter endorse it when $\rho(X\,|\,C) = \rho(C\,\Box\!\!\rightarrow A)$, which makes $\mathcal{V}(A\,|\,A)$ equal A's instrumental expected utility. Thus, EDT and CDT are both instances of abstract conditional utility theory. The difference between them has to do not with the basic form of the utility function or with the connection between expected utility and choiceworthiness, but with the correct type of supposition to use in decision making contexts.

Once we recognize this, it becomes clear that the problem of proving a representation theorem for CDT can be subsumed under the more general problem of proving a representation theorem for an abstract conditional utility theory. And, since the function $\mathcal{V}(\bullet\,|\,C)$ obeys equation (2.3) relative to any fixed condition C, this latter problem can be solved by extending the Bolker/Jeffrey axioms for unconditional preferences to conditional preferences, and showing that anyone who satisfies the axioms is sure to have conditional preferences that can be represented by some function $\mathcal{V}(A\,|\,C)$ of form (6.2) that is defined relative to a supposition function $\rho(\bullet\,|\,\bullet)$ for her subjective probability ρ.

Joyce was able to accomplish this. We refer to reader to Joyce (forthcoming) for the details. These turn out to be rather complicated, but the basic idea is straightforward. One starts by imagining an agent with a system of conditional preferences of the form: X on the supposition that B is weakly preferable to Y on the supposition that C, written $X\,|\,B \geq Y\,|\,C$. One assumes that this ranking obeys the usual axioms: transitivity, connectedness, a continuity principle, an Archimedean axiom, and so on. One also requires each *section* of the ranking $X\,|\,C \geq Y\,|\,C$, for C fixed, to satisfy the Bolker/Jeffrey axioms. Bolker's theorem then ensures that each section will be associated with a family $\mathcal{R}_C$ of $(\mathcal{V}_C, \rho_C)$ pairs that satisfy equation (2.3) and that represent $X\,|\,C \geq Y\,|\,C$. Different $\mathcal{R}_C$-pairs will be related by the equations $\rho_C^*(X) = \rho_C(X)[1 + k\mathcal{V}_C(X)]$ and $\mathcal{V}_C^*(X) = \mathcal{V}_C(X)[(k+1)/(1 + k\mathcal{V}_C(X)]$, where k is any real number such that $[1 + k\mathcal{V}_C(X)] > 0$ for all propositions X such that $\mathcal{V}_C(X)$ is defined. The trick to proving a representation theorem for conditional decision theory is to find further constraints on conditional preferences under which it is possible to select a unique $(\mathcal{V}_C, \rho_C)$ pair from each $\mathcal{R}_C$ in such a way that $\mathcal{V}_B(X) \geq \mathcal{V}_C(X)$ is guaranteed to hold whenever $X \mid B \geq Y \mid C$. The main axiom that is needed is the following generalization of Impartiality:

■ Let X_1, X_2, and X_3, and Y_1, Y_2, and Y_3, be mutually incompatible, and suppose that

$$X_1 \mid B \approx Y_1 \mid C > (X_1 \vee X_2) \mid B \approx (Y_1 \vee Y_2) \mid C > X_2 \mid B \approx Y_2 \mid C \quad (6.3)$$

holds for some conditions B and C. Then, if

$$X_1 \mid B \approx Y_1 \mid C \not\approx X_3 \mid B \approx Y_3 \mid C \not\approx (X_1 \vee X_3) \mid B \approx (Y_1 \vee Y_3) \mid C \quad (6.4)$$

then

$$(X_1 \vee X_2 \vee X_3) \mid B \approx (Y_1 \vee Y_2 \vee Y_3) \mid C. \quad (6.5)$$

This is not as complicated as it looks. If clause (6.3) holds, the only $(\rho, \mathcal{V})$ pairs that will represent $X \mid C \geq Y \mid B$ will be one in which $\rho(X_1 \mid B)/\rho(X_1 \vee X_2 \mid B) = \rho(Y_1 \mid C)/\rho(Y_1 \vee Y_2 \mid C)$. Likewise, if (6.4) holds, then the representation must be one in which $\rho(X_1 \mid B)/\rho(X_1 \vee X_3 \mid B) = \rho(Y_1 \mid C)/\rho(Y_1 \vee Y_3 \mid C)$. Together these two equalities entail that $\rho(X_1 \mid B)/\rho(X_1 \vee X_2 \vee X_3 \mid B) = \rho(Y_1 \mid C)/\rho(Y_1 \vee Y_2 \vee Y_3 \mid C)$, and this is just what (6.5) guarantees.

Using this axiom as the main formal tool, Joyce is able to construct a full conditional expected utility representation for the ranking $X \mid C \geq Y \mid B$. By adding further conditions, one can ensure either that the representation's supposition function will be Bayesian or that it will arise via imaging from some similarity relation among possible worlds. In this way, both EDT and CDT are seen to have a common foundation in the abstract theory of conditional expected utility.

7 Conclusion

While the classical theory of Ramsey, de Finetti and Savage remains our best account of rational choice, its development has yet to be completed. An adequate theory should explain the role in decision making of causal thinking. True, a decision theory that did without causal propositions would have been nice: Cause and effect have long puzzled and divided philosophers and scientists, and theoretical discussion of causal methodology remains underdeveloped. In decision making, though, we are stuck with causal thinking. Rational choice always involves judgements of how likely an option is to have various desirable consequences—and such judgements, we have argued, require the decision maker to have views, explicit or implicit, about causal or counterfactual relationships.

Nothing else can substitute for these causal beliefs. The conditional credences employed by evidential decision theory cannot, because they are unable to distinguish causation from correlation. More refined "screening" techniques, while better at capturing causal connections, fail to apply in a important class of cases. To specify the kind of case to which they do apply, we must, one way or another, invoke causal relations.

We should not find this need for causal notions distressing. We draw causal conclusions all the time, after all, and scientists are able to glean causal tendencies from experiment and statistical data, using methods of high sophistication. Still, no one theory of causal notions has the precision and orthodox status of, say, the standard theory of subjective probability. Thus, an adequate decision theory, if we are right, must depend on new advances in our understanding of causation and its relation to rational belief. We might have wished that theoretical life had turned out easier, but as matters stand, important work on the foundations of utility theory remains to be done.

References

Adams, E. W. (1975). *The Logic of Conditionals*. D. Reidel, Dordrecht.

Armendt, B. (1986). A Foundation for Causal Decision Theory. *Topoi*, 5:3–19.

Aumann, R. (1974). Subjectivity and Correlation in Randomized Strategies. *Journal of Mathematical Economics*, 1:67–96.

Aumann, R. (1987). Correlated Equilibrium as an Expression of Bayesian Rationality. *Econometrica*, 55:1–18.

Binmore, K. (1987). Modeling Rational Players I. *Economics and Philosophy*, 3:179–212. Reprinted in Binmore, 1990.

Binmore, K. (1988). Modeling Rational Players II. *Economics and Philosophy*, 4:9–55. Reprinted in Binmore, 1990.

Binmore, K. (1990). *Essays on the Foundations of Game Theory*. Blackwell, Oxford.

Bolker, E. (1966). Functions Resembling Quotients of Measures. *Transactions of the American Mathematical Society*, 124:292–312.

Eells, E. (1982). *Rational Decision and Causality*. Cambridge University Press, Cambridge.

Fine, K. (1975). Review of Lewis, 1973. *Mind*, 84:451–458.

Fishburn, P. C. (1974). A Mixture-set Axiomatization of Conditional Subjective Expected Utility. *Econometrica*, 41:1–25.

Gibbard, A. (1986). A Characterization of Decision Matrices that Yield Instrumental Expected Utility. In Daboni, L., Montesano, A., and Lines, M., editors, *Recent Developments in the Foundations of Utility and Risk Theory*, pages 139–148. D. Reidel, Dordrecht.

Gibbard, A. and Harper, W. L. (1978). Counterfactuals and Two Kinds of Expected Utility. In Hooker, C. A., Leach, J. J., and McClennen, E. F., editors, *Foundations and Applications of Decision Theory*, volume I, pages 125–162. D. Reidel, Dordrecht.

Hammond, P. J. (1994). Elementary Non-Archimedean Representations of Probability for Decision Theory and Games. In Humphries, P., editor, *Patrick Suppes: Scientific Philosopher*, volume 1, pages 25–61. Kluwer Academic Publishers, Dordrecht.

Harper, W. L. (1986). Mixed Strategies and Ratifiability in Causal Decision Theory. *Erkenntnis*, 24:25–26.

Harper, W. L. (1991). Ratifiability and Refinements in Two-person Noncooperative Games. In Bacharach, M. and Hurley, S., editors, *Foundations of Decision Theory*, pages 263–293. Basil Blackwell, Oxford.

Harsanyi, J. and Selten, R. (1988). *A General Theory of Equilibrium Selection in Games*. MIT Press, Cambridge, Mass.

Horgan, T. (1981). Counterfactuals and Newcomb's Problem. *Journal of Philosophy*, 68:331–356.

Howard, J. V. (1988). Cooperation in the Prisoner's Dilemma. *Theory and Decision*, 24:203–213.

Jeffrey, R. (1967). *The Logic of Decision*. McGraw Hill, New York.

Jeffrey, R. (1983). *The Logic of Decision*. University of Chicago Press, Chicago, 2nd edition.

Joyce, J. M. (forthcoming). *The Foundations of Causal Decision Theory*. Cambridge University Press, Cambridge.

Kohlberg, E. and Mertens, J. (1986). On the Strategic Stability of Equilibria. *Econometrica*, 54:1003–1037.

Lewis, D. K. (1973). *Counterfactuals*. Harvard University Press, Cambridge, Mass.

Lewis, D. K. (1976). Probabilities of Conditionals and Conditional Probabilities. *Philosophical Review*, 85:297–315. Reprinted in Lewis, 1986, pages 133–152.

Lewis, D. K. (1979a). Counterfactual Dependence and Time's Arrow. *Noûs*, 13:455–476. Reprinted in Lewis, 1986, pages 32–52.

Lewis, D. K. (1979b). Prisoner's Dilemma is a Newcomb Problem. *Philosophy and Public Affairs*, 8:235–240. Reprinted in Lewis, 1986, pages 299–304.

Lewis, D. K. (1980). A Subjectivist's Guide to Objective Chance. In Jeffrey, R. C., editor, *Studies in Inductive Logic and Probability*, volume 2. University of California Press, Berkeley. Reprinted in Lewis, 1986, pages 83–113.

Lewis, D. K. (1981). Causal Decision Theory. *Australasian Journal of Philosophy*, 59:5–30. Reprinted in Lewis, 1986, pages 305–337.

Lewis, D. K. (1986). *Philosophical Papers*, volume 2. Oxford University Press, Oxford.

Luce, R. D. and Krantz, D. H. (1971). Conditional Expected Utility. *Econometrica*, 39:253–271.

McGee, V. (1994). Learning the Impossible. In Eells, E. and Skyrms, B., editors, *Probability and Conditionals*, pages 179–197. Cambridge University Press, Cambridge.

Nozick, R. (1969). Newcomb's Problem and Two Principles of Choice. In Rescher, N., editor, *Essays in Honor of Carl G. Hempel*, pages 107–133. D. Reidel, Dordrecht-Holland.

Piccione, M. and Rubinstein, A. (1997). On the Interpretation of Decision Problems with Imperfect Recall. *Games and Economic Behavior*, 20:3–24.

Popper, K. (1934). *Logik der Forschung*. Springer Verlag, Vienna. Translated as: the Logic of Scientific Discovery (London: Hutchinson, 1959).

Renyi, A. (1955). On a New Axiomatic Theory of Probability. *Acta Mathematica Academiae Scientiarium Hungaricae*, 6:285–335.

Savage, L. J. (1972). *The Foundations of Statistics*. Dover, New York. First edition 1954.

Shin, H. S. (1991a). A Reconstruction of Jeffrey's Notion of Ratifiability in Terms of Counterfactual Beliefs. *Theory and Decision*, 31:21–47.

Shin, H. S. (1991b). Two Notions of Ratifiability and Equilibrium in Games. In Bacharach, M. and Hurley, S., editors, *Foundations of Decision Theory*, pages 242–262. Basil Blackwell, Oxford.

Simon, H. A. (1957). *Models of Man*. John Wiley & Sons, New York.

Skyrms, B. (1980). *Causal Necessity*. Yale University Press, New Haven.

Skyrms, B. (1984). *Pragmatics and Empiricism*. Yale University Press, New Haven.

Skyrms, B. (1990). Ratifiability and the Logic of Decision. *Midwest Studies in Philosophy*, 15:44–56.

Sobel, J. H. (1989). Partition Theorems for Causal Decision Theories. *Philosophy of Science*, 56:70–95.

Stalnaker, R. (1968). A Theory of Conditionals. *Studies in Logical Theory*, 2. American Philosophical Quarterly Monograph Series.

Stalnaker, R. (1981). Letter to David Lewis of May 21, 1972. In Harper, W. L., Stalnaker, R., and Pearce, G., editors, *Ifs: Conditionals, Belief, Decision, Chance, and Time*, pages 153–190. D. Reidel, Dordrecht-Holland.

Stalnaker, R. and Thomason, R. (1970). A Semantic Analysis of Conditional Logic. *Theoria*, 36:23–42.

Van Fraassen, B. (1995). Fine-grained Opinion, Probability, and the Logic of Belief. *Journal of Philosophical Logic*, 24:349–377.

absolute magnitude effect, 610
abstinence, 571
act, 164, 219, 307
act set, 279
actual behaviour, 167
additive price aggregation, 69
additive utility, 96, 105, 112
additive-difference model, 294
additivity, 135
additivity and duality, 75
additivity in a two-group partition, 74
adjacent gaps, 22
admissible equilibrium, 117
admissible value function, 102
aggregation, 555
aggregator, 96, 110
Allen index, 518, 520, 522
Allen quantity index, 524
almost unrestricted domain, 173, 176,
    177, 179, 182, 185, 238, 241, 244
α-rationality, 595
Anscombe and Aumann framework, 254
Anscombe and Aumann theory, 217
Anscombe and Aumann's axioms, 228
Antonelli equation, 511
Antonelli matrix, 494
arc-length, 11
Archimedean axiom, 155, 346
Archimedean Property, 360
Arrow-Hahn theorem, 17, 27
asymptotic discount factor, 108
atomistic quantity index, 518
atomistic welfare measures, 512
average growth factor, 115
axiom of choice, 188

backwards induction, 654
bargaining problems, 347
base set, 280
Bayesianism, 404, 438, 440, 441, 444
behavioral life cycle hypothesis, 612
behaviour set, 164, 167, 237
belief revision, 638
belief system, 362
Bellman's equation, 101, 102, 111, 112
Bellman's operator, 102, 111
bequeath value, 549

bequest motive, 571
Bernoulli utility function, 24
biconvergence, 98, 105, 109, 112
bidding game method, 550
binary choice probabilities, 291
binary simple scalability, 292
Bolzano-Weierstrass theorem, 15
Boolean algebra, 281
Borel measurability, 201
Borel sets, 298
Borel σ-algebra, 203
Borel σ-field, 201
bounded expected utility, 188
bounded preferences, 187, 254
bounded utility, 218
boundedness, 147, 187
boundedness condition, 187, 254
bounding condition, 12

capital accumulation, 571
cardinal equivalence class, 151, 163, 229
cardinality, 385, 411, 412
cardinally equivalent utility function, 151
Cauchy-Bochner integral, 32
causal act-independence, 632
causal decision theory, 632
causal dependency, 629
causal ratifiability, 645
cautious choice, 594
chance nodes, 165, 172, 223, 237
changing tastes, 118, 571
characteristic step function, 196
choice correspondence, 354
choice function, 148, 329
choice probabilities, 276
choice set, 148
choice space, 148
chosen probabilities, 247
circularity criterion, 487, 503, 509,
    517–520, 531
closed gap, 22
closed graph property, 179
commodity aggregation, 51
commodity space, 98
common difference effect, 577
Common Prior Assumption, 363
compatible complete order, 353
compatible complete preorders, 352

compatible order, 353
compatible preorders, 353
compensated demands, 129
compensated inverse demand functions, 494, 510
competitive equilibrium, 460, 461, 463, 464
complete preorder, 347
complete separability, 71
completely ordered set, 353
compound lottery, 148, 158, 174, 231
computability criterion, 488, 503
condition (B), 187, 190, 254
condition (C*), 155, 180, 192, 230
condition (C), 155, 230
condition (CB), 179
condition (CP*), 201
condition (CP), 191, 201
condition (D*), 153, 189
condition (D), 189, 190, 203, 254
condition (EC), 255, 258, 259
condition (ED*), 256
condition (ED), 256, 258
condition (FD*), 153, 189
condition (GSI), 251, 253
condition (I*), 153, 174, 230, 238
condition (I'), 153
condition (I), 153, 230
condition (I^0), 153
condition (M*), 201
condition (M), 197, 256
condition (O), 152, 219, 220, 230
condition (OE), 222, 226
condition (PD), 190, 197, 201, 203, 256, 258
condition (PM), 197
condition (RO), 231, 235, 238, 240
condition (SI), 220, 221, 232, 245, 258
condition (STP), 232
conditional Archimedean Property, 359
conditional cost function, 137
conditional expected utility, 243
conditional indirect utility function, 58
conditional lexicographic probability system, 361
conditional lottery, 232
conditional objectively expected utility, 232
conditional preferences, 359
conditional probability, 634
conditional probability measure, 203
conditional subjective probability, 243
conjugate Banach space, 32
conscious choice, 168
consequence domain, 164, 169, 218

consequence lotteries, 174
consequence mapping, 165, 223
consequentialism, 164, 167, 168, 174, 177, 203, 217, 224, 226
consequentialist, 177, 179, 215
consequentialist analysis, 217
consequentialist approach, 216
consequentialist axioms, 168, 176, 194, 206, 216, 217, 222
consequentialist behaviour, 177, 179, 185, 226, 241, 244
consequentialist choice, 168
consequentialist choice function, 164, 224
consequentialist foundations, 146, 164, 217, 222, 237
consequentialist hypothesis, 205, 224, 238
consequentialist justification, 195, 216
consequentialist motivation, 193
consequentialist normal form invariance, 239, 240, 244
consequentialist principle, 164, 167
conservative sequence, 601
consistent plan, 570
constant acts, 218
constant marginal utility of income, 497
constant valuation acts, 245
constant-ratio rule, 295
constant utility models, 286
construction of a utility function, 161
consumer choice theory, 354
contingent choice function (CCF), 217, 219, 238
    chosen, 223
    feasible, 223
contingent consequence functions, 219
contingent expected utility, 220, 231
contingent orderings, 224, 226, 246, 258
contingent preference orderings, 216, 220, 225
contingent preferences, 219, 231, 241
contingent securities, 219
contingent utilities, 238
contingent valuation methods, 549
continuation subtrees, 166, 182, 224
continuity, 146, 230, 266
continuity condition, 155, 185, 191
continuity hypothesis, 238
continuity of behaviour, 217
continuity of expected utility, 147, 200
continuous behaviour, 179, 243, 244
continuous preference condition, 147, 191, 201
contraction mapping, 100, 103, 108, 109

convex combination, 148
convex hull, 192
convex preferences, 124
correlated equilibrium, 647
cost function, 124
cost-of-living indices, 516, 523
cost-of-utility function, 491
countable basis, 7
countable events, 254
countable mixture, 188
countable mixture preservation property
    (MP*), 188, 198
countably infinite decision tree, 193
countably infinite lottery, 185
counterfactual conditionals, 636
cyclic preference, 277

Deaton index, 519, 520, 522
Debreu's Gap Lemma, 17–19
Debreu's theorem, 23, 29
decentralized decision making, 51
decision nodes, 165, 223
decision theory, 165, 355
decision trees, 146, 173, 217, 222
decomposition of utility, 110
degenerate lottery, 229
delay gratification, 614
delay-speedup asymmetry, 610
deliberate randomization, 311
dichotomous choice method, 551
diffeomorphism, 35
differential geometry, 35
dimensionality axiom, 523
direct methods of preference revelation,
    547
direct money-metric utility function, 492
direct question method, 550
direct utility function, 489
discard probability, 305
discrete lotteries, 185, 186, 201
discrete order, 27
distance function, 51, 132, 493
distance variation, 508, 519
dogmatic choice, 593
dominance, 147, 187, 189, 193, 220, 266,
    630
dominance condition, 254
dynamic consistency, 166, 167, 169, 171,
    185, 224, 244, 570
dynamic inconsistency, 571
dynamic programming, 93, 181, 182, 243

editing, 608
Eilenberg theorem, 23, 29
elementary consequence, 164, 165

elimination by aspects, 289
Ellsberg paradox, 215, 232
empirical distributions, 202
envelope property, 129
equivalence relation, 4, 280
equivalent chance node, 244
equivalent consequence domains, 249
equivalent variation, 514, 518, 539, 547,
    610
Euclidean spaces, 10
Euler equation, 104, 589
evaluation functions, 218, 244
evaluation stage, 608
even chance event, 216
event, 219, 256, 307
event continuity, 218, 254, 258, 266
event correspondence, 223
event dominance, 218, 255, 258, 266
event-contingent choice function, 224
evidential decision theorists, 629
evidential decision theory, 631
evidential ratifiability, 644
exact choice, 329
existence value, 549
expected consumer's surplus, 554
expected loss, 309
expected surplus, 554
expected utility, 145, 148, 215, 258, 307,
    346, 355, 553, 606, 630
expected utility function, 149
expected utility (EU) hypothesis, 145,
    147, 148, 186, 215
expected utility theory, 24
expenditure function, 17, 51, 491
exponential discounting, 570
extended lottery, 248
extended sure thing principle, 215
extensive form game, 240
extensive game, 240

facet defining inequalities, 301
Falmagne's theorem, 297
Farkas theorem, 351
feasible set, 148, 224, 237
felicity function, 106, 118
finite decision trees, 173, 223
finite dominance, 153, 189, 193
finitely additive probability measure, 281
forced choice paradigm, 281
form invariance, 244
forward induction, 654
frame of reference, 570
framing effects, 571
Fubini's theorem, 257
functional quantity index, 518

functional welfare measures, 495
fuzzy aggregation rule, 336
fuzzy preference, 323

gain-loss asymmetry, 610
game theory, 355, 361
generalized state independence, 251
Glueing Lemma, 13
Gorman Polar Form, 62
    generalized, 62

habit formation (addiction), 600
half-open half-closed gap, 18
hedonic price method, 548
Heine-Borel theorem, 8
hemispaces, 352
Herrnstein's matching law, 579
heuristics, 621
Hicks-Kaldor compensation test, 557
Hicksian compensating variation, 502,
    514, 518
Hicksian demand function, 491, 529
Hicksian equivalent variation, 501, 546
homothetic preference ordering, 498, 524
homothetic separability, 68
horse lotteries, 217, 228
Hotelling-Wold Identity, 491
hypothetical choices of probabilities, 248
hyperbolic discount function, 570
hypothetical behaviour, 248
hypothetical probabilities, 218, 248

identity axiom, 523
immediate successor, 165, 173, 223
impartiality axiom, 657
implicit choice function, 168
implicit choice set, 164
implicit homothetic separability, 86
implicit preference, 170, 174, 177, 179,
    185, 195, 205
implicit separability, 82
implicit-function theorem, 36
in-kind subsidy programs, 526
income-compensated demand function,
    491
income-compensated shadow price
    functions, 529, 546
increasing set, 6
incremental expected utility (EU)
    advantage model, 309
independence, 146, 153, 172, 174, 230,
    266
independence axiom, 146, 153, 225, 308,
    606
independence condition, 153, 355

index measures, 515
index numbers, 515
index of ophelimity, 3
indicative conditionals, 636
indicator criterion, 487, 502, 509, 513,
    514, 517–520, 531
indifference function, 3
indifference relation, 170, 219, 355
indifference subspace, 353
indirect methods of preference revelation,
    547
indirect money-metric utility function,
    492
indirect utility function, 51, 129, 489
infinite decision trees, 204, 206
infinite dimensional spaces, 30
infinite dominance, 153
infinite-dimensional Banach space, 32
information bias, 549
information set, 240
initial nodes, 165, 223
instantaneous compensating variations,
    540
instantaneous equivalent variations, 540
instantaneous expenditure functions, 540
instantaneous utility functions, 540
instrumental act independence, 658
instrumental expected utility, 633
intangible goods, 550
integrability conditions, 506
integrability problem, 35
integrable selections, 204
intergenerational models, 116
internal conflict, 613
interpersonal welfare comparisons, 556
intertemporal choice, 570
intertemporal compensating variation,
    539
intertemporal inelasticity, 107, 118
intertemporal substitution, 570
intertemporal welfare effects, 538
interval order, 33
interval-valued representations, 33
inverse compensated demand functions,
    536
inverse demand functions, 490
isotone function, 27

jointly continuous utility functions, 36
Jordan arc, 11

Klein-Rubin-Stone-Geary linear
    expenditure system, 599
Konüs indices, 524, 525
Koopmans' equation, 99, 110

$L^\infty(\mu)$, 30
Laspeyres price index, 525
Laspeyres quantity indices, 521, 525
Laspeyres variation, 513
Lebesgue integration, 196
Lebesgue-Tietze-Urysohn extension
    theorem, 27
lenient choice, 593
lexicographic additive model, 346
lexicographic domination, 364
lexicographic expected utility, 346, 360
lexicographic function space, 353
lexicographic index, 351
lexicographic linear utility choice
    correspondences, 358
lexicographic linear utility rational, 358
lexicographic Nash equilibrium, 346, 362
lexicographic optimization, 346
lexicographic order in $\mathbf{R}^n$, 346
lexicographic orders, 346
lexicographic preferences, 154, 156, 346
lexicographic preorders, 346, 347
lexicographic probability systems, 359,
    362
lexicographic product, 37
lexicographic relation, 9
lexicographic representation theorem,
    356
lexicographic subjective expected utility,
    346, 360, 362
lexicographic utility, 346
lexicographic utility functions, 353
lexicographic utility rationality, 354
lexicographically nonnegative matrices,
    350
leximin, 416–418, 459, 465, 467
leximin rule, 347
lifetime expenditure function, 538
lifetime utility function, 538, 540
likelihood ordering, 221, 228
limit tree, 179
linear axiom of revealed preference, 358
linear expenditure system, 532
linear order, 280
linear ordering polytope, 299, 300
linear-homogeneity axiom, 523
liquidity constraints, 615
local non-satiation rules, 14
long run utility, 600
long term demands, 600
lotteries, 148, 165, 355
lottery set, 279
lower convergence, 98, 110
lower hemi-continuity, 183
lower preference set, 147, 218

lower section (lower contour set), 5
lower semicontinuous function, 13
Luce's choice axiom, 282, 295

Malmquist index, 520, 522
marginal distributions, 231, 238, 240, 245
marginal probabilities, 231
marginal rate of substitution (MRS), 145,
    150, 229
marginal utility of income, 489
Marschak triangle, 149
Marshallian demand functions, 489, 528
Marshallian measure, 497, 546
maximum theorem, 183
measurability, 197, 218, 256, 266
measurable expected utility, 256
measurable lotteries, 218
measurable space, 195, 218, 256
measurable subsets, 24
measurable trees, 205
measure theory, 147, 218
mechanical index numbers, 522
mental accounts, 608, 684
metric space, 200
metric topology, 192
mixed strategies, 179
mixture continuity, 155
mixture preservation property (MP), 149,
    188, 234, 235
mixture set, 357
mixture space, 148, 186, 257, 357
moderate stochastic transitivity, 282
monotonic preorder, 10
monotonicity axiom, 523
moral expectation, 145
moral hazard, 248
moral philosophy, 164
multi-person game, 179
multi-person game theory, 173
multiattributed structures, 279
multiplicative inequality, 299

Nachbin extension theorem, 27
Nachbin separation theorem, 27
naive plan, 584
Nash equilibrium, 179, 355, 362, 647
natural nodes, 217, 222, 223, 225, 226,
    237, 242
natural topology, 8
negative dynamic programming, 103
node valuation, 181
node valuation function, 243
non-additive utility, 96, 108
non-Archimedean utility, 354
non-expected utility, 164

non-null event, 216, 258
non-null state independence, 258, 360
noncontradictory trade-offs, 216
noncooperative games, 346
nonexcludability property, 543
Nonstandard Analysis, 354
nontransitive preferences, 310
nonuse values, 549
normal forms, 240
normal form invariance, 217
normal space, 27
normalized version of the indirect utility
    function, 490
normative behaviour, 164
normative principle, 164
normed linear spaces, 30
notion of duality, 124
null events, 216, 217

objective conditional chance, 639
objective independence, 359
objective probabilities, 215, 223
open decreasing subsets, 28
open gap, 18, 22
open sets, 6
ophelimity, 3
optimal control, 104
optimal growth factor, 108
option price, 554
option value, 549, 555
order, 347
order embedding, 8
order homomorphism, 8
order interval, 161
order isomorphism, 8
order monomorphism, 8
order topology, 8, 36
order-preserving function, 2
order-separable in the sense of Birkhoff, 6
order-separable in the sense of Cantor, 5
order-separable in the sense of Debreu, 6
order-separable in the sense of Jaffray, 6
ordered vector space, 335
ordering condition, 152
ordering of events, 215, 217, 222, 226,
    233
ordinal representations, 286
ordinality, 146, 164, 169, 265
ordinally fuzzy aggregation rule, 338
ordinally fuzzy strict binary relation, 337
outcome set, 307
overlapping separable sets, 72

Paasche quantity index, 521, 525
Paasche variation, 514

Pareto criterion, 555
Pareto-inefficiency, 595
partial compositions, 108
partial order, 4, 280
partial preorder, 347
path monotonicity, 12
path-connected topological space, 31
path-independence, 498
payment card method, 550
Peleg's theorem, 29
perfect equilibrium, 363
perfect recall, 223
planned behaviour, 167
point-summable measure, 281
policy correspondence, 101, 111
positive affine transformations, 285
positive dynamic programming, 103
possible worlds, 635
potential Pareto improvement criterion,
    556
potential Pareto improvement test, 555
precommitment behavior, 574
preference, 2
preference intervals, 356
preference measurability, 197
preference ordering, 146, 152, 170, 176,
    217, 219, 225, 489, 500
preference relation, 14, 324, 346, 347
preference reversal, 611
preference satisfaction, 373, 376, 382,
    384–390
preference sets, 191, 197
preorder, 4, 347
preordered vector spaces, 352
preservation property, 188
price aggregation, 51
primitive domain, 281
principle of optimality, 182, 243
Prisoner's Dilemma with Twin, 628
prize-state lotteries, 245
probabilistic choice, 276
probabilistic product, 237
probability distribution, 173
probability dominance, 190, 197, 203,
    218, 256, 258, 266
probability measures, 147, 195, 218
probability of a conditional, 635
probability space, 286
product lottery, 231
profit function, 132
proper equilibrium, 363
proportionality property, 290
proportionality transformations, 285
prospect theory, 571
prudence, 571

public goods, 543
pure-accumulation consumption, 106

qualitative fuzziness, 337
qualitative probabilities, 215
quantity constraints, 526
quantity index, 516
quasi-linearity, 105

r-conditionally homogeneous of degree
    zero, 80
random consequence, 164
random disutility model, 303
random expected utility (EU) model, 309
random moves, 223
random utility, 275
random utility model, 286
random-elimination model, 289
range bias, 551
rank dependent structure, 609
ranking, 280
ranking condition, 518
ranking criterion, 487, 503, 509,
    517–520, 531
ranking domain, 280
rankings from choice probabilities, 302
ratificationism, 642
rationed compensating variation, 531
rationed equivalent variation, 531
rationed goods, 527
rationed households, 527
rationing theory, 527
ratios of utility differences, 229
real-income index, 516
recomposition of utility, 100, 111
recursive utility, 94
reduced decision tree, 169
reduction of compound lotteries, 174
reference bundle, 600
reference consumption bundle, 619
reference date, 575, 619
reference lottery, 619
referendum method, 551
regularity, 296
rejection probability, 303
relative likelihood, 217
relativity principle, 570
representation theorem, 284, 656
resolute choice, 612
restricted expenditure function, 528
restricted indirect utility function, 528
revealed preference, 149
revealed subjective probability, 259
revealed weak preference relation, 354
reversal of order, 230, 266

risk aversion, 118
risk-neutral agent, 215
roulette lotteries, 217, 228
Roy's Identity, 490

sagacious choice, 593
Savage's approach, 222
Savage's axiom system, 216
Savage-null, 360
savings behavior, 571
second countable, 7
second-best rules, 614
self-control, 571
semiorder, 33
separability, 51, 169, 399, 402, 417
separating system, 38
separation and extension problem, 26
separation theorems for convex sets, 353
sequence functions, 219
sequential equilibrium, 364
shadow price function, 491
shadow prices, 529, 547
Shephard's Duality Theorem, 493
Shephard's Lemma, 491
Shephard-Hanoch Lemma, 494, 536
short run demand, 600
σ-additivity, 195
σ-algebra, 24, 195
σ-field, 195, 256
σ-finite measure space, 30
σ-ring, 196
similarity mapping, 8
simple finite decision trees, 165, 172
simple lotteries, 147, 185
simple scalability, 294
single-person decision theory, 173
Slutsky equation, 34, 132
Slutsky matrix, 491
smooth preference relation, 36
social choice, 335
social choice lotteries, 306
social choice theory, 347
social welfare functional (SWFL), 375,
    408–415, 417–419, 422–424, 427,
    429–432, 458
social welfare functions, 556
soft preference, 327
Sono independent, 74
sophisticated plan, 584
split-and-splice, 305
St. Petersburg game, 145
St. Petersburg paradox, 145, 147, 186
starting point bias, 550
state contingent consequence, 223

state contingent consequence functions,
    217
state dependent lotteries, 215
state independence, 217, 221, 232, 245,
    258, 266, 361
state independent consequence domain,
    251
state independent preferences, 221, 233,
    256
state invariance, 245
state-consequence pairs, 245
state-contingent value function, 114, 115
state-dependent consequence domains,
    245, 247
state-dependent utilities, 245, 247
state-dependent utility function, 249
state-independent consequence
    preference, 251
state-independent utilities, 226, 250
states of nature, 218
states of the world, 219
step function, 195, 198
stochastic dominance arguments, 147
stochastic monotonicity, 157, 180
stochastic transitivity, 282, 291
stochastic utility, 275, 279
Stone-Geary utility function, 532
strategic game, 217
strict partial order, 5
strict preference, 170, 219
strict total order, 5
strict utility model, 285
strict weak order, 5, 291
strong continuity, 230
strong dominance, 189
strong event dominance, 256
strong independence, 153, 177, 179, 193,
    230, 238, 363
strong sure thing principle (STP*), 217,
    221, 226
Strotz-Pollak equilibrium, 583
subgame perfect Nash equilibrium, 583
subjective expected utility, 219, 228, 358
subjective probabilities, 215, 219, 228,
    255
subjective probability measures, 256
subjectively expected utility (SEU), 216,
    219, 221, 228, 233, 257, 358
    stronger version (SEU*), 216, 221,
    228, 233
subjunctive conditionals, 636
subset choice, 288
subset random utility model, 288
substitutability, 292
successive approximations, 103

superlative index numbers, 522
sure consequence, 221
sure thing principle (STP), 217, 219, 220,
    225, 226, 231, 232, 238, 266
Szpilrajn's extension theorem, 353

terminal nodes, 165, 223, 237
theory of cardinal and ordinal numbers,
    37
time-additivity, 105, 216
topological space, 6, 203
topological subspace, 7
topological vector space, 32
topology of closed convergence, 36
topology of weak convergence, 201
total (or complete or linear) preorder, 5
total ordering, 155
totally ordered set, 354
tournament, 280
transition probabilities, 173, 180, 238,
    239
transversality condition, 104
travel cost method, 547
tree structure, 165
triangle inequality, 277, 299
true equilibrium, 116
true index of the cost of living, 524
two-stage budgeting, 51

unbounded expected utility, 188
unbounded utilities, 147, 186
uncertain lifetime, 571
uncertainty, 606
uncompensated demand functions, 131
underlying set, 148
uniformity axiom, 216
uniformly convergent sequence, 20
union domain, 245, 250
unique cardinal equivalence class, 145,
    185, 190, 236, 238, 244
universal domain, 245, 250
universal indifference, 219, 221, 222,
    234, 258
universal state-consequence domain, 248
unordered events, 226
unrestricted domain, 166, 169, 171, 173
upper convergence, 98, 105, 110, 112
upper hemi-continuity, 179, 183
upper preference set, 147, 187, 218
upper section (upper contour set), 5
upper semicontinuous function, 13
Urysohn extension theorem
    (Lebesgue-Tietze-Urysohn
    extension theorem), 27

Urysohn separation theorem (Urysohn's lemma), 26
Urysohn-Nachbin separation and extension theorems, 26
use value, 548
utilitarianism, 374, 377, 379, 380, 391, 415–422, 425, 427, 430–432, 434, 436, 454, 465, 467
utility, 2
utility differences, 149, 187
utility extension problem, 30
utility for gambling, 174
utility function, 2, 8, 346
utility representation problem, 30

vague preferences, 276
value function, 101, 111
Vartia algorithm, 510, 546
Vartia method, 535
virtual income, 530
virtual price system, 530
von Neumann-Morgenstern (VNM), 403–407, 410, 425, 426, 428–430, 432, 434–436, 453–455, 464
    axioms, 373, 403, 406, 413, 437, 451
von Neumann-Morgenstern utility, 219
von Neumann-Morgenstern utility function (NMUF), 24, 146, 148, 181, 219, 229, 236, 238, 244
    unbounded, 188

vote differential function, 306

weak *-topology, 32
weak axiom of revealed preference, 354
weak factor-reversal test, 516
weak order, 280, 355
weak order domain, 280
weak preference, 169
weak separability, 57
weak stochastic transitivity, 284
weak topology, 201
weakly monotonic preorder, 10
Weierstrass's M-test, 16
welfare measurement under uncertainty, 554
welfare measures, 486
welfarism, 375, 394, 395, 401, 410, 411, 413, 414, 418–420, 424, 434, 458, 466, 467
well ordered set, 347
well-being, 373, 376, 387–392, 395, 396, 398, 434, 466, 467
Well-Ordering theorem of Zermelo, 38
willingness to accept, 549
willingness to pay, 491, 549
willpower, 571
Wold's theorem, 32

zone of ignorance, 515, 522
Zorn's Lemma, 36

NAME INDEX

Aczél, J., 582
Adams, E.W., 636
Afriat, S.N., 87
Ahlheim, M., 510, 511, 530, 553
Ainslie, G., 578, 580, 614
Albon, R., 527
Aliprantis, C., 13
Allais, M., 146, 307, 308, 310, 386, 403
Allen, R.G.D., 518, 524
Alwang, J., 87
Amemiya, T., 278
Anscombe, F., 215–218, 228, 229, 233,
    254, 266, 359, 360, 404–407, 438,
    443, 449, 455
Anscombe, G.E.M., 165
Antonelli, G.B., 35, 125
Apostol, T.M., 12, 13, 496, 498
Arneson, R.J., 394
Aristotle, 164, 377, 397
Armendt, B., 658–660
Arnsperger, C., 459
Arrow, K.J., 10, 14, 16, 17, 24, 28, 30,
    32, 37, 147, 148, 165, 170, 215,
    219, 329, 335, 336, 354, 385, 408,
    413–416, 418, 422, 423, 431, 439,
    434, 443, 444, 450, 454, 455, 459,
    485, 556
Aubin, J., 13
Aumann, R.J., 215–218, 228, 229, 233,
    254, 266, 357, 359, 360, 404–407,
    438, 444, 449, 455, 647, 648,
    650–652, 653

Babington Smith, A., 303
Banach, S., 32, 100, 103
Banerjee, A., 326, 331, 337
Banks, J., 131
Barberá, S., 288, 297, 306, 347
Bar-Hillel, M., 448
Barnett, W.A. 87, 131
Barrett, C.R., 329, 332, 333, 335, 336,
    338
Barry, B., 420
Bartle, R., 15
Basu, K., 326, 327, 334, 341
Bateman, I., 553
Bayes, T., 215, 404, 661
Bearden, A.F., 10, 18, 19

Beccaria, C., 381
Becker, G.M., 307–309, 600
Becker, R.A., 96
Behringer, F.A., 347
Bellman, R., 101–104, 107, 112, 114, 117
Bentham, J., 374, 380–382, 384, 413, 433
Berge, C., 101, 102, 183
Bergson, A., 70, 78, 423
Berliant, M., 24
Berndt, E.R., 87
Bernheim, D., 116
Bernoulli, D., 24, 145
Bertrand, J., 215
Billingsley, P., 195, 201
Billot, A., 325, 326
Binmore, K., 375, 448, 654
Bishop, R.C., 551, 554
Bjornstad, D., 553
Black, D., 289
Blackorby, C., 57–63, 65, 67–69, 71,
    73–76, 80–84, 86, 87, 95, 124, 125,
    402, 409, 413, 19–422, 429, 485,
    489, 490, 492, 493, 539, 556, 557
Blackwell, D., 103, 146, 147, 153, 155,
    189, 205
Blaug, M., 385
Bliss, C., 95
Block, H.D., 277, 278, 285–288, 291,
    293, 296, 303, 304
Blume, L., 232, 346, 359–362, 364
Blundell, R., 131
Boadway, R.W., 82, 557
Bockstael, N.E., 547
Böhm–Bawerk, E.v. 572, 573, 616
Bolker, E., 656, 657, 662
Border, K.C., 146
Borel, E., 201, 257
Borwein, J.M., 353
Bosi, G., 34
Bossert, W., 409, 419, 422
Bouyssou, D., 435
Bowen, R., 19
Bowring, J., 381
Boyce, R., 62
Boyd, J.H., 100, 109
Bradley, R.A., 285
Brams, S.J., 289

Brandenburger, A., 232, 346, 359–362, 364
Brandt, R., 377, 398
Breslaw, J.A., 506, 527
Bridges, D., 32, 34–37, 418
Broome, J., 380, 388, 397, 399, 405, 420, 425, 431, 432, 436, 437, 440, 443, 453
Brown, D., 13
Brown, T.C., 551
Browning, M.J., 65, 87, 132, 136, 138, 540
Buchanan, J.M., 444
Burkinshaw, O., 13
Burns, C., 322
Busemeyer, J.R., 289

Campbell, D.E., 485, 556
Campello de Souza, F.M., 300
Candeal, J.C., 9, 32
Cantor, G.A., 6, 25, 34, 348, 394
Canto-Sperber, M., 375
Carrol, J.D., 278, 293, 295
Carson, R.T., 549–551, 553
Champ, P.A., 551
Chateauneuf, A., 34
Chavas, J.P., 555
Chernoff, H., 215
Chichilnisky, G., 36
Chipman, J.S., 2, 35, 37, 329, 354, 355, 386, 503
Choi, S., 87
Christenson, L.R., 87
Chritchlow, D.E., 278, 302, 305
Chun, Y., 347
Clark, S.A., 306, 311, 346, 354, 355, 357, 358
Cobb, C.W., 78, 461
Cohen, M.A., 290, 298, 299, 300
Collard, D., 398, 446
Collonius, H., 278, 288
Conlon, J.R., 87
Cook, P.J., 131
Cooper, R.J., 87, 135
Corbin, R., 288, 289, 297
Cornes, R., 125,132, 139, 489, 493, 527
Coulhon, T., 426
Cowen, T., 420
Cramer, G., 145, 147
Croom, F., 4, 13, 16
Cubitt, R., 206
Cuesta Dutari, 353

Dagsvik, J.K., 278, 299
Daniels, H.E., 287, 303

Dasgupta, M., 326, 333, 335, 341
d'Aspremont, C., 165, 347, 408, 409, 411, 413, 415, 417, 418, 424, 431, 451
David, H.A., 285
Davidson, R., 83, 84, 86, 87
De Borger, B., 527, 530
De Finetti, B., 215, 216, 404, 640, 663
De Meyer, B., 428
De Soete, G., 278, 293, 295
Deaton, A., 63, 70, 77, 86, 125, 131, 132, 133, 136, 493, 518, 527, 530, 532
Deb, R., 326, 327, 329, 333, 334, 441
Debreu, G., 3, 6, 9, 11, 17–19, 23, 24, 28, 30, 34–36, 55, 57, 219, 282, 284, 285, 293, 341, 348, 353, 354, 401, 493
DeGroot, M., 215, 307–309
Dekel, E., 232, 346, 359–362, 364, 526
Denardo, E.V., 103
Denny, M., 87
Dérathé, R., 448
Deschamps, R., 347, 417, 418
Devlin, K., 37
Diamond, P.A., 96, 109, 436, 552
Diewert, W.E., 65, 87, 125, 131, 133, 489, 493, 522
Dixit, A., 129
Donaldson, D., 409, 413, 419–422, 429, 485, 492, 539, 556, 557
Douglas, P.H., 78, 461
Drèze, J., 218, 248
Dridi, T., 300
Driscoll, P.J., 87
Droste, M., 19
Dubois, D., 324
Dummett, M., 322
Dupuit, J., 497
Dutta, B., 326, 333, 357
Dworkin, R., 394, 462–464, 466

Eastman, C., 550
Edgeworth, F.Y., 3, 381, 382, 515
Edwards, W., 307–309
Eells, E., 642, 645, 659
Eichorn, W., 523
Eilenberg, S., 17, 23, 24, 28, 30, 31
Eisler, H., 289
Ellsberg, D., 215, 232, 307, 407
Epicurus, 381
Epstein, L.G., 97, 118, 436, 443
Euler, L., 61, 85, 104, 496, 587, 589

Falmagne, J.-C., 278, 288, 290, 294, 296, 297–300

Farkas, J., 351
Farquharson, R., 289
Fechner, G., 285
Field, C.A., 493
Fine, K., 637
Fine, T., 404
Fishburn, P.C., 33, 34, 146, 147, 153, 188,
    215–217 233, 255, 257, 278, 277,
    279, 280, 282, 286, 289, 291–293,
    299, 300, 301, 305–310, 326, 346,
    348, 349, 350, 354–361, 403, 404,
    407, 408, 434, 435, 659–661
Fisher, F., 487, 523
Fisher, I., 573, 617, 619
Fleetwood, W., 515
Fleurbaey, M., 375, 394
Fligner, M.A., 278, 302, 305
Foley, D., 459, 461
Forsyth, B., 289
Frank, R., 579, 580, 613
Frankel, A., 25
Freeman, A.M., 547, 548, 555
Freeman, S., 549
Frisch, R., 136, 137, 487, 512, 523
Fubini, G., 257
Fudenberg, D., 363
Fuss, M., 87

Gaertner, W., 448
Gauthier, D., 447, 4488
Geary, P.T., 75, 532
Gehrlein, W.V., 306
Gensemer, S., 33
Gérard-Varet, L.A., 451
Gevers, L., 347, 414, 417, 418, 431
Gibbard, A., 335, 336, 398, 629, 632,
    641, 658, 659
Gilboa, I., 301
Girshick, M.A., 146, 147, 153, 155, 189,
    205
Glannon, W., 419
Goguen, J., 327
Goldman, S.M., 87, 584, 590, 596
Goodin, R.E., 392
Gorman, W.M., 55, 57, 59, 60, 61, 62, 68,
    71, 72, 82, 95, 124, 125, 132, 137,
    402, 600
Gorokhovik, V., 353
Gossen, H.H., 70
Graaf, J.d.v., 387, 397
Graham, D.A., 553–555
Grandmont, J.-M., 24, 201
Graves, P.E., 550
Green, J., 461
Green, R.D., 87

Grötschel, M., 299, 301
Griffin, J., 396, 397
Guilbaud, G.T., 299
Gul, F., 216

Hacking, I., 145, 215
Hagen, O., 386
Hahn, F., 10, 14, 16, 17, 28, 30, 32, 37
Hakansson, N.H., 116
Halévy, E., 381
Hall, R.E., 136
Halmos, P., 195, 257
Hammond, P.J., 99, 118, 146, 165, 169,
    170, 217, 237, 239, 347, 398, 403,
    407, 413, 417, 420, 422, 425, 427,
    431, 436, 434, 437, 441, 442, 485,
    556, 557, 592, 594, 595, 601, 603,
    606, 661, 662
Hanemann, M., 552
Haque, W., 79, 80, 82
Hare, R.M., 377, 378, 391, 434, 446, 447
Harper, W.L., 629, 632, 640, 650, 654,
    656, 659
Harris, C., 116
Harris, R., 82
Harrod, R.F., 377
Harsanyi, J.C., 215, 375, 377, 378, 386,
    392, 400, 403, 418, 425–429,
    431–437, 441, 443, 444, 446, 447,
    449–455, 457, 464, 465, 466,
    654–656
Haslam, N., 580, 614
Hausdorff, F., 36
Hausman, D., 375, 394, 443, 506, 552,
    553
Hausner, M., 348, 353, 355–357
Heberlein, T.A., 551
Heckman, J.J., 136
Herden, G., 19, 26, 29, 30
Herrnstein, R., 579
Herstein, I.N., 146, 148, 149, 153, 155,
    157, 307, 357, 403, 427, 580
Herzberger, H.G., 148
Hicks, J.R., 4, 55, 78–79, 81, 82, 126,
    129, 136, 383, 385, 386, 486, 502,
    512, 557
Hild, M., 443
Hildenbrand, W., 36, 183, 201, 204
Hobbes, T., 215, 447
Hoevenagel, R., 551
Holman, E., 296
Homer, 574
Horgan, T., 642
Horowitz, J.K., 578
Hotelling, H., 125

Houston, A., 293
Houthakker, H.S., 63, 78, 81, 329, 527
Howard, J.V., 306, 629
Howson, C., 407
Hu, S., 14, 16
Huber, P.J., 201
Hume, D., 445
Hurwicz, L., 329, 386
Hutcheson, F., 445
Hylland, A., 437
Hynes, J.A., 97

Imai, H., 347
Indow, I., 278
Induráin, E., 9, 32
Intriligator, M.D., 306
Irish, M., 132, 136
Isermann, H., 347
Isler, R., 34
Ives, B., 550

Jackson, M.O., 347
Jackson, W.A, 527
Jacobsen, S.E., 493
Jaffray, J., 9, 19
Jain, N., 326, 333
Jamison–Waldner, R.E., 352
Jeffrey, R.C., 383, 404, 405, 443, 630,
    631, 642–645, 652, 656, 657, 658,
    662
Jensen, N.E., 146, 153, 157
Jevons, S., 2, 381, 382, 572, 573, 575
Jewitt, I., 82, 83
Johansson, P.-O., 556
Jordan, C., 13
Jorgenson, D.C., 87
Joyce, J.M., 660–662
Judd, K.L., 103
Jünger, M., 299, 301

Kadane, J.B., 248, 407, 437, 444
Kagan, S., 395
Kahn, J., 553
Kahneman, D., 307, 308, 310, 381, 604,
    607–609
Kalai, E., 448
Kaldor, N., 557
Kamke, E., 25
Kaneko, M., 453
Kannai, Y., 36, 357
Kant, I., 376–378, 391, 445, 446, 449
Karni, E., 146, 155, 215, 218, 245, 248,
    282, 436, 454
Keen, M., 539, 542
Kelley, J., 4

Kelsey, D., 411
Keynes, J.M., 215
Kirman, A.P., 195, 201
Klee, V., 353
Klemisch-Ahlert, M., 448
Kohlberg, E., 655, 656
Kolm, S.C., 375, 398, 417, 443, 450, 453,
    454, 459
Konüs, A., 524
Koopmans, T., 95, 96, 99, 100, 109, 111,
    117, 574, 578
Koppen, M., 301
Krantz, D.H., 278, 279, 291, 293, 299,
    294–296, 298, 326, 385, 406, 630,
    631
Krause, U., 347
Kreps, D.M., 118, 364
Kreweras, G., 306, 310
Krutilla, J., 548

La Fontaine, J. de, 453
Lady, G., 69
Laibson, D., 589
Laisney, F., 556
Lancaster, K.J., 282, 289
Lange, O., 387
Lankford, R.H., 527
Larsson, S., 277, 307
Laspeyres, E., 512–515, 521, 522, 525,
    526
Lau, L.J., 78, 79, 81, 87, 131
Lauwers, L., 422
LaValle, I.H., 146, 168, 176, 206, 310,
    357–359, 360
Lebesgue, H., 19, 196
Leclerc, B., 337
Lee, J., 299, 301
Lee, W., 307
Lee, Y.W., 131
Legendre, A.-M., 128
Leininger, W., 116
Leonard, R.J., 146
Leontief, W.W., 56, 65
Lerner, A., 450
Leung, J., 299, 301
Levi, I., 444
Lewbel, A., 131
Lewis, D.K., 629, 638–640, 658, 660
Lichtenstein, S., 307
Lindley, D.V., 215
Little, I.M.D., 380, 423
Locke, J., 447
Loève, M., 298
Loewenstein, G., 577, 578, 581, 610, 611
Loomes, G., 310, 386

Lucas, R.E., 96, 100, 103, 109
Luce, R.D., 32, 174, 277–279, 282, 283, 285, 286, 290–296, 298, 303– 305, 306, 307–309, 326, 346, 348, 350, 385, 403, 406, 435, 630, 631
Lukasiewicz, 324
Luptáčik, M., 347
Lyons, D., 377

MacCrimmon, K.R., 277, 307
Machina, M., 145, 149, 169, 278, 311
Mackay, R.J., 527
MaCurdy, T., 136
Madden, P., 527
Mak, K.T., 87, 95
Malinvaud, E., 153
Mallows, C.L., 303
Malmquist, S., 63, 134, 519, 520
Manski, C.F., 295
Markov, A.A., 113
Marley, A.A.J., 196, 278, 286, 288, 289, 296, 297–299, 303, 305, 306
Marschak, J., 146, 149, 150, 153, 154, 277, 278, 285–288, 291, 293, 296, 299, 303, 304, 307–309
Marshall, A., 486, 497
Marshall, J.M., 555
Martínez-Legaz, J.E., 351–353
Mas-Colell, A., 31, 35, 36, 335, 461
Maskin, E., 415
McClennen, E.F., 169, 403, 604, 607, 612
McCollum, D.W., 551
McFadden, D., 68, 278, 295, 299, 300
McGee, V., 661
McGuirk, A.M., 87
McKay, A.F., 453
McKenzie, G.W., 504–506, 534
McKenzie, L.W., 131, 492
McLennan, A., 36, 206, 301, 302
McPherson, M., 375, 394, 443
Meghir, C., 87, 138
Mehta, G.B., 4, 10, 18, 19, 26, 30, 32, 36, 37, 152
Meier, C.E., 555
Menger, K., 147, 186, 187
Mertens, J., 655, 656
Milgram, A., 37
Mill, J.S., 164, 381, 382
Milnor, J., 146, 148, 153, 155, 157, 307, 357, 403, 427
Mirrlees, J.A., 463
Mischel, W., 614
Mitchell, R.C., 549, 553
Moloney, D., 485, 539
Monderer, D., 297, 301

Mongin, P., 165, 248, 380, 400, 402, 408, 411, 425, 428–431, 437, 438, 440, 444
Monjardet, B., 291, 337
Monroe, D.H., 446
Monteiro, P.K., 31, 32
Moore, G.E., 164, 398, 433
Moore, J.C., 503
Morgenstern, O., 24, 146, 153, 174, 219, 282, 306–308, 311, 355, 373, 374, 402, 403, 466
Morishima, M., 75
Moro, D., 87
Moroney, M., 375,515
Morris, S., 440
Moschini, G., 87
Moulin, H., 409, 459, 462
Muellbauer, J., 97, 125, 131, 493
Munier, B., 169
Myers, J.L., 307
Myerson, R.B., 215, 217, 218, 245, 363, 443
Nachbin, L., 26–28

Narens, L., 216, 282, 283, 285, 290, 354, 355
Nash, J.F., 146, 355, 362, 364, 448, 583, 591, 592
Neary, J.P., 527, 530
Nelson, M., 422
Newcomb, W., 629
Nieto, J., 347
Nissen, D., 69
Nozawa, G., 289
Nozick, R., 379, 449, 629

Ok, E.A., 329
Okada, A., 364
O'Neill, B., 12
Orlovsky, S., 326, 331
Osborne, M.J., 363
Osherson, D.N., 286
Ovchinnikov, S., 326, 337
Ozaki, H., 114, 118

Paasche, H., 512, 515, 521, 522, 525, 526
Palmquist, R.B., 548
Panda, C., 326, 333
Pareto, V., 3, 83, 384, 385, 387, 413, 417, 422, 423, 425, 428, 429, 438, 441, 442, 460, 555, 556, 571, 595, 597, 623
Parfit, D., 374, 420
Parkin, C., 87
Parthasarathy, K.R., 201, 202

Pascal, B., 145
Pattanaik, P.K., 288, 297, 326, 327–329, 332–336, 338, 341, 347, 450, 453, 455
Pauwels, W., 527
Pazner, E.A., 461, 462
Pearce, I.F., 504
Peleg, B., 24, 25, 28–30, 347, 590
Peston, M., 600
Peters, H., 347
Phelps, E.S., 589
Picavet, E., 378
Piccione, M., 646
Pierson, N., 515
Pigou, A.C., 387, 389, 515
Plato, 377
Pollak, R.A., 87, 523, 582–585, 589–591, 599, 601, 614
Pommerehne, W.W., 547
Ponsard, C., 326
Popper, K.R., 661
Porteus, E.L., 118
Portney, P.R., 552
Prade, H., 324
Pratt, J.W., 216, 434
Prelec, D., 577, 578, 581, 610, 611
Primont, D., 57, 58, 59, 61, 62, 65, 67, 68, 69, 71, 73, 74, 75, 76, 87, 95, 124, 125, 402, 489, 490, 493
Puppe, C., 335
Puterman, M.L., 103

Quiggin, J., 609

Rae, J., 571–573, 614, 616
Raiffa, H., 174, 216, 232, 282, 306, 403, 435
Ramsey, F.P., 215, 216, 404, 634, 663
Randall, A., 535, 550
Rapoport, A., 578
Rawls, J., 375, 376, 379, 388, 392, 393, 396, 400, 417, 418, 419, 425, 432, 436, 446, 448, 449, 455–459, 463–465, 467
Ray, D., 97, 116
Ready, R., 555
Reilly, R.E., 307
Reinelt, G., 299, 301
Renyi, A., 661
Restle, F., 289
Richter, M.K., 299, 300, 329, 386, 402
Riley, J., 382
Risse, M., 443
Robbins, L., 384
Roberts, A.V., 127

Roberts, F.S., 4, 32, 33, 291
Roberts, K.W.S., 411, 424, 527, 530, 556
Rockafellar, R.T., 127
Rodriguez, M., 614
Roemer, J.E., 375, 394, 448, 463, 464
Rosen, H.S., 548
Rosenstein, J.G., 298
Rothbarth, E., 527, 530
Rotundo, J., 286
Roubens, N., 326
Rousseau, J.J., 447, 448
Roy, R., 59, 60, 131, 490
Royden, H.L., 195, 196
Ruben, H., 215
Rubinstein, A., 363, 422, 646
Rudin, W., 11
Russell, R.R., 57–63, 65, 67–69, 71, 73–76, 80–82, 87, 95, 124, 125, 402, 489, 490, 493
Russo, J.E., 291, 293
Rustichini, A., 218

Safra, Z., 146
Sainsbury, R.M., 322
Salles, M., 329, 332, 333, 335, 336, 338
Samuelson, P.A., 70, 78, 79, 81, 145, 146, 153, 176, 329, 386, 423, 487, 492, 497, 516, 543, 573, 574
Sattath, S., 292, 298, 299
Savage, L.J., 146, 165, 215, 216, 217, 218, 219, 220, 221, 222, 227, 228, 233, 254, 255, 256, 282, 307, 310, 358, 373, 404–407, 427, 436, 438, 440, 442, 449, 629–636, 656–658, 663
Scanlon, T.M., 393
Schelling, T., 615
Schervish, M.J., 248, 407, 437, 444
Schlaifer, R., 216
Schmachtenberg, R., 556
Schmeidler, D., 155, 215, 218, 248, 282, 361, 461, 462
Schumpeter, J.A., 381, 384
Schwab, R.M., 527, 535
Schwartz, T., 329
Schworm, W., 83, 84, 86, 87
Scitovsky, T., 557
Scott, D., 33, 284
Screpanti, E., 385
Segal, U., 311, 436, 443
Seidenfeld, T., 248, 407, 437, 444
Selten, R., 653, 654, 655, 656
Sen, A.K., 148, 322, 323, 329, 335, 347, 375, 379, 382, 386, 388–391, 393–396, 398, 408, 409, 417, 418,

422, 425, 427, 428, 432, 434–436, 444, 450, 453, 454, 465, 595
Senior, N.W., 572, 573
Shafer, W., 31
Shafir, E.B., 286
Shapley, L.S., 145
Shechter, M., 549
Sheffler, S., 400
Shefrin, H., 612, 614
Shephard, R.W., 85, 129, 493
Shin, H.S., 638, 645, 650, 653
Shipley, E.F., 307
Shoda, Y., 614
Sidgwick, H., 388
Sierpiński, 353
Sikora, R., 420
Simmons, P., 86, 322
Simon, H., 641
Singer, I., 351–353
Singer, P., 375, 377
Sinn, H.-W., 145
Skala, H.J., 354, 361
Skryms, B., 640, 650, 658
Slesnick, D.T., 485, 556
Slovic, P., 307
Slutsky, E., 34, 86, 87, 131
Smart, J.J.C., 377
Smith, A., 2, 306, 445, 446, 449, 571
Smith, E.E., 286
Smith, J.B., 506, 527
Smorodinsky, M., 448
Sobel, J.H., 640, 659
Sonnenschein, H., 306, 329, 335, 386
Sono, M., 56, 65, 73, 74
Sorensen, A., 322
Stalnaker, R., 629, 632, 635, 636–640
Stephen, L., 381
Stern, H., 285
Stigler, G.J., 381, 600
Stokey, N.L., 96, 100, 103, 109
Stone, R., 532, 599
Strasnick, S., 417
Strauch, R., 103
Strauss, D., 299, 305
Streufert, P.A., 87, 97, 100–102, 109, 114, 116, 118
Strotz, R.H., 59, 61, 570, 574, 575–577, 583–585, 590, 591, 607, 614
Subramanian, S., 335
Suck, R., 299
Sugden, R., 310, 386
Suppes, P., 33, 215, 277–279, 284, 285, 286, 289, 290, 291–296, 298, 304, 307–309, 326, 385, 386, 406, 416, 435, 450

Suydam, M.M., 307, 309
Suzumura, K., 329, 416, 450–453, 455
Svento, R., 555
Swamy, S., 487, 492, 516
Swofford, J.L., 87
Szpilrajn, E., 353

Taub, H.A., 307
Taylor, A.E., 525
Tempkin, L., 399, 419
Terry, M.E., 285
Thaler, R.H., 578, 611, 612, 614
Thomas Aquinas, St., 164
Thomason, R., 637
Thompson, W., 448, 459
Thurstone, L.L., 287, 303
Tinbergen, J., 459
Tirole, J., 363
Tobin, J., 527
Train, K., 278
Turner, R., 553
Turnovec, F., 347
Tversky, A., 277, 278, 279, 289–295, 296, 298, 299, 307, 308, 310, 326, 348, 349, 381, 385, 406, 604, 607–609, 611, 612

Ulph, D., 506, 534
Urquhart, A., 324
Urysohn, P., 26–28
Uzawa, H., 87, 97, 329

Vallentyne, P., 422
Van Fraassen, B., 645, 661
Van Liederkerke, L., 422
Van Parijs, P., 463
Vansnick, J., 435
Varberg, D.E., 127
Varian, H., 459, 460, 463
Vartia, Y., 506, 510, 534, 535
Verducci, J.S., 278, 302, 305
Verneaux, R., 377
Vickrey, W.S., 450
Villegas, C., 215
Vind, K., 218, 248
Viner, J., 381
Voeller, J., 523
von Auer, L. 592, 593, 594, 606
von Neumann, J., 24, 146, 148, 153, 174, 219, 282, 306, 307, 308, 311, 355, 361, 373, 374, 402, 403, 466
von Stengel, B., 95
von Weizsäcker, C.C., 584, 600, 601

Wagenhals, G., 510

Wakker, P.P., 146, 148, 188, 216, 228, 279, 293, 406
Wales, T.J., 131
Wapman, K., 146, 148, 176
Wasserman, D., 436
Weierstrass, K.T.W., 10, 16
Weisbrod, B.A., 548
Wendel, J.G., 353
Weyl, H., 361
Weymark, J., 409, 413, 425, 428, 429, 432, 434, 435, 454, 492
Whinston, M. 461
Whitney, G.A., 87, 527
Wicksell, K., 421
Williams, B., 400, 435
Williamson, R.E., 96,109
Williamson, T., 322
Wilson, R.B., 218, 245, 364
Winet, M., 386, 435

Wold, H., 3, 10, 11, 13, 14, 17, 19, 20, 22, 30, 32
Wolfe, M.D., 131
Woodland, A.D., 87

Yaari, M.E., 448, 590, 596, 597
Yagil, J., 558
Yellot, J.I., 296, 299
Yuhn, K.H. 87

Zabell, S.L., 145
Zadeh, L.A., 324
Zamagni, S., 385
Zank, H., 228
Zeckhauser, R., 306, 437
Zermelo, E., 38
Zhou, L., 429
Zimmerman, H.-K. 324
Zin, S.E., 118
Zorn, M., 188, 354